DON'T THROW THIS CARD AWAY!
THIS MAY BE REQUIRED FOR YOUR COURSE!

THOMSON ONE | Business School Edition

Congratulations!

Your purchase of this NEW textbook includes complimentary access to THOMSON ONE – Business School Edition for Finance. THOMSON ONE – Business School Edition is a Web-based portal product that provides integrated access to Thomson Financial content for the purpose of financial analysis. This is an educational version of the same financial resources used by Wall Street analysts on a daily basis!

For hundreds of companies, this online resource provides seamless access to:

- **Current and Past Company Data:** Worldscope which includes company profiles, financials and accounting results, market per-share data, annual information, and monthly prices going back to 1980.

- **Financial Analyst Data and Forecasts:** I/B/E/S Consensus Estimates which provides consensus estimates, analyst-by-analyst earnings coverage, and analysts' forecasts.

- **SEC Disclosure Statements:** Disclosure SEC Database which includes company profiles, annual and quarterly company financials, pricing information, and earnings.

- **And More!**

© 2008 South-Western, a part of Cengage Learning.

ISBN-13: 978-0-324-23596-8
ISBN-10: 0-324-23596-8

SOUTH-WESTERN
CENGAGE Learning

THOMSON ONE
Business School Edition

ACCESS CODE

PX9Ø8BTPPQSS2H

HOW TO REGISTER YOUR ACCESS CODE

1. Launch a web browser and go to **http://academic.cengage.com/thomsonone**

2. Click the "Register" button to enter your access code.

3. Enter your access code **exactly** as it appears here and create a unique User ID, or enter an existing User ID if you have previously registered for a different South-Western product via an access code.

4. When prompted, create a password (or enter an existing password, if you have previously registered for a different product via an access code.) Submit the necessary information when prompted. **Record your User ID and password in a secure location.**

5. Once registered, return to the URL above and select the "Enter" button; have your User ID and password handy.

NOTE: The duration of your access to the product begins when registration is complete.

For technical support, cgo to **academic.cengage.com/support**

Discover the FUNDAMENTAL DIFFERENCE

Which Choice is Best for You?

Determine which Brigham/Houston Fundamentals text is best for your course:

LENGTH

Which length is ideal for your course?

Concise, 6e

17 CHAPTERS

Fundamentals, 12e

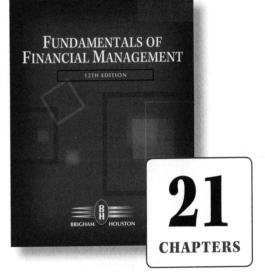

21 CHAPTERS

DEPTH OF COVERAGE

What depth of coverage is best for your course?

If you want a brief version of the text but still want to cover important topics such as **time value of money**, **basics of capital budgeting**, **working capital management**, and more, then *Concise, 6e* is the choice for you.

If you want to cover **real options** and **capital budgeting** in more depth; **derivatives** and **risk management**; **hybrid financing**, including **preferred stock**, **leading**, **warrants** and **convertibles**; or **mergers and acquisitions**, *Fundamentals, 12e* is the choice for you.

FULL CUSTOM CONTENT

Or create the unique combination of content that is best for your course with a Cengage Learning Custom Solution. This Personalized Instructor's Edition is an ideal example of the power you have to create a custom product perfectly tailored to your needs. Visit **www.cengage.com/custom** or contact your Cengage Learning representative for more information.

Still not sure? **See the next two pages for a full Table of Contents for both texts...**

Discover the FUNDAMENTAL DIFFERENCE

Fundamentals of Financial Management: Concise, 6e

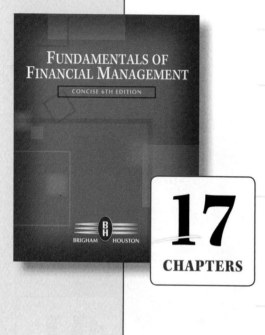

FUNDAMENTALS OF FINANCIAL MANAGEMENT

CONCISE 6TH EDITION

BRIGHAM HOUSTON

17 CHAPTERS

Chapter 12 in Concise, 6e does not include the "Incorporating Risk Into Capital Budgeting" section, but **does** include three sections: "Introduction to Real Options," "Abandonment/Shutdown Options," and "The Optimal Capital Budget", that are found in Fundamentals, 12e.

Briefer Coverage!
The Concise, 6e text does not include chapters 13, 18, 20, and 21 from the Fundamentals 12e text.

First in Finance With Either Choice!

Whether you choose Brigham/Houston's *Concise, 6e* or *Fundamentals, 12e*, you'll be first in finance with the power of Aplia™ for Finance, a comprehensive supplemental package—written by the text author team—as well as access to Thomson ONE - BSE, the professional database that Wall Street professionals use every day. So take a moment and see for yourself how to place you and your students *first in finance* every time!

Fundamentals of Financial Management, 12e

FUNDAMENTALS OF FINANCIAL MANAGEMENT
12TH EDITION
BRIGHAM · HOUSTON

21 CHAPTERS

More Coverage!
Fundamentals, 12e
includes chapters
13, 18, 20, and 21.

FUNDAMENTALS OF FINANCIAL MANAGEMENT

Concise Sixth Edition/Twelfth Edition

Eugene F. Brigham
UNIVERSITY OF FLORIDA

Joel F. Houston
UNIVERSITY OF FLORIDA

SOUTH-WESTERN
CENGAGE Learning™

Australia • Brazil • Japan • Korea • Mexico • Singapore • Spain • United Kingdom • United States

SOUTH-WESTERN
CENGAGE Learning

Fundamentals of Financial Management, 12ᵗʰ edition

Fundamentals of Financial Management: Concise Edition, 6ᵗʰ edition
Eugene F. Brigham, Joel F. Houston

Vice President of Editorial, Business: Jack W. Calhoun

Editor-in-Chief: Alex von Rosenberg

Executive Editor: Michael R. Reynolds

Development Editor: Michael Guendelsberger

Marketing Manager: Nathan Anderson

Senior Marketing Communications Manager: Jim Overly

Marketing Coordinator: Suellen Ruttkay

Frontlist Buyer, Manufacturing: Kevin Kluck

Senior Art Director: Michelle Kunkler

Content Project Manager: Jennifer A. Ziegler

Director of Production: Sharon Smith

Media Editor: Scott Fidler

Senior Editorial Assistant: Adele T. Scholtz

Production Service: Litten Editing and Publishing

Compositor: ICC MacMillan Inc.

Cover and Internal Designer: Grannan Graphic Design

Photography Manager: Sheri Blaney

South-Western Cengage Learning
5191 Natorp Boulevard
Mason, OH 45040
USA

Cengage Learning products are represented in Canada by Nelson Education, Ltd.

For your course and learning solutions, visit **academic.cengage.com**
Purchase any of our products at your local college store or at our preferred online store **www.ichapters.com**

Printed in the United States of America
1 2 3 4 5 6 7   14 13 12 11 10

BRIGHAM *first in* FINANCE

first in CONTENT

- First Introductory book to cover CAPM
- First to differentiate expected and required returns
- First to discuss the intrinsic value of stocks

first in PRESENTATION

- First timelines to explain TVM
- First financial calculators to solve TVM problems
- First NPV profiles in capital budgeting analysis
- First Mini-Cases to integrate chapter concepts
- First Spreadsheet Problems

first in SUPPORT

- First with Aplia™ for Finance
- First Lecture Presentation software
- First with WordPerfect Test Bank
- First with Blueprints

FUNDAMENTALS OF FINANCIAL MANAGEMENT
12TH EDITION

FUNDAMENTALS OF FINANCIAL MANAGEMENT
CONCISE 6TH EDITION

BRIGHAM HOUSTON

Brigham/Houston, the first name in finance education today, is the last name you need to remember. Because for Brigham/Houston, **First in Finance** is not a mere description of who we are, but a promise of what we deliver, edition after edition, course after course, to keep you and your students on the forefront of financial management success.

Whether it's *Fundamentals of Financial Management* or one of the many other leading Brigham products, you can depend on the remarkable authorship team that reshaped financial education over the years to provide the latest innovations, unforgettable content, and exceptional learning tools and support you won't find anywhere else. **Trust Brigham/Houston to place you and your students** *first in finance* every time.

BRIGHAM HOUSTON

Brigham/Houston's
Fundamentals of Financial Management, 12e & Concise, 6e

Concise. Complete. A True Contemporary Classic.

Like each of Brigham/Houston's market-leading solutions, *Fundamentals of Financial Management* brings you the best in finance first with a classic combination of hallmark strengths and contemporary innovations. You'll find everything you and your students need to remain on the forefront of today's financial management education with this leading text's unique balance of contemporary theory and practical applications.

The renowned author team's emphasis on Time Value of Money (TVM) is now repositioned to allow students to *immediately* use the concepts after learning them. A compact, strong foundation in the basics is punctuated with timely examples, meaningful applications, Integrated Cases, and Spreadsheet Models. Supplements, prepared by the text authors to mirror the quality consistent within the text, are now strengthened with yet another first, Aplia™ for Finance.

Count on this contemporary classic for *first in finance* coverage today!

First-Rate Presentation with First-Class Support

First to Offer the Aplia™ Advantage

Engage. Prepare. Educate.

Aplia has two interactive learning solutions to help your students succeed in the classroom:

Aplia for Finance

Aplia for Finance is an interactive learning solution that makes finance relevant and engaging, while ensuring that students practice the application of course concepts on a regular basis. Aplia assignments are automatically graded and include detailed feedback on every question.

- Problem Sets
- Preparing for Finance Tutorials
- News Analyses
- Course Management System
- Digital Textbook

Aplia's Preparing for Finance

Make sure your students have the fundamental skills to succeed in finance with Aplia's Preparing for Finance tutorials. These interactive tutorials ensure that students confront and overcome deficiencies in prerequisite math, accounting, economics, and statistics. A tutorial on using financial calculators is also included.

For more information on how Aplia could benefit you, visit **www.aplia.com/finance** today!

Proven Test Bank Stronger
Than Ever with Algorithmic Flexibility

Test your students' knowledge of critical finance concepts and techniques simply and efficiently with this thoroughly revised, substantial test bank that offers 1,200 class-tested questions and problems, including new true/false and multiple-choice questions.

ExamView™ Computerized Testing Software allows you to easily *algorithmically modify problems* to create unlimited versions of the test or specific problems—ideal for instructors who teach a large number of students.

FIRST IN CONTENT. BEST IN STRENGTH.

Time Value of Money (TVM) Allows Students to Immediately Practice Concepts

Based on your feedback, the authors have relocated TVM coverage from Chapter 2 to Chapter 5 to provide a stronger foundation and seamless flow into concepts that follow. Students no longer have to wait, but are able to begin applying TVM concepts *immediately* after learning them, which deepens their understanding.

> **SELF TEST**
>
> The U.S. Treasury offers to sell you a bond for $585.43. No payments will be made until the bond matures 10 years from now, at which time it will be redeemed for $1,000. What interest rate would you earn if you bought this bond for $585.43? What rate would you earn if you could buy the bond for $550? for $600? **(5.5%; 6.16%; 5.24%)**
>
> Microsoft earned $0.33 per share in 1997. Ten years later in 2007 it earned $1.42. What was the growth rate in Microsoft's earnings per share (EPS) over the 10-year period? If EPS in 2007 had been $0.90 rather than $1.42, what would the growth rate have been? **(15.71%; 10.55%)**

New Self-Test Problems Ensure Immediate Understanding

New focused Self-Test Problems now appear immediately after each major section of the chapter, allowing students to check their comprehension right away rather than waiting until the end of the chapter.

Ethics Coverage Expanded for Today's Times

Additional coverage of ethics in this new edition allows you to easily and time-efficiently locate and integrate critical ethics discussions at appropriate points within your course.

Consistent Strengths of a Contemporary Classic

Unique Balance of Theory and Practice Leads Today's Learning

A hallmark strength of these leading finance texts, both versions clearly introduce important financial theories using a unique, practically focused presentation. Students apply the text's theories and trends using proven learning features, a wealth of real-world examples, practical problem sets, and Integrated Mini-Cases.

Integrated Spreadsheet Models Help Perfect Problem-Solving Skills

More than just Excel templates, these unique Integrated Spreadsheet Models accompany each chapter (except Ch. 1) to assist students in developing effective techniques for financial problem solving. Spreadsheet Models serve as focused tutorials that show students how to maximize Excel as a powerful finance tool.

Renowned Contemporary Author Team Ensures Innovative Approach

The premier Brigham/Houston authorship team combines Gene Brigham's extensive teaching background and more than 40 years of text writing experience, with Joel Houston's recognized contemporary scholarship and forward thinking, to deliver a consistently innovative approach that's first in finance today.

INTEGRATED CASE

SMYTH BARRY & COMPANY

2-1   **FINANCIAL MARKETS AND INSTITUTIONS**   Assume that you recently graduated with a degree in finance and have just reported to work as an investment adviser at the brokerage firm of Smyth Barry & Co. Your first assignment is to explain the nature of the U.S. financial markets to Michelle Varga, a professional tennis player who recently came to the United States from Mexico. Varga is a highly ranked tennis player who expects to invest substantial amounts of money through Smyth Barry. She is very bright; therefore, she would like to understand in general terms what will happen to her money. Your boss has developed the following questions that you must use to explain the U.S. financial system to Varga.

   a.   What are the three primary ways in which capital is transferred between savers and borrowers? Describe each one.

   b.   What is a market? Differentiate between the following types of markets: physical asset markets versus financial markets, spot markets versus futures markets, money markets versus capital markets, primary markets versus secondary markets, and public markets versus private markets.

   c.   Why are financial markets essential for a healthy economy and economic growth?

   d.   What are derivatives? How can derivatives be used to reduce risk? Can derivatives be used to increase risk? Explain.

   e.   Briefly describe each of the following financial institutions: commercial banks, investment banks, mutual funds, hedge funds, and private equity companies.

Author-Written Support Mirrors Text Quality and Consistency

Since the first edition, all supplements have been written by the text authors to ensure the same level of accuracy and precision crafting that has made this text a leader.

FIRST-CLASS SUPPLEMENT SUPPORT IN AUTHOR-WRITTEN PACKAGE

Instructor's Resource CD-ROM (IRCD)

Place teaching resources at your fingertips with this all-in-one resource that includes the Instructor's Manual, Word Test Bank, Spreadsheet Models, solutions to Spreadsheet Problems, and PowerPoint® slides. These supplements can also be found on the text Companion Web site: www.cengage.com/brigham.

PowerPoint® Lecture Presentation Software

Bring lectures to life as new, colorful PowerPoint slides cover the essential topics for each chapter. Graphs, tables, lists, and calculations are developed sequentially for your convenience. Easily modify slides for your specific needs. Slides are available on the IRCD or Companion Web site: www.cengage.com/brigham.

Spreadsheet Models for Excel

Easily illustrate the application of spreadsheets to finance concepts using Spreadsheet Models and the book's Integrated Case data. Spreadsheet models show students how to best utilize Excel as a finance tool. Spreadsheet models are available on the IRCD or Companion Web site: www.cengage.com/brigham.

Instructor's Manual

Save time with this tool's answers to all text questions and problems, detailed solutions to the Integrated Cases, descriptions of how to best use all available supplements, sample syllabus and course schedule. A digital version is available on the IRCD or password-protected Companion Web site: www.cengage.com/brigham.

Fundamentals of Financial Management Companion Web site

www.cengage.com/brigham

Place your students *first in finance* with the leading learning tools and convenient, password-protected resources found on this dynamic companion Web site. Easily access digital versions of the author-written supplements.

Study Guide

Give your students essential support as this invaluable tool, written by the text authors, lists learning objectives for each chapter, outlines key sections, provides self-test questions, and offers an additional set of problems with fully completed solutions.

Strengthened Test Bank

This edition's significantly revised Test Bank provides more than 1,200 class-tested questions and problems. Each question includes information regarding the topic, degree of difficulty, correct answers, and completed numerical solutions.

ExamView™ Electronic Testing with Algorithmic Convenience

Make test preparation, scoring and grading easy with this reliable testing software. This fully-customizable algorithmic test bank allows you to create unlimited variations of each test or specific problems, which is particularly useful for large class enrollments.

iChapters.com

iChapters.com, Cengage Learning's online store, is a single destination for more than 10,000 new print textbooks, e-books, single e-chapters, and print, digital and audio supplements. Students have the freedom to purchase *a-la-carte* exactly what they need when they need it. **Save your students time and money. Tell them about www.iChapters.com for choice, savings . . . and a better chance to succeed in your class.**

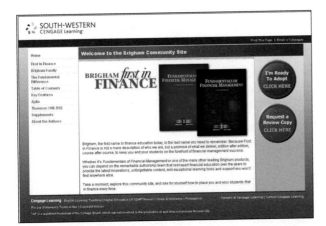

Brigham/Houston Community Web site

www.cengage.com/community/brigham

Be *first in finance* with the latest financial innovations for you and your students. Download demonstrations of the latest Brigham/Houston technology. Discover how the valuable tools and technology offered in this leading family of products will keep you *first in finance* throughout the year!

aplia™
Engage. Prepare. Educate.

Help your students learn finance with Aplia's online, interactive homework solution. Trusted by over 3,400 instructors and 900,000 students worldwide, Aplia has become an industry leader in online learning solutions.

Aplia™ for Finance

- **Problem Sets:** Chapter-specific problem sets ensure that students are completing finance assignments on a regular basis.

- **Preparing for Finance Tutorials:** Interactive tutorials help students overcome skill deficiencies in prerequisite subjects that would otherwise prevent them from learning finance. Aplia also includes tutorials on using financial calculators.

- **News Analyses:** Students connect course concepts to real-world events by reading relevant news articles and answering graded questions about them.

- **Course Management System**

- **Digital Textbook**

Preparing for Finance

- Interactive tutorials ensure that students overcome skill deficiencies in prerequisite subjects

- Reviews accounting, economics, math, and statistics

- Teaches students how to use a financial calculator

For more information on how Aplia could benefit you, visit **www.aplia.com/finance**.

Eugene F. Brigham
University of Florida

Dr. Eugene F. Brigham is a Graduate Research Professor Emeritus at the University of Florida where he has taught since 1971. Dr. Brigham received his M.B.A. and Ph.D. from the University of California-Berkeley and his undergraduate degree from the University of North Carolina. Prior to coming to the University of Florida, Dr. Brigham held teaching positions at the University of Connecticut, the University of Wisconsin, and the University of California-Los Angeles. Dr. Brigham served as president of the Financial Management Association and has written more than 40 journal articles on the cost of capital, capital structure, and other aspects of financial management. The ten textbooks on managerial finance and managerial economics that he authored or co-authored are used at more than 1,000 universities in the United States and have been translated into 11 languages for worldwide use. Dr. Brigham has testified in numerous electric, gas, and telephone rate cases at both federal and state levels. He has served as a consultant to many corporations and government agencies, including the Federal Reserve Board, the Federal Home Loan Bank Board, the U.S. Office of Telecommunications Policy, and the RAND Corporation. Dr. Brigham continues to teach, consult, and do research, as well as continue his work on textbooks. He spends his spare time on the golf course, enjoying his family and dogs, and tackling outdoor adventure activities such as biking through Alaska.

Joel F. Houston
University of Florida

Dr. Joel F. Houston is a Bank of America Professor of Finance at the University of Florida. He received his M.A. and Ph.D. from the Wharton School at the University of Pennsylvania and his undergraduate degree from Franklin and Marshall College. Prior to his appointment at the University of Florida, Dr. Houston was an economist at the Federal Reserve Bank of Philadelphia. Dr. Houston has published widely in the areas of corporate finance and commercial banking. His research focuses primarily on the role of financial institutions in the capital acquisition process and mergers in the banking industry. In addition to co-authoring the leading textbooks in financial management, Dr. Houston has participated in management education programs for the World Bank, Southern Company, and Service America Corporation. Dr. Houston received the College of Business Teacher of the Year Award in 1992, 1997, and 1999 and was a recipient of the Teaching Incentive Program Award in 1993 and 1996. In his spare time, Dr. Houston coaches baseball and enjoys spending time at the beach with his wife and two children. He is an avid sports fan and loyally follows the Florida Gators and Pittsburgh Steelers.

Here's What's Ahead!

This Personalized Instructor's Edition contains all 21 chapters—the entire 12th Edition of Fundamentals of Financial Management. It also includes a separate chapter 12 from the Concise text since Concise does not share the exact same content as chapter 12 from the *full* Fundamentals text.

Remember, the Concise, 6e text does not include chapters 13, 18, 20, and 21 from the full Fundamentals text.

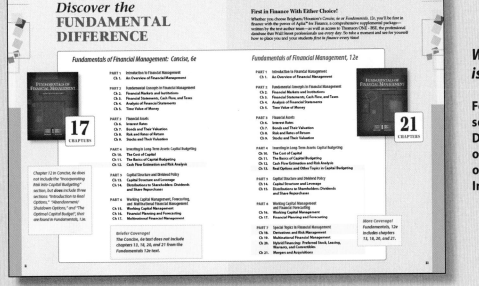

Which Choice is Best for You?

For more information, see The Fundamental Difference section on pages i, ii, and iii of this Personalized Instructor's Edition.

So take a moment and see for yourself how to place you and your students first in finance every time!

FUNDAMENTALS OF FINANCIAL MANAGEMENT

Twelfth Edition

Eugene F. Brigham
UNIVERSITY OF FLORIDA

Joel F. Houston
UNIVERSITY OF FLORIDA

SOUTH-WESTERN
CENGAGE Learning

Australia • Brazil • Japan • Korea • Mexico • Singapore • Spain • United Kingdom • United States

SOUTH-WESTERN
CENGAGE Learning

Fundamentals of Financial Management, 12th edition
Eugene F. Brigham, Joel F. Houston

Vice President of Editorial, Business:
Jack W. Calhoun

Editor-in-Chief: Alex von Rosenberg

Executive Editor: Michael R. Reynolds

Development Editor:
Michael Guendelsberger

Executive Marketing Manager:
Brian Joyner

Marketing Manager: Nathan Anderson

Senior Marketing Communications
Manager: Jim Overly

Marketing Coordinator: Suellen Ruttkay

Web site Project Manager: Brian Courter

Frontlist Buyer, Manufacturing:
Kevin Kluck

Senior Art Director: Michelle Kunkler

Content Project Manager: Jennifer A.
Ziegler

Director of Production: Sharon Smith

Media Editor: Scott Fidler

Senior Editorial Assistant: Adele T.
Scholtz

Production Service: Litten Editing
and Publishing

Compositor: Macmillan Publishing
Solutions

Cover and Internal Designer:
Grannan Graphic Design

Photography Manager: Sheri Blaney

For product information and technology assistance, contact us at
Cengage Learning Customer & Sales Support, 1-800-354-9706

For permission to use material from this text or product,
submit all requests online at **www.cengage.com/permissions**
Further permissions questions can be emailed to
permissionrequest@cengage.com

Exam*View*® is a registered trademark of eInstruction Corp.

© 2009 Cengage Learning. All Rights Reserved.

Library of Congress Control Number: 2008941113

ISBN 13: 978-0-324-59771-4

ISBN 10: 0-324-59771-1

Student Edition ISBN 13: 978-0-324-59770-7

Student Edition ISBN 10: 0-324-59770-3

South-Western Cengage Learning
5191 Natorp Boulevard
Mason, OH 45040
USA

Cengage Learning products are represented in Canada by Nelson Education, Ltd.

For your course and learning solutions, visit **academic.cengage.com**
Purchase any of our products at your local college store or at our preferred online store **www.ichapters.com**

Printed in the United States of America
1 2 3 4 5 6 7 12 11 10 09 08

When the first edition of *Fundamentals* was published 31 years ago, we wanted to provide an introductory text that students would find interesting and easy to understand. *Fundamentals* immediately became the leading undergraduate finance text, and it has maintained that position ever since. Our goal with this edition was to produce a book and ancillary package that would maintain its lead and set a new standard for finance textbooks.

Important changes in the financial environment have occurred since the last edition. New technology and increased globalization continue to transform practices and markets. Continued improvements in communications and transportation have made it easier for businesses to operate on a worldwide basis—a company can be headquartered in New York, develop products in India, manufacture them in China, and sell them anywhere in the world. This has led to major changes in the labor markets, especially to an increase in outsourcing, which has resulted in generally lower consumer prices; but it has caused job losses for some U.S. workers and gains for others. There have also been dramatic rises and falls in the stock market, and interest rates have remained low even as energy prices continue to rise. Corporate scandals have led to important changes in the laws governing corporate management and financial reporting, as well as to equally important changes in managerial compensation. These issues are discussed in this edition of *Fundamentals*, where we analyze them from financial and ethical perspectives.

Our target audience is undergraduate students taking their first, and often only, finance course. Some students will decide to major in finance and go on to take courses in investments, money and capital markets, and advanced corporate finance. Others will choose marketing, management, or some other nonfinance major. Still others will major in areas other than business and take finance and a few other business courses to gain information that will help them in law, real estate, and other fields.

Our challenge was to provide a book that serves all of these audiences well. Our conclusion was that we should focus on the core principles of finance (i.e., on basic topics such as the time value of money, risk analysis, and valuation). Moreover, we concluded that we should address these topics from two points of view: (1) as an investor who is seeking to make intelligent investment choices and (2) as a business manager trying to maximize the value of his or her firm's stock. Note that both investors and managers need to know the same set of principles, so the core topics are important to students regardless of what they choose to do after they finish the course.

THE FINANCIAL CRISIS OF 2008

As everyone knows, the financial markets experienced a meltdown in the fall of 2008. The average stock's price declined by about 50%, which wiped out trillions of dollars of savings. The (sick) joke was that 401 (k) retirement plans were becoming 201 (k) plans. These market losses delayed many retirements and also caused many retirees to go back to work. Housing construction virtually ceased, and home prices plunged by about 20% nationwide and by as much as 50% in some parts of the country, wiping out trillions more of savings. Millions of homeowners found that their mortgages exceeded the value of their homes, and defaults and foreclosures followed. This led to huge losses by banks and other lenders, which in turn led to bankruptcies, restructuring, and massive layoffs. Three years ago, there were many strong, old, and independent global investment banks. Today, all of those in the U.S. are gone—icons like Merrill Lynch and

Morgan Stanley have either gone bankrupt, sold out at rock bottom prices, or been forced to convert into regulated banks that are partially owned by the federal government.

The credit markets literally froze up. Banks needed to conserve their cash to meet withdrawals; hence they refused to make loans even to strong industrial and retail companies, or home and auto purchasers. This quickly led to a severe slowdown in non-financial businesses, accompanied by still more bankruptcies and layoffs. This happened all over the world, and the specter of a 1930s type depression was on the minds of central bankers and treasury officials worldwide. As a result, coordinated government rescue plans were put into operation in most developed nations. We don't know at this point what will happen next. The best bet is that a depression will be avoided but a bad recession will occur. Going forward, companies and individuals will recognize that an excessive use of debt was the root cause of the financial meltdown, hence there will be a smaller and more responsible use of debt in the future—at least until memories of 2008 fade.

How should the 2008 Crisis affect the contents of this textbook? Here is our conclusion:

- The fundamental concepts of finance are unchanged; hence all the concepts covered in the book are still applicable.
- The problems of 2008 resulted largely because businesses, individuals, and government officials did not pay sufficient attention to the basic principles of finance as covered in the book.
- Therefore, there is no reason to change most of the book.
- We should, however, use the 2008 experience to illustrate the basic points made in the book. For example, we talk about risk, and 2008 can and should be used to drive home how risk can be measured and dealt with.

The economic situation is fluid and dynamic. We may have a rapid recovery, which would be great, but, we might have a long, deep, and painful recession. We plan to use the Internet in the years ahead, while the book is in use, to update the situation on a chapter-by-chapter basis. As events related to the different chapters occur, we will provide updated vignettes and other information on the book' web site. We anticipate many important developments, hence a lot of updates. Still, the good news is that the basic, fundamental contents of the book will remain the same.

ORGANIZATION OF THE CHAPTERS: A VALUATION FOCUS

As we discuss in Chapter 1, in an enterprise system such as that of the United States, the primary goal of financial management is to help managers maximize their firms' values, subject to constraints such as not polluting the environment, not engaging in unfair labor practices, and not engaging in antitrust activities. Therefore, valuation underlies everything in *Fundamentals*. In Chapter 1, we discuss the concept of valuation, explain how it depends on future cash flows and risk, and show why value maximization is good for society in general. The valuation theme runs throughout the text.

Values are not established in a vacuum—stock and bond values are determined in the financial markets, so an understanding of those markets is essential to anyone involved with finance. Therefore, Chapter 2 covers the major types of financial markets, the returns that investors have historically earned, and the risks inherent in different types of securities. This information is important for anyone working in finance. It is also important for anyone who has or hopes to own financial assets.

Asset values depend in a fundamental way on earnings and cash flows as reported in the accounting statements. Therefore, we review those statements in Chapter 3. Then in Chapter 4, we show how accounting data can be analyzed and used to measure how well a company has operated in the past and how it is likely to perform in the future.

Chapter 5 covers the time value of money (TVM), perhaps the most fundamental concept in finance. The basic valuation model, which ties together cash flows, risk, and interest rates, is based on TVM concepts; and these concepts are used throughout the remainder of the book. Therefore, students should allocate plenty of time to Chapter 5.

Chapter 6 deals with interest rates, a key determinant of asset values. We discuss how interest rates are affected by risk, inflation, liquidity, the supply of and demand for capital in the economy, and the actions of the Federal Reserve.

The discussion of interest rates leads directly to bonds in Chapter 7 and stocks in Chapters 8 and 9. We show how stocks and bonds (and all other financial assets) are valued using the basic TVM model.

Chapters 1 through 9 provide background information that is essential to investors and corporate managers. These are "finance" topics, not "business" or "corporate finance" topics as those terms are commonly used. Thus, Chapters 1 through 9 discuss the concepts and models used to establish values, and we go on in Chapters 10 through 21 to discuss specific actions managers can take to maximize their firms' values.

As noted previously, most business students don't plan to specialize in finance, so they might not think the "business finance" chapters are relevant to them. This is not true, and in the later chapters, we show that all important business decisions involve all of a firm's departments—marketing, accounting, production, and so forth. Thus, while capital budgeting can be thought of as a financial decision, marketing people provide input on likely unit sales and sales prices, manufacturing people provide inputs on costs, and so forth. Moreover, capital budgeting decisions influence the size of the firm, its products, and its profits; and those factors affect all the firm's employees, from the CEO to the mail room staff.

STRUCTURAL CHANGES

We made two important structural changes in this new edition:

1. We moved the material on financial markets and institutions from Chapter 5 to Chapter 2. Markets and institutions follow naturally from Chapter 1, and this material provides useful background information for the remainder of the book.

2. We moved the time value of money (TVM) chapter from Chapter 2 to Chapter 5. Under the previous structure, we covered TVM concepts, then covered the accounting and financial markets chapters before applying TVM concepts to bond and stock valuation. We liked the idea of covering TVM early, but we concluded that it was pedagogically better to cover TVM concepts and then immediately focus on applications, as we do now.

These changes improve the flow of the text significantly—there is a much smoother transition from chapter to chapter in the first part of the book.

OTHER CHANGES

We made many other changes, but the following are the most significant:

1. *Editing*. We edit each new edition to improve clarity, but we did more in this edition than ever before. We put the entire text on digital files, which

facilitated shifting things around to improve transitions and flow. Students will find it easier to read the book than in the past.

2. *Beginning-of-Chapter Vignettes and Within-Chapter Boxes.* Many events have transpired in the financial markets during the past three years—for example, in 2008 credit markets tightened almost to the point of collapse, the housing and auto markets are in terrible shape, the major investment banks all failed or were forced to reorganize as regulated commercial banks, and the heads of a number of major corporations were fired. We use these events as the subjects of many vignettes and boxes, and they illustrate very well the points made in the chapters.

3. *Learning Objectives.* To help students see what we expect them to take away from the chapters, we added a set of learning objectives at the beginning of each chapter.

4. *Excel.* Spreadsheets, especially Excel, are becoming increasingly important in business; and students who are familiar with Excel have a significant advantage in the job market and later on the job. We used Excel in two ways. First, we worked all the in-text examples, end-of-chapter problems, and test bank problems with both Excel and a calculator, using the calculator to make sure the problem was workable with a calculator and using Excel to check for accuracy. Second, we used Excel to create many of the tables and graphs in the text, we displayed them as Excel pictures, and we have made available the models we used. Students do not need to know how to use Excel to go through the book, but if they are somewhat familiar with this software, they will see how many common financial problems can be set up and solved efficiently with Excel. Students who are not familiar with Excel may also be motivated to learn something about it.

5. *Tie-In between Self-Test Questions, End-of-Chapter Questions, and the Test Bank.* Because testing is important, we spent a great deal of time improving the test bank. Every question and problem was reviewed for clarity, accuracy, and consistency with the text. Also, we set up self-test questions at the end of each major section within the text to enable students to take real-time tests on their own before moving on. The end-of-chapter (EOC) questions and problems are similar to, but often go beyond, the self-test questions, and the test bank questions and problems are similar to the EOC materials. If students read the text, do the self-test questions as they go along, and then work a sampling of the EOC questions and problems, they should do well on exams drawn from the test bank.

6. *Accounting Statements and Free Cash Flow.* Most students in the basic finance course are familiar with balance sheets and income statements, but many don't understand the statement of cash flows and its relationship to free cash flows. Reviewers told us that in the last edition we tried to do too many things—such as present alternative ways to calculate free cash flow—and that we should delete some of those items and better explain what remained. We agreed, and this edition does a much better job in this regard.

7. *Cash Flows and Risk in Capital Budgeting.* In the last edition, the first two chapters on capital budgeting (Chapters 11 and 12) were not tied together very well. In that edition, we used relatively simple and straightforward illustrative projects in Chapter 11 but switched to entirely different and more complex projects in Chapter 12. For this edition, we rewrote Chapter 12, continuing with the Chapter 11 examples. We also reordered materials to present them in a more logical sequence. One reviewer stated that this chapter was the single biggest improvement in the twelfth edition.

8. *Financial Forecasting.* As we were rewriting Chapter 17, GE's chairman announced that he expected to report higher earnings shortly, but two weeks later he announced a significant earnings decline, which led to a sharp drop in

GE's stock price. We used this example to illustrate the importance of accurate forecasts and to liven up our discussion of strategic financial planning. In addition, we used an improved Excel model to streamline our illustrative forecast and to make the forecasting process simpler and clearer to students.

9. *Capital Budgeting.* We moved the analysis of projects with unequal lives back from Chapter 13 to Chapter 12 because unequal life analysis is more closely related to the other topics in Chapter 12. An additional benefit is that Chapter 13 is now more streamlined and focuses on real options.

10. *Derivatives.* We rearranged some of the sections to improve the discussion in Chapter 18. More specifically, we moved the "Using Derivatives to Reduce Risk" section so that it immediately follows the discussion of "Other Types of Derivatives." We also received feedback suggesting that we focused too much on call options. With that in mind, we added a new Appendix 18A entitled "Valuation of Put Options." Finally, we added some problems related to option pricing using the riskless hedge approach.

11. *Mergers.* We eliminated the discussion of purchase/pooling accounting treatment from Chapter 21 since all mergers are now accounted for as purchases. We also moved the discussion of merger regulation to a Web Appendix to help streamline the chapter.

We could continue to list changes in this edition, but these items provide instructors (particularly those familiar with the last edition) with a good idea of the kinds of revisions that were made to this text. It also lets students know how authors try to improve their texts.

ACKNOWLEDGMENTS

The book reflects the efforts of a great many people—those who worked on *Fundamentals* and our related books in the past and those who worked on this twelfth edition. First, we would like to thank Dana Aberwald Clark, who worked closely with us at every stage of the revision—her assistance was absolutely invaluable. Second, Susan Whitman provided great typing and logistical support.

Our colleagues Roy Crum, Jim Keys, Andy Naranjo, M. Nimalendran, Jay Ritter, Mike Ryngaert, Craig Tapley, and Carolyn Takeda gave us many useful suggestions regarding the ancillaries and many parts of the book, including the integrated cases. We also benefited from the work of Mike Ehrhardt and Phillip Daves of the University of Tennessee and Roy Crum of the University of Florida, who worked with us on companion books. Also, Christopher Buzzard did an outstanding job helping us develop the Excel models, the web site, and the PowerPoint® presentations.

Next, we would like to thank the following professors who reviewed this edition in detail and provided many useful comments and suggestions:

Rebecca Abraham—*Nova Southeastern University*
Kavous Ardalan—*Marist College*
Tom Arnold—*University of Richmond*
Deborah Bauer—*University of Oregon*
Gary Benesh—*Florida State University*
Mark S. Bettner—*Bucknell University*
Elizabeth Booth—*Michigan State University*
Brian Boscaljon—*Penn State University, Erie*
Rajesh Chakrabarti—*Georgia Institute of Technology*
Brent Dalrymple—*University of Central Florida*
Jim DeMello—*Western Michigan University*
Anne M. Drougas—*Dominican University*

Scott Ehrhorn—*Liberty University*
David Feller—*Brevard Community College*
Jennifer Foo—*Stetson University*
Partha Gangopadhyay—*St. Cloud State University*
Sharon H. Garrison—*University of Arizona*
Robert P. Hoffman—*College of St. Scholastica*
Benjamas Jirasakuldech—*University of the Pacific*
Ashok Kapoor—*Augsburg College*
Howard Keen—*Temple University*
Christopher J. Lambert, J.D.—*Fairmont State University*
Alice Lee—*San Francisco State University*
Denise Letterman—*Robert Morris University*
Yulong Ma—*California State University, Long Beach*
Barry Marchman—*Florida A&M*
Brian Maris—*Northern Arizona University*
Matthew Morey—*Pace University*
Tom C. Nelson—*Leeds School of Business, University of Colorado at Boulder*
Darshana Palkar—*Minnesota State University, Mankato*
Narendar V. Rao—*Northeastern Illinois University*
Charles R. Rayhorn—*Northern Michigan University*
Oliver Schnusenberg—*University of North Florida*
Dean S. Sommers—*University of Delaware*
Michal Spivey—*Clemson University*
Glenn L. Stevens—*Franklin & Marshall College*
Lowell E. Stockstill—*Wittenberg University*
Samantha Thapa—*Western Kentucky University*
David O. Vang—*University of St. Thomas*
Sheng Yang—*Black Hills State University*
David Zalewski—*Providence College*
Sijing Zong—*California State University—Stanislaus*

We would also like to thank the following professors, whose reviews and comments on our earlier books contributed to this edition:

Robert Adams	Charles Barngrover	Geof Booth	Alva Butcher
Mike Adler	Sam Basu	Waldo Born	Bill Campsey
Sharif Ahkam	Greg Bauer	Steven Bouchard	Bob Carlson
Syed Ahmad	Bill Beedles	Kenneth Boudreaux	Severin Carlson
Ed Altman	Brian Belt	Rick Boulware	David Cary
Bruce Anderson	Moshe Ben-Horim	Helen Bowers	Steve Celec
Ron Anderson	Bill Beranek	Oswald Bowlin	Mary Chaffin
Tom Anderson	Tom Berry	Don Boyd	Charles Chan
John Andrews	Will Bertin	G. Michael Boyd	Don Chance
Bob Angell	Scott Besley	Pat Boyer	Antony Chang
Vince Apilado	Dan Best	Joe Brandt	Susan Chaplinsky
Harvey Arbalaez	Roger Bey	Elizabeth Brannigan	K. C. Chen
Henry Arnold	Gilbert W. Bickum	Mary Broske	Jay Choi
Bob Aubey	Dalton Bigbee	Christopher Brown	S. K. Choudhary
Gil Babcock	John Bildersee	David T. Brown	Lal Chugh
Peter Bacon	Laurence E. Blose	Kate Brown	Maclyn Clouse
Kent Baker	Russ Boisjoly	Larry Brown	Bruce Collins
Robert Balik	Bob Boldin	Bill Brueggeman	Mitch Conover
Tom Bankston	Keith Boles	Paul Bursik	Margaret Considine
Babu Baradwaj	Michael Bond		Phil Cooley
Les Barenbaum			Joe Copeland

David Cordell
Marsha Cornett
M. P. Corrigan
John Cotner
Charles Cox
David Crary
John Crockett, Jr.
Bill Damon
Morris Danielson
Joel Dauten
Steve Dawson
Sankar De
Fred Dellva
Chad Denson
James
  Desreumaux
Bodie Dickerson
Bernard Dill
Gregg Dimkoff
Les Dlabay
Mark Dorfman
Tom Downs
Frank Draper
Gene Drzycimski
Dean Dudley
David Durst
Ed Dyl
Fred J. Ebeid
Daniel Ebels
Richard Edelman
Charles Edwards
U. Elike
John Ellis
George Engler
Suzanne Erickson
Dave Ewert
John Ezzell
L. Franklin Fant
Richard J. Fendler
Michael Ferri
Jim Filkins
John Finnerty
Robert Fiore
Susan Fischer
Peggy Fletcher
Steven Flint
Russ Fogler
Jennifer Frazier
Dan French
Michael
  Garlington
David Garraty
Jim Garven
Adam Gehr, Jr.
Jim Gentry

Wafica Ghoul
Erasmo
  Giambona
Armand Gilinsky,
  Jr.
Philip Glasgo
Rudyard Goode
Raymond
  Gorman
Walt Goulet
Bernie
  Grablowsky
Theoharry
  Grammatikos
Owen Gregory
Ed Grossnickle
John Groth
Alan Grunewald
Manak Gupta
Darryl Gurley
Sam Hadaway
Don Hakala
Gerald
  Hamsmith
William Hardin
John Harris
Paul Hastings
Bob Haugen
Steve Hawke
Stevenson
  Hawkey
Del Hawley
Eric M. Haye
Robert Hehre
Kath Henebry
David Heskel
George
  Hettenhouse
Hans Heymann
Kendall Hill
Roger Hill
Tom Hindelang
Linda Hittle
Ralph Hocking
J. Ronald
  Hoffmeister
Robert Hollinger
Jim Horrigan
John Houston
John Howe
Keith Howe
Steve Isberg
Jim Jackson
Keith Jakob
Vahan Janjigian

Narayanan
  Jayaraman
Zhenhn Jin
Kose John
Craig Johnson
Keith Johnson
Ramon Johnson
Steve Johnson
Ray Jones
Frank Jordan
Manuel Jose
Sally Joyner
Alfred Kahl
Gus Kalogeras
Rajiv Kalra
Ravi Kamath
John Kaminarides
Michael Keenan
Bill Kennedy
Peppi M. Kenny
Carol Kiefer
Joe Kiernan
Richard Kish
Robert Kleiman
Erich Knehans
Don Knight
Ladd Kochman
Dorothy Koehl
Jaroslaw
  Komarynsky
Duncan Kretovich
Harold Krogh
Charles Kroncke
Don Kummer
Robert A. Kunkel
Reinhold Lamb
Joan Lamm
Larry Lang
David Lange
P. Lange
Howard Lanser
Edward Lawrence
Martin Lawrence
Wayne Lee
Jim LePage
David E.
  LeTourneau
Jules Levine
John Lewis
Jason Lin
Chuck Linke
Bill Lloyd
Susan Long
Judy Maese
Bob Magee

Ileen Malitz
Bob Malko
Phil Malone
Abbas
  Mamoozadeh
Terry Maness
Chris Manning
Surendra
  Mansinghka
Timothy Manuel
Terry Martell
David Martin
D. J. Masson
John Mathys
Ralph May
John McAlhany
Andy
  McCollough
Ambrose McCoy
Thomas McCue
Bill McDaniel
John McDowell
Charles
  McKinney
Robyn
  McLaughlin
James McNulty
Jeanette
  Medewitz-
  Diamond
Jamshid Mehran
Larry Merville
Rick Meyer
Jim Millar
Ed Miller
John Miller
John Mitchell
Carol Moerdyk
Bob Moore
Scott Moore
Barry Morris
Gene Morris
Dianne R.
  Morrison
Chris Muscarella
David Nachman
Tim Nantell
Don Nast
Edward Nelling
Bill Nelson
Bob Nelson
William Nelson
Bob Niendorf
Bruce Niendorf
Ben Nonnally, Jr.

Tom O'Brien
William O'Connell
Dennis O'Connor
John O'Donnell
Jim Olsen
Robert Olsen
Dean Olson
Jim Pappas
Stephen Parrish
Helen Pawlowski
Barron Peake
Michael Pescow
Glenn Petry
Jim Pettijohn
Rich Pettit
Dick Pettway
Aaron Phillips
Hugo Phillips
H. R. Pickett
John Pinkerton
Gerald Pogue
Eugene Poindexter
R. Potter
Franklin Potts
R. Powell
Dianna Preece
Chris Prestopino
John Primus
Jerry Prock
Howard Puckett
Herbert Quigley
George Racette
Bob Radcliffe
David Rakowski
Allen Rappaport
Bill Rentz
Ken Riener
Charles Rini
John Ritchie

Bill Rives
Pietra Rivoli
Antonio Rodriguez
James Rosenfeld
Stuart Rosenstein
E. N. Roussakis
Dexter Rowell
Arlyn R. Rubash
Marjorie Rubash
Bob Ryan
Jim Sachlis
Abdul Sadik
Travis Sapp
Thomas Scampini
Kevin Scanlon
Frederick Schadeler
Patricia L. Schaeff
David Schalow
Mary Jane Scheuer
David Schirm
Robert Schwebach
Carol Schweser
John Settle
Alan Severn
James Sfiridis
Sol Shalit
Frederic Shipley
Dilip Shome
Ron Shrieves
Neil Sicherman
J. B. Silvers
Clay Singleton
Joe Sinkey
Stacy Sirmans
Jaye Smith
Patricia Smith

Patricia Matisz Smith
Don Sorensen
David Speairs
Ken Stanley
Kenneth Stanton
Ed Stendardi
Alan Stephens
Don Stevens
Jerry Stevens
Glen Strasburg
David Suk
Katherine Sullivan
Timothy Sullivan
Philip Swensen
Bruce Swenson
Ernest Swift
Paul Swink
Eugene Swinnerton
Gary Tallman
Dular Talukdar
Dennis Tanner
Russ Taussig
John Teall
Richard Teweles
Ted Teweles
Madeline Thimmes
Francis D. Thomas
Andrew Thompson
John Thompson
Arlene Thurman
Dogan Tirtirogu
Janet Todd
Holland J. Toles
William Tozer
Emery Trahan

George Trivoli
George Tsetsekos
David Upton
Howard Van Auken
Pretorious Van den Dool
Pieter Vandenberg
Paul Vanderheiden
JoAnn Vaughan
Jim Verbrugge
Patrick Vincent
Steve Vinson
Susan Visscher
John Wachowicz
Joe Walker
Mike Walker
Sam Weaver
Marsha Weber
Al Webster
Shelton Weeks
Kuo-Chiang Wei
Bill Welch
Fred Weston
Richard Whiston
Norm Williams
Tony Wingler
Ed Wolfe
Criss Woodruff
Don Woods
Yangru Wu
Robert Wyatt
Steve Wyatt
Michael Yonan
John Zietlow
Dennis Zocco
Kent Zumwalt

Special thanks are due to Chris Barry, Texas Christian University, and Shirley Love, Idaho State University, who wrote many of the boxes relating to small-business issues that are on the Web; to Emery Trahan and Paul Bolster, Northeastern University, who developed and wrote the summaries and questions for NewsWire; to Dilip Shome, Virginia Polytechnic Institute, who helped greatly with the capital structure chapter; to Dave Brown and Mike Ryngaert, University of Florida, who helped us with the bankruptcy and merger material; to Roy Crum, Andy Naranjo, and Subu Venkataraman, who worked with us on the international materials; to Scott Below, East Carolina University, who developed the web site information and references; to Laurie and Stan Eakins of East Carolina, who developed the materials on Excel for the *Technology Supplement*; and to Larry Wolken, Texas A&M University, who offered his hard work and advice for the development of the *Lecture Presentation Software*. Finally, the Cengage and LEAP

Publishing staffs, especially Mike Guendelsberger, Erin Shelton, Jennifer Ziegler, Scott Fidler, Mike Reynolds, Mike Roche, Adele Scholtz, Suellen Ruttkay, and Alex von Rosenberg, helped greatly with all phases of the textbook's development and production.

ERRORS IN THE TEXTBOOK

At this point, most authors make a statement such as this: "We appreciate all the help we received from the people listed above; but any remaining errors are, of course, our own responsibility." And generally there are more than enough remaining errors! Having experienced difficulties with errors ourselves, both as students and instructors, we resolved to avoid this problem in *Fundamentals*. As a result of our detection procedures, we are convinced that few errors remain, but primarily because we want to detect any errors that may have slipped by so that we can correct them in subsequent printings, we decided to offer a reward of $10 per error to the first person who reports it to us. For purpose of this reward, errors are defined as misspelled words, nonrounding numerical errors, incorrect statements, and any other error that inhibits comprehension. Typesetting problems such as irregular spacing and differences of opinion regarding grammatical or punctuation conventions do not qualify for this reward. Given the ever-changing nature of the World Wide Web, changes in web addresses also do not qualify as errors, although we would like to learn about them. Finally, any qualifying error that has follow-through effects is counted as two errors only. Please report any errors to Joel Houston through e-mail at **fundamentals@joelhouston.com** or by regular mail at the address below.

CONCLUSION

Finance is, in a real sense, the cornerstone of the enterprise system—good financial management is vitally important to the economic health of all firms and hence to the nation and the world. Because of its importance, finance should be widely and thoroughly understood, but this is easier said than done. The field is complex, and it undergoes constant change due to shifts in economic conditions. All of this makes finance stimulating and exciting, but challenging and sometimes perplexing. We sincerely hope that this twelfth edition of *Fundamentals* will meet its own challenge by contributing to a better understanding of our financial system.

EUGENE F. BRIGHAM
JOEL F. HOUSTON
4723 N.W. 53rd Ave., Suite A
Gainesville, Florida 32653

fundamentals@joelhouston.com

September 2008

BRIEF CONTENTS

Appendixes

CONTENTS

PART 5

Capital Structure and Dividend Policy 415

PART 7

Special Topics in Financial Management 551

PART 1

INTRODUCTION TO FINANCIAL MANAGEMENT

An Overview of Financial Management

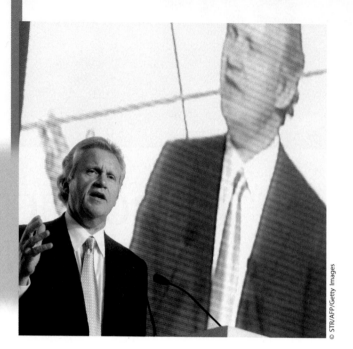

CHAPTER 1

An Overview of Financial Management

Striking the Right Balance

In 1776, Adam Smith described how an "invisible hand" guides companies as they strive for profits; and that hand leads them to decisions that benefit society. Smith's insights led him to conclude that profit maximization is the right goal for a business and that the free enterprise system is best for society. But the world has changed since 1776. Firms today are much larger, they operate globally, they have thousands of employees, and they are owned by millions of stockholders. This makes us wonder if the "invisible hand" still provides reliable guidance. Should companies still try to maximize profits; or should they take a broader view and take more balanced actions designed to benefit customers, employees, suppliers, and society as a whole?

Most academics today subscribe to the following modified version of Adam Smith's theory:

- *A firm's principal goal should be to maximize the wealth of its stockholders, which means maximizing the value of its stock.*

- *Free enterprise is still the best economic system for the country as a whole.*
- *However, some constraints are needed—firms should not be allowed to pollute the air and water, engage in unfair employment practices, or create monopolies that exploit consumers.*

Profits depend on sales; and sales require that firms develop desirable products and services, produce them efficiently, and sell them at competitive prices, all of which benefit society. So the view today is that management should try to maximize stock prices, but their actions should be subject to government-imposed constraints.

Still, some argue that the constrained maximization theory is inadequate. For example, GE Chief Executive Officer (CEO) Jeffrey Immelt believes that just obeying the law is not enough. GE is the world's most valuable company, and it has an excellent reputation.[1] Immelt argues that value and reputation go hand in hand and that

---

[1] Marc Gunther, "Money and Morals at GE," *Fortune*, November 15, 2004, pp. 176–182.

having a good reputation with customers, suppliers, employees, and regulators is essential if value is to be maximized. According to Immelt, "The reason people come to work for GE is that they want to be part of something bigger than themselves. They want to work hard, win promotions, and be well compensated, but they also want to work for a company that makes a difference, a company that's doing great things in the world. . . . It's up to GE to be a good citizen. Not only is that a nice thing to do, it's good for business and thus the price of our stock."

GE is by no means alone. An increasing number of companies see their mission as more than just making money for their shareholders. Google Inc.'s well-known corporate motto is "Don't Be Evil." Taking things a step further, the company recently announced that it was setting aside another $30 million to be used for philanthropic ventures worldwide. The company's in-house foundation now has assets in excess of $2 billion. Days later Microsoft Corporation's chairperson, Bill Gates, gave a speech to the World Economic Forum in which he made the case for a "creative capitalism." Gates stated that, "Such a system would have a twin mission: making profits and also improving lives for those who don't fully benefit from market forces."

Gates has certainly been true to his word. In 2000, he and his wife established the Bill & Melinda Gates Foundation. Today the fund has assets totaling $37.6 billion. It received a notable boost in 2006 when famed investor Warren Buffett announced that he would donate a huge share of his fortune to the Foundation. To date, Buffett has contributed more than $3 billion; and over time, he is scheduled to contribute additional shares of stock that are now worth in excess of $40 million. These efforts show that while there is more to life than money, it often takes money to do good things.

Sources: Patricia Sellers, "Melinda Gates Goes Public," CNNMoney.com, January 7, 2008; Kevin J. Delaney, "Google: From 'Don't Be Evil' to How to Do Good," *The Wall Street Journal,* January 18, 2008, p. B1; and Robert A. Guth, "Bill Gates Issues Call for Kinder Capitalism," *The Wall Street Journal,* January 24, 2008, p. A1.

PUTTING THINGS IN PERSPECTIVE

This chapter will give you an idea of what financial management is all about. We begin the chapter by describing how finance is related to the overall business and by discussing the different forms of business organization. For corporations, management's goal should be to maximize shareholder wealth, which means maximizing the value of the stock. When we say "maximizing the value of the stock," we mean the "true, long-run value," which may be different from the current stock price. Good managers understand the importance of ethics, and they recognize that maximizing long-run value is consistent with being socially responsible. We conclude the chapter by discussing how firms must provide the right incentives if they are to get managers to focus on long-run value maximization. When you finish this chapter, you should be able to:

- Explain the role of finance and the different types of jobs in finance.
- Identify the advantages and disadvantages of different forms of business organization.
- Explain the links between stock price, intrinsic value, and executive compensation.
- Discuss the importance of business ethics and the consequences of unethical behavior.
- Identify the potential conflicts that arise within the firm between stockholders and managers and between stockholders and bondholders and discuss the techniques that firms can use to mitigate these potential conflicts.

1-1 WHAT IS FINANCE?

It's hard to define *finance*—the term has many facets, which makes it difficult to provide a clear and concise definition. The discussion in this section will give you an idea of what finance people do and what you might do if you enter the finance field after you graduate.

1-1a Finance versus Economics and Accounting

Finance as we know it today grew out of economics and accounting. Economists developed the notion that an asset's value is based on the future cash flows the asset will provide, and accountants provided information regarding the likely size of those cash flows. Finance then grew out of and lies between economics and accounting, so people who work in finance need knowledge of those two fields. Also, as discussed next, in the modern corporation, the accounting department falls under the control of the chief financial officer (CFO).

1-1b Finance within an Organization

Most businesses and not-for-profit organizations have an organization chart similar to the one shown in Figure 1-1.

The board of directors is the top governing body, and the chairperson of the board is generally the highest-ranking individual. The CEO comes next, but note that the chairperson of the board often serves as the CEO as well. Below the CEO comes the chief operating officer (COO), who is often also designated as a firm's president. The COO directs the firm's operations, which include marketing, manufacturing, sales, and other operating departments. The CFO, who is generally a senior vice president and the third ranking officer, is in charge of accounting,

---

FIGURE 1-1 Finance within an Organization

financing, credit policy, decisions regarding asset acquisitions, and investor relations, which involves communications with stockholders and the press.

If the firm is publicly owned, the CEO and the CFO must both certify to the Securities and Exchange Commission (SEC) that reports released to stockholders, and especially the annual report, are accurate. If inaccuracies later emerge, the CEO and the CFO could be fined or even jailed. This requirement was instituted in 2002 as a part of the **Sarbanes-Oxley Act**. The Act was passed by Congress in the wake of a series of corporate scandals involving now-defunct companies such as Enron and WorldCom, where investors, workers, and suppliers lost billions of dollars due to false information released by those companies.

Sarbanes-Oxley Act
A law passed by Congress that requires the CEO and CFO to certify that their firm's financial statements are accurate.

1-1c Corporate Finance, Capital Markets, and Investments

Finance as taught in universities is generally divided into three areas: (1) financial management, (2) capital markets, and (3) investments.

Financial management, also called corporate finance, focuses on decisions relating to how much and what types of assets to acquire, how to raise the capital needed to buy assets, and how to run the firm so as to maximize its value. The same principles apply to both for-profit and not-for-profit organizations; and as the title suggests, much of this book is concerned with financial management.

Capital markets relate to the markets where interest rates, along with stock and bond prices, are determined. Also studied here are the financial institutions that supply capital to businesses. Banks, investment banks, stockbrokers, mutual funds, insurance companies, and the like bring together "savers" who have money to invest and businesses, individuals, and other entities that need capital for various purposes. Governmental organizations such as the Federal Reserve System, which regulates banks and controls the supply of money, and the SEC, which regulates the trading of stocks and bonds in public markets, are also studied as part of capital markets.

Investments relate to decisions concerning stocks and bonds and include a number of activities: (1) *Security analysis* deals with finding the proper values of individual securities (i.e., stocks and bonds). (2) *Portfolio theory* deals with the best way to structure portfolios, or "baskets," of stocks and bonds. Rational investors want to hold diversified portfolios in order to limit risks, so choosing a properly balanced portfolio is an important issue for any investor. (3) *Market analysis* deals with the issue of whether stock and bond markets at any given time are "too high," "too low," or "about right." *Behavioral finance,* where investor psychology is examined in an effort to determine if stock prices have been bid up to unreasonable heights in a speculative bubble or driven down to unreasonable lows in a fit of irrational pessimism, is a part of market analysis.

Although we separate these three areas, they are closely interconnected. Banking is studied under capital markets, but a bank lending officer evaluating a business' loan request must understand corporate finance to make a sound decision. Similarly, a corporate treasurer negotiating with a banker must understand banking if the treasurer is to borrow on "reasonable" terms. Moreover, a security analyst trying to determine a stock's true value must understand corporate finance and capital markets to do his or her job. In addition, financial decisions of all types depend on the level of interest rates; so all people in corporate finance, investments, and banking must know something about interest rates and the way they are determined. Because of these interdependencies, we cover all three areas in this book.

What is the relationship between economics, finance, and accounting?

Who is the CFO, where does this individual fit into the corporate hierarchy, and what are some of his or her responsibilities?

Does it make sense for not-for-profit organizations such as hospitals and universities to have CFOs?

What three areas of finance does this book cover? Are these areas independent of one another, or are they interrelated in the sense that someone working in one area should know something about each of the other areas?

1-2 JOBS IN FINANCE

*To find information about different finance careers, go to **www.careers-in-finance. com**. This web site provides information about different finance areas and recommends different books about jobs in finance.*

Next to health care, jobs in finance have been growing faster than any other area. Finance prepares students for jobs in banking, investments, insurance, corporations, and the government. Accounting students need to know finance, marketing, management, and human resources; they also need to understand finance, for it affects decisions in all those areas. For example, marketing people propose advertising programs, but those programs are examined by finance people to judge the effects of the advertising on the firm's profitability. So to be effective in marketing, one needs to have a basic knowledge of finance. The same holds for management—indeed, most important management decisions are evaluated in terms of their effects on the firm's value. This is called value-based management, and it is the "in" thing today.

It is also worth noting that finance is important to individuals regardless of their jobs. Some years ago most businesses provided pensions to their employees, so managing one's personal investments was not critically important. That's no longer true. Most firms today provide what's called "defined contribution" pension plans, where each year the company puts a specified amount of money into an account that belongs to the employee. The employee must decide how those funds are to be invested—how much should be divided among stocks, bonds, or money funds and how risky the stocks and bonds should be. These decisions have a major effect on people's lives, and the concepts covered in this book can improve decision-making skills.

1-3 FORMS OF BUSINESS ORGANIZATION

The basics of financial management are the same for all businesses, large or small, regardless of how they are organized. Still, a firm's legal structure affects its operations and thus should be recognized. There are four main forms of business organizations: (1) sole proprietorships, (2) partnerships, (3) corporations, and (4) limited liability companies (LLCs) and limited liability partnerships (LLPs). In terms of numbers, most businesses are sole proprietorships. However, based on the dollar value of sales, about 80% of all business is done by corporations. Because corporations conduct the most business and because most successful businesses eventually convert to corporations, we concentrate on them in this book. Still, it is important to understand the legal differences between firms.

Proprietorship
An unincorporated business owned by one individual.

A **proprietorship** is an unincorporated business owned by one individual. Going into business as a sole proprietor is easy—a person begins business operations. Proprietorships have three important advantages: (1) They are easily and inexpensively formed, (2) they are subject to few government regulations, and

(3) they are subject to lower income taxes than are corporations. However, proprietorships also have three important limitations: (1) Proprietors have unlimited personal liability for the business's debts, so they can lose more than the amount of money they invested in the company. You might invest $10,000 to start a business but be sued for $1 million if, during company time, one of your employees runs over someone with a car. (2) The life of the business is limited to the life of the individual who created it; and to bring in new equity, investors require a change in the structure of the business. (3) Because of the first two points, proprietorships have difficulty obtaining large sums of capital; hence, proprietorships are used primarily for small businesses. However, businesses are frequently started as proprietorships and then converted to corporations when their growth results in the disadvantages outweighing their advantages.

A **partnership** is a legal arrangement between two or more people who decide to do business together. Partnerships are similar to proprietorships in that they can be established relatively easily and inexpensively. Moreover, the firm's income is allocated on a pro rata basis to the partners and is taxed on an individual basis. This allows the firm to avoid the corporate income tax. However, all of the partners are generally subject to unlimited personal liability, which means that if a partnership goes bankrupt and any partner is unable to meet his or her pro rata share of the firm's liabilities, the remaining partners will be responsible for making good on the unsatisfied claims. Thus, the actions of a Texas partner can bring ruin to a millionaire New York partner who had nothing to do with the actions that led to the downfall of the company. Unlimited liability makes it difficult for partnerships to raise large amounts of capital.[2]

A **corporation** is a legal entity created by a state, and it is separate and distinct from its owners and managers. It is this separation that limits stockholders' losses to the amount they invested in the firm—the corporation can lose all of its money, but its owners can lose only the funds that they invested in the company. Corporations also have unlimited lives, and it is easier to transfer shares of stock in a corporation than one's interest in an unincorporated business. These factors make it much easier for corporations to raise the capital necessary to operate large businesses. Thus, companies such as Hewlett-Packard and Microsoft generally begin as proprietorships or partnerships, but at some point they find it advantageous to become a corporation.

A major drawback to corporations is taxes. Most corporations' earnings are subject to double taxation—the corporation's earnings are taxed; and then when its after-tax earnings are paid out as dividends, those earnings are taxed again as personal income to the stockholders. However, as an aid to small businesses, Congress created **S corporations**, which are taxed as if they were partnerships; thus, they are exempt from the corporate income tax. To qualify for S corporation status, a firm can have no more than 75 stockholders, which limits their use to relatively small, privately owned firms. Larger corporations are known as C corporations. The vast majority of small corporations elect S status and retain that status until they decide to sell stock to the public, at which time they become C corporations.

A **limited liability company (LLC)** is a relatively new type of organization that is a hybrid between a partnership and a corporation. A **limited liability partnership (LLP)** is similar to an LLC; but LLPs are used for professional firms in

Partnership
An unincorporated business owned by two or more persons.

Corporation
A legal entity created by a state, separate and distinct from its owners and managers, having unlimited life, easy transferability of ownership, and limited liability.

S Corporation
A special designation that allows small businesses that meet qualifications to be taxed as if they were a proprietorship or a partnership rather than a corporation.

Limited Liability Company (LLC)
A relatively new type of organization that is a hybrid between a partnership and a corporation.

Limited Liability Partnership (LLP)
Similar to an LLC but used for professional firms in the fields of accounting, law, and architecture. It has limited liability like corporations but is taxed like partnerships.

---

[2]Originally, there were just "plain vanilla" partnerships; but over the years, lawyers have created a number of variations. We leave the variations to courses on business law, but we note that the variations are generally designed to limit the liabilities of some of the partners. For example, a "limited partnership" has a general partner, who has unlimited liability, and one or more limited partners, whose liability is limited to the amount of their investment. This sounds great from the standpoint of limited liability; but the limited partners must cede sole control to the general partner, which means that they have almost no say in the way the firm is managed. With a corporation, the owners (stockholders) have limited liability, but they also have the right to vote and thus change management if they think that a change is in order. Note too that LLCs and LLPs, discussed later in this section, are increasingly used in lieu of partnerships.

the fields of accounting, law, and architecture, while LLCs are used by other businesses. Both LLCs and LLPs have limited liability like corporations but are taxed like partnerships. Further, unlike limited partnerships, where the general partner has full control of the business, the investors in an LLC or LLP have votes in proportion to their ownership interest. LLCs and LLPs have been gaining in popularity in recent years, but large companies still find it advantageous to be C corporations because of the advantages in raising capital to support growth. LLCs/LLPs were dreamed up by lawyers, and it is necessary to hire a good lawyer when establishing one.[3]

When deciding on its form of organization, a firm must trade off the advantages of incorporation against a possibly higher tax burden. However, for the following reasons, the value of any business other than a relatively small one will probably be maximized if it is organized as a corporation:

1. Limited liability reduces the risks borne by investors; and other things held constant, the lower the firm's risk, the higher its value.

2. A firm's value is dependent on its growth opportunities, which are dependent on its ability to attract capital. Because corporations can attract capital more easily than other types of businesses, they are better able to take advantage of growth opportunities.

3. The value of an asset also depends on its liquidity, which means the time and effort it takes to sell the asset for cash at a fair market value. Because the stock of a corporation is easier to transfer to a potential buyer than is an interest in a proprietorship or partnership and because more investors are willing to invest in stocks than in partnerships (with their potential unlimited liability), a corporate investment is relatively liquid. This too enhances the value of a corporation.

SELF TEST

What are the key differences between proprietorships, partnerships, and corporations?

How are LLCs and LLPs related to the other forms of organization?

What is an S corporation, and what is its advantage over a C corporation? Why don't firms such as IBM, GE, and Microsoft choose S corporation status?

What are some reasons the value of a business other than a small one is generally maximized when it is organized as a corporation?

Suppose you are relatively wealthy and are looking for a potential investment. You do not plan to be active in the business. Would you be more interested in investing in a partnership or in a corporation? Why or why not?

1-4 STOCK PRICES AND SHAREHOLDER VALUE

The primary goal of a corporation should be to maximize its owners' value, but a proprietor's goal might be quite different. Consider Larry Jackson, the proprietor of a local sporting goods store. Jackson is in business to make money, but he likes to take time off to play golf on Fridays. He also has a few employees who are no longer very productive, but he keeps them on the payroll out of friendship and loyalty. Jackson is running the business in a way that is consistent with his own

---

[3]LLCs and LLPs are relatively complicated structures, and what they can do and how they must be set up varies by state. Moreover, they are still evolving. If you are interested in learning more about them, we recommend that you go to Google (or another search engine), enter *LLC* or *LLP*, and see the many references that are available.

personal goals. He knows that he could make more money if he didn't play golf or if he replaced some of his employees. But he is comfortable with his choices; and since it is his business, he is free to make those choices.

By contrast, Linda Smith is CEO of a large corporation. Smith manages the company; but most of the stock is owned by shareholders who purchased it because they were looking for an investment that would help them retire, send their children to college, pay for a long-anticipated trip, and so forth. The shareholders elected a board of directors, which then selected Smith to run the company. Smith and the firm's other managers are working on behalf of the shareholders, and they were hired to pursue policies that enhance shareholder value. At the same time, the managers know that this does not mean maximize shareholder value "at all costs." Managers have an obligation to behave ethically, and they must follow the laws and other society-imposed constraints that we discussed in the opening vignette to this chapter. Throughout this book, we focus primarily on publicly owned companies; hence, we operate on the assumption that management's primary goal is **shareholder wealth maximization**. That translates into this rule:

> *A manager should try to maximize the price of the firm's stock, subject to the constraints discussed in the opening vignette.*

If a manager is to maximize shareholder wealth, he or she must know how that wealth is determined. Essentially, shareholder wealth is the number of shares outstanding times the market price per share. For example, if you own 100 shares of GE's stock and the price is $40 per share, your wealth in GE is $4,000. The wealth of all of GE's stockholders can be summed; and that is the value of the firm's stock, the item that management should maximize. The number of shares outstanding is a given, so what really determines shareholder wealth is the price of the stock.

Throughout this book, we will see that the value of any asset is the present value of the stream of cash flows the asset provides to its owners. We discuss stock valuation in depth in Chapter 9, where we will see that a stock's price at any given time depends on the cash flows a "marginal" investor expects to receive after buying the stock. To illustrate, suppose investors are aware that GE earned $2.20 per share in 2007 and paid out 52% of that amount, or $1.15 per share, in dividends. Suppose further that most investors expect earnings, dividends, and the stock price to increase by about 6% per year. It might turn out that these expectations are met exactly. However, management might make a prudent decision that causes profits to rise at a 12% rate, causing the stock price to jump from $40 to $60 per share. Of course, management might make a big mistake, profits might suffer, and the stock price might decline to $20. Thus, investors are exposed to risk when they buy GE stock or any other company's stock. If, instead, the investor bought a U.S. Treasury bond, he or she would receive a guaranteed interest payment every 6 months plus the bond's par value when it matures; so his or her risk would be minimal.

We see then that if GE's management makes good decisions, its stock price will increase; however, if its managers make bad decisions, the stock price will decrease. *Management's goal should be to make decisions designed to maximize the stock's price.* Note, though, that factors beyond management's control also affect stock prices. Thus, after the 9/11 terrorist attacks on the World Trade Center, the price of most stocks fell no matter how effective their management may have been.

Firms have a number of different departments, including marketing, accounting, production, human resources, and finance. The finance department's principal task is to evaluate proposed decisions and judge how they will affect the stock price and thus shareholder wealth. For example, suppose the production manager wants to replace some old equipment with new automated machinery that will reduce labor costs. The finance staff will evaluate that proposal and determine whether the savings seem to be worth the cost. Similarly, if marketing wants to sign a contract with Tiger Woods that will cost $10 million per year for

Shareholder Wealth Maximization
The primary goal for managers of publicly owned companies implies that decisions should be made to maximize the long-run value of the firm's common stock.

5 years, the financial staff will evaluate the proposal, look at the probable increase in sales, and reach a conclusion as to whether signing Tiger will lead to a higher stock price. Most significant decisions are evaluated in terms of their financial consequences.

Note too that stock prices change over time as conditions change and as investors obtain new information about a company's prospects. For example, Apple Computer's stock ranged from $77 to $193 per share during a recent 12-month period, rising and falling as good and bad news was released. Wal-Mart, which is in a more stable industry, had a narrower price range—from $42 to $52. Investors can predict future results for Wal-Mart more accurately than for Apple; thus, Wal-Mart is thought to be less risky. Also, some projects are relatively straightforward and easy to evaluate and, hence, not very risky. For example, if Wal-Mart were considering a proposed new store, the revenues, costs, and profits for this project would be easier to estimate than for an Apple project related to a new voice-activated computer. The success or lack thereof of projects such as these determine the stock prices of Wal-Mart, Apple, and other companies.

SELF TEST

What is management's primary goal?

What do investors expect to receive when they buy a share of stock? Do investors know for sure how much they will receive? Explain.

Based just on the name, which company would you expect to be riskier—General Foods or South Seas Oil Exploration? Explain.

When Boeing decides to invest $5 billion in a new jet airliner, are its managers certain of the project's effects on Boeing's future profits and stock price? Explain.

Who would be better able to judge the effect of a new airliner on Boeing's profits—its managers or its stockholders? Explain.

Would all Boeing stockholders expect the same outcome from a given new project, and how would those expectations affect the stock's price? Explain.

1-5 INTRINSIC VALUES, STOCK PRICES, AND EXECUTIVE COMPENSATION

As noted in the preceding section, stock prices are based on cash flows expected in future years, not just in the current year. Thus, stock price maximization requires us to take a long-run view of operations. Academics have generally assumed that managers adhere to this long-run focus, but it is now clear that the focus for many companies shifted to the short run in recent years. To give managers an incentive to focus on stock prices, stockholders (acting through boards of directors) awarded executives stock options that could be exercised on a specified future date. An executive could exercise the option on that date, receive stock, immediately sell it, and earn a profit. The profit was based on the stock price on the option exercise date, which led some managers to try to maximize the stock price on that specific date, not over the long run. That, in turn, led to some horrible abuses. Projects that looked good from a long-run perspective were turned down because they would penalize profits in the short run and thus lower the stock price on the option exercise day. Even worse, some managers deliberately overstated profits, temporarily boosted the stock price, exercised their options, sold the inflated stock, and left outside stockholders "holding the bag" when the true situation was revealed. Enron and WorldCom are examples of companies whose managers did this, but there were many others.

Other companies have also used aggressive but legal accounting practices that boosted current profits but lowered profits in future years. For example, knowing that an asset would be usable for only 5 years, management might depreciate it over a 10-year life. This reduces reported costs—and raises reported income—for the next 5 years but raises costs and lowers income during the following 5 years. Many other legal but questionable accounting procedures have been used, all in an effort to boost reported profits and the stock price on the option exercise day. Obviously, all this can make it difficult for investors to decide how much a stock is really worth, and it helps explain why a firm's reputation is an important determinant of its stock price.

Fortunately, most executives are honest. But even for honest companies, it is hard for investors to determine the proper price of a stock. Figure 1-2 illustrates the situation. The top box indicates that managerial actions, combined with the economy, taxes, and political conditions, determine stock prices and thus investors' returns. Remember that no one knows for sure what those future returns will be—we can estimate them, but expected and realized returns are often quite different. Investors like high returns, but they dislike risk; so the larger the expected profits and the lower the perceived risk, the higher the stock's price.

The second row of boxes differentiates what we call "true expected returns" and "true risk" from "perceived" returns and "perceived" risk. By "true," we mean the returns and risk that investors would expect if they had all of the information that existed about a company. "Perceived" means what investors expect, given the limited information they actually have. To illustrate, in early 2001, investors had information that caused them to think that Enron was highly profitable and would enjoy high and rising future profits. They also thought that actual results would be close to the expected levels and hence, that Enron's risk was low. However, true estimates of Enron's profits, which were known by its executives but not the investing public, were much lower; and Enron's true situation was extremely risky.

FIGURE 1-2   Determinants of Intrinsic Values and Stock Prices

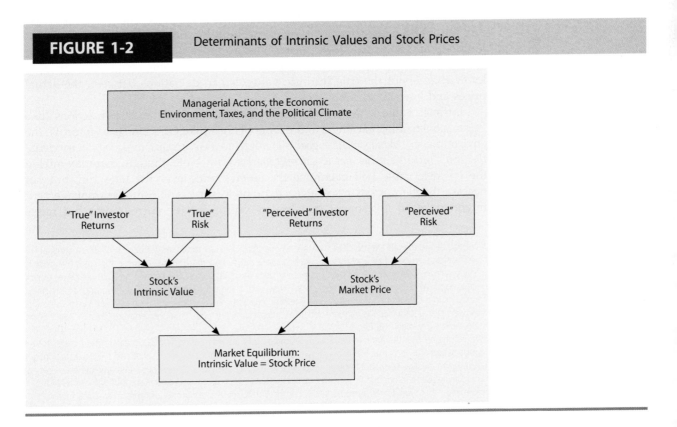

Intrinsic Value
An estimate of a stock's "true" value based on accurate risk and return data. The intrinsic value can be estimated but not measured precisely.

Market Price
The stock value based on perceived but possibly incorrect information as seen by the marginal investor.

Marginal Investor
An investor whose views determine the actual stock price.

Equilibrium
The situation in which the actual market price equals the intrinsic value, so investors are indifferent between buying or selling a stock.

The third row of boxes shows that each stock has an **intrinsic value**, which is an estimate of the stock's "true" value as calculated by a competent analyst who has the best available risk and return data, and a **market price**, which is the actual market price based on perceived but possibly incorrect information as seen by the **marginal investor**.[4] Not all investors agree, so it is the "marginal" investor who determines the actual price. For example, investors at the margin might expect a firm to pay a $1.00 dividend with a 5% growth rate thereafter; and on that basis, they might set the firm's stock price at $45 per share. However, if they had all of the available facts, they might conclude that the dividend would be $1.30 with a 7% growth rate, which would lead to a price of $50 per share. In this case, the actual market price would be $45 versus an intrinsic value of $50.

When a stock's actual market price is equal to its intrinsic value, the stock is in **equilibrium**, which is shown in the bottom box in Figure 1-2; and when equilibrium exists, there is no pressure for a change in the stock's price. Market prices can and do differ from intrinsic values; but eventually, as the future unfolds, the two values tend to converge.

Actual stock prices are easy to determine—they can be found on the Internet and are published in newspapers every day. However, intrinsic values are estimates; and different analysts with different data and different views about the future form different estimates of a stock's intrinsic value. *Indeed, estimating intrinsic values is what security analysis is all about and is what distinguishes successful from unsuccessful investors.* Investing would be easy, profitable, and essentially riskless if we knew all stocks' intrinsic values; but, of course, we don't. We can estimate intrinsic values, but we can't be sure that we are right. A firm's managers have the best information about the firm's future prospects, so managers' estimates of intrinsic values are generally better than those of outside investors. However, even managers can be wrong.

Figure 1-3 graphs a hypothetical company's actual price and intrinsic value as estimated by its management over time.[5] The intrinsic value rises because the firm retains and reinvests earnings each year, which tends to increase profits. The value jumped dramatically in 2003, when a research and development (R&D) breakthrough raised management's estimate of future profits before investors had this information. The actual stock price tended to move up and down with the estimated intrinsic value; but investor optimism and pessimism, along with imperfect knowledge about the true intrinsic value, led to deviations between the actual prices and intrinsic values.

Intrinsic value is a long-run concept. It reflects both improper actions (like Enron's overstating earnings) and proper actions (like GE's efforts to improve the environment). *Management's goal should be to take actions designed to maximize the firm's intrinsic value, not its current market price.* Note, though, that maximizing the intrinsic value will maximize the *average* price over the long run, but not necessarily the current price at each point in time. For example, management might make an investment that lowers profits for the current year but raises

[4]Investors at the margin are the ones who actually set stock prices. Some stockholders think that a stock at its current price is a good deal, and they would buy more if they had more money. Others think that the stock is priced too high, so they would not buy it unless the price dropped sharply. Still others think that the current stock price is about where it should be; so they would buy more if the price fell slightly, sell it if the price rose slightly, and maintain their current holdings unless something were to change. These are the marginal investors, and it is their view that determines the current stock price. We discuss this point in more depth in Chapter 9, where we discuss the stock market in detail.

[5]We emphasize that the intrinsic value is an estimate and that different analysts have different estimates for a company at any given time. Managers should also estimate their firm's intrinsic value and then take actions to maximize that value. They should try to help outside security analysts improve their intrinsic value estimates by providing accurate information about the company's financial position and operations, but without releasing information that would help its competitors. Enron, WorldCom, and a number of other companies tried to deceive analysts; and they succeeded all too well.

FIGURE 1-3	Graph of Actual Prices versus Intrinsic Values

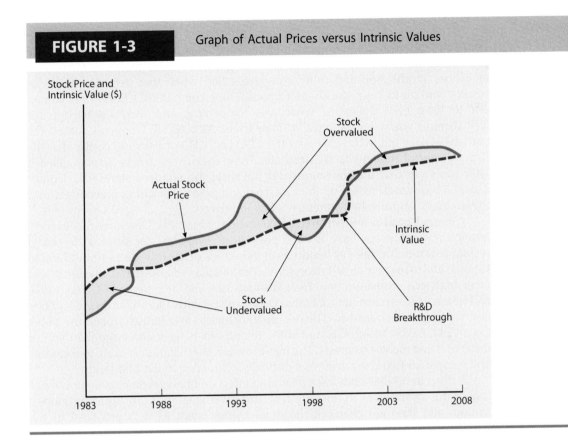

expected future profits. If investors are not aware of the true situation, the stock price will be held down by the low current profit even though the intrinsic value was actually raised. Management should provide information that helps investors make better estimates of the firm's intrinsic value, which will keep the stock price closer to its equilibrium level. However, there are times when management cannot divulge the true situation because doing so would provide information that helps its competitors.[6]

SELF TEST

What's the difference between a stock's current market price and its intrinsic value?

Do stocks have known and "provable" intrinsic values, or might different people reach different conclusions about intrinsic values? Explain.

Should managers estimate intrinsic values or leave that to outside security analysts? Explain.

If a firm could maximize either its current market price or its intrinsic value, what would stockholders (as a group) want managers to do? Explain.

Should a firm's managers help investors improve their estimates of the firm's intrinsic value? Explain.

---

[6]As we discuss in Chapter 2, many academics believe that stock prices embody all publicly available information—hence, that stock prices are typically reasonably close to their intrinsic values and thus at or close to an equilibrium. However, almost no one doubts that managers have better information than the public at large, that at times stock prices and equilibrium values diverge, and thus that stocks can be temporarily undervalued or overvalued (as we suggest in Figure 1-3).

1-6 IMPORTANT BUSINESS TRENDS

Four important business trends should be noted. First, the points discussed in the preceding section have led to profound changes in business practices. Executives at Enron, WorldCom, and other companies lied when they reported financial results, leading to huge stockholder losses. These companies' CEOs later claimed not to have been aware of what was happening, and their knowledge (or lack thereof) was a central issue in their trials. As a result, Congress passed the Sarbanes-Oxley bill, which requires the CEO and CFO of a firm to certify that the firm's financial statements are accurate. These executives can be sent to jail if it later turns out that the statements did not meet the required standards. Consequently, businesses beefed up their internal and external auditing procedures, and the accuracy of published statements has improved.

A second trend is the increased globalization of business. Developments in communications technology have made it possible for Wal-Mart, for example, to obtain real-time data on the sales of hundreds of thousands of items in stores from China to Chicago and to manage all of its stores from Bentonville, Arkansas. IBM, Microsoft, and other high-tech companies now have research labs and help desks in China, India, and Romania; and customers of Home Depot and other retailers have their telephone and e-mail questions answered by call center operators in countries around the globe. Coca-Cola, Exxon Mobil, GE, and IBM, among others, generate more than half of their sales and income overseas. The trend toward globalization is likely to continue, and companies that resist will have difficulty competing in the 21st century.[7]

A third trend that's having a profound effect on financial management is ever-improving information technology (IT). Improvements in IT are spurring globalization, and they are changing financial management as it is practiced in the

GLOBAL PERSPECTIVES

IS SHAREHOLDER WEALTH MAXIMIZATION A WORLDWIDE GOAL?

Most academics agree that shareholder wealth maximization should be a firm's primary goal, but it's not clear that people elsewhere really know how to implement it. PricewaterhouseCoopers (PWC), a global consulting firm, conducted a survey of 82 Singapore companies to test their understanding and implementation of shareholder value concepts. Ninety percent of the respondents said their firm's primary goal was to enhance shareholder value, but only 44% had taken steps to achieve this goal. Moreover, almost half of the respondents who had shareholder value programs in place said they were dissatisfied with the results achieved thus far. Even so, respondents who focused on shareholder value were more likely to believe that their stock was fairly valued than those with other focuses, and 50% of those without a specific program said they wanted to learn more and would probably adopt the goal of shareholder wealth maximization eventually.

The study found that firms measure performance primarily with accounting-based measures such as the return on assets, equity, or invested capital. These measures are easy to understand and thus to implement, even though they are not the best conceptually. When compensation was tied to shareholder value, this was only for mid-level managers and above.

It is unclear how closely these results correspond to U.S. firms, but firms in the United States and Singapore would certainly agree on one thing: It is easier to set the goal of shareholder wealth maximization than it is to figure out how to achieve it.

Source: Kalpana Rashiwala, "Low Adoption of Shareholder Value Concepts Here," *The Business Times* (Singapore), February 14, 2002.

---

[7]To give you an idea of the prevalence of globalization, the computer programming that causes the test bank problems for this book to vary randomly was outsourced to programmers in Moscow, Russia. Our books have been translated into 11 languages, and they are sold throughout the world. Globalization is alive and well!

United States and elsewhere. Firms are collecting massive amounts of data and using it to take much of the guesswork out of financial decisions. For example, when Wal-Mart is considering a potential site for a new store, it can draw on historical results from thousands of other stores to predict results at the proposed site. This lowers the risk of investing in new stores.

A fourth trend relates to *corporate governance*, or the way the top managers operate and interface with stockholders. Some years ago the chairperson of the board of directors was almost always also the CEO, and this individual decided who would be elected to the board. That made it almost impossible for stockholders to replace a poor management team. Today, though, active investors who control huge pools of capital (hedge funds and private equity groups) are constantly looking for underperforming firms; and they will quickly pounce on laggards, take control, and replace managers. At the same time, the SEC, which has jurisdiction over the way stockholders vote and the information they must be given, has been making it easier for activist stockholders to change the way things are done within firms. For example, the SEC is forcing companies to provide more transparent information on CEO compensation, which is affecting managers' actions.

SELF TEST   What four trends affect business management in general and financial management in particular?

1-7 BUSINESS ETHICS

As a result of the Enron scandal and other recent scandals, there has been a strong push to improve *business ethics*. This is occurring on several fronts—actions begun by former New York attorney general and former governor Elliot Spitzer and others who sued companies for improper acts; Congress' passing of the Sarbanes Oxley bill to impose sanctions on executives who sign financial statements later found to be false; and business schools trying to inform students about proper versus improper business actions.

As noted earlier, companies benefit from having good reputations and are penalized by having bad ones; the same is true for individuals. Reputations reflect the extent to which firms and people are ethical. *Ethics* is defined in *Webster's Dictionary* as "standards of conduct or moral behavior." **Business ethics** can be thought of as a company's attitude and conduct toward its employees, customers, community, and stockholders. A firm's commitment to business ethics can be measured by the tendency of its employees, from the top down, to adhere to laws, regulations, and moral standards relating to product safety and quality, fair employment practices, fair marketing and selling practices, the use of confidential information for personal gain, community involvement, and illegal payments to obtain business.

Business Ethics
A company's attitude and conduct toward its employees, customers, community, and stockholders.

1-7a What Companies Are Doing

Most firms today have strong written codes of ethical behavior; companies also conduct training programs to ensure that employees understand proper behavior in different situations. When conflicts arise involving profits and ethics, ethical considerations sometimes are so obviously important that they dominate. In other cases, however, the right choice is not clear. For example, suppose that Norfolk Southern's managers know that its coal trains are polluting the air; but the amount of pollution is within legal limits, and further reduction would be costly. Are the managers ethically bound to reduce pollution? Similarly, several years ago Merck's research indicated that its Vioxx pain medicine might be causing heart attacks. However, the evidence was not overly strong, and the product was clearly helping some patients. Over time, additional tests produced stronger evidence that Vioxx did pose a health risk. What should Merck have done, and when should Merck have done it? If the company released negative but perhaps incorrect information, this announcement would have hurt sales and possibly prevented some patients who could have benefit from using the product. If the company delayed the release of this additional information, more patients might have suffered irreversible harm. At what point should Merck have made the potential problem known to the public? There are no obvious answers to questions such as these; but companies must deal with them, and a failure to handle them properly can lead to severe consequences.

1-7b Consequences of Unethical Behavior

Over the past few years, ethical lapses have led to a number of bankruptcies. The recent collapses of Enron and WorldCom as well as the accounting firm Arthur Andersen dramatically illustrate how unethical behavior can lead to a firm's rapid decline. In all three cases, top executives came under fire because of misleading accounting practices that led to overstated profits. Enron and WorldCom executives were busily selling their stock at the same time they were recommending the stock to employees and outside investors. These executives reaped millions before the stock declined, while lower-level employees and outside investors were left "holding the bag." Some of these executives are now in jail, and Enron's CEO had a fatal heart attack while awaiting sentencing after being found guilty of conspiracy and fraud. Moreover, Merrill Lynch and Citigroup, which were accused of facilitating these frauds, were fined hundreds of millions of dollars.

These frauds also severely damaged other companies and even whole industries. For example, WorldCom understated its costs by billions of dollars. It then used those artificially low costs when it set prices for its customers. Not knowing that WorldCom's results were built on lies, AT&T's CEO put pressure on his own managers to match WorldCom's costs and prices. AT&T cut back on important projects, put far too much stress on its employees, acquired other companies at high prices, and ended up ruining a successful 100-year-old company.[8] A similar situation occurred in the energy industry as a result of Enron's cheating.

These and other improper actions caused many investors to lose faith in American business and to turn away from the stock market, which made it difficult for firms to raise the capital they needed to grow, create jobs, and stimulate the economy. So unethical actions can have adverse consequences far beyond the companies that perpetrate them.

All this raises a question: Are *companies* unethical, or is it just a few of their employees? That was a central issue that came up in the case of Arthur Andersen, the accounting firm that audited Enron, WorldCom, and several other companies that committed accounting fraud. Evidence showed that relatively few of Andersen's accountants helped perpetrate the frauds. Its top managers argued that while a few rogue employees did bad things, most of the firm's 85,000 employees, and the firm itself, were innocent. The U.S. Justice Department disagreed, concluding that the firm was guilty because it fostered a climate where unethical behavior was permitted and that Andersen used an incentive system

---

[8]The original AT&T was reorganized into a manufacturing company (Lucent), 8 regional telephone companies, and a long-distance company that retained the AT&T name. WorldCom was in the long-distance business and thus competed with the surviving AT&T. Partly as the result of its efforts to match WorldCom's phony costs and prices, AT&T lost billions. In the end, AT&T was acquired by the smallest of the 8 regional companies, which then took the AT&T name.

that made such behavior profitable to both the perpetrators and the firm. As a result, Andersen was put out of business, its partners lost millions of dollars, and its 85,000 employees lost their jobs. In most other cases, individuals rather than firms were tried; and while the firms survived, they suffered damage to their reputations, which greatly lowered their future profit potential and value.

1-7c How Should Employees Deal with Unethical Behavior?

Far too often the desire for stock options, bonuses, and promotions drives managers to take unethical actions such as fudging the books to make profits in the manager's division look good, holding back information about bad products that would depress sales, and failing to take costly but needed measures to protect the environment. Generally, these acts don't rise to the level of an Enron or a World-Com, but they are still bad. If questionable things are going on, who should take action and what should that action be? Obviously, in situations such as Enron and WorldCom, where fraud was being perpetrated at or close to the top, senior managers knew about the illegal activities. In other cases, the problem is caused by a mid-level manager trying to boost his or her unit's profits and thus his or her bonus. In all cases, though, at least some lower-level employees are aware of what's happening; they may even be ordered to take fraudulent actions. Should the lower-level employees obey their boss's orders; refuse to obey those orders; or report the situation to a higher authority, such as the company's board of directors, the company's auditors, or a federal prosecutor?

In the WorldCom and Enron cases, it was clear to a number of employees that unethical and illegal acts were being committed; but in cases such as Merck's Vioxx product, the situation was less clear. Because early evidence that Vioxx led to heart attacks was weak and evidence of its pain reduction was strong, it was probably not appropriate to sound an alarm early on. However, as evidence accumulated, at some point the public needed to be given a strong warning or the product should have been taken off the market. But judgment comes into play when deciding on what action to take and when to take it. If a lower-level employee thinks that a product should be pulled but the boss disagrees, what should the employee do? If an employee decides to report the problem, trouble may ensue regardless of the merits of the case. If the alarm is false, the company will have been harmed and nothing will have been gained. In that case, the employee will probably be fired. Even if the employee is right, his or her career may still be ruined because many companies (or at least bosses) don't like "disloyal, troublemaking" employees.

PROTECTION FOR WHISTLE-BLOWERS

As a result of the recent accounting and other frauds, in 2002, Congress passed the Sarbanes-Oxley Act, which codified certain rules pertaining to corporate behavior. One provision in the bill was designed to protect whistle-blowers, or lower-level employees who sound an alarm over actions by their superiors. Employees who report improper actions are often fired or otherwise penalized, which keeps many people from reporting activities that should be investigated. The Sarbanes-Oxley provision was designed to alleviate this problem. If someone reports a corporate wrongdoing and is later penalized, he or she can ask the Occupational Safety & Health Administration (OSHA) to investigate the situation; if the employee was improperly penalized, the company can be required to reinstate the person, along with back pay and a sizable penalty award. According to *The Wall Street Journal*, some big awards have been handed out and a National Whistle-Blower Center has been established to help people sue companies. It's still dangerous to blow the whistle, but less so than before the Sarbanes-Oxley Act was passed.

Source: Deborah Solomon and Kara Scannell, "SEC Is Urged to Enforce 'Whistle-Blower' Provision," *The Wall Street Journal,* November 15, 2004, p. A6.

Such situations arise fairly often in contexts ranging from accounting fraud to product liability and environmental cases. Employees jeopardize their jobs if they come forward over their bosses' objections. However, if they don't speak up, they may suffer emotional problems and contribute to the downfall of their companies and the accompanying loss of jobs and savings. Moreover, if employees obey orders regarding actions they know are illegal, they may end up going to jail. Indeed, in most of the scandals that have gone to trial, the lower-level people who physically entered the bad data received longer jail sentences than the bosses who presumably gave the directives. So employees can be "stuck between a rock and a hard place," that is, doing what they should do and possibly losing their jobs versus going along with the boss and possibly ending up in jail.

This discussion shows why ethics is such an important consideration in business and in business schools—and why we are concerned with it in this book.

SELF TEST

How would you define "business ethics"?

Can a firm's executive compensation plan lead to unethical behavior? Explain.

Unethical acts are generally committed by unethical people. What are some things companies can do to help ensure that their employees act ethically?

1-8 CONFLICTS BETWEEN MANAGERS, STOCKHOLDERS, AND BONDHOLDERS[9]

1-8a Managers versus Stockholders

It has long been recognized that managers' personal goals may compete with shareholder wealth maximization. In particular, managers might be more interested in maximizing their own wealth than their stockholders' wealth; therefore, managers might pay themselves excessive salaries. For example, Disney paid its former president Michael Ovitz $140 million as a severance package after just 14 months on the job—$140 million to go away—because he and Disney CEO Michael Eisner were having disagreements. Eisner was also handsomely compensated the year Ovitz was fired—a $750,000 base salary plus a $9.9 million bonus plus $565 million in profits from stock options, for a total of just over $575 million. As another example of corporate excesses, Tyco CEO Dennis Kozlowski (who is now in jail) spent more than $1 million of the company's money on a birthday party for his wife.

Neither the Disney executives' pay nor Kozlowski's birthday party seem consistent with shareholder wealth maximization. Still, good executive compensation plans can motivate managers to act in their stockholders' best interests. Useful motivational tools include (1) reasonable compensation packages, (2) firing of managers who don't perform well, and (3) the threat of hostile takeovers.

Compensation packages should be sufficient to attract and retain able managers, but they should not go beyond what is needed. Also, compensation should be structured so that managers are rewarded on the basis of the stock's performance over the long run, not the stock's price on an option exercise date. This means that options (or direct stock awards) should be phased in over a number of years so that managers have an incentive to keep the stock price high over time. When the

---

[9]These conflicts are studied under the heading of *agency theory* in finance literature. The classic work on agency theory is Michael C. Jensen and William H. Meckling, "Theory of the Firm, Managerial Behavior, Agency Costs, and Ownership Structure," *Journal of Financial Economics,* October 1976, pp. 305–360.

intrinsic value can be measured in an objective and verifiable manner, performance pay can be based on changes in intrinsic value. However, because intrinsic value is not observable, compensation must be based on the stock's market price—but the price used should be an average over time rather than on a specific date.

Stockholders can intervene directly with managers. Years ago most stock was owned by individuals. Today, however, the majority of stock is owned by institutional investors such as insurance companies, pension funds, hedge funds, and mutual funds; and private equity groups are ready and able to step in and take over underperforming firms. These institutional money managers have the clout to exercise considerable influence over firms' operations. First, they can talk with managers and make suggestions about how the business should be run. In effect, institutional investors such as CalPERS (California Public Employees' Retirement System, with $165 billion of assets) and TIAA-CREF (Teachers Insurance and Annuity Association–College Retirement Equity Fund, a retirement plan originally set up for professors at private colleges that now has more than $300 billion of assets) act as lobbyists for the body of stockholders. When such large stockholders speak, companies listen. Second, any shareholder who has owned $2,000 of a company's stock for one year can sponsor a proposal that may be voted on at the annual stockholders' meeting, even if management opposes the proposal.[10] Although shareholder-sponsored proposals are nonbinding, the results of such votes are heard by top management. There is an ongoing debate regarding how much influence shareholders should have through the proxy process. For example, shareholder activists sharply criticized a recent SEC vote that continued to allow companies to exclude shareholder proposals related to director elections.[11]

Until recently, the probability of a large firm's management being ousted by its stockholders was so remote that it posed little threat. Most firms' shares were so widely distributed and the CEO had so much control over the voting mechanism that it was virtually impossible for dissident stockholders to get the votes needed to overthrow a management team. However, that situation has changed. In recent years, the top executives of AT&T, Coca-Cola, Fannie Mae, General Motors, IBM, and Xerox, to name a few, have been forced out. All of these departures were due to the firm's poor performance.

If a firm's stock is undervalued, **corporate raiders** will see it as a bargain and will attempt to capture the firm in a **hostile takeover**. If the raid is successful, the target's executives will almost certainly be fired. This situation gives managers a strong incentive to take actions to maximize their stock's price. In the words of one executive, "If you want to keep your job, never let your stock become a bargain."

Again, note that the price managers should be trying to maximize is not the price on a specific day. Rather, it is the average price over the long run, which will be maximized if management focuses on the stock's intrinsic value. However, managers must communicate effectively with stockholders (without divulging information that would aid their competitors) to keep the actual price close to the intrinsic value. It's bad for stockholders and managers when the intrinsic value is high but the actual price is low. In that situation, a raider may swoop in, buy the company at a bargain price, and fire the managers. To repeat our earlier message:

Managers should try to maximize their stock's intrinsic value and then communicate effectively with stockholders. That will cause the intrinsic value to be high and the actual stock price to remain close to the intrinsic value over time.

Corporate Raider
An individual who targets a corporation for takeover because it is undervalued.

Hostile Takeover
The acquisition of a company over the opposition of its management.

---

[10]Under current guidelines, shareholder proposals are restricted to governance issues and shareholders are not allowed to vote directly on items that are considered to be "operating issues."
[11]Kara Scannell, "Cox, in Denying Proxy Access, Puts His Legacy on the Line," *The Wall Street Journal Online*, November 29, 2007, p. C1.

Because the intrinsic value cannot be observed, it is impossible to know whether it is really being maximized. Still, as we will discuss in Chapter 9, there are procedures for estimating a stock's intrinsic value. Managers can use these valuation models to analyze alternative courses of action and thus see how these actions are likely to impact the firm's value. This type of value-based management is not as precise as we would like, but it is the best way to run a business.

1-8b Stockholders versus Bondholders

Conflicts can also arise between stockholders and bondholders. Bondholders generally receive fixed payment regardless of how well the company does, while stockholders do better when the company does better. This situation leads to conflicts between these two groups.[12] To illustrate the problem, suppose a company has the chance to make an investment that will result in a profit of $10 billion if it is successful but the company will be worthless and go bankrupt if the investment is unsuccessful. The firm has bonds that pay an 8% annual interest rate and have a value of $1,000 per bond and stock that sells for $10 per share. If the new project—say, a cure for the common cold—is successful, the price of the stock will jump to $2,000 per share, but the value of the bonds will remain just $1,000 per bond. The probability of success is 50% and the probability of failure is 50%, so the expected stock price is

$$\text{Expected stock price} = 0.5(\$2,000) + 0.5(\$0) = \$1,000$$

versus a current price of $10. The expected percentage gain on the stock is

$$\text{Expected percentage gain on stock} = (\$1,000 - \$10)/\$10 \times 100\% = 9,900\%$$

The project looks wonderful from the stockholders' standpoint but lousy for the bondholders. They just break even if the project is successful, but they lose their entire investment if it is a failure.

Another type of bondholder/stockholder conflict arises over the use of additional debt. As we will see later in this book, the more debt a firm uses to finance a given amount of assets, the riskier the firm is. For example, if a firm has $100 million of assets and finances them with $5 million of bonds and $95 million of common stock, things will have to go terribly bad before the bondholders will suffer a loss. On the other hand, if the firm uses $95 million of bonds and $5 million of stock, the bondholders will suffer a loss even if the value of the assets declines only slightly.

Bondholders attempt to protect themselves by including covenants in the bond agreements that limit firms' use of additional debt and constrain managers' actions in other ways. We will address these issues later in this book, but they are quite important and everyone should be aware of them.

SELF TEST

What are three techniques stockholders can use to motivate managers to maximize their stock's long-run price?

Should managers focus directly on the stock's actual market price or its intrinsic value, or are both important? Explain.

Why might conflicts arise between stockholders and bondholders?

---

[12]Managers represent stockholders; so saying "stockholders versus bondholders" is the same as saying "managers versus bondholders."

TYING IT ALL TOGETHER

This chapter provides a broad overview of financial management. *Management's primary goal should be to maximize the long-run value of the stock, which means the intrinsic value as measured by the stock's price over time.* To maximize value, firms must develop products that consumers want, produce the products efficiently, sell them at competitive prices, and observe laws relating to corporate behavior. If firms are successful at maximizing the stock's value, they will also be contributing to social welfare and citizens' well-being.

Businesses can be organized as proprietorships, partnerships, corporations, limited liability companies (LLCs), or limited liability partnerships (LLPs). The vast majority of all business is done by corporations, and the most successful firms end up as corporations, which explains the focus on corporations in this book. We also discussed four important business trends: (1) the focus on business ethics that resulted from a series of scandals in the late 1990s, (2) the trend toward globalization, (3) the ever-improving information technology, and (4) the changes in corporate governance. These four trends are changing the way business is done.

The primary tasks of the CFO are (1) to make sure the accounting system provides "good" numbers for internal decision making and for investors, (2) to ensure that the firm is financed in the proper manner, (3) to evaluate the operating units to make sure they are performing in an optimal manner, and (4) to evaluate all proposed capital expenditures to make sure they will increase the firm's value. In the remainder of this book, we discuss exactly how financial managers carry out these tasks.

SELF-TEST QUESTION AND PROBLEM
(Solutions Appear in Appendix A)

ST-1　**KEY TERMS**　Define each of the following terms:

a. Sarbanes-Oxley Act

b. Proprietorship; partnership; corporation

c. S corporations; limited liability companies (LLCs); limited liability partnerships (LLPs)

d. Stockholder wealth maximization

e. Intrinsic value; market price

f. Equilibrium; marginal investor

g. Business ethics

h. Corporate raider; hostile takeover

QUESTIONS

1-1　If you bought a share of stock, what would you expect to receive, when would you expect to receive it, and would you be certain that your expectations would be met?

1-2　If most investors expect the same cash flows from Companies A and B but are more confident that A's cash flows will be closer to their expected value, which company should have the higher stock price? Explain.

1-3   What is a firm's intrinsic value? its current stock price? Is the stock's "true long-run value" more closely related to its intrinsic value or to its current price?

1-4   When is a stock said to be in equilibrium? At any given time, would you guess that most stocks are in equilibrium as you defined it? Explain.

1-5   Suppose three honest individuals gave you their estimates of Stock X's intrinsic value. One person is your current roommate, the second person is a professional security analyst with an excellent reputation on Wall Street, and the third person is Company X's CFO. If the three estimates differed, in which one would you have the most confidence? Why?

1-6   Is it better for a firm's actual stock price in the market to be under, over, or equal to its intrinsic value? Would your answer be the same from the standpoints of stockholders in general and a CEO who is about to exercise a million dollars in options and then retire? Explain.

1-7   If a company's board of directors wants management to maximize shareholder wealth, should the CEO's compensation be set as a fixed dollar amount, or should the compensation depend on how well the firm performs? If it is to be based on performance, how should performance be measured? Would it be easier to measure performance by the growth rate in reported profits or the growth rate in the stock's intrinsic value? Which would be the better performance measure? Why?

1-8   What are the four forms of business organization? What are the advantages and disadvantages of each?

1-9   Should stockholder wealth maximization be thought of as a long-term or a short-term goal? For example, if one action increases a firm's stock price from a current level of $20 to $25 in 6 months and then to $30 in 5 years but another action keeps the stock at $20 for several years but then increases it to $40 in 5 years, which action would be better? Think of some specific corporate actions that have these general tendencies.

1-10   What are some actions that stockholders can take to ensure that management's and stockholders' interests are aligned?

1-11   The president of Southern Semiconductor Corporation (SSC) made this statement in the company's annual report: "SSC's primary goal is to increase the value of our common stockholders' equity." Later in the report, the following announcements were made:

   a. The company contributed $1.5 million to the symphony orchestra in Birmingham, Alabama, its headquarters city.

   b. The company is spending $500 million to open a new plant and expand operations in China. No profits will be produced by the Chinese operation for 4 years, so earnings will be depressed during this period versus what they would have been had the decision been made not to expand in China.

   c. The company holds about half of its assets in the form of U.S. Treasury bonds, and it keeps these funds available for use in emergencies. In the future, though, SSC plans to shift its emergency funds from Treasury bonds to common stocks.

   Discuss how SSC's stockholders might view each of these actions and how the actions might affect the stock price.

1-12   Investors generally can make one vote for each share of stock they hold. TIAA-CREF is the largest institutional shareholder in the United States; therefore, it holds many shares and has more votes than any other organization. Traditionally, this fund has acted as a passive investor, just going along with management. However, in 1993, it mailed a notice to all 1,500 companies whose stocks it held that henceforth, it planned to actively intervene if, in its opinion, management was not performing well. Its goal was to improve corporate performance to boost the prices of the stocks it held. It also wanted to encourage corporate boards to appoint a majority of independent (outside) directors; and it stated that it would vote against any directors of firms that "don't have an effective, independent board that can challenge the CEO."
   In the past, TIAA-CREF responded to poor performance by "voting with its feet," which means selling stocks that were not doing well. However, by 1993, that position had become difficult to maintain for two reasons. First, the fund invested a large part of its assets in "index funds," which hold stocks in accordance with their percentage value in the broad stock market. Furthermore, TIAA-CREF owns such large blocks of stocks in many companies that if it tried to sell out, doing so would severely depress the prices of those stocks. Thus, TIAA-CREF is locked in to a large extent, which led to its decision to become a more active investor.

   a. Is TIAA-CREF an ordinary shareholder? Explain.

   b. Due to its asset size, TIAA-CREF owns many shares in a number of companies. The fund's management plans to vote those shares. However, TIAA-CREF is owned by many thousands of investors. Should the fund's managers vote its shares; or should it pass those votes, on a pro rata basis, back to its own shareholders? Explain.

1-13   Edmund Enterprises recently made a large investment to upgrade its technology. While these improvements won't have much effect on performance in the short run, they are expected to reduce future costs significantly. What effect will this investment have on Edmund Enterprises' earnings per share this year? What effect might this investment have on the company's intrinsic value and stock price?

1-14   Suppose you were a member of Company X's board of directors and chairperson of the company's compensation committee. What factors should your committee consider when setting the CEO's compensation? Should the compensation consist of a dollar salary, stock options that depend on the firm's performance, or a mix of the two? If "performance" is to be considered, how should it be measured? Think of both theoretical and practical (that is, measurement) considerations. If you were also a vice president of Company X, might your actions be different than if you were the CEO of some other company?

1-15   Suppose you are a director of an energy company that has three divisions—natural gas, oil, and retail (gas stations). These divisions operate independently from one another, but all division managers report to the firm's CEO. If you were on the compensation committee as discussed in Question 1–14 and your committee was asked to set the compensation for the three division managers, would you use the same criteria as that used for the firm's CEO? Explain your reasoning.

© HIROKO MASUIKE/GETTY IMAGES

CHAPTER 2
Financial Markets and Institutions

Efficient Financial Markets Are Necessary for a Growing Economy

Over the past few decades, changing technology and improving communications have increased cross-border transactions and expanded the scope and efficiency of the global financial system. Companies routinely raise funds throughout the world; and with the click of a mouse, an investor can buy GE stock on the New York Stock Exchange, deposit funds in a European bank, or purchase a mutual fund that invests in Chinese securities.

This globalization was dramatically illustrated in the fall of 2007. The U.S. housing market had been exceedingly strong, which bolstered the entire economy. Rising home values enabled people to borrow on home equity loans to buy everything from autos to Caribbean vacations. However, lenders had been making loans that required no down payment, that had "teaser" rates programmed to rise sharply after a year or two, and that were made to borrowers whose credit had not been carefully checked. These relaxed lending standards enabled people who could not have bought homes in the past to buy

a home now; but the loans were getting riskier, and about 30% were classified as "subprime."

The risk buildup was obscured by fancy "financial engineering." A few years ago people obtained mortgage loans primarily from local banks. The banks kept the mortgages, collected the interest, and likely knew how risky the loans were. In recent years, the situation has changed. Now mortgage brokers originate, for example, 500 loans for $200,000 each, or $100 million in total, and then sell them to an investment bank. The bank uses the loans as collateral for $100 million of bonds, which are divided into classes such as A, B, and C. The A bonds have first claim on cash from the mortgages and are rated AAA; the Bs are next, which are also highly rated; and even the Cs are rated "investment grade." Initially, times were good; the interest and repayment of principal from the mortgages were sufficient to cover required payments to all of the bonds. However, recently, some of the mortgages began going into default, and inflows were no longer sufficient to cover required payments to all of the bonds.

When home prices are rising, borrowers' equity also rises. That enables borrowers who cannot keep up with their payments to refinance—or sell the house for enough to pay off the mortgage. But when home prices start falling, refinancings and profitable sales are impossible. That triggers mortgage defaults, which, in turn, triggers defaults on the riskiest bonds. People become worried about the B and even the A bonds, so their values also fall. The banks and other institutions that own the bonds are forced to write them down on their balance sheets.

Institutions that hold mortgage-backed bonds—many of which are subsidiaries of banks—raised the money to buy the bonds by borrowing on a 3-month basis from money market funds of similar lenders. As risks became more apparent, the short-term lenders refused to roll over these loans; thus, the bondholders were forced to sell bonds to repay their short-term loans. Those sales depressed the bond market even further, causing further bond sales, lower bond prices, and more write-downs. A downward spiral and a severe credit crunch began.

Banks across the globe had invested in these bonds; and huge losses were reported by Citigroup, Deutsche Bank (Germany's largest), and UBS (Switzerland's largest). These losses reduced banks' willingness and ability to make new loans, which threatened economies in many nations. The Federal Reserve and other central banks lowered interest rates and eased the terms under which they extended credit to banks, and the banks themselves joined forces to head off a downward spiral. The headline in *The Wall Street Journal* on October 13, 2007, read as follows: "Big Banks Push $100 Billion Plan to Avert Credit Crunch." The article described how government officials are working with bankers to head off an impending crisis. However, working things out will be difficult. Many think that the banks whose actions contributed to the problems—especially Citigroup—should not be bailed out. Others think that the crisis must be averted because the U.S. economy and other economies will be badly damaged if the downward spiral continues.

All of this demonstrates the extent to which markets are interconnected, the impact markets can have on countries and on individual companies, and the complexity of capital markets.

Source: Carrick Mollenkamp, Ian McDonald, and Deborah Solomon, "Big Banks Push $100 Billion Plan to Avert Crunch: Fund Seeks to Prevent Mortgage-Debt Selloff; Advice from Treasury," *The Wall Street Journal*, October 13, 2007, p. A1.

PUTTING THINGS IN PERSPECTIVE

In Chapter 1, we saw that a firm's primary goal is to maximize the price of its stock. Stock prices are determined in the financial markets; so if financial managers are to make good decisions, they must understand how these markets operate. In addition, individuals make personal investment decisions; so they too need to know something about financial markets and the institutions that operate in those markets. Therefore, in this chapter, we describe the markets where capital is raised, securities are traded, and stock prices are established and the institutions that operate in these markets.

When you finish this chapter, you should be able to:

- Identify the different types of financial markets and financial institutions and explain how these markets and institutions enhance capital allocation.
- Explain how the stock market operates and list the distinctions between the different types of stock markets.
- Explain how the stock market has performed in recent years.
- Discuss the importance of market efficiency and explain why some markets are more efficient than others.

2-1 THE CAPITAL ALLOCATION PROCESS

Businesses, individuals, and governments often need to raise capital. For example, Carolina Power & Light (CP&L) forecasts an increase in the demand for electricity in North and South Carolina, so it will build a new power plant to meet those needs. Because CP&L's bank account does not contain the $1 billion necessary to pay for the plant, the company must raise this capital in the financial markets. Similarly, Mr. Fong, the proprietor of a San Francisco hardware store, wants to expand into appliances. Where will he get the money to buy the initial inventory of TV sets, washers, and freezers? Or suppose the Johnson family wants to buy a home that costs $200,000, but they have only $50,000 in savings. Where will they get the additional $150,000? The city of New York needs $200 million to build a new sewer plant. Where can it obtain this money? Finally, the federal government needs more money than it receives from taxes. Where will the extra money come from?

On the other hand, some individuals and firms have incomes that exceed their current expenditures, in which case they have funds available to invest. For example, Carol Hawk has an income of $36,000, but her expenses are only $30,000. That leaves her with $6,000 to invest. Similarly, Microsoft has accumulated roughly $23.5 billion of cash. What can Microsoft do with this money until it is needed in the business?

People and organizations with surplus funds are saving today in order to accumulate funds for some future use. Members of a household might save to pay for their children's education and the parents' retirement, while a business might save to fund future investments. Those with surplus funds expect to earn a return on their investments, while people and organizations that need capital understand that they must pay interest to those who provide that capital.

In a well-functioning economy, capital flows efficiently from those with surplus capital to those who need it. This transfer can take place in the three ways described in Figure 2-1.

1. *Direct transfers* of money and securities, as shown in the top section, occur when a business sells its stocks or bonds directly to savers, without going

---

FIGURE 2-1   Diagram of the Capital Formation Process

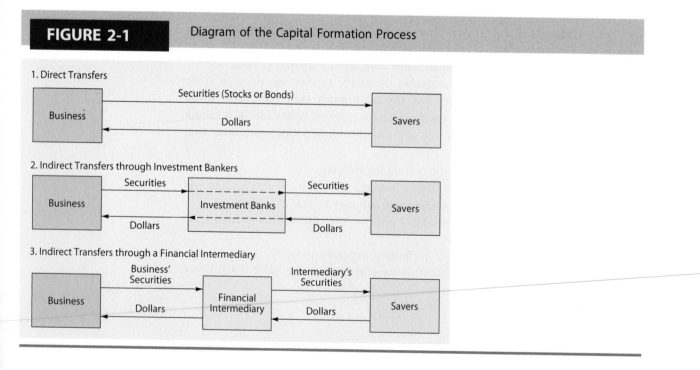

1. Direct Transfers

2. Indirect Transfers through Investment Bankers

3. Indirect Transfers through a Financial Intermediary

through any type of financial institution. The business delivers its securities to savers, who, in turn, give the firm the money it needs. This procedure is used mainly by small firms, and relatively little capital is raised by direct transfers.

2. As shown in the middle section, transfers may also go through an investment bank (iBank) such as Citigroup, which *underwrites* the issue. An underwriter serves as a middleman and facilitates the issuance of securities. The company sells its stocks or bonds to the investment bank, which then sells these same securities to savers. The businesses' securities and the savers' money merely "pass through" the investment bank. However, because the investment bank buys and holds the securities for a period of time, it is taking a risk—it may not be able to resell the securities to savers for as much as it paid. Because new securities are involved and the corporation receives the proceeds of the sale, this transaction is called a *primary market transaction*.

3. Transfers can also be made through a *financial intermediary* such as a bank, an insurance company, or a mutual fund. Here the intermediary obtains funds from savers in exchange for its securities. The intermediary uses this money to buy and hold businesses' securities, while the savers hold the intermediary's securities. For example, a saver deposits dollars in a bank, receiving a certificate of deposit; then the bank lends the money to a business in the form of a mortgage loan. Thus, intermediaries literally create new forms of capital—in this case, certificates of deposit, which are safer and more liquid than mortgages and thus are better for most savers to hold. The existence of intermediaries greatly increases the efficiency of money and capital markets.

Often the entity needing capital is a business (and specifically a corporation); but it is easy to visualize the demander of capital being a home purchaser, a small business, or a government unit. For example, if your uncle lends you money to help you fund a new business, a direct transfer of funds will occur. Alternatively, if you borrow money to purchase a home, you will probably raise the funds through a financial intermediary such as your local commercial bank or mortgage banker. That banker could sell your mortgage to an investment bank, which then might use it as collateral for a bond that is bought by a pension fund.

In a global context, economic development is highly correlated with the level and efficiency of financial markets and institutions.[1] It is difficult, if not impossible, for an economy to reach its full potential if it doesn't have access to a well-functioning financial system. In a well-developed economy like that of the United States, an extensive set of markets and institutions has evolved over time to facilitate the efficient allocation of capital. To raise capital efficiently, managers must understand how these markets and institutions work; and individuals need to know how the markets and institutions work to get high rates of returns on their savings.

Name three ways capital is transferred between savers and borrowers.

Why are efficient capital markets necessary for economic growth?

---

[1]For a detailed review of the evidence linking financial development to economic growth, see Ross Levine, "Finance and Growth: Theory and Evidence," NBER Working Paper No. 10766, September 2004.

2-2 FINANCIAL MARKETS

People and organizations wanting to borrow money are brought together with those who have surplus funds in the *financial markets*. Note that *markets* is plural; there are many different financial markets in a developed economy such as that of the United States. We describe some of these markets and some trends in their development.

2-2a Types of Markets

Different financial markets serve different types of customers or different parts of the country. Financial markets also vary depending on the maturity of the securities being traded and the types of assets used to back the securities. For these reasons, it is useful to classify markets along the following dimensions:

1. *Physical asset markets versus financial asset markets.* Physical asset markets (also called "tangible" or "real" asset markets) are for products such as wheat, autos, real estate, computers, and machinery. *Financial asset markets*, on the other hand, deal with stocks, bonds, notes, and mortgages. Financial markets also deal with *derivative securities* whose values are *derived* from changes in the prices of other assets. A share of Ford stock is a "pure financial asset," while an option to buy Ford shares is a derivative security whose value depends on the price of Ford stock. The bonds backed by subprime mortgages discussed at the beginning of this chapter are another type of derivative, as the values of these bonds are derived from the values of the underlying mortgages.

2. *Spot markets versus futures markets.* **Spot markets** are markets in which assets are bought or sold for "on-the-spot" delivery (literally, within a few days). **Futures markets** are markets in which participants agree today to buy or sell an asset at some future date. For example, a farmer may enter into a futures contract in which he agrees today to sell 5,000 bushels of soybeans 6 months from now at a price of $5 a bushel. To continue that example, a food processor that needs soybeans in the future may enter into a futures contract in which it agrees to buy soybeans 6 months from now. Such a transaction can reduce, or *hedge*, the risks faced by both the farmer and the food processor.

3. *Money markets versus capital markets.* **Money markets** are the markets for short-term, highly liquid debt securities. The New York, London, and Tokyo money markets are among the world's largest. **Capital markets** are the markets for intermediate- or long-term debt and corporate stocks. The New York Stock Exchange, where the stocks of the largest U.S. corporations are traded, is a prime example of a capital market. There is no hard-and-fast rule, but in a description of debt markets, *short-term* generally means less than 1 year, *intermediate-term* means 1 to 10 years, and *long-term* means more than 10 years.

4. *Primary markets versus secondary markets.* **Primary markets** are the markets in which corporations raise new capital. If GE were to sell a new issue of common stock to raise capital, a primary market transaction would take place. The corporation selling the newly created stock, GE, receives the proceeds from the sale in a primary market transaction. **Secondary markets** are markets in which existing, already outstanding securities are traded among investors. Thus, if Jane Doe decided to buy 1,000 shares of GE stock, the purchase would occur in the secondary market. The New York Stock Exchange is a secondary market because it deals in outstanding, as opposed to newly issued, stocks and bonds. Secondary markets also exist for mortgages, other types of loans, and other financial assets. The corporation whose securities are being traded is not involved in a secondary market transaction and thus does not receive funds from such a sale.

Spot Markets
The markets in which assets are bought or sold for "on-the-spot" delivery.

Futures Markets
The markets in which participants agree today to buy or sell an asset at some future date.

Money Markets
The financial markets in which funds are borrowed or loaned for short periods (less than one year).

Capital Markets
The financial markets for stocks and for intermediate- or long-term debt (one year or longer).

Primary Markets
Markets in which corporations raise capital by issuing new securities.

Secondary Markets
Markets in which securities and other financial assets are traded among investors after they have been issued by corporations.

5. *Private markets versus public markets.* **Private markets**, where transactions are negotiated directly between two parties, are differentiated from **public markets**, where standardized contracts are traded on organized exchanges. Bank loans and private debt placements with insurance companies are examples of private market transactions. Because these transactions are private, they may be structured in any manner to which the two parties agree. By contrast, securities that are traded in public markets (for example, common stock and corporate bonds) are held by a large number of individuals. These securities must have fairly standardized contractual features because public investors do not generally have the time and expertise to negotiate unique, nonstandardized contracts. Broad ownership and standardization result in publicly traded securities being more liquid than tailor-made, uniquely negotiated securities.

Private Markets
Markets in which transactions are worked out directly between two parties.

Public Markets
Markets in which standardized contracts are traded on organized exchanges.

Other classifications could be made, but this breakdown shows that there are many types of financial markets. Also note that the distinctions among markets are often blurred and unimportant except as a general point of reference. For example, it makes little difference if a firm borrows for 11, 12, or 13 months, that is, whether the transaction is a "money" or "capital" market transaction. You should be aware of the important differences among types of markets, but don't be overly concerned about trying to distinguish them at the boundaries.

A healthy economy is dependent on efficient funds transfers from people who are net savers to firms and individuals who need capital. Without efficient transfers, the economy could not function: Carolina Power & Light could not raise capital, so Raleigh's citizens would have no electricity; the Johnson family would not have adequate housing; Carol Hawk would have no place to invest her savings; and so forth. Obviously, the level of employment and productivity (i.e., the standard of living) would be much lower. Therefore, it is essential that financial markets function efficiently—not only quickly, but also inexpensively.[2]

Table 2-1 is a listing of the most important instruments traded in the various financial markets. The instruments are arranged in ascending order of typical length of maturity. As we go through this book, we will look in more detail at many of the instruments listed in Table 2-1. For example, we will see that there are many varieties of corporate bonds, ranging from "plain vanilla" bonds to bonds that can be converted to common stocks to bonds whose interest payments vary depending on the inflation rate. Still, the table provides an overview of the characteristics and costs of the instruments traded in the major financial markets.

2-2b Recent Trends

Financial markets have experienced many changes in recent years. Technological advances in computers and telecommunications, along with the globalization of banking and commerce, have led to deregulation, which has increased competition throughout the world. As a result, there are more efficient, internationally linked markets, which are far more complex than what existed a few years ago. While these developments have been largely positive, they have also created problems for policy makers. At one conference, former Federal Reserve Board Chairperson Alan Greenspan stated that modern financial markets "expose national economies to shocks from new and unexpected sources and with little if any lag." He went on to say that central banks must develop new ways to evaluate and limit risks to the financial system. Large amounts of capital move quickly

[2]As the countries of the former Soviet Union and other Eastern European nations move toward capitalism, as much attention must be paid to the establishment of cost-efficient financial markets as to electrical power, transportation, communications, and other infrastructure systems. Economic efficiency is impossible without a good system for allocating capital within the economy.

Table 2-1 Summary of Major Market Instruments, Market Participants, and Security Characteristics

SECURITY CHARACTERISTICS

Instrument (1)	Market (2)	Major Participants (3)	Riskiness (4)	Original Maturity (5)	Interest Rate on 2/5/08[a] (6)
U.S. Treasury bills	Money	Sold by U.S. Treasury to finance federal expenditures	Default-free, close to riskless	91 days to 1 year	2.23%
Bankers' acceptances	Money	A firm's note, but one guaranteed by a bank	Low degree of risk if guaranteed by a strong bank	Up to 180 days	3.11%
Dealer commercial paper	Money	Issued by financially secure firms to large investors	Low default risk	Up to 270 days	3.05%
Negotiable certificates of deposit (CDs)	Money	Issued by major money-center commercial banks to large investors	Default risk depends on the strength of the issuing bank	Up to 1 year	3.10%
Money market mutual funds	Money	Invest in Treasury bills, CDs, and commercial paper; held by individuals and businesses	Low degree of risk	No specific maturity (instant liquidity)	2.84%
Eurodollar market time deposits	Money	Issued by banks outside the United States	Default risk depends on the strength of the issuing bank	Up to 1 year	3.10%
Consumer credit, including credit card debt	Money	Issued by banks, credit unions, and finance companies to individuals	Risk is variable	Variable	Variable, but goes up to 20% or more
U.S. Treasury notes and bonds	Capital	Issued by U.S. government	No default risk, but price will decline if interest rates rise; hence, there is some risk	2 to 30 years	1.919% on 2-year to 4.327% on 30-year bonds
Mortgages	Capital	Loans to individuals and businesses secured by real estate; bought by banks and other institutions	Risk is variable; risk is high in the case of subprime loans	Up to 30 years	5.14% adjustable 5-year rate, 5.62% 30-year fixed rate
State and local government bonds	Capital	Issued by state and local governments; held by individuals and institutional investors	Riskier than U.S. government securities but exempt from most taxes	Up to 30 years	4.63% to 5.03% for A-rated, 20- to 40-year bonds
Corporate bonds	Capital	Issued by corporations; held by individuals and institutional investors	Riskier than U.S. government securities but less risky than preferred and common stocks; varying degree of risk within bonds depends on strength of issuer	Up to 40 years[b]	5.38% on AAA bonds, 6.63% on BBB bonds
Leases	Capital	Similar to debt in that firms can lease assets rather than borrow and then buy the assets	Risk similar to corporate bonds	Generally 3 to 20 years	Similar to bond yields
Preferred stocks	Capital	Issued by corporations to individuals and institutional investors	Generally riskier than corporate bonds but less risky than common stock	Unlimited	5.5% to 9%
Common stocks[c]	Capital	Issued by corporations to individuals and institutional investors	Riskier than bonds and preferred stock; risk varies from company to company	Unlimited	NA

[a]The yields reported are from the web site of *The Wall Street Journal* on February 5, 2008, http://online.wsj.com. Money market rates assume a 3-month maturity.
[b]A few corporations have issued 100-year bonds; however, the majority have issued bonds with maturities that are less than 40 years.
[c]While common stocks do not pay interest, they are expected to provide a "return" in the form of dividends and capital gains. As you will see in Chapter 8, historically, stock returns have averaged between 9% and 12% a year, but they can be much higher or lower in a given year. Of course, if you purchase a stock, your actual return may be considerably higher or lower than these historical averages.

around the world in response to changes in interest and exchange rates, and these movements can disrupt local institutions and economies. The subprime mortgage crisis discussed in the opening chapter vignette illustrates how problems in one country quickly affect the economies of other nations.

Globalization has exposed the need for greater cooperation among regulators at the international level, but the task is not easy. Factors that complicate coordination include (1) the different structures in nations' banking and securities industries; (2) the trend toward financial services conglomerates, which obscures developments in various market segments; and (3) the reluctance of individual countries to give up control over their national monetary policies. Still, regulators are unanimous about the need to close the gaps in the supervision of worldwide markets.

Another important trend in recent years has been the increased use of **derivatives**. A derivative is any security whose value is *derived* from the price of some other "underlying" asset. An option to buy IBM stock is a derivative, as is a contract to buy Japanese yen 6 months from now or a bond backed by subprime mortgages. The value of the IBM option depends on the price of IBM's stock, the value of the Japanese yen "future" depends on the exchange rate between yen and dollars, and the value of the bond depends on the value of the underlying mortgages. The market for derivatives has grown faster than any other market in recent years, providing investors with new opportunities, but also exposing them to new risks.

Derivatives can be used to reduce risks or to speculate. Suppose a wheat processor's costs rise and its net income falls when the price of wheat rises. The processor could reduce its risk by purchasing derivatives—wheat futures—whose value increases when the price of wheat rises. This is a *hedging operation*, and its purpose is to reduce risk exposure. Speculation, on the other hand, is done in the hope of high returns; but it raises risk exposure. For example, several years ago Procter & Gamble disclosed that it lost $150 million on derivative investments. More recently, losses on mortgage-related derivatives helped contribute to the credit collapse in 2008.

The values of most derivatives are subject to more volatility than the values of the underlying assets. For example, someone might pay $500 for an option to buy 100 shares of IBM stock at $120 per share when the stock is selling for $120. If the stock rose by $5 per share, a gain of 4.17% would result. However, the options would be worth somewhere between $25 and $30; so the percentage gain would be between 400% and 500%.[3] Of course, if IBM stayed at $120 or fell, the options would be worthless and the option purchaser would have a 100% loss. Many other derivatives have similar characteristics and are equally as risky or even more risky.

If a bank or any other company reports that it invests in derivatives, how can one tell if the derivatives are held as a hedge against something like an increase in the price of wheat or as a speculative bet that wheat prices will rise? The answer is that it is very difficult to tell how derivatives are affecting the risk profile of the firm. In the case of financial institutions, things are even more complicated—the derivatives are generally based on changes in interest rates, foreign exchange rates, or stock prices; and a large international bank might have tens of thousands of separate derivative contracts. The size and complexity of these transactions concern regulators, academics, and members of Congress. Former Fed Chairperson Greenspan noted that in theory, derivatives should allow companies to better manage risk but that it is not clear whether recent innovations have "increased or decreased the inherent stability of the financial system."

Derivative
Any financial asset whose value is derived from the value of some other "underlying" asset.

---

[3]For a discussion on options and option pricing, refer to Chapter 18 in this text.

Distinguish between physical asset markets and financial asset markets.

What's the difference between spot markets and futures markets?

Distinguish between money markets and capital markets.

What's the difference between primary markets and secondary markets?

Differentiate between private and public markets.

Why are financial markets essential for a healthy economy and economic growth?

2-3 FINANCIAL INSTITUTIONS

Direct funds transfers are common among individuals and small businesses and in economies where financial markets and institutions are less developed. But large businesses in developed economies generally find it more efficient to enlist the services of a financial institution when it comes time to raise capital.

In the United States and other developed nations, a set of highly efficient financial intermediaries has evolved. Their original roles were generally quite specific, and regulation prevented them from diversifying. However, in recent years, regulations against diversification have been largely removed; and today the differences between institutions have become blurred. Still, there remains a degree of institutional identity. Therefore, it is useful to describe the major categories of financial institutions here. Keep in mind, though, that one company can own a number of subsidiaries that engage in the different functions described next.

Investment Bank
An organization that underwrites and distributes new investment securities and helps businesses obtain financing.

1. **Investment banks** traditionally help companies raise capital. They (a) help corporations design securities with features that are currently attractive to investors, (b) buy these securities from the corporation, and (c) resell them to savers. Since the investment bank generally guarantees that the firm will raise the needed capital, the investment bankers are also called *underwriters*. The recent credit crisis has had a dramatic effect on the investment banking industry. Bear Stearns collapsed and was later acquired by J.P. Morgan, Lehman Brothers went bankrupt, and Merrill Lynch was forced to sell out to Bank of America. Moreover, the two "surviving" major investment banks (Morgan Stanley and Goldman Sachs) received Federal Reserve approval to become commercial bank holding companies. Their future remains uncertain.

Commercial Bank
The traditional department store of finance serving a variety of savers and borrowers.

2. **Commercial banks,** such as Bank of America, Citibank, Wells Fargo, Wachovia, and JPMorgan Chase, are the traditional "department stores of finance" because they serve a variety of savers and borrowers. Historically, commercial banks were the major institutions that handled checking accounts and through which the Federal Reserve System expanded or contracted the money supply. Today, however, several other institutions also provide checking services and significantly influence the money supply. Note, too, that the larger banks are generally part of financial services corporations as described next.[4]

Financial Services Corporation
A firm that offers a wide range of financial services, including investment banking, brokerage operations, insurance, and commercial banking.

3. **Financial services corporations** are large conglomerates that combine many different financial institutions within a single corporation. Most financial services corporations started in one area but have now diversified to cover most of the financial spectrum. For example, Citigroup owns Citibank (a commercial bank), Smith Barney (an investment bank and securities brokerage organization), insurance companies, and leasing companies.

---

[4]Two other institutions that were important a few years ago were *savings and loan associations* and *mutual savings banks*. Most of these organizations have now been merged into commercial banks.

4. *Credit unions* are cooperative associations whose members are supposed to have a common bond, such as being employees of the same firm. Members' savings are loaned only to other members, generally for auto purchases, home improvement loans, and home mortgages. Credit unions are often the cheapest source of funds available to individual borrowers.

5. *Pension funds* are retirement plans funded by corporations or government agencies for their workers and administered primarily by the trust departments of commercial banks or by life insurance companies. Pension funds invest primarily in bonds, stocks, mortgages, and real estate.

6. *Life insurance companies* take savings in the form of annual premiums; invest these funds in stocks, bonds, real estate, and mortgages; and make payments to the beneficiaries of the insured parties. In recent years, life insurance companies have also offered a variety of tax-deferred savings plans designed to provide benefits to participants when they retire.

7. **Mutual funds** are corporations that accept money from savers and then use these funds to buy stocks, long-term bonds, or short-term debt instruments issued by businesses or government units. These organizations pool funds and thus reduce risks by diversification. They also achieve economies of scale in analyzing securities, managing portfolios, and buying and selling securities. Different funds are designed to meet the objectives of different types of savers. Hence, there are bond funds for those who prefer safety, stock funds for savers who are willing to accept significant risks in the hope of higher returns, and still other funds that are used as interest-bearing checking accounts (**money market funds**). There are literally thousands of different mutual funds with dozens of different goals and purposes.

    Mutual funds have grown more rapidly than most other institutions in recent years, in large part because of a change in the way corporations provide for employees' retirement. Before the 1980s, most corporations said, in effect, "Come work for us; and when you retire, we will give you a retirement income based on the salary you were earning during the last five years before you retired." The company was then responsible for setting aside funds each year to make sure it had the money available to pay the agreed-upon retirement benefits. That situation is changing rapidly. Today new employees are likely to be told, "Come work for us, and we will give you some money each payday that you can invest for your future retirement. You can't get the money until you retire (without paying a huge tax penalty); but if you invest wisely, you can retire in comfort." Most workers recognize that they don't know how to invest wisely, so they turn their retirement funds over to a mutual fund. Hence, mutual funds are growing rapidly. Excellent information on the objectives and past performances of the various funds are provided in publications such as *Value Line Investment Survey* and *Morningstar Mutual Funds*, which are available in most libraries and on the Internet.

8. *Exchange Traded Funds* (ETFs) are similar to regular mutual funds and are often operated by mutual fund companies. ETFs buy a portfolio of stocks of a certain type—for example, the S&P 500 or media companies or Chinese companies—and then sell their own shares to the public. ETF shares are generally traded in the public markets, so an investor who wants to invest in the Chinese market, for example, can buy shares in an ETF that holds stocks in that particular market.

9. *Hedge funds* are also similar to mutual funds because they accept money from savers and use the funds to buy various securities, but there are some important differences. While mutual funds (and ETFs) are registered and regulated by the Securities and Exchange Commission (SEC), hedge funds are largely unregulated. This difference in regulation stems from the fact that

Mutual Funds
Organizations that pool investor funds to purchase financial instruments and thus reduce risks through diversification.

Money Market Funds
Mutual funds that invest in short-term, low-risk securities and allow investors to write checks against their accounts.

mutual funds typically target small investors, whereas hedge funds typically have large minimum investments (often exceeding $1 million) and are marketed primarily to institutions and individuals with high net worths. Hedge funds received their name because they traditionally were used when an individual was trying to hedge risks. For example, a hedge fund manager who believes that interest rate differentials between corporate and Treasury bonds are too large might simultaneously buy a portfolio of corporate bonds and sell a portfolio of Treasury bonds. In this case, the portfolio would be "hedged" against overall movements in interest rates, but it would perform especially well if the spread between these securities were to narrow.

However, some hedge funds take on risks that are considerably higher than that of an average individual stock or mutual fund. For example, in 1998, Long-Term Capital Management (LTCM), a high-profile hedge fund whose managers included several well-respected practitioners as well as two Nobel Prize–winning professors who were experts in investment theory, made some incorrect assumptions and "blew up."[5] LTCM had many billions of dollars under management, and it owed large amounts of money to a number of banks. To avert a worldwide crisis, the Federal Reserve orchestrated a buyout of the firm by a group of New York banks.

As hedge funds have become more popular, many of them have begun to lower their minimum investment requirements. Perhaps not surprisingly, their rapid growth and shift toward smaller investors have also led to a call for more regulation.

10. *Private equity companies* are organizations that operate much like hedge funds; but rather than buying some of the stock of a firm, private equity players buy and then manage entire firms. Most of the money used to buy the target companies is borrowed. Recent examples include Cerberus Capital's buyout of Chrysler and private equity company JC Flowers' proposed $25 billion purchase of Sallie Mae, the largest student loan company. The Sallie Mae deal is in jeopardy—Flowers planned to borrow most of the money for the purchase, but the subprime situation has made borrowing more difficult and expensive. Flowers tried to back out of the deal, but Sallie Mae executives insisted that it complete the transaction or pay a $900 million "breakup fee."

With the exception of hedge funds and private equity companies, financial institutions are regulated to ensure the safety of these institutions and to protect investors. Historically, many of these regulations—which have included a prohibition on nationwide branch banking, restrictions on the types of assets the institutions could buy, ceilings on the interest rates they could pay, and limitations on the types of services they could provide—tended to impede the free flow of capital and thus hurt the efficiency of the capital markets. Recognizing this fact, policy makers took several steps during the 1980s and 1990s to deregulate financial services companies. For example, the restriction barring nationwide branching by banks was eliminated in 1999.

Panel A of Table 2-2 lists the 10 largest U.S. bank holding companies, while Panel B shows the leading world banking companies. Among the world's 10 largest, only two (Citigroup and Bank of America) are based in the United States. While U.S. banks have grown dramatically as a result of recent mergers, they are still small by global standards. Panel C of the table lists the 10 leading underwriters in terms of dollar volume of new debt and equity issues. Six of the top underwriters are also major commercial banks or are part of bank holding companies, which confirms the continued blurring of distinctions between different types of financial institutions.

---

[5]See Franklin Edwards, "Hedge Funds and the Collapse of Long-Term Capital Management," *Journal of Economic Perspectives*, Vol. 13, no. 2 (Spring 1999), pp. 189–210, for a thoughtful review of the implications of Long-Term Capital Management's collapse.

CITIGROUP BUILT TO COMPETE IN A CHANGING ENVIRONMENT

The financial environment has been undergoing tremendous changes, including breakthroughs in technology, increased globalization, and shifts in the regulatory environment. All of these factors have presented financial managers and investors with opportunities, but those opportunities are accompanied by substantial risks.

Consider the case of Citigroup Inc., which was created in 1998 when Citicorp and Travelers Group (which included the investment firm Salomon Smith Barney) merged. Citigroup today operates in more than 100 countries, has roughly 200 million customers and 275,000 employees, and holds more than $2.2 trillion (that's over two thousand billion!) worth of assets.

Citigroup resulted from three important trends:

1. Regulatory changes made it possible for U.S. corporations to engage in commercial banking, investment banking, insurance, and other activities.

2. Increased globalization made it essential for financial institutions to follow their clients and thus operate in many countries.

3. Changing technology led to increased economies of scale and scope, both of which increased the relative efficiency of huge diversified companies such as Citigroup.

Citigroup has grown, and it is now the largest financial institution in the world. But as the chapter opening vignette indicated, Citigroup has been hit hard by the mortgage debacle; and its chairperson, Charles Prince, recently lost his job. When you read this, you might access the Internet to find the extent to which Citigroup has been able to rebound from its recent difficulties.

Table 2-2   Largest Banks and Underwriters

Panel A U.S. Bank Holding Companies[a]	Panel B World Banking Companies[b]	Panel C Leading Global Underwriters[c]
Citigroup Inc.	UBS AG (Zurich)	Citigroup Inc.
Bank of America Corp.	Barclays PLC (London)	JPMorgan
JPMorgan Chase & Co.	BNP Paribas (Paris)	Deutsche Bank AG
Wachovia Corp.	Citigroup Inc. (New York)	Merrill Lynch
Taunus Corp.	HSBC Holdings PLC (London)	Morgan Stanley
Wells Fargo & Co.	Royal Bank of Scotland Group PLC (Edinburgh)	Lehman Brothers
HSBC North America Holdings Inc.	Credit Agricole (Paris)	Goldman Sachs
U.S. Bancorp	Mitsubishi UFJ Financial Group (Tokyo)	Barclays Capital
Bank of New York, The Mellon Corp.	Deutsche Bank AG (Frankfurt)	UBS AG
SunTrust Banks, Inc.	Bank of America Corp. (Charlotte)	Credit Suisse

Notes:
[a]Ranked by total assets as of December 31, 2007. *Source:* National Information Center, www.ffiec.gov/nicpubweb/nicweb/Top50Form.aspx.
[b]Ranked by total assets as of December 31, 2007. *Source:* Thomson One Banker.
[c]Ranked by dollar amount raised through new issues (stocks and bonds) in 2007. For this ranking, the lead underwriter (manager) is given credit for the entire issue. *Source:* Adapted from *The Wall Street Journal*, January 2, 2008, p. R18.

2-4 THE STOCK MARKET

As noted earlier, outstanding, previously issued securities are traded in the secondary markets. By far, the most active secondary market—and the most important one to financial managers—is the *stock market*, where the prices of firms' stocks are established. Because the primary goal of financial managers is to maximize their firms' stock prices, knowledge of the stock market is important to anyone involved in managing a business.

There are a number of different stock markets. The two leaders are the New York Stock Exchange (NYSE) and the Nasdaq stock market. Stocks are traded using a variety of market procedures, but there are just two basic types: (1) *physical location exchanges,* which include the NYSE, the American Stock Exchange (AMEX), and several regional stock exchanges, and (2) *electronic dealer-based markets,* which include the Nasdaq, the less formal over-the-counter market, and the recently developed electronic communications networks (ECNs). (See the box entitled, "The NYSE and Nasdaq Go Global.") Because the physical location exchanges are easier to describe and understand, we discuss them first.

GLOBAL PERSPECTIVES

THE NYSE AND NASDAQ GO GLOBAL

Advances in computers and telecommunications that spurred consolidation in the financial services industry have also promoted online trading systems that bypass the traditional exchanges. These systems, which are known as *electronic communications networks (ECNs),* use electronic technology to bring buyers and sellers together. The rise of ECNs accelerated the move toward 24-hour trading. U.S. investors who wanted to trade after the U.S. markets closed could utilize an ECN, thus bypassing the NYSE and Nasdaq.

Recognizing the new threat, the NYSE and Nasdaq took action. First, both exchanges went public, which enabled them to use their stock as "currency" that could be used to buy ECNs and other exchanges across the globe. For example, Nasdaq acquired the American Stock Exchange

(AMEX), several ECNs, and 25% of the London Stock Exchange; and it is actively seeking to merge with other exchanges around the world. The NYSE has taken similar actions, including a merger with the largest European exchange, Euronext, to form NYSE Euronext.

These actions illustrate the growing importance of global trading, especially electronic trading. Indeed, many pundits have concluded that the floor traders who buy and sell stocks on the NYSE and other physical exchanges will soon become a thing of the past. That may or may not be true, but it is clear that stock trading will continue to undergo dramatic changes in the upcoming years.

To find a wealth of up-to-date information on the NYSE and Nasdaq, go to Google (or another search engine) and do NYSE history and Nasdaq history searches.

2-4a Physical Location Stock Exchanges

Physical location exchanges are tangible entities. Each of the larger ones occupies its own building, allows a limited number of people to trade on its floor, and has an elected governing body—its board of governors. Members of the NYSE formerly had "seats" on the exchange, although everybody stood up. Today the seats have been exchanged for trading licenses, which are auctioned to member organizations and cost about $50,000 per year. Most of the larger investment banks operate *brokerage departments*. They purchase seats on the exchanges and designate one or more of their officers as members. The exchanges are open on all normal working days, with the members meeting in a large room equipped with telephones and other electronic equipment that enable each member to communicate with his or her firm's offices throughout the country.

Like other markets, security exchanges facilitate communication between buyers and sellers. For example, Merrill Lynch (the fourth largest brokerage firm) might receive an order in its Atlanta office from a customer who wants to buy shares of GE stock. Simultaneously, the Denver office of Morgan Stanley (the fifth largest brokerage firm) might receive an order from a customer wanting to sell shares of GE. Each broker communicates electronically with the firm's representative on the NYSE. Other brokers throughout the country are also communicating with their own exchange members. The exchange members with *sell orders* offer the shares for sale, and they are bid for by the members with *buy orders*. Thus, the exchanges operate as *auction markets*.[6]

2-4b Over-the-Counter (OTC) and the Nasdaq Stock Markets

While the stocks of most large companies trade on the NYSE, a larger number of stocks trade off the exchange in what was traditionally referred to as the **over-the-counter (OTC) market.** An explanation of the term *over-the-counter* will help clarify how this term arose. As noted earlier, the exchanges operate as auction markets—buy and sell orders come in more or less simultaneously, and exchange members match these orders. When a stock is traded infrequently, perhaps because the firm is new or small, few buy and sell orders come in and matching them within a reasonable amount of time is difficult. To avoid this problem, some brokerage firms maintain an inventory of such stocks and stand prepared to make a market for them. These "dealers" buy when individual investors want to sell, and they sell part of their inventory when investors want to buy. At one time, the inventory of securities was kept in a safe; and the stocks, when bought and sold, were literally passed over the counter.

Physical Location Exchanges
Formal organizations having tangible physical locations that conduct auction markets in designated ("listed") securities.

Over-the-Counter (OTC) Market
A large collection of brokers and dealers, connected electronically by telephones and computers, that provides for trading in unlisted securities.

---

[6] The NYSE is actually a modified auction market wherein people (through their brokers) bid for stocks. Originally —in 1792—brokers would literally shout, "I have 100 shares of Erie for sale; how much am I offered?" and then sell to the highest bidder. If a broker had a buy order, he or she would shout, "I want to buy 100 shares of Erie; who'll sell at the best price?" The same general situation still exists, although the exchanges now have members known as *specialists* who facilitate the trading process by keeping an inventory of shares of the stocks in which they specialize. If a buy order comes in at a time when no sell order arrives, the specialist will sell off some inventory. Similarly, if a sell order comes in, the specialist will buy and add to inventory. The specialist sets a *bid price* (the price the specialist will pay for the stock) and an *ask price* (the price at which shares will be sold out of inventory). The bid and ask prices are set at levels designed to keep the inventory in balance. If many buy orders start coming in because of favorable developments or many sell orders come in because of unfavorable events, the specialist will raise or lower prices to keep supply and demand in balance. Bid prices are somewhat lower than ask prices, with the difference, or *spread*, representing the specialist's profit margin.

Special facilities are available to help institutional investors such as mutual or pension funds sell large blocks of stock without depressing their prices. In essence, brokerage houses that cater to institutional clients will purchase blocks (defined as 10,000 or more shares) and then resell the stock to other institutions or individuals. Also, when a firm has a major announcement that is likely to cause its stock price to change sharply, it will ask the exchange to halt trading in its stock until the announcement has been made and the resulting information has been digested by investors.

Dealer Market
Includes all facilities that are needed to conduct security transactions not conducted on the physical location exchanges.

Today these markets are often referred to as **dealer markets.** A dealer market includes all facilities that are needed to conduct security transactions, but the transactions are not made on the physical location exchanges. The dealer market system consists of (1) the relatively few *dealers* who hold inventories of these securities and who are said to "make a market" in these securities; (2) the thousands of brokers who act as *agents* in bringing the dealers together with investors; and (3) the computers, terminals, and electronic networks that provide a communication link between dealers and brokers. The dealers who make a market in a particular stock quote the price at which they will pay for the stock (the *bid price*) and the price at which they will sell shares (the *ask price*). Each dealer's prices, which are adjusted as supply and demand conditions change, can be seen on computer screens across the world. The *bid-ask spread,* which is the difference between bid and ask prices, represents the dealer's markup, or profit. The dealer's risk increases when the stock is more volatile or when the stock trades infrequently. Generally, we would expect volatile, infrequently traded stocks to have wider spreads in order to compensate the dealers for assuming the risk of holding them in inventory.

Brokers and dealers who participate in the OTC market are members of a self-regulatory body known as the *National Association of Securities Dealers (NASD),* which licenses brokers and oversees trading practices. The computerized network used by the NASD is known as the NASD Automated Quotation System (Nasdaq).

Nasdaq started as just a quotation system, but it has grown to become an organized securities market with its own listing requirements. Over the past decade, the competition between the NYSE and Nasdaq has become increasingly fierce. As noted earlier, the Nasdaq has invested in the London Stock Exchange and other market makers, while the NYSE merged with Euronext. Since most of the larger companies trade on the NYSE, the market capitalization of NYSE-traded stocks is much higher than for stocks traded on Nasdaq. However, reported volume (number of shares traded) is often larger on Nasdaq, and more companies are listed on Nasdaq.[7]

Interestingly, many high-tech companies such as Microsoft, Google, and Intel have remained on Nasdaq even though they meet the listing requirements of the NYSE. At the same time, however, other high-tech companies have left Nasdaq for the NYSE. Despite these defections, Nasdaq's growth over the past decade has been impressive. In the years ahead, competition between Nasdaq and NYSE Euronext will no doubt remain fierce.

SELF TEST

What are the differences between the physical location exchanges and the Nasdaq stock market?

What is the bid-ask spread?

2-5 THE MARKET FOR COMMON STOCK

Closely Held Corporation
A corporation that is owned by a few individuals who are typically associated with the firm's management.

Some companies are so small that their common stocks are not actively traded; they are owned by relatively few people, usually the companies' managers. These firms are said to be *privately owned,* or **closely held, corporations;** and their stock is called *closely held stock.* In contrast, the stocks of most large companies are owned

---

[7]One transaction on Nasdaq generally shows up as two separate trades (the buy and the sell). This "double counting" makes it difficult to compare the volume between stock markets.

by thousands of investors, most of whom are not active in management. These companies are called **publicly owned corporations**, and their stock is called *publicly held stock*.

A recent study found that institutional investors owned about 46% of all publicly held common stocks. Included are pension plans (26%), mutual funds (10%), foreign investors (6%), insurance companies (3%), and brokerage firms (1%). However, because these institutions buy and sell relatively actively, they account for about 75% of all transactions. Thus, institutional investors have a significant influence on the prices of individual stocks.

2-5a Types of Stock Market Transactions

We can classify stock market transactions into three distinct categories:

1. *Outstanding shares of established publicly owned companies that are traded: the secondary market.* Allied Food Products, the company we will study in Chapters 3 and 4, has 50 million shares of stock outstanding. If the owner of 100 shares sells his or her stock, the trade is said to have occurred in the *secondary market*. Thus, the market for outstanding shares, or *used shares*, is the secondary market. The company receives no new money when sales occur in this market.

2. *Additional shares sold by established publicly owned companies: the primary market.* If Allied Food decides to sell (or issue) an additional 1 million shares to raise new equity capital, this transaction is said to occur in the *primary market*.[8]

3. *Initial public offerings made by privately held firms: the IPO market.* In the summer of 2004, Google sold shares to the public for the first time at $85 per share. By February 2008, the stock was selling for $495, so it had increased by over 480%. In 2006, McDonald's owned Chipotle Mexican Grill. McDonald's then sold its shares to the public for about $47.50 to raise capital to support its core business; and by February 2008, Chipotle's stock price was $117. Making these types of offerings is called **going public**. Whenever stock in a closely held corporation is offered to the public for the first time, the company is said to be going public. The market for stock that is just being offered to the public is called the **initial public offering (IPO) market**.[9]

The number of new IPOs rises and falls with the stock market. When the market is strong, many companies go public to bring in new capital and to give their founders an opportunity to cash out some of their shares. Table 2-3 lists the largest, the best performing, and the worst performing IPOs of 2007 and shows how they performed from their offering dates through year-end 2007. As the table shows, not all IPOs are as well received as Google and Chipotle. Moreover, even if you are able to identify a "hot" issue, it is often difficult to purchase shares in the initial offering. These deals are often *oversubscribed*, which means that the demand for shares at the offering price exceeds the number of shares issued. In such instances, investment bankers favor large institutional investors (who are their best customers); and small investors find it hard, if not impossible, to get in on the ground floor. They can buy the stock in the aftermarket; but evidence suggests

Publicly Owned Corporation
A corporation that is owned by a relatively large number of individuals who are not actively involved in the firm's management.

Going Public
The act of selling stock to the public at large by a closely held corporation or its principal stockholders.

Initial Public Offering (IPO) Market
The market for stocks of companies that are in the process of going public.

---

[8]Allied has 60 million shares authorized but only 50 million outstanding; thus, it has 10 million authorized but unissued shares. If it had no authorized but unissued shares, management could increase the authorized shares by obtaining stockholders' approval, which would generally be granted without any arguments.

[9]A number of years ago Coors, the beer company, offered some of its shares to the public. These shares were designated Class B, and they were nonvoting. The Coors family retained the founders' shares, called Class A stock, which carried full voting privileges. This illustrates how the managers of a company can use different classes of shares to maintain control. However, the nonvoting shares always sell for less than the voting shares, so using nonvoting shares does not maximize the value of the firm.

Table 2-3	Initial Public Offerings in 2007

THE BIGGEST IPOs

Issuer	Issue Date	U.S. Proceeds (Millions)	PERCENT CHANGE FROM OFFER	
			First-Day Trading	Through 12/31/07
Blackstone	06/21/07	$4,753.3	+13.1%	−28.6%
MF Global	07/18/07	2,921.4	−8.2	+4.9
MetroPCS Communications	04/18/07	1,322.5	+19.1	−15.4
Cosan	08/16/07	1,172.7	unch.	+20.0
Och-Ziff Capital Management Group	11/13/07	1,152.0	−4.2	−17.9
VMware	08/13/07	1,100.6	+75.9	+193.1
Giant Interactive Group	10/31/07	1,019.5	+17.6	−16.3
National CineMedia	02/07/07	882.0	+22.2	+20.0
AECOM Technology	05/09/07	808.5	+5.5	+42.9
Energy Solutions	11/14/07	765.9	+0.04	+17.3

THE BEST PERFORMERS

Issuer	Issue Date	Offer Price	U.S. Proceeds (Millions)	PERCENT CHANGE FROM OFFER	
				First-Day Trading	Through 12/31/07
JA Solar Holdings	02/06/07	$15.00	$ 258.8	+18.7%	+365.4%
MercadoLibre	08/09/07	18.00	332.8	+58.3	+310.4
Yingli Green Energy Holding	06/07/07	11.00	324.5	−4.6	+251.8
VMware	08/13/07	29.00	1,100.6	+75.9	+193.1
Lululemon Athletica	07/26/07	18.00	376.7	+55.6	+163.2
Masimo	08/07/07	17.00	233.0	+22.9	+132.1
MSCI	11/14/07	18.00	289.8	+38.7	+113.3
American Public Education	11/08/07	20.00	107.8	+79.6	+108.9
WuXi PharmaTech (Cayman)	08/08/07	14.00	212.3	+40.0	+108.9
Dolan Media	08/01/07	14.50	224.4	+22.2	+101.2

THE WORST PERFORMERS

Issuer	Issue Date	Offer Price	U.S. Proceeds (Millions)	PERCENT CHANGE FROM OFFER	
				First-Day Trading	Through 12/31/07
Superior Offshore International	04/19/07	$15.00	$175.4	+16.9%	−66.5%
VeriChip	02/09/07	6.50	20.2	unch.	−65.4
ImaRx Therapeutics	07/25/07	5.00	15.0	−4.2	−61.4
BigBand Networks	03/14/07	13.00	160.0	+30.8	−60.5
Meruelo Maddux Properties	01/24/07	10.00	455.5	+6.0	−60.0
HFF	01/30/07	18.00	296.0	+3.9	−57.0
Glu Mobile	03/21/07	11.50	86.2	+6.9	−54.6
Limelight Networks	06/07/07	15.00	276.0	+47.9	−54.1
Xinhua Finance Media	03/08/07	13.00	300.0	−12.7	−53.8
GSI Technology	03/29/07	5.50	35.4	−3.8	−53.6

Source: Lynn Cowan, "IPOs Tally Record Amount of Cash," *The Wall Street Journal,* January 2, 2008, p. R10.

that when an investor does not get in on the ground floor, IPOs often underperform the overall market over the long run.[10]

Google Inc.'s highly publicized IPO attracted attention because of its size (Google raised $1.67 billion in stock) and because of the way the sale was conducted. Rather than having the offer price set by its investment bankers, Google conducted a Dutch auction, where individual investors placed bids for shares directly. In a *Dutch auction,* the actual transaction price is set at the highest price (the clearing price) that causes all of the offered shares to be sold. All investors who set their bids at or above the clearing price received all of the shares they subscribed to at the offer price, which turned out to be $85. While Google's IPO was in many ways precedent-setting, few companies going public since then have been willing or able to use the Dutch auction method to allocate their IPO shares.

It is important to recognize that firms can go public without raising any additional capital. For example, the Ford Motor Company was once owned exclusively by the Ford family. When Henry Ford died, he left a substantial part of his stock to the Ford Foundation. When the Foundation later sold some of the stock to the general public, the Ford Motor Company went public, even though the company itself raised no capital in the transaction.

SELF TEST

Differentiate between closely held and publicly owned corporations.

Differentiate between primary and secondary markets.

What is an IPO?

What is a Dutch auction, and what company used this procedure for its IPO?

2-6 STOCK MARKETS AND RETURNS

Anyone who has invested in the stock market knows that there can be (and generally are) large differences between *expected* and *realized* prices and returns. Figure 2-2 shows how total realized portfolio returns have varied from year to year. As logic would suggest (and as is demonstrated in Chapter 8), a stock's expected return as estimated by investors at the margin is always positive; otherwise, investors would not buy the stock. However, as Figure 2-2 shows, in some years, actual returns are negative.

2-6a Stock Market Reporting

Up until a few years ago, the best source of stock quotations was the business section of daily newspapers such as *The Wall Street Journal.* One problem with newspapers, however, is that they report yesterday's prices. Now it is possible to obtain real-time quotes throughout the day from a wide variety of Internet sources.[11] One of the best is Yahoo!, and Figure 2-3 shows a detailed quote for GlaxoSmithKline PLC (GSK). As the heading shows, GlaxoSmithKline is traded on the NYSE under the symbol GSK. (The NYSE is just one of many world markets on which the stock trades.) The first two rows of information show that GSK had last traded at $45.89 and that the stock had traded thus far on this day from as low as $45.42 to as high as $46.23. (Note that the price is reported in decimals rather than fractions, reflecting a recent change in trading conventions.) The last trade

---

[10]See Jay R. Ritter, "The Long-Run Performance of Initial Public Offerings," *Journal of Finance*, Vol. 46, no. 1 (March 1991), pp. 3–27.

[11]Most free sources provide quotes that are delayed 15 minutes. Real-time quotes can be obtained for a fee.

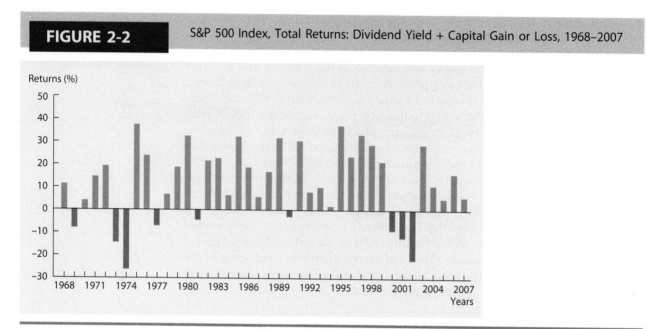

| FIGURE 2-2 | S&P 500 Index, Total Returns: Dividend Yield + Capital Gain or Loss, 1968–2007 |

Source: Data taken from various issues of *The Wall Street Journal* "Investment Scoreboard" section.

| FIGURE 2-3 | Stock Quote for GlaxoSmithKline, February 5, 2008 |

GLAXOSMITHKLINE PLC (NYSE:GSK)   [Edit]

Last Trade:	**45.89**	Day's Range:	45.42 - 46.23
Trade Time:	2.20PM ET	52wk Range:	45.89 - 59.98
Change:	↓0.98 (2.09%)	Volume:	1,835,434
Prev Close:	46.87	Avg Vol (3m):	1,968,960
Open:	46.07	Market Cap:	125.39B
Bid:	N/A	P/E (ttm):	12.30
Ask:	N/A	EPS (ttm):	3.73
1y Target Est:	56.10	Div & Yield:	2.13 (4.50%)

Add Quotes to Your Web Site   ▢ Add GSK to Portfolio   ⚲ Set Alert   ⬇ Download Data

Source: http://finance.yahoo.com.

shown was at 2:20 p.m. ET on February 5, 2008; and its price range during the past 52 weeks was between $45.89 and $59.98.

The next three lines show that GSK opened trading on February 5 at $46.07, that it closed on February 4 at $46.87, and that its price fell by $0.98 (or a 2.09% decrease) from the previous close to the current price. So far during the day, 1,835,434 shares had traded hands. GSK's average daily trading volume (based on the past three months) was 1,968,960 shares, so trading so far that day was close to the average. The total value of all of GSK's stock, called its market cap, was $125.39 billion.

The last three lines report other market information for GSK. If it were trading on Nasdaq rather than a listed exchange, the most recent bid and ask quotes from dealers would have been shown. However, because it trades on the NYSE, these data are not available. GSK's P/E ratio (price per share divided by the most recent 12 months' earnings) was 12.30, and its earnings per share for the most recent 12 months was $3.73 (*ttm* stands for "trailing 12 months"—in other words, the

MEASURING THE MARKET

Stock market indexes are designed to show the performance of the stock market. However, there are many stock indexes, and it is difficult to determine which index best reflects market actions. Some are designed to represent the entire stock market, some track the returns of certain industry sectors, and others track the returns of small-cap, mid-cap, or large-cap stocks. In addition, there are indexes for different countries. We discuss here the three leading U.S. indexes. These indexes are used as a benchmark for comparing individual stocks with the overall market, for measuring the trend in stock prices over time, and for determining how various economic factors affect the market.

Dow Jones Industrial Average

Unveiled in 1896 by Charles H. Dow, the Dow Jones Industrial Average (DJIA) began with just 10 stocks, was expanded in 1916 to 20 stocks, and then was increased to 30 stocks in 1928, when the editors of *The Wall Street Journal* began adjusting the index for stock splits and making periodic substitutions. Today the DJIA still includes 30 companies. They represent almost a fifth of the market value of all U.S. stocks, and all are leading companies in their industries and widely held by individual and institutional investors. Visit www.dowjones.com to get more information about the DJIA. You can find out how it is calculated, the companies that make up the DJIA, and more history about the DJIA. In addition, a DJIA time line shows various historical events.

S&P 500 Index

Created in 1926, the S&P 500 Index is widely regarded as the standard for measuring large-cap U.S. stock market performance. The stocks in the S&P 500 are selected by the Standard & Poor's Index Committee, and they are the leading companies in the leading industries. It is weighted by each stock's market value, so the largest companies have the greatest influence. The S&P 500 is used for benchmarking by 97% of all U.S. money managers and pension plan sponsors, and approximately $700 billion is held in index funds designed to mirror the same performance of the index.

Nasdaq Composite Index

The Nasdaq Composite Index measures the performance of all stocks listed on the Nasdaq. Currently, it includes more than 5,000 companies; and because many companies in the technology sector are traded on the computer-based Nasdaq exchange, this index is generally regarded as an economic indicator of the high-tech industry. Microsoft, Intel, Google, and Cisco Systems are the four largest Nasdaq companies, and they make up a high percentage of the index's value-weighted market capitalization. For this reason, substantial movements in the same direction by these four companies can move the entire index.

Recent Performance

The accompanying figure plots the value that an investor would now have if he or she had invested $1 in each of the three indexes on January 1, 1995. The returns on the three indexes are compared with an investment strategy that invests only in 1-year T-bills. Each of these indexes performed quite well through 1999. However, for a couple of years, each index stumbled before beginning to rebound again in 2003. During the last 13 years, the average annualized returns of these indexes ranged from 8.8% for the S&P 500 to 9.6% for the Dow. Nasdaq experienced a huge bubble in 1999, reflecting overly optimistic valuations of technology companies. However, in 2000, the bubble burst and technology stock valuations spiraled downward, causing the Nasdaq Index to revert back to a level comparable to the S&P 500 and Dow Jones Industrial Average Index.

Growth of a $1 Investment Made on January 1, 1995

most recent 12 months). The mean of the analysts' one-year target price for GSK was $56.10. GSK's dividend was $2.13 per share, so the quarterly dividend was $0.5325 per share; and the dividend yield, which is the annual dividend divided by the previous closing price, is 4.50%.

In Figure 2-3, the chart to the right plots the stock price during the day; however, the links below the chart allow you to pick different time intervals for plotting data. As you can see, Yahoo! provides a great deal of information in its detailed quote; and even more detail is available on the screen page below the basic quote information.

2-6b Stock Market Returns

In Chapters 8 and 9, we will discuss in detail how a stock's rate of return is calculated, what the connection is between risk and returns, and what techniques analysts use to value stocks. However, it is useful at this point to give you a rough idea of how stocks have performed in recent years. Figure 2-2 shows how the returns on large U.S. stocks have varied over the past years, and the box entitled "Measuring the Market" provides information on the major U.S. stock market indices and their performances since the mid-1990s.

The market trend has been strongly up since 1968, but by no means does it go up every year. Indeed, as we can see from Figure 2-2, the overall market was down in 9 of the 40 years, including the three consecutive years of 2000–2002. The stock prices of individual companies have likewise gone up and down.[12] Of course, even in bad years, some individual companies do well; so "the name of the game" in security analysis is to pick the winners. Financial managers attempt to do this, but they don't always succeed. In subsequent chapters, we will examine the decisions managers make to increase the odds that their firms will perform well in the marketplace.

Would you expect a portfolio that consisted of the NYSE stocks to be more or less risky than a portfolio of Nasdaq stocks?

If we constructed a chart like Figure 2-2 for an average S&P 500 stock, do you think it would show more or less volatility? Explain.

2-7 STOCK MARKET EFFICIENCY

To begin this section, consider the following definitions:

Market price: The current price of a stock. For example, the Internet showed that on one day, GSK's stock traded at $45.89. The market price had varied from $45.42 to $46.23 during that same day as buy and sell orders came in.

Intrinsic value: The price at which the stock would sell if all investors had all knowable information about a stock. This concept was discussed in Chapter 1, where we saw that a stock's intrinsic value is based on its expected future cash flows and its risk. Moreover, the market price tends to fluctuate around the

---

[12]If we constructed a graph like Figure 2-2 for individual stocks rather than for the index, far greater variability would be shown. Also, if we constructed a graph like Figure 2-2 for bonds, it would have similar ups and downs, but the bars would be far smaller, indicating that gains and losses on bonds are generally much smaller than those on stocks. Above-average bond returns occur in years when interest rates decline, losses occur when interest rates rise sharply, but interest payments tend to stabilize bonds' total returns. We will discuss bonds in detail in Chapter 7.

intrinsic value; and the intrinsic value changes over time as the company succeeds or fails with new projects, competitors enter or exit the market, and so forth. We can guess (or estimate) GSK's intrinsic value, but different analysts will reach somewhat different conclusions.

Equilibrium price: The price that balances buy and sell orders at any given time. When a stock is in equilibrium, the price remains relatively stable until new information becomes available and causes the price to change. For example, GSK's equilibrium price appears to be about $45.89, as it has been fluctuating narrowly around this amount.

Efficient market: A market in which prices are close to intrinsic values and stocks seem to be in equilibrium.

When markets are efficient, investors can buy and sell stocks and be confident that they are getting good prices. When markets are inefficient, investors may be afraid to invest and may put their money "under the pillow," which will lead to a poor allocation of capital and economic stagnation. So from an economic standpoint, market efficiency is good.

Academics and financial professionals have studied the issue of market efficiency extensively.[13] As generally happens, some people think that markets are highly efficient, others think that markets are highly inefficient, and others think that the issue is too complex for a simple answer.

Those who believe that markets are efficient note that there are 100,000 or so full-time, highly trained professional analysts and traders operating in the market. Many have PhDs in physics, chemistry, and other technical fields in addition to advanced degrees in finance. Moreover, there are fewer than 3,000 major stocks; so if each analyst followed 30 stocks (which is about right, as analysts tend to focus on a specific industry), on average, 1,000 analysts would be following each stock. Further, these analysts work for organizations such as Goldman Sachs, Merrill Lynch, Citigroup, and Deutsche Bank or for Warren Buffett and other billionaire investors who have billions of dollars available to take advantage of bargains. Also, the SEC has disclosure rules which, combined with electronic information networks, means that new information about a stock is received by all analysts at about the same time, causing almost instantaneous revaluations. All of these factors help markets be efficient and cause stock prices to move toward their intrinsic values.

However, other people point to data that suggests that markets are not very efficient. For example, on October 15, 1987, the S&P 500 lost 25% of its value. Many of the largest U.S. companies did worse, watching their prices get cut in half. In 2000, Internet stocks rose to phenomenally high prices, then fell to zero or close to it the following year. No truly important news was announced that could have caused either of these changes; and if the market was efficient, it's hard to see how such drastic changes could have occurred. Another situation that causes people to question market efficiency is the apparent ability of some analysts to consistently outperform the market over long periods. Warren Buffett comes to mind, but there are others. If markets are truly efficient, then each stock's price

---

[13]The general name for these studies is the efficient markets hypothesis, or EMH. It was, and still is, a hypothesis that needs to be proved or disproved empirically. In the literature, researchers identified three levels of efficiency: *weak form*, which contends that information on past stock price movements cannot be used to predict future stock prices; *semi-strong form*, which contends that all publicly available information is immediately incorporated into stock prices (i.e., that one cannot analyze published reports and then beat the market); and *strong form*, which contends that even company insiders, with inside information, cannot earn abnormally high returns. Few people believe the strong form today, as a number of insiders have made large profits, been caught (it's illegal to trade on inside information), and gone to jail. Martha Stewart is one, and she helped disprove the strong form of the EMH.

should be close to its intrinsic value. That would make it hard for any analyst to consistently pick stocks that outperform the market.

The following diagram sums up where most observers seem to be today. There is an "efficiency continuum," with the market for some companies' stocks being highly efficient and the market for other stocks being highly inefficient. The key factor is the size of the company—the larger the firm, the more analysts tend to follow it and thus the faster new information is likely to be reflected in the stock's price. Also, different companies communicate better with analysts and investors; and the better the communications, the more efficient the market for the stock.

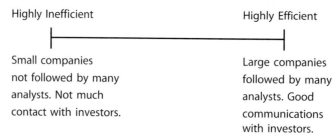

As an investor, would you prefer to purchase a stock whose price was determined in an efficient or an inefficient market? If you thought you knew something that others didn't know, you might prefer inefficient markets. But if you thought that those physics PhDs with unlimited buying power and access to company CEOs might know more than you, you would probably prefer efficient markets, where the price you paid was likely to be the "right" price. From an economic standpoint, it is good to have efficient markets in which everyone is willing to participate. So the SEC and other regulatory agencies should do everything they can to encourage market efficiency.

Thus far we have been discussing the market for individual stocks. There is also a market for entire companies, where other companies, private equity groups, and large investors like Warren Buffett buy the entire company or a controlling stake in it. Suppose, for example, that Company X is in equilibrium, selling at a price that is close to its intrinsic value but where the intrinsic value is based on it being operated by its current managers, who own 51% of the stock. However, suppose that astute analysts study the company and conclude that it could produce much higher earnings and cash flows under a different management team or if it were combined with some other company or if it were broken up into a number of separate pieces. In this case, the stock might be thought of as trading in an efficient market while the company as a whole was not efficiently priced.

Some years ago, quite a few companies were inefficiently priced. But then along comes Warren Buffett, the private equity players, and hedge fund managers who are willing to contest entrenched managers. For example, Dow Jones, the owner of *The Wall Street Journal,* was controlled by its founding family, the Bancrofts. Dow Jones's stock lagged the market for years. Then Rupert Murdoch, who controls News Corporation, arguably the largest media company in the world, offered $60 per share for Dow Jones, which was then selling for about $35 per share. Murdoch planned to change *The Wall Street Journal* and combine its content with his Fox News and new financial channel. To Murdoch, Dow Jones' intrinsic value was $60. Without him or someone else who would operate the company differently, the intrinsic value was about $35. One could, of course, argue that Dow Jones' intrinsic value was $60 all along; but it was hard to know that until Murdoch came along and made his offer. Alternatively, one could argue that Murdoch raised the intrinsic value from $35 to $60. Finally, you can bet that many analysts on Wall Street are looking for the next Dow Jones. If they succeed, they will surely beat the market!

A CLOSER LOOK AT BEHAVIORAL FINANCE THEORY

The *efficient markets hypothesis (EMH)* remains one of the cornerstones of modern finance theory. It implies that, on average, asset prices are about equal to their intrinsic values. The logic behind the EMH is straightforward. If a stock's price is "too low," rational traders will quickly take advantage of this opportunity and buy the stock, pushing prices up to the proper level. Likewise, if prices are "too high," rational traders will sell the stock, pushing the price down to its equilibrium level. Proponents of the EMH argue that these forces keep prices from being systematically wrong.

While the logic behind the EMH is compelling, many events in the real world seem inconsistent with the hypothesis, which has spurred a growing field called *behavioral finance.* Rather than assuming that investors are rational, behavioral finance theorists borrow insights from psychology to better understand how irrational behavior can be sustained over time. Pioneers in this field include psychologists Daniel Kahneman, Amos Tversky, and Richard Thaler. Their work has encouraged a growing number of scholars to work in this promising area of research.[14]

Professor Thaler and his colleague Nicholas Barberis summarized much of this research in the article cited below. They argue that behavioral finance's criticism of the EMH rests on two key points. First, it is often difficult or risky for traders to take advantage of mispriced assets. For example, even if you know that a stock's price is too low because investors have overreacted to recent bad news, a trader with limited capital may be reluctant to buy the stock for fear that the same forces that pushed the price down may work to keep it artificially low for a long time. Similarly, during the recent stock market bubble, many traders who believed (correctly) that stock prices were too high lost a great deal of money selling stocks short in the early stages of the bubble, because prices went even higher before they eventually collapsed. Thus, mispricings may persist.

The second point deals with why mispricings can occur in the first place. Here insights from psychology come into play. For example, Kahneman and Tversky suggested that individuals view potential losses and gains differently. If you ask average individuals whether they would rather have $500 with certainty or flip a fair coin and receive $1,000 if a head comes up and nothing if a tail comes up, most would prefer the certain $500, which suggests an aversion to risk. However, if you ask people whether they would rather pay $500 with certainty or flip a coin and pay $1,000 if it's a head and nothing if it's a tail, most would indicate that they prefer to flip the coin. Other studies suggest that people's willingness to take a gamble depends on recent performance. Gamblers who are ahead tend to take on more risks, whereas those who are behind tend to become more conservative.

These experiments suggest that investors and managers behave differently in down markets than they do in up markets, which might explain why those who made money early in the stock market bubble continued to invest their money in the market even as prices went ever higher. Other evidence suggests that individuals tend to overestimate their true abilities. For example, a large majority (upward of 90% in some studies) of people believe that they have above-average driving ability and above-average ability to get along with others. Barberis and Thaler point out that:

> Overconfidence may in part stem from two other biases, self-attribution bias and hindsight bias. Self-attribution bias refers to people's tendency to ascribe any success they have in some activity to their own talents, while blaming failure on bad luck rather than on their ineptitude. Doing this repeatedly will lead people to the pleasing, but erroneous, conclusion that they are very talented. For example, investors might become overconfident after several quarters of investing success [Gervais and Odean (2001)]. Hindsight bias is the tendency of people to believe, after an event has occurred, that they predicted it before it happened. If people think they predicted the past better than they actually did, they may also believe that they can predict the future better than they actually can.

Behavioral finance has been studied in both the corporate finance and investments areas. Ulrike Malmendier of Stanford and Geoffrey Tate of Wharton found that overconfidence leads managers to overestimate their ability and thus the profitability of their projects. This result may explain why so many corporate projects fail to live up to their stated expectations.

Sources: Nicholas Barberis and Richard Thaler, "A Survey of Behavioral Finance," Chapter 18, *Handbook of the Economics of Finance,* edited by George Constantinides, Milt Harris, and René Stulz, part of the *Handbooks in Economics Series* (New York: Elsevier/North-Holland, 2003); and Ulrike Malmendier and Geoffrey Tate, "CEO Overconfidence and Corporate Investment," Stanford Graduate School of Business Research Paper #1799, June 2004.

---

[14]Three noteworthy sources for students interested in behavioral finance are Richard H. Thaler, Editor, *Advances in Behavioral Finance* (New York: Russell Sage Foundation, 1993); Hersh Shefrin, "Behavioral Corporate Finance," *Journal of Applied Corporate Finance,* Vol. 14.3, Fall 2001, pp. 113–125; and Nicholas Barberis and Richard Thaler, "A Survey of Behavioral Finance," Chapter 18, *Handbook of the Economics of Finance,* edited by George Constantinides, Milt Harris, and René Stulz, part of the *Handbooks in Economics Series* (New York: Elsevier/North-Holland, 2003). Students interested in learning more about the efficient markets hypothesis should consult Burton G. Malkiel, *A Random Walk Down Wall Street: The Time-Tested Strategy for Successful Investing,* 9th ed., (New York: W.W. Norton & Company, 2007).

2-7a Conclusions about Market Efficiency

As noted previously, if the stock market is efficient, it is a waste of time for most people to seek bargains by analyzing published data on stocks. That follows because if stock prices already reflect all publicly available information, they will be fairly priced; and a person can beat the market only with luck or inside information. So rather than spending time and money trying to find undervalued stocks, it would be better to buy an index fund designed to match the overall market as reflected in an index such as the S&P 500. However, if we worked for an institution with billions of dollars, we would try to find undervalued stocks or companies because even a small undervaluation would amount to a great deal of money when investing millions rather than thousands. Also, markets are more efficient for individual stocks than for entire companies; so for investors with enough capital, it does make sense to seek out badly managed companies that can be acquired and improved. Note, though, that a number of private equity players are doing exactly that; so the market for entire companies may soon be as efficient as that for individual stocks.

However, even if markets are efficient and all stocks and companies are fairly priced, an investor should still be careful when selecting stocks for his or her portfolio. Most importantly, the portfolio should be diversified, with a mix of stocks from various industries along with some bonds and other fixed income securities. We will discuss diversification in greater detail in Chapter 8, but it is an important consideration for most individual investors.

SELF TEST

What does it mean for a market to be "efficient"?

Is the market for all stocks equally efficient? Explain.

Why is it good for the economy that markets be efficient?

Is it possible that the market for individual stocks could be highly efficient but the market for whole companies could be less efficient?

What is behavioral finance? What are the implications of behavioral finance for market efficiency?

TYING IT ALL TOGETHER

In this chapter, we provided a brief overview of how capital is allocated and discussed the financial markets, instruments, and institutions used in the allocation process. We discussed physical location exchanges and electronic markets for common stocks, stock market reporting, and stock indexes. We demonstrated that security prices are volatile—investors expect to make money, which they generally do over time; but losses can be large in any given year. Finally, we discussed the efficiency of the stock market and developments in behavioral finance. After reading this chapter, you should have a general understanding of the financial environment in which businesses and individuals operate, realize that actual returns are often different from expected returns, and be able to read stock market quotations from business newspapers or various Internet sites. You should also recognize that the theory of financial markets is a "work in progress," and much work remains to be done.

SELF-TEST QUESTION AND PROBLEM
(Solutions Appear in Appendix A)

ST-1   **KEY TERMS**   Define each of the following terms:

   a.   Spot markets; futures markets

   b.   Money markets; capital markets

   c.   Primary markets; secondary markets

   d.   Private markets; public markets

   e.   Derivatives

   f.   Investment banks (iBanks); commercial banks; financial services corporations

   g.   Mutual funds; money market funds

   h.   Physical location exchanges; over-the-counter (OTC) market; dealer market

   i.   Closely held corporation; publicly owned corporation

   j.   Going public; initial public offering (IPO) market

   k.   Efficient markets hypothesis (EMH)

   l.   Behavioral finance

QUESTIONS

2-1   How does a cost-efficient capital market help reduce the prices of goods and services?

2-2   Describe the different ways in which capital can be transferred from suppliers of capital to those who are demanding capital.

2-3   Is an initial public offering an example of a primary or a secondary market transaction? Explain.

2-4   Indicate whether the following instruments are examples of money market or capital market securities.

   a.   U.S. Treasury bills

   b.   Long-term corporate bonds

   c.   Common stocks

   d.   Preferred stocks

   e.   Dealer commercial paper

2-5   What would happen to the U.S. standard of living if people lost faith in the safety of the financial institutions? Explain.

2-6   What types of changes have financial markets experienced during the last two decades? Have they been perceived as positive or negative changes? Explain.

2-7   Differentiate between dealer markets and stock markets that have a physical location.

2-8   Identify and briefly compare the two leading stock exchanges in the United States today.

2-9   Describe the three different forms of market efficiency.

2-10   Investors expect a company to announce a 10% increase in earnings; instead, the company announces a 1% increase. If the market is semi-strong form efficient, which of the following would you expect to happen? (Hint: Refer to Footnote 13 in this chapter.)

   a.   The stock's price will increase slightly because the company had a slight increase in earnings.

   b.   The stock's price will fall because the earnings increase was less than expected.

   c.   The stock's price will stay the same because earnings announcements have no effect if the market is semi-strong form efficient.

2-11   Briefly explain what is meant by the term *efficiency continuum*.

2-12   Explain whether the following statements are true or false.

   a.   Derivative transactions are designed to increase risk and are used almost exclusively by speculators who are looking to capture high returns.

b.   Hedge funds typically have large minimum investments and are marketed to institutions and individuals with high net worths.

c.   Hedge funds have traditionally been highly regulated.

d.   The New York Stock Exchange is an example of a stock exchange that has a physical location.

e.   A larger bid-ask spread means that the dealer will realize a lower profit.

f.   The efficient markets hypothesis assumes that all investors are rational.

INTEGRATED CASE

SMYTH BARRY & COMPANY

2-1   **FINANCIAL MARKETS AND INSTITUTIONS**   Assume that you recently graduated with a degree in finance and have just reported to work as an investment adviser at the brokerage firm of Smyth Barry & Co. Your first assignment is to explain the nature of the U.S. financial markets to Michelle Varga, a professional tennis player who recently came to the United States from Mexico. Varga is a highly ranked tennis player who expects to invest substantial amounts of money through Smyth Barry. She is very bright; therefore, she would like to understand in general terms what will happen to her money. Your boss has developed the following questions that you must use to explain the U.S. financial system to Varga.

a.   What are the three primary ways in which capital is transferred between savers and borrowers? Describe each one.

b.   What is a market? Differentiate between the following types of markets: physical asset markets versus financial asset markets, spot markets versus futures markets, money markets versus capital markets, primary markets versus secondary markets, and public markets versus private markets.

c.   Why are financial markets essential for a healthy economy and economic growth?

d.   What are derivatives? How can derivatives be used to reduce risk? Can derivatives be used to increase risk? Explain.

e.   Briefly describe each of the following financial institutions: commercial banks, investment banks, mutual funds, hedge funds, and private equity companies.

f.   What are the two leading stock markets? Describe the two basic types of stock markets.

g.   If Apple Computer decided to issue additional common stock and Varga purchased 100 shares of this stock from Smyth Barry, the underwriter, would this transaction be a primary or a secondary market transaction? Would it make a difference if Varga purchased previously outstanding Apple stock in the dealer market? Explain.

h.   What is an initial public offering (IPO)?

i.   What does it mean for a market to be efficient? Explain why some stock prices may be more efficient than others.

j.   After your consultation with Michelle, she asks to discuss these two scenarios with you:

(1)   While in the waiting room of your office, she overheard an analyst on a financial TV network say that a particular medical research company just received FDA approval for one of its products. On the basis of this "hot" information, Michelle wants to buy many shares of that company's stock. Assuming the stock market is highly efficient, what advice would you give her?

(2)   She has read a number of newspaper articles about a huge IPO being carried out by a leading technology company. She wants to get as many shares in the IPO as possible and would even be willing to buy the shares in the open market immediately after the issue. What advice do you have for her?

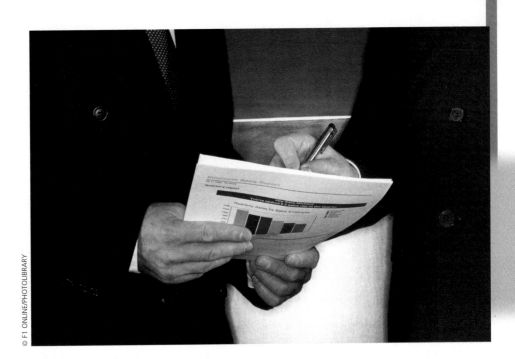

© F1 ONLINE/PHOTOLIBRARY

Financial Statements, Cash Flow, and Taxes

The "Quality" of Financial Statements

The financial statements presented in a typical company's annual report look quite official. They are signed by the firm's top executives and are certified by a Big Four accounting firm, so one would think that they must be accurate. That may not be true, though, for three reasons: legitimate misjudgments in valuing assets and measuring costs, "flexible" accounting rules that result in differently reported results for similar companies, and outright cheating.

One blatant example of cheating involved WorldCom, which reported asset values that exceeded their true value by about $11 billion. This led to an understatement of costs and a corresponding overstatement of profits. Enron is another example. That company overstated the value of certain assets, reported those artificial value increases as profits, and transferred the assets to subsidiary companies to hide the true facts. Enron's and WorldCom's investors eventually learned what was happening, the companies were forced into bankruptcy, their top executives went to jail, the accounting firm that

audited their books was forced out of business, and millions of investors lost billions of dollars.

After the Enron and WorldCom blowups, Congress passed the Sarbanes-Oxley Act (SOX), which required companies to improve their internal auditing standards and required the CEO and CFO to certify that the financial statements were properly prepared. The SOX bill also created a new watchdog organization to help make sure that the outside accounting firms were doing their job. From all indications, financial statements are generally more accurate and clearer than they were in the past.

But the world is dynamic, and a new accounting problem surfaced in 2007. Big banks, most notably Citigroup, owned many risky but high-yielding subprime mortgages. The banks invented a complex legal procedure that they called a structured investment vehicle (SIV) to conceal the fact that they held all of these risky mortgages. They correctly feared that people wouldn't want to do business with a risky bank. But when the subprime market fell apart in 2007, the banks had to acknowledge their losses, which ran into many billions of dollars.

It turns out that the banks had tried to avoid writing down their mortgages; but a newly formed organization set up by the Big Four accounting firms, called the Center for Audit Quality, took a hard line and forced the write-downs. That led Lynn Turner, former chief accountant for the SEC and a frequent critic of the accounting profession, to state, "The accounting firms are doing a much better job than they did in the past."[1]

---

[1]David Reilly, "Behind Bank's Credit Rescue Fund: "With New, United Voice, Auditors Stand Ground on How to Treat Crunch," *The Wall Street Journal*, October 17, 2007, p. C1.

PUTTING THINGS IN PERSPECTIVE

A manager's primary goal is to maximize the value of his or her firm's stock, and value is based on the firm's future cash flows. But how do managers decide which actions are most likely to increase those flows, and how do investors estimate future cash flows? The answers to both questions lie in a study of financial statements that publicly traded firms must provide to investors. Here *investors* include both institutions (banks, insurance companies, pension funds, and the like) and individuals like you.

Much of the material in this chapter deals with concepts you covered in a basic accounting course. However, the information is important enough to warrant a review. Also, in accounting, you probably focused on how accounting statements are made; the focus here is on how investors and managers *interpret* and *use* them. Accounting is the basic language of business, so everyone engaged in business needs a good working knowledge of it. It is used to "keep score"; and if investors and managers do not know the score, they won't know whether their actions are appropriate. If you took midterm exams but were not told your scores, you would have a difficult time knowing whether you needed to improve. The same idea holds in business. If a firm's managers—whether they are in marketing, personnel, pro-duction, or finance—do not understand financial statements, they will not be able to judge the effects of their actions, which will make it hard for the firm to survive, much less to have a maximum value.

When you finish this chapter you should be able to:

- List each of the key financial statements and identify the kinds of information they provide to corporate managers and investors.
- Estimate a firm's free cash flow and explain why free cash flow has such an important effect on firm value.
- Discuss the major features of the federal income tax system.

3-1 FINANCIAL STATEMENTS AND REPORTS

Annual Report
A report issued annually by a corporation to its stockholders. It contains basic financial statements as well as management's analysis of the firm's past operations and future prospects.

The **annual report** is the most important report that corporations issue to stock-holders, and it contains two types of information.[2] First, there is a verbal section, often presented as a letter from the chairperson, which describes the firm's operating

---

[2]Firms also provide quarterly reports, but these are much less comprehensive than the annual report. In addition, larger firms file even more detailed statements with the Securities and Exchange Commission (SEC), giving breakdowns for each major division or subsidiary. These reports, called *10-K reports*, are made available to stockholders upon request to a company's corporate secretary. In this chapter, we focus on annual data—balance sheets at the ends of years and income statements for entire years rather than for shorter periods.

results during the past year and discusses new developments that will affect future operations. Second, the report provides these four basic financial statements:

1. The *balance sheet*, which shows what assets the company owns and who has claims on those assets as of a given date—for example, December 31, 2008.

2. The *income statement*, which shows the firm's sales and costs (and thus profits) during some past period—for example, 2008.

3. The *statement of cash flows*, which shows how much cash the firm began the year with, how much cash it ended up with, and what it did to increase or decrease its cash.

4. The *statement of stockholders' equity*, which shows the amount of equity the stockholders had at the start of the year, the items that increased or decreased equity, and the equity at the end of the year.

These statements are related to one another; and taken together, they provide an accounting picture of the firm's operations and financial position.

The quantitative and verbal materials are equally important. The firm's financial statements report *what has actually happened* to its assets, earnings, and dividends over the past few years, whereas management's verbal statements attempt to explain why things turned out the way they did and what might happen in the future.

For discussion purposes, we use data for Allied Food Products, a processor and distributor of a wide variety of food products, to illustrate the basic financial statements. Allied was formed in 1981, when several regional firms merged; and it has grown steadily while earning a reputation as one of the best firms in its industry. Allied's earnings dropped from $121.8 million in 2007 to $117.5 million in 2008. Management reported that the drop resulted from losses associated with a drought as well as increased costs due to a three-month strike. However, management then went on to describe a more optimistic picture for the future, stating that full operations had been resumed, that several unprofitable businesses had been eliminated, and that 2009 profits were expected to rise sharply. Of course, an increase in profit-ability may not occur; and analysts should compare management's past statements with subsequent results. In any event, *the information contained in the annual report can be used to help forecast future earnings and dividends*. Therefore, investors are very interested in this report.

We should note that Allied's financial statements are relatively simple and straightforward; we also omitted some details often shown in the statements. Allied finances with only debt and common stock—it has no preferred stock, convertibles, or complex derivative securities. Also, the firm has made no acquisitions that resulted in goodwill that must be carried on the balance sheet. Finally, all of its assets are used in its basic business operations; hence, no nonoperating assets must be pulled out when we evaluate its operating performance. We deliberately chose such a company because this is an introductory text; as such, we want to explain the basics of financial analysis, not wander into arcane accounting matters that are best left to accounting and security analysis courses. We do point out some of the pitfalls that can be encountered when trying to interpret accounting statements, but we leave it to advanced courses to cover the intricacies of accounting.

SELF TEST

What is the annual report, and what two types of information does it provide?

What four financial statements are typically included in the annual report?

Why is the annual report of great interest to investors?

3-2 THE BALANCE SHEET

Balance Sheet
A statement of a firm's financial position at a specific point in time.

The balance sheet is a "snapshot" of a firm's position at a specific point in time. Figure 3-1 shows the layout of a typical **balance sheet**. The left side of the statement shows the assets that the company owns, while the right side shows the firm's liabilities and stockholders' equity, which are claims against the firm's assets.

As Figure 3-1 indicates, assets are divided into two major categories: current assets and fixed, or long-term, assets. Current assets consist of assets that should be converted to cash within one year; and they include cash and cash equivalents, accounts receivable, and inventory.[3] Long-term assets are assets expected to be used for more than one year; they include plant and equipment in addition to intellectual property such as patents and copyrights. Plant and equipment is generally reported net of accumulated depreciation. Allied's long-term assets consist entirely of net plant and equipment, and we often refer to them as "net fixed assets."

FIGURE 3-1	A Typical Balance Sheet

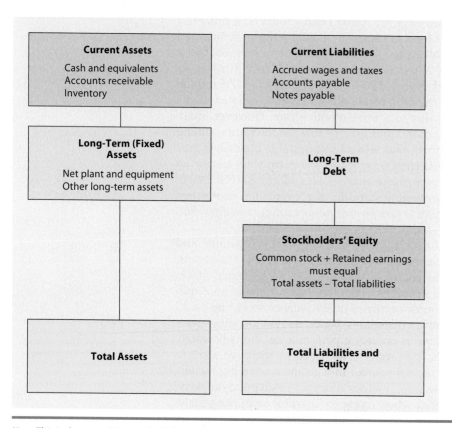

Note: This is the typical layout of a balance sheet for one year. When balance sheets for two or more years are shown, assets are listed in the top section; liabilities and equity, in the bottom section. See Table 3-1.

---

[3]Allied and most other companies hold some currency in addition to a bank checking account. They may also hold short-term interest-bearing securities that can be sold and thus converted to cash immediately with a simple telephone call. These securities are called "cash equivalents," and they are generally included with checking account balances for financial reporting purposes. If a company owns stocks or other marketable securities that it regards as short-term investments, these items will be shown separately on the balance sheet. Allied does not hold any marketable securities other than cash equivalents.

The claims against assets are of two basic types—liabilities (or money the company owes to others) and stockholders' equity. Liabilities consist of claims that must be paid off within one year (current liabilities), including accounts payable, accruals (total of accrued wages and accrued taxes), and notes payable to banks that are due within one year. Long-term debt includes bonds that mature in more than a year.

Stockholders' equity can be thought of in two ways. First, it is the amount that stockholders paid to the company when they bought shares the company sold to raise capital, in addition to all of the earnings the company has retained over the years:

$$\text{Stockholders' equity} = \text{Paid-in capital} + \text{Retained earnings}$$

The retained earnings are not just the earnings retained in the latest year—they are the cumulative total of all of the earnings the company has earned during its life.

Stockholders' equity can also be thought of as a residual:

$$\text{Stockholders' equity} = \text{Total assets} - \text{Total liabilities}$$

If Allied had invested surplus funds in bonds backed by subprime mortgages and the bonds' value fell below their purchase price, the true value of the firm's assets would have declined. The amount of its liabilities would not have changed—the firm would still owe the amount it had promised to pay its creditors. Therefore, the reported value of the common equity must decline. The accountants would make a series of entries, and the result would be a reduction in retained earnings—and thus in common equity. In the end, assets would equal liabilities and equity and the balance sheet would balance. This example shows why common stock is more risky than bonds—any mistake that management makes has a big impact on the stockholders. Of course, gains from good decisions also go to the stockholders; so with risk comes possible rewards.

Assets on the balance sheet are listed by the length of time before they will be converted to cash (inventories and accounts receivable) or used by the firm (fixed assets). Similarly, claims are listed in the order in which they must be paid: Accounts payable must generally be paid within a few days, accruals must also be paid promptly, notes payable to banks must be paid within one year, and so forth, down to the stockholders' equity accounts, which represent ownership and need never be "paid off."

3-2a Allied's Balance Sheet

Table 3-1 shows Allied's year-end balance sheets for 2008 and 2007. From the 2008 statement, we see that Allied had $2 billion of assets—half current and half long term. These assets were financed with $310 million of current liabilities, $750 million of long-term debt, and $940 million of common equity. Comparing the balance sheets for 2008 and 2007, we see that Allied's assets grew by $320 million and its liabilities and equity necessarily grew by that same amount. Assets must, of course, equal liabilities and equity; otherwise, the balance sheet does not balance.

Several additional points about the balance sheet should be noted:

1. *Cash versus other assets.* Although assets are reported in dollar terms, only the cash and equivalents account represents actual spendable money. Accounts receivable represents credit sales that have not yet been collected. Inventories show the cost of raw materials, work in process, and finished goods. Net fixed assets represent the cost of the buildings and equipment used in operations minus the depreciation that has been taken on these assets. At the end of 2008, Allied has $10 million of cash; hence, it could write checks totaling that amount. The noncash assets should generate cash over time, but they do not represent cash in hand. And the cash they would bring in if they were sold today could be higher or lower than the values reported on the balance sheet.

Table 3-1	Allied Food Products: December 31 Balance Sheets (Millions of Dollars)	

	2008	2007
Assets		
Current assets:		
Cash and equivalents	$ 10	$ 80
Accounts receivable	375	315
Inventories	615	415
Total current assets	$1,000	$ 810
Net fixed assets:		
Net plant and equipment (cost minus depreciation)	1,000	870
Other assets expected to last more than a year	0	0
Total assets	$2,000	$1,680
Liabilities and Equity		
Current liabilities:		
Accounts payable	$ 60	$ 30
Accruals	140	130
Notes payable	110	60
Total current liabilities	$ 310	$ 220
Long-term bonds	750	580
Total debt	$1,060	$ 800
Common equity:		
Common stock (50,000,000 shares)	$ 130	$ 130
Retained earnings	810	750
Total common equity	$ 940	$ 880
Total liabilities and equity	$2,000	$1,680

Notes:

1. Inventories can be valued by several different methods, and the method chosen can affect both the balance sheet value and the cost of goods sold, and thus net income, as reported on the income statement. Similarly, companies can use different depreciation methods. The methods used must be reported in the notes to the financial statements, and security analysts can make adjustments when they compare companies if they think the differences are material.
2. Book value per share: Total common equity/Shares outstanding = $940/50 = $18.80.
3. Also note that a relatively few firms use preferred stock, which we discuss in Chapter 9. Preferred stock can take several different forms, but it is generally like debt because it pays a fixed amount each year. However, it is like common stock because a failure to pay the preferred dividend does not expose the firm to bankruptcy. If a firm does use preferred stock, it is shown on the balance sheet between Total debt and Common stock. There is no set rule on how preferred stock should be treated when financial ratios are calculated—it could be considered as debt or as equity. Bondholders often think of it as equity, while stockholders think of it as debt because it is a fixed charge. In truth, it is a hybrid, somewhere between debt and common equity.

Working Capital
Current assets.

2. *Working capital.* Current assets are often called **working capital** because these assets "turn over"; that is, they are used and then replaced throughout the year.[4]

3. *Net working capital.* When Allied buys inventory items on credit, its suppliers, in effect, lend it the money used to finance the inventory items. Allied could have borrowed from its bank or sold stock to obtain the money, but it received the funds from its suppliers. These loans are shown as accounts payable, and they typically are "free" in the sense that they do not bear interest. Similarly, Allied pays its workers every two weeks and it pays taxes quarterly; so

---

[4]Any current assets not used in normal operations, such as excess cash held to pay for a plant under construction, are deducted and thus not included in working capital. Allied requires all of its current assets for operations.

Allied's labor force and tax authorities provide it with loans equal to its accrued wages and taxes. If we subtract the sum of payables plus accruals from current assets, the difference is called **net working capital**. That represents the amount of money that Allied must obtain from non-free sources to carry its current assets, $800 million in 2008:

$$\text{Net working capital} = \text{Current assets} - (\text{Payables} + \text{Accruals})$$
$$= \$1,000 - (\$60 + \$140) = \$800$$

Net Working Capital
Current assets minus accounts payable and accruals.

4. *Other sources of funds.* Most companies (including Allied) finance their assets with a combination of current liabilities, long-term debt, and common equity. Some companies also use "hybrid" securities such as preferred stock, convertible bonds, and long-term leases. Preferred stock is a hybrid between common stock and debt, while convertible bonds are debt securities that give the bondholder an option to exchange their bonds for shares of common stock. In the event of bankruptcy, debt is paid off first, then preferred stock. Common stock is last, receiving a payment only when something remains after the debt and preferred stock are paid off.[5]

5. *Depreciation.* Most companies prepare two sets of financial statements—one is based on Internal Revenue Service (IRS) rules and is used to calculate taxes; the other is based on generally accepted accounting principles (GAAP) and is used for reporting to investors. Firms often use accelerated depreciation for tax purposes but straight line depreciation for stockholder reporting. Allied uses accelerated depreciation for both.[6]

6. *Market values versus book values.* Companies generally use GAAP to determine the values reported on their balance sheets. In most cases, these accounting numbers (or "book values") are different from what the assets would sell for if they were put up for sale (or "market values"). For example, Allied purchased its headquarters in Chicago in 1988. Under GAAP, the company must report the value of this asset at its historical cost (what it originally paid for the building in 1988) less accumulated depreciation. Given that Chicago real estate prices have increased over the last 20 years, the market value of the building is higher than its book value. Other assets' market values also differ from their book values.

We can also see from Table 3-1 that the book value of Allied's common equity at the end of 2008 was $940 million. Because 50 million shares were outstanding, the book value per share was $940/50 = $18.80. However, the market value of the common stock was $23.06. As is true for most companies in 2008, shareholders are willing to pay more than book value for Allied's stock. This occurs in part because the values of assets have increased due to inflation and in part because shareholders expect earnings to grow. Allied, like most other companies, has learned how to make investments that will increase future profits.

Apple provides an example of the effect of growth on the stock price. When Apple first introduced the iPod and iPhone, its balance sheet didn't budge;

---

[5]Other forms of financing are discussed in Brigham and Daves, *Intermediate Financial Management,* 9th ed., (Mason, OH: Thomson/South-Western, 2007), Chapter 20. In *Fundamentals of Financial Management,* 12th ed., readers should refer to Chapter 20.

[6]Depreciation over an asset's life is equal to the asset's cost, but accelerated depreciation results in higher initial depreciation charges—and thus lower taxable income—than straight line. Due to the time value of money, it is better to delay taxes; so most companies use accelerated depreciation for tax purposes. Either accelerated or straight line can be used for stockholder reporting. Allied is a relatively conservative company; hence, it uses accelerated depreciation for stockholder reporting. Had Allied elected to use straight line for stockholder reporting, its 2008 depreciation expense would have been $25 million lower, the $1 billion shown for "net plant" on its balance sheet would have been $25 million higher, and its reported income would also have been higher.

Depreciation is also important in capital budgeting, where we make decisions regarding new investments in fixed assets. We will have more to say about depreciation in Chapter 12, when we take up capital budgeting.

but investors recognized that these were great products that would lead to higher future profits. So Apple's stock quickly rose above its book value—it now (Spring 2008) has a stock price of $185 versus a $20 book value.

If a company has problems, its stock price can fall below its book value. For example, Countrywide Financial, the largest originator of subprime mortgages, saw its stock price fall to $13 versus a book value of $25 when the sub-prime market blew up in 2007.

7. *The time dimension.* The balance sheet is a snapshot of the firm's financial position *at a point in time*—for example, on December 31, 2008. Thus, we see that on December 31, 2007, Allied had $80 million of cash; but that balance fell to $10 million by year-end 2008. The balance sheet changes every day as inventories rise and fall, as bank loans are increased or decreased, and so forth. A company such as Allied, whose business is seasonal, experiences especially large balance sheet changes during the year. Its inventories are low just before the harvest season but high just after the fall crops have been harvested and processed. Similarly, most retailers have large inventories just before Christmas but low inventories (and high accounts receivable) just after Christmas. We will examine the effects of these changes in Chapter 4, when we compare companies' financial statements and evaluate their performance.

SELF TEST

What is the balance sheet, and what information does it provide?

How is the order in which items are shown on the balance sheet determined?

What was Allied's net working capital on December 31, 2007? **($650 million)**

What items on Allied's December 31 balance sheet would probably be different from its June 30 values? Would these differences be as large if Allied were a grocery chain rather than a food processor? Explain. **(Inventories, accounts receivable, and accounts payable would experience seasonal fluctuations; no—less seasonality)**

3-3 THE INCOME STATEMENT

Income Statement
A report summarizing a firm's revenues, expenses, and profits during a reporting period, generally a quarter or a year.

Table 3-2 shows Allied's 2007 and 2008 **income statements**. Net sales are shown at the top of the statement; then operating costs, interest, and taxes are subtracted to obtain the net income available to common shareholders. We also show earnings and dividends per share, in addition to some other data, at the bottom of Table 3-2. Earnings per share (EPS) is often called "the bottom line," denoting that of all items on the income statement, EPS is the one that is most important to stockholders. Allied earned $2.35 per share in 2008, down from $2.44 in 2007. In spite of the decline in earnings, the firm still increased the dividend from $1.06 to $1.15.

A typical stockholder focuses on the reported EPS, but professional security analysts and managers differentiate between *operating* and *non-operating* income. **Operating income** is derived from the firm's regular core business—in Allied's case, from producing and selling food products. Moreover, it is calculated before deducting interest expenses and taxes, which are considered to be non-operating costs. Operating income is also called EBIT, or earnings before interest and taxes. Here is its equation:

Operating Income
Earnings from operations before interest and taxes (i.e., EBIT).

3-1

$$\text{Operating income (or EBIT)} = \text{Sales revenues} - \text{Operating costs}$$
$$= \$3,000.0 - \$2,716.2$$
$$= \$283.8$$

This figure must, of course, match the one reported on the income statement.

Table 3-2	**Allied Food Products: Income Statements for Years Ending December 31 (Millions of Dollars, Except for Per-Share Data)**	
	2008	**2007**
Net sales	$3,000.0	$2,850.0
Operating costs except depreciation and amortization	2,616.2	2,497.0
Depreciation and amortization	100.0	90.0
Total operating costs	$2,716.2	$2,587.0
Operating income, or earnings before interest and taxes (EBIT)	283.8	263.0
Less interest	88.0	60.0
Earnings before taxes (EBT)	$ 195.8	$ 203.0
Taxes (40%)	78.3	81.2
Net income	$ 117.5	$ 121.8
Here are some related items:		
Total dividends	$ 57.5	$ 53.0
Addition to retained earnings = Net income – Total dividends	$ 60.0	$ 68.8
Per-share data:		
Common stock price	$ 23.06	$ 26.00
Earnings per share (EPS)[a]	$ 2.35	$ 2.44
Dividends per share (DPS)[a]	$ 1.15	$ 1.06
Book value per share (BVPS)	$ 18.80	$ 17.60

[a]Allied has 50 million shares of common stock outstanding. Note that EPS is based on net income available to common stockholders. Calculations of EPS and DPS for 2008 are as follows:

$$\text{Earnings per share} = \text{EPS} = \frac{\text{Net income}}{\text{Common shares outstanding}} = \frac{\$117,500,000}{50,000,000} = \$2.35$$

$$\text{Dividends per share} = \text{DPS} = \frac{\text{Dividends paid to common stockholders}}{\text{Common shares outstanding}} = \frac{\$57,500,000}{50,000,000} = \$1.15$$

When a firm has options or convertibles outstanding or it recently issued new common stock, a more comprehensive EPS, "diluted EPS," must be calculated. Its calculation is a bit more complicated, but you may refer to any financial accounting text for a discussion.

Different firms have different amounts of debt, different tax carry-backs and carry-forwards, and different amounts of non-operating assets such as marketable securities. These differences can cause two companies with identical operations to report significantly different net incomes. For example, suppose two companies have identical sales, operating costs, and assets. However, one company uses some debt and the other uses only common equity. Despite their identical operating performances, the company with no debt (and therefore no interest expense) would report a higher net income because no interest was deducted from its operating income. Consequently, if you want to compare two companies' operating performances, it is best to focus on their operating income.[7]

From Allied's income statement, we see that its operating income increased from $263.0 million in 2007 to $283.8 million in 2008, or by $20.8 million. However,

---

[7]Operating income is important for several reasons. First, as we noted in Chapter 1, managers are generally compensated based on the performance of the units they manage. A division manager can control his or her division's performance but not the firm's capital structure policy or other corporate decisions. Second, if one firm is considering acquiring another, it will be interested in the value of the target firm's operations; and that value is determined by the target firm's operating income. Third, operating income is normally more stable than total income, as total income can be heavily influenced by write-offs of bonds backed by subprime mortgages and the like. Therefore, analysts focus on operating income when they estimate firms' long-run stock values.

Depreciation
The charge to reflect the cost of assets used up in the production process. Depreciation is not a cash outlay.

Amortization
A noncash charge similar to depreciation except that it is used to write off the costs of intangible assets.

EBITDA
Earnings before interest, taxes, depreciation, and amortization.

its 2008 net income declined. This decline occurred because it increased its debt in 2008, and the $28 million interest increase lowered its net income.

Taking a closer look at the income statement, we see that depreciation and amortization are important components of operating costs. Recall from accounting that **depreciation** is an annual charge against income that reflects the estimated dollar cost of the capital equipment and other tangible assets that were used up in the production process. **Amortization** amounts to the same thing except that it represents the decline in value of intangible assets such as patents, copyrights, trademarks, and goodwill. Because depreciation and amortization are so similar, they are generally lumped together for purposes of financial analysis on the income statement and for other purposes. They both write off, or allocate, the costs of assets over their useful lives.

Even though depreciation and amortization are reported as costs on the income statements, they are not cash expenses—cash was spent in the past, when the assets being written off were acquired, but no cash is paid out to cover depreciation. Therefore, managers, security analysts, and bank loan officers who are concerned with the amount of cash a company is generating often calculate **EBITDA**, an acronym for earnings before interest, taxes, depreciation, and amortization. Allied has no amortization charges, so Allied's depreciation and amortization consist entirely of depreciation. In 2008, Allied's EBITDA was $383.8 million.

While the balance sheet represents a snapshot in time, the income statement reports on operations *over a period of time*. For example, during 2008, Allied had sales of $3 billion and its net income was $117.5 million. Income statements are prepared monthly, quarterly, and annually. The quarterly and annual statements are reported to investors, while the monthly statements are used internally for planning and control purposes.

Finally, note that the income statement is tied to the balance sheet through the retained earnings account on the balance sheet. Net income as reported on the income statement, less dividends paid, is the retained earnings for the year (e.g., 2008). Those retained earnings are added to the cumulative retained earnings from prior years to obtain the year-end 2008 balance for retained earnings. The retained earnings for the year are also reported in the statement of stockholders' equity. All four of the statements provided in the annual report are tied together.

SELF TEST

Why is earnings per share called "the bottom line"?

What is EBIT, or operating income?

What is EBITDA?

Which is more like a snapshot of the firm's operations—the balance sheet or the income statement? Explain your answer.

3-4 STATEMENT OF CASH FLOWS

Statement of Cash Flows
A report that shows how things that affect the balance sheet and income statement affect the firm's cash flows.

Net income as reported on the income statement is not cash; and in finance, "cash is king." Management's goal is to maximize the price of the firm's stock; and the value of any asset, including a share of stock, is based on the cash flows the asset is expected to produce. Therefore, managers strive to maximize the cash flows available to investors. The **statement of cash flows** as shown in Table 3-3 is the accounting report that shows how much cash the firm is generating. The statement is divided into four sections, and we explain it on a line-by-line basis.[8]

---

[0]Our statement of cash flows is relatively simple because Allied is a relatively uncomplicated company. Many cash flow statements are more complicated; but if you understand Table 3-3, you should be able to follow more complicated statements.

Table 3-3	**Allied Food Products: Statement of Cash Flows for 2008 (Millions of Dollars)**	
		2008
a.	**I. Operating Activities**	
b.	Net income	$ 117.5
c.	Depreciation and amortization	100.0
d.	Increase in inventories	(200.0)
e.	Increase in accounts receivable	(60.0)
f.	Increase in accounts payable	30.0
g.	Increase in accrued wages and taxes	10.0
h.	Net cash provided by (used in) operating activities	($ 2.5)
i.	**II. Long-Term Investing Activities**	
j.	Additions to property, plant, and equipment	($ 230.0)
k.	Net cash used in investing activities	($ 230.0)
l.	**III. Financing Activities**	
m.	Increase in notes payable	$ 50.0
n.	Increase in bonds outstanding	170.0
o.	Payment of dividends to stockholders	(57.5)
p.	Net cash provided by financing activities	$ 162.5
q.	**IV. Summary**	
r.	Net decrease in cash (Net sum of I, II, and III)	($ 70.0)
s.	Cash and equivalents at the beginning of the year	80.0
t.	Cash and equivalents at the end of the year	$ 10.0

Note: Here and throughout the book, parentheses are sometimes used to denote negative numbers.

Here is a line-by-line explanation of the statement shown in Table 3-3:

a. *Operating Activities.* This section deals with items that occur as part of normal ongoing operations.

b. *Net income.* The first operating activity is net income, which is the first source of cash. If all sales were for cash, if all costs required immediate cash payments, and if the firm were in a static situation, net income would equal cash from operations. However, these conditions don't hold; so net income is not equal to cash from operations. Adjustments shown in the remainder of the statement must be made.

c. *Depreciation and amortization.* The first adjustment relates to depreciation and amortization. Allied's accountants subtracted depreciation (it has no amortization expense), which is a noncash charge, when they calculated net income. Therefore, depreciation must be added back to net income when net cash flow is determined.

d. *Increase in inventories.* To make or buy inventory items, the firm must use cash. It may get some of this cash as loans from its suppliers and workers (payables and accruals); but ultimately, any increase in inventories requires cash. Allied increased its inventories by $200 million in 2008. That amount is shown in parentheses on Line d because it is negative (i.e., a use of cash). If Allied had reduced its inventories, it would have generated positive cash.

e. *Increase in accounts receivable.* If Allied chooses to sell on credit, when it makes a sale, it will not immediately get the cash that it would have received had it not extended credit. To stay in business, it must replace the inventory that it sold on credit; but it won't yet have received cash from the credit sale. So if the firm's accounts receivable increase, this will amount to a use of cash. Allied's receivables rose by $60 million in 2008, and that use of cash is shown as a negative on Line e. If Allied had reduced its receivables, this would have showed up as a positive cash flow. (Once cash is received for the sale, the accompanying accounts receivable will be eliminated.)

f. *Increase in accounts payable.* Accounts payable represent a loan from suppliers. Allied bought goods on credit, and its payables increased by $30 million this year. That is treated as a $30 million increase in cash on Line f. If Allied had reduced its payables, that would have required, or used, cash. Note that as Allied grows, it will purchase more inventories. That will give rise to additional payables, which will reduce the amount of new outside funds required to finance inventory growth.

g. *Increase in accrued wages and taxes.* The same logic applies to accruals as to accounts payable. Allied's accruals increased by $10 million this year, which means that in 2008, it borrowed an additional $10 million from its workers and tax authorities. So this represents a $10 million cash inflow.

h. *Net cash provided by operating activities.* All of the previous items are part of normal operations—they arise as a result of doing business. When we sum them, we obtain the net cash flow from operations. Allied had positive flows from net income, depreciation, and increases in payables and accruals; but it used cash to increase inventories and to carry receivables. The net result was that operations led to a $2.5 million net outflow of cash.

i. *Long-Term Investing Activities.* All activities involving long-term assets are covered in this section. Allied had only one long-term investment activity—the acquisition of some fixed assets, as shown on Line j. If Allied had sold some fixed assets, its accountants would have reported it in this section as a positive amount (i.e., as a source of cash).

j. *Additions to property, plant, and equipment.* Allied spent $230 million on fixed assets during the current year. This is an outflow; therefore, it is shown in parentheses. If Allied had sold some of its fixed assets, this would have been a cash inflow.[9]

k. *Net cash used in investing activities.* Since Allied had only one investment activity, the total on this line is the same as that on the previous line.

l. *Financing Activities.* Allied's financing activities are shown in this section.

m. *Increase in notes payable.* Allied borrowed an additional $50 million from its bank this year, which was a cash inflow. When Allied repays the loan, this will be an outflow.

n. *Increase in bonds (long-term debt).* Allied borrowed an additional $170 million from long-term investors this year, giving them newly issued bonds in exchange for cash. This is shown as an inflow. When the bonds are repaid some years hence, this will be an outflow.

o. *Payment of dividends to stockholders.* Dividends are paid in cash, and the $57.5 million that Allied paid out is shown as a negative amount.

p. *Net cash provided by financing activities.* The sum of the three financing entries, which is a positive $162.5 million, is shown here. These funds were used to help pay for the $230 million of new plant and equipment and to help cover the deficit resulting from operations.

q. *Summary.* This section summarizes the change in cash and cash equivalents over the year.

---

[9]The number on Line j is "gross" investment, or total expenditures. It is also equal to the change in net plant and equipment (from the balance sheet) plus depreciation as shown on Line c: Gross investment = Net investment + Depreciation = $130 + $100 = $230.

MASSAGING THE CASH FLOW STATEMENT

Profits as reported on the income statement can be "massaged" by changes in depreciation methods, inventory valuation procedures, and so on, but "cash is cash," so management can't mess with the cash flow statement, right? Nope—wrong. A recent article in *The Wall Street Journal* described how Ford, General Motors, and several other companies overstated their operating cash flows, the most important section of the cash flow statement. Indeed, GM reported more than twice as much cash from operations as it really generated, $7.6 billion versus a true $3.5 billion. What happened is that when GM sold cars to a dealer on credit, it created an account receivable, which should be shown in the "Operating Activities" section as a use of cash. However, GM classified these receivables as loans to dealers and reported them as a financing activity. That decision more than doubled the reported cash flow from operations. It didn't affect the end-of-year cash balance, but it made operations look stronger than they really were.

If Allied Foods, in Table 3-3, had done this, the $60 million increase in receivables, which is correctly shown as a use of cash, would have been shifted to the "Financing Activities" section, causing Allied's cash provided by operations to rise from $2.5 million to +$57.5 million. That would have made Allied look better to investors and credit analysts, but it would have been just smoke and mirrors.

GM's treatment was first reported by Charles Mulford, a professor at Georgia Tech. The SEC then sent GM a letter that basically required it to change its procedures. The company issued a statement saying that it thought at the time that it was acting in accordance with GAAP but that it would reclassify its accounts in the future. GM's action was not in the league of WorldCom's or Enron's fraudulent accounting, but it does show that companies sometimes do things to make their statements look better than they really are.

Source: Diya Gullapalli, "Little Campus Lab Shakes Big Firms," *The Wall Street Journal*, March 1, 2005, p. C3.

r. *Net decrease in cash.* The net sum of the operating activities, investing activities, and financing activities is shown here. These activities resulted in a $70 million net decrease in cash during 2008, mainly due to expenditures on new fixed assets.

s. *Cash and equivalents at the beginning of the year.* Allied began the year with the $80 million of cash, which is shown here.

t. *Cash and equivalents at the end of the year.* Allied ended the year with $10 million of cash, the $80 million it started with minus the $70 million net decrease as shown previously. Clearly, Allied's cash position is weaker than it was at the beginning of the year.

Allied's statement of cash flows should be of concern to its managers and investors. The company was able to cover the small operating deficit and the large investment in fixed assets by borrowing and reducing its beginning balances of cash and equivalents. However, that can't continue indefinitely. In the long run, Section I needs to show positive operating cash flows. In addition, we would expect Section II to show expenditures on fixed assets that are about equal to (1) its depreciation charges (to replace worn out fixed assets) along with (2) some additional spending to provide for growth. Section III would normally show some net borrowing in addition to a "reasonable" amount of dividends.[10] Finally, Section IV should show a reasonably stable cash balance from year to year. These conditions don't hold for Allied, so something should be done to correct the situation. We will consider corrective actions in Chapter 4, when we analyze the firm's financial statements.

---

[10]The average company pays out about one third of its earnings as dividends, but there is a great deal of variation between companies depending on each company's needs for retained earnings to support its growth. We cover dividends in detail later in the text in Distributions to Shareholders: Dividends and Share Repurchases.

What is the statement of cash flows, and what are some questions it answers?

Identify and briefly explain the three types of activities shown in the statement of cash flows.

If a company has high cash flows from operations, does this mean that cash as shown on its balance sheet will also be high? Explain. **(Not necessarily. The company may have invested heavily in working capital and/or fixed assets, it may have borrowed a great deal, or it may not have had much initial cash.)**

3-5 STATEMENT OF STOCKHOLDERS' EQUITY

Statement of Stockholders' Equity
A statement that shows by how much a firm's equity changed during the year and why this change occurred.

Changes in stockholders' equity during the accounting period are reported in the **statement of stockholders' equity**. Table 3-4 shows that Allied earned $117.5 million during 2008, paid out $57.5 million in common dividends, and plowed $60 million back into the business. Thus, the balance sheet item "Retained earnings" increased from $750 million at year-end 2007 to $810 million at year-end 2008.[11]

Note that "retained earnings" represents a *claim against assets,* not assets per se. Stockholders allowed management to retain earnings and reinvest them in the business, using the retained earnings to increase plant and equipment, add to inventories, and the like. Companies *do not* just pile up cash in a bank account. *Thus, retained earnings as reported on the balance sheet do not represent cash and are not "available" for dividends or anything else.*[12]

What is the statement of stockholders' equity designed to tell us?

Why do changes in retained earnings occur?

Explain why the following statement is true: The retained earnings account reported on the balance sheet does not represent cash and is not "available" for dividend payments or anything else.

| Table 3-4 | Statement of Stockholders' Equity, December 31, 2008 (Millions of Dollars) |

| | COMMON STOCK | | | |
	Shares (000)	Amount	Retained Earnings	Total Stockholders' Equity
Balances, December 31, 2007	50,000	$130.0	$750.0	$880.0
2008 Net Income			$117.5	
Cash Dividends			($ 57.5)	
Addition to Retained Earnings			$ 60.0	$ 60.0
Balances, December 31, 2008	50,000	$130.0	$810.0	$940.0

---

[11]If they had been applicable, columns would have been used to show Additional Paid-in Capital and Treasury Stock. Also, additional rows would have contained information on such things as new issues of stock, treasury stock acquired or reissued, stock options exercised, and unrealized foreign exchange gains or losses.

[12]Cash (as of the balance sheet date) is found in the cash account, an asset account. A positive number in the retained earnings account indicates only that the firm has in the past earned income and has not paid it all out as dividends. Even though a company reports record earnings and shows an increase in retained earnings, it still may be short of cash if it is using its available cash to purchase current and fixed assets to support growth. The same situation holds for individuals. You might own a new BMW (no loan), many clothes, and an expensive stereo (hence, have a high net worth); but if you had only $0.23 in your pocket plus $5.00 in your checking account, you would still be short of cash.

FINANCIAL ANALYSIS ON THE INTERNET

A wide range of valuable financial information is available on the Internet. With just a couple of clicks, an investor can find the key financial statements for most publicly traded companies.

Suppose you are thinking of buying some Disney stock, and you want to analyze its recent performance. Here's a partial (but by no means complete) list of sites you can access to get started:

- One source is Yahoo!'s finance web site, http://finance.yahoo.com. Here you will find updated market information along with links to a variety of interesting research sites. Enter a stock's ticker symbol, click "Go," and you will see the stock's current price along with recent news about the company. Click "Key Statistics" to find a report on the company's key financial ratios. Links to the company's financials (income statement, balance sheet, and statement of cash flows) can also be found. The Yahoo! site also has a list of insider transactions that will tell you whether a company's CEO and other key insiders are buying or selling the company's stock. In addition, the site has a message board where investors share opinions about the company and a link is provided to the company's filings with the Securities and Exchange Commission (SEC). Note also that, in most cases, a more complete listing of SEC filings can be found at www.sec.gov.

- Two other web sites with similar information are Google Finance (http://finance.google.com) and MSN Money (http://moneycentral.msn.com). After entering a stock's ticker symbol, you will see the current stock price and a list of recent news stories. At either of these sites, you will find links to a company's financial statements and key ratios, as well as other information including analyst ratings, historical charts, earnings estimates, and a summary of insider transactions. Google Finance, MSN Money, and Yahoo! Finance allow you to export the financial statements and historical prices to an Excel spreadsheet.

- Other sources for up-to-date market information are http://money.cnn.com and www.marketwatch.com. On these sites, you also can obtain stock quotes, financial statements, links to Wall Street research and SEC filings, company profiles, and charts of a firm's stock price over time.

- After accumulating all of this information, you may want to look at a site that provides opinions regarding the direction of the overall market and a particular stock. Two popular sites are The Motley Fool's web site, www.fool.com, and the site for TheStreet.com, www.thestreet.com.

- A popular source is the online web site of *The Wall Street Journal*, http://online.wsj.com. It is a great resource, but you have to subscribe to access the full range of materials.

Keep in mind that this list is just a small subset of the information available online. Also, sites come and go and change their content over time. New and interesting sites are constantly being added to the Internet.

3-6 FREE CASH FLOW

Thus far, we have focused on financial statements as they are prepared by accountants. However, accounting statements are designed primarily for use by creditors and tax collectors, not for managers and stock analysts. Therefore, corporate decision makers and security analysts often modify accounting data to meet their needs. The most important modification is the concept of **free cash flow (FCF)**, defined as "the amount of cash that could be withdrawn without harming a firm's ability to operate and to produce future cash flows." Here is the equation used to calculate free cash flow:

Free Cash Flow (FCF)
The amount of cash that could be withdrawn from a firm without harming its ability to operate and to produce future cash flows.

$$FCF = EBIT\ (1-T) + Depreciation - \left[\left(\begin{array}{c} Capital \\ expenditures \end{array} + \begin{array}{c} Increase\ in\ net \\ working\ capital \end{array}\right)\right]$$

$$= \$283.8(1-0.4) + 100 - \left[\$230 + \left(\begin{array}{c} Change\ in \\ current\ assets \end{array} - \begin{array}{c} Change\ in \\ payables\ and\ accruals \end{array}\right)\right]$$

$$= \$170.3 + \$100 - (\$230 + [(\$1,000 - \$810) - (\$200 - \$160)])$$

$$= \$170.3 + \$100 - \$230 - \$150$$

$$= -\$109.7\ million$$

FREE CASH FLOW IS IMPORTANT FOR SMALL BUSINESSES

Free cash flow is important to large companies like Allied Foods. Security analysts use FCF to help estimate the value of the stock, and Allied's managers use it to assess the value of proposed capital budgeting projects and potential merger candidates. Note, though, that the concept is also relevant for small businesses.

Let's assume that your aunt and uncle own a small pizza shop and that they have an accountant who prepares their financial statements. The income statement shows their accounting profit for each year. While they are certainly interested in this number, what they probably care more about is how much money they can take out of the business each year to maintain their standard of living. Let's assume that the shop's net income for 2008 was $75,000. However, your aunt and uncle had to spend $50,000 to refurbish the kitchen and restrooms.

So while the business is generating a great deal of "profit," your aunt and uncle can't take much money out because they have to put money back into the pizza shop. Stated another way, their free cash flow is much less than their net income. The required investments could be so large that they even exceed the money made from selling pizza. In this case, your aunt and uncle's free cash flow would be negative. If so, this means they must find funds from other sources just to maintain the pizza business.

As astute businesspeople, your aunt and uncle recognize that investments in the restaurant, such as updating the kitchen and restrooms, are nonrecurring; and if nothing else comes up unexpectedly, your aunt and uncle should be able to take more out of the business in upcoming years, when their free cash flow increases. But some businesses never seem to produce cash for their owners—they consistently generate positive net income, but this net income is swamped by the amount of cash that has to be plowed back into the business. Thus, when it comes to valuing the pizza shop (or any business small or large), what really matters is the amount of free cash flow that the business generates over time.

Looking ahead, your aunt and uncle face competition from national chains that are moving into the area. To meet the competition, your aunt and uncle will have to modernize the dining room. This will again drain cash from the business and reduce its free cash flow, although the hope is that it will enable them to increase sales and free cash flow in the years ahead. As we will see when we discuss capital budgeting, evaluating projects requires us to estimate whether the future increases in free cash flow are sufficient to more than offset the initial project cost. And this comes down to free cash flows.

EBIT(1 − T) is the after-tax operating income that would exist if the firm had no debt and therefore no interest payments.[13] For Allied, EBIT(1 − T) = $283.8(1 − 0.4) = $170.3. Depreciation is then added back because it is a noncash expense. Allied's business plan called for $230 million of capital expenditures plus a $150 million increase in net working capital. Those investments are necessary to sustain ongoing operations.

Allied's FCF is negative, which is not good. Note, though, that the negative FCF is largely attributable to the $230 million expenditure for a new processing plant. This plant is large enough to meet production for several years, so another new plant will not be needed until 2012. Therefore, Allied's FCF for 2009 and the next few years should increase, which means that things are not as bad as the negative FCF might suggest.

Note also that most rapidly growing companies have negative FCFs—the fixed assets and working capital needed to support rapid growth generally exceed cash flows from existing operations. This is not bad, provided the new investments are eventually profitable and contribute to FCF.

Many analysts regard FCF as being the single most important number that can be developed from accounting statements, even more important than net income.

---

[13]After tax operating income = EBIT − Taxes = EBIT − EBIT(T) = EBIT(1 − T), where T is the firm's marginal tax rate.

After all, FCF shows how much the firm can distribute to its investors. We will discuss FCF again in Chapter 9, which deals with stock valuation, and in Chapter 11 and Chapter 12, which deal with capital budgeting.

SELF TEST

What is free cash flow (FCF)?

Why is FCF an important determinant of a firm's value?

A company has EBIT of $30 million, depreciation of $5 million, and a 40% tax rate. It needs to spend $10 million on new fixed assets and $15 million to increase its current assets, and it expects its payables to increase by $2 million and its accruals to increase by $3 million. What is its free cash flow? **($3 million)**

3-7 INCOME TAXES

Individuals and corporations pay out a significant portion of their income as taxes, so taxes are important in both personal and corporate decisions. We summarize the key aspects of the U.S. tax system for individuals in this section and for corporations in the next section, using 2008 data. The details of our tax laws change fairly often—annually for things that are indexed for inflation—but the basic nature of the tax system is likely to remain intact.

3-7a Individual Taxes

Individuals pay taxes on wages and salaries, on investment income (dividends, interest, and profits from the sale of securities), and on the profits of proprietorships and partnerships. The tax rates are **progressive**—that is, the higher one's income, the larger the percentage paid in taxes. Table 3-5 gives the tax rates that were in effect April 2008.

Taxable income is defined as "gross income less a set of exemptions and deductions." When filing a tax return in 2008 for the tax year 2007, taxpayers received an exemption of $3,400 for each dependent, including the taxpayer, which reduces taxable income. However, this exemption is indexed to rise with inflation, and the exemption is phased out (taken away) for high-income taxpayers. Also, certain expenses, including mortgage interest paid, state and local income taxes paid, and charitable contributions, can be deducted and thus be used to reduce taxable income; but again, high-income taxpayers lose most of these deductions.

The **marginal tax** rate is defined as "the tax rate on the last dollar of income." Marginal rates begin at 10% and rise to 35%. Note, though, that when consideration is given to the phase-out of exemptions and deductions, to Social Security and Medicare taxes, and to state taxes, the marginal tax rate may actually exceed 50%. Average tax rates can be calculated from the data in Table 3-5. For example, if a single individual had taxable income of $35,000, his or her tax bill would be $4,386.25 + ($35,000 − $31,850)(0.25) = $4,386.25 + $787.50 = $5,173.75. Her **average tax rate** would be $5,173.75/$35,000 = 14.78% versus a marginal rate of 25%. If she received a raise of $1,000, bringing her income to $36,000, she would have to pay $250 of it as taxes; so her after-tax raise would be $750.

Note too that *interest income* received by individuals from corporate securities is added to other income and thus is taxed at federal rates going up to 35%, plus state taxes.[14] *Capital gains and losses*, on the other hand, are treated differently.

Progressive Tax
A tax system where the tax rate is higher on higher incomes. The personal income tax in the United States, which ranges from 0% on the lowest incomes to 35% on the highest incomes, is progressive.

Marginal Tax Rate
The tax rate applicable to the last unit of a person's income.

Average Tax Rate
Taxes paid divided by taxable income.

---

[14]Under U.S. tax laws, interest on most state and local government bonds, called municipals or "munis," is not subject to federal income taxes. This has a significant effect on the values of munis and on their rates of return. We discuss rates and returns in Chapter 8.

Table 3-5   **Individual Tax Rates in April 2008**

SINGLE INDIVIDUALS

If Your Taxable Income Is	You Pay This Amount on the Base of the Bracket	Plus This Percentage on the Excess over the Base (Marginal Rate)	Average Tax Rate at Top of Bracket
Up to $7,825	$ 0	10.0%	10.0%
$7,825–$31,850	782.50	15.0	13.8
$31,850–$77,100	4,386.25	25.0	20.4
$77,100–$160,850	15,698.75	28.0	24.3
$160,850–$349,700	39,148.75	33.0	29.0
Over $349,700	101,469.25	35.0	35.0

MARRIED COUPLES FILING JOINT RETURNS

If Your Taxable Income Is	You Pay This Amount on the Base of the Bracket	Plus This Percentage on the Excess over the Base (Marginal Rate)	Average Tax Rate at Top of Bracket
Up to $15,650	$ 0	10.0%	10.0%
$15,650–$63,700	1,565.00	15.0	13.8
$63,700–$128,500	8,772.50	25.0	19.4
$128,500–$195,850	24,972.50	28.0	22.4
$195,850–$349,700	43,830.50	33.0	27.0
Over $349,700	94,601.00	35.0	35.0

Notes:
a. These are the tax rates as of April 2008. The income ranges at which each tax rate takes effect are indexed with inflation, so they change each year.
b. The average tax rates are always below the marginal rates, but the average at the top of the brackets approaches 35% as taxable income rises without limit.
c. In 2007, a *personal exemption* of $3,400 per person or dependent could be deducted from gross income to determine taxable income. Thus, a husband and wife with two children would have a 2007 exemption of 4 × $3,400 = $13,600. The exemption increases with inflation; but if gross income exceeds certain limits, the exemption is phased out, which has the effect of raising the effective tax rate on incomes over the specified limit. In addition, taxpayers can claim *itemized deductions* for charitable contributions and certain other items, but these deductions are also phased out for high-income taxpayers. In addition, there are Social Security and Medicare taxes. All of this pushes the effective tax rate to well above 35%.

Capital Gain or Loss
The profit (loss) from the sale of a capital asset for more (less) than its purchase price.

Assets such as stocks, bonds, and real estate are defined as *capital assets*. When you buy a capital asset and later sell it for more than you paid, you earn a profit that is called a **capital gain;** when you suffer a loss, it is called a **capital loss**. If you held the asset for less than one year, you will have a *short-term gain or loss,* while if you held it for more than a year, you will have a *long-term gain or loss.* Thus, if you buy 100 shares of Disney stock for $42 per share and sell it for $52 per share, you make a capital gain of 100 × $10, or $1,000. However, if you sell the stock for $32 per share, you will have a $1,000 capital loss. Depending on how long you hold the stock, you will have a short-term or long-term gain or loss.[15] If you sell the stock for exactly $42 per share, you make neither a gain nor a loss; so no tax is due.

A short-term capital gain is added to such ordinary income as wages and interest, then is taxed at the same rate as ordinary income. However, long-term capital gains are taxed differently. The top rate on long-term gains in 2008 is 15%. Thus, if in 2008, you were in the 35% tax bracket, any short-term gains you earned would be taxed just like ordinary income; but your long-term gains would be taxed at 15%. Thus, capital gains on assets held for more than 12 months are better than ordinary income for many people because the tax bite is smaller. However,

---

[15]If you have a *net* capital loss (your capital losses exceed your capital gains) for the year, you can deduct up to $3,000 of this loss against your other income (for example, salary, interest, and dividends).

the 15% maximum rate is scheduled to increase to 20% after 2010. That's still better than 35%, though; so from a tax standpoint, capital gains income is good.

Dividends received by individuals in 2008 are also taxed at the same 15% rate as long-term capital gains. However, the rate is scheduled to rise after 2010. Note that since corporations pay dividends out of earnings that have already been taxed, there is *double taxation of corporate income*—income is first taxed at the corporate rate; and when what is left is paid out as dividends, it is taxed again. This double taxation motivated Congress to reduce the tax rate on dividends.

Tax rates on dividends and capital gains have varied over time, but they have generally been lower than rates on ordinary income. Congress wants the economy to grow. For growth, we need investment in productive assets; and low capital gains and dividend tax rates encourage investment. Individuals with money to invest understand the tax advantages associated with making equity investments in newly formed companies versus buying bonds, so new ventures have an easier time attracting capital under the tax system. All in all, lower capital gains and dividend tax rates stimulate capital formation and investment.

One other tax feature should be addressed—the **Alternative Minimum Tax (AMT)**. The AMT was created in 1969 because Congress learned that 155 million-aires with high incomes paid no taxes because they had so many tax shelters from items such as depreciation on real estate and municipal bond interest. Under the AMT law, people must calculate their tax under the "regular" system and then under the AMT system, where many deductions are added back to income and then taxed at a special AMT rate. The law was not indexed for inflation; and by 2007, literally millions of taxpayers' found themselves subject to this very complex tax.[16]

> **Alternative Minimum Tax (AMT)**
> *Created by Congress to make it more difficult for wealthy individuals to avoid paying taxes through the use of various deductions.*

3-7b Corporate Taxes

The corporate tax structure, shown in Table 3-6, is relatively simple. To illustrate, if a firm had $65,000 of taxable income, its tax bill would be $11,250.

$$\text{Taxes} = \$7,500 + 0.25(\$15,000)$$
$$= \$7,500 + \$3,750 = \$11,250$$

Its average tax rate would be $11,250/$65,000 = 17.3%. Note that corporate income above $18,333,333 has an average and marginal tax rate of 35%.

Table 3-6	Corporate Tax Rates as of January 2008		
If a Corporation's Taxable Income Is	**It Pays This Amount on the Base of the Bracket**	**Plus This Percentage on the Excess over the Base (Marginal Rate)**	**Average Tax Rate at Top of Bracket**
Up to $50,000	$ 0	15%	15.0%
$50,000–$75,000	7,500	25	18.3
$75,000–$100,000	13,750	34	22.3
$100,000–$335,000	22,250	39	34.0
$335,000–$10,000,000	113,900	34	34.0
$10,000,000–$15,000,000	3,400,000	35	34.3
$15,000,000–$18,333,333	5,150,000	38	35.0
Over $18,333,333	6,416,667	35	35.0

[16]On December 26, 2007, President Bush signed legislation that (1) increases the AMT exemption amounts for 2007 to $44,350 for single taxpayers and $66,250 for joint filers and (2) allows taxpayers to take several tax credits for AMT purposes through 2007.

Interest and Dividends Received by a Corporation

Corporations earn most of their income from operations, but they may also own securities—bonds and stocks—and receive interest and dividend income. Interest income received by a corporation is taxed as ordinary income at regular corporate tax rates. *However, dividends are taxed more favorably: 70% of dividends received is excluded from taxable income, while the remaining 30% is taxed at the ordinary tax rate.*[17] Thus, a corporation earning more than \$18,333,333 and paying a 40% marginal federal plus state tax rate would normally pay only $(0.30)(0.4) = 0.12 = 12\%$ of its dividend income as taxes. If this firm had \$10,000 in pretax dividend income, its after-tax dividend income would be \$8,800.

$$\text{A-T income} = \text{B-T income}(1 - T) = \$10{,}000(1 - 0.12) = \$8{,}800$$

The reason for this exclusion is that when a corporation receives dividends and then pays out its own after-tax income as dividends to its stockholders, the dividends received are subjected to triple taxation: (1) The original corporation is taxed, (2) the second corporation is taxed on the dividends it receives, and (3) the individuals who receive the final dividends are taxed again. This explains the 70% intercorporate dividend exclusion.

Suppose a firm has excess cash that it does not need for operations, and it plans to invest this cash in marketable securities. The tax factor favors stocks, which pay dividends, rather than bonds, which pay interest. For example, suppose Allied had \$100,000 to invest, and it could buy bonds that paid 8% interest, or \$8,000 per year, or stock that paid 7% in dividends, or \$7,000. Allied is in the 40% federal-plus-state tax bracket. Therefore, if Allied bought bonds and received interest, its tax on the \$8,000 of interest would be $0.4(\$8,000) = \$3,200$ and its after-tax income would be \$4,800. If it bought stock, its tax would be $\$7,000(0.12) = \$840$ and its after-tax income would be \$6,160. *Other factors might lead Allied to invest in bonds, but the tax factor favors stock investments when the investor is a corporation.*

Interest and Dividends Paid by a Corporation

A firm like Allied can finance its operations with either debt or stock. If a firm uses debt, it must pay interest, whereas if it uses stock, it is expected to pay dividends. *Interest paid can be deducted from operating income to obtain taxable income, but dividends paid cannot be deducted.* Therefore, Allied would need \$1 of pretax income to pay \$1 of interest; but since it is in the 40% federal-plus-state tax bracket, it must earn \$1.67 of pretax income to pay \$1 of dividends:

$$\begin{array}{c}\text{Pretax income needed} \\ \text{to pay \$1 of dividends}\end{array} = \frac{\$1}{1 - \text{Tax rate}} = \frac{\$1}{0.60} = \$1.67$$

Working backward, if Allied has \$1.67 in pretax income, it must pay \$0.67 in taxes $[(0.4)(\$1.67) = \$0.67]$. This leaves it with after-tax income of \$1.00.

Table 3-7 shows the situation for a firm with \$10 million of assets, sales of \$5 million, and \$1.5 million of earnings before interest and taxes (EBIT). As shown in Column 1, if the firm were financed entirely by bonds and if it made interest payments of \$1.5 million, its taxable income would be zero, taxes would be zero, and its investors would receive the entire \$1.5 million. (The term *investors* includes both stockholders and bondholders.) However, as shown in Column 2, if the firm had no debt and was therefore financed entirely by stock, all of the \$1.5 million of EBIT would be taxable income to the corporation, the tax would be $\$1,500,000(0.40) = \$600,000$, and investors would receive only \$0.9 million versus \$1.5 million under debt financing. Therefore, the rate of return to investors on their \$10 million investment is much higher when debt is used.

---

[17]The exclusion depends on the percentage of the paying company's stock the receiving company owns. If it owns 100% (hence, the payer is a subsidiary), all of the dividend will be excluded. If it owns less than 20%, which is the case if the stock held is just an investment, 70% will be excluded. Also, state tax rules vary; but in our example, we assume that Allied also has a state tax exclusion.

Table 3-7	Returns to Investors under Bond and Stock Financing	
	Use Bonds **(1)**	**Use Stock** **(2)**
Sales	$ 5,000,000	$5,000,000
Operating costs	3,500,000	3,500,000
Earnings before interest and taxes (EBIT)	$ 1,500,000	$1,500,000
Interest	1,500,000	0
Taxable income	$ 0	$1,500,000
Federal-plus-state taxes (40%)	0	600,000
After-tax income	$ 0	$ 900,000
Income to investors	$1,500,000	$ 900,000
Rate of return on $10 million of assets	15.0%	9.0%

Of course, it is generally not possible to finance exclusively with debt; and the risk of doing so would offset the benefits of the higher expected income. *Still, the fact that interest is a deductible expense has a profound effect on the way businesses are financed—the corporate tax system favors debt financing over equity financing.* This point is discussed in more detail in the chapters on cost of capital and capital structure.[18]

Corporate Capital Gains

Before 1987, corporate long-term capital gains were taxed at lower rates than corporate ordinary income; so the situation was similar for corporations and individuals. Currently, though, corporations' capital gains are taxed at the same rates as their operating income.

Corporate Loss Carry-Back and Carry-Forward

Ordinary corporate operating losses can be carried back (**carry-back**) to each of the preceding 2 years and carried forward (**carry-forward**) for the next 20 years and used to offset taxable income in those years. For example, an operating loss in 2008 could be carried back and used to reduce taxable income in 2006 and 2007; it also could be carried forward, if necessary, and used in 2009, 2010, up until 2028. The loss is applied to the earliest year first, then to the next earliest year, and so forth, until losses have been used up or the 20-year carry-forward limit has been reached.

To illustrate, suppose Company X had $2 million of pretax profits (taxable income) in 2006 and 2007 and then in 2008, it lost $12 million. Its federal-plus-state tax rate is 40%. As shown in Table 3-8, Company X would use the carry-back feature to recompute its taxes for 2006, using $2 million of the 2008 operating losses to reduce the 2006 pretax profit to zero. This would permit it to recover the taxes paid in 2006. Therefore, in 2008, it would receive a refund of its 2006 taxes because of the loss experienced in 2008. Because $10 million of the unrecovered losses would still be available, X would repeat this procedure for 2007. Thus, in 2008, the company would pay zero taxes for 2008 and would receive a refund for taxes paid in 2006 and 2007. It would still have $8 million of unrecovered losses to carry forward, subject to the 20-year limit. This $8 million could be used until the entire $12 million loss had been used to offset taxable income. The purpose of permitting this loss treatment is to avoid penalizing corporations whose incomes fluctuate substantially from year to year.

Consolidated Corporate Tax Returns

If a corporation owns 80% or more of another corporation's stock, it can aggregate income and file one consolidated tax return. This allows the losses of one company to

Tax Loss Carry-Back or Carry-Forward
Ordinary corporate operating losses can be carried backward for 2 years and carried forward for 20 years to offset taxable income in a given year.

---

[18]A company could, in theory, refrain from paying dividends to help prevent its stockholders from having to pay taxes on dividends received. The IRS has a rule against the *improper accumulation of retained earnings* that would permit this. However, in our experience, it is easy for firms to justify retaining earnings; and we have never seen a firm have a problem with the improper accumulation rule.

Table 3-8	Calculation of Loss Carry-Back and Carry-Forward for 2006–2007 Using a $12 Million 2008 Loss

	2006	2007
Original taxable income	$ 2,000,000	$ 2,000,000
Carry-back credit	−2,000,000	−2,000,000
Adjusted profit	$ 0	$ 0
Taxes previously paid (40%)	800,000	800,000
Difference = Tax refund	$ 800,000	$ 800,000

Total refund check received in 2009: $800,000 + $800,000 = $1,600,000
Amount of loss carry-forward available for use in 2009–2028:

2008 loss	$12,000,000	
Carry-back losses used	4,000,000	
Carry-forward losses still available	$ 8,000,000	

be used to offset the profits of another. (Similarly, one division's losses can be used to offset another division's profits.) No business wants to incur losses; but tax offsets make it more feasible for large, multidivisional corporations to undertake risky new ventures or ventures that will suffer losses during a developmental period.

Taxation of Small Businesses: S Corporations

S Corporation

A small corporation that, under Subchapter S of the Internal Revenue Code, elects to be taxed as a proprietorship or a partnership yet retains limited liability and other benefits of the corporate form of organization.

As we noted in Chapter 1, the Tax Code allows small businesses that meet certain conditions to be set up as corporations and thus receive the benefits of the corporate form of organization—especially limited liability—yet still be taxed as proprietorships or partnerships rather than as corporations. These corporations are called **S corporations**. (Regular corporations are called C corporations.) If a corporation elects S, all of its income is reported as personal income by its stockholders, on a pro rata basis, and thus is taxed at the stockholders' individual rates. Because the income is taxed only once, this is an important benefit to the owners of small corporations in which all or most of the income earned each year will be distributed as dividends. The situation is similar for LLCs.

Depreciation

Depreciation plays an important role in income tax calculations—the larger the depreciation, the lower the taxable income, the lower the tax bill, and thus the higher the operating cash flow. Congress specifies the life over which assets can be depreciated for tax purposes and the depreciation methods that can be used. We will discuss in detail how depreciation is calculated and how it affects income and cash flows when we study capital budgeting.

SELF TEST

Explain this statement: Our tax rates are progressive.

What's the difference between marginal and average tax rates?

What's the AMT, and why was it instituted?

What's a muni bond, and how are these bonds taxed?

What are long-term capital gains? Are they taxed like other income? Explain.

How does our tax system influence the use of debt financing by corporations?

What is the logic behind allowing tax loss carry-backs/carry-forwards?

Differentiate between S and C corporations.

TYING IT ALL TOGETHER

The primary purposes of this chapter were to describe the basic financial statements, to present background information on cash flows, to differentiate between cash flow and accounting income, and to provide an overview of the federal income tax system. In the next chapter, we build on this information to analyze a firm's financial statements and to determine its financial health.

SELF-TEST QUESTIONS AND PROBLEMS
(Solutions Appear in Appendix A)

ST-1 **KEY TERMS**   Define each of the following terms:

    a.   Annual report; balance sheet; income statement; statement of cash flows; statement of stockholders' equity

    b.   Stockholders' equity; retained earnings; working capital; net working capital

    c.   Depreciation; amortization; operating income; EBITDA; free cash flow

    d.   Progressive tax; marginal tax rate; average tax rate

    e.   Tax loss carry-back; carry-forward; AMT

    f.   Capital gain (loss)

    g.   S corporation

ST-2 **NET INCOME AND CASH FLOW**   Last year Rattner Robotics had $5 million in operating income (EBIT). Its depreciation expense was $1 million, its interest expense was $1 million, and its corporate tax rate was 40%. At year-end, it had $14 million in current assets, $3 million in accounts payable, $1 million in accruals, and $15 million in net plant and equipment. Assume that Rattner's only noncash item was depreciation.

    a.   What was the company's net income?

    b.   What was its net working capital (NWC)?

    c.   Rattner had $12 million in net plant and equipment the prior year. Its net working capital has remained constant over time. What is the company's free cash flow (FCF) for the year that just ended?

    d.   If the firm had $4.5 million in retained earnings at the beginning of the year and paid out total dividends of $1.2 million, what was its retained earnings at the end of the year? Assume that all dividends declared were actually paid.

QUESTIONS

3-1   What four financial statements are contained in most annual reports?

3-2   Who are some of the basic users of financial statements, and how do they use them?

3-3   If a "typical" firm reports $20 million of retained earnings on its balance sheet, could its directors declare a $20 million cash dividend without having any qualms about what they were doing? Explain your answer.

3-4   Explain the following statement: While the balance sheet can be thought of as a snapshot of a firm's financial position *at a point in time,* the income statement reports on operations *over a period of time.*

3-5 Financial statements are based on generally accepted accounting principles (GAAP) and are audited by CPA firms. Therefore, do investors need to worry about the validity of those statements? Explain your answer.

3-6 What is free cash flow? If you were an investor, why might you be more interested in free cash flow than net income?

3-7 Would it be possible for a company to report *negative* free cash flow and still be highly valued by investors; that is, could a negative free cash flow ever be a good thing in the eyes of investors? Explain your answer.

3-8 What is meant by the following statement: Our tax rates are progressive.

3-9 What does *double taxation of corporate income* mean? Could income ever be subject to *triple* taxation? Explain your answer.

3-10 How does the deductibility of interest and dividends by the *paying corporation* affect the choice of financing (that is, the use of debt versus equity)?

PROBLEMS

Easy Problems 1–3

3-1 **INCOME STATEMENT** Little Books Inc. recently reported $3 million of net income. Its EBIT was $6 million, and its tax rate was 40%. What was its interest expense? [Hint: Write out the headings for an income statement and fill in the known values. Then divide $3 million of net income by $(1 - T) = 0.6$ to find the pretax income. The difference between EBIT and taxable income must be the interest expense. Use this same procedure to complete similar problems.]

3-2 **INCOME STATEMENT** Pearson Brothers recently reported an EBITDA of $7.5 million and net income of $1.8 million. It had $2.0 million of interest expense, and its corporate tax rate was 40%. What was its charge for depreciation and amortization?

3-3 **STATEMENT OF STOCKHOLDERS' EQUITY** In its most recent financial statements, Newhouse Inc. reported $50 million of net income and $810 million of retained earnings. The previous retained earnings were $780 million. How much in dividends were paid to shareholders during the year? Assume that all dividends declared were actually paid.

Intermediate Problems 4–7

3-4 **BALANCE SHEET** Which of the following actions are most likely to directly increase cash as shown on a firm's balance sheet? Explain and state the assumptions that underlie your answer.

a. It issues $2 million of new common stock.

b. It buys new plant and equipment at a cost of $3 million.

c. It reports a large loss for the year.

d. It increases the dividends paid on its common stock.

3-5 **STATEMENT OF STOCKHOLDERS' EQUITY** Computer World Inc. paid out $22.5 million in total common dividends and reported $278.9 million of retained earnings at year-end. The prior year's retained earnings were $212.3 million. What was the net income? Assume that all dividends declared were actually paid.

3-6 **STATEMENT OF CASH FLOWS** W.C. Cycling had $55,000 in cash at year-end 2007 and $25,000 in cash at year-end 2008. Cash flow from long-term investing activities totaled −$250,000, and cash flow from financing activities totaled +$170,000.

a. What was the cash flow from operating activities?

b. If accruals increased by $25,000, receivables and inventories increased by $100,000, and depreciation and amortization totaled $10,000, what was the firm's net income?

3-7 **FREE CASH FLOW** Bailey Corporation's financial statements (dollars and shares are in millions) are provided here.

Balance Sheets as of December 31

	2008	2007
Assets		
Cash and equivalents	$ 14,000	$ 13,000
Accounts receivable	30,000	25,000
Inventories	28,125	21,000
Total current assets	$ 72,125	$ 59,000
Net plant and equipment	50,000	47,000
Total assets	$122,125	$106,000
Liabilities and Equity		
Accounts payable	$ 10,800	$ 9,000
Notes payable	6,700	5,150
Accruals	7,600	6,000
Total current liabilities	$ 25,100	$ 20,150
Long-term bonds	15,000	15,000
Total debt	$ 40,100	$ 35,150
Common stock (5,000 shares)	50,000	50,000
Retained earnings	32,025	20,850
Common equity	$ 82,025	$ 70,850
Total liabilities and equity	$122,125	$106,000

Income Statement for Year Ending December 31, 2008

Sales	$214,000
Operating costs excluding depreciation and amortization	170,000
EBITDA	$ 44,000
Depreciation & amortization	5,000
EBIT	$ 39,000
Interest	1,750
EBT	$ 37,250
Taxes (40%)	14,900
Net income	$ 22,350
Dividends paid	$ 11,175

a. What was net working capital for 2007 and 2008?

b. What was Bailey's 2008 free cash flow?

c. Construct Bailey's 2008 statement of stockholders' equity.

Challenging Problems 8–10

3-8   **INCOME STATEMENT**   Hermann Industries is forecasting the following income statement:

Sales	$8,000,000
Operating costs excluding depr. & amort.	4,400,000
EBITDA	$3,600,000
Depreciation & amortization	800,000
EBIT	$2,800,000
Interest	600,000
EBT	$2,200,000
Taxes (40%)	880,000
Net income	$1,320,000

The CEO would like to see higher sales and a forecasted net income of $2,500,000. Assume that operating costs (excluding depreciation and amortization) are 55% of sales and that depreciation and amortization and interest expenses will increase by 10%. The tax rate, which is 40%, will remain the same. What level of sales would generate $2,500,000 in net income?

3-9 **FINANCIAL STATEMENTS** The Davidson Corporation's balance sheet and income statement are provided here.

Davidson Corporation: Balance Sheet as of December 31, 2008
(Millions of Dollars)

Assets		Liabilities and Equity	
Cash and equivalents	$ 15	Accounts payable	$ 120
Accounts receivable	515	Notes payable	220
Inventories	880	Accruals	280
Total current assets	$1,410	Total current liabilities	$ 620
Net plant and equipment	2,590	Long-term bonds	1,520
		Total debt	$ 2,140
		Common stock (100 million shares)	260
		Retained earnings	1,600
		Common equity	$ 1,860
Total assets	$4,000	Total liabilities and equity	$ 4,000

Davidson Corporation: Income Statement
For Year Ending December 31, 2008 (Millions of Dollars)

Sales	$6,250
Operating costs excluding depreciation and amortization	5,230
EBITDA	$1,020
Depreciation & amortization	220
EBIT	$ 800
Interest	180
EBT	$ 620
Taxes (40%)	248
Net income	$ 372
Common dividends paid	$ 146
Earnings per share	$ 3.72

a. Construct the statement of stockholders' equity for December 31, 2008.

b. How much money has been reinvested in the firm over the years?

c. At the present time, how large a check could be written without it bouncing?

d. How much money must be paid to current creditors within the next year?

3-10 **FREE CASH FLOW** Financial information for Powell Panther Corporation is shown here.

Powell Panther Corporation: Income Statements
For Year Ending December 31 (Millions of Dollars)

	2008	2007
Sales	$1,200.0	$1,000.0
Operating costs excluding depreciation and amortization	1,020.0	850.0
EBITDA	$ 180.0	$ 150.0
Depreciation & amortization	30.0	25.0
Earnings before interest and taxes	$ 150.0	$ 125.0
Interest	21.7	20.2
Earnings before taxes	$ 128.3	$ 104.8
Taxes (40%)	51.3	41.9
Net income	$ 77.0	$ 62.9
Common dividends	$ 60.5	$ 46.4

Powell Panther Corporation: Balance Sheets as of December 31 (Millions of Dollars)

	2008	2007
Assets		
Cash and equivalents	$ 12.0	$ 10.0
Accounts receivable	180.0	150.0
Inventories	180.0	200.0
Total current assets	$372.0	$360.0
Net plant and equipment	300.0	250.0
Total assets	$672.0	$610.0
Liabilities and Equity		
Accounts payable	$108.0	$ 90.0
Notes payable	67.0	51.5
Accruals	72.0	60.0
Total current liabilities	$247.0	$201.5
Long-term bonds	150.0	150.0
Total debt	$397.0	$351.5
Common stock (50 million shares)	50.0	50.0
Retained earnings	225.0	208.5
Common equity	$275.0	$258.5
Total liabilities and equity	$672.0	$610.0

a. What was net working capital for 2007 and 2008?

b. What was the 2008 free cash flow?

c. How would you explain the large increase in 2008 dividends?

COMPREHENSIVE/SPREADSHEET PROBLEM

3-11 **FINANCIAL STATEMENTS, CASH FLOW, AND TAXES** Laiho Industries' 2007 and 2008 balance sheets (in thousands of dollars) are shown.

	2008	2007
Cash	$102,850	$ 89,725
Accounts receivable	103,365	85,527
Inventories	38,444	34,982
Total current assets	$244,659	$210,234
Net fixed assets	67,165	42,436
Total assets	$311,824	$252,670
Accounts payable	$ 30,761	$ 23,109
Accruals	30,477	22,656
Notes payable	16,717	14,217
Total current liabilities	$ 77,955	$ 59,982
Long-term debt	76,264	63,914
Total liabilities	$154,219	$123,896
Common stock	100,000	90,000
Retained earnings	57,605	38,774
Total common equity	$157,605	$128,774
Total liabilities and equity	$311,824	$252,670

a. Sales for 2008 were $455,150,000, and EBITDA was 15% of sales. Furthermore, depreciation and amortization were 11% of net fixed assets, interest was $8,575,000, the corporate tax rate was 40%, and Laiho pays 40% of its net income in dividends. Given this information, construct the firm's 2008 income statement.

    b.   Construct the statement of stockholders' equity for the year ending December 31, 2008, and the 2008 statement of cash flows.

    c.   Calculate 2007 and 2008 net working capital and 2008 free cash flow.

    d.   If Laiho increased its dividend payout ratio, what effect would this have on corporate taxes paid? What effect would this have on taxes paid by the company's shareholders?

INTEGRATED CASE

D'LEON INC., PART I

3-1   **FINANCIAL STATEMENTS AND TAXES**   Donna Jamison, a 2003 graduate of the University of Florida with 4 years of banking experience, was recently brought in as assistant to the chairperson of the board of D'Leon Inc., a small food producer that operates in north Florida and whose specialty is high-quality pecan and other nut products sold in the snack foods market. D'Leon's president, Al Watkins, decided in 2007 to undertake a major expansion and to "go national" in competition with Frito-Lay, Eagle, and other major snack foods companies. Watkins believed that D'Leon's products were of higher quality than the competition's; that this quality differential would enable it to charge a premium price; and that the end result would be greatly increased sales, profits, and stock price.

    The company doubled its plant capacity, opened new sales offices outside its home territory, and launched an expensive advertising campaign. D'Leon's results were not satisfactory, to put it mildly. Its board of directors, which consisted of its president, vice president, and major stockholders (who were all local businesspeople), was most upset when directors learned how the expansion was going. Unhappy suppliers were being paid late; and the bank was complaining about the deteriorating situation, threatening to cut off credit. As a result, Watkins was informed that changes would have to be made—and quickly; otherwise, he would be fired. Also, at the board's insistence, Donna Jamison was brought in and given the job of assistant to Fred Campo, a retired banker who was D'Leon's chairperson and largest stockholder. Campo agreed to give up a few of his golfing days and help nurse the company back to health, with Jamison's help.

    Jamison began by gathering the financial statements and other data given in Tables IC 3-1, IC 3-2, IC 3-3, and IC 3-4. Assume that you are Jamison's assistant. You must help her answer the following questions for Campo. (Note: We will continue with this case in Chapter 4, and you will feel more comfortable with the analysis there. But answering these questions will help prepare you for Chapter 4. Provide clear explanations.)

    a.   What effect did the expansion have on sales, after-tax operating income, net working capital (NWC), and net income?

    b.   What effect did the company's expansion have on its free cash flow?

    c.   D'Leon purchases materials on 30-day terms, meaning that it is supposed to pay for purchases within 30 days of receipt. Judging from its 2008 balance sheet, do you think that D'Leon pays suppliers on time? Explain, including what problems might occur if suppliers are not paid in a timely manner.

    d.   D'Leon spends money for labor, materials, and fixed assets (depreciation) to make products—and spends still more money to sell those products. Then the firm makes sales that result in receivables, which eventually result in cash inflows. Does it appear that D'Leon's sales price exceeds its costs per unit sold? How does this affect the cash balance?

    e.   Suppose D'Leon's sales manager told the sales staff to start offering 60-day credit terms rather than the 30-day terms now being offered. D'Leon's competitors react by offering similar terms, so sales remain constant. What effect would this have on the cash account? How would the cash account be affected if sales doubled as a result of the credit policy change?

    f.   Can you imagine a situation in which the sales price exceeds the cost of producing and selling a unit of output, yet a dramatic increase in sales volume causes the cash balance to decline? Explain.

    g.   Did D'Leon finance its expansion program with internally generated funds (additions to retained earnings plus depreciation) or with external capital? How does the choice of financing affect the company's financial strength?

    h.   Refer to Tables IC 3-2 and IC 3-4. Suppose D'Leon broke even in 2008 in the sense that sales revenues equaled total operating costs plus interest charges. Would the asset expansion have caused the company to experience a cash shortage that required it to raise external capital? Explain.

    i.   If D'Leon starts depreciating fixed assets over 7 years rather than 10 years, would that affect (1) the physical stock of assets, (2) the balance sheet account for fixed assets, (3) the company's reported net income, and (4) the company's cash position? Assume that the same depreciation method is used for stockholder reporting and for tax calculations and that the accounting change has no effect on assets' physical lives.

    j.   Explain how earnings per share, dividends per share, and book value per share are calculated and what they mean. Why does the market price per share not equal the book value per share?

    k.   Explain briefly the tax treatment of (1) interest and dividends paid, (2) interest earned and dividends received, (3) capital gains, and (4) tax loss carry-back and carry-forward. How might each of these items affect D'Leon's taxes?

Table IC 3-1	Balance Sheets	
	2008	**2007**
Assets		
Cash	$ 7,282	$ 57,600
Accounts receivable	632,160	351,200
Inventories	1,287,360	715,200
Total current assets	$1,926,802	$1,124,000
Gross fixed assets	1,202,950	491,000
Less accumulated depreciation	263,160	146,200
Net fixed assets	$ 939,790	$ 344,800
Total assets	$2,866,592	$1,468,800
Liabilities and Equity		
Accounts payable	$ 524,160	$ 145,600
Notes payable	636,808	200,000
Accruals	489,600	136,000
Total current liabilities	$1,650,568	$ 481,600
Long-term debt	723,432	323,432
Common stock (100,000 shares)	460,000	460,000
Retained earnings	32,592	203,768
Total equity	$ 492,592	$ 663,768
Total liabilities and equity	$2,866,592	$1,468,800

Table IC 3-2	Income Statements	
	2008	**2007**
Sales	$6,034,000	$3,432,000
Cost of goods sold	5,528,000	2,864,000
Other expenses	519,988	358,672
Total operating costs excluding depreciation and amortization	$6,047,988	$3,222,672
Depreciation and amortization	116,960	18,900
EBIT	($ 130,948)	$ 190,428
Interest expense	136,012	43,828
EBT	($ 266,960)	$ 146,600
Taxes (40%)	(106,784)[a]	58,640
Net income	($ 160,176)	$ 87,960
EPS	($ 1.602)	$ 0.880
DPS	$ 0.110	$ 0.220
Book value per share	$ 4.926	$ 6.638
Stock price	$ 2.25	$ 8.50
Shares outstanding	100,000	100,000
Tax rate	40.00%	40.00%
Lease payments	40,000	40,000
Sinking fund payments	0	0

Note:
[a]The firm had sufficient taxable income in 2006 and 2007 to obtain its full tax refund in 2008.

Table IC 3-3 — Statement of Stockholders' Equity, 2008

	COMMON STOCK		Retained Earnings	Total Stockholders' Equity
	Shares	Amount		
Balances, 12/31/07	100,000	$460,000	$ 203,768	$663,768
2008 Net Income			(160,176)	
Cash Dividends			(11,000)	
Addition (Subtraction) to Retained Earnings			(171,176)	(171,176)
Balances, 12/31/08	100,000	$460,000	$ 32,592	$492,592

Table IC 3-4 — Statement of Cash Flows, 2008

Operating Activities	
Net income	($160,176)
Depreciation and amortization	116,960
Increase in accounts payable	378,560
Increase in accruals	353,600
Increase in accounts receivable	(280,960)
Increase in inventories	(572,160)
Net cash provided by operating activities	($164,176)
Long-Term Investing Activities	
Additions to property, plant, and equipment	($711,950)
Net cash used in investing activities	($711,950)
Financing Activities	
Increase in notes payable	$436,808
Increase in long-term debt	400,000
Payment of cash dividends	(11,000)
Net cash provided by financing activities	$825,808
Summary	
Net decrease in cash	($ 50,318)
Cash at beginning of year	57,600
Cash at end of year	$ 7,282

THOMSON ONE | Business School Edition

Access the Thomson ONE problems through the CengageNOW™ web site. Use the Thomson ONE—Business School Edition online database to answer this chapter's questions.

Exploring Starbucks' Financial Statements

Over the past decade, Starbucks coffee shops have become an increasingly familiar part of the urban landscape. Currently (2008), the company operates more than 8,000 coffee shops in all 50 states, in the District of Columbia, and in international markets; and in 2008, it had approximately 145,000 employees.

Thomson ONE can access a wealth of financial information for companies such as Starbucks. To find some background information, begin by entering the company's ticker symbol, SBUX, and then selecting "GO." On the opening screen, you will see a great deal of useful information, including a summary of what Starbucks does, a chart of its recent stock price, EPS estimates, recent news stories, and a list of key financial data and ratios.

In researching a company's operating performance, a good place to start is the recent stock price performance. At the top of the Stock Price Chart, click on the section labeled "Interactive Chart." From this point, you can obtain a chart of the company's stock price performance relative to the overall market (as measured by the S&P 500) between 1998 and 2008. To obtain a 10-year chart, go to "Time Frame," click on the down arrow, and select "10 years." Then click on "Draw"; a 10-year price chart should appear.

As you can see, Starbucks has had its ups and downs. But the company's overall performance has been quite strong, and it has beaten the overall market handily.

You can also find Starbucks' recent financial statements. Click on Financials to find the company's annual balance sheets for the past 5 years. Selecting Thomson Financials provides balance sheets, income statements, and statements of cash flows for various time periods. Clicking on the Microsoft Excel icon downloads these statements directly to a spreadsheet.

Discussion Questions

1. Looking at the most recent year available, what is the amount of total assets on Starbucks' balance sheet? What percentage is fixed assets, such as plant and equipment? What percentage is current assets? How much has the company grown over the years that are shown?
2. Does Starbucks have very much long-term debt? What are the chief ways in which Starbucks has financed assets?
3. Looking at the statement of cash flows, what factors can explain the change in the company's cash position over the last couple of years?
4. Looking at the income statement, what are the company's most recent sales and net income? Over the past several years, what has been the sales growth rate? What has been the growth rate in net income?
5. Over the past few years, has there been a strong correlation between stock price performance and reported earnings? Explain.

CHIP SOMODEVILLA/GETTY IMAGES

CHAPTER

4 Analysis of Financial Statements

Can You Make Money Analyzing Stocks?

For the past 40 years, a debate has raged over the question posed above. Some argue that the stock market is highly efficient and that all available information regarding a stock is already reflected in its price. The "efficient market advocates" point out that there are thousands of smart, well-trained analysts working for institutions with billions of dollars. These analysts have access to the latest information, and they spring into action—buying or selling—as soon as a firm releases any information that has a bearing on its future profits. The "efficient markets advocates" also point out that few mutual funds, which hire good people and pay them well, actually beat the averages. If these experts earn only average returns, how can the rest of us expect to beat the market?

Others disagree, arguing that analysis can pay off. They point out that some fund managers perform better than average year after year. Also, they note that some "activist" investors analyze firms carefully, identify those with weaknesses that appear to be correctable, and then persuade

their managers to take actions to improve the firms' performances. One such investor is Warren Buffett, perhaps the best known U.S. investor. Another is Carl Icahn—not a household name, but someone whose investments have made him the 18th wealthiest American. Buffett and Icahn now have billions of dollars to work with, and those billions give them better access to corporate managers than most of us have. However, neither of them started as billionaires—they worked their way up, doing careful analysis of the type described in this chapter.

When investors learn that an activist investor such as Icahn has bought a stock, the price of that stock generally rises. Thus, in the fall of 2007, Icahn began buying shares in BEA Systems, a billion dollar software company, that had been selling for about $10.50. Once investors learned of Icahn's interest, the price jumped to $18.94. You can bet that Icahn and his staff went through the type of analysis discussed in this chapter, identified BEA's strengths and weaknesses, and concluded that managerial actions could boost the

84

firm's cash flows and value. Icahn's views were shared by Larry Ellison, chairperson of Oracle Corporation, a $17 billion software company. As we write this, Oracle and Icahn have combined forces and are trying to force a change in BEA's operations. Thousands of analysts are doing similar analyses of thousands of other companies, trying to find the next BEA and becoming the next Buffett or Icahn. It's fun; and unless the efficient markets folks are correct, it can be profitable.

PUTTING THINGS IN PERSPECTIVE

The primary goal of financial management is to maximize shareholders' wealth, not accounting measures such as net income or EPS. However, accounting data influence stock prices, and this data can be used to see why a company is performing the way it is and where it is heading. Chapter 3 described the key financial statements and showed how they change as a firm's operations change. Now, in Chapter 4, we show how the statements are used by managers to improve the firm's stock price; by lenders to evaluate the likelihood that borrowers will be able to pay off loans; and by security analysts to forecast earnings, dividends, and stock prices.

If management is to maximize a firm's value, it must take advantage of the firm's strengths and correct its weaknesses. Financial analysis involves (1) comparing the firm's performance to that of other firms in the same industry and (2) evaluating trends in the firm's financial position over time. These studies help managers identify deficiencies and then take corrective actions. In this chapter, we focus on how managers and investors evaluate a firm's financial position. Then, in later chapters, we examine the types of actions managers can take to improve future performance and thus increase the firm's stock price.

The most important ratio is the ROE, or return on equity, which tells us how much stockholders are earning on the funds they provide to the firm. When ROE is high, the stock price also tends to be high; so actions that increase ROE generally increase the stock price. Other ratios provide information about how well assets such as inventory, accounts receivable, and fixed assets are managed and about the firm's capital structure. Managers use ratios related to these factors to help develop plans to improve ROE.

When you finish this chapter, you should be able to:

- Explain what ratio analysis is.
- List the 5 groups of ratios and identify, calculate, and interpret the key ratios in each group. In addition, discuss each ratio's relationship to the balance sheet and income statement.
- Discuss why ROE is the key ratio under management's control, how the other ratios affect ROE, and explain how to use the DuPont equation to see how the ROE can be improved.
- Compare a firm's ratios with those of other firms (benchmarking) and analyze a given firm's ratios over time (trend analysis).
- Discuss the tendency of ratios to fluctuate over time, which may or may not be problematic. Explain how they can be influenced by accounting practices and other factors and why they must be used with care.

4-1 RATIO ANALYSIS

Ratios help us evaluate financial statements. For example, at the end of 2008, Allied Food Products had $1,060 million of debt and interest charges of $88 million while Midwest Products had $52 million of debt and interest charges of $4 million. Which company is stronger? The burden of these debts and the companies' ability to repay them can best be evaluated by comparing each firm's debt to its assets and comparing interest expense to the income and cash available to pay that interest. Ratios are used to make such comparisons. We calculate Allied's ratios for 2008 using data from the balance sheets and income statements given in Tables 3-1 and 3-2. We also evaluate the ratios relative to food industry averages, using data in millions of dollars.[1] As you will see, we can calculate many different ratios, with different ones used to examine different aspects of the firm's operations. You will get to know some ratios by name, but it's better to understand what they are designed to do than to memorize names and equations.

We divide the ratios into five categories:

1. *Liquidity ratios,* which give us an idea of the firm's ability to pay off debts that are maturing within a year.
2. *Asset management ratios,* which give us an idea of how efficiently the firm is using its assets.
3. *Debt management ratios,* which give us an idea of how the firm has financed its assets as well as the firm's ability to repay its long-term debt.
4. *Profitability ratios,* which give us an idea of how profitably the firm is operating and utilizing its assets.
5. *Market value ratios,* which bring in the stock price and give us an idea of what investors think about the firm and its future prospects.

Satisfactory liquidity ratios are necessary if the firm is to continue operating. Good asset management ratios are necessary for the firm to keep its costs low and thus its net income high. Debt management ratios give us an idea of how risky the firm is and how much of its operating income must be paid to bondholders rather than stockholders. Profitability ratios bring together the asset and debt management ratios and show their effects on ROE. Finally, market value ratios tell us what investors think about the company and its prospects.

All of the ratios are important, but different ones are more important for some companies than for others. For example, if a firm borrowed too much in the past and its debt now threatens to drive it into bankruptcy, the debt ratios are key. Similarly, if a firm expanded too rapidly and now finds itself with excess inventory and manufacturing capacity, the asset management ratios take center stage. The ROE is always important; but a high ROE depends on maintaining liquidity, on efficient asset management, and on the proper use of debt. Managers are, of

---

[1] Financial statement data for most publicly traded firms can be obtained from the Internet. A couple of free sites that provide this information include Google Finance and Yahoo Finance. These sites provide the financial statements, which can be copied to an Excel file and used to create your own ratios; but the web sites also provide calculated ratios.

In addition to the ratios discussed in this chapter, financial analysts often employ a tool known as *common size analysis.* To form a common size balance sheet, simply divide each asset, liability, and equity item by total assets and then express the results as percentages. To develop a common size income statement, divide each income statement item by sales. The resultant percentage statements can be compared with statements of larger or smaller firms or with those of the same firm over time. One would normally obtain the basic statements from a source such as Google Finance and copy them to Excel, so constructing common size statements is quite easy. Note too that industry average data are generally given as percentages, which makes them easy to compare with a firm's own common size statements.

course, vitally concerned with the stock price; but managers have little direct control over the stock market while they do have control over their firm's ROE. So ROE tends to be the main focal point.

4-2 LIQUIDITY RATIOS

The liquidity ratios help answer this question: Will the firm be able to pay off its debts as they come due and thus remain a viable organization? If the answer is no, liquidity must be the first order of business.

A **liquid asset** is one that trades in an active market and thus can be quickly converted to cash at the going market price. As shown in Table 3-1 in Chapter 3, Allied has $310 million of debt that must be paid off within the coming year. Will it have trouble meeting that obligation? A full liquidity analysis requires the use of a cash budget, which we discuss in the working capital management chapter; however, by relating cash and other current assets to current liabilities, ratio analysis provides a quick and easy-to-use measure of liquidity. Two of the most commonly used **liquidity ratios** are discussed below.

4-2a Current Ratio

The primary liquidity ratio is the **current ratio**, which is calculated by dividing current assets by current liabilities:

$$\text{Current ratio} = \frac{\text{Current assets}}{\text{Current liabilities}}$$

$$= \frac{\$1,000}{\$310} = 3.2\times$$

$$\text{Industry average} = 4.2\times$$

Current assets include cash, marketable securities, accounts receivable, and inventories. Allied's current liabilities consist of accounts payable, accrued wages and taxes, and short-term notes payable to its bank, all of which are due within one year.

If a company is having financial difficulty, it typically begins to pay its accounts payable more slowly and to borrow more from its bank, both of which increase current liabilities. If current liabilities are rising faster than current assets, the current ratio will fall; and this is a sign of possible trouble. Allied's current ratio is 3.2, which is well below the industry average of 4.2. Therefore, its liquidity position is somewhat weak but by no means desperate.[2]

Although industry average figures are discussed later in some detail, note that an industry average is not a magic number that all firms should strive to maintain; in fact, some very well-managed firms may be above the average while other good firms are below it. However, if a firm's ratios are far removed from the averages for its industry, an analyst should be concerned about why this variance occurs. Thus, a deviation from the industry average should signal the analyst (or management) to check further. Note too that a high current ratio generally indicates a very strong, safe liquidity position; it might also indicate that the firm has too much old inventory that will have to be written off and too many old accounts receivable that may turn into bad debts. Or the high current ratio might indicate that the firm has too much cash, receivables, and inventory relative to its sales, in

Liquid Asset
An asset that can be converted to cash quickly without having to reduce the asset's price very much.

Liquidity Ratios
Ratios that show the relationship of a firm's cash and other current assets to its current liabilities.

Current Ratio
This ratio is calculated by dividing current assets by current liabilities. It indicates the extent to which current liabilities are covered by those assets expected to be converted to cash in the near future.

[2]Since current assets should be convertible to cash within a year, it is likely that they could be liquidated at close to their stated value. With a current ratio of 3.2, Allied could liquidate current assets at only 31% of book value and still pay off current creditors in full: 1/3.2 = 0.31, or 31%. Note also that 0.31($1,000) = $310, the current liabilities balance.

which case these assets are not being managed efficiently. So it is always necessary to look deeply into the full set of ratios before forming a judgment as to how well the firm is performing.

4-2b Quick, or Acid Test, Ratio

Quick (Acid Test) Ratio
This ratio is calculated by deducting inventories from current assets and then dividing the remainder by current liabilities.

The second liquidity ratio is the **quick,** or **acid test, ratio**, which is calculated by deducting inventories from current assets and then dividing the remainder by current liabilities:

$$\text{Quick, or acid test, ratio} = \frac{\text{Current assets} - \text{Inventories}}{\text{Current liabilities}}$$

$$= \frac{\$385}{\$310} = 1.2\times$$

Industry average $= 2.2\times$

Inventories are typically the least liquid of a firm's current assets; and if sales slow down, they might not be converted to cash as quickly as expected. Also, inventories are the assets on which losses are most likely to occur in the event of liquidation. Therefore, the quick ratio, which measures the firm's ability to pay off short-term obligations without relying on the sale of inventories, is important.

The industry average quick ratio is 2.2, so Allied's 1.2 ratio is relatively low. Still, if the accounts receivable can be collected, the company can pay off its current liabilities even if it has trouble disposing of its inventories.

SELF TEST

What are the characteristics of a liquid asset? Give examples of some liquid assets.

What question are the two liquidity ratios designed to answer?

Which is the least liquid of the firm's current assets?

A company has current liabilities of $500 million, and its current ratio is 2.0. What is the total of its current assets? **($1,000 million)** If this firm's quick ratio is 1.6, how much inventory does it have? **($200 million)** (Hint: To answer this problem and some of the other problems in this chapter, write out the equation for the ratio in the question, insert the given data, and solve for the missing value.)

Examples:

Current ratio = 2.0 = CA/CL = CA/$500, so CA = 2($500) = $1,000

Quick ratio = 1.6 = (CA − Inventories)/CL = ($1,000 − Inventories)/$500, so $1,000 − Inventories = 1.6($500) and Inventories = $1,000 − $800 = $200

4-3 ASSET MANAGEMENT RATIOS

Asset Management Ratios
A set of ratios that measure how effectively a firm is managing its assets.

The second group of ratios, the **asset management ratios**, measure how effectively the firm is managing its assets. These ratios answer this question: Does the amount of each type of asset seem reasonable, too high, or too low in view of current and projected sales? These ratios are important because when Allied and other companies acquire assets, they must obtain capital from banks or other sources and capital is expensive. Therefore, if Allied has too many assets, its cost of capital will be too high, which will depress its profits. On the other hand, if its assets are too low, profitable sales will be lost. So Allied must strike a balance between too many and too few assets, and the asset management ratios will help it strike this proper balance.

4-3a Inventory Turnover Ratio

"Turnover ratios" divide sales by some asset: Sales/Various assets. As the name implies, these ratios show how many times the particular asset is "turned over" during the year. Here is the **inventory turnover ratio**:

$$\text{Inventory turnover ratio} = \frac{\text{Sales}}{\text{Inventories}}$$

$$= \frac{\$3,000}{\$615} = 4.9\times$$

$$\text{Industry average} = 10.9\times$$

As a rough approximation, each item of Allied's inventory is sold and restocked, or "turned over," 4.9 times per year. *Turnover* is a term that originated many years ago with the old Yankee peddler who would load up his wagon with pots and pans, then go off on his route to peddle his wares. The merchandise was called working capital because it was what he actually sold, or "turned over," to produce his profits, whereas his "turnover" was the number of trips he took each year. Annual sales divided by inventory equaled turnover, or trips per year. If he made 10 trips per year, stocked 100 pots and pans, and made a gross profit of $5 per item, his annual gross profit was (100)($5)(10) = $5,000. If he went faster and made 20 trips per year, his gross profit doubled, other things held constant. So his turnover directly affected his profits.

Allied's inventory turnover of 4.9 is much lower than the industry average of 10.9. This suggests that it is holding too much inventory. Excess inventory is, of course, unproductive and represents an investment with a low or zero rate of return. Allied's low inventory turnover ratio also makes us question the current ratio. With such a low turnover, the firm may be holding obsolete goods that are not worth their stated value.[3]

Note that sales occur over the entire year, whereas the inventory figure is for one point in time. For this reason, it might be better to use an average inventory measure.[4] If the business is highly seasonal or if there has been a strong upward or downward sales trend during the year, it is especially useful to make an adjustment. Allied's sales are not growing especially rapidly though; and to maintain comparability with industry averages, we used year-end rather than average inventories.

4-3b Days Sales Outstanding

Accounts receivable are evaluated by the **days sales outstanding (DSO) ratio**, also called the average collection period (ACP).[5] It is calculated by dividing accounts receivable by the average daily sales to find how many days' sales are tied up in

Inventory Turnover Ratio
This ratio is calculated by dividing sales by inventories.

Days Sales Outstanding (DSO)
This ratio is calculated by dividing accounts receivable by average sales per day; it indicates the average length of time the firm must wait after making a sale before it receives cash.

---

[3]Our measure of inventory turnover is frequently used by established compilers of financial ratio statistics such as Value Line and Dun & Bradstreet. However, you should recognize that other sources calculate inventory using cost of goods sold in place of sales in the formula's numerator. The rationale for this alternative measure is that sales are stated at market prices; so if inventories are carried at cost, as they generally are, the calculated turnover overstates the true turnover ratio. Therefore, it might be more appropriate to use cost of goods sold in place of sales in the formula's numerator. When evaluating and comparing financial ratios from various sources, it is important to understand how those sources are specifically calculating financial ratios.

[4]Preferably, the average inventory value should be calculated by summing the monthly figures during the year and dividing by 12. If monthly data are not available, the beginning and ending figures can be added and then divided by 2. Both methods adjust for growth but not for seasonal effects.

[5]We could use the receivables turnover to evaluate receivables. Allied's receivables turnover is $3,000/$375 = 8×. However, the DSO ratio is easier to interpret and judge.

receivables. Thus, the DSO represents the average length of time the firm must wait after making a sale before receiving cash. Allied has 46 days sales outstanding, well above the 36-day industry average:

$$\text{Days sales outstanding (DSO)} = \frac{\text{Receivables}}{\text{Average sales per day}} = \frac{\text{Receivables}}{\text{Annual sales}/365}$$

$$= \frac{\$375}{\$3,000/365} = \frac{\$375}{\$8.2192} = 45.625 \text{ days} \approx 46 \text{ days}$$

Industry average = 36 days

The DSO can be compared with the industry average, but it is also evaluated by comparing it with Allied's credit terms. Allied's credit policy calls for payment within 30 days. So the fact that 46 days' sales are outstanding, not 30 days', indicates that Allied's customers, on average, are not paying their bills on time. This deprives the company of funds that could be used to reduce bank loans or some other type of costly capital. Moreover, the high average DSO indicates that if some customers are paying on time, quite a few must be paying very late. Late-paying customers often default, so their receivables may end up as bad debts that can never be collected.[6] Note too that the trend in the DSO over the past few years has been rising, but the credit policy has not been changed. This reinforces our belief that Allied's credit manager should take steps to collect receivables faster.

4-3c Fixed Assets Turnover Ratio

Fixed Assets Turnover Ratio
The ratio of sales to net fixed assets.

The **fixed assets turnover ratio**, which is the ratio of sales to net fixed assets, measures how effectively the firm uses its plant and equipment:

$$\text{Fixed assets turnover ratio} = \frac{\text{Sales}}{\text{Net fixed assets}}$$

$$= \frac{\$3,000}{\$1,000} = 3.0\times$$

Industry average = 2.8×

Allied's ratio of 3.0 times is slightly above the 2.8 industry average, indicating that it is using its fixed assets at least as intensively as other firms in the industry. Therefore, Allied seems to have about the right amount of fixed assets relative to its sales.

Potential problems may arise when interpreting the fixed assets turnover ratio. Recall that fixed assets are shown on the balance sheet at their historical costs less depreciation. Inflation has caused the value of many assets that were purchased in the past to be seriously understated. Therefore, if we compare an old firm whose fixed assets have been depreciated with a new company with similar operations that acquired its fixed assets only recently, the old firm will probably have the higher fixed assets turnover ratio. However, this would be more reflective of the age of the assets than of inefficiency on the part of the new firm. The accounting profession is trying to develop procedures for making financial statements reflect current values rather than historical values, which would help us make better comparisons. However, at the moment, the problem still exists; so financial analysts must recognize this problem and deal with it judgmentally. In Allied's case, the issue is not serious because all firms in the industry have been

---

[6]For example, if further analysis along the lines suggested in Part 6 of this text indicates that 85% of the customers pay in 30 days, for the DSO to average 46 days, the remaining 15% must be paying, on average, in 136.67 days. Paying that late suggests financial difficulties. A DSO of 46 days would alert a good analyst of the need to dig deeper.

expanding at about the same rate; hence, the balance sheets of the comparison firms are reasonably comparable.[7]

4-3d Total Assets Turnover Ratio

The final asset management ratio, the **total assets turnover ratio**, measures the turnover of all of the firm's assets; and it is calculated by dividing sales by total assets:

$$\text{Total assets turnover ratio} = \frac{\text{Sales}}{\text{Total assets}}$$

$$= \frac{\$3,000}{\$2,000} = 1.5\times$$

$$\text{Industry average} = 1.8\times$$

Allied's ratio is somewhat below the industry average, indicating that it is not generating enough sales given its total assets. We just saw that Allied's fixed assets turnover is in line with the industry average; so the problem is with its current assets, inventories and accounts receivable, whose ratios were below the industry standards. Inventories should be reduced and receivables collected faster, which would improve operations.

> **Total Assets Turnover Ratio**
> *This ratio is calculated by dividing sales by total assets.*

SELF TEST

Write the equations for four ratios that are used to measure how effectively a firm manages its assets.

If one firm is growing rapidly and another is not, how might this distort a comparison of their inventory turnover ratios?

If you wanted to evaluate a firm's DSO, with what could you compare it? **(Other companies and the same company over time)**

How might different ages distort comparisons of different firms' fixed assets turnover ratios?

A firm has annual sales of $100 million, $20 million of inventory, and $30 million of accounts receivable. What is its inventory turnover ratio? **(5×)** What is its DSO? **(109.5 days)**

4-4 DEBT MANAGEMENT RATIOS

The use of debt will increase, or "leverage up," a firm's ROE if the firm earns more on its assets than the interest rate it pays on debt. However, debt exposes the firm to more risk than if it financed only with equity. In this section we discuss **debt management ratios**.

Table 4-1 illustrates the potential benefits and risks associated with debt.[8] Here we analyze two companies that are identical except for how they are financed. Firm U (for *Unleveraged*) has no debt; thus, it uses 100% common equity. Firm L (for *Leveraged*) obtained 50% of its capital as debt at an interest rate of 10%. Both firms have $100 of assets, and their sales are expected to range from a high of $150 down to $75 depending on business conditions. Some of their operating costs

> **Debt Management Ratios**
> *A set of ratios that measure how effectively a firm manages its debt.*

---

[7]See FASB #89, *Financial Reporting and Changing Prices* (December 1986), for a discussion of the effects of inflation on financial statements. The report's age indicates how difficult it has been to solve this problem.

[8]We discuss ROE in more depth later in this chapter, and we examine the effects of leverage in detail in the capital structure and leverage chapter.

| Table 4-1 | **Effects of Financial Leverage on Stockholder Returns** |

FIRM U [UNLEVERAGED (NO DEBT)]

Current assets	$ 50	Debt		$ 0
Fixed assets	50	Common equity		100
Total assets	$100	Total liabilities and equity		$100

	STATE OF THE ECONOMY		
	Good	**Expected**	**Bad**
Sales revenues	$150.0	$100.0	$75.0
Operating costs Fixed	45.0	45.0	45.0
Variable	60.0	40.0	30.0
Total operating costs	105.0	85.0	75.0
Operating income (EBIT)	$ 45.0	$ 15.0	$ 0.0
Interest (Rate = 10%)	0.0	0.0	0.0
Earnings before taxes (EBT)	$ 45.0	$ 15.0	$ 0.0
Taxes (Rate = 40%)	18.0	6.0	0.0
Net income (NI)	$ 27.0	$ 9.0	$ 0.0
ROE_U	27.0%	9.0%	0.0%

FIRM L [LEVERAGED (SOME DEBT)]

Current assets	$ 50	Debt		$ 50
Fixed assets	50	Common equity		50
Total assets	$100	Total liabilities and equity		$100

	STATE OF THE ECONOMY		
	Good	**Expected**	**Bad**
Sales revenues	$150.0	$100.0	$75.0
Operating costs Fixed	45.0	45.0	45.0
Variable	60.0	40.0	30.0
Total operating costs	105.0	85.0	75.0
Operating income (EBIT)	$ 45.0	$ 15.0	$ 0.0
Interest (Rate = 10%)	5.0	5.0	5.0
Earnings before taxes (EBT)	$ 40.0	$ 10.0	−$ 5.0
Taxes (Rate = 40%)	16.0	4.0	0.0
Net income (NI)	$ 24.0	$ 6.0	−$ 5.0
ROE_L	48.0%	12.0%	−10.0%

(e.g., rent and the president's salary) are fixed and will be the same regardless of the level of sales, while other costs (e.g., manufacturing labor and materials costs) vary with sales.[9]

---

[9]The financial statements do not show the breakdown between fixed and variable operating costs, but companies can and do make this breakdown for internal purposes. Of course, the distinction is not always clear because what's a fixed cost in the very short run can become a variable cost over a longer time horizon. It's interesting to note that companies are moving toward making more of their costs variable, using such techniques as increasing bonuses rather than base salaries, switching to profit-sharing plans rather than fixed pension plans, and outsourcing various operations.

Notice that everything is the same in the table for the leveraged and unleveraged firms down through operating income—thus, their EBITs are the same in each state of the economy. However, things differ below operating income. Firm U has no debt, it pays no interest, its taxable income is the same as its operating income, it pays a 40% state and federal tax rate, and its net income ranges from $27 under good conditions down to $0 under bad conditions. When U's net income is divided by its common equity, its ROEs range from 27% to 0% depending on the state of the economy.

Firm L has the same EBIT as U under each state of the economy, but L uses $50 of debt with a 10% interest rate; so it has $5 of interest charges regardless of the economy. This $5 is deducted from EBIT to arrive at taxable income; taxes are taken out; and the result is net income, which ranges from $24 to –$5 depending on conditions.[10] At first, it looks as though Firm U is better off under all conditions; but this is not correct—we need to consider how much the two firms' stockholders have invested. Firm L's stockholders have put up only $50; so when that investment is divided into net income, we see that their ROE under good conditions is a whopping 48% (versus 27% for U) and is 12% (versus 9% for U) under expected conditions. However, L's ROE falls to –10% under bad conditions, which means that Firm L would go bankrupt if those conditions persisted for several years.

There are two reasons for the leveraging effect: (1) Interest is deductible, so the use of debt lowers the tax bill and leaves more of the firm's operating income available to its investors. (2) If the rate of return on assets exceeds the interest rate on debt, as is generally expected, a company can use debt to acquire assets, pay the interest on the debt, and have something left over as a "bonus" for its stockholders. Under the expected conditions, our hypothetical firms expect to earn 15% on assets versus a 10% cost of debt. This, combined with the tax benefit of debt, pushes L's expected ROE far above that of U.

Thus, firms with relatively high debt ratios typically have higher expected returns when the economy is normal but lower returns and possibly bankruptcy if the economy goes into a recession. Therefore, decisions about the use of debt require firms to balance higher expected returns against increased risk. Determining the optimal amount of debt is a complicated process, and we defer a discussion of that subject until the capital structure chapter. For now, we simply look at two procedures that analysts use to examine the firm's debt: (1) They check the balance sheet to determine the proportion of total funds represented by debt, and (2) they review the income statement to see the extent to which interest is covered by operating profits.

4-4a Total Debt to Total Assets

The ratio of total debt to total assets, generally called the **debt ratio**, measures the percentage of funds provided by creditors:

Debt Ratio
The ratio of total debt to total assets.

$$\text{Debt ratio} = \frac{\text{Total debt}}{\text{Total assets}}$$

$$= \frac{\$310 + \$750}{\$2,000} = \frac{\$1,060}{\$2,000} = 53.0\%$$

Industry average = 40.0%

Total debt includes all current liabilities and long-term debt. Creditors prefer low debt ratios because the lower the ratio, the greater the cushion against creditors' losses in the event of liquidation. Stockholders, on the other hand, may want more leverage because it can magnify expected earnings, as we saw in Table 4-1.

---

[10]As we discussed in the last chapter, firms can carry losses back or forward for several years. Therefore, if Firm L had profits and thus paid taxes in recent 2007, it could carry back the 2008 loss under bad conditions and receive a credit (a check from the government). In Table 4-1, we disregard the carry-back/carry-forward provision.

Allied's debt ratio is 53.0%, which means that its creditors have supplied more than half of its total funds. As we will discuss in the capital structure chapter, a number of factors affect a company's optimal debt ratio. Nevertheless, the fact that Allied's debt ratio exceeds the industry average by a fairly large amount raises a red flag, and this will make it relatively costly for Allied to borrow additional funds without first raising more equity. Creditors will be reluctant to lend the firm more money, and management would probably be subjecting the firm to too high a risk of bankruptcy if it sought to borrow a substantial amount of additional funds.[11]

4-4b Times-Interest-Earned Ratio

Times-Interest-Earned (TIE) Ratio

The ratio of earnings before interest and taxes (EBIT) to interest charges; a measure of the firm's ability to meet its annual interest payments.

The **times-interest-earned (TIE) ratio** is determined by dividing earnings before interest and taxes (EBIT in Table 3-2) by the interest charges:

$$\text{Times-interest-earned (TIE) ratio} = \frac{\text{EBIT}}{\text{Interest charges}}$$
$$= \frac{\$283.8}{\$88} = 3.2\times$$
$$\text{Industry average} = 6.0\times$$

The TIE ratio measures the extent to which operating income can decline before the firm is unable to meet its annual interest costs. Failure to pay interest will bring legal action by the firm's creditors and probably result in bankruptcy. Note that earnings before interest and taxes, rather than net income, is used in the numerator. Because interest is paid with pretax dollars, the firm's ability to pay current interest is not affected by taxes.

Allied's interest is covered 3.2 times. The industry average is 6 times, so Allied is covering its interest charges by a relatively low margin of safety. Thus, the TIE ratio reinforces our conclusion from the debt ratio, namely, that Allied would face difficulties if it attempted to borrow much additional money.[12]

SELF TEST

How does the use of financial leverage affect stockholders' control position?

How does the U.S. tax structure influence a firm's willingness to finance with debt?

How does the decision to use debt involve a risk-versus-return trade-off?

Explain the following statement: Analysts look at both balance sheet and income statement ratios when appraising a firm's financial condition.

Name two ratios that are used to measure financial leverage and write their equations.

---

[11]The ratio of debt to equity is also used in financial analysis. The debt-to-assets (D/A) and debt-to-equity (D/E) ratios are simply transformations of each other:

$$D/E = \frac{D/A}{1 - D/A} \quad \text{and} \quad D/A = \frac{D/E}{1 + D/E}$$

With a D/A ratio of 53%, or 0.53, Allied's Debt/Equity ratio is 0.53/(1 − 0.53) = 1.13.

[12]Another commonly used debt management ratio is the following:

$$\text{EBITDA coverage} = \frac{\text{EBITDA} + \text{Lease payments}}{\text{Interest} + \text{Principal payments} + \text{Lease payments}}$$

This ratio is more complete than the TIE ratio in that it recognizes that depreciation and amortization expenses are not cash charges and thus are available to service debt and that lease payments and principal repayments on debt are fixed charges. For more on this ratio, see E. F. Brigham and P. R. Daves, *Intermediate Financial Management,* 9th ed., (Mason, OH: Thomson/South-Western, 2007), p. 258.

4-5 PROFITABILITY RATIOS

Accounting statements reflect events that happened in the past, but they also provide clues about what's really important—what's likely to happen in the future. The liquidity, asset management, and debt ratios covered thus far tell us something about the firm's policies and operations. Now we turn to the **profitability ratios**, which reflect the net result of all of the financing policies and operating decisions.

4-5a Operating Margin

The **operating margin**, calculated by dividing operating income (EBIT) by sales, gives the operating profit per dollar of sales:

$$\text{Operating margin} = \frac{\text{Operating income (EBIT)}}{\text{Sales}}$$

$$= \frac{\$283.8}{\$3,000} = 9.5\%$$

Industry average $= 10.0\%$

Allied's 9.5% operating margin is below the industry average of 10.0%. This subpar result indicates that Allied's operating costs are too high. This is consistent with the low inventory turnover and high days' sales outstanding ratios that we calculated earlier.

4-5b Profit Margin

The **profit margin**, also sometimes called the net profit margin, is calculated by dividing net income by sales:

$$\text{Profit margin} = \frac{\text{Net income}}{\text{Sales}}$$

$$= \frac{\$117.5}{\$3,000} = 3.9\%$$

Industry average $= 5.0\%$

Allied's 3.9% profit margin is below the industry average of 5.0%, and this subpar result occurred for two reasons. First, Allied's operating margin was below the industry average because of the firm's high operating costs. Second, the profit margin is negatively impacted by Allied's heavy use of debt. To see this second point, recognize that net income is *after interest*. Suppose two firms have identical operations in the sense that their sales, operating costs, and operating income are identical. However, one firm uses more debt; hence, it has higher interest charges. Those interest charges pull down its net income; and since sales are constant, the result is a relatively low net profit margin for the firm with more debt. We see then that Allied's operating inefficiency and its high debt ratio combine to lower its net profit margin below the food processing industry average. It also follows that when two companies have the same operating margin but different debt ratios, we can expect the company with a higher debt ratio to have a lower profit margin.

Note too that while a high return on sales is good, other things held constant, other things may not be held constant—we must also be concerned with turnover. If a firm sets a very high price on its products, it may get a high return on each sale but fail to make many sales. That strategy might result in a high profit margin, low sales, and hence a low net income. We will see shortly how, through the use of the DuPont equation, profit margins, the use of debt, and turnover ratios interact to affect overall stockholder returns.

Profitability Ratios
A group of ratios that show the combined effects of liquidity, asset management, and debt on operating results.

Operating Margin
This ratio measures operating income, or EBIT, per dollar of sales; it is calculated by dividing operating income by sales.

Profit Margin
This ratio measures net income per dollar of sales and is calculated by dividing net income by sales.

GLOBAL PERSPECTIVES

GLOBAL ACCOUNTING STANDARDS: CAN ONE SIZE FIT ALL?

These days you must be a good financial detective to analyze financial statements, especially when the company operates overseas. Despite attempts to standardize accounting practices, there are still many differences in financial reporting in different countries; and those differences create headaches for investors making cross-border company comparisons. However, as businesses become more global and as more foreign companies list on U.S. stock exchanges, accountants and regulators are realizing the need for a global convergence of accounting standards. As a result, the "writing is on the wall" regarding accounting standards and differences are disappearing.

The effort to internationalize accounting standards began in 1973 with the formation of the International Accounting Standards Committee. However, in 1998, it became apparent that a full-time rule-making body with global representation was necessary; so the International Accounting Standards Board (IASB), with members representing 9 major countries, was established. The IASB was charged with the responsibility for creating a set of International Financial Reporting Standards (IFRS).

A survey of senior executives from 85 financial institutions worldwide found that 92% of those responding favored a single set of international standards. The U.S. SEC has proposed allowing non-U.S. companies that operate in the United States to base their reports on IFRS rather than GAAP, and it is considering requiring U.S. companies to shift to IFRS. Obviously, the globalization of accounting standards is a huge endeavor—one that will involve compromises between the IASB and FASB. The main problem is that U.S. GAAP takes a rules-based approach, while the IASB insists on using a principles-based approach. With a rules-based system, companies can tell whether they are in compliance, but they can also devise ways to get around a rule and thus subvert its intent. With a principles-based system, there is more uncertainty about whether certain borderline procedures will be allowed; but such a system makes it easier to prosecute on the basis of intent.

A global accounting structure would enable investors and practitioners around the world to read and understand financial reports produced anywhere in the world. According to SEC Chairman Christopher Cox, "Having a set of globally accepted accounting standards is critical to the rapidly accelerating global integration of the world's capital markets." Even the chairman of the U.S. Financial Accounting Standards Board, Robert Herz, has recommended that a target date be set for U.S. companies to transition from GAAP to IFRS. So it seems that the issue is when, not if, all companies will be playing by the same set of accounting rules.

Sources: "All Accountants Soon May Speak the Same Language," *The Wall Street Journal,* August 29, 1995, p. A15; "For and Against; Standards Need Time to Work," *Accountancy Age,* June 5, 2003, p. 16; and James Turley (CEO, Ernst & Young), "Mind the GAAP," *The Wall Street Journal,* November 9, 2007, p. A18.

4-5c Return on Total Assets

Return on Total Assets (ROA)

The ratio of the net income to total assets.

Net income divided by total assets gives us the **return on total assets (ROA)**:

$$\text{Return on total assets (ROA)} = \frac{\text{Net income}}{\text{Total assets}}$$

$$= \frac{\$117.5}{\$2,000} = 5.9\%$$

Industry average $= 9.0\%$

Allied's 5.9% return is well below the 9.0% industry average. This is not good—it is obviously better to have a higher than a lower return on assets. Note, though, that a low ROA can result from a conscious decision to use a great deal of debt, in which case high interest expenses will cause net income to be relatively low. That is part of the reason for Allied's low ROA. Never forget—you must look at a number of ratios, see what each suggests, and then look at the overall situation when you judge the performance of a company and consider what actions it should undertake to improve.

4-5d Basic Earning Power (BEP) Ratio

The **basic earning power (BEP) ratio** is calculated by dividing operating income (EBIT) by total assets:

$$\text{Basic earning power (BEP)} = \frac{\text{EBIT}}{\text{Total assets}}$$

$$= \frac{\$283.8}{\$2,000} = 14.2\%$$

$$\text{Industry average} = 18.0\%$$

Basic Earning Power (BEP) Ratio
This ratio indicates the ability of the firm's assets to generate operating income; it is calculated by dividing EBIT by total assets.

This ratio shows the raw earning power of the firm's assets before the influence of taxes and debt, and it is useful when comparing firms with different debt and tax situations. Because of its low turnover ratios and poor profit margin on sales, Allied has a lower BEP ratio than the average food processing company.[13]

4-5e Return on Common Equity

The most important, or bottom-line, accounting ratio is the **return on common equity (ROE)**, found as follows:

$$\text{Return on common equity (ROE)} = \frac{\text{Net income}}{\text{Common equity}}$$

$$= \frac{\$117.5}{\$940} = 12.5\%$$

$$\text{Industry average} = 15.0\%$$

Return on Common Equity (ROE)
The ratio of net income to common equity; measures the rate of return on common stockholders' investment.

Stockholders expect to earn a return on their money, and this ratio tells how well they are doing in an accounting sense. Allied's 12.5% return is below the 15.0% industry average, but not as far below as the return on total assets. This somewhat better ROE results from the company's greater use of debt, a point discussed earlier in the chapter.

SELF TEST

Identify five profitability ratios and write their equations.

Why does the use of debt lower the profit margin and the ROA?

Using more debt lowers profits and thus the ROA. Why doesn't debt have the same negative effect on the ROE? **(Debt lowers net income, but it also lowers the firm's equity; and the equity reduction can offset the lower net income.)**

A company has $20 billion of sales and $1 billion of net income. Its total assets are $10 billion, financed half by debt and half by common equity. What is its profit margin? **(5%)** What is its ROA? **(10%)** What is its ROE? **(20%)** Would this firm's ROA increase if it used less leverage? **(yes)** Would its ROE increase? **(no)**

---

[13]A related ratio is the return on investors' capital, defined as follows:

$$\text{Return on investors' capital (ROIC)} = \frac{\text{Net income} + \text{Interest}}{\text{Debt} + \text{Equity}}$$

The numerator shows the dollar returns to all investors, the denominator shows the money investors have put up, and the resulting ratio shows the rate of return on total investor capital. This ratio is especially important in regulated industries such as electric utilities, where regulators are concerned about companies using their monopoly power to earn excessive returns on investors' capital. In fact, regulators often try to set electricity prices at a level that will force the return on investors' capital to equal a company's cost of capital, as defined in Chapter 10.

4-6 MARKET VALUE RATIOS

Market Value Ratios
Ratios that relate the firm's stock price to its earnings and book value per share.

ROE reflects the effects of all of the other ratios, and it is the single best accounting measure of performance. Investors like a high ROE, and high ROEs are correlated with high stock prices. However, other things come into play. For example, financial leverage generally increases the ROE but also increases the firm's risk; so if a high ROE is achieved by using a great deal of debt, the stock price might end up lower than if the firm had been using less debt and had a lower ROE. We use the final set of ratios—the **market value ratios**, which relate the stock price to earnings and book value price—to help address this situation. If the liquidity, asset management, debt management, and profitability ratios all look good and if investors think these ratios will continue to look good in the future, the market value ratios will be high, the stock price will be as high as can be expected, and management will be judged to have been doing a good job.

The market value ratios are used in three primary ways: (1) by investors when they are deciding to buy or sell a stock, (2) by investment bankers when they are setting the share price for a new stock issue (an IPO), and (3) by firms when they are deciding how much to offer for another firm in a potential merger.

4-6a Price/Earnings Ratio

Price/Earnings (P/E) Ratio
The ratio of the price per share to earnings per share; shows the dollar amount investors will pay for $1 of current earnings.

The **price/earnings (P/E) ratio** shows how much investors are willing to pay per dollar of reported profits. Allied's stock sells for $23.06; so with an EPS of $2.35, its P/E ratio is 9.8×:

$$\text{Price/Earnings (P/E) ratio} = \frac{\text{Price per share}}{\text{Earnings per share}}$$

$$= \frac{\$23.06}{\$2.35} = 9.8\times$$

$$\text{Industry average} = 11.3\times$$

As we will see in Chapter 9, P/E ratios are relatively high for firms with strong growth prospects and little risk but low for slowly growing and risky firms. Allied's P/E ratio is below its industry average; so this suggests that the company is regarded as being relatively risky, as having poor growth prospects, or both.

There is no "correct" P/E ratio; but the S&P 500's historical average is 15.9×, and it has ranged from 48.1× to 7.1× over the last 30 years. In the winter of 2008, the S&P's ratio was 21.7× versus 37.8× for Google. Countrywide Financial, which was badly hurt by the subprime mortgage debacle, had negative earnings and thus a negative P/E. The Google and Countrywide data demonstrate that strong companies with good growth prospects have high P/Es while weaker companies with poor prospects have low ratios.[14]

4-6b Market/Book Ratio

The ratio of a stock's market price to its book value gives another indication of how investors regard the company. Companies that are well regarded by

---

[14]Security analysts also look at the Price-to-Free-Cash-Flow ratio. In addition, analysts consider the PEG, or P/E to growth, ratio where the P/E is divided by the firm's forecasted growth rate. Allied's growth rate as forecasted by a number of security analysts for the next 5 years is 7.0%, so its PEG = 9.8/7.0 = 1.4×. The lower the ratio, the better; and most firms have ratios in the range of 1.0x to 2.0x. We note, though, that P/E ratios jump around from year to year because earnings and forecasted growth rates fluctuate. Like other ratios, PEG ratios are interesting, but must be interpreted with care and judgment.

investors—which means low risk and high growth—have high M/B ratios. For Allied, we first find its book value per share:

$$\text{Book value per share} = \frac{\text{Common equity}}{\text{Shares outstanding}}$$

$$= \frac{\$940}{50} = \$18.80$$

We then divide the market price per share by the book value per share to get the **market/book (M/B) ratio**, which for Allied is 1.2×:

$$\text{Market/book (M/B) ratio} = \frac{\text{Market price per share}}{\text{Book value per share}}$$

$$= \frac{\$23.06}{\$18.80} = 1.2\times$$

Industry average $= 1.7\times$

Investors are willing to pay less for a dollar of Allied's book value than for one of an average food processing company. This is consistent with our other findings.

M/B ratios typically exceed 1.0, which means that investors are willing to pay more for stocks than the accounting book values of the stocks. This situation occurs primarily because asset values, as reported by accountants on corporate balance sheets, do not reflect either inflation or goodwill. Assets purchased years ago at pre-inflation prices are carried at their original costs even though inflation might have caused their actual values to rise substantially; and successful companies' values rise above their historical costs, whereas unsuccessful ones have low M/B ratios.[15] This point is demonstrated by Google and Countrywide: In the winter of 2008, Google's M/B ratio was 6.9×, while Countrywide's was only 0.26×. Google's stockholders now have $6.90 in market value per $1.00 of equity, whereas Countrywide's stockholders have only $0.26 for each dollar they invested.

Market/Book (M/B) Ratio
The ratio of a stock's market price to its book value.

SELF TEST

Describe two ratios that relate a firm's stock price to its earnings and book value per share and write their equations.

In what sense do these market value ratios reflect investors' opinions about a stock's risk and expected future growth?

What does the price/earnings (P/E) ratio show? If one firm's P/E ratio is lower than that of another firm, what factors might explain the difference?

How is book value per share calculated? Explain how inflation and R&D programs might cause book values to deviate from market values.

4-7 TREND ANALYSIS

It is important to analyze trends in ratios as well as their absolute levels, for trends give clues as to whether a firm's financial condition is likely to improve or to deteriorate. To do a **trend analysis**, simply plot a ratio over time, as shown in Figure 4-1. This graph shows that Allied's ROE has been declining since 2005 even though the industry average has been relatively stable. All of the other ratios could be analyzed similarly, and such an analysis can be quite useful in gaining insights as to why the ROE behaved as it did.

Trend Analysis
An analysis of a firm's financial ratios over time; used to estimate the likelihood of improvement or deterioration in its financial condition.

[15]The second point is known as *"survivor bias."* Successful companies survive and are reflected in the averages, whereas unsuccessful companies vanish and their low numbers are not reflected in the averages.

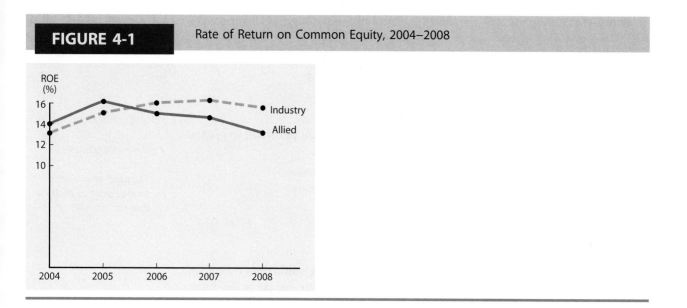

FIGURE 4-1   Rate of Return on Common Equity, 2004–2008

SELF TEST

How is a trend analysis done?

What important information does a trend analysis provide?

4-8 THE DuPONT EQUATION

DuPont Equation

A formula that shows that the rate of return on equity can be found as the product of profit margin, total assets turnover, and the equity multiplier. It shows the relationships among asset management, debt management, and profitability ratios.

We have discussed many ratios, so it would be useful to see how they work together to determine the ROE. For this, we use the **DuPont equation**, a formula developed by the chemical giant's financial staff in the 1920s. It is shown here for Allied and the food processing industry.

4-1

$$
\begin{aligned}
\text{ROE} &= \text{Profit margin} \times \text{Total assets turnover} \times \text{Equity multiplier} \\
&= \frac{\text{Net income}}{\text{Sales}} \times \frac{\text{Sales}}{\text{Total assets}} \times \frac{\text{Total assets}}{\text{Total common equity}} \\
&= \frac{\$117.5}{\$3,000} \times \frac{\$3,000}{\$2,000} \times \frac{\$2,000}{\$940} \\
&= 3.92\% \times 1.5 \text{ times} \times 2.13 \text{ times} = 12.5\%
\end{aligned}
$$

Industry	=	5.0%	×	1.8 times	×	1.67 times	=	15.0%

- The first term, the profit margin, tells us how much the firm earns on its sales. This ratio depends primarily on costs and sales prices—if a firm can command a premium price and hold down its costs, its profit margin will be high, which will help its ROE.

- The second term is the total assets turnover. It is a "multiplier" that tells us how many times the profit margin is earned each year—Allied earned 3.92% on each dollar of sales, and its assets were turned over 1.5 times each year; so its return on assets was 3.92% × 1.5 = 5.9%. Note, though, that this entire 5.9% belongs to the common stockholders—the bondholders earned a return in the form of interest, and that interest was deducted before we calculated net income to stockholders. Therefore, the whole 5.9% return on assets belongs to the stockholders. Therefore, the return on assets must be adjusted upward to obtain the return on equity.

- That brings us to the third term, the equity multiplier, which is the adjustment factor. Allied's assets are 2.13 times its equity, so we must multiply the 5.9% return on assets by the 2.13× equity multiplier to arrive at its ROE of 12.5%.

Note that ROE as calculated using the DuPont equation is identical to Allied's ROE, 12.5%, which we calculated earlier. What's the point of going through all of the steps required to implement the DuPont equation to find ROE? The answer is that the DuPont equation helps us see *why* Allied's ROE is only 12.5% versus 15.0% for the industry. First, its profit margin is below average, which indicates that its costs are not being controlled as well as they should be and that it cannot charge premium prices. In addition, because it uses more debt than most companies, its high interest charges also reduce the net profit margin. Second, its total assets turnover is below the industry average, which indicates that it has more assets than it needs. Finally, because its equity multiplier is relatively high, its heavy use of debt offsets to some extent its low profit margin and turnover. However, the high debt ratio exposes Allied to above-average bankruptcy risk; so it might want to cut back on its financial leverage. But if it reduced its debt to the same level as the average firm in its industry, its ROE would decline significantly, to $3.92\% \times 1.5 \times 1.67 = 9.8\%$.[16]

Allied's management can use the DuPont equation to help identify ways to improve its performance. Focusing on the profit margin, its marketing people can study the effects of raising sales prices or of introducing new products with higher margins. Its cost accountants can study various expense items and, working with engineers, purchasing agents, and other operating personnel, seek ways to cut costs. The credit manager can investigate ways to speed up collections, which would reduce accounts receivable and therefore improve the quality of the total assets turnover ratio. And the financial staff can analyze the effects of alternative debt policies, showing how changes in leverage would affect both the expected ROE and the risk of bankruptcy.

As a result of this analysis, Ellen Jackson, Allied's chief executive officer (CEO), undertook a series of moves that are expected to cut operating costs by more than 20%. Jackson and Allied's other executives have a strong incentive to improve the firm's financial performance—their compensation depends on how well the company operates. If Allied meets or exceeds its growth and profit targets, Jackson and the other executives—and the stockholders—will do well. Otherwise, someone like Warren Buffett or Carl Icahn, whom we discussed at the beginning of the chapter, may come calling.

SELF TEST

Write the equation for the basic DuPont equation.

What is the equity multiplier, and why is it used?

How can management use the DuPont equation to analyze ways of improving the firm's performance?

---

[16]The ROE reduction would actually be somewhat less because if debt were lowered, interest payments would also decline, which would raise the profit margin. Allied's analysts determined that the net effect of a reduction in debt would still be a significant reduction in ROE.

4-9 RATIOS IN DIFFERENT INDUSTRIES

Table 4-2 provides a list of the ratios for a number of different industries in early 2008. ROEs vary across industries, ranging from 45.7% for education and training services to 0.9% for newspapers. The education and training services industry has been positively impacted by enrollment growth of online operations in schools. The newspaper industry has been in decline because the proportion of the population that reads newspapers has been in a long-term decline, which has a negative impact on the demand for newspaper advertising. Industry rankings change from year to year because firms and industries go through cycles of good and bad times. When times are good, companies often overexpand, which leads to hard times. Note too that there are huge differences between individual companies in a given industry. That point isn't illustrated in Table 4-2 but it shows up dramatically in Table 4-4 in Section 4-11.

SELF TEST

Why might railroads have such low total assets turnovers and food wholesalers and grocery stores such high turnovers? **(Railroads require many long-term assets; while grocery companies have more perishable products and thus high turnovers.)**

If competition causes all companies to have similar ROEs in the long run, would companies with high turnovers tend to have high or low profit margins? Explain your answer. **(Low)**

Table 4-2

DuPont Financial Ratios for Selected Industries[a]

Industry Name	ROE	=	Profit Margin	×	Total Assets Turnover	×	Equity Multiplier[b]
Aerospace/defense—major diversified	41.4%		6.8%		1.0		6.1
Apparel stores	37.2		6.7		1.8		3.1
Auto mfg.—major	12.9		3.9		0.8		4.1
Beverage (soft drink)	21.6		14.1		0.8		1.9
Education and training services	45.7		13.0		1.4		2.5
Electronics—equipment	6.8		4.7		0.9		1.6
Food wholesaling	17.8		1.5		3.3		3.6
Grocery stores	19.1		3.7		2.5		2.1
Lodging	30.6		12.6		0.9		2.7
Medical instruments and supplies	9.6		4.5		0.7		3.0
Metals and minerals—industrial	34.8		10.9		0.7		4.6
Newspapers	0.9		8.5		0.3		0.4
Paper and paper products	15.1		13.5		0.8		1.4
Railroad	15.3		15.0		0.4		2.6
Restaurant	15.3		8.1		0.7		2.7
Retail—department stores	18.4		4.8		1.7		2.3
Scientific and technical instruments	12.9		9.0		0.8		1.8
Sporting goods	15.2		4.1		1.7		2.2
Steel and iron	36.3		23.5		0.8		1.9
Telecommunications services—domestic	11.9		10.1		0.4		2.9
Tobacco (cigarettes)	14.4		15.4		0.3		3.1

[a]The ratios presented are averages for each industry. Ratios for the individual companies are also available.
[b]Calculated as ROE/ROA.
Source: Data obtained from the Key Ratios section, http://moneycentral.msn.com, February 7, 2008.

4-10 SUMMARY OF ALLIED'S RATIOS

Table 4-3 provides a summary of the ratios we have discussed in the chapter. This table is useful as a quick reference for the formulas, for calculations, and for the ratios of Allied and the average food processing company.

Table 4-3	Allied Food Products: Summary of Financial Ratios (Millions of Dollars)				
Ratio	**Formula**	**Calculation**	**Ratio**	**Industry Average**	**Comment**
Liquidity					
Current	$\dfrac{\text{Current assets}}{\text{Current liabilities}}$	$\dfrac{\$1,000}{\$310}$	= 3.2×	4.2×	Poor
Quick	$\dfrac{\text{Current assets} - \text{Inventories}}{\text{Current liabilities}}$	$\dfrac{\$385}{\$310}$	= 1.2×	2.2×	Poor
Asset Management					
Inventory turnover	$\dfrac{\text{Sales}}{\text{Inventories}}$	$\dfrac{\$3,000}{\$615}$	= 4.9×	10.9×	Poor
Days sales outstanding (DSO)	$\dfrac{\text{Receivables}}{\text{Annual sales}/365}$	$\dfrac{\$375}{\$8.2192}$	= 46 days	36 days	Poor
Fixed assets turnover	$\dfrac{\text{Sales}}{\text{Net fixed assets}}$	$\dfrac{\$3,000}{\$1,000}$	= 3.0×	2.8×	OK
Total assets turnover	$\dfrac{\text{Sales}}{\text{Total assets}}$	$\dfrac{\$3,000}{\$2,000}$	= 1.5×	1.8×	Somewhat low
Debt Management					
Total debt to total assets	$\dfrac{\text{Total debt}}{\text{Total assets}}$	$\dfrac{\$1,060}{\$2,000}$	= 53.0%	40.0%	High (risky)
Times interest earned (TIE)	$\dfrac{\text{Earnings before interest and taxes (EBIT)}}{\text{Interest charges}}$	$\dfrac{\$283.8}{\$88}$	= 3.2×	6.0×	Low (risky)
Profitability					
Operating margin	$\dfrac{\text{Operating income (EBIT)}}{\text{Sales}}$	$\dfrac{\$283.8}{\$3,000}$	= 9.5%	10.0%	Low
Profit margin	$\dfrac{\text{Net income}}{\text{Sales}}$	$\dfrac{\$117.5}{\$3,000}$	= 3.9%	5.0%	Poor
Return on total assets (ROA)	$\dfrac{\text{Net income}}{\text{Total assets}}$	$\dfrac{\$117.5}{\$2,000}$	= 5.9%	9.0%	Poor
Basic earning power (BEP)	$\dfrac{\text{Earnings before interest and taxes (EBIT)}}{\text{Total assets}}$	$\dfrac{\$283.8}{\$2,000}$	= 14.2%	18.0%	Poor
Return on common equity (ROE)	$\dfrac{\text{Net income}}{\text{Common equity}}$	$\dfrac{\$117.5}{\$940}$	= 12.5%	15.0%	Poor
Market Value					
Price/earnings (P/E)	$\dfrac{\text{Price per share}}{\text{Earnings per share}}$	$\dfrac{\$23.06}{\$2.35}$	= 9.8×	11.3×	Low
Market/book (M/B)	$\dfrac{\text{Market price per share}}{\text{Book value per share}}$	$\dfrac{\$23.06}{\$18.80}$	= 1.2×	1.7×	Low

4-11 BENCHMARKING

Benchmarking

The process of comparing a particular company with a set of benchmark companies.

Ratio analysis involves comparisons with industry average figures, but Allied and many other firms also compare themselves with the top firms in their industry. This is called **benchmarking**, and the companies used for the comparison are called benchmark companies. Table 4-4 provides data for Allied and its seven benchmarks. The companies are ranked by ROE, and the other ratios used in a DuPont analysis are shown in the table as well. The ROE makes it easy for Allied's managers to see where the firm stands relative to top food processors, and the other data give management an idea of why Allied's ROE ranking compares unfavorably with most of the other benchmark companies.

Perhaps the most interesting feature of Table 4-4 is the wide range of ROEs. This range is caused primarily by variations in profit margins and equity multipliers. These companies also have the most widely recognized brands—their excellent marketing programs enabled them to charge relatively high prices, which boosted their profit margins and thus their ROEs. Their high and stable profits enable them to use a great deal of debt, which boosted their equity multipliers and provided another boost to their ROEs.

Note too that the averages for Allied and its benchmark companies differ significantly from the averages for its industry. The benchmarks are all very large companies, while there are many small food processing companies whose data are included in the industry averages. Since Allied is a relatively large company, its chief financial officer (CFO) believes it makes more sense to compare Allied to other large companies than to industry averages.

Table 4-4

Benchmark Companies Ranked by ROE

	ROE	=	Profit Margin	×	Turnover	×	Equity Multiplier
Campbell Soup	59.4%		10.3%		1.1		5.24
H.J. Heinz	39.3		8.8		0.9		4.96
Hershey Foods	33.6		4.3		1.2		6.51
Sara Lee	21.9		4.8		1.1		4.15
Dean Foods	17.4		1.6		1.6		6.80
Flowers Foods	15.5		4.8		2.2		1.47
Allied Foods	**12.5**		**3.9**		**1.5**		**2.13**
Del Monte Foods	8.0		3.2		0.7		3.57
Averages	25.9%		5.2%		1.3		4.35
Averages for entire food industry	26.8%		10.5%		1.1		2.32

Note: Rounding causes some variations in the numbers.
Source: Data on the benchmark companies were obtained from http://moneycentral.msn.com, February 11, 2008. Similar data can be obtained from Yahoo, Google, and a number of other online and print sources.

SELF TEST   Why are comparative ratio analyses useful?

LOOKING FOR WARNING SIGNS WITHIN THE FINANCIAL STATEMENTS

Enron's decline spurred a renewed interest in financial accounting, and analysts now scour companies' financial statements to see if trouble is lurking. This renewed interest has led to a list of red flags to consider when reviewing a company's financial statements. For example, after conferring with New York University Accounting Professor Baruch Lev, *Fortune* magazine's Shawn Tully identified the following warning signs:

- Year after year a company reports restructuring charges and/or write-downs. This practice raises concerns because companies can use write-downs to mask operating expenses, which results in overstated earnings.

- A company's earnings have been propped up through a series of acquisitions. Acquisitions can increase earnings if the acquiring company has a higher P/E than the acquired firm, but such "growth" cannot be sustained over the long run.

- A company depreciates its assets more slowly than the industry average. Lower depreciation boosts current earnings, but again this cannot be sustained because eventually depreciation must be recognized.

- A company routinely has high earnings but low cash flow. As Tully points out, this warning sign would have exposed Enron's problems. In the second quarter of 2001 (a few months before its problems began to unfold), Enron reported earnings of $423 million versus a cash flow of minus $527 million.

Along similar lines, after consulting with various professionals, Ellen Simon of the *Newark Star Ledger* came up with her list of red flags:

- You wouldn't buy the stock at today's price.

- You don't really understand the company's financial statements.

- The company is in a business that lends itself to "creative accounting."

- The company keeps taking nonrecurring charges.

- Accounts receivable and inventory are increasing faster than sales revenues.

- The company's insiders are selling their stock.

- The company is making aggressive acquisitions, especially in unrelated fields.

There is some overlap between these two lists. Also, none of these items automatically means there is something wrong with the company—instead, the items should be viewed as warning signs that cause you to take a closer look at the company's performance before making an investment.

4-12 USES AND LIMITATIONS OF RATIOS

As noted earlier, ratio analysis is used by three main groups: (1) *managers*, who use ratios to help analyze, control, and thus improve their firms' operations; (2) *credit analysts*, including bank loan officers and bond rating analysts, who analyze ratios to help judge a company's ability to repay its debts; and (3) *stock analysts*, who are interested in a company's efficiency, risk, and growth prospects. In later chapters, we will look more closely at the basic factors that underlie each ratio. Note, though, that while ratio analysis can provide useful information concerning a company's operations and financial condition, it does have limitations. Some potential problems are listed here:

1. Many firms have divisions that operate in different industries; and for such companies, it is difficult to develop a meaningful set of industry averages. Therefore, ratio analysis is more useful for narrowly focused firms than for multidivisional ones.

2. Most firms want to be better than average, so merely attaining average performance is not necessarily good. As a target for high-level performance, it is best to focus on the industry leaders' ratios. Benchmarking helps in this regard.

3. Inflation has distorted many firms' balance sheets—book values are often different from market values. Market values would be more appropriate for most purposes, but we cannot generally get market value figures because

To find information about a company quickly, link to www.reuters.com. Here you can find company profiles and snapshots, stock price quotes and share information, key ratios, and comparative ratios.

assets such as used machinery are not traded in the marketplace. Further, inflation affects asset values, depreciation charges, inventory costs, and thus profits. Therefore, a ratio analysis for one firm over time or a comparative analysis of firms of different ages must be interpreted with care and judgment.

4. Seasonal factors can also distort a ratio analysis. For example, the inventory turnover ratio for a food processor will be radically different if the balance sheet figure used for inventory is the one just before versus just after the close of the canning season. This problem can be mitigated by using monthly averages for inventory (and receivables) when calculating turnover ratios.

"Window Dressing" Techniques
Techniques employed by firms to make their financial statements look better than they really are.

5. Firms can employ **"window dressing" techniques** to improve their financial statements. To illustrate, people tend to think that larger hedge funds got large because their high returns attracted many investors. However, we learned in 2007 that some funds simply borrowed and invested money to increase their apparent size. One fund, Wharton Asset Management, reported $2 billion "under management," but it had actually attracted less than $100 million of investors' capital.

6. Different accounting practices can distort comparisons. As noted earlier, inventory valuation and depreciation methods can affect financial statements and thus distort comparisons among firms. Also, if one firm leases much of its productive equipment, its fixed assets turnover may be artificially high because leased assets often do not appear on the balance sheet. At the same time, the liability associated with the lease may not appear as debt, keeping the debt ratio low even though failure to make lease payments can bankrupt the firm. Therefore, leasing can artificially improve both turnover and the debt ratios. The accounting profession has taken steps to reduce this problem, but it still can cause distortions.

7. It is difficult to generalize about whether a particular ratio is "good" or "bad." For example, a high current ratio may indicate a strong liquidity position, which is good, but it can also indicate excessive cash, which is bad because excess cash in the bank is a nonearning asset. Similarly, a high fixed assets turnover ratio may indicate that the firm uses its assets efficiently, but it could also indicate that the firm is short of cash and cannot afford to make needed fixed asset investments.

8. Firms often have some ratios that look "good" and others that look "bad," making it difficult to tell whether the company is, on balance, strong or weak. To deal with this problem, banks and other lending organizations often use statistical procedures to analyze the *net effects* of a set of ratios and to classify firms according to their probability of getting into financial trouble.[17]

We see then that ratio analysis is useful, but analysts should be aware of the problems just listed and make adjustments as necessary. Ratio analysis conducted in a mechanical, unthinking manner is dangerous; but used intelligently and with good judgment, it can provide useful insights into firms' operations. Your judgment in interpreting ratios is bound to be weak at this point, but it will improve as you go through the remainder of the book.

SELF TEST

List three types of users of ratio analysis. Would the different users emphasize the same or different types of ratios? Explain.

List several potential difficulties with ratio analysis.

---

[17]The technique used is discriminant analysis. The seminal work on this subject was undertaken by Edward I. Altman, "Financial Ratios, Discriminant Analysis, and the Prediction of Corporate Bankruptcy," *Journal of Finance*, September 1968, pp. 589–609.

ECONOMIC VALUE ADDED (EVA) VERSUS NET INCOME

Economic Value Added (EVA) is a measure of how much management has added to shareholders' wealth during the year. To better understand the idea behind EVA, let's look at Allied's 2008 numbers (in millions). All of the firm's capital was supplied by investors except for $60 of accounts payable and $140 of accruals, or $200 in total; so its investor-supplied capital consists of $110 of notes payable, $750 of long-term debt, and $940 of common equity, totaling $1,800. Debt represents 47.78% of this total, and equity is 52.22%. Later in the text we will discuss how to calculate the cost of Allied's capital; but for now, to simplify things, we will estimate its capital cost at 10%. Thus, the firm's total dollar cost of capital (which includes both debt and equity) per year is 0.10($1,800) = $180.

Now let's look at Allied's income statement. Its operating income, EBIT, is $283.8; and its interest expense is $88.0. Therefore, its taxable income is $283.8 − $88.0 = $195.8. Taxes equal 40% of taxable income, or 0.4($195.8) = $78.3; so the firm's net income is $117.5. Its return on equity, ROE, is $117.5/$940 = 12.5%.

Given this data, we can now calculate Allied's EVA. The basic formula for EVA is as follows:

$$
\begin{aligned}
\text{EVA} &= \text{EBIT } (1 - \text{Corporate tax rate}) \\
&\quad -[(\text{Total investors' capital}) \times (\text{After} - \text{tax} \\
&\quad \text{cost of capital})] \\
&= \$283.8(1 - 0.40) - (\$1,800)(0.10) \\
&= \$170.3 - \$180 \\
&= -\$9.7
\end{aligned}
$$

This negative EVA indicates that Allied's shareholders actually earned $9.7 million less than they could have earned elsewhere by investing in other stocks with the same risk as Allied. To see where this −$9.7 comes from, let's trace what happened to the money.

- The firm generated $283.8 of operating income.
- $78.3 went to the government to pay taxes, leaving $205.5 available for investors—stockholders and bondholders.

- $88.0 went to the bondholders in the form of interest payments, thus leaving $117.5 for the stockholders.
- However, Allied's shareholders must also earn a return on the equity capital they have invested in the firm because they could have invested in other companies of comparable risk. We call this the cost of Allied's equity.
- Once Allied's shareholders are "paid" their return, the firm comes up $9.7 million short—that's the economic value management added, and it is negative. In a sense, Allied's management created *negative* wealth because it provided shareholders with a lower return than they could have earned on alternative investments with the same risk as Allied's stock.
- In practice, it is often necessary to make several adjustments to arrive at a "better" measure of EVA. The adjustments deal with nonoperating assets, leased assets, depreciation, and other accounting details that we leave to advanced finance courses.

The Connection between ROE and EVA

EVA is different from traditional accounting profit *because EVA reflects the cost of equity as well as the cost of debt.* Indeed, using the previous example, we could also express EVA as net income minus the dollar cost of equity:

$$
\text{EVA} = \frac{\text{Net}}{\text{Income}} - \left[\frac{\text{Equity}}{\text{capital}} \times \frac{\text{Cost of}}{\text{equity capital}} \right]
$$

That expression could be rewritten as follows:

$$
\text{EVA} = \frac{\text{Equity}}{\text{capital}} \times \left[\frac{\text{Net income}}{\text{Equity capital}} - \frac{\text{Cost of}}{\text{equity capital}} \right]
$$

which can be rewritten as

$$
\text{EVA} = (\text{Equity capital})(\text{ROE} - \text{Cost of equity capital})
$$

This last expression implies that EVA depends on three factors: rate of return, as reflected in ROE; risk, which affects the cost of equity; and size, which is measured by the equity employed. Recall that earlier in this chapter, we said that shareholder value depends on risk, return, and capital invested. This final equation illustrates that point.

4-13 POTENTIAL MISUSES OF ROE

We know that managers should strive to maximize shareholder wealth. If a firm takes steps that improve its ROE, does that mean that shareholder wealth will also be increased? The answer is, "not necessarily." Indeed, three problems are likely to arise if a firm relies too heavily on ROE to measure performance.

First, ROE does not consider risk. Shareholders care about ROE, but they also care about risk. To illustrate, consider two divisions within the same firm. Division S has stable cash flows and a predictable 15% ROE. Division R has a 16% expected ROE, but its cash flows are quite risky; so the expected ROE may not materialize. If managers were compensated solely on the basis of ROE and if the expected ROEs were actually achieved during the coming year, Division R's manager would receive a higher bonus than S's even though S might actually be creating more value for shareholders as a result of its lower risk. Similarly, financial leverage can increase expected ROE, but more leverage means higher risk; so raising ROE through the use of leverage may not be good.

Second, ROE does not consider the amount of invested capital. To illustrate, consider a company that is choosing between two mutually exclusive projects. Project A calls for investing $50,000 at an expected ROE of 50%, while Project B calls for investing $1,000,000 at a 45% ROE. The projects are equally risky, and the company's cost of capital is 10%. Project A has the higher ROE, but it is much smaller. Project B should be chosen because it would add more to shareholder wealth.

Third, a focus on ROE can cause managers to turn down profitable projects. For example, suppose you manage a division of a large firm and the firm determines bonuses solely on the basis of ROE. You project that your division's ROE for the year will be an impressive 45%. Now you have an opportunity to invest in a large, low-risk project with an estimated ROE of 35%, which is well above the firm's 10% cost of capital. Even though this project is extremely profitable, you might still be reluctant to undertake it because it would reduce your division's average ROE and therefore your year-end bonus.

These three examples suggest that a project's ROE must be combined with its size and risk to determine its effect on the firm's stock price:

$$\text{Contribution of a project to stock price} = f(\text{ROE, Risk, Size})$$

We will discuss this in more depth when we consider capital budgeting, where we look in detail at how projects are selected so as to maximize stock prices.

SELF TEST   If a firm takes steps that increase its expected future ROE, does this necessarily mean that the stock price will also increase? Explain.

4-14 LOOKING BEYOND THE NUMBERS

Working through this chapter should increase your ability to understand and interpret financial statements. This is critically important for anyone making business decisions or forecasting stock prices. However, sound financial analysis involves more than just numbers—good analysis requires that certain qualitative factors also be considered. These factors, as summarized by the American Association of Individual Investors (AAII), include the following:

*Students might want to refer to AAII's educational web site at **www.aaii.com**. The site provides information on investing basics, financial planning, portfolio management, and the like, so that individuals can manage their own assets more effectively.*

1. Are the company's revenues tied to one key customer? If so, the company's performance may decline dramatically if that customer goes elsewhere. On the other hand, if the customer has no alternative to the company's products, this might actually stabilize sales.

2. To what extent are the company's revenues tied to one key product? Firms that focus on a single product are often efficient, but a lack of diversification

also increases risk because having revenues from several products stabilizes profits and cash flows in a volatile world.

3. To what extent does the company rely on a single supplier? Depending on a single supplier may lead to an unanticipated shortage and a hit to sales and profits.

4. What percentage of the company's business is generated overseas? Companies with a large percentage of overseas business are often able to realize higher growth and larger profit margins. However, overseas operations may expose the firm to political risks and exchange rate problems.

5. How much competition does the firm face? Increases in competition tend to lower prices and profit margins; so when forecasting future performance, it is important to assess the likely actions of current competitors and the entry of new ones.

6. Is it necessary for the company to continually invest in research and development? If so, its future prospects will depend critically on the success of new products in the pipeline. For example, investors in a pharmaceutical company want to know whether the company has a strong pipeline of potential blockbuster drugs and whether those products are doing well in the required tests.

7. Are changes in laws and regulations likely to have important implications for the firm? For example, when the future of electric utilities are forecasted, it is crucial to factor in the effects of proposed regulations affecting the use of coal, nuclear, and gas-fired plants.

SELF TEST What are some qualitative factors that analysts should consider when evaluating a company's likely future financial performance?

TYING IT ALL TOGETHER

In the last chapter, we discussed the key financial statements; and in this one, we described how ratios are used to analyze the statements to identify weaknesses that need to be strengthened to maximize the stock price. Ratios are grouped into five categories:

- Liquidity
- Asset management
- Debt management
- Profitability
- Market value

The firm's ratios are compared with averages for its industry and with the leading firms in the industry (benchmarking), and these comparisons are used to help formulate policies that will lead to improved future performance. Similarly, the firm's own ratios can be analyzed over time to see if its financial situation is getting better or worse (trend analysis).

The single most important ratio over which management has control is the ROE—the other ratios are also important, but mainly because they affect the ROE. One tool used to show how ROE is determined is the DuPont equation: ROE = Profit margin × Total assets turnover × Equity multiplier. If the firm's ROE is below the industry average and that of the benchmark companies, a DuPont analysis can help identify problem areas that should be strengthened. In later chapters, we consider specific actions that can be taken to improve ROE and thus a firm's stock price. One closing note: Although ratio analysis is useful, it must be applied with care and good judgment. Actions taken to improve one ratio can have negative effects on some other ratio or ratios. For example, it might be possible to improve the ROE by using more debt, but the risk of the additional debt may lead to a decrease in the P/E ratio and thus in the firm's stock price. Quantitative analysis such as ratio analysis can be useful, but thinking through the results is even more important.

SELF-TEST QUESTIONS AND PROBLEMS
(Solutions Appear in Appendix A)

ST-1   **KEY TERMS**   Define each of the following terms:
   a.   Liquidity ratios: current ratio; acid test ratio
   b.   Asset management ratios: inventory turnover ratio; days sales outstanding (DSO); fixed assets turnover ratio; total assets turnover ratio
   c.   Debt management ratios: debt ratio; times-interest-earned (TIE) ratio
   d.   Profitability ratios: operating margin; profit margin; basic earning power (BEP) ratio; return on total assets (ROA); return on common equity (ROE)
   e.   Market value ratios: price/earnings (P/E) ratio; market/book (M/B) ratio
   f.   Trend analysis
   g.   DuPont equation
   h.   Benchmarking
   i.   "Window dressing" techniques

ST-2   **DEBT RATIO**   Last year K. Billingsworth & Co. had earnings per share of $4 and dividends per share of $2. Total retained earnings increased by $12 million during the year, while book value per share at year-end was $40. Billingsworth has no preferred stock, and no new common stock was issued during the year. If its year-end total debt was $120 million, what was the company's year-end debt/assets ratio?

ST-3   **RATIO ANALYSIS**   The following data apply to A.L. Kaiser & Company (millions of dollars):

Cash and equivalents	$100.00
Fixed assets	283.50
Sales	1,000.00
Net income	50.00
Current liabilities	105.50
Current ratio	3.00×
DSO[a]	40.55 days
ROE	12.00%

[a]This calculation is based on a 365-day year.

Kaiser has no preferred stock—only common equity, current liabilities, and long-term debt.

a. Find Kaiser's (1) accounts receivable, (2) current assets, (3) total assets, (4) ROA, (5) common equity, (6) quick ratio, and (7) long-term debt.

b. In Part a, you should have found that Kaiser's accounts receivable (A/R) = $111.1 million. If Kaiser could reduce its DSO from 40.55 days to 30.4 days while holding other things constant, how much cash would it generate? If this cash were used to buy back common stock (at book value), thus reducing common equity, how would this affect (1) the ROE, (2) the ROA, and (3) the total debt/total assets ratio?

QUESTIONS

4-1 Financial ratio analysis is conducted by three main groups of analysts: credit analysts, stock analysts, and managers. What is the primary emphasis of each group, and how would that emphasis affect the ratios they focus on?

4-2 Why would the inventory turnover ratio be more important for someone analyzing a grocery store chain than an insurance company?

4-3 Over the past year, M. D. Ryngaert & Co. had an increase in its current ratio and a decline in its total assets turnover ratio. However, the company's sales, cash and equivalents, DSO, and fixed assets turnover ratio remained constant. What balance sheet accounts must have changed to produce the indicated changes?

4-4 Profit margins and turnover ratios vary from one industry to another. What differences would you expect to find between the turnover ratios, profit margins, and DuPont equations for a grocery chain and a steel company?

4-5 How does inflation distort ratio analysis comparisons for one company over time (trend analysis) and for different companies that are being compared? Are only balance sheet items or both balance sheet and income statement items affected?

4-6 If a firm's ROE is low and management wants to improve it, explain how using more debt might help.

4-7 Give some examples that illustrate how (a) seasonal factors and (b) different growth rates might distort a comparative ratio analysis. How might these problems be alleviated?

4-8 Why is it sometimes misleading to compare a company's financial ratios with those of other firms that operate in the same industry?

4-9 Suppose you were comparing a discount merchandiser with a high-end merchandiser. Suppose further that both companies had identical ROEs. If you applied the DuPont equation to both firms, would you expect the three components to be the same for each company? If not, explain what balance sheet and income statement items might lead to the component differences.

4-10 Indicate the effects of the transactions listed in the following table on total current assets, current ratio, and net income. Use (+) to indicate an increase, (−) to indicate a decrease, and (0) to indicate either no effect or an indeterminate effect. Be prepared to state any necessary assumptions and assume an initial current ratio of more than 1.0. (Note: A good accounting background is necessary to answer some of these questions; if yours is not strong, answer just the questions you can.)

	Total Current Assets	Current Ratio	Effect on Net Income
a. Cash is acquired through issuance of additional common stock.	_____	_____	_____
b. Merchandise is sold for cash.	_____	_____	_____
c. Federal income tax due for the previous year is paid.	_____	_____	_____
d. A fixed asset is sold for less than book value.	_____	_____	_____
e. A fixed asset is sold for more than book value.	_____	_____	_____
f. Merchandise is sold on credit.	_____	_____	_____
g. Payment is made to trade creditors for previous purchases.	_____	_____	_____
h. A cash dividend is declared and paid.	_____	_____	_____

	Total Current Assets	Current Ratio	Effect on Net Income
i. Cash is obtained through short-term bank loans.	_____	_____	_____
j. Short-term notes receivable are sold at a discount.	_____	_____	_____
k. Marketable securities are sold below cost.	_____	_____	_____
l. Advances are made to employees.	_____	_____	_____
m. Current operating expenses are paid.	_____	_____	_____
n. Short-term promissory notes are issued to trade creditors in exchange for past due accounts payable.	_____	_____	_____
o. 10-year notes are issued to pay off accounts payable.	_____	_____	_____
p. A fully depreciated asset is retired.	_____	_____	_____
q. Accounts receivable are collected.	_____	_____	_____
r. Equipment is purchased with short-term notes.	_____	_____	_____
s. Merchandise is purchased on credit.	_____	_____	_____
t. The estimated taxes payable are increased.	_____	_____	_____

PROBLEMS

Easy Problems 1–6

4-1 DAYS SALES OUTSTANDING Baker Brothers has a DSO of 40 days, and its annual sales are $7,300,000. What is its accounts receivable balance? Assume that it uses a 365-day year.

4-2 DEBT RATIO Bartley Barstools has an equity multiplier of 2.4, and its assets are financed with some combination of long-term debt and common equity. What is its debt ratio?

4-3 DuPONT ANALYSIS Doublewide Dealers has an ROA of 10%, a 2% profit margin, and an ROE of 15%. What is its total assets turnover? What is its equity multiplier?

4-4 MARKET/BOOK RATIO Jaster Jets has $10 billion in total assets. Its balance sheet shows $1 billion in current liabilities, $3 billion in long-term debt, and $6 billion in common equity. It has 800 million shares of common stock outstanding, and its stock price is $32 per share. What is Jaster's market/book ratio?

4-5 PRICE/EARNINGS RATIO A company has an EPS of $2.00, a cash flow per share of $3.00, and a price/cash flow ratio of 8.0×. What is its P/E ratio?

4-6 DuPONT AND ROE A firm has a profit margin of 2% and an equity multiplier of 2.0. Its sales are $100 million, and it has total assets of $50 million. What is its ROE?

Intermediate Problems 7–18

4-7 DuPONT AND NET INCOME Ebersoll Mining has $6 million in sales, its ROE is 12%, and its total assets turnover is 3.2×. The company is 50% equity financed. What is its net income?

4-8 BASIC EARNING POWER Duval Manufacturing recently reported the following information:

Net income	$600,000
ROA	8%
Interest expense	$225,000

Duval's tax rate is 35%. What is its basic earning power (BEP)?

4-9 M/B AND SHARE PRICE You are given the following information: Stockholders' equity = $3.75 billion, price/earnings ratio = 3.5, common shares outstanding = 50 million, and market/book ratio = 1.9. Calculate the price of a share of the company's common stock.

4-10 RATIO CALCULATIONS Assume the following relationships for the Brauer Corp.:

Sales total assets	1.5×
Return on assets (ROA)	3%
Return on equity (ROE)	5%

Calculate Brauer's profit margin and debt ratio.

4-11 RATIO CALCULATIONS Graser Trucking has $12 billion in assets, and its tax rate is 40%. Its basic earning power (BEP) ratio is 15%, and its return on assets (ROA) is 5%. What is its times-interest-earned (TIE) ratio?

4-12   **TIE RATIO**   The H.R. Pickett Corp. has $500,000 of debt outstanding, and it pays an annual interest rate of 10%. Its annual sales are $2 million, its average tax rate is 30%, and its net profit margin is 5%. What is its TIE ratio?

4-13   **RETURN ON EQUITY**   Midwest Packaging's ROE last year was only 3%; but its management has developed a new operating plan that calls for a total debt ratio of 60%, which will result in annual interest charges of $300,000. Management projects an EBIT of $1,000,000 on sales of $10,000,000, and it expects to have a total assets turnover ratio of 2.0. Under these conditions, the tax rate will be 34%. If the changes are made, what will be the company's return on equity?

4-14   **RETURN ON EQUITY AND QUICK RATIO**   Lloyd Inc. has sales of $200,000, a net income of $15,000, and the following balance sheet:

Cash	$ 10,000	Accounts payable	$ 30,000
Receivables	50,000	Other current liabilities	20,000
Inventories	150,000	Long-term debt	50,000
Net fixed assets	90,000	Common equity	200,000
Total assets	$300,000	Total liabilities and equity	$300,000

The new owner thinks that inventories are excessive and can be lowered to the point where the current ratio is equal to the industry average, 2.5×, without affecting sales or net income. If inventories are sold off and not replaced (thus reducing the current ratio to 2.5×), if the funds generated are used to reduce common equity (stock can be repurchased at book value), and if no other changes occur, by how much will the ROE change? What will be the firm's new quick ratio?

4-15   **RETURN ON EQUITY**   Central City Construction (CCC) needs $1 million of assets to get started, and it expects to have a basic earning power ratio of 20%. CCC will own no securities, so all of its income will be operating income. If it so chooses, CCC can finance up to 50% of its assets with debt, which will have an 8% interest rate. Assuming a 40% tax rate on all taxable income, what is the *difference* between CCC's expected ROE if it finances with 50% debt versus its expected ROE if it finances entirely with common stock?

4-16   **CONCEPTUAL: RETURN ON EQUITY**   Which of the following statements is most correct? (Hint: Work Problem 4-15 before answering 4-16 and consider the solution setup for 4-15 as you think about 4-16.)
   a. If a firm's expected basic earning power (BEP) is constant for all of its assets and exceeds the interest rate on its debt, adding assets and financing them with debt will raise the firm's expected return on common equity (ROE).
   b. The higher a firm's tax rate, the lower its BEP ratio, other things held constant.
   c. The higher the interest rate on a firm's debt, the lower its BEP ratio, other things held constant.
   d. The higher a firm's debt ratio, the lower its BEP ratio, other things held constant.
   e. Statement a is false; but statements b, c, and d are true.

4-17   **TIE RATIO**   AEI Incorporated has $5 billion in assets, and its tax rate is 40%. Its basic earning power (BEP) ratio is 10%, and its return on assets (ROA) is 5%. What is AEI's times-interest-earned (TIE) ratio?

4-18   **CURRENT RATIO**   The Petry Company has $1,312,500 in current assets and $525,000 in current liabilities. Its initial inventory level is $375,000, and it will raise funds as additional notes payable and use them to increase inventory. How much can its short-term debt (notes payable) increase without pushing its current ratio below 2.0?

Challenging Problems 19–23

4-19   **DSO AND ACCOUNTS RECEIVABLE**   Harrelson Inc. currently has $750,000 in accounts receivable, and its days sales outstanding (DSO) is 55 days. It wants to reduce its DSO to 35 days by pressuring more of its customers to pay their bills on time. If this policy is adopted, the company's average sales will fall by 15%. What will be the level of accounts receivable following the change? Assume a 365-day year.

4-20   **P/E AND STOCK PRICE**   Fontaine Inc. recently reported net income of $2 million. It has 500,000 shares of common stock, which currently trades at $40 a share. Fontaine continues to expand and anticipates that 1 year from now, its net income will be $3.25 million. Over the next year, it also anticipates issuing an additional 150,000 shares of stock so that 1 year from now it will have 650,000 shares of common stock. Assuming Fontaine's price/earnings ratio remains at its current level, what will be its stock price 1 year from now?

4-21   **BALANCE SHEET ANALYSIS** Complete the balance sheet and sales information using the following financial data:

> Debt ratio: 50%
>
> Current ratio: 1.8×
>
> Total assets turnover: 1.5×
>
> Days sales outstanding: 36.5 days[a]
>
> Gross profit margin on sales: (Sales − Cost of goods sold)/Sales = 25%
>
> Inventory turnover ratio: 5×
>
> [a]Calculation is based on a 365-day year.

Balance Sheet

Cash	————	Accounts payable	————
Accounts receivable	————	Long-term debt	60,000
Inventories	————	Common stock	————
Fixed assets	————	Retained earnings	97,500
Total assets	$300,000	Total liabilities and equity	————
Sales	————	Cost of goods sold	————

4-22   **RATIO ANALYSIS** Data for Barry Computer Co. and its industry averages follow.

a. Calculate the indicated ratios for Barry.

b. Construct the DuPont equation for both Barry and the industry.

c. Outline Barry's strengths and weaknesses as revealed by your analysis.

d. Suppose Barry had doubled its sales as well as its inventories, accounts receivable, and common equity during 2008. How would that information affect the validity of your ratio analysis? (Hint: Think about averages and the effects of rapid growth on ratios if averages are not used. No calculations are needed.)

Barry Computer Company: Balance Sheet as of December 31, 2008 (In Thousands)

Cash	$ 77,500	Accounts payable	$129,000
Receivables	336,000	Notes payable	84,000
Inventories	241,500	Other current liabilities	117,000
Total current assets	$655,000	Total current liabilities	$330,000
		Long-term debt	256,500
Net fixed assets	292,500	Common equity	361,000
Total assets	$947,500	Total liabilities and equity	$947,500

Barry Computer Company: Income Statement for Year Ended December 31, 2008 (In Thousands)

Sales		$1,607,500
Cost of goods sold		
Materials	$ 717,000	
Labor	453,000	
Heat, light, and power	68,000	
Indirect labor	113,000	
Depreciation	41,500	1,392,500
Gross profit		$ 215,000
Selling expenses		115,000
General and administrative expenses		30,000
Earnings before interest and taxes (EBIT)		$ 70,000
Interest expense		24,500
Earnings before taxes (EBT)		$ 45,500
Federal and state income taxes (40%)		18,200
Net income		$ 27,300

Ratio	Barry	Industry Average
Current	————	2.0×
Quick	————	1.3×
Days sales outstanding[a]	————	35.0 days
Inventory turnover	————	6.7×
Total assets turnover	————	3.0×
Profit margin	————	1.2%
ROA	————	3.6%
ROE	————	9.0%
Total debt/total assets	————	60.0%

[a]Calculation is based on a 365-day year.

4-23 **DuPONT ANALYSIS** A firm has been experiencing low profitability in recent years. Perform an analysis of the firm's financial position using the DuPont equation. The firm has no lease payments but has a $2 million sinking fund payment on its debt. The most recent industry average ratios and the firm's financial statements are as follows:

Industry Average Ratios

Current ratio	2×	Fixed assets turnover		6×
Debt/total assets	30%	Total assets turnover		3×
Times interest earned	7×	Profit margin		3%
EBITDA coverage	9×	Return on total assets		9%
Inventory turnover	10×	Return on common equity		12.86%
Days sales outstanding[a]	24 days			

[a]Calculation is based on a 365-day year.

Balance Sheet as of December 31, 2008 (Millions of Dollars)

Cash and equivalents	$ 78	Accounts payable	$ 45
Net receivables	66	Notes payable	45
Inventories	159	Other current liabilities	21
Total current assets	$303	Total current liabilities	$111
		Long-term debt	24
		Total liabilities	$135
Gross fixed assets	225		
Less depreciation	78	Common stock	114
Net fixed assets	$147	Retained earnings	201
		Total stockholders' equity	$315
Total assets	$450	Total liabilities and equity	$450

Income Statement for Year Ended December 31, 2008 (Millions of Dollars)

Net sales	$795.0
Cost of goods sold	660.0
Gross profit	$135.0
Selling expenses	73.5
EBITDA	$ 61.5
Depreciation expense	12.0
Earnings before interest and taxes (EBIT)	$ 49.5
Interest expense	4.5
Earnings before taxes (EBT)	$ 45.0
Taxes (40%)	18.0
Net income	$ 27.0

a. Calculate those ratios that you think would be useful in this analysis.

b. Construct a DuPont equation and compare the company's ratios to the industry average ratios.

c. Do the balance sheet accounts or the income statement figures seem to be primarily responsible for the low profits?

d. Which specific accounts seem to be most out of line relative to other firms in the industry?

e. If the firm had a pronounced seasonal sales pattern or if it grew rapidly during the year, how might that affect the validity of your ratio analysis? How might you correct for such potential problems?

COMPREHENSIVE/SPREADSHEET PROBLEM

4-24 **RATIO ANALYSIS** The Corrigan Corporation's 2007 and 2008 financial statements follow, along with some industry average ratios.

a. Assess Corrigan's liquidity position and determine how it compares with peers and how the liquidity position has changed over time.

b. Assess Corrigan's asset management position and determine how it compares with peers and how its asset management efficiency has changed over time.

c. Assess Corrigan's debt management position and determine how it compares with peers and how its debt management has changed over time.

d. Assess Corrigan's profitability ratios and determine how they compare with peers and how its profitability position has changed over time.

e. Assess Corrigan's market value ratios and determine how its valuation compares with peers and how it has changed over time.

f. Calculate Corrigan's ROE as well as the industry average ROE using the DuPont equation. From this analysis, how does Corrigan's financial position compare with the industry average numbers?

g. What do you think would happen to its ratios if the company initiated cost-cutting measures that allowed it to hold lower levels of inventory and substantially decreased the cost of goods sold? No calculations are necessary. Think about which ratios would be affected by changes in these two accounts.

Corrigan Corporation: Balance Sheets as of December 31

	2008	2007
Cash	$ 72,000	$ 65,000
Accounts receivable	439,000	328,000
Inventories	894,000	813,000
Total current assets	$1,405,000	$1,206,000
Land and building	238,000	271,000
Machinery	132,000	133,000
Other fixed assets	61,000	57,000
Total assets	$1,836,000	$1,667,000
Accounts and notes payable	$ 432,000	$ 409,500
Accrued liabilities	170,000	162,000
Total current liabilities	$ 602,000	$ 571,500
Long-term debt	404,290	258,898
Common stock	575,000	575,000
Retained earnings	254,710	261,602
Total liabilities and equity	$1,836,000	$1,667,000

Corrigan Corporation: Income Statements for Years Ending December 31

	2008	2007
Sales	$4,240,000	$3,635,000
Cost of goods sold	3,680,000	2,980,000
Gross operating profit	$ 560,000	$ 655,000
General administrative and selling expenses	236,320	213,550
Depreciation	159,000	154,500
Miscellaneous	134,000	127,000
Earnings before taxes (EBT)	$ 30,680	$ 159,950
Taxes (40%)	12,272	63,980
Net income	$ 18,408	$ 95,970

Per-Share Data

	2008	2007
EPS	$0.80	$4.17
Cash dividends	$1.10	$0.95
Market price (average)	$12.34	$23.57
P/E ratio	15.4×	5.65×
Number of shares outstanding	23,000	23,000

Industry Financial Ratios[a]

	2008
Current ratio	2.7×
Inventory turnover[b]	7.0×
Days sales outstanding[c]	32.0 days
Fixed assets turnover[b]	13.0×
Total assets turnover[b]	2.6×
Return on assets	9.1%
Return on equity	18.2%
Debt ratio	50.0%
Profit margin	3.5%
P/E ratio	6.0×
Price/cash flow ratio	3.5×

[a]Industry average ratios have been constant for the past 4 years.
[b]Based on year-end balance sheet figures.
[c]Calculation is based on a 365-day year.

INTEGRATED CASE

D'LEON INC., PART II

4-25   **FINANCIAL STATEMENT ANALYSIS**   Part I of this case, presented in Chapter 3, discussed the situation of D'Leon Inc., a regional snack foods producer, after an expansion program. D'Leon had increased plant capacity and undertaken a major marketing campaign in an attempt to "go national." Thus far, sales have not been up to the forecasted level, costs have been higher than were projected, and a large loss occurred in 2008 rather than the expected profit. As a result, its managers, directors, and investors are concerned about the firm's survival.

Donna Jamison was brought in as assistant to Fred Campo, D'Leon's chairman, who had the task of getting the company back into a sound financial position. D'Leon's 2007 and 2008 balance sheets and income statements, together with projections for 2009, are given in Tables IC 4-1 and IC 4-2. In addition, Table IC 4-3 gives the company's 2007 and 2008 financial ratios, together with industry average data. The 2009 projected financial statement data represent Jamison's and Campo's best guess for 2009 results, assuming that some new financing is arranged to get the company "over the hump."

Jamison examined monthly data for 2008 (not given in the case), and she detected an improving pattern during the year. Monthly sales were rising, costs were falling, and large losses in the early months had turned to a small profit by December. Thus, the annual data look somewhat worse than final monthly data. Also, it appears to be taking longer for the advertising program to get the message out, for the new sales offices to generate sales, and for the new manufacturing facilities to operate efficiently. In other words, the lags between spending money and deriving benefits were longer than D'Leon's managers had anticipated. For these reasons, Jamison and Campo see hope for the company—provided it can survive in the short run.

Jamison must prepare an analysis of where the company is now, what it must do to regain its financial health, and what actions should be taken. Your assignment is to help her answer the following questions. Provide clear explanations, not yes or no answers.

a. Why are ratios useful? What are the five major categories of ratios?

b. Calculate D'Leon's 2009 current and quick ratios based on the projected balance sheet and income statement data. What can you say about the company's liquidity positions in 2007, in 2008, and as projected for 2009? We often think of ratios as being useful (1) to managers to help run the business, (2) to bankers for credit analysis, and (3) to stockholders for stock valuation. Would these different types of analysts have an equal interest in the company's liquidity ratios?

c. Calculate the 2009 inventory turnover, days sales outstanding (DSO), fixed assets turnover, and total assets turnover. How does D'Leon's utilization of assets stack up against other firms in the industry?

d. Calculate the 2009 debt and times-interest-earned ratios. How does D'Leon compare with the industry with respect to financial leverage? What can you conclude from these ratios?

e. Calculate the 2009 operating margin, profit margin, basic earning power (BEP), return on assets (ROA), and return on equity (ROE). What can you say about these ratios?

f. Calculate the 2009 price/earnings ratio and market/book ratio. Do these ratios indicate that investors are expected to have a high or low opinion of the company?

g. Use the DuPont equation to provide a summary and overview of D'Leon's financial condition as projected for 2009. What are the firm's major strengths and weaknesses?

h. Use the following simplified 2009 balance sheet to show, in general terms, how an improvement in the DSO would tend to affect the stock price. For example, if the company could improve its collection procedures and thereby lower its DSO from 45.6 days to the 32-day industry average without affecting sales, how would that change "ripple through" the financial statements (shown in thousands below) and influence the stock price?

Accounts receivable	$ 878	Debt	$1,545
Other current assets	1,802		
Net fixed assets	817	Equity	1,952
Total assets	$3,497	Liabilities plus equity	$3,497

i. Does it appear that inventories could be adjusted? If so, how should that adjustment affect D'Leon's profitability and stock price?

j. In 2008, the company paid its suppliers much later than the due dates; also, it was not maintaining financial ratios at levels called for in its bank loan agreements. Therefore, suppliers could cut the company off, and its bank could refuse to renew the loan when it comes due in 90 days. On the basis of data provided, would you, as a credit manager, continue to sell to D'Leon on credit? (You could demand cash on delivery—that is, sell on terms of COD—but that might cause D'Leon to stop buying from your company.) Similarly, if you were the bank loan officer, would you recommend renewing the loan or demand its repayment? Would your actions be influenced if in early 2009 D'Leon showed you its 2009 projections along with proof that it was going to raise more than $1.2 million of new equity?

k. In hindsight, what should D'Leon have done in 2007?

l. What are some potential problems and limitations of financial ratio analysis?

m. What are some qualitative factors that analysts should consider when evaluating a company's likely future financial performance?

Table IC 4-1   Balance Sheets

	2009E	2008	2007
Assets			
Cash	$ 85,632	$ 7,282	$ 57,600
Accounts receivable	878,000	632,160	351,200
Inventories	1,716,480	1,287,360	715,200
Total current assets	$2,680,112	$1,926,802	$1,124,000
Gross fixed assets	1,197,160	1,202,950	491,000
Less accumulated depreciation	380,120	263,160	146,200
Net fixed assets	$ 817,040	$ 939,790	$ 344,800
Total assets	$3,497,152	$2,866,592	$1,468,800
Liabilities and Equity			
Accounts payable	$ 436,800	$ 524,160	$ 145,600
Notes payable	300,000	636,808	200,000
Accruals	408,000	489,600	136,000
Total current liabilities	$1,144,800	$1,650,568	$ 481,600
Long-term debt	400,000	723,432	323,432
Common stock	1,721,176	460,000	460,000
Retained earnings	231,176	32,592	203,768
Total equity	$1,952,352	$ 492,592	$ 663,768
Total liabilities and equity	$3,497,152	$2,866,592	$1,468,800

Note: E indicates estimated. The 2009 data are forecasts.

Table IC 4-2   Income Statements

	2009E	2008	2007
Sales	$7,035,600	$6,034,000	$3,432,000
Cost of goods sold	5,875,992	5,528,000	2,864,000
Other expenses	550,000	519,988	358,672
Total operating costs excluding depreciation & amortization	$6,425,992	$6,047,988	$3,222,672
EBITDA	$ 609,608	($ 13,988)	$ 209,328
Depreciation & amortization	116,960	116,960	18,900
EBIT	$ 492,648	($ 130,948)	$ 190,428
Interest expense	70,008	136,012	43,828
EBT	$ 422,640	($ 266,960)	$ 146,600
Taxes (40%)	169,056	(106,784)[a]	58,640
Net income	$ 253,584	($ 160,176)	$ 87,960
EPS	$1.014	($1.602)	$0.880
DPS	$0.220	$0.110	$0.220
Book value per share	$7.809	$4.926	$6.638
Stock price	$12.17	$2.25	$8.50
Shares outstanding	250,000	100,000	100,000
Tax rate	40.00%	40.00%	40.00%
Lease payments	$40,000	$40,000	$40,000
Sinking fund payments	0	0	0

Note: E indicates estimated. The 2009 data are forecasts.
[a]The firm had sufficient taxable income in 2006 and 2007 to obtain its full tax refund in 2008.

Table IC 4-3	Ratio Analysis			
	2009E	**2008**	**2007**	**Industry Average**
Current		1.2×	2.3×	2.7×
Quick		0.4×	0.8×	1.0×
Inventory turnover		4.7×	4.8×	6.1×
Days sales outstanding (DSO)[a]		38.2	37.4	32.0
Fixed assets turnover		6.4×	10.0×	7.0×
Total assets turnover		2.1×	2.3×	2.6×
Debt ratio		82.8%	54.8%	50.0%
TIE		−1.0×	4.3×	6.2×
Operating margin		−2.2%	5.6%	7.3%
Profit margin		−2.7%	2.6%	3.5%
Basic earning power		−4.6%	13.0%	19.1%
ROA		−5.6%	6.0%	9.1%
ROE		−32.5%	13.3%	18.2%
Price/earnings		−1.4×	9.7×	14.2×
Market/book		0.5×	1.3×	2.4×
Book value per share		$4.93	$6.64	n.a.

Note: E indicates estimated. The 2009 data are forecasts.
[a]Calculation is based on a 365-day year.

THOMSON ONE | Business School Edition

Access the Thomson ONE problems through the CengageNOW™ web site. Use the Thomson ONE—Business School Edition online database to answer this chapter's questions.

Conducting a Financial Ratio Analysis on Ford Motor Company

In Chapter 3, we looked at Starbucks' financial statements. Now we use Thomson ONE to analyze Ford Motor Company.

Enter Ford's ticker symbol (F) and select "GO." Select "Financial Statements" and "Thomson Financials" to find Ford's key financial statements for the past several years. Click on "Financial Ratios" and then "SEC Ratios." From here you can select either annual or quarterly ratios.

Under annual ratios, there is an in-depth summary of Ford's various ratios over the past 3 years. This information enables you to evaluate Ford's performance over time for each of the ratio categories mentioned in the text (liquidity, asset management, debt management, profitability, and market-based ratios).

The text mentions that financial statement analysis has two major components: a trend analysis, where we evaluate changes in the key ratios over time, and a peer analysis, where we compare financial ratios with firms that are in the same industry and/or line of business. We have already used Thomson ONE to conduct a trend analysis—next, we use this tool to conduct a peer analysis. Click on "Comparables" to find some summary financial information for Ford and a few of its peers. By clicking on the Peer Sets, you can modify the list of peer firms. The default setup is "Peers set by SIC Code." To obtain a comparison of many of the key ratios presented in the text, click on "Financials" and select "Key Financial Ratios."

Discussion Questions

1. What has happened to Ford's liquidity position over the past 3 years? How does Ford's liquidity compare with that of its peers? (Hint: You may use both the peer key financial ratios and liquidity comparison to answer this question.)
2. Take a look at Ford's inventory turnover ratio. How does this ratio compare with that of its peers? Have there been any interesting changes over time in this measure? Do you consider Ford's inventory management to be a strength or a weakness? Explain.
3. Construct a DuPont analysis for Ford and its peers. What are Ford's strengths and weaknesses compared to those of its competitors?

© REIMAR/ALAMY

5 Time Value of Money

Will You Be Able to Retire?

Your reaction to that question is probably, "First things first! I'm worried about getting a job, not about retiring!" However, understanding the retirement situation can help you land a job because (1) this is an important issue today, (2) employers like to hire people who know what's happening in the real world, and (3) professors often test on the time value of money with problems related to saving for future purposes (including retirement).

A recent *Fortune* article began with some interesting facts: (1) The U.S. savings rate is the lowest of any industrial nation. (2) The ratio of U.S. workers to retirees, which was 17 to 1 in 1950, is now down to 3 to 1; and it will decline to less than 2 to 1 after 2020. (3) With so few people paying into the Social Security system and so

many drawing funds out, Social Security is going to be in serious trouble. The article concluded that even people making $85,000 per year will have trouble maintaining a reasonable standard of living after they retire, and many of today's college students will have to support their parents.

This is an important issue for millions of Americans, but many don't know how to deal with it. When *Fortune* studied the retirement issue, using the tools and techniques described in this chapter, they concluded that most Americans have been ignoring what is most certainly going to be a huge personal and social problem. However, if you study this chapter carefully, you can avoid the trap that is likely to catch so many people.

PUTTING THINGS IN PERSPECTIVE

Time value analysis has many applications, including planning for retirement, valuing stocks and bonds, setting up loan payment schedules, and making corporate decisions regarding investing in new plant and equipment. *In fact, of all financial concepts, time value of money is the single most important concept. Indeed, time value analysis is used throughout the book; so it is vital that you understand this chapter before continuing.*

    You need to understand basic time value concepts, but conceptual knowledge will do you little good if you can't do the required calculations. Therefore, this chapter is heavy on calculations. Most students studying finance have a financial or scientific calculator; some also own or have access to a computer. One of these tools is necessary to work many finance problems in a reasonable length of time. However, when students start on this chapter, many of them don't know how to use the time value functions on their calculator or computer. If you are in that situation, you will find yourself simultaneously studying concepts and trying to learn to use your calculator, and you will need more time to cover this chapter than you might expect.[1]

    When you finish this chapter, you should be able to:

- Explain how the time value of money works and discuss why it is such an important concept in finance.
- Calculate the present value and future value of lump sums.
- Identify the different types of annuities and calculate the present value and future value of both an ordinary annuity and an annuity due. You should also be able to calculate relevant annuity payments.
- Calculate the present value and future value of an uneven cash flow stream. You will use this knowledge in later chapters that show how to value common stocks and corporate projects.
- Explain the difference between nominal, periodic, and effective interest rates.
- Discuss the basics of loan amortization.

*Excellent retirement calculators are available at **www.ssa.gov** and **www.choosetosave.org/ calculators**. These calculators allow you to input hypothetical retirement savings information; the program then shows if current retirement savings will be sufficient to meet retirement needs.*

5-1 TIME LINES

The first step in time value analysis is to set up a **time line**, which will help you visualize what's happening in a particular problem. As an illustration, consider the following diagram, where PV represents $100 that is on hand today and FV is the value that will be in the account on a future date:

Periods	0		1	2	3
		5%			
Cash	PV = $100				FV = ?

Time Line

An important tool used in time value analysis; it is a graphical representation used to show the timing of cash flows.

The intervals from 0 to 1, 1 to 2, and 2 to 3 are time periods such as years or months. Time 0 is today, and it is the beginning of Period 1; Time 1 is one period from today, and it is both the end of Period 1 and the beginning of Period 2; and

---

[1]Calculator manuals tend to be long and complicated, partly because they cover a number of topics that aren't required in the basic finance course. Therefore, on the textbook's web site, we provide tutorials for the most commonly used calculators. The tutorials are keyed to this chapter, and they show exactly how to do the required calculations. If you don't know how to use your calculator, go to the textbook's web site, find the relevant tutorial, and work through it as you study the chapter.

so forth. Although the periods are often years, periods can also be quarters or months or even days. Note that each tick mark corresponds to both the *end* of one period and the *beginning* of the next one. Thus, if the periods are years, the tick mark at Time 2 represents the *end* of Year 2 and the *beginning* of Year 3.

Cash flows are shown directly below the tick marks, and the relevant interest rate is shown just above the time line. Unknown cash flows, which you are trying to find, are indicated by question marks. Here the interest rate is 5%; a single cash outflow, $100, is invested at Time 0; and the Time 3 value is an unknown inflow. In this example, cash flows occur only at Times 0 and 3, with no flows at Times 1 or 2. Note that in our example, the interest rate is constant for all 3 years. That condition is generally true; but if it were not, we would show different interest rates for the different periods.

Time lines are essential when you are first learning time value concepts, but even experts use them to analyze complex finance problems; and we use them throughout the book. We begin each problem by setting up a time line to show what's happening, after which we provide an equation that must be solved to find the answer. Then we explain how to use a regular calculator, a financial calculator, and a spreadsheet to find the answer.

SELF TEST

Do time lines deal only with years, or can other periods be used?

Set up a time line to illustrate the following situation: You currently have $2,000 in a 3-year certificate of deposit (CD) that pays a guaranteed 4% annually.

5-2 FUTURE VALUES

A dollar in hand today is worth more than a dollar to be received in the future because if you had it now, you could invest it, earn interest, and end up with more than a dollar in the future. The process of going to **future values (FVs)** from **present values (PVs)** is called **compounding**. For an illustration, refer back to our 3-year time line and assume that you plan to deposit $100 in a bank that pays a guaranteed 5% interest each year. How much would you have at the end of Year 3? We first define some terms, after which we set up a time line and show how the future value is calculated.

Future Value (FV)
The amount to which a cash flow or series of cash flows will grow over a given period of time when compounded at a given interest rate.

Present Value (PV)
The value today of a future cash flow or series of cash flows.

Compounding
The arithmetic process of determining the final value of a cash flow or series of cash flows when compound interest is applied.

PV = Present value, or beginning amount. In our example, PV = $100.

FV_N = Future value, or ending amount, of your account after N periods. Whereas PV is the value now, or the *present value*, FV_N is the value N periods into the *future*, after the interest earned has been added to the account.

CF_t = Cash flow. Cash flows can be positive or negative. The cash flow for a particular period is often given as a subscript, CF_t, where t is the period. Thus, CF_0 = PV = the cash flow at Time 0, whereas CF_3 is the cash flow at the end of Period 3.

I = Interest rate earned per year. Sometimes a lowercase *i* is used. Interest earned is based on the balance at the beginning of each year, and we assume that it is paid at the end of the year. Here I = 5% or, expressed as a decimal, 0.05. Throughout this chapter, we designate the interest rate as *I* because that symbol (or I/YR, for interest rate per year) is used on most financial calculators. Note, though, that in later chapters, we use the symbol *r* to denote rates because r (for rate of return) is used more often in the finance literature. Note too that in this chapter, we generally assume that interest payments are guaranteed by the U.S. government; hence, they are certain. In later chapters, we will consider risky investments, where the interest rate earned might differ from its expected level.

INT = Dollars of interest earned during the year = Beginning amount × I. In our example, INT = $100(0.05) = $5.

N = Number of periods involved in the analysis. In our example, N = 3. Sometimes the number of periods is designated with a lowercase *n*, so both N and n indicate a number of periods.

We can use four different procedures to solve time value problems.[2] These methods are described in the following sections.

5-2a Step-by-Step Approach

The time line used to find the FV of $100 compounded for 3 years at 5%, along with some calculations, is shown.

Multiply the initial amount and each succeeding amount by (1 + I) = (1.05):

Time	0		1	2	3
		5%			
Amount at beginning of period	$100.00 ----▶		$105.00 ----▶	$110.25 ----▶	$115.76

SIMPLE VERSUS COMPOUND INTEREST

As noted in the text, interest earned on the interest earned in prior periods, as was true in our example and is always true when we apply Equation 5-1, is called **compound interest**. If interest is not earned on interest, we have **simple interest**. The formula for FV with simple interest is FV = PV + PV(I)(N); so in our example, FV would have been $100 + $100(0.05)(3) = $100 + $15 = $115 based on simple interest. Most financial contracts are based on compound interest; but in legal proceedings, the law often specifies that simple interest must be used. For example, Maris Distributing, a company founded by home run king Roger Maris, won a lawsuit against Anheuser-Busch (A-B)

because A-B had breached a contract and taken away Maris's franchise to sell Budweiser beer. The judge awarded Maris $50 million plus interest at 10% from 1997 (when A-B breached the contract) until the payment is actually made. The interest award was based on simple interest, which as of 2008 had raised the total from $50 million to $50 million + 0.10($50 million)(11 years) = $105 million. If the law had allowed compound interest, the award would have totaled ($50 million)$(1.10)^{11}$ = $142.66 million, or $37.66 million more. This legal procedure dates back to the days before calculators and computers. The law moves slowly!

Compound Interest
Occurs when interest is earned on prior periods' interest.

Simple Interest
Occurs when interest is not earned on interest.

---

[2]A fifth procedure, using tables that show "interest factors," was used before financial calculators and computers became available. Now, though, calculators and spreadsheets such as Excel are programmed to calculate the specific factor needed for a given problem and then to use it to find the FV. This is more efficient than using the tables. Moreover, calculators and spreadsheets can handle fractional periods and fractional interest rates, such as the FV of $100 after 3.75 years when the interest rate is 5.375%, whereas tables provide numbers only for whole periods and rates. For these reasons, tables are not used in business today; hence, we do not discuss them in the text.

You start with $100 in the account—this is shown at t = 0:

- You earn $100(0.05) = $5 of interest during the first year, so the amount at the end of Year 1 (or t = 1) is $100 + $5 = $105.
- You begin the second year with $105, earn 0.05($105) = $5.25 on the now larger beginning-of-period amount, and end the year with $110.25. Interest during Year 2 is $5.25; and it is higher than the first year's interest, $5.00, because you earned $5(0.05) = $0.25 interest on the first year's interest. This is called compounding, and interest earned on interest is called compound interest.
- This process continues; and because the beginning balance is higher each successive year, the interest earned each year increases.
- The total interest earned, $15.76, is reflected in the final balance, $115.76.

The step-by-step approach is useful because it shows exactly what is happening. However, this approach is time-consuming, especially when a number of years are involved; so streamlined procedures have been developed.

5-2b Formula Approach

In the step-by-step approach, we multiply the amount at the beginning of each period by $(1 + I) = (1.05)$. If N = 3, we multiply by $(1 + I)$ three different times, which is the same as multiplying the beginning amount by $(1 + I)^3$. This concept can be extended, and the result is this key equation:

| 5-1 |

$$FV_N = PV(1 + I)^N$$

We can apply Equation 5-1 to find the FV in our example:

$$FV_3 = \$100(1.05)^3 = \$115.76$$

Equation 5-1 can be used with any calculator that has an exponential function, making it easy to find FVs no matter how many years are involved.

5-2c Financial Calculators

Financial calculators are extremely helpful in working time value problems. Their manuals explain calculators in detail; and on the textbook's web site, we provide summaries of the features needed to work the problems in this book for several popular calculators. Also see the box entitled "Hints on Using Financial Calculators," on page 128, for suggestions that will help you avoid common mistakes. If you are not yet familiar with your calculator, we recommend that you work through the tutorial as you study this chapter.

First, note that financial calculators have five keys that correspond to the five variables in the basic time value equations. We show the inputs for our example above the keys and the output, the FV, below its key. Because there are no periodic payments, we enter 0 for PMT. We describe the keys in more detail below the diagram.

3	5	−100	0	
N	I/YR	PV	PMT	FV
				115.76

N = Number of periods. Some calculators use n rather than N.

I/YR = Interest rate per period. Some calculators use i or I rather than I/YR.

PV = Present value. In our example, we begin by making a deposit, which is an outflow; so the PV should be entered with a negative sign. On most calculators, you must enter the 100, then press the +/− key to switch from +100 to −100. If you enter −100 directly, 100 will be subtracted from the last number in the calculator, giving you an incorrect answer.

PMT = Payment. This key is used when we have a series of equal, or constant, payments. Because there are no such payments in our illustrative problem, we enter PMT = 0. We will use the PMT key when we discuss annuities later in this chapter.

FV = Future value. In this example, the FV is positive because we entered the PV as a negative number. If we had entered the 100 as a positive number, the FV would have been negative.

As noted in our example, you first enter the known values (N, I/YR, PMT, and PV) and then press the FV key to get the answer, 115.76. Again, note that if you enter the PV as 100 without a minus sign, the FV will be given as a negative. The calculator *assumes* that either the PV or the FV is negative. This should not be confusing if you think about what you are doing.

5-2d Spreadsheets[3]

Students generally use calculators for homework and exam problems; but in business, people generally use spreadsheets for problems that involve the time value of money (TVM). Spreadsheets show in detail what is happening, and they help reduce both conceptual and data-entry errors. The spreadsheet discussion can be skipped without loss of continuity; but if you understand the basics of Excel and have access to a computer, we recommend that you read through this section. Even if you aren't familiar with spreadsheets, the discussion will still give you an idea of how they operate.

We used Excel to create Table 5-1, which summarizes the four methods of finding the FV and shows the spreadsheet formulas toward the bottom. Note that spreadsheets can be used to do calculations; but they can also be used like a word processor to create exhibits like Table 5-1, which includes text, drawings, and calculations. The letters across the top designate columns, the numbers to the left designate rows, and the rows and columns jointly designate cells. Thus, C14 is the cell in which we specify the −$100 investment, C15 shows the interest rate, and C16 shows the number of periods. We then created a time line on Rows 17 to 19; and on Row 21, we have Excel go through the step-by-step calculations, multiplying the beginning-of-year values by (1 + I) to find the compounded value at the end of each period. Cell G21 shows the final result. Then on Row 23, we illustrate the formula approach, using Excel to solve Equation 5-1, and find the FV, $115.76. Next, on Rows 25 to 27, we show a picture of the calculator solution. Finally, on Rows 29 and 30, we use Excel's built-in FV function to find the answers given in Cells G29 and G30. The G29 answer is based on fixed inputs, while the G30 answer is based on cell references, which makes it easy to change inputs and see the effects on the output.

Table 5-1 demonstrates that all four methods get the same result, but they use different calculating procedures. It also shows that with Excel, all inputs are

[3]If you have never worked with spreadsheets, you may choose to skip this section. However, you might want to read through it and refer to this chapter's Excel model to get an idea of how spreadsheets work.

Table 5-1

| Table 5-1 | | Summary of Future Value Calculations | | | | | |

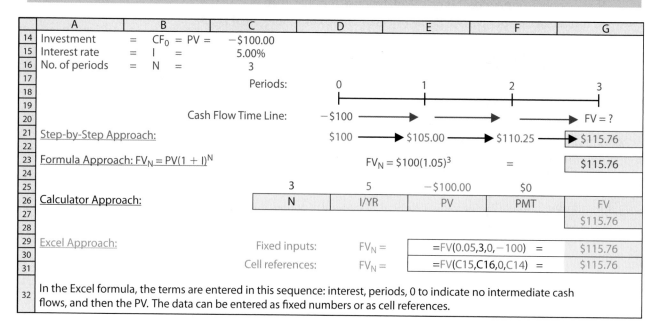

	A	B	C	D	E	F	G
14	Investment	= CF$_0$ = PV =	−$100.00				
15	Interest rate	= I =	5.00%				
16	No. of periods	= N =	3				
17				Periods:	0	1	2	3
18								
19								
20			Cash Flow Time Line:	−$100 ——→	——→	——→	FV = ?
21	Step-by-Step Approach:			$100 ——→	$105.00 ——→	$110.25 ——→	$115.76
22								
23	Formula Approach: FV$_N$ = PV(1 + I)^N			FV$_N$ = $100(1.05)^3		=	$115.76
24								
25				3	5	−$100.00	$0	
26	Calculator Approach:		N	I/YR	PV	PMT	FV
27							$115.76
28								
29	Excel Approach:		Fixed inputs:	FV$_N$ =	=FV(0.05,3,0,−100) =		$115.76
30			Cell references:	FV$_N$ =	=FV(C15,C16,0,C14) =		$115.76
31								
32	In the Excel formula, the terms are entered in this sequence: interest, periods, 0 to indicate no intermediate cash flows, and then the PV. The data can be entered as fixed numbers or as cell references.						

shown in one place, which makes checking data entries relatively easy. Finally, it shows that Excel can be used to create exhibits, which are quite important in the real world. In business, it's often as important to explain what you are doing as it is to "get the right answer" because if decision makers don't understand your analysis, they may reject your recommendations.

HINTS ON USING FINANCIAL CALCULATORS

When using a financial calculator, make sure your machine is set up as indicated here. Refer to your calculator manual or to our calculator tutorial on the text's web site for information on setting up your calculator.

- *One payment per period.* Many calculators "come out of the box" assuming that 12 payments are made per year; that is, they assume monthly payments. However, in this book, we generally deal with problems in which only one payment is made each year. *Therefore, you should set your calculator at one payment per year and leave it there. See our tutorial or your calculator manual if you need assistance.*

- *End mode.* With most contracts, payments are made at the end of each period. However, some contracts call for payments at the beginning of each period. You can switch between "End Mode" and "Begin Mode" depending on the problem you are solving. *Because most of the problems in this book call for end-of-period payments, you should return your calculator to End Mode after you work a problem where payments are made at the beginning of periods.*

- *Negative sign for outflows.* Outflows must be entered as negative numbers. This generally means typing the outflow as a positive number and then pressing the +/− key to convert from + to − before hitting the enter key.

- *Decimal places.* With most calculators, you can specify from 0 to 11 decimal places. When working with dollars, we generally specify two decimal places. When dealing with interest rates, we generally specify two places when the rate is expressed as a percentage (e.g., 5.25%), but we specify four places when the rate is expressed as a decimal (e.g., 0.0525).

- *Interest rates.* For arithmetic operations with a nonfinancial calculator, the 0.0525 must be used; but with a financial calculator, you must enter 5.25, not .0525, because financial calculators assume that rates are stated as percentages.

5-2e Graphic View of the Compounding Process

Figure 5-1 shows how a $1 investment grows over time at different interest rates. We made the curves by solving Equation 5-1 with different values for N and I. The interest rate is a growth rate: If a sum is deposited and earns 5% interest per year, the funds on deposit will grow by 5% per year. Note also that time value concepts can be applied to anything that grows—sales, population, earnings per share, or future salary.

SELF TEST

Explain why this statement is true: A dollar in hand today is worth more than a dollar to be received next year.

What is compounding? What's the difference between simple interest and compound interest? What would the future value of $100 be after 5 years at 10% *compound* interest? at 10% *simple* interest? **($161.05; $150.00)**

Suppose you currently have $2,000 and plan to purchase a 3-year certificate of deposit (CD) that pays 4% interest compounded annually. How much will you have when the CD matures? How would your answer change if the interest rate were 5% or 6% or 20%? **($2,249.73; $2,315.25; $2,382.03; $3,456.00) (Hint: With a calculator, enter N = 3, I/YR = 4, PV = −2000, and PMT = 0; then press FV to get 2,249.73. Enter I/YR = 5 to override the 4% and press FV again to get the second answer. In general, you can change one input at a time to see how the output changes.)**

A company's sales in 2008 were $100 million. If sales grow at 8%, what will they be 10 years later, in 2018? **($215.89 million)**

How much would $1, growing at 5% per year, be worth after 100 years? What would FV be if the growth rate was 10%? **($131.50; $13,780.61)**

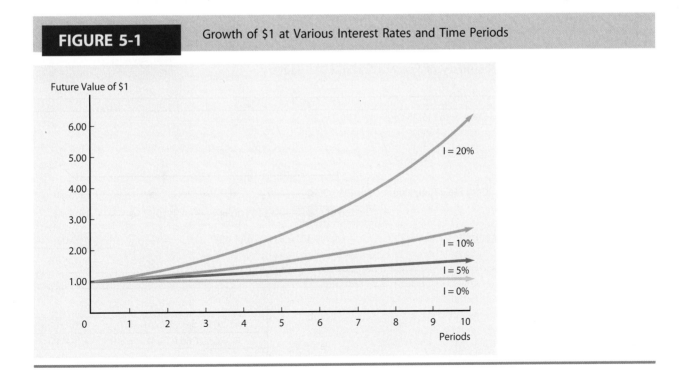

FIGURE 5-1   Growth of $1 at Various Interest Rates and Time Periods

5-3 PRESENT VALUES

Finding a present value is the reverse of finding a future value. Indeed, we simply solve Equation 5-1, the formula for the future value, for the PV to produce the basic present value Equation, 5-2:

5-1
$$\text{Future value} = FV_N = PV(1 + I)^N$$

5-2
$$\text{Present value} = PV = \frac{FV_N}{(1 + I)^N}$$

We illustrate PVs with the following example. A broker offers to sell you a Treasury bond that will pay $115.76 in 3 years from now. Banks are currently offering a guaranteed 5% interest on 3-year certificates of deposit (CDs); and if you don't buy the bond, you will buy a CD. The 5% rate paid on the CDs is defined as your **opportunity cost**, or the rate of return you could earn on an alternative investment of similar risk. Given these conditions, what's the most you should pay for the bond? We answer this question using the four methods discussed in the last section—step-by-step, formula, calculator, and spreadsheet. Table 5-2 summarizes the results.

Opportunity Cost
The rate of return you could earn on an alternative investment of similar risk.

First, recall from the future value example in the last section that if you invested $100 at 5%, it would grow to $115.76 in 3 years. You would also have $115.76 after 3 years if you bought the T-bond. Therefore, the most you should pay for the bond is $100—this is its "fair price." If you could buy the bond for *less than* $100, you should buy it rather than invest in the CD. Conversely, if its price was *more than* $100, you should buy the CD. If the bond's price was exactly $100, you should be indifferent between the T-bond and the CD.

The $100 is defined as the present value, or PV, of $115.76 due in 3 years when the appropriate interest rate is 5%. In general, *the present value of a cash flow due N years in the future is the amount which, if it were on hand today, would grow to equal the given future amount.* Because $100 would grow to $115.76 in 3 years at a 5% interest rate, $100 is the present value of $115.76 due in 3 years at a 5% rate. Finding present values is called **discounting**; and as noted above, it is the reverse of compounding—if you know the PV, you can compound to find the FV, while if you know the FV, you can discount to find the PV.

Discounting
The process of finding the present value of a cash flow or a series of cash flows; discounting is the reverse of compounding.

Table 5-2   **Summary of Present Value Calculations**

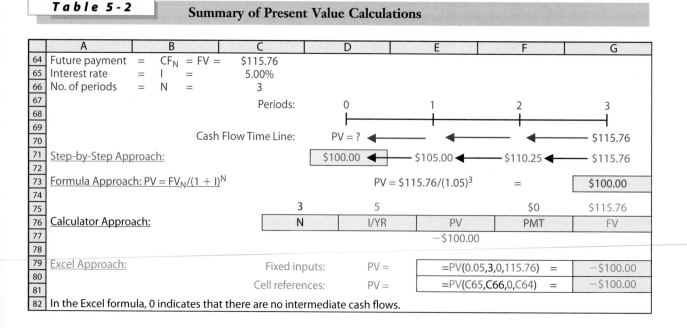

	A	B	C	D	E	F	G
64	Future payment	= CF_N = FV =	$115.76				
65	Interest rate	= I =	5.00%				
66	No. of periods	= N =	3				
67			Periods:	0	1	2	3
68							
69							
70			Cash Flow Time Line:	PV = ?			$115.76
71	Step-by-Step Approach:			$100.00	$105.00	$110.25	$115.76
72							
73	Formula Approach: PV = FV_N/(1 + I)^N			PV = $115.76/(1.05)³		=	$100.00
74							
75				3	5	$0	$115.76
76	Calculator Approach:			N	I/YR	PV	PMT	FV
77						−$100.00		
78								
79	Excel Approach:		Fixed inputs:	PV =	=PV(0.05,3,0,115.76) =		−$100.00
80							
81			Cell references:	PV =	=PV(C65,C66,0,C64) =		−$100.00
82	In the Excel formula, 0 indicates that there are no intermediate cash flows.						

The top section of Table 5-2 calculates the PV using the step-by-step approach. When we found the future value in the previous section, we worked from left to right, multiplying the initial amount and each subsequent amount by $(1 + I)$. To find present values, we work backward, or from right to left, dividing the future value and each subsequent amount by $(1 + I)$. This procedure shows exactly what's happening, which can be quite useful when you are working complex problems. However, it's inefficient, especially when you are dealing with a number of years.

With the formula approach, we use Equation 5-2, simply dividing the future value by $(1 + I)^N$. This is more efficient than the step-by-step approach, and it gives the same result. Equation 5-2 is built into financial calculators; and as shown in Table 5-2, we can find the PV by entering values for N, I/YR, PMT, and FV and then pressing the PV key. Finally, spreadsheets have a function that's essentially the same as the calculator, which also solves Equation 5-2.

The fundamental goal of financial management is to maximize the firm's value, and the value of a business (or any asset, including stocks and bonds) is the *present value* of its expected future cash flows. Because present value lies at the heart of the valuation process, we will have much more to say about it in the remainder of this chapter and throughout the book.

5-3a Graphic View of the Discounting Process

Figure 5-2 shows that the present value of a sum to be received in the future decreases and approaches zero as the payment date is extended further into the future and that the present value falls faster at higher interest rates. At relatively high rates, funds due in the future are worth very little today; and even at relatively low rates, present values of sums due in the very distant future are quite small. For example, at a 20% discount rate, $1 million due in 100 years would be worth only $0.0121 today. This is because $0.0121 would grow to $1 million in 100 years when compounded at 20%.

FIGURE 5-2	Present Value of $1 at Various Interest Rates and Time Periods

What is discounting, and how is it related to compounding? How is the future value equation (5-1) related to the present value equation (5-2)?

How does the present value of a future payment change as the time to receipt is lengthened? as the interest rate increases?

Suppose a U.S. government bond promises to pay $2,249.73 three years from now. If the going interest rate on three-year government bonds is 4%, how much is the bond worth today? How would your answer change if the bond matured in 5 years rather than 3? What if the interest rate on the 5-year bond was 6% rather than 4%? **($2,000; $1,849.11; $1,681.13)**

How much would $1,000,000 due in 100 years be worth today if the discount rate was 5%? if the discount rate was 20%? **($7,604.49; $0.0121)**

5-4 FINDING THE INTEREST RATE, I

Thus far we have used Equations 5-1 and 5-2 to find future and present values. Those equations have four variables; and if we know three of the variables, we can solve for the fourth. Thus, if we know PV, I, and N, we can solve 5-1 for FV, while if we know FV, I, and N, we can solve 5-2 to find PV. That's what we did in the preceding two sections.

Now suppose we know PV, FV, and N and we want to find I. For example, suppose we know that a given bond has a cost of $100 and that it will return $150 after 10 years. Thus, we know PV, FV, and N; and we want to find the rate of return we will earn if we buy the bond. Here's the situation:

$$FV = PV(1 + I)^N$$
$$\$150 = \$100(1 + I)^{10}$$
$$\$150/\$100 = (1 + I)^{10}$$
$$1.5 = (1 + I)^{10}$$

Unfortunately, we can't factor I out to produce as simple a formula as we could for FV and PV—we can solve for I, but it requires a bit more algebra.[4] However, financial calculators and spreadsheets can find interest rates almost instantly. Here's the calculator setup:

10		−100	0	150
N	I/YR	PV	PMT	FV
	4.14			

Enter N = 10, PV = −100, PMT = 0 because there are no payments until the security matures, and FV = 150. Then when you press the I/YR key, the calculator gives the answer, 4.14%. You would get this same answer with a spreadsheet.

---

[4]Raise the left side of the equation, the 1.5, to the power 1/N = 1/10 = 0.1, getting 1.0414. That number is 1 plus the interest rate, so the interest rate is 0.0414 = 4.14%.

The U.S. Treasury offers to sell you a bond for $585.43. No payments will be made until the bond matures 10 years from now, at which time it will be redeemed for $1,000. What interest rate would you earn if you bought this bond for $585.43? What rate would you earn if you could buy the bond for $550? for $600? **(5.5%; 6.16%; 5.24%)**

Microsoft earned $0.33 per share in 1997. Ten years later in 2007 it earned $1.42. What was the growth rate in Microsoft's earnings per share (EPS) over the 10-year period? If EPS in 2007 had been $0.90 rather than $1.42, what would the growth rate have been? **(15.71%; 10.55%)**

5-5 FINDING THE NUMBER OF YEARS, N

We sometimes need to know how long it will take to accumulate a certain sum of money, given our beginning funds and the rate we will earn on those funds. For example, suppose we believe that we could retire comfortably if we had $1 million. We want to find how long it will take us to acquire $1 million, assuming we now have $500,000 invested at 4.5%. We cannot use a simple formula—the situation is like that with interest rates. We can set up a formula that uses logarithms, but calculators and spreadsheets find N very quickly. Here's the calculator setup:

	4.5	−500000	0	1000000
N	I/YR	PV	PMT	FV
15.7473				

Enter I/YR = 4.5, PV = −500000, PMT = 0, and FV = 1000000. Then when you press the N key, you get the answer, 15.7473 years. If you plug N = 15.7473 into the FV formula, you can prove that this is indeed the correct number of years:

$$FV = PV(1 + I)^N = \$500,000(1.045)^{15.7473} = \$1,000,000$$

You would also get N = 15.7473 with a spreadsheet.

How long would it take $1,000 to double if it was invested in a bank that paid 6% per year? How long would it take if the rate was 10%? **(11.9 years; 7.27 years)**

Microsoft's 2007 earnings per share were $1.42, and its growth rate during the prior 10 years was 15.71% per year. If that growth rate was maintained, how long would it take for Microsoft's EPS to double? **(4.75 years)**

5-6 ANNUITIES

Thus far we have dealt with single payments, or "lump sums." However, many assets provide a series of cash inflows over time; and many obligations, such as auto, student, and mortgage loans, require a series of payments. When the payments are equal and are made at fixed intervals, the series is an **annuity**. For example, $100 paid at the *end* of each of the next 3 years is a 3-year annuity. If the payments occur at the end of each year, the annuity is an **ordinary (or deferred)**

Annuity
A series of equal payments at fixed intervals for a specified number of periods.

Ordinary (Deferred) Annuity
An annuity whose payments occur at the end of each period.

Annuity Due
An annuity whose payments occur at the beginning of each period.

annuity. If the payments are made at the *beginning* of each year, the annuity is an **annuity due**. Ordinary annuities are more common in finance; so when we use the term *annuity* in this book, assume that the payments occur at the ends of the periods unless otherwise noted.

Here are the time lines for a $100, 3-year, 5% ordinary annuity and for the same annuity on an annuity due basis. With the annuity due, each payment is shifted to the left by one year. A $100 deposit will be made each year, so we show the payments with minus signs:

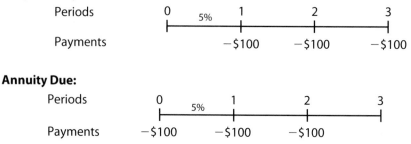

Ordinary Annuity:

Annuity Due:

As we demonstrate in the following sections, we can find an annuity's future and present values, the interest rate built into annuity contracts, and the length of time it takes to reach a financial goal using an annuity. Keep in mind that annuities must have *constant payments* and a *fixed number of periods*. If these conditions don't hold, we don't have an annuity.

SELF TEST

What's the difference between an ordinary annuity and an annuity due?

Why would you prefer to receive an annuity due for $10,000 per year for 10 years than an otherwise similar ordinary annuity?

5-7 FUTURE VALUE OF AN ORDINARY ANNUITY

FVA_N
The future value of an annuity over N periods.

The future value of an annuity can be found using the step-by-step approach or using a formula, a financial calculator, or a spreadsheet. As an illustration, consider the ordinary annuity diagrammed earlier, where you deposit $100 at the end of each year for 3 years and earn 5% per year. How much will you have at the end of the third year? The answer, $315.25, is defined as the future value of the annuity, **FVA_N**; it is shown in Table 5-3.

As shown in the step-by-step section of the table, we compound each payment out to Time 3, then sum those compounded values to find the annuity's FV, $FVA_3 = \$315.25$. The first payment earns interest for two periods, the second payment earns interest for one period, and the third payment earns no interest at all because it is made at the end of the annuity's life. This approach is straightforward; but if the annuity extends out for many years, the approach is cumbersome and time-consuming.

As you can see from the time line diagram, with the step-by-step approach, we apply the following equation, with N = 3 and I = 5%:

$$FVA_N = PMT(1+I)^{N-1} + PMT(1+I)^{N-2} + PMT(1+I)^{N-3}$$
$$= \$100(1.05)^2 + \$100(1.05)^1 + \$100(1.05)^0$$
$$= \$315.25$$

	A	B	C	D	E	F	G
131	Payment amount	= PMT =	$100.00				
132	Interest rate	= I =	5.00%				
133	No. of periods	= N =	3				
134							
135		Periods:	0	1	2	3	
136							
137		Cash Flow Time Line:		−$100	−$100	−$100	
138	Step-by-Step Approach.						
139	Multiply each payment by						
140	$(1+I)^{N-t}$ and sum these FVs to					−$100.00	
141	find FVA_N:					−$105.00	
142						−$110.25	
143						−$315.25	
144	Formula Approach:						
145		FVA_N =	$PMT \times \left(\dfrac{(1+I)^N - 1}{I}\right)$		=	$315.25	
146							
147							
148			3	5	$0	−$100.00	
149	Calculator Approach:		N	I/YR	PV	PMT	FV
150							
151							$315.25
152	Excel Function Approach:		Fixed inputs:	FVA_N =	=FV(0.05,3,−100,0) =		$315.25
153							
154			Cell references:	FVA_N =	=FV(C132,C133,−C131,0) =		$315.25
155		Excel entries correspond with these calculator keys:			I/YR N PMT PV		FV

We can generalize and streamline the equation as follows:

$$FVA_N = PMT(1+I)^{N-1} + PMT(1+I)^{N-2}$$
$$+ PMT(1+I)^{N-3} + \ldots + PMT(1+I)^0$$
$$= PMT\left[\frac{(1+I)^N - 1}{I}\right] \qquad \text{5-3}$$

The first line shows the equation in its long form. It can be transformed to the second form, which can be used to solve annuity problems with a nonfinancial calculator.[5] This equation is also built into financial calculators and spreadsheets. With an annuity, we have recurring payments; hence, the PMT key is used. Here's the calculator setup for our illustrative annuity:

3	5	0	−100		End Mode
N	I/YR	PV	PMT	FV	
				315.25	

We enter PV = 0 because we start off with nothing, and we enter PMT = −100 because we plan to deposit this amount in the account at the end of each year. When we press the FV key, we get the answer, $FVA_3 = 315.25$.

Because this is an ordinary annuity, with payments coming at the *end* of each year, we must set the calculator appropriately. As noted earlier, calculators "come out of the box" set to assume that payments occur at the end of each period, that is, to deal with ordinary annuities. However, there is a key that enables us to switch between ordinary annuities and annuities due. For ordinary annuities, the

---

[5]The long form of the equation is a geometric progression that can be reduced to the second form.

designation is "End Mode" or something similar, while for annuities due, the designation is "Begin" or "Begin Mode" or "Due" or something similar. If you make a mistake and set your calculator on Begin Mode when working with an ordinary annuity, each payment will earn interest for one extra year. That will cause the compounded amounts, and thus the FVA, to be too large.

The last approach in Table 5-3 shows the spreadsheet solution using Excel's built-in function. We can put in fixed values for N, I, and PMT or set up an Input Section, where we assign values to those variables, and then input values into the function as cell references. Using cell references makes it easy to change the inputs to see the effects of changes on the output.

SELF TEST

For an ordinary annuity with five annual payments of $100 and a 10% interest rate, how many years will the first payment earn interest? What will this payment's value be at the end? Answer this same question for the fifth payment. **(4 years, $146.41; 0 years, $100)**

Assume that you plan to buy a condo 5 years from now, and you estimate that you can save $2,500 per year. You plan to deposit the money in a bank that pays 4% interest, and you will make the first deposit at the end of the year. How much will you have after 5 years? How will your answer change if the interest rate is increased to 6% or lowered to 3%? **($13,540.81; $14,092.73; $13,272.84)**

5-8 FUTURE VALUE OF AN ANNUITY DUE

Because each payment occurs one period earlier with an annuity due, all of the payments earn interest for one additional period. Therefore, the FV of an annuity due will be greater than that of a similar ordinary annuity. If you went through the step-by-step procedure, you would see that our illustrative annuity due has an FV of $331.01 versus $315.25 for the ordinary annuity.

With the formula approach, we first use Equation 5-3; but since each payment occurs one period earlier, we multiply the Equation 5-3 result by $(1 + I)$:

5-4
$$FVA_{due} = FVA_{ordinary}(1 + I)$$

Thus, for the annuity due, $FVA_{due} = \$315.25(1.05) = \$331.01$, which is the same result when the period-by-period approach is used. With a calculator, we input the variables just as we did with the ordinary annuity; but now we set the calculator to Begin Mode to get the answer, $331.01.

SELF TEST

Why does an annuity due always have a higher future value than an ordinary annuity?

If you calculated the value of an ordinary annuity, how could you find the value of the corresponding annuity due?

Assume that you plan to buy a condo 5 years from now and you need to save for a down payment. You plan to save $2,500 per year (with the first deposit made *immediately*), and you will deposit the funds in a bank account that pays 4% interest. How much will you have after 5 years? How much will you have if you make the deposits at the end of each year? **($14,082.44; $13,540.81)**

5-9 PRESENT VALUE OF AN ORDINARY ANNUITY

The present value of an annuity, **PVA$_N$**, can be found using the step-by-step, formula, calculator, or spreadsheet method. Look back at Table 5-3. To find the FV of the annuity, we compounded the deposits. To find the PV, we discount them, dividing each payment by $(1 + I)$. The step-by-step procedure is diagrammed as follows:

PVA$_N$
The present value of an annuity of N periods.

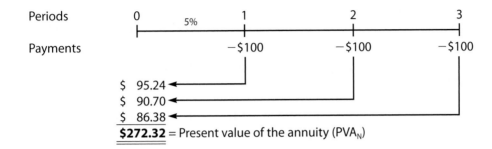

Equation 5-5 expresses the step-by-step procedure in a formula. The bracketed form of the equation can be used with a scientific calculator, and it is helpful if the annuity extends out for a number of years:

$$PVA_N = PMT/(1+I)^1 + PMT/(1+I)^2 + \cdots + PMT/(1+I)^N$$

$$= PMT \left[\frac{1 - \dfrac{1}{(1+I)^N}}{I} \right] \qquad \text{5-5}$$

$$= \$100 \times [1 - 1/(1.05)^3]/0.05 = \$272.32$$

Calculators are programmed to solve Equation 5-5; so we merely input the variables and press the PV key, *making sure the calculator is set to End Mode.* The calculator setup follows for both an ordinary annuity and an annuity due. Note that the PV of the annuity due is larger because each payment is discounted back one less year. Note too that you can find the PV of the ordinary annuity and then multiply by $(1 + I) = 1.05$, getting $\$272.32(1.05) = \$285.94$, the PV of the annuity due.

3	5		−100	0	End Mode
N	I/YR	PV	PMT	FV	(Ordinary
		272.32			Annuity)

3	5		−100	0	Begin Mode
N	I/YR	PV	PMT	FV	(Annuity
		285.94			Due)

Compared to an ordinary annuity, why does an annuity due have a higher present value?

If you know the present value of an ordinary annuity, how can you find the PV of the corresponding annuity due?

What is the PVA of an ordinary annuity with 10 payments of $100 if the appropriate interest rate is 10%? What would the PVA be if the interest rate was 4%? What if the interest rate was 0%? How would the PVA values differ if we were dealing with annuities due? **($614.46; $811.09; $1,000.00; $675.90; $843.53; $1,000.00)**

Assume that you are offered an annuity that pays $100 at the end of each year for 10 years. You could earn 8% on your money in other investments with equal risk. What is the most you should pay for the annuity? If the payments began immediately, how much would the annuity be worth? **($671.01; $724.69)**

5-10 FINDING ANNUITY PAYMENTS, PERIODS, AND INTEREST RATES

We can find payments, periods, and interest rates for annuities. Here five variables come into play: N, I, PMT, FV, and PV. If we know any four, we can find the fifth.

5-10a Finding Annuity Payments, PMT

Suppose we need to accumulate $10,000 and have it available 5 years from now. Suppose further that we can earn a return of 6% on our savings, which are currently zero. Thus, we know that FV = 10,000, PV = 0, N = 5, and I/YR = 6. We can enter these values in a financial calculator and press the PMT key to find how large our deposits must be. The answer will, of course, depend on whether we make deposits at the end of each year (ordinary annuity) or at the beginning (annuity due). Here are the results for each type of annuity:

5	6	0		10000	End Mode
N	I/YR	PV	PMT	FV	(Ordinary Annuity)
			−1,773.96		

5	6	0		10000	Begin Mode
N	I/YR	PV	PMT	FV	(Annuity Due)
			−1,673.55		

Thus, you must save $1,773.96 per year if you make payments at the *end* of each year, but only $1,673.55 if the payments begin *immediately*. Note that the required payment for the annuity due is the ordinary annuity payment divided by $(1 + I)$: $1,773.96/1.06 = $1,673.55. Spreadsheets can also be used to find annuity payments.

5-10b Finding the Number of Periods, N

Suppose you decide to make end-of-year deposits, but you can save only $1,200 per year. Again assuming that you would earn 6%, how long would it take to reach your $10,000 goal? Here is the calculator setup:

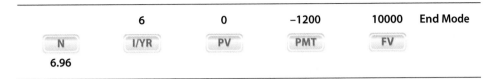

	6		0	−1200	10000	End Mode
N	I/YR	PV	PMT	FV		
6.96						

With these smaller deposits, it would take 6.96 years to reach the $10,000 target. If you began the deposits immediately, you would have an annuity due and N would be a bit less, 6.63 years.

5-10c Finding the Interest Rate, I

Now suppose you can save only $1,200 annually, but you still want to have the $10,000 in 5 years. What rate of return would enable you to achieve your goal? Here is the calculator setup:

5			0	−1200	10000	End Mode
N	I/YR	PV	PMT	FV		
	25.78					

You would need to earn a whopping 25.78%. About the only way to earn such a high return would be to invest in speculative stocks or head to the casinos in Las Vegas. Of course, investing in speculative stocks and gambling aren't like making deposits in a bank with a guaranteed rate of return, so there's a good chance you'd end up with nothing. You might consider changing your plans—save more, lower your $10,000 target, or extend your time horizon. It might be appropriate to seek a somewhat higher return, but trying to earn 25.78% in a 6% market would require taking on more risk than would be prudent.

It's easy to find rates of return using a financial calculator or a spreadsheet. However, without one of these tools, you would have to go through a trial-and-error process, which would be very time-consuming if many years were involved.

SELF TEST

Suppose you inherited $100,000 and invested it at 7% per year. How much could you withdraw at the *end* of each of the next 10 years? How would your answer change if you made withdrawals at the *beginning* of each year? **($14,237.75; $13,306.31)**

If you had $100,000 that was invested at 7% and you wanted to withdraw $10,000 at the end of each year, how long would your funds last? How long would they last if you earned 0%? How long would they last if you earned the 7% but limited your withdrawal to $7,000 per year? **(17.8 years; 10 years; forever)**

Your rich uncle named you beneficiary of his life insurance policy. The insurance company gives you a choice of $100,000 today or a 12-year annuity of $12,000 at the end of each year. What rate of return is the insurance company offering? **(6.11%)**

Assume that you just inherited an annuity that will pay you $10,000 per year for 10 years, with the first payment being made today. A friend of your mother offers to give you $60,000 for the annuity. If you sell it, what rate of return would your mother's friend earn on his investment? If you think a "fair" return would be 6%, how much should you ask for the annuity? **(13.70%; $78,016.92)**

5-11 PERPETUITIES

Consol

A perpetual bond issued by the British government to consolidate past debts; in general, any perpetual bond.

Perpetuity

A stream of equal payments at fixed intervals expected to continue forever.

In the last section, we dealt with annuities whose payments continue for a specific number of periods—for example, $100 per year for 10 years. However, some securities promise to make payments forever. For example, in 1749, the British government issued bonds whose proceeds were used to pay off other British bonds; and since this action consolidated the government's debt, the new bonds were called **consols**. Because consols promise to pay interest forever, they are "perpetuities." The interest rate on the consols was 2.5%, so a bond with a face value of $1,000 would pay $25 per year in perpetuity.[6]

A **perpetuity** is simply an annuity with an extended life. Because the payments go on forever, you can't apply the step-by-step approach. However, it's easy to find the PV of a perpetuity with a formula found by solving Equation 5-5 with N set at infinity:[7]

5-6
$$\text{PV of a perpetuity} = \frac{PMT}{I}$$

Now we can use Equation 5-6 to find the value of a British consol with a face value of $1,000 that pays $25 per year in perpetuity. The answer depends on the interest rate. In 1888, the "going rate" as established in the financial marketplace was 2.5%; so at that time, the consol's value was $1,000:

$$\text{Consol value}_{1888} = \$25/0.025 = \$1,000$$

In 2008, 120 years later, the annual payment was still $25, but the going interest rate had risen to 4.3%, causing the consol's value to fall to $581.40:

$$\text{Consol value}_{2008} = \$25/0.043 = \$581.40$$

Note, though, that if interest rates decline in the future (say, to 2%), the value of the consol will rise:

$$\text{Consol value if rates decline to 2\%} = \$25/0.02 = \$1,250.00$$

These examples demonstrate an important point: *When interest rates change, the prices of outstanding bonds also change. Bond prices decline when rates rise and increase when rates fall.* We will discuss this point in more detail in Chapter 7, where we cover bonds in depth.

Figure 5-3 gives a graphic picture of how much each payment contributes to the value of an annuity. Here we analyze an annuity that pays $100 per year when the market interest rate is 10%. We found the PV of each payment for the first 100 years and graphed those PVs. We also found the value of the annuity with a 25-year, 50-year, 100-year, and infinite life. Here are some points to note:

1. The value of an ordinary annuity is the sum of the present values of its payments.

2. We can construct graphs for annuities of any length—for 3 years or 25 years or 50 years or any other period. The fewer the years, the fewer the bars in the graph.

3. As the years increase, the PV of each additional payment—which represents the amount the payment contributes to the annuity's value—decreases. This occurs because each payment is divided by $(1 + I)^t$, and that term increases exponentially with t. Indeed, in our graph, the payments after 62 years are too small to be noticed.

---

[6]The consols actually pay interest in pounds, but we discuss them in dollar terms for simplicity.
[7]Equation 5-6 was found by letting *N* in Equation 5-5 approach infinity. The result is Equation 5-6.

| FIGURE 5-3 | Contribution of Payments to Value of $100 Annuity at 10% Interest Rate |

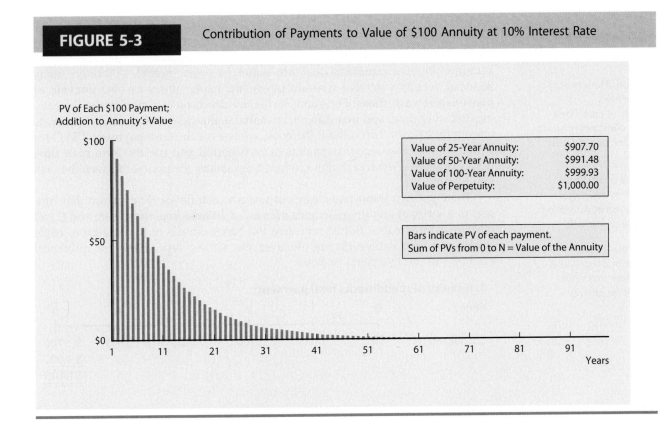

PV of Each $100 Payment;
Addition to Annuity's Value

Value of 25-Year Annuity:	$907.70
Value of 50-Year Annuity:	$991.48
Value of 100-Year Annuity:	$999.93
Value of Perpetuity:	$1,000.00

Bars indicate PV of each payment.
Sum of PVs from 0 to N = Value of the Annuity

4. The data to the right of the graph show the value of a $100 annuity when the interest rate is 10% and the annuity lasts for 25, 50, and 100 years and forever. The difference between these values shows how much the additional years contribute to the annuity's value. The payments for distant years are worth very little today, so the value of the annuity is determined largely by the payments to be received in the near term. Note, though, that the discount rate affects the values of distant cash flows and thus the graph. The higher the discount rate, the steeper the decline and thus the smaller the values of the distant flows.

Figure 5-3 highlights some important implications for financial issues. For example, if you win a $10 million lottery that pays $500,000 per year for 20 years beginning immediately, the lottery is really worth much less than $10 million. Each cash flow must be discounted, and the sum of the cash flows is much less than $10 million. At a 10% discount rate, the "$10 million" is worth only $4,682,460; and that's before taxes. Not bad, but not $10 million.

SELF TEST

What's the present value of a perpetuity that pays $1,000 per year beginning one year from now if the appropriate interest rate is 5%? What would the value be if payments on the annuity began immediately? **($20,000, $21,000. Hint: Just add the $1,000 to be received immediately to the value of the annuity.)**

Would distant payments contribute more to the value of an annuity if interest rates were high or low? **(Hint: When answering conceptual questions, it often helps to make up an example and use it to formulate your answer. PV of $100 at 5% after 25 years = $29.53; PV at 20% = $1.05. So distant payments contribute more at low rates.)**

5-12 UNEVEN CASH FLOWS

Uneven (Nonconstant) Cash Flows
A series of cash flows where the amount varies from one period to the next.

Payment (PMT)
This term designates equal cash flows coming at regular intervals.

Cash Flow (CF$_t$)
This term designates a cash flow that's not part of an annuity.

The definition of an annuity includes the words *constant payment*—in other words, annuities involve payments that are equal in every period. Although many financial decisions involve constant payments, many others involve **uneven, or nonconstant, cash flows**. For example, the dividends on common stocks typically increase over time, and investments in capital equipment almost always generate uneven cash flows. Throughout the book, we reserve the term **payment (PMT)** for annuities with their equal payments in each period and use the term **cash flow (CF$_t$)** to denote uneven cash flows, where t designates the period in which the cash flow occurs.

There are two important classes of uneven cash flows: (1) a stream that consists of a series of annuity payments plus an additional final lump sum and (2) all other uneven streams. Bonds represent the best example of the first type, while stocks and capital investments illustrate the second type. Here are numerical examples of the two types of flows:

1. Annuity plus additional final payment:

Periods	0	1	2	3	4	5
I = 12%						
Cash flows	$0	$100	$100	$100	$100	$ 100
						$ 1,000
						$1,100

2. Irregular cash flows:

Periods	0	1	2	3	4	5
I = 12%						
Cash flows	$0	$100	$300	$300	$300	$500

We can find the PV of either stream by using Equation 5-7 and following the step-by-step procedure, where we discount each cash flow and then sum them to find the PV of the stream:

5-7
$$PV = \frac{CF_1}{(1+I)^1} + \frac{CF_2}{(1+I)^2} + \cdots + \frac{CF_N}{(1+I)^N} = \sum_{t=1}^{N} \frac{CF_t}{(1+I)^t}$$

If we did this, we would find the PV of Stream 1 to be $927.90 and the PV of Stream 2 to be $1,016.35.

The step-by-step procedure is straightforward; but if we have a large number of cash flows, it is time-consuming. However, financial calculators speed up the process considerably. First, consider Stream 1; notice that we have a 5-year, 12% ordinary annuity plus a final payment of $1,000. We could find the PV of the annuity, then find the PV of the final payment and sum them to obtain the PV of the stream. Financial calculators do this in one simple step—use the five TVM keys, enter the data as shown below, and press the PV key to obtain the answer, $927.90.

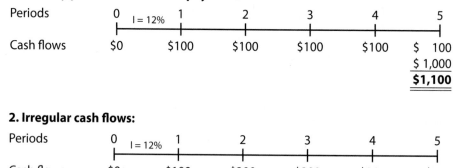

5	12		100	1000
N	I/YR	PV	PMT	FV
		−927.90		

The solution procedure is different for the second uneven stream. Here we must use the step-by-step approach as shown in Figure 5-4. Even calculators and spreadsheets solve the problem using the step-by-step procedure, but they do it

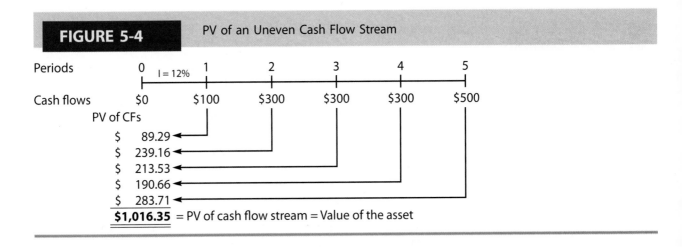

FIGURE 5-4   PV of an Uneven Cash Flow Stream

quickly and efficiently. First, you enter all of the cash flows and the interest rate; then the calculator or computer discounts each cash flow to find its present value and sums these PVs to produce the PV of the stream. You must enter the cash flows in the calculator's "cash flow register," enter the interest rate, and then press the NPV key to find the PV of the stream. NPV stands for "net present value." We cover the calculator mechanics in the tutorial, and we discuss the process in more detail in Chapters 9 and 11, where we use the NPV calculation to analyze stocks and proposed capital budgeting projects. If you don't know how to do the calculation with your calculator, it would be worthwhile to go to the tutorial or your calculator manual, learn the steps, and make sure you can do this calculation. Since you will have to learn to do it eventually, now is a good time to begin.

SELF TEST

How could you use Equation 5-2 to find the PV of an uneven stream of cash flows?

What's the present value of a 5-year ordinary annuity of $100 plus an additional $500 at the end of Year 5 if the interest rate is 6%? What is the PV if the $100 payments occur in Years 1 through 10 and the $500 comes at the end of Year 10? **($794.87; $1,015.21)**

What's the present value of the following uneven cash flow stream: $0 at Time 0, $100 in Year 1 (or at Time 1), $200 in Year 2, $0 in Year 3, and $400 in Year 4 if the interest rate is 8%? **($558.07)**

Would a typical common stock provide cash flows more like an annuity or more like an uneven cash flow stream? Explain.

5-13 FUTURE VALUE OF AN UNEVEN CASH FLOW STREAM

We find the future value of uneven cash flow streams by compounding rather than discounting. Consider Cash Flow Stream 2 in the preceding section. We discounted those cash flows to find the PV, but we would compound them to find the FV. Figure 5-5 illustrates the procedure for finding the FV of the stream using the step-by-step approach.

FIGURE 5-5	FV of an Uneven Cash Flow Stream

Periods

0		1	2	3	4	5
	I = 12%					

Cash flows

$0	$100	$300	$300	$300	$500

$ 500.00
$ 336.00
$ 376.32
$ 421.48
$ 157.35
$ 0.00
$1,791.15

The values of all financial assets—stocks, bonds, and business capital investments—are found as the present values of their expected future cash flows. Therefore, we need to calculate present values very often, far more often than future values. As a result, all financial calculators provide automated functions for finding PVs, but they generally do not provide automated FV functions. On the relatively few occasions when we need to find the FV of an uneven cash flow stream, we generally use the step-by-step procedure shown in Figure 5-5. That approach works for all cash flow streams, even those for which some cash flows are zero or negative.

SELF TEST

Why are we more likely to need to calculate the PV of cash flow streams than the FV of streams?

What is the future value of this cash flow stream: $100 at the end of 1 year, $150 due after 2 years, and $300 due after 3 years if the appropriate interest rate is 15%? **($604.75)**

5-14 SOLVING FOR I WITH UNEVEN CASH FLOWS[8]

Before financial calculators and spreadsheets existed, it was *extremely difficult* to find I when the cash flows were uneven. With spreadsheets and financial calculators, though, it's relatively easy to find I. If you have an annuity plus a final lump sum, you can input values for N, PV, PMT, and FV into the calculator's TVM registers and then press the I/YR key. Here is the setup for Stream 1 from Section 5-12, assuming we must pay $927.90 to buy the asset. The rate of return on the $927.90 investment is 12%.

5		−927.90	100	1000
N	I/YR	PV	PMT	FV
	12.00			

[8]This section is relatively technical. It can be deferred at this point, but the calculations will be required in Chapter 11.

Finding the interest rate for an uneven cash flow stream such as Stream 2 is a bit more complicated. First, note that there is no simple procedure—finding the rate requires a trial-and-error process, which means that a financial calculator or a spreadsheet is needed. With a calculator, we enter the CFs into the cash flow register and then press the IRR key to get the answer. IRR stands for "internal rate of return," and it is the rate of return the investment provides. The investment is the cash flow at Time 0, and it must be entered as a negative. As an illustration, consider the cash flows given here, where $CF_0 = -\$1,000$ is the cost of the asset.

Periods	0	1	2	3	4	5
Cash flows	−$1,000	$100	$300	$300	$300	$500
IRR = I =	12.55%					

When we enter those cash flows into the calculator's cash flow register and press the IRR key, we get the rate of return on the $1,000 investment, 12.55%. You get the same answer using Excel's IRR function. The process is covered in the calculator tutorial; it is also discussed in Chapter 11, where we study capital budgeting.

SELF TEST

An investment costs $465 and is expected to produce cash flows of $100 at the end of each of the next 4 years, then an extra lump sum payment of $200 at the end of the fourth year. What is the expected rate of return on this investment? **(9.05%)**

An investment costs $465 and is expected to produce cash flows of $100 at the end of Year 1, $200 at the end of Year 2, and $300 at the end of Year 3. What is the expected rate of return on this investment? **(11.71%)**

5-15 SEMIANNUAL AND OTHER COMPOUNDING PERIODS

In all of our examples thus far, we assumed that interest was compounded once a year, or annually. This is called **annual compounding**. Suppose, however, that you deposit $100 in a bank that pays a 5% annual interest rate but credits interest each 6 months. So in the second 6-month period, you earn interest on your original $100 plus interest on the interest earned during the first 6 months. This is called **semiannual compounding**. Note that banks generally pay interest more than once a year; virtually all bonds pay interest semiannually; and most mortgages, student loans, and auto loans require monthly payments. Therefore, it is important to understand how to deal with nonannual compounding.

For an illustration of semiannual compounding, assume that we deposit $100 in an account that pays 5% and leave it there for 10 years. First, consider again what the future value would be under *annual* compounding:

$$FV_N = PV(1 + I)^N = \$100(1.05)^{10} = \$162.89$$

We would, of course, get the same answer using a financial calculator or a spreadsheet.

How would things change in this example if interest was paid semiannually rather than annually? First, whenever payments occur more than once a year, you must make two conversions: (1) Convert the stated interest rate into a "periodic rate" and (2) convert the number of years into "number of periods." The

Annual Compounding
The arithmetic process of determining the final value of a cash flow or series of cash flows when interest is added once a year.

Semiannual Compounding
The arithmetic process of determining the final value of a cash flow or series of cash flows when interest is added twice a year.

conversions are done as follows, where I is the stated annual rate, M is the number of compounding periods per year, and N is the number of years:

| 5-8 | $$\text{Periodic rate}(I_{PER}) = \frac{\text{Stated annual rate}}{\text{Number of payments per year}} = I/M$$ |

With a stated annual rate of 5% compounded semiannually, the periodic rate is 2.5%:

$$\text{Periodic rate} = 5\%/2 = 2.5\%$$

The number of compounding periods per year is found with Equation 5-9:

| 5-9 | $$\text{Number of periods} = (\text{Number of years})(\text{Periods per year}) = NM$$ |

With 10 years and semiannual compounding, there are 20 periods:

$$\text{Number of periods} = 10(2) = 20 \text{ periods}$$

Under semiannual compounding, our $100 investment will earn 2.5% every 6 months for 20 semiannual periods, not 5% per year for 10 years. The periodic rate and number of periods, not the annual rate and number of years, must be shown on time lines and entered into the calculator or spreadsheet whenever you are working with nonannual compounding.[9]

With this background, we can find the value of $100 after 10 years if it is held in an account that pays a stated annual rate of 5.0% but with semiannual compounding. Here's the time line and the future value:

Periods	0		1	2		19	20
		$I = 2.5\%$			$\cdots$		
Cash flows	$-\$100$						

$$\rightarrow PV\,(1+I)^N = \$100(1.025)^{20} = FV_{20} = \$163.86$$

With a financial calculator, we get the same result using the periodic rate and number of periods:

20	2.5	−100	0	
N	I/YR	PV	PMT	FV
				163.86

The future value under semiannual compounding, $163.86, exceeds the FV under annual compounding, $162.89, because interest starts accruing sooner; thus, you earn more interest on interest.

How would things change in our example if interest was compounded quarterly or monthly or daily? With quarterly compounding, there would be $NM = 10(4) = 40$ periods and the periodic rate would be $I/M = 5\%/4 = 1.25\%$ per quarter. Using those values, we would find FV = $164.36. If we used monthly compounding, we would have $10(12) = 120$ periods, the monthly rate would be $5\%/12 = 0.416667\%$, and the FV would rise to $164.70. If we went to daily compounding, we would have $10(365) = 3{,}650$ periods, the daily rate would be $5\%/365 = 0.0136986\%$ per day, and the FV would be $164.87 (based on a 365-day year).

---

[9]With some financial calculators, you can enter the annual (nominal) rate and the number of compounding periods per year rather than make the conversions we recommend. We prefer the conversions because they must be used on time lines and because it is easy to forget to reset your calculator after you change its settings, which may lead to an error on your next problem.

The same logic applies when we find present values under semiannual compounding. Again, we use Equation 5-8 to convert the stated annual rate to the periodic (semiannual) rate and Equation 5-9 to find the number of semiannual periods. We then use the periodic rate and number of periods in the calculations. For example, we can find the PV of $100 due after 10 years when the stated annual rate is 5%, with semiannual compounding:

$$\text{Periodic rate} = 5\%/2 = 2.5\% \text{ per period}$$
$$\text{Number of periods} = 10(2) = 20 \text{ periods}$$
$$\text{PV of }\$100 = \$100/(1.025)^{20} = \$61.03$$

We would get this same result with a financial calculator:

20	2.5		0	−100
N	I/YR	PV	PMT	FV
		61.03		

If we increased the number of compounding periods from 2 (semiannual) to 12 (monthly), the PV would decline to $60.72; and if we went to daily compounding, the PV would fall to $60.66.

SELF TEST

Would you rather invest in an account that pays 7% with annual compounding or 7% with monthly compounding? Would you rather borrow at 7% and make annual or monthly payments? Why?

What's the *future value* of $100 after 3 years if the appropriate interest rate is 8% compounded annually? compounded monthly? **($125.97; $127.02)**

What's the *present value* of $100 due in three years if the appropriate interest rate is 8% compounded annually? compounded monthly? **($79.38; $78.73)**

5-16 COMPARING INTEREST RATES

Different compounding periods are used for different types of investments. For example, bank accounts generally pay interest daily; most bonds pay interest semiannually; stocks pay dividends quarterly; and mortgages, auto loans, and other instruments require monthly payments.[10] If we are to compare investments or loans with different compounding periods properly, we need to put them on a common basis. Here are some terms you need to understand:

- The **nominal interest rate (I_{NOM})**, also called the **annual percentage rate (APR)** (or **quoted** or **stated rate**), is the rate that credit card companies, student loan officers, auto dealers, and so forth, tell you they are charging on loans. Note that if two banks offer loans with a stated rate of 8% but one requires monthly payments and the other quarterly payments, they are not charging the same "true" rate—the one that requires monthly payments is charging more than the one with quarterly payments because it will get your

Nominal (Quoted, or Stated) Interest Rate, I_{NOM}
The contracted (or quoted or stated) interest rate.

Annual Percentage Rate (APR)
The periodic rate times the number of periods per year.

[10]Some banks even pay interest compounded continuously. Continuous compounding is discussed in Web Appendix 5A.

money sooner. So to compare loans across lenders, or interest rates earned on different securities, you should calculate effective annual rates as described here.[11]

Effective (Equivalent) Annual Rate (EFF% or EAR)

The annual rate of interest actually being earned, as opposed to the quoted rate. Also called the "equivalent annual rate."

- The **effective annual rate,** abbreviated **EFF%,** is also called the **equivalent annual rate (EAR)**. This is the rate that would produce the same future value under annual compounding as would more frequent compounding at a given nominal rate.

- If a loan or an investment uses annual compounding, its nominal rate is also its effective rate. However, if compounding occurs more than once a year, the EFF% is higher than I_{NOM}.

- To illustrate, a nominal rate of 10% with semiannual compounding is equivalent to a rate of 10.25% with annual compounding because both rates will cause $100 to grow to the same amount after 1 year. The top line in the following diagram shows that $100 will grow to $110.25 at a nominal rate of 10.25%. The lower line shows the situation if the nominal rate is 10% but semiannual compounding is used.

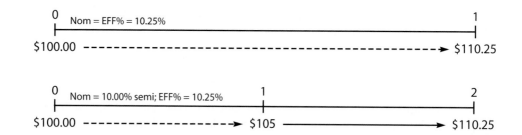

Given the nominal rate and the number of compounding periods per year, we can find the effective annual rate with this equation:

5-10 $$\text{Effective annual rate (EFF\%)} = \left(1 + \frac{I_{NOM}}{M}\right)^M - 1.0$$

Here I_{NOM} is the nominal rate expressed as a decimal and M is the number of compounding periods per year. In our example, the nominal rate is 10%; but with semiannual compounding, $I_{NOM} = 10\% = 0.10$ and M = 2. This results in EFF% = 10.25%:[12]

$$\text{Effective annual rate (EFF\%)} = \left(1 + \frac{0.10}{2}\right)^2 - 1 = 0.1025 = 10.25\%$$

Thus, if one investment promises to pay 10% with semiannual compounding and an equally risky investment promises 10.25% with annual compounding, we would be indifferent between the two.

---

[11]Note, though, that if you are comparing two bonds that both pay interest semiannually, it's OK to compare their nominal rates. Similarly, you can compare the nominal rates on two money funds that pay interest daily. But don't compare the nominal rate on a semiannual bond with the nominal rate on a money fund that compounds daily because that will make the money fund look worse than it really is.

[12]Most financial calculators are programmed to find the EFF% or, given the EFF%, to find the nominal rate. This is called interest rate conversion. You enter the nominal rate and the number of compounding periods per year and then press the EFF% key to find the effective annual rate. However, we generally use Equation 5-10 because it's as easy to use as the interest conversion feature and the equation reminds us of what we are really doing. If you use the interest rate conversion feature on your calculator, don't forget to reset your calculator settings. Interest rate conversion is discussed in the calculator tutorials. Interest rate conversion is also very easy using Excel. For details, look at the spreadsheet model that accompanies this chapter.

Define the terms *annual percentage rate (APR)*, *effective annual rate (EFF%)*, and *nominal interest rate* (I_{NOM}).

A bank pays 5% with daily compounding on its savings accounts. Should it advertise the nominal or effective rate if it is seeking to attract new deposits?

By law, credit card issuers must print their annual percentage rate on their monthly statements. A common APR is 18% with interest paid monthly. What is the EFF% on such a loan? [**EFF% = $(1 + 0.18/12)^{12} - 1 = 0.1956 = 19.56\%$**]

Some years ago banks didn't have to reveal the rates they charged on credit cards. Then Congress passed the Truth in Lending Act that required banks to publish their APRs. Is the APR really the "most truthful" rate, or would the EFF% be "more truthful"? Explain.

5-17 FRACTIONAL TIME PERIODS

Thus far we have assumed that payments occur at the beginning or the end of periods but not *within* periods. However, we often encounter situations that require compounding or discounting over fractional periods. For example, suppose you deposited $100 in a bank that pays a nominal rate of 10% but adds interest daily, based on a 365-day year. How much would you have after 9 months? The answer is $107.79, found as follows:[13]

$$\text{Periodic rate} = I_{PER} = 0.10/365 = 0.000273973 \text{ per day}$$
$$\text{Number of days} = (9/12)(365) = 0.75(365) = 273.75 \text{ rounded to } 274$$
$$\text{Ending amount} = \$100(1.000273973)^{274} = \$107.79$$

Now suppose you borrow $100 from a bank whose nominal rate is 10% per year simple interest, which means that interest is not earned on interest. If the loan is outstanding for 274 days, how much interest would you have to pay? Here we would calculate a daily interest rate, I_{PER}, as just shown, but multiply it by 274 rather than use the 274 as an exponent:

$$\text{Interest owed} = \$100(0.000273973)(274) = \$7.51$$

You would owe the bank a total of $107.51 after 274 days. This is the procedure that most banks use to calculate interest on loans, except that they require borrowers to pay the interest on a monthly basis rather than after 274 days.

Suppose a company borrowed $1 million at a rate of 9%, simple interest, with interest paid at the end of each month. The bank uses a 360-day year. How much interest would the firm have to pay in a 30-day month? What would the interest be if the bank used a 365-day year? [**$(0.09/360)(30)(\$1,000,000) = \$7,500$ interest for the month. For the 365-day year, $(0.09/365)(30)(\$1,000,000) = \$7,397.26$ of interest. The use of a 360-day year raises the interest cost by $102.74, which is why banks like to use it on loans.**]

Suppose you deposited $1,000 in a credit union that pays 7% with daily compounding and a 365-day year. What is the EFF%, and how much could you withdraw after seven months, assuming this is seven-twelfths of a year? [**EFF% = $(1 + 0.07/365)^{365} - 1 = 0.07250098 = 7.250098\%$. Thus, your account would grow from $1,000 to $1,000(1.07250098)^{0.583333} = \$1,041.67$, and you could withdraw that amount.**]

---

[13]Bank loan contracts specifically state whether they are based on a 360- or a 365-day year. If a 360-day year is used, the daily rate is higher, which means that the effective rate is also higher. Here we assumed a 365-day year. Also note that in real-world calculations, banks' computers have built-in calendars so they can calculate the exact number of days, taking account of 30-day, 31-day, and 28- or 29-day months.

5-18 AMORTIZED LOANS[14]

Amortized Loan

A loan that is repaid in equal payments over its life.

An important application of compound interest involves loans that are paid off in installments over time. Included are automobile loans, home mortgage loans, student loans, and many business loans. A loan that is to be repaid in equal amounts on a monthly, quarterly, or annual basis is called an **amortized loan**.[15]

Table 5-4 illustrates the amortization process. A homeowner borrows $100,000 on a mortgage loan, and the loan is to be repaid in five equal payments at the end of each of the next 5 years.[16] The lender charges 6% on the balance at the beginning of each year.

Our first task is to determine the payment the homeowner must make each year. Here's a picture of the situation:

0	I = 6%	1	2	3	4	5
$100,000		PMT	PMT	PMT	PMT	PMT

The payments must be such that the sum of their PVs equals $100,000:

$$\$100{,}000 = \frac{PMT}{(1.06)^1} + \frac{PMT}{(1.06)^2} + \frac{PMT}{(1.06)^3} + \frac{PMT}{(1.06)^4} + \frac{PMT}{(1.06)^5} = \sum_{t=1}^{5} \frac{PMT}{(1.06)^t}$$

We could insert values into a calculator as follows to get the required payments, $23,739.64:[17]

5	6	100000		0
N	I/YR	PV	PMT	FV
			−23,739.64	

Table 5-4

Loan Amortization Schedule, $100,000 at 6% for 5 Years

Amount borrowed: $100,000
Years: 5
Rate: 6%
PMT: −$23,739.64

Year	Beginning Amount (1)	Payment (2)	Interest[a] (3)	Repayment of Principal[b] (4)	Ending Balance (5)
1	$100,000.00	$23,739.64	$6,000.00	$17,739.64	$82,260.36
2	82,260.36	23,739.64	4,935.62	18,804.02	63,456.34
3	63,456.34	23,739.64	3,807.38	19,932.26	43,524.08
4	43,524.08	23,739.64	2,611.44	21,128.20	22,395.89
5	22,395.89	23,739.64	1,343.75	22,395.89	0.00

[a]Interest in each period is calculated by multiplying the loan balance at the beginning of the year by the interest rate. Therefore, interest in Year 1 is $100,000.00(0.06) = $6,000; in Year 2, it is $4,935.62; and so forth.
[b]Repayment of principal is equal to the payment of $23,739.64 minus the interest charge for the year.

---

[14]Amortized loans are important, but this section can be omitted without loss of continuity.
[15]The word *amortized* comes from the Latin *mors*, meaning "death"; so an amortized loan is one that is "killed off" over time.
[16]Most mortgage loans call for monthly payments over 10 to 30 years, but we use a shorter period to reduce the calculations.
[17]You could also factor out the PMT term; find the value of the remaining summation term (4.212364); and divide it into the $100,000 to find the payment, $23,739.64.

Therefore, the borrower must pay the lender $23,739.64 per year for the next 5 years.

Each payment will consist of two parts—interest and repayment of principal. This breakdown is shown on an **amortization schedule** such as the one in Table 5-4. The interest component is relatively high in the first year, but it declines as the loan balance decreases. For tax purposes, the borrower would deduct the interest component while the lender would report the same amount as taxable income.

Amortization Schedule
A table showing precisely how a loan will be repaid. It gives the required payment on each payment date and a breakdown of the payment, showing how much is interest and how much is repayment of principal.

> **SELF TEST**
>
> Suppose you borrowed $30,000 on a student loan at a rate of 8% and must repay it in three equal installments at the end of each of the next 3 years. How large would your payments be, how much of the first payment would represent interest, how much would be principal, and what would your ending balance be after the first year? **(PMT = $11,641.01; Interest = $2,400; Principal = $9,241.01; Balance at end of Year 1 = $20,758.99)**

TYING IT ALL TOGETHER

In this chapter, we worked with single payments, ordinary annuities, annuities due, perpetuities, and uneven cash flow streams. One fundamental equation, Equation 5-1, is used to calculate the future value of a given amount. The equation can be transformed to Equation 5-2 and then used to find the present value of a given future amount. We used time lines to show when cash flows occur; and we saw that time value problems can be solved in a step-by-step manner when we work with individual cash flows, with formulas that streamline the approach, with financial calculators, and with spreadsheets.

As we noted at the outset, TVM is the single most important concept in finance and the procedures developed in Chapter 5 are used throughout this book. Time value analysis is used to find the values of stocks, bonds, and capital budgeting projects. It is also used to analyze personal finance problems, such as the retirement issue set forth in the opening vignette. You will become more familiar with time value analysis as you go through the book, but we *strongly recommend* that you get a good handle on Chapter 5 before you continue.

SELF-TEST QUESTIONS AND PROBLEMS
(Solutions Appear in Appendix A)

ST-1 **KEY TERMS** Define each of the following terms:
   a. Time line
   b. FV_N; PV; I; INT; N; FVA_N; PMT; PVA_N
   c. Compounding; discounting
   d. Simple interest; compound interest
   e. Opportunity cost
   f. Annuity; ordinary (deferred) annuity; annuity due
   g. Consol; perpetuity

h.   Uneven cash flow; payment; cash flow (CFt)

i.   Annual compounding; semiannual compounding

j.   Nominal (quoted) interest rate; annual percentage rate (APR); effective (equivalent) annual rate (EAR or EFF%)

k.   Amortized loan; amortization schedule

ST-2   **FUTURE VALUE**   It is now January 1, 2009. Today you will deposit $1,000 into a savings account that pays 8%.

a.   If the bank compounds interest annually, how much will you have in your account on January 1, 2012?

b.   What will your January 1, 2012, balance be if the bank uses quarterly compounding?

c.   Suppose you deposit $1,000 in three payments of $333.333 each on January 1 of 2010, 2011, and 2012. How much will you have in your account on January 1, 2012, based on 8% annual compounding?

d.   How much will be in your account if the three payments begin on January 1, 2009?

e.   Suppose you deposit three equal payments into your account on January 1 of 2010, 2011, and 2012. Assuming an 8% interest rate, how large must your payments be to have the same ending balance as in Part a?

ST-3   **TIME VALUE OF MONEY**   It is now January 1, 2009; and you will need $1,000 on January 1, 2013, in 4 years. Your bank compounds interest at an 8% annual rate.

a.   How much must you deposit today to have a balance of $1,000 on January 1, 2013?

b.   If you want to make four equal payments on each January 1 from 2010 through 2013 to accumulate the $1,000, how large must each payment be? (Note that the payments begin a year from today.)

c.   If your father offers to make the payments calculated in Part b ($221.92) or to give you $750 on January 1, 2010 (a year from today), which would you choose? Explain.

d.   If you have only $750 on January 1, 2010, what interest rate, compounded annually for 3 years, must you earn to have $1,000 on January 1, 2013?

e.   Suppose you can deposit only $200 each January 1 from 2010 through 2013 (4 years). What interest rate, with annual compounding, must you earn to end up with $1,000 on January 1, 2013?

f.   Your father offers to give you $400 on January 1, 2010. You will then make six additional equal payments each 6 months from July 2010 through January 2013. If your bank pays 8% compounded semiannually, how large must each payment be for you to end up with $1,000 on January 1, 2013?

g.   What is the EAR, or EFF%, earned on the bank account in Part f? What is the APR earned on the account?

ST-4   **EFFECTIVE ANNUAL RATES**   Bank A offers loans at an 8% nominal rate (its APR) but requires that interest be paid quarterly; that is, it uses quarterly compounding. Bank B wants to charge the same effective rate on its loans but it wants to collect interest on a monthly basis, that is, use monthly compounding. What nominal rate must Bank B set?

QUESTIONS

5-1   What is an *opportunity cost?* How is this concept used in TVM analysis, and where is it shown on a time line? Is a single number used in all situations? Explain.

5-2   Explain whether the following statement is true or false: $100 a year for 10 years is an annuity; but $100 in Year 1, $200 in Year 2, and $400 in Years 3 through 10 does *not* constitute an annuity. However, the second series *contains* an annuity.

5-3   If a firm's earnings per share grew from $1 to $2 over a 10-year period, the *total growth* would be 100%, but the *annual growth rate* would be *less than* 10%. True or false? Explain. (Hint: If you aren't sure, plug in some numbers and check it out.)

5-4   Would you rather have a savings account that pays 5% interest compounded semiannually or one that pays 5% interest compounded daily? Explain.

5-5   To find the present value of an uneven series of cash flows, you must find the PVs of the individual cash flows and then sum them. Annuity procedures can never be of use, even when some of the cash flows constitute an annuity because the entire series is not an annuity. True or false? Explain.

5-6   The present value of a perpetuity is equal to the payment on the annuity, PMT, divided by the interest rate, I: $PV - PMT/I$. What is the *future value* of a perpetuity of PMT dollars per year? (Hint: The answer is infinity, but explain why.)

5-7   Banks and other lenders are required to disclose a rate called the APR. What is this rate? Why did Congress require that it be disclosed? Is it the same as the effective annual rate? If you were comparing the costs of loans from different lenders, could you use their APRs to determine the loan with the lowest effective interest rate? Explain.

5-8   What is a loan amortization schedule, and what are some ways these schedules are used?

PROBLEMS

Easy Problems 1–8

5-1   **FUTURE VALUE**   If you deposit $10,000 in a bank account that pays 10% interest annually, how much will be in your account after 5 years?

5-2   **PRESENT VALUE**   What is the present value of a security that will pay $5,000 in 20 years if securities of equal risk pay 7% annually?

5-3   **FINDING THE REQUIRED INTEREST RATE**   Your parents will retire in 18 years. They currently have $250,000, and they think they will need $1,000,000 at retirement. What annual interest rate must they earn to reach their goal, assuming they don't save any additional funds?

5-4   **TIME FOR A LUMP SUM TO DOUBLE**   If you deposit money today in an account that pays 6.5% annual interest, how long will it take to double your money?

5-5   **TIME TO REACH A FINANCIAL GOAL**   You have $42,180.53 in a brokerage account, and you plan to deposit an additional $5,000 at the end of every future year until your account totals $250,000. You expect to earn 12% annually on the account. How many years will it take to reach your goal?

5-6   **FUTURE VALUE: ANNUITY VERSUS ANNUITY DUE**   What's the future value of a 7%, 5-year ordinary annuity that pays $300 each year? If this was an annuity due, what would its future value be?

5-7   **PRESENT AND FUTURE VALUES OF A CASH FLOW STREAM**   An investment will pay $100 at the end of each of the next 3 years, $200 at the end of Year 4, $300 at the end of Year 5, and $500 at the end of Year 6. If other investments of equal risk earn 8% annually, what is its present value? its future value?

5-8   **LOAN AMORTIZATION AND EAR**   You want to buy a car, and a local bank will lend you $20,000. The loan will be fully amortized over 5 years (60 months), and the nominal interest rate will be 12% with interest paid monthly. What will be the monthly loan payment? What will be the loan's EAR?

Intermediate Problems 9–26

5-9   **PRESENT AND FUTURE VALUES FOR DIFFERENT PERIODS**   Find the following values *using the equations* and then a financial calculator. Compounding/discounting occurs annually.

a.   An initial $500 compounded for 1 year at 6%

b.   An initial $500 compounded for 2 years at 6%

c.   The present value of $500 due in 1 year at a discount rate of 6%

d.   The present value of $500 due in 2 years at a discount rate of 6%

5-10   **PRESENT AND FUTURE VALUES FOR DIFFERENT INTEREST RATES**   Find the following values. Compounding/discounting occurs annually.

a.   An initial $500 compounded for 10 years at 6%

b.   An initial $500 compounded for 10 years at 12%

c.   The present value of $500 due in 10 years at 6%

d.   The present value of $1,552.90 due in 10 years at 12% and at 6%

e.   Define *present value* and illustrate it using a time line with data from Part d. How are present values affected by interest rates?

5-11 **GROWTH RATES** Shalit Corporation's 2008 sales were $12 million. Its 2003 sales were $6 million.

a. At what rate have sales been growing?

b. Suppose someone made this statement: "Sales doubled in 5 years. This represents a growth of 100% in 5 years; so dividing 100% by 5, we find the growth rate to be 20% per year." Is that statement correct?

5-12 **EFFECTIVE RATE OF INTEREST** Find the interest rates earned on each of the following:

a. You *borrow* $700 and promise to pay back $749 at the end of 1 year.

b. You *lend* $700 and the borrower promises to pay you $749 at the end of 1 year.

c. You *borrow* $85,000 and promise to pay back $201,229 at the end of 10 years.

d. You *borrow* $9,000 and promise to make payments of $2,684.80 at the end of each year for 5 years.

5-13 **TIME FOR A LUMP SUM TO DOUBLE** How long will it take $200 to double if it earns the following rates? Compounding occurs once a year.

a. 7%

b. 10%

c. 18%

d. 100%

5-14 **FUTURE VALUE OF AN ANNUITY** Find the *future values* of these *ordinary annuities*. Compounding occurs once a year.

a. $400 per year for 10 years at 10%

b. $200 per year for 5 years at 5%

c. $400 per year for 5 years at 0%

d. Rework Parts a, b, and c assuming they are *annuities due*.

5-15 **PRESENT VALUE OF AN ANNUITY** Find the *present values* of these *ordinary annuities*. Discounting occurs once a year.

a. $400 per year for 10 years at 10%

b. $200 per year for 5 years at 5%

c. $400 per year for 5 years at 0%

d. Rework Parts a, b, and c assuming they are *annuities due*.

5-16 **PRESENT VALUE OF A PERPETUITY** What is the present value of a $100 perpetuity if the interest rate is 7%? If interest rates doubled to 14%, what would its present value be?

5-17 **EFFECTIVE INTEREST RATE** You borrow $85,000; the annual loan payments are $8,273.59 for 30 years. What interest rate are you being charged?

5-18 **UNEVEN CASH FLOW STREAM**

a. Find the present values of the following cash flow streams at 8% compounded annually.

	0	1	2	3	4	5
Stream A	$0	$100	$400	$400	$400	$300
Stream B	$0	$300	$400	$400	$400	$100

b. What are the PVs of the streams at 0% compounded annually?

5-19 **FUTURE VALUE OF AN ANNUITY** Your client is 40 years old; and she wants to begin saving for retirement, with the first payment to come one year from now. She can save $5,000 per year; and you advise her to invest it in the stock market, which you expect to provide an average return of 9% in the future.

a. If she follows your advice, how much money will she have at 65?

b. How much will she have at 70?

c. She expects to live for 20 years if she retires at 65 and for 15 years if she retires at 70. If her investments continue to earn the same rate, how much will she be able to withdraw at the end of each year after retirement at each retirement age?

5-20   **PV OF A CASH FLOW STREAM**   A rookie quarterback is negotiating his first NFL contract. His opportunity cost is 10%. He has been offered three possible 4-year contracts. Payments are guaranteed, and they would be made at the end of each year. Terms of each contract are as follows:

	1	2	3	4
Contract 1	$3,000,000	$3,000,000	$3,000,000	$3,000,000
Contract 2	$2,000,000	$3,000,000	$4,000,000	$5,000,000
Contract 3	$7,000,000	$1,000,000	$1,000,000	$1,000,000

As his adviser, which contract would you recommend that he accept?

5-21   **EVALUATING LUMP SUMS AND ANNUITIES**   Crissie just won the lottery, and she must choose between three award options. She can elect to receive a lump sum today of $61 million, to receive 10 end-of-year payments of $9.5 million, or to receive 30 end-of-year payments of $5.5 million.

    a.   If she thinks she can earn 7% annually, which should she choose?

    b.   If she expects to earn 8% annually, which is the best choice?

    c.   If she expects to earn 9% annually, which option would you recommend?

    d.   Explain how interest rates influence the optimal choice.

5-22   **LOAN AMORTIZATION**   Jan sold her house on December 31 and took a $10,000 mortgage as part of the payment. The 10-year mortgage has a 10% nominal interest rate, but it calls for semiannual payments beginning next June 30. Next year Jan must report on Schedule B of her IRS Form 1040 the amount of interest that was included in the two payments she received during the year.

    a.   What is the dollar amount of each payment Jan receives?

    b.   How much interest was included in the first payment? How much repayment of principal was included? How do these values change for the second payment?

    c.   How much interest must Jan report on Schedule B for the first year? Will her interest income be the same next year?

    d.   If the payments are constant, why does the amount of interest income change over time?

5-23   **FUTURE VALUE FOR VARIOUS COMPOUNDING PERIODS**   Find the amount to which $500 will grow under each of these conditions:

    a.   12% compounded annually for 5 years

    b.   12% compounded semiannually for 5 years

    c.   12% compounded quarterly for 5 years

    d.   12% compounded monthly for 5 years

    e.   12% compounded daily for 5 years

    f.   Why does the observed pattern of FVs occur?

5-24   **PRESENT VALUE FOR VARIOUS DISCOUNTING PERIODS**   Find the present value of $500 due in the future under each of these conditions:

    a.   12% nominal rate, semiannual compounding, discounted back 5 years

    b.   12% nominal rate, quarterly compounding, discounted back 5 years

    c.   12% nominal rate, monthly compounding, discounted back 1 year

    d.   Why do the differences in the PVs occur?

5-25   **FUTURE VALUE OF AN ANNUITY**   Find the future values of the following ordinary annuities:

    a.   FV of $400 paid each 6 months for 5 years at a nominal rate of 12% compounded semiannually

    b.   FV of $200 paid each 3 months for 5 years at a nominal rate of 12% compounded quarterly

    c.   These annuities receive the same amount of cash during the 5-year period and earn interest at the same nominal rate, yet the annuity in Part b ends up larger than the one in Part a. Why does this occur?

5-26 **PV AND LOAN ELIGIBILITY** You have saved $4,000 for a down payment on a new car. The largest monthly payment you can afford is $350. The loan will have a 12% APR based on end-of-month payments. What is the most expensive car you can afford if you finance it for 48 months? for 60 months?

Challenging Problems 27–40

5-27 **EFFECTIVE VERSUS NOMINAL INTEREST RATES** Bank A pays 4% interest compounded annually on deposits, while Bank B pays 3.5% compounded daily.

    a. Based on the EAR (or EFF%), which bank should you use?

    b. Could your choice of banks be influenced by the fact that you might want to withdraw your funds during the year as opposed to at the end of the year? Assume that your funds must be left on deposit during an entire compounding period in order to receive any interest.

5-28 **NOMINAL INTEREST RATE AND EXTENDING CREDIT** As a jewelry store manager, you want to offer credit, with interest on outstanding balances paid monthly. To carry receivables, you must borrow funds from your bank at a nominal 6%, monthly compounding. To offset your overhead, you want to charge your customers an EAR (or EFF%) that is 2% more than the bank is charging you. What APR rate should you charge your customers?

5-29 **BUILDING CREDIT COST INTO PRICES** Your firm sells for cash only; but it is thinking of offering credit, allowing customers 90 days to pay. Customers understand the time value of money, so they would all wait and pay on the 90th day. To carry these receivables, you would have to borrow funds from your bank at a nominal 12%, daily compounding based on a 360-day year. You want to increase your base prices by exactly enough to offset your bank interest cost. To the closest whole percentage point, by how much should you raise your product prices?

5-30 **REACHING A FINANCIAL GOAL** Erika and Kitty, who are twins, just received $30,000 each for their 25th birthday. They both have aspirations to become millionaires. Each plans to make a $5,000 annual contribution to her "early retirement fund" on her birthday, beginning a year from today. Erika opened an account with the Safety First Bond Fund, a mutual fund that invests in high-quality bonds whose investors have earned 6% per year in the past. Kitty invested in the New Issue Bio-Tech Fund, which invests in small, newly issued bio-tech stocks and whose investors have earned an average of 20% per year in the fund's relatively short history.

    a. If the two women's funds earn the same returns in the future as in the past, how old will each be when she becomes a millionaire?

    b. How large would Erika's annual contributions have to be for her to become a millionaire at the same age as Kitty, assuming their expected returns are realized?

    c. Is it rational or irrational for Erika to invest in the bond fund rather than in stocks?

5-31 **REQUIRED LUMP SUM PAYMENT** Starting next year, you will need $10,000 annually for 4 years to complete your education. (One year from today you will withdraw the first $10,000.) Your uncle deposits an amount *today* in a bank paying 5% annual interest, which will provide the needed $10,000 payments.

    a. How large must the deposit be?

    b. How much will be in the account immediately after you make the first withdrawal?

5-32 **REACHING A FINANCIAL GOAL** Six years from today you need $10,000. You plan to deposit $1,500 annually, with the first payment to be made a year from today, in an account that pays an 8% effective annual rate. Your last deposit, which will occur at the end of Year 6, will be for less than $1,500 if less is needed to reach $10,000. How large will your last payment be?

5-33 **FV OF UNEVEN CASH FLOW** You want to buy a house within 3 years, and you are currently saving for the down payment. You plan to save $5,000 at the end of the first year, and you anticipate that your annual savings will increase by 10% annually thereafter. Your expected annual return is 7%. How much will you have for a down payment at the end of Year 3?

5-34 **AMORTIZATION SCHEDULE**

    a. Set up an amortization schedule for a $25,000 loan to be repaid in equal installments at the end of each of the next 3 years. The interest rate is 10% compounded annually.

    b. What percentage of the payment represents interest and what percentage represents principal for each of the 3 years? Why do these percentages change over time?

5-35 **AMORTIZATION SCHEDULE WITH A BALLOON PAYMENT** You want to buy a house that costs $100,000. You have $10,000 for a down payment, but your credit is such that mortgage companies will not lend you the required $90,000. However, the realtor persuades the seller to take a $90,000 mortgage (called a seller take-back mortgage) at a rate of 7%, provided the loan is paid off in full in 3 years. You expect to inherit $100,000 in 3 years; but right now all you have is $10,000, and you can afford to make payments of no more than $7,500 per year given your salary. (The loan would call for monthly payments, but assume end-of-year annual payments to simplify things.)

a.   If the loan was amortized over 3 years, how large would each annual payment be? Could you afford those payments?

b.   If the loan was amortized over 30 years, what would each payment be? Could you afford those payments?

c.   To satisfy the seller, the 30-year mortgage loan would be written as a balloon note, which means that at the end of the third year, you would have to make the regular payment plus the remaining balance on the loan. What would the loan balance be at the end of Year 3, and what would the balloon payment be?

5-36   NONANNUAL COMPOUNDING

a.   You plan to make five deposits of $1,000 each, one every 6 months, with the first payment being made in 6 months. You will then make no more deposits. If the bank pays 4% nominal interest, compounded semiannually, how much will be in your account after 3 years?

b.   One year from today you must make a payment of $10,000. To prepare for this payment, you plan to make two equal quarterly deposits (at the end of Quarters 1 and 2) in a bank that pays 4% nominal interest compounded quarterly. How large must each of the two payments be?

5-37   PAYING OFF CREDIT CARDS   Simon recently received a credit card with an 18% nominal interest rate. With the card, he purchased a new stereo for $350. The minimum payment on the card is only $10 per month.

a.   If Simon makes the minimum monthly payment and makes no other charges, how many months will it be before he pays off the card? Round to the nearest month.

b.   If Simon makes monthly payments of $30, how many months will it be before he pays off the debt? Round to the nearest month.

c.   How much more in total payments will Simon make under the $10-a-month plan than under the $30-a-month plan? Make sure you use three decimal places for N.

5-38   PV AND A LAWSUIT SETTLEMENT   It is now December 31, 2008 (t = 0), and a jury just found in favor of a woman who sued the city for injuries sustained in a January 2007 accident. She requested recovery of lost wages plus $100,000 for pain and suffering plus $20,000 for legal expenses. Her doctor testified that she has been unable to work since the accident and that she will not be able to work in the future. She is now 62, and the jury decided that she would have worked for another 3 years. She was scheduled to have earned $34,000 in 2007. (To simplify this problem, assume that the entire annual salary amount would have been received on December 31, 2007.) Her employer testified that she probably would have received raises of 3% per year. The actual payment will be made on December 31, 2009. The judge stipulated that all dollar amounts are to be adjusted to a present value basis on December 31, 2009, using a 7% annual interest rate and using compound, not simple, interest. Furthermore, he stipulated that the pain and suffering and legal expenses should be based on a December, 31, 2008, date. How large a check must the city write on December 31, 2009?

5-39   REQUIRED ANNUITY PAYMENTS   Your father is 50 years old and will retire in 10 years. He expects to live for 25 years after he retires, until he is 85. He wants a fixed retirement income that has the same purchasing power at the time he retires as $40,000 has today. (The real value of his retirement income will decline annually after he retires.) His *retirement income will begin the day he retires*, 10 years from today, at which time he will receive 24 additional annual payments. Annual inflation is expected to be 5%. He currently has $100,000 saved, and he expects to earn 8% annually on his savings. How much must he save during each of the next 10 years (end-of-year deposits) to meet his retirement goal?

5-40   REQUIRED ANNUITY PAYMENTS   A father is now planning a savings program to put his daughter through college. She is 13, she plans to enroll at the university in 5 years, and she should graduate in 4 years. Currently, the annual cost (for everything—food, clothing, tuition, books, transportation, and so forth) is $15,000, but these costs are expected to increase by 5% annually. The college requires that this amount be paid at the start of the year. She now has $7,500 in a college savings account that pays 6% annually. Her father will make six equal annual deposits into her account; the first deposit today and the sixth on the day she starts college. How large must each of the six payments be? [Hint: Calculate the cost (inflated at 5%) for each year of college and find the total present value of those costs, discounted at 6%, as of the day she enters college. Then find the compounded value of her initial $7,500 on that same day. The difference between the PV costs and the amount that would be in the savings account must be made up by the father's deposits, so find the six equal payments (starting immediately) that will compound to the required amount.]

COMPREHENSIVE/SPREADSHEET PROBLEM

5-41   **TIME VALUE OF MONEY**   Answer the following questions:

a. Assuming a rate of 10% annually, find the FV of $1,000 after 5 years.

b. What is the investment's FV at rates of 0%, 5%, and 20% after 0, 1, 2, 3, 4, and 5 years?

c. Find the PV of $1,000 due in 5 years if the discount rate is 10%.

d. What is the rate of return on a security that costs $1,000 and returns $2,000 after 5 years?

e. Suppose California's population is 30 million people and its population is expected to grow by 2% annually. How long will it take for the population to double?

f. Find the PV of an ordinary annuity that pays $1,000 each of the next 5 years if the interest rate is 15%. What is the annuity's FV?

g. How will the PV and FV of the annuity in (f) change if it is an annuity due?

h. What will the FV and the PV be for $1,000 due in 5 years if the interest rate is 10%, semiannual compounding?

i. What will the annual payments be for an ordinary annuity for 10 years with a PV of $1,000 if the interest rate is 8%? What will the payments be if this is an annuity due?

j. Find the PV and the FV of an investment that pays 8% annually and makes the following end-of-year payments:

k. Five banks offer nominal rates of 6% on deposits; but A pays interest annually, B pays semiannually, C pays quarterly, D pays monthly, and E pays daily.

(1) What effective annual rate does each bank pay? If you deposit $5,000 in each bank today, how much will you have at the end of 1 year? 2 years?

(2) If all of the banks are insured by the government (the FDIC) and thus are equally risky, will they be equally able to attract funds? If not (and the TVM is the only consideration), what nominal rate will cause all of the banks to provide the same effective annual rate as Bank A?

(3) Suppose you don't have the $5,000 but need it at the end of 1 year. You plan to make a series of deposits—annually for A, semiannually for B, quarterly for C, monthly for D, and daily for E—with payments beginning today. How large must the payments be to each bank?

(4) Even if the five banks provided the same effective annual rate, would a rational investor be indifferent between the banks? Explain.

l. Suppose you borrow $15,000. The loan's annual interest rate is 8%, and it requires four equal end-of-year payments. Set up an amortization schedule that shows the annual payments, interest payments, principal repayments, and beginning and ending loan balances.

INTEGRATED CASE

FIRST NATIONAL BANK

5-42   **TIME VALUE OF MONEY ANALYSIS**   You have applied for a job with a local bank. As part of its evaluation process, you must take an examination on time value of money analysis covering the following questions:

a. Draw time lines for (1) a $100 lump sum cash flow at the end of Year 2; (2) an ordinary annuity of $100 per year for 3 years; and (3) an uneven cash flow stream of –$50, $100, $75, and $50 at the end of Years 0 through 3.

b. (1)   What's the future value of $100 after 3 years if it earns 10%, annual compounding?

(2)   What's the present value of $100 to be received in 3 years if the interest rate is 10%, annual compounding?

c. What annual interest rate would cause $100 to grow to $125.97 in 3 years?

d. If a company's sales are growing at a rate of 20% annually, how long will it take sales to double?

e. What's the difference between an ordinary annuity and an annuity due? What type of annuity is shown here? How would you change it to the other type of annuity?

f. (1) What is the future value of a 3-year, $100 ordinary annuity if the annual interest rate is 10%?

   (2) What is its present value?

   (3) What would the future and present values be if it was an annuity due?

g. A 5-year $100 ordinary annuity has an annual interest rate of 10%.

   (1) What is its present value?

   (2) What would the present value be if it was a 10-year annuity?

   (3) What would the present value be if it was a 25-year annuity?

   (4) What would the present value be if this was a perpetuity?

h. A 20-year-old student wants to save $3 a day for her retirement. Every day she places $3 in a drawer. At the end of each year, she invests the accumulated savings ($1,095) in a brokerage account with an expected annual return of 12%.

   (1) If she keeps saving in this manner, how much will she have accumulated at age 65?

   (2) If a 40-year-old investor began saving in this manner, how much would he have at age 65?

   (3) How much would the 40-year-old investor have to save each year to accumulate the same amount at 65 as the 20-year-old investor?

i. What is the present value of the following uneven cash flow stream? The annual interest rate is 10%.

j. (1) Will the future value be larger or smaller if we compound an initial amount more often than annually (e.g., semiannually, holding the stated (nominal) rate constant)? Why?

   (2) Define (a) the stated (or quoted or nominal) rate, (b) the periodic rate, and (c) the effective annual rate (EAR or EFF%).

   (3) What is the EAR corresponding to a nominal rate of 10% compounded semiannually? compounded quarterly? compounded daily?

   (4) What is the future value of $100 after 3 years under 10% semiannual compounding? quarterly compounding?

k. When will the EAR equal the nominal (quoted) rate?

l. (1) What is the value at the end of Year 3 of the following cash flow stream if interest is 10% compounded semiannually? (Hint: You can use the EAR and treat the cash flows as an ordinary annuity or use the periodic rate and compound the cash flows individually.)

   (2) What is the PV?

   (3) What would be wrong with your answer to Parts l(1) and l(2) if you used the nominal rate, 10%, rather than the EAR or the periodic rate, $I_{NOM}/2 = 10\%/2 = 5\%$, to solve the problems?

m. (1) Construct an amortization schedule for a $1,000, 10% annual interest loan with three equal installments.

   (2) What is the annual interest expense for the borrower and the annual interest income for the lender during Year 2?

PART 3

FINANCIAL ASSETS

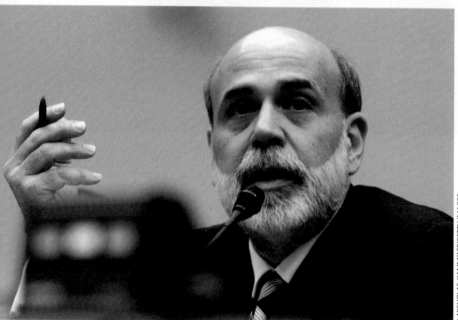

© NICHOLAS KAMM/AFP/GETTY IMAGES

6 Interest Rates

Low Interest Rates Encourage Investment and Stimulate Consumer Spending

The U.S. economy performed well from the early 1990s through 2007. Economic growth was positive, unemployment was fairly low, and inflation remained under control. One reason for the economy's good performance was the low level of interest rates over most of that period, with the rate on 10-year Treasury bonds generally at or below 5%, a level last seen in the 1960s, and rates on most other bonds correspondingly low. These low interest rates reduced the cost of capital for businesses, which encouraged corporate investment. They also stimulated consumer spending and helped produce a massive growth in the housing market.

The drop in interest rates was due to a number of factors—low inflation, foreign investors' purchases of U.S. securities (which drove their rates down), and effective management of the economy by the Federal Reserve and other government policy makers. However, some shocks hit the system in 2007, including $100 per barrel oil and massive write-offs by banks and other institutions that resulted from the subprime mortgage debacle. Higher oil prices and a weakening dollar could lead to higher inflation, which, in turn, would push interest rates up. Likewise, the growing federal budget deficit, combined with the weakening dollar, could cause foreigners to sell U.S. bonds, which would put more upward pressure on rates. At the same time, though, the economy seems to be weakening, which has led the Federal Reserve to lower its key short-term rate in hopes of staving off a general recession. So some forces are trying to drive rates higher, but other forces are operating to keep rates low.

Because corporations and individuals are greatly affected by interest rates, this chapter takes a closer look at the major factors that determine those rates. As we will see, there is no single interest rate—various factors determine the rate that each borrower pays—and in some cases, rates on different types of debt move in different directions. For example, in the aftermath of the recent subprime mortgage crisis, investors rushed to put their money in liquid securities with little or no default risk. This "flight to quality" led to a decline in the rate the government had to pay when it borrowed. At the same time, investors demanded much higher rates from corporate borrowers—particularly those thought to be especially risky.

The subprime mortgage crisis demonstrates how major shocks to the economy can have profound effects on interest rates in a wide number of markets, all of which are interconnected. Looking ahead, it will be interesting to see if interest rates can continue to remain low and if not, whether the economy can continue to perform as well as it has in the past.

PUTTING THINGS IN PERSPECTIVE

Companies raise capital in two main forms: debt and equity. In a free economy, capital, like other items, is allocated through a market system, where funds are transferred and prices are established. The interest rate is the price that lenders receive and borrowers pay for debt capital. Similarly, equity investors expect to receive dividends and capital gains, the sum of which represents the cost of equity. We will take up the cost of equity in a later chapter, but our focus in this chapter is on the cost of debt. We begin by examining the factors that affect the supply of and demand for capital, which, in turn, affects the cost of money. We will see that there is no single interest rate—interest rates on different types of debt vary depending on the borrower's risk, the use of the funds borrowed, the type of collateral used to back the loan, and the length of time the money is needed. In this chapter, we concentrate mainly on how these various factors affect the cost of debt for individuals; but in later chapters, we delve into cost of debt for a business and its role in investment decisions. As you will see in Chapters 7 and 9, the cost of debt is a key determinant of bond and stock prices; it is also an important component of the cost of corporate capital, which we take up in Chapter 10.

When you finish this chapter, you should be able to:

- List the various factors that influence the cost of money.
- Discuss how market interest rates are affected by borrowers' need for capital, expected inflation, different securities' risks, and securities' liquidity.
- Explain what the yield curve is, what determines its shape, and how you can use the yield curve to help forecast future interest rates.

Production Opportunities
The investment opportunities in productive (cash-generating) assets.

Time Preferences for Consumption
The preferences of consumers for current consumption as opposed to saving for future consumption.

6-1 THE COST OF MONEY

The four most fundamental factors affecting the cost of money are (1) **production opportunities**, (2) **time preferences for consumption**, (3) **risk**, and (4) **inflation**. To see how these factors operate, visualize an isolated island community where people live on fish. They have a stock of fishing gear that permits them to survive reasonably well, but they would like to have more fish. Now suppose one of the island's inhabitants, Mr. Crusoe, had a bright idea for a new type of fishnet that would enable him to double his daily catch. However, it would take him a year to perfect the design, build the net, and learn to use it efficiently. Mr. Crusoe would probably starve before he could put his new net into operation. Therefore, he might suggest to Ms. Robinson, Mr. Friday, and several others that if they would give him one fish each day for a year, he would return two fish a day the next year. If someone accepted the offer, the fish that Ms. Robinson and the others gave to Mr. Crusoe would constitute *savings*, these savings would be *invested* in the

Risk
In a financial market context, the chance that an investment will provide a low or negative return.

Inflation
The amount by which prices increase over time.

fishnet, and the extra fish the net produced would constitute a *return on the investment*.

Obviously, the more productive Mr. Crusoe thought the new fishnet would be, the more he could afford to offer potential investors for their savings. In this example, we assume that Mr. Crusoe thought he would be able to pay (and thus he offered) a 100% rate of return—he offered to give back two fish for every one he received. He might have tried to attract savings for less—for example, he might have offered only 1.5 fish per day next year for every one he received this year, which would represent a 50% rate of return to Ms. Robinson and the other potential savers.

How attractive Mr. Crusoe's offer appeared to a potential saver would depend in large part on the saver's *time preference for consumption*. For example, Ms. Robinson might be thinking of retirement, and she might be willing to trade fish today for fish in the future on a one-for-one basis. On the other hand, Mr. Friday might have a wife and several young children and need his current fish; so he might be unwilling to "lend" a fish today for anything less than three fish next year. Mr. Friday would be said to have a high time preference for current consumption; Ms. Robinson, a low time preference. Note also that if the entire population was living right at the subsistence level, time preferences for current consumption would necessarily be high, aggregate savings would be low, interest rates would be high, and capital formation would be difficult.

The *risk* inherent in the fishnet project (and thus in Mr. Crusoe's ability to repay the loan) also affects the return that investors require: The higher the perceived risk, the higher the required rate of return. Also, in a more complex society, there are many businesses like Mr. Crusoe's, many goods other than fish, and many savers like Ms. Robinson and Mr. Friday. Therefore, people use money as a medium of exchange rather than barter with fish. When money is used, its value in the future, which is affected by *inflation*, comes into play: The higher the expected rate of inflation, the larger the required dollar return. We discuss this point in detail later in the chapter.

Thus, we see that the interest rate paid to savers depends (1) on the rate of return that producers expect to earn on invested capital, (2) on savers' time preferences for current versus future consumption, (3) on the riskiness of the loan, and (4) on the expected future rate of inflation. Producers' expected returns on their business investments set an upper limit to how much they can pay for savings, while consumers' time preferences for consumption establish how much consumption they are willing to defer and, hence, how much they will save at different interest rates.[1] Higher risk and higher inflation also lead to higher interest rates.

SELF TEST

What is the price paid to borrow debt capital called?

What are the two items whose sum is the cost of equity?

What four fundamental factors affect the cost of money?

---

[1] The term *producers* is too narrow. A better word might be *borrowers*, which would include corporations, home purchasers, people borrowing to go to college, and even people borrowing to buy autos or to pay for vacations. Also, the wealth of a society and its demographics influence its people's ability to save and thus their time preferences for current versus future consumption.

6-2 INTEREST RATE LEVELS

Borrowers bid for the available supply of debt capital using interest rates: The firms with the most profitable investment opportunities are willing and able to pay the most for capital, so they tend to attract it away from inefficient firms and firms whose products are not in demand. Of course, the economy is not completely free in the sense of being influenced only by market forces. For example, the federal government has agencies that help designated individuals or groups obtain credit on favorable terms. Among those eligible for this kind of assistance are small businesses, certain minorities, and firms willing to build plants in areas with high unemployment. Still, most capital in the United States is allocated through the price system, where the interest rate is the price.

Figure 6-1 shows how supply and demand interact to determine interest rates in two capital markets. Markets L and H represent two of the many capital markets in existence. The supply curve in each market is upward-sloping, which indicates that investors are willing to supply more capital the higher the interest rate they receive on their capital. Likewise, the downward-sloping demand curve indicates that borrowers will borrow more if interest rates are lower. The interest rate in each market is the point where the supply and demand curves intersect. The going interest rate, designated as r, is initially 5% for the low-risk securities in Market L. Borrowers whose credit is strong enough to participate in this market can obtain funds at a cost of 5%, and investors who want to put their money to work without much risk can obtain a 5% return. Riskier borrowers must obtain higher-cost funds in Market H, where investors who are more willing to take risks expect to earn a 7% return but also realize that they might receive much less. In this scenario, investors are willing to accept the higher risk in Market H in exchange for a *risk premium* of 7% − 5% = 2%.

Now let's assume that because of changing market forces, investors perceive that Market H has become relatively more risky. This changing perception will induce many investors to shift toward safer investments—along the lines of the recent "flight to quality" discussed in the opening vignette to this chapter. As investors move their money from Market H to Market L, this supply of funds is increased in Market L from S_1 to S_2; and the increased availability of capital will push down interest rates in this market from 5% to 4%. At the same time, as investors move their money out of Market H, there will be a decreased supply in that market; and tighter credit in that market will force interest rates up from 7% to 8%. In this new environment, money is transferred from Market H to Market L and the risk premium rises from 2% to 8% − 4% = 4%.

FIGURE 6-1	Interest Rates as a Function of Supply and Demand for Funds

There are many capital markets in the United States, and Figure 6-1 highlights the fact that they are interconnected. U.S. firms also invest and raise capital throughout the world, and foreigners both borrow and lend in the United States. There are markets for home loans; farm loans; business loans; federal, state, and local government loans; and consumer loans. Within each category, there are regional markets as well as different types of submarkets. For example, in real estate, there are separate markets for first and second mortgages and for loans on single-family homes, apartments, office buildings, shopping centers, and vacant land. And, of course, there are separate markets for prime and subprime mortgage loans. Within the business sector, there are dozens of types of debt securities and there are several different markets for common stocks.

There is a price for each type of capital, and these prices change over time as supply and demand conditions change. Figure 6-2 shows how long- and short-term interest rates to business borrowers have varied since the early 1970s. Notice that short-term interest rates are especially volatile, rising rapidly during booms and falling equally rapidly during recessions. (The shaded areas of the chart indicate recessions.) When the economy is expanding, firms need capital; and this demand pushes rates up. Also, inflationary pressures are strongest during business booms, also exerting upward pressure on rates. Conditions are reversed during recessions: Slack business reduces the demand for credit, inflation falls, and the Federal Reserve increases the supply of funds to help stimulate the economy. The result is a decline in interest rates.

| FIGURE 6-2 | Long- and Short-Term Interest Rates, 1971–2007 |

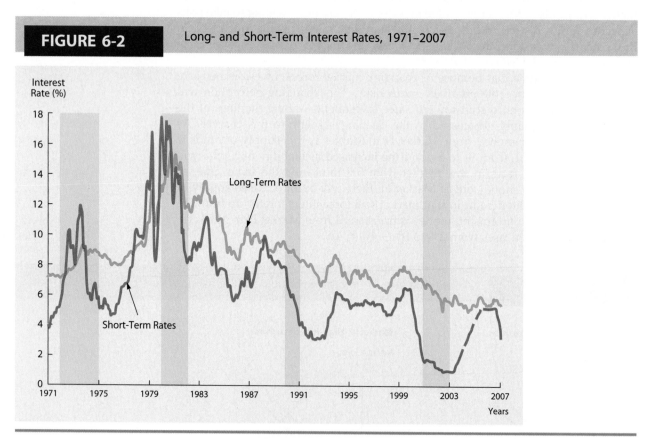

Notes:

a. The shaded areas designate business recessions.

b. Short-term rates are measured by 3- to 6-month loans to very large, strong corporations; and long-term rates are measured by AAA corporate bonds.

Source: St. Louis Federal Reserve web site, FRED database, **http://research.stlouisfed.org/fred2**.

These tendencies do not hold exactly, as demonstrated by the period after 1984. Oil prices fell dramatically in 1985 and 1986, reducing inflationary pressures on other prices and easing fears of serious long-term inflation. Earlier these fears had pushed interest rates to record levels. The economy from 1984 to 1987 was strong, but the declining fears of inflation more than offset the normal tendency for interest rates to rise during good economic times; the net result was lower interest rates.[2]

The relationship between inflation and long-term interest rates is highlighted in Figure 6-3, which plots inflation over time along with long-term interest rates. In the early 1960s, inflation averaged 1% per year and interest rates on high-quality long-term bonds averaged 4%. Then the Vietnam War heated up, leading to an increase in inflation; and interest rates began an upward climb. When the war ended in the early 1970s, inflation dipped a bit; but then the 1973 Arab oil embargo led to rising oil prices, much higher inflation rates, and sharply higher interest rates.

Inflation peaked at about 13% in 1980. But interest rates continued to increase into 1981 and 1982, and they remained quite high until 1985 because people feared another increase in inflation. Thus, the "inflationary psychology" created during the 1970s persisted until the mid-1980s. People gradually realized that the Federal Reserve was serious about keeping inflation down, that global competition was keeping U.S. auto producers and other corporations from raising prices as they

FIGURE 6-3	Relationship between Annual Inflation Rates and Long-Term Interest Rates, 1972–2007

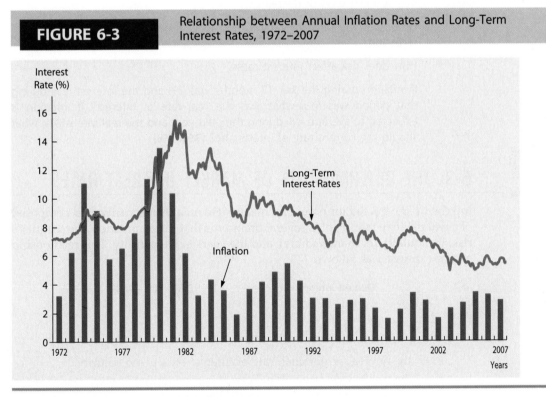

Notes:

a.   Interest rates are rates on AAA long-term corporate bonds.

b.   Inflation is measured as the annual rate of change in the consumer price index (CPI).

Source: St. Louis Federal Reserve web site, FRED database, **http://research.stlouisfed.org/fred2**.

[2]Short-term rates are responsive to current economic conditions, whereas long-term rates primarily reflect long-run expectations for inflation. As a result, short-term rates are sometimes above and sometimes below long-term rates. The relationship between long-term and short-term rates is called the *term structure of interest rates*, and it is discussed later in this chapter.

had in the past, and that constraints on corporate price increases were diminishing labor unions' ability to push through cost-increasing wage hikes. As these real-izations set in, interest rates declined.

The current interest rate minus the current inflation rate (which is also the gap between the inflation bars and the interest rate curve in Figure 6-3) is defined as the "current real rate of interest." It is called a "real rate" because it shows how much investors really earned after the effects of inflation were removed. The real rate was extremely high during the mid-1980s, but it has generally been in the range of 3% to 4% since 1987.

In recent years, inflation has been about 2% a year. However, long-term interest rates have been volatile because investors are not sure if inflation is truly under control or is about to jump back to the higher levels of the 1980s. In the years ahead, we can be sure of two things: (1) Interest rates will vary, and (2) they will increase if inflation appears to be headed higher or decrease if inflation is expected to decline. We don't know where interest rates will go, but we do know they will vary.

SELF TEST

What role do interest rates play in allocating capital to different potential borrowers?

What happens to market-clearing, or equilibrium, interest rates in a capital market when the supply of funds declines? What happens when expected inflation increases or decreases?

How does the price of capital tend to change during a boom? during a recession?

How does risk affect interest rates?

If inflation during the last 12 months was 2% and the interest rate during that period was 5%, what was the real rate of interest? If inflation is expected to average 4% during the next year and the real rate is 3%, what should the current rate of interest be? **(3%; 7%)**

6-3 THE DETERMINANTS OF MARKET INTEREST RATES

In general, the quoted (or nominal) interest rate on a debt security, r, is composed of a real risk-free rate, r*, plus several premiums that reflect inflation, the security's risk, its liquidity (or marketability), and the years to its maturity. This relationship can be expressed as follows:

6-1 $$\text{Quoted interest rate} = r = r^* + IP + DRP + LP + MRP$$

Here

> r = the quoted, or nominal, rate of interest on a given security.[3]
>
> r^* = the real risk-free rate of interest. r^* is pronounced "r-star," and it is the rate that would exist on a riskless security in a world where no inflation was expected.

---

[3]The term *nominal* as it is used here means the *stated* rate as opposed to the *real* rate, where the real rate is adjusted to remove inflation's effects. If you had bought a 10-year Treasury bond in January 2008, the quoted, or nominal, rate would have been about 3.7%; but if inflation averages 2.5% over the next 10 years, the real rate would turn out to be about 3.7% − 2.5% = 1.2%.

Also note that in later chapters, when we discuss both debt and equity, we use the subscripts *d* and *s* to designate returns on debt and stock, that is, r_d and r_s.

r_{RF} = r^* + IP. It is the quoted rate on a risk-free security such as a U.S. Treasury bill, which is very liquid and is free of most types of risk. Note that the premium for expected inflation, IP, is included in r_{RF}.

IP = inflation premium. IP is equal to the average expected rate of inflation over the life of the security. The expected future inflation rate is not necessarily equal to the current inflation rate, so IP is not necessarily equal to current inflation as shown in Figure 6-3.

DRP = default risk premium. This premium reflects the possibility that the issuer will not pay the promised interest or principal at the stated time. DRP is zero for U.S. Treasury securities, but it rises as the riskiness of the issuer increases.

LP = liquidity (or marketability) premium. This is a premium charged by lenders to reflect the fact that some securities cannot be converted to cash on short notice at a "reasonable" price. LP is very low for Treasury securities and for securities issued by large, strong firms; but it is relatively high on securities issued by small, privately held firms.

MRP = maturity risk premium. As we will explain later, longer-term bonds, even Treasury bonds, are exposed to a significant risk of price declines due to increases in inflation and interest rates; and a maturity risk premium is charged by lenders to reflect this risk.

Because r_{RF} = r^* + IP, we can rewrite Equation 6-1 as follows:

$$\text{Nominal, or quoted, rate} = r = r_{RF} + DRP + LP + MRP$$

We discuss the components whose sum makes up the quoted, or nominal, rate on a given security in the following sections.

6-3a The Real Risk-Free Rate of Interest, r^*

The **real risk-free rate of interest, r^***, is the interest rate that would exist on a riskless security if no inflation were expected. It may be thought of as the rate of interest on short-term U.S. Treasury securities in an inflation-free world. The real risk-free rate is not static—it changes over time depending on economic conditions, especially on (1) the rate of return that corporations and other borrowers expect to earn on productive assets and (2) people's time preferences for current versus future consumption. Borrowers' expected returns on real assets set an upper limit on how much borrowers can afford to pay for funds, while savers' time preferences for consumption establish how much consumption savers will defer—hence, the amount of money they will lend at different interest rates. It is difficult to measure the real risk-free rate precisely, but most experts think that r^* has fluctuated in the range of 1% to 5% in recent years.[4] The best estimate of r^* is the rate of return on indexed Treasury bonds, which are discussed later in the chapter.

Real Risk-Free Rate of Interest, r^*
The rate of interest that would exist on default-free U.S. Treasury securities if no inflation were expected.

---

[4]The real rate of interest as discussed here is different from the *current* real rate as discussed in connection with Figure 6-3. The current real rate is the current interest rate minus the current (or latest past) inflation rate, while the real rate (without the word *current*) is the current interest rate minus the *expected future* inflation rate over the life of the security. For example, suppose the current quoted rate for a one-year Treasury bill is 2.7%, inflation during the latest year was 1.2%, and inflation expected for the coming year is 2.2%. The *current* real rate would be 2.7% − 1.2% = 1.5%, but the *expected* real rate would be 2.7% − 2.2% = 0.5%. The rate on a 10-year bond would be related to the average expected inflation rate over the next 10 years, and so on. In the press, the term *real rate* generally means the current real rate; but in economics and finance (hence, in this book unless otherwise noted), the real rate means the one based on *expected* inflation rates.

6-3b The Nominal, or Quoted, Risk-Free Rate of Interest, $r_{RF} = r^* + IP$

Nominal (Quoted) Risk-Free Rate, r_{RF}
The rate of interest on a security that is free of all risk; r_{RF} is proxied by the T-bill rate or the T-bond rate. r_{RF} includes an inflation premium.

The **nominal**, or **quoted, risk-free rate, r_{RF},** is the real risk-free rate plus a premium for expected inflation: $r_{RF} = r^* + IP$. To be strictly correct, the risk-free rate should be the interest rate on a totally risk-free security—one that has no default risk, no maturity risk, no liquidity risk, no risk of loss if inflation increases, and no risk of any other type. There is no such security; hence, there is no observable truly risk-free rate. However, one security is free of most risks—a Treasury Inflation Protected Security (TIPS), whose value increases with inflation. TIPS are free of default, maturity, and liquidity risks and of risk due to changes in the general level of interest rates. However, they are not free of changes in the real rate.[5]

If the term *risk-free rate* is used without the modifiers *real* or *nominal*, people generally mean the quoted (or nominal) rate; and we follow that convention in this book. Therefore, when we use the term *risk-free rate, r_{RF},* we mean the nominal risk-free rate, which includes an inflation premium equal to the average expected inflation rate over the remaining life of the security. In general, we use the T-bill rate to approximate the short-term risk-free rate and the T-bond rate to approximate the long-term risk-free rate. So whenever you see the term *risk-free rate,* assume that we are referring to the quoted U.S. T-bill rate or to the quoted T-bond rate.

6-3c Inflation Premium (IP)

Inflation Premium (IP)
A premium equal to expected inflation that investors add to the real risk-free rate of return.

Inflation has a major impact on interest rates because it erodes the real value of what you receive from the investment. To illustrate, suppose you saved $1,000 and invested it in a Treasury bill that pays a 3% interest rate and matures in one year. At the end of the year, you will receive $1,030—your original $1,000 plus $30 of interest. Now suppose the inflation rate during the year turned out to be 3.5%, and it affected all goods equally. If heating oil had cost $1 per gallon at the beginning of the year, it would cost $1.035 at the end of the year. Therefore, your $1,000 would have bought $1,000/$1 = 1,000 gallons at the beginning of the year, but only $1,030/$1.035 = 995 gallons at the end. In real terms, you would be worse off —you would receive $30 of interest, but it would not be sufficient to offset inflation. You would thus be better off buying 1,000 gallons of heating oil (or some other storable asset such as land, timber, apartment buildings, wheat, or gold) than buying the Treasury bill.

Investors are well aware of all this; so when they lend money, they build an **inflation premium (IP)** equal to the average expected inflation rate over the life of the security into the rate they charge. As discussed previously, the actual interest rate on a short-term default-free U.S. Treasury bill, r_{T-bill}, would be the real risk-free rate, r^*, plus the inflation premium (IP):

$$r_{T-bill} = r_{RF} = r^* + IP$$

Therefore, if the real risk-free rate was $r^* = 1.7\%$ and if inflation was expected to be 1.5% (and hence IP = 1.5%) during the next year, the quoted rate of interest on one-year T-bills would be 1.7% + 1.5% = 3.2%.

It is important to note that the inflation rate built into interest rates is the *inflation rate expected in the future,* not the rate experienced in the past. Thus, the

---

[5]Indexed Treasury securities are the closest thing we have to a riskless security, but even they are not totally riskless because r^* can change and cause a decline in the prices of these securities. For example, between its issue date in February 1998 and December 2004, the TIPS that matures on February 15, 2028 first declined from 100 to 89, or by almost 10%, but it then rose; and in February 2008, the bond sold for 130. The cause of the initial price decline was an *increase* in the real rate on long-term securities from 3.625% to 4.4%, and the cause of the subsequent price increase was a *decline* in real rates to 2.039%.

AN ALMOST RISKLESS TREASURY BOND

Investors who purchase bonds must constantly worry about inflation. If inflation turns out to be greater than expected, bonds will provide a lower-than-expected real return. To protect themselves against expected increases in inflation, investors build an inflation risk premium into their required rate of return. This raises borrowers' costs.

To provide investors with an inflation-protected bond and to reduce the cost of debt to the government, the U.S. Treasury issues Treasury Inflation Protected Securities (TIPS), which are bonds that are indexed to inflation. For example, in 2004, the Treasury issued 10-year TIPS with a 2% coupon. These bonds pay an interest rate of 2% plus an additional amount that is just sufficient to offset inflation. At the end of each 6-month period, the principal (originally set at par or $1,000) is adjusted by the inflation rate. To understand how TIPS work, consider that during the first 6-month interest period, inflation (as measured by the CPI) was 2.02%. The inflation-adjusted principal was then calculated as $1,000(1 + Inflation) = $1,000 × 1.0202 = $1,020.20. So on July 15, 2004, each bond paid interest of 0.02/2 × $1,020.20 = $10.202. Note that the interest rate is divided by 2 because interest on Treasury (and most other) bonds is paid twice a year. This same adjustment process will continue each year until the bonds mature on January 15, 2014, at which time they will pay the adjusted maturity value. Thus, the cash income provided by the bonds rises by exactly enough to cover inflation, producing a real inflation-adjusted rate of 2% for those who hold the bond from the beginning to the end. Further, since the principal also rises by the inflation rate, it too is protected from inflation.

Both the annual interest received and the increase in principal are taxed each year as interest income even though cash from the appreciation will not be received until the bond matures. Therefore, these bonds are not good for accounts subject to current income taxes; but they are excellent for individual retirement accounts (IRAs) and 401 (k) plans, which are not taxed until funds are withdrawn.

The Treasury regularly conducts auctions to issue indexed bonds. The 2% rate was based on the relative supply and demand for the issue, and it will remain fixed over the life of the bond. However, after the bonds are issued, they continue to trade in the open market; and their price will vary as investors' perceptions of the real rate of interest changes. Indeed, as we can see in the following graph, the real rate of interest on this bond has varied quite a bit since it was issued; and as the real rate changes, so does the price of the bond. Real rates fell in 2005, causing the bond's price to rise; rates then rose to a peak in 2007, at which point the bond sold below its par value. They fell again in late 2007 and 2008 as investors sought safety in Treasury securities. Thus, despite their protection against inflation, indexed bonds are not completely riskless. The real rate can change; and if r* rises, the prices of indexed bonds will decline. This confirms again that there is no such thing as a free lunch or a riskless security.

Source: St. Louis Federal Reserve web site, FRED database, **http://research.stlouisfed.org/fred2**.

latest reported figures might show an annual inflation rate of 3% over the past 12 months, but that is for the *past* year. If people, on average, expect a 4% inflation rate in the future, 4% would be built into the current interest rate. Note also that the inflation rate reflected in the quoted interest rate on any security is the *average inflation rate expected over the security's life.* Thus, the inflation rate built into a 1-year bond is the expected inflation rate for the next year, but the inflation rate built into a 30-year bond is the average inflation rate expected over the next 30 years.[6]

Expectations for future inflation are closely, but not perfectly, correlated with rates experienced in the recent past. Therefore, if the inflation rate reported for last month increased, people would tend to raise their expectations for future inflation; and this change in expectations would cause an increase in current rates. Also, consumer prices change with a lag following changes at the producer level. Thus, if the price of oil increases this month, gasoline prices are likely to increase in the coming months. This lagged situation between final product and producer goods prices exists throughout the economy.

Note that Germany, Japan, and Switzerland have, over the past several years, had lower inflation rates than the United States; hence, their interest rates have generally been lower than those of the United States. Italy and most South American countries have experienced higher inflation, so their rates have been higher than those of the United States.

Students should go to **www. bloomberg.com/markets/ rates** *to find current interest rates in the United States as well as in Australia, Brazil, Germany, Japan, and Great Britain.*

6-3d Default Risk Premium (DRP)

The risk that a borrower will *default*, which means the borrower will not make scheduled interest or principal payments, also affects the market interest rate on a bond: The greater the bond's risk of default, the higher the market rate. Treasury securities have no default risk; hence, they carry the lowest interest rates on taxable securities in the United States. For corporate bonds, the higher the bond's rating, the lower its default risk and, consequently, the lower its interest rate.[7] Here are some representative interest rates on long-term bonds in January 2008:

	Rate	DRP
U.S. Treasury	4.28%	—
AAA corporate	4.83	0.55
AA corporate	4.93	0.65
A corporate	5.18	0.90
BBB corporate	6.03	1.75

Default Risk Premium (DRP)

The difference between the interest rate on a U.S. Treasury bond and a corporate bond of equal maturity and marketability.

The difference between the quoted interest rate on a T-bond and that on a corporate bond with similar maturity, liquidity, and other features is the **default risk premium (DRP)**. Therefore, if the bonds previously listed have the same maturity, liquidity, and so forth, the default risk premium will be DRP = 4.83% − 4.28% = 0.55% for AAAs, 4.93% − 4.28% = 0.65% for AAs, 5.18% − 4.28% = 0.90% for A corporate bonds, and so forth. If we had gone down into "junk bond" territory, we would have seen DRPs of as much as 8%. Default risk premiums vary somewhat over time, but the January 2008 figures are representative of levels in recent years.

6-3e Liquidity Premium (LP)

A "liquid" asset can be converted to cash quickly at a "fair market value." Real assets are generally less liquid than financial assets, but different financial assets

---

[6]To be theoretically precise, we should use a *geometric average*. Also, since millions of investors are active in the market, it is impossible to determine exactly the consensus-expected inflation rate. Survey data are available, however, that give us a reasonably good idea of what investors expect over the next few years. For example, in 1980, the University of Michigan's Survey Research Center reported that people expected inflation during the next year to be 11.9% and that the average rate of inflation expected over the next 5 to 10 years was 10.5%. Those expectations led to record-high interest rates. However, the economy cooled thereafter; and as Figure 6-3 showed, actual inflation dropped sharply. This led to a gradual reduction in the *expected future* inflation rate; and as inflationary expectations dropped, so did quoted market interest rates.

[7]Bond ratings and bonds' riskiness in general are discussed in detail in Chapter 7. For now, merely note that bonds rated AAA are judged to have less default risk than bonds rated AA, while AA bonds are less risky than A bonds, and so forth. Ratings are designated AAA or Aaa, AA or Aa, and so forth, depending on the rating agency. In this book, the designations are used interchangeably.

A 20% LIQUIDITY PREMIUM ON A HIGH-GRADE BOND

Since the yield curve is normally upward-sloping, short-term debt is normally less expensive than long-term debt. However, it's dangerous to finance long-term assets with short-term debt. To get around this problem, investment bankers created a new instrument, *auction rate securities (ARS)*, which are long-term bonds with this wrinkle: Weekly (or monthly for some) auctions are held. The borrower buys back at par the bonds of holders who want to get out and simultaneously sells those reclaimed bonds to new lenders. Potential new lenders indicate the lowest interest rate they will accept, and the actual rate paid on the entire issue is the lowest rate that causes the auction to clear. Most of the bonds were insured by AAA insurance companies, which gave them a AAA rating.

To illustrate, the total issue might be for $100 million and the initial rate might be 3%. One week later holders of $5 million of bonds might turn in their bonds, which would then be offered in an auction to potential buyers. To get the bonds resold, an annual rate of 3.1% might be required. Then for the next week, all $100 million of the bonds would earn 3.1%. There was a cap on the interest rate tied to an index of rates on regular long-term bonds.

Investors liked the ARS because they paid a somewhat higher rate than money market funds and they were equally safe and almost as liquid. They were underwritten by major financial institutions such as Goldman Sachs, Merrill Lynch, and Citigroup, which would buy the excess if more bonds were turned in than were bid for at rates below the cap. The institutions would hold repurchased bonds in inventory and then sell them to their customers.

Everything worked fine until the credit market meltdown of 2008. The banks who back-stopped the auction had lost billions in the subprime mortgage debacle, and they didn't have the capital to step in. After a couple of failed auctions, many ARS holders became concerned about liquidity and tried to turn in their bonds. That rush to the exits caused the whole market to freeze up. Highly liquid securities suddenly became totally illiquid. Penalty rates for frozen securities kicked in, some as high as 20%. That's much higher than "normal" liquidity premiums, but it does demonstrate that liquidity is valuable and that high liquidity premiums are built into illiquid securities' rates.

Source: Stan Rosenberg and Romy Varghese, "Auction-Rate Bonds May Come to Rescue," *The Wall Street Journal,* February 15, 2008, p. C2.

vary in their liquidity. Because liquidity is important, investors include a **liquidity premium (LP)** in the rates charged on different debt securities. Although it is difficult to measure liquidity premiums accurately, a differential of at least two and probably four or five percentage points exists between the least liquid and the most liquid financial assets of similar default risk and maturity.

Liquidity Premium (LP)
A premium added to the equilibrium interest rate on a security if that security cannot be converted to cash on short notice and at close to its "fair market value."

6-3f Interest Rate Risk and the Maturity Risk Premium (MRP)

U.S. Treasury securities are free of default risk in the sense that one can be virtually certain that the federal government will pay interest on its bonds and pay them off when they mature. Therefore, the default risk premium on Treasury securities is essentially zero. Further, active markets exist for Treasury securities, so their liquidity premiums are close to zero. Thus, as a first approximation, the rate of interest on a Treasury security should be the risk-free rate, r_{RF}, which is the real risk-free rate plus an inflation premium, $r_{RF} = r^* + IP$. However, the prices of long-term bonds decline whenever interest rates rise; and because interest rates can and do occasionally rise, all long-term bonds, even Treasury bonds, have an element of risk called **interest rate risk.** As a general rule, the bonds of any organization, from the U.S. government to Delta Airlines, have more interest rate risk the longer the maturity of the bond.[8] Therefore, a **maturity risk premium (MRP)**,

Interest Rate Risk
The risk of capital losses to which investors are exposed because of changing interest rates.

Maturity Risk Premium (MRP)
A premium that reflects interest rate risk.

---

[8]For example, if someone had bought a 20-year Treasury bond for $1,000 in October 1998, when the long-term interest rate was 5.3%, and sold it in May 2002, when long-term T-bond rates were about 5.8%, the value of the bond would have declined to about $942. That would represent a loss of 5.8%; and it demonstrates that long-term bonds, even U.S. Treasury bonds, are not riskless. However, had the investor purchased short-term T-bills in 1998 and subsequently reinvested the principal each time the bills matured, he or she would still have had the original $1,000. This point is discussed in detail in Chapter 7.

which is higher the greater the years to maturity, is included in the required interest rate.

The effect of maturity risk premiums is to raise interest rates on long-term bonds relative to those on short-term bonds. This premium, like the others, is difficult to measure; but (1) it varies somewhat over time, rising when interest rates are more volatile and uncertain, then falling when interest rates are more stable and (2) in recent years, the maturity risk premium on 20-year T-bonds has generally been in the range of one to two percentage points.[9]

Reinvestment Rate Risk
The risk that a decline in interest rates will lead to lower income when bonds mature and funds are reinvested.

We should also note that although long-term bonds are heavily exposed to interest rate risk, short-term bills are heavily exposed to **reinvestment rate risk.** When short-term bills mature and the principal must be reinvested, or "rolled over," a decline in interest rates would necessitate reinvestment at a lower rate, which would result in a decline in interest income. To illustrate, suppose you had $100,000 invested in T-bills and you lived on the income. In 1981, short-term Treasury rates were about 15%, so your income would have been about $15,000. However, your income would have declined to about $9,000 by 1983 and to just $2,700 by January 2008. Had you invested your money in long-term T-bonds, your income (but not the value of the principal) would have been stable.[10] Thus, although "investing short" preserves one's principal, the interest income provided by short-term T-bills is less stable than that on long-term bonds.

SELF TEST

Write an equation for the nominal interest rate on any security.

Distinguish between the *real* risk-free rate of interest, r*, and the *nominal*, or *quoted*, risk-free rate of interest, r_{RF}.

How do investors deal with inflation when they determine interest rates in the financial markets?

Does the interest rate on a T-bond include a default risk premium? Explain.

Distinguish between liquid and illiquid assets and list some assets that are liquid and some that are illiquid.

Briefly explain the following statement: Although long-term bonds are heavily exposed to interest rate risk, short-term T-bills are heavily exposed to reinvestment rate risk. The maturity risk premium reflects the net effects of those two opposing forces.

Assume that the real risk-free rate is r* = 2% and the average expected inflation rate is 3% for each future year. The DRP and LP for Bond X are each 1%, and the applicable MRP is 2%. What is Bond X's interest rate? Is Bond X (1) a Treasury bond or a corporate bond and (2) more likely to have a 3-month or a 20-year maturity? **(9%, corporate, 20-year)**

---

[9]The MRP for long-term bonds has averaged 1.4% over the last 82 years. See *Stocks, Bonds, Bills, and Inflation: (Valuation Edition) 2008 Yearbook* (Chicago: Morningstar Inc., 2008).

[10]Most long-term bonds also have some reinvestment rate risk. If a person is saving and investing for some future purpose (say, to buy a house or to retire), to actually earn the quoted rate on a long-term bond, each interest payment must be reinvested at the quoted rate. However, if interest rates fall, the interest payments would be reinvested at a lower rate; so the realized return would be less than the quoted rate. Note, though, that reinvestment rate risk is lower on long-term bonds than on short-term bonds because only the interest payments (rather than interest plus principal) on a long-term bond are exposed to reinvestment rate risk. Non-callable zero coupon bonds, which are discussed in Chapter 7, are completely free of reinvestment rate risk during their lifetime.

6-4 THE TERM STRUCTURE OF INTEREST RATES

The **term structure of interest rates** describes the relationship between long- and short-term rates. The term structure is important to corporate treasurers deciding whether to borrow by issuing long- or short-term debt and to investors who are deciding whether to buy long- or short-term bonds. Therefore, both borrowers and lenders should understand (1) how long- and short-term rates relate to each other and (2) what causes shifts in their relative levels.

Interest rates for bonds with different maturities can be found in a variety of publications, including *The Wall Street Journal* and the *Federal Reserve Bulletin*, and on a number of web sites, including Bloomberg, Yahoo!, CNN Financial, and the Federal Reserve Board. Using interest rate data from these sources, we can determine the term structure at any given point in time. For example, the tabular section below Figure 6-4 presents interest rates for different maturities on three different dates. The set of data for a given date, when plotted on a graph such as Figure 6-4, is called the **yield curve** for that date.

Term Structure of Interest Rates
The relationship between bond yields and maturities.

Yield Curve
A graph showing the relationship between bond yields and maturities.

FIGURE 6-4	U.S. Treasury Bond Interest Rates on Different Dates

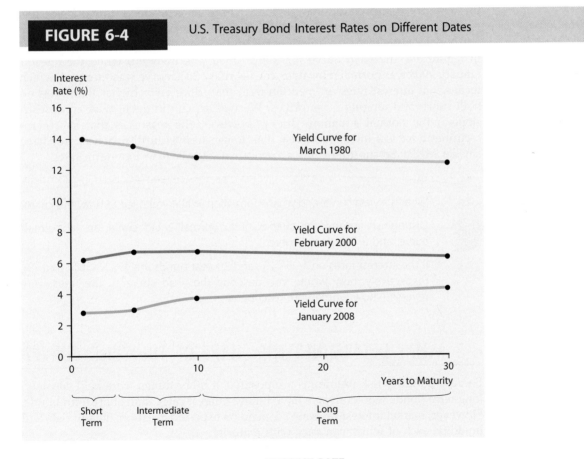

	INTEREST RATE		
Term to Maturity	**March 1980**	**February 2000**	**January 2008**
1 year	14.0%	6.2%	2.7%
5 years	13.5	6.7	3.0
10 years	12.8	6.7	3.7
30 years	12.3	6.3	4.3

As the figure shows, the yield curve changes in position and in slope over time. In March 1980, all rates were quite high because high inflation was expected. However, the rate of inflation was expected to decline; so short-term rates were higher than long-term rates, and the yield curve was thus *downward-sloping*. By February 2000, inflation had indeed declined; thus, all rates were lower, and the yield curve had become *humped*—medium-term rates were higher than either short- or long-term rates. By January 2008, all rates had fallen below the 2000 levels; and because short-term rates had dropped below long-term rates, the yield curve was *upward-sloping*.

Figure 6-4 shows yield curves for U.S. Treasury securities; but we could have constructed curves for bonds issued by GE, IBM, Delta Air Lines, or any other company that borrows money over a range of maturities. Had we constructed such corporate yield curves and plotted them on Figure 6-4, they would have been above those for Treasury securities because corporate yields include default risk premiums and somewhat higher liquidity premiums. Even so, the corporate yield curves would have had the same general shape as the Treasury curves. Also, the riskier the corporation, the higher its yield curve; so Delta, which has been flirting with bankruptcy, would have a higher yield curve than GE or IBM.

Historically, long-term rates are generally above short-term rates because of the maturity risk premium; so all yield curves usually slope upward. For this reason, people often call an upward-sloping yield curve a **"normal" yield curve** and a yield curve that slopes downward an **inverted** or **"abnormal" curve.** Thus, in Figure 6-4, the yield curve for March 1980 was inverted, while the one for January 2008 was normal. However, the February 2000 curve was **humped,** which means that interest rates on medium-term maturities were higher than rates on both short- and long-term maturities. We will explain in detail why an upward slope is the normal situation. Briefly, however, the reason is that short-term securities have less interest rate risk than longer-term securities; hence, they have smaller MRPs. So short-term rates are normally lower than long-term rates.

"Normal" Yield Curve
An upward-sloping yield curve.

Inverted ("Abnormal") Yield Curve
A downward-sloping yield curve.

Humped Yield Curve
A yield curve where interest rates on medium-term maturities are higher than rates on both short-and long-term maturities.

What is a yield curve, and what information would you need to draw this curve?

Distinguish among the shapes of a "normal" yield curve, an "abnormal" curve, and a "humped" curve.

If the interest rates on 1-, 5-, 10-, and 30-year bonds are 4%, 5%, 6%, and 7%, respectively, how would you describe the yield curve? If the rates were reversed, how would you describe it?

6-5 WHAT DETERMINES THE SHAPE OF THE YIELD CURVE?

Because maturity risk premiums are positive, if other things were held constant, long-term bonds would always have higher interest rates than short-term bonds. However, market interest rates also depend on expected inflation, default risk, and liquidity, each of which can vary with maturity.

Expected inflation has an especially important effect on the yield curve's shape, especially the curve for U.S. Treasury securities. Treasuries have essentially no default or liquidity risk, so the yield on a Treasury bond that matures in t years can be expressed as follows:

$$\text{T-bond yield} = r_t^* + IP_t + MRP_t$$

While the real risk-free rate, r*, varies somewhat over time because of changes in the economy and demographics, these changes are random rather than predictable. Therefore, the best forecast for the future value of r* is its current value. However, the inflation premium, IP, varies significantly over time and in a somewhat predictable manner. Recall that the inflation premium is the average level of expected inflation over the life of the bond. Thus, if the market expects inflation to increase in the future (say, from 3% to 4% to 5% over the next 3 years), the inflation premium will be higher on a 3-year bond than on a 1-year bond. On the other hand, if the market expects inflation to decline in the future, long-term bonds will have a smaller inflation premium than will short-term bonds. Finally, since investors consider long-term bonds to be riskier than short-term bonds because of interest rate risk, the maturity risk premium always increases with maturity.

Panel a of Figure 6-5 shows the yield curve when inflation is expected to increase. Here long-term bonds have higher yields for two reasons: (1) Inflation is expected to be higher in the future, and (2) there is a positive maturity risk premium. Panel b shows the yield curve when inflation is expected to decline. Such a downward-sloping yield curve often foreshadows an economic downturn because

---

FIGURE 6-5   Illustrative Treasury Yield Curves

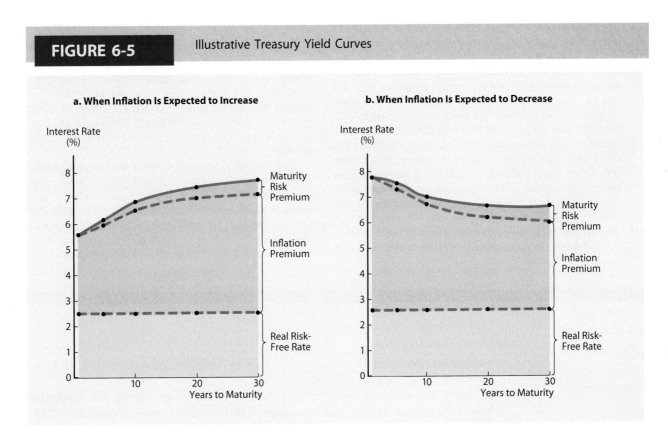

Maturity	WITH INFLATION EXPECTED TO INCREASE				Maturity	WITH INFLATION EXPECTED TO DECREASE			
	r*	IP	MRP	Yield		r*	IP	MRP	Yield
1 year	2.50%	3.00%	0.00%	5.50%	1 year	2.50%	5.00%	0.00%	7.50%
5 years	2.50	3.40	0.18	6.08	5 years	2.50	4.60	0.18	7.28
10 years	2.50	4.00	0.28	6.78	10 years	2.50	4.00	0.28	6.78
20 years	2.50	4.50	0.42	7.42	20 years	2.50	3.50	0.42	6.42
30 years	2.50	4.67	0.53	7.70	30 years	2.50	3.33	0.53	6.36

THE LINKS BETWEEN EXPECTED INFLATION AND INTEREST RATES: A CLOSER LOOK

Throughout the text, we use the following equation to describe the link between expected inflation and the nominal risk-free rate of interest, r_{RF}:

$$r_{RF} = r^* + IP$$

Recall that r^* is the real risk-free interest rate and IP is the corresponding inflation premium. This equation suggests that there is a simple link between expected inflation and nominal interest rates.

It turns out, however, that this link is a bit more complex. To fully understand this relationship, first recognize that individuals get utility through the consumption of real goods and services such as bread, water, haircuts, pizza, and textbooks. When we save money, we are giving up the opportunity to consume these goods today in return for being able to consume more of them in the future. Our gain from waiting is measured by the real rate of interest, r^*.

To illustrate this point, consider the following example. Assume that a loaf of bread costs $1 today. Also assume that the real rate of interest is 3% and that inflation is expected to be 5% over the next year. The 3% real rate indicates that the average consumer is willing to trade 100 loaves of bread today for 103 loaves next year. If a "bread bank" were available, consumers who wanted to defer consumption until next year could deposit 100 loaves today and withdraw 103 loaves next year. In practice, most of us do not directly trade real goods such as bread—instead, we purchase these goods with money because in a well-functioning economy, it is more efficient to exchange money than goods. However, when we lend money over time, we worry that borrowers might pay us back with dollars that aren't worth as much due to inflation. To compensate for this risk, lenders build in a premium for expected inflation.

With these concerns in mind, let's compare the dollar cost of 100 loaves of bread today to the cost of 103 loaves next year. Given the current price, 100 loaves of bread today would cost $100. Since expected inflation is 5%, this means that a loaf of bread is expected to cost $1.05 next year. Consequently, 103 loaves of bread are expected to cost $108.15 next year (103 × $1.05). So if consumers were to deposit $100 in a bank today, they would need to earn 8.15% to realize a real return of 3%.

Putting this all together, we see that the 1-year nominal interest rate can be calculated as follows:

$$
\begin{aligned}
r_{RF} &= (1 + r^*)(1 + I) - 1 \\
&= (1.03)(1.05) - 1 = 0.0815 = 8.15\%
\end{aligned}
$$

Note that this expression can be rewritten as follows:

$$r_{RF} = r^* + I + (r^* \times I)$$

That equation is identical to our original expression for the nominal risk-free rate except that it includes a "cross-term," $r^* \times I$. When real interest rates and expected inflation are relatively low, the cross-term turns out to be quite small and thus is often ignored. Because it is normally insignificant we disregard the cross-term in the text unless stated otherwise.

One last point—you should recognize that while it may be reasonable to ignore the cross-term when interest rates are low (as they are in the United States today), it is a mistake to do so when investing in a market where interest rates and inflation are quite high, as is often the case in many emerging markets. In these markets, the cross-term can be significant and thus should not be disregarded.

weaker economic conditions generally lead to declining inflation, which, in turn, results in lower long-term rates.[11]

Now let's consider the yield curve for corporate bonds. Recall that corporate bonds include a default risk premium (DRP) and a liquidity premium (LP). Therefore, the yield on a corporate bond that matures in t years can be expressed as follows:

$$\text{Corporate bond yield} = r_t^* + IP_t + MRP_t + DRP_t + LP_t$$

Corporate bonds' default and liquidity risks are affected by their maturities. For example, the default risk on Coca-Cola's short-term debt is very small since

---

[11]Note that yield curves tend to rise or fall relatively sharply over the first 5 to 10 years and then flatten out. One reason this occurs is that when forecasting future interest rates, people often predict relatively high or low inflation for the next few years, after which they assume an average long-run inflation rate. Consequently, the short end of the yield curve tends to have more curvature and the long end of the yield curve tends to be more stable.

there is almost no chance that Coca-Cola will go bankrupt over the next few years. However, Coke has some bonds that have a maturity of almost 100 years; and while the odds of Coke defaulting on those bonds might not be very high, there is still a higher probability of default risk on Coke's long-term bonds than its short-term bonds.

Longer-term corporate bonds also tend to be less liquid than shorter-term bonds. Since short-term debt has less default risk, someone can buy a short-term bond without doing as much credit checking as would be necessary for a long-term bond. Thus, people can move in and out of short-term corporate debt relatively rapidly. As a result, a corporation's short-term bonds are typically more liquid and thus have lower liquidity premiums than its long-term bonds.

Figure 6-6 shows yield curves for two hypothetical corporate bonds—an AA-rated bond with minimal default risk and a BBB-rated bond with more default risk—along with the yield curve for Treasury securities taken from Panel a of Figure 6-5. Here we assume that inflation is expected to increase, so the Treasury yield curve is upward-sloping. Because of their additional default and liquidity risk, corporate bonds yield more than Treasury bonds with the same maturity and BBB-rated bonds yield more than AA-rated bonds. Finally, note that the yield spread between corporate and Treasury bonds is larger the longer the maturity. This occurs because

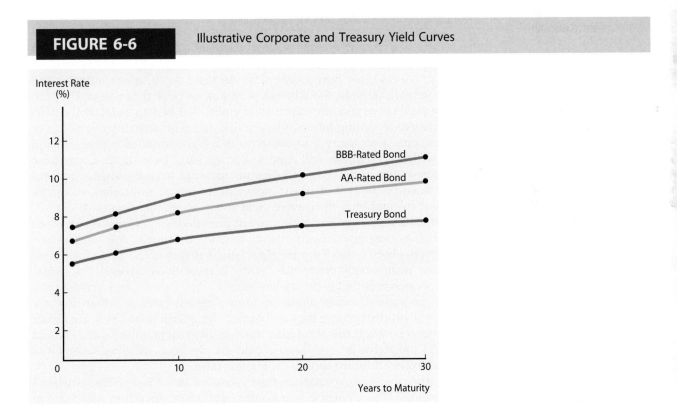

FIGURE 6-6   Illustrative Corporate and Treasury Yield Curves

Term to Maturity	INTEREST RATE		
	Treasury Bond	AA-Rated Bond	BBB-Rated Bond
1 year	5.5%	6.7%	7.4%
5 years	6.1	7.4	8.1
10 years	6.8	8.2	9.1
20 years	7.4	9.2	10.2
30 years	7.7	9.8	11.1

longer-term corporate bonds have more default and liquidity risk than shorter-term bonds, and both of these premiums are absent in Treasury bonds.

How do maturity risk premiums affect the yield curve?

If the inflation rate is expected to increase, would this increase or decrease the slope of the yield curve?

If the inflation rate is expected to remain constant at the current level in the future, would the yield curve slope up, slope down, or be horizontal? Consider all factors that affect the yield curve, not just inflation.

Explain why corporate bonds' default and liquidity premiums are likely to increase with their maturity.

Explain why corporate bonds always yield more than Treasury bonds and why BBB-rated bonds always yield more than AA-rated bonds.

6-6 USING THE YIELD CURVE TO ESTIMATE FUTURE INTEREST RATES[12]

Pure Expectations Theory

A theory that states that the shape of the yield curve depends on investors' expectations about future interest rates.

In the last section, we saw that the slope of the yield curve depends primarily on two factors: (1) expectations about future inflation and (2) effects of maturity on bonds' risk. We also saw how to calculate the yield curve, given inflation and maturity-related risks. Note, though, that people can reverse the process: They can look at the yield curve and use information embedded in it to estimate the market's expectations regarding future inflation, risk, and short-term interest rates. For example, suppose a company is in the midst of a 5-year expansion program and the treasurer knows that she will need to borrow short-term funds a year from now. She knows the current cost of 1-year money, read from the yield curve, but she wants to know the cost of 1-year money next year. That information can be "backed out" by analyzing the current yield curve, as will be discussed.

The estimation process is straightforward provided we (1) focus on Treasury bonds and (2) assume that Treasury bonds contain no maturity risk premiums.[13] This position has been called the **pure expectations theory** of the term structure of interest rates, often simply referred to as the "expectations theory." The expectations theory assumes that bond traders establish bond prices and interest rates strictly on the basis of expectations for future interest rates and that they are indifferent to maturity because they do not view long-term bonds as being riskier than short-term bonds. If this were true, the maturity risk premium (MRP) would be zero and long-term interest rates would simply be a weighted average of current and expected future short-term interest rates.

To illustrate the pure expectations theory, assume that a 1-year Treasury bond currently yields 5.00% while a 2-year bond yields 5.50%. Investors who want to invest for a 2-year horizon have two primary options:

Option 1: *Buy a two-year security and hold it for 2 years.*

---

[12]This section is relatively technical, but instructors can omit it without loss of continuity.

[13]Although most evidence suggests that there is a positive maturity risk premium, some academics and practitioners contend that this second assumption is reasonable, at least as an approximation. They argue that the market is dominated by large bond traders who buy and sell securities of different maturities each day, that these traders focus only on short-term returns, and that they are not concerned with maturity risk. According to this view, a bond trader is just as willing to buy a 20-year bond to pick up a short-term profit as he or she is to buy a 3-month security. Proponents of this view argue that the shape of the Treasury yield curve is therefore determined only by market expectations about future interest rates. Later we show what happens when we include the effects of maturity risk premiums.

Option 2: *Buy a 1-year security; hold it for 1 year; and then at the end of the year, reinvest the proceeds in another 1-year security.*

If they select Option 1, for every dollar they invest today, they will have accumulated $1.113025 by the end of Year 2:

$$\text{Funds at end of Year 2} = \$1 \times (1.055)^2 = \$1.113025$$

If they select Option 2, they should end up with the same amount; but this equation is used to find the ending amount:

$$\text{Funds at end of Year 2} = \$1 \times (1.05) \times (1 + X)$$

Here X is the expected interest rate on a 1-year Treasury security 1 year from now.

If the expectations theory is correct, each option must provide the same amount of cash at the end of 2 years, which implies the following:

$$(1.05)(1 + X) = (1.055)^2$$

We can rearrange this equation and then solve for X:

$$1 + X = (1.055)^2/1.05$$
$$X = (1.055)^2/1.05 - 1 = 0.0600238 = 6.00238\%$$

Therefore, X, the 1-year rate 1 year from today, must be 6.00238%; otherwise, one option will be better than the other and the market will not be in equilibrium. However, if the market is not in equilibrium, buying and selling will quickly bring about equilibrium. For example, suppose investors expect the 1-year Treasury rate to be 6.00238% a year from now but a 2-year bond now yields 5.25%, not the 5.50% rate required for equilibrium. Bond traders could earn a profit by adopting the following strategy:

1. Borrow money for 2 years at the 2-year rate, 5.25% per year.
2. Invest the money in a series of 1-year securities, expecting to earn 5.00% this year and 6.00238% next year, for an overall expected return over the 2 years of $[(1.05) \times (1.0600238)]^{1/2} - 1 = 5.50\%$.

Borrowing at 5.25% and investing to earn 5.50% is a good deal, so bond traders would rush to borrow money (demand funds) in the 2-year market and invest (or supply funds) in the 1-year market.

Recall from Figure 6-1 that a decline in the supply of funds raises interest rates, while an increase in the supply lowers rates. Likewise, an increase in the demand for funds raises rates, while a decline in demand lowers rates. Therefore, bond traders would push up the 2-year yield and simultaneously lower the yield on 1-year bonds. This buying and selling would cease when the 2-year rate becomes a weighted average of expected future 1-year rates.[14]

The preceding analysis was based on the assumption that the maturity risk premium is zero. However, most evidence suggests that a positive maturity risk premium exists. For example, assume once again that 1- and 2-year maturities yield 5.00% and 5.50%, respectively; so we have a rising yield curve. However,

---

[14]In our calculations, we used the geometric average of the current and expected 1-year rates: $[(1.05) \times (1.0600238)]^{1/2} - 1 = 0.055$ or 5.50%. The arithmetic average of the two rates is $(5\% + 6.00238\%)/2 = 5.50119\%$. The geometric average is theoretically correct, but the difference is only 0.00119%. With interest rates at the levels they have been in the United States and most other nations in recent years, the geometric and arithmetic averages are so close that many people use the arithmetic average, especially given the other assumptions that underlie the estimation of future 1-year rates.

now assume that the maturity risk premium on the 2-year bond is 0.20% versus zero for the 1-year bond. This premium means that in equilibrium, the expected annual return on a 2-year bond (5.50%) must be 0.20% higher than the expected return on a series of two 1-year bonds (5.00% and X%). Therefore, the expected return on the series must be 5.50% − 0.20% = 5.30%:

$$\text{Expected return on 2-year series} = \text{Rate on 2-year bond} - \text{MRP}$$
$$= 0.055 - 0.002 = 0.053 = 5.30\%$$

Now recall that the annual expected return from the series of two 1-year bonds can be expressed as follows, where X is the 1-year rate next year:

$$(1.05)(1 + X) = (1 + \text{Expected return on 2-year series})^2 = (1.053)^2$$
$$1.05X = (1.053)^2 - 1.05$$
$$X = \frac{0.0588090}{1.05} = 0.0560086 = 5.60086\%$$

Under these conditions, equilibrium requires that market participants expect the 1-year rate next year to be 5.60086%.

Note that the rate read from the yield curve rises by 0.50% when the years to maturity increase from one to two: 5.50% − 5.00% = 0.50%. Of this 0.50% increase, 0.20% is attributable to the MRP and the remaining 0.30% is due to the increase in expected 1-year rates next year.

Putting all of this together, we see that one can use the yield curve to estimate what the market expects the short-term rate to be next year. However, this requires an estimate of the maturity risk premium; and if our estimated MRP is incorrect, then so will our yield-curve-based interest rate forecast. Thus, while the yield curve can be used to obtain insights into what the market thinks future interest rates will be, we calculate out these expectations with precision unless the pure expectations theory holds or we know with certainty the exact maturity risk premium. Since neither of these conditions holds, it is difficult to know for sure what the market is forecasting.

Note too that even if we could determine the market's consensus forecast for future rates, the market is not always right. So a forecast of next year's rate based on the yield curve could be wrong. Therefore, obtaining an accurate forecast of rates for next year—or even for next month—is extremely difficult.

SELF TEST

What key assumption underlies the pure expectations theory?

Assuming that the pure expectations theory is correct, how are expected short-term rates used to calculate expected long-term rates?

According to the pure expectations theory, what would happen if long-term rates were not an average of expected short-term rates?

Most evidence suggests that a positive maturity risk premium exists. How would this affect your calculations when determining interest rates?

Assume that the interest rate on a 1-year T-bond is currently 7% and the rate on a 2-year bond is 9%. If the maturity risk premium is zero, what is a reasonable forecast of the rate on a 1-year bond next year? What would the forecast be if the maturity risk premium on the 2-year bond was 0.5% versus zero for the 1-year bond? **(11.04%; 10.02%)**

6-7 MACROECONOMIC FACTORS THAT INFLUENCE INTEREST RATE LEVELS

We described how key components such as expected inflation, default risk, maturity risk, and liquidity concerns influence the level of interest rates over time and across different markets. On a day-to-day basis, a variety of macroeconomic factors may influence one or more of these components; hence, macroeconomic factors have an important effect on both the general level of interest rates and the shape of the yield curve. The primary factors are (1) Federal Reserve policy; (2) the federal budget deficit or surplus; (3) international factors, including the foreign trade balance and interest rates in other countries; and (4) the level of business activity.

*The home page for the Board of Governors of the Federal Reserve System can be found at **www.federalreserve.gov**. You can access general information about the Federal Reserve, including press releases, speeches, and monetary policy.*

6-7a Federal Reserve Policy

As you probably learned in your economics courses, (1) the money supply has a significant effect on the level of economic activity, inflation, and interest rates, and (2) in the United States, the Federal Reserve Board controls the money supply. If the Fed wants to stimulate the economy, it increases the money supply. The Fed buys and sells short-term securities, so the initial effect of a monetary easing would be to cause short-term rates to decline. However, a larger money supply might lead to an increase in expected future inflation, which would cause long-term rates to rise even as short-term rates fell. The reverse holds if the Fed tightens the money supply.

As you can see from Figure 6-2, interest rates in recent years have been relatively low, with short-term rates especially low in 2003 and 2004. Those low rates enabled mortgage banks to write adjustable rate mortgage loans with very favorable rates, and that helped stimulate a huge housing boom along with growth of the economy. The Fed became concerned that the economy would overheat; so from 2004 to 2006, it raised its target rate 17 times, going from 2.0% to 5.25% in 2006. Long-term rates remained relatively stable during those years.

The Fed left its target rate unchanged from June 2006 to September 2007, but the subprime credit crunch that began in 2007 caused increasing concerns about a possible recession. Those fears led the Fed to cut rates five times from September 2007 to February 2008, taking the target rate down from 5.25% to 3.00%. The Fed also signaled that more cuts were likely in the coming few months.

Actions that lower short-term rates won't necessarily lower long-term rates. This point was made in the following quote from the online edition of *Investors' Business Daily* on February 15, 2008:

> *U.S. government debt prices ended mostly lower Thursday, led by long-dated issues, as traders turned their focus to potential inflation risks resulting from additional interest rate cuts signaled by the Federal Reserve.*
>
> *It was a rough day for the Treasuries market, as traders concluded that more Fed rate cuts and the government's fiscal stimulus program would come at the expense of higher long-term inflation.*
>
> *"Fiscal and monetary stimuli are focused on the current strain in the financial markets and its effect on the economy, but there are fears about what these actions may do to inflation down the road," said Tom Sapio, a managing director at Cantor Fitzgerald in New York.*

Lower rates could also cause foreigners to sell their holdings of U.S. bonds. These investors would be paid with dollars, which they would then sell to buy their own currencies. The sale of dollars and the purchase of other currencies would lower the value of the dollar relative to other currencies, which would make U.S. goods less expensive, which would help manufacturers and thus lower the trade deficit. Note also that during periods when the Fed is actively intervening in the markets, the yield curve may be temporarily distorted. Short-term rates may be driven below the long-run equilibrium level if the Fed is easing credit and above the equilibrium rate if the Fed is tightening credit. Long-term rates are not affected as much by Fed intervention.

6-7b Federal Budget Deficits or Surpluses

If the federal government spends more than it takes in as taxes, it runs a deficit; and that deficit must be covered by additional borrowing (selling more Treasury bonds) or by printing money. If the government borrows, this increases the demand for funds and thus pushes up interest rates. If the government prints money, investors recognize that with "more money chasing a given amount of goods," the result will be increased inflation, which will also increase interest rates. So the larger the federal deficit, other things held constant, the higher the level of interest rates.

Over the past several decades, the federal government has generally run large budget deficits. There were some surpluses in the late 1990s; but the September 11, 2001, terrorist attacks, the subsequent recession, and the Iraq war all boosted government spending and caused the deficits to return. It is difficult to tell where fiscal policy will go and consequently what effect it will have on interest rates.

6-7c International Factors

Foreign Trade Deficit
The situation that exists when a country imports more than it exports.

Businesses and individuals in the United States buy from and sell to people and firms all around the globe. If they buy more than they sell (that is, if there are more imports than exports), they are said to be running a **foreign trade deficit**. When trade deficits occur, they must be financed; and this generally means borrowing from nations with export surpluses. Thus, if the United States imported $200 billion of goods but exported only $100 billion, it would run a trade deficit of $100 billion while other countries would have a $100 billion trade surplus. The United States would probably borrow the $100 billion from the surplus nations.[15] At any rate, the larger the trade deficit, the higher the tendency to borrow. Note that foreigners will hold U.S. debt if and only if the rates on U.S. securities are competitive with rates in other countries. This causes U.S. interest rates to be highly dependent on rates in other parts of the world.

All this interdependency limits the ability of the Federal Reserve to use monetary policy to control economic activity in the United States. For example, if the Fed attempts to lower U.S. interest rates and this causes rates to fall below rates abroad, foreigners will begin selling U.S. bonds. Those sales will depress bond prices, which will push up rates in the United States. Thus, the large U.S. trade deficit (and foreigners' holdings of U.S. debt that resulted from many years of deficits) hinders the Fed's ability to combat a recession by lowering interest rates.

For about 25 years following World War II, the United States ran large trade surpluses and the rest of the world owed it many billions of dollars. However, the situation changed, and the United States has been running trade deficits since the mid-1970s. The cumulative effect of these deficits has been to change the United States from being the largest creditor nation to being the largest debtor nation of

---

[15]The deficit could also be financed by selling assets, including gold, corporate stocks, entire companies, and real estate. The United States has financed its massive trade deficits by all of these means in recent years. Although the primary method has been by borrowing from foreigners, in recent years, there has been a sharp increase in foreign purchases of U.S. assets, especially oil exporters' purchases of U.S. businesses.

all time. As a result, interest rates are very much influenced by interest rates in other countries—higher or lower rates abroad lead to higher or lower U.S. rates. Because of all of this, U.S. corporate treasurers and everyone else who is affected by interest rates should keep up with developments in the world economy.

6-7d Business Activity

You can examine Figure 6-2 to see how business conditions influence interest rates. Here are the key points revealed by the graph:

1. Because inflation increased from 1972 to 1981, the general tendency during that period was toward higher interest rates. However, since the 1981 peak, the trend has generally been downward.

2. The shaded areas in the graph represent recessions, during which (a) the demand for money and the rate of inflation tended to fall and (b) the Federal Reserve tended to increase the money supply in an effort to stimulate the economy. As a result, there is a tendency for interest rates to decline during recessions. For example, the economy began to slow down in 2000, and the country entered a mild recession in 2001. In response, the Federal Reserve cut interest rates. In 2004, the economy began to rebound; so the Fed began to raise rates. However, the subprime debacle hit in 2007; so the Fed began lowering rates in September 2007. By February, the Fed's target rate had fallen from 5.25% to 3.00%, with indications that more reductions were likely.

3. During recessions, short-term rates decline more sharply than long-term rates. This occurs for two reasons: (a) The Fed operates mainly in the short-term sector, so its intervention has the strongest effect there. (b) Long-term rates reflect the average expected inflation rate over the next 20 to 30 years; and this expectation generally does not change much, even when the current inflation rate is low because of a recession or high because of a boom. So short-term rates are more volatile than long-term rates. Taking another look at Figure 6-2, we see that short-term rates did decline recently by much more than long-term rates.

SELF TEST

Identify some macroeconomic factors that influence interest rates and explain the effects of each.

How does the Fed stimulate the economy? How does the Fed affect interest rates?

Does the Fed have complete control over U.S. interest rates? That is, can it set rates at any level it chooses? Why or why not?

6-8 INTEREST RATES AND BUSINESS DECISIONS

The yield curve for January 2008 shown earlier in Figure 6-4 indicates how much the U.S. government had to pay in January 2008 to borrow money for 1 year, 5 years, 10 years, and so forth. A business borrower would have paid somewhat more, but assume for the moment that it is January 2008 and the yield curve shown for that year applies to your company. Now suppose you decide to build a new plant with a 30-year life that will cost $1 million and you will raise the $1 million by borrowing rather than by issuing new stock. If you borrowed in January 2008 on a short-term basis—say for 1 year—your annual interest cost would be only 2.7%, or $27,000. On the other hand, if you used long-term financing, your annual cost would be 4.3%, or $43,000. Therefore, at first glance, it would seem that you should use short-term debt.

However, this could prove to be a horrible mistake. If you use short-term debt, you will have to renew your loan every 6 months; and the rate charged on each new loan will reflect the then-current short-term rate. Interest rates could return to their previous highs, in which case you would be paying 14%, or $140,000, per year. Those high interest payments would cut into and perhaps eliminate your profits. Your reduced profitability could increase your firm's risk to the point where your bond rating was lowered, causing lenders to increase the risk premium built into your interest rate. That would further increase your interest payments, which would further reduce your profitability, worry lenders still more, and make them reluctant to renew your loan. If your lenders refused to renew the loan and demanded its repayment, as they would have every right to do, you might have to sell assets at a loss, which could result in bankruptcy.

On the other hand, if you used long-term financing in 2008, your interest costs would remain constant at $43,000 per year; so an increase in interest rates in the economy would not hurt you. You might even be able to acquire some of your bankrupt competitors at bargain prices—bankruptcies increase dramatically when interest rates rise, primarily because many firms use so much short-term debt.

Does all of this suggest that firms should avoid short-term debt? Not at all. If inflation falls over the next few years, so will interest rates. If you had borrowed on a long-term basis for 4.3% in January 2008, your company would be at a disadvantage if it was locked into 4.3% debt while its competitors (who used short-term debt in 2008) had a borrowing cost of only 2.7%.

Financing decisions would be easy if we could make accurate forecasts of future interest rates. Unfortunately, predicting interest rates with consistent accuracy is nearly impossible. However, although it is difficult to predict future interest rate *levels*, it is easy to predict that interest rates will *fluctuate*—they always have, and they always will. That being the case, sound financial policy calls for using a mix of long- and short-term debt as well as equity to position the firm so that it can survive in any interest rate environment. Further, the optimal financial policy depends in an important way on the nature of the firm's assets—the easier it is to sell off assets to generate cash, the more feasible it is to use more short-term debt. This makes it logical for a firm to finance current assets such as inventories and receivables with short-term debt and to finance fixed assets such as buildings and equipment with long-term debt. We will return to this issue later in the book when we discuss capital structure and financing policy.

Changes in interest rates also have implications for savers. For example, if you had a 401(k) plan—and someday most of you will—you would probably want to invest some of your money in a bond mutual fund. You could choose a fund that had an average maturity of 25 years, 20 years, on down to only a few months (a money market fund). How would your choice affect your investment results and hence your retirement income? First, your decision would affect your annual interest income. For example, if the yield curve was upward- sloping, as it normally is, you would earn more interest if you chose a fund that held long-term bonds. Note, though, that if you chose a long-term fund and interest rates then rose, the market value of your fund would decline. For example, as we will see in Chapter 7, if you had $100,000 in a fund whose average bond had a maturity of 25 years and a coupon rate of 6% and if interest rates then rose from 6% to 10%, the market value of your fund would decline from $100,000 to about $63,500. On the other hand, if rates declined, your fund would increase in value. If you invested in a short-term fund, its value would be stable, but it would probably provide less interest per year. In any event, your choice of maturity would have a major effect on your investment performance and hence on your future income.

SELF TEST

If short-term interest rates are lower than long-term rates, why might a borrower still choose to finance with long-term debt?

Explain the following statement: The optimal financial policy depends in an important way on the nature of the firm's assets.

TYING IT ALL TOGETHER

In this chapter, we discussed the way interest rates are determined, the term structure of interest rates, and some of the ways interest rates affect business decisions. We saw that the interest rate on a given bond, r, is based on this equation:

$$r = r^* + IP + DRP + LP + MRP$$

Here r* is the real risk-free rate, IP is the premium for expected inflation, DRP is the premium for potential default risk, LP is the premium for lack of liquidity, and MRP is the premium to compensate for the risk inherent in bonds with long maturities. Both r* and the various premiums can and do change over time depending on economic conditions, Federal Reserve actions, and the like. Since changes in these factors are difficult to predict, it is hard to forecast the future direction of interest rates.

The yield curve, which relates bonds' interest rates to their maturities, usually has an upward slope; but it can slope up or down, and both its slope and level change over time. The main determinants of the slope of the curve are expectations for future inflation and the MRP. We can analyze yield curve data to estimate what market participants think future interest rates are likely to be.

We will use the insights gained from this chapter in later chapters, when we analyze the values of bonds and stocks and when we examine various corporate investment and financing decisions.

SELF-TEST QUESTIONS AND PROBLEMS
(Solutions Appear in Appendix A)

ST-1 **KEY TERMS** Define each of the following terms:
a. Production opportunities; time preferences for consumption; risk; inflation
b. Real risk-free rate of interest, r*; nominal (quoted) risk-free rate of interest, r_{RF}
c. Inflation premium (IP)
d. Default risk premium (DRP)
e. Liquidity premium (LP); maturity risk premium (MRP)
f. Interest rate risk; reinvestment rate risk
g. Term structure of interest rates; yield curve
h. "Normal" yield curve; inverted ("abnormal") yield curve; humped yield curve
i. Pure expectations theory

ST-2   **INFLATION AND INTEREST RATES**   The real risk-free rate of interest, r*, is 3%; and it is expected to remain constant over time. Inflation is expected to be 2% per year for the next 3 years and 4% per year for the next 5 years. The maturity risk premium is equal to 0.1 (t − 1)%, where t = the bond's maturity. The default risk premium for a BBB-rated bond is 1.3%.

    a.   What is the average expected inflation rate over the next 4 years?

    b.   What is the yield on a 4-year Treasury bond?

    c.   What is the yield on a 4-year BBB-rated corporate bond with a liquidity premium of 0.5%?

    d.   What is the yield on an 8-year Treasury bond?

    e.   What is the yield on an 8-year BBB-rated corporate bond with a liquidity premium of 0.5%?

    f.   If the yield on a 9-year Treasury bond is 7.3%, what does that imply about expected inflation in 9 years?

ST-3   **PURE EXPECTATIONS THEORY**   The yield on 1-year Treasury securities is 6%, 2-year securities yield 6.2%, and 3-year securities yield 6.3%. There is no maturity risk premium. Using expectations theory, forecast the yields on the following securities:

    a.   A 1-year security, 1 year from now

    b.   A 1-year security, 2 years from now

    c.   A 2-year security, 1 year from now

QUESTIONS

6-1   Suppose interest rates on residential mortgages of equal risk are 5.5% in California and 7.0% in New York. Could this differential persist? What forces might tend to equalize rates? Would differentials in borrowing costs for businesses of equal risk located in California and New York be more or less likely to exist than differentials in residential mortgage rates? Would differentials in the cost of money for New York and California firms be more likely to exist if the firms being compared were very large or if they were very small? What are the implications of all of this with respect to nationwide branching?

6-2   Which fluctuate more—long-term or short-term interest rates? Why?

6-3   Suppose you believe that the economy is just entering a recession. Your firm must raise capital immediately, and debt will be used. Should you borrow on a long-term or a short-term basis? Why?

6-4   Suppose the population of Area Y is relatively young and the population of Area O is relatively old but everything else about the two areas is the same.
    a.   Would interest rates likely be the same or different in the two areas? Explain.
    b.   Would a trend toward nationwide branching by banks and the development of nationwide diversified financial corporations affect your answer to part a? Explain.

6-5   Suppose a new process was developed that could be used to make oil out of seawater. The equipment required is quite expensive; but it would, in time, lead to low prices for gasoline, electricity, and other types of energy. What effect would this have on interest rates?

6-6   Suppose a new and more liberal Congress and administration are elected. Their first order of business is to take away the independence of the Federal Reserve System and to force the Fed to greatly expand the money supply. What effect will this have:
    a.   On the level and slope of the yield curve immediately after the announcement?
    b.   On the level and slope of the yield curve that would exist two or three years in the future?

6-7   It is a fact that the federal government (1) encouraged the development of the savings and loan industry, (2) virtually forced the industry to make long-term fixed-interest-rate mortgages, and (3) forced the savings and loans to obtain most of their capital as deposits that were withdrawable on demand.
    a.   Would the savings and loans have higher profits in a world with a "normal" or an inverted yield curve?

b. Would the savings and loan industry be better off if the individual institutions sold their mortgages to federal agencies and then collected servicing fees or if the institutions held the mortgages that they originated?

6-8 Suppose interest rates on Treasury bonds rose from 5% to 9% as a result of higher interest rates in Europe. What effect would this have on the price of an average company's common stock?

6-9 What does it mean when it is said that the United States is running a trade deficit? What impact will a trade deficit have on interest rates?

PROBLEMS

Easy Problems 1–7

6-1 **YIELD CURVES** The following yields on U.S. Treasury securities were taken from a recent financial publication:

Term	Rate
6 months	5.1%
1 year	5.5
2 years	5.6
3 years	5.7
4 years	5.8
5 years	6.0
10 years	6.1
20 years	6.5
30 years	6.3

a. Plot a yield curve based on these data.

b. What type of yield curve is shown?

c. What information does this graph tell you?

d. Based on this yield curve, if you needed to borrow money for longer than 1 year, would it make sense for you to borrow short-term and renew the loan or borrow long-term? Explain.

6-2 **REAL RISK-FREE RATE** You read in *The Wall Street Journal* that 30-day T-bills are currently yielding 5.5%. Your brother-in-law, a broker at Safe and Sound Securities, has given you the following estimates of current interest rate premiums:

- Inflation premium = 3.25%
- Liquidity premium = 0.6%
- Maturity risk premium = 1.8%
- Default risk premium = 2.15%

On the basis of these data, what is the real risk-free rate of return?

6-3 **EXPECTED INTEREST RATE** The real risk-free rate is 3%. Inflation is expected to be 2% this year and 4% during the next 2 years. Assume that the maturity risk premium is zero. What is the yield on 2-year Treasury securities? What is the yield on 3-year Treasury securities?

6-4 **DEFAULT RISK PREMIUM** A Treasury bond that matures in 10 years has a yield of 6%. A 10-year corporate bond has a yield of 8%. Assume that the liquidity premium on the corporate bond is 0.5%. What is the default risk premium on the corporate bond?

6-5 **MATURITY RISK PREMIUM** The real risk-free rate is 3%, and inflation is expected to be 3% for the next 2 years. A 2-year Treasury security yields 6.2%. What is the maturity risk premium for the 2-year security?

6-6 **INFLATION CROSS-PRODUCT** An analyst is evaluating securities in a developing nation where the inflation rate is very high. As a result, the analyst has been warned not to ignore the cross-product between the real rate and inflation. If the real risk-free rate is 5% and inflation is expected to be 16% each of the next 4 years, what is the yield on a 4-year security with no maturity, default, or liquidity risk? (Hint: Refer to "The Links between Expected Inflation and Interest Rates: A Closer Look" on Page 178.)

6-7 **EXPECTATIONS THEORY** One-year Treasury securities yield 5%. The market anticipates that 1 year from now, 1-year Treasury securities will yield 6%. If the pure expectations theory is correct, what is the yield today for 2-year Treasury securities?

6-8 **EXPECTATIONS THEORY** Interest rates on 4-year Treasury securities are currently 7%, while 6-year Treasury securities yield 7.5%. If the pure expectations theory is correct, what does the market believe that 2-year securities will be yielding 4 years from now?

6-9 **EXPECTED INTEREST RATE** The real risk-free rate is 3%. Inflation is expected to be 3% this year, 4% next year, and 3.5% thereafter. The maturity risk premium is estimated to be $0.05 \times (t - 1)\%$, where t = number of years to maturity. What is the yield on a 7-year Treasury note?

6-10 **INFLATION** Due to a recession, expected inflation this year is only 3%. However, the inflation rate in Year 2 and thereafter is expected to be constant at some level above 3%. Assume that the expectations theory holds and the real risk-free rate is $r^* = 2\%$. If the yield on 3-year Treasury bonds equals the 1-year yield plus 2%, what inflation rate is expected after Year 1?

6-11 **DEFAULT RISK PREMIUM** A company's 5-year bonds are yielding 7.75% per year. Treasury bonds with the same maturity are yielding 5.2% per year, and the real risk-free rate (r^*) is 2.3%. The average inflation premium is 2.5%; and the maturity risk premium is estimated to be $0.1 \times (t - 1)\%$, where t = number of years to maturity. If the liquidity premium is 1%, what is the default risk premium on the corporate bonds?

6-12 **MATURITY RISK PREMIUM** An investor in Treasury securities expects inflation to be 2.5% in Year 1, 3.2% in Year 2, and 3.6% each year thereafter. Assume that the real risk-free rate is 2.75% and that this rate will remain constant. Three-year Treasury securities yield 6.25%, while 5-year Treasury securities yield 6.80%. What is the difference in the maturity risk premiums (MRPs) on the two securities; that is, what is $MRP_5 - MRP_3$?

6-13 **DEFAULT RISK PREMIUM** The real risk-free rate, r^*, is 2.5%. Inflation is expected to average 2.8% a year for the next 4 years, after which time inflation is expected to average 3.75% a year. Assume that there is no maturity risk premium. An 8-year corporate bond has a yield of 8.3%, which includes a liquidity premium of 0.75%. What is its default risk premium?

6-14 **EXPECTATIONS THEORY AND INFLATION** Suppose 2-year Treasury bonds yield 4.5%, while 1-year bonds yield 3%. r^* is 1%, and the maturity risk premium is zero.
a. Using the expectations theory, what is the yield on a 1-year bond 1 year from now?
b. What is the expected inflation rate in Year 1? Year 2?

6-15 **EXPECTATIONS THEORY** Assume that the real risk-free rate is 2% and that the maturity risk premium is zero. If the 1-year bond yield is 5% and a 2-year bond (of similar risk) yields 7%, what is the 1-year interest rate that is expected for Year 2? What inflation rate is expected during Year 2? Comment on why the average interest rate during the 2-year period differs from the 1-year interest rate expected for Year 2.

6-16 **INFLATION CROSS-PRODUCT** An analyst is evaluating securities in a developing nation where the inflation rate is very high. As a result, the analyst has been warned not to ignore the cross-product between the real rate and inflation. A 6-year security with no maturity, default, or liquidity risk has a yield of 20.84%. If the real risk-free rate is 6%, what average rate of inflation is expected in this country over the next 6 years? (Hint: Refer to "The Links between Expected Inflation and Interest Rates: A Closer Look" on Page 178.)

6-17 **INTEREST RATE PREMIUMS** A 5-year Treasury bond has a 5.2% yield. A 10-year Treasury bond yields 6.4%, and a 10-year corporate bond yields 8.4%. The market expects that inflation will average 2.5% over the next 10 years (IP_{10} = 2.5%). Assume that there is no maturity risk premium (MRP = 0) and that the annual real risk-free rate, r^*, will remain constant over the next 10 years. (Hint: Remember that the default risk premium and the liquidity premium are zero for Treasury securities: DRP = LP = 0.) A 5-year corporate bond has the same default risk premium and liquidity premium as the 10-year corporate bond described. What is the yield on this 5-year corporate bond?

6-18   **YIELD CURVES**   Suppose the inflation rate is expected to be 7% next year, 5% the following year, and 3% thereafter. Assume that the real risk-free rate, r*, will remain at 2% and that maturity risk premiums on Treasury securities rise from zero on very short-term bonds (those that mature in a few days) to 0.2% for 1-year securities. Furthermore, maturity risk premiums increase 0.2% for each year to maturity, up to a limit of 1.0% on 5-year or longer-term T-bonds.

   a.   Calculate the interest rate on 1-, 2-, 3-, 4-, 5-, 10-, and 20-year Treasury securities and plot the yield curve.

   b.   Suppose a AAA-rated company (which is the highest bond rating a firm can have) had bonds with the same maturities as the Treasury bonds. Estimate and plot what you believe a AAA-rated company's yield curve would look like on the same graph with the Treasury bond yield curve. (Hint: Think about the default risk premium on its long-term versus its short-term bonds.)

   c.   On the same graph, plot the approximate yield curve of a much riskier lower-rated company with a much higher risk of defaulting on its bonds.

6-19   **INFLATION AND INTEREST RATES**   In late 1980, the U.S. Commerce Department released new data showing inflation was 15%. At the time, the prime rate of interest was 21%, a record high. However, many investors expected the new Reagan administration to be more effective in controlling inflation than the Carter administration had been. Moreover, many observers believed that the extremely high interest rates and generally tight credit, which resulted from the Federal Reserve System's attempts to curb the inflation rate, would lead to a recession, which, in turn, would lead to a decline in inflation and interest rates. Assume that at the beginning of 1981, the expected inflation rate for 1981 was 13%; for 1982, 9%; for 1983, 7%; and for 1984 and thereafter, 6%.

   a.   What was the average expected inflation rate over the 5-year period 1981–1985? (Use the arithmetic average.)

   b.   Over the 5-year period, what average *nominal* interest rate would be expected to produce a 2% real risk-free return on 5-year Treasury securities? Assume MRP = 0.

   c.   Assuming a real risk-free rate of 2% and a maturity risk premium that equals $0.1 \times (t)$%, where t is the number of years to maturity, estimate the interest rate in January 1981 on bonds that mature in 1, 2, 5, 10, and 20 years. Draw a yield curve based on these data.

   d.   Describe the general economic conditions that could lead to an upward-sloping yield curve.

   e.   If investors in early 1981 expected the inflation rate for every future year to be 10% (that is, $I_t = I_{t+1} = 10\%$ for t = 1 to ∞), what would the yield curve have looked like? Consider all the factors that are likely to affect the curve. Does your answer here make you question the yield curve you drew in part c?

COMPREHENSIVE/SPREADSHEET PROBLEM

6-20   **INTEREST RATE DETERMINATION AND YIELD CURVES**

   a.   What effect would each of the following events likely have on the level of nominal interest rates?

   (1)   Households dramatically increase their savings rate.

   (2)   Corporations increase their demand for funds following an increase in investment opportunities.

   (3)   The government runs a larger-than-expected budget deficit.

   (4)   There is an increase in expected inflation.

   b.   Suppose you are considering two possible investment opportunities: a 12-year Treasury bond and a 7-year, A-rated corporate bond. The current real risk-free rate is 4%; and inflation is expected to be 2% for the next 2 years, 3% for the following 4 years, and 4% thereafter. The maturity risk premium is estimated by this formula: MRP = 0.1 (t – 1)%. The liquidity premium for the corporate bond is estimated to be 0.7%. Finally, you may determine the default risk premium, given the company's bond rating, from the default risk premium table in the text. What yield would you predict for each of these two investments?

c. Given the following Treasury bond yield information from a recent financial publication, construct a graph of the yield curve.

Maturity	Yield
1 year	5.37%
2 years	5.47
3 years	5.65
4 years	5.71
5 years	5.64
10 years	5.75
20 years	6.33
30 years	5.94

d. Based on the information about the corporate bond provided in part b, calculate yields and then construct a new yield curve graph that shows both the Treasury and the corporate bonds.

e. Which part of the yield curve (the left side or right side) is likely to be most volatile over time?

f. Using the Treasury yield information in part c, calculate the following rates:

(1) The 1-year rate 1 year from now

(2) The 5-year rate 5 years from now

(3) The 10-year rate 10 years from now

(4) The 10-year rate 20 years from now

INTEGRATED CASE

MORTON HANDLEY & COMPANY

6-21   **INTEREST RATE DETERMINATION**   Maria Juarez is a professional tennis player, and your firm manages her money. She has asked you to give her information about what determines the level of various interest rates. Your boss has prepared some questions for you to consider.

a. What are the four most fundamental factors that affect the cost of money, or the general level of interest rates, in the economy?

b. What is the real risk-free rate of interest (r^*) and the nominal risk-free rate (r_{RF})? How are these two rates measured?

c. Define the terms *inflation premium (IP)*, *default risk premium (DRP)*, *liquidity premium (LP)*, and *maturity risk premium (MRP)*. Which of these premiums is included in determining the interest rate on (1) short-term U.S. Treasury securities, (2) long-term U.S. Treasury securities, (3) short-term corporate securities, and (4) long-term corporate securities? Explain how the premiums would vary over time and among the different securities listed.

d. What is the term structure of interest rates? What is a yield curve?

e. Suppose most investors expect the inflation rate to be 5% next year, 6% the following year, and 8% thereafter. The real risk-free rate is 3%. The maturity risk premium is zero for bonds that mature in 1 year or less and 0.1% for 2-year bonds; then the MRP increases by 0.1% per year thereafter for 20 years, after which it is stable. What is the interest rate on 1-, 10-, and 20-year Treasury bonds? Draw a yield curve with these data. What factors can explain why this constructed yield curve is upward-sloping?

f. At any given time, how would the yield curve facing a AAA-rated company compare with the yield curve for U.S. Treasury securities? At any given time, how would the yield curve facing a BB-rated company compare with the yield curve for U.S. Treasury securities? Draw a graph to illustrate your answer.

g. What is the pure expectations theory? What does the pure expectations theory imply about the term structure of interest rates?

h. Suppose you observe the following term structure for Treasury securities:

Maturity	Yield
1 year	6.0%
2 years	6.2
3 years	6.4
4 years	6.5
5 years	6.5

Assume that the pure expectations theory of the term structure is correct. (This implies that you can use the yield curve provided to "back out" the market's expectations about future interest rates.) What does the market expect will be the interest rate on 1-year securities 1 year from now? What does the market expect will be the interest rate on 3-year securities 2 years from now?

CHAPTER

7 Bonds and Their Valuation

Sizing Up Risk in the Bond Market

Many people view Treasury securities as a lackluster but ultra-safe investment. From a default standpoint, Treasuries are indeed our safest investments; but their prices can still decline in any given year if interest rates increase. This is especially true for long-term bonds, which lost nearly 9% in 1999. However, bonds can perform well—in fact, they outgained stocks in 5 of the 8 years between 2000 and 2007.

All bonds aren't alike, and they don't necessarily all move in the same direction. For example, corporate bonds are callable and they can default, whereas Treasury bonds are not exposed to these risks. This results in higher nominal yields on corporates, but the spread between corporate and Treasury yields differs widely depending on the risk of the particular corporate bond. Moreover, yield spreads vary substantially over time, especially for lower-rated securities. For example, as information about WorldCom's deteriorating condition began coming out in 2002, the spread on its 5-year bonds jumped from 1.67% to over 20% in mid-2002. These

bonds subsequently defaulted, so greedy people who bought them expecting a high return ended up with a large loss.

When the economy is strong, corporate bonds generally produce higher returns than Treasuries—their promised returns are higher, and most make their promised payments because few go into default. However, when the economy weakens, concerns about defaults rise, which leads to declines in corporate bond prices. For example, from the beginning of 2000 to the end of 2002, a sluggish economy and a string of accounting scandals led to some major corporate defaults, which worried investors. All corporate bond prices then declined relative to Treasuries, and the result was an increase in yield spreads. As the economy rebounded in 2003, yield spreads declined to their former levels, which resulted in good gains in corporate bond prices. The situation is once again worrisome in 2008. The subprime mortgage crisis has led to fears of recession; and this has caused spreads to rise dramatically, especially for lower-rated bonds.

For example, the spread on junk bonds over Treasuries rose from 2.4% to 7.5% in the 6 months from mid-2007 to January 2008.

Bond investors are rightly worried today. If a recession does occur, this will lead to increased defaults on corporate bonds. A recession might benefit investors in Treasury bonds. However, because there have already been several rounds of Federal Reserve rate cuts, Treasury rates may not have much room to fall. Also, there is concern that recent Fed easing is sowing the seeds for higher inflation down the road, which would lead to higher rates and lower bond prices.

In the face of similar risks in 2001, a *BusinessWeek Online* article gave investors the following advice, which is still applicable today:

Take the same diversified approach to bonds as you do with stocks. Blend in U.S. government, corporate— both high-quality and high-yield—and perhaps even some foreign government debt. If you're investing taxable dollars, consider tax-exempt municipal bonds. And it doesn't hurt to layer in some inflation-indexed bonds.

Sources: Scott Patterson, "Ahead of the Tape: Junk Yields Flashing Back to '01 Slump," *The Wall Street Journal*, January 30, 2008, p. C1; *Stocks, Bonds, Bills, and Inflation: (Valuation Edition) 2008 Yearbook* (Chicago: Morningstar, Inc., 2008); and Susan Scherreik, "Getting the Most Bang Out of Your Bonds," *BusinessWeek Online*, November 12, 2001.

PUTTING THINGS IN PERSPECTIVE

In previous chapters, we noted that companies raise capital in two main forms: debt and equity. In this chapter, we examine the characteristics of bonds and discuss the various factors that influence bond prices. In Chapter 9, we will turn our attention to stocks and their valuation.

If you skim through *The Wall Street Journal*, you will see references to a wide variety of bonds. This variety may seem confusing; but in actuality, only a few characteristics distinguish the various types of bonds.

When you finish this chapter, you should be able to:

- Identify the different features of corporate and government bonds.
- Discuss how bond prices are determined in the market, what the relationship is between interest rates and bond prices, and how a bond's price changes over time as it approaches maturity.
- Calculate a bond's yield to maturity and its yield to call if it is callable and determine the "true" yield.
- Explain the different types of risk that bond investors and issuers face and the way a bond's terms and collateral can be changed to affect its interest rate.

7-1 WHO ISSUES BONDS?

A **bond** is a long-term contract under which a borrower agrees to make payments of interest and principal on specific dates to the holders of the bond. Bonds are issued by corporations and government agencies that are looking for long-term debt capital. For example, on January 3, 2009, Allied Food Products borrowed $50 million by issuing $50 million of bonds. For convenience, we assume that Allied sold 50,000 individual bonds for $1,000 each. Actually, it could have sold one $50 million bond, 10 bonds each with a $5 million face value, or any other combination that totaled $50 million. In any event, Allied received the $50 million; and in exchange, it promised to make annual interest payments and to repay the $50 million on a specified maturity date.

Bond
A long-term debt instrument.

Treasury Bonds
Bonds issued by the federal government, sometimes referred to as government bonds.

Corporate Bonds
Bonds issued by corporations.

Municipal Bonds
Bonds issued by state and local governments.

Foreign Bonds
Bonds issued by foreign governments or by foreign corporations.

Until the 1970s, most bonds were beautifully engraved pieces of paper and their key terms, including their face values, were spelled out on the bonds. Today, though, virtually all bonds are represented by electronic data stored in secure computers, much like the "money" in a bank checking account.

Bonds are grouped in several ways. One grouping is based on the issuer: the U.S. Treasury, corporations, state and local governments, and foreigners. Each bond differs with respect to risk and consequently its expected return.

Treasury bonds, generally called Treasuries and sometimes referred to as government bonds, are issued by the federal government.[1] It is reasonable to assume that the U.S. government will make good on its promised payments, so Treasuries have no default risk. However, these bonds' prices do decline when interest rates rise; so they are not completely riskless.

Corporate bonds are issued by business firms. Unlike Treasuries, corporates are exposed to default risk—if the issuing company gets into trouble, it may be unable to make the promised interest and principal payments and bondholders may suffer losses. Different corporate bonds have different levels of default risk depending on the issuing company's characteristics and the terms of the specific bond. Default risk is often referred to as "credit risk"; and as we saw in Chapter 6, the larger this risk, the higher the interest rate investors demand.

Municipal bonds, or munis, is the term given to bonds issued by state and local governments. Like corporates, munis are exposed to some default risk; but they have one major advantage over all other bonds: As we discussed in Chapter 3, the interest earned on most munis is exempt from federal taxes and from state taxes if the holder is a resident of the issuing state. Consequently, the market interest rate on a muni is considerably lower than on a corporate of equivalent risk.

Foreign bonds are issued by a foreign government or a foreign corporation. All foreign corporate bonds are exposed to default risk, as are some foreign government bonds. An additional risk exists when the bonds are denominated in a currency other than that of the investor's home currency. Consider, for example, a U.S. investor who purchases a corporate bond denominated in Japanese yen. At some point, the investor will want to close out his investment and convert the yen back to U.S. dollars. If the Japanese yen unexpectedly falls relative to the dollar, the investor will have fewer dollars than he originally expected to receive. Consequently, the investor could still lose money even if the bond does not default.

What is a bond?

What are the four main issuers of bonds?

Why are U.S. Treasury bonds not completely riskless?

In addition to default risk, what key risk do investors in foreign bonds face?

7-2 KEY CHARACTERISTICS OF BONDS

Although all bonds have some common characteristics, different bonds can have different contractual features. For example, most corporate bonds have provisions that allow the issuer to pay them off early ("call" features), but the specific call

[1]The U.S. Treasury actually calls its debt "bills," "notes," or "bonds." T-bills generally have maturities of 1 year or less at the time of issue, notes generally have original maturities of 2 to 7 years, and bonds originally mature in 8 to 30 years. There are technical differences between bills, notes, and bonds; but they are not important for our purposes. So we generally call all Treasury securities "bonds." Note too that a 30-year T-bond at the time of issue becomes a 29-year bond the next year, and it is a 1-year bond after 29 years.

provisions vary widely among different bonds. Similarly, some bonds are backed by specific assets that must be turned over to the bondholders if the issuer defaults, while other bonds have no such collateral backup. Differences in contractual provisions (and in the fundamental underlying financial strength of the companies backing the bonds) lead to differences in bonds' risks, prices, and expected returns. To understand bonds, it is essential that you understand the following terms.

7-2a Par Value

The **par value** is the stated face value of the bond; for illustrative purposes, we generally assume a par value of $1,000, although any multiple of $1,000 (e.g., $5,000 or $5 million) can be used. The par value generally represents the amount of money the firm borrows and promises to repay on the maturity date.

7-2b Coupon Interest Rate

Allied Food Products' bonds require the company to pay a fixed number of dollars of interest each year. This payment, generally referred to as the **coupon payment,** is set at the time the bond is issued and remains in force during the bond's life.[2] Typically, at the time a bond is issued, its coupon payment is set at a level that will induce investors to buy the bond at or near its par value. Most of the examples and problems throughout this text will focus on bonds with fixed coupon rates.

When this annual coupon payment is divided by the par value, the result is the **coupon interest rate.** For example, Allied's bonds have a $1,000 par value, and they pay $100 in interest each year. The bond's coupon payment is $100, so its coupon interest rate is $100/$1,000 = 10%. In this regard, the $100 is the annual income that an investor receives when he or she invests in the bond.

Allied's bonds are **fixed-rate bonds** because the coupon rate is fixed for the life of the bond. In some cases, however, a bond's coupon payment is allowed to vary over time. These **floating-rate bonds** work as follows: The coupon rate is set for an initial period, often 6 months, after which it is adjusted every 6 months based on some open market rate. For example, the bond's rate may be adjusted so as to equal the 10-year Treasury bond rate plus a "spread" of 1.5 percentage points. Other provisions can be included in corporate bonds. For example, some can be converted at the holders' option into fixed-rate debt, and some floaters have upper limits (caps) and lower limits (floors) on how high or low the rate can go.

Some bonds pay no coupons at all, but are offered at a discount below their par values and hence provide capital appreciation rather than interest income. These securities are called **zero coupon bonds** (*zeros*). Other bonds pay some coupon interest, but not enough to induce investors to buy them at par. In general, any bond originally offered at a price significantly below its par value is called an **original issue discount (OID) bond.** Some of the details associated with issuing or investing in zero coupon bonds are discussed more fully in Web Appendix 7A.

7-2c Maturity Date

Bonds generally have a specified **maturity date** on which the par value must be repaid. Allied's bonds, which were issued on January 3, 2009, will mature on

---

Par Value
The face value of a bond.

Coupon Payment
The specified number of dollars of interest paid each year.

Coupon Interest Rate
The stated annual interest rate on a bond.

Fixed-Rate Bond
A bond whose interest rate is fixed for its entire life.

Floating-Rate Bond
A bond whose interest rate fluctuates with shifts in the general level of interest rates.

Zero Coupon Bond
A bond that pays no annual interest but is sold at a discount below par, thus compensating investors in the form of capital appreciation.

Original Issue Discount (OID) Bond
Any bond originally offered at a price below its par value.

Maturity Date
A specified date on which the par value of a bond must be repaid.

---

[2]Back when bonds were ornate, they were engraved pieces of paper rather than electronic information stored on a computer. Each bond had a number of small (1/2- by 2-inch) dated coupons attached to them; and on each interest payment date, the owner would "clip the coupon" for that date, send it to the company's paying agent, and receive a check for the interest. A 30-year semiannual bond would start with 60 coupons, whereas a 5-year annual payment bond would start with only 5 coupons. Today no physical coupons are involved, and interest checks are mailed or deposited automatically to the bonds' registered owners on the payment date. Even so, people continue to use the terms *coupon* and *coupon interest rate* when discussing bonds. You can think of the coupon interest rate as the *promised rate.*

January 2, 2024; thus, they had a 15-year maturity at the time they were issued. Most bonds have **original maturities** (the maturity at the time the bond is issued) ranging from 10 to 40 years, but any maturity is legally permissible.[3] Of course, the effective maturity of a bond declines each year after it has been issued. Thus, Allied's bonds had a 15-year original maturity. But in 2010, a year later, they will have a 14-year maturity; a year after that, they will have a 13-year maturity; and so forth.

7-2d Call Provisions

Most corporate and municipal bonds, but not Treasuries, contain a **call provision** that gives the issuer the right to call the bonds for redemption.[4] The call provision generally states that the issuer must pay the bondholders an amount greater than the par value if they are called. The additional sum, which is termed a *call premium,* is often equal to one year's interest. For example, the call premium on a 10-year bond with a 10% annual coupon and a par value of $1,000 might be $100, which means that the issuer would have to pay investors $1,100 (the par value plus the call premium) if it wanted to call the bonds. In most cases, the provisions in the bond contract are set so that the call premium declines over time as the bonds approach maturity. Also, while some bonds are immediately callable, in most cases, bonds are often not callable until several years after issue, generally 5 to 10 years. This is known as a *deferred call,* and such bonds are said to have *call protection.*

Companies are not likely to call bonds unless interest rates have declined significantly since the bonds were issued. Suppose a company sold bonds when interest rates were relatively high. Provided the issue is callable, the company could sell a new issue of low-yielding securities if and when interest rates drop, use the proceeds of the new issue to retire the high-rate issue, and thus reduce its interest expense. This process is called a *refunding operation.* Thus, the call privilege is valuable to the firm but detrimental to long-term investors, who will need to reinvest the funds they receive at the new and lower rates. Accordingly, the interest rate on a new issue of callable bonds will exceed that on the company's new noncallable bonds. For example, on February 29, 2008, Pacific Timber Company sold a bond issue yielding 8% that was callable immediately. On the same day, Northwest Milling Company sold an issue with similar risk and maturity that yielded only 7.5%; but its bonds were noncallable for 10 years. Investors were willing to accept a 0.5% lower coupon interest rate on Northwest's bonds for the assurance that the 7.5% interest rate would be earned for at least 10 years. Pacific, on the other hand, had to incur a 0.5% higher annual interest rate for the option of calling the bonds in the event of a decline in rates.

Note that the refunding operation is similar to a homeowner refinancing his or her home mortgage after a decline in rates. Consider, for example, a homeowner with an outstanding mortgage at 8%. If mortgage rates have fallen to 5%, the homeowner will probably find it beneficial to refinance the mortgage. There may

---

Original Maturity

The number of years to maturity at the time a bond is issued.

Call Provision

A provision in a bond contract that gives the issuer the right to redeem the bonds under specified terms prior to the normal maturity date.

---

[3]In July 1993, The Walt Disney Company, attempting to lock in a low interest rate, stretched the meaning of "long-term bond" by issuing the first 100-year bonds sold by any borrower in modern times. Soon after, Coca-Cola became the second company to sell 100-year bonds. A number of other companies have followed.

[4]The number of new corporate issues with call provisions has declined somewhat in recent years. In the 1980s, nearly 80% of new issues contained call provisions; but in recent years, this number has fallen to about 35%. The use of call provisions also varies with credit quality. Roughly 25% of investment-grade bonds in recent years have call provisions versus about 75% of non-investment-grade bonds. Interest rates were historically high in the 1980s, so issuers wanted to be able to refund their debt if and when rates fell. Similarly, companies with low ratings hoped their ratings would rise, lowering their market rates and giving them an opportunity to refund. For more information on the use of callable bonds, see Levent Güntay, N. R. Prabhala, and Haluk Unal, "Callable Bonds, Interest-Rate Risk, and the Supply Side of Hedging," May 2005, a Wharton Financial Institutions Center working paper.

be some fees involved in the refinancing, but the lower rate may be more than enough to offset those fees. The analysis required is essentially the same for homeowners and corporations.

7-2e Sinking Funds

Some bonds include a **sinking fund provision** that facilitates the orderly retirement of the bond issue. Years ago firms were required to deposit money with a trustee, which invested the funds and then used the accumulated sum to retire the bonds when they matured. Today, though, sinking fund provisions require the issuer to buy back a specified percentage of the issue each year. A failure to meet the sinking fund requirement constitutes a default, which may throw the company into bankruptcy. Therefore, a sinking fund is a mandatory payment.

Suppose a company issued $100 million of 20-year bonds and it is required to call 5% of the issue, or $5 million of bonds, each year. In most cases, the issuer can handle the sinking fund requirement in either of two ways:

1. It can call in for redemption, at par value, the required $5 million of bonds. The bonds are numbered serially, and those called for redemption would be determined by a lottery administered by the trustee.
2. The company can buy the required number of bonds on the open market.

The firm will choose the least-cost method. If interest rates have fallen since the bond was issued, the bond will sell for more than its par value. In this case, the firm will use the call option. However, if interest rates have risen, the bonds will sell at a price below par; so the firm can and will buy $5 million par value of bonds in the open market for less than $5 million. Note that a call for sinking fund purposes is generally different from a refunding call because most sinking fund calls require no call premium. However, only a small percentage of the issue is normally callable in a given year.

Although sinking funds are designed to protect investors by ensuring that the bonds are retired in an orderly fashion, these funds work to the detriment of bondholders if the bond's coupon rate is higher than the current market rate. For example, suppose the bond has a 10% coupon but similar bonds now yield only 7.5%. A sinking fund call at par would require a long-term investor to give up a bond that pays $100 of interest and then to reinvest in a bond that pays only $75 per year. This is an obvious disadvantage to those bondholders whose bonds are called. On balance, however, bonds that have a sinking fund are regarded as being safer than those without such a provision; so at the time they are issued, sinking fund bonds have lower coupon rates than otherwise similar bonds without sinking funds.

7-2f Other Features

Several other types of bonds are used sufficiently often to warrant mention.[5] First, **convertible bonds** are bonds that are exchangeable into shares of common stock at a fixed price at the option of the bondholder. Convertibles offer investors the chance for capital gains if the stock increases, but that feature enables the issuing company to set a lower coupon rate than on nonconvertible debt with similar credit risk. Bonds issued with **warrants** are similar to convertibles; but instead of giving the investor an option to exchange the bonds for stock, warrants give the holder an option to buy stock for a stated price, thereby providing a capital gain if the stock's price rises. Because of this factor, bonds issued with warrants, like convertibles, carry lower coupon rates than otherwise similar nonconvertible bonds.

Sinking Fund Provision
A provision in a bond contract that requires the issuer to retire a portion of the bond issue each year.

Convertible Bond
A bond that is exchangeable at the option of the holder for the issuing firm's common stock.

Warrant
A long-term option to buy a stated number of shares of common stock at a specified price.

[5]A recent article by John D. Finnerty and Douglas R. Emery reviews new types of debt (and other) securities that have been created in recent years. See "Corporate Securities Innovations: An Update," *Journal of Applied Finance: Theory, Practice, Education*, Vol. 12, no. 1 (Spring/Summer 2002), pp. 21–47.

Putable Bond

A bond with a provision that allows its investors to sell it back to the company prior to maturity at a prearranged price.

Income Bond

A bond that pays interest only if it is earned.

Indexed (Purchasing Power) Bond

A bond that has interest payments based on an inflation index so as to protect the holder from inflation.

Whereas callable bonds give the *issuer* the right to retire the debt prior to maturity, **putable bonds** allow *investors* to require the company to pay in advance. If interest rates rise, investors will put the bonds back to the company and reinvest in higher coupon bonds. Yet another type of bond is the **income bond**, which pays interest only if the issuer has earned enough money to pay the interest. Thus, income bonds cannot bankrupt a company; but from an investor's standpoint, they are riskier than "regular" bonds. Yet another bond is the **indexed,** or **purchasing power, bond.** The interest rate is based on an inflation index such as the consumer price index; so the interest paid rises automatically when the inflation rate rises, thus protecting bondholders against inflation. As we mentioned in Chapter 6, the U.S. Treasury is the main issuer of indexed bonds. Recall that these Treasury Inflation Protected Securities (TIPS) generally pay a real return varying from 1% to 3%, plus the rate of inflation during the past year.

SELF TEST

Define floating-rate bonds, zero coupon bonds, callable bonds, putable bonds, income bonds, convertible bonds, and inflation-indexed bonds (TIPS).

Which is riskier to an investor, other things held constant—a callable bond or a putable bond?

In general, how is the rate on a floating-rate bond determined?

What are the two ways sinking funds can be handled? Which alternative will be used if interest rates have risen? if interest rates have fallen?

7-3 BOND VALUATION

The value of any financial asset—a stock, a bond, a lease, or even a physical asset such as an apartment building or a piece of machinery—is the present value of the cash flows the asset is expected to produce.

The cash flows for a standard coupon-bearing bond, like those of Allied Foods, consist of interest payments during the bond's 15-year life plus the amount borrowed (generally the par value) when the bond matures. In the case of a floating-rate bond, the interest payments vary over time. For zero coupon bonds, there are no interest payments; so the only cash flow is the face amount when the bond matures. For a "regular" bond with a fixed coupon, like Allied's, here is the situation:

0	r_d%	1	2	3	N
Bond's value		INT	INT	INT	INT M

Here

r_d = the market rate of interest on the bond, 10%. This is the discount rate used to calculate the present value of the cash flows, which is also the bond's price. In Chapter 6, we discussed in detail the various factors that determine market interest rates. Note that r_d is *not* the coupon interest rate. However, r_d is equal to the coupon rate at times, especially the day the bond is issued; and when the two rates are equal, as in this case, the bond sells at par.

> N = the number of years before the bond matures = 15. N declines over time after the bond has been issued; so a bond that had a maturity of 15 years when it was issued (original maturity = 15) will have N = 14 after 1 year, N = 13 after 2 years, and so forth. At this point, we assume that the bond pays interest once a year, or annually; so N is measured in years. Later on we will analyze semiannual payment bonds, which pay interest every 6 months.
>
> INT = dollars of interest paid each year = Coupon rate × Par value = 0.10 ($1,000) = $100. In calculator terminology, INT = PMT = 100. If the bond had been a semiannual payment bond, the payment would have been $50 every 6 months. The payment would have been zero if Allied had issued zero coupon bonds, and it would have varied over time if the bond had been a "floater."
>
> M = the par, or maturity, value of the bond = $1,000. This amount must be paid at maturity. Back in the 1970s and before, when paper bonds with paper coupons were used, most bonds had a $1,000 value. Now with computer-entry bonds, the par amount purchased can vary; but we use $1,000 for simplicity.

We can now redraw the time line to show the numerical values for all variables except the bond's value (and price, assuming an equilibrium exists), V_B:

The following general equation can be solved to find the value of any bond:

$$\text{Bond's value} = V_B = \frac{INT}{(1+r_d)^1} + \frac{INT}{(1+r_d)^2} + \cdots + \frac{INT}{(1+r_d)^N} + \frac{M}{(1+r_d)^N}$$

$$= \sum_{t=1}^{N} \frac{INT}{(1+r_d)^t} + \frac{M}{(1+r_d)^N} \qquad \text{7-1}$$

Inserting values for the Allied bond, we have

$$V_B = \sum_{t=1}^{15} \frac{\$100}{(1.10)^t} + \frac{\$1,000}{(1.10)^{15}}$$

The cash flows consist of an annuity of N years plus a lump sum payment at the end of Year N, and this fact is reflected in Equation 7-1.

We could simply discount each cash flow back to the present and sum those PVs to find the bond's value; see Figure 7-1 for an example. However, this procedure is not very efficient, especially when the bond has many years to maturity. Therefore, we use a financial calculator to solve the problem. Here is the setup:

Inputs:	15	10		100	1000
	N	I/YR	PV	PMT	FV
Output:			= −1,000		

Simply input N = 15, r_d = I/YR = 10, INT = PMT = 100, and M = FV = 1000; then press the PV key to find the bond's value, $1,000.[6] Since the PV is an outflow to the

---

[6]Spreadsheets can also be used to solve for the bond's value, as we show in the Excel model for this chapter.

FIGURE 7-1	Time Line for Allied Food Products' Bonds, 10% Interest Rate

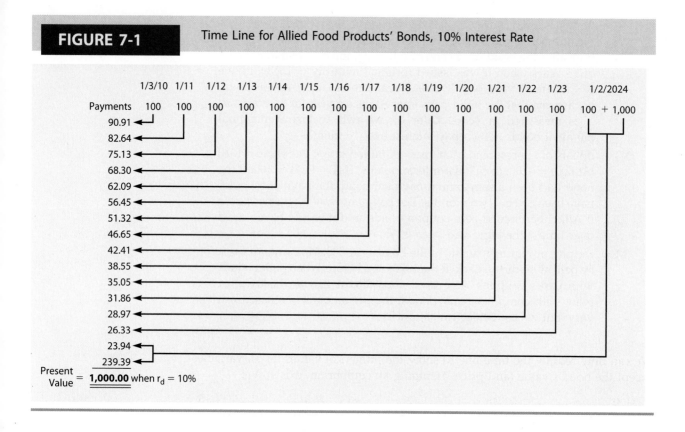

investor, it is shown with a negative sign. The calculator is programmed to solve Equation 7-1: It finds the PV of an annuity of $100 per year for 15 years discounted at 10%; then it finds the PV of the $1,000 maturity payment; then it adds those two PVs to find the bond's value.

In this example, the bond is selling at a price equal to its par value. Whenever the bond's market, or going, rate, r_d, is equal to its coupon rate, a *fixed-rate* bond will sell at its par value. Normally, the coupon rate is set at the going rate in the market the day a bond is issued, causing it to sell at par initially.

The coupon rate remains fixed after the bond is issued, but interest rates in the market move up and down. Looking at Equation 7-1, we see that an *increase* in the market interest rate (r_d) causes the price of an outstanding bond to *fall*, whereas a *decrease* in the rate causes the bond's price to *rise*. For example, if the market interest rate on Allied's bond increased to 15% immediately after it was issued, we would recalculate the price with the new market interest rate as follows:

Inputs:	15	15		100	1000
	N	I/YR	PV	PMT	FV
Output:			= −707.63		

Discount Bond

A bond that sells below its par value; occurs whenever the going rate of interest is above the coupon rate.

The bond's price would fall to $707.63, well below par, as a result of the increase in interest rates. Whenever the going rate of interest *rises above* the coupon rate, a fixed-rate bond's price will fall *below* its par value; this type of bond is called a **discount bond**.

On the other hand, bond prices rise when market interest rates fall. For example, if the market interest rate on Allied's bond decreased to 5% immediately after it was issued, we would once again recalculate its price as follows:

Inputs:	15	5		100	1000
	N	I/YR	PV	PMT	FV
Output:			= −1,518.98		

In this case, the price rises to $1,518.98. In general, whenever the going interest rate *falls below* the coupon rate, a fixed-rate bond's price will rise *above* its par value; this type of bond is called a **premium bond**.

To summarize, here is the situation:

r_d = coupon rate, fixed-rate bond sells at par; hence, it is a *par bond*

r_d > coupon rate, fixed-rate bond sells below par; hence, it is a *discount bond*

r_d < coupon rate, fixed-rate bond sells above par; hence, it is a *premium bond*

SELF TEST

A bond that matures in 8 years has a par value of $1,000 and an annual coupon payment of $70; its market interest rate is 9%. What is its price? **($889.30)**

A bond that matures in 12 years has a par value of $1,000 and an annual coupon of 10%; the market interest rate is 8%. What is its price? **($1,150.72)**

Which of those two bonds is a discount bond, and which is a premium bond?

7-4 BOND YIELDS

If you examine the bond market table of *The Wall Street Journal* or a price sheet put out by a bond dealer, you will typically see information regarding each bond's maturity date, price, and coupon interest rate. You will also see a reported yield. Unlike the coupon interest rate, which is fixed, the bond's yield varies from day to day depending on current market conditions.

To be most useful, the bond's yield should give us an estimate of the rate of return we would earn if we bought the bond today and held it over its remaining life. If the bond is not callable, its remaining life is its years to maturity. If it is callable, its remaining life is the years to maturity if it is not called or the years to the call if it is called. In the following sections, we explain how to calculate those two possible yields and which one is likely to occur.

7-4a Yield to Maturity

Suppose you were offered a 14-year, 10% annual coupon, $1,000 par value bond at a price of $1,494.93. What rate of interest would you earn on your investment if you bought the bond, held it to maturity, and received the promised interest and maturity payments? This rate is called the bond's **yield to maturity (YTM)**, and it is the interest rate generally discussed by investors when they talk about rates of return and the rate reported by *The Wall Street Journal* and other publications. To find the YTM, all you need to do is solve Equation 7-1 for r_d as follows:

$$V_B = \frac{INT}{(1 + r_d)^1} + \frac{INT}{(1 + r_d)^2} + \cdots + \frac{INT}{(1 + r_d)^N} + \frac{M}{(1 + r_d)^N}$$

$$\$1,494.93 = \frac{\$100}{(1 + r_d)^1} + \cdots + \frac{\$100}{(1 + r_d)^{14}} + \frac{\$1,000}{(1 + r_d)^{14}}$$

You can substitute values for r_d until you find a value that "works" and force the sum of the PVs in the equation to equal $1,494.93. However, finding r_d = YTM by trial and error would be a tedious, time-consuming process. However, as you might guess, the calculation is easy with a financial calculator.[7] Here is the setup:

Inputs:	14		−1494.93	100	1000
	N	I/YR	PV	PMT	FV
Output:		= 5			

Simply enter N = 14, PV = −1494.93, PMT = 100, and FV = 1000; then press the I/YR key. The answer, 5%, will appear.

The yield to maturity can also be viewed as the bond's *promised rate of return*, which is the return that investors will receive if all of the promised payments are made. However, the yield to maturity equals the *expected rate of return* only when (1) the probability of default is zero and (2) the bond cannot be called. If there is some default risk or the bond may be called, there is some chance that the promised payments to maturity will not be received, in which case the calculated yield to maturity will exceed the expected return.

Note also that a bond's calculated yield to maturity changes whenever interest rates in the economy change, which is almost daily. An investor who purchases a bond and holds it until it matures will receive the YTM that existed on the purchase date, but the bond's calculated YTM will change frequently between the purchase date and the maturity date.

7-4b Yield to Call

If you purchase a bond that is callable and the company calls it, you do not have the option of holding it to maturity. Therefore, the yield to maturity would not be earned. For example, if Allied's 10% coupon bonds were callable and if interest rates fell from 10% to 5%, the company could call in the 10% bonds, replace them with 5% bonds, and save $100 − $50 = $50 interest per bond per year. This would be beneficial to the company but not to its bondholders.

If current interest rates are well below an outstanding bond's coupon rate, a callable bond is likely to be called; and investors will estimate its most likely rate of return as the **yield to call (YTC)** rather than the yield to maturity. To calculate the YTC, we modify Equation 7-1, using years to call as N and the call price rather than the maturity value as the ending payment. Here's the modified equation:

Yield to Call (YTC)
The rate of return earned on a bond when it is called before its maturity date.

7-2

$$\text{Price of bond} = \sum_{t=1}^{N} \frac{INT}{(1 + r_d)^t} + \frac{\text{Call price}}{(1 + r_d)^N}$$

Here N is the number of years until the company can call the bond; call price is the price the company must pay in order to call the bond (it is often set equal to the par value plus one year's interest); and r_d is the YTC.

---

[7]You can also find the YTM with a spreadsheet. In Excel, you use the Rate function, inputting N_{per} = 14, Pmt = 100, Pv = −1494.93, Fv = 1000, and 0 for Type and leaving Guess blank.

To illustrate, suppose Allied's bonds had a provision that permitted the company, if it desired, to call them 10 years after their issue date at a price of $1,100. Suppose further that interest rates had fallen and that 1 year after issuance, the going interest rate had declined, causing their price to rise to $1,494.93. Here is the time line and the setup for finding the bonds' YTC with a financial calculator:

The YTC is 4.21%—this is the return you would earn if you bought an Allied bond at a price of $1,494.93 and it was called 9 years from today. (It could not be called until 10 years after issuance. One year has gone by, so there are 9 years left until the first call date.)

Do you think Allied *will* call its 10% bonds when they become callable? Allied's action will depend on what the going interest rate is when they become callable. If the going rate remains at $r_d = 5\%$, Allied could save $10\% - 5\% = 5\%$, or $50 per bond per year; so it would call the 10% bonds and replace them with a new 5% issue. There would be some cost to the company to refund the bonds; but because the interest savings would most likely be worth the cost, Allied would probably refund them. Therefore, you should expect to earn the YTC = 4.21% rather than the YTM = 5% if you bought the bond under the indicated conditions.

In the balance of this chapter, we assume that bonds are not callable unless otherwise noted. However, some of the end-of-chapter problems deal with yield to call.[8]

SELF TEST

Explain the difference between yield to maturity and yield to call.

Halley Enterprises' bonds currently sell for $975. They have a 7-year maturity, an annual coupon of $90, and a par value of $1,000. What is their yield to maturity? **(9.51%)**

The Henderson Company's bonds currently sell for $1,275. They pay a $120 annual coupon and have a 20-year maturity, but they can be called in 5 years at $1,120. What are their YTM and their YTC, and which is "more relevant" in the sense that investors should expect to earn it? **(8.99%; 7.31%; YTC)**

---

[8]Brokerage houses occasionally report a bond's *current yield*, defined as the annual interest payment divided by the current price. For example, if Allied's 10% coupon bonds were selling for $985, the current yield would be $100/$985 = 10.15%. Unlike the YTM or YTC, the current yield *does not* represent the actual return that investors should expect because it does not account for the capital gain or loss that will be realized if the bond is held until it matures or is called. The current yield was popular before calculators and computers came along because it was easy to calculate. However, it can be misleading, and now it's easy enough to calculate the YTM and YTC.

7-5 CHANGES IN BOND VALUES OVER TIME

When a coupon bond is issued, the coupon is generally set at a level that causes the bond's market price to equal its par value. If a lower coupon were set, investors would not be willing to pay $1,000 for the bond; but if a higher coupon were set, investors would clamor for it and bid its price up over $1,000. Investment bankers can judge quite precisely the coupon rate that will cause a bond to sell at its $1,000 par value.

A bond that has just been issued is known as a *new issue.* Once it has been issued, it is an *outstanding bond,* also called a *seasoned issue.* Newly issued bonds generally sell at prices very close to par, but the prices of outstanding bonds can vary widely from par. Except for floating-rate bonds, coupon payments are constant; so when economic conditions change, a bond with a $100 coupon that sold at its $1,000 par value when it was issued will sell for more or less than $1,000 thereafter.

Among its outstanding bonds, Allied currently has three equally risky issues that will mature in 15 years:

- Allied's just-issued 15-year bonds have a 10% annual coupon. They were issued at par, which means that the market interest rate on their issue date was also 10%. Because the coupon rate equals the market interest rate, these bonds are trading at par, or $1,000.

- Five years ago Allied issued 20-year bonds with a 7% annual coupon. These bonds currently have 15 years remaining until maturity. They were originally issued at par, which means that 5 years ago the market interest rate was 7%. Currently, this bond's coupon rate is less than the 10% market rate, so they sell at a discount. Using a financial calculator or spreadsheet, we can quickly find that they have a price of $771.82. (Set N = 15, I/YR = 10, PMT = 70, and FV = 1000 and solve for the PV to get the price.)

- Ten years ago Allied issued 25-year bonds with a 13% coupon rate. These bonds currently have 15 years remaining until maturity. They were originally issued at par, which means that 10 years ago the market interest rate must have been 13%. Because their coupon rate is greater than the current market rate, they sell at a premium. Using a financial calculator or spreadsheet, we can find that their price is $1,228.18. (Set N = 15, I/YR = 10, PMT = 130, and FV = 1000 and solve for the PV to get the price.)

Each of these three bonds has a 15-year maturity; each has the same credit risk; and thus each has the same market interest rate, 10%. However, the bonds have different prices because of their different coupon rates.

Now let's consider what would happen to the prices of these three bonds over the 15 years until they mature, assuming that market interest rates remain constant at 10% and Allied does not default on its payments. Table 7-1 demonstrates how the prices of each of these bonds will change over time if market interest rates remain at 10%. One year from now each bond will have a maturity of 14 years—that is, N = 14. With a financial calculator, override N = 15 with N = 14 and press the PV key; that gives you the value of each bond 1 year from now. Continuing, set N = 13, N = 12, and so forth, to see how the prices change over time.

Table 7-1 also shows the current yield (which is the coupon interest divided by the bond's price), the capital gains yield, and the total return over time. For any given year, the *capital gains yield* is calculated as the bond's annual change in price divided by the beginning-of-year price. For example, if a bond was selling for $1,000 at the beginning of the year and $1,035 at the end of the year, its capital gains yield for the year would be $35/$1,000 = 3.5%. (If the bond was selling at a premium, its price would decline over time. Then the capital gains yield would be negative, but it would be offset by a high current yield.) A bond's total return is

Table 7-1　Calculation of Current Yields, Capital Gains Yields, and Total Returns for 7%, 10%, and 13% Coupon Bonds When the Market Rate Remains Constant at 10%

Number of Years Until Maturity	7% COUPON BOND				10% COUPON BOND				13% COUPON BOND			
	Price[a]	Expected Current Yield[b]	Expected Capital Gains Yield[c]	Expected Total Return[d]	Price[a]	Expected Current Yield[b]	Expected Capital Gains Yield[c]	Expected Total Return[d]	Price[a]	Expected Current Yield[b]	Expected Capital Gains Yield[c]	Expected Total Return[d]
15	$ 771.82	9.1%	0.9%	10.0%	$1,000.00	10.0%	0.0%	10.0%	$1,228.18	10.6%	−0.6%	10.0%
14	779.00	9.0	1.0	10.0	1,000.00	10.0	0.0	10.0	1,221.00	10.6	−0.6	10.0
13	786.90	8.9	1.1	10.0	1,000.00	10.0	0.0	10.0	1,213.10	10.7	−0.7	10.0
12	795.59	8.8	1.2	10.0	1,000.00	10.0	0.0	10.0	1,204.41	10.8	−0.8	10.0
11	805.15	8.7	1.3	10.0	1,000.00	10.0	0.0	10.0	1,194.85	10.9	−0.9	10.0
10	815.66	8.6	1.4	10.0	1,000.00	10.0	0.0	10.0	1,184.34	11.0	−1.0	10.0
9	827.23	8.5	1.5	10.0	1,000.00	10.0	0.0	10.0	1,172.77	11.1	−1.1	10.0
8	839.95	8.3	1.7	10.0	1,000.00	10.0	0.0	10.0	1,160.05	11.2	−1.2	10.0
7	853.95	8.2	1.8	10.0	1,000.00	10.0	0.0	10.0	1,146.05	11.3	−1.3	10.0
6	869.34	8.1	1.9	10.0	1,000.00	10.0	0.0	10.0	1,130.66	11.5	−1.5	10.0
5	886.28	7.9	2.1	10.0	1,000.00	10.0	0.0	10.0	1,113.72	11.7	−1.7	10.0
4	904.90	7.7	2.3	10.0	1,000.00	10.0	0.0	10.0	1,095.10	11.9	−1.9	10.0
3	925.39	7.6	2.4	10.0	1,000.00	10.0	0.0	10.0	1,074.61	12.1	−2.1	10.0
2	947.93	7.4	2.6	10.0	1,000.00	10.0	0.0	10.0	1,052.07	12.4	−2.4	10.0
1	972.73	7.2	2.8	10.0	1,000.00	10.0	0.0	10.0	1,027.27	12.7	−2.7	10.0
0	1,000.00				1,000.00				1,000.00			

Notes:
[a]Using a financial calculator, the price of each bond is calculated by entering the data for N, I/YR, PMT, and FV, then solving for PV = the bond's value.
[b]The expected current yield is calculated as the annual interest divided by the price of the bond.
[c]The expected capital gains yield is calculated as the differece between the end-of-year bond price and the beginning-of-year bond price divided by the beginning-of-year price.
[d]The expected total return is the sum of the expected current yield and the expected capital gains yield.

equal to the current yield plus the capital gains yield. In the absence of default risk and assuming market equilibrium, the total return is also equal to YTM and the market interest rate, which in our example is 10%.

Figure 7-2 plots the three bonds' predicted prices as calculated in Table 7-1. Notice that the bonds have very different price paths over time but that at maturity, all three will sell at their par value of $1,000. Here are some points about the prices of the bonds over time:

- The price of the 10% coupon bond trading at par will remain at $1,000 if the market interest rate remains at 10%. Therefore, its current yield will remain at 10% and its capital gains yield will be zero each year.

- The 7% bond trades at a discount; but at maturity, it must sell at par because that is the amount the company will give to its holders. Therefore, its price must rise over time.

- The 13% coupon bond trades at a premium. However, its price must be equal to its par value at maturity; so the price must decline over time.

While the prices of the 7% and 13% coupon bonds move in opposite directions over time, each bond provides investors with the same total return, 10%, which is also the total return on the 10% coupon bond that sells at par. The discount bond has a low coupon rate (and therefore a low current yield), but it provides a capital gain each year. In contrast, the premium bond has a high current yield, but it has an expected capital loss each year.[9]

FIGURE 7-2	Time Paths of 7%, 10%, and 13% Coupon Bonds When the Market Rate Remains Constant at 10%

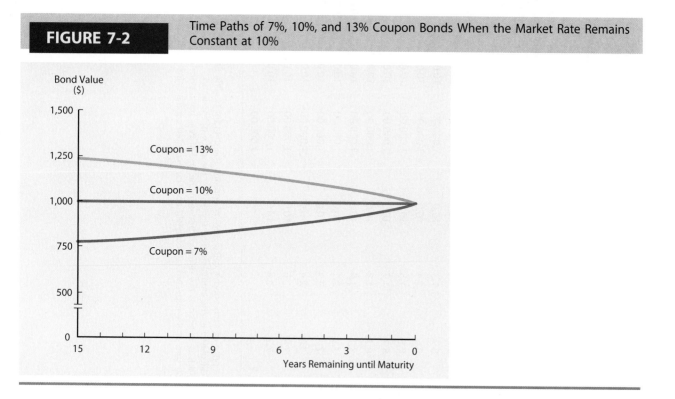

---

[9]In this example (and throughout the text), we ignore the tax effects associated with purchasing different types of bonds. For coupon bonds, under the current Tax Code, coupon payments are taxed as ordinary income, whereas capital gains are taxed at the capital gains tax rate. As we mentioned in Chapter 3, for most investors, the capital gains tax rate is lower than the personal tax rate. Moreover, while coupon payments are taxed each year, capital gains taxes are deferred until the bond is sold or matures. Consequently, all else equal, investors end up paying lower taxes on discount bonds because a greater percentage of their total return comes in the form of capital gains. For details on the tax treatment of zero coupon bonds, see Web Appendix 7A.

What is meant by the terms *new issue* and *seasoned issue*?

Last year a firm issued 20-year, 8% annual coupon bonds at a par value of $1,000.

(1) Suppose that one year later the going rate drops to 6%. What is the new price of the bonds assuming they now have 19 years to maturity? **($1,223.16)**

(2) Suppose that one year after issue, the going interest rate is 10% (rather than 6%). What would the price have been? **($832.70)**

Why do the prices of fixed-rate bonds fall if expectations for inflation rise?

7-6 BONDS WITH SEMIANNUAL COUPONS

Although some bonds pay interest annually, the vast majority actually make payments semiannually. To evaluate semiannual bonds, we must modify the valuation model (Equation 7-1) as follows:

1. Divide the annual coupon interest payment by 2 to determine the dollars of interest paid each six months.

2. Multiply the years to maturity, N, by 2 to determine the number of semi-annual periods.

3. Divide the nominal (quoted) interest rate, r_d, by 2 to determine the periodic (semiannual) interest rate.

On a time line, there would be twice as many payments, but each would be half as large as with an annual payment bond. Making the indicated changes results in the following equation for finding a semiannual bond's value:

$$V_B = \sum_{t=1}^{2N} \frac{INT/2}{(1 + r_d/2)^t} + \frac{M}{(1 + r_d/2)^{2N}} \qquad \text{7-1a}$$

To illustrate, assume that Allied Food's 15-year bonds as discussed in Section 7-3 pay $50 of interest each 6 months rather than $100 at the end of each year. Thus, each interest payment is only half as large but there are twice as many of them. We would describe the coupon rate as "10% with semiannual payments."[10]

When the going (nominal) rate is $r_d = 5\%$ with semiannual compounding, the value of a 15-year, 10% semiannual coupon bond that pays $50 interest every 6 months is found as follows:

Inputs:	30	2.5		50	1000
	N	I/YR	PV	PMT	FV
Output:			= −1,523.26		

Enter N = 30, r_d = I/YR = 2.5, PMT = 50, and FV = 1000; then press the PV key to obtain the bond's value, $1,523.26. The value with semiannual interest payments is slightly larger than $1,518.98, the value when interest is paid annually as we

---

[10]In this situation, the coupon rate of "10% paid semiannually" is the rate that bond dealers, corporate treasurers, and investors generally discuss. Of course, if this bond were issued at par, its *effective annual rate* would be higher than 10%.

$$EAR = EFF\% = \left(1 + \frac{r_{NOM}}{M}\right)^M - 1 = \left(1 + \frac{0.10}{2}\right)^2 - 1 = (1.05)^2 - 1 = 10.25\%$$

Since 10% with annual payments is quite different from 10% with semiannual payments, we have assumed a change in effective rates in this section from the situation in Section 7-3, where we assumed 10% with annual payments.

calculated in Section 7-3. This higher value occurs because each interest payment is received somewhat faster under semiannual compounding.

Alternatively, when we know the price of a semiannual bond, we can easily back out the bond's nominal yield to maturity. In the previous example, if you were told that a 15-year bond with a 10% semiannual coupon was selling for $1,523.26, you could solve for the bond's periodic interest rate as follows:

Inputs:	30			−1,523.26	50	1000
	N		I/YR	PV	PMT	FV
Output:			= 2.5			

In this case, enter N = −30, PV = −1523.26, PMT = 50, and FV = 1000; then press the I/YR key to obtain the interest rate per semiannual period, 2.5%. Multiplying by 2, we calculate the bond's nominal yield to maturity to be 5%.[11]

SELF TEST

Describe how the annual payment bond valuation formula is changed to evaluate semiannual coupon bonds and write the revised formula.

Hartwell Corporation's bonds have a 20-year maturity, an 8% semiannual coupon, and a face value of $1,000. The going interest rate (r_d) is 7% based on semiannual compounding. What is the bond's price? **($1,106.78)**

7-7 ASSESSING A BOND'S RISKINESS

In this section, we identify and explain the two key factors that impact a bond's riskiness. Once those factors are identified, we differentiate between them and discuss how you can minimize these risks.

7-7a Interest Rate Risk

Interest Rate (Price) Risk
The risk of a decline in a bond's price due to an increase in interest rates.

As we saw in Chapter 6, interest rates fluctuate over time and when they rise, the value of outstanding bonds decline. This risk of a decline in bond values due to an increase in interest rates is called **interest rate risk** (or **interest rate price risk**). To illustrate, refer back to Allied's bonds; assume once more that they have a 10% annual coupon; and assume that you bought one of these bonds at its par value, $1,000. Shortly after your purchase, the going interest rate rises from 10 to 15%.[12] As we saw in Section 7-3, this interest rate increase would cause the bond's price to fall from $1,000 to $707.63; so you would have a loss of $292.37 on the bond.[13] Since interest rates can and do rise, rising rates cause losses to bondholders; people or firms who invest in bonds are exposed to risk from increasing interest rates.

---

[11]We can use a similar process to calculate the nominal yield to call for a semiannual bond. The only difference would be that N should represent the number of semiannual periods until the bond is callable and FV should be the bond's call price rather than its par value.

[12]An immediate increase in rates from 10% to 15% would be quite unusual, and it would occur only if something quite bad were revealed about the company or happened in the economy. Smaller but still significant rate increases that adversely affect bondholders do occur fairly often.

[13]You would have an accounting (and tax) loss only if you sold the bond; if you held it to maturity, you would not have such a loss. However, even if you did not sell, you would still have suffered a real economic loss in an opportunity cost sense because you would have lost the opportunity to invest at 15% and would be stuck with a 10% bond in a 15% market. In an economic sense, "paper losses" are just as bad as realized accounting losses.

Interest rate risk is higher on bonds that have long maturities than on bonds that will mature in the near future.[14] This follows because the longer the maturity, the longer before the bond will be paid off and the bondholder can replace it with another bond with a higher coupon. This point can be demonstrated by showing how the value of a 1-year bond with a 10% annual coupon fluctuates with changes in r_d and then comparing those changes with changes on a 15-year bond. The 1-year bond's values at different interest rates are shown here:

Value of a 1-year bond at

r_d = 5%:	Inputs:	1	5		100	1000
		N	I/YR	PV	PMT	FV
Output (Bond Value):				−1,047.62		

r_d = 10%:	Inputs:	1	10		100	1000
		N	I/YR	PV	PMT	FV
Output (Bond Value):				−1,000.00		

r_d = 15%:	Inputs:	1	15		100	1000
		N	I/YR	PV	PMT	FV
Output (Bond Value):				−956.52		

You would obtain the first value with a financial calculator by entering N = 1, I/YR = 5, PMT = 100, and FV = 1000 and then pressing PV to get $1,047.62. With everything still in your calculator, enter I/YR = 10 to override the old I/YR = 5 and press PV to find the bond's value at a 10% rate; it drops to $1,000. Then enter I/YR = 15 and press the PV key to find the last bond value, $956.52.

The effects of increasing rates on the 15-year bond as found earlier can be compared with the just-calculated effects for the 1-year bond. This comparison is shown in Figure 7-3, where we show bond prices at several rates and then plot those prices on the graph. Compared to the 1-year bond, the 15-year bond is far more sensitive to changes in rates. At a 10% interest rate, both the 15-year and 1-year bonds are valued at $1,000. When rates rise to 15%, the 15-year bond falls to $707.63, but the 1-year bond falls only to $956.52. The price decline for the 1-year bond is only 4.35%, while that for the 15-year bond is 29.24%.

For bonds with similar coupons, this differential interest rate sensitivity always holds true—the longer its maturity, the more its price changes in response to a given change in interest rates. Thus, even if the risk of default on two bonds is exactly the same, the

---

[14]Actually, a bond's maturity and coupon rate both affect interest rate risk. Low coupons mean that most of the bond's return will come from repayment of principal, whereas on a high-coupon bond with the same maturity, more of the cash flows will come in during the early years due to the relatively large coupon payments. A measurement called *duration*, which finds the average number of years the bond's PV of cash flows remain outstanding, has been developed to combine maturity and coupons. A zero coupon bond, which has no interest payments and whose payments all come at maturity, has a duration equal to its maturity. All coupon bonds have durations that are shorter than their maturity; and the higher the coupon rate, the shorter the duration. Bonds with longer duration are exposed to more interest rate risk. A discussion of duration would go beyond the scope of this book, but see any investments text for a discussion of the concept.

FIGURE 7-3	Values of Long- and Short-Term 10% Annual Coupon Bonds at Different Market Interest Rates

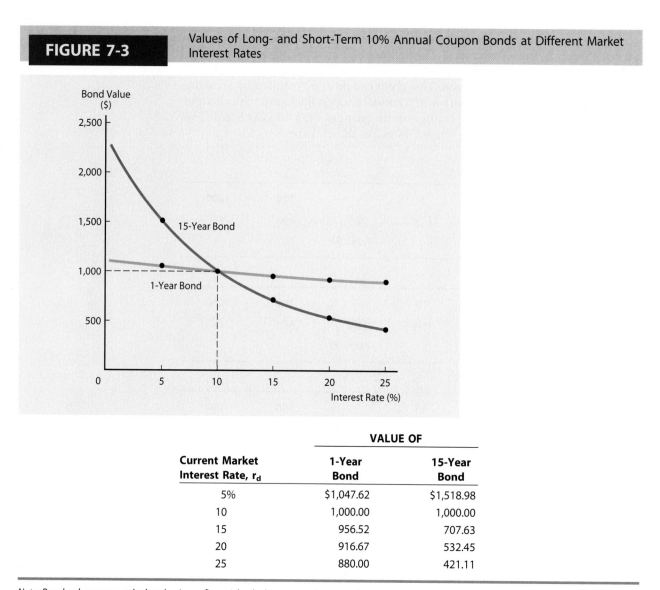

	VALUE OF	
Current Market Interest Rate, r_d	**1-Year Bond**	**15-Year Bond**
5%	$1,047.62	$1,518.98
10	1,000.00	1,000.00
15	956.52	707.63
20	916.67	532.45
25	880.00	421.11

Note: Bond values were calculated using a financial calculator assuming annual, or once-a-year, compounding.

one with the longer maturity is typically exposed to more risk from a rise in interest rates.[15]

The logical explanation for this difference in interest rate risk is simple. Suppose you bought a 15-year bond that yielded 10%, or $100 a year. Now suppose interest rates on comparable-risk bonds rose to 15%. You would be stuck with only $100 of interest for the next 15 years. On the other hand, had you bought a 1-year bond, you would have had a low return for only 1 year. At the end of the year, you would have received your $1,000 back; then you could have reinvested it and earned 15%, or $150 per year, for the next 14 years.

[15]If a 10-year bond were plotted on the graph in Figure 7-3, its curve would lie between those of the 15-year and the 1-year bonds. The curve of a 1-month bond would be almost horizontal, indicating that its price would change very little in response to an interest rate change; but a 100-year bond would have a very steep slope, and the slope of a perpetuity would be even steeper. Also, a zero coupon bond's price is quite sensitive to interest rate changes; and the longer its maturity, the greater its price sensitivity. Therefore, a 30-year zero coupon bond would have a huge amount of interest rate risk.

7-7b Reinvestment Rate Risk

As we saw in the preceding section, an *increase* in interest rates hurts bondholders because it leads to a decline in the current value of a bond portfolio. But can a *decrease* in interest rates also hurt bondholders? Actually, the answer is yes because if interest rates fall, long-term investors will suffer a reduction in income. For example, consider a retiree who has a bond portfolio and lives off the income it produces. The bonds in the portfolio, on average, have coupon rates of 10%. Now suppose interest rates decline to 5%. Many of the bonds will mature or be called; as this occurs, the bondholder will have to replace 10% bonds with 5% bonds. Thus, the retiree will suffer a reduction of income.

The risk of an income decline due to a drop in interest rates is called **reinvestment rate risk**, and its importance has been demonstrated to all bond-holders in recent years as a result of the sharp drop in rates since the mid-1980s. Reinvestment rate risk is obviously high on callable bonds. It is also high on short-term bonds because the shorter the bond's maturity, the fewer the years before the relatively high old-coupon bonds will be replaced with the new low-coupon issues. Thus, retirees whose primary holdings are short-term bonds or other debt securities will be hurt badly by a decline in rates, but holders of noncallable long-term bonds will continue to enjoy the old high rates.

Reinvestment Rate Risk
The risk that a decline in interest rates will lead to a decline in income from a bond portfolio.

7-7c Comparing Interest Rate and Reinvestment Rate Risk

Note that interest rate risk relates to the *current market value* of the bond portfolio, while reinvestment rate risk relates to the *income* the portfolio produces. If you hold long-term bonds, you will face significant interest rate price risk because the value of your portfolio will decline if interest rates rise, but you will not face much reinvestment rate risk because your income will be stable. On the other hand, if you hold short-term bonds, you will not be exposed to much interest rate price risk, but you will be exposed to significant reinvestment rate risk.

Which type of risk is "more relevant" to a given investor depends critically on how long the investor plans to hold the bonds—this is often referred to as his or her **investment horizon.** To illustrate, consider an investor who has a relatively short 1-year investment horizon—say, the investor plans to go to graduate school a year from now and needs money for tuition and expenses. Reinvestment rate risk is of minimal concern to this investor because there is little time for rein-vestment. The investor could eliminate interest rate risk by buying a 1-year Treasury security since he would be assured of receiving the face value of the bond 1 year from now (the investment horizon). However, if this investor were to buy a long-term Treasury security, he would bear a considerable amount of interest rate risk because, as we have seen, long-term bond prices decline when interest rates rise. Consequently, investors with shorter investment horizons should view long-term bonds as being more risky than short-term bonds.

Investment Horizon
The period of time an investor plans to hold a particular investment.

By contrast, the reinvestment risk inherent in short-term bonds is especially relevant to investors with longer investment horizons. Consider a retiree who is living on income from her portfolio. If this investor buys 1-year bonds, she will have to "roll them over" every year; and if rates fall, her income in sub-sequent years will likewise decline. A younger couple saving for their retire-ment or their children's college costs, for example, would be affected similarly because if they buy short-term bonds, they too will have to roll over their portfolio at possibly much lower rates. Since there is uncertainty today about the rates that will be earned on these reinvested cash flows, long-term investors should be especially concerned about the reinvestment rate risk inherent in short-term bonds.

One way to manage both interest rate and reinvestment rate risk is to buy a zero coupon Treasury bond with a maturity that matches the investor's investment horizon. For example, assume your investment horizon is 10 years. If you buy a 10-year zero, you will receive a guaranteed payment in 10 years equal to the bond's face value.[16] Moreover, as there are no coupons to reinvest, there is no reinvestment rate risk. This explains why investors with specific goals often invest in zero coupon bonds.[17]

Recall from Chapter 6 that maturity risk premiums are generally positive. Moreover, a positive maturity risk premium implies that investors, on average, regard longer-term bonds as being riskier than shorter-term bonds. That, in turn, suggests that the average investor is most concerned with interest rate price risk. Still, it is appropriate for each investor to consider his or her own situation, to recognize the risks inherent in bonds with different maturities, and to construct a portfolio that deals best with the investor's most relevant risk.

SELF TEST

Differentiate between interest rate risk and reinvestment rate risk.

To which type of risk are holders of long-term bonds more exposed? short-term bondholders?

What type of security can be used to minimize both interest rate and reinvestment rate risk for an investor with a fixed investment horizon?

7-8 DEFAULT RISK

Potential default is another important risk that bondholders face. If the issuer defaults, investors will receive less than the promised return. Recall from Chapter 6 that the quoted interest rate includes a default risk premium—the higher the probability of default, the higher the premium and thus the yield to maturity. Default risk on Treasuries is zero, but this risk is substantial for lower-grade corporate and municipal bonds.

To illustrate, suppose two bonds have the same promised cash flows—their coupon rates, maturities, liquidity, and inflation exposures are identical; but one has more default risk than the other. Investors will naturally pay more for the one with less chance of default. As a result, bonds with higher default risk have higher market rates: $r_d = r^* + IP + DRP + LP + MRP$. If a bond's default risk changes, r_d and thus the price will be affected. Thus, if the default risk on Allied's bonds increases, their price will fall and the yield to maturity (YTM = r_d) will increase.

---

[16]Note that in this example, the 10-year zero technically has a considerable amount of interest rate risk since its *current* price is highly sensitive to changes in interest rates. However, the year-to year movements in price should not be of great concern to an investor with a 10-year horizon. The reason is that the investor knows that regardless of what happens to interest rates, the bond's price will still be $1,000 when it matures.

[17]Two words of caution about zeros are in order. First, as we show in Web Appendix 7A, investors in zeros must pay taxes each year on their accrued gain in value even though the bonds don't pay any cash until they mature. Second, buying a zero coupon with a maturity equal to your investment horizon enables you to lock in a nominal cash payoff, but the *real* value of that payment still depends on what happens to inflation during your investment horizon. What we need is an inflation-indexed zero coupon Treasury bond; but to date, no such bond exists.

Also, the fact that maturity risk premiums are positive suggests that most investors have relatively short investment horizons, or at least worry about short-term changes in their net worth. See *Stocks, Bonds, Bills, and Inflation: (Valuation Edition) 2008 Yearbook* (Chicago: Morningstar, Inc., 2008), which finds that the maturity risk premium for long-term bonds has averaged 1.4% over the past 82 years.

7-8a Various Types of Corporate Bonds

Default risk is influenced by the financial strength of the issuer and the terms of the bond contract, including whether collateral has been pledged to secure the bond. The characteristics of some key types of bonds are described in this section.

Mortgage Bonds

Under a **mortgage bond**, the corporation pledges specific assets as security for the bond. To illustrate, in 2008, Billingham Corporation needed $10 million to build a regional distribution center. Bonds in the amount of $4 million, secured by a *first mortgage* on the property, were issued. (The remaining $6 million was financed with equity capital.) If Billingham defaults on the bonds, the bondholders can foreclose on the property and sell it to satisfy their claims.

If Billingham had chosen to, it could have issued *second mortgage bonds* secured by the same $10 million of assets. In the event of liquidation, the holders of the second mortgage bonds would have a claim against the property, but only after the first mortgage bondholders had been paid off in full. Thus, second mortgages are sometimes called *junior mortgages* because they are junior in priority to the claims of *senior mortgages,* or *first mortgage bonds.*

All mortgage bonds are subject to an **indenture**, which is a legal document that spells out in detail the rights of the bondholders and the corporation. The indentures of many major corporations were written 20, 30, 40, or more years ago. These indentures are generally "open-ended," meaning that new bonds can be issued from time to time under the same indenture. However, the amount of new bonds that can be issued is usually limited to a specified percentage of the firm's total "bondable property," which generally includes all land, plant, and equipment. And, of course, the coupon interest rate on the newly issued bonds changes over time, along with the market rate on the older bonds.

Debentures

A **debenture** is an unsecured bond; and as such, it provides no specific collateral as security for the obligation. Therefore, debenture holders are general creditors whose claims are protected by property not otherwise pledged. In practice, the use of debentures depends on the nature of the firm's assets and on its general credit strength. Extremely strong companies such as General Electric and ExxonMobil can use debentures because they do not need to put up property as security for their debt. Debentures are also issued by weak companies that have already pledged most of their assets as collateral for mortgage loans. In this case, the debentures are quite risky and that risk will be reflected in their interest rates.

Subordinated Debentures

The term *subordinate* means "below" or "inferior to"; and in the event of bankruptcy, subordinated debt has a claim on assets only after senior debt has been paid in full. **Subordinated debentures** may be subordinated to designated notes payable (usually bank loans) or to all other debt. In the event of liquidation or reorganization, holders of subordinated debentures receive nothing until all senior debt, as named in the debentures' indenture, has been paid. Precisely how subordination works and how it strengthens the position of senior debtholders are explained in detail in Web Appendix 7B.

7-8b Bond Ratings

Since the early 1900s, bonds have been assigned quality ratings that reflect their probability of going into default. The three major rating agencies are Moody's Investors Service (Moody's), Standard & Poor's Corporation (S&P), and Fitch

Mortgage Bond
A bond backed by fixed assets. First mortgage bonds are senior in priority to claims of second mortgage bonds.

Indenture
A formal agreement between the issuer and the bondholders.

Debenture
A long-term bond that is not secured by a mortgage on specific property.

Subordinated Debenture
A bond having a claim on assets only after the senior debt has been paid off in the event of liquidation.

Investment-Grade Bond
Bonds rated triple-B or higher; many banks and other institutional investors are permitted by law to hold only investment-grade bonds.

Junk Bond
A high-risk, high-yield bond.

Investor's Service. Moody's and S&P's rating designations are shown in Table 7-2.[18] The triple- and double-A bonds are extremely safe. Single-A and triple-B bonds are also strong enough to be called **investment-grade bonds**, and they are the lowest-rated bonds that many banks and other institutional investors are permitted by law to hold. Double-B and lower bonds are speculative, or **junk, bonds**; and they have a significant probability of going into default.

Bond Rating Criteria

Bond ratings are based on financial ratios such as those discussed in Chapter 4 and on various qualitative factors. The ratios, especially the debt and interest coverage ratios, are generally the most important ratings determinants; but at times, other factors that are expected to affect the ratios in the future take center stage. In 2008, firms' exposures to subprime mortgages are leading to downgrades of firms whose ratios still look "reasonable." Published ratios are, of course, historical—they show the firm's condition in the past, whereas bond investors are more interested in the firm's condition in the future. The qualitative factors can be divided into two groups: factors that are related to the bond contract and all other factors. Following is an outline of the determinants of bond ratings:

1. *Financial Ratios.* All of the ratios are potentially important, but the debt and interest coverage ratios are key. The rating agencies' analysts go through a financial analysis along the lines discussed in Chapter 4 and forecast future ratios along the lines described in the financial planning and forecasting chapter. For the forecasts, the qualitative factors discussed next are important.

2. *Qualitative Factors: Bond Contract Terms.* Every bond is covered by a contract, often called an indenture, between the issuer and the bondholders. The indenture spells out all the terms related to the bond. Included in the indenture are the maturity, the coupon interest rate, a statement of whether the bond is secured by a mortgage on specific assets, any sinking fund provisions, and a statement of whether the bond is guaranteed by some other party with a high credit ranking. Other provisions might include *restrictive covenants* such as requirements that the firm not let its debt ratio exceed a stated level and that it keep its times-interest-earned ratio at or above a given level. Some bond indentures are hundreds of pages long, while others are quite short and cover just the terms of the loan.

3. *Miscellaneous Qualitative Factors.* Included here are issues like the sensitivity of the firm's earnings to the strength of the economy, the way it is affected by inflation, a statement of whether it is having or likely to have labor problems, the extent of its international operations (including the stability of the countries in which it operates), potential environmental problems, and potential antitrust problems. Today the most important factor is exposure to subprime loans, including the difficulty to determine the extent of this exposure as a result of the complexity of the assets backed by such loans.

Table 7-2	**Moody's and S&P Bond Ratings**							
	INVESTMENT GRADE				**JUNK BONDS**			
Moody's	Aaa	Aa	A	Baa	Ba	B	Caa	C
S&P	AAA	AA	A	BBB	BB	B	CCC	C

Note: Both Moody's and S&P use "modifiers" for bonds rated below triple A. S&P uses a plus and minus system. Thus, A+ designates the strongest A-rated bonds; A-, the weakest. Moody's uses a 1, 2, or 3 designation, with 1 denoting the strongest and 3 denoting the weakest; thus, within the double-A category, Aa1 is the best, Aa2 is average, and Aa3 is the weakest.

---

[18]In the discussion to follow, reference to the S&P rating is intended to imply the Moody's and Fitch's ratings as well. Thus, triple-B bonds mean both BBB and Baa bonds; double-B bonds mean both BB and Ba bonds; and so forth.

We see that bond ratings are determined by a great many factors, some quantitative and some qualitative (or subjective). Also, the rating process is dynamic—at times, one factor is of primary importance; at other times, some other factor is key. Nevertheless, as we can see from Table 7-3, there is a strong correlation between bond ratings and many of the ratios that we described in Chapter 4. Not surprisingly, companies with lower debt ratios, higher free cash flow to debt, higher returns on invested capital, higher EBITDA coverage ratios, and higher TIE ratios typically have higher bond ratings.

Importance of Bond Ratings

Bond ratings are important to both firms and investors. First, because a bond's rating is an indicator of its default risk, the rating has a direct, measurable influence on the bond's interest rate and the firm's cost of debt. Second, most bonds are purchased by institutional investors rather than individuals and many institutions are restricted to investment-grade securities. Thus, if a firm's bonds fall below BBB, it will have a difficult time selling new bonds because many potential purchasers will not be allowed to buy them.

As a result of their higher risk and more restricted market, lower-grade bonds have higher required rates of return, r_d, than high-grade bonds. Figure 7-4 illustrates this point. In each of the years shown on the graph, U.S. government bonds have had the lowest yields, AAA bonds have been next, and BBB bonds have had the highest yields. The figure also shows that the gaps between yields on the three types of bonds vary over time, indicating that the cost differentials, or yield spreads, fluctuate from year to year. This point is highlighted in Figure 7-5, which gives the yields on the three types of bonds and the yield spreads for AAA and BBB bonds over Treasuries in January 1994 and January 2008.[19] Note first from

Table 7-3	Bond Rating Criteria: Three-Year (2002–2004) Median Financial Ratios for Different Bond Rating Classifications of Industrial Companies[a]						
	AAA	**AA**	**A**	**BBB**	**BB**	**B**	**CCC**
Times interest earned (EBIT/Interest)	23.8×	19.5×	8.0×	4.7×	2.5×	1.2×	0.4×
EBITDA interest coverage (EBITDA/Interest)	25.5	24.6	10.2	6.5	3.5	1.9	0.9
Net cash flow/Total debt	203.3%	79.9%	48.0%	35.9%	22.4%	11.5%	5.0%
Free cash flow/Total debt	127.6	44.5	25.0	17.3	8.3	2.8	(2.1)
Return on capital	27.6	27.0	17.5	13.4	11.3	8.7	3.2
Total debt/EBITDA	0.4	0.9	1.6	2.2	3.5	5.3	7.9
Total debt/Total capital	12.4	28.3	37.5	42.5	53.7	75.9	113.5

[a]Somewhat different criteria are applied to firms in different industries, such as utilities and financial corporations. This table pertains to industrial companies, which include manufacturers, retailers, and service firms.
Source: Adapted from "CreditStats Adjusted Key Industrial Financial Ratios," *Standard & Poor's 2006 Corporate Ratings Criteria*, September 10, 2007, p. 43.

[19]A yield spread is related to but not identical to risk premiums on corporate bonds. The true *risk premium* reflects only the difference in expected (and required) returns between two securities that results from differences in their risk. However, yield spreads reflect (1) a true risk premium; (2) a liquidity premium, which reflects the fact that U.S. Treasury bonds are more readily marketable than most corporate bonds; (3) a call premium because most Treasury bonds are not callable whereas corporate bonds are; and (4) an expected loss differential, which reflects the probability of loss on the corporate bonds. As an example of the last point, suppose the yield to maturity on a BBB bond was 6.0% versus 4.8% on government bonds but there was a 5% probability of total default loss on the corporate bond. In this case, the *expected* return on the BBB bond would be 0.95(6.0%) + 0.05(0%) = 5.7% and the yield spread would be 0.9%, not the full 1.2 percentage points difference in "promised" yields to maturity.

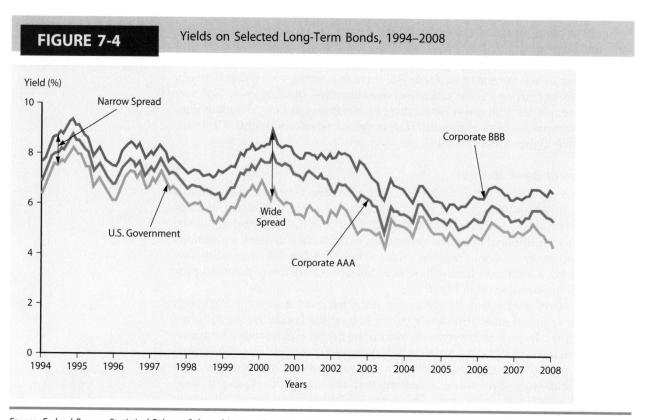

Source: Federal Reserve Statistical Release, Selected Interest Rates (Historical Data), www.federalreserve.gov/releases/H15/data.htm.

Figure 7-5 that the risk-free rate, or vertical axis intercept, was lower in January 2008 than it was in January 1994, primarily reflecting the decline in both rates and expected inflation over the past few years. Second, the slope of the line has increased, indicating an increase in investors' risk aversion largely due to the sub-prime mortgage problem and growing fears of a possible recession. Thus, the penalty for having a low credit rating varies over time. Occasionally, as in 2008, the penalty is quite large; but at times, as in 1994 (shown in Figures 7-4 and 7-5), it is small. These spread differences reflect investors' risk aversion and their optimism or pessimism regarding the economy and corporate profits. In 2008, as more and more homeowners default on their loans and poor economic news continues, investors were both pessimistic and risk-averse; so spreads were quite high.

Changes in Ratings

Changes in a firm's bond rating affect its ability to borrow funds capital and its cost of that capital. Rating agencies review outstanding bonds on a periodic basis, occasionally upgrading or downgrading a bond as a result of its issuer's changed circumstances. For example, on March 4, 2008, S&P upgraded Reliant Energy's secured debt facilities from B to BB–; however, the firm's "B" corporate credit rating remained unchanged. The secured debt's upgrade was due to the firm's refinancing the secured debt with unsecured debt, reducing the size of its secured revolving loan, and paying down the senior secured notes. On the other hand, on March 6, 2008, S&P downgraded Airborne Health Inc.'s corporate credit rating from B– to CCC+. The downgrade was largely due to S&P's concern about the company's future sales following negative publicity from its recent settlement of a class action lawsuit. (The lawsuit came about from the company's claims that its product helped prevent the common cold, a fact that was proved to be untrue.)

| FIGURE 7-5 | Relationship between Bond Ratings and Bond Yields, 1994 and 2008 |

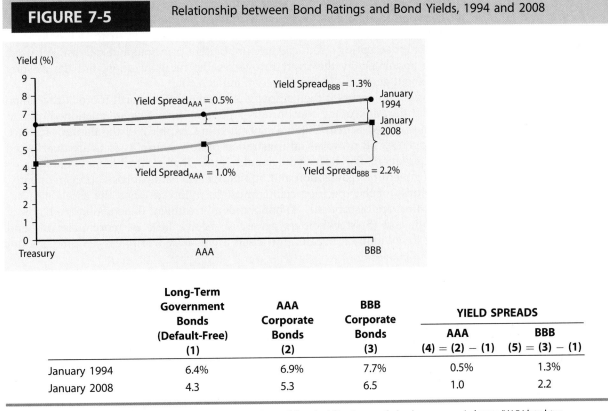

| | Long-Term Government Bonds (Default-Free) (1) | AAA Corporate Bonds (2) | BBB Corporate Bonds (3) | YIELD SPREADS | |
				AAA (4) = (2) − (1)	BBB (5) = (3) − (1)
January 1994	6.4%	6.9%	7.7%	0.5%	1.3%
January 2008	4.3	5.3	6.5	1.0	2.2

Source: Federal Reserve Statistical Release, Selected Interest Rates (Historical Data), www.federalreserve.gov/releases/H15/data.htm.

Over the long run, rating agencies have done a reasonably good job of measuring the average credit risk of bonds and of changing ratings whenever there is a significant change in credit quality. However, it is important to understand that ratings do not adjust immediately to changes in credit quality; and in some cases, there can be a considerable lag between a change in credit quality and a change in rating. For example, Enron's bonds still carried an investment-grade rating on a Friday in December 2001, but the company declared bankruptcy 2 days later, on Sunday. Many other abrupt downgrades occurred in 2007 and 2008, leading to calls by Congress and the SEC for changes in rating agencies and the way they rate bonds. Improvements can clearly be made, but there will always be surprises when we learn that supposedly strong bonds were in fact quite weak.

7-8c Bankruptcy and Reorganization

When a business becomes *insolvent*, it doesn't have enough cash to meet its interest and principal payments. A decision must then be made whether to dissolve the firm through *liquidation* or to permit it to *reorganize* and thus continue to operate. These issues are addressed in Chapter 7 and Chapter 11 of the federal bankruptcy statutes, and the final decision is made by a federal bankruptcy court judge.

The decision to force a firm to liquidate versus permitting it to reorganize depends on whether the value of the reorganized business is likely to be greater than the value of its assets if they were sold off piecemeal. In a reorganization, the firm's creditors negotiate with management on the terms of a potential reorganization. The reorganization plan may call for *restructuring* the debt, in which case the interest rate may be reduced, the term to maturity lengthened, or some of the debt exchanged for equity. The point of the restructuring is to reduce the financial charges to a level that is supportable by the firm's projected cash flows. Of course, the common stockholders also have to "take a haircut"—they generally see their position diluted as a result of additional shares being given to debtholders in exchange for accepting a reduced amount of debt principal and interest. A trustee may be appointed by the court to oversee the reorganization, but the existing management generally is allowed to retain control.

Liquidation occurs if the company is deemed to be worth more "dead" than "alive." If the bankruptcy court orders a liquidation, assets are auctioned off and the cash obtained is distributed as specified in Chapter 7 of the Bankruptcy Act. Web Appendix 7B provides an illustration of how a firm's assets are distributed after liquidation. For now, you should know that (1) the federal bankruptcy statutes govern reorganization and liquidation, (2) bankruptcies occur frequently, (3) a priority of the specified claims must be followed when the assets of a liquidated firm are distributed, (4) bondholders' treatment depends on the terms of the bond, and (5) stockholders generally receive little in reorganizations and nothing in liquidations because the assets are usually worth less than the amount of debt outstanding.

SELF TEST

Differentiate between mortgage bonds and debentures.

Name the major rating agencies and list some factors that affect bond ratings.

Why are bond ratings important to firms and investors?

Do bond ratings adjust immediately to changes in credit quality? Explain.

Differentiate between Chapter 7 liquidations and Chapter 11 reorganizations. In general, when should each be used?

7-9 BOND MARKETS

Corporate bonds are traded primarily in the over-the-counter market. Most bonds are owned by and traded among large financial institutions (for example, life insurance companies, mutual funds, hedge funds, and pension funds, all of which deal in very large blocks of securities), and it is relatively easy for over-the-counter bond dealers to arrange the transfer of large blocks of bonds among the relatively few holders of the bonds. It would be more difficult to conduct similar operations in the stock market among the literally millions of large and small stockholders, so a higher percentage of stock trades occur on the exchanges.

The Wall Street Journal routinely reports key developments in the Treasury, corporate, and municipal bond markets. The online edition of *The Wall Street Journal* also lists for each trading day the most actively traded investment-grade bonds, high-yield bonds, and convertible bonds. Table 7-4 reprints portions of the online edition's "Corporate Bonds Data" section which shows the most active issues that traded on March 6, 2008, in descending order of sales volume.

Looking at Table 7-4, you will see the coupon rate, maturity date, bond rating, high and low prices for the day, closing (last) price, change in price, and yield to maturity. The table assumes that each bond has a par value of $100. Not surprisingly, the high-yield bonds have much higher yields to maturity because of their higher default risk and the convertible bonds have much lower yields because investors are willing to accept lower yields in return for the option to convert their bonds to common stock.

If you examine the table closely, you will also see that the bonds with a yield to maturity above their coupon rate trade at a discount, whereas bonds with a

Table 7-4	Most Active Investment-Grade, High-Yield, and Convertible Corporate Bonds, March 6, 2008

CORPORATE BONDS

Last updated: 3/6/2008 at 6:35 PM ET

Market Breadth

	All Issues	Investment Grade	High Yield	Convertibles
Total Issues Traded	3,774	2,587	942	245
Advances	1,457	1,083	299	75
Declines	1,873	1,187	532	154
Unchanged	126	53	68	5
52 Week High	170	161	8	1
52 Week Low	344	191	117	36
Dollar Volume *	15,640	7,350	4,989	3,301

About This Information:
End of Day data. Activity as reported to FINRA TRACE (Trade Reporting and Compliance Engine). The Market breadth information represents activity in all TRACE eligible publicly traded securities. The most active information represents the most active fixed-coupon bonds (ranked by par value traded). Inclusion in Investment Grade or High Yield tables based on TRACE dissemination criteria. "C" indicates yield is unavailable because of issues call criteria.

* Par value in millions.

Most Active Investment Grade Bonds

Issuer Name	Symbol	Coupon	Maturity	Rating Moody's/S&P/ Fitch	High	Low	Last	Change	Yield %
MERRILL LYNCH	MER.GDW	4.125%	Jan 2009	A1/A+/A+	100.886	99.500	100.886	0.910	3.051
BANK OF AMERICA CORP	BAC.HBM	5.750%	Dec 2017	Aa1/AA/AA	103.143	99.280	99.280	−1.339	5.847
JPMORGAN CHASE & CO	JPM.JPF	6.000%	Jan 2018	Aa2/AA−/AA−	104.566	100.632	101.587	−0.413	5.784
SPRINT CAPITAL	S.GJ	6.875%	Nov 2028	Baa3/BBB−/BB+	74.000	69.000	72.563	0.063	10.048
GOLDMAN SACHS GP	GS.YL	5.950%	Jan 2018	Aa3/AA−/AA−	100.516	95.956	98.520	0.576	6.151
GENERAL ELECTRIC CAPITAL	GE.HEE	5.250%	Dec 2017	Aaa/AAA/--	101.750	97.678	98.770	−0.335	5.413
SPRINT CAPITAL	S.HK	8.750%	Mar 2032	Baa3/BBB−/BB+	81.120	76.063	80.000	0.000	11.159
TELECOM ITALIA CAPITAL	TI.GK	5.250%	Nov 2013	Baa2/BBB+/BBB+	100.834	95.908	95.908	−1.949	6.112
UNITED PARCEL SERVICE	UPS.QE	4.500%	Jan 2013	Aa2/AA−/--	103.964	103.617	103.734	1.053	3.651
SPRINT CAPITAL	S.GM	6.900%	May 2019	Baa3/BBB−/BB+	76.313	73.950	76.313	0.563	10.565

Most Active High Yield Bonds

Issuer Name	Symbol	Coupon	Maturity	Rating Moody's/S&P/ Fitch	High	Low	Last	Change	Yield %
THORNBURG MORTGAGE	TMA.GB	8.000%	May 2013	Caa2/CCC+/CCC−	49.000	35.500	40.000	−23.750	32.807
GENERAL MOTORS	GM.HB	8.375%	Jul 2033	Caa1/B−/B−	79.750	74.000	75.938	−1.063	11.262
E TRADE FINANCIAL	ET.GF	8.000%	Jun 2011	Ba3/B/--	86.000	85.000	86.000	0.500	13.429
CCH I	CHTR.HM	11.000%	Oct 2015	Caa2/CCC/CCC	70.125	69.688	70.070	−0.430	18.517
BLOCKBUSTER	BBI.GB	9.000%	Sep 2012	Caa2/CCC/CC	87.500	83.000	83.500	1.625	14.096
COMMUNITY HEALTH SYSTEMS	CYH.GI	8.875%	Jul 2015	B3/B−/CCC+	99.500	98.750	98.750	−0.750	9.108
HERTZ CORP	F.GRY	8.875%	Jan 2014	B1/B/BB−	99.000	94.750	97.086	0.586	9.535
GENERAL MOTORS ACCEPTANCE	GMA.HE	6.875%	Sep 2011	B1/B+/BB	81.710	79.000	80.516	−0.484	14.099
NEIMAN MARCUS GP	NMGA.GD	9.000%	Oct 2015	B2/B/B−	98.250	97.000	97.250	−0.688	9.511
INTELSAT(BERMUDA)	INTEL.GR	9.250%	Jun 2016	B3/B−/BB−	101.250	100.875	100.875	0.000	9.093

Most Active Convertible Bonds

Issuer Name	Symbol	Coupon	Maturity	Rating Moody's/S&P/ Fitch	High	Low	Last	Change	Yield %
AMGEN	AMGN.GM	0.125%	Feb 2011	A2/--/--	92.438	91.813	91.883	−0.745	3.083
SANDISK CORP	SNDK.GC	1.000%	May 2013	--/BB−/--	74.000	72.690	74.000	−0.116	7.086
NABORS INDUSTRIES	NBR.GP	0.940%	May 2011	--/BBB+/A−	100.500	96.000	100.000	−0.750	0.940
PROTEIN DESIGN LABS	PDLI.GF	2.000%	Feb 2012	--/--/--	80.608	78.882	79.443	0.203	8.231
AMGEN	AMGN.GN	0.375%	Feb 2013	A2/--/--	88.467	87.000	87.587	−0.663	3.133

Source: FINRA TRACE data. Reference information from Reuters DataScope Data. Credit ratings from Moody's, Standard & Poor's, and Fitch Ratings.

Source: http://online.wsj.com, "Corporate Bonds," *The Wall Street Journal Online*, March 7, 2008.

yield below their coupon rate trade at a premium above par. We see that the large majority of high-yield bonds trade at a discount to par, which suggests that because of increased default risk, most of these bonds now trade at higher yields relative to when they were issued. (Recall that most bonds are issued at par, so the coupon rate tells us what the bond's yield was at the time it was issued.) You should also note that when bonds with similar ratings are compared, bonds with longer maturities tend to have higher yields, which is consistent with the upward-sloping yield curve during this time period.

SELF TEST

Why do most bond trades occur in the over-the-counter market?

If a bond issue is to be sold at par, at what rate must its coupon rate be set? Explain.

TYING IT ALL TOGETHER

This chapter described the different types of bonds governments and corporations issue, explained how bond prices are established, and discussed how investors estimate rates of return on bonds. It also discussed various types of risks that investors face when they purchase bonds.

When an investor purchases a company's bonds, the investor is providing the company with capital. Moreover, when a firm issues bonds, *the return that investors require on the bonds represents the cost of debt capital to the firm.* This point is extended in Chapter 10, where the ideas developed in this chapter are used to help determine a company's overall cost of capital, which is a basic component of the capital budgeting process.

In recent years, many companies have used zero coupon bonds to raise billions of dollars, while bankruptcy is an important consideration for companies that issue debt and for investors. Therefore, these two related issues are discussed in detail in Web Appendixes 7A and 7B. Go to the textbook's web site to access these appendixes.

SELF-TEST QUESTIONS AND PROBLEMS
(Solutions Appear in Appendix A)

ST-1 **KEY TERMS** Define each of the following terms:

a. Bond; treasury bond; corporate bond; municipal bond; foreign bond

b. Par value; maturity date; original maturity

c. Coupon payment; coupon interest rate

d. Fixed-rate bond; floating-rate bond; zero coupon bond; original issue discount (OID) bond

e. Call provision; sinking fund provision

f. Convertible bond; warrant; putable bond; income bond; indexed, or purchasing power, bond

  g. Discount bond; premium bond

  h. Yield to maturity (YTM); yield to call (YTC); total return; yield spread

  i. Interest rate risk; reinvestment rate risk; investment horizon; default risk

  j. Mortgage bond; indenture; debenture; subordinated debenture

  k. Investment-grade bond; junk bond

ST-2 **BOND VALUATION** The Pennington Corporation issued a new series of bonds on January 1, 1985. The bonds were sold at par ($1,000); had a 12% coupon; and mature in 30 years, on December 31, 2014. Coupon payments are made semiannually (on June 30 and December 31).

  a. What was the YTM on January 1, 1985?

  b. What was the price of the bonds on January 1, 1990, 5 years later, assuming that interest rates had fallen to 10%?

  c. Find the current yield, capital gains yield, and total return on January 1, 1990, given the price as determined in Part b.

  d. On July 1, 2008, 6½ years before maturity, Pennington's bonds sold for $916.42. What were the YTM, the current yield, the capital gains yield, and the total return at that time?

  e. Now assume that you plan to purchase an outstanding Pennington bond on March 1, 2008, when the going rate of interest given its risk was 15.5%. How large a check must you write to complete the transaction? This is a difficult question.

ST-3 **SINKING FUND** The Vancouver Development Company (VDC) is planning to sell a $100 million, 10-year, 12%, semiannual payment bond issue. Provisions for a sinking fund to retire the issue over its life will be included in the indenture. Sinking fund payments will be made at the end of each year, and each payment must be sufficient to retire 10% of the original amount of the issue. The last sinking fund payment will retire the last of the bonds. The bonds to be retired each period can be purchased on the open market or obtained by calling up to 5% of the original issue at par, at VDC's option.

  a. How large must each sinking fund payment be if the company (1) uses the option to call bonds at par or (2) decides to buy bonds on the open market? For Part (2), you can only answer in words.

  b. What will happen to debt service requirements per year associated with this issue over its 10-year life?

  c. Now consider an alternative plan where VDC sets up its sinking fund so that *equal annual amounts* are paid into a sinking fund trust held by a bank, with the proceeds being used to buy government bonds that are expected to pay 7% annual interest. The payments, plus accumulated interest, must total $100 million at the end of 10 years, when the proceeds will be used to retire the issue. How large must the annual sinking fund payments be? Is this amount known with certainty, or might it be higher or lower?

  d. What are the annual cash requirements for covering bond service costs under the trusteeship arrangement described in Part c? (Note: Interest must be paid on Vancouver's outstanding bonds but not on bonds that have been retired.) Assume level interest rates for purposes of answering this question.

  e. What would have to happen to interest rates to cause the company to buy bonds on the open market rather than call them under the plan where some bonds are retired each year?

QUESTIONS

7-1 A sinking fund can be set up in one of two ways:

  a. The corporation makes annual payments to the trustee, who invests the proceeds in securities (frequently government bonds) and uses the accumulated total to retire the bond issue at maturity.

  b. The trustee uses the annual payments to retire a portion of the issue each year, calling a given percentage of the issue by a lottery and paying a specified price per bond or buying bonds on the open market, whichever is cheaper.

   What are the advantages and disadvantages of each procedure from the viewpoint of (a) the firm and (b) the bondholders?

7-2   Is it true that the following equation can be used to find the value of a bond with N years to maturity that pays interest once a year? Assume that the bond was issued several years ago.

$$V_B = \sum_{t=1}^{N} \frac{\text{Annual interest}}{(1 + r_d)^t} + \frac{\text{Par value}}{(1 + r_d)^N}$$

7-3   The values of outstanding bonds change whenever the going rate of interest changes. In general, short-term interest rates are more volatile than long-term interest rates. Therefore, short-term bond prices are more sensitive to interest rate changes than are long-term bond prices. Is that statement true or false? Explain. (Hint: Make up a "reasonable" example based on a 1-year and a 20-year bond to help answer the question.)

7-4   If interest rates rise after a bond issue, what will happen to the bond's price and YTM? Does the time to maturity affect the extent to which interest rate changes affect the bond's price? (Again, an example might help you answer this question.)

7-5   If you buy a *callable* bond and interest rates decline, will the value of your bond rise by as much as it would have risen if the bond had not been callable? Explain.

7-6   Assume that you have a short investment horizon (less than 1 year). You are considering two investments: a 1-year Treasury security and a 20-year Treasury security. Which of the two investments would you view as being riskier? Explain.

7-7   Indicate whether each of the following actions will increase or decrease a bond's yield to maturity:

   a.   The bond's price increases.

   b.   The bond is downgraded by the rating agencies.

   c.   A change in the bankruptcy code makes it more difficult for bondholders to receive payments in the event the firm declares bankruptcy.

   d.   The economy seems to be shifting from a boom to a recession. Discuss the effects of the firm's credit strength in your answer.

   e.   Investors learn that the bonds are subordinated to another debt issue.

7-8   Why is a call provision advantageous to a bond issuer? When would the issuer be likely to initiate a refunding call?

7-9   Are securities that provide for a sinking fund more or less risky from the bondholder's perspective than those without this type of provision? Explain.

7-10   What's the difference between a call for sinking fund purposes and a refunding call?

7-11   Why are convertibles and bonds with warrants typically offered with lower coupons than similarly rated straight bonds?

7-12   Explain whether the following statement is true or false: Only weak companies issue debentures.

7-13   Would the yield spread on a corporate bond over a Treasury bond with the same maturity tend to become wider or narrower if the economy appeared to be heading toward a recession? Would the change in the spread for a given company be affected by the firm's credit strength? Explain.

7-14   A bond's expected return is sometimes estimated by its YTM and sometimes by its YTC. Under what conditions would the YTM provide a better estimate, and when would the YTC be better?

PROBLEMS

**Easy
Problems
1–4**

7-1   **BOND VALUATION**   Callaghan Motors' bonds have 10 years remaining to maturity. Interest is paid annually, they have a $1,000 par value, the coupon interest rate is 8%, and the yield to maturity is 9%. What is the bond's current market price?

7-2   **YIELD TO MATURITY AND FUTURE PRICE**   A bond has a $1,000 par value, 10 years to maturity, and a 7% annual coupon and sells for $985.

   a.   What is its yield to maturity (YTM)?

   b.   Assume that the yield to maturity remains constant for the next 3 years. What will the price be 3 years from today?

7-3 **BOND VALUATION**   Nungesser Corporation's outstanding bonds have a $1,000 par value, a 9% semiannual coupon, 8 years to maturity, and an 8.5% YTM. What is the bond's price?

7-4 **YIELD TO MATURITY**   A firm's bonds have a maturity of 10 years with a $1,000 face value, have an 8% semiannual coupon, are callable in 5 years at $1,050, and currently sell at a price of $1,100. What are their nominal yield to maturity and their nominal yield to call? What return should investors expect to earn on these bonds?

Intermediate Problems 5–14

7-5 **BOND VALUATION**   An investor has two bonds in his portfolio that have a face value of $1,000 and pay a 10% annual coupon. Bond L matures in 15 years, while Bond S matures in 1 year.

 a. What will the value of each bond be if the going interest rate is 5%, 8%, and 12%? Assume that only one more interest payment is to be made on Bond S at its maturity and that 15 more payments are to be made on Bond L.

 b. Why does the longer-term bond's price vary more than the price of the shorter-term bond when interest rates change?

7-6 **BOND VALUATION**   An investor has two bonds in her portfolio, Bond C and Bond Z. Each bond matures in 4 years, has a face value of $1,000, and has a yield to maturity of 9.6%. Bond C pays a 10% annual coupon, while Bond Z is a zero coupon bond.

 a. Assuming that the yield to maturity of each bond remains at 9.6% over the next 4 years, calculate the price of the bonds at each of the following years to maturity:

Years to Maturity	Price of Bond C	Price of Bond Z
4	_____	_____
3	_____	_____
2	_____	_____
1	_____	_____
0	_____	_____

 b. Plot the time path of prices for each bond.

7-7 **INTEREST RATE SENSITIVITY**   An investor purchased the following 5 bonds. Each bond had a par value of $1,000 and an 8% yield to maturity on the purchase day. Immediately after the investor purchased them, interest rates fell and each then had a new YTM of 7%. What is the percentage change in price for each bond after the decline in interest rates? Fill in the following table:

	Price @ 8%	Price @ 7%	Percentage Change
10-year, 10% annual coupon	_____	_____	_____
10-year zero	_____	_____	_____
5-year zero	_____	_____	_____
30-year zero	_____	_____	_____
$100 perpetuity	_____	_____	_____

7-8 **YIELD TO CALL**   Six years ago the Singleton Company issued 20-year bonds with a 14% annual coupon rate at their $1,000 par value. The bonds had a 9% call premium, with 5 years of call protection. Today Singleton called the bonds. Compute the realized rate of return for an investor who purchased the bonds when they were issued and held them until they were called. Explain why the investor should or should not be happy that Singleton called them.

7-9 **YIELD TO MATURITY**   Heymann Company bonds have 4 years left to maturity. Interest is paid annually, and the bonds have a $1,000 par value and a coupon rate of 9%.

 a. What is the yield to maturity at a current market price of (1) $829 and (2) $1,104?

 b. Would you pay $829 for each bond if you thought that a "fair" market interest rate for such bonds was 12%—that is, if $r_d = 12\%$? Explain your answer.

7-10 **CURRENT YIELD, CAPITAL GAINS YIELD, AND YIELD TO MATURITY**   Hooper Printing Inc. has bonds outstanding with 9 years left to maturity. The bonds have an 8% annual coupon rate and were issued 1 year ago at their par value of $1,000. However, due to changes in interest rates, the bond's market price has fallen to $901.40. The capital gains yield last year was −9.86%.

a. What is the yield to maturity?

b. For the coming year, what are the expected current and capital gains yields? (Hint: Refer to Footnote 8 for the definition of the current yield and to Table 7-1.)

c. Will the actual realized yields be equal to the expected yields if interest rates change? If not, how will they differ?

7-11 **BOND YIELDS** Last year Clark Company issued a 10-year, 12% semiannual coupon bond at its par value of $1,000. Currently, the bond can be called in 4 years at a price of $1,060 and it sells for $1,100.

a. What are the bond's nominal yield to maturity and its nominal yield to call? Would an investor be more likely to earn the YTM or the YTC?

b. What is the current yield? Is this yield affected by whether the bond is likely to be called? (Hint: Refer to Footnote 8 for the definition of the current yield and to Table 7-1.)

c. What is the expected capital gains (or loss) yield for the coming year? Is this yield dependent on whether the bond is expected to be called?

7-12 **YIELD TO CALL** It is now January 1, 2009, and you are considering the purchase of an outstanding bond that was issued on January 1, 2007. It has a 9.5% annual coupon and had a 30-year original maturity. (It matures on December 31, 2036.) There is 5 years of call protection (until December 31, 2011), after which time it can be called at 109—that is, at 109% of par, or $1,090. Interest rates have declined since it was issued; and it is now selling at 116.575% of par, or $1,165.75.

a. What is the yield to maturity? What is the yield to call?

b. If you bought this bond, which return would you actually earn? Explain your reasoning.

c. Suppose the bond had been selling at a discount rather than a premium. Would the yield to maturity have been the most likely return, or would the yield to call have been most likely?

7-13 **PRICE AND YIELD** An 8% semiannual coupon bond matures in 5 years. The bond has a face value of $1,000 and a current yield of 8.21%. What are the bond's price and YTM? (Hint: Refer to Footnote 8 for the definition of the current yield and to Table 7-1.)

7-14 **EXPECTED INTEREST RATE** Lloyd Corporation's 14% coupon rate, semiannual payment, $1,000 par value bonds, which mature in 30 years, are callable 5 years from today at $1,050. They sell at a price of $1,353.54, and the yield curve is flat. Assume that interest rates are expected to remain at their current level.

a. What is the best estimate of these bonds' remaining life?

b. If Lloyd plans to raise additional capital and wants to use debt financing, what coupon rate would it have to set in order to issue new bonds at par?

Challenging Problems 15–19

7-15 **BOND VALUATION** Bond X is noncallable and has 20 years to maturity, a 9% annual coupon, and a $1,000 par value. Your required return on Bond X is 10%; and if you buy it, you plan to hold it for 5 years. You (and the market) have expectations that in 5 years, the yield to maturity on a 15-year bond with similar risk will be 8.5%. How much should you be willing to pay for Bond X today? (Hint: You will need to know how much the bond will be worth at the end of 5 years.)

7-16 **BOND VALUATION** You are considering a 10-year, $1,000 par value bond. Its coupon rate is 9%, and interest is paid semiannually. If you require an "effective" annual interest rate (not a nominal rate) of 8.16%, how much should you be willing to pay for the bond?

7-17 **BOND RETURNS** Last year Joan purchased a $1,000 face value corporate bond with an 11% annual coupon rate and a 10-year maturity. At the time of the purchase, it had an expected yield to maturity of 9.79%. If Joan sold the bond today for $1,060.49, what rate of return would she have earned for the past year?

7-18 **BOND REPORTING** Look back at Table 7-4 and examine United Parcel Service and Telecom Italia Capital bonds that mature in 2013.

a. If these companies were to sell new $1,000 par value long-term bonds, approximately what coupon interest rate would they have to set if they wanted to bring them out at par?

b. If you had $10,000 and wanted to invest in United Parcel Service bonds, what return would you expect to earn? What about Telecom Italia Capital bonds? Based just on the data in the table, would you have more confidence about earning your expected rate of return if you bought United Parcel Service or Telecom Italia Capital bonds? Explain.

7-19   **YIELD TO MATURITY AND YIELD TO CALL**   Kaufman Enterprises has bonds outstanding with a $1,000 face value and 10 years left until maturity. They have an 11% annual coupon payment, and their current price is $1,175. The bonds may be called in 5 years at 109% of face value (Call price = $1,090).

a.   What is the yield to maturity?

b.   What is the yield to call if they are called in 5 years?

c.   Which yield might investors expect to earn on these bonds? Why?

d.   The bond's indenture indicates that the call provision gives the firm the right to call the bonds at the end of each year beginning in Year 5. In Year 5, the bonds may be called at 109% of face value; but in each of the next 4 years, the call percentage will decline by 1%. Thus, in Year 6, they may be called at 108% of face value; in Year 7, they may be called at 107% of face value; and so forth. If the yield curve is horizontal and interest rates remain at their current level, when is the latest that investors might expect the firm to call the bonds?

COMPREHENSIVE/SPREADSHEET PROBLEM

7-20   **BOND VALUATION**   Clifford Clark is a recent retiree who is interested in investing some of his savings in corporate bonds. His financial planner has suggested the following bonds:

- Bond A has a 7% annual coupon, matures in 12 years, and has a $1,000 face value.
- Bond B has a 9% annual coupon, matures in 12 years, and has a $1,000 face value.
- Bond C has an 11% annual coupon, matures in 12 years, and has a $1,000 face value.

Each bond has a yield to maturity of 9%.

a.   Before calculating the prices of the bonds, indicate whether each bond is trading at a premium, at a discount, or at par.

b.   Calculate the price of each of the three bonds.

c.   Calculate the current yield for each of the three bonds. (Hint: Refer to Footnote 8 for the definition of the current yield and to Table 7-1.)

d.   If the yield to maturity for each bond remains at 9%, what will be the price of each bond 1 year from now? What is the expected capital gains yield for each bond? What is the expected total return for each bond?

e.   Mr. Clark is considering another bond, Bond D. It has an 8% semiannual coupon and a $1,000 face value (i.e., it pays a $40 coupon every 6 months). Bond D is scheduled to mature in 9 years and has a price of $1,150. It is also callable in 5 years at a call price of $1,040.

(1)   What is the bond's nominal yield to maturity?

(2)   What is the bond's nominal yield to call?

(3)   If Mr. Clark were to purchase this bond, would he be more likely to receive the yield to maturity or yield to call? Explain your answer.

f.   Explain briefly the difference between interest rate (or price) risk and reinvestment rate risk. Which of the following bonds has the most interest rate risk?

- A 5-year bond with a 9% annual coupon
- A 5-year bond with a zero coupon
- A 10-year bond with a 9% annual coupon
- A 10-year bond with a zero coupon

g.   Only do this part if you are using a spreadsheet. Calculate the price of each bond (A, B, and C) at the end of each year until maturity, assuming interest rates remain constant. Create a graph showing the time path of each bond's value similar to Figure 7-2.

(1)   What is the expected interest yield for each bond in each year?

(2)   What is the expected capital gains yield for each bond in each year?

(3)   What is the total return for each bond in each year?

INTEGRATED CASE

WESTERN MONEY MANAGEMENT INC.

7-21   **BOND VALUATION**   Robert Black and Carol Alvarez are vice presidents of Western Money Management and codirectors of the company's pension fund management division. A major new client, the California League of Cities, has requested that Western present an investment seminar to the mayors of the represented cities. Black and Alvarez, who will make the presentation, have asked you to help them by answering the following questions.

a.   What are a bond's key features?

b.   What are call provisions and sinking fund provisions? Do these provisions make bonds more or less risky?

c.   How is the value of any asset whose value is based on expected future cash flows determined?

d.   How is a bond's value determined? What is the value of a 10-year, $1,000 par value bond with a 10% annual coupon if its required return is 10%?

e.   (1)   What is the value of a 13% coupon bond that is otherwise identical to the bond described in Part d? Would we now have a discount or a premium bond?

   (2)   What is the value of a 7% coupon bond with these characteristics? Would we now have a discount or premium bond?

   (3)   What would happen to the values of the 7%, 10%, and 13% coupon bonds over time if the required return remained at 10%? [Hint: With a financial calculator, enter PMT, I/YR, FV, and N; then change (override) N to see what happens to the PV as it approaches maturity.]

f.   (1)   What is the yield to maturity on a 10-year, 9%, annual coupon, $1,000 par value bond that sells for $887.00? that sells for $1,134.20? What does the fact that it sells at a discount or at a premium tell you about the relationship between r_d and the coupon rate?

   (2)   What are the total return, the current yield, and the capital gains yield for the discount bond? Assume that it is held to maturity and the company does not default on it. (Hint: Refer to Footnote 8 for the definition of the current yield and to Table 7-1.)

g.   What is *interest rate* (or *price*) *risk*? Which has more interest rate risk, an annual payment 1-year bond or a 10-year bond? Why?

h.   What is *reinvestment rate risk*? Which has more reinvestment rate risk, a 1-year bond or a 10-year bond?

i.   How does the equation for valuing a bond change if semiannual payments are made? Find the value of a 10-year, semiannual payment, 10% coupon bond if nominal $r_d = 13\%$.

j.   Suppose for $1,000 you could buy a 10%, 10-year, annual payment bond or a 10%, 10-year, semiannual payment bond. They are equally risky. Which would you prefer? If $1,000 is the proper price for the semiannual bond, what is the equilibrium price for the annual payment bond?

k.   Suppose a 10-year, 10%, semiannual coupon bond with a par value of $1,000 is currently selling for $1,135.90, producing a nominal yield to maturity of 8%. However, it can be called after 4 years for $1,050.

   (1)   What is the bond's *nominal yield to call* (YTC)?

   (2)   If you bought this bond, would you be more likely to earn the YTM or the YTC? Why?

l.   Does the yield to maturity represent the promised or expected return on the bond? Explain.

m.   These bonds were rated AA- by S&P. Would you consider them investment-grade or junk bonds?

n.   What factors determine a company's bond rating?

o.   If this firm were to default on the bonds, would the company be immediately liquidated? Would the bondholders be assured of receiving all of their promised payments? Explain.

CHAPTER

8   Risk and Rates of Return

A Tale of Three Markets—or Is It Four?

The purpose of this vignette is to give you some additional perspective on the stock market. Refer to Figure 8-1 on page 232 as you read the following paragraphs.

Market 1: 1975–2000. These were great years, especially the last five. Only 3 years saw losses; and toward the end of the run, most investors and money managers had never experienced a really bad market and acted as though bad markets had been banished and would never reappear again. However, Alan Greenspan, Chairman of the Federal Reserve Board at that time, knew the wild ride couldn't continue. In 1995, he stated that investors were exhibiting "irrational exuberance"; but the market ignored him and kept roaring ahead.

Market 2: 2000–2003. Greenspan was right. In 2000, the bubble started to leak and the market fell by 10%. Then in 2001, the 9/11 terrorist attacks on the World Trade Center knocked stocks down another 14%. Finally, in 2002, fears of another attack in addition to a recession led to a gut-wrenching 24% decline. Those 3 years cost the average investor almost 50% of his or her beginning-of-2000 market value. People planning to retire rich and young had to rethink those plans.

Market 3: 2003–2007. Investors had overreacted; so in 2003, the market rebounded, rising by just over 25%. The market remained strong through 2007—the economy was robust, profits were rising rapidly, and the Federal Reserve encouraged a bull market by cutting interest rates 11 times. In 2007, the Dow Jones and other stock averages hit all-time highs. But the debt markets were suffering from the subprime mortgage debacle, and institutions such as Merrill Lynch and Citigroup were writing off tens of billions of dollars of bad loans. Oil prices hit $100 per barrel, gasoline prices hit new highs, and unemployment rates were creeping up. With this backdrop, some observers wondered if we were again suffering from irrational exuberance.

<u>Market 4: 2008 and Thereafter: Bull or Bear?</u> In early 2008, the big question is this: Will the bull market continue; or are we entering another bear market? It turned out that the bears were right—by October 2008, the market had fallen nearly 30% from its high earlier in the year in the aftermath of a credit crisis on Wall Street, the collapse of several leading financial firms, and fears of a sharp economic decline. In response, Congress passed an unprecedented $700 billion plan to rescue the financial system. What's next? Will the market stabilize or will it continue to see further declines? We wish we knew! By the time you read this, you will know, but it will be too late to profit from that knowledge.

PUTTING THINGS IN PERSPECTIVE

We start this chapter from the basic premise that investors like returns and dislike risk; hence, they will invest in risky assets only if those assets offer higher expected returns. We define what risk means as it relates to investments, examine procedures that are used to measure *risk,* and discuss the relationship between risk and return. Investors should understand these concepts, as should corporate managers as they develop the plans that will shape their firms' futures.

Risk can be measured in different ways, and different conclusions about an asset's riskiness can be reached depending on the measure used. Risk analysis can be confusing, but it will help if you keep the following points in mind:

1. All business assets are expected to produce *cash flows*, and the riskiness of an asset is based on the riskiness of its cash flows. The riskier the cash flows, the riskier the asset.

2. Assets can be categorized as *financial assets*, especially stocks and bonds, and as *real assets,* such as trucks, machines, and whole businesses. In theory, risk analysis for all types of assets is similar and the same fundamental concepts apply to all assets. However, in practice, differences in the types of available data lead to different procedures for stocks, bonds, and real assets. Our focus in this chapter is on financial assets, especially stocks. We considered bonds in Chapter 7; and we take up real assets in the capital budgeting chapters, especially Chapter 12.

3. A stock's risk can be considered in two ways: (a) on a *stand-alone, or single-stock, basis,* or (b) in a *portfolio context,* where a number of stocks are combined and their consolidated cash flows are analyzed.[1] There is an important difference between stand-alone and portfolio risk, and a stock that has a great deal of risk held by itself may be much less risky when held as part of a larger portfolio.

4. In a portfolio context, a stock's risk can be divided into two components: (a) *diversifiable risk,* which can be diversified away and is thus of little concern to diversified investors, and (b) *market risk,* which reflects the risk of a general stock market decline and cannot be eliminated by diversification (hence, does concern investors). Only market risk is *relevant* to rational investors because diversifiable risk can and will be eliminated.

5. A stock with high market risk must offer a relatively high expected rate of return to attract investors. Investors in general are *averse to risk,* so they will not buy risky assets unless they are compensated with high expected returns.

6. If investors, on average, think a stock's expected return is too low to compensate for its risk, they will start selling it, driving down its price and boosting its expected

---

[1]A *portfolio* is a collection of investment securities. If you owned stock in General Motors, ExxonMobil, and IBM, you would be holding a three-stock portfolio. Because diversification lowers risk without sacrificing much if any expected return, most stocks are held in portfolios.

return. Conversely, if the expected return on a stock is more than enough to compensate for the risk, people will start buying it, raising its price and thus lowering its expected return. The stock will be in equilibrium, with neither buying nor selling pressure, when its expected return is exactly sufficient to compensate for its risk.

7. Stand-alone risk, the topic of Section 8-2, is important in stock analysis primarily as a lead-in to portfolio risk analysis. However, stand-alone risk is extremely important when analyzing real assets such as capital budgeting projects.

When you finish this chapter, you should be able to:

- Explain the difference between stand-alone risk and risk in a portfolio context.
- Explain how risk aversion affects a stock's required rate of return.
- Discuss the difference between diversifiable risk and market risk, and explain how each type of risk affects well-diversified investors.
- Explain what the CAPM is and how it can be used to estimate a stock's required rate of return.
- Discuss how changes in the general stock and the bond markets could lead to changes in the required rate of return on a firm's stock.
- Discuss how changes in a firm's operations might lead to changes in the required rate of return on the firm's stock.

8-1 STOCK PRICES OVER THE LAST 20 YEARS

Figure 8-1 gives you an idea about how stocks have performed over the period from 1988 through 2007.[2] The top graph compares General Electric (GE), the broad stock market as measured by the S&P 500, and General Motors (GM). GE illustrates companies that have done well, GM illustrates those that have not done well, and the S&P 500 shows how an average company has performed. Most stocks climbed sharply until 2000 (Market 1 in the vignette), then dropped equally sharply during Market 2, then rose nicely through most of Market 3. Since there are thousands of stocks, we could have shown many different pictures, with some rising much faster than GE and others falling much faster than GM—with some going to zero and vanishing. Most of the indexes rise and fall together; but if we had shown the Nasdaq index, it would have looked a great deal like GE, rising much faster than the S&P but then falling faster later on. Also note that the beginning and ending dates can lead to totally different "pictures" of stocks' performances. If we had started in 1990 and ended in 2000, it would have looked as though stocks were wonderful investments. On the other hand, if we had started in 2000 and ended in 2003, it would have looked as though stocks were a terrible place to put our money. It would be great if we knew when to get in and out of the market.

The lower graph shows GE's P/E ratio. The P/E ratio depends on a number of factors, including fundamental factors such as interest rates and earnings growth rates; but it also reflects investors' optimism or pessimism—or in Alan Greenspan's words, their "irrational exuberance" or pessimism. Security analysts and investors forecast the future, but they seem to be overly optimistic at certain times and overly pessimistic at other times. Looking back, we can see that they were overly optimistic in 2000. But what about in 1997? There had been a sharp run-up to that time, and some "experts" thought the market was at a top and recommended getting out. Those experts turned out to be wrong, and they "left a lot of money on the table."

---

[2]The graph reflects stock prices; dividends are not included. If dividends were included, the percentage gains would be somewhat higher.

FIGURE 8-1   Stock Performance, 1988–2007

© BigCharts.com

Source: http://online.wsj.com, *The Wall Street Journal Online*, January 12, 2008.

Note also that if you had bought and held GE stock you would have done quite well; but if you had bought GM stock, you wouldn't have done well at all. If you had formed a portfolio with some GM and some GE stocks, you would have had "average" performance. The portfolio would have limited your potential gain but also would have limited your low-end returns. We will have more to say about portfolios later, but keep this in mind as you go through the chapter.

8-2 STAND-ALONE RISK

Risk
The chance that some unfavorable event will occur.

Risk is defined by *Webster* as "a hazard; a peril; exposure to loss or injury." Thus, risk refers to the chance that some unfavorable event will occur. If you engage in skydiving, you are taking a chance with your life—skydiving is risky. If you bet on the horses, you are risking your money.

As we saw in previous chapters, individuals and firms invest funds today with the expectation of receiving additional funds in the future. Bonds offer relatively low returns, but with relatively little risk—at least if you stick to Treasury and high-grade corporate bonds. Stocks offer the chance of higher returns, but stocks are generally riskier than bonds. If you invest in speculative stocks (or, really, *any* stock), you are taking a significant risk in the hope of making an appreciable return.

An asset's risk can be analyzed in two ways: (1) on a stand-alone basis, where the asset is considered by itself, and (2) on a portfolio basis, where the asset is held as one of a number of assets in a portfolio. Thus, an asset's **stand-alone risk** is the risk an investor would face if he or she held only this one asset. Most financial assets, and stocks in particular, are held in portfolios; but it is necessary to understand stand-alone risk to understand risk in a portfolio context.

To illustrate stand-alone risk, suppose an investor buys $100,000 of short-term Treasury bills with an expected return of 5%. In this case, the investment's return, 5%, can be estimated quite precisely; and the investment is defined as being essentially *risk-free*. This same investor could also invest the $100,000 in the stock of a company just being organized to prospect for oil in the mid-Atlantic. Returns on the stock would be much harder to predict. In the worst case, the company would go bankrupt and the investor would lose all of his or her money, in which case the return would be −100%. In the best-case scenario, the company would discover huge amounts of oil and the investor would receive a 1,000% return. When evaluating this investment, the investor might analyze the situation and conclude that the *expected* rate of return, in a statistical sense, is 20%; but the *actual* rate of return could range from, say, +1,000% to −100%. Because there is a significant danger of earning much less than the expected return, such a stock would be relatively risky.

No investment should be undertaken unless the expected rate of return is high enough to compensate for the perceived risk. In our example, it is clear that few if any investors would be willing to buy the oil exploration stock if its expected return didn't exceed that of the T-bill. This is an extreme example. Generally, things are much less obvious; and we need to measure risk in order to decide whether a potential investment should be undertaken. Therefore, we need to define risk more precisely.

As you will see, the risk of an asset is different when the asset is held by itself versus when it is held as a part of a group, or portfolio, of assets. We look at stand-alone risk in this section, then at portfolio risk in later sections. It's necessary to know something about stand-alone risk in order to understand portfolio risk. Also, stand-alone risk is important to the owners of small businesses and in our examination of physical assets in the capital budgeting chapters. For stocks and most financial assets, though, it is portfolio risk that is most important. Still, you need to understand the key elements of both types of risk.

8-2a Statistical Measures of Stand-Alone Risk

This is not a statistics book, and we won't spend a great deal of time on statistics. However, you do need an intuitive understanding of the relatively simple statistics presented in this section. All of the calculations can be done easily with a calculator or with Excel; and while we show pictures of the Excel setup, Excel is not needed for the calculations.

Here are the five key items that are covered:

- Probability distributions
- Expected rates of return, $\hat{r}$ ("r hat")
- Historical, or past realized, rates of return, $\bar{r}$ ("r bar")
- Standard deviation, σ (sigma)
- Coefficient of variation (CV)

Table 8-1 gives the **probability distributions** for Martin Products, which makes engines for long-haul trucks (18-wheelers), and for U.S. Water, which supplies an essential product and thus has very stable sales and profits. Three possible states of the economy are shown in Column 1; and the probabilities of these outcomes, expressed as decimals rather than percentages, are given in Column 2 and then repeated in Column 5. There is a 30% chance of a strong economy and thus strong demand, a 40% probability of normal demand, and a 30% probability of weak demand.

Stand-Alone Risk
The risk an investor would face if he or she held only one asset.

Probability Distribution
A listing of possible outcomes or events with a probability (chance of occurrence) assigned to each outcome.

| Table 8-1 | Probability Distributions and Expected Returns |

	A	B	C	D	E	F	G
			Martin Products			U.S. Water	
	Economy, Which Affects Demand (1)	Probability of This Demand Occurring (2)	Rate of Return If This Demand Occurs (3)	Product (2)×(3) (4)	Probability of This Demand Occurring (5)	Rate of Return If This Demand Occurs (6)	Product (5)×(6) (7)
12	Strong	0.30	80%	24%	0.30	15%	4.5%
13	Normal	0.40	10	4	0.40	10	4.0
14	Weak	0.30	-60	-18	0.30	5	1.5
15		1.00	Expected return =	10%	1.00	Expected return =	10.0%

Columns 3 and 6 show the returns for the two companies under each state of the economy. Returns are relatively high when demand is strong and low when demand is weak. Notice, though, that Martin's rate of return could vary far more widely than U.S. Water's. Indeed, there is a fairly high probability that Martin's stock will suffer a 60% loss, while at worst, U.S. Water should have a 5% return.[3]

Columns 4 and 7 show the products of the probabilities times the returns under the different demand levels. When we sum these products, we obtain the **expected rates of return, $\hat{r}$** "r-hat," for the stocks. Both stocks have an expected return of 10%.[4]

We can graph the data in Table 8-1 as we do in Figure 8-2. The height of each bar indicates the probability that a given outcome will occur. The range of possible returns for Martin is from −60% to +80%, and the expected return is 10%. The expected return for U.S. Water is also 10%, but its possible range (and thus maximum loss) is much narrower.

In Figure 8-2, we assumed that only three economic states could occur: strong, normal, and weak. Actually, the economy can range from a deep depression to a fantastic boom; and there are an unlimited number of possibilities in between. Suppose we had the time and patience to assign a probability to each possible level of demand (with the sum of the probabilities still equaling 1.0) and to assign a rate of return to each stock for each level of demand. We would have a table similar to Table 8-1 except that it would have many more demand levels. This table could be used to calculate expected rates of return as shown previously, and the probabilities and outcomes could be represented by continuous curves such as those shown in Figure 8-3. Here we changed the assumptions so that there is essentially no chance that Martin's return will be less than −60% or more than 80% or that

Expected Rate of Return, $\hat{r}$

The rate of return expected to be realized from an investment; the weighted average of the probability distribution of possible results.

---

[3]It is completely unrealistic to think that any stock has no chance of a loss. Only in hypothetical examples could this occur. To illustrate, the price of Countrywide Financial's stock dropped from $45.26 to $4.43 in the 12 months ending January 2008.

[4]The expected return can also be calculated with an equation that does the same thing as the table:

$$\text{Expected rate of return} = \hat{r} = P_1 r_1 + P_2 r_2 + \cdots + P_N r_N$$

8-1

$$\hat{r} = \sum_{i=1}^{N} P_i r_i$$

The second form of the equation is a shorthand expression in which sigma (Σ) means "sum up," or add the values of n factors. If $i = 1$, then $P_i r_i = P_1 r_1$; if $i = 2$, then $P_i r_i = P_2 r_2$; and so forth; until $i = N$, the last possible outcome.

The symbol $\sum_{i=1}^{N}$ simply says, "Go through the following process: First, let $i = 1$ and find the first product; then let $i = 2$ and find the second product; then continue until each individual product up to N has been found. Add these individual products to find the expected rate of return."

| FIGURE 8-2 | Probability Distributions of Martin Products' and U.S. Water's Rates of Return |

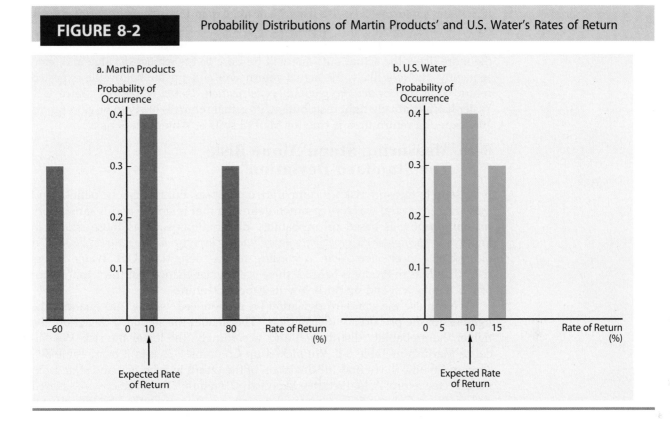

| FIGURE 8-3 | Continuous Probability Distributions of Martin Products' and U.S. Water's Rates of Return |

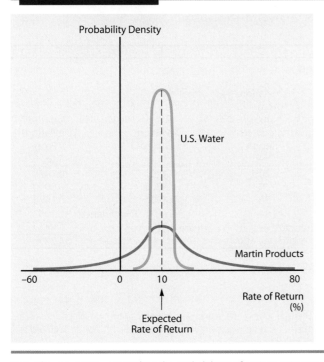

Note: The assumptions regarding the probabilities of various outcomes have been changed from those in Figure 8-2. There the probability of obtaining exactly 10% was 40%; here it is *much smaller* because there are many possible outcomes instead of just three. With continuous distributions, it is more appropriate to ask what the probability is of obtaining at least some specified rate of return than to ask what the probability is of obtaining exactly that rate. This topic is covered in detail in statistics courses.

U.S. Water's return will be less than 5% or more than 15%. However, virtually any return within these limits is possible.

The tighter (or more peaked) the probability distributions shown in Figure 8-3, the more likely the actual outcome will be close to the expected value and, consequently, the less likely the actual return will end up far below the expected return. *Thus, the tighter the probability distribution, the lower the risk.* Since U.S. Water has a relatively tight distribution, its actual return is likely to be closer to its 10% expected return than is true for Martin; so U.S. Water is less risky.[5]

8-2b Measuring Stand-Alone Risk: The Standard Deviation[6]

It is useful to measure risk for comparative purposes, but risk can be defined and measured in several ways. A common definition that is simple and is satisfactory for our purpose is based on probability distributions such as those shown in Figure 8-3: *The tighter the probability distribution of expected future returns, the smaller the risk of a given investment.* According to this definition, U.S. Water is less risky than Martin Products because there is a smaller chance that the actual return of U.S. Water will end up far below its expected return.

We can use the standard deviation (σ, pronounced "sigma") to quantify the tightness of the probability distribution.[7] The smaller the standard deviation, the tighter the probability distribution and, accordingly, the lower the risk. We calculate Martin's in Table 8-2. We picked up Columns 1, 2, and 3 from Table 8-1. Then in Column 4, we find the deviation of the return in each demand state from the expected return: Actual return – Expected 10% return. The deviations are squared and shown in Column 5. Each squared deviation is then multiplied by the relevant probability and shown in Column 6. The sum of the products in Column 6 is the *variance* of the distribution. Finally, we find the square root of the variance—this is

Table 8-2	**Calculating Martin Products' Standard Deviation**

	A	B	C	D	E	F
19						
20						
21			Rate of	Deviation:		
22	Economy,	Probability	Return	Actual -		
23	Which	of This	If This	10%		Squared
24	Affects	Demand	Demand	Expected	Deviation	Deviation
25	Demand	Occurring	Occurs	Return	Squared	x Prob.
26	(1)	(2)	(3)	(4)	(5)	(6)
27	Strong	0.30	80%	70%	0.4900	0.1470
28	Normal	0.40	10	0	0.0000	0.0000
29	Weak	0.30	-60	-70	0.4900	0.1470
30		1.00			Σ = Variance:	0.2940
31				Standard deviation = square root of variance: σ =		0.5422
32				Standard deviation expressed as a percentage: σ =		54.22%

---

[5] In this example, we implicitly assume that the state of the economy is the only factor that affects returns. In reality, many factors, including labor, materials, and development costs, influence returns. This is discussed at greater length in the chapters on capital budgeting.

[6] This section is relatively technical, but it can be omitted without loss of continuity.

[7] There are actually two types of standard deviations, one for complete distributions and one for situations that involve only a sample. Different formulas and notations are used. Also, the standard deviation should be modified if the distribution is not normal, or bell-shaped. Since our purpose is simply to get the general idea across, we leave the refinements to advanced finance and statistics courses.

the *standard deviation*, and it is shown at the bottom of Column 6 as a fraction and a percentage.[8]

The **standard deviation** is a measure of how far the actual return is likely to deviate from the expected return. Martin's standard deviation is 54.2%, so its actual return is likely to be quite different from the expected 10%.[9] U.S. Water's standard deviation is 3.9%, so its actual return should be much closer to the expected return of 10%. The average publicly traded firm's has been in the range of 20% to 30% in recent years; so Martin is more risky than most stocks, while U.S. Water is less risky.

Standard Deviation, σ (sigma)
A statistical measure of the variability of a set of observations.

8-2c Using Historical Data to Measure Risk[10]

In the last section, we found the mean and standard deviation based on a subjective probability distribution. If we had actual historical data instead, the standard deviation of returns could be found as shown in Table 8-3.[11] Because past results are often repeated in the future, the historical σ is often used as an estimate of future risk.[12] A key question that arises when historical data is used to forecast the future is how far back in time we should go. Unfortunately, there is no simple answer. Using a longer historical time series has the benefit of giving more information, but some of that information may be misleading if you believe that the level of risk in the future is likely to be very different than the level of risk in the past.

Table 8-3		**Finding σ Based On Historical Data**			
	A	B	C	D	E	F

	A	B	C	D	E	F
35						
36						
37				Deviation from		Squared
38				Average		Deviation
39	Year	Return		(3)		(4)
40	(1)	(2)				
41	2005	30.0%		19.8%		3.9%
42	2006	-10.0		-20.3		4.1
43	2007	-19.0		-29.3		8.6
44	2008	40.0		29.8		8.9
45	Average	10.3%			Variance = Σ:	25.4%
46						
47				Variance/(N–1) = Variance/3:		8.5%
48				Standard deviation = Square root of variance: σ =		29.1%

---

[8]This formula summarizes what we did in Table 8-2:

$$\text{Standard deviation} = \sigma = \sqrt{\sum_{i=1}^{N} (r_i - \hat{r})^2 P_i} \qquad \text{8-2}$$

[9]With a normal (bell-shaped) distribution, the actual return should be within one σ about 68% of the time.

[10]Again, this section is relatively technical, but it can be omitted without loss of continuity.

[11]The 4 years of historical data are considered to be a "sample" of the full (but unknown) set of data, and the procedure used to find the standard deviation is different from the one used for probabilistic data. Here is the equation for sample data, and it is the basis for Table 8-3:

$$\text{Estimated } \sigma = \sqrt{\frac{\sum_{t=1}^{N} (\bar{r}_t - \bar{r}_{Avg})^2}{N-1}} \qquad \text{8-2a}$$

Here $\bar{r}_t$ ("r bar t") denotes the past realized rate of return in Period t, and $\bar{r}_{Avg}$ is the average annual return earned over the last N years.

[12]The average return for the past period (10.3% in our example) may also be used as an estimate of future returns, but this is problematic because the average historical return varies widely depending on the period examined. In our example, if we went from 2005 to 2007, we would get a different average from the 10.3%. The average historical return stabilizes with more years of data, but that brings into question whether data from many years ago is still relevant today.

All financial calculators (and Excel) have easy-to-use functions for finding σ based on historical data.[13] Simply enter the rates of return and press the key marked S (or S_x) to obtain the standard deviation. However, neither calculators nor Excel have a built-in formula for finding σ where probabilistic data are involved. In those cases, you must go through the process outlined in Table 8-2.

8-2d Measuring Stand-Alone Risk: The Coefficient of Variation

If a choice has to be made between two investments that have the same expected returns but different standard deviations, most people would choose the one with the lower standard deviation and, therefore, the lower risk. Similarly, given a choice between two investments with the same risk (standard deviation) but different expected returns, investors would generally prefer the investment with the higher expected return. To most people, this is common sense—return is "good" and risk is "bad"; consequently, investors want as much return and as little risk as possible. But how do we choose between two investments if one has the higher expected return but the other has the lower standard deviation? To help answer that question, we use another measure of risk, the **coefficient of variation (CV)**, which is the standard deviation divided by the expected return:

Coefficient of Variation (CV)

The standardized measure of the risk per unit of return; calculated as the standard deviation divided by the expected return.

8-3
$$\text{Coefficient of variation} = CV = \frac{\sigma}{\hat{r}}$$

The coefficient of variation shows the risk per unit of return, and it provides a more meaningful risk measure when the expected returns on two alternatives are not the same. Since U.S. Water and Martin Products have the same expected return, the coefficient of variation is not necessary in this case. Here the firm with the larger standard deviation, Martin, must have the larger coefficient of variation. In fact, the coefficient of variation for Martin is 54.22/10 = 5.42 and the coefficient of variation for U.S. Water is 3.87/10 = 0.39. Thus, Martin is about 14 times riskier than U.S. Water on the basis of this criterion.

8-2e Risk Aversion and Required Returns

Suppose you inherited $1 million, which you plan to invest and then retire on the income. You can buy a 5% U.S. Treasury bill, and you will be sure of earning $50,000 of interest. Alternatively, you can buy stock in R&D Enterprises. If R&D's research programs are successful, your stock will increase to $2.1 million. However, if the research is a failure, the value of your stock will be zero and you will be penniless. You regard R&D's chances of success or failure as 50-50, so the expected value of the stock a year from now is 0.5($0) + 0.5($2,100,000) = $1,050,000. Subtracting the $1 million cost leaves an expected $50,000 profit and a 5% rate of return, the same as for the T-bill:

$$\text{Expected rate of return} = \frac{\text{Expected ending value} - \text{Cost}}{\text{Cost}}$$
$$= \frac{\$1,050,000 - \$1,000,000}{\$1,000,000}$$
$$= \frac{\$50,000}{\$1,000,000} = 5\%$$

Given the choice of the sure $50,000 profit (and 5% rate of return) and the risky expected $50,000 profit and 5% return, which one would you choose? *If you choose the*

---

[13]See our tutorials on the text's web site (http://academic.cengage.com/finance/brigham) or your calculator manual for instructions on calculating historical standard deviations.

less risky investment, you are risk-averse. Most investors are risk-averse, and certainly the average investor is with regard to his or her "serious money." Because this is a well-documented fact, we assume **risk aversion** *in our discussions throughout the remainder of the book.*

What are the implications of risk aversion for security prices and rates of return? *The answer is that, other things held constant, the higher a security's risk, the higher its required return; and if this situation does not hold, prices will change to bring about the required condition.* To illustrate this point, look back at Figure 8-3 and consider again the U.S. Water and Martin Products stocks. Suppose each stock sells for $100 per share and each has an expected rate of return of 10%. Investors are averse to risk; so under those conditions, there would be a general preference for U.S. Water. People with money to invest would bid for U.S. Water, and Martin's stockholders would want to sell and use the money to buy U.S. Water. Buying pressure would quickly drive U.S. Water's stock up, and selling pressure would simultaneously cause Martin's price to fall.

These price changes, in turn, would change the expected returns of the two securities. Suppose, for example, that U.S. Water's stock was bid up from $100 to $125 and Martin's stock declined from $100 to $77. These price changes would cause U.S. Water's expected return to fall to 8% and Martin's return to rise to 13%.[14] The difference in returns, 13% − 8% = 5%, would be a **risk premium (RP)**, which represents the additional compensation investors require for bearing Martin's higher risk.

This example demonstrates a very important principle: *In a market dominated by risk-averse investors, riskier securities compared to less risky securities must have higher expected returns as estimated by the marginal investor. If this situation does not exist, buying and selling will occur until it does exist.* Later in the chapter we will consider the question of how much higher the returns on risky securities must be, after we see how diversification affects the way risk should be measured.

Risk Aversion
Risk-averse investors dislike risk and require higher rates of return as an inducement to buy riskier securities.

Risk Premium (RP)
The difference between the expected rate of return on a given risky asset and that on a less risky asset.

THE TRADE-OFF BETWEEN RISK AND RETURN

The table accompanying this box summarizes the historical trade-off between risk and return for different classes of investments from 1926 through 2007. As the table shows, those assets that produced the highest average returns also had the highest standard deviations and the widest ranges of returns. For example, small-company stocks had the highest average annual return, 17.1%, but the standard deviation of their returns, 32.6%, was also the highest. By contrast, U.S. Treasury bills had the lowest standard deviation, 3.1%, but they also had the lowest average return, 3.8%. While there is no guarantee that history will repeat itself, the returns and standard deviations observed in the past are often used as a starting point for estimating future returns.

Selected Realized Returns, 1926–2007

	Average Return	Standard Deviation
Small-company stocks	17.1%	32.6%
Large-company stocks	12.3	20.0
Long-term corporate bonds	6.2	8.4
Long-term government bonds	5.8	9.2
U.S. Treasury bills	3.8	3.1

Source: Based on *Stocks, Bonds, Bills, and Inflation: (Valuation Edition) 2008 Yearbook* (Chicago: Morningstar, Inc., 2008), p. 28.

---

[14]We assume that each stock is expected to pay shareholders $10 a year in perpetuity. The price of this perpetuity can be found by dividing the annual cash flow by the stock's return. Thus, if the stock's expected return is 10%, the price must be $10/0.10 = $100. Likewise, an 8% expected return would be consistent with a $125 stock price ($10/0.08 = $125) and a 13% return with a $77 stock price ($10/0.13 = $77).

SELF TEST

What does *investment risk* mean?

Set up an illustrative probability distribution table for an investment with probabilities for different conditions, returns under those conditions, and the expected return.

Which of the two stocks graphed in Figure 8-3 is less risky? Why?

Explain why you agree or disagree with this statement: Most investors are risk-averse.

How does risk aversion affect rates of return?

An investment has a 50% chance of producing a 20% return, a 25% chance of producing an 8% return, and a 25% chance of producing a −12% return. What is its expected return? **(9%)**

8-3 RISK IN A PORTFOLIO CONTEXT: THE CAPM

Capital Asset Pricing Model (CAPM)
A model based on the proposition that any stock's required rate of return is equal to the risk-free rate of return plus a risk premium that reflects only the risk remaining after diversification.

In this section, we discuss the risk of stocks when they are held in portfolios rather than as stand-alone assets. Our discussion is based on an extremely important theory, the **Capital Asset Pricing Model,** or **CAPM**, that was developed in the 1960s.[15] We do not attempt to cover the CAPM in detail—rather, we simply use its intuition to explain how risk should be considered in a world where stocks and other assets are held in portfolios. If you go on to take a course in investments, you will cover the CAPM in detail.

Thus far in the chapter we have considered the riskiness of assets when they are held in isolation. This is generally appropriate for small businesses, many real estate investments, and capital budgeting projects. However, the risk of a stock held in a portfolio is typically lower than the stock's risk when it is held alone. Since investors dislike risk and since risk can be reduced by holding portfolios, most stocks are held in portfolios. Banks, pension funds, insurance companies, mutual funds, and other financial institutions are required by law to hold diversified portfolios. Most individual investors—at least those whose security holdings constitute a significant part of their total wealth—also hold portfolios. Therefore, the fact that one particular stock's price goes up or down is not important—*what is important is the return on the portfolio and the portfolio's risk. Logically, then, the risk and return of an individual stock should be analyzed in terms of how the security affects the risk and return of the portfolio in which it is held.*

To illustrate, Pay Up Inc. is a collection agency that operates nationwide through 37 offices. The company is not well known, its stock is not very liquid, and its earnings have experienced sharp fluctuations in the past. This suggests that Pay Up is risky and that its required rate of return, r, should be relatively high. However, Pay Up's required return in 2008 (and all other years) was quite low in comparison to most other companies. This indicates that investors think Pay Up is a low-risk company in spite of its uncertain profits. *This counterintuitive finding has to do with diversification and its effect on risk.* Pay Up's earnings rise during recessions, whereas most other companies' earnings decline when the economy slumps. Thus, Pay Up's stock is like insurance—it pays off when other things go bad—so adding Pay Up to a portfolio of "regular" stocks stabilizes the portfolio's returns and makes it less risky.

---

[15]The CAPM was originated by Professor William F. Sharpe in his article "Capital Asset Prices: A Theory of Market Equilibrium Under Conditions of Risk," *Journal of Finance*, 1964. Literally thousands of articles exploring various aspects of the CAPM have been published subsequently, and it is very widely used in investment analysis.

8-3a Expected Portfolio Returns, $\hat{r}_p$

The **expected return on a portfolio, $\hat{r}_p$**, is the weighted average of the expected returns of the individual assets in the portfolio, with the weights being the percentage of the total portfolio invested in each asset :

$$\hat{r}_p = w_1\hat{r}_1 + w_2\hat{r}_2 + \cdots + w_N\hat{r}_N$$

$$= \sum_{i=1}^{N} w_i\hat{r}_i \qquad\qquad 8\text{-}4$$

Here $\hat{r}_i$ is the expected return on the *i*th stock; the w_i's are the stocks' weights, or the percentage of the total value of the portfolio invested in each stock; and N is the number of stocks in the portfolio.

Table 8-4 can be used to implement the equation. Here we assume that an analyst estimated returns on the four stocks shown in Column 1 for the coming year, as shown in Column 2. Suppose further that you had $100,000 and you planned to invest $25,000, or 25% of the total, in each stock. You could multiply each stock's percentage weight as shown in Column 4 by its expected return; get the product terms in Column 5; and then sum Column 5 to get the expected portfolio return, 10.75%.

If you added a fifth stock with a higher expected return, the portfolio's expected return would increase, and vice versa if you added a stock with a lower expected return. *The key point to remember is that the expected return on a portfolio is a weighted average of expected returns on the stocks in the portfolio.*

Several additional points should be made:

1. The expected returns in Column 2 would be based on a study of some type, but they would still be essentially subjective and judgmental because different analysts could look at the same data and reach different conclusions. Therefore, this type of analysis must be viewed with a critical eye. Nevertheless, it is useful, indeed necessary, if one is to make intelligent investment decisions.

2. If we added companies such as Delta Airlines and Ford, which are generally considered to be relatively risky, their expected returns as estimated by the marginal investor would be relatively high; otherwise, investors would sell them, drive down their prices, and force the expected returns above the returns on safer stocks.

3. After the fact and a year later, the actual **realized rates of return, $\bar{r}_i$**, on the individual stocks—the r_i, or "r-bar," values—would almost certainly be different from the initial expected values. That would cause the portfolio's actual return, r_p, to differ from the expected return, $\hat{r}_p = 10.75\%$. For example, Microsoft's price might double and thus provide a return of +100%, whereas IBM might have a terrible year, fall sharply, and have a return of −75%. Note, though, that those two events would be offsetting; so the portfolio's return still might be close to its expected return even though the returns on the individual stocks were far from their expected values.

Expected Return on a Portfolio, $\hat{r}_p$
The weighted average of the expected returns on the assets held in the portfolio.

Realized Rate of Return, $\bar{r}$
The return that was actually earned during some past period. The actual return ($\bar{r}$) usually turns out to be different from the expected return ($\hat{r}$) except for riskless assets.

| Table 8-4 | | Expected Return on a Portfolio, $\hat{r}_p$ | | | |

	A	B	C	D	E	F
52						
53						
54						
55		Expected	Dollars	Percent of	Product:	
56	Stock	Return	Invested	Total (w_i)	(2)×(4)	
57	(1)	(2)	(3)	(4)	(5)	
58	Microsoft	12.00%	$ 25,000	25.0%	3.000%	
59	IBM	11.50	25,000	25.0	2.875	
60	GE	10.00	25,000	25.0	2.500	
61	Exxon	9.50	25,000	25.0	2.375	
62		10.75%	$100,000	100.0%	10.750%	= Expected r_p

8-3b Portfolio Risk

Although the expected return on a portfolio is simply the weighted average of the expected returns on its individual stocks, the portfolio's risk, σ_p, is *not* the weighted average of the individual stocks' standard deviations. The portfolio's risk is generally *smaller* than the average of the stocks' σs because diversification lowers the portfolio's risk.

To illustrate this point, consider the situation in Figure 8-4. The bottom section gives data on Stocks W and M individually and data on a portfolio with 50% in each stock. The left graph plots the data in a time series format, and it shows that the returns on the individual stocks vary widely from year to year. Therefore, the individual stocks are risky. However, the portfolio's returns are constant at 15%, indicating that it is not risky at all. The probability distribution graphs to the right show the same thing—the two stocks would be quite risky if they were held in isolation; but when they are combined to form Portfolio WM, they have no risk whatsoever.

If you invested all of your money in Stock W, you would have an expected return of 15%, but you would face a great deal of risk. The same thing would hold if you invested entirely in Stock M. However, if you invested 50% in each stock, you would have the same expected return of 15%, but with no risk whatsoever. Being rational and averse to risk, you and all other rational investors would choose to hold the portfolio, not the stocks individually.

FIGURE 8-4   Returns With Perfect Negative Correlation, $\rho = -1.0$

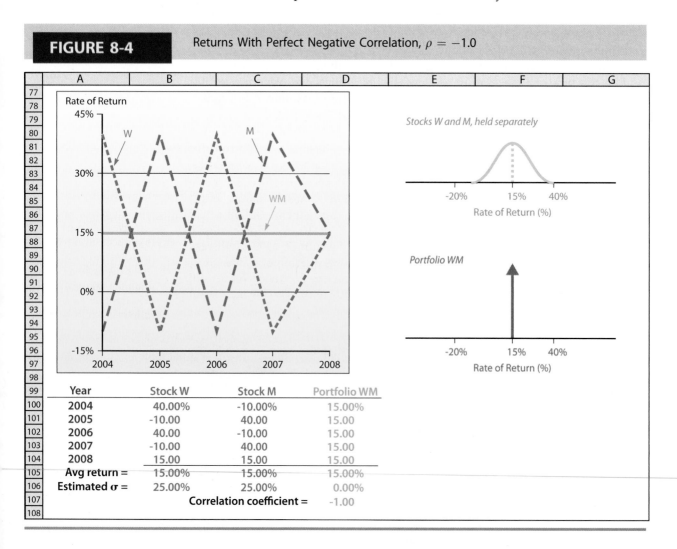

Year	Stock W	Stock M	Portfolio WM
2004	40.00%	-10.00%	15.00%
2005	-10.00	40.00	15.00
2006	40.00	-10.00	15.00
2007	-10.00	40.00	15.00
2008	15.00	15.00	15.00
Avg return =	15.00%	15.00%	15.00%
Estimated σ =	25.00%	25.00%	0.00%
	Correlation coefficient =		-1.00

Stocks W and M can be combined to form a riskless portfolio because their returns move countercyclically to each other—when W's fall, M's rise, and vice versa. The tendency of two variables to move together is called **correlation**, and the **correlation coefficient,** ρ (pronounced "rho"), measures this tendency.[16] In statistical terms, we say that the returns on Stocks W and M are *perfectly negatively correlated*, with $\rho = -1.0$. The opposite of perfect negative correlation is *perfect positive correlation*, with $\rho = +1.0$. If returns are not related to one another at all, they are said to be *independent* and $\rho = 0$.

The returns on two perfectly positively correlated stocks with the same expected return would move up and down together, and a portfolio consisting of these stocks would be exactly as risky as the individual stocks. If we drew a graph like Figure 8-4, we would see just one line because the two stocks and the portfolio would have the same return at each point in time. *Thus, diversification is completely useless for reducing risk if the stocks in the portfolio are perfectly positively correlated.*

We see then that when stocks are perfectly negatively correlated ($\rho = -1.0$), all risk can be diversified away; but when stocks are perfectly positively correlated ($\rho = +1.0$), diversification does no good. In reality, most stocks are positively correlated but not perfectly so. Past studies have estimated that on average, the correlation coefficient between the returns of two randomly selected stocks is about 0.30.[17] *Under this condition, combining stocks into portfolios reduces risk but does not completely eliminate it.*[18] Figure 8-5 illustrates this point using two stocks whose correlation coefficient is $\rho = +0.35$. The portfolio's average return is 15%, which is the same as the average return for the two stocks; but its standard deviation is 18.62%, which is below the stocks' standard deviations and their average σ. Again, a rational, risk-averse investor would be better off holding the portfolio rather than just one of the individual stocks.

In our examples, we considered portfolios with only two stocks. What would happen if we increased the number of stocks in the portfolio?

As a rule, portfolio risk declines as the number of stocks in a portfolio increases.

If we added enough partially correlated stocks, could we completely eliminate risk? In general, the answer is no. For an illustration, see Figure 8-5 on page 244 which shows that a portfolio's risk declines as stocks are added. Here are some points to keep in mind about the figure:

1. The portfolio's risk declines as stocks are added, but at a decreasing rate; and once 40 to 50 stocks are in the portfolio, additional stocks do little to reduce risk.
2. The portfolio's total risk can be divided into two parts, **diversifiable risk** and **market risk**.[19] Diversifiable risk is the risk that is eliminated by adding stocks. Market risk is the risk that remains even if the portfolio holds every stock in

---

Correlation
The tendency of two variables to move together.

Correlation Coefficient, ρ
A measure of the degree of relationship between two variables.

Diversifiable Risk
That part of a security's risk associated with random events; it can be eliminated by proper diversification. This risk is also known as company-specific, or unsystematic, risk.

Market Risk
The risk that remains in a portfolio after diversification has eliminated all company-specific risk. This risk is also known as nondiversifiable or systematic or beta risk.

---

[16]The correlation coefficient, ρ, can range from +1.0, denoting that the two variables move up and down in perfect synchronization, to −1.0, denoting that the variables move in exactly opposite directions. A correlation coefficient of zero indicates that the two variables are not related to each other—that is, changes in one variable are independent of changes in the other. It is easy to calculate correlation coefficients with a financial calculator. Simply enter the returns on the two stocks and press a key labeled "r." For W and M, $\rho = -1.0$. See our tutorial on the text's web site or your calculator manual for the exact steps. Also note that the correlation coefficient is often denoted by the term *r*. We use ρ here to avoid confusion with r used to denote the rate of return.

[17]A study by Chan, Karceski, and Lakonishok (1999) estimated that the average correlation coefficient between two randomly selected stocks was 0.28, while the average correlation coefficient between two large-company stocks was 0.33. The time period of their sample was 1968 to 1998. See Louis K. C. Chan, Jason Karceski, and Josef Lakonishok, "On Portfolio Optimization: Forecasting Covariance and Choosing the Risk Model," *The Review of Financial Studies*, Vol. 12, no. 5 (Winter 1999), pp. 937–974.

[18]If we combined a large number of stocks with $\rho = 0$, we could form a riskless portfolio. However, there are not many stocks with $\rho = 0$—stocks' returns tend to move together, not to be independent of one another.

[19]Diversifiable risk is also known as *company-specific*, or *unsystematic*, risk. Market risk is also known as *nondiversifiable* or *systematic* or *beta* risk; it is the risk that remains in the portfolio after diversification has eliminated all company-specific risk.

FIGURE 8-5	Returns with Partial Correlation, $\rho = +0.35$

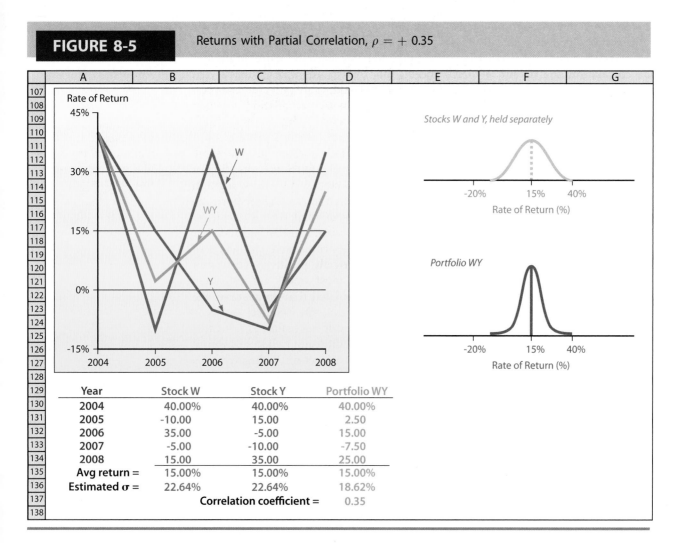

Year	Stock W	Stock Y	Portfolio WY
2004	40.00%	40.00%	40.00%
2005	-10.00	15.00	2.50
2006	35.00	-5.00	15.00
2007	-5.00	-10.00	-7.50
2008	15.00	35.00	25.00
Avg return =	15.00%	15.00%	15.00%
Estimated σ =	22.64%	22.64%	18.62%
Correlation coefficient =			0.35

the market. Market risk is the risk that we discussed in the opening vignette and in our discussion of Figure 8-1.

3. Diversifiable risk is caused by such random, unsystematic events as lawsuits, strikes, successful and unsuccessful marketing and R&D programs, the winning or losing of a major contract, and other events that are unique to the particular firm. Because these events are random, their effects on a portfolio can be eliminated by diversification—bad events for one firm will be offset by good events for another. Market risk, on the other hand, stems from factors that systematically affect most firms: war, inflation, recessions, high interest rates, and other macro factors. Because most stocks are affected by macro factors, market risk cannot be eliminated by diversification.

4. If we carefully selected the stocks included in the portfolio rather than adding them randomly, the graph would change. In particular, if we chose stocks with low correlations with one another and with low stand-alone risk, the portfolio's risk would decline faster than if random stocks were added. The reverse would hold if we added stocks with high correlations and high σs.

5. Most investors are rational in the sense that they dislike risk, other things held constant. That being the case, why would an investor ever hold one (or a few) stocks? Why not hold a **market portfolio** consisting of all stocks? There are several reasons. First, high administrative costs and commissions would more than offset

Market Portfolio
A portfolio consisting of all stocks.

the benefits for individual investors. Second, index funds can diversify for investors, and many individuals can and do get broad diversification through these funds. Third, some people think that they can pick stocks that will "beat the market"; so they buy them rather than the broad market. And fourth, some people can, through superior analysis, beat the market; so they find and buy undervalued stocks and sell overvalued ones and, in the process, cause most stocks to be properly valued, with their expected returns consistent with their risks.

6. One key question remains: How should the risk of an individual stock be measured? The standard deviation of expected returns, σ, is not appropriate because it includes risk that can be eliminated by holding the stock in a portfolio. How then should we measure a stock's risk in a world where most people hold portfolios? That's the subject of the next section.

8-3c Risk in a Portfolio Context: The Beta Coefficient

When a stock is held by itself, its risk can be measured by the standard deviation of its expected returns. However, σ is not appropriate when the stock is held in a portfolio, as stocks generally are. So how do we measure a stock's **relevant risk** in a portfolio context?

First, note that all risk except that related to broad market movements can and will be diversified away by most investors—rational investors will hold enough stocks to move down the risk curve in Figure 8-6 to the point where only market risk remains in their portfolios.

> *The risk that remains once a stock is in a diversified portfolio is its contribution to the portfolio's market risk, and that risk can be measured by the extent to which the stock moves up or down with the market.*

The tendency of a stock to move with the market is measured by its **beta coefficient, b.** Ideally, when estimating a stock's beta, we would like to have a crystal ball that tells us how the stock is going to move relative to the overall stock market in the future. But since we can't look into the future, we often use historical data and assume that the stock's historical beta will give us a reasonable estimate of how the stock will move relative to the market in the future.

To illustrate the use of historical data, consider Figure 8-7, which shows the historical returns on three stocks and a market index. In Year 1, "the market," as defined by a portfolio containing all stocks, had a total return (dividend yield plus capital gains yield) of 10%, as did the three individual stocks. In Year 2, the market went up sharply and its return was 20%. Stocks H (for high) soared by 30%; A (for average) returned 20%, the same as the market; and L (for low) returned 15%. In Year 3, the market dropped sharply; its return was −10%. The three stocks' returns also fell—H's return was −30%, A's was −10%, and L broke even with a 0% return. In Years 4 and 5, the market returned 0% and 5%, respectively, and the three stocks' returns were as shown in the figure.

A plot of the data shows that the three stocks moved up or down with the market but that H was twice as volatile as the market, A was exactly as volatile as the market, and L had only half the market's volatility. It is apparent that the steeper a stock's line, the greater its volatility and thus the larger its loss in a down market. *The slopes of the lines are the stocks' beta coefficients.* We see in the figure that the slope coefficient for H is 2.0; for A, it is 1.0; and for L, it is 0.5.[20] Thus, beta measures a given stock's volatility relative to the market, and an **average stock's beta, $b_A = 1.0$.**

Relevant Risk
The risk that remains once a stock is in a diversified portfolio is its contribution to the portfolio's market risk. It is measured by the extent to which the stock moves up or down with the market.

Beta Coefficient, b
A metric that shows the extent to which a given stock's returns move up and down with the stock market. Beta thus measures market risk.

Average Stock's Beta, b_A
By definition, $b_A = 1$ because an average-risk stock is one that tends to move up and down in step with the general market.

---

[20]For more on calculating betas, see Brigham and Daves, *Intermediate Financial Management*, 9th ed., (Mason, OH: Thomson/South-Western, 2007), pp. 55–58 and pp. 89–94.

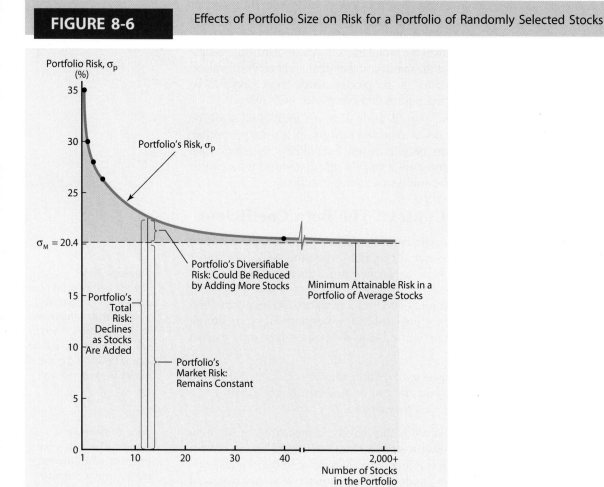

FIGURE 8-6   Effects of Portfolio Size on Risk for a Portfolio of Randomly Selected Stocks

Note: This graph assumes that stocks in the portfolio are randomly selected from the universe of large, publicly-traded stocks listed on the NYSE.

Stock A is defined as an *average-risk stock* because it has a beta of $b = 1.0$ and thus moves up and down in step with the general market. Thus, an average stock will, in general, move up by 10% when the market moves up by 10% and fall by 10% when the market falls by 10%. A large portfolio of such $b = 1.0$ stocks would (1) have all of its diversifiable risk removed but (2) would still move up and down with the broad market averages and thus have a degree of risk.

Stock H, which has $b = 2.0$, is twice as volatile as an average stock, which means that it is twice as risky. The value of a portfolio consisting of $b = 2.0$ stocks could double—or halve—in a short time; and if you held such a portfolio, you could quickly go from being a millionaire to being a pauper. Stock L, on the other hand, with $b = 0.5$, is only half as volatile as the average stock, and a portfolio of such stocks would rise and fall only half as rapidly as the market. Thus, its risk would be half that of an average-risk portfolio with $b = 1.0$.

Betas for literally thousands of companies are calculated and published by Merrill Lynch, Value Line, Yahoo, Google, and numerous other organizations; and the beta coefficients of some well-known companies are shown in Table 8-5. Most stocks have betas in the range of 0.50 to 1.50; and the average beta for all stocks is 1.0, which indicates that the average stock moves in sync with the market.[21]

---

[21]While fairly uncommon, it is possible for a stock to have a negative beta. In that case, the stock's returns would tend to rise whenever the returns on other stocks fell.

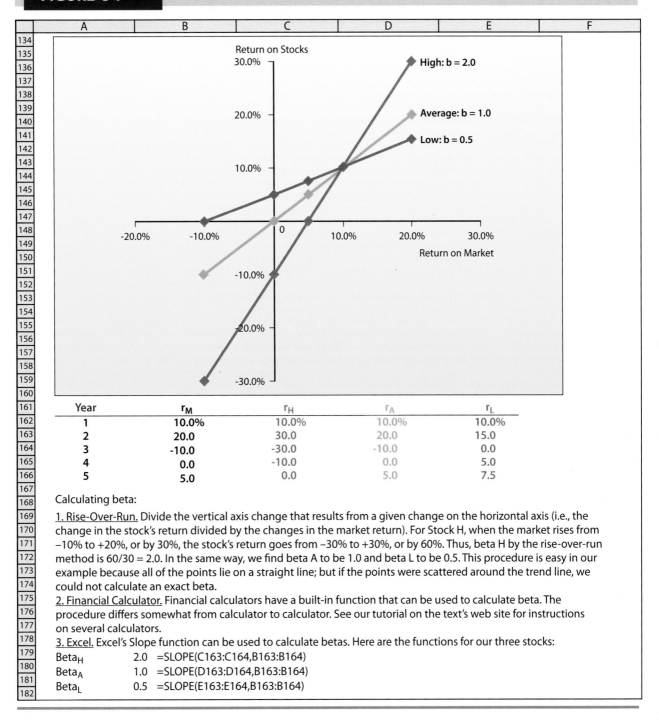

FIGURE 8-7   Betas: Relative Volatility of Stocks H, A, and L

Year	r_M	r_H	r_A	r_L
1	10.0%	10.0%	10.0%	10.0%
2	20.0	30.0	20.0	15.0
3	-10.0	-30.0	-10.0	0.0
4	0.0	-10.0	0.0	5.0
5	5.0	0.0	5.0	7.5

Calculating beta:

1. Rise-Over-Run. Divide the vertical axis change that results from a given change on the horizontal axis (i.e., the change in the stock's return divided by the changes in the market return). For Stock H, when the market rises from −10% to +20%, or by 30%, the stock's return goes from −30% to +30%, or by 60%. Thus, beta H by the rise-over-run method is 60/30 = 2.0. In the same way, we find beta A to be 1.0 and beta L to be 0.5. This procedure is easy in our example because all of the points lie on a straight line; but if the points were scattered around the trend line, we could not calculate an exact beta.

2. Financial Calculator. Financial calculators have a built-in function that can be used to calculate beta. The procedure differs somewhat from calculator to calculator. See our tutorial on the text's web site for instructions on several calculators.

3. Excel. Excel's Slope function can be used to calculate betas. Here are the functions for our three stocks:

Beta$_H$ 2.0   =SLOPE(C163:C164,B163:B164)
Beta$_A$ 1.0   =SLOPE(D163:D164,B163:B164)
Beta$_L$ 0.5   =SLOPE(E163:E164,B163:B164)

If a stock whose beta is greater than 1.0 (say 1.5) is added to a $b_p = 1.0$ portfolio, the portfolio's beta and consequently its risk will increase. Conversely, if a stock whose beta is less than 1.0 is added to a $b_p = 1.0$ portfolio, the portfolio's beta and risk will decline. *Thus, because a stock's beta reflects its contribution to the riskiness of a portfolio, beta is the theoretically correct measure of the stock's riskiness.*

Table 8-5	Illustrative List of Beta Coefficients

Stock	Beta
Merrill Lynch	1.35
Best Buy	1.25
eBay	1.20
General Electric	0.95
Microsoft	0.95
ExxonMobil	0.90
Heinz	0.80
Coca-Cola	0.75
FPL Group	0.75
Procter & Gamble	0.65

Source: Adapted from *Value Line,* February 2008.

We can summarize our discussion up to this point as follows:

1. A stock's risk has two components, diversifiable risk and market risk.

2. Diversifiable risk can be eliminated; and most investors do eliminate it, either by holding very large portfolios or by buying shares in a mutual fund. We are left, then, with market risk, which is caused by general movements in the stock market and reflects the fact that most stocks are systematically affected by events such as wars, recessions, and inflation. Market risk is the only risk that should matter to a rational, diversified investor.

3. Investors must be compensated for bearing risk—the greater the risk of a stock, the higher its required return. However, compensation is required only for risk that cannot be eliminated by diversification. If risk premiums existed on a stock due to its diversifiable risk, that stock would be a bargain to well-diversified investors. They would start buying it and bid up its price, and the stock's final (equilibrium) price would be consistent with an expected return that reflected only its market risk.

   To illustrate this point, suppose half of Stock B's risk is market risk (it occurs because the stock moves up and down with the market), while the other half is diversifiable. You are thinking of buying Stock B and holding it in a one-stock portfolio, so you would be exposed to all of its risk. As compensation for bearing so much risk, you want a risk premium of 8% over the 6% T-bond rate; so your required return is $r_A = 6\% + 8\% = 14\%$. But other investors, including your professor, are well diversified. They are also looking at Stock B; but they would hold it in diversified portfolios, eliminate its diversifiable risk, and thus be exposed to only half as much risk as you. Therefore, their required risk premium would be half as large as yours, and their required rate of return would be $r_B = 6\% + 4\% = 10\%$.

   If the stock was priced to yield the 14% you require, those diversified investors, including your professor, would buy it, push its price up and its yield down, and prevent you from getting the stock at a price low enough to provide the 14% return. In the end, you would have to accept a 10% return or keep your money in the bank.

4. The market risk of a stock is measured by its beta coefficient, which is an index of the stock's relative volatility. Here are some benchmark betas:

   $b = 0.5$: Stock is only half as volatile, or risky, as an average stock.
   $b = 1.0$: Stock is of average risk.
   $b = 2.0$: Stock is twice as risky as an average stock.

5. A portfolio consisting of low-beta stocks will also have a low beta because the beta of a portfolio is a weighted average of its individual securities' betas, found using this equation:

$$b_p = w_1 b_1 + w_2 b_2 + \cdots + w_N b_N$$

$$= \sum_{i=1}^{N} w_i b_i. \qquad \text{8-5}$$

Here b_p is the beta of the portfolio, and it shows how volatile the portfolio is relative to the market; w_i is the fraction of the portfolio invested in the ith stock; and b_i is the beta coefficient of the ith stock. To illustrate, if an investor holds a $100,000 portfolio consisting of $33,333.33 invested in each of three stocks and if each of the stocks has a beta of 0.70, the portfolio's beta will be $b_p = 0.70$:

$$b_p = 0.333(0.70) + 0.333(0.70) + 0.333(0.70) = 0.70.$$

Such a portfolio would be less risky than the market, so it should experience relatively narrow price swings and have relatively small rate-of-return fluctuations. In terms of Figure 8-7, the slope of its regression line would be 0.70, which is less than that for a portfolio of average stocks.

Now suppose one of the existing stocks is sold and replaced by a stock with $b_i = 2.00$. This action will increase the portfolio's beta from $b_{p1} = 0.70$ to $b_{p2} = 1.13$:

$$b_{p2} = 0.333(0.70) + 0.333(0.70) + 0.333(2.00) = 1.13.$$

Had a stock with $b_i = 0.20$ been added, the portfolio's beta would have declined from 0.70 to 0.53. Adding a low-beta stock would therefore reduce the portfolio's riskiness. Consequently, changing the stocks in a portfolio can change the riskiness of that portfolio.

6. Because a stock's beta coefficient determines how the stock affects the riskiness of a diversified portfolio, beta is, in theory, the most relevant measure of a stock's risk.

SELF TEST

Explain the following statement: An asset held as part of a portfolio is generally less risky than the same asset held in isolation.

What is meant by *perfect positive correlation, perfect negative correlation,* and *zero correlation?*

In general, can the riskiness of a portfolio be reduced to zero by increasing the number of stocks in the portfolio? Explain.

What is an average-risk stock? What is the beta of such a stock?

Why is it argued that beta is the best measure of a stock's risk?

If you plotted a particular stock's returns versus those on the S&P 500 Index over the past five years, what would the slope of the regression line indicate about the stock's risk?

An investor has a two-stock portfolio with $25,000 invested in Stock X and $50,000 invested in Stock Y. X's beta is 1.50, and Y's beta is 0.60. What is the beta of the investor's portfolio? **(0.90)**

GLOBAL PERSPECTIVES

THE BENEFITS OF DIVERSIFYING OVERSEAS

The increasing availability of international securities is making it possible to achieve a better risk-return trade-off than could be obtained by investing only in U.S. securities. So investing overseas might result in a portfolio with less risk but a higher expected return. This result occurs because of low correlations between the returns on U.S. and international securities, along with potentially high returns on overseas stocks.

Figure 8-6, presented earlier, demonstrated that an investor can reduce the risk of his or her portfolio by holding a number of stocks. The figure that follows suggests that investors may be able to reduce risk even further by holding a portfolio of stocks from all around the world, given the fact that the returns on domestic and international stocks are not perfectly correlated.

Even though foreign stocks represent roughly 60% of the worldwide equity market and despite the apparent benefits from investing overseas, the typical U.S. investor still puts less than 10% of his or her money in foreign stocks. One possible explanation for this reluctance to invest overseas is that investors prefer domestic stocks because of lower transactions costs. However, this explanation is questionable because recent studies reveal that investors buy and sell overseas stocks more frequently than they trade their domestic stocks. Other explanations for the domestic bias include the additional risks from investing overseas (for example, exchange rate risk) and the fact that the typical U.S. investor is uninformed about international investments and/or thinks that international investments are extremely risky. It has been argued that world capital markets have become more integrated, causing the correlation of returns between different countries to increase, which reduces the benefits from international diversification. In addition, U.S. corporations are investing more internationally, providing U.S. investors with international diversification even if they purchase only U.S. stocks.

Whatever the reason for their relatively small holdings of international assets, our guess is that in the future U.S. investors will shift more of their assets to overseas investments.

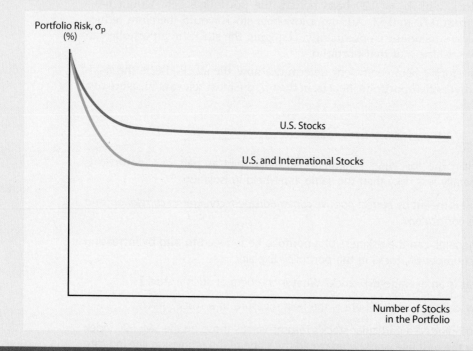

Source: For further reading, see also Kenneth Kasa, "Measuring the Gains from International Portfolio Diversification," *Federal Reserve Bank of San Francisco Weekly Letter*, Number 94–14, April 8, 1994.

8-4 THE RELATIONSHIP BETWEEN RISK AND RATES OF RETURN

The preceding section demonstrated that under the CAPM theory, beta is the most appropriate measure of a stock's relevant risk. The next issue is this: For a given level of risk as measured by beta, what rate of return is required to compensate investors for bearing that risk? To begin, let us define the following terms:

$\hat{r}_i =$ *expected* rate of return on the ith stock.

$r_i =$ *required* rate of return on the ith stock. Note that if $\hat{r}_i$ is less than r_i, the typical investor will not purchase this stock or will sell it if he or she owns it. If $\hat{r}_i$ is greater than r_i, the investor will purchase the stock because it looks like a bargain. Investors will be indifferent if $\hat{r}_i = r_i$. Buying and selling by investors tends to force the expected return to equal the required return, although the two can differ from time to time before the adjustment is completed.

$\bar{r} =$ realized, after-the-fact return. A person obviously does not know $\bar{r}$ at the time he or she is considering the purchase of a stock.

$r_{RF} =$ risk-free rate of return. In this context, r_{RF} is generally measured by the return on U.S. Treasury securities. Some analysts recommend that short-term T-bills be used; others recommend long-term T-bonds. We generally use T-bonds because their maturity is closer to the average investor's holding period of stocks.

$b_i =$ beta coefficient of the ith stock. The beta of an average stock is $b_A = 1.0$.

$r_M =$ required rate of return on a portfolio consisting of all stocks, which is called the *market portfolio*. r_M is also the required rate of return on an average ($b_A = 1.0$) stock.

$RP_M =$ $(r_M - r_{RF})$ = risk premium on "the market" and the premium on an average stock. This is the additional return over the risk-free rate required to compensate an average investor for assuming an average amount of risk. Average risk means a stock where $b_i = b_A = 1.0$.

$RP_i =$ $(r_M - r_{RF})b_i = (RP_M)b_i$ = risk premium on the ith stock. A stock's risk premium will be less than, equal to, or greater than the premium on an average stock, RP_M, depending on whether its beta is less than, equal to, or greater than 1.0. If $b_i = b_A = 1.0$, then $RP_i = RP_M$.

The **market risk premium, RP_M,** shows the premium that investors require for bearing the risk of an average stock. The size of this premium depends on how risky investors think the stock market is and on their degree of risk aversion. Let us assume that at the current time, Treasury bonds yield $r_{RF} = 6\%$ and an average share of stock has a required rate of return of $r_M = 11\%$. Therefore, the market risk premium is 5%, calculated as follows:

Market Risk Premium, RP_M

The additional return over the risk-free rate needed to compensate investors for assuming an average amount of risk.

$$RP_M = r_M - r_{RF} = 11\% - 6\% = 5\%$$

It should be noted that the risk premium of an average stock, $r_M - r_{RF}$, is actually hard to measure because it is impossible to obtain a precise estimate of the expected future return of the market, r_M.[22] Given the difficulty of estimating future

---

[22]This concept, as well as other aspects of the CAPM, is discussed in more detail in Chapter 3 of Eugene F. Brigham and Philip R. Daves, *Intermediate Financial Management*, 9th ed., (Mason, OH: Thomson/South-Western, 2007). That chapter also discusses the assumptions embodied in the CAPM framework. Some of those assumptions are unrealistic; and because of this, the theory does not hold exactly.

ESTIMATING THE MARKET RISK PREMIUM

The Capital Asset Pricing Model (CAPM) is more than a theory describing the trade-off between risk and return—it is also widely used in practice. As we will see later, investors use the CAPM to determine the discount rate for valuing stocks and corporate managers use it to estimate the cost of equity capital.

The market risk premium is a key component of the CAPM, and it should be the difference between the *expected future return on the overall stock market and the expected future return on a riskless investment*. However, we cannot obtain investors' expectations; instead, academicians and practitioners often use a historical risk premium as a proxy for the expected risk premium. The historical premium is found by taking the difference between the actual return on the overall stock market and the risk-free rate during a number of different years and then averaging the annual results. Morningstar (through its recent purchase of Ibbotson Associates) may provide the most comprehensive estimates of historical risk premiums. It reports that the annual premiums have averaged 7.1% over the past 82 years.

However, there are three potential problems with historical risk premiums. First, what is the proper number of years over which to compute the average? Morningstar goes back to 1926, when good data first became available; but that is an arbitrary choice, and the starting and ending points make a major difference in the calculated premium.

Second, historical premiums are likely to be misleading at times when the market risk premium is changing. To illustrate, the stock market was very strong from 1995 through 1999, *in part because investors were becoming less risk-averse, which means that they applied a lower risk premium when they valued stocks*. The strong market resulted in stock returns of about 30% per year; and when bond yields were subtracted from the high stock returns, the calculated risk premiums averaged 22.3% a year. When those high numbers were added to data from prior years, they caused the long-run historical risk premium as reported by Morningstar to increase. Thus, a declining "true" risk premium led to very high stock returns, which, in turn, led to an increase in the calculated historical risk premium. That's a worrisome result, to say the least.

The third concern is that historical estimates may be biased upward because they include only the returns of firms that have survived—they do not reflect the losses incurred on investments in failed firms. Stephen Brown, William Goetzmann, and Stephen Ross discussed the implications of this *"survivorship bias"* in a 1995 *Journal of Finance* article. Putting these ideas into practice, Tim Koller, Marc Goedhart, and David Wessels recently suggested that survivorship bias increases historical returns by 1% to 2% a year. Therefore, they suggest that practitioners subtract 1% to 2% from the historical estimates to obtain the risk premium used in the CAPM.

Sources: Stocks, Bonds, Bills, and Inflation: (Valuation Edition) 2008 Yearbook (Chicago: Morningstar, Inc., 2008); Stephen J. Brown, William N. Goetzmann, and Stephen A. Ross, "Survival," Journal of Finance, Vol. 50, no. 3 (July 1995), pp. 853–873; and Tim Koller, Marc Goedhart, and David Wessels, Valuation: Measuring and Managing the Value of Companies, 4th edition (New York: McKinsey & Company, 2005).

market returns, analysts often look to historical data to estimate the market risk premium. Historical data suggest that the market risk premium varies somewhat from year to year due to changes in investors' risk aversion but that it has generally ranged from 4% to 8%.

While historical estimates might be a good starting point for estimating the market risk premium, those estimates would be misleading if investors' attitudes toward risk changed considerably over time. (See "Estimating the Market Risk Premium" box above.) Indeed, many analysts have argued that the market risk premium has fallen in recent years. If this claim is correct, the market risk premium is considerably lower than one based on historical data.

The risk premium on individual stocks varies in a systematic manner from the market risk premium. For example, if one stock is twice as risky as another stock as measured by their beta coefficients, its risk premium should be twice as high. Therefore, if we know the market risk premium, RP_M, and the stock's beta, b_i, we can find its risk premium as the product $(RP_M)b_i$. For example, if beta for Stock L = 0.5 and RP_M = 5%, RP_L will be 2.5%:

8-6 Risk premium for Stock L $= RP_i = (RP_M)b_i$
$= (5\%)(0.5)$
$= 2.5\%$

As the discussion in Chapter 6 implied, the required return for any stock can be found as follows:

Required return on a stock = Risk-free return + Premium for the stock's risk

Here the risk-free return includes a premium for expected inflation; and if we assume that the stocks under consideration have similar maturities and liquidity, the required return on Stock L can be found using the **Security Market Line (SML) equation**:

$$\begin{array}{l} \text{Required return} \\ \text{on Stock L} \end{array} = \begin{array}{l} \text{Risk-free} \\ \text{return} \end{array} + \left(\begin{array}{l} \text{Market risk} \\ \text{premium} \end{array}\right)\left(\begin{array}{l} \text{Stock L's} \\ \text{beta} \end{array}\right)$$

$$\begin{aligned} r_L &= r_{RF} + (r_M - r_{RF})b_L \qquad\qquad \text{8-7} \\ &= r_{RF} + (RP_M)b_L \\ &= 6\% + (11\% - 6\%)(0.5) \\ &= 6\% + 2.5\% \\ &= 8.5\% \end{aligned}$$

Security Market Line (SML) Equation
An equation that shows the relationship between risk as measured by beta and the required rates of return on individual securities.

Stock H had $b_H = 2.0$, so its required rate of return is 16%:

$$r_H = 6\% + (5\%)2.0 = 16\%$$

An average stock, with $b = 1.0$, would have a required return of 11%, the same as the market return:

$$r_A = 6\% + (5\%)1.0 = 11\% = r_M$$

The SML equation is plotted in Figure 8-8 using the data shown below the graph on Stocks L, A, and H and assuming that $r_{RF} = 6\%$ and $r_M = 11\%$. Note the following points:

1. Required rates of return are shown on the vertical axis, while risk as measured by beta is shown on the horizontal axis. This graph is quite different from the one shown in Figure 8-7, where we calculated betas. In the earlier graph, the returns on individual stocks were plotted on the vertical axis and returns on the market index were shown on the horizontal axis. The betas found in Figure 8-7 were then plotted as points on the horizontal axis of Figure 8-8.

2. Riskless securities have $b_i = 0$; so the return on the riskless asset, $r_{RF} = 6.0\%$, is shown as the vertical axis intercept in Figure 8-8.

3. The slope of the SML in Figure 8-8 can be found using the rise-over-run procedure. When beta goes from 0 to 1.0, the required return goes from 6% to 11%, or 5%; so the slope is 5%/1.0 = 5%. Thus, a 1-unit increase in beta causes a 5% increase in the required rate of return.

4. The slope of the SML reflects the degree of risk aversion in the economy—the greater the average investor's risk aversion, (a) the steeper the slope of the line and (b) the greater the risk premium for all stocks—hence, the higher the required rate of return on all stocks.

Both the SML and a company's position on it change over time due to changes in interest rates, investors' risk aversion, and individual companies' betas. Such changes are discussed in the following sections.

8-4a The Impact of Expected Inflation

As we discussed in Chapter 6, interest amounts to "rent" on borrowed money, or the price of money. Thus, r_{RF} is the price of money to a riskless borrower. We also

FIGURE 8-8   The Security Market Line (SML)

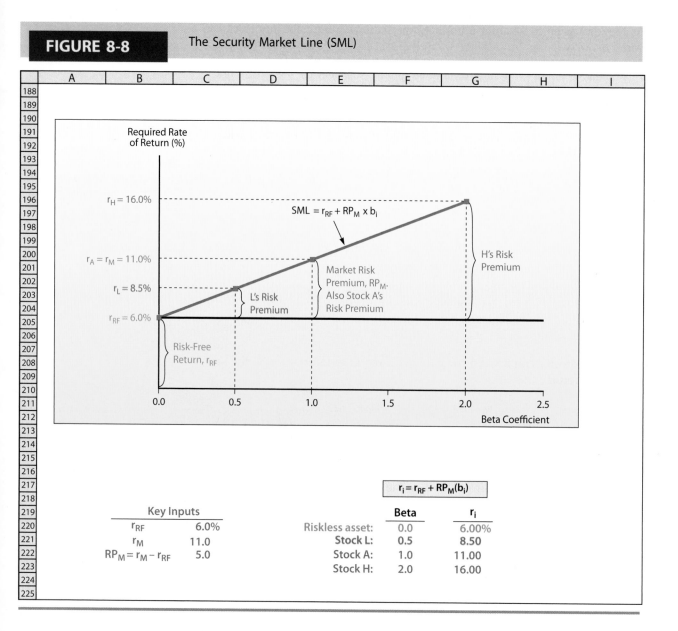

	Key Inputs	
r_{RF}	6.0%
r_M	11.0
$RP_M = r_M - r_{RF}$	5.0

$$r_i = r_{RF} + RP_M(b_i)$$

	Beta	r_i
Riskless asset:	0.0	6.00%
Stock L:	0.5	8.50
Stock A:	1.0	11.00
Stock H:	2.0	16.00

saw that the risk-free rate as measured by the rate on U.S. Treasury securities is called the *nominal*, or *quoted*, *rate*; and it consists of two elements: (1) a *real inflation-free rate of return*, r^* and (2) an *inflation premium, IP*, equal to the antici- pated rate of inflation.[23] Thus, $r_{RF} = r^* + IP$. The real rate on long-term Treasury bonds has historically ranged from 2% to 4%, with a mean of about 3%. Therefore, if no inflation were expected, long-term Treasury bonds would yield about 3%. However, as the expected rate of inflation increases, a premium must be added to the real risk-free rate of return to compensate investors for the loss of purchasing power that results from inflation. Therefore, the 6% r_{RF} shown in Figure 8-8 might be thought of as consisting of a 3% real risk-free rate of return plus a 3% inflation premium: $r_{RF} = r^* + IP = 3\% + 3\% = 6\%$.

---

[23]Long-term Treasury bonds also contain a maturity risk premium, MRP. We include the MRP in r^* to simplify the discussion.

If the expected inflation rate rose by 2%, to 3% + 2% = 5%, r_{RF} would rise to 8%. Such a change is shown in Figure 8-9. Notice that the increase in r_{RF} leads to an *equal* increase in the rates of return on all risky assets because the same inflation premium is built into required rates of return on both riskless and risky assets.[24] Therefore, the rate of return on our illustrative average stock, r_A, increases from 11% to 13%. Other risky securities' returns also rise by two percentage points.

8-4b Changes in Risk Aversion

The slope of the SML reflects the extent to which investors are averse to risk—the steeper the slope of the line, the more the average investor requires as compensation for bearing risk. Suppose investors were indifferent to risk; that is, they were not at all risk-averse. If r_{RF} was 6%, risky assets would also have a required return of 6% because if there were no risk aversion, there would be no risk premium. In that case, the SML would plot as a horizontal line. However, because investors are risk-averse, there is a risk premium; and the greater the risk aversion, the steeper the slope of the SML.

FIGURE 8-9   Shift in the SML Caused by an Increase in Expected Inflation

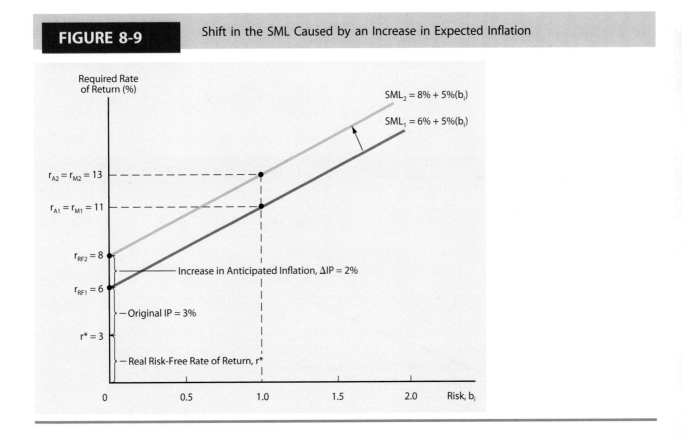

---

[24]Recall that the inflation premium for any asset is the average expected rate of inflation over the asset's life. Thus, in this analysis, we must assume that all securities plotted on the SML graph have the same life or that the expected rate of future inflation is constant.

   It should also be noted that r_{RF} in a CAPM analysis can be proxied by either a long-term rate (the T-bond rate) or a short-term rate (the T-bill rate). Traditionally, the T-bill rate was used; but in recent years, there has been a movement toward use of the T-bond rate because there is a closer relationship between T-bond yields and stocks' returns than between T-bill yields and stocks' returns. See *Stocks, Bonds, Bills, and Inflation: (Valuation Edition) 2008 Yearbook* (Chicago: Morningstar, Inc., 2008) for a discussion.

Figure 8-10 illustrates an increase in risk aversion. The market risk premium rises from 5% to 7.5%, causing r_M to rise from $r_{M1} = 11\%$ to $r_{M2} = 13.5\%$. The returns on other risky assets also rise, and the effect of this shift in risk aversion is more pronounced on riskier securities. For example, the required return on Stock L with $b_A = 0.5$ increases by only 1.25 percentage points, from 8.5% to 9.75%, whereas the required return on a stock with a beta of 1.5 increases by 3.75 percentage points, from 13.5% to 17.25%.

8-4c Changes in a Stock's Beta Coefficient

As we will see later in the book, a firm can influence its market risk (hence, its beta) through changes in the composition of its assets and through changes in the amount of debt it uses. A company's beta can also change as a result of external factors such as increased competition in its industry and expiration of basic patents. When such changes occur, the firm's required rate of return also changes; and as we will see in Chapter 9, this change will affect its stock price. For example, consider Allied Food Products, with a beta of 1.48. Now suppose some action occurred that caused Allied's beta to increase from 1.48 to 2.0. If the conditions depicted in Figure 8-8 held, Allied's required rate of return would increase from 13.4% to 16%:

$$
\begin{aligned}
r_1 &= r_{RF} + (r_M - r_{RF})b_i \\
&= 6\% + (11\% - 6\%)1.48 \\
&= 13.4\%
\end{aligned}
$$

to

$$
\begin{aligned}
r_2 &= 6\% + (11\% - 6\%)2.0 \\
&= 16.0\%
\end{aligned}
$$

FIGURE 8-10	Shift in the SML Caused by Increased Risk Aversion

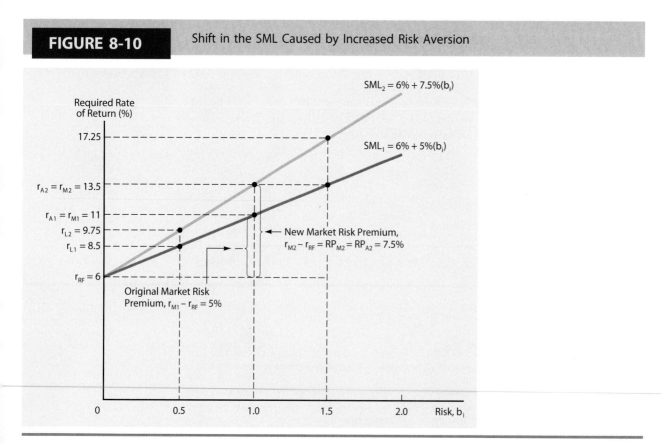

As we will see in Chapter 9, this change would have a negative effect on Allied's stock price.[25]

SELF TEST

Differentiate between a stock's expected rate of return ($\hat{r}$); required rate of return (r); and realized, after-the-fact historical return ($\bar{r}$). Which would have to be larger to induce you to buy the stock, $\hat{r}$ or r? At a given point in time, would $\hat{r}$, r, and $\bar{r}$ typically be the same or different? Explain.

What are the differences between the relative volatility graph (Figure 8-7), where "betas are made," and the SML graph (Figure 8-8), where "betas are used"? Explain how both graphs are constructed and what information they convey.

What would happen to the SML graph in Figure 8-8 if expected inflation increased or decreased?

What happens to the SML graph when risk aversion increases or decreases?

What would the SML look like if investors were indifferent to risk, that is, if they had zero risk aversion?

How can a firm influence the size of its beta?

A stock has a beta of 1.2. Assume that the risk-free rate is 4.5% and the market risk premium is 5%. What is the stock's required rate of return? **(10.5%)**

8-5 SOME CONCERNS ABOUT BETA AND THE CAPM

The Capital Asset Pricing Model (CAPM) is more than just an abstract theory described in textbooks—it has great intuitive appeal and is widely used by analysts, investors, and corporations. However, a number of recent studies have raised concerns about its validity. For example, a study by Eugene Fama of the University of Chicago and Kenneth French of Dartmouth found no historical relationship between stocks' returns and their market betas, confirming a position long held by some professors and stock market analysts.[26]

As an alternative to the traditional CAPM, researchers and practitioners are developing models with more explanatory variables than just beta. These multivariable models represent an attractive generalization of the traditional CAPM model's insight that market risk—risk that cannot be diversified away—underlies the pricing of assets. In the multivariable models, risk is assumed to be caused by a number of different factors, whereas the CAPM gauges risk only relative to returns on the market portfolio. These multivariable models represent a potentially important step forward in finance theory; they also have some deficiencies

Kenneth French's web site **http://mba.tuck.dartmouth. edu/pages/faculty/ken. french/index.html** *is an excellent resource for information regarding factors related to stock returns.*

---

[25]The concepts covered in this chapter are obviously important to investors, but they are also important for managers in two key ways. First, as we will see in the next chapter, the risk of a stock affects the required rate of return on equity capital, and that feeds directly into the important subject of capital budgeting. Second, and also related to capital budgeting, the "true" risk of individual projects is impacted by their correlation with the firm's other projects and with other assets that the firm's stockholders might hold. We will discuss these topics in later chapters.

[26]See Eugene F. Fama and Kenneth R. French, "The Cross-Section of Expected Stock Returns," *Journal of Finance*, Vol. 47 (1992), pp. 427–465; and Eugene F. Fama and Kenneth R. French, "Common Risk Factors in the Returns on Stocks and Bonds," *Journal of Financial Economics*, Vol. 33 (1993), pp. 3–56. They found that stock returns are related to firm size and market/book ratios. Small firms and firms with low market/book ratios had higher returns; however, they found no relationship between returns and beta.

when applied in practice. As a result, the basic CAPM is still the most widely used method for estimating required rates of return on stocks.

SELF TEST   Have there been any studies that question the validity of the CAPM? Explain.

8-6 SOME CONCLUDING THOUGHTS: IMPLICATIONS FOR CORPORATE MANAGERS AND INVESTORS

The connection between risk and return is an important concept, and it has numerous implications for both corporate managers and investors. As we will see in later chapters, corporate managers spend a great deal of time assessing the risk and returns on individual projects. Indeed, given their concerns about the risk of individual projects, it might be fair to ask why we spend so much time discussing the riskiness of stocks. Why not begin by looking at the riskiness of such business assets as plant and equipment? *The reason is that for management whose primary goal is stock price maximization, the overriding consideration is the riskiness of the firm's stock, and the relevant risk of any physical asset must be measured in terms of its effect on the stock's risk as seen by investors.* For example, suppose Goodyear, the tire company, is considering a major investment in a new product, recapped tires. Sales of recaps (hence, earnings on the new operation) are highly uncertain; so on a stand-alone basis, the new venture appears to be quite risky. However, suppose returns in the recap business are negatively correlated with Goodyear's other operations—when times are good and people have plenty of money, they buy new cars with new tires; but when times are bad, they tend to keep their old cars and buy recaps for them. Therefore, returns would be high on regular operations and low on the recap division during good times, but the opposite would be true during recessions. The result might be a pattern like that shown earlier in Figure 8-4 for Stocks W and M. Thus, what appears to be a risky investment when viewed on a stand-alone basis might not be very risky when viewed within the context of the company as a whole.

This analysis can be extended to the corporation's stockholders. Because Goodyear's stock is owned by diversified stockholders, the real issue each time management makes an investment decision is this: How will this investment affect the risk of our stockholders? Again, the stand-alone risk of an individual project may look quite high; however, viewed in the context of the project's effect on stockholder risk, it may not be very large. We will address this issue again in Chapter 12, where we examine the effects of capital budgeting on companies' beta coefficients and thus on stockholders' risks.

While these concepts are obviously important for individual investors, they are also important for corporate managers. We summarize some key ideas that all investors should consider:

1. There is a trade-off between risk and return. The average investor likes higher returns but dislikes risk. It follows that higher-risk investments need to offer investors higher expected returns. Put another way—if you are seeking higher returns, you must be willing to assume higher risks.

2. Diversification is crucial. By diversifying wisely, investors can dramatically reduce risk without reducing their expected returns. Don't put all of your money in one or two stocks or in one or two industries. A huge mistake that many people make is to invest a high percentage of their funds in their employer's stock. If the company goes bankrupt, they not only lose their job but also their invested capital. While no stock is completely riskless, you can smooth out the bumps by holding a well-diversified portfolio.

3. Real returns are what matters. All investors should understand the difference between nominal and real returns. When assessing performance, the real return (what you have left over after inflation) is what matters. It follows that as expected inflation increases, investors need to receive higher nominal returns.

4. The risk of an investment often depends on how long you plan to hold the investment. Common stocks, for example, can be extremely risky for short-term investors. However, over the long haul, the bumps tend to even out; thus, stocks are less risky when held as part of a long-term portfolio. Indeed, in his best-selling book *Stocks for the Long Run,* Jeremy Siegel of the University of Pennsylvania concludes that "[t]he safest long-term investment for the preservation of purchasing power has clearly been stocks, not bonds."

5. While the past gives us insights into the risk and returns on various investments, there is no guarantee that the future will repeat the past. Stocks that have performed well in recent years might tumble, while stocks that have struggled may rebound. The same thing may hold true for the stock market as a whole. Even Jeremy Siegel, who has preached that stocks have historically been good long-term investments, also has argued that there is no assurance that returns in the future will be as strong as they have been in the past. More importantly, when purchasing a stock, you always need to ask, "Is this stock fairly valued, or is it currently priced too high?" We discuss this issue more completely in the next chapter.

SELF TEST

Explain the following statement: The stand-alone risk of an individual corporate project may be quite high; but viewed in the context of its effect on stockholders' risk, the project's true risk may not be very large.

How does the correlation between returns on a project and returns on the firm's other assets affect the project's risk?

What are some important concepts for individual investors to consider when evaluating the risk and returns of various investments?

TYING IT ALL TOGETHER

In this chapter, we described the relationship between risk and return. We discussed how to calculate risk and return for individual assets and for portfolios. In particular, we differentiated between stand-alone risk and risk in a portfolio context and we explained the benefits of diversification. We also discussed the CAPM, which describes how risk should be measured and how risk affects rates of return. In the chapters that follow, we will give you the tools needed to estimate the required rates of return on a firm's common stock and explain how that return and the yield on its bonds are used to develop the firm's cost of capital. As you will see, the cost of capital is a key element in the capital budgeting process.

SELF-TEST QUESTIONS AND PROBLEMS
(Solutions Appear in Appendix A)

ST-1   **KEY TERMS**   Define the following terms using graphs or equations to illustrate your answers whenever feasible:
   a.   Risk; stand-alone risk; probability distribution
   b.   Expected rate of return, $\hat{r}$
   c.   Standard deviation, σ; coefficient of variation (CV)
   d.   Risk aversion; risk premium (RP); realized rate of return, $\bar{r}$
   e.   Risk premium for Stock i, RP_i; market risk premium, RP_M
   f.   Expected return on a portfolio, $\hat{r}_p$; market portfolio
   g.   Correlation; correlation coefficient, ρ
   h.   Market risk; diversifiable risk; relevant risk
   i.   Capital Asset Pricing Model (CAPM)
   j.   Beta coefficient, b; average stock's beta, b_A
   k.   Security Market Line (SML) equation

ST-2   **REALIZED RATES OF RETURN**   Stocks A and B have the following historical returns:

Year	Stock A's Returns, r_A	Stock B's Returns, r_B
2004	(24.25%)	5.50%
2005	18.50	26.73
2006	38.67	48.25
2007	14.33	(4.50)
2008	39.13	43.86

   a.   Calculate the average rate of return for each stock during the period 2004 through 2008. Assume that someone held a portfolio consisting of 50% of Stock A and 50% of Stock B. What would the realized rate of return on the portfolio have been in each year from 2004 through 2008? What would the average return on the portfolio have been during that period?
   b.   Calculate the standard deviation of returns for each stock and for the portfolio. Use Equation 8-2a.
   c.   Looking at the annual returns on the two stocks, would you guess that the correlation coefficient between the two stocks is closer to +0.8 or to –0.8?
   d.   If more randomly selected stocks had been included in the portfolio, which of the following is the most accurate statement of what would have happened to σ_p?

      (1) σ_p would have remained constant.
      (2) σ_p would have been in the vicinity of 20%.
      (3) σ_p would have declined to zero if enough stocks had been included.

ST-3   **BETA AND THE REQUIRED RATE OF RETURN**   ECRI Corporation is a holding company with four main subsidiaries. The percentage of its capital invested in each of the subsidiaries (and their respective betas) are as follows:

Subsidiary	Percentage of Capital	Beta
Electric utility	60%	0.70
Cable company	25	0.90
Real estate development	10	1.30
International/special projects	5	1.50

a. What is the holding company's beta?

b. If the risk-free rate is 6% and the market risk premium is 5%, what is the holding company's required rate of return?

c. ECRI is considering a change in its strategic focus; it will reduce its reliance on the electric utility subsidiary, so the percentage of its capital in this subsidiary will be reduced to 50%. At the same time, it will increase its reliance on the international/special projects division, so the percentage of its capital in that subsidiary will rise to 15%. What will the company's required rate of return be after these changes?

QUESTIONS

8-1 Suppose you owned a portfolio consisting of $250,000 of long-term U.S. government bonds.
a. Would your portfolio be riskless? Explain.

b. Now suppose the portfolio consists of $250,000 of 30-day Treasury bills. Every 30 days your bills mature, and you will reinvest the principal ($250,000) in a new batch of bills. You plan to live on the investment income from your portfolio, and you want to maintain a constant standard of living. Is the T-bill portfolio truly riskless? Explain.

c. What is the least risky security you can think of? Explain.

8-2 The probability distribution of a less risky expected return is more peaked than that of a riskier return. What shape would the probability distribution be for (a) completely certain returns and (b) completely uncertain returns?

8-3 A life insurance policy is a financial asset, with the premiums paid representing the investment's cost.
a. How would you calculate the expected return on a 1-year life insurance policy?

b. Suppose the owner of a life insurance policy has no other financial assets—the person's only other asset is "human capital," or earnings capacity. What is the correlation coefficient between the return on the insurance policy and the return on the human capital?

c. Life insurance companies must pay administrative costs and sales representatives' commissions; hence, the expected rate of return on insurance premiums is generally low or even negative. Use portfolio concepts to explain why people buy life insurance in spite of low expected returns.

8-4 Is it possible to construct a portfolio of real-world stocks that has an expected return equal to the risk-free rate?

8-5 Stock A has an expected return of 7%, a standard deviation of expected returns of 35%, a correlation coefficient with the market of –0.3, and a beta coefficient of –0.5. Stock B has an expected return of 12%, a standard deviation of returns of 10%, a 0.7 correlation with the market, and a beta coefficient of 1.0. Which security is riskier? Why?

8-6 A stock had a 12% return last year, a year when the overall stock market declined. Does this mean that the stock has a negative beta and thus very little risk if held in a portfolio? Explain.

8-7 If investors' aversion to risk increased, would the risk premium on a high-beta stock increase by more or less than that on a low-beta stock? Explain.

8-8 If a company's beta were to double, would its required return also double?

8-9 In Chapter 7, we saw that if the market interest rate, r_d, for a given bond increased, the price of the bond would decline. Applying this same logic to stocks, explain (a) how a decrease in risk aversion would affect stocks' prices and earned rates of return, (b) how this would affect risk premiums as measured by the historical difference between returns on stocks and returns on bonds, and (c) what the implications of this would be for the use of historical risk premiums when applying the SML equation.

PROBLEMS

8-1   **EXPECTED RETURN**   A stock's returns have the following distribution:

Demand for the Company's Products	Probability of This Demand Occurring	Rate of Return If This Demand Occurs
Weak	0.1	(50%)
Below average	0.2	(5)
Average	0.4	16
Above average	0.2	25
Strong	0.1	60
	1.0	

Calculate the stock's expected return, standard deviation, and coefficient of variation.

8-2   **PORTFOLIO BETA**   An individual has $35,000 invested in a stock with a beta of 0.8 and another $40,000 invested in a stock with a beta of 1.4. If these are the only two investments in her portfolio, what is her portfolio's beta?

8-3   **REQUIRED RATE OF RETURN**   Assume that the risk-free rate is 6% and the expected return on the market is 13%. What is the required rate of return on a stock with a beta of 0.7?

8-4   **EXPECTED AND REQUIRED RATES OF RETURN**   Assume that the risk-free rate is 5% and the market risk premium is 6%. What is the expected return for the overall stock market? What is the required rate of return on a stock with a beta of 1.2?

8-5   **BETA AND REQUIRED RATE OF RETURN**   A stock has a required return of 11%, the risk-free rate is 7%, and the market risk premium is 4%.

a.   What is the stock's beta?

b.   If the market risk premium increased to 6%, what would happen to the stock's required rate of return? Assume that the risk-free rate and the beta remain unchanged.

8-6   **EXPECTED RETURNS**   Stocks X and Y have the following probability distributions of expected future returns:

Probability	X	Y
0.1	(10%)	(35%)
0.2	2	0
0.4	12	20
0.2	20	25
0.1	38	45

a.   Calculate the expected rate of return, $\hat{r}_Y$, for Stock Y ($\hat{r}_X = 12\%$).

b.   Calculate the standard deviation of expected returns, σ_X, for Stock X ($\sigma_Y = 20.35\%$). Now calculate the coefficient of variation for Stock Y. Is it possible that most investors will regard Stock Y as being less risky than Stock X? Explain.

8-7   **PORTFOLIO REQUIRED RETURN**   Suppose you are the money manager of a $4 million investment fund. The fund consists of four stocks with the following investments and betas:

Stock	Investment	Beta
A	$ 400,000	1.50
B	600,000	(0.50)
C	1,000,000	1.25
D	2,000,000	0.75

If the market's required rate of return is 14% and the risk-free rate is 6%, what is the fund's required rate of return?

8-8   **BETA COEFFICIENT**   Given the following information, determine the beta coefficient for Stock J that is consistent with equilibrium: $\hat{r}_J = 12.5\%$; $r_{RF} = 4.5\%$; $r_M = 10.5\%$.

8-9   **REQUIRED RATE OF RETURN**   Stock R has a beta of 1.5, Stock S has a beta of 0.75, the expected rate of return on an average stock is 13%, and the risk-free rate of return is 7%. By how much does the required return on the riskier stock exceed the required return on the less risky stock?

8-10   **CAPM AND REQUIRED RETURN**   Bradford Manufacturing Company has a beta of 1.45, while Farley Industries has a beta of 0.85. The required return on an index fund that holds the entire stock market is 12.0%. The risk-free rate of interest is 5%. By how much does Bradford's required return exceed Farley's required return?

8-11   **CAPM AND REQUIRED RETURN**   Calculate the required rate of return for Manning Enterprises assuming that investors expect a 3.5% rate of inflation in the future. The real risk-free rate is 2.5%, and the market risk premium is 6.5%. Manning has a beta of 1.7, and its realized rate of return has averaged 13.5% over the past 5 years.

8-12   **REQUIRED RATE OF RETURN**   Suppose $r_{RF} = 9\%$, $r_M = 14\%$, and $b_i = 1.3$.

a.   What is r_i, the required rate of return on Stock i?

b.   Now suppose that r_{RF} (1) increases to 10% or (2) decreases to 8%. The slope of the SML remains constant. How would this affect r_M and r_i?

c.   Now assume that r_{RF} remains at 9% but r_M (1) increases to 16% or (2) falls to 13%. The slope of the SML does not remain constant. How would these changes affect r_i?

**Challenging
Problems
13–21**

8-13   **CAPM, PORTFOLIO RISK, AND RETURN**   Consider the following information for three stocks, Stocks X, Y, and Z. The returns on the three stocks are positively correlated, but they are not perfectly correlated. (That is, each of the correlation coefficients is between 0 and 1.)

Stock	Expected Return	Standard Deviation	Beta
X	9.00%	15%	0.8
Y	10.75	15	1.2
Z	12.50	15	1.6

Fund Q has one-third of its funds invested in each of the three stocks. The risk-free rate is 5.5%, and the market is in equilibrium. (That is, required returns equal expected returns.)

a.   What is the market risk premium $(r_M - r_{RF})$?

b.   What is the beta of Fund Q?

c.   What is the expected return of Fund Q?

d.   Would you expect the standard deviation of Fund Q to be less than 15%, equal to 15%, or greater than 15%? Explain.

8-14   **PORTFOLIO BETA**   Suppose you held a diversified portfolio consisting of a $7,500 investment in each of 20 different common stocks. The portfolio's beta is 1.12. Now suppose you decided to sell one of the stocks in your portfolio with a beta of 1.0 for $7,500 and use the proceeds to buy another stock with a beta of 1.75. What would your portfolio's new beta be?

8-15   **CAPM AND REQUIRED RETURN**   HR Industries (HRI) has a beta of 1.8, while LR Industries' (LRI) beta is 0.6. The risk-free rate is 6%, and the required rate of return on an average stock is 13%. The expected rate of inflation built into r_{RF} falls by 1.5 percentage points, the real risk-free rate remains constant, the required return on the market falls to 10.5%, and all betas remain constant. After all of these changes, what will be the difference in the required returns for HRI and LRI?

8-16   **CAPM AND PORTFOLIO RETURN**   You have been managing a $5 million portfolio that has a beta of 1.25 and a required rate of return of 12%. The current risk-free rate is 5.25%. Assume that you receive another $500,000. If you invest the money in a stock with a beta of 0.75, what will be the required return on your $5.5 million portfolio?

8-17   **PORTFOLIO BETA**   A mutual fund manager has a $20 million portfolio with a beta of 1.5. The risk-free rate is 4.5%, and the market risk premium is 5.5%. The manager expects to receive an additional $5 million, which she plans to invest in a number of stocks. After investing the additional funds, she wants the fund's required return to be 13%. What should be the average beta of the new stocks added to the portfolio?

8-18   **EXPECTED RETURNS**   Suppose you won the lottery and had two options: (1) receiving $0.5 million or (2) taking a gamble in which at the flip of a coin you receive $1 million if a head comes up but receive zero if a tail comes up.

a.   What is the expected value of the gamble?

b.   Would you take the sure $0.5 million or the gamble?

c. If you chose the sure $0.5 million, would that indicate that you are a risk averter or a risk seeker?

d. Suppose the payoff was actually $0.5 million—that was the only choice. You now face the choice of investing it in a U.S. Treasury bond that will return $537,500 at the end of a year or a common stock that has a 50-50 chance of being worthless or worth $1,150,000 at the end of the year.

(1) The expected profit on the T-bond investment is $37,500. What is the expected dollar profit on the stock investment?

(2) The expected rate of return on the T-bond investment is 7.5%. What is the expected rate of return on the stock investment?

(3) Would you invest in the bond or the stock? Why?

(4) Exactly how large would the expected profit (or the expected rate of return) have to be on the stock investment to make you invest in the stock, given the 7.5% return on the bond?

(5) How might your decision be affected if, rather than buying one stock for $0.5 million, you could construct a portfolio consisting of 100 stocks with $5,000 invested in each? Each of these stocks has the same return characteristics as the one stock—that is, a 50-50 chance of being worth zero or $11,500 at year-end. Would the correlation between returns on these stocks matter? Explain.

8-19   **EVALUATING RISK AND RETURN**   Stock X has a 10% expected return, a beta coefficient of 0.9, and a 35% standard deviation of expected returns. Stock Y has a 12.5% expected return, a beta coefficient of 1.2, and a 25% standard deviation. The risk-free rate is 6%, and the market risk premium is 5%.

a. Calculate each stock's coefficient of variation.

b. Which stock is riskier for a diversified investor?

c. Calculate each stock's required rate of return.

d. On the basis of the two stocks' expected and required returns, which stock would be more attractive to a diversified investor?

e. Calculate the required return of a portfolio that has $7,500 invested in Stock X and $2,500 invested in Stock Y.

f. If the market risk premium increased to 6%, which of the two stocks would have the larger increase in its required return?

8-20   **REALIZED RATES OF RETURN**   Stocks A and B have the following historical returns:

Year	Stock A's Returns, r_A	Stock B's Returns, r_B
2004	(18.00%)	(14.50%)
2005	33.00	21.80
2006	15.00	30.50
2007	(0.50)	(7.60)
2008	27.00	26.30

a. Calculate the average rate of return for each stock during the period 2004 through 2008.

b. Assume that someone held a portfolio consisting of 50% of Stock A and 50% of Stock B. What would the realized rate of return on the portfolio have been each year? What would the average return on the portfolio have been during this period?

c. Calculate the standard deviation of returns for each stock and for the portfolio.

d. Calculate the coefficient of variation for each stock and for the portfolio.

e. Assuming you are a risk-averse investor, would you prefer to hold Stock A, Stock B, or the portfolio? Why?

8-21   **SECURITY MARKET LINE**   You plan to invest in the Kish Hedge Fund, which has total capital of $500 million invested in five stocks:

Stock	Investment	Stock's Beta Coefficient
A	$160 million	0.5
B	120 million	1.2
C	80 million	1.8
D	80 million	1.0
E	60 million	1.6

Kish's beta coefficient can be found as a weighted average of its stocks' betas. The risk-free rate is 6%, and you believe the following probability distribution for future market returns is realistic:

Probability	Market Return
0.1	−28%
0.2	0
0.4	12
0.2	30
0.1	50

a. What is the equation for the Security Market Line (SML)? (Hint: First, determine the expected market return.)

b. Calculate Kish's required rate of return.

c. Suppose Rick Kish, the president, receives a proposal from a company seeking new capital. The amount needed to take a position in the stock is $50 million, it has an expected return of 15%, and its estimated beta is 1.5. Should Kish invest in the new company? At what expected rate of return should Kish be indifferent to purchasing the stock?

COMPREHENSIVE/SPREADSHEET PROBLEM

8-22 **EVALUATING RISK AND RETURN** Bartman Industries' and Reynolds Inc.'s stock prices and dividends, along with the Winslow 5000 Index, are shown here for the period 2003–2008. The Winslow 5000 data are adjusted to include dividends.

	BARTMAN INDUSTRIES		REYNOLDS INC.		WINSLOW 5000
Year	Stock Price	Dividend	Stock Price	Dividend	Includes Dividends
2008	$17.250	$1.15	$48.750	$3.00	$11,663.98
2007	14.750	1.06	52.300	2.90	8,785.70
2006	16.500	1.00	48.750	2.75	8,679.98
2005	10.750	0.95	57.250	2.50	6,434.03
2004	11.375	0.90	60.000	2.25	5,602.28
2003	7.625	0.85	55.750	2.00	4,705.97

a. Use the data to calculate annual rates of return for Bartman, Reynolds, and the Winslow 5000 Index. Then calculate each entity's average return over the 5-year period. (Hint: Remember, returns are calculated by subtracting the beginning price from the ending price to get the capital gain or loss, adding the dividend to the capital gain or loss, and dividing the result by the beginning price. Assume that dividends are already included in the index. Also, you cannot calculate the rate of return for 2003 because you do not have 2002 data.)

b. Calculate the standard deviations of the returns for Bartman, Reynolds, and the Winslow 5000. (Hint: Use the sample standard deviation formula, Equation 8-2a in this chapter, which corresponds to the STDEV function in Excel.)

c. Calculate the coefficients of variation for Bartman, Reynolds, and the Winslow 5000.

d. Construct a scatter diagram that shows Bartman's and Reynolds' returns on the vertical axis and the Winslow 5000 Index's returns on the horizontal axis.

e. Estimate Bartman's and Reynolds' betas by running regressions of their returns against the index's returns. (Hint: Refer to Web Appendix 8A.) Are these betas consistent with your graph?

f. Assume that the risk-free rate on long-term Treasury bonds is 6.04%. Assume also that the average annual return on the Winslow 5000 is *not* a good estimate of the market's required return—it is too high. So use 11% as the expected return on the market. Use the SML equation to calculate the two companies' required returns.

g. If you formed a portfolio that consisted of 50% Bartman and 50% Reynolds, what would the portfolio's beta and required return be?

h. Suppose an investor wants to include Bartman Industries' stock in his portfolio. Stocks A, B, and C are currently in the portfolio; and their betas are 0.769, 0.985, and 1.423, respectively. Calculate the new portfolio's required return if it consists of 25% of Bartman, 15% of Stock A, 40% of Stock B, and 20% of Stock C.

INTEGRATED CASE

MERRILL FINCH INC.

8-23 **RISK AND RETURN** Assume that you recently graduated with a major in finance. You just landed a job as a financial planner with Merrill Finch Inc., a large financial services corporation. Your first assignment is to invest $100,000 for a client. Because the funds are to be invested in a business at the end of 1 year, you have been instructed to plan for a 1-year holding period. Further, your boss has restricted you to the investment alternatives in the following table, shown with their probabilities and associated outcomes. (For now, disregard the items at the bottom of the data; you will fill in the blanks later.)

RETURNS ON ALTERNATIVE INVESTMENTS

ESTIMATED RATE OF RETURN

State of the Economy	Probability	T-Bills	High Tech	Collections	U.S. Rubber	Market Portfolio	2-Stock Portfolio
Recession	0.1	5.5%	(27.0%)	27.0%	6.0%[a]	(17.0%)	0.0%
Below average	0.2	5.5	(7.0)	13.0	(14.0)	(3.0)	
Average	0.4	5.5	15.0	0.0	3.0	10.0	7.5
Above average	0.2	5.5	30.0	(11.0)	41.0	25.0	
Boom	0.1	5.5	45.0	(21.0)	26.0	38.0	12.0
$\hat{r}$				1.0%	9.8%	10.5%	
σ		0.0		13.2	18.8	15.2	3.4
CV				13.2	1.9	1.4	0.5
b				−0.87	0.88		

[a]Note that the estimated returns of U.S. Rubber do not always move in the same direction as the overall economy. For example, when the economy is below average, consumers purchase fewer tires than they would if the economy were stronger. However, if the economy is in a flat-out recession, a large number of consumers who were planning to purchase a new car may choose to wait and instead purchase new tires for the car they currently own. Under these circumstances, we would expect U.S. Rubber's stock price to be higher if there was a recession than if the economy was just below average.

Merrill Finch's economic forecasting staff has developed probability estimates for the state of the economy; and its security analysts have developed a sophisticated computer program, which was used to estimate the rate of return on each alternative under each state of the economy. High Tech Inc. is an electronics firm, Collections Inc. collects past-due debts, and U.S. Rubber manufactures tires and various other rubber and plastics products. Merrill Finch also maintains a "market portfolio" that owns a market-weighted fraction of all publicly traded stocks; you can invest in that portfolio and thus obtain average stock market results. Given the situation described, answer the following questions:

a. (1) Why is the T-bill's return independent of the state of the economy? Do T-bills promise a completely risk-free return? Explain.

   (2) Why are High Tech's returns expected to move with the economy, whereas Collections' are expected to move counter to the economy?

b. Calculate the expected rate of return on each alternative and fill in the blanks on the row for $\hat{r}$ in the previous table.

c. You should recognize that basing a decision solely on expected returns is appropriate only for risk-neutral individuals. Because your client, like most people, is risk-averse, the riskiness of each alternative is an important aspect of the decision. One possible measure of risk is the standard deviation of returns.

   (1) Calculate this value for each alternative and fill in the blank on the row for σ in the table.

   (2) What type of risk is measured by the standard deviation?

(3) Draw a graph that shows *roughly* the shape of the probability distributions for High Tech, U.S. Rubber, and T-bills.

d. Suppose you suddenly remembered that the coefficient of variation (CV) is generally regarded as being a better measure of stand-alone risk than the standard deviation when the alternatives being considered have widely differing expected returns. Calculate the missing CVs and fill in the blanks on the row for CV in the table. Does the CV produce the same risk rankings as the standard deviation? Explain.

e. Suppose you created a two-stock portfolio by investing $50,000 in High Tech and $50,000 in Collections.

(1) Calculate the expected return ($\hat{r}_p$), the standard deviation (σ_p), and the coefficient of variation (CV_p) for this portfolio and fill in the appropriate blanks in the table.

(2) How does the riskiness of this two-stock portfolio compare with the riskiness of the individual stocks if they were held in isolation?

f. Suppose an investor starts with a portfolio consisting of one randomly selected stock. What would happen:

(1) To the riskiness and to the expected return of the portfolio as more randomly selected stocks were added to the portfolio?

(2) What is the implication for investors? Draw a graph of the two portfolios to illustrate your answer.

g. (1) Should the effects of a portfolio impact the way investors think about the riskiness of individual stocks?

(2) If you decided to hold a 1-stock portfolio (and consequently were exposed to more risk than diversified investors), could you expect to be compensated for all of your risk; that is, could you earn a risk premium on the part of your risk that you could have eliminated by diversifying?

h. The expected rates of return and the beta coefficients of the alternatives supplied by Merrill Finch's computer program are as follows:

Security	Return ($\hat{r}$)	Risk (Beta)
High Tech	12.4%	1.32
Market	10.5	1.00
U.S. Rubber	9.8	0.88
T-bills	5.5	0.00
Collections	1.0	(0.87)

(1) What is a beta coefficient, and how are betas used in risk analysis?

(2) Do the expected returns appear to be related to each alternative's market risk?

(3) Is it possible to choose among the alternatives on the basis of the information developed thus far? Use the data given at the start of the problem to construct a graph that shows how the T-bill's, High Tech's, and the market's beta coefficients are calculated. Then discuss what betas measure and how they are used in risk analysis.

i. The yield curve is currently flat; that is, long-term Treasury bonds also have a 5.5% yield. Consequently, Merrill Finch assumes that the risk-free rate is 5.5%.

(1) Write out the Security Market Line (SML) equation, use it to calculate the required rate of return on each alternative, and graph the relationship between the expected and required rates of return.

(2) How do the expected rates of return compare with the required rates of return?

(3) Does the fact that Collections has an expected return that is less than the T-bill rate make any sense? Explain.

(4) What would be the market risk and the required return of a 50-50 portfolio of High Tech and Collections? of High Tech and U.S. Rubber?

j. (1) Suppose investors raised their inflation expectations by 3 percentage points over current estimates as reflected in the 5.5% risk-free rate. What effect would higher inflation have on the SML and on the returns required on high- and low-risk securities?

(2) Suppose instead that investors' risk aversion increased enough to cause the market risk premium to increase by 3 percentage points. (Inflation remains constant.) What effect would this have on the SML and on returns of high- and low-risk securities?

THOMSON ONE | Business School Edition

Access the Thomson ONE problems through the CengageNOW™ web site. Use the Thomson ONE—Business School Edition online database to work this chapter's questions.

Using Past Information to Estimate Required Returns

Chapter 8 discussed the basic trade-off between risk and return. In the Capital Asset Pricing Model (CAPM) discussion, beta was identified as the correct measure of risk for diversified shareholders. Recall that beta measures the extent to which the returns of a given stock move with the stock market. When using the CAPM to estimate required returns, we would like to know how the stock will move with the market in the future; but since we don't have a crystal ball, we generally use historical data to estimate this relationship with beta.

As mentioned in the Web Appendix for this chapter, beta can be estimated by regressing the individual stock's returns against the returns of the overall market. As an alternative to running our own regressions, we can rely on reported betas from a variety of sources. These published sources make it easy for us to readily obtain beta estimates for most large publicly traded corporations. However, a word of caution is in order. Beta estimates can often be quite sensitive to the time period in which the data are estimated, the market index used, and the frequency of the data used. Therefore, it is not uncommon to find a wide range of beta estimates among the various published sources. Indeed, Thomson One reports multiple beta estimates. These multiple estimates reflect the fact that Thomson One puts together data from a variety of different sources.

Discussion Questions

1. Begin by looking at the historical performance of the overall stock market. If you want to see, for example, the performance of the S&P 500, select "INDICES" and enter S&PCOMP. Click on "PERFORMANCE." You will see a quick summary of the market's performance in recent months and years. How has the market performed over the past year? the past 3 years? the past 5 years? the past 10 years?

2. Now let's take a closer look at the stocks of four companies: Colgate Palmolive (Ticker = CL), Campbell Soup (CPB), Motorola (MOT), and Tiffany & Co (TIF). Before looking at the data, which of these companies would you expect to have a relatively high beta (greater than 1.0) and which of these companies would you expect to have a relatively low beta (less than 1.0)?

3. Select one of the four stocks listed in Question 2 by selecting "COMPANY ANALYSIS," entering the company's ticker symbol in the blank companies box, and clicking "GO." On the company overview page, you should see a chart that summarizes how the stock has done relative to the S&P 500 over the past 6 months. Has the stock outperformed or underperformed the overall market during this time period?

4. If you scroll down the company overview page, you should see an estimate of the company's beta. What is the company's beta? What was the source of the estimated beta?

5. Click on "PRICES" on the left-hand side of the screen. What is the company's current dividend yield? What has been its total return to investors over the past 6 months? over the past year? over the past 3 years? (Remember that total return includes the dividend yield plus any capital gains or losses.)

6. Assume that the risk-free rate is 5% and the market risk premium is 6%. What is the required return on the company's stock?

7. Repeat the same exercise for each of the 3 remaining companies. Do the reported betas confirm your earlier intuition? In general, do you find that the higher-beta stocks tend to do better in up markets and worse in down markets? Explain.

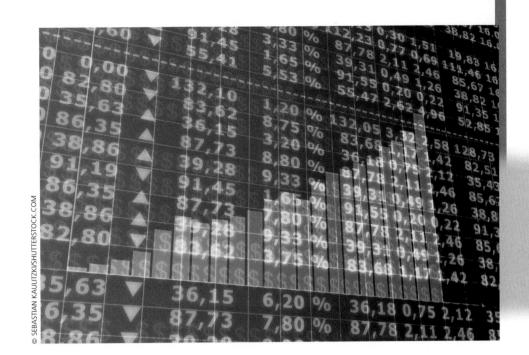

SEBASTIAN KAULITZKI/SHUTTERSTOCK.COM

CHAPTER
9 Stocks and Their Valuation

Searching for the Right Stock

A recent study by the securities industry found that roughly half of all U.S. households have invested in common stocks. As noted in Chapter 8, over the long run, returns in the U.S. stock market have been quite strong, averaging 12% per year. However, the market's performance recently has been less than stellar. Trying to put things in perspective, *Fortune* magazine's senior editor Allan Sloan offered the following comments about the market's performance:

> When the greatest bull market in U.S. history started in the summer of 1982, only a relative handful of people owned stocks, which were cheap because they were considered highly risky. But by the time the Standard & Poor's 500 peaked in March 2000 amid a fully inflated stock bubble, the masses were in the market. Stocks were magical, a supposedly can't-miss way to pay for your kids' college, save for retirement, enrich employees by giving them options, and regrow hair. (Just kidding about the hair. Alas.)

Stocks might go down in any given year, the mantra went, but in the long term they'd produce double-digit returns. However, one of the lessons of the past eight years is that the long run can be . . . really long. As I write this in late February 2008, the U.S. market—which I'm defining as the Standard & Poor's 500—is well below the high that it set on March 24, 2000. Even after you include dividends, which have run a bit below 2% a year, you've barely broken even, according to calculations for Fortune *by Aronson & Johnson & Ortiz, a Philadelphia money manager.*

One month later in March 2008 the stock market fell further in the aftermath of the startling collapse of Wall Street giant Bear Stearns. While most experts believe the stock market will ultimately rebound, most doubt that investors will average double-digit returns from common stock returns in the years ahead.

As we discussed in Chapter 8, the returns of individual stocks are more volatile than the

269

returns of the overall market. For example, in 2007, the overall market (as measured by the S&P 500 Index) was up slightly (+5.49%). That same year some individual stocks realized huge gains while others declined sharply. On the plus side, Research in Motion was up 166%, Amazon.com rose 135%, and Apple Computer climbed 133%. On the down side, E*Trade Financial plummeted 84%; Circuit City, 78%; and Starbucks, 42%. This wide range in individual stocks' returns shows, first, that diversification is important and, second, that when it comes to picking stocks, it is not enough to simply pick a good company—the stock must also be "fairly" priced.

To determine whether a stock is fairly priced, you first need to estimate the stock's true value, or "intrinsic value," a concept first discussed in Chapter 1. With this objective in mind, in this chapter, we describe some models that analysts have used to estimate intrinsic values. As you will see, while it is difficult to predict stock prices, we are not completely in the dark. Indeed, after studying this chapter, you should have a reasonably good understanding of the factors that influence stock prices; and with that knowledge—plus a little luck—you should be able to successfully navigate the market's often-treacherous ups and downs.

Sources: Allan Sloan, "The Incredible Shrinking Bull," *Fortune,* March 17, 2008, p. 24 and Alexandra Twin, "Best and Worst Stocks of 2007," CNNMoney.com, December 31, 2007.

PUTTING THINGS IN PERSPECTIVE

Key trends in the securities industry are listed and explained at www.sifma.org/ research/statistics/ key_industry_trends.html.

In Chapter 7, we examined bonds. We now turn to stocks, both common and preferred. Since the cash flows provided by bonds are set by contract, it is generally easy to predict their cash flows. Preferred stock returns are also set by contract, which makes them similar to bonds; and they are valued in much the same way. However, common stock returns are not contractual—they depend on the firm's earnings, which in turn depend on many random factors, making their valuation more difficult. Two fairly straightforward models are used to estimate stocks' intrinsic (or "true") values: (1) the discounted dividend model and (2) the corporate valuation model. A stock should, of course, be bought if its price is less than its estimated intrinsic value and sold if its price exceeds its intrinsic value. By the time you finish this chapter, you should be able to:

- Discuss the legal rights of stockholders.
- Explain the distinction between a stock's price and its intrinsic value.
- Identify the two models that can be used to estimate a stock's intrinsic value: the discounted dividend model and the corporate model.
- List the key characteristics of preferred stock and explain how to estimate the value of preferred stock.

Stock valuation is interesting in its own right; but you also need to understand valuation when you estimate the cost of capital for use in capital budgeting, which is probably a firm's most important task.

9-1 LEGAL RIGHTS AND PRIVILEGES OF COMMON STOCKHOLDERS

A corporation's common stockholders are the owners of the corporation; and as such, they have certain rights and privileges, as discussed in this section.

9-1a Control of the Firm

A firm's common stockholders have the right to elect its directors, who, in turn, elect the officers who manage the business. In a small firm, usually the major stockholder is also the president and chair of the board of directors. In large, publicly owned firms, the managers typically have some stock, but their personal holdings are generally insufficient to give them voting control. Thus, the managements of most publicly owned firms can be removed by the stockholders if the management team is not effective.

State and federal laws stipulate how stockholder control is to be exercised. First, corporations must hold elections of directors periodically, usually once a year, with the vote taken at the annual meeting. Each share of stock has one vote; thus, the owner of 1,000 shares has 1,000 votes for each director.[1] Stockholders can appear at the annual meeting and vote in person, but typically they transfer their right to vote to another person by means of a **proxy**. Management always solicits stockholders' proxies and usually receives them. However, if earnings are poor and stockholders are dissatisfied, an outside group may solicit the proxies in an effort to overthrow management and take control of the business. This is known as a **proxy fight**.

The question of control has become a central issue in finance in recent years. The frequency of proxy fights has increased, as have attempts by one corporation to take over another by purchasing a majority of the outstanding stock. These actions are called **takeovers**. Some well-known examples of takeover battles in past years include KKR's acquisition of RJR Nabisco, Chevron's acquisition of Gulf Oil, and the QVC/Viacom fight to take over Paramount. More recently, in February 2008, Microsoft made an unsolicited offer for Yahoo; but thus far Yahoo's management has resisted.

Managers without more than 50% of their firms' stock are very much concerned about proxy fights and takeovers, and many of them have attempted to obtain stockholder approval for changes in their corporate charters that would make takeovers more difficult. For example, a number of companies have gotten their stockholders to agree (1) to elect only one-third of the directors each year (rather than electing all directors each year), (2) to require 75% of the stockholders (rather than 50%) to approve a merger, and (3) to vote in a "poison pill" provision that would allow the stockholders of a firm that is taken over by another firm to buy shares in the second firm at a reduced price. The poison pill makes the acquisition unattractive and thus helps ward off hostile takeover attempts. Managers seeking such changes generally cite a fear that the firm will be picked up at a bargain price, but it often appears that the managers' concern about their own positions is the primary consideration.

Managers' moves to make takeovers more difficult have been countered by stockholders, especially large institutional stockholders, who do not like barriers erected to protect incompetent managers. To illustrate, the California Public Employees Retirement System (CalPERS), which is one of the largest institutional investors, has led proxy fights with several corporations whose financial performances were poor in CalPERS' judgment. CalPERS wants companies to increase outside (non-management) directors' ability to force managers to be more responsive to stockholder complaints.

Proxy
A document giving one person the authority to act for another, typically the power to vote shares of common stock.

Proxy Fight
An attempt by a person or group to gain control of a firm by getting its stockholders to grant that person or group the authority to vote its shares to replace the current management.

Takeover
An action whereby a person or group succeeds in ousting a firm's management and taking control of the company.

---

[1]In the situation described, a 1,000-share stockholder could cast 1,000 votes for each of three directors if there were three contested seats on the board. An alternative procedure that may be prescribed in the corporate charter calls for *cumulative voting*. There the 1,000-share stockholder would get 3,000 votes if there were three vacancies, and he or she could cast all of them for one director. Cumulative voting helps small groups obtain representation on the board.

Managers' pay is another contentious issue. It has been asserted, with considerable support, that CEOs tend to pick other CEOs to serve on their boards, with "you-scratch-my-back-and-I'll-scratch-yours" behavior resulting in excessive compensation packages to top managers. Boards have tried to conceal the facts by making it extremely difficult for stockholders to know what the top managers are being paid. Investors are galled to see CEOs such as Stan O'Neil of Merrill Lynch, who was fired because of his firm's multibillion-dollar loss, walk away with stock and cash worth hundreds of millions. CalPERS and other institutional investors have weighed in on this issue, and most firms today have been forced to make their compensation packages more transparent.

For many years, SEC rules prohibited large investors such as CalPERS from getting together to force corporate managers to institute policy changes. However, the SEC began changing its rules in 1993, and now large investors can work together to force management changes. These rulings have helped keep managers focused on stockholder concerns, which means the maximization of stock prices.

9-1b The Preemptive Right

Preemptive Right
A provision in the corporate charter or bylaws that gives common stockholders the right to purchase on a pro rata basis new issues of common stock (or convertible securities).

Common stockholders often have the right, called the **preemptive right**, to purchase on a pro rata basis any additional shares sold by the firm. In some states, the preemptive right is automatically included in every corporate charter; in other states, it must be specifically inserted into the charter.

The purpose of the preemptive right is twofold. First, it prevents the management of a corporation from issuing a large number of additional shares and purchasing those shares itself. Management could use this tactic to seize control of the corporation and frustrate the will of the current stockholders. The second, and far more important, reason for the preemptive right is to protect stockholders from a dilution of value. For example, suppose 1,000 shares of common stock, each with a price of $100, were outstanding, making the total market value of the firm $100,000. If an additional 1,000 shares were sold at $50 a share, or for $50,000, this would raise the firm's total market value to $150,000. When the new total market value is divided by the 2,000 total shares now outstanding, a value of $75 a share is obtained. The old stockholders would thus lose $25 per share, and the new stockholders would have an instant profit of $25 per share. Thus, selling common stock at a price below the market value would dilute a firm's price and transfer wealth from its present stockholders to those who were allowed to purchase the new shares. The preemptive right prevents this.

SELF TEST

Identify some actions that companies have taken to make takeovers more difficult.

What is the preemptive right, and what are the two primary reasons for its existence?

9-2 TYPES OF COMMON STOCK

Classified Stock
Common stock that is given a special designation such as Class A or Class B to meet special needs of the company.

Although most firms have only one type of common stock, in some instances, **classified stock** is used to meet special needs. Generally, when special classifications are used, one type is designated *Class A*, another *Class B*, and so forth. Small, new companies seeking funds from outside sources frequently use different types of common stock. For example, when Google went public, it sold Class A stock to the public while its Class B stock was retained by the company's insiders.

The key difference is that the Class B stock has 10 votes per share while the Class A stock has 1 vote per share. Google's Class B shares are predominantly held by the company's two founders and its current CEO. The use of classified stock thus enables the company's founders to maintain control over the company without having to own a majority of the common stock. For this reason, Class B stock of this type is sometimes called **founders' shares**. Since *dual-class* share structures of this type give special voting privileges to key insiders, these structures are sometimes criticized because they may enable insiders to make decisions that are counter to the interests of the majority of stockholders.

Founders' Shares
Stock owned by the firm's founders that has sole voting rights but restricted dividends for a specified number of years.

Note that "Class A," "Class B," and so forth, have no standard meanings. Most firms have no classified shares; but a firm that does could designate its Class B shares as founders' shares and its Class A shares as those sold to the public, while another could reverse those designations. Still other firms could use stock classifications for entirely different purposes. For example, when General Motors acquired Hughes Aircraft for $5 billion, it paid in part with a new Class H common, GMH, which had limited voting rights and whose dividends were tied to Hughes's performance as a GM subsidiary. The reasons for the new stock were that (1) GM wanted to limit voting privileges on the new classified stock because of management's concern about a possible takeover and (2) Hughes's employees wanted to be rewarded more directly on Hughes's own performance than would have been possible through regular GM stock. These Class H shares disappeared in 2003 when GM decided to sell off the Hughes unit.

SELF TEST   What are some reasons a company might use classified stock?

9-3 STOCK PRICE VS. INTRINSIC VALUE

We saw in Chapter 1 that a manager should seek to maximize the value of his or her firm's stock. In that chapter, we also emphasized the difference between stock price and intrinsic value. The stock price is simply the current market price, and it is easily observed for publicly traded companies. By contrast, intrinsic value, which represents the "true" value of the company's stock, cannot be directly observed and must instead be estimated. Figure 9-1 illustrates once again the connection between stock price and intrinsic value.

As the figure suggests, market equilibrium occurs when the stock's price equals its intrinsic value. If the stock market is reasonably efficient, gaps between the stock price and intrinsic value should not be very large and they should not persist for very long. However, in some cases, an individual stock price may be much higher or lower than its intrinsic value. During several years leading up to the credit crunch of 2007–2008, most of the large investment banks were reporting record profits and selling at record prices. However, much of those earnings were illusory in that they did not reflect the huge risks that existed in the mortgage-backed securities they were buying. So with hindsight, we now know that the market prices of most financial firms' stocks exceeded their intrinsic values just prior to 2007. Then when the market realized what was happening, those stock prices crashed. Citigroup, Merrill Lynch, and others lost over 60% of their value in a few short months; and Bear Stearns, the fifth largest investment bank, saw its

| FIGURE 9-1 | Determinants of Intrinsic Values and Stock Prices |

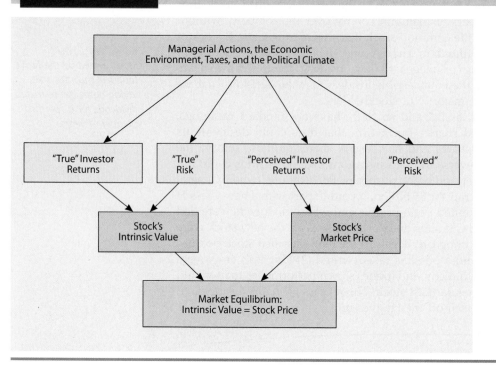

stock price drop from $171 in 2007 to $2 in mid-March 2008. It clearly pays to question market prices at times!

9-3a Why Do Investors and Companies Care About Intrinsic Value?

The remainder of this chapter focuses primarily on different approaches for estimating a stock's intrinsic value. Before these approaches are described, it is worth asking why it is important for investors and companies to understand how to calculate intrinsic value.

When investing in common stocks, one's goal is to purchase stocks that are undervalued (i.e., the price is below the stock's intrinsic value) and avoid stocks that are overvalued. Consequently, Wall Street analysts, institutional investors who control mutual funds and pension funds, and many individual investors are interested in finding reliable models that help predict intrinsic value.

Investors obviously care about intrinsic value, but managers also need to understand how intrinsic value is estimated. First, managers need to know how alternative actions are likely to affect stock prices; and the models of intrinsic value that we cover help demonstrate the connection between managerial decisions and firm value. Second, managers should consider whether their stock is significantly undervalued or overvalued before making certain decisions. For example, firms should consider carefully the decision to issue new shares if they believe their stock is undervalued; and an estimate of their stock's intrinsic value is the key to such decisions.

Two basic models are used to estimate intrinsic values: the *discounted dividend model* and the *corporate valuation model*. The dividend model focuses on dividends, while the corporate model goes beyond dividends and focuses on sales, costs, and free cash flows. In the following sections, we describe these approaches in more detail.

What is the difference between a stock's price and its intrinsic value?

Why do investors and managers need to understand how to estimate a firm's intrinsic value?

What are two commonly used approaches for estimating a stock's intrinsic value?

9-4 THE DISCOUNTED DIVIDEND MODEL

The value of a share of common stock depends on the cash flows it is expected to provide, and those flows consist of two elements: (1) the dividends the investor receives each year while he or she holds the stock and (2) the price received when the stock is sold. The final price includes the original price paid plus an expected capital gain. Keep in mind that there are many different investors in the market and thus many different sets of expectations. Therefore, different investors will have different opinions about a stock's true intrinsic value and thus proper price. The analysis as performed by the **marginal investor**, whose actions actually determine the equilibrium stock price, is critical; but every investor, marginal or not, implicitly goes through the same type of analysis.

The following terms are used in our analysis:[2]

> Marginal investor = the investor (or group of investors with similar views) who is at the margin and would be willing to buy if the stock price was slightly lower or to sell if the price was slightly higher. It is this investor's expectations about dividends, growth, and risk that are key in the valuation process.
>
> Other investors = all except the marginal investor. Some will be more optimistic than the marginal investor; others, more pessimistic. These investors will place new buy or sell orders if events occur to cause them to change their current expectations.
>
> D_t = the dividend a stockholder expects to receive at the end of each Year t. D_0 is the last dividend the company paid. Since it has already been paid, a buyer of the stock will not receive D_0. The first dividend a new buyer will receive is D_1, which is paid at the end of Year 1. D_2 is the dividend expected at the end of Year 2; D_3, at the end of Year 3; and so forth. D_0 is known with certainty; but D_1, D_2, and all other future dividends are *expected values;* and different investors can have different expectations.[3] Our primary concern is with D_t as forecasted by the *marginal investor.*
>
> P_0 = actual **market price** of the stock today. P_0 is known with certainty, but predicted future prices are subject to uncertainty.

Marginal Investor
A representative investor whose actions reflect the beliefs of those people who are currently trading a stock. It is the marginal investor who determines a stock's price.

Market Price, P_0
The price at which a stock sells in the market.

---

[2]Many terms are described here, and students sometimes get concerned about having to memorize all of them. We tell our students that we will provide formula sheets for use on exams, so they don't have to try to memorize everything. With their minds thus eased, they end up learning what the terms are rather than memorizing them.

[3]Stocks generally pay dividends quarterly, so theoretically we should evaluate them on a quarterly basis. However, most analysts actually work with annual data because forecasted stock data are not precise enough to warrant the use of a quarterly model. For additional information on the quarterly model, see Charles M. Linke and J. Kenton Zumwalt, "Estimation Biases in Discounted Cash Flow Analysis of Equity Capital Costs in Rate Regulation," *Financial Management*, Autumn 1984, pp. 15–21.

$\hat{P}_t = $ both the expected price and the expected intrinsic value of the stock at the end of each Year t (pronounced "P hat t") as seen by the investor doing the analysis. $\hat{P}_t$ is based on the investor's estimates of the dividend stream and the riskiness of that stream. There are many investors in the market, so there can be many estimates for $\hat{P}_t$. However, for the marginal investor, P_0 must equal $\hat{P}_0$. Otherwise, a disequilibrium would exist, and buying and selling in the market would soon result in P_0 equaling $\hat{P}_0$ as seen by the marginal investor.

Growth Rate, g
The expected rate of growth in dividends per share.

$g = $ expected **growth rate** in dividends as predicted by an investor. If dividends are expected to grow at a constant rate, g should also equal the expected growth rate in earnings and the stock's price. Different investors use different g's to evaluate a firm's stock; but the market price, P_0, is based on g as estimated by the marginal investor.

Required Rate of Return, r_s
The minimum rate of return on a common stock that a stockholder considers acceptable.

$r_s = $ **required,** or minimum acceptable, **rate of return** on the stock considering its riskiness and the returns available on other investments. Different investors typically have different opinions, but the key is again the marginal investor. The determinants of r_s include factors discussed in Chapter 8, including the real rate of return, expected inflation, and risk.

Expected Rate of Return, $\hat{r}_s$
The rate of return on a common stock that a stockholder expects to receive in the future.

$\hat{r}_s = $ **expected rate of return** (pronounced "r hat s") that an investor believes the stock will provide in the future. The expected return can be above or below the required return; but a rational investor will buy the stock if $\hat{r}_s$ exceeds r_s, sell the stock if $\hat{r}_s$ is less than r_s, and simply hold the stock if these returns are equal. Again, the key is the marginal investor, whose views determine the actual stock price.

Actual (Realized) Rate of Return, $\bar{r}_s$
The rate of return on a common stock actually received by stockholders in some past period. $\bar{r}_s$ may be greater or less than $\hat{r}_s$ and/or r_s.

$\bar{r}_s = $ **actual,** or **realized,** *after-the-fact* **rate of return,** pronounced "r bar s." You can *expect* to obtain a return of $\bar{r}_s = 10\%$ if you buy a stock today; but if the market goes down, you may end up with an actual realized return that is much lower, perhaps even negative.

Dividend Yield
The expected dividend divided by the current price of a share of stock.

$D_1/P_0 = $ **dividend yield** expected during the coming year. If Company X's stock is expected to pay a dividend of $D_1 = \$1$ during the next 12 months and if X's current price is $P_0 = \$20$, the expected dividend yield will be $\$1/\$20 = 0.05 = 5\%$. Different investors could have different expectations for D_1; but again, the marginal investor is the key.

Capital Gains Yield
The capital gain during a given year divided by the beginning price.

$(\hat{P}_1 - P_0)/P_0 = $ expected **capital gains yield** on the stock during the coming year. If the stock sells for $20.00 today and if it is expected to rise to $21.00 by the end of the year, the expected capital gain will be $\hat{P}_1 - P_0 = \$21.00 - \$20.00 = \$1.00$ and the expected capital gains yield will be $\$1.00/\$20.00 = 0.05 = 5\%$. Different investors can have different expectations for $\hat{P}_1$, but the marginal investor is key.

Expected Total Return
The sum of the expected dividend yield and the expected capital gains yield.

Expected total return $= \hat{r}_s = $ expected dividend yield (D_1/P_0) plus expected capital gains yield $[(\hat{P}_1 - P_0)/P_0]$. In our example, the **expected total return** $= \hat{r}_s = 5\% + 5\% = 10\%$.

All active investors hope to be better than average—they hope to identify stocks whose intrinsic values exceed their current prices and whose expected returns (expected by this investor) exceed the required rate of return. Note, though, that about half of all investors are likely to be disappointed. A good understanding of the points made in this chapter can help you avoid being disappointed.

9-4a Expected Dividends as the Basis for Stock Values

In our discussion of bonds, we used Equation 7-1 to find the value of a bond; the equation is the present value of interest payments over the bond's life plus the present value of its maturity (or par) value:

$$V_B = \frac{INT}{(1+r_d)^1} + \frac{INT}{(1+r_d)^2} + \cdots + \frac{INT}{(1+r_d)^N} + \frac{M}{(1+r_d)^N}$$

Stock prices are likewise determined as the present value of a stream of cash flows, and the basic stock valuation equation is similar to the one for bonds. What are the cash flows that a corporation will provide to its stockholders? To answer that question, think of yourself as an investor who buys the stock of a company that is expected to go on indefinitely (for example, GE). You intend to hold it (in your family) forever. In this case, all you (and your heirs) will receive is a stream of dividends; and the value of the stock today can be calculated as the present value of an infinite stream of dividends:

$$\text{Value of stock} = \hat{P}_0 = \text{PV of expected future dividends}$$

$$= \frac{D_1}{(1+r_s)^1} + \frac{D_2}{(1+r_s)^2} + \cdots + \frac{D_\infty}{(1+r_s)^\infty}$$

$$= \sum_{t=1}^{\infty} \frac{D_t}{(1+r_s)^t} \qquad \text{9-1}$$

What about the more typical case, where you expect to hold the stock for a finite period and then sell it—what will be the value of $\hat{P}_0$ in this case? Unless the company is likely to be liquidated or sold and thus disappears, *the value of the stock is again determined by Equation 9-1.* To see this, recognize that for any individual investor, the expected cash flows consist of expected dividends plus the expected sale price of the stock. However, the sale price to the current investor depends on the dividends some future investor expects, and that investor's expected sale price is also dependent on some future dividends, and so forth. Therefore, for all present and future investors in total, expected cash flows must be based on expected future dividends. Put another way, unless a firm is liquidated or sold to another concern, the cash flows it provides to its stockholders will consist only of a stream of dividends. Therefore, the value of a share of stock must be established as the present value of the stock's expected dividend stream.[4]

[4] The general validity of Equation 9-1 can also be confirmed by asking yourself the following question: Suppose I buy a stock and expect to hold it for 1 year. I will receive dividends during the year plus the value $\hat{P}_1$ when I sell it at the end of the year. But what will determine the value of $\hat{P}_1$? The answer is that it will be determined as the present value of the dividends expected during Year 2 plus the stock price at the end of that year, which, in turn, will be determined as the present value of another set of future dividends and an even more distant stock price. This process can be continued ad infinitum, and the ultimate result is Equation 9-1.

We should note that investors periodically lose sight of the long-run nature of stocks as investments and forget that in order to sell a stock at a profit, one must find a buyer who will pay the higher price. If you analyze a stock's value in accordance with Equation 9-1, conclude that the stock's market price exceeds a reasonable value, and buy the stock anyway, you would be following the "bigger fool" theory of investment—you think you may be a fool to buy the stock at its excessive price; but you also believe that when you get ready to sell it, you can find someone who is an even bigger fool. The bigger fool theory was widely followed in the summer of 2000, just before the stock market crashed.

Explain the following statement: Whereas a bond contains a promise to pay interest, a share of common stock typically provides an expectation of, but no promise of, dividends plus capital gains.

What are the two parts of most stocks' expected total return?

If $D_1 = \$2.00$, $g = 6\%$, and $P_0 = \$40.00$, what are the stock's expected dividend yield, capital gains yield, and total expected return for the coming year? **(5%, 6%, 11%)**

Is it necessary for all investors to have the same expectations regarding a stock for the stock to be in equilibrium? **(No, but explain.)** What would happen to a stock's price if the "marginal investor" examined a stock and concluded that its intrinsic value was greater than its current market price? **(P_0 would rise.)**

9-5 CONSTANT GROWTH STOCKS

Equation 9-1 is a generalized stock valuation model in the sense that the time pattern of D_t can be anything: D_t can be rising, falling, or fluctuating randomly; or it can be zero for several years. Equation 9-1 can be applied in any of these situations; and with a computer spreadsheet, we can easily use the equation to find a stock's intrinsic value—provided we have an estimate of the future dividends. However, it is not easy to obtain accurate estimates of future dividends.

Still, for many companies it is reasonable to predict that dividends will grow at a constant rate. In this case, Equation 9-1 may be rewritten as follows:

9-2
$$\hat{P}_0 = \frac{D_0(1+g)^1}{(1+r_s)^1} + \frac{D_0(1+g)^2}{(1+r_s)^2} + \cdots + \frac{D_0(1+g)^\infty}{(1+r_s)^\infty}$$
$$= \frac{D_0(1+g)}{r_s - g} = \frac{D_1}{r_s - g}$$

Constant Growth (Gordon) Model
Used to find the value of a constant growth stock.

The last term of Equation 9-2 is the **constant growth model,** or **Gordon model,** named after Myron J. Gordon, who did much to develop and popularize it.[5]

The term r_s in Equation 9-2 is the *required rate of return,* which is a riskless rate plus a risk premium. However, we know that if the stock is in equilibrium, the required rate of return must equal the expected rate of return, which is the expected dividend yield plus an expected capital gains yield. So we can solve Equation 9-2 for r_s, but now using the hat to indicate that we are dealing with an expected rate of return:[6]

$$\begin{array}{ccccc} \text{Expected rate} & = & \text{Expected} & + & \text{Expected growth rate, or} \\ \text{of return} & & \text{dividend yield} & & \text{capital gains yield} \end{array}$$

9-3
$$\hat{r}_s \qquad = \qquad \frac{D_1}{P_0} \qquad + \qquad g$$

We illustrate Equations 9-2 and 9-3 in the following section.

---

[5]The last term in Equation 9-2 is derived in the Web/CD Extension of Chapter 5 of Eugene F. Brigham and Phillip R. Daves, *Intermediate Financial Management,* 9th ed. (Mason, OH: Thomson/South-Western, 2007). In essence, Equation 9-2 is the sum of a geometric progression, and the final result is the solution value of the progression.
[6]The r_s value in Equation 9-2 is a *required* rate of return; but when we transform Equation 9-2 to obtain Equation 9-3, we are finding an *expected* rate of return. Obviously, the transformation requires that $r_s = \hat{r}_s$. This equality must hold if the stock is in equilibrium, as most normally are.

9-5a Illustration of a Constant Growth Stock

Table 9-1 presents an analysis of Allied Food Products' stock as performed by a security analyst after a meeting for analysts and other investors presided over by Allied's CFO. The table looks complicated, but it is really quite straightforward.[7] Part I, in the upper left corner, provides some basic data. The last dividend, which was just paid, was $1.15; the stock's last closing price was $23.06; and it is in equilibrium. Based on an analysis of Allied's history and likely future, the analyst forecasts that earnings and dividends will grow at a constant rate of 8.3% per year and that the stock's price will grow at this same rate. Moreover, the analyst believes that the most appropriate required rate of return is 13.7%. Different analysts might use different inputs; but we assume for now that since this analyst is widely followed, her results represent those of the marginal investor.

Now look at Part IV, where we show the predicted stream of dividends and stock prices along with annual values for the dividend yield, the capital gains yield, and the expected total return. Notice that the total return shown in Column 6 is equal to the required rate of return shown in Part I. This indicates that the stock

Table 9-1	Analysis of a Constant Growth Stock

	A	B	C	D	E	F	G	H	I
1									
2									
3	**I. Basic Information**			**II. Formulas Used in the Analysis:**					
4	D_0	= $1.15			Dividend in Year t, D_t, in Col. 2				$D_{t-1}(1+g)$
5	P_0	= $23.06			Intrinsic value (and price) in Year t, P_t, in Col. 3				$D_{t+1}/(r_s - g)$
6	g	= 8.30%			Dividend yield (constant), in Col. 4				D_t/P_{t-1}
7	r_s	= 13.70%			Capital gains yield (constant), in Col. 5				$(P_t - P_{t-1})/P_{t-1}$
8					Total return (constant), in Col. 6				Div. yield + CG yield
9					PV of dividends, discounted at 13.7% Col. 7				$D_t/(1+r_s)_t$
10	**III. Examples:**								
11			Col. 2	$D_1 = \$1.1500(1.083)$					$1.25
12			Col. 3	$P_0 = \$1.25/(0.137 - 0.083)$					$23.06
13			Col. 4	Dividend yield, Year 1: $1.25/$23.06					5.40%
14			Col. 5	Cap gains yield, Year 1: ($24.98 − $23.06)/$23.06					8.30%
15			Col. 6	Total return, Year 1: 5.4% + 8.3%					13.70%
16			Col. 7	PV of D_1 discounted at 13.7%					$1.10
17									
18	**IV. Table: Forecasted Results over Time**								PV of dividend
19			**At end**			Dividend	Capital	Total		at 13.7%
20			**of year:**	Dividend	Price	yield	gain yield	returns		
21			**(1)**	(2)	(3)	(4)	(5)	(6)		(7)
22			2008	$1.15	$23.06					
23			2009	1.25	24.98	5.40%	8.30%	13.70%		$1.10
24			2010	1.35	27.05	5.40	8.30	13.70		1.04
25			2011	1.46	29.30	5.40	8.30	13.70		0.99
26			2012	1.58	31.73	5.40	8.30	13.70		0.95
27			2013	1.71	34.36	5.40	8.30	13.70		0.90
28			2014	1.86	37.21	5.40	8.30	13.70		0.86
29			2015	2.01	40.30	5.40	8.30	13.70		0.82
30			2016	2.18	43.65	5.40	8.30	13.70		0.78
31			2017	2.36	47.27	5.40	8.30	13.70		0.74
32			2018	2.55	51.19	5.40	8.30	13.70		0.71
33			↓							↓
34			∞					Sum of PVs from 1 to ∞ = $P_0 =$		$23.06

[7]You may notice some minor "errors" in the table. These are not errors—they are simply differences caused by rounding.

analyst thinks that the stock is fairly priced; hence, it is in equilibrium. She forecasted out 10 years, but she could have forecasted out to infinity.

Part II shows the formulas used to calculate the data in Part IV, and Part III gives examples of the calculations. For example, D_1, the first dividend a purchaser would receive, is forecasted to be $D_1 = \$1.15(1.083) = \$1.25$, and the other forecasted dividends in Column 2 were calculated similarly.

The estimated intrinsic values shown in Column 3 are based on Equation 9-2, the constant growth model: $P_0 = D_1/(r_s - g) = \$1.25/(0.137 - 0.083) = \$23.06$ (corrected for rounding), $P_1 = \$24.98$, and so forth.

Column 4 shows the dividend yield, which for 2009 is $D_1/P_0 = 5.40\%$; and this number is constant thereafter. The capital gain expected during 2009 is $P_1 - P_0 = \$24.98 - \$23.06 = \$1.92$, which when divided by P_0 gives the expected capital gains yield, $\$1.92/\$23.06 = 8.3\%$, again corrected for rounding. The total return is found as the dividend yield plus the capital gains yield, 13.7%; and it is both constant and equal to the required rate of return given in Part I.

Finally, look at Column 7 in the table. Here we find the present value of each of the dividends shown in Column 2, discounted at the required rate of return. For example, the PV of $D_1 = \$1.25/(1.137)^1 = \$1.10$, the PV of $D_2 = \$1.35/(1.137)^2 = \$1.04$, and so forth. If you extended the table out to about 170 years (with Excel, this is easy), then summed the PVs of the dividends, you would get the same value as that found using Equation 9-2, $\$23.06$.[8] Figure 9-2 shows graphically what's happening. We extended the table out 20 years and then plotted dividends from Column 2 in the upper step function curve and the PV of those dividends in the lower curve. The sum of the PVs is an estimate of the stock's forecasted intrinsic value.

Note that in Table 9-1, the forecasted intrinsic value is equal to the current stock price and the expected total return is equal to the required rate of return. In this situation, the analysis would call the stock a "Hold" and would recommend that investors not buy or sell it. However, if the analyst were somewhat more optimistic and thought the growth rate would be 10.0% rather than 8.3%, the forecasted intrinsic value would be (by Equation 9-2) $34.19 and the analyst would call it a "Buy." At $g = 6\%$, the intrinsic value would be $15.83 and the stock would be a "Sell." Changes in the required rate of return would produce similar changes in the forecasted intrinsic value and thus the equilibrium current price.

9-5b Dividends Versus Growth

The discounted dividend model as expressed in Equation 9-2 shows that, other things held constant, a higher value for D_1 increases a stock's price. However, Equation 9-2 shows that a higher growth rate also increases the stock's price. But now recognize the following:

- Dividends are paid out of earnings.
- Therefore, growth in dividends requires growth in earnings.
- Earnings growth in the long run occurs primarily because firms retain earnings and reinvest them in the business.
- Therefore, the higher the percentage of earnings retained, the higher the growth rate.

To illustrate all this, suppose you inherit a business that has $1,000,000 of assets, no debt, and thus $1,000,000 of equity. The expected return on equity (ROE)

---

[8]The dividends get quite large, but the discount rate exceeds the growth rate; so the PVs of the dividends become quite small. In theory, you would have to go out to infinity to find the exact price of a constant growth stock, but the difference between the Equation 9-2 value and the sum of the PVs can't be seen out to 2 decimal places if you go out about 170 periods.

FIGURE 9-2	Present Values of Dividends of a Constant Growth Stock where $D_0 = \$1.15$, $g = 8.3\%$, $r_s = 13.7\%$

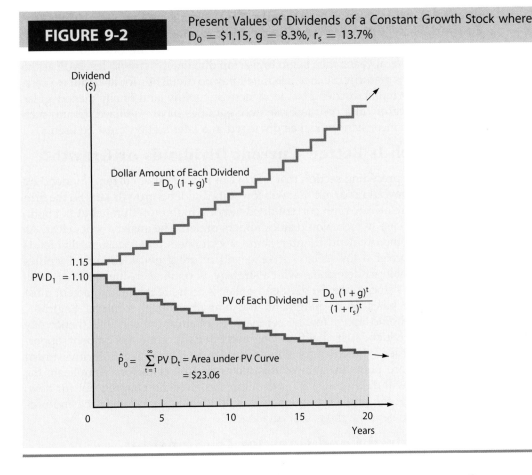

equals 10.0%, so its expected earnings for the coming year are $(0.10)\$1,000,000 = \$100,000$. You could take out the entire \$100,000 of earnings in dividends, or you could reinvest some or all of the \$100,000 in the business. If you pay out all the earnings, you will have \$100,000 of dividend income this year, but dividends will not grow because assets and therefore earnings will not grow.

However, suppose you decide to have the firm pay out 40% and retain 60%. Now your dividend income in Year 1 will be \$40,000; but assets will rise by \$60,000, and earnings and dividends will likewise increase:

$$\text{Next year's earnings} = \text{Prior earnings} + \text{ROE(Retained earnings)}$$
$$= \$100,000 + 0.1(\$60,000)$$
$$= \$106,000$$
$$\text{Next year's dividends} = 0.4(\$106,000) = \$42,400$$

Moreover, your dividend income will continue to grow by 6% per year thereafter:

$$\text{Growth rate} = (1 - \text{Payout ratio})\text{ROE} \qquad \text{9-4}$$
$$= (1 - 0.4)10.0\%$$
$$= 0.6(10.0\%) = 60\%$$

This demonstrates that in the long run, growth in dividends depends primarily on the firm's payout ratio and its ROE.

In our example, we assumed that other things remain constant. This is often but not always a logical assumption. For example, suppose the firm develops a successful new product or hires a better CEO or makes some other change that increased the ROE. Any of these actions could cause the ROE and thus the growth rate to increase. Also note that the earnings of new firms are often low or even negative for several years, then begin to rise rapidly; finally, growth levels off as the firm approaches maturity. Such a firm might pay no dividends for its first few years, then pay a low initial dividend but let it increase rapidly, and finally make regular payments that grow at a constant rate once earnings have stabilized. In any such situation, the nonconstant model as discussed in a later section must be used.

9-5c Which Is Better: Current Dividends or Growth?

We saw in the preceding section that a firm can pay a higher current dividend by increasing its payout ratio, but that will lower its dividend growth rate. So the firm can provide a relatively high current dividend or a high growth rate but not both. This being the case, which would stockholders prefer? The answer is not clear. As we will see in the dividend chapter, some stockholders prefer current dividends while others prefer a lower payout ratio and future growth. Empirical studies have been unable to determine which strategy is optimal in the sense of maximizing a firm's stock price. So dividend policy is an issue that management must decide on the basis of its judgment, not a mathematical formula. Logically, shareholders should prefer for the company to retain more earnings (hence pay less current dividends) if the firm has exceptionally good investment opportunities; however, shareholders should prefer a high payout if investment opportunities are poor. In spite of this, taxes and other factors complicate the situation. We will discuss all this in detail in the dividend chapter; but for now, just assume that the firm's management has decided on a payout policy and uses that policy to determine the actual dividend.

9-5d Required Conditions for the Constant Growth Model

Several conditions are necessary for Equation 9-2 to be used. First, the required rate of return, r_s, must be greater than the long-run growth rate, g. *If the equation is used in situations where g is greater than r_s, the results will be wrong, meaningless, and misleading.* For example, if the forecasted growth rate in our example was 15% and thus exceeded the 13.7% required rate of return, stock price as calculated by Equation 9-2 would be a *negative* $101.73. That would be nonsense—stocks can't have negative prices. Moreover, in Table 9-1, the PV of each future dividend would exceed that of the prior year. If this situation was graphed in Figure 9-2, the step-function curve for the PV of dividends would be increasing, not decreasing; so the sum would be infinitely high, which would indicate an infinitely high stock price. Obviously, stock prices cannot be either infinite or negative, so Equation 9-2 cannot be used unless $r_s > g$.

Second, the constant growth model as expressed in Equation 9-2 is not appropriate unless a company's growth rate is expected to remain constant in the future. This condition almost never holds for new start-up firms, but it does exist for many mature companies. Indeed, mature firms such as Allied and GE are generally expected to grow at about the same rate as nominal gross domestic product (that is, real GDP plus inflation). On this basis, one might expect the dividends of an average, or "normal," company to grow at a rate of 5% to 8% a year.

Note too that Equation 9-2 is sufficiently general to handle the case of a **zero growth stock**, where the dividend is expected to remain constant over time. If g = 0, Equation 9-2 reduces to Equation 9-5:

Zero Growth Stock
A common stock whose future dividends are not expected to grow at all; that is, g = 0.

9-5

$$\hat{P}_0 = \frac{D}{r_s}$$

This is the same equation as the one we developed in Chapter 5 for a perpetuity, and it is simply the current dividend divided by the discount rate.

Finally, as we discuss later in the chapter, most firms, even rapidly growing startups and others that pay no dividends at present, can be expected to pay dividends at some point in the future, at which time the constant growth model will be appropriate. For such firms, Equation 9-2 is used as one part of a more complicated valuation equation that we discuss next.

SELF TEST

Write out and explain the valuation formula for a constant growth stock.

Explain how the formula for a zero growth stock can be derived from that for a normal constant growth stock.

Firm A is expected to pay a dividend of $1.00 at the end of the year. The required rate of return is $r_s = 11\%$. Other things held constant, what would the stock's price be if the growth rate was 5%? What if g was 0%? **($16.67; $9.09)**

Firm B has a 12% ROE. Other things held constant, what would its expected growth rate be if it paid out 25% of its earnings as dividends? 75%? **(9%, 3%)**

If Firm B had a 75% payout ratio but then lowered it to 25%, causing its growth rate to rise from 3% to 9%, would that action necessarily increase the price of its stock? Why or why not?

9-6 VALUING NONCONSTANT GROWTH STOCKS

For many companies, it is not appropriate to assume that dividends will grow at a constant rate. Indeed, most firms go through *life cycles* where they experience different growth rates during different parts of the cycle. In their early years, most firms grow much faster than the economy as a whole; then they match the economy's growth; and finally they grow at a slower rate than the economy.[9] Automobile manufacturers in the 1920s, computer software firms such as Microsoft in the 1990s, and Google in the 2000s are examples of firms in the early part of their cycle. These firms are defined as **supernormal, or nonconstant growth**, firms. Figure 9-3 illustrates nonconstant growth and compares it with normal growth, zero growth, and negative growth.[10]

In the figure, the dividends of the supernormal growth firm are expected to grow at a 30% rate for three years, after which the growth rate is expected to fall to 8%, the assumed average for the economy. The value of this firm's stock, like any other asset, is the present value of its expected future dividends as determined by

Supernormal (Nonconstant) Growth
The part of the firm's life cycle in which it grows much faster than the economy as a whole.

---

[9] The concept of life cycles could be broadened to *product cycle*, which would include both small start-up companies and large companies such as Microsoft and Procter & Gamble, which periodically introduce new products that give sales and earnings a boost. We should also mention *business cycles*, which alternately depress and boost sales and profits. The growth rate just after a major new product has been introduced (or just after a firm emerges from the depths of a recession) is likely to be much higher than the "expected long-run average growth rate," which is the proper number for use in the discounted dividend model.

[10] A negative growth rate indicates a declining company. A mining company whose profits are falling because of a declining ore body is an example. Someone buying such a company would expect its earnings (and consequently its dividends and stock price) to decline each year, which would lead to capital losses rather than capital gains. Obviously, a declining company's stock price is relatively low, and its dividend yield must be high enough to offset the expected capital loss and still produce a competitive total return. Students sometimes argue that they would never be willing to buy a stock whose price was expected to decline. However, if the present value of the expected dividends exceeds the stock price, the stock is still a good investment that would provide a good return.

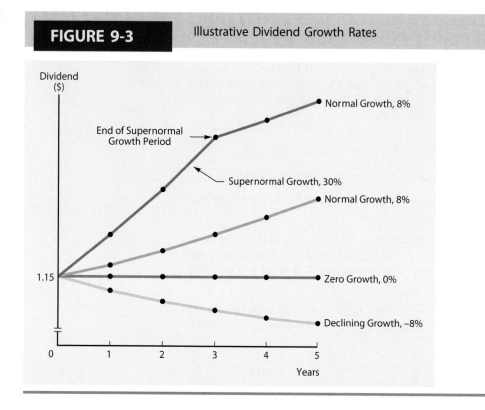

FIGURE 9-3 Illustrative Dividend Growth Rates

Dividend
($)

End of Supernormal
Growth Period

Normal Growth, 8%

Supernormal Growth, 30%

Normal Growth, 8%

1.15

Zero Growth, 0%

Declining Growth, –8%

0   1   2   3   4   5

Years

Equation 9-1. When D_t is growing at a constant rate, we can simplify Equation 9-1 to Equation 9-2, $\hat{P}_0 = D_1/(r_s - g)$. In the supernormal case, however, the expected growth rate is not a constant. In our example, there are two distinctly different rates.

Because Equation 9-2 requires a constant growth rate, we obviously cannot use it to value stocks that are not growing at a constant rate. However, assuming that a company currently enjoying supernormal growth will eventually slow down and become a constant growth stock, we can combine Equations 9-1 and 9-2 to construct a new formula, Equation 9-6, for valuing the stock.

First, we assume that the dividend will grow at a nonconstant rate (generally a relatively high rate) for N periods, after which it will grow at a constant rate, g. N is often called the **terminal**, or **horizon**, **date**. Second, we can use the constant growth formula, Equation 9-2, to determine what the stock's **horizon**, or **terminal**, **value** will be N periods from today:

Terminal (Horizon) Date
The date when the growth rate becomes constant. At this date, it is no longer necessary to forecast the individual dividends.

$$\text{Horizon Value} = \hat{P}_N = \frac{D_{N+1}}{r_s - g}$$

The stock's intrinsic value today, $\hat{P}_0$, is the present value of the dividends during the nonconstant growth period plus the present value of the horizon value:

Horizon (Terminal) Value
The value at the horizon date of all dividends expected thereafter.

$$\hat{P}_0 = \underbrace{\frac{D_1}{(1+r_s)^1} + \frac{D_2}{(1+r_s)^2} + \cdots + \frac{D_N}{(1+r_s)^N}}_{\substack{\text{PV of dividends during the} \\ \text{nonconstant growth} \\ \text{Period, } t = 1, \cdots N}} + \underbrace{\frac{D_{N+1}}{(1+r_s)^{N+1}} + \cdots + \frac{D^\infty}{(1+r_s)^\infty}}_{\substack{\text{Horizon value} = \text{PV of dividends} \\ \text{during the constant growth} \\ \text{Period, } t = N+1, \cdots \infty}}$$

$$\hat{P}_0 = \underbrace{\frac{D_1}{(1 + r_s)^1} + \frac{D_2}{(1 + r_s)^2} + \cdots + \frac{D_N}{(1 + r_s)^N}}_{\substack{\text{PV of dividends during the} \\ \text{nonconstant growth period} \\ t = 1, \cdots N}} + \underbrace{\frac{\hat{P}_N}{(1 + r_s)^N}}_{\substack{\text{PV of horizon} \\ \text{value, } \hat{P}_N: \\ \frac{[(D_{N+1})/(r_s - g)]}{(1 + r_s)^N}}} \qquad \text{9-6}$$

To implement Equation 9-6, we go through the following three steps:

1. Find the PV of each dividend during the period of nonconstant growth and sum them.

2. Find the expected stock price at the end of the nonconstant growth period, at which point it has become a constant growth stock so it can be valued with the constant growth model, and discount this price back to the present.

3. Add these two components to find the stock's intrinsic value, $\hat{P}_0$.

Figure 9-4 illustrates the process for valuing nonconstant growth stocks. Here we use a new company, Firm M, and we assume that the following five facts exist:

r_s = stockholders' required rate of return = 13.4%. This rate is used to discount the cash flows.

N = years of nonconstant growth = 3.

g_s = rate of growth in both earnings and dividends during the nonconstant growth period = 30%. This rate is shown directly on the time line. (Note: The growth rate during the nonconstant growth period could vary from year to year. Also, there could be several different nonconstant growth periods—for example, 30% for three years, 20% for the next three years, and a constant 8% thereafter).

g_n = rate of normal, constant growth after the nonconstant period = 8.0%. This rate is also shown on the time line, after Period 3, when it is in effect.

D_0 = last dividend the company paid = $1.15.

The valuation process diagrammed in Figure 9-4 is explained in the steps set forth below the time line. The value of the nonconstant growth stock is calculated to be $39.21.

Note that in this example, we assumed a relatively short 3-year horizon to keep things simple. When evaluating stocks, most analysts use a longer horizon (for example, 5 years) to estimate intrinsic values. This requires a few more calculations; but because analysts use spreadsheets, the arithmetic is not a problem. In practice, the real limitation is obtaining reliable forecasts for future growth.

SELF TEST

Explain how one would find the value of a nonconstant growth stock.

Explain what is meant by terminal (horizon) date and horizon (terminal) value.

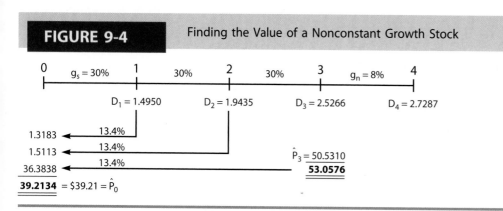

FIGURE 9-4   Finding the Value of a Nonconstant Growth Stock

Notes to Figure 9-4:

Step 1. Calculate the dividends expected at the end of each year during the nonconstant growth period. Calculate the first dividend, $D_1 = D_0(1 + g_s) = \$1.15(1.30) = \$1.4950$. Here g_s is the growth rate during the 3-year nonconstant growth period, 30%. Show the $1.4950 on the time line as the cash flow at Time 1. Calculate $D_2 = D_1(1 + g_s) = \$1.4950(1.30) = \$1.9435$, then $D_3 = D_2(1 + g_s) = \$1.9435(1.30) = \$2.5266$. Show these values on the time line as the cash flows at Times 2 and 3. Note that D_0 is used only to calculate D_1.

Step 2. The price of the stock is the PV of dividends from Time 1 to infinity; so in theory, we could project each future dividend, with the normal growth rate, $g_n = 8\%$, used to calculate D_4 and subsequent dividends. However, we know that after D_3 has been paid at Time 3, the stock becomes a constant growth stock. Therefore, we can use the constant growth formula to find $\hat{P}_3$, which is the PV of the dividends from Time 4 to infinity as evaluated at Time 3.

First, we determine $D_4 = \$2.5266(1.08) = \$2.7287$ for use in the formula; then we calculate $\hat{P}_3$ as follows:

$$\hat{P}_3 = \frac{D_4}{r_s - g_n} = \frac{\$2.7287}{0.134 - 0.08} = \$50.5310$$

We show this $50.5310 on the time line as a second cash flow at Time 3. The $50.5310 is a Time 3 cash flow in the sense that the stockholder could sell the stock for $50.5310 at Time 3 and in the sense that $50.5310 is the present value of the dividend cash flows from Time 4 to infinity. Note that the total cash flow at Time 3 consists of the sum of $D_3 + \hat{P}_3 = \$2.5266 + \$50.5310 = \$53.0576$.

Step 3. Now that the cash flows have been placed on the time line, we can discount each cash flow at the required rate of return, $r_s = 13.4\%$. We could discount each cash flow by dividing by $(1.134)^t$, where $t = 1$ for Time 1, $t = 2$ for Time 2, and $t = 3$ for Time 3. This produces the PVs shown to the left below the time line; and the sum of the PVs is the value of the nonconstant growth stock, $39.21.

With a financial calculator, you can find the PV of the cash flows as shown on the time line with the cash flow (CFLO) register of your calculator. Enter 0 for CF_0 because you receive no cash flow at Time 0, $CF_1 = 1.495$, $CF_2 = 1.9435$, and $CF_3 = 2.5266 + 50.5310 = 53.0576$. Then enter I/YR = 13.4 and press the NPV key to find the value of the stock, $39.21.

9-7 VALUING THE ENTIRE CORPORATION[11]

Corporate Valuation Model

A valuation model used as an alternative to the discounted dividend model to determine a firm's value, especially one with no history of dividends, or the value of a division of a larger firm. The corporate model first calculates the firm's free cash flows, then finds their present values to determine the firm's value.

Thus far we have discussed the discounted dividend model for valuing a firm's common stock. This procedure is widely used, but it is based on the assumption that the analyst can forecast future dividends reasonably well. This is often true for mature companies that have a history of steadily growing dividends. However, dividends are dependent on earnings; so a really reliable dividend forecast must be based on an underlying forecast of the firm's future sales, costs, and capital requirements. This recognition has led to an alternative stock valuation approach, the **corporate valuation model**.

---

[11] The corporate valuation model presented in this section is widely used by analysts, and it is in many respects superior to the discounted dividend model. However, it is rather involved as it requires the estimation of sales, costs, and cash flows on out into the future before the discounting process is begun. Therefore, in the introductory course, some instructors may prefer to omit Section 9-7 and skip to Section 9-8.

EVALUATING STOCKS THAT DON'T PAY DIVIDENDS

The discounted dividend model assumes that the firm is currently paying a dividend. However, many firms, even highly profitable ones, including Google, Dell, and Apple, have never paid a dividend. If a firm is expected to begin paying dividends in the future, we can modify the equations presented in the chapter and use them to determine the value of the stock.

A new business often expects to have low sales during its first few years of operation as it develops its product. Then if the product catches on, sales will grow rapidly for several years. Sales growth brings with it the need for additional assets—a firm cannot increase sales without also increasing its assets, and asset growth requires an increase in liability and/or equity accounts. Small firms can generally obtain some bank credit, but they must maintain a reasonable balance between debt and equity. Thus, additional bank borrowings require increases in equity, and getting the equity capital needed to support growth can be difficult for small firms. They have limited access to the capital markets; and even when they can sell common stock, their owners are reluctant to do so for fear of losing voting control. Therefore, the best source of equity for most small businesses is retained earnings; for this reason most small firms pay no dividends during their rapid growth years. Eventually, though, successful small firms do pay dividends, and those dividends generally grow rapidly at first but slow down to a sustainable constant rate once the firm reaches maturity.

If a firm currently pays no dividends but is expected to pay future dividends, the value of its stock can be found as follows:

1. Estimate at what point dividends will be paid, the amount of the first dividend, the growth rate during the supernormal growth period, the length of the supernormal period, the long-run (constant) growth rate, and the rate of return required by investors.

2. Use the constant growth model to determine the price of the stock after the firm reaches a stable growth situation.

3. Set out on a time line the cash flows (dividends during the supernormal growth period and the stock price once the constant growth state is reached); then find the present value of these cash flows. That present value represents the value of the stock today.

To illustrate this process, consider the situation for Marvel-Lure Inc., a company that was set up in 2007 to produce and market a new high-tech fishing lure. Marvel-Lure's sales are currently growing at a rate of 200% per year. The company expects to experience a high but declining rate of growth in sales and earnings during the next 10 years, after which analysts estimate that it will grow at a steady 10% per year. The firm's management has announced that it will pay no dividends for 5 years but that if earnings materialize as forecasted, it will pay a dividend of $0.20 per share at the end of Year 6, $0.30 in Year 7, $0.40 in Year 8, $0.45 in Year 9, and $0.50 in Year 10. After Year 10, current plans are to increase dividends by 10% per year.

MarvelLure's investment bankers estimate that investors require a 15% return on similar stocks. Therefore, we find the value of a share of MarvelLure's stock as follows:

$$P_0 = \frac{\$0}{(1.15)^1} + \cdots + \frac{\$0}{(1.15)^5} + \frac{\$0.20}{(1.15)^6} + \frac{\$0.30}{(1.15)^7} + \frac{\$0.40}{(1.15)^8}$$
$$+ \frac{\$0.45}{(1.15)^9} + \frac{\$0.50}{(1.15)^{10}} + \left(\frac{\$0.50(1.10)}{0.15 - 0.10}\right)\left(\frac{1}{(1.15)^{10}}\right)$$
$$= \$3.30$$

The last term finds the expected stock price in Year 10 and then finds the present value of that price. Thus, we see that the discounted dividend model can be applied to firms that currently pay no dividends, provided we can estimate future dividends with a fair degree of confidence. However, in many cases, we can have more confidence in the forecasts of free cash flows; and in these situations, it is better to use the corporate valuation model.

Rather than starting with a forecast of dividends, the corporate valuation model focuses on the firm's future free cash flows. We discussed free cash flow (FCF) in Chapter 3, where we developed the following equation:

$$FCF = \left[EBIT(1 - T) + \frac{Depreciation}{and\ amortizaton} \right] - \left[\frac{Capital}{expenditures} + \frac{\Delta Net}{working\ capital} \right]$$

EBIT is earnings before interest and taxes, and free cash flow represents the cash generated from current operations, less the cash that must be spent on investments in fixed assets and working capital to support future growth. Consider the case of Home Depot (HD). The first term in brackets in the preceding equation represents the amount of cash that HD is generating from its existing stores. The second term represents the amount of cash the company plans to spend this period to construct new stores. To open a new store, HD must spend cash to purchase the land and construct the building—these are the capital expenditures, and they lead to a corresponding increase in the firm's fixed assets as shown on the balance sheet. But HD also needs to increase its working capital, especially inventory. Putting everything together, HD generates positive free cash flow for its investors if and only if the money from its existing stores exceeds the money required to build and equip its new stores.

9-7a The Corporate Valuation Model

In Chapter 3, we explained that a firm's value is determined by its ability to generate cash flow both now and in the future. Therefore, its market value can be expressed as follows:

$$\text{Market value of company} = V_{company} = \text{PV of expected future free cash flows}$$

9-7
$$= \frac{FCF_1}{(1 + WACC)^1} + \frac{FCF_2}{(1 + WACC)^2} + \cdots + \frac{FCF_\infty}{(1 + WACC)^\infty}$$

Here FCF_t is the free cash flow in Year t; and the discount rate, the WACC, is the weighted average cost of all the firm's capital. When thinking about the WACC, note these two points:

1. The firm finances with debt, preferred stock, and common equity. The WACC is the weighted average of these three types of capital, and we discuss it in detail in Chapter 10.

2. Free cash flow is the cash generated *before any payments are made to any investors; so it must be used to compensate common stockholders, preferred stockholders, and bondholders*. Moreover, each type of investor has a required rate of return; and the weighted average of those returns is the WACC, which is used to discount the free cash flows.

Free cash flows are generally forecasted for 5 to 10 years, after which it is assumed that the final explicitly forecasted FCF will grow at some long-run constant rate. Once the company reaches its horizon date, when cash flows begin to grow at a constant rate, we can use the following formula to calculate the market value of the company as of that date:

9-8
$$\text{Horizon value} = V_{\text{Company at } t=N} = FCF_{N+1}/(WACC - g_{FCF})$$

The corporate model is applied internally by the firm's financial staff and by outside security analysts. For illustrative purposes, we discuss an analysis conducted by Susan Buskirk, senior food analyst for the investment banking firm Morton Staley and Company. Her analysis is summarized in Table 9-2, which was reproduced from the chapter *Excel* model.

- Based on Allied's history and Buskirk's knowledge of the firm's business plan, she estimated sales, costs, and cash flows on an annual basis for 5 years. Growth will vary during those years, but she assumes that things will stabilize and growth will be constant after the fifth year. She would have made explicit forecasts for more years if she thought it would take longer to reach a steady-state, constant growth situation.

- Buskirk next calculated the expected free cash flows (FCFs) for each of the 5 nonconstant growth years, and she found the PV of those cash flows discounted at the WACC.

- After Year 5, she assumed that FCF growth would be constant; hence, the constant growth model could be used to find Allied's total market value at Year 5. This "horizon, or terminal, value" is the sum of the PVs of the FCFs from Year 6 on out into the future, discounted back to Year 5 at the WACC. It

Table 9-2			**Allied Food Products: Free Cash Flow Valuation**				

	A	B	C	D	E	F	G	H
133	Part 1. Key Inputs				**Forecasted Years**			
134				2009	2010	2011	2012	2013
135	Sales growth rate			10.0%	9.0%	9.0%	9.0%	8.0%
136	Operating costs as a % of sales			87.0	87.0	86.0	85.0	85.0
137	Growth in operating capital			8.0	8.0	8.0	8.0	8.0
138	Depr'n as a % of operating capital			6.0	8.0	7.0	7.0	7.0
139	Tax rate			40.0				
140	WACC			10.0				
141	Long-run FCF growth, g_{LR}			6.0				
142								
143	Part 2. Forecast of Cash Flows During Period of Nonconstant Growth							
144				Historical		**Forecasted Years**		
145				2008	2009	2010	2011	2012	2013
146								
147	Sales			$3,000.0	$3,300.0	$3,597.0	$3,920.7	$4,273.6	$4,615.5
148	Operating costs			2,616.2	2,871.0	3,129.4	3,371.8	3,632.6	3,923.2
149	Depreciation			100.0	116.6	168.0	158.7	171.4	185.1
150	EBIT			$283.8	$312.4	$299.6	$390.2	$469.6	$507.2
151	EBIT × (1 - T)			$170.3	$187.4	$179.8	$234.1	$281.8	$304.3
152								
153	Total operating capital			$1,800.0	$1,944.0	$2,099.5	$2,267.5	$2,448.9	$2,644.8
154	Net new operating cap			280	144.0	155.5	168.0	181.4	195.9
155	Free Cash Flow, FCF			-$109.7	$43.4	$24.3	$66.1	$100.4	$108.4
156	PV of FCFs			N.A.	$39.5	$20.1	$49.7	$68.6	$67.3

Part 3. Terminal Value and Intrinsic Value Estimation

158	Part 3. Terminal Value and Intrinsic Value Estimation
159	*Estimated Value at the Horizon, 2013*
160	Free Cash Flow (2014)	$114.9
161	Terminal Value at 2013, TV	$2,872.7
162	PV of the 2013 TV	$1,783.7
163	
164	*Calculation of Firm's Intrinsic Value*
165	Sum of PVs of FCFs, 2009-2013	$245.1
166	PV of 2013 TV	1,783.7
167	Total corporate value	$2,028.8
168	Less: market value of debt and pfd	860.0
169	Intrinsic value of common equity	$1,168.8
170	Shares outstanding (millions)	50.0
171	
172	Intrinsic Value Per Share	$23.38

Formulas at right of Part 3:

$$FCF_{2013}(1 + g_{LR})$$

$$TV_{2013} = \frac{FCF_{2014}}{WACC - g}$$

$$TV / (1 + WACC)^N$$

follows that: Horizon Value at $t = 5 = FCF_6/(WACC - g_{FCF})$, where g_{FCF} represents the long-run growth rate of free cash flow.

- Next, she discounted the Year 5 terminal value back to the present to find its PV at Year 0.
- She then summed all the PVs, the annual cash flows during the nonconstant period plus the PV of the horizon value, to find the firm's estimated total market value.
- Then she subtracted the value of the debt and preferred stock to find the value of the common equity.
- Finally, she divided the equity value by the number of shares outstanding, and the result was her estimate of Allied's intrinsic value per share. This value was quite close to the stock's market price, so she concluded that Allied's stock is priced at its equilibrium level. Consequently, she issued a "Hold" recommendation on the stock. If the estimated intrinsic value had been significantly below the market price, she would have issued a "Sell" recommendation; if the estimated intrinsic value had been well above the market price, she would have called the stock a "Buy."

OTHER APPROACHES TO VALUING COMMON STOCKS

While the dividend growth and the corporate valuation models presented in this chapter are the most widely used methods for valuing common stocks, they are by no means the only approaches. Analysts often use a number of different techniques to value stocks. Two of these alternative approaches are described here.

The P/E Multiple Approach

Investors have long looked for simple rules of thumb to determine whether a stock is fairly valued. One such approach is to look at the stock's price-to-earnings (P/E) ratio. Recall from Chapter 4 that a company's P/E ratio shows how much investors are willing to pay for each dollar of reported earnings. As a starting point, you might conclude that stocks with low P/E ratios are undervalued since their price is "low" given current earnings, while stocks with high P/E ratios are overvalued.

Unfortunately, however, valuing stocks is not that simple. We should not expect all companies to have the same P/E ratio. P/E ratios are affected by risk—investors discount the earnings of riskier stocks at a higher rate. Thus, all else equal, riskier stocks should have lower P/E ratios. In addition, when you buy a stock, you have a claim not only on current earnings but also on all future earnings. All else equal, companies with stronger growth opportunities will generate larger future earnings and thus should trade at higher P/E ratios. Therefore, eBay is not necessarily overvalued just because its P/E ratio is 121.2 at a time when the median firm has a P/E of 19.7. Investors believe that eBay's growth potential is well above average. Whether the stock's future prospects justify its P/E ratio remains to be seen; but in and of itself, a high P/E ratio does not mean that a stock is overvalued.

Nevertheless, P/E ratios can provide a useful starting point in stock valuation. If a stock's P/E ratio is well above its industry average and if the stock's growth potential and risk are similar to other firms in the industry, the stock's price may be too high. Likewise, if a company's P/E ratio falls well below its historical average, the stock may be undervalued —particularly if the company's growth prospects and risk are unchanged and if the overall P/E for the market has remained constant or increased.

One obvious drawback of the P/E approach is that it depends on reported accounting earnings. For this reason, some analysts choose to rely on other multiples to value stocks. For example, some analysts look at a company's price-to-cash-flow ratio, while others look at the price-to-sales ratio.

The EVA Approach

In recent years, analysts have looked for more rigorous alternatives to the discounted dividend model. More than a quarter of all stocks listed on the NYSE pay no dividends. This proportion is even higher on Nasdaq. While the discounted dividend model can still be used for these stocks (see "Evaluating Stocks That Don't Pay Dividends"), this approach requires that analysts forecast when the stock will begin paying dividends, what the dividend will be once it is established, and what the future dividend growth rate will be. In many cases, these forecasts contain considerable errors.

An alternative approach is based on the concept of Economic Value Added (EVA), which we discussed in Chapter 4 in "Economic Value Added (EVA) versus Net Income," that can be written as follows:

$$\text{EVA} = (\textbf{Equity capital})(\textbf{ROE} - \textbf{Cost of equity capital})$$

This equation suggests that companies can increase their EVA by investing in projects that provide shareholders with returns that are above their cost of equity capital, which is the return they could expect to earn on alternative investments with the same level of risk. When you purchase stock in a company, you receive more than just the book value of equity—you also receive a claim on all future value that is created by the firm's managers (the present value of all future EVAs). It follows that a company's market value of equity can be written as follows:

$$\textbf{Market value of equity} = \textbf{Book value} + \textbf{PV of all future EVAs}$$

We can find the "fundamental" value of the stock, P_0, by simply dividing the preceding expression by the number of shares outstanding.

As is the case with the discounted dividend model, we can simplify the expression by assuming that at some point in time, annual EVA becomes a perpetuity, or grows at some constant rate over time.[a]

---

[a]What we have presented here is a simplified version of what is often referred to as the Edwards-Bell-Ohlson (EBO) model. For a more complete description of this technique and an excellent summary of how it can be used in practice, read the article "Measuring Wealth," by Charles M. C. Lee, in *CA Magazine,* April 1996, pp. 32–37.

9-7b Comparing the Corporate Valuation and Discounted Dividend Models

Analysts use both the discounted dividend model and the corporate valuation model when valuing mature, dividend-paying firms; and they generally use the corporate model when valuing divisions and firms that do not pay dividends. In principle, we should find the same intrinsic value using either model, but differences are often observed. When a conflict exists, the assumptions embedded in the corporate model can be reexamined; and once the analyst is convinced they are reasonable, the results of that model are used. In our Allied example, the estimates were extremely close—the discounted dividend model predicted a price of $23.06 per share versus $23.38 using the corporate model; both are essentially equal to Allied's actual $23.06 price.

In practice, intrinsic value estimates based on the two models normally deviate from one another and from actual stock prices, leading different analysts to reach different conclusions about the attractiveness of a given stock. The better the analyst, the more often his or her valuations turn out to be correct; but no one can make perfect predictions because too many things can change randomly and unpredictably in the future. Given all this, does it matter whether you use the corporate model or the discounted dividend model to value stocks? We would argue that it does. If we had to value, for example, 100 mature companies whose dividends were expected to grow steadily in the future, we would probably use the discounted dividend model. Here we would estimate only the growth rate in dividends, not the entire set of pro forma financial statements; hence, it would be more feasible to use the dividend model.

However, if we were studying just one company or a few companies, especially companies still in the high-growth stage of their life cycles, we would want to project future financial statements before estimating future dividends. Because we would already have projected future financial statements, we would go ahead and apply the corporate model. Intel, which pays a dividend of $0.56 versus earnings of about $1.17, is an example of a company where either model could be used; but we think the corporate model is better.

Now suppose you were trying to estimate the value of a company such as eBay that, to date (2008), has never paid a dividend or a new firm that is about to go public. In either situation, you would be better off using the corporate valuation model. Actually, even if a company is paying steady dividends, much can be learned from the corporate model; so analysts today use it for all types of valuations. The process of projecting future financial statements can reveal a great deal about a company's operations and financing needs. Also, such an analysis can provide insights into actions that might be taken to increase the company's value; and for this reason, it is integral to the planning and forecasting process, as we discuss in a later chapter.

SELF TEST

Write out the equation for free cash flows and explain it.

Why might someone use the corporate valuation model for companies that have a history of paying dividends?

What steps are taken to find a stock price using the corporate model?

Why might the calculated intrinsic value differ from the stock's current market price? Which would be "correct," and what does "correct" mean?

9-8 PREFERRED STOCK[12]

Preferred stock is a *hybrid*—it is similar to a bond in some respects and to common stock in others. This hybrid nature becomes apparent when we try to classify preferred stock in relation to bonds and common stock. Like bonds, preferred

---

[12]Preferred stock is discussed in more detail in Chapter 20 of *Fundamentals of Financial Management*, 12th ed., (Mason, OH: Cengage Learning, 2010) and in Chapter 20 of Brigham & Daves, *Intermediate Financial Management*, 9th ed., (Mason, OH: Thomson/South-Western, 2007).

stock has a par value and a fixed dividend that must be paid before dividends can be paid on the common stock. However, the directors can omit (or "pass") the preferred dividend without throwing the company into bankruptcy. So although preferred stock calls for a fixed payment like bonds, skipping the payment will not lead to bankruptcy.

As noted earlier, a preferred stock entitles its owners to regular, fixed dividend payments. If the payments last forever, the issue is a *perpetuity* whose value, V_p, is found as follows:

9-9
$$V_p = \frac{D_p}{r_p}$$

V_p is the value of the preferred stock, D_p is the preferred dividend, and r_p is the required rate of return on the preferred. Allied Food has no preferred outstanding, but discussions about such an issue suggested that its preferred should pay a dividend of $10 per year. If its required return was 10.3%, the preferred's value would be $97.09, found as follows:

$$V_p = \frac{\$10.00}{0.103} = \$97.09$$

In equilibrium, the expected return, $\hat{r}_p$, must be equal to the required return, r_p. Thus, if we know the preferred's current price and dividend, we can solve for the expected rate of return as follows:

9-9a
$$\hat{r}_p = \frac{D_p}{V_p}$$

Some preferreds have a stated maturity, often 50 years. Assume that our illustrative preferred matured in 50 years, paid a $10 annual dividend, and had a required return of 8%. We could then find its price as follows: Enter N = 50, I/YR = 8, PMT = 10, and FV = 100. Then press PV to find the price, $V_p = \$124.47$. If r_p rose to 10%, change I/YR to 10, in which case $V_p = PV = \$100$. If you know the price of a share of preferred stock, you can solve for I/YR to find the expected rate of return, $\hat{r}_p$.

SELF TEST

Explain the following statement: Preferred stock is a hybrid security.

Is the equation used to value preferred stock more like the one used to evaluate a bond or the one used to evaluate a "normal" constant growth common stock? Explain.

TYING IT ALL TOGETHER

Corporate decisions should be analyzed in terms of how alternative courses of action are likely to affect a firm's value. However, it is necessary to know how stock prices are established before attempting to measure how a given decision will affect a specific firm's value. This chapter discussed the rights and privileges of common stockholders, showed how stock values are determined, and explained how investors estimate stocks' intrinsic values and expected rates of return.

Two types of stock valuation models were discussed: the discounted dividend model and the corporate valuation model. The discounted dividend model is useful for mature, stable companies. It is easier to use, but the corporate valuation model is more flexible and better for use with companies that do not pay dividends or whose dividends would be especially hard to predict.

We also discussed preferred stock, which is a hybrid security that has some characteristics of a common stock and some of a bond. Preferreds are valued using models similar to those for perpetual and "regular" bonds.

SELF-TEST QUESTIONS AND PROBLEMS
(Solutions Appear in Appendix A)

ST-1   **KEY TERMS**   Define the following terms:

a. Proxy; proxy fight; takeover

b. Preemptive right

c. Classified stock; founders' shares

d. Marginal investor; intrinsic value ($\hat{P}_0$); market price (P_0)

e. Required rate of return, r_s; expected rate of return, $\hat{r}_s$; actual (realized) rate of return, $\bar{r}_s$

f. Capital gains yield; dividend yield; expected total return; growth rate, g

g. Zero growth stock

h. Constant growth (Gordon) model; supernormal (nonconstant) growth

i. Corporate valuation model

j. Terminal (horizon) date; horizon (terminal) value

k. Preferred stock

ST-2   **STOCK GROWTH RATES AND VALUATION**   You are considering buying the stocks of two companies that operate in the same industry. They have very similar characteristics except for their dividend payout policies. Both companies are expected to earn $3 per share this year; but Company D (for "dividend") is expected to pay out all of its earnings as dividends, while Company G (for "growth") is expected to pay out only one-third of its earnings, or $1 per share. D's stock price is $25. G and D are equally risky. Which of the following statements is most likely to be true?

a. Company G will have a faster growth rate than Company D. Therefore, G's stock price should be greater than $25.

b. Although G's growth rate should exceed D's, D's current dividend exceeds that of G, which should cause D's price to exceed G's.

c. A long-term investor in Stock D will get his or her money back faster because D pays out more of its earnings as dividends. Thus, in a sense, D is like a short-term bond and G is like a long-term bond. Therefore, if economic shifts cause r_d and r_s to increase and if the expected dividend streams from D and G remain constant, both Stocks D and G will decline, but D's price should decline further.

d. D's expected and required rate of return is $\hat{r}_s = r_s = 12\%$. G's expected return will be higher because of its higher expected growth rate.

e. If we observe that G's price is also $25, the best estimate of G's growth rate is 8%.

ST-3   **CONSTANT GROWTH STOCK VALUATION**   Fletcher Company's current stock price is $36.00, its last dividend was $2.40, and its required rate of return is 12%. If dividends are expected to grow at a constant rate, g, in the future and if r_s is expected to remain at 12%, what is Fletcher's expected stock price 5 years from now?

ST-4   **NONCONSTANT GROWTH STOCK VALUATION**   Snyder Computers Inc. is experiencing rapid growth. Earnings and dividends are expected to grow at a rate of 15% during the next 2 years, at 13% the following year, and at a constant rate of 6% during Year 4 and thereafter. Its last dividend was $1.15, and its required rate of return is 12%.

a. Calculate the value of the stock today.

b. Calculate $\hat{P}_1$ and $\hat{P}_2$.

c. Calculate the dividend and capital gains yields for Years 1, 2, and 3.

QUESTIONS

9-1 It is frequently stated that the one purpose of the preemptive right is to allow individuals to maintain their proportionate share of the ownership and control of a corporation.

a. How important do you suppose control is for the average stockholder of a firm whose shares are traded on the New York Stock Exchange?

b. Is the control issue likely to be of more importance to stockholders of publicly owned or closely held (private) firms? Explain.

9-2 Is the following equation correct for finding the value of a constant growth stock? Explain.

$$\hat{P}_0 = \frac{D_0}{r_s + g}$$

9-3 If you bought a share of common stock, you would probably expect to receive dividends plus an eventual capital gain. Would the distribution between the dividend yield and the capital gains yield be influenced by the firm's decision to pay more dividends rather than to retain and reinvest more of its earnings? Explain.

9-4 Two investors are evaluating GE's stock for possible purchase. They agree on the expected value of D_1 and on the expected future dividend growth rate. Further, they agree on the riskiness of the stock. However, one investor normally holds stocks for 2 years, while the other holds stocks for 10 years. On the basis of the type of analysis done in this chapter, should they both be willing to pay the same price for GE's stock? Explain.

9-5 A bond that pays interest forever and has no maturity is a perpetual bond. In what respect is a perpetual bond similar to a no-growth common stock? Are there preferred stocks that are evaluated similarly to perpetual bonds and other preferred stocks that are more like bonds with finite lives? Explain.

PROBLEMS

Easy Problems 1–6

9-1 **DPS CALCULATION** Warr Corporation just paid a dividend of $1.50 a share (that is, $D_0 = \$1.50$). The dividend is expected to grow 7% a year for the next 3 years and then at 5% a year thereafter. What is the expected dividend per share for each of the next 5 years?

9-2 **CONSTANT GROWTH VALUATION** Thomas Brothers is expected to pay a $0.50 per share dividend at the end of the year (that is, $D_1 = \$0.50$). The dividend is expected to grow at a constant rate of 7% a year. The required rate of return on the stock, r_s, is 15%. What is the stock's current value per share?

9-3 **CONSTANT GROWTH VALUATION** Harrison Clothiers' stock currently sells for $20.00 a share. It just paid a dividend of $1.00 a share (that is, $D_0 = \$1.00$). The dividend is expected to grow at a constant rate of 6% a year. What stock price is expected 1 year from now? What is the required rate of return?

9-4 **NONCONSTANT GROWTH VALUATION** Hart Enterprises recently paid a dividend, D_0, of $1.25. It expects to have nonconstant growth of 20% for 2 years followed by a constant rate of 5% thereafter. The firm's required return is 10%.

a. How far away is the terminal, or horizon, date?

b. What is the firm's horizon, or terminal, value?

c. What is the firm's intrinsic value today, $\hat{P}_0$?

9-5 **CORPORATE VALUATION** Smith Technologies is expected to generate $150 million in free cash flow next year, and FCF is expected to grow at a constant rate of 5% per year indefinitely. Smith has no debt or preferred stock, and its WACC is 10%. If Smith has 50 million shares of stock outstanding, what is the stock's value per share?

9-6   **PREFERRED STOCK VALUATION**   Fee Founders has perpetual preferred stock outstanding that sells for $60 a share and pays a dividend of $5 at the end of each year. What is the required rate of return?

Intermediate
Problems
7–15

9-7   **PREFERRED STOCK RATE OF RETURN**   What will be the nominal rate of return on a perpetual preferred stock with a $100 par value, a stated dividend of 8% of par, and a current market price of (a) $60, (b) $80, (c) $100, and (d) $140?

9-8   **PREFERRED STOCK VALUATION**   Ezzell Corporation issued perpetual preferred stock with a 10% annual dividend. The stock currently yields 8%, and its par value is $100.
  a.   What is the stock's value?
  b.   Suppose interest rates rise and pull the preferred stock's yield up to 12%. What is its new market value?

9-9   **PREFERRED STOCK RETURNS**   Bruner Aeronautics has perpetual preferred stock outstanding with a par value of $100. The stock pays a quarterly dividend of $2, and its current price is $80.
  a.   What is its nominal annual rate of return?
  b.   What is its effective annual rate of return?

9-10   **VALUATION OF A DECLINING GROWTH STOCK**   Martell Mining Company's ore reserves are being depleted, so its sales are falling. Also, because its pit is getting deeper each year, its costs are rising. As a result, the company's earnings and dividends are declining at the constant rate of 5% per year. If $D_0 = \$5$ and $r_s = 15\%$, what is the value of Martell Mining's stock?

9-11   **VALUATION OF A CONSTANT GROWTH STOCK**   A stock is expected to pay a dividend of $0.50 at the end of the year (that is, $D_1 = 0.50$), and it should continue to grow at a constant rate of 7% a year. If its required return is 12%, what is the stock's expected price 4 years from today?

9-12   **VALUATION OF A CONSTANT GROWTH STOCK**   Investors require a 15% rate of return on Levine Company's stock (that is, $r_s = 15\%$).
  a.   What is its value if the previous dividend was $D_0 = \$2$ and investors expect dividends to grow at a constant annual rate of (1) –5%, (2) 0%, (3) 5%, or (4) 10%?
  b.   Using data from Part a, what would the Gordon (constant growth) model value be if the required rate of return was 15% and the expected growth rate was (1) 15% or (2) 20%? Are these reasonable results? Explain.
  c.   Is it reasonable to think that a constant growth stock could have $g > r_s$? Explain.

9-13   **CONSTANT GROWTH**   You are considering an investment in Keller Corp's stock, which is expected to pay a dividend of $2.00 a share at the end of the year ($D_1 = \$2.00$) and has a beta of 0.9. The risk-free rate is 5.6%, and the market risk premium is 6%. Keller currently sells for $25.00 a share, and its dividend is expected to grow at some constant rate g. Assuming the market is in equilibrium, what does the market believe will be the stock price at the end of 3 years? (That is, what is $\hat{P}_3$?)

9-14   **NONCONSTANT GROWTH**   Microtech Corporation is expanding rapidly and currently needs to retain all of its earnings; hence, it does not pay dividends. However, investors expect Microtech to begin paying dividends, beginning with a dividend of $1.00 coming 3 years from today. The dividend should grow rapidly—at a rate of 50% per year—during Years 4 and 5; but after Year 5, growth should be a constant 8% per year. If the required return on Microtech is 15%, what is the value of the stock today?

9-15   **CORPORATE VALUATION**   Dozier Corporation is a fast-growing supplier of office products. Analysts project the following free cash flows (FCFs) during the next 3 years, after which FCF is expected to grow at a constant 7% rate. Dozier's WACC is 13%.

Year	0	1	2	3
FCF ($ millions)	NA	−$20	$30	$40

  a.   What is Dozier's terminal, or horizon, value? (Hint: Find the value of all free cash flows beyond Year 3 discounted back to Year 3.)
  b.   What is the firm's value today?
  c.   Suppose Dozier has $100 million of debt and 10 million shares of stock outstanding. What is your estimate of the current price per share?

Challenging
Problems
16–21

9-16 **NONCONSTANT GROWTH** Mitts Cosmetics Co.'s stock price is $58.88, and it recently paid a $2.00 dividend. This dividend is expected to grow by 25% for the next 3 years, then grow forever at a constant rate, g; and r_s = 12%. At what constant rate is the stock expected to grow after Year 3?

9-17 **CONSTANT GROWTH** Your broker offers to sell you some shares of Bahnsen & Co. common stock that paid a dividend of $2.00 *yesterday*. Bahnsen's dividend is expected to grow at 5% per year for the next 3 years. If you buy the stock, you plan to hold it for 3 years and then sell it. The appropriate discount rate is 12%.

    a. Find the expected dividend for each of the next 3 years; that is, calculate D_1, D_2, and D_3. Note that D_0 = $2.00.

    b. Given that the first dividend payment will occur 1 year from now, find the present value of the dividend stream; that is, calculate the PVs of D_1, D_2, and D_3 and then sum these PVs.

    c. You expect the price of the stock 3 years from now to be $34.73; that is, you expect $\hat{P}_3$ to equal $34.73. Discounted at a 12% rate, what is the present value of this expected future stock price? In other words, calculate the PV of $34.73.

    d. If you plan to buy the stock, hold it for 3 years, and then sell it for $34.73, what is the most you should pay for it today?

    e. Use Equation 9-2 to calculate the present value of this stock. Assume that g = 5% and that it is constant.

    f. Is the value of this stock dependent upon how long you plan to hold it? In other words, if your planned holding period was 2 years or 5 years rather than 3 years, would this affect the value of the stock today, $\hat{P}_0$? Explain.

9-18 **NONCONSTANT GROWTH STOCK VALUATION** Taussig Technologies Corporation (TTC) has been growing at a rate of 20% per year in recent years. This same growth rate is expected to last for another 2 years, then decline to g_n = 6%.

    a. If D_0 = $1.60 and r_s = 10%, what is TTC's stock worth today? What are its expected dividend and capital gains yields at this time, that is, during Year 1?

    b. Now assume that TTC's period of supernormal growth is to last for 5 years rather than 2 years. How would this affect the price, dividend yield, and capital gains yield? Answer in words only.

    c. What will TTC's dividend and capital gains yields be once its period of supernormal growth ends? (Hint: These values will be the same regardless of whether you examine the case of 2 or 5 years of supernormal growth; the calculations are very easy.)

    d. Of what interest to investors is the changing relationship between dividend and capital gains yields over time?

9-19 **CORPORATE VALUATION** Barrett Industries invests a large sum of money in R&D; as a result, it retains and reinvests all of its earnings. In other words, Barrett does not pay any dividends and it has no plans to pay dividends in the near future. A major pension fund is interested in purchasing Barrett's stock. The pension fund manager has estimated Barrett's free cash flows for the next 4 years as follows: $3 million, $6 million, $10 million, and $15 million. After the fourth year, free cash flow is projected to grow at a constant 7%. Barrett's WACC is 12%, its debt and preferred stock total $60 million, and it has 10 million shares of common stock outstanding.

    a. What is the present value of the free cash flows projected during the next 4 years?

    b. What is the firm's terminal value?

    c. What is the firm's total value today?

    d. What is an estimate of Barrett's price per share?

9-20 **CORPORATE VALUE MODEL** Assume that today is December 31, 2008, and that the following information applies to Vermeil Airlines:

- After-tax operating income [EBIT(1 – T)] for 2009 is expected to be $500 million.

- The depreciation expense for 2009 is expected to be $100 million.

- The capital expenditures for 2009 are expected to be $200 million.

- No change is expected in net working capital.

- The free cash flow is expected to grow at a constant rate of 6% per year.

- The required return on equity is 14%.

- The WACC is 10%.

- The market value of the company's debt is $3 billion.

- 200 million shares of stock are outstanding.

  Using the corporate valuation model approach, what should be the company's stock price today?

9-21 **NONCONSTANT GROWTH** Assume that it is now January 1, 2009. Wayne-Martin Electric Inc. (WME) has developed a solar panel capable of generating 200% more electricity than any other solar panel currently on the market. As a result, WME is expected to experience a 15% annual growth rate for the next 5 years. Other firms will have developed comparable technology at the end of 5 years, and WME's growth rate will slow to 5% per year indefinitely. Stockholders require a return of 12% on WME's stock. The most recent annual dividend (D_0), which was paid yesterday, was $1.75 per share.

a. Calculate WME's expected dividends for 2009, 2010, 2011, 2012, and 2013.

b. Calculate the value of the stock today, $\hat{P}_0$. Proceed by finding the present value of the dividends expected at the end of 2009, 2010, 2011, 2012, and 2013 plus the present value of the stock price that should exist at the end of 2013. The year-end 2013 stock price can be found by using the constant growth equation. Notice that to find the December 31, 2013, price, you must use the dividend expected in 2014, which is 5% greater than the 2013 dividend.

c. Calculate the expected dividend yield (D_1/P_0), capital gains yield, and total return (dividend yield plus capital gains yield) expected for 2009. (Assume that $\hat{P}_0 = P_0$ and recognize that the capital gains yield is equal to the total return minus the dividend yield.) Then calculate these same three yields for 2014.

d. How might an investor's tax situation affect his or her decision to purchase stocks of companies in the early stages of their lives, when they are growing rapidly, versus stocks of older, more mature firms? When does WME's stock become "mature" for purposes of this question?

e. Suppose your boss tells you she believes that WME's annual growth rate will be only 12% during the next 5 years and that the firm's long-run growth rate will be only 4%. Without doing any calculations, what general effect would these growth rate changes have on the price of WME's stock?

f. Suppose your boss also tells you that she regards WME as being quite risky and that she believes the required rate of return should be 14%, not 12%. Without doing any calculations, determine how the higher required rate of return would affect the price of the stock, the capital gains yield, and the dividend yield. Again, assume that the long-run growth rate is 4%.

COMPREHENSIVE/SPREADSHEET PROBLEM

9-22 **NONCONSTANT GROWTH AND CORPORATE VALUATION** Rework Problem 9-18, Parts a, b, and c, using a spreadsheet model. For Part b, calculate the price, dividend yield, and capital gains yield as called for in the problem. After completing Parts a through c, answer the following additional question using the spreadsheet model.

d. TTC recently introduced a new line of products that has been wildly successful. On the basis of this success and anticipated future success, the following free cash flows were projected:

Year	1	2	3	4	5	6	7	8	9	10
FCF	$5.5	$12.1	$23.8	$44.1	$69.0	$88.8	$107.5	$128.9	$147.1	$161.3

After the tenth year, TTC's financial planners anticipate that its free cash flow will grow at a constant rate of 6%. Also, the firm concluded that the new product caused the WACC to fall to 9%. The market value of TTC's debt is $1,200 million, it uses no preferred stock, and there are 20 million shares of common stock outstanding. Use the corporate valuation model approach to value the stock.

INTEGRATED CASE

MUTUAL OF CHICAGO INSURANCE COMPANY

9-23   **STOCK VALUATION**   Robert Balik and Carol Kiefer are senior vice presidents of the Mutual of Chicago Insurance Company. They are codirectors of the company's pension fund management division, with Balik having responsibility for fixed-income securities (primarily bonds) and Kiefer being responsible for equity investments. A major new client, the California League of Cities, has requested that Mutual of Chicago present an investment seminar to the mayors of the represented cities; and Balik and Kiefer, who will make the actual presentation, have asked you to help them.

To illustrate the common stock valuation process, Balik and Kiefer have asked you to analyze the Bon Temps Company, an employment agency that supplies word processor operators and computer programmers to businesses with temporarily heavy workloads. You are to answer the following questions:

a. Describe briefly the legal rights and privileges of common stockholders.

b. (1) Write a formula that can be used to value any stock, regardless of its dividend pattern.

   (2) What is a constant growth stock? How are constant growth stocks valued?

   (3) What are the implications if a company forecasts a constant g that exceeds its r_s? Will many stocks have expected $g > r_s$ in the short run (that is, for the next few years)? in the long run (that is, forever)?

c. Assume that Bon Temps has a beta coefficient of 1.2, that the risk-free rate (the yield on T-bonds) is 7%, and that the required rate of return on the market is 12%. What is Bon Temps's required rate of return?

d. Assume that Bon Temps is a constant growth company whose last dividend (D_0, which was paid yesterday) was $2.00 and whose dividend is expected to grow indefinitely at a 6% rate.

   (1) What is the firm's expected dividend stream over the next 3 years?

   (2) What is its current stock price?

   (3) What is the stock's expected value 1 year from now?

   (4) What are the expected dividend yield, capital gains yield, and total return during the first year?

e. Now assume that the stock is currently selling at $30.29. What is its expected rate of return?

f. What would the stock price be if its dividends were expected to have zero growth?

g. Now assume that Bon Temps is expected to experience nonconstant growth of 30% for the next 3 years, then return to its long-run constant growth rate of 6%. What is the stock's value under these conditions? What are its expected dividend and capital gains yields in Year 1? Year 4?

h. Suppose Bon Temps is expected to experience zero growth during the first 3 years and then resume its steady-state growth of 6% in the fourth year. What would be its value then? What would be its expected dividend and capital gains yields in Year 1? in Year 4?

i. Finally, assume that Bon Temps's earnings and dividends are expected to decline at a constant rate of 6% per year, that is, $g = -6\%$. Why would anyone be willing to buy such a stock, and at what price should it sell? What would be its dividend and capital gains yields in each year?

j. Suppose Bon Temps embarked on an aggressive expansion that requires additional capital. Management decided to finance the expansion by borrowing $40 million and by halting dividend payments to increase retained earnings. Its WACC is now 10%, and the projected free cash flows for the next 3 years are -$5 million, $10 million, and $20 million. After Year 3, free cash flow is projected to grow at a constant 6%. What is Bon Temps's total value? If it has 10 million shares of stock and $40 million of debt and preferred stock combined, what is the price per share?

k. Suppose Bon Temps decided to issue preferred stock that would pay an annual dividend of $5.00 and that the issue price was $50.00 per share. What would be the stock's expected return? Would the expected rate of return be the same if the preferred was a perpetual issue or if it had a 20-year maturity?

THOMSON ONE | Business School Edition

Access the Thomson ONE problems through the CengageNOW™ web site. Use the Thomson ONE—Business School Edition online database to work this chapter's questions.

Estimating ExxonMobil's Intrinsic Stock Value

In this chapter, we described the various factors that influence stock prices and the approaches that analysts use to estimate a stock's intrinsic value. By comparing these intrinsic value estimates to the current price, an investor can assess whether it makes sense to buy or sell a particular stock. Stocks trading at a price far below their estimated intrinsic values may be good candidates for purchase, whereas stocks trading at prices far in excess of their intrinsic value may be good stocks to avoid or sell.

While estimating a stock's intrinsic value is a complex exercise that requires reliable data and good judgment, we can use the data available in Thomson ONE to arrive at a quick "back-of-the-envelope" calculation of intrinsic value.

Discussion Questions

1. For purposes of this exercise, let's take a closer look at the stock of ExxonMobil Corporation (XOM). Looking at the COMPANY ANALYSIS OVERVIEW, we can see the company's current stock price and its performance relative to the overall market in recent months. What is ExxonMobil's current stock price? How has the stock performed relative to the market over the past few months?

2. Click on "NEWS & EVENTS" on the left-hand side of your screen to see the company's recent news stories for the company. Have there been any recent events impacting the company's stock price, or have things been relatively quiet?

3. To provide a starting point for gauging a company's relative valuation, analysts often look at a company's price-to-earnings (P/E) ratio. Return to the COMPANY OVERVIEW page. Here you can see XOM's forward P/E ratio, which uses XOM's next 12-month estimate of earnings in the calculation. To see its current P/E ratio, click on "FINANCIALS" (on the left-hand side of your screen), scroll down to "WORLDSCOPE" (under Financial Ratios on the left-hand side of your screen), and click on "ANNUAL INCOME STATE-MENT RATIOS." The firm's current P/E ratio is shown at the top right of your screen. What is the firm's current P/E ratio?

4. To put XOM's P/E ratio in perspective, it is useful to see how this ratio has varied over time. Scroll down to the Stock Performance section of this screen. The first two lines of this section show the firm's P/E ratio using the end-of-year closing price and the 5-year average over time. Is XOM's current P/E ratio well above or well below its latest 5-year average? Do you have any explanation for why the current P/E deviates from its historical trend? Explain. On the basis of this information, does XOM's current P/E suggest that the stock is undervalued or overvalued? Explain.

5. To put the firm's current P/E ratio in perspective, it is useful to compare this ratio with that of other companies in the same industry. To see how XOM's P/E ratio stacks up to its peers, click on "COMPARABLES" (left-hand side of your screen). Select "KEY FINANCIAL RATIOS." Toward the bottom of the table, you should see information on the P/E ratio in the section titled "Market Value Ratios." For the most part, is XOM's P/E ratio above or below that of its peers? In Chapter 4, we discussed the various factors that may influence P/E ratios. Can any of these factors explain why XOM's P/E ratio differs from its peers? Explain. If you want to compare XOM to a different set of firms, click on "CLICK TO SELECT NEW PEER SET." (This appears toward the top of the screen.)

6. In the text, we discussed using the discounted dividend model to estimate a stock's intrinsic value. To keep things as simple as possible, let's assume at first that XOM's dividend is expected to grow at some constant rate over time. If so, the intrinsic value equals $D_1/(r_s - g)$, where D_1 is the expected annual dividend 1 year from now, r_s is the stock's required rate of return, and g is the dividend's constant growth rate. To estimate the dividend growth rate, it's helpful to look at XOM's dividend history. Go back to the COMPANY OVERVIEW page. Select "FINANCIALS"; and under "FINANCIAL RATIOS," select "WORLDSCOPE" and "ANNUAL INCOME STATEMENT RATIOS." On your screen at the bottom of the Per Share Data section, you should see

the firm's annual dividend over the past several years. On the basis of this information, what has been the average annual dividend growth rate? Another way to obtain estimates of dividend growth rates is to look at analysts' forecasts for future dividends, which can be found under "ESTIMATES" (on the left-hand side of your screen). Near the top of your screen, you should see an area marked "Consensus Estimates." Use the scroll bar to change from EPS estimates to DPS estimates. What is the median year-end dividend forecast? You can use this as an estimate of D_1 in your measure of intrinsic value. Also notice that the last line of this area shows the long-term growth rate. What is the median forecast of the company's long-term growth rate? You can use this as a forecast of the firm's dividend growth rate, g.

7. The required return on equity, r_s, is the final input needed to estimate intrinsic value. For our purposes, you can assume a number (say, 8% or 9%) or you can use the CAPM to calculate an estimate of the cost of equity using the data available in Thomson ONE. (For more details, look at the Thomson ONE exercise for Chapter 8.) Having decided on your best estimates for D_1, r_s, and g, you can calculate XOM's intrinsic value. How does this estimate compare with the current stock price? Does your preliminary analysis suggest that XOM is under-valued or overvalued? Explain.

8. It is often useful to perform a sensitivity analysis, where you show how your estimate of intrinsic value varies according to different estimates of D_1, r_s, and g. To do so, recalculate your intrinsic value estimate for a range of different estimates for each of these key inputs. One convenient way to do this is to set up a simple data table in *Excel*. Refer to the *Excel* tutorial accessed through the CengageNOW™ web site for instructions on data tables. On the basis of this analysis, what inputs justify the current stock price?

9. On the basis of the dividend history you uncovered in Question 6 and your assessment of XOM's future dividend payout policies, do you think it is reasonable to assume that the constant growth model is a good proxy for intrinsic value? If not, how would you use the available data in Thomson ONE to estimate intrinsic value using the nonconstant growth model?

10. Finally, you can also use the information in Thomson ONE to value the entire corporation. This approach requires that you estimate XOM's annual free cash flows. Once you estimate the value of the entire corporation, you subtract the value of debt and preferred stock to arrive at an estimate of the company's equity value. By dividing this number by the number of shares of common stock outstanding, you calculate an alternative estimate of the stock's intrinsic value. While this approach may take additional time and involves more judgment concerning forecasts of future free cash flows, you can use the financial statements and growth forecasts in Thomson ONE as useful starting points. Go to Worldscope's Cash Flow Ratios Report (which you find by clicking on "FINANCIALS, WORLDSCOPE"—under "FINAN-CIAL RATIOS"—and "ANNUAL CASH FLOW RATIOS"). There you will find an estimate of free cash flow per share. While this number is useful, Worldscope's definition of free cash flow subtracts out dividends per share; therefore, to make it comparable to the measure in this text, you must add back dividends. To see Worldscope's definition of free cash flow (or any term), go to the top of your screen and click on "GLOSSARY". In the middle of your screen on the right-hand side, you will see a dialog box with terms. Use the down arrow to scroll through the terms, highlighting the term for which you would like to see a definition. Then click the SELECT button immediately below the dialog box.

APPENDIX 9A

Stock Market Equilibrium

Recall that r_X, the required return on Stock X, can be found using the Security Market Line (SML) equation from the Capital Asset Pricing Model (CAPM) as discussed in Chapter 8:

$$r_X = r_{RF} + (r_M - r_{RF})b_X = r_{RF} + (RP_M)b_X$$

If the risk-free rate is 6%, the market risk premium is 5%, and Stock X has a beta of 2, the marginal investor will require a return of 16% on the stock:

$$r_X = 6\% + (5\%)2.0$$
$$= 16\%$$

This 16% required return is shown as the point on the SML in Figure 9A-1 associated with beta = 2.0.

A marginal investor will purchase Stock X if its expected return is more than 16%, will sell it if the expected return is less than 16%, and will be indifferent (will hold but not buy or sell) if the expected return is exactly 16%. Now suppose the investor's portfolio contains Stock X; he or she analyzes its prospects and concludes that its earnings, dividends, and price can be expected to grow at a constant rate of 5% per year. The last dividend was $D_0 = \$2.8571$, so the next expected dividend is as follows:

$$D_1 = \$2.8571(1.05) = \$3$$

The investor observes that the present price of the stock, P_0, is \$30. Should he or she buy more of Stock X, sell the stock, or maintain the present position?

The investor can calculate Stock X's *expected rate of return* as follows:

$$\hat{r}_X = \frac{D_1}{P_0} + g = \frac{\$3}{\$30} + 5\% = 15\%$$

FIGURE 9A-1	Expected and Required Returns on Stock X

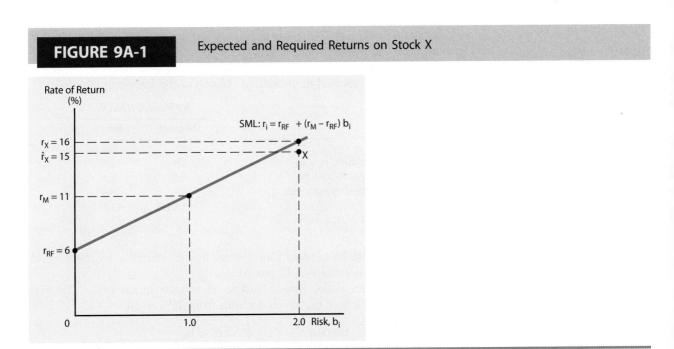

This value is plotted on Figure 9A-1 as Point X, which is below the SML. Because the expected rate of return is less than the required return, he or she (and many other investors) would want to sell the stock. However, few people would want to buy at the $30 price; so the present owners would be unable to find buyers unless they cut the price of the stock. Thus, the price would decline, and the decline would continue until the price hit $27.27. At that point, the stock would be in **equilibrium**, defined as the price at which the expected rate of return, 16%, is equal to the required rate of return:

Equilibrium
The condition under which the expected return on a security is just equal to its required return, $\hat{r} = r$. Also, $\hat{P}_0 = P_0$, and the price is stable.

$$\hat{r}_x = \frac{\$3.00}{\$27.27} + 5\% = 11\% + 5\% = 16\% = r_x$$

Had the stock initially sold for less than $27.27 (say, $25), events would have been reversed. Investors would have wanted to purchase the stock because its expected rate of return would have exceeded its required rate of return, buy orders would have come in, and the stock's price would have been driven up to $27.27.

To summarize, in equilibrium, two related conditions must hold:

1. A stock's expected rate of return as seen by the marginal investor must equal its required rate of return: $\hat{r}_i = r_i$.
2. The actual market price of the stock must equal its intrinsic value as estimated by the marginal investor: $P_0 = \hat{P}_0$.

Of course, some individual investors may believe that $\hat{r}_i > r_i$ and $\hat{P}_0 > P_0$ (hence, they would invest most of their funds in the stock), while other investors might have an opposite view and sell all of their shares. However, investors at the margin establish the actual market price; and for these investors, we must have $\hat{r}_i = r_i$ and $\hat{P}_0 = P_0$. If these conditions do not hold, trading will occur until they do.

9A-1 CHANGES IN EQUILIBRIUM STOCK PRICES

Stock prices are not constant—they undergo violent changes at times. For example, on October 27, 1997, the Dow Jones Industrials fell 554 points, a 7.18% drop in value. Even worse, on October 19, 1987, the Dow lost 508 points, causing an average stock to lose 23% of its value on that one day, and some individual stocks lost more than 70%. To see what could cause such changes to occur, assume that Stock X is in equilibrium, selling at a price of $27.27 per share. If all expectations were met exactly, during the next year the price would gradually rise to $28.63, or by 5%. However, suppose conditions changed as indicated in the second column of the following table:

	VARIABLE VALUE	
	Original	**New**
Risk-free rate, r_{RF}	6%	5%
Market risk premium, $r_M - r_{RF}$	5%	4%
Stock X's beta coefficient, b_X	2.0	1.25
Stock X's expected growth rate, g_X	5%	6%
D_0	$2.8571	$2.8571
Price of Stock X	$27.27	?

Now give yourself a test: How would the change in each variable, by itself, affect the price; and what new price would result?

Every change, taken alone, would lead to an *increase* in the price. The first three changes together lower r_X, which declines from 16% to 10%:

$$\text{Original } r_x = 6\% + 5\%(2.0) = 16\%$$
$$\text{New } r_x = 5\% + 4\%(1.25) = 10\%$$

Using these values, together with the new g, we find that $\hat{P}_0$ rises from $27.27 to $75.71, or by 178%:[1]

$$\text{Original } \hat{P}_0 = \frac{\$2.8571(1.05)}{0.16 - 0.05} = \frac{\$3.00}{0.11} = \$27.27$$

$$\text{New } \hat{P}_0 = \frac{\$2.8571(1.06)}{0.10 - 0.06} = \frac{\$3.0285}{0.04} = \$75.71$$

Note too that at the new price, the expected and required rates of return will be equal:[2]

$$\hat{r}_x = \frac{\$3.0285}{\$75.71} + 6\% = 10\% = r_x$$

Evidence suggests that stocks, especially those of large companies, adjust rapidly when their fundamental positions change. Such stocks are followed closely by a number of security analysts; so as soon as things change, so does the stock price. Consequently, equilibrium ordinarily exists for any given stock, and required and expected returns are generally close to equal. Stock prices certainly change, sometimes violently and rapidly; but this simply reflects changing conditions and expectations. There are, of course, times when a stock will continue to react for several months to unfolding favorable or unfavorable developments. However, this does not signify a long adjustment period; rather, it simply indicates that as more new information about the situation becomes available, the market adjusts to it.

QUESTIONS

9A-1   For a stock to be in equilibrium, what two conditions must hold?

9A-2   If a stock is not in equilibrium, explain how financial markets adjust to bring it into equilibrium.

PROBLEMS

9A-1   **RATES OF RETURN AND EQUILIBRIUM**   Stock C's beta coefficient is $b_C = 0.4$, while Stock D's is $b_D = -0.5$. (Stock D's beta is negative, indicating that its return rises when returns on most other stocks fall. There are very few negative beta stocks, although collection agency stocks are sometimes cited as an example.)

a.   If the risk-free rate is 7% and the expected rate of return on an average stock is 11%, what are the required rates of return on Stocks C and D?

b.   For Stock C, suppose the current price, P_0, is $25.00; the next expected dividend, D_1, is $1.50; and the stock's expected constant growth rate is 4%. Is the stock in equilibrium? Explain and describe what will happen if the stock is not in equilibrium.

---

[1]A price change of this magnitude is by no means rare. The prices of *many* stocks double or halve during a year. For example, during 2007, Amazon.com, a large online retailer of books, music, and videos, increased in value by 134.8%. On the other hand, E*Trade Financial, a discount brokerage firm, fell in value by 84.2%.

[2]It should be obvious by now that *actual realized* rates of return are not necessarily equal to expected and required returns. Thus, an investor might have expected to receive a return of 15% if he or she had bought Amazon.com or E*Trade Financial stock in 2007; but after the fact, the realized return on Amazon.com was far above 15%, whereas the return on E*Trade Financial was far below.

9A-2   **EQUILIBRIUM STOCK PRICE**   The risk-free rate of return, r_{RF}, is 6%; the required rate of return on the market, r_M, is 10%; and Upton Company's stock has a beta coefficient of 1.5.

    a.   If the dividend expected during the coming year, D_1, is $2.25 and if $g =$ a constant 5%, at what price should Upton's stock sell?

    b.   Now suppose the Federal Reserve Board increases the money supply, causing the risk-free rate to drop to 5% and r_M to fall to 9%. What would happen to Upton's price?

    c.   In addition to the change in Part b, suppose investors' risk aversion declines and this, combined with the decline in r_{RF}, causes r_M to fall to 8%. Now what is Upton's price?

    d.   Suppose Upton has a change in management. The new group institutes policies that increase the expected constant growth rate from 5% to 6%. Also, the new management smoothes out fluctuations in sales and profits, causing beta to decline from 1.5 to 1.3. Assume that r_{RF} and r_M are equal to the values in Part c. After all these changes, what is its new equilibrium price? (Note: D_1 is now $2.27.)

9A-3   **BETA COEFFICIENTS**   Suppose Chance Chemical Company's management conducted a study and concluded that if it expands its consumer products division (which is less risky than its primary business, industrial chemicals), its beta will decline from 1.2 to 0.9. However, consumer products have a somewhat lower profit margin, and this would cause its constant growth rate in earnings and dividends to fall from 6% to 4%. The following also apply: $r_M = 9\%$, $r_{RF} = 6\%$, and $D_0 = \$2.00$.

    a.   Should management expand the consumer products division? Explain.

    b.   Assume all the facts given except the change in the beta coefficient. How low would the beta have to fall to cause the expansion to be a good one? (Hint: Set $\hat{P}_0$ under the new policy equal to $\hat{P}_0$ under the old one and find the new beta that will produce this equality.)

PART 4

INVESTING IN LONG-TERM ASSETS: CAPITAL BUDGETING

© STAN HONDA/AFP/GETTY IMAGES

General Electric

CHAPTER
10 The Cost of Capital

Creating Value at GE

General Electric (GE) is one of the world's best-managed companies, and it has rewarded its shareholders with outstanding returns. GE creates shareholder value by investing in assets that earn more than the cost of the capital used to acquire them. For example, if a project earns 20% but the capital invested in it costs only 10%, taking on the project will increase the firm's value and thus its stock price.

Capital is obtained in three primary forms: debt, preferred stock, and common equity, with equity acquired by retaining earnings and by the issuance of new stock. The investors who provide capital to GE expect to earn at least their required rate of return on that capital, and the required return represents the firm's cost of capital.[1] A variety of factors influence the cost of capital. Some—including interest rates, state

and federal tax policies, and general economic conditions—are outside the firm's control. However, the firm's decisions regarding how it raises capital and how it invests those funds also have a profound effect on its cost of capital.

Estimating the cost of capital for a company such as GE is conceptually straightforward. GE's capital comes largely from debt plus common equity obtained by retaining earnings, so its cost of capital depends largely on the level of interest rates in the economy and the marginal stockholder's required rate of return on equity. However, GE operates many different divisions throughout the world; so the corporation is similar to a portfolio that contains a number of different stocks, each with a different risk. Recall that portfolio risk is a weighted average of the relevant risks of the different stocks in the portfolio.

---

[1]Recall from earlier chapters that expected and required returns as seen by the marginal investor must be equal; otherwise, the security will not be in equilibrium. Therefore, buying and selling will force this equality to hold, except for short periods immediately following the release of new information. Since expected and required returns are normally equal, we use the two terms interchangeably.

Similarly, each of GE's divisions has its own level of risk (hence, its own cost of capital). GE's overall cost of capital is an average of its divisions' costs. For example, GE's NBC subsidiary probably has a different cost of capital than its aircraft engine division; and even within divisions, some projects are riskier than others. Moreover, overseas projects may have different risks and thus different costs of capital than similar domestic projects.

As we will see in this chapter, the cost of capital is an essential element in the capital budgeting process. This process is the primary determinant of the firm's long-run stock price.

PUTTING THINGS IN PERSPECTIVE

In the last four chapters, we explained how risk influences prices and required rates of return on bonds and stocks. A firm's primary objective is to maximize its shareholders' value. The principal way value is increased is by investing in projects that earn more than their cost of capital. In the next two chapters, we will see that a project's future cash flows can be forecasted and that those cash flows can be discounted to find their present value. Then if the PV of the future cash flows exceeds the project's cost, the firm's value will increase if the project is accepted. However, we need a discount rate to find the PV of the future cash flows, and that discount rate is the firm's cost of capital. Finding the cost of the capital required to take on new projects is the primary focus of this chapter.[2]

Most formulas used in this chapter were developed earlier, when we examined the required rates of return on bonds and stocks. *Indeed, the rates of return that investors require on bonds and stocks represent the costs of those securities to the firm.* As we shall see, companies estimate the required returns on their securities, calculate a weighted average of the costs of their different types of capital, and use this average cost for capital budgeting purposes.

When you finish this chapter, you should be able to:

- Explain why the weighted average cost of capital (WACC) is used in capital budgeting.
- Estimate the costs of different capital components—debt, preferred stock, retained earnings, and common stock.
- Combine the different component costs to determine the firm's WACC.

These concepts are necessary to understand the firm's capital budgeting process.

10-1 AN OVERVIEW OF THE WEIGHTED AVERAGE COST OF CAPITAL (WACC)

Table 10-1 shows Allied Food Products' balance sheet as presented in Chapter 3, with two additions: (1) the actual capital supplied by investors (banks, bondholders, and stockholders) and (2) the capital structure that Allied plans to use in the future. Allied's overall cost of capital is an average of the costs of the various types of capital it uses. Allied's debt costs 10%, it currently uses no preferred stock

---

[2]If projects differ in risk, risk-adjusted costs of capital should be used, not one single corporate cost of capital. We discuss this point later in the chapter.

Table 10-1	Allied Food Products: Capital Structure Used to Calculate the WACC					

REGULAR BALANCE SHEET: at 12/31/08			All Liabilities & Equity		Actual Investor-Supplied Capital		Target Capital Structure
Cash	$ 10	Accounts payable	$ 60	3.0%			
Receivables	375	Accruals	140	7.0			
Inventories	615	Spontaneous debt	$ 200	10.0%			
Total C.A.	$1,000	Notes payable	110	5.5	$ 110		
		Total C.L.	$ 310	15.5%			
Net fixed assets	$1,000	Long-term debt	750	37.5	750		
		Total debt	$1,060	53.0%	$ 860	47.8%	45.0%
		Preferred stock	0	0.0	0	0.0	2.0
		Common stock	130	6.5	130		
		Retained earnings	810	40.5	810		
		Total equity	$ 940	47.0%	$ 940	52.2	53.0
Total	$2,000	Total	$2,000	100.0%	$1,800	100.0%	100.0%

but plans to use a small amount of preferred in the future, and its common equity costs about 13.5%. (This is the return that stockholders require on the stock.)[3] Now assume that Allied has made the decision to finance all of next year's projects with debt. The argument is sometimes made that the cost of capital for next year's projects will be 10% because only debt will be used to finance them. However, this position is incorrect. If Allied finances this set of projects with debt, it will be using up some of its future borrowing capacity. As expansion occurs in subsequent years, the firm will at some point have to raise more equity to prevent the debt ratio from getting too high.

Our concern is with capital that must be provided by *investors*—interest-bearing debt, preferred stock, and common equity. Accounts payable and accruals increase automatically when capital budgeting projects are taken on, so increases in these items are deducted from projects' costs. This point is discussed in detail in Chapter 12, but the result is that we are concerned only with investor-supplied capital when we calculate the cost of capital.

To illustrate, suppose Allied borrows heavily at 10% during 2009 and, in the process, uses up its capacity to borrow, to finance projects yielding 11%. In 2010, it has new projects available that yield 13% (well above the return on 2009 projects), but it could not accept them because they would have to be financed with 13.5% equity. *To avoid this problem, Allied and other firms take a long-run view; and the cost of capital is calculated as a weighted average, or composite, of the various types of funds used over time, regardless of the specific financing used in a given year.*

We explore the weights in more detail in the capital structure chapter, where we see how the optimal capital structure is estimated. As we will see, there is an optimal capital structure—one where the percentages of debt, preferred stock, and common equity maximize the firm's value. As shown in the last column of Table 10-1, Allied Foods has concluded that it should use 45% debt, 2% preferred stock, and 53% common equity; and it plans to raise capital in those proportions in

---

[3] We estimate this 13.5% later in the chapter. It differs slightly from the number we found in an earlier chapter. As you will see, there are several ways to estimate r_s and those methods generally produce different estimates. Allied concluded that its r_s is somewhere in the range of 13% to 14%, and it compromised by using 13.5%. The costs of debt and preferred stock are set by contract, so they can be estimated with relatively little error; but the cost of equity cannot be measured precisely.

the future. Therefore, we use those target weights when we calculate Allied's weighted average cost of capital.

Why should the cost of capital be calculated as a weighted average of the various types of funds that a firm generally uses, not as the cost of the specific type of capital used during a given year?

What is the riskiest and thus highest-cost type of capital? least-cost type?

Why can't a firm finance with only the lowest-cost type of capital?

10-2 BASIC DEFINITIONS

The investor-supplied items—debt, preferred stock, and common equity—are called **capital components**. Increases in assets must be financed by increases in these capital components. The cost of each component is called its *component cost;* for example, Allied can borrow money at 10%, so its component cost of debt is 10%.[4] These costs are then combined to form a weighted average cost of capital, which is used in the capital budgeting process. Throughout this chapter, we concentrate on the three major capital components. The following symbols identify the cost and weight of each:

Capital Component
One of the types of capital used by firms to raise funds.

r_d = interest rate on the firm's new debt = before-tax component cost of debt. It can be found in several ways, including calculating the yield to maturity on the firm's currently outstanding bonds.

$r_d(1 - T)$ = after-tax component cost of debt, where T is the firm's marginal tax rate. $r_d(1 - T)$ *is the debt cost used to calculate the weighted average cost of capital.* As we shall see, the after-tax cost of debt is lower than its before-tax cost because interest is tax deductible.

r_p = component cost of preferred stock, found as the yield investors expect to earn on the preferred stock. Preferred dividends are not tax-deductible; hence, the before- and after-tax costs of preferred are equal.

r_s = component cost of common equity raised by retaining earnings, or *internal equity.* It is the r_s developed in Chapters 8 and 9 and defined there as the rate of return that investors require on a firm's common stock. Most firms, once they have become well established, obtain all of their new equity as retained earnings; hence, r_s is their cost of all new equity.

r_e = component cost of *external equity,* or common equity raised by issuing new stock. As we will see, r_e is equal to r_s plus a factor that reflects the cost of issuing new stock. Note, though, that established firms such as Allied Foods rarely issue new stock; hence, r_e is rarely a relevant consideration except for very young, rapidly growing firms.

---

[4]We will see shortly that there is a before-tax and an after-tax cost of debt; for now, it is sufficient to know that 10% is the before-tax component cost of debt. Also, for simplicity, we assume that long- and short-term debt have the same cost; hence, we deal with just one type of debt.

$w_d, w_p, w_s, w_e =$ target weights of debt, preferred stock, retained earnings (internal equity), and new common stock (external equity). The weights are the percentages of the different types of capital the firm plans to use when it raises capital in the future. Target weights may differ from actual current weights.[5]

WACC = the firm's weighted average, or overall, cost of capital.

Weighted Average Cost of Capital (WACC)
A weighted average of the component costs of debt, preferred stock, and common equity.

The target proportions of debt (w_d), preferred stock (w_p), and common equity (w_c), along with the costs of those components, are used to calculate the firm's **weighted average cost of capital, WACC**. We assume at this point that all new common equity is raised as retained earnings, as is true for most companies; hence, the cost of common equity is r_s.

$$\text{WACC} = \begin{pmatrix} \% \\ \text{of} \\ \text{debt} \end{pmatrix}\begin{pmatrix} \text{After-tax} \\ \text{cost of} \\ \text{debt} \end{pmatrix} + \begin{pmatrix} \% \text{ of} \\ \text{preferred} \\ \text{stock} \end{pmatrix}\begin{pmatrix} \text{Cost of} \\ \text{preferred} \\ \text{stock} \end{pmatrix} + \begin{pmatrix} \% \text{ of} \\ \text{common} \\ \text{equity} \end{pmatrix}\begin{pmatrix} \text{Cost of} \\ \text{common} \\ \text{equity} \end{pmatrix}$$

10-1

$$= \quad w_d r_d(1 - T) \quad + \quad w_p r_p \quad + \quad w_c r_s$$

Note that only debt has a tax adjustment factor, $(1 - T)$. As discussed in the next section, this is because interest on debt is tax-deductible but preferred dividends and the returns on common stock (dividends and capital gains) are not.

These definitions and concepts are discussed in the remainder of the chapter, using Allied Foods for illustrative purposes. Later in the capital structure chapter, we extend the discussion to show how the optimal mix of securities minimizes the firm's cost of capital and maximizes its value.

SELF TEST

Identify the firm's three major capital structure components and give their respective component cost and weight symbols.

Why might there be two different component costs for common equity? Which one is generally relevant, and for what type of firm is the second one likely to be relevant?

If a firm now has a debt ratio of 50% but plans to finance with only 40% debt in the future, what should it use as w_d when it calculates its WACC?

10-3 COST OF DEBT, $r_d(1 - T)$

Before-Tax Cost of Debt, r_d
The interest rate the firm must pay on new debt.

The interest rate a firm must pay on its *new* debt is defined as its **before-tax cost of debt, r_d**. Firms can estimate r_d by asking their bankers what it will cost to borrow or by finding the yield to maturity (or yield to call if the debt is likely to be

---

[5]We should also note that the weights could be based on the book values of the capital components or on their market values. The market value of the equity is found by multiplying the stock's price by the number of shares outstanding. Market value weights are theoretically superior; but accountants show assets on a book-value basis, bond rating agencies and security analysts generally focus on book values, and market value weights are quite unstable because stock prices fluctuate widely. If a firm's book and market values differ widely, the firm may set its *target* weights as a blend of book and market weights. We will discuss this at greater length in the capital structure chapter; but for now, just take the target weights provided in this chapter as management determined.

called) on their currently outstanding debt (see Chapter 7).[6] *However, the* **after-tax cost of debt, $r_d(1 - T)$,** *should be used to calculate the weighted average cost of capital.* This is the interest rate on new debt, r_d, less the tax savings that result because interest is tax deductible:[7]

After-Tax Cost of Debt, $r_d(1 - T)$
The relevant cost of new debt, taking into account the tax deductibility of interest; used to calculate the WACC.

$$\text{After-tax cost of debt} = \text{Interest rate on new debt} - \text{Tax savings}$$
$$= r_d - r_d T$$
$$= r_d(1 - T) \qquad \text{10-2}$$

In effect, the government pays part of the cost of debt because interest is tax deductible. Therefore, if Allied can borrow at an interest rate of 10% and its marginal federal-plus-state tax rate is 40%, its after-tax cost of debt will be 6%:[8]

$$\text{After-tax cost of debt} = r_d(1 - T) = 10\%(1.0 - 0.4)$$
$$= 10\%(0.6)$$
$$= 6.0\%$$

We use the after-tax cost of debt in calculating the WACC because we are interested in maximizing the value of the firm's stock, and the stock price depends on *after-tax* cash flows. Because we are concerned with after-tax cash flows and because cash flows and rates of return should be calculated on a comparable basis, we adjust the interest rate downward due to debt's preferential tax treatment.

Note that the cost of debt is the interest rate on *new* debt, not on already outstanding debt. We are interested in the cost of new debt because our primary concern with the cost of capital is its use in capital budgeting decisions. For example, would a new machine earn a return greater than the cost of the capital needed to acquire the machine? The rate at which the firm has borrowed in the past is irrelevant when answering this question because we need to know the cost of *new capital.*[9]

SELF TEST

Why is the after-tax cost of debt rather than the before-tax cost used to calculate the WACC?

Why is the relevant cost of debt the interest rate on *new* debt, not that on already outstanding, or *old*, debt?

How can the yield to maturity on a firm's outstanding debt be used to estimate its before-tax cost of debt?

---

[6]If the yield curve is sharply upward- or downward-sloping, the costs of long- and short-term debt will differ. In this case, the firm should calculate an average of its debt costs based on the proportions of long- and short-term debt that it plans to use.

[7]If Allied borrowed $100,000 at 10%, it would have to write a check for $10,000 to pay interest charges for a year. However, that $10,000 would be a tax deduction, which at a 40% tax rate would save $4,000 in taxes.

[8]Note that in 2008, the federal tax rate for most large corporations is 35%. However, most corporations are also subject to state income taxes; so for illustrative purposes, we assume that the effective federal-plus-state tax rate on marginal income is 40%.

[9]Three additional points should also be noted: (1) The tax rate is *zero* for a firm with losses. Therefore, for a company that does not pay taxes, the cost of debt is not reduced. That is, in Equation 10-2, the tax rate equals zero; so the after-tax cost of debt is equal to the interest rate. (2) Strictly speaking, the after-tax cost of debt should reflect the *expected* cost of debt, which is very slightly below the promised 10% yield. (3) Allied raises most of its debt from commercial banks and sells bonds directly to financial institutions; but if it sold new bonds through investment bankers, a flotation cost would be incurred. We can adjust for flotation costs by deducting the dollar flotation costs from the issue price (par value) of the bond and calculating an adjusted YTM. If the bonds had a flotation cost of 0.5% (or $5 per $1,000 bond), an annual interest rate of 10%, and a 20-year maturity, the calculated YTM would be 10.06% versus 10.00% with no flotation costs. Because the difference is so small, most firms ignore bond flotation costs.

A company has outstanding 20-year non-callable bonds with a face value of $1,000, an 11% annual coupon, and a market price of $1,294.54. If the company was to issue new debt, what would be a reasonable estimate of the interest rate on that debt? If the company's tax rate is 40%, what is its after-tax cost of debt? **(8.0%; 4.8%)**

10-4 COST OF PREFERRED STOCK, r_p

Cost of Preferred Stock, r_p
The rate of return investors require on the firm's preferred stock. r_p is calculated as the preferred dividend, D_p, divided by the current price, P_p.

The component **cost of preferred stock** used to calculate the weighted average cost of capital, r_p, is the preferred dividend, D_p, divided by the current price of the preferred stock, P_p.

10-3
$$\text{Component cost of preferred stock} = r_p = \frac{D_p}{P_p}$$

Allied does not have any preferred stock outstanding, but the company plans to issue some in the future and therefore has included it in its target capital structure. Allied would sell this stock to a few large hedge funds, the stock would have a $10.00 dividend per share, and it would be priced at $97.50 a share. Therefore, Allied's cost of preferred stock would be 10.3%:[10]

$$r_p = \$10.00/\$97.50 = 10.3\%$$

As we can see from Equation 10-3, calculating the cost of preferred stock is easy. This is particularly true for traditional "plain vanilla" preferred that pays a fixed dividend in perpetuity. However, in Chapter 9, we noted that some preferred issues have a specified maturity date and we described how to calculate the expected return on these issues. Also, preferred stock may include an option to convert to common stock, which adds another layer of complexity. We leave these more complicated situations for advanced classes. Finally, note that no tax adjustments are made when calculating r_p because preferred dividends, unlike interest on debt, are *not* tax deductible; so no tax savings are associated with preferred stock.

SELF TEST

Is a tax adjustment made to the cost of preferred stock? Why or why not?

A company's preferred stock currently trades at $80 per share and pays a $6 annual dividend per share. Ignoring flotation costs, what is the firm's cost of preferred stock? **(7.50%)**

10-5 THE COST OF RETAINED EARNINGS, r_s

The costs of debt and preferred stock are based on the returns that investors require on these securities. Similarly, the cost of common equity is based on the rate of return that investors require on the company's common stock. Note, though, that new common equity is raised in two ways: (1) by retaining some of

---

[10]This preferred stock would be sold directly to a group of hedge funds, so no flotation costs would be incurred. If significant flotation costs were involved, the cost of the preferred should be adjusted upward, as we explain in a later section.

the current year's earnings and (2) by issuing new common stock.[11] We use the symbol r_s to designate the **cost of retained earnings** and r_e to designate the **cost of new common stock**, or external equity. Equity raised by issuing stock has a higher cost than equity from retained earnings due to the flotation costs required to sell new common stock. Therefore, once firms get beyond the startup stage, they normally obtain all of their new equity by retaining earnings.

Some have argued that retained earnings should be "free" because they represent money that is "left over" after dividends are paid. While it is true that no direct costs are associated with retained earnings, this capital still has a cost, an *opportunity cost*. The firm's after-tax earnings belong to its stockholders. Bondholders are compensated by interest payments; preferred stockholders, by preferred dividends. But the net earnings remaining after interest and preferred dividends belong to the common stockholders, and these earnings serve to compensate them for the use of their capital. The managers, who work for the stockholders, can either pay out earnings in the form of dividends or retain earnings for reinvestment in the business. When managers make this decision, they should recognize that there is an opportunity cost involved—stockholders could have received the earnings as dividends and invested this money in other stocks, in bonds, in real estate, or in anything else. *Therefore, the firm needs to earn at least as much on any earnings retained as the stockholders could earn on alternative investments of comparable risk.*

What rate of return can stockholders expect to earn on equivalent-risk investments? First, recall from Chapter 9 that stocks are normally in equilibrium, with expected and required rates of return being equal: $\hat{r}_s = r_s$. Thus, Allied's stockholders expect to be able to earn r_s on their money. *Therefore, if the firm cannot invest retained earnings to earn at least r_s, it should pay those funds to its stockholders and let them invest directly in stocks or other assets that will provide that return.*

Whereas debt and preferred stocks are contractual obligations whose costs are clearly stated on the contracts, stocks have no comparable stated cost rate. That makes it difficult to measure r_s. However, we can employ the techniques developed in Chapters 8 and 9 to produce reasonably good estimates of the cost of equity from retained earnings. To begin, recall that if a stock is in equilibrium, its *required rate of return, r_s,* must be equal to its *expected rate of return, $\hat{r}_s$.* Further, its *required return* is equal to a risk-free rate, r_{RF}, plus a risk premium, RP, whereas the expected return on the stock is its dividend yield, D_1/P_0, plus its expected growth rate, g. Thus, we can write the following equation and estimate r_s using the left term, the right term, or both terms:

$$\text{Required rate of return} = \text{Expected rate of return}$$
$$r_s = r_{RF} + RP = \hat{D}_1/P_0 + g = \hat{r}_s \qquad \text{10-4}$$

The left term is based on the Capital Asset Pricing Model (CAPM) as discussed in Chapter 8, and the right term is based on the discounted dividend model as developed in Chapter 9. We discuss these two procedures, in addition to one based on the firm's own cost of debt, in the following sections.

Cost of Retained Earnings, r_s
The rate of return required by stockholders on a firm's common stock.

Cost of New Common Stock, r_e
The cost of external equity based on the cost of retained earnings but increased for flotation costs.

[11]The term *retained earnings* can be interpreted to mean the balance sheet item *retained earnings,* consisting of all the earnings retained in the business throughout its history or the income statement item *addition to retained earnings.* The income statement item is relevant in this chapter; for our purpose, *retained earnings* refers to that part of the current year's earnings not paid as dividends (hence, available for reinvestment in the business this year). If this is not clear, look back at Allied's balance sheet shown in Table 3-1 and note that at the end of 2007, Allied had $750 million of retained earnings; but that figure rose to $810 million by the end of 2008. Then look at the 2008 income statement, where you will see that Allied retained $60 million of its 2008 income. This $60 million was the new equity from retained earnings that was used, along with some additional debt, to fund the 2008 capital budgeting projects. Also, you can see from the 2007 and 2008 balance sheets that Allied had $130 million of common stock at the end of both years. This indicates that it did not sell any new common stock to raise capital during 2008.

10-5a The CAPM Approach

The most widely used method for estimating the cost of common equity is the Capital Asset Pricing Model (CAPM) as developed in Chapter 8.[12] Here are the steps used to find r_s:

Step 1: Estimate the risk-free rate, r_{RF}. We generally use the 10-year Treasury bond rate as the measure of the risk-free rate, but some analysts use the short-term Treasury bill rate.

Step 2: Estimate the stock's beta coefficient, b_i, and use it as an index of the stock's risk. The i signifies the ith company's beta.

Step 3: Estimate the expected market risk premium. Recall that the market risk premium is the difference between the return that investors require on an average stock and the risk-free rate.[13]

Step 4: Substitute the preceding values in the CAPM equation to estimate the required rate of return on the stock in question:

10-5

$$r_s = r_{RF} + (RP_M)b_i$$
$$= r_{RF} + (r_M - r_{RF})b_i$$

Thus, the CAPM estimate of r_s is equal to the risk-free rate, r_{RF}, plus a risk premium that is equal to the risk premium on an average stock, $(r_M - r_{RF})$, scaled up or down to reflect the particular stock's risk as measured by its beta coefficient.

Assume that in today's market, $r_{RF} = 5.6\%$, the market risk premium is $RP_M = 5.0\%$, and Allied's beta is 1.48. Using the CAPM approach, Allied's cost of equity is estimated to be 13.0%:

$$r_s = 5.6\% + (5.0\%)(1.48)$$
$$= 13.0\%$$

Although the CAPM appears to produce an accurate, precise estimate of r_s, several potential problems exist. First, as we saw in Chapter 8, if a firm's stockholders are not well diversified, they may be concerned with *stand-alone risk* rather than just market risk. In that case, the firm's true investment risk would not be measured by its beta and the CAPM estimate would understate the correct value of r_s. Further, even if the CAPM theory is valid, it is hard to obtain accurate estimates of the required inputs because (1) there is controversy about whether to use long-term or short-term Treasury yields for r_{RF}, (2) it is hard to estimate the beta that investors expect the company to have in the future, and (3) it is difficult to estimate the proper market risk premium. As we indicated earlier, the CAPM approach is used most often; but because of the just-noted problems, analysts also estimate the cost of equity using the other approaches discussed in the following sections.

---

[12]A recent survey by John Graham and Campbell Harvey indicates that the CAPM approach is most often used to estimate the cost of equity. More than 70% of the surveyed firms used the CAPM approach. In some cases, they used beta from the CAPM as one determinant of r_s, but they also added other factors thought to improve the estimate. For more details, see John R. Graham and Campbell R. Harvey, "The Theory and Practice of Corporate Finance: Evidence from the Field," *Journal of Financial Economics*, Vol. 60, nos. 2 and 3 (May–June 2001), pp. 187–243, for the survey and Eugene F. Fama and Kenneth R. French, "Common Risk Factors in the Return on Stocks and Bonds," *Journal of Financial Economics*, 1993, pp. 3–56.

[13]It is important to be consistent in the use of a long-term versus a short-term rate for r_{RF} and for the market risk premium. The market risk premium ($RP_M = r_M - r_{RF}$) depends on the measure used for the risk-free rate. The yield curve is normally upward-sloping, so the 10-year Treasury bond rate normally exceeds the short-term Treasury bill rate. In this case, it follows that one will obtain a lower estimate of the market risk premium if the higher longer-term bond rate is used as the risk-free rate. At any rate, the r_{RF} used to find the market risk premium should be the same as the r_{RF} used as the first term in the CAPM equation.

10-5b Bond-Yield-plus-Risk-Premium Approach

In situations where reliable inputs for the CAPM approach are not available, as would be true for a closely held company, analysts often use a somewhat subjective procedure to estimate the cost of equity. Empirical studies suggest that the risk premium on a firm's stock over its own bonds generally ranges from 3 to 5 percentage points.[14] Based on this evidence, one might simply add a judgmental risk premium of 3% to 5% to the interest rate on the firm's own long-term debt to estimate its cost of equity. Firms with risky, low-rated, and consequently high-interest-rate debt also have risky, high-cost equity; and the procedure of basing the cost of equity on the firm's own readily observable debt cost utilizes this logic. For example, given that Allied's bonds yield 10%, its cost of equity might be estimated as follows:

$$r_s = \text{Bond yield} + \text{Risk premium} = 10.0\% + 4.0\% = 14.0\%$$

The bonds of a riskier company might have a higher yield, 12%, in which case the estimated cost of equity would be 16%:

$$r_s = 12.0\% + 4.0\% = 16.0\%$$

Because the 4% risk premium is a judgmental estimate, the estimated value of r_s is also judgmental. Therefore, one might use a range of 3% to 5% for the risk premium and obtain a range of 13% to 15% for Allied. While this method does not produce a precise cost of equity, it should "get us in the right ballpark."

10-5c Dividend-Yield-plus-Growth-Rate, or Discounted Cash Flow (DCF), Approach

In Chapter 9, we saw that both the price and the expected rate of return on a share of common stock depend, ultimately, on the stock's expected cash flows. For companies that are expected to remain in business indefinitely, the cash flows are the dividends; on the other hand, if investors expect the firm to be acquired by some other company or to be liquidated, the cash flows will be dividends for some number of years plus a terminal price when the firm is expected to be acquired or liquidated. Like most firms, Allied is expected to continue indefinitely, in which case the following equation applies:

$$P_0 = \frac{D_1}{(1 + r_s)^1} + \frac{D_2}{(1 + r_s)^2} + \cdots + \frac{D_\infty}{(1 + r_s)^\infty}$$
$$= \sum_{t=1}^{\infty} \frac{D_t}{(1 + r_s)^t} \qquad \text{10-6}$$

Here P_0 is the current stock price, D_t is the dividend expected to be paid at the end of Year t, and r_s is the required rate of return. If dividends are expected to grow at a constant rate, as we saw in Chapter 9, Equation 10-6 reduces to this important formula:[15]

$$P_0 = \frac{D_1}{r_s - g} \qquad \text{10-7}$$

---

[14]Ibbotson Associates, a well-known research firm, has calculated the historical returns on common stocks and on corporate bonds and used the differential as an estimate of the *historical risk premium* of stocks over corporate bonds. Historical risk premiums vary from year to year, but a range of 3% to 5% is common. Also, analysts have calculated the CAPM-required return on equity for publicly traded firms in a given industry, averaged them, subtracted those firms' average bond yield, and used the differential as an *expected risk premium*. Again, these risk premium estimates are often generally in the 3% to 5% range.

[15]If the growth rate is not expected to be constant, the DCF procedure can still be used to estimate r; but in this case, it is necessary to calculate an average growth rate using the procedures described in this chapter's Excel model.

We can solve for r_s to obtain the required rate of return on common equity, which for the marginal investor is also equal to the expected rate of return:

10-8
$$r_s = \hat{r}_s = \frac{D_1}{P_0} + \text{Expected g}$$

Thus, investors expect to receive a dividend yield, D_1/P_0, plus a capital gain, g, for a total expected return of $\hat{r}_s$; and in equilibrium, this expected return is also equal to the required return, r_s. This method of estimating the cost of equity is called the *discounted cash flow, or DCF, method*. Henceforth, we will assume that equilibrium exists, which permits us to use the terms r_s and $\hat{r}_s$ interchangeably.

It is easy to calculate the dividend yield; but since stock prices fluctuate, the yield varies from day to day, which leads to fluctuations in the DCF cost of equity. Also, it is difficult to determine the proper growth rate. If past growth rates in earnings and dividends have been relatively stable and if investors expect a continuation of past trends, g may be based on the firm's historic growth rate. *However, if the company's past growth has been abnormally high or low because of its own unique situation or because of general economic fluctuations, investors will not project historical growth rates into the future.* In this case, which applies to Allied, g must be obtained in some other manner.

Security analysts regularly forecast growth rates for earnings and dividends, looking at such factors as projected sales, net profit margins, and competition. For example, *Value Line*, which is available in most libraries, provides growth rate forecasts for 1,700 companies; and Merrill Lynch, Citi Smith Barney, and other organizations make similar forecasts. Averages of these forecasts are available on Yahoo Finance and other web sites. Therefore, someone estimating a firm's cost of equity can obtain analysts' forecasts and use them as a proxy for the growth expectations of investors in general. Then they can combine this g with the current dividend yield to estimate $\hat{r}_s$:

$$\hat{r}_s = \frac{D_1}{P_0} + \text{Growth rate as projected by security analysts}$$

Again, note that this estimate of $\hat{r}_s$ is based on the assumption that g is expected to remain constant in the future. Otherwise, we must use an average of expected future rates.[16]

To illustrate the DCF approach, Allied's stock sells for $23.06, its next expected dividend is $1.25, and analysts expect its growth rate to be 8.3%. Thus, Allied's expected and required rates of return (hence, its cost of retained earnings) are estimated to be 13.7%:

$$\hat{r}_s = r_s = \frac{\$1.25}{\$23.06} + 8.3\%$$
$$= 5.4\% + 8.3\%$$
$$= 13.7\%$$

Based on the DCF method, 13.7% is the minimum rate of return that should be earned on retained earnings to justify plowing earnings back into the business

---

[16]Analysts' growth rate forecasts are usually for 5 years into the future, and the rates provided represent the average growth rate over that 5-year horizon. Studies have shown that analysts' forecasts represent the best source of growth rate data for DCF cost of capital estimates. See Robert Harris, "Using Analysts' Growth Rate Forecasts to Estimate Shareholder Required Rates of Return," *Financial Management*, Spring 1986.

Two organizations—IBES and Zacks—collect the forecasts of leading analysts for most larger companies, average these forecasts, and publish the averages. The IBES and Zacks data are available through online computer data services.

rather than paying them out as dividends. Put another way, since investors are thought to have an *opportunity* to earn 13.7% if earnings are paid out as dividends, the *opportunity cost* of equity from retained earnings is 13.7%.

10-5d Averaging the Alternative Estimates

In our examples, Allied's estimated cost of equity was 13.0% by the CAPM, 14.0% by the bond-yield-plus-risk premium method, and 13.7% by the DCF method. Which method should the firm use? If management is highly confident of one method, it would probably use that method's estimate. Otherwise, it might use an average of the three methods, which for Allied is 13.6%:

$$\text{Average} = (13.0\% + 13.7\% + 14.0\%)/3 = 13.6\%$$

One could, of course, give different weights to the different methods and thus calculate a weighted average.

As consultants, we have estimated companies' costs of capital on numerous occasions. We generally use all three methods and average them, but we rely most heavily on the method that seems best under the circumstances. Judgment is important and comes into play here, as is true for most of finance. Also, we recognize that our final estimate will almost certainly be incorrect to some extent.[17] Therefore, we always provide a range and state that in our judgment, the cost of equity is within that range. For Allied, we used a range of 13% to 14%; the company then used 13.5% as the cost of retained earnings when it calculated its WACC:

Final estimate of r_s used to calculate the WACC: 13.5%.

Why must a cost be assigned to retained earnings?

What three approaches are used to estimate the cost of common equity? Which approach is most commonly used in practice?

Identify some potential problems with the CAPM.

Which of the two components of the DCF formula, the dividend yield or the growth rate, do you think is more difficult to estimate? Why?

What's the logic behind the bond-yield-plus-risk-premium approach?

Suppose you are an analyst with the following data: $r_{RF} = 5.5\%$, $r_M - r_{RF} = 6\%$, $b = 0.8$, $D_1 = \$1.00$, $P_0 = \$25.00$, $g = 6\%$, and $r_d =$ firm's bond yield $= 6.5\%$. What is this firm's cost of equity using the CAPM, DCF, and bond-yield-plus-risk-premium approaches? Use the midrange of the judgmental risk premium for the bond-yield-plus-risk-premium approach. (**CAPM = 10.3%; DCF = 10%; Bond yield + RP = 10.5%**)

---

[17]Investment bankers are generally regarded as experts on concepts such as the cost of capital, and they are paid big salaries for their analysis. But those investment bankers aren't always too accurate. To illustrate, the stock price of the fifth-largest investment bank, Bear Stearns, closed on Friday, March 14, 2008, at $30. Its employees owned 33% of the stock. On Sunday, in a special meeting, its board of directors agreed to sell the company to JP Morgan for $2 per share. Even investment bankers don't always get it right, so don't expect too much precision unless you are given a set of numbers and told to do some relatively simple calculations. As of this writing, JP Morgan has since increased its offer for Bear Stearns to $10 per share.

10-6 COST OF NEW COMMON STOCK, r_e

Companies generally use an investment banker when they issue new common stock and sometimes when they issue preferred stock or bonds. In return for a fee, investment bankers help the company structure the terms, set a price for the issue, and sell the issue to investors. The bankers' fees are called *flotation costs,* and the total cost of the capital raised is the investors' required return plus the flotation cost.

For most firms at most times, equity flotation costs are not an issue because most equity comes from retained earnings. Therefore, in our discussion to this point, we have ignored flotation costs. However, as you can see in "How Much Does It Cost to Raise External Capital," which follows, flotation costs can be substantial. So if a firm does plan to issue new stock, these costs should not be ignored. When firms use investment bankers to raise capital, two approaches can be used to account for flotation costs.[18] We describe them next.

10-6a Add Flotation Costs to a Project's Cost

In the next chapter, we show that capital budgeting projects typically involve an initial cash outlay followed by a series of cash inflows. One approach to handling flotation costs, found as the sum of the flotation costs for the debt, preferred, and common stock used to finance the project, is to add this sum to the initial investment cost. Because the investment cost is increased, the project's expected rate of return is reduced. For example, consider a 1-year project with an initial cost (not including flotation costs) of $100 million. After 1 year, the project is expected to produce an inflow of $115 million. Therefore, its expected rate of return is $115/$100 − 1 = 0.15 = 15.0%. However, if the project requires the company to raise $100 million of new capital and incur $2 million of flotation costs, the total up-front cost will rise to $102 million, which will lower the expected rate of return to $115/$102 − 1 = 0.1275 = 12.75%.

10-6b Increase the Cost of Capital

The second approach involves adjusting the cost of capital rather than increasing the project's investment cost. If the firm plans to continue using the capital in the future, as is generally true for equity, this second approach theoretically will be better. The adjustment process is based on the following logic. If there are flotation costs, the issuing firm receives only a portion of the capital provided by investors, with the remainder going to the underwriter. To provide investors with their required rate of return on the capital they contributed, each dollar the firm actually receives must "work harder"; that is, each dollar must earn a higher rate of return than the investors' required rate of return. For example, suppose investors require a 13.7% return on their investment, but flotation costs represent 10% of the funds raised. Therefore, the firm actually keeps and invests only 90% of the amount that investors supplied. In that case, the firm must earn about 14.3% on the available funds in order to provide investors with a 13.7% return on their investment. This higher rate of return is the flotation-adjusted cost of equity.

The DCF approach can be used to estimate the effects of flotation costs. Here is the equation for the *cost of new common stock, r_e:*

10-9
$$\text{Cost of equity from new stock} = r_e = \frac{D_1}{P_0(1 - F)} + g$$

---

[18]A more complete discussion of flotation cost adjustments can be found in Brigham and Daves, *Intermediate Financial Management,* 9th ed. (Mason, OH: Thomson/South-Western, 2007), and other advanced texts.

HOW MUCH DOES IT COST TO RAISE EXTERNAL CAPITAL?

A study by four professors provides some insights into how much it costs U.S. corporations to raise external capital. Using information from the Securities Data Company, they found the average flotation cost for equity and debt as presented below.

The common stock flotation costs are for established firms, not for firms raising funds in IPOs. Costs associated with IPOs are much higher—flotation costs are about 17%

of gross proceeds for common equity if the amount raised in the IPO is less than $10 million and about 6% if more than $500 million is raised. The data shown include both utility and nonutility companies. If utilities were excluded, flotation costs would be somewhat higher. Also, the debt costs are for debt raised using investment bankers. Most debt is actually obtained from banks and other creditors, in which case flotation costs are generally quite small or nonexistent.

Amount of Capital Raised (Millions of Dollars)	Average Flotation Cost for Common Stock (% of Total Capital Raised)	Average Flotation Cost for New Debt (% of Total Capital Raised)
2–9.99	13.28	4.39
10–19.99	8.72	2.76
20–39.99	6.93	2.42
40–59.99	5.87	1.32
60–79.99	5.18	2.34
80–99.99	4.73	2.16
100–199.99	4.22	2.31
200–499.99	3.47	2.19
500 and up	3.15	1.64

Source: Inmoo Lee, Scott Lochhead, Jay Ritter, and Quanshui Zhao, "The Costs of Raising Capital," *The Journal of Financial Research*, Vol. XIX, no. 1 (Spring 1996), pp. 59–74. Reprinted with permission.

Here **F** is the percentage **flotation cost** required to sell the new stock, so $P_0(1 - F)$ is the net price per share received by the company.

Assuming that Allied has a flotation cost of 10%, its cost of new common equity, r_e, would be computed as follows:

$$r_e = \frac{\$1.25}{\$23.06(1 - 0.10)} + 8.3\%$$

$$= \frac{\$1.25}{\$20.75} + 8.3\%$$

$$= 6.0\% + 8.3\% = 14.3\%$$

> **Flotation Cost, F**
> *The percentage cost of issuing new common stock.*

This is 0.6% higher than the previously estimated 13.7% DCF cost of equity, so the **flotation cost adjustment** is 0.6%:

Flotation adjustment = Adjusted DCF cost − Pure DCF cost = 14.3% − 13.7% = 0.6%

> **Flotation Cost Adjustment**
> *The amount that must be added to r_s to account for flotation costs to find r_e.*

The 0.6% adjustment factor can be added to the previously estimated $r_s = 13.5\%$ (Allied management's estimate), resulting in a cost of equity from new common stock, or external equity, of 14.1%:

Cost of external equity = r_s + Adjustment factor = 13.5% + 0.6% = 14.1%

If Allied earns 14.1% on funds obtained from selling new stock, the investors who purchased that stock will end up earning 13.5%, their required rate of return, on the money they invested. If Allied earns more than 14.1%, its stock price should rise; but the price should fall if Allied earns less than 14.1%.[19]

10-6c When Must External Equity Be Used?

Retained Earnings Breakpoint

The amount of capital raised beyond which new common stock must be issued.

Because of flotation costs, dollars raised by selling new stock must "work harder" than dollars raised by retaining earnings. Moreover, because no flotation costs are involved, retained earnings cost less than new stock. Therefore, firms should utilize retained earnings to the greatest extent possible. However, if a firm has more good investment opportunities than can be financed with retained earnings plus the debt and preferred stock supported by those retained earnings, it may need to issue new common stock. The total amount of capital that can be raised before new stock must be issued is defined as the **retained earnings breakpoint**, and it can be calculated as follows:

10-10 $$\text{Retained earnings breakpoint} = \frac{\text{Addition to retained earnings for the year}}{\text{Equity fraction}}$$

Allied's addition to retained earnings in 2009 is expected to be $66 million; and its target capital structure consists of 45% debt, 2% preferred, and 53% equity. Therefore, its retained earnings breakpoint for 2009 is as follows:

$$\text{Retained earnings breakpoint} = \$66/0.53 = \$124.5 \text{ million}$$

To prove that this is correct, note that a capital budget of $124.5 million could be financed as 0.45($124.5) = $56 million of debt, 0.02($124.5) = $2.5 million of preferred stock, and 0.53($124.5) = $66 million of equity raised from retained earnings. Up to a total of $124.5 million of new capital, equity would have a cost of $r_s = 13.5\%$. However, if the capital budget exceeded $124.5 million, Allied would have to obtain equity by issuing new common stock at a cost of $r_e = 14.1\%$.[20]

SELF TEST

What are the two approaches that can be used to adjust for flotation costs?

Would a firm that has many good investment opportunities be likely to have a higher or a lower dividend payout ratio than a firm with few good investment opportunities? Explain.

A firm's common stock has $D_1 = \$1.50$, $P_0 = \$30.00$, $g = 5\%$, and $F = 4\%$. If the firm must issue new stock, what is its cost of new external equity? **(10.21%)**

Suppose Firm A plans to retain $100 million of earnings for the year. It wants to finance using its current target capital structure of 46% debt, 3% preferred, and 51% common equity. How large could its capital budget be before it must issue new common stock? **($196.08 million)**

---

[19]Flotation costs for preferred stock and bonds are handled similarly to common stock. In both cases, the dollars of flotation costs are deducted from the price of the security, P_P for preferred stock and $1,000 for bonds issued at par. Then for preferred, the cost is found using Equation 10-9 with $g = 0$. For bonds, we find the YTM based on $1,000 − Flotation costs (say, $970 if flotation costs are 3% of the issue price).

[20]This breakpoint is only suggestive—it is not written in stone. For example, rather than issuing new common stock, the company could use more debt (hence, increase its debt ratio) or it could increase its addition to retained earnings by reducing its dividend payout ratio. Both actions would change the retained earnings breakpoint. Also, breakpoints could occur due to increases in the costs of debt and preferred. Indeed, all manner of changes could occur; and the end result would be a large number of potential breakpoints. All of this is discussed in more detail in Brigham and Ehrhardt, *Financial Management Theory and Practice*, 12th ed. (Mason, OH: Thomson/South-Western, 2008), Web Extension 11B.

10-7 COMPOSITE, OR WEIGHTED AVERAGE, COST OF CAPITAL, WACC

Allied's target capital structure calls for 45% debt, 2% preferred stock, and 53% common equity. Earlier we saw that its before-tax cost of debt is 10.0%, its after-tax cost of debt is $r_d(1 - T) = 10\%(0.6) = 6.0\%$, its cost of preferred stock is 10.3%, its cost of common equity from retained earnings is 13.5%, and its marginal tax rate is 40%. Equation 10-1, presented earlier, can be used to calculate its WACC when all of the new common equity comes from retained earnings:

$$WACC = w_d r_d(1 - T) \quad + \quad w_p r_p \quad + \quad w_c r_s$$
$$= 0.45(10\%)(0.6) + 0.02(10.3\%) + 0.53(13.5\%)$$
$$= 10.1\% \text{ if equity comes from retained earnings}$$

Under these conditions, every dollar of new capital that Allied raises would consist of 45 cents of debt with an after-tax cost of 6%, 2 cents of preferred stock with a cost of 10.3%, and 53 cents of common equity from additions to retained earnings with a cost of 13.5%. The average cost of each whole dollar, or the WACC, would be 10.1%.

This estimate of Allied's WACC assumes that common equity comes exclusively from retained earnings. If, instead, Allied was to issue new common stock, its WACC would be slightly higher because of the additional flotation costs.

$$WACC = w_d r_d(1 - T) \quad + \quad w_p r_p \quad + \quad w_c r_e$$
$$= 0.45(10\%)(0.6) + 0.02(10.3\%) + 0.53(14.1\%)$$
$$= 10.4\% \text{ with equity raised by selling new stock}$$

In the Web Appendix 10A, we discuss in more detail the connection between the WACC and the costs of issuing new common stock.

SELF TEST

Write the equation for the WACC.

Firm A has the following data: Target capital structure of 46% debt, 3% preferred, and 51% common equity; Tax rate = 40%; $r_d = 7\%$; $r_p = 7.5\%$; $r_s = 11.5\%$; and $r_e = 12.5\%$. What is the firm's WACC if it does not issue any new stock? **(8.02%)**

What is Firm A's WACC if it issues new common stock? **(8.53%)**

Firm A has 11 equally risky capital budgeting projects, each costing $19.608 million and each having an expected rate of return of 8.25%. Firm A's retained earnings breakpoint is $196.08 million. How much capital should Firm A raise and invest? Why? **($196.08 million; the 11th project would have a higher WACC than its expected rate of return. This question anticipates some of the analysis in Chapter 11.)**

10-8 FACTORS THAT AFFECT THE WACC

The cost of capital is affected by a number of factors. Some are beyond the firm's control, but others can be influenced by its financing and investment decisions.

10-8a Factors the Firm Cannot Control

The three most important factors that the firm cannot directly control are *interest rates in the economy, the general level of stock prices,* and *tax rates.* If interest rates in the economy rise, the cost of debt increases because the firm must pay bond-holders more when it borrows. Similarly, if stock prices in general decline, pulling the firm's stock price down, its cost of equity will rise. Also, since tax rates are used in the calculation of the component cost of debt, they have an important effect on the firm's cost of capital. Taxes also affect the cost of capital in other less apparent ways. For example, when tax rates on dividends and capital gains were lowered relative to rates on interest income, stocks became relatively more attractive than debt; consequently, the cost of equity and WACC declined.

10-8b Factors the Firm Can Control

A firm can directly affect its cost of capital in three primary ways: (1) by changing its *capital structure*, (2) by changing its *dividend payout ratio*, and (3) by *altering its capital budgeting decision rules* to accept projects with more or less risk than projects previously undertaken.

Capital structure impacts a firm's cost of capital. So far we have assumed that Allied has a given target capital structure, and we used the target weights to calculate its WACC. However, if the firm changes its target capital structure, the weights used to calculate the WACC will change. Other things held constant, an increase in the target debt ratio tends to lower the WACC (and vice versa if the debt ratio is lowered) because the after-tax cost of debt is lower than the cost of equity. However, other things are not likely to remain constant. An increase in the use of debt will increase the riskiness of both the debt and the equity, and these increases in component costs might more than offset the effects of the changes in the weights and raise the WACC. In the capital structure chapter, we will discuss how a firm can try to balance these effects to reach its optimal capital structure.

Dividend policy affects the amount of retained earnings available to the firm and thus the need to sell new stock and incur flotation costs. This suggests that the higher the dividend payout ratio, the smaller the addition to retained earnings and thus the higher the cost of equity and therefore the WACC. However, investors may prefer dividends to retained earnings, in which case reducing dividends

GLOBAL PERSPECTIVES

GLOBAL VARIATIONS IN THE COST OF CAPITAL

For U.S. firms to be competitive in world markets, they must have capital costs similar to those their international competitors face. In the past, many experts argued that U.S. firms were at a disadvantage. In particular, Japanese firms enjoyed lower costs of capital, which lowered their total costs and made it harder for U.S. firms to compete. Recent events, however, have considerably narrowed cost of capital differences between U.S. and Japanese firms. In particular, despite its recent decline, the U.S. stock market has outperformed the Japanese market over the past decade, which has made it relatively easy for U.S. firms to raise equity capital.

As capital markets become increasingly integrated, cross-country differences in the costs of capital are disappearing. Today most large corporations raise capital throughout the world; hence, we are moving toward one global capital market rather than distinct capital markets in each country. Although government policies and market conditions can affect the costs of capital within a given country, this affects primarily smaller firms that do not have access to global capital markets. However, even these differences are becoming less important as time goes by. What matters most to investors is the risk of the individual firm, not the market in which it raises capital.

might lead to an increase in both r_s and r_e. As we will see in the dividend chapter, the optimal dividend policy is a complicated issue, but one that can have an important effect on the cost of capital.

The firm's capital budgeting decisions can also affect its cost of capital. When we estimate the firm's cost of capital, we use as the starting point the required rates of return on its outstanding stock and bonds. These cost rates reflect the riskiness of the firm's existing assets. Therefore, we have been implicitly assuming that new capital will be invested in assets that have the same risk as existing assets. This assumption is generally correct, as most firms do invest in assets similar to ones they currently operate. However, if the firm decides to invest in an entirely new and risky line of business, its component costs of debt and equity (and thus its WACC) will increase. To illustrate, in 1996 when ITT Corporation sold off its finance company and purchased Caesar's World, which operates gambling casinos, its dramatic shift in corporate focus almost certainly affected ITT's cost of capital. (Subsequently, ITT's hospitality and entertainment division has become part of Starwood Hotels & Resorts.) The effects of such investment decisions are discussed in Chapter 12.

SELF TEST

Name three factors that affect the cost of capital and that are beyond the firm's control.

What are three factors under the firm's control that can affect its cost of capital?

Suppose interest rates in the economy increase. How would such a change affect the costs of both debt and common equity based on the CAPM?

10-9 ADJUSTING THE COST OF CAPITAL FOR RISK

As you will see in the chapters on capital budgeting that follow, the cost of capital is a key element in the capital budgeting process. Projects should be accepted if and only if their estimated returns exceed their costs of capital. Thus, the cost of capital is a "hurdle rate"—a project's expected rate of return must "jump the hurdle" for it to be accepted. Moreover, investors require higher returns on riskier investments. Consequently, companies that are raising capital to take on risky projects will have higher costs of capital than companies that are investing in safer projects.

Figure 10-1 illustrates the trade-off between risk and the cost of capital. Firm L is in a low-risk business and has a WACC of 8%. Firm A is an average-risk business with a WACC of 10%, while Firm H's business is exposed to greater risk and consequently has a WACC of 12%. Thus, Firm L will accept a typical project if its expected return is above 8%. Firm A's hurdle rate is 10%, while the corresponding hurdle rate for Firm H is 12%.

It's important to remember that the costs of capital for Firms L, A, and H in Figure 10-1 represent the overall, or composite, WACCs for the three firms and thus apply only to "typical" projects for each firm. However, different projects often have different risks, even for a given firm. *Therefore, each project's hurdle rate should reflect the risk of the project, not the risk associated with the firm's average project as reflected in its composite WACC.* Empirical studies do indicate that firms consider the risks of individual projects, but the studies also indicate that most firms regard most projects as having about the same risk as the firm's average existing assets. Therefore, the WACC is used to evaluate most projects; but if a project has an especially high or low risk, the WACC will be adjusted up or down to account for the risk differential.

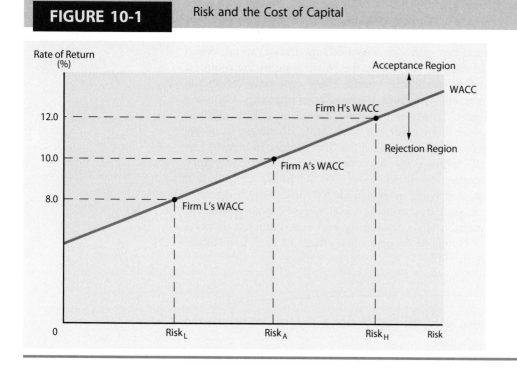

FIGURE 10-1 Risk and the Cost of Capital

For example, assume that Firm A (the average-risk firm with a composite WACC of 10%) has two divisions, L and H. Division L has relatively little risk; and if it were operated as a separate firm, its WACC would be 7%. Division H has higher risk, and its divisional cost of capital is 13%. Since the two divisions are of equal size, Firm A's composite WACC is calculated as 0.50(7%) + 0.50(13%) = 10%. However, it would be a mistake to use this 10% WACC for either division. To see this point, assume that Division L is considering a relatively low-risk project with an expected return of 9%, while Division H is considering a higher-risk project with an expected return of 11%. As shown in Figure 10-2, Division L's project should be accepted because its return is above its risk-based cost of capital, whereas Division H's project should be rejected. If the 10% corporate WACC was used by each division, the decision would be reversed: Division H would incorrectly accept its project, and Division L would incorrectly reject its project. In general, failing to adjust for differences in risk would lead the firm to accept too many risky projects and reject too many safe ones. Over time, the firm would become riskier, its WACC would increase, and its shareholder value would suffer. We will return to these issues in Chapter 12, when we consider different approaches for measuring project risk.

SELF TEST

Why is the cost of capital sometimes referred to as a "hurdle rate"?

How should firms evaluate projects with different risks?

Should all divisions within the same firm use the firm's composite WACC for evaluating all capital budgeting projects? Explain.

FIGURE 10-2   Divisional Cost of Capital

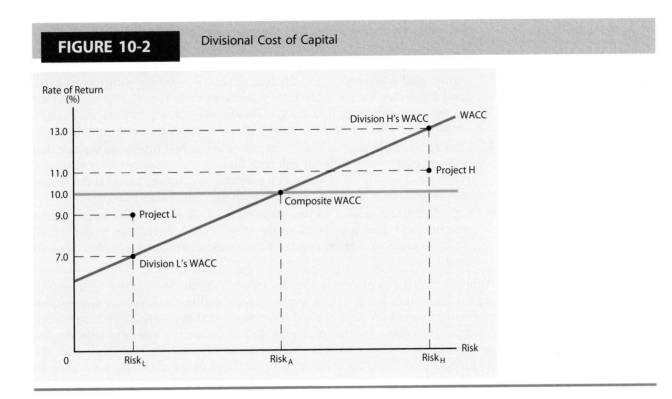

10-10 SOME OTHER PROBLEMS WITH COST OF CAPITAL ESTIMATES

A number of issues related to the cost of capital have not been mentioned or were glossed over in this chapter. These topics are covered in advanced finance courses, but they deserve mention now to alert you to potential dangers and to provide a preview of some matters covered in advanced courses.

1. *Depreciation-generated funds.*[21] The largest single source of capital for many firms is depreciation, yet we have not discussed how the cost of this capital is determined. In brief, depreciation cash flows can either be reinvested or returned to investors (stockholders *and* creditors). The cost of depreciation-generated funds is thus an opportunity cost; and it is approximately equal to the WACC from retained earnings, preferred stock, and debt. Therefore, we can ignore it in our estimate of the WACC.

2. *Privately owned firms.* Our discussion of the cost of equity focused on publicly owned corporations, and we have concentrated on the rate of return required by public stockholders. However, there is a serious question about how to measure the cost of equity for a firm whose stock is not traded. Tax issues are also especially important in these cases. As a general rule, the same principles of cost of capital estimation apply to both privately held

---

[21]See Table 3-3, the statement of cash flows, for an illustration of the cash flows provided from depreciation. Refer to advanced finance textbooks for a discussion on the treatment of depreciation-generated funds.

and publicly owned firms, but the problems of obtaining input data are somewhat different.

3. *Measurement problems.* We cannot overemphasize the practical difficulties encountered when estimating the cost of equity. It is very difficult to obtain good input data for the CAPM, for g in the formula $\hat{r}_s = D_1/P_0 + g$, and for the risk premium in the formula $r_s = $ Bond yield $+$ Risk premium. As a result, we can never be sure of the accuracy of our estimated cost of capital.

4. *Costs of capital for projects of differing risk.* We touched briefly on the fact that different projects can differ in risk and, thus, in their required rates of return. However, it is difficult to measure a project's risk (hence, to adjust the cost of capital for capital budgeting projects with different risks).

5. *Capital structure weights.* In this chapter, we took as given the target capital structure and used it to calculate the WACC. As we shall see in the capital structure chapter, establishing the target capital structure is a major task in itself.

Although this list of problems appears formidable, the state of the art in cost of capital estimation is not in bad shape. The procedures outlined in this chapter can be used to obtain costs of capital estimates that are sufficiently accurate for practical purposes, so the problems listed previously merely indicate the desirability of refinements. The refinements are not unimportant, but the problems noted do not invalidate the usefulness of the procedures outlined in this chapter.

SELF TEST

Identify some problem areas in cost of capital analysis. Do these problems invalidate the cost of capital procedures discussed in this chapter? Explain.

TYING IT ALL TOGETHER

We began this chapter by discussing the concept of the weighted average cost of capital. We then discussed the four capital components (debt, preferred stock, retained earnings, and new common equity) and the procedures used to estimate each component's cost. Next, we calculated the WACC, which is a key element in capital budgeting. A key issue here is the weights that should be used to find the WACC. In general, companies consider a number of factors, then establish a target capital structure that is used to calculate the WACC. We discuss the target capital structure and its affect on the WACC in more detail in the capital structure chapter.

The cost of capital is a key element in capital budgeting decisions, our focus in the following chapters. Indeed, capital budgeting as it should be done is impossible without a good estimate of the cost of capital; so you need to have a good understanding of cost of capital concepts before you move on.

SELF-TEST QUESTIONS AND PROBLEMS
(Solutions Appear in Appendix A)

ST-1   **KEY TERMS**   Define the following terms:

   a.   Capital components

   b.   Before-tax cost of debt, r_d; after-tax cost of debt, $r_d(1 - T)$

   c.   Cost of preferred stock, r_p

   d.   Cost of retained earnings, r_s; cost of new common stock, r_e

   e.   Weighted average cost of capital, WACC

   f.   Flotation cost, F; flotation cost adjustment; retained earnings breakpoint

ST-2   **WACC**   Lancaster Engineering Inc. (LEI) has the following capital structure, which it considers to be optimal:

Debt	25%
Preferred stock	15
Common equity	60
	100%

LEI's expected net income this year is $34,285.72; its established dividend payout ratio is 30%; its federal-plus-state tax rate is 40%; and investors expect future earnings and dividends to grow at a constant rate of 9%. LEI paid a dividend of $3.60 per share last year, and its stock currently sells for $54.00 per share.

LEI can obtain new capital in the following ways:

*   Preferred: New preferred stock with a dividend of $11.00 can be sold to the public at a price of $95.00 per share.

*   Debt: Debt can be sold at an interest rate of 12%.

   a.   Determine the cost of each capital component.

   b.   Calculate the WACC.

   c.   LEI has the following investment opportunities that are average-risk projects:

Project	Cost at t = 0	Rate of Return
A	$10,000	17.4%
B	20,000	16.0
C	10,000	14.2
D	20,000	13.7
E	10,000	12.0

Which projects should LEI accept? Why?

QUESTIONS

10-1   How would each of the following scenarios affect a firm's cost of debt, $r_d(1 - T)$; its cost of equity, r_s; and its WACC? Indicate with a plus (+), a minus (–), or a zero (0) if the factor would raise, would lower, or would have an indeterminate effect on the item in question. Assume for each answer that other things are held constant even though in some instances this would probably not be true. Be prepared to justify your answer but recognize that several of the parts have no single correct answer. These questions are designed to stimulate thought and discussion.

	EFFECT ON		
	$r_d(1 - T)$	r_s	WACC
a. The corporate tax rate is lowered.	_____	_____	_____
b. The Federal Reserve tightens credit.	_____	_____	_____
c. The firm uses more debt; that is, it increases its debt/assets ratio.	_____	_____	_____
d. The dividend payout ratio is increased.	_____	_____	_____
e. The firm doubles the amount of capital it raises during the year.	_____	_____	_____
f. The firm expands into a risky new area.	_____	_____	_____
g. The firm merges with another firm whose earnings are countercyclical both to those of the first firm and to the stock market.	_____	_____	_____
h. The stock market falls drastically, and the firm's stock price falls along with the rest of the stocks.	_____	_____	_____
i. Investors become more risk-averse.	_____	_____	_____
j. The firm is an electric utility with a large investment in nuclear plants. Several states are considering a ban on nuclear power generation.	_____	_____	_____

10-2 Assume that the risk-free rate increases. What impact would this have on the cost of debt? What impact would it have on the cost of equity?

10-3 How should the capital structure weights used to calculate the WACC be determined?

10-4 Suppose a firm estimates its WACC to be 10%. Should the WACC be used to evaluate all of its potential projects, even if they vary in risk? If not, what might be "reasonable" costs of capital for average-, high-, and low-risk projects?

10-5 The WACC is a weighted average of the costs of debt, preferred stock, and common equity. Would the WACC be different if the equity for the coming year came solely in the form of retained earnings versus some equity from the sale of new common stock? Would the calculated WACC depend in any way on the size of the capital budget? How might dividend policy affect the WACC?

PROBLEMS

Easy Problems 1–5

10-1 **AFTER-TAX COST OF DEBT** The Heuser Company's currently outstanding bonds have a 10% coupon and a 12% yield to maturity. Heuser believes it could issue new bonds at par that would provide a similar yield to maturity. If its marginal tax rate is 35%, what is Heuser's after-tax cost of debt?

10-2 **COST OF PREFERRED STOCK** Tunney Industries can issue perpetual preferred stock at a price of $47.50 a share. The stock would pay a constant annual dividend of $3.80 a share. What is the company's cost of preferred stock, r_p?

10-3 **COST OF COMMON EQUITY** Percy Motors has a target capital structure of 40% debt and 60% common equity, with no preferred stock. The yield to maturity on the company's outstanding bonds is 9%, and its tax rate is 40%. Percy's CFO estimates that the company's WACC is 9.96%. What is Percy's cost of common equity?

10-4 **COST OF EQUITY WITH AND WITHOUT FLOTATION** Javits & Sons' common stock currently trades at $30.00 a share. It is expected to pay an annual dividend of $3.00 a share at the end of the year ($D_1 = 3.00), and the constant growth rate is 5% a year.

a. What is the company's cost of common equity if all of its equity comes from retained earnings?

b. If the company issued new stock, it would incur a 10% flotation cost. What would be the cost of equity from new stock?

10-5   **PROJECT SELECTION**   Midwest Water Works estimates that its WACC is 10.5%. The company is considering the following capital budgeting projects:

Project	Size	Rate of Return
A	$1 million	12.0%
B	2 million	11.5
C	2 million	11.2
D	2 million	11.0
E	1 million	10.7
F	1 million	10.3
G	1 million	10.2

Assume that each of these projects is just as risky as the firm's existing assets and that the firm may accept all the projects or only some of them. Which set of projects should be accepted? Explain.

**Intermediate
Problems
6–13**

10-6   **COST OF COMMON EQUITY**   The future earnings, dividends, and common stock price of Carpetto Technologies Inc. are expected to grow 7% per year. Carpetto's common stock currently sells for $23.00 per share; its last dividend was $2.00; and it will pay a $2.14 dividend at the end of the current year.

a. Using the DCF approach, what is its cost of common equity?

b. If the firm's beta is 1.6, the risk-free rate is 9%, and the average return on the market is 13%, what will be the firm's cost of common equity using the CAPM approach?

c. If the firm's bonds earn a return of 12%, based on the bond-yield-plus-risk-premium approach, what will be r_s? Use the midpoint of the risk premium range discussed in Section 10-5 in your calculations.

d. If you have equal confidence in the inputs used for the three approaches, what is your estimate of Carpetto's cost of common equity?

10-7   **COST OF COMMON EQUITY WITH AND WITHOUT FLOTATION**   The Evanec Company's next expected dividend, D_1, is $3.18; its growth rate is 6%; and its common stock now sells for $36.00. New stock (external equity) can be sold to net $32.40 per share.

a. What is Evanec's cost of retained earnings, r_s?

b. What is Evanec's percentage flotation cost, F?

c. What is Evanec's cost of new common stock, r_e?

10-8   **COST OF COMMON EQUITY AND WACC**   Patton Paints Corporation has a target capital structure of 40% debt and 60% common equity, with no preferred stock. Its before-tax cost of debt is 12%, and its marginal tax rate is 40%. The current stock price is $P_0 = \$22.50$. The last dividend was $D_0 = \$2.00$, and it is expected to grow at a 7% constant rate. What is its cost of common equity and its WACC?

10-9   **WACC**   The Patrick Company's cost of common equity is 16%, its before-tax cost of debt is 13%, and its marginal tax rate is 40%. The stock sells at book value. Using the following balance sheet, calculate Patrick's WACC.

Assets		Liabilities and Equity	
Cash	$ 120		
Accounts receivable	240		
Inventories	360	Long-term debt	$1,152
Plant and equipment, net	2,160	Common equity	1,728
Total assets	$2,880	Total liabilities and equity	$2,880

10-10   **WACC**   Klose Outfitters Inc. believes that its optimal capital structure consists of 60% common equity and 40% debt, and its tax rate is 40%. Klose must raise additional capital to fund its upcoming expansion. The firm will have $2 million of new retained earnings with a cost of $r_s = 12\%$. New common stock in an amount up to $6 million would have a cost of $r_e = 15\%$. Furthermore, Klose can raise up to $3 million of debt at an interest rate of $r_d = 10\%$ and an additional $4 million of debt at $r_d = 12\%$. The CFO estimates that a proposed expansion would require an investment of $5.9 million. What is the WACC for the last dollar raised to complete the expansion?

10-11   **WACC AND PERCENTAGE OF DEBT FINANCING**   Hook Industries' capital structure consists solely of debt and common equity. It can issue debt at $r_d = 11\%$, and its common stock currently pays a $2.00 dividend per share ($D_0 = \$2.00$). The stock's price is currently $24.75, its dividend is expected to grow at a constant rate of 7% per year, its tax rate is 35%, and its WACC is 13.95%. What percentage of the company's capital structure consists of debt?

10-12   **WACC**   Midwest Electric Company (MEC) uses only debt and common equity. It can borrow unlimited amounts at an interest rate of $r_d = 10\%$ as long as it finances at its target capital structure, which calls for 45% debt and 55% common equity. Its last dividend was $2, its expected constant growth rate is 4%, and its common stock sells for $20. MEC's tax rate is 40%. Two projects are available: Project A has a rate of return of 13%, while Project B's return is 10%. These two projects are equally risky and about as risky as the firm's existing assets.

a.   What is its cost of common equity?

b.   What is the WACC?

c.   Which projects should Midwest accept?

10-13   **COST OF COMMON EQUITY WITH FLOTATION**   Ballack Co.'s common stock currently sells for $46.75 per share. The growth rate is a constant 12%, and the company has an expected dividend yield of 5%. The expected long-run dividend payout ratio is 25%, and the expected return on equity (ROE) is 16%. New stock can be sold to the public at the current price, but a flotation cost of 5% would be incurred. What would be the cost of new equity?

Challenging Problems 14–20   **10-14**   **COST OF PREFERRED STOCK INCLUDING FLOTATION**   Trivoli Industries plans to issue perpetual preferred stock with an $11.00 dividend. The stock is currently selling for $97.00; but flotation costs will be 5% of the market price, so the net price will be $92.15 per share. What is the cost of the preferred stock, including flotation?

10-15   **WACC AND COST OF COMMON EQUITY**   Kahn Inc. has a target capital structure of 60% common equity and 40% debt to fund its $10 billion in operating assets. Furthermore, Kahn Inc. has a WACC of 13%, a before-tax cost of debt of 10%, and a tax rate of 40%. The company's retained earnings are adequate to provide the common equity portion of its capital budget. Its expected dividend next year (D_1) is $3, and the current stock price is $35.

a.   What is the company's expected growth rate?

b.   If the firm's net income is expected to be $1.1 billion, what portion of its net income is the firm expected to pay out as dividends? (Hint: Refer to Equation 9-4 in Chapter 9.)

10-16   **COST OF COMMON EQUITY**   The Bouchard Company's EPS was $6.50 in 2008, up from $4.42 in 2003. The company pays out 40% of its earnings as dividends, and its common stock sells for $36.00.

a.   Calculate the past growth rate in earnings. (Hint: This is a 5-year growth period.)

b.   The last dividend was $D_0 = 0.4(\$6.50) = \$2.60$. Calculate the next expected dividend, D_1, assuming that the past growth rate continues.

c.   What is Bouchard's cost of retained earnings, r_s?

10-17   **CALCULATION OF g AND EPS**   Sidman Products' common stock currently sells for $60.00 a share. The firm is expected to earn $5.40 per share this year and to pay a year-end dividend of $3.60, and it finances only with common equity.

a.   If investors require a 9% return, what is the expected growth rate?

b.   If Sidman reinvests retained earnings in projects whose average return is equal to the stock's expected rate of return, what will be next years' EPS? (Hint: Refer to Equation 9-4 in Chapter 9.)

10-18   **WACC AND OPTIMAL CAPITAL BUDGET**   Adams Corporation is considering four average-risk projects with the following costs and rates of return:

Project	Cost	Expected Rate of Return
1	$2,000	16.00%
2	3,000	15.00
3	5,000	13.75
4	2,000	12.50

The company estimates that it can issue debt at a rate of $r_d = 10\%$, and its tax rate is 30%. It can issue preferred stock that pays a constant dividend of $5.00 per year at $49.00 per share. Also, its common stock currently sells for $36.00 per share; the next expected dividend, D_1, is $3.50; and the dividend is expected to grow at a constant rate of 6% per year. The target capital structure consists of 75% common stock, 15% debt, and 10% preferred stock.
   a.   What is the cost of each of the capital components?
   b.   What is Adams' WACC?
   c.   Only projects with expected returns that exceed WACC will be accepted. Which projects should Adams accept?

10-19   **ADJUSTING COST OF CAPITAL FOR RISK**   Ziege Systems is considering the following independent projects for the coming year:

Project	Required Investment	Rate of Return	Risk
A	$4 million	14.0%	High
B	5 million	11.5	High
C	3 million	9.5	Low
D	2 million	9.0	Average
E	6 million	12.5	High
F	5 million	12.5	Average
G	6 million	7.0	Low
H	3 million	11.5	Low

Ziege's WACC is 10%, but it adjusts for risk by adding 2% to the WACC for high-risk projects and subtracting 2% for low-risk projects.
   a.   Which projects should Ziege accept if it faces no capital constraints?
   b.   If Ziege can only invest a total of $13 million, which projects should it accept and what would be the dollar size of its capital budget?
   c.   Suppose Ziege can raise additional funds beyond the $13 million, but each new increment (or partial increment) of $5 million of new capital will cause the WACC to increase by 1%. Assuming that Ziege uses the same method of risk adjustment, which projects should it now accept and what would be the dollar size of its capital budget?

10-20   **WACC**   The following table gives Foust Company's earnings per share for the last 10 years. The common stock, 7.8 million shares outstanding, is now (1/1/09) selling for $65.00 per share. The expected dividend at the end of the current year (12/31/09) is 55% of the 2008 EPS. Because investors expect past trends to continue, g may be based on the historical earnings growth rate. (Note that 9 years of growth are reflected in the 10 years of data.)

Year	EPS	Year	EPS
1999	$3.90	2004	$5.73
2000	4.21	2005	6.19
2001	4.55	2006	6.68
2002	4.91	2007	7.22
2003	5.31	2008	7.80

The current interest rate on new debt is 9%; Foust's marginal tax rate is 40%; and its capital structure, considered to be optimal, is as follows:

Debt	$104,000,000
Common equity	156,000,000
Total liabilities and equity	$260,000,000

a. Calculate Foust's after-tax cost of debt and common equity. Calculate the cost of equity as $r_s = D_1/P_0 + g$.

b. Find Foust's WACC.

COMPREHENSIVE/SPREADSHEET PROBLEM

10-21 **CALCULATING THE WACC** Here is the condensed 2008 balance sheet for Skye Computer Company (in thousands of dollars):

	2008
Current assets	$2,000
Net fixed assets	3,000
Total assets	$5,000
Current liabilities	$ 900
Long-term debt	1,200
Preferred stock	250
Common stock	1,300
Retained earnings	1,350
Total common equity	$2,650
Total liabilities and equity	$5,000

Skye's earnings per share last year were $3.20, the common stock sells for $55.00, last year's dividend was $2.10, and a flotation cost of 10% would be required to sell new common stock. Security analysts are projecting that the common dividend will grow at a rate of 9% per year. Skye's preferred stock pays a dividend of $3.30 per share, and new preferred could be sold at a price to net the company $30.00 per share. The firm can issue long-term debt at an interest rate (or before-tax cost) of 10%, and its marginal tax rate is 35%. The market risk premium is 5%, the risk-free rate is 6%, and Skye's beta is 1.516. In its cost of capital calculations, the company considers only long-term capital; hence, it disregards current liabilities.

a. Calculate the cost of each capital component, that is, the after-tax cost of debt, the cost of preferred stock, the cost of equity from retained earnings, and the cost of newly issued common stock. Use the DCF method to find the cost of common equity.

b. Now calculate the cost of common equity from retained earnings using the CAPM method.

c. What is the cost of new common stock based on the CAPM? (Hint: Find the difference between r_e and r_s as determined by the DCF method and add that differential to the CAPM value for r_s.)

d. If Skye continues to use the same capital structure, what is the firm's WACC assuming that (1) it uses only retained earnings for equity? (2) If it expands so rapidly that it must issue new common stock?

INTEGRATED CASE

COLEMAN TECHNOLOGIES INC.

10-22   **COST OF CAPITAL**   Coleman Technologies is considering a major expansion program that has been proposed by the company's information technology group. Before proceeding with the expansion, the company must estimate its cost of capital. Assume that you are an assistant to Jerry Lehman, the financial vice president. Your first task is to estimate Coleman's cost of capital. Lehman has provided you with the following data, which he believes may be relevant to your task.

    (1)   The firm's tax rate is 40%.

    (2)   The current price of Coleman's 12% coupon, semiannual payment, noncallable bonds with 15 years remaining to maturity is $1,153.72. Coleman does not use short-term interest-bearing debt on a permanent basis. New bonds would be privately placed with no flotation cost.

    (3)   The current price of the firm's 10%, $100.00 par value, quarterly dividend, perpetual preferred stock is $111.10.

    (4)   Coleman's common stock is currently selling for $50.00 per share. Its last dividend (D_0) was $4.19, and dividends are expected to grow at a constant rate of 5% in the foreseeable future. Coleman's beta is 1.2, the yield on T-bonds is 7%, and the market risk premium is estimated to be 6%. For the bond-yield-plus-risk-premium approach, the firm uses a risk premium of 4%.

    (5)   Coleman's target capital structure is 30% debt, 10% preferred stock, and 60% common equity.

To structure the task somewhat, Lehman has asked you to answer the following questions.

a.   (1)   What sources of capital should be included when you estimate Coleman's WACC?

    (2)   Should the component costs be figured on a before-tax or an after-tax basis?

    (3)   Should the costs be historical (embedded) costs or new (marginal) costs?

b.   What is the market interest rate on Coleman's debt and its component cost of debt?

c.   (1)   What is the firm's cost of preferred stock?

    (2)   Coleman's preferred stock is riskier to investors than its debt, yet the preferred's yield to investors is lower than the yield to maturity on the debt. Does this suggest that you have made a mistake? (Hint: Think about taxes.)

d.   (1)   Why is there a cost associated with retained earnings?

    (2)   What is Coleman's estimated cost of common equity using the CAPM approach?

e.   What is the estimated cost of common equity using the DCF approach?

f.   What is the bond-yield-plus-risk-premium estimate for Coleman's cost of common equity?

g.   What is your final estimate for r_s?

h.   Explain in words why new common stock has a higher cost than retained earnings.

i.   (1)   What are two approaches that can be used to adjust for flotation costs?

    (2)   Coleman estimates that if it issues new common stock, the flotation cost will be 15%. Coleman incorporates the flotation costs into the DCF approach. What is the estimated cost of newly issued common stock, considering the flotation cost?

j.   What is Coleman's overall, or weighted average, cost of capital (WACC)? Ignore flotation costs.

k.   What factors influence Coleman's composite WACC?

l.   Should the company use the composite WACC as the hurdle rate for each of its projects? Explain.

THOMSON ONE | Business School Edition

Access the Thomson ONE problems through the CengageNOW™ web site. Use the Thomson ONE—Business School Edition online database to work this chapter's questions.

Calculating 3M's Cost of Capital

In this chapter, we described how to estimate a company's WACC, which is the weighted average of its costs of debt, preferred stock, and common equity. Most of the data we need to do this can be found in Thomson ONE. Here we walk through the steps used to calculate Minnesota Mining & Manufacturing's (MMM) WACC.

Discussion Questions

1. As a first step, we need to estimate what percentage of MMM's capital comes from long-term debt, preferred stock, and common equity. If we click on "FINANCIALS," we can see from the balance sheet the amount of MMM's long-term debt and common equity. (As of year-end 2007, MMM had no preferred stock.) Alternatively, under "Financial Ratios," you can click on "WORLDSCOPE" and "ANNUAL BALANCE SHEET RATIOS." Here you will find a recent measure of long-term debt as a percentage of total capital. Recall that the weights used in the WACC are based on the company's target capital structure. If we assume that the company wants to maintain the same mix of capital that it currently has on its balance sheet, what weights should you use to estimate the WACC for MMM? (In the capital structure and leverage chapter, we might arrive at different estimates for these weights if we assume that MMM bases its target capital structure on the market values of debt and equity rather than on the book values.)

2. Once again we can use the CAPM to estimate MMM's cost of equity. Thomson ONE provides various estimates of beta—select the measure that you believe is best and combine this with your estimates of the risk-free rate and the market risk premium to obtain an estimate of its cost of equity. (See the Thomson ONE exercise in Chapter 8 for more details.) What is your estimate for MMM's cost of equity? Why might it not make much sense to use the DCF approach to estimate MMM's cost of equity?

3. Next, we need to calculate MMM's cost of debt. Unfortunately, Thomson ONE doesn't provide a direct measure of the cost of debt. However, we can use different approaches to estimate it. One approach is to take the company's long-term interest expense and divide it by the amount of long-term debt. This approach only works if the historical cost of debt equals the yield to maturity in today's market (that is, if MMM's outstanding bonds are trading at close to par). This approach may produce misleading estimates in years in which MMM issues a significant amount of new debt. For example, if a company issues a great deal of debt at the end of the year, the full amount of debt will appear on the year-end balance sheet, yet we still may not see a sharp increase in interest expense on the annual income statement because the debt was outstanding for only a small portion of the entire year. When this situation occurs, the estimated cost of debt will likely understate the true cost of debt. Another approach is to try to find this number in the notes to the company's annual report by accessing the company's home page and its Investor Relations section. Alternatively, you can go to other external sources, such as www.bondsonline.com, for corporate bond spreads, which can be used to find estimates of the cost of debt. Remember that you need the after-tax cost of debt to calculate a firm's WACC, so you will need MMM's tax rate (which has averaged about 32% in recent years). What is your estimate of MMM's after-tax cost of debt?

4. Putting all this information together, what is your estimate of MMM's WACC? How confident are you in this estimate? Explain your answer.

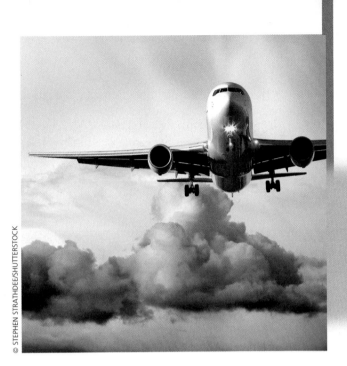
© STEPHEN STRATHDEE/SHUTTERSTOCK

CHAPTER 11 The Basics of Capital Budgeting

Competition in the Aircraft Industry: Airbus vs. Boeing

In early 2008, Boeing was involved in a titanic struggle with European consortium Airbus SAS for dominance of the commercial aircraft industry.[1] Several years ago Airbus committed to spend $16 billion to develop the A380, the largest plane ever built. Boeing countered by announcing that it would spend $6 billion on a super-efficient new plane, the 7E7 Dreamliner. Airbus then announced plans to spend another $6 billion on the A350, a competitor to the 7E7. Many detailed calculations went into these multibillion-dollar investment decisions— development costs were estimated, the cost of each plane was forecasted, a sales price per plane was established, and the number of planes that would be sold through 2025 was predicted.

Both companies projected negative cash flows for 5 or 6 years, then positive cash flows for the following 20 years. Given their forecasted cash flows, both managements decided that taking on the projects would increase each company's intrinsic value. Because the planes will compete with one another, either Boeing's or Airbus's forecast is probably incorrect. One will probably be a winner and the other a loser, and one set of stockholders will likely be happy and the other unhappy. As of the winter of 2008, both companies received orders for their planes, but both have encountered problems that have delayed the actual introduction of the aircraft. The winner is still undecided.

Projects such as the A350, A380, and 7E7 receive a great deal of attention; but Boeing, Airbus, and other companies make a great many routine investment decisions every year, ranging from buying new trucks or machinery

---

[1] Airbus SAS is owned by European Aeronautics Defense & Space Company (EADS), which is owned by the French government and several large European companies. Airbus was formed because the Europeans wanted to create an organization large enough to compete with Boeing.

to purchasing computers and software to optimize inventory management. The techniques described in this chapter are required to analyze projects of all types and sizes.

Sources: John Newhouse, *Boeing Versus Airbus: The Inside Story of the Greatest International Competition in Business* (New York: Random House, 2007).

PUTTING THINGS IN PERSPECTIVE

Capital Budgeting
The process of planning expenditures on assets with cash flows that are expected to extend beyond one year.

In the last chapter, we discussed the cost of capital. Now we turn to investment decisions involving fixed assets, or *capital budgeting*. Here *capital* refers to long-term assets used in production, while a *budget* is a plan that outlines projected expenditures during some future period. Thus, the *capital budget* is a summary of planned investments in long-term assets, and *capital budgeting* is the whole process of analyzing projects and deciding which ones to include in the capital budget. Boeing, Airbus, and other companies use the techniques in this chapter when deciding to accept or reject proposed capital expenditures.

When you finish this chapter, you should be able to:

- Discuss capital budgeting.
- Calculate and use the major capital budgeting decision criteria, which are NPV, IRR, MIRR, and payback.
- Explain why NPV is the best criterion and how it overcomes problems inherent in the other methods.

With an understanding of the theory of capital budgeting developed in this chapter, which uses simplified examples, you will be ready for the next chapter, where we discuss how cash flows are estimated, how risk is measured, and how capital budgeting decisions are made.

11-1 AN OVERVIEW OF CAPITAL BUDGETING

The same concepts used in security valuation are also used in capital budgeting, but there are two major differences. First, stocks and bonds exist in the security markets, and investors select from the available set; firms, however, create capital budgeting projects. Second, for most securities, investors have no influence on the cash flows produced by their investments, whereas corporations have a major influence on projects' results. Still, in both security valuation and capital budgeting, we forecast a set of cash flows, find the present value of those flows, and make the investment only if the PV of the inflows exceeds the investment's cost.

A firm's growth, and even its ability to remain competitive and to survive, depends on a constant flow of ideas relating to new products, to improvements in existing products, and to ways of operating more efficiently. Accordingly, well-managed firms go to great lengths to develop good capital budgeting proposals. For example, the executive vice president of one successful corporation said that his company takes the following steps to generate projects:

> *Our R&D department constantly searches for new products and ways to improve existing products. In addition, our Executive Committee, which consists of senior executives in marketing, production, and finance, identifies the*

products and markets in which our company should compete, and the Committee sets long-run targets for each division. These targets, which are spelled out in the corporation's **strategic business plan**, *provide a general guide to the operating executives who must meet them. The operating executives then seek new products, set expansion plans for existing products, and look for ways to reduce production and distribution costs. Since bonuses and promotions are based on each unit's ability to meet or exceed its targets, these economic incentives encourage our operating executives to seek out profitable investment opportunities.*

While our senior executives are judged and rewarded on the basis of how well their units perform, people further down the line are given bonuses and stock options for suggestions that lead to profitable investments. Additionally, a percentage of our corporate profit is set aside for distribution to nonexecutive employees, and we have an Employees' Stock Ownership Plan (ESOP) to provide further incentives. Our objective is to encourage employees at all levels to keep an eye out for good ideas, especially those that lead to capital investments.

Strategic Business Plan
A long-run plan that outlines in broad terms the firm's basic strategy for the next 5 to 10 years.

Analyzing capital expenditure proposals is not costless—benefits can be gained, but analysis does have a cost. For certain types of projects, an extremely detailed analysis may be warranted, while for other projects, simpler procedures are adequate. Accordingly, firms generally categorize projects and then analyze them in each category somewhat differently:

1. *Replacement: needed to continue current operations.* One category consists of expenditures to replace worn-out or damaged equipment required in the production of profitable products. The only questions here are should the operation be continued and if so, should the firm continue to use the same production processes? If the answers are yes, the project will be approved without going through an elaborate decision process.

2. *Replacement: cost reduction.* This category includes expenditures to replace serviceable but obsolete equipment and thereby to lower costs. These decisions are discretionary, and a fairly detailed analysis is generally required.

3. *Expansion of existing products or markets.* These are expenditures to increase output of existing products or to expand retail outlets or distribution facilities in markets now being served. Expansion decisions are more complex because they require an explicit forecast of growth in demand, so a more detailed analysis is required. The go/no-go decision is generally made at a higher level within the firm.

4. *Expansion into new products or markets.* These investments relate to new products or geographic areas, and they involve strategic decisions that could change the fundamental nature of the business. Invariably, a detailed analysis is required, and the final decision is generally made at the top level of management.

5. *Safety and/or environmental projects.* Expenditures necessary to comply with government orders, labor agreements, or insurance policy terms fall into this category. How these projects are handled depends on their size, with small ones being treated much like the Category 1 projects.

6. *Other projects.* This catch-all includes items such as office buildings, parking lots, and executive aircraft. How they are handled varies among companies.

7. *Mergers.* In a merger, one firm buys another one. Buying a whole firm is different from buying an asset such as a machine or investing in a new airplane, but the same principles are involved. The concepts of capital budgeting underlie merger analysis.

In general, relatively simple calculations, and only a few supporting documents, are required for replacement decisions, especially maintenance investments in profitable plants. More detailed analyses are required for cost-reduction projects, for expansion of existing product lines, and especially for investments in new products or areas. Also, within each category, projects are grouped by their dollar costs: Larger investments require increasingly detailed analysis and approval at higher levels. Thus, a plant manager might be authorized to approve maintenance expenditures up to $10,000 using a relatively unsophisticated analysis, but the full board of directors might have to approve decisions that involve amounts greater than $1 million or expansions into new products or markets.

If a firm has capable and imaginative executives and employees and if its incentive system is working properly, many ideas for capital investment will be advanced. Some ideas will be good ones, but others will not. Therefore, procedures must be established for screening projects. Companies use, and we discuss, the following criteria for deciding to accept or reject projects:[2]

1. Net Present Value (NPV)
2. Internal Rate of Return (IRR)
3. Modified Internal Rate of Return (MIRR)
4. Regular Payback
5. Discounted Payback

The NPV is the best method, primarily because it addresses directly the central goal of financial management—maximizing shareholder wealth. However, all of the methods provide useful information, and all are used in practice at least to some extent.

SELF TEST

How is capital budgeting similar to security valuation? How is it different?

What are some ways that firms generate ideas for capital projects?

Identify the major project classification categories and explain how and why they are used.

What is the single best capital budgeting decision criterion?

11-2 NET PRESENT VALUE (NPV)

Net Present Value (NPV)
A method of ranking investment proposals using the NPV, which is equal to the present value of future net cash flows, discounted at the cost of capital.

The **net present value (NPV)** tells us how much a project contributes to shareholder wealth—the larger the NPV, the more value the project adds; and added value means a higher stock price.[3] Thus, NPV is the best selection criterion. We use the data for Projects S and L shown in Table 11-1 to illustrate the calculation. The S stands for *Short*; the L, for *Long*. Project S is a short-term project in the sense that its cash inflows come in relatively soon, while L has more total cash inflows but they come in later in its life. The projects are equally risky, and they both have a 10% cost of capital. Furthermore, the cash flows have been adjusted to reflect

---

[2]Two other rarely used criteria, the Profitability Index and the Accounting Rate of Return, are covered in Chapter 12 and its Web Extension of Eugene F. Brigham and Phillip R. Daves, *Intermediate Financial Management*, 9th ed. (Mason, OH: Thomson/South-Western, 2007).

[3]We could divide the NPV by the number of shares outstanding to estimate a project's effect on the stock price. However, given the lag between project acceptance and visible effects on earnings, this is rarely done for routine projects. However, for major projects, this procedure is useful.

	A	B	C	D	E	F	G
1							
2							
3	WACC for both projects:		10%				
4							
5		Initial Cost:	After-Tax, End of Year Net Cash Inflows, CF$_t$:				Total Inflows
6	Years:	0	1	2	3	4	
7	Project S:	-$1,000	$500	$400	$300	$100	$1,300
8	Project L:	-$1,000	$100	$300	$400	$675	$1,475

Table 11-1   Data on Projects S and L

depreciation, taxes, and salvage values.[4] The investment outlays shown as CF$_0$ include fixed assets and any necessary investments in working capital, and cash flows come in at the end of the year. Finally, we show the table with an "Excel look," which simply means adding row and column headings to a "regular" table. All of the calculations can be done easily with a financial calculator; but since some students may want to work with Excel, we show how problems would be set up in Excel. Do keep in mind, though, that Excel is not necessary.

We find the NPVs as follows:

1. The present value of each cash flow is calculated, discounted at the project's risk-adjusted cost of capital, r = 10% in our example.

2. The sum of the discounted cash flows is defined as the project's NPV.

The equation for the NPV, set up with input data for Project S, is as follows:

$$NPV = CF_0 + \frac{CF_1}{(1 + r)^1} + \frac{CF_2}{(1 + r)^2} + \cdots + \frac{CF_N}{(1 + r)^N}$$

$$= \sum_{t=0}^{N} \frac{CF_t}{(1 + r)^t}$$

11-1

$$NPV_s = -\$1,000 + \frac{\$500}{(1.10)^1} + \frac{\$400}{(1.10)^2} + \frac{\$300}{(1.10)^3} + \frac{\$100}{(1.10)^4}$$

Here CF$_t$ is the expected net cash flow at Time t, r is the project's risk-adjusted cost of capital (or WACC), and N is its life. Projects generally require an initial investment—for example, developing the product, buying the equipment needed to make it, building a factory, and stocking inventory. The initial investment is a negative cash flow. For Projects S and L, only CF$_0$ is negative; but for a large project such as Boeing's 7E7, outflows occur for several years before cash inflows begin.

Figure 11-1 shows the cash flow time line for Project S; the PV of each cash flow; and the sum of the PVs, which is by definition the NPV.

The cost, at t = 0, is –$1,000. The first positive cash flow is $500; and with a regular calculator, you could find its PV as $500/(1.10)^1 = $454.55. You could also find the PV of the $500 with a financial calculator. Other PVs could be found similarly, and the end result would be the numbers in the left column of the diagram. When we sum those numbers, the result is $78.82, which is NPV$_S$. Note that the initial cost, the –$1,000, is not discounted because it occurs at Time 0. The NPV for Project L, $100.40, could be found similarly.

---

[4]The most difficult aspect of capital budgeting is estimating the relevant cash flows. For simplicity, the net cash flows are treated as a given in this chapter, which allows us to focus on the rules for making capital budgeting decisions. However, in Chapter 12, we discuss cash flow estimation in detail. Also note that *net working capital* is defined as the increase in current assets required for a project minus the associated increases in payables and accruals. Thus, in capital budgeting, investment in working capital means the *net amount* that must be financed by investors.

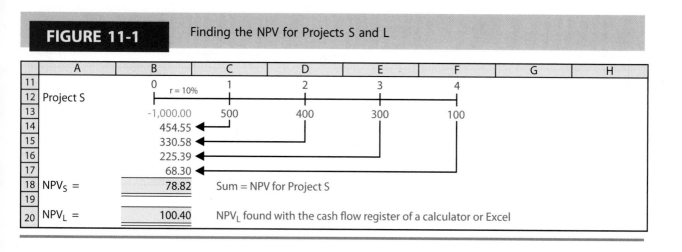

FIGURE 11-1   Finding the NPV for Projects S and L

The step-by-step procedure shown in Figure 11-1 is useful for illustrating how the NPV is calculated; but in practice (and on exams), it is far more efficient to use a financial calculator or Excel. Different calculators are set up somewhat differently; but as we discussed in Chapter 5, they all have a "cash flow register" that can be used to evaluate uneven cash flows such as those for Projects S and L. Equation 11-1 is programmed into these calculators, and all you must do is enter the cash flows (with the correct signs) along with $r = I/YR = 10$. Once the data have been entered and you press the NPV key, the answer, 78.82, appears on the screen.[5]

If you are familiar with Excel, you can use it to find the NPVs for S and L:

$$NPV_S = \$78.82$$
$$NPV_L = \$100.40$$

The model used to obtain these values is provided in the chapter's Excel model. If you want to know something about Excel, you should look at the model, as this is the way most people in practice find NPVs.

Before using these NPVs in the decision process, we need to know whether Projects S and L are **independent** or **mutually exclusive**. Independent projects are projects whose cash flows are not affected by one another. If Wal-Mart was considering a new store in Boise and another in Atlanta, the projects would be independent; and if both had positive NPVs, Wal-Mart should accept both. Mutually exclusive projects, on the other hand, are projects where if one project is accepted, the other must be rejected. A conveyor belt system to move goods in a warehouse and a fleet of forklifts used for the same purpose would be mutually exclusive—accepting one implies rejecting the other.

What should be the decision if Projects S and L are independent? In this case, both should be accepted because both have positive NPVs and thus add value to the firm. However, if they are mutually exclusive, Project L should be chosen because it has the higher NPV and thus adds more value than S. Here is a summary of the NPV decision rules:

Independent projects: If NPV exceeds zero, accept the project.

Mutually exclusive projects: Accept the project with the highest positive NPV. If no project has a positive NPV, reject them all.

Independent Projects
Projects with cash flows that are not affected by the acceptance or nonacceptance of other projects.

Mutually Exclusive Projects
A set of projects where only one can be accepted.

---

[5]The keystrokes for finding the NPV are shown for several calculators in the calculator tutorials provided on the text's web site.

Since projects must be either independent or mutually exclusive, one or the other of these rules applies to every project.

Why is the NPV the primary capital budgeting decision criterion?

What is the difference between independent and mutually exclusive projects?

Projects SS and LL have the following cash flows:

END-OF-YEAR CASH FLOWS

	0	1	2	3	
					WACC = r = 10%
SS	−$700	$500	$300	$100	
LL	−$700	$100	$300	$600	

If a 10% cost of capital is appropriate for both projects, what are their NPVs? (NPV$_{SS}$ = **$77.61**; NPV$_{LL}$ = **$89.63**)

Which project(s) would you accept if SS and LL were (a) independent? (b) mutually exclusive?

11-3 INTERNAL RATE OF RETURN (IRR)

In Chapter 7, we discussed the yield to maturity on a bond and we explained that if you hold it to maturity, you will earn the YTM on your investment. The YTM is found as the discount rate that forces the PV of the cash inflows to equal the price of the bond. This same concept is involved in capital budgeting when we calculate a project's **internal rate of return (IRR)**:

A project's IRR is the discount rate that forces the PV of the inflows to equal the cost. This is equivalent to forcing the NPV to equal zero. The IRR is an estimate of the project's rate of return, and it is comparable to the YTM on a bond.

Internal Rate of Return (IRR)
The discount rate that forces a project's NPV to equal zero.

To calculate the IRR, we begin with Equation 11-1 for the NPV, replace r in the denominator with the term IRR, and set the NPV equal to zero. This transforms Equation 11-1 into Equation 11-2, the one used to find the IRR. The rate that forces NPV to equal zero is the IRR.[6]

$$NPV = CF_0 + \frac{CF_1}{(1 + IRR)^1} + \frac{CF_2}{(1 + IRR)^2} + \cdots + \frac{CF_N}{(1 + IRR)^N} = 0$$

$$0 = \sum_{t=0}^{N} \frac{CF_t}{(1 + IRR)^t}$$

11-2

$$NPV_s = 0 = -\$1,000 + \frac{\$500}{(1 + IRR)^1} + \frac{\$400}{(1 + IRR)^2} + \frac{\$300}{(1 + IRR)^3} + \frac{\$100}{(1 + IRR)^4}$$

Figure 11-2 illustrates the process of finding the IRR for Project S.

Three procedures can be used:

1. *Trial and Error.* We could use a trial-and-error procedure—try a discount rate; see if the equation solves to zero; and if it doesn't, try a different rate. We could

---

[6]For a large, complex project like Boeing's 7E7 jetliner, costs are incurred for several years before cash inflows begin. That means that we have a number of negative cash flows before the positive cash flows begin.

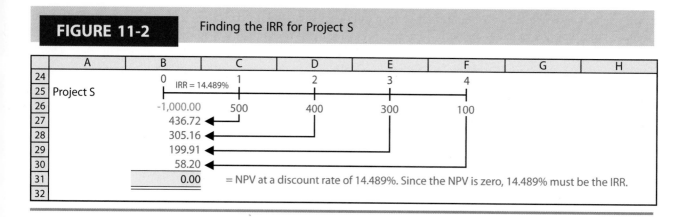

FIGURE 11-2 Finding the IRR for Project S

then continue until we found the rate that forces the NPV to zero; that rate would be the IRR. For Project S, the IRR is 14.489%. Note, though, that the trial-and-error procedure is so time-consuming that before computers and financial calculators were available, the IRR was rarely used. It's useful to think about the trial-and-error procedure, but it's far better to use a calculator or Excel to do the actual calculations.

2. *Calculator Solution.* Enter the cash flows in the calculator's cash flow register just as we did to find the NPV; then press the button labeled "IRR." Instantly, you get the IRR. Here are the values for Projects S and L:[7]

$$IRR_S = 14.489\%$$
$$IRR_L = 13.549\%$$

3. *Excel Solution.* It is even easier to find IRR_S using Excel, as we demonstrate in the chapter model.

Why is the discount rate that causes a project's NPV to equal zero so special? The reason is that the IRR is an estimate of the project's rate of return. If this return exceeds the cost of the funds used to finance the project, the difference will be a bonus that goes to the firm's stockholders and causes the stock price to rise. Project S has an estimated return of 14.489% versus a 10% cost of capital, so its bonus is 4.489%. On the other hand, if the IRR is less than the cost of capital, stockholders must make up the shortfall, which will hurt the stock price.

Note again that the IRR formula, Equation 11-2, is simply the NPV formula, Equation 11-1, solved for the particular discount rate that forces the NPV to zero. Thus, the same basic equation is used for both methods. The only difference is that with the NPV method, the discount rate is given and we find the NPV; with the IRR method, however, the NPV is set equal to zero and we find the interest rate that produces this equality.

As we noted earlier, projects should be accepted or rejected depending on whether their NPVs are positive. However, the IRR is sometimes used (improperly

---

[7]See the calculator tutorials on the text's web site. Note that once the cash flows have been entered in the cash flow register, you can find the NPV and the IRR. To find the NPV, enter the interest rate (I/YR) and then press the NPV key. Then with no further entries, press the IRR key to find the IRR. Thus, once you set up the calculator to find the NPV, it is trivially easy to find the IRR. This is one reason most firms calculate the NPV and the IRR. If you calculate one, it is easy to calculate the other; and both provide information that decision makers find useful. The same is true with Excel.

WHY NPV IS BETTER THAN IRR

Buffett University recently hosted a seminar on business methods for managers. A finance professor covered capital budgeting, explaining how to calculate the NPV and stating that it should be used to screen potential projects. In the Q&A session, Ed Wilson, the treasurer of an electronics firm, said that his firm used the IRR primarily because the CFO and the directors understood the selection of projects based on their rates of return but didn't understand the NPV. Ed had tried to explain why the NPV was better, but he simply confused everyone; so the company stuck with the IRR. Now a meeting on the firm's capital budget is coming up, and Ed asked the professor for a simple, easy-to-understand explanation of why the NPV was better.

The professor recommended the following extreme example. A firm with adequate access to capital and a 10% WACC is choosing between two equally risky, mutually exclusive projects. Project Large calls for investing $100,000 and then receiving $50,000 per year for 10 years, while Project Small calls for investing $1 and receiving $0.60 per year for 10 years. Here is each project's NPV and IRR:

The IRR says choose S, but the NPV says take L. Intuitively, it's obvious that the firm would be better off choosing the large project in spite of its lower IRR. With a cost of capital of only 10%, a 49% rate of return on a $100,000 investment is more profitable than a 59% return on a $1 investment.

When Ed gave this example in his firm's executive meeting on the capital budget, the CFO argued that this example was extreme and unrealistic and that no one would choose S in spite of its higher IRR. Ed agreed, but he asked the CFO where the line should be drawn between realistic and unrealistic examples. When Ed received no answer, he went on to say that (1) it's hard to draw this line and (2) the NPV is always better because it tells us how much value each project will add, which is what the firm should maximize. The president was listening, and he declared Ed the winner. The company switched from IRR to NPV, and Ed is now the CFO.

Project Large (L)	Project Small (S)
NPV$_L$: $207,228.36	NPV$_S$: $2.69
IRR$_L$: 49.1%	IRR$_S$: 59.4%

we believe) to rank projects and make capital budgeting decisions. When this is done, here are the decision rules:

Independent projects: If IRR exceeds the project's WACC, accept the project. If IRR is less than the project's WACC, reject it.

Mutually exclusive projects. Accept the project with the highest IRR, provided that IRR is greater than WACC. Reject all projects if the best IRR does not exceed WACC.

The IRR is logically appealing—it is useful to know the rates of return on proposed investments. However, as we demonstrate in a later section, NPV and IRR can produce conflicting conclusions when a choice is being made between mutually exclusive projects; and when conflicts occur, the NPV is generally better.

SELF TEST

In what sense is a project's IRR similar to the YTM on a bond?

The cash flows for projects SS and LL are as follows:

	END-OF-YEAR CASH FLOWS				
	0	**1**	**2**	**3**	**WACC = r = 10%**
SS	−$700	$500	$300	$100	
LL	−$700	$100	$300	$600	

What are the projects' IRRs, and which one would the IRR method select if the firm had a 10% cost of capital and the projects were (a) independent or (b) mutually exclusive? ($IRR_{SS} = 18.0\%$; $IRR_{LL} = 15.6\%$)

11-4 MULTIPLE INTERNAL RATES OF RETURN[8]

A problem with the IRR is that under certain conditions, a project may have more than one IRR. First, note that a project is said to have *normal* cash flows if it has one or more cash outflows (costs) followed by a series of cash inflows. If, however, a cash *outflow* occurs sometime after the inflows have commenced, meaning that the signs of the cash flows change *more than once*, the project is said to have *nonnormal* cash flows.

Examples:

Normal:	−	+	+	+	+	+	or	−	−	−	+	+	+	+	+
Nonnormal:	−	+	+	+	+	−	or	−	+	+	+	−	+	+	+

Multiple IRRs
The situation where a project has two or more IRRs.

An example of nonnormal flows would be a strip coal mine where the company spends money to buy the property and prepare the site for mining, has positive inflows for several years, and spends more money to return the land to its original condition. In such a case, the project might have two IRRs, that is, **multiple IRRs**.[9]

To illustrate multiple IRRs, suppose a firm is considering a potential strip mine (Project M) that has a cost of $1.6 million and will produce a cash flow of $10 million at the end of Year 1. Then at the end of Year 2, the firm must spend $10 million to restore the land to its original condition. Therefore, the project's expected net cash flows are as follows (in millions):

	Year 0	End of Year 1	End of Year 2
Cash flows	−$1.6	+$10	−$10

We can substitute these values into Equation 11-2 and solve for the IRR:

$$NPV = \frac{-\$1.6 \text{ million}}{(1 + IRR)^0} + \frac{\$10 \text{ million}}{(1 + IRR)^1} + \frac{-\$10 \text{ million}}{(1 + IRR)^2} = 0$$

NPV equals 0 when IRR = 25%, but it also equals 0 when IRR = 400%.[10] Therefore, Project M has an IRR of 25% and another of 400%, and we don't know which one to use. This relationship is depicted graphically in Figure 11-3.[11] The graph is constructed by plotting the project's NPV at different discount rates.

Note that no dilemma regarding Project M would arise if the NPV method was used; we would simply find the NPV and use it to evaluate the project.

---

[8]This section is relatively technical, but it can be omitted without loss of continuity.

[9]Equation 11-2 is a polynomial of degree n; so it has n different roots, or solutions. All except one of the roots is an imaginary number when investments have normal cash flows (one or more cash outflows followed by cash inflows). So in the normal case, only one value of IRR appears. However, the possibility of multiple real roots (hence multiple IRRs) arises when negative net cash flows occur after the project has been placed in operation.

[10]If you attempt to find Project M's IRR with an HP calculator, you will get an error message, while TI calculators give only the IRR that's closest to zero. When you encounter either situation, you can find the approximate IRRs by calculating NPVs using several different values for r = I/YR, plotting NPV on the vertical axis with the corresponding discount rate on the horizontal axis of a graph, and seeing about where NPV = 0. The intersection with the x-axis provides a rough idea of the IRRs' values. With some calculators and with Excel, you can find both IRRs by entering guesses, as explained in the calculator and Excel tutorials.

[11]Figure 11-3 is called an NPV profile. Profiles are discussed in more detail in Section 11-7.

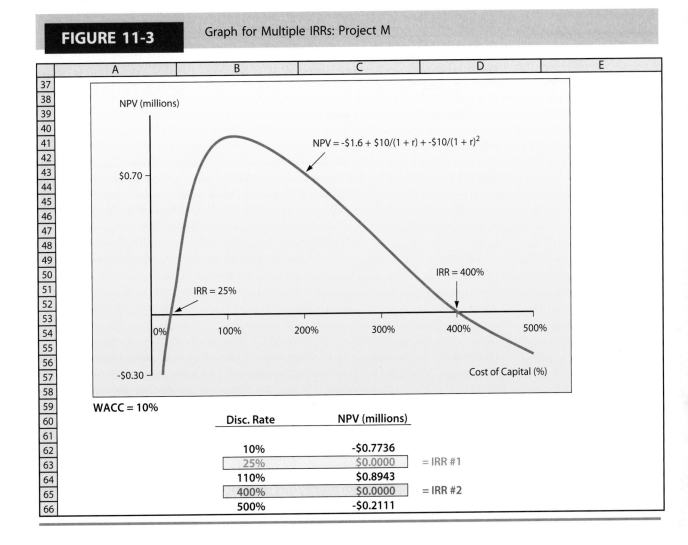

FIGURE 11-3   Graph for Multiple IRRs: Project M

Disc. Rate	NPV (millions)	
10%	-$0.7736	
25%	$0.0000	= IRR #1
110%	$0.8943	
400%	$0.0000	= IRR #2
500%	-$0.2111	

We would see that if Project M's cost of capital was 10%, its NPV would be –$0.7736 million and the project should be rejected. However, if r was between 25% and 400%, NPV would be positive, but those numbers would not be realistic or useful for anything.

SELF TEST

What condition regarding cash flows would cause more than one IRR to exist?

Project MM has the following cash flows:

END-OF-YEAR CASH FLOWS

0	1	2	3
–$1,000	$2,000	$2,000	–$3,350

Calculate MM's NPV at discount rates of 0%, 10%, 12.2258%, 25%, 122.1470%, and 150%. What are MM's IRRs? If the cost of capital is 10%, should the project be accepted or rejected? **(NPVs range from –$350 to +$164 and then back down to –$94; the IRRs are 12.23% and 122.15%.)**

11-5 REINVESTMENT RATE ASSUMPTIONS[12]

The NPV calculation is based on the assumption that cash inflows can be reinvested at the project's risk-adjusted WACC, whereas the IRR calculation is based on the assumption that cash flows can be reinvested at the IRR. To see why this is so, consider the following diagram, which was first used in Chapter 5 to illustrate the future value of $100 when the interest rate was 5%.

```
       0    5%    1    5%    2    5%    3
       |----------|----------|----------|
```

Going from PV to FV: PV = $100.00 ⟶ $105.00 ⟶ $110.25 ⟶ $115.76 = FV

Observe that the FV calculation assumes that the interest earned during each year can be reinvested to earn the same 5% in each succeeding year.

Now recall that when we found the PV, we reversed the process, discounting rather than compounding at the 5% rate. This diagram was used to demonstrate this point:

```
       0    5%    1    5%    2    5%    3
       |----------|----------|----------|
```

Going from FV to PV: PV = $100.00 ⟵ $105.00 ⟵ $110.25 ⟵ $115.76 = FV

This led to the following conclusion: *When we calculate a present value, we are implicitly assuming that cash flows can be reinvested at a specified interest rate, 5% in our example.* This applies to Projects S and L: When we calculated their NPVs, we discounted at the WACC, 10%, which means that we were assuming that their cash flows could be reinvested at 10%.

Now consider the IRR. In Section 11-3 we presented a cash flow diagram set up to show the PVs of the cash flows when discounted at the IRR. We saw that the sum of the PVs is equal to the cost at a discount rate of 14.489%; so by definition, 14.489% is the IRR. Now we can ask this question: What reinvestment rate is built into the IRR?

> *Since discounting at a given rate assumes that cash flows can be reinvested at that same rate, the IRR assumes that cash flows are reinvested at the IRR.*

The NPV assumes reinvestment at the WACC, while the IRR assumes reinvestment at the IRR. Which assumption is more reasonable? For most firms, assuming reinvestment at the WACC is more reasonable for the following reasons:

- If a firm has reasonably good access to the capital markets, it can raise all the capital it needs at the going rate, which in our example is 10%.
- Since the firm can obtain capital at 10%, if it has investment opportunities with positive NPVs, it should take them on and it can finance them at a 10% cost.
- If the firm uses internally generated cash flows from past projects rather than external capital, this will save it the 10% cost of capital. Thus, 10% is the *opportunity cost* of the cash flows, and that is the effective return on reinvested funds.

To illustrate all this, suppose a project's IRR is 50%, the firm's WACC is 10%, and the firm has adequate access to the capital markets. Thus, the firm can raise all the capital it needs at the 10% rate. Unless the firm is a monopoly, the 50% return would attract competition, which would make it hard to find new projects with a similar high return, which is what the IRR assumes. Moreover, even if the firm

---

[12]This section gives a theoretical explanation of the key difference between NPV and IRR. However, it is relatively technical; so if time is a constraint, professors may decide to have students skip it and just read the box titled, "Why NPV Is Better Than IRR," which appears earlier in the chapter.

does find such projects, it could take them on with external capital that costs 10%. The logical conclusion is that the original project's cash flows will save the 10% cost of the external capital, and that is the effective return on those flows.

If a firm does not have good access to external capital and if it has many potential projects with high IRRs, it might be reasonable to assume that a project's cash flows could be reinvested at rates close to their IRRs. However, that situation rarely exists: Firms with good investment opportunities generally *do* have good access to debt and equity markets.

Our conclusion is that the assumption built into the IRR—that cash flows can be reinvested at the IRR—is flawed, whereas the assumption built into the NPV— that cash flows can be reinvested at the WACC—is generally correct. Moreover, if the true reinvestment rate is less than the IRR, the true rate of return on the investment must be less than the calculated IRR; thus, the IRR is misleading as a measure of projects' profitability. This point is discussed further in the next section.

SELF TEST

Why is it true that a reinvestment rate is implicitly assumed whenever we find the present value of a future cash flow? Would it be possible to find the PV of a FV without specifying an implicit reinvestment rate? **(PVs are the reverse of FVs. We need r to find FV; hence, we need r to find the PV.)**

What reinvestment rate is built into the NPV calculation? the IRR calculation? **(WACC, IRR)**

For a firm that has adequate access to capital markets, is it more reasonable to assume reinvestment at the WACC or the IRR? **(WACC)**

11-6 MODIFIED INTERNAL RATE OF RETURN (MIRR)[13]

It is logical for managers to want to know the expected rate of return on investments, and this is what the IRR is supposed to tell them. However, the IRR is based on the assumption that projects' cash flows can be reinvested at the IRR. *This assumption is generally* incorrect, *and this causes the IRR to overstate the project's true return.*[14] Given this fundamental flaw, is there a percentage evaluator that is better than the regular IRR? The answer is yes—we can modify the IRR to make it a better measure of profitability.

This new measure, the **Modified IRR (MIRR)**, is illustrated for Project S in Figure 11-4. It is similar to the regular IRR except that it is based on the assumption that cash flows are reinvested at the WACC (or some other explicit rate if that is a more reasonable assumption). Refer to Figure 11-4 as you read about its construction.

1. Project S has just one outflow, the minus $1,000 at t = 0. Since it occurs at Time 0, it is not discounted and its PV is –$1,000. If the project had additional outflows, we would find the PV at t = 0 for each one and sum them for use in the MIRR calculation.

2. Next, we find the future value of each *inflow* compounded at the WACC out to the "terminal year," which is the year the last inflow is received. We assume that cash flows are reinvested at the WACC. For Project S, the first cash flow,

Modified IRR (MIRR)
The discount rate at which the present value of a project's cost is equal to the present value of its terminal value, where the terminal value is found as the sum of the future values of the cash inflows, compounded at the firm's cost of capital.

---

[13]Again, this section is relatively technical, but it too can be omitted without loss of continuity.
[14]The IRR overstates the expected return for accepted projects because cash flows cannot generally be reinvested at the IRR. Therefore, the average IRR for accepted projects is greater than the true expected rate of return. This imparts an upward bias on corporate projections based on IRRs.

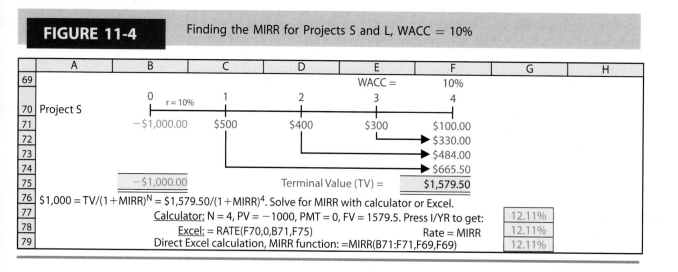

FIGURE 11-4 Finding the MIRR for Projects S and L, WACC = 10%

$500, is compounded at WACC = 10% for 3 years and it grows to $665.50. The second inflow, $400, grows to $484.00; the third, to $330.00. The last inflow is received at the end, so it is not compounded at all. The sum of the future values, $1,579.50, is called the "terminal value," or TV.

3. We now have the cost at t = 0, –$1,000, and the TV at Year 4, $1,579.50. There is some discount rate that will cause the PV of the terminal value to equal the cost. *That interest rate is defined as the MIRR.* In a calculator, enter N = 4, PV = –1000, PMT = 0, and FV = 1579.50. Then when you press the I/YR key, you get the MIRR, 12.11%.

4. The MIRR can be found in a number of ways. Figure 11-4 illustrates how the MIRR is calculated: We compound each cash inflow, sum them to determine the TV, and then find the rate that causes the PV of the TV to equal the cost. That rate is 12.11%. However, some of the better calculators have a built-in MIRR function that streamlines the process, as does Excel. We explain how to use the calculator function in the calculator tutorials, and we explain how to find MIRR with Excel in the chapter Excel model.[15]

The MIRR has two significant advantages over the regular IRR. First, whereas the regular IRR assumes that the cash flows from each project are reinvested at the

---

[15]Equation 11-2a summarizes these steps.

11-2a

$$\sum_{t=0}^{N} \frac{COF_t}{(1+r)^t} = \frac{\sum_{t=0}^{N} CIF_t (1+r)^{N-t}}{(1+MIRR)^N}$$

$$PV\ costs = \frac{TV}{(1+MIRR)^N}$$

COF_t is the cash outflow at time t, and CIF_t is the cash inflow at time t. The left term is the PV of the investment outlays when discounted at the cost of capital; the numerator of the second term is the compounded value of the inflows, assuming the inflows are reinvested at the cost of capital. The MIRR is the discount rate that forces the PV of the TV to equal the PV of the costs.

Also note that there are alternative definitions for the MIRR. One difference relates to whether negative cash flows, after the positive cash flows begin, should be compounded and treated as part of the TV or discounted and treated as a cost. A related issue is whether negative and positive flows in a given year should be netted or treated separately. For a complete discussion, see William R. McDaniel, Daniel E. McCarty, and Kenneth A. Jessell, "Discounted Cash Flow with Explicit Reinvestment Rates: Tutorial and Extension," *The Financial Review,* August 1988, pp. 369–385 and David M. Shull, "Interpreting Rates of Return: A Modified Rate of Return Approach," *Financial Practice and Education,* Fall 1993, pp. 67–71.

IRR, the MIRR assumes that cash flows are reinvested at the cost of capital (or some other explicit rate). Since reinvestment at the IRR is generally not correct, the MIRR is generally a better indicator of a project's true profitability. Second, the MIRR eliminates the multiple IRR problem—there can never be more than one MIRR, and it can be compared with the cost of capital when deciding to accept or reject projects.

Our conclusion is that the MIRR is better than the regular IRR; however, this question remains: Is MIRR as good as the NPV? Here are our conclusions:

- For *independent* projects, the NPV, IRR, and MIRR always reach the same accept/reject conclusion; so the three criteria are equally good when evaluating independent projects.

- However, if projects are *mutually exclusive* and they differ in size, conflicts can arise. In such cases, the NPV is best because it selects the project that maximizes value.[16]

- Our overall conclusions are that (1) the MIRR is superior to the regular IRR as an indicator of a project's "true" rate of return but that (2) NPV is better than IRR and MIRR when choosing among competing projects.

SELF TEST

What's the primary difference between the MIRR and the regular IRR? **(reinvestment rate)**

Which provides a better estimate of a project's "true" rate of return, the MIRR or the regular IRR? Explain.

Projects A and B have the following cash flows:

	0	1	2
A	−$1,000	$1,150	$ 100
B	−$1,000	$ 100	$1,300

Their cost of capital is 10%. What are the projects' IRRs, MIRRs, and NPVs? Which project would each method select? (**IRR$_A$ = 23.1%, IRR$_B$ = 19.1%; MIRR$_A$ = 16.8%, MIRR$_B$ =18.7%; NPV$_A$ = $128.10, NPV$_B$ = $165.29**)

11-7 NPV PROFILES

Figure 11-5 presents the **net present value profile** for Project S. To make the profile, we find the project's NPV at a number of different discount rates and then plot those values to create a graph. Note that at a zero cost of capital, the NPV is simply the net total of the undiscounted cash flows, $1,300 − $1,000 = $300. This value is plotted as the vertical axis intercept. Also recall that the IRR is the discount rate that causes the NPV to equal zero, so the discount rate at which the profile line crosses the horizontal axis is the project's IRR. When we connect the data points, we have the NPV profile.[17]

Net Present Value Profile
A graph showing the relationship between a project's NPV and the firm's cost of capital.

---

[16]See Brigham and Daves, *Intermediate Financial Management,* 9th ed. (Mason, OH: South-Western, 2007), pp. 412–413.

[17]Notice that the NPV profile is curved—it is *not* a straight line. NPV approaches CF$_0$, which is the −$1,000 project cost, as the discount rate increases toward infinity. The reason is that at an infinitely high cost of capital, all the PVs of the inflows would be zero; so NPV at r = ∞ must be CF$_0$. We should also note that under certain conditions, the NPV profiles can cross the horizontal axis several times or never cross it. This point was discussed in Section 11-4.

FIGURE 11-5	NPV Profile for Project S

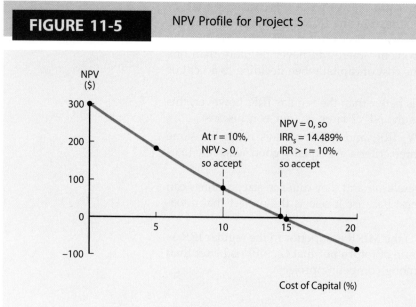

	Cost of Capital	NPV$_s$
	0%	$300.00
	5	180.00
	10	78.82
IRR$_s$ =	14.489	0.00
	15	−8.33
	20	−83.72

Now consider Figure 11-6, which shows two NPV profiles—one for Project S and one for L—and note the following points:

- The IRRs are fixed, and S has the higher IRR regardless of the cost of capital.
- However, the NPVs vary depending on the actual cost of capital.
- The two NPV profile lines cross at a cost of capital of 11.975%, which is called the **crossover rate**. The crossover rate can be found by calculating the IRR of the differences in the projects' cash flows, as demonstrated:

Crossover Rate
The cost of capital at which the NPV profiles of two projects cross and, thus, at which the projects' NPVs are equal.

	0	1	2	3	4
Project S	−$1,000	$500	$400	$300	$100
Project L	−$1,000	$100	$300	$400	$675
ΔCFs − CF$_L$	$ 0	$400	$100	−$100	−$575
IRR Δ =	11.975% = Crossover Rate				

- Project L has the higher NPV if the cost of capital is less than the crossover rate, but S has the higher NPV if the cost of capital is greater than that rate.

Notice that Project L has the steeper slope, indicating that a given increase in the cost of capital causes a larger decline in NPV$_L$ than in NPV$_S$. To see why this is so, recall that L's cash flows come in later than those of S. Therefore, L is a long-term project and S is a short-term project. Next, recall the equation for the NPV:

$$NPV = CF_0 + \frac{CF_1}{(1 + r)^1} + \frac{CF_2}{(1 + r)^2} + \cdots + \frac{CF_N}{(1 + r)^N}$$

FIGURE 11-6	NPV Profiles for Projects S and L

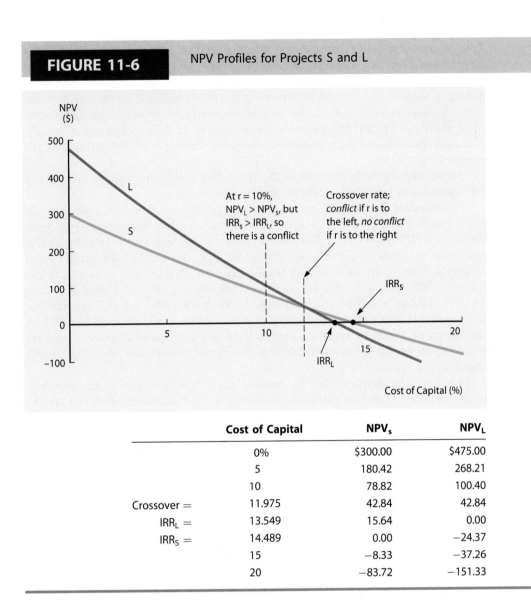

	Cost of Capital	NPV$_s$	NPV$_L$
	0%	$300.00	$475.00
	5	180.42	268.21
	10	78.82	100.40
Crossover =	11.975	42.84	42.84
IRR$_L$ =	13.549	15.64	0.00
IRR$_S$ =	14.489	0.00	−24.37
	15	−8.33	−37.26
	20	−83.72	−151.33

Now recognize that the impact of an increase in the cost of capital is much greater on distant than near-term cash flows, as we demonstrate here:

Effect of doubling r on a Year 1 cash flow:

$$\text{PV of } \$100 \text{ due in 1 year @ } r = 5\%: \frac{\$100}{(1.05)^1} = \$95.24$$

$$\text{PV of } \$100 \text{ due in 1 year @ } r = 10\%: \frac{\$100}{(1.10)^1} = \$90.91$$

$$\text{Percentage decline due to higher } r = \frac{\$95.24 - \$90.91}{\$95.24} = 4.5\%$$

Effect of doubling r on a Year 20 cash flow:

$$\text{PV of } \$100 \text{ due in 20 years @ } r = 5\%: \frac{\$100}{(1.05)^{20}} = \$37.69$$

$$\text{PV of } \$100 \text{ due in 20 years @ } r = 10\%: \frac{\$100}{(1.10)^{20}} = \$14.86$$

$$\text{Percentage decline due to higher } r = \frac{\$37.69 - \$14.86}{\$37.69} = 60.6\%$$

Thus, a doubling of the discount rate results in only a 4.5% decline in the PV of a Year 1 cash flow, but the same discount rate increase causes the PV of a Year 20 cash flow to fall by more than 60%. *Therefore, if a project has most of its cash flows coming in the later years, its NPV will decline sharply if the cost of capital increases; but a project whose cash flows come earlier will not be severely penalized by high capital costs.* Most of Project L's cash flows come in its later years; so if the cost of capital is high, L is hurt much worse than Project S. Therefore, Project L's NPV profile has the steeper slope.

Sometimes the NPV and IRR methods produce conflicting results. We can use NPV profiles to see when conflicts can and cannot arise.

Independent Projects. If an independent project with normal cash flows is being evaluated, the NPV and IRR criteria always lead to the same accept/reject decision: If NPV says accept, IRR also says accept, and vice versa. To see why this is so, look at Figure 11-5 and notice that (1) the IRR says accept if the project's cost of capital is less than (or to the left of) the IRR and (2) if the cost of capital is less than the IRR, the NPV will be positive. Thus, at any cost of capital less than 14.489%, Project S will be recommended by both the NPV and IRR criteria; but both methods reject the project if the cost of capital is greater than 14.489%. A similar graph could be used for Project L or any other normal project, and we would always reach the same conclusion: *For normal, independent projects, if the IRR says accept, so will the NPV.*

Mutually Exclusive Projects. Assume that Projects S and L are mutually exclusive rather than independent. Therefore, we can choose either S or L, or we can reject both; but we can't accept both. Now look at Figure 11-6 and note these points:

- As long as the cost of capital is *greater than* the crossover rate, 11.975%, both methods agree that Project S is better: $NPV_S > NPV_L$ and $IRR_S > IRR_L$. Therefore, if r is *greater* than the crossover rate, no conflict occurs.

- However, if the cost of capital is *less than* the crossover rate, a conflict arises: NPV ranks L higher, but IRR ranks S higher.

Two basic conditions cause NPV profiles to cross and thus lead to conflicts:[18]

1. *Timing differences.* If most of the cash flows from one project come in early while most of those from the other project come in later, as occurred with Projects S and L, the NPV profiles may cross and result in a conflict.

2. *Project size (or scale) differences.* If the amount invested in one project is larger than the other, this too can lead to profiles crossing and a resulting conflict.

When size or timing differences occur, the firm will have different amounts of funds to invest in the various years depending on which of the two mutually exclusive projects it chooses. If it chooses S, it will have more funds to invest in Year 1 because S has a higher inflow that year. Similarly, if one project costs more than the other, the firm will have more money to invest at t = 0 if it selects the smaller project.

Given this situation, the rate of return at which differential cash flows can be reinvested is a critical issue. We saw earlier that the NPV assumes reinvestment at the cost of capital and that this is generally the best assumption. Therefore, *when conflicts exist between mutually exclusive projects, use the NPV method.*

---

[18]Of course, mutually exclusive projects can differ with respect to both scale and timing. Also, if mutually exclusive projects have different lives (as opposed to different cash flow patterns over a common life), this introduces further complications; and for meaningful comparisons, some mutually exclusive projects must be evaluated over a common life. This point is discussed later in the text and in an appendix on the text's web site.

Describe in words how an NPV profile is constructed. How are the intercepts of the x- and y-axes determined?

What is the crossover rate, and how does its value relative to the cost of capital determine whether a conflict exists between NPV and IRR?

What two characteristics can lead to conflicts between the NPV and the IRR when evaluating mutually exclusive projects?

11-8 PAYBACK PERIOD

NPV is the most commonly used method today; but historically, the first selection criterion was the **payback period**, defined as the number of years required to recover the funds invested in a project from its operating cash flows. Equation 11-3 is used for the calculation, and the process is diagrammed in Figure 11-7. We start with the project's cost, a negative, and then add the cash inflow for each year until the cumulative cash flow turns positive. The payback year is the year prior to full recovery plus a fraction equal to the shortfall at the end of that year divided by the cash flow during the full recovery year:[19]

Payback Period
The length of time required for an investment's net revenues to cover its cost.

$$\text{Payback} = \begin{array}{c}\text{Number of} \\ \text{years prior to} \\ \text{full recovery}\end{array} + \dfrac{\begin{array}{c}\text{Unrecovered cost} \\ \text{at start of year}\end{array}}{\begin{array}{c}\text{Cash flow during} \\ \text{full recovery year}\end{array}} \qquad \text{11-3}$$

The shorter the payback, the better the project. Therefore, if the firm requires a payback of three years or less, S would be accepted, but L would be rejected. If the projects were mutually exclusive, S would be ranked over L because of its shorter payback.

FIGURE 11-7	Payback Calculations					
Project S	Years	0	1	2	3	4
	Cash flow	−1,000	500	400	300	100
	Cumulative cash flow	−1,000	−500	−100	200	300
Payback S = 2 + 100/300 =	2.33					
Project L	Years	0	1	2	3	4
	Cash flow	−1,000	100	300	400	675
	Cumulative cash flow	−1,000	−900	−600	−200	475
Payback L = 3 + 200/675 =	3.30					

---

[19]Equation 11-3 assumes that cash flows come in uniformly during the full recovery year.

The payback has three flaws: (1) All dollars received in different years are given the same weight (i.e., the time value of money is ignored). (2) Cash flows beyond the payback year are given no consideration regardless of how large they might be. (3) Unlike the NPV, which tells us how much wealth a project adds, and the IRR, which tells us how much a project yields over the cost of capital, the payback merely tells us when we recover our investment. There is no necessary relationship between a given payback and investor wealth maximization, so we do not know what an acceptable payback is. The firm might use 2 years, 3 years, or any other number as the minimum acceptable payback; but the choice is purely arbitrary.

Discounted Payback

The length of time required for an investment's cash flows, discounted at the investment's cost of capital, to cover its cost.

To counter the first criticism, analysts developed the **discounted payback**. Here cash flows are discounted at the WACC; then those discounted cash flows are used to find the payback. In Figure 11-8, we calculate the discounted paybacks for S and L assuming that both have a 10% cost of capital. Each inflow is divided by $(1 + r)^t = (1.10)^t$, where t is the year in which the cash flow occurs and r is the project's cost of capital; and those PVs are used to find the payback. Project S's discounted payback is 2.95, while L's is 3.78.

Note that the payback is a "break-even" calculation in the sense that if cash flows come in at the expected rate, the project will break even. However, since the regular payback doesn't consider the cost of capital, it doesn't specify the true break-even year. The discounted payback does consider capital costs; but it still disregards cash flows beyond the payback year, which is a serious flaw. Further, if mutually exclusive projects vary in size, both payback methods can conflict with the NPV, which might lead to a poor choice. Finally, there is no way of telling how low the paybacks must be to justify project acceptance.

Although the payback methods have faults as ranking criteria, they do provide information about *liquidity* and *risk*. The shorter the payback, other things held constant, the greater the project's liquidity. This factor is often important for smaller firms that don't have ready access to the capital markets. Also, cash flows expected in the distant future are generally riskier than near-term cash flows, so the payback is used as one *risk indicator*.

FIGURE 11-8	Discounted Payback Calculations at 10% Cost of Capital

Project S

	Years	0	1	2	3	4
Cash flow		−1,000	500	400	300	100
Discounted cash flow		−1,000	455	331	225	68
Cumulative discounted CF		−1,000	−545	−215	11	79

Discounted payback S = 2 + 215/225 = 2.95

Project L

	Years	0	1	2	3	4
Cash flow		−1,000	100	300	400	675
Discounted cash flow		−1,000	91	248	301	461
Cumulative discounted CF		−1,000	−909	−661	−361	100

Discounted payback L = 3 + 361/461 = 3.78

What information does the payback convey that is absent from the other capital budgeting decision methods?

What three flaws does the regular payback have? Does the discounted payback correct all of these flaws? Explain.

Project P has a cost of $1,000 and cash flows of $300 per year for three years plus another $1,000 in Year 4. The project's cost of capital is 15%. What are P's regular and discounted paybacks? **(3.10, 3.55)** If the company requires a payback of three years or less, would the project be accepted? Would this be a good accept/reject decision considering the NPV and/or the IRR? **(NPV = $256.72, IRR = 24.78%)**

11-9 CONCLUSIONS ON CAPITAL BUDGETING METHODS

We have discussed five capital budgeting decision criteria—NPV, IRR, MIRR, payback, and discounted payback. We compared these methods with one another and highlighted their strengths and weaknesses. In the process, we may have created the impression that "sophisticated" firms should use only one method, the NPV. However, virtually all capital budgeting decisions are analyzed by computer, so it is easy to calculate all five decision criteria. In making the accept/reject decision, large, sophisticated firms such as GE, Boeing, and Airbus generally calculate and consider all five measures because each provides a somewhat different piece of information about the decision.

NPV is the single best criterion because it provides a direct measure of value the project adds to shareholder wealth. IRR and MIRR measure profitability expressed as a percentage rate of return, which is interesting to decision makers. Further, IRR and MIRR contain information concerning a project's "safety margin." To illustrate, consider a firm whose WACC is 10% that must choose between these two mutually exclusive projects: SS (for small), which costs $10,000 and is expected to return $16,500 at the end of one year, and LL (for large), which costs $100,000 and has an expected payoff of $115,550 after one year. SS has a huge IRR, 65%, while LL's IRR is a more modest 15.6%. The NPV paints a somewhat different picture—at the 10% cost of capital, SS's NPV is $5,000 while LL's is $5,045. By the NPV rule, we would choose LL. However, SS's IRR indicates that it has a much larger margin for error: Even if its cash flow was 39% below the $16,500 forecast, the firm would still recover its $10,000 investment. On the other hand, if LL's inflows fell by only 13.5% from its forecasted $115,550, the firm would not recover its investment. Further, if neither project generated any cash flows, the firm would lose only $10,000 on SS but $100,000 if it accepted LL.

The Modified IRR has all the virtues of the IRR, but it incorporates a better reinvestment rate assumption and avoids the multiple rate of return problem. So if decision makers want to know projects' rates of return, the MIRR is a better indicator than the regular IRR.

Payback and discounted payback provide indications of a project's *liquidity* and *risk*. A long payback means that investment dollars will be locked up for a long time; hence, the project is relatively illiquid. In addition, a long payback means that cash flows must be forecasted far out into the future, and that probably makes the project riskier than one with a shorter payback. A good analogy for this is bond valuation. An investor should never compare the yields to maturity on two bonds without also considering their terms to maturity because a bond's risk is significantly influenced by its maturity. The same holds true for capital projects.

In summary, the different measures provide different types of information. Since it is easy to calculate all of them, all should be considered when capital budgeting decisions are being made. For most decisions, the greatest weight should be given to the NPV, but it would be foolish to ignore the information provided by the other criteria.

SELF TEST

Describe the advantages and disadvantages of the five capital budgeting methods discussed in this chapter.

Should capital budgeting decisions be made solely on the basis of a project's NPV? Explain.

11-10 DECISION CRITERIA USED IN PRACTICE

Surveys designed to find out which of the criteria managers actually use have been taken over the years. Surveys prior to 1999 asked companies to indicate which method they gave the most weight, while the most recent survey, in 1999, asked what method(s) managers actually calculated and used. A summary of all these surveys is shown in Table 11-2, and it reveals some interesting trends.

First, the NPV criterion was not used significantly before 1980; but by 1999, it was close to the top in usage. Moreover, informal discussions with companies suggest that if a survey were to be taken in 2008, NPV would be at the top of this list. Second, the IRR method is widely used, but its recent growth is less dramatic than that of NPV. Third, payback was the most important criterion years ago, but its use as the primary criterion had fallen drastically by 1980. Companies still use payback because it is easy to calculate and it does provide some information, but it is rarely used today as the primary criterion. Fourth, "other methods," primarily the accounting rate of return and the profitability index, have been fading due to the increased use of IRR and especially NPV.

These trends are consistent with our evaluation of the various methods. NPV is the best single criterion, but all of the methods provide useful information and all are easy to calculate; thus, all are used, along with judgment and common sense. We will have more to say about all this in the next chapter.

Table 11-2	**Capital Budgeting Methods Used in Practice**				
	PRIMARY CRITERION			**CALCULATE AND USE**	
	1960	**1970**	**1980**	**1999**	
NPV	0%	0%	15%	75%	
IRR	20	60	65	76	
Payback	35	15	5	57	
Discounted Payback	NA	NA	NA	29	
Other	45	25	15	NA	
Totals	100%	100%	100%		

Source: The 1999 data are from John R. Graham and Campbell R. Harvey, "The Theory and Practice of Corporate Finance: Evidence from the Field," *Journal of Financial Economics,* 2001, pp. 187–244. Data from prior years are our estimates based on averaging data from these studies: J. S. Moore and A. K. Reichert, "An Analysis of the Financial Management Techniques Currently Employed by Large U.S. Corporations," *Journal of Business Finance and Accounting,* Winter 1983, pp. 623–645; and M. T. Stanley and S. R. Block, "A Survey of Multinational Capital Budgeting," *The Financial Review,* March 1984, pp. 36–51.

What trends in capital budgeting methodology can be seen from Table 11-2?

TYING IT ALL TOGETHER

In this chapter, we described five techniques—NPV, IRR, MIRR, payback, and discounted payback—that are used to evaluate proposed capital budgeting projects. NPV is the best single measure as it tells us how much value each project contributes to shareholder wealth. Therefore, NPV is the method that should be given the greatest weight in decisions. However, the other approaches provide useful information; and in this age of computers, it is easy to calculate all of them. Therefore, managers generally look at all five criteria when deciding to accept or reject projects and when choosing among mutually exclusive projects.

In this chapter, we took the cash flows given and used them to illustrate the different capital budgeting methods. As you will see in the next chapter, estimating cash flows is a major task. Still, the framework established in this chapter is critically important for sound capital budgeting analyses; and at this point, you should:

- Understand capital budgeting.
- Know how to calculate and use the major capital budgeting decision criteria, which are NPV, IRR, MIRR, and payback.
- Understand why NPV is the best criterion and how it overcomes problems inherent in the other methods.
- Recognize that while NPV is the best method, the other methods do provide information that decision makers find useful.

SELF-TEST QUESTIONS AND PROBLEMS
(Solutions Appear in Appendix A)

ST-1   **KEY TERMS**   Define the following terms:
     a.   Capital budgeting; strategic business plan
     b.   Net present value (NPV)
     c.   Internal rate of return (IRR)
     d.   NPV profile; crossover rate
     e.   Mutually exclusive projects; independent projects
     f.   Nonnormal cash flows; normal cash flows; multiple IRRs
     g.   Modified internal rate of return (MIRR)
     h.   Payback period; discounted payback

ST-2   **CAPITAL BUDGETING CRITERIA**   You must analyze two projects, X and Y. Each project costs $10,000, and the firm's WACC is 12%. The expected net cash flows are as follows:

	0	1	2	3	4
Project X	−$10,000	$6,500	$3,000	$3,000	$1,000
Project Y	−$10,000	$3,500	$3,500	$3,500	$3,500

a.   Calculate each project's NPV, IRR, MIRR, payback, and discounted payback.

b.   Which project(s) should be accepted if they are independent?

c.   Which project(s) should be accepted if they are mutually exclusive?

d.   How might a change in the WACC produce a conflict between the NPV and IRR rankings of the two projects? Would there be a conflict if WACC were 5%? (Hint: Plot the NPV profiles. The crossover rate is 6.21875%.)

e.   Why does the conflict exist?

QUESTIONS

11-1   How are project classifications used in the capital budgeting process?

11-2   What are three potential flaws with the regular payback method? Does the discounted payback method correct all three flaws? Explain.

11-3   Why is the NPV of a relatively long-term project (one for which a high percentage of its cash flows occurs in the distant future) more sensitive to changes in the WACC than that of a short-term project?

11-4   What is a mutually exclusive project? How should managers rank mutually exclusive projects?

11-5   If two mutually exclusive projects were being compared, would a high cost of capital favor the longer-term or the shorter-term project? Why? If the cost of capital declined, would that lead firms to invest more in longer-term projects or shorter-term projects? Would a decline (or an increase) in the WACC cause changes in the IRR ranking of mutually exclusive projects?

11-6   Discuss the following statement: If a firm has only independent projects, a constant WACC, and projects with normal cash flows, the NPV and IRR methods will always lead to identical capital budgeting decisions. What does this imply about the choice between IRR and NPV? If each of the assumptions were changed (one by one), how would your answer change?

11-7   Why might it be rational for a small firm that does not have access to the capital markets to use the payback method rather than the NPV method?

11-8   Project X is very risky and has an NPV of $3 million. Project Y is very safe and has an NPV of $2.5 million. They are mutually exclusive, and project risk has been properly considered in the NPV analyses. Which project should be chosen? Explain.

11-9   What reinvestment rate assumptions are built into the NPV, IRR, and MIRR methods? Give an explanation (other than "because the text says so") for your answer.

11-10   A firm has a $100 million capital budget. It is considering two projects, each costing $100 million. Project A has an IRR of 20%; has an NPV of $9 million; and will be terminated after 1 year at a profit of $20 million, resulting in an immediate increase in EPS. Project B, which cannot be postponed, has an IRR of 30% and an NPV of $50 million. However, the firm's short-run EPS will be reduced if it accepts Project B because no revenues will be generated for several years.

a.   Should the short-run effects on EPS influence the choice between the two projects?

b.   How might situations like this influence a firm's decision to use payback?

PROBLEMS

11-1 **NPV** Project K costs $52,125, its expected net cash inflows are $12,000 per year for 8 years, and its WACC is 12%. What is the project's NPV?

11-2 **IRR** Refer to Problem 11-1. What is the project's IRR?

11-3 **MIRR** Refer to Problem 11-1. What is the project's MIRR?

11-4 **PAYBACK PERIOD** Refer to Problem 11-1. What is the project's payback?

11-5 **DISCOUNTED PAYBACK** Refer to Problem 11-1. What is the project's discounted payback?

11-6 **NPV** Your division is considering two projects with the following net cash flows (in millions):

	0	1	2	3
Project A	−$25	$5	$10	$17
Project B	−$20	$10	$9	$6

a. What are the projects' NPVs assuming the WACC is 5%? 10%? 15%?

b. What are the projects' IRRs at each of these WACCs?

c. If the WACC was 5% and A and B were mutually exclusive, which project would you choose? What if the WACC was 10%? 15%? (Hint: The crossover rate is 7.81%.)

11-7 **CAPITAL BUDGETING CRITERIA** A firm with a 14% WACC is evaluating two projects for this year's capital budget. After-tax cash flows, including depreciation, are as follows:

	0	1	2	3	4	5
Project A	−$6,000	$2,000	$2,000	$2,000	$2,000	$2,000
Project B	−$18,000	$5,600	$5,600	$5,600	$5,600	$5,600

a. Calculate NPV, IRR, MIRR, payback, and discounted payback for each project.

b. Assuming the projects are independent, which one(s) would you recommend?

c. If the projects are mutually exclusive, which would you recommend?

d. Notice that the projects have the same cash flow timing pattern. Why is there a conflict between NPV and IRR?

11-8 **CAPITAL BUDGETING CRITERIA: ETHICAL CONSIDERATIONS** A mining company is considering a new project. Because the mine has received a permit, the project would be legal; but it would cause significant harm to a nearby river. The firm could spend an additional $10 million at Year 0 to mitigate the environmental problem, but it would not be required to do so. Developing the mine (without mitigation) would cost $60 million, and the expected net cash inflows would be $20 million per year for 5 years. If the firm does invest in mitigation, the annual inflows would be $21 million. The risk-adjusted WACC is 12%.

a. Calculate the NPV and IRR with and without mitigation.

b. How should the environmental effects be dealt with when this project is evaluated?

c. Should this project be undertaken? If so, should the firm do the mitigation?

11-9 **CAPITAL BUDGETING CRITERIA: ETHICAL CONSIDERATIONS** An electric utility is considering a new power plant in northern Arizona. Power from the plant would be sold in the Phoenix area, where it is badly needed. Because the firm has received a permit, the plant would be legal; but it would cause some air pollution. The company could spend an additional $40 million at Year 0 to mitigate the environmental problem, but it would not be required to do so. The plant without mitigation would cost $240 million, and the expected net cash inflows would be $80 million per year for 5 years. If the firm does invest in mitigation, the annual inflows would be $84 million. Unemployment in the area where the plant would be built is high, and the plant would provide about 350 good jobs. The risk-adjusted WACC is 17%.

a. Calculate the NPV and IRR with and without mitigation.

b. How should the environmental effects be dealt with when evaluating this project?

c. Should this project be undertaken? If so, should the firm do the mitigation?

11-10 **CAPITAL BUDGETING CRITERIA: MUTUALLY EXCLUSIVE PROJECTS** A firm with a WACC of 10% is considering the following mutually exclusive projects:

	0	1	2	3	4	5
Project A	−$400	$55	$55	$55	$225	$225
Project B	−$600	$300	$300	$50	$50	$49

Which project would you recommend? Explain.

11-11 **CAPITAL BUDGETING CRITERIA: MUTUALLY EXCLUSIVE PROJECTS** Project S costs $15,000, and its expected cash flows would be $4,500 per year for 5 years. Mutually exclusive Project L costs $37,500, and its expected cash flows would be $11,100 per year for 5 years. If both projects have a WACC of 14%, which project would you recommend? Explain.

11-12 **IRR AND NPV** A company is analyzing two mutually exclusive projects, S and L, with the following cash flows:

	0	1	2	3	4
Project S	−$1,000	$900	$250	$10	$10
Project L	−$1,000	$0	$250	$400	$800

The company's WACC is 10%. What is the IRR of the *better* project? (Hint: The better project may or may not be the one with the higher IRR.)

11-13 **MIRR** A firm is considering two mutually exclusive projects, X and Y, with the following cash flows:

	0	1	2	3	4
Project X	−$1,000	$100	$300	$400	$700
Project Y	−$1,000	$1,000	$100	$50	$50

The projects are equally risky, and their WACC is 12%. What is the MIRR of the project that maximizes shareholder value?

Challenging Problems 14–22

11-14 **CHOOSING MANDATORY PROJECTS ON THE BASIS OF LEAST COST** K. Kim Inc. must install a new air conditioning unit in its main plant. Kim must install one or the other of the units; otherwise, the highly profitable plant would have to shut down. Two units are available, HCC and LCC (for high and low capital costs, respectively). HCC has a high capital cost but relatively low operating costs, while LCC has a low capital cost but higher operating costs because it uses more electricity. The costs of the units are shown here. Kim's WACC is 7%.

	0	1	2	3	4	5
HCC	−$600,000	−$50,000	−$50,000	−$50,000	−$50,000	−$50,000
LCC	−$100,000	−$175,000	−$175,000	−$175,000	−$175,000	−$175,000

a. Which unit would you recommend? Explain.

b. If Kim's controller wanted to know the IRRs of the two projects, what would you tell him?

c. If the WACC rose to 15% would this affect your recommendation? Explain your answer and the reason this result occurred.

11-15 **NPV PROFILES: TIMING DIFFERENCES** An oil drilling company must choose between two mutually exclusive extraction projects, and each costs $12 million. Under Plan A, all the oil would be extracted in 1 year, producing a cash flow at $t = 1$ of $14.4 million. Under Plan B, cash flows would be $2.1 million per year for 20 years. The firm's WACC is 12%.

a. Construct NPV profiles for Plans A and B, identify each project's IRR, and show the approximate crossover rate.

b. Is it logical to assume that the firm would take on all available independent, average-risk projects with returns greater than 12%? If all available projects with returns greater than 12% have been undertaken, does this mean that cash flows from past investments have an opportunity cost of only 12% because all the company can do with these cash flows is to replace money that has a cost of 12%? Does this imply that the WACC is the correct reinvestment rate assumption for a project's cash flows?

11-16 **NPV PROFILES: SCALE DIFFERENCES** A company is considering two mutually exclusive expansion plans. Plan A requires a $40 million expenditure on a large-scale integrated plant that would provide expected cash flows of $6.4 million per year for 20 years. Plan B requires a $12 million expenditure to build a somewhat less efficient, more labor-intensive plant with expected cash flows of $2.72 million per year for 20 years. The firm's WACC is 10%.

    a. Calculate each project's NPV and IRR.

    b. Graph the NPV profiles for Plan A and Plan B and approximate the crossover rate.

    c. Why is NPV better than IRR for making capital budgeting decisions that add to shareholder value?

11-17 **CAPITAL BUDGETING CRITERIA** A company has a 12% WACC and is considering two mutually exclusive investments (that cannot be repeated) with the following net cash flows:

	0	1	2	3	4	5	6	7
Project A	−$300	−$387	−$193	−$100	$600	$600	$850	−$180
Project B	−$405	$134	$134	$134	$134	$134	$134	$0

    a. What is each project's NPV?

    b. What is each project's IRR?

    c. What is each project's MIRR? (Hint: Consider Period 7 as the end of Project B's life.)

    d. From your answers to Parts a, b, and c, which project would be selected? If the WACC was 18%, which project would be selected?

    e. Construct NPV profiles for Projects A and B.

    f. What is each project's MIRR at a WACC of 18%?

11-18 **NPV AND IRR** A store has 5 years remaining on its lease in a mall. Rent is $2,000 per month, 60 payments remain, and the next payment is due in 1 month. The mall's owner plans to sell the property in a year and wants rent at that time to be high so that the property will appear more valuable. Therefore, the store has been offered a "great deal" (owner's words) on a new 5-year lease. The new lease calls for no rent for 9 months, then payments of $2,600 per month for the next 51 months. The lease cannot be broken, and the store's WACC is 12% (or 1% per month).

    a. Should the new lease be accepted? (Hint: Make sure you use 1% per month.)

    b. If the store owner decided to bargain with the mall's owner over the new lease payment, what new lease payment would make the store owner indifferent between the new and old leases? (Hint: Find FV of the old lease's original cost at $t = 9$; then treat this as the PV of a 51-period annuity whose payments represent the rent during months 10 to 60.)

    c. The store owner is not sure of the 12% WACC—it could be higher or lower. At what *nominal* WACC would the store owner be indifferent between the two leases? (Hint: Calculate the differences between the two payment streams; then find its IRR.)

11-19 **MULTIPLE IRRS AND MIRR** A mining company is deciding whether to open a strip mine, which costs $2 million. Net cash inflows of $13 million would occur at the end of Year 1. The land must be returned to its natural state at a cost of $12 million, payable at the end of Year 2.

    a. Plot the project's NPV profile.

    b. Should the project be accepted if WACC = 10%? if WACC = 20%? Explain your reasoning.

    c. Think of some other capital budgeting situations in which negative cash flows during or at the end of the project's life might lead to multiple IRRs.

    d. What is the project's MIRR at WACC = 10%? at WACC = 20%? Does MIRR lead to the same accept/reject decision for this project as the NPV method? Does the MIRR method *always* lead to the same accept/reject decision as NPV? (Hint: Consider mutually exclusive projects that differ in size.)

11-20 **NPV** A project has annual cash flows of $7,500 for the next 10 years and then $10,000 each year for the following 10 years. The IRR of this 20-year project is 10.98%. If the firm's WACC is 9%, what is the project's NPV?

11-21 **MIRR** Project X costs $1,000, and its cash flows are the same in Years 1 through 10. Its IRR is 12%, and its WACC is 10%. What is the project's MIRR?

11-22 **MIRR** A project has the following cash flows:

0	1	2	3	4	5
−$500	$202	−$X	$196	$350	$451

This project requires two outflows at Years 0 and 2, but the remaining cash flows are positive. Its WACC is 10%, and its MIRR is 14.14%. What is the Year 2 cash outflow?

COMPREHENSIVE/SPREADSHEET PROBLEM

11-23 **CAPITAL BUDGETING CRITERIA** Your division is considering two projects. Its WACC is 10%, and the projects' after-tax cash flows (in millions of dollars) would be as follows:

	0	1	2	3	4
Project A	−$30	$5	$10	$15	$20
Project B	−$30	$20	$10	$8	$6

a. Calculate the projects' NPVs, IRRs, MIRRs, regular paybacks, and discounted paybacks.

b. If the two projects are independent, which project(s) should be chosen?

c. If the two projects are mutually exclusive and the WACC is 10%, which project(s) should be chosen?

d. Plot NPV profiles for the two projects. Identify the projects' IRRs on the graph.

e. If the WACC was 5%, would this change your recommendation if the projects were mutually exclusive? If the WACC was 15%, would this change your recommendation? Explain your answers.

f. The crossover rate is 13.5252%. Explain what this rate is and how it affects the choice between mutually exclusive projects.

g. Is it possible for conflicts to exist between the NPV and the IRR when *independent* projects are being evaluated? Explain your answer.

h. Now look at the regular and discounted paybacks. Which project looks better when judged by the paybacks?

i. If the payback was the only method a firm used to accept or reject projects, what pay-back should it choose as the cutoff point, that is, reject projects if their payouts are not below the chosen cutoff? Is your selected cutoff based on some economic criteria, or is it more or less arbitrary? Are the cutoff criteria equally arbitrary when firms use the NPV and/or the IRR as the criteria? Explain.

j. Define the MIRR. What's the difference between the IRR and the MIRR, and which generally gives a better idea of the rate of return on the investment in a project?

k. Why do most academics and financial executives regard the NPV as being the single best criterion and better than the IRR? Why do companies still calculate IRRs?

INTEGRATED CASE

ALLIED COMPONENTS COMPANY

11-24 **BASICS OF CAPITAL BUDGETING** You recently went to work for Allied Components Company, a supplier of auto repair parts used in the after-market with products from Daimler, Chrysler, Ford, and other automakers. Your boss, the chief financial officer (CFO), has just handed you the estimated cash flows for two proposed projects. Project L involves adding a new item to the firm's ignition system line; it would take some time to build up the market for this product, so the cash inflows would increase over time. Project S involves an add-on to an existing line, and its cash flows would decrease over time. Both projects have 3-year lives because Allied is planning to introduce entirely new models after 3 years.

Here are the projects' net cash flows (in thousands of dollars):

	0	1	2	3
Project L	−$100	$10	$60	$80
Project S	−$100	$70	$50	$20

Depreciation, salvage values, net working capital requirements, and tax effects are all included in these cash flows. The CFO also made subjective risk assessments of each project, and he concluded that both projects have risk characteristics that are similar to the firm's average project. Allied's WACC is 10%. You must determine whether one or both of the projects should be accepted.

a. What is capital budgeting? Are there any similarities between a firm's capital budgeting decisions and an individual's investment decisions?

b. What is the difference between independent and mutually exclusive projects? Between projects with normal and nonnormal cash flows?

c. (1) Define the term *net present value (NPV)*. What is each project's NPV?

   (2) What is the rationale behind the NPV method? According to NPV, which project(s) should be accepted if they are independent? mutually exclusive?

   (3) Would the NPVs change if the WACC changed? Explain.

d. (1) Define the term *internal rate of return (IRR)*. What is each project's IRR?

   (2) How is the IRR on a project related to the YTM on a bond?

   (3) What is the logic behind the IRR method? According to IRR, which project(s) should be accepted if they are independent? mutually exclusive?

   (4) Would the projects' IRRs change if the WACC changed?

e. (1) Draw NPV profiles for Projects L and S. At what discount rate do the profiles cross?

   (2) Look at your NPV profile graph without referring to the actual NPVs and IRRs. Which project(s) should be accepted if they are independent? mutually exclusive? Explain. Are your answers correct at any WACC less than 23.6%?

f. (1) What is the underlying cause of ranking conflicts between NPV and IRR?

   (2) What is the reinvestment rate assumption, and how does it affect the NPV versus IRR conflict?

   (3) Which method is best? Why?

g. (1) Define the term *modified IRR (MIRR)*. Find the MIRRs for Projects L and S.

   (2) What are the MIRR's advantages and disadvantages vis-à-vis the NPV?

h. (1) What is the payback period? Find the paybacks for Projects L and S.

   (2) What is the rationale for the payback method? According to the payback criterion, which project(s) should be accepted if the firm's maximum acceptable payback is 2 years, if Projects L and S are independent, if Projects L and S are mutually exclusive?

   (3) What is the difference between the regular and discounted payback methods?

   (4) What are the two main disadvantages of discounted payback? Is the payback method of any real usefulness in capital budgeting decisions? Explain.

i. As a separate project (Project P), the firm is considering sponsoring a pavilion at the upcoming World's Fair. The pavilion would cost $800,000, and it is expected to result in $5 million of incremental cash inflows during its 1 year of operation. However, it would then take another year, and $5 million of costs, to demolish the site and return it to its original condition. Thus, Project P's expected net cash flows look like this (in millions of dollars):

	0	1	2
	−$0.8	$5.0	−$5.0

The project is estimated to be of average risk, so its WACC is 10%.

   (1) What is Project P's NPV? What is its IRR? its MIRR?

   (2) Draw Project P's NPV profile. Does Project P have normal or nonnormal cash flows? Should this project be accepted? Explain.

CHAPTER 12 Cash Flow Estimation and Risk Analysis

Home Depot Keeps Growing

Home Depot Inc. (HD) has grown phenomenally in recent years, and that growth continues. At the beginning of 1990, HD had 118 stores with annual sales of $2.8 billion. By early 2008, it had 2,234 stores and annual sales of $77 billion. Stockholders have benefited mightily from this growth as the stock's price has increased from a split-adjusted $1.87 in 1990 to $40 in early 2007, or by 2,039%.

However, the more recent news has not been as good. In the face of a declining housing market, the company has struggled. In May 2008, it announced the closing of 12 underperforming stores. Still, despite the poor housing market, the company continues to open new stores in areas it thinks the stores will do well. It costs, on average, over $20 million to purchase land, construct a new store, and stock it with inventory. Therefore, it is critical that the company perform a financial analysis to determine whether a potential store's expected cash flows will cover its costs.

Home Depot uses information from its existing stores to forecast its new stores' expected cash flows. Thus far, its forecasts have been outstanding, but there are always risks. First, a store's sales might be less than projected, especially if the economy weakens. Second, some of HD's customers might bypass the store altogether and buy directly from manufacturers through the Internet. Third, its new stores could "cannibalize," or take sales away from, its existing stores. To avoid cannibalization while still opening enough new stores to generate substantial growth, HD has been developing complementary formats. For example, it recently rolled out its Expo Design Center chain, which offers one-stop sales and service for kitchen, bath, and other remodeling and renovation work; and in 2007, it acquired a Chinese home improvement chain to jump-start its operations in that nation.

Rational expansion decisions require detailed assessments of the forecasted cash flows, along with a measure of the risk that forecasted sales might not be realized. That information can then be used to determine the risk-adjusted NPV associated with each potential project. In this chapter, we describe techniques for estimating projects' cash flows, as well as projects' risks. Companies such as Home Depot use these techniques on a regular basis when making capital budgeting decisions.

PUTTING THINGS IN PERSPECTIVE

The basic principles of capital budgeting were covered in Chapter 11. Given a project's expected cash flows, it is easy to calculate the primary decision criterion—the NPV—as well as the supplemental criteria, IRR, MIRR, payback, and discounted payback. However, in the real world, cash flow numbers are not just handed to you—rather, they must be estimated based on information from various sources. Moreover, uncertainty surrounds the forecasted cash flows, and some projects are more uncertain and thus riskier than others. In this chapter, we review examples that illustrate how project cash flows are estimated, discuss techniques for measuring and then dealing with risk, and discuss how projects are evaluated once they go into operation. Finally, we discuss techniques to use when evaluating mutually exclusive projects that have unequal lives.

When you finish this chapter, you should be able to:

- Identify "relevant" cash flows that should and should not be included in a capital budgeting analysis.
- Estimate a project's relevant cash flows and put them into a time line format that can be used to calculate a project's NPV, IRR, and other capital budgeting metrics.
- Explain how risk is measured and use this measure to adjust the firm's WACC to account for differential project riskiness.
- Correctly calculate the NPV of mutually exclusive projects that have unequal lives.

12-1 CONCEPTUAL ISSUES IN CASH FLOW ESTIMATION

Before the cash flow estimation process is illustrated, we need to discuss several important conceptual issues. A failure to handle these issues properly can lead to incorrect NPVs and thus bad capital budgeting decisions.

12-1a Cash Flow versus Accounting Income

We saw in Chapter 3 that there is a difference between cash flows and accounting income. We also saw that *cash* is what people and firms spend or reinvest; so the present value of *cash flows*, not accounting income, is the basis of a firm's value. That's why, in the last chapter, we discounted net cash flows, not net income, to find projects' NPVs.

Many things can lead to differences between net cash flows and net income. First, depreciation is not a cash outlay, but it is deducted when net income is calculated. Second, net income is based on the depreciation rate the firm's accountants decide to use, not necessarily on the depreciation rate allowed by the IRS, and it is the IRS rate that determines cash flows. Moreover, if a project requires an addition to working capital, this directly affects cash flows but not net income. Other factors also differentiate net income from cash flow, but the important thing to keep in mind is this: *For capital budgeting purposes, the project's cash flows, not its accounting income, is the key item.*

12-1b Timing of Cash Flows

In theory, capital budgeting analyses should deal with cash flows exactly when they occur; hence, daily cash flows theoretically would be better than annual flows. However, it would be costly to estimate and analyze daily cash flows, and they would probably be no more accurate than annual estimates because we simply cannot accurately forecast at a daily level out 10 years or so into the future. Therefore, we generally assume that all cash flows occur at the end of the year. Note, though, for projects with highly predictable cash flows, it might be useful to assume that cash flows occur at midyear (or even quarterly or monthly); but for most purposes, we assume end-of-year flows.

12-1c Incremental Cash Flows

Incremental Cash Flow
A cash flow that will occur if and only if the firm takes on a project.

Incremental cash flows are flows that will occur *if and only if* some specific event occurs. In capital budgeting, the event is the firm's acceptance of a project and the project's incremental cash flows are ones that occur as a result of this decision. Cash flows such as investments in buildings, equipment, and working capital needed for the project are obviously incremental, as are sales revenues and operating costs associated with the project. However, some items are not so obvious, as we explain later in this section.

12-1d Replacement Projects

Two types of projects can be distinguished: expansion projects, where the firm makes an investment, such as a new Home Depot store, and replacement projects, where the firm replaces existing assets, generally to reduce costs. For example, suppose Home Depot is considering replacing some of its delivery trucks. The benefit would be lower fuel and maintenance expenses, and the shiny new trucks also might improve the company's image and reduce pollution. Replacement analysis is complicated by the fact that almost all of the cash flows are incremental, found by subtracting the new cost numbers from the old numbers. Thus, the fuel bill for a more efficient new truck might be $10,000 per year versus $15,000 for the old truck. The $5,000 savings is the incremental cash flow that would be used in the replacement analysis. Similarly, we would need to find the difference in depreciation and other factors that affect cash flows. Once we have found the incremental cash flows, we use them in a "regular" NPV analysis to decide whether to replace the asset or to continue using it.

12-1e Sunk Costs

Sunk Cost
A cash outlay that has already been incurred and that cannot be recovered regardless of whether the project is accepted or rejected.

A **sunk cost** is an outlay that was incurred in the past and cannot be recovered in the future regardless of whether the project under consideration is accepted. In capital budgeting, we are concerned with *future incremental cash flows*—we want to know if the *new* investment will produce enough incremental cash flow to justify the incremental investment. *Because sunk costs were incurred in the past and cannot be recovered regardless of whether the project is accepted or rejected, they are not relevant in the capital budgeting analysis.*

To illustrate this concept, suppose Home Depot spent $2 million to investigate a potential new store and obtain the permits required to build it. That $2 million would be a sunk cost—the money is gone, and it won't come back regardless of whether or not the new store is built.

Not handling sunk costs properly can lead to incorrect decisions. For example, suppose Home Depot completed the analysis and found that it must spend an additional $17 million, on top of the $2 million site study, to open the store. Suppose it then used as the required investment $19 million and found a projected NPV of *negative* $1 million. This would indicate that HD should reject the new store. *However, that would be a bad decision.* The real issue is whether the *incremental* $17 million would result in *incremental* cash inflows sufficient to produce a positive NPV. If the $2 million sunk cost is disregarded, as it should be, the true NPV will be a *positive* $1 million. Therefore, the failure to deal properly with the sunk cost would lead to turning down a project that would add $1 million to stockholders' value.

12-1f Opportunity Costs Associated with Assets the Firm Owns

Another issue relates to **opportunity costs** associated with assets the firm already owns. For example, suppose Home Depot owns land with a market value of $2 million and that land will be used for the new store if HD decides to build it. If HD decides to go forward with the project, only another $15 million will be required, not the typical $17 million because HD would not need to buy the required land. Does this mean that HD should use $15 million as the cost of the new store? The answer is no. If the new store is not built, HD could sell the land and receive a cash flow of $2 million. This $2 million is an *opportunity cost*— something that HD would not receive if the land was used for the new store. Therefore, the $2 million must be charged to the new project, and a failure to do so would artificially and incorrectly increase the new project's NPV.

> **Opportunity Cost**
> *The best return that can be earned on assets the firm already owns if those assets are not used for the new project.*

If this is not clear, consider the following example. Assume that a firm owns a building and equipment with a market (resale) value of $10 million. The property is not being used, and the firm is considering using it for a new project. The only required additional investment would be $100,000 for working capital, and the new project would produce a cash inflow of $50,000 forever. If the firm has a WACC of 10% and evaluates the project using only the $100,000 of working capital as the required investment, it would find an NPV of $50,000/0.10 = $500,000. Does this mean that the project is a good one? The answer is no. The firm can sell the property for $10 million, which is a much larger amount than $500,000.

12-1g Externalities

Another potential problem involves **externalities**, which are defined as the effects of a project on other parts of the firm or the environment. The three types of externalities—negative within-firm externalities, positive within-firm externalities, and environmental externalities—are explained next.

> **Externality**
> *An effect on the firm or the environment that is not reflected in the project's cash flows.*

Negative Within-Firm Externalities

As noted earlier, when retailers such as Home Depot open new stores that are too close to their existing stores, this takes customers away from their existing stores. In this case, even though the new store has positive cash flows, its existence reduces some of the firm's current cash flows. This type of externality is called **cannibalization** because the new business eats into the company's existing business. Manufacturers also can experience cannibalization. Thus, if Cengage Learning, the publisher of this book, decides to publish another introductory finance text, that new book will presumably reduce sales of this one. Those lost cash flows should be taken into account, and that means charging them as a cost when analyzing the proposed new book.

> **Cannibalization**
> *The situation when a new project reduces cash flows that the firm would otherwise have had.*

Dealing properly with negative externalities can be tricky. If Cengage decides not to publish the new book because of its cannibalization effects, might another publisher publish it, causing our book to lose sales regardless of what Cengage does? Logically, Cengage must examine the total situation, which is more than a simple mechanical analysis. Experience and knowledge of the industry is required to make good decisions.

One of the best examples of a company fouling up as a result of not dealing correctly with cannibalization effects was IBM's response when transistors made personal computers possible in the 1970s. IBM's mainframe computers were the biggest game in town, and they generated huge profits. But IBM also had the technology, entered into the PC market, and for a time was the leading PC company. However, top management decided to rein back the PC division because managers were afraid it would hurt the more profitable mainframe business. That decision opened the door for Microsoft, Intel, Dell, Hewlett-Packard, and others; and IBM went from being the most profitable firm in the world to one whose very survival was threatened. This experience highlights the fact that while it is essential to understand the theory of finance, it is equally important to understand the business environment, including how competitors are likely to react to a firm's actions. A great deal of judgment goes into making good financial decisions.

Positive Within-Firm Externalities

Cannibalization occurs when new products compete with old ones. However, a new project also can be *complementary* to an old one, in which case cash flows in the old operation will be *increased* when the new one is introduced. For example, Apple's iPod was a profitable product; but when Apple made an investment in another project, its music store, that investment boosted sales of the iPod. So if an analysis of the proposed music store indicated a negative NPV, the analysis would not be complete unless the incremental cash flows that would occur in the iPod division were credited to the music store. That might well change the project's NPV from negative to positive.

Environmental Externalities

The most common type of negative externality is a project's impact on the environment. Government rules and regulations constrain what companies can do, but firms have some flexibility in dealing with the environment. For example, suppose a manufacturer is studying a proposed new plant. The company could meet the environmental regulations at a cost of $1 million, but the plant would still emit fumes that might cause ill feelings in its neighborhood. Those ill feelings would not show up in the cash flow analysis, but they still should be considered. Perhaps a relatively small additional expenditure would reduce the emissions substantially, make the plant look good relative to other plants in the area, and provide goodwill that would help the firm's sales and negotiations with governmental agencies in the future.

Of course, everyone's profits depend on the earth remaining healthy, so companies have an incentive to do things to protect the environment even though those actions are not required. However, if one firm decides to take actions that are good for the environment but costly, its products must reflect the higher costs. If its competitors decide to get by with less costly but less environmentally friendly processes, they can price their products lower and make more money. Of course, more environmentally friendly companies can advertise their environmental efforts, and this might—or might not—offset the higher costs. All of this illustrates why government regulations are necessary, both nationally and internationally. Finance, politics, and the environment are all interconnected.

SELF TEST Why should companies use a project's cash flows rather than accounting income when determining a project's NPV?

Explain the following terms: incremental cash flow, sunk cost, opportunity cost, externality, and cannibalization.

Provide an example of a "good" externality, that is, one that increases a project's true NPV.

12-2 ANALYSIS OF AN EXPANSION PROJECT

In Chapter 11, we analyzed two projects, S and L. We were given the cash flows and used them to illustrate how the NPV, IRR, MIRR, and payback are calculated. Now we demonstrate how cash flows are actually estimated, using our old Project S to demonstrate the procedure. We explain the process in Table 12-1. Look at it as we discuss the analysis. Note that the dollars are in thousands; we omitted

| **Table 12-1** | **Cash Flow Estimation and Analysis for Expansion Project S** |

	A	B	C	D	E	F	G	H	I
1									
2					0	1	2	3	4
3	*Investment Outlays at Time = 0*								
4	Equipment				-$ 900				
5	Net WC				-100				
6	*Net Cash Flows Over the Project's Life*								
7	Unit sales					537	520	505	490
8	Sales price					$10.00	$10.00	$10.00	$10.00
9	Variable cost per unit					$5.092	$5.391	$5.228	$6.106
10	Sales revenues = Units × Price					$5,370	$5,200	$5,050	$4,900
11	Variable costs = Units × Cost/unit					2,735	2,803	2,640	2,992
12	Fixed operating costs except depreciation					2,000	2,000	2,000	2,000
13	Depreciation: <u>Accelerated</u> from table below					297	405	135	63
14	Total operating costs					$5,032	$5,208	$4,775	$5,055
15	EBIT (or operating income)					$ 338	-$ 8	$ 275	-$ 155
16	Taxes on operating income		40%			135	-3	110	-62
17	After-tax project operating income					$ 203	-$ 5	$ 165	-$ 93
18	Add back depreciation					297	405	135	63
19	Salvage value (taxed as ordinary income)								50
20	Tax on salvage value (SV is taxed at 40%)								-20
21	Recovery of net working capital								100
22	Project net cash flows (Time Line)				-$1,000	$ 500	$ 400	$ 300	$ 100
23	*Depreciation*			<u>Accelerated</u>		1	2	3	4
24		Cost:	$900	Rate		33%	45%	15%	7%
25				Depreciation		$297	$405	$135	$63
26	Alternative *depreciation*			<u>Straight line</u>					
27		Cost:	$900	Rate		25%	25%	25%	25%
28				Depreciation		$225	$225	$225	$225
29	*Project Evaluation @ WACC =*				10%				
30			Accelerated			Formulas		Straight line	
31		NPV	$78.82		=NPV(D29,F22:I22)+E22			$64.44	
32		IRR	14.489%		=IRR(E22:I22)			13.437%	
33		MIRR	12.106%		=MIRR(E22:I22,D29,D29)			11.731%	
34		Payback	2.33		=G2+(-E22-F22-G22)/H22			2.60	

35. 1. Accelerated depreciation rates are set by Congress. We show the <u>approximate</u> rates for a 4-year asset in 2008. Companies also have the option of using straight-line depreciation. Under IRS rules, salvage value is not deducted when establishing the depreciable basis. However, if a salvage payment is received, it is called a recapture of depreciation and is taxed at the 40% rate.

36. 2. If the firm owned assets that would be used for the project but would be sold if the project is not accepted, the after-tax value of those assets would be shown as an "opportunity cost" in the "Investment Outlays" section.

37. 3. If this project would reduce sales and cash flows from one of the firm's other divisions, then the after-tax cannibalization effect, or "externality," would be deducted from the net cash flows shown on Row 22.

38. 4. If the firm had previously incurred costs associated with this project, but those costs could not be recovered regardless of whether this project is accepted, then they are "sunk costs" and should not enter the analysis.

three zeros to streamline the presentation. Also note that we used Excel to make Table 12-1. We could have used a calculator and plain paper, but Excel is much better in dealing with arithmetic. You don't need to know Excel to understand the discussion; but if you plan to work in finance—or in almost any business function—you should learn something about it.

The column headers in the table, the A through I, and the row headers, 1 through 38, designate cells, which contain the data. For example, the equipment needed for Project S will cost $900, and that number is shown in Cell E4 as a negative. The equipment is expected to have a salvage value of $50 at the end of the project's 4-year life; this is shown in Cell I19.[1] The new project will require $100 of working capital; this is shown in Cell E5 as a negative number because it is a cost and then as a positive number in Cell I21 because it is recovered at the end of Year 4. The total investment at Time 0 is $1,000, which is shown in Cell E22.

Unit sales of Project S are shown on Row 7; they are expected to decline somewhat over the project's 4-year life. The sales price, a constant $10, is shown on Row 8. The projected variable cost per unit is given on Row 9; it generally increases over time due to expected increases in materials and labor. Sales revenues, which are calculated as units multiplied by price, are given on Row 10. Variable costs, equal to units multiplied by VC/unit, are given on Row 11; and fixed costs excluding depreciation, which are a constant $2,000, are shown on Row 12.

Depreciation is found as the annual rate allowed by the IRS times the depreciable basis. As noted in Chapter 3, Congress sets the depreciation rates that can be used for tax purposes and these are the tax rates used in the capital budgeting analysis. Congress permits firms to depreciate assets by the straight-line method or by an accelerated method. As we will see, profitable firms are better off using accelerated depreciation. We discuss depreciation more fully in Appendix 12A; but to simplify things for this chapter, we assume that the applicable accelerated rates for a project with a 4-year life are as given on Row 24 of the depreciation section of the table and that straight-line rates are as given on Row 27. Thus, we assume that if the firm uses accelerated depreciation, it will write off 33% of the basis during Year 1, another 45% in Year 2, and so forth. These are the rates used to obtain the cash flows shown in the table.

The depreciable basis is the cost of the equipment including any shipping or installation costs, or $900 as shown in Cells E4, C24, and C27. The total depreciation over the 4 years equals the cost of the equipment.

If for some reason the firm decided to use straight-line depreciation, it could write off a constant $225 per year. Its total cash flows over the entire 4 years would be the same as under accelerated depreciation; but under straight line, those cash flows would come in a bit slower because the firm would have higher tax payments in the early years and lower tax payments later on.

We calculate the annual cash flows for Project S over the 4 years in Columns F, G, H, and I, ending with the net cash flows shown on Row 22. The numbers in Cells E22 through I22 amount to a cash flow time line, and they are the same numbers used in Chapter 11 for Project S. Since the numbers are the same, the NPV, IRR, MIRR, and Payback shown in Cells C31 through C34 are the same as those we calculated in Chapter 11.

The Excel model used to create Table 12-1 is part of the chapter Excel model available on the text's web site. We recommend that anyone with a computer and

---

[1]The equipment will be fully depreciated after 4 years. Therefore, the $50 estimated salvage value will exceed the book value, which will be zero. This $50 gain is classified as a recapture of depreciation, and it is taxed at the same rate as ordinary income.

some familiarity with Excel access the model and work through it to see how the table was generated. Anyone doing real-world capital budgeting today would use such a model; and our model provides a good template, or starting point, if and when you need to analyze an actual project.

12-2a Effect of Different Depreciation Rates

If we replaced the accelerated depreciation numbers in Table 12-1 with the constant $225 values that would exist under straight line, the result would be a cash flow time line on Row 22 that has the same total flows. However, in the early years, the cash flows resulting from straight-line depreciation would be lower than those now in the table; and the later years' cash flows would show higher numbers. You know that dollars received earlier have a higher present value than dollars received later. Therefore, Project S's NPV is higher if the firm uses accelerated depreciation. The exact effect is shown in the Project Evaluation section of Table 12-1—the NPV is $78.82 under accelerated depreciation and $64.44, or 18% less, with straight line.

Now suppose Congress wants to encourage companies to increase their capital expenditures to boost economic growth and employment. What change in depreciation would have the desired effect? The answer is to make accelerated depreciation even more accelerated. For example, if the firm could write off this 4-year equipment at rates of 50%, 35%, 10%, and 5%, its early tax payments would be lower, early cash flows would be higher, and the project's NPV would be higher than that shown in Table 12-1.

12-2b Cannibalization

Project S does not involve any cannibalization effects. Suppose, however, that Project S would reduce the net after-tax cash flows of another division by $50 per year. No other firm would take on this project if our firm turns it down. In this case, we would add a row at about Row 18 and deduct $50 for each year. If this were done, Project S would end up with a negative NPV; hence, it would be rejected. On the other hand, if Project S would cause additional flows in some other division (a positive externality), those after-tax inflows should be attributed to Project S.

12-2c Opportunity Costs

Now suppose the $900 initial cost shown in Table 12-1 was based on the assumption that the project would save money by using some equipment the company now owns and that equipment would be sold for $100, after taxes, if the project is rejected. The $100 is an opportunity cost, and it should be reflected in our calculations. We would add $100 to the project's cost. The result would be an NPV of $78.82 − $100 = −$21.18, so the project would be rejected.

12-2d Sunk Costs

Now suppose the firm had spent $150 on a marketing study to estimate potential sales. This $150 could not be recovered regardless of whether the project is accepted or rejected. Should the $150 be charged to Project S when determining its NPV for capital budgeting purposes? The answer is no. We are interested only in *incremental costs*. The $150 is not an incremental cost; it is a *sunk cost*. Therefore, it should not enter into the analysis.

One additional point should be made about sunk costs. If the $150 expenditure was actually made, in the final analysis, Project S would turn out to be a loser: Its NPV would be $78.82 − $150 = −$71.18. If we could somehow back up and reconsider the project *before* the $150 had been spent, we would see that the project should be rejected. However, we can't back up—at this point, we can either abandon the project or spend $1,000 and go forward with it. If we go forward, we will receive an incremental NPV of $78.82, which would reduce the loss from −$150 to −$71.18.

12-2e Other Changes to the Inputs

Variables other than depreciation also could be varied, and these changes would alter the calculated cash flows and thus NPV and IRR. For example, we could increase or decrease the projected unit sales, the sales price, the variable and/or the fixed costs, the initial investment cost, the working capital requirements, the salvage value, and even the tax rate if we thought Congress was likely to raise or lower taxes. Such changes could be made easily in an Excel model, making it possible to see the resulting changes in NPV and IRR immediately. This is called *sensitivity analysis,* and we discuss it later in the chapter when we take up procedures for measuring projects' risks.

SELF TEST

In what ways is the setup for finding a project's cash flows similar to the projected income statements for a new single-product firm? In what ways would the two statements be different? **(One would find cash flows; the other, net income.)**

Would a project's NPV for a typical firm be higher or lower if the firm used accelerated rather than straight-line depreciation? Why?

How could the analysis in Table 12-1 be modified to consider cannibalization, opportunity costs, and sunk costs?

Why does working capital appear as both a negative and a positive number in Table 12-1?

12-3 REPLACEMENT ANALYSIS[2]

In the last section, we assumed that Project S was an entirely new project. So all of its cash flows were incremental—they occurred only if the firm accepted the project. This is true for expansion projects; but for replacement projects, we must find cash flow *differentials* between the new and old projects and these differentials are the incremental flows that we analyze.

We evaluate a replacement decision in Table 12-2, which is set up much like Table 12-1, but with data on both a new, highly efficient machine (which will be depreciated on an accelerated basis) and the old machine (which is depreciated on a straight-line basis). Here we find the firm's cash flows when it continues using the old machine, then the cash flows when it decides to use the new one. Finally, we subtract the old flows from the new to arrive at the *incremental cash flows.* We used Excel in our analysis; but again, we could have used a calculator or pencil and paper. Here are the key inputs used in the analysis. No additional working capital is needed.

---

[2]This section is somewhat technical, but it can be omitted without loss of continuity.

Data applicable to both machines:

Sales revenues, which would remain constant	$2,500
Expected life of the new and old machines	4 years
WACC for the analysis	10%
Tax rate	40%

Data for old machine:

Market (salvage) value of the old machine today	$400
Old labor, materials, and other costs per year	$1,000
Old machine's annual depreciation	$100

Data for new machine:

Cost of new machine	$2,000
New labor, materials, and other costs per year	$400

The key here is to find the *incremental* cash flows. As noted previously, we find the cash flows from the operation with the old machine, then find the cash flows with the new machine, then find the differences in the cash flows. This is what we do in Parts I, II, and III of Table 12-2. Since there will be an additional expenditure to buy the new machine, that cost is shown in Cell E13. However, we can sell the old machine for $400, so that is shown as an inflow in Cell E14. The net cash outlay at Time 0 is $1,600, as shown in Cell E23.

The net cash flows based on the old machine are shown on Row 11, and those for the new one are on Row 23. Then on Row 25, we show the differences in the cash flows with and without replacement—these are the incremental cash flows used to find the replacement NPV. When we evaluate the incremental cash flows, we see that the replacement has an NPV of $80.28, so the old machine should be replaced.[3]

In some instances, replacements add capacity as well as lower operating costs. When this is the case, sales revenues in Part II would be increased; and if that led to a need for more working capital, that number would be shown as a Time 0 expenditure along with a recovery at the end of the project's life. These changes would, of course, be reflected in the differential cash flows on Row 25.

SELF TEST

What role do incremental cash flows play in a replacement analysis?

If you were analyzing a replacement project and you suddenly learned that the old equipment could be sold for $1,000 rather than $100, would this new information make the replacement look better or worse? **(Better; the net initial investment would be lower.)**

In Table 12-2, we assumed that output would not change if the old machine was replaced. Suppose output would actually double. How would this change be dealt with in the framework of Table 12-2?

---

[3]We could have found the incremental cash flows by calculating the differences in the only factors that change, the net cost of the new machine, operating cost savings reduced for the taxes, and the differences in depreciation, which save some taxes. This procedure is shown in the lower section of the table. The two procedures produce the same incremental cash flows and NPV, as they must.

Table 12-2   Replacement Project R

	A	B	C	D	E	F	G	H	I
1					0	1	2	3	4
2	Part I. Net Cash Flows Before Replacement								
3	Sales revenues					$2,500	$2,500	$2,500	$2,500
4	Costs except depreciation					1,000	1,000	1,000	1,000
5	Depreciation					100	100	100	100
6	Total operating costs					$1,100	$1,100	$1,100	$1,100
7	Operating income					$1,400	$1,400	$1,400	$1,400
8	Taxes 40%					560	560	560	560
9	After-tax operating income					$ 840	$ 840	$ 840	$ 840
10	Add back depreciation					100	100	100	100
11	Net cash flows before replacement					$ 940	$ 940	$ 940	$ 940
12	Part II. Net Cash Flows After Replacement								
13	New machine cost				-$2,000				
14	After-tax salvage value, old machine				$ 400				
15	Sales revenues					$2,500	$2,500	$2,500	$2,500
16	Costs except depreciation					400	400	400	400
17	Depreciation					660	900	300	140
18	Total operating costs					$1,060	$1,300	$ 700	$ 540
19	Operating income					$1,440	$1,200	$1,800	$1,960
20	Taxes @ 40%					576	480	720	784
21	After-tax operating income					$ 864	$ 720	$1,080	$1,176
22	Add back depreciation					660	900	300	140
23	Net cash flows after replacement				-$1,600	$1,524	$1,620	$1,380	$1,316
24	Part III. Incremental Cash Flows and Evaluation								
25	Incremental CFs = CF After - CF Before				-$1,600	$584	$680	$440	$376
26									
27	Project Evaluation @ WACC = 10%								
28				NPV =	$80.28				
29				IRR =	12.51%				
30				MIRR =	11.35%				
31				Payback =	2.76				
32	Part IV. Alternative (Streamlined) Calculation for NCF								
33	New machine cost				-$2,000				
34	Salvage value, old machine				400				
35	Net cost of new machine				-$1,600				
36	Cost savings = Old - New					$600	$600	$600	$600
37	A-T savings = Cost savings × (1 - Tax rate)					360	360	360	360
38	△ Depreciation = (New - Old)					560	800	200	40
39	Depr'n tax savings = △ Depreciation × Tax rate					224	320	80	16
40	NCF = A-T cost savings + Depr'n tax savings				-$1,600	$584	$680	$440	$376

12-4 RISK ANALYSIS IN CAPITAL BUDGETING[4]

Projects differ in risk, and risk should be reflected in capital budgeting decisions. However, it is difficult to measure risk, especially for new projects where no history exists. For this reason, managers deal with risk in many different ways, ranging from almost totally subjective adjustments to highly sophisticated analyses that involve computer simulation and high-powered statistics.

---

[4]Some professors may choose to cover some of the risk sections (12-4 through 12-6) and skip others. We offer a range of choices, and we tried to make the exposition clear enough that interested and self-motivated students can read sections on their own even if the sections are not assigned.

Three separate and distinct types of risk are involved:

1. **Stand-alone risk**, which is a project's risk assuming (a) that it is the only asset the firm has and (b) that the firm is the only stock in each investor's portfolio. Stand-alone risk is measured by the variability of the project's expected returns. *Diversification is totally ignored.*

2. **Corporate, or within-firm, risk**, which is a project's risk to the corporation as opposed to its investors. Within-firm risk takes account of the fact that the project is only one asset in the firm's portfolio of assets; hence, some of its risk will be eliminated by diversification within the firm. This type of risk is measured by the project's impact on uncertainty about the firm's future returns.

3. **Market, or beta, risk**, which is the riskiness of the project as seen by a well-diversified stockholder who recognizes (a) that the project is only one of the firm's assets and (b) that the firm's stock is but one part of his or her stock portfolio. The project's market risk is measured by its effect on the firm's beta coefficient.

Taking on a project with a great deal of stand-alone or corporate risk will not necessarily affect the firm's beta. However, if the project has high stand-alone risk and if its returns are highly correlated with returns on the firm's other assets and with returns on most other stocks in the economy, the project will have a high degree of all three types of risk. Market risk is theoretically the most relevant of the three because it is the one reflected in stock prices. Unfortunately, market risk is also the most difficult to estimate, primarily because new projects don't have "market prices" that can be related to stock market returns. Therefore, most decision makers do a *quantitative* analysis of stand-alone risk and then consider the other two risk measures in a *qualitative* manner.

Projects are generally classified into several categories. Then with the firm's overall WACC as a starting point, a **risk-adjusted cost of capital** is assigned to each category. For example, a firm might establish three risk classes, assign the corporate WACC to average-risk projects, add a 5% risk premium for higher-risk projects, and subtract 2% for low-risk projects. Under this setup, if the company's overall WACC was 10%, 10% would be used to evaluate average-risk projects, 15% for high-risk projects, and 8% for low-risk projects. While this approach is probably better than not making any risk adjustments, these adjustments are highly subjective and difficult to justify. Unfortunately, there's no perfect way to specify how high or low the adjustments should be.[5]

Stand-Alone Risk
The risk an asset would have if it was a firm's only asset and if investors owned only one stock. It is measured by the variability of the asset's expected returns.

Corporate (Within-Firm) Risk
Risk considering the firm's diversification but not stockholder diversification. It is measured by a project's effect on uncertainty about the firm's expected future returns.

Market (Beta) Risk
Considers both firm and stockholder diversification. It is measured by the project's beta coefficient.

Risk-Adjusted Cost of Capital
The cost of capital appropriate for a given project, given the riskiness of that project. The greater the risk, the higher the cost of capital.

SELF TEST

What are the three types of project risk?

Which type is theoretically the most relevant? Why?

What is one classification scheme that firms often use to obtain risk-adjusted costs of capital?

---

[5]We should note that the CAPM approach can be used for projects provided there are specialized publicly traded firms in the same business as that of the project under consideration. For further information on estimating the risk-adjusted cost of capital, see Web Appendix 12C; and for more information on measuring market (or beta) risk, see Web Appendix 12D.

12-5 MEASURING STAND-ALONE RISK

A project's stand-alone risk reflects uncertainty about its cash flows. The required investment, unit sales, sales prices, and operating costs shown in Table 12-1 for Project S are subject to uncertainty. First-year sales were projected at 537 units (actually, 537,000, but we shortened it to 537 to streamline the analysis) to be sold at a price of $10 per unit. However, unit sales would almost certainly be somewhat higher or lower than 537, and the price would probably turn out to be different from the projected $10 per unit. Similarly, the other variables would probably differ from their indicated values. *Indeed, all the inputs are expected values, and actual values can vary from expected values.*

Three techniques are used to assess stand-alone risk: (1) sensitivity analysis, (2) scenario analysis, and (3) Monte Carlo simulation. We discuss them in the following sections.

12-5a Sensitivity Analysis

Sensitivity Analysis
Percentage change in NPV resulting from a given percentage change in an input variable, other things held constant.

Intuitively, we know that a change in a key input variable such as units sold or sales price will cause the NPV to change. **Sensitivity analysis** *measures the percentage change in NPV that results from a given percentage change in an input, other variables held at their expected values.* This is by far the most commonly used type of risk analysis, and it is used by most firms. It begins with a *base-case* situation, where the project's NPV is found using the base-case value for each input variable. Here's a list of the key inputs for Project S:

- Equipment cost
- Required working capital
- Unit sales
- Sales price
- Variable cost per unit
- Fixed operating costs
- Tax rate
- WACC

Base-Case NPV
The NPV when sales and other input variables are set equal to their most likely (or base-case) values.

The data we used back in Table 12-1 were the *most likely, or base-case, values;* and the resulting NPV, $78.82, is the **base-case NPV**. It's easy to imagine changes in the inputs, and those changes would result in different NPVs.

When senior managers review capital budgeting studies, they are interested in the base-case NPV, but they always go on to ask the financial analyst a series of "what if" questions: What if unit sales turn out to be 25% below the base-case level? What if market conditions force us to price the product at $9, not $10? What if variable costs are higher than we forecasted? Sensitivity analysis is designed to provide answers to such questions. Each variable is increased or decreased from its expected value, holding other variables constant at their base-case levels. Then the NPV is calculated using the changed input. Finally, the resulting set of NPVs is plotted to show how sensitive NPV is to changes in each variable.

Figure 12-1 shows Project S's sensitivity graph for six key variables. The table below the graph gives the NPVs based on different values of the inputs, and those NPVs were then plotted to make the graph. Figure 12-1 shows that as unit sales and price increase, the project's NPV increases, whereas the opposite is true for the other four input variables. An increase in variable costs, fixed costs, equipment costs, and WACC lowers the project's NPV. The ranges shown at the bottom of the table and the slopes of the lines in the graph indicate how sensitive NPV is to changes in each input. When the data are plotted in

| FIGURE 12-1 | Sensitivity Graph for Project S |

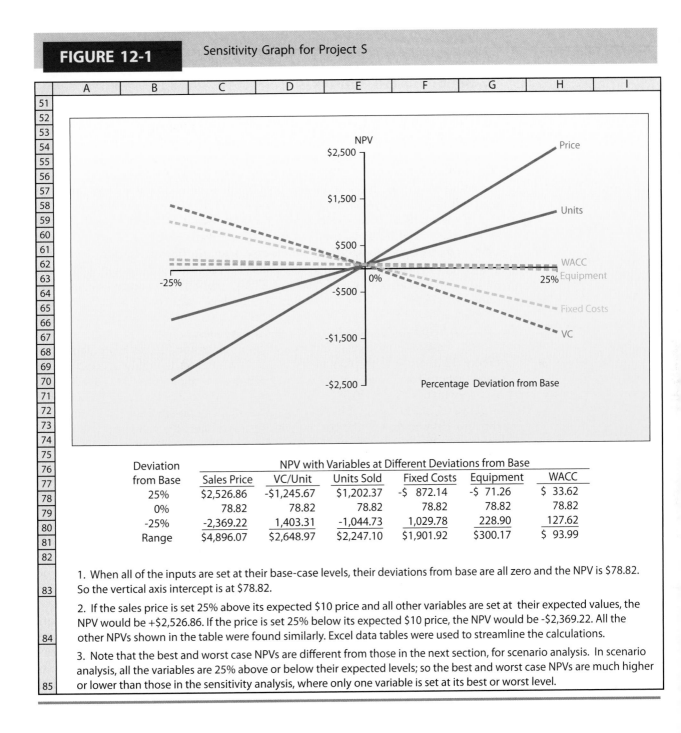

Deviation	NPV with Variables at Different Deviations from Base					
from Base	Sales Price	VC/Unit	Units Sold	Fixed Costs	Equipment	WACC
25%	$2,526.86	-$1,245.67	$1,202.37	-$ 872.14	-$ 71.26	$ 33.62
0%	78.82	78.82	78.82	78.82	78.82	78.82
-25%	-2,369.22	1,403.31	-1,044.73	1,029.78	228.90	127.62
Range	$4,896.07	$2,648.97	$2,247.10	$1,901.92	$300.17	$ 93.99

1. When all of the inputs are set at their base-case levels, their deviations from base are all zero and the NPV is $78.82. So the vertical axis intercept is at $78.82.

2. If the sales price is set 25% above its expected $10 price and all other variables are set at their expected values, the NPV would be +$2,526.86. If the price is set 25% below its expected $10 price, the NPV would be -$2,369.22. All the other NPVs shown in the table were found similarly. Excel data tables were used to streamline the calculations.

3. Note that the best and worst case NPVs are different from those in the next section, for scenario analysis. In scenario analysis, all the variables are 25% above or below their expected levels; so the best and worst case NPVs are much higher or lower than those in the sensitivity analysis, where only one variable is set at its best or worst level.

Figure 12-1, the slopes of the lines in the graph indicate how sensitive NPV is to each input: *The larger the range, the steeper the variable's slope and the more sensitive the NPV is to this variable.* We see that NPV is very sensitive to changes in the sales price, fairly sensitive to changes in variable costs, a bit less sensitive to units sold and fixed costs, but not very sensitive to changes in the equipment cost or the WACC.

If we were comparing two projects, the one with the steeper sensitivity lines would be riskier, other things held constant, because relatively small changes in the input variables would produce large changes in the NPV. Thus, sensitivity analysis provides useful insights into a project's risk.[6]

12-5b Scenario Analysis

In sensitivity analysis, we change one variable at a time. However, it is useful to know what would happen to the project's NPV if all of the inputs turned out to be better or worse than expected. Also, we can assign probabilities to the good, bad, and most likely (or base-case) scenarios, then find the expected value and the standard deviation of the NPV. **Scenario analysis** allows for these extensions—it allows us to change more than one variable at a time, and it incorporates the probabilities of changes in the key variables.

In a scenario analysis, we begin with the **base-case scenario**, which uses the most likely set of input values. We then ask marketing, engineering, and other operating managers to specify a **worst-case scenario** (low unit sales, low sales price, high variable costs, and so forth) and a **best-case scenario**. Often the best and worst cases are defined as having a 25% probability of conditions being that good or bad, with a 50% probability for the base-case conditions. Obviously, conditions can take on many more than three values, but such a scenario setup is useful to help in understanding the project's riskiness.

The best-case, base-case, and worst-case values for Project S are shown in Figure 12-2, along with plots of the data. If the project is highly successful, the combination of a high sales price, low production costs, and high unit sales will result in a very high NPV, $7,450.38. However, if things turn out badly, the NPV will be a negative $4,782.40. The graphs show the wide range of possibilities, suggesting that this is a risky project. If the bad conditions materialize, the company will not go bankrupt—this is just one project for a large company. Still, losing $4,782.40 (or $4,782,400 since we are working in thousands) would hurt the stock price.

If we multiply each scenario's probability by the NPV under that scenario and then sum the products, we will have the project's expected NPV, $706.40 as shown in Figure 12-2. Note that the *expected* NPV differs from the *base-case* NPV. This is not an error—mathematically, they are not equal. We also calculate the standard deviation of the expected NPV; it is $5,028.94. When we divide the standard deviation by the expected NPV, we get the coefficient of variation, 7.12, which is a measure of stand-alone risk. The firm's average-risk project has a coefficient of variation of about 2.0, so the CV of 7.12 indicates that this project is much riskier than most of the firm's other projects.

Our firm's WACC is 10%, so that rate should be used to find the NPV of an average-risk project. Project S is riskier than average, so a higher discount rate should be used to find its NPV. There is no way to determine the "correct" discount rate—this is a judgment call. However, some firms increase the corporate WACC when they evaluate projects deemed to be relatively risky and reduce it for low-risk projects. When the NPV was recalculated using a 12.5% WACC, the base-case NPV fell from $78.82 to $33.62; so the project still passed the NPV test.

Note that the base-case results are the same in our sensitivity and scenario analyses; but in the scenario analysis, the worst case is much worse than in the sensitivity analysis and the best case is much better. This is because in scenario analysis, all of the variables are set at their best or worst levels, while in sensitivity analysis, only one variable is adjusted and all the others are left at their base-case levels.

---

[6]Sensitivity analysis is tedious using a regular calculator but easy using a spreadsheet. We used the chapter's Excel model to calculate the NPVs and to draw the graph in Figure 12-1. To conduct such an analysis by hand would be quite time-consuming, and if the basic data were changed even slightly—say the cost of the equipment was increased slightly—all of the calculations would have to be redone. With a spreadsheet, by simply typing over the old input with the new one, the analysis is changed instantaneously.

Scenario Analysis

A risk analysis technique in which "bad" and "good" sets of financial circumstances are compared with a most likely, or base-case, situation.

Base-Case Scenario

An analysis in which all of the input variables are set at their most likely values.

Worst-Case Scenario

An analysis in which all of the input variables are set at their worst reasonably forecasted values.

Best-Case Scenario

An analysis in which all of the input variables are set at their best reasonably forecasted values.

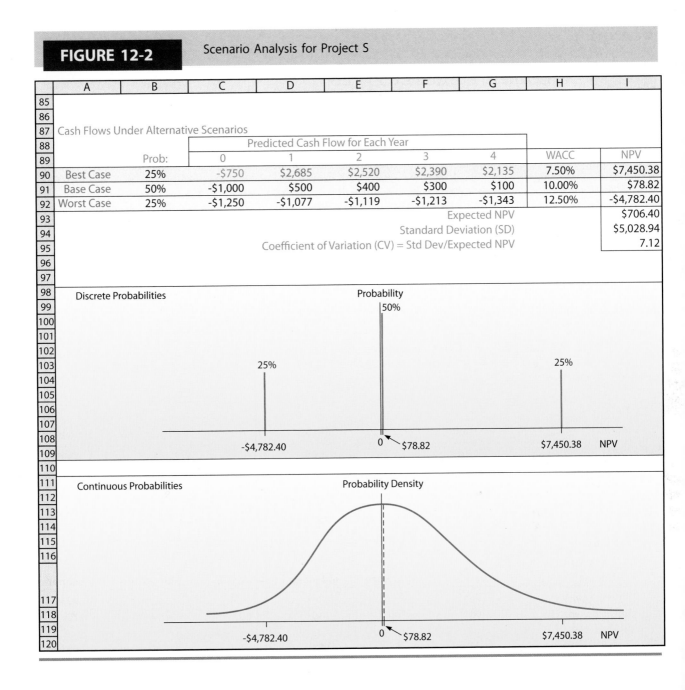

FIGURE 12-2   Scenario Analysis for Project S

	A	B	C	D	E	F	G	H	I
85									
86									
87	Cash Flows Under Alternative Scenarios								
88			Predicted Cash Flow for Each Year						
89		Prob:	0	1	2	3	4	WACC	NPV
90	Best Case	25%	-$750	$2,685	$2,520	$2,390	$2,135	7.50%	$7,450.38
91	Base Case	50%	-$1,000	$500	$400	$300	$100	10.00%	$78.82
92	Worst Case	25%	-$1,250	-$1,077	-$1,119	-$1,213	-$1,343	12.50%	-$4,782.40
93							Expected NPV		$706.40
94							Standard Deviation (SD)		$5,028.94
95						Coefficient of Variation (CV) = Std Dev/Expected NPV			7.12
96									
97									

12-5c Monte Carlo Simulation

Monte Carlo simulation, so named because this type of analysis grew out of work on the mathematics of casino gambling, is a sophisticated version of scenario analysis. Here the project is analyzed under a large number of scenarios, or "runs." In the first run, the computer randomly picks a value for each variable—units sold, sales price, variable costs per unit, and so forth. Those values are then used to calculate an NPV, and that NPV is stored in the computer's memory. Next, a second set of input values is selected at random and a second NPV is calculated. This process is repeated perhaps 1,000 times, generating 1,000 NPVs. The mean of the 1,000 NPVs is determined and used as a measure of the project's expected profitability, and the standard deviation (or perhaps the coefficient of variation) of the NPVs is used as a measure of risk.

Monte Carlo Simulation
A risk analysis technique in which probable future events are simulated on a computer, generating estimated rates of return and risk indexes.

GLOBAL PERSPECTIVES

CAPITAL BUDGETING PRACTICES IN THE ASIAN/PACIFIC REGION

A recent survey of executives in Australia, Hong Kong, Indonesia, Malaysia, the Philippines, and Singapore asked several questions about companies' capital budgeting practices. The study yielded the results summarized here.

Techniques for Evaluating Corporate Projects
Consistent with U.S. companies, most companies in this region evaluate projects using IRR, NPV, and payback. IRR usage ranged from 96% (in Australia) to 86% (in Hong Kong). NPV usage ranged from 96% (in Australia) to 81% (in the Philippines). Payback usage ranged from 100% (in Hong Kong and the Philippines) to 81% (in Indonesia).

Techniques for Estimating the Cost of Equity Capital
Recall from Chapter 10 that three basic approaches can be used to estimate the cost of equity: CAPM, dividend yield

plus growth rate (DCF), and cost of debt plus a risk premium. The use of these methods varied considerably from country to country. (See Table A.) The CAPM is used most often by U.S. firms. This is also true for Australian firms, but not for the other Asian/Pacific firms, which instead are more likely to use the DCF and risk premium approaches.

Techniques for Assessing Risk
Firms in the Asian/Pacific region rely heavily on scenario and sensitivity analyses. They also use decision trees and Monte Carlo simulation, but less frequently. (See Table B.)

Table A

Method	Australia	Hong Kong	Indonesia	Malaysia	Philippines	Singapore
CAPM	72.7%	26.9%	0.0%	6.2%	24.1%	17.0%
Dividend yield plus growth rate	16.4	53.8	33.3	50.0	34.5	42.6
Cost of debt plus risk premium	10.9	23.1	53.4	37.5	58.6	42.6

Table B

Risk Assessment Technique	Australia	Hong Kong	Indonesia	Malaysia	Philippines	Singapore
Scenario analysis	96%	100%	94%	80%	97%	90%
Sensitivity analysis	100	100	88	83	94	79
Decision tree analysis	44	58	50	37	33	46
Monte Carlo simulation	38	35	25	9	24	35

Source: Adapted from George W. Kester et al., "Capital Budgeting Practices in the Asia-Pacific Region: Australia, Hong Kong, Indonesia, Malaysia, Philippines, and Singapore," *Financial Practice and Education*, Vol. 9, No. 1 (Spring/Summer 1999), pp. 25–33.

Monte Carlo simulation is technically more complex than scenario analysis, but simulation software makes the process manageable. Simulation is useful; but because of its complexity, a detailed discussion is best left for advanced finance courses.[7]

---

[7]To use Monte Carlo simulation, one needs probability distributions for the inputs and correlation coefficients between each pair of inputs. It is often difficult to obtain "reasonable" values for the correlations, especially for new projects where no historical data are available. This limits the use of simulation analysis.

SELF TEST

Explain briefly how a sensitivity analysis is done and what the analysis is designed to show.

What is a scenario analysis, what is it designed to show, and how does it differ from a sensitivity analysis?

What is Monte Carlo simulation? How does a simulation analysis differ from a regular scenario analysis?

12-6 WITHIN-FIRM AND BETA RISK[8]

Sensitivity analysis, scenario analysis, and Monte Carlo simulation as described in the preceding section dealt with stand-alone risk. They provide useful information about a project's risk; but if the project is negatively correlated with the firm's other projects, it might stabilize the firm's total earnings and thus be relatively safe. Similarly, if a project is negatively correlated with returns on most stocks, it might reduce the firm's beta and thus be correctly evaluated with a relatively low WACC. So in theory, we should be more concerned with within-firm and beta risk than with stand-alone risk.

Although managers recognize the importance of within-firm and beta risk, they generally end up dealing with these risks subjectively, or judgmentally, rather than quantitatively. The problem is that to measure diversification's effects on risk, we need the *correlation coefficient between a project's returns and returns on the firm's other assets,* which requires historical data that obviously do not exist for new projects. Experienced managers generally have a "feel" for how a project's returns will relate to returns on the firm's other assets. Generally, positive correlation is expected; and if the correlation is high, stand-alone risk will be a good proxy for within-firm risk. Similarly, managers can make judgmental estimates about whether a project's returns will be high when the economy and the stock market are strong (hence, what the project's beta should be). But for the most part, those estimates are subjective, not based on actual data.

However, projects occasionally involve an entirely new product line, such as a steel company going into iron ore mining. In such cases, the firm may be able to obtain betas for *"pure-play"* companies in the new area. For example, this steel company might get the average beta for a group of mining companies such as Rio Tinto and BHP, assume that its mining subsidiary has similar characteristics, and use the average beta of the "comparables" to calculate a WACC for the mining subsidiary. While the pure-play approach makes sense for some projects, it is rare. Just think about it. How would you find a pure-play proxy for a new inventory control system, machine tool, truck, or most other projects? The answer is, you couldn't.

Our conclusions regarding risk analysis are as follows:

- It is very difficult, if not impossible, to quantitatively measure projects' within-firm and beta risks.
- Most projects' returns are positively correlated with returns on the firm's other assets and with returns on the stock market. This being the case, because stand-alone risk is correlated with within-firm and market risk, not much is lost by focusing just on stand-alone risk.

---

[8]This section is relatively technical, but it can be omitted without a loss of continuity.

- Experienced managers make many judgmental assessments, including those related to risk; and they work them into the capital budgeting process. Introductory students like neat, precise answers; and they want to make decisions on the basis of calculated NPVs. Experienced managers consider quantitative NPVs, but they also bring subjective judgment into the decision process.

- If a firm does not use the types of analyses covered in this book, it will have trouble. On the other hand, if a firm tries to quantify everything and let a computer make its decisions, it too will have trouble. Good managers understand and use the theory of finance, but they apply it with judgment.

SELF TEST Is it easier to measure the stand-alone, within-firm, or beta risk for projects such as a new delivery truck or a Home Depot warehouse?

If a firm cannot measure a potential project's risk with precision, should it abandon the project? Explain your answer.

12-7 UNEQUAL PROJECT LIVES

If a company is choosing between two projects and those projects (1) have *significantly different lives*, (2) are *mutually exclusive*, and (3) *can be repeated*, the "regular" NPV method may not indicate the better project. For example, suppose Home Depot is planning to modernize a distribution center; it is choosing between a conveyor system (Project C) and a fleet of forklift trucks (Project F). The projects are mutually exclusive—choosing one means rejecting the other. Also, the distribution center will be used for many years, so the equipment will be replaced when it wears out.

Part I of Figure 12-3 shows the analysis that traditionally would be used to analyze the two projects. We see that Project C, when discounted at a 12% WACC, has the higher NPV and thus appears to be the better project. *However, the traditional analysis is incomplete, and the decision to choose Project C is actually incorrect.* If we choose Project F, we will have an opportunity to make a similar investment in 3 years; and if costs and revenues remain at the Part I levels, this second investment also will be profitable. If we choose Project C, we will not have the option to make this second investment. Therefore, to make a proper comparison between C and F we must make an adjustment. We discuss the two methods for making the adjustment in the remainder of this section.

12-7a Replacement Chains

Replacement Chain (Common Life) Approach
A method of comparing projects with unequal lives that assumes that each project can be repeated as many times as necessary to reach a common life. The NPVs over this life are then compared, and the project with the higher common-life NPV is chosen.

First, we can apply the **replacement chain (common life) approach** as shown in Part II of Figure 12-3. This involves finding the NPV of Project F over 6 years, which is also the life of Project C, and then comparing this extended NPV with the NPV of Project C over the same 6 years. We see that on a common-life basis, F turns out to be the better project.[9]

---

[9]In this case, we need to extend F's life out for only one replacement. However, if C had a life of 7 years and F had a life of 3 years, it would have been necessary to go out to Year 21, using three replacements for C and seven for F, to reach a common life span. Also note that the adjusted NPVs are based on a 6-year life. If the selected project were to be used longer—say, for 24 years—the firm's NPV would be much larger—4 times larger on a 24-year total life.

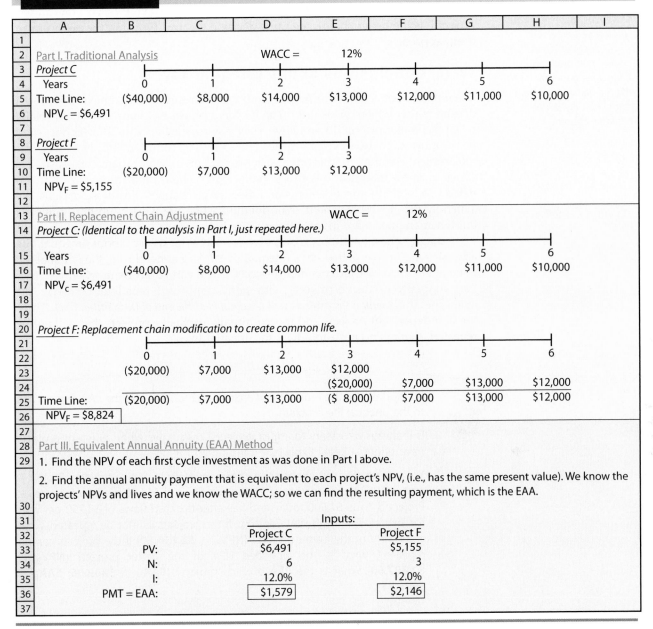

FIGURE 12-3   Mutually Exclusive and Repeatable Projects with Unequal Lives

12-7b Equivalent Annual Annuities (EAA)

Electrical engineers designing power plants and distribution lines were the first to encounter the unequal life problem. They could use transformers that had a relatively low initial cost but a short life, or they could use transformers that had higher initial costs but longer lives. Transformers would be required on into the indefinite future, so this was the issue: Which choice would result in the higher NPV over the long run? The engineers first found the NPV of each project over its stated life and then found the constant annual cash flow that this NPV would provide over the project's initial life. Since the projects would presumably be repeated indefinitely, those annuity payments would continue indefinitely and the project that provided the higher payment stream was the better option. This

Equivalent Annual Annuity (EAA) Method
A method that calculates the annual payments that a project will provide if it is an annuity. When comparing projects with unequal lives, the one with the higher equivalent annual annuity (EAA) should be chosen.

procedure was called the **equivalent annual annuity (EAA) method**. The EAAs of Projects C and F are calculated in Part III of Figure 12-3. We first find the projects' traditional NPVs and then find the EAAs of those NPVs. As you can see, Project F is the better choice, the same decision reached by using the replacement chain approach.

12-7c Conclusions about Unequal Lives

The replacement chain and EAA methods always result in the same decision, so it doesn't matter which one is used. The EAA is a bit easier to implement, especially when the longer project doesn't have exactly twice the life of the shorter one—and hence more than two cycles are needed to find a common life. However, the replacement chain method is often easier to explain to senior managers. Also, it is easier to make modifications to the replacement chain data to deal with anticipated productivity improvements and asset price changes. For those reasons, we generally use the replacement chain method when we work with nonengineers; but when engineers are involved, we show both results.

Another question often arises: Do we have to worry about unequal life analysis for all projects that have unequal lives? As a general rule, the unequal life issue never arises for independent projects, but it can be an issue when we compare mutually exclusive projects with significantly different lives. *However, the issue arises if and only if the projects will be repeated at the end of their initial lives.* Thus, for all independent projects and those mutually exclusive projects that will not be repeated, there is no need to adjust for unequal lives.

SELF TEST

Briefly describe the replacement chain (common life) and the EAA approaches to the unequal life problem.

Is it always necessary to adjust projects' cash flows when different projects have unequal lives? Explain.

Your company must choose one of two mutually exclusive projects. Project A costs $2,000 today and has after-tax cash flows of $1,500 per year for 4 years. Project B costs $1,500 today and has after-tax cash flows of $1,750 per year for 2 years. The firm's WACC is 10%. If the projects cannot be repeated, what is the NPV of the better project? (**NPV_A = $2,754.80**) If the projects can be repeated, what is the extended NPV of the better project? (**NPV_B = $2,807.60**) What is the EAA of each project? (**EAA_A = $869.06; EAA_B = $885.71**)

TYING IT ALL TOGETHER

This chapter focused on estimating the cash flows that are used in a capital budgeting analysis, appraising the riskiness of those flows, finding NPVs when risk is present, and calculating the NPVs of mutually exclusive projects having unequal lives. Here is a summary of our primary conclusions:

- Some cash flows are *relevant* (hence, should be included in a capital budgeting analysis), while others should not be included. The key question is this: Is the cash flow *incremental* in the sense that it will occur if and only if the project is accepted?

- *Sunk costs* are not incremental costs—they are not affected by accepting or rejecting the project. *Cannibalization* and other *externalities*, on the other hand, are incremental—they will occur if and only if the project is accepted.

- The cash flows used to analyze a project are different from a project's *net income.* One important factor is that *depreciation* is deducted when accountants calculate net income; but because it is a noncash charge, it must be added back to find cash flows.

- Many projects require additional *net working capital.* Net working capital is a negative flow when the project is started but a positive flow at the end of the project's life, when the capital is recovered.

- We considered two types of projects—expansion and replacement. For a replacement project, we find the difference in the cash flows when the firm continues to use the old asset versus the new asset. If the NPV of the differential flows is positive, the replacement should be made.

- The forecasted cash flows (and hence NPV and other outputs) are only estimates—they may turn out to be incorrect, and this means *risk.*

- There are three types of risk: *stand-alone, within-firm, and market (or beta) risk.* In theory, market risk is most relevant; but since it cannot be measured for most projects, stand-alone risk is the one on which we generally focus. However, firms subjectively consider within-firm and market risk, which they definitely should not ignore. Note, though, that since the three types of risk are generally positively correlated, stand-alone risk is often a good proxy for the other risks.

- Stand-alone risk can be analyzed using *sensitivity analysis, scenario analysis, and/or Monte Carlo simulation.*

- Once a decision has been made about a project's relative risk, we determine a *risk-adjusted WACC* for evaluating it.

- If *mutually exclusive projects* have *unequal lives* and are *repeatable,* a traditional NPV analysis may lead to incorrect results. In this case, we should use *replacement chain or equivalent annual annuity (EAA) analysis.*

SELF-TEST QUESTIONS AND PROBLEMS
(Solutions Appear in Appendix A)

ST-1   **KEY TERMS**   Define the following terms:

    a.   Incremental cash flow; sunk cost; opportunity cost; externality; cannibalization

    b.   Stand-alone risk; corporate (within-firm) risk; market (beta) risk

    c.   Risk-adjusted cost of capital

    d.   Sensitivity analysis; base-case NPV

    e.   Scenario analysis; base-case scenario; worst-case scenario; best-case scenario

    f.   Monte Carlo simulation

    g.   Replacement chain (common life) approach; equivalent annual annuity (EAA) method

ST-2   **PROJECT AND RISK ANALYSIS**   As a financial analyst, you must evaluate a proposed project to produce printer cartridges. The equipment would cost $55,000, plus $10,000 for installation. Annual sales would be 4,000 units at a price of $50 per cartridge, and the project's life would be 3 years. Current assets would increase by $5,000 and payables by

$3,000. At the end of 3 years, the equipment could be sold for $10,000. Depreciation would be based on the MACRS 3-year class; so the applicable depreciation rates would be 33%, 45%, 15%, and 7%. Variable costs (VC) would be 70% of sales revenues, fixed costs excluding depreciation would be $30,000 per year, the marginal tax rate is 40%, and the corporate WACC is 11%.

a. What is the required investment, that is, the Year 0 project cash flow?

b. What are the annual depreciation charges?

c. What are the project's annual net cash flows?

d. If the project is of average risk, what is its NPV? Should it be accepted?

e. Suppose management is uncertain about the exact unit sales. What would the project's NPV be if unit sales turned out to be 20% below forecast but other inputs were as forecasted? Would this change the decision? Explain.

f. The CFO asks you to do a scenario analysis using these inputs:

	Probability	Unit Sales	VC%
Best case	25%	4,800	65%
Base case	50	4,000	70
Worst case	25	3,200	75

Other variables are unchanged. What are the expected NPV, its standard deviation, and the coefficient of variation? [Hint: To do the scenario analysis, you must change unit sales and VC% to the values specified for each scenario, get the scenario cash flows, and then find each scenario's NPV. Then you must calculate the project's expected NPV, standard deviation (SD), and coefficient of variation (CV). This is not difficult, but it requires many calculations. You might want to look at the answer, but make sure you understand how it was computed.]

g. The firm's project CVs generally range from 1.0 to 1.5. A 3% risk premium is added to the WACC if the initial CV exceeds 1.5, and the WACC is reduced by 0.5% if the CV is 0.75 or less. Then a revised NPV is calculated. What WACC should be used for this project? What are the revised values for the expected NPV, standard deviation, and coefficient of variation? Would you recommend that the project be accepted? Why or why not?

ST-3 **PROJECTS WITH UNEQUAL LIVES** Wisconsin Dairy Inc. is deciding on its capital budget for the upcoming year. Among the projects being considered are two machines, W and WW. W costs $500,000 and will produce expected after-tax cash flows of $300,000 during the next 2 years. WW also costs $500,000, but it will produce after-tax cash flows of $165,000 during the next 4 years. Both projects have a 10% WACC.

a. If the projects are independent and not repeatable, which project(s) should the company accept?

b. If the projects are mutually exclusive but are not repeatable, which project should the company accept?

c. Assume that the projects are mutually exclusive and can be repeated indefinitely.

(1) Use the replacement chain method to determine the NPV of the project selected.

(2) Use the equivalent annual annuity method to determine the annuity of the project selected.

d. Could a replacement chain analysis be modified for use when the project's cash flows are different each time it is repeated? Explain.

QUESTIONS

12-1 Operating cash flows rather than accounting income are listed in Table 12-1. Why do we focus on cash flows as opposed to net income in capital budgeting?

12-2 Explain why sunk costs should not be included in a capital budgeting analysis but opportunity costs and externalities should be included. Give an example of each.

12-3   Explain why working capital is included in a capital budgeting analysis and how it is recovered at the end of a project's life.

12-4   Why are interest charges not deducted when a project's cash flows for use in a capital budgeting analysis are calculated?

12-5   Most firms generate cash inflows every day, not just once at the end of the year. In capital budgeting, should we recognize this fact by estimating daily project cash flows and then using them in the analysis? If we do not, are our results biased? If so, would the NPV be biased up or down? Explain.

12-6   What are some differences in the analysis for a replacement project versus that for a new expansion project?

12-7   Distinguish among beta (or market) risk, within-firm (or corporate) risk, and stand-alone risk for a project being considered for inclusion in a firm's capital budget.

12-8   In theory, market risk should be the only "relevant" risk. However, companies focus as much on stand-alone risk as on market risk. What are the reasons for the focus on stand-alone risk?

12-9   Define (a) sensitivity analysis, (b) scenario analysis, and (c) simulation analysis. If GE was considering two projects (one for $500 million to develop a satellite communications system and the other for a $30,000 new truck) on which project would the company be more likely to use a simulation analysis?

12-10   If you were the CFO of a company that had to decide on hundreds of potential projects every year, would you want to use sensitivity analysis and scenario analysis as described in the chapter or would the amount of arithmetic required take too much time and thus not be cost-effective? What involvement would nonfinancial people such as those in marketing, accounting, and production have in the analysis?

12-11   What is a "replacement chain?" When and how should replacement chains be used in capital budgeting?

12-12   What is an "equivalent annual annuity (EAA)?" When and how are EAAs used in capital budgeting?

12-13   Suppose a firm is considering two mutually exclusive projects. One project has a life of 6 years; the other, a life of 10 years. Both projects can be repeated at the end of their lives. Might the failure to employ a replacement chain or EAA analysis bias the decision toward one of the projects? If so, which one and why?

PROBLEMS

Easy Problems 1–5

12-1   **REQUIRED INVESTMENT**   Truman Industries is considering an expansion. The necessary equipment would be purchased for $9 million, and the expansion would require an additional $3 million investment in working capital. The tax rate is 40%.

   a.   What is the initial investment outlay?

   b.   The company spent and expensed $50,000 on research related to the project last year. Would this change your answer? Explain.

   c.   The company plans to use another building that it owns to house the project. The building could be sold for $1 million after taxes and real estate commissions. How would that fact affect your answer?

12-2   **PROJECT CASH FLOW**   Eisenhower Communications is trying to estimate the first-year net cash flow (at Year 1) for a proposed project. The financial staff has collected the following information on the project:

Sales revenues	$10 million
Operating costs (excluding depreciation)	7 million
Depreciation	2 million
Interest expense	2 million

The company has a 40% tax rate, and its WACC is 10%.

a.   What is the project's net cash flow for the first year (t = 1)?

b.   If this project would cannibalize other projects by $1 million of cash flow before taxes per year, how would this change your answer to Part a?

c.   Ignore Part b. If the tax rate dropped to 30%, how would that change your answer to Part a?

12-3   **NET SALVAGE VALUE**   Kennedy Air Services is now in the final year of a project. The equipment originally cost $20 million, of which 80% has been depreciated. Kennedy can sell the used equipment today for $5 million, and its tax rate is 40%. What is the equipment's after-tax net salvage value?

12-4   **REPLACEMENT ANALYSIS**   The Chang Company is considering the purchase of a new machine to replace an obsolete one. The machine being used for the operation has a book value and a market value of zero. However, the machine is in good working order and will last at least another 10 years. The proposed replacement machine will perform the operation so much more efficiently that Chang's engineers estimate that it will produce after-tax cash flows (labor savings and depreciation) of $9,000 per year. The new machine will cost $40,000 delivered and installed, and its economic life is estimated to be 10 years. It has zero salvage value. The firm's WACC is 10%, and its marginal tax rate is 35%. Should Chang buy the new machine? Explain.

12-5   **EQUIVALENT ANNUAL ANNUITY**   Corcoran Consulting is deciding which of two computer systems to purchase. It can purchase state-of-the-art equipment (System A) for $20,000, which will generate cash flows of $6,000 at the end of each of the next 6 years. Alternatively, the company can spend $12,000 for equipment that can be used for 3 years and will generate cash flows of $6,000 at the end of each year (System B). If the company's WACC is 10% and both projects can be repeated indefinitely, which system should be chosen and what is its EAA?

Intermediate
Problems
6–17

12-6   **DEPRECIATION METHODS**   Kristin is evaluating a capital budgeting project that should last 4 years. The project requires $800,000 of equipment. She is unsure what depreciation method to use in her analysis, straight-line or the 3-year MACRS accelerated method. Under straight-line depreciation, the cost of the equipment would be depreciated evenly over its 4-year life. (Ignore the half-year convention for the straight-line method.) The applicable MACRS depreciation rates are 33%, 45%, 15%, and 7% as discussed in Appendix 12A. The company's WACC is 10%, and its tax rate is 40%.

a.   What would the depreciation expense be each year under each method?

b.   Which depreciation method would produce the higher NPV, and how much higher would it be?

12-7   **SCENARIO ANALYSIS**   Huang Industries is considering a proposed project whose estimated NPV is $12 million. This estimate assumes that economic conditions will be "average." However, the CFO realizes that conditions could be better or worse, so she performed a scenario analysis and obtained these results:

Economic Scenario	Probability of Outcome	NPV
Recession	0.05	($70 million)
Below average	0.20	(25 million)
Average	0.50	12 million
Above average	0.20	20 million
Boom	0.05	30 million

Calculate the project's expected NPV, standard deviation, and coefficient of variation.

12-8   **NEW PROJECT ANALYSIS**   You must evaluate a proposed spectrometer for the R&D Department. The base price is $140,000, and it would cost another $30,000 to modify the equipment for special use by the firm. The equipment falls into the MACRS 3-year class and would be sold after 3 years for $60,000. The applicable depreciation rates are 33%, 45%, 15%, and 7% as discussed in Appendix 12A. The equipment would require an $8,000 increase in working capital (spare parts inventory). The project would have no effect on revenues, but it should save the firm $50,000 per year in before-tax labor costs. The firm's marginal federal-plus-state tax rate is 40%.

a.   What is the net cost of the spectrometer; that is, what is the Year 0 project cash flow?

b.   What are the project's annual net cash flows in Years 1, 2, and 3?

c.   If the WACC is 12%, should the spectrometer be purchased? Explain.

12-9   **NEW PROJECT ANALYSIS**   You must evaluate a proposal to buy a new milling machine. The base price is $108,000, and shipping and installation costs would add another $12,500. The machine falls into the MACRS 3-year class, and it would be sold after 3 years for $65,000. The applicable depreciation rates are 33%, 45%, 15%, and 7% as discussed in Appendix 12A. The machine would require a $5,500 increase in working capital (increased inventory less increased accounts payable). There would be no effect on revenues, but pretax labor costs would decline by $44,000 per year. The marginal tax rate is 35%, and the WACC is 12%. Also, the firm spent $5,000 last year investigating the feasibility of using the machine.

a.   How should the $5,000 spent last year be handled?

b.   What is the net cost of the machine for capital budgeting purposes, that is, the Year 0 project cash flow?

c.   What are the project's annual net cash flows during Years 1, 2, and 3?

d.   Should the machine be purchased? Explain your answer.

12-10   **REPLACEMENT ANALYSIS**   The Dauten Toy Corporation uses an injection molding machine that was purchased 2 years ago. This machine is being depreciated on a straight-line basis, and it has 6 years of remaining life. Its current book value is $2,100, and it can be sold for $2,500 at this time. Thus, the annual depreciation expense is $2,100/6 = $350 per year. If the old machine is not replaced, it can be sold for $500 at the end of its useful life.
      Dauten is offered a replacement machine that has a cost of $8,000, an estimated useful life of 6 years, and an estimated salvage value of $800. This machine falls into the MACRS 5-year class; so the applicable depreciation rates are 20%, 32%, 19%, 12%, 11%, and 6%. The replacement machine would permit an output expansion, so sales would rise by $1,000 per year. Even so, the new machine's greater efficiency would cause operating expenses to decline by $1,500 per year. The new machine would require that inventories be increased by $2,000, but accounts payable would simultaneously increase by $500. Dauten's marginal federal-plus-state tax rate is 40%, and its WACC is 15%. Should the company replace the old machine?

12-11   **REPLACEMENT ANALYSIS**   Mississippi River Shipyards is considering replacing an 8-year-old riveting machine with a new one that will increase earnings before depreciation from $27,000 to $54,000 per year. The new machine will cost $82,500, and it will have an estimated life of 8 years and no salvage value. The new machine will be depreciated over its 5-year MACRS recovery period; so the applicable depreciation rates are 20%, 32%, 19%, 12%, 11%, and 6%. The applicable corporate tax rate is 40%, and the firm's WACC is 12%. The old machine has been fully depreciated and has no salvage value. Should the old riveting machine be replaced by the new one? Explain your answer.

12-12   **PROJECT RISK ANALYSIS**   The Butler-Perkins Company (BPC) must decide between two mutually exclusive projects. Each costs $6,750 and has an expected life of 3 years. Annual project cash flows begin 1 year after the initial investment and are subject to the following probability distributions:

PROJECT A		PROJECT B	
Probability	**Cash Flows**	**Probability**	**Cash Flows**
0.2	$6,000	0.2	$ 0
0.6	6,750	0.6	6,750
0.2	7,500	0.2	18,000

BPC has decided to evaluate the riskier project at 12% and the less risky project at 10%.

a.   What is each project's expected annual cash flow? Project B's standard deviation (σ_B) is $5,798, and its coefficient of variation (CV_B) is 0.76. What are the values of σ_A and CV_A?

b.   Based on the risk-adjusted NPVs, which project should BPC choose?

c.   If you knew that Project B's cash flows were negatively correlated with the firm's other cash flows whereas Project A's flows were positively correlated, how might this affect the decision? If Project B's cash flows were negatively correlated with gross domestic product (GDP) while A's flows were positively correlated, would that influence your risk assessment? Explain.

12-13   **UNEQUAL LIVES** Haley's Graphic Designs Inc. is considering two mutually exclusive projects. Both projects require an initial investment of $10,000 and are typical average-risk projects for the firm. Project A has an expected life of 2 years with after-tax cash inflows of $6,000 and $8,000 at the end of Years 1 and 2, respectively. Project B has an expected life of 4 years with after-tax cash inflows of $4,000 at the end of each of the next 4 years. The firm's WACC is 10%.

a.   If the projects cannot be repeated, which project should be selected if Haley uses NPV as its criterion for project selection?

b.   Assume that the projects can be repeated and that there are no anticipated changes in the cash flows. Use the replacement chain analysis to determine the NPV of the project selected.

c.   Make the same assumptions as in Part b. Using the equivalent annual annuity (EAA) method, what is the EAA of the project selected?

12-14   **UNEQUAL LIVES** Cotner Clothes Inc. is considering the replacement of its old, fully depreciated knitting machine. Two new models are available: (a) Machine 190-3, which has a cost of $190,000, a 3-year expected life, and after-tax cash flows (labor savings and depreciation) of $87,000 per year, and (b) Machine 360-6, which has a cost of $360,000, a 6-year life, and after-tax cash flows of $98,300 per year. Assume that both projects can be repeated. Knitting machine prices are not expected to rise because inflation will be offset by cheaper components (microprocessors) used in the machines. Assume that Cotner's WACC is 14%. Using the replacement chain and EAA approaches, which model should be selected? Why?

12-15   **REPLACEMENT CHAIN** Zappe Airlines is considering two alternative planes. Plane A has an expected life of 5 years, will cost $100 million, and will produce after-tax cash flows of $30 million per year. Plane B has a life of 10 years, will cost $132 million, and will produce after-tax cash flows of $25 million per year. Zappe plans to serve the route for 10 years. The company's WACC is 12%. If Zappe needs to purchase a new Plane A, the cost will be $105 million, but cash inflows will remain the same. Should Zappe acquire Plane A or Plane B? Explain your answer.

12-16   **REPLACEMENT CHAIN** The Fernandez Company has an opportunity to invest in one of two mutually exclusive machines that will produce a product the company will need for the next 8 years. Machine A costs $10 million but will provide after-tax inflows of $4 million per year for 4 years. If Machine A was replaced, its cost would be $12 million due to inflation and its cash inflows would increase to $4.2 million due to production efficiencies. Machine B costs $15 million and will provide after-tax inflows of $3.5 million per year for 8 years. If the WACC is 10%, which machine should be acquired? Explain.

12-17   **EQUIVALENT ANNUAL ANNUITY** A firm has two mutually exclusive investment projects to evaluate; both can be repeated indefinitely. The projects have the following cash flows:

Time	Size	IRR
0	$100,000	$70,000
1	30,000	30,000
2	50,000	30,000
3	70,000	30,000
4	—	30,000
5	—	10,000

Projects X and Y are equally risky and may be repeated indefinitely. If the firm's WACC is 12%, what is the EAA of the project that adds the most value to the firm? (Round your final answer to the nearest whole dollar.)

Challenging
Problems
18–21

12-18   **SCENARIO ANALYSIS** Your firm, Agrico Products, is considering a tractor that would have a net cost of $36,000, would increase pretax operating cash flows before taking account of depreciation by $12,000 per year, and would be depreciated on a straight-line basis to zero over 5 years at the rate of $7,200 per year beginning the first year. (Thus, annual cash flows would be $12,000 before taxes plus the tax savings that result from $7,200 of depreciation.) The managers are having a heated debate about whether the tractor would last 5 years. The controller insists that she knows of tractors that have lasted only 4 years. The treasurer agrees with the controller, but he argues that most tractors do give 5 years of service. The service manager then states that some last as long as 8 years.

Given this discussion, the CFO asks you to prepare a scenario analysis to determine the importance of the tractor's life on the NPV. Use a 40% marginal federal-plus-state tax rate, a zero salvage value, and a 10% WACC. Assuming each of the indicated lives has the same probability of occurring (probability = 1/3), what is the tractor's expected NPV? (Hint: Use the 5-year straight-line depreciation for all analyses and ignore the MACRS half-year convention for this problem.)

12-19   **NEW PROJECT ANALYSIS**   Holmes Manufacturing is considering a new machine that costs $250,000 and would reduce pretax manufacturing costs by $90,000 annually. Holmes would use the 3-year MACRS method to depreciate the machine, and management thinks the machine would have a value of $23,000 at the end of its 5-year operating life. The applicable depreciation rates are 33%, 45%, 15%, and 7% as discussed in Appendix 12A. Working capital would increase by $25,000 initially, but it would be recovered at the end of the project's 5-year life. Holmes's marginal tax rate is 40%, and a 10% WACC is appropriate for the project.

a. Calculate the project's NPV, IRR, MIRR, and payback.

b. Assume that management is unsure about the $90,000 cost savings—this figure could deviate by as much as plus or minus 20%. What would the NPV be under each of these situations?

c. Suppose the CFO wants you to do a scenario analysis with different values for the cost savings, the machine's salvage value, and the working capital (WC) requirement. She asks you to use the following probabilities and values in the scenario analysis:

Scenario	Probability	Cost Savings	Salvage Value	WC
Worst case	0.35	$ 72,000	$18,000	$30,000
Base case	0.35	90,000	23,000	25,000
Best case	0.30	108,000	28,000	20,000

Calculate the project's expected NPV, its standard deviation, and its coefficient of variation. Would you recommend that the project be accepted? Why or why not?

12-20   **REPLACEMENT ANALYSIS**   The Erley Equipment Company purchased a machine 5 years ago at a cost of $90,000. The machine had an expected life of 10 years at the time of purchase, and it is being depreciated by the straight-line method by $9,000 per year. If the machine is not replaced, it can be sold for $10,000 at the end of its useful life.

A new machine can be purchased for $150,000, including installation costs. During its 5-year life, it will reduce cash operating expenses by $50,000 per year. Sales are not expected to change. At the end of its useful life, the machine is estimated to be worthless. MACRS depreciation will be used. The machine will be depreciated over its 3-year class life rather than its 5-year economic life; so the applicable depreciation rates are 33%, 45%, 15%, and 7%.

The old machine can be sold today for $55,000. The firm's tax rate is 35%. The appropriate WACC is 16%.

a. If the new machine is purchased, what is the amount of the initial cash flow at Year 0?

b. What are the incremental net cash flows that will occur at the end of Years 1 through 5?

c. What is the NPV of this project? Should Erley replace the old machine? Explain.

12-21   **REPLACEMENT ANALYSIS**   The Bigbee Bottling Company is contemplating the replacement of one of its bottling machines with a newer and more efficient one. The old machine has a book value of $600,000 and a remaining useful life of 5 years. The firm does not expect to realize any return from scrapping the old machine in 5 years, but it can sell it now to another firm in the industry for $265,000. The old machine is being depreciated by $120,000 per year using the straight-line method.

The new machine has a purchase price of $1,175,000, an estimated useful life and MACRS class life of 5 years, and an estimated salvage value of $145,000. The applicable depreciation rates are 20%, 32%, 19%, 12%, 11%, and 6%. The machine is expected to economize on electric power usage, labor, and repair costs as well as to reduce the number of defective bottles. In total, an annual savings of $255,000 will be realized if the new machine is installed. The company's marginal tax rate is 35%, and it has a 12% WACC.

a. What initial cash outlay is required for the new machine?

b. Calculate the annual depreciation allowances for both machines and compute the change in the annual depreciation expense if the replacement is made.

c. What are the incremental net cash flows in Years 1 through 5?

d. Should the firm purchase the new machine? Support your answer.

e. In general, how would each of the following factors affect the investment decision, and how should each be treated?

(1) The expected life of the existing machine decreases.

(2) The WACC is not constant but is increasing as Bigbee adds more projects to its capital budget for the year.

COMPREHENSIVE/SPREADSHEET PROBLEM

12-22 **NEW PROJECT ANALYSIS AND UNEQUAL LIVES** You must analyze a potential new product—a caulking compound that Cory Materials' R&D people developed for use in the residential construction industry. Cory's marketing manager thinks the company can sell 115,000 tubes per year for 3 years at a price of $3.25 each, after which the product will be obsolete. The required equipment would cost $150,000, plus another $25,000 for shipping and installation. Current assets (receivables and inventories) would increase by $35,000, while current liabilities (accounts payable and accruals) would rise by $15,000. Variable costs would be 60% of sales revenues, fixed costs (exclusive of depreciation) would be $70,000 per year, and fixed assets would be depreciated under MACRS with a 3-year life. (Refer to Appendix 12A for MACRS depreciation rates.) When production ceases after 3 years, the equipment should have a market value of $15,000. Cory's tax rate is 40%, and it uses a 10% WACC for average-risk projects.

a. Find the required Year 0 investment and the project's annual net cash flows. Then calculate the project's NPV, IRR, MIRR, and payback. Assume at this point that the project is of average risk.

b. Suppose you now learn that R&D costs for the new product were $30,000 and that those costs were incurred and expensed for tax purposes last year. How would this affect your estimate of NPV and the other profitability measures?

c. If the new project would reduce cash flows from Cory's other projects and if the new project would be housed in an empty building that Cory owns and could sell, how would those factors affect the project's NPV?

d. Are this project's cash flows likely to be positively or negatively correlated with returns on Cory's other projects and with the economy, and should this matter in your analysis? Explain.

e. Unrelated to the new product, Cory is analyzing two mutually exclusive machines that will upgrade its manufacturing plant. These machines are considered average-risk projects, so management will evaluate them at the firm's 10% WACC. Machine X has a life of 4 years, while Machine Y has a life of 2 years. The cost of each machine is $60,000; however, Machine X provides after-tax cash flows of $25,000 per year for 4 years and Machine Y provides after-tax cash flows of $42,000 per year for 2 years. The manufacturing plant is very successful, so the machines will be repurchased at the end of each machine's useful life. In other words, the machines are "repeatable" projects.

(1) Using the replacement chain approach, what is the NPV of the better machine?

(2) Using the EAA approach, what is the EAA of the better machine?

f. **Spreadsheet assignment: at instructor's option** Disregard Part e for the remaining parts of this problem. Construct a spreadsheet that calculates the caulking compound's cash flows, NPV, IRR, payback, and MIRR.

g. The CEO expressed concern that some of the base-case inputs might be too optimistic or too pessimistic. He wants to know how the caulking product's NPV would be affected if these 6 variables were 20% better or 20% worse than the base-case level: unit sales, sales price, variable costs, fixed costs, WACC, and equipment cost. Hold other things constant when you consider each variable and construct a sensitivity graph to illustrate your results.

h. Do a scenario analysis based on the assumption that there is a 25% probability that each of the 6 variables itemized in Part g will turn out to have their best-case values as calculated in Part g, a 50% probability that all will have their base-case values, and a 25% probability that all will have their worst-case values. The other variables remain at base-case levels. Calculate the caulking compound's expected NPV, the standard deviation of NPV, and the coefficient of variation.

i. Does Cory's management use the risk-adjusted discount rate to adjust for project risk? Explain.

INTEGRATED CASE

ALLIED FOOD PRODUCTS

12-23 **CAPITAL BUDGETING AND CASH FLOW ESTIMATION** Allied Food Products is considering expanding into the fruit juice business with a new fresh lemon juice product. Assume that you were recently hired as assistant to the director of capital budgeting and you must evaluate the new project.

The lemon juice would be produced in an unused building adjacent to Allied's Fort Myers plant; Allied owns the building, which is fully depreciated. The required equipment would cost $200,000, plus an additional $40,000 for shipping and installation. In addition, inventories would rise by $25,000, while accounts payable would increase by $5,000. All of these costs would be incurred at t = 0. By a special ruling, the machinery could be depreciated under the MACRS system as 3-year property. The applicable depreciation rates are 33%, 45%, 15%, and 7%.

The project is expected to operate for 4 years, at which time it will be terminated. The cash inflows are assumed to begin 1 year after the project is undertaken, or at t = 1, and to continue out to t = 4. At the end of the project's life (t = 4), the equipment is expected to have a salvage value of $25,000.

Unit sales are expected to total 100,000 units per year, and the expected sales price is $2.00 per unit. Cash operating costs for the project (total operating costs less depreciation) are expected to total 60% of dollar sales. Allied's tax rate is 40%, and its WACC is 10%. Tentatively, the lemon juice project is assumed to be of equal risk to Allied's other assets.

You have been asked to evaluate the project and to make a recommendation as to whether it should be accepted or rejected. To guide you in your analysis, your boss gave you the following set of tasks/questions:

a. Allied has a standard form that is used in the capital budgeting process. (See Table IC12-1.) Part of the table has been completed, but you must replace the blanks with the missing numbers. Complete the table using the following steps:

   (1) Fill in the blanks under Year 0 for the initial investment outlay.

   (2) Complete the table for unit sales, sales price, total revenues, and operating costs excluding depreciation.

   (3) Complete the depreciation data.

   (4) Complete the table down to after-tax operating income and then down to the project's operating cash flows.

   (5) Fill in the blanks under Year 4 for the terminal cash flows and complete the project cash flow line. Discuss working capital. What would have happened if the machinery had been sold for less than its book value?

b. (1) Allied uses debt in its capital structure, so some of the money used to finance the project will be debt. Given this fact, should the projected cash flows be revised to show projected interest charges? Explain.

   (2) Suppose you learned that Allied had spent $50,000 to renovate the building last year, expensing these costs. Should this cost be reflected in the analysis? Explain.

   (3) Suppose you learned that Allied could lease its building to another party and earn $25,000 per year. Should that fact be reflected in the analysis? If so, how?

   (4) Assume that the lemon juice project would take profitable sales away from Allied's fresh orange juice business. Should that fact be reflected in your analysis? If so, how?

c. Disregard all the assumptions from Part b and assume there is no alternative use for the building over the next 4 years. Now calculate the project's NPV, IRR, MIRR, and payback. Do these indicators suggest that the project should be accepted? Explain.

d. If this project had been a replacement rather than an expansion project, how would the analysis have changed? Think about the changes that would have to occur in the cash flow table.

e. (1) What three levels, or types, of project risk are normally considered?

   (2) Which type is most relevant?

   (3) Which type is easiest to measure?

   (4) Are the three types of risk generally highly correlated?

f. (1) What is sensitivity analysis?

   (2) How would you perform a sensitivity analysis on the unit sales, salvage value, and WACC for the project? Assume that each of these variables deviates from its base-case, or expected, value by plus or minus 10%, 20%, and 30%. Explain how you would calculate the NPV, IRR, MIRR, and payback for each case; but don't do the analysis unless your instructor asks you to.

   (3) What is the primary weakness of sensitivity analysis? What are its primary advantages?

Table IC 12-1   Allied's Lemon Juice Project (Total Cost in Thousands)

End of Year:	0	1	2	3	4
I. Investment Outlay					
Equipment cost					
Installation					
Increase in inventory					
Increase in accounts payable	_____				
Total net investment	=====				
II. Project Operating Cash Flows					
Unit sales (thousands)			100		
Price/unit		$ 2.00	$ 2.00	_____	_____
Total revenues		_____	_____	_____	$ 200.0
Operating costs excluding depreciation			$120.0		
Depreciation		_____	_____	36.0	16.8
Total costs		$199.2	$228.0	_____	_____
Operating income before taxes (EBIT)				$44.0	
Taxes on operating income		0.3	_____	_____	25.3
After-tax operating income				$26.4	
Depreciation		79.2	_____	36.0	
Project operating cash flows	$ 0.0	$ 79.7	=====	=====	$ 54.7
III. Project Termination Cash Flows					
Return of net working capital					
Salvage value					
Tax on salvage value					_____
Total project termination cash flows					=====
IV. Project Net Cash Flows					
Project net cash flows	($ 260.0)	=====	=====	=====	$ 89.7
V. Results					
NPV =					
IRR =					
MIRR =					
Payback =					

g. Unrelated to the lemon juice project, Allied is upgrading its plant and must choose between two machines that are mutually exclusive. The plant is highly successful, so whichever machine is chosen will be repurchased after its useful life is over. Both machines cost $50,000; however, Machine A provides after-tax savings of $17,500 per year for 4 years, while Machine B provides after-tax savings of $34,000 in Year 1 and $27,500 in Year 2.

   (1) Using the replacement chain method, what is the NPV of the better machine?

   (2) Using the EAA method, what is the EAA of the better machine?

Work out quantitative answers to the remaining questions only if your instructor asks you to. Also note that it will take a *long time* to do the calculations unless you are using an *Excel* model.

h. Assume that inflation is expected to average 5% over the next 4 years and that this expectation is reflected in the WACC. Moreover, inflation is expected to increase revenues and variable costs by this same 5%. Does it appear that inflation has been dealt with properly in the lemon juice project's initial analysis to this point? If not, what should be done and how would the required adjustment affect the decision?

i. The lemon juice project's expected cash flows, considering inflation (in thousands of dollars), are given in Table IC12-2. Allied's WACC is 10%. Assume that you are confident about the estimates of all the variables

Table IC 12-2	**Allied's Lemon Juice Project Considering 5% Inflation (in Thousands)**				
	YEAR				
	0	**1**	**2**	**3**	**4**
Investment in:					
Fixed assets	($240)				
Net working capital	(20)				
Unit sales (thousands)		100	100	100	100
Sales price (dollars)		$ 2.100	$ 2.205	$ 2.315	$ 2.431
Total revenues		$ 210.0	$ 220.5	$ 231.5	$ 243.1
Cash operating costs (60%)		126.0	132.3	138.9	145.9
Depreciation		79.2	108.0	36.0	16.8
Operating income before taxes (EBIT)		$ 4.8	($ 19.8)	$ 56.6	$ 80.4
Taxes on operating income (40%)		1.9	(7.9)	22.6	32.1
After-tax operating income		$ 2.9	($ 11.9)	$ 34.0	$ 48.3
Plus depreciation		79.2	108.0	36.0	16.8
Project operating cash flows		$ 82.1	$ 96.1	$ 70.0	$ 65.1
Salvage value					25.0
Tax on SV (40%)					(10.0)
Recovery of NWC					20.0
Project net cash flows	($260)	$ 82.1	$ 96.1	$ 70.0	$100.1
Cumulative cash flows for payback:	(260.0)	(177.9)	(81.8)	(11.8)	88.3
Compounded inflows for MIRR:		109.2	116.3	77.0	100.1
Sum of compounded inflows:					402.6

$$\text{NPV} = \$15.0$$
$$\text{IRR} = 12.6\%$$
$$\text{MIRR} = 11.6\%$$

that affect the cash flows except unit sales. If product acceptance is poor, sales will be only 75,000 units a year, while a strong consumer response will produce sales of 125,000 units. In either case, cash costs will still amount to 60% of revenues. You believe that there is a 25% chance of poor acceptance, a 25% chance of excellent acceptance, and a 50% chance of average acceptance (the base case). Provide numbers only if you are using a computer model.

(1) What is the worst-case NPV? the best-case NPV?

(2) Use the worst-case, most likely case (or base-case), and best-case NPVs with their probabilities of occurrence to find the lemon juice project's expected NPV, standard deviation, and coefficient of variation.

j. Assume that Allied's average project has a coefficient of variation (CV) in the range of 1.25 to 1.75. Would the lemon juice project be classified as a high risk, an average risk, or a low risk? What type of risk is being measured here?

k. Based on common sense, how highly correlated do you think the lemon juice project would be with the firm's other assets? (Give a correlation coefficient or range of coefficients based on your judgment.)

l. How would the correlation coefficient and the previously calculated σ combine to affect the lemon juice project's contribution to corporate, or within-firm, risk? Explain.

m. Based on your judgment, what do you think the lemon juice project's correlation coefficient will be with respect to the general economy and thus with returns on "the market"? How will correlation with the economy affect the project's market risk?

n. Allied typically adds or subtracts 3% to its WACC to adjust for risk. After adjusting for risk, should the lemon juice project be accepted? Should any subjective risk factors be considered before the final decision is made? Explain.

APPENDIX 12A

Tax Depreciation

Because depreciation is covered in detail in accounting courses, here we provide only some basic information that is needed for capital budgeting. First, note that accountants generally calculate each asset's depreciation in two ways—they use straight line to figure the depreciation used for reporting profits to investors; but they use depreciation rates provided by the Internal Revenue Service (IRS), called MACRS (Modified Accelerated Cost Recovery System) rates, when they calculate depreciation for tax purposes. In capital budgeting, we are concerned with tax depreciation; so the relevant rates are the MACRS rates.

Class Life
The specified life of assets under the MACRS system.

Under MACRS, each type of fixed asset is assigned to a "class" and is then depreciated over the asset's **class life.** Table 12A-1 provides class lives for different types of assets as they existed in 2008. Next, as shown in Table 12A-2, MACRS specifies **annual depreciation rates** for assets in each class life. Real properties (buildings) are depreciated on a straight-line basis over 27.5 or 39 years; but all other assets are depreciated over shorter periods and on an accelerated basis, with high depreciation charges in the early years and less depreciation in the later years. The IRS tables are based on the **half-year convention,** where it is assumed that the asset is placed in service halfway through the first year and is taken out of service halfway through the year after its class life.

Annual Depreciation Rates
The annual expense accountants charge against income for "wear and tear" of an asset. For tax purposes, the IRS provides that appropriate MACRS rates be used that are dependent on an asset's class life.

In the following example, we calculate depreciation on equipment that would be classified as a 5-year asset with a cost of $8 million. In developing the tables, the IRS assumes that the machinery would be used for only 6 months of the year in which it is acquired, for 12 months in each of the next 4 years, and then for 6 months of the sixth year. Here are the depreciation charges, in thousands, that could be deducted for tax purposes based on MACRS:

Half-Year Convention
Assumes that assets are used for half the first year and half the last year.

Year	1	2	3	4	5	6
Rate	20%	32%	19%	12%	11%	6%
Depreciation	$1,600	$2,560	$1,520	$960	$880	$480

The total of the annual depreciation charges equals the $8 million cost of the asset, but it would be taken over 6 years and thus would affect cash flows over those 6 years.

Table 12A-1	**Major Classes and Asset Lives for MACRS**

Class	Type of Property
3-year	Certain special manufacturing tools
5-year	Automobiles, light-duty trucks, computers, and certain special manufacturing equipment
7-year	Most industrial equipment, office furniture, and fixtures
10-year	Certain longer-lived types of equipment
27.5-year	Residential rental real property such as apartment buildings
39-year	All nonresidential real property, including commercial and industrial buildings

| Table 12A-2 | Recovery Allowance Percentage for Personal Property |

CLASS OF INVESTMENT

Ownership Year	3-Year	5-Year	7-Year	10-Year
1	33%	20%	14%	10%
2	45	32	25	18
3	15	19	17	14
4	7	12	13	12
5		11	9	9
6		6	9	7
7			9	7
8			4	7
9				7
10				6
11				3
	100%	100%	100%	100%

Notes:

a. We developed these recovery allowance percentages based on the 200% declining balance method prescribed by MACRS, with a switch to straight-line depreciation at some point in the asset's life. For example, consider the 5-year recovery allowance percentages. The straight-line percentage would be 20% per year, so the 200% declining balance multiplier is 2.0(20%) = 40% = 0.4. However, because the half-year convention applies, the MACRS percentage for Year 1 is 20%. For Year 2, 80% of the depreciable basis remains to be depreciated; so the recovery allowance percentage is 0.40(80%) = 32%. In Year 3, 20% + 32% = 52% of the depreciation has been taken, leaving 48%; so the percentage is 0.4(48%) = 19%. In Year 4, the percentage is 0.4(29%) = 12%. After 4 years, straight-line depreciation exceeds the declining balance depreciation; so a switch is made to straight-line. (This is permitted under the law.) However, the half-year convention must also be applied at the end of the class life, and the remaining 17% of depreciation must be taken (amortized) over 1.5 years. Thus, the percentage in Year 5 is 17%/1.5 ≈ 11% and in Year 6 is 17% − 11% = 6%. Although the tax tables carry out the allowance percentages to two decimal places, we have rounded to the nearest whole number for ease of illustration.

b. Residential rental property (apartments) is depreciated over a 27.5-year life, whereas commercial and industrial structures are depreciated over 39 years. In both cases, straight-line depreciation must be used. The depreciation allowance for the first year is based, pro rata, on the month the asset was placed in service, with the remainder of the first year's depreciation being taken in the 28th or 40th year.

CHAPTER 13 Real Options and Other Topics in Capital Budgeting

Anheuser-Busch Used Real Options to Enhance Its Value[1]

Anheuser-Busch (AB) recently made headlines when it agreed to be acquired by InBev, a large international brewer headquartered in Belgium. The proposed merger dramatically illustrates the continued globalization of the brewery business and represents the culmination of AB's ongoing attempt to increase its presence in foreign markets.

AB was founded in 1875; by 1990, it was the largest U.S. beer company. However, eventually, its growth slowed and it had almost no foreign sales. In the mid-1990s, though, something changed—AB made modest investments in several foreign countries; and those investments led to a huge spurt of growth and profitability.

Most capital investments, especially when a firm invests outside of its home country, are risky. AB approached "going international" cautiously. Large-scale operations are essential in the beer industry; and to set up large enough operations

in Argentina, Brazil, Chile, and other nations would require hundreds of millions of dollars to build the necessary breweries, to establish the distribution systems, and to do the marketing necessary to establish the brand. Also, time would be required to get up to speed; so it would be several years before the investment could begin producing substantial cash flows. Finally, mistakes are often made when a company attempts to break into a new market, and those mistakes can be costly.

AB's management recognized these problems; and it concluded that it should not make a direct, large-scale push into the target markets. Rather, it decided to make relatively small investments—in the $2 to $3 million range—in small, local brewers and to form joint ventures with those companies. AB would provide expertise in making and marketing beer; and the new partner would provide expertise about the

---

[1]Tom Arnold and R. L. Shockley, Jr., "Value Creation at Anheuser-Busch: A Real Options Example," *Journal of Applied Corporate Finance*, Vol. 14, Summer 2001, pp. 41–50.

country, its culture, and its political system. Thus, AB would be learning about the country and its customs at the same time it was teaching its partner about making and marketing beer. As the bugs were worked out—and this occurs rapidly when the right partner is chosen—AB planned to increase its investment, locate additional breweries around the country, and engage in the kinds of marketing programs that had led to its success in the United States.

When AB invested in foreign companies, it bought certain tangible assets, but the most important item it received was a *real option*—the right, but not the obligation, to make further investments if things worked out well. Some of its initial investments looked questionable, and a "regular" capital budgeting analysis would show a low or even negative NPV. However, when the value of the real option was considered, AB's executives could see that they were getting a very attractive potential return with only a modest amount of risk.

AB's initial investments provided it with *growth options*. Other types of real options include the option to *abandon* an operation if its cash flows turn out to be low, to *delay* a potential investment until more information is available, and to switch inputs or outputs (*flexibility options*) after a project has gone into operation. As we will see, all of these options have the potential for increasing a project's expected NPV and for simultaneously reducing its risk.

PUTTING THINGS IN PERSPECTIVE

Chapters 11 and 12 covered the basic principles of capital budgeting. Now we examine three important extensions. First, we discuss real options, presenting some examples to demonstrate their importance. Next, we discuss the effect of the size of the capital budget on the WACC. The WACC tends to increase as the firm raises larger and larger amounts of capital, creating a feedback relationship between project acceptance, the size of the capital budget, and the WACC. Finally, we discuss the post-audit and its role in capital budgeting.

When you finish this chapter, you should be able to:

- **Explain what real options are, how they influence capital budgeting, and how they can be analyzed.**
- **Discuss how projects' NPVs are affected by the size of the firm's total capital budget and how to deal with this situation.**
- **Describe the post-audit, which is an important part of the capital budgeting process, and discuss its relevance in capital budgeting decisions.**

13-1 INTRODUCTION TO REAL OPTIONS

Traditional discounted cash flow (DCF) analysis—where a project's cash flows are estimated and then discounted to obtain an expected NPV—has been the cornerstone of capital budgeting since the 1950s. However, in recent years, it has been demonstrated that DCF techniques do not always lead to proper capital budgeting decisions.[2]

DCF techniques were originally developed to value securities such as stocks and bonds. They are *passive investments*—once the investment has been made,

---

[2]For an early but excellent discussion of the problems inherent in discounted cash flow valuation techniques as applied to capital budgeting, see Avinash K. Dixit and Robert S. Pindyck, "The Options Approach to Capital Investment," *Harvard Business Review*, May–June 1995, pp. 105–115. For more information on the option value inherent in investment timing decisions, see Stephen A. Ross, "Uses, Abuses, and Alternatives to the Net-Present-Value Rule," *Financial Management*, Autumn 1995, pp. 96–101. Also, the summer 2001 issue of the *Journal of Applied Corporate Finance* contains several interesting articles on the use of option concepts in capital budgeting.

Real Option

The right but not the obligation to take some future action.

most investors have no influence over the cash flows that result.[3] However, real assets are not passive investments—managers often can take actions to alter the cash flow stream even after the project is in operation. Such opportunities are called **real options**—"real" to distinguish them from financial options, such as an option to buy shares of GE stock, and "options" because they provide the right but not the obligation to take some future action. Real options are valuable, but that value is not captured by a traditional NPV analysis. Therefore, real options must be considered separately.

There are several types of real options: (1) *growth (or expansion)*, where the project can be expanded if demand turns out to be stronger than expected; (2) *abandonment*, where the project can be shut down if its cash flows are low; (3) *investment timing (or delay)*, where a project can be postponed until more information about demand and/or costs is available; (4) *output flexibility*, where the output can be changed if market conditions change; and (5) *input flexibility*, where the inputs used in the production process (e.g., oil versus natural gas for generating electricity) can be changed if input prices change.

SELF TEST

What is a real option?

Why might DCF techniques not lead to proper capital budgeting decisions?

Why might recognizing the existence of a real option raise, but not lower, a project's NPV as found in the traditional manner?

Name the five types of real options. Which one best describes the Anheuser-Busch situation discussed in the preceding section?

13-2 GROWTH (EXPANSION) OPTIONS

Growth Option

If an investment creates the opportunity to make other potentially profitable investments that would not otherwise be possible, then the investment is said to contain a growth option.

Anheuser-Busch's investment strategy in South America illustrates a **growth option**. Another example is a "strategic investment" such as a new process for desalinating seawater. Suppose GRE Inc. is considering the investment shown in Figure 13-1. Part I looks at the investment without considering an embedded real option to expand the project. GRE would invest $3 million at Time 0. Because this is considered a relatively risky investment, a WACC of 12% is used. There is a 50% probability of success, in which case the project will yield positive cash inflows of $1.5 million per year for 3 years. There is also a 50% probability of poor results, in which case inflows will be only $1.1 million per year for 3 years. If the project is successful, the NPV will be $603,000; but the NPV will be −$358,000 if the project is unsuccessful. The expected NPV, found by multiplying each NPV by its 50% probability, is $122,000; so it appears that the project should be accepted. However, the project is quite risky as measured by its coefficient of variation, so it might still be rejected.[4]

Now consider Part II, where we recognize the existence of the growth option. The firm would know if conditions are good at the end of Year 1, so it would then invest another $1 million to expand at Time 2. The expansion would produce cash flows on out in future years; and the present value of those flows, at the end of Year 3, is estimated to be $5 million. We then add the new cash flows to the original flows to obtain the "total good scenario cash flows" as shown on Row 19.

---

[3]Large investors such as Warren Buffett and some hedge fund operators can buy stocks in companies and then influence firms' operations and cash flows. However, the average stockholder does not have such influence.
[4]The standard deviation and coefficient of variation both indicate what is already obvious—the project is quite risky.

| FIGURE 13-1 | Analysis of a Growth Option (Dollars in Thousands) |

	A	B	C	D	E	F	G	H
3								
4								
5	Part I. Project without the Growth Option							
6						Cash Flow at End of Period		NPV@
7		Outcome	Prob.	0	1	2	3	12%
8		Good	50%	-$3,000	$1,500	$1,500	$1,500	$603
9		Bad	50%	-$3,000	$1,100	$1,100	$1,100	-$358
10							Expected NPV	$122
11							Standard Deviation (σ)	$480
12						Coefficient of Variation = CV = σ / Expected NPV		3.93
13								
14	Part II. Project with the Growth Option							
15						Cash Flow at End of Period		NPV@
16				0	1	2	3	12%
17		Cash flows, initial investment		-$3,000	$1,500	$1,500	$1,500	
18		Cash flows, growth investment				-$1,000	$5,000	
19		Good	50%	-$3,000	$1,500	$500	$6,500	$3,364
20		Bad	50%	-$3,000	$1,100	$1,100	$1,100	-$358
21							Expected NPV	$1,503
22							Standard Deviation (σ)	$1,861
23						Coefficient of Variation = CV = σ / Expected NPV		1.24
24								
25	Part III. Value of the Option						NPV considering the growth option	$1,503
26							NPV not considering the growth option	$122
27			Value of the option: If NPV without option is negative, value of option = NPV with option. Otherwise, value of option = NPV with option - NPV without option.					$1,381

The NPV under good conditions is $3.364 million. The bad-case cash flows are the same as in Part I, and their NPV is −$358,000. Now when we find the expected value of the project, it is $1.503 million. The standard deviation and coefficient of variation are much lower, indicating that the project is much less risky compared to the project in the absence of the option.

Part III shows the **option value**, which is the additional value of the project if the option exists. If the expected NPV of the project with and without the option is positive, as it is in our example, the value of the option will be the additional NPV resulting from the option:

> **Value of option = Expected NPV with option − Expected NPV without option**
>
> = $1.503 − $0.122 = $1.381 million

If the NPV without the option had been negative but the NPV with the option was positive, the value of the option would have been the full expected NPV under the with-option analysis. This is the value of the option because without it, the project would have been rejected and there would have been no positive NPV.

One final point: Once we have done the analysis as in Figure 13-1, we must consider any costs that might be required to obtain the option. For example, suppose that to be able to undertake the expansion, GRE would have to spend an extra $300,000 at Time 0 for an option on land that would be needed for the expansion. We could have built this cost into the analysis in Part II. However, we choose to disregard this cost initially, find the value of the option without accounting for any additional cost to acquire it, and then compare the value of the option to its cost. Either procedure can be used, but we prefer the second one.

Option Value
The difference between the expected NPVs with and without the relevant option. It is the value that is not accounted for in a traditional NPV analysis. A positive option value expands the firm's opportunities.

Note, though, that the true expected value of the project would be the expected NPV minus the cost of obtaining the option, or $1.081 million.

SELF TEST

If a firm fails to consider growth options, would this cause it to underestimate or overestimate projects' NPVs? Explain.

13-3 ABANDONMENT/SHUTDOWN OPTIONS

Abandonment Option
The option of stopping a project if operating cash flows turn out to be lower than expected. This option can raise expected profitability and lower project risk.

In capital budgeting, we generally assume that a firm will undertake a project for the project's full physical life. However, this is not always the best course of action. If the firm's project has an **abandonment option** that allows the project to be stopped before the end of its physical life, this can increase expected profitability and lower risk. For example, suppose GRE is considering another project and it is negotiating with a key supplier regarding the cost and availability of electricity. Typically, the utility requires a guarantee for the purchase of a minimum amount of power before it will bring in the required lines because it wants assurance that its investment will not be stranded. The result is that if GRE undertakes the project, GRE will be forced to operate the project for its full 4-year life.

The details on GRE's project are provided in Figure 13-2, Part I. The initial investment would be $1 million at t = 0. Three possible outcomes are considered: (1) A best-case outcome that will result in the cash inflows shown on Row 6, (2) a base-case (or average) outcome with the cash flows shown on Row 7, and (3) a worst-case outcome with annual losses as shown on Row 8. There is a 50% probability of the base-case results and a 25% probability of both the best-case and worst-case outcomes. Initially, the project was considered to have a relatively low risk, so its cost of capital is 10%. The NPV under each possibility is shown in Column H, and the expected value is $14,000. Therefore, the project is barely acceptable.

Now consider Part II, the analysis where abandonment is possible. The best-case and base-case data are reproduced from Part I and shown on Rows 16 and 17. Also, we show on Row 18 the same worst-case information as was given in Part I. However, we now show on Row 19 the situation that would exist if GRE could abandon the project. We assume that it could decide, once it saw the bad results in Year 1, to close the operation and that it could sell the equipment for $200,000 in Year 2. There would be no cash flows in Years 3 and 4, and the new worst-case #2 NPV would be −$1,089—bad but still much better than worst-case #1, the "can't abandon" situation.

Given the option to abandon, GRE would never choose Worst #1; so if things turned out badly, it would choose Worst #2 and abandon the project. Therefore, when we calculate the expected NPV, we assign a zero probability to Worst #1 and a 25% probability to Worst #2. The result is an expected NPV of $214,000, up from $14,000 when abandonment was not a possibility. Note too that there is a dramatic decrease in the project's risk as measured by the coefficient of variation. This is to be expected because the possibility of abandonment greatly lowers the worst-case results, which lowers the project's risk.

In Part III, we calculate the value of the abandonment option. This value is the increase in NPV, $200,000. It would pay GRE to pay the utility up to $200,000 to be able to get out of the required purchases and thus be able to abandon the project if things turn out badly.

FIGURE 13-2		Abandonment Option (Dollars in Thousands)						

	A	B	C	D	E	F	G	H	I
1									
2									
3	Part I. Cannot Abandon								
4					Cash Flow at End of Period				NPV@
5		Prob.	0	1	2	3	4	10%	
6	Best Case	25%	-$1,000	$400	$600	$800	$1,300	$1,348	
7	Base Case	50%	-$1,000	$200	$400	$500	$600	$298	
8	Worst Case	25%	-$1,000	-$280	-$280	-$280	-$280	-$1,888	
9							Expected NPV	$14	
10							Standard Deviation (σ)	$1,179	
11						Coefficient of Variation = CV = σ / Expected NPV		83.3	
12									
13	Part II. Can Abandon								
14					Cash Flow at End of Period				NPV@
15		Prob.	0	1	2	3	4	10%	
16	Best Case	25%	-$1,000	$400	$600	$800	$1,300	$1,348	
17	Base Case	50%	-$1,000	$200	$400	$500	$600	$298	
18	Worst #1	0%	-$1,000	-$280	-$280	-$280	-$280	-$1,888	Disregard
19	Worst #2	25%	-$1,000	-$280	$200	$0	$0	-$1,089	Use
20							Expected NPV	$214	
21							Standard Deviation (σ)	$866	
22						Coefficient of Variation = CV = σ / Expected NPV		4.1	
23									
24	Part III. Value of the Option								
25					NPV considering the abandonment option			$214	
26					NPV not considering the abandonment option			$14	
27	Value of the option: If NPV without option is negative, value of option = NPV with option. Otherwise, value of option = NPV with option - NPV without option.							$200	

SELF TEST

Would you expect an abandonment option to increase or decrease a project's NPV and risk (as measured by the coefficient of variation)? Explain.

Suppose a project's expected "cannot abandon" NPV is −$14 and its "can abandon" expected NPV is $214. How much is the abandonment option worth? **($214)**

13-4 INVESTMENT TIMING OPTIONS

Traditionally, an NPV analysis assumes that projects will be accepted or rejected, which implies that they will be undertaken now or never. However, in practice, companies sometimes have a third choice—delay the decision until later, when more information will be available. Such **investment timing options** can affect projects' estimated profitability and risk.

To illustrate a timing option, suppose GRE Inc. is considering a project with the data shown in Figure 13-3. It requires an initial investment of $3 million at t = 0. It will generate positive net cash flows for 3 years, and it is considered to have above-average risk; hence, a 12% WACC is used. The size of the annual cash

Investment Timing Option
An option as to when to begin a project. Often, if a firm can delay a decision, it can increase a project's expected NPV.

FIGURE 13-3	Analysis of a Timing Option (Dollars in Thousands)

	A	B	C	D	E	F	G	H
1								
2								
3	Part I. Project Without the Timing Option							
4				Cash Flow at End of Period				NPV@
5		Outcome	Prob.	0	1	2	3	12%
6		Good	50%	-$3,000	$2,000	$2,000	$2,000	$1,804
7		Bad	50%	-$3,000	$450	$450	$450	-$1,919
8							Expected NPV	-$58
9							Standard Deviation (σ)	$1,861
10						Coefficient of Variation = CV = σ / Expected NPV		-32.23
11								
12	Part II. Delay the Decision Until We Know the Market Conditions							
13				Cash Flow at End of Period				NPV@
14				0	1	2	3	12%
15		Good	50%	$0	-$3,000	$2,000	$2,000	$339
16		Bad	50%	$0	$0	$0	$0	$0
17							Expected NPV	$170
18							Standard Deviation (σ)	$170
19						Coefficient of Variation = CV = σ / Expected NPV		1.00
20								
21	Part III. Value of the Option					NPV considering the growth option		$170
22						NPV not considering the growth option		-$58
23			Value of the option: If NPV without option is negative, value of option = NPV with option. Otherwise, value of option = NPV with option - NPV without option.					$170
24								
25	Note: Under the Delay situation, we must find the NPV as of t = 0. If we set the cash flow for t = 0 at $0, then using a calculator or Excel we automatically find the t = 0 NPV. However, if we let PV = -3000, PMT = 2000, N = 2, and I = 12, we get an NPV = $380 under the Good outcome and an expected NPV of $190. Note, though, that these NPVs are as of t = 1, so we must discount them back one year at 12% to achieve comparability and get the correct answer.							

flows will depend on what happens to market conditions in the future. As shown in Part I, there is a 50% probability that market conditions will be strong, in which case the project will generate cash flows of $2 million per year. There is also a 50% probability that demand will be weak, in which case the annual cash flows will be only $450,000. If the market is strong, the NPV will be $1.804 million; but if demand is weak, the NPV will be −$1.919 million. The expected value, assuming the project is undertaken today, is −$58,000; so it appears that the project should be rejected.

Now look at Part II. Here we assume that GRE can delay the decision until next year, when more information will be available about market conditions. Delaying the decision also will mean giving up 1 year of positive cash flows. But if conditions are good, the firm will proceed and realize an NPV of $339,000, while if conditions are bad, it simply will not make the investment and thus will have a zero NPV. The probability of each outcome is 50%; and the expected NPV, as of t = 0, is $170,000, indicating that the project should be accepted.

Several other factors should also be considered before reaching the final accept/reject decision. First, if GRE decides to wait, it may lose the strategic advantage of being the first to enter a new business. Also, costs may increase, which could lower the calculated NPV. In general, the more uncertainty there is about future market conditions, the more attractive it is to wait. However, this risk reduction may be offset by the loss of the "first mover advantage."

Briefly describe what an investment timing, or delay, option is and why such options are valuable.

Explain why the following statement is true: In general, the more uncertainty there is about future market conditions, the more attractive a "delay" option will be, other things held constant.

13-5 FLEXIBILITY OPTIONS

Many projects offer **flexibility options**, which permit the firm to change after operations have commenced—either the inputs it uses or the output it produces. BMW's Spartanburg, South Carolina, auto assembly plant provides a good example. When BMW built the plant, it planned to produce sports coupes. If it built the plant configured to produce just those vehicles, the construction cost would be minimized, which would maximize the NPV. However, BMW recognized that the demand for different types of autos changes over time, which meant that at some point, it might want to switch production to another type of vehicle. Such a shift would be difficult if the plant was designed strictly for coupes. Therefore, BMW decided to spend additional money to construct a more flexible plant, one that could produce several different models should demand patterns shift. Sure enough, things did change. The demand for coupes dropped, while the demand for convertibles soared. But BMW was ready, and the Spartanburg plant is now spewing out hot-selling convertibles. Consequently, the plant's cash flows are much higher than they would have been without the flexibility option that BMW obtained by building a more flexible plant.

Electric utilities such as Florida Power & Light (FPL) provide an example of building input flexibility into capital budgeting projects. FPL can build plants that generate electricity by burning oil or natural gas. The prices of those fuels change over time depending on developments in places such as Iraq and Iran, on changing environmental policies, and the like. Some years ago virtually all power plants were designed to burn one type of fuel because this resulted in the lowest construction cost. However, as fuel price volatility increased, power companies began to build higher-cost but more flexible plants to permit switching from oil to gas and back again depending on relative fuel prices.

Figure 13-4 illustrates the analysis for a flexibility option. Part I shows a negative expected NPV if demand for the product—say, sedans—turns out to be low. However, as we see in Part II, if the plant is sufficiently flexible to switch production to another product—say, convertibles—the expected NPV will be positive. The setup would be similar if we were analyzing input flexibility—say, a switch from oil to natural gas if oil prices rose more than gas prices. Flexibility options do have costs, but those costs can be compared with the calculated values of the options.

Flexibility Option
An option that permits operations to be altered depending on how conditions change during a project's life.

What are input flexibility options and output flexibility options?

How do flexibility options affect projects' NPVs and risk?

FIGURE 13-4		Flexibility Option (Dollars in Thousands)							

	A	B	C	D	E	F	G	H	I	J
1										
2										
3	Part I. Project without the Flexibility Option						Cash Flow at End of Period			NPV@
4						0	1	2	3	12%
5	Strong demand				50%	-$5,000	$2,500	$2,500	$2,500	$1,005
6	Weak demand				50%	-$5,000	$1,500	$1,500	$1,500	-$1,397
7									Expected NPV	-$196
8										
9	Part II. Project with the Flexibility Option						Cash Flow at End of Period			NPV@
10						0	1	2	3	12%
11	Strong demand				50%	-$5,100	$2,500	$2,500	$2,500	$905
12	Weak demand		Switch products		50%	-$5,100	$1,500	$2,250	$2,250	-$366
13									Expected NPV	$270
14										
15	Part III. Value of the Option								NPV with the option	$270
16									NPV without the option	-$196
17		Value of the option: If NPV without option is negative, value of option = NPV with option. Otherwise, value of option = NPV with option - NPV without option.								$270

13-6 THE OPTIMAL CAPITAL BUDGET

Thus far we have described various factors that managers consider when they evaluate individual projects. For planning purposes, managers must also forecast the total capital budget because the amount of capital raised affects the WACC. If the capital budget is small, the firm's WACC might be 10%, while with a larger capital budget, the overall WACC might be 12%. Furthermore, accepting one large project might change the WACC from 10% to 12%.

We can use GRE Inc. to illustrate how this process works in theory.

Step 1. The treasurer estimated the firm's overall composite WACC at different amounts of capital raised. As we discussed in Chapter 10, the cost of equity from retained earnings is lower than the cost of external equity; so once the retained earnings for the year have been exhausted, the WACC will rise. Similarly, as the firm raises more and more capital, its costs of debt and preferred stock are likely to rise. Therefore, a graph that shows the firm's WACC plotted against the amount of funds raised will look like the WACC line in Figure 13-5.

Step 2. The firm's different divisions have reasonably good ideas about the projects they are likely to undertake during the coming year and the IRRs on those projects. Obviously, some projects are better than others in the sense that they have higher IRRs—and probably higher NPVs once the WACC is known and the NPVs can be calculated. At any rate, the divisions provide the treasurer with schedules showing their likely capital projects, ranked from the highest IRR to the lowest IRR. This information is also plotted on Figure 13-5 as the **IRR schedule**.

Step 3. The WACC schedule tells us the firm's **marginal cost of capital** (i.e., the cost of each dollar raised), which will consist of a certain percentage of debt and a certain percentage of equity). Similarly, the IRR schedule shows the rate of return on each project; hence, the IRR schedule amounts

IRR Schedule
A graph of the marginal rates of return on investment at different levels of investment, ranked from highest to lowest IRR.

Marginal Cost of Capital
The cost of each dollar raised.

FIGURE 13-5	Optimal Capital Budget: Marginal IRR = Marginal WACC

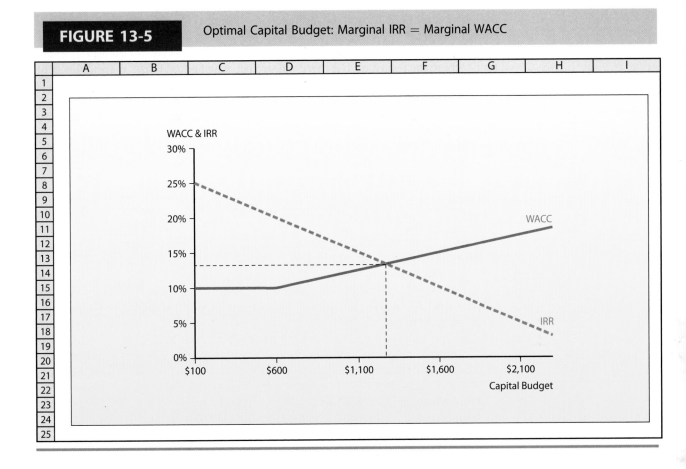

to a schedule of the marginal rates of return on investment at different levels of investment, ranked from highest to lowest IRR.

Step 4. We know from economics that value is maximized when investment is taken to the point where marginal returns are just equal to marginal costs. In Figure 13-5, this means that the **optimal capital budget** calls for the investment of about $1,200 million.

Step 5. The WACC at the optimal cost of capital is approximately 13.5%. The treasurer would report that number to the various divisions, and they would then make appropriate risk adjustments depending on the risk factors assigned to the divisions. For example, as we saw in Chapter 10, firms often have protocols where low-risk divisions begin with a cost rate that is 90% of the corporate WACC, use that rate for average-risk projects, and then use higher or lower rates for relatively high- or low-risk projects in the division. A high-risk division might use a base WACC of 110% of the corporate WACC for an average-risk project in that division and then adjust up or down for individual project risk.

Step 6. The divisions would find the NPVs of their various projects, using the risk- and size-adjusted costs of capital as we just found.

Optimal Capital Budget
The size of the capital budget where the rate of return on the marginal project is equal to the marginal cost of capital.

In practice, the previous six steps are rarely followed precisely. However, the CFO, CEO, and other top executives understand the concepts involved; and they do make adjustments in a judgmental manner. For example, if things are proceeding in a stable, routine, manner, the treasurer will simply estimate the corporate WACC for use in capital budgeting. However, if the firm is contemplating a very large project or so many smaller projects that the firm is moving out the WACC schedule as shown in Figure 13-5, a more detailed study will be done and the corporate WACC will be adjusted to account for the larger-than-normal capital budget.

Thus far in this section, we have assumed that the firm would invest out to the point where the return on the marginal project is just equal to the marginal cost of capital. This procedure maximizes the firm's intrinsic value; and the assumption is reasonable for most large, mature firms with good track records. However, smaller firms, new firms, and firms with dubious track records may have difficulty raising capital, even for projects that appear to have highly positive NPVs. Also, the owners of some businesses may not want to expand rapidly—they may prefer to grow at a more leisurely pace. In such circumstances, the size of the firm's capital budget may be *constrained,* a situation called **capital rationing**. If capital is constrained for whatever reason, it should be used in the most efficient way possible. Procedures have been explored for allocating capital to maximize the firm's aggregate NPV subject to the constraint that the capital rationing ceiling is not exceeded. However, these procedures are extremely complicated, so they are best left for advanced finance courses.

The procedures discussed in this section cannot be implemented with much precision. However, they do force the firm to think carefully about each division's relative risk, about the risk of each project within each division, and about the relationship between the total amount of capital raised and the cost of that capital. Further, the process forces the firm to adjust its capital budget to reflect capital market conditions. If the costs of debt and equity rise, this fact will be reflected in the cost of capital used to evaluate projects. Thus, projects that would be marginally acceptable when capital costs were low would (correctly) be ruled unacceptable when capital costs become high.

Capital Rationing

The situation in which a firm can raise only a specified, limited amount of capital regardless of how many good projects it has.

Why is a firm's value maximized if it invests to the point where its marginal return on new investment is equal to its marginal cost of capital?

Explain how a financial manager might estimate his or her firm's optimal capital budget.

What is capital rationing?

In terms of Figure 13-5, how would an event such as the credit crisis of 2008, where interest rates for many corporate borrowers climbed quite high, affect the size of the capital budget?

13-7 THE POST-AUDIT

Post-Audit

A comparison of actual versus expected results for a given capital project.

One final aspect of the capital budgeting process is the **post-audit**, which involves (1) comparing actual results with those predicted by the project's sponsors and (2) explaining why any differences occurred. For example, many firms require that the operating divisions send a monthly report for the first 6 months after a project goes into operation and a quarterly report thereafter until the project's results meet expectations. From then on, reports on the operation are reviewed on a regular basis like those of other operations. The post-audit has two main purposes:

1. *Improve forecasts.* When decision makers are forced to compare their projections with actual outcomes, there is a tendency for estimates to improve. Conscious or unconscious biases are observed and eliminated; new forecasting methods are sought as the need for them becomes apparent; and people tend to do everything better, including forecasting, if they know that their actions are being monitored.

2. *Improve operations.* Businesses are run by people, and people can perform at higher or lower levels of efficiency. When a divisional team has made a forecast about an investment, the team members are, in a sense, putting their reputations on the line. Accordingly, if costs are above and sales are below predicted levels, executives in production, marketing, and other areas will strive to improve operations and to bring results in line with forecasts. In a discussion related to this point, one executive made this statement: "You academics only worry about making good decisions. In business, we also worry about making decisions good."

The post-audit is not a simple, mechanical process. First, we must recognize that each element of the cash flow forecast is subject to uncertainty; so a percentage of all projects undertaken by any reasonably aggressive firm will necessarily go awry. This fact must be considered when the performances of the operating executives who sponsor projects are appraised. Second, projects sometimes fail to meet expectations for reasons beyond the control of their sponsors and for reasons that no one could be expected to anticipate. For example, the unanticipated run-up in commodity prices in 2008 adversely affected many projects. Third, it is often difficult to separate the operating results of one investment from those of a larger system. Although some projects stand alone and permit ready identification of costs and revenues, the cost savings that result from assets such as new computers may be very hard to measure. Fourth, it is often difficult to hand out blame or praise because the executives who were responsible for launching a given investment have moved on by the time the results are known.

Because of these difficulties, some firms play down the post-audit's importance. However, observations of businesses and governmental units suggest that the best-run and most successful organizations put a great deal of emphasis on post-audits. Accordingly, we regard the post-audit as an important element in a good capital budgeting system.

SELF TEST

What is done in the post-audit?

Identify several benefits of the post-audit.

What are some factors that complicate the post-audit process?

TYING IT ALL TOGETHER

This chapter focused on three aspects of capital budgeting: (1) real options and their effects on projects' values; (2) the size of the optimal capital budget and the relationship between the budget's size and the firm's WACC; and (3) the post-audit, where the results of projects are examined and compared with their forecasted results. We also discussed capital rationing, which occurs when a firm constrains its capital budget in a manner that requires it to reject some projects that have positive NPVs.

In the following chapters, we go on to discuss how the target capital structure is established and what effect the capital structure has on the firm's cost of capital and optimal capital budget. Then we discuss a related topic, dividend policy.

SELF-TEST QUESTIONS AND PROBLEMS
(Solutions Appear in Appendix A)

ST-1 **KEY TERMS** Define each of the following terms:

   a. Real option; option value

   b. Growth option; abandonment option

   c. Investment timing option; flexibility option

   d. Marginal cost of capital; IRR schedule

   e. Optimal capital budget

   f. Capital rationing

   g. Post-audit

ST-2 **ABANDONMENT OPTION** Your firm is considering a project with the following cash flows:

		PREDICTED CASH FLOW FOR EACH YEAR			
		0	**1**	**2**	**3**
Best Case	25%	($25,000)	$18,000	$18,000	$18,000
Base Case	50%	(25,000)	12,000	12,000	12,000
Worst Case	25%	(25,000)	(8,000)	(8,000)	(8,000)

You learn that the firm can abandon the project, if it so chooses, after one year of operation, in which case it can sell the asset and receive $15,000 in cash at the end of Year 2. Assume that all cash flows are after-tax amounts. The WACC is 12%.

   a. What is the project's NPV if the abandonment option is not considered?

   b. What is the NPV considering abandonment?

   c. What is the value of the abandonment option?

QUESTIONS

13-1 Explain in general terms what each of the following real options is and how it could change projects' NPVs and their corresponding risk relative to what would have been estimated if the options had not been considered.

   a. abandonment

   b. timing

   c. growth

   d. flexibility

13-2 Would a failure to recognize growth options tend to cause a firm's actual capital budget to be above or below the optimal level? Would your answer be the same for abandonment, timing, and flexibility options? Explain.

13-3 Companies often have to increase their initial investment costs to obtain real options. Why might this be so, and how could a firm decide if it was worth the cost to obtain a given real option?

13-4 How might a firm's corporate WACC be affected by the size of its capital budget?

13-5 What is a post-audit, why do firms use them, and what problems can arise when they are used?

PROBLEMS

**Easy
Problems
1–2**

13-1   **GROWTH OPTION**   Martin Development Co. is deciding whether to proceed with Project X. The cost would be $9 million in Year 0. There is a 50% chance that X would be hugely successful and would generate annual after-tax cash flows of $6 million per year during Years 1, 2, and 3. However, there is a 50% chance that X would be less successful and would generate only $1 million per year for the 3 years. If Project X is hugely successful, it would open the door to another investment, Project Y, which would require an outlay of $10 million at the end of Year 2. Project Y would then be sold to another company at a price of $20 million at the end of Year 3. Martin's WACC is 11%.

a.   If the company does not consider real options, what is Project X's NPV?

b.   What is X's NPV considering the growth option?

c.   How valuable is the growth option?

13-2   **OPTIMAL CAPITAL BUDGET**   Marble Construction estimates that its WACC is 10% if equity comes from retained earnings. However, if the company issues new stock to raise new equity, it estimates that its WACC will rise to 10.8%. The company believes that it will exhaust its retained earnings at $2,500,000 of capital due to the number of highly profitable projects available to the firm and its limited earnings. The company is considering the following seven investment projects:

Project	Size	IRR
A	$ 650,000	14.0%
B	1,050,000	13.5
C	1,000,000	11.2
D	1,200,000	11.0
E	500,000	10.7
F	650,000	10.3
G	700,000	10.2

Assume that each of these projects is independent and that each is just as risky as the firm's existing assets. Which set of projects should be accepted, and what is the firm's optimal capital budget?

**Intermediate
Problems
3–4**

13-3   **INVESTMENT TIMING OPTION**   Digital Inc. is considering production of a new cell phone. The project will require an investment of $20 million. If the phone is well-received, the project will produce cash flows of $10 million a year for 3 years; but if the market does not like the product, the cash flows will be only $5 million per year. There is a 50% probability of both good and bad market conditions. Digital can delay the project a year while it conducts a test to determine whether demand will be strong or weak. The delay will not affect the project's cost or its cash flows. Digital's WACC is 10%. What action do you recommend?

13-4   **ABANDONMENT OPTION**   The Scampini Supplies Company recently purchased a new delivery truck. The new truck costs $22,500; and it is expected to generate after-tax cash flows, including depreciation, of $6,250 per year. The truck has a 5-year expected life. The expected year-end abandonment values (salvage values after tax adjustments) for the truck are given here. The company's WACC is 10%.

Year	Annual After-Tax Cash Flow	Abandonment Value
0	($22,500)	—
1	6,250	$17,500
2	6,250	14,000
3	6,250	11,000
4	6,250	5,000
5	6,250	0

a.   Should the firm operate the truck until the end of its 5-year physical life; if not, what is the truck's optimal economic life?

b.   Would the introduction of abandonment values, in addition to operating cash flows, ever *reduce* the expected NPV and/or IRR of a project? Explain.

Challenging
Problems
5–7

13-5 **OPTIMAL CAPITAL BUDGET** Hampton Manufacturing estimates that its WACC is 12% if equity comes from retained earnings. However, if the company issues new stock to raise new equity, it estimates that its WACC will rise to 12.5%. The company believes that it will exhaust its retained earnings at $3,250,000 of capital due to the number of highly profitable projects available to the firm and its limited earnings. The company is considering the following seven investment projects:

Project	Size	IRR
A	$ 750,000	14.0%
B	1,250,000	13.5
C	1,250,000	13.2
D	1,250,000	13.0
E	750,000	12.7
F	750,000	12.3
G	750,000	12.2

a. Assume that each of these projects is independent and that each is just as risky as the firm's existing assets. Which set of projects should be accepted, and what is the firm's optimal capital budget?

b. Now assume that Projects C and D are mutually exclusive. Project D has an NPV of $400,000, whereas Project C has an NPV of $350,000. Which set of projects should be accepted, and what is the firm's optimal capital budget?

c. Ignore Part b and assume that each of the projects is independent but that management decides to incorporate project risk differentials. Management judges Projects B, C, D, and E to have average risk; Project A to have high risk; and Projects F and G to have low risk. The company adds 2% to the WACC of those projects that are significantly more risky than average, and it subtracts 2% from the WACC of those projects that are substantially less risky than average. Which set of projects should be accepted, and what is the firm's optimal capital budget?

13-6 **INVESTMENT TIMING OPTION** The Bush Oil Company is deciding whether to drill for oil on a tract of land that the company owns. The company estimates that the project will cost $8 million today. Bush estimates that once drilled, the oil will generate positive net cash flows of $4 million a year at the end of each of the next 4 years. While the company is fairly confident about its cash flow forecast, it recognizes that if it waits 2 years, it will have more information about the local geology as well as the price of oil. Bush estimates that if it waits 2 years, the project will cost $9 million. Moreover, if it waits 2 years, there is a 90% chance that the net cash flows will be $4.2 million a year for 4 years, and there is a 10% chance that the cash flows will be $2.2 million a year for 4 years. Assume that all cash flows are discounted at 10%.

a. If the company chooses to drill today, what is the project's net present value?

b. Would it make sense to wait 2 years before deciding whether to drill? Explain.

c. What is the value of the investment timing option?

d. What disadvantages might arise from delaying a project such as this drilling project?

13-7 **REAL OPTIONS** Nevada Enterprises is considering buying a vacant lot that sells for $1.2 million. If the property is purchased, the company's plan is to spend another $5 million today (t = 0) to build a hotel on the property. The after-tax cash flows from the hotel will depend critically on whether the state imposes a tourism tax in this year's legislative session. If the tax is imposed, the hotel is expected to produce after-tax cash inflows of $600,000 at the end of each of the next 15 years. If the tax is not imposed, the hotel is expected to produce after-tax cash inflows of $1,200,000 at the end of each of the next 15 years. The project has a 12% WACC. Assume at the outset that the company does not have the option to delay the project.

a. What is the project's expected NPV if the tax is imposed?

b. What is the project's expected NPV if the tax is not imposed?

c. Given that there is a 50% chance that the tax will be imposed, what is the project's expected NPV if management proceeds with it today?

d. While the company does not have an option to delay construction, it does have the option to abandon the project 1 year from now if the tax is imposed. If it abandons the project, it will sell the complete property 1 year from now at an expected price of $6 million. Once the project is abandoned, the company will no longer receive any cash inflows from it. Assuming that all cash flows are discounted at 12%, will the existence of this abandonment option affect the company's decision to proceed with the project today? Explain.

e. Finally, assume that there is no option to abandon or delay the project, but that the company has an option to purchase an adjacent property in 1 year at a price of $1.5 million. If the tourism tax is imposed, the net present value of developing this property (as of t = 1) will be only $300,000 (so it doesn't make sense to purchase the property for $1.5 million). However, if the tax is not imposed, the net present value of the future opportunities from developing the property will be $4 million (as of t = 1). Thus, under this scenario, it makes sense to purchase the property for $1.5 million. Assume that these cash flows are discounted at 12% and that the probability that the tax will be imposed is still 50%. How much will the company pay today for the option to purchase this property 1 year from now for $1.5 million?

COMPREHENSIVE/SPREADSHEET PROBLEMS

13-8 **REAL OPTIONS** Use a spreadsheet model to evaluate the project analyzed in Problem 13-7.

13-9 **REAL OPTIONS** Bankers' Services Inc. (BSI) is considering a project that has a cost of $10 million and an expected life of 3 years. There is a 30% probability of good conditions, in which case the project will provide a cash flow of $9 million at the end of each year for 3 years. There is a 40% probability of average conditions, in which case the annual cash flows will be $4.5 million, and there is a 30% probability of bad conditions and a cash flow of −$1.5 million per year. BSI can, if it chooses, close down the project at the end of any year and sell the related assets for 90% of the book value. The asset sale price will be received at the end of the year the project is shut down. The related assets will be depreciated by the straight-line method over 3 years, and the value at the end of Year 3 is zero. (Don't worry about IRS regulations for this problem.) BSI uses a 12% WACC to evaluate projects such as this one.

a. Find the project's expected NPV with and without the abandonment option.

b. How sensitive is the NPV to changes in the company's WACC? to the percentage of book value at which the asset can be sold?

c. Now assume that the project cannot be shut down. However, expertise gained by taking it on will lead to an opportunity at the end of Year 3 to undertake a venture that has the same cost as the original project and will be undertaken if the best-case scenario develops. If the project is wildly successful (the good conditions), the firm will go ahead with the project but will not go ahead with the other two scenarios (because consumer demand will still be considered too difficult to determine). As a result, the new project will generate the same cash flows as the original project in the best-case scenario. In other words, there will be a second $10 million cost at the end of Year 3 and then cash flows of $9 million for the following 3 years. Also, this new project cannot be abandoned if it is undertaken. How does this new information affect the original project's expected NPV? At what WACC will the project break even in the sense that NPV = $0?

d. Now suppose the original (no abandonment) project can be delayed a year. All of the cash flows remain unchanged, but information obtained during that year will tell the company exactly which set of demand conditions exist. How does this option to delay the project affect its NPV?

INTEGRATED CASE

21st CENTURY EDUCATIONAL PRODUCTS

13-10 **OTHER TOPICS IN CAPITAL BUDGETING** 21st Century Educational Products (21st Century) is a rapidly growing software company; and consistent with its growth, it has a relatively large capital budget. While most of the company's projects are fairly easy to evaluate, a handful of projects involve more complex evaluations.

John Keller, a senior member of the company's finance staff, coordinates the evaluation of these more complex projects. His group brings their recommendations directly to the company's CFO and CEO, Kristin Riley and Bob Stevens, respectively.

a. In recent months, Keller's group has begun to focus on real option analysis.

(1) What is real option analysis?

(2) What are some examples of projects with real options?

b. Considering real options, one of Keller's colleagues, Barbara Hudson, has suggested that instead of investing in Project X today, it might make sense to wait a year because 21st Century would learn more about market conditions and would be better able to forecast the project's cash flows. Right now 21st Century forecasts that Project X will generate expected annual net cash flows of $33,500 for 4 years. However, if the company waits a year, it will learn more about market conditions. There is a 50% chance that the market will be strong and a 50% chance that it will be weak. If the market is strong, the annual cash flows will be $43,500. If the market is weak, the annual cash flows will be only $23,500. If 21st Century chooses to wait a year, the initial investment will remain $100,000 and cash flows will continue for 4 years after the initial investment is made. Assume that all cash flows are discounted at 10%. Should 21st Century invest in Project X today, or should it wait a year before deciding whether to invest in the project?

c. Now assume that there is more uncertainty about the future cash flows. More specifically, assume that the annual cash flows are $53,500 if the market is strong and $13,500 if the market is weak. Assume that the up-front cost is still $100,000 and that the WACC is still 10%. Will this increased uncertainty make the firm more or less willing to invest in the project today? Explain.

d. 21st Century is considering another project, Project Y. Project Y has an up-front cost of $200,000 and an economic life of three years. If the company develops the project, its after-tax operating costs will be $100,000 a year; however, the project is expected to produce after-tax cash inflows of $180,000 a year. Thus, the project's estimated cash flows are as follows:

Year	Cash Outflows	Cash Inflows	Net Cash Flows
0	($200,000)	$ 0	($200,000)
1	(100,000)	180,000	80,000
2	(100,000)	180,000	80,000
3	(100,000)	180,000	80,000

(1) The project has an estimated WACC of 10%. What is the project's NPV?

(2) While the project's operating costs are fairly certain at $100,000 per year, the estimated cash inflows depend critically on whether 21st Century's largest customer uses the product. Keller estimates that there is a 60% chance that the customer will use the product, in which case the project will produce after-tax cash inflows of $250,000. Thus, its net cash flows will be $150,000 per year. However, there is a 40% chance that the customer will not use the product, in which case the project will produce after-tax cash inflows of only $75,000. Thus, its net cash flows will be -$25,000. Write out the estimated cash flows and calculate the project's NPV under each of the two scenarios.

(3) While 21st Century does not have the option to delay the project, it will know one year from now whether the key customer has selected the product. If the customer chooses not to adopt the product, 21st Century has the option to abandon the project. If 21st Century abandons the project, it will not receive any cash flows after Year 1 and it will not incur any operating costs after Year 1. Thus, if the company chooses to abandon the project, its estimated cash flows will be as follows:

Again, assuming a WACC of 10%, what is the project's expected NPV if it abandons the project? Should 21st Century invest in Project Y today, realizing it has the option to abandon the project at t = 1?

(4) Up until now, we have assumed that the abandonment option has not affected the project's WACC. Is this assumption reasonable? How might the abandonment option affect the WACC?

e. Finally, 21st Century is also considering Project Z. Project Z has an up-front cost of $500,000, and it is expected to produce after-tax cash inflows of $100,000 at the end of each of the next five years (t = 1, 2, 3, 4, and 5). Because Project Z has a WACC of 12%, it clearly has a negative NPV. However, Keller and his group recognize that if 21st Century goes ahead with Project Z today, there is a 10% chance that this will lead to subsequent opportunities that have a net present value at t = 5 equal to $3,000,000. At the same time, there is a 90% chance that the subsequent opportunities will have a negative net present value (-$1,000,000) at t = 5. On the basis of their knowledge of real options, Keller and his group understand that the company will choose to develop these subsequent opportunities only if they appear to be profitable at t = 5. Given this information, should 21st Century invest in Project Z today? Explain your answer.

PART 5

CAPITAL STRUCTURE AND DIVIDEND POLICY

© PHOTO BY TIM BOYLE/GETTY IMAGES

CHAPTER

14 Capital Structure and Leverage

Debt: Rocket Booster or Anchor?

If it is to grow, a firm needs capital; and capital comes primarily in the form of debt or equity. Debt financing has two important advantages: (1) The interest paid is tax deductible whereas dividends paid on stock are not deductible, which lowers debt's relative cost. (2) The return on debt is fixed, so stockholders do not have to share the firm's profits if the firm turns out to be extremely successful.

However, debt also has disadvantages: (1) Using more debt increases the firm's risk, and that raises the costs of debt and equity. (2) If the company falls on hard times and its operating income is not sufficient to cover interest charges, the firm may go bankrupt. Good times may be just around the corner, but too much debt can bankrupt the company before it reaches that corner.

Because of the risk of using debt, companies with volatile earnings and operating cash flows tend to limit its use. On the other hand, companies with relatively little business risk and stable operating cash flows can benefit from taking on more debt. Kellogg Co., the world's largest cereal manufacturer, is a good example of such a company. Indeed, just after its 2001 acquisition of Keebler Foods Co., Kellogg's book value capital structure consisted of 86% debt and 14% equity. An 86% debt ratio is quite high, and Kellogg's management was well aware that excessive debt can push an otherwise well-regarded company into bankruptcy. Accordingly, Kellogg's management began to pay down its debt and restore its balance sheet to a more "reasonable" debt level so that by early 2008, its debt ratio had fallen to around 70%.

For many companies, a 70% debt ratio would still be too high. However, because Kellogg's business is so stable, this ratio is not too bad. After all, the consumption of Frosted Flakes, Froot Loops, and Pop Tarts has remained stable even during economic downturns. Moreover, if we examine Kellogg's capital structure in more detail, it soon becomes apparent that there is more than meets the eye. According to its balance sheet, Kellogg has about $5.86 billion of total debt versus stockholders' equity of about

$2.23 billion. But in May 2008, the market capitalization of Kellogg's equity (which is the stock price times the number of shares outstanding) was approximately $19.30 billion. From a market value perspective, Kellogg's debt ratio is only $5.86/($5.86 + $19.30) = 23.3%, which is actually conservative and helps explain why the company has a relatively strong BBB+ bond rating.

Kellogg and other companies can finance with debt or equity. Is one better than the other? If so, should firms finance with all debt or with all equity? Or if the best solution is some mix of debt and equity, what is the optimal mix? As you read this chapter, think about those questions and consider how you would answer them.

PUTTING THINGS IN PERSPECTIVE

When we calculated the weighted average cost of capital (WACC) in Chapter 10, we assumed that the firm had a specific target capital structure. However, target capital structures often change over time, such changes affect the risk and cost of each type of capital, and all this can change the WACC. Moreover, a change in the WACC will affect capital budgeting decisions and, ultimately, the stock price.

Many factors influence capital structure decisions; and as we will see, determining the optimal capital structure is not an exact science. Therefore, even firms in the same industry often have dramatically different capital structures. In this chapter, we consider the effects of debt on risk and on the optimal capital structure.

When you finish this chapter, you should be able to:

- Identify the trade-offs that firms must consider when they determine their target capital structure.
- Distinguish between business risk and financial risk and explain the effects that debt financing has on the firm's expected return and risk.
- Discuss the analytical framework used when determining the optimal capital structure.
- Discuss capital structure theory and use it to explain why firms in different industries tend to have different capital structures.

Two video clips of Steve Walsh, Assistant Treasurer at JCPenney, talking about capital structure are available at **http://fisher.osu.edu/fin/clips.htm.** *The first clip on capital structure discusses the cost of capital and debt, while the second clip discusses the optimal capital structure as seen by JCPenney relative to capital structure theory as seen by Modigliani/Miller.*

14-1 THE TARGET CAPITAL STRUCTURE

A firm's **optimal capital structure** is defined as the structure that would maximize its stock price. It is useful to analyze the situation and attempt to determine the optimal structure; but in practice, it is difficult to do this with much confidence. As a result, in practice, many managers think of the optimal capital structure more as a range (e.g., from 40% to 50% debt) rather than as a precise number (e.g., 45%). Other firms study the situation; reach a conclusion as to the optimal structure; and then set a **target capital structure**, such as 45% debt.[1] If the actual debt ratio is significantly below the target level, management will raise capital by issuing debt, whereas if the debt ratio is above the target, equity will be used. The target may

Optimal Capital Structure
The capital structure that maximizes a firm's stock price.

Target Capital Structure
The mix of debt, preferred stock, and common equity the firm wants to have.

---

[1] A recent study by Graham and Harvey surveyed corporate managers and asked whether their firms established a target capital structure. Only 19% of the respondents indicated that their firm did not have a target capital structure. Ten percent of the respondents said that they had a strict target debt ratio, 34% indicated that they had a somewhat tight range for their target debt ratio, and 37% of the respondents indicated that they had a flexible target. Refer to John R. Graham and Campbell R. Harvey, "The Theory and Practice of Corporate Finance: Evidence from the Field," *Journal of Financial Economics*, Volume 60 (May 2001), pp. 187–243.

change over time as conditions change; but at any given moment, management generally has a specific debt ratio in mind.

Setting the capital structure involves a trade-off between risk and return:

- Using more debt will raise the risk borne by stockholders.
- However, using more debt generally increases the expected return on equity.

The higher risk associated with using more debt tends to lower the stock price, but the higher debt-induced expected rate of return raises it. *Therefore, we seek to find the capital structure that strikes a balance between risk and return so as to maximize the stock price.*

Four primary factors influence capital structure decisions:

1. *Business risk,* or the riskiness inherent in the firm's operations if it used no debt. The greater the firm's business risk, the lower its optimal debt ratio.

2. The firm's *tax position.* A major reason for using debt is that interest is tax deductible, which lowers the effective cost of debt. However, if most of a firm's income is already sheltered from taxes by depreciation tax shields or interest on currently outstanding debt or tax loss carry-forwards, its tax rate will be low. In this case, additional debt would not be as advantageous as it would be to a firm with a higher effective tax rate.

3. *Financial flexibility,* or the ability to raise capital on reasonable terms even under adverse market conditions. Corporate treasurers know that a steady supply of capital is necessary for stable operations, which is vital for long-run success. They also know that when money is tight in the economy or when a firm is experiencing operating difficulties, it is easier to raise debt than equity capital and lenders are more willing to accommodate companies with strong balance sheets. Therefore, the firm's potential future need for funds and the consequences of a funds shortage combine to influence its target capital structure—the greater the probability that capital will be needed and the worse the consequences of not being able to obtain it, the less debt the firm should have on its balance sheet.

4. *Managerial conservatism or aggressiveness.* Some managers are more aggressive than others; hence, they are more willing to use debt in an effort to boost profits. This factor does not affect the true optimal, or value-maximizing, capital structure; but it does influence the firm's target capital structure.

Those four points largely determine a firm's target capital structure, but operating conditions can cause its actual capital structure to vary from the target. For example, a company's actual stock price might for some reason be well below the intrinsic value as seen by management. In this case, management would be reluctant to issue new stock to raise capital; so it might use debt financing even though this would cause the debt ratio to rise above the target level. However, the company would probably take steps to return the capital structure to its target level as soon as the stock price approached its intrinsic value.

SELF TEST   Define the optimal capital structure and differentiate it from the target capital structure.

Name four factors that influence a firm's target capital structure.

In what sense does setting the target capital structure involve a trade-off between risk and return?

Why might market conditions cause a firm's actual capital structure to vary from its target level?

14-2 BUSINESS AND FINANCIAL RISK

In Chapter 8, we examined risk from the viewpoint of an individual investor and we distinguished between *risk on a stand-alone basis*, where an asset's cash flows are analyzed by themselves, and *risk in a portfolio context*, where cash flows from a number of assets are combined and consolidated cash flows are analyzed. In a portfolio context, we saw that an asset's risk can be divided into two components: *diversifiable risk*, which can be diversified away and hence is of little concern to most investors, and *market risk*, which is measured by the beta coefficient and reflects broad market movements that cannot be eliminated by diversification and therefore is of concern to investors. Then in Chapter 12, we examined risk from the viewpoint of the corporation and we considered how capital budgeting decisions affect the firm's riskiness.

Now we introduce two new dimensions of risk:

1. *Business risk,* which is the riskiness of the firm's assets if no debt is used.
2. *Financial risk,* which is the additional risk placed on the common stockholders as a result of using debt.

14-2a Business Risk

Business risk is the single most important determinant of capital structure, and it represents the amount of risk that is inherent in the firm's operations even if it uses no debt financing. Consider Bigbee Electronics Company, a *debt-free (unlevered)* firm. Because the company has no debt, its ROE is equal to its ROA and either can be used to estimate business risk. Figure 14-1 gives some clues about the

Business Risk
The riskiness inherent in the firm's operations if it uses no debt.

FIGURE 14-1	Bigbee Electronics: Trend in ROE, 1998–2008, and Estimated Probability Distribution of ROE, 2008

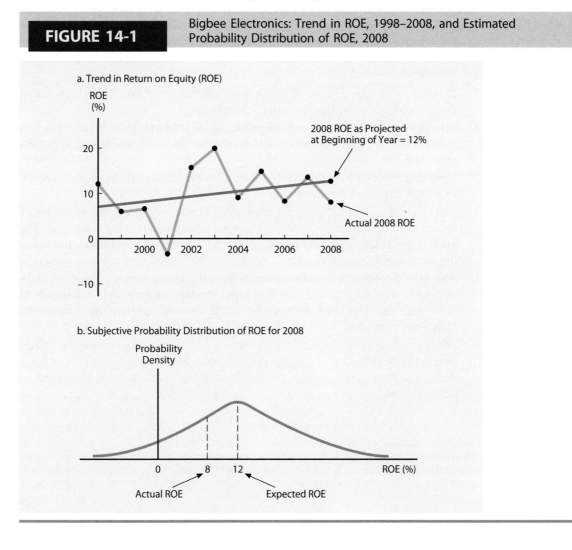

company's business risk. The top graph shows the trend in ROE from 1998 through 2008; this graph gives both security analysts and Bigbee's management an idea of the degree to which ROE has varied in the past and might vary in the future. The lower graph shows the beginning-of-year subjectively estimated probability distribution of Bigbee's ROE for 2008 based on the trend line in the top section of Figure 14-1. As the graphs indicate, Bigbee's actual ROE in 2008 (8%) fell below the expected value (12%); so the forecast had been too optimistic.

Bigbee's past fluctuations in ROE were caused by many factors—booms and recessions in the national economy, successful new product introductions by Bigbee and by its competitors, labor strikes, and a fire in Bigbee's main plant. Similar events will doubtless occur in the future; and when they do, the realized ROE will be higher or lower than the projected level. Further, there is always the possibility that a long-term disaster will strike, permanently depressing the company's earning power. For example, a competitor might introduce a new product that makes Bigbee's products obsolete and puts the company out of business. Automobiles did this to buggy manufacturers about a century ago. The more uncertainty there is about future ROEs, the greater the company's *business risk*. Bigbee uses no debt, so this is the risk its stockholders face. As we shall see, the stockholders face more risk if the company chooses to finance with both debt and equity.

Business risk varies from industry to industry and among firms in a given industry. Further, business risk can change over time. For example, for many years, the electric utilities were regarded as having little business risk; but a combination of events in recent years altered the utilities' situation, producing sharp declines in their ROEs and greatly increasing the industry's risk. Today food processors and health care firms are examples of industries with low business risk, while cyclical manufacturing industries such as autos and steel, as well as many small start-up companies, are regarded as having especially high business risks.[2]

Business risk depends on a number of factors, the more important of which are listed here:

1. *Demand variability.* The more stable the demand for a firm's products, other things held constant, the lower its business risk.

2. *Sales price variability.* Firms whose products are sold in highly volatile markets are exposed to more business risk than similar firms whose output prices are more stable.

3. *Input cost variability.* Firms whose input costs are highly uncertain are exposed to a high degree of business risk.

4. *Ability to adjust output prices for changes in input costs.* Some firms are better able than others to raise their own output prices when input costs rise. The greater the ability to adjust output prices to reflect cost conditions, the lower the degree of business risk.

5. *Ability to develop new products in a timely, cost-effective manner.* Firms in high-tech industries such as drugs and computers depend on a constant stream of new products. The faster a firm's products become obsolete, the greater the firm's business risk.

6. *Foreign risk exposure.* Firms that generate a high percentage of their earnings overseas are subject to earnings declines due to exchange rate fluctuations. Also, if a firm operates in a politically unstable area, it may be subject to political risk.

---

[2]We have avoided any discussion of market versus company-specific risk in this section. We note now (1) that any action that increases business risk in the sense of stand-alone risk will generally increase a firm's beta coefficient and (2) that a part of business risk as we define it will generally be company-specific and hence subject to elimination as a result of diversification by the firm's stockholders.

7. *The extent to which costs are fixed: operating leverage.* If a high percentage of its costs are fixed (and hence do not decline when demand falls), the firm will be exposed to a relatively high degree of business risk. This factor is called *operating leverage,* and it is discussed at length in the next section.

Each of those factors is determined partly by the firm's industry characteristics, but each factor also is controllable to some extent by management. For example, most firms can, through their marketing policies, take actions to stabilize both unit sales and sales prices. However, this stabilization may require spending a great deal on advertising and/or making price concessions to obtain commitments from customers to purchase fixed quantities at fixed prices in the future. Similarly, firms such as Bigbee Electronics can reduce the volatility of future input costs by negotiating long-term labor and materials supply contracts, but they may have to pay prices above the current spot price to obtain those contracts. Many firms are also using hedging techniques to reduce business risk, as we discuss in Chapter 18.

14-2b Operating Leverage

As noted earlier, business risk depends in part on the extent to which a firm builds fixed costs into its operations—if fixed costs are high, even a small decline in sales can lead to a large decline in ROE. So other things held constant, the higher a firm's fixed costs, the greater its business risk. Higher fixed costs are generally associated with more highly automated, capital-intensive firms and industries. However, businesses that employ highly skilled workers who must be retained and paid even during recessions also have relatively high fixed costs, as do firms with high product development costs, because the amortization of development costs is a fixed cost.

When a high percentage of total costs are fixed, the firm is said to have a high degree of **operating leverage**. In physics, leverage implies the use of a lever to raise a heavy object with a small force. In politics, if people have leverage, their smallest word or action can accomplish a great deal. *In business terminology, a high degree of operating leverage, other factors held constant, implies that a relatively small change in sales results in a large change in ROE.*

Operating Leverage
The extent to which fixed costs are used in a firm's operations.

Figure 14-2 illustrates the concept of operating leverage by comparing the results that Bigbee could expect if it used different degrees of operating leverage. Plan A calls for a relatively small amount of fixed costs, $20,000. Here the firm would not have much automated equipment; so its depreciation, maintenance, property taxes, and so forth, would be low. However, the total operating costs line has a relatively steep slope, indicating that variable costs per unit are higher than they would be if the firm used more operating leverage. Plan B calls for a higher level of fixed costs, $60,000. Here the firm uses automated equipment (with which one operator can turn out a few or many units at the same labor cost) to a much larger extent. The breakeven point is higher under Plan B—breakeven occurs at 60,000 units under Plan B versus only 40,000 units under Plan A.

We can calculate the breakeven quantity by recognizing that **operating breakeven** occurs when earnings before interest and taxes (EBIT) = 0:[3]

Operating Breakeven
The output quantity at which EBIT = 0.

$$\text{EBIT} = PQ - VQ - F = 0 \qquad \text{14-1}$$

Here P is average sales price per unit of output, Q is units of output, V is variable cost per unit, and F is fixed operating costs. If we solve for the break-even quantity, Q_{BE}, we get this expression:

$$Q_{BE} = \frac{F}{P - V} \qquad \text{14-1a}$$

[3]This definition of breakeven does not include any fixed financial costs. If there were fixed financial costs, the firm would suffer an accounting loss at the operating breakeven point. We will introduce financial costs shortly.

| FIGURE 14-2 | Illustration of Operating Leverage |

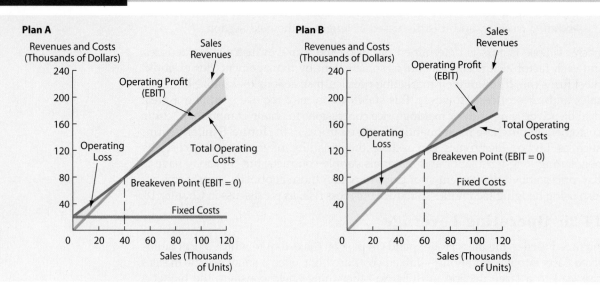

	Plan A	Plan B
Price	$ 2.00	$ 2.00
Variable costs	$ 1.50	$ 1.00
Fixed costs	$ 20,000	$ 60,000
Assets	$200,000	$200,000
Tax rate	40%	40%

					PLAN A					PLAN B			
Demand	Probability	Units Sold	Dollar Sales	Operating Costs	Operating Profits (EBIT)	Net Income	ROE	Operating Costs	Operating Profits (EBIT)	Net Income	ROE
Terrible	0.05	0	$ 0	$ 20,000	($20,000)	($12,000)	(6.00)%	$ 60,000	($ 60,000)	($36,000)	(18.00)%
Poor	0.20	40,000	80,000	80,000	0	0	0.00	100,000	(20,000)	(12,000)	(6.00)
Normal	0.50	100,000	200,000	170,000	30,000	18,000	9.00	160,000	40,000	24,000	12.00
Good	0.20	160,000	320,000	260,000	60,000	36,000	18.00	220,000	100,000	60,000	30.00
Wonderful	0.05	200,000	400,000	320,000	80,000	48,000	24.00	260,000	140,000	84,000	42.00
Expected value		100,000	$200,000	$170,000	$30,000	$18,000	9.00%	$160,000	$ 40,000	$24,000	12.00%
Standard deviation					$24,698		7.41%		$ 49,396		14.82%
Coefficient of variation					0.82		0.82		1.23		1.23

Notes:

a. Operating costs = Variable costs + Fixed costs.

b. The federal-plus-state tax rate is 40%, so NI = EBIT(1 − Tax rate) = EBIT(0.6).

c. ROE = NI/Equity. The firm has no debt, so Assets = Equity = $200,000.

d. The breakeven sales level for Plan B is not shown in the table, but it is 60,000 units or $120,000.

e. The expected values, standard deviations, and coefficients of variation were found using procedures discussed in Chapter 8.

Thus, for Plan A,

$$Q_{BE} = \frac{\$20,000}{\$2.00 - \$1.50} = 40,000 \text{ units}$$

And for Plan B,

$$Q_{BE} = \frac{\$60,000}{\$2.00 - \$1.00} = 60,000 \text{ units}$$

How does operating leverage affect business risk? *Other things held constant, the higher a firm's operating leverage, the higher its business risk.* This point is demonstrated in Figure 14-3, where we develop probability distributions for ROE under Plans A and B.

The top section of Figure 14-3 graphs the probability distribution of sales that was presented in tabular form in Figure 14-2. The sales probability distribution depends on how demand for the product varies, not on whether the product is

FIGURE 14-3	Analysis of Business Risk

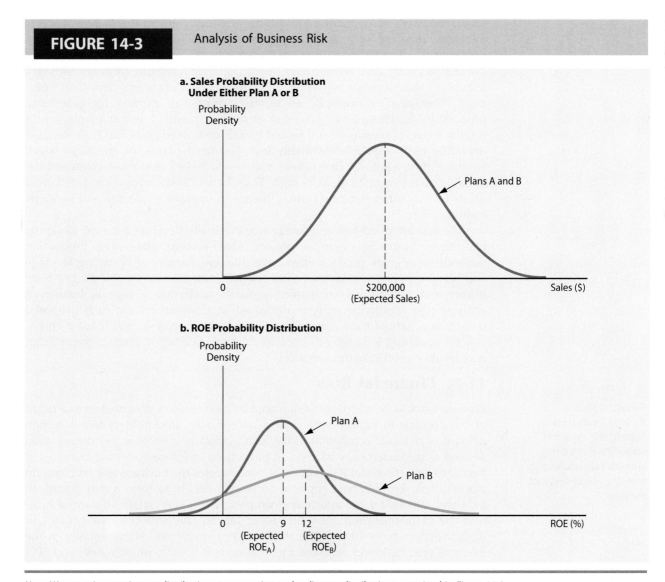

Note: We are using continuous distributions to approximate the discrete distributions contained in Figure 14-2.

manufactured by Plan A or by Plan B. Therefore, the same sales probability distribution applies to both production plans. This distribution has expected sales of $200,000; and it ranges from zero to about $400,000, with a standard deviation of $\sigma_{Sales} = \$98,793$.

We use the sales probability distribution, together with the operating costs at each sales level, to develop graphs of the ROE probability distributions under Plans A and B. These are shown in the lower section of Figure 14-3. Plan B has a higher expected ROE, but this plan also entails a much higher probability of losses. Plan B, the one with more fixed costs and a higher degree of operating leverage, is clearly riskier. *In general, holding other factors constant, the higher the degree of operating leverage, the greater the firm's business risk.* In the discussion that follows, we assume that Bigbee has decided to go ahead with Plan B because its management believes that the higher expected return is sufficient to compensate for the higher risk.

To what extent can firms control their operating leverage? To a large extent, operating leverage is determined by technology. Electric utilities, telephone companies, airlines, steel mills, and chemical companies must have large investments in fixed assets; and this results in high fixed costs and operating leverage. Similarly, pharmaceutical, auto, computer, and other companies must spend heavily to develop new products; and product-development costs increase operating leverage. Grocery stores and service businesses such as accounting and consulting firms, on the other hand, generally have significantly lower fixed costs and hence lower operating leverage. Still, although industry factors do exert a major influence, all firms have some control over their operating leverage. For example, an electric utility can expand its generating capacity by building either gas-fired or nuclear plants. Nuclear plants would require a larger investment and would have higher fixed costs, but their variable operating costs would be relatively low. Gas-fired plants, on the other hand, would require a smaller investment and would have lower fixed costs; but the variable costs (for gas) would be high. Thus, by its capital budgeting decisions, a utility (or any other company) can influence its operating leverage and hence its business risk.

The concept of operating leverage was originally developed for use in capital budgeting. Mutually exclusive projects that involve alternative production methods for a given product often have different degrees of operating leverage and hence different breakeven points and different degrees of risk. Bigbee Electronics and many other companies regularly undertake a type of breakeven analysis (the sensitivity analysis discussed in Chapter 12) for each proposed project as a part of their regular capital budgeting process. Still, once a corporation's operating leverage has been established, this factor exerts a major influence on its capital structure decision.

14-2c Financial Risk

Financial Risk

An increase in stockholders' risk, over and above the firm's basic business risk, resulting from the use of financial leverage.

Financial risk is the additional risk placed on the common stockholders as a result of the decision to finance with debt. Conceptually, stockholders face a certain amount of risk that is inherent in the firm's operations—this is its business risk, defined as the uncertainty inherent in projections of future operating income. If a firm uses debt (financial leverage), this concentrates the business risk on common stockholders. To illustrate, suppose 10 people decide to form a corporation to own and operate a large apartment complex. There is a certain amount of business risk in the operation. If the firm is capitalized only with common equity and if each person buys 10% of the stock, each investor will share equally in the business risk. However, suppose the firm is capitalized with 50% debt and 50% equity, with 5 of the investors putting up their capital as debt and the other 5 putting up their money as equity. The debtholders will receive a fixed payment, and it will come before the stockholders receive anything. Also, if the firm goes bankrupt, the debtholders must be paid off before the stockholders get anything. In this case, the 5 investors who put up the equity will have to bear all of the business risk; so the common stock will be twice as risky as it would have been had the firm been financed only with equity. *Thus, the use of debt, or* **financial leverage**, *concentrates the firm's business risk on the stockholders*. (In Web Appendix 14A, we describe in more detail the interaction between operating leverage and financial leverage.)

To illustrate the business risk concentration, we can extend the Bigbee Electronics example. To date, the company has never used debt, but the treasurer is now considering a possible change in its capital structure. Changes in the use of debt would cause changes in earnings per share (EPS) as well as changes in risk—both would affect the stock price. To understand the relationship between financial leverage and EPS, first consider Table 14-1, which shows how Bigbee's cost of debt would vary if it used different amounts of debt to finance a fixed amount of assets. The higher the percentage of debt in the capital structure, the riskier the debt and hence the higher the interest rate lenders would charge.

For now, assume that only two financing choices are being considered—remain at 100% equity or shift to 50% debt and 50% equity. We also assume that with no debt, Bigbee has 10,000 shares of common stock outstanding and if it decides to change its capital structure, common stock would be repurchased at the $20 current stock price. Now consider Table 14-2, which shows how the financing choice would affect Bigbee's profitability and risk.

First, focus on Section I, which assumes that Bigbee uses no debt. Because debt is zero, interest is also zero; hence, pretax income is equal to EBIT. Taxes at 40% are deducted to obtain net income, which is then divided by the $200,000 of equity to calculate ROE. Note that Bigbee will receive a tax credit if net income is negative (when demand is terrible or poor). Here we assume that Bigbee's losses can be carried back to offset income earned in the prior year, thus resulting in a tax credit. The ROE at each sales level is then multiplied by the probability of that sales level to calculate the 12% expected ROE. Note that this 12% is the same as that found in Figure 14-2 for Plan B.

Section I of the table also calculates Bigbee's earnings per share (EPS) for each scenario under the assumption that the company continues to use no debt. Net income is divided by the 10,000 common shares outstanding to obtain EPS. If demand is terrible, the EPS will be −$3.60; but if demand is wonderful, the EPS will rise to $8.40. The EPS at each sales level is then multiplied by the probability of that level to calculate the expected EPS, which is $2.40 if Bigbee uses no debt. We also calculate the standard deviation of EPS and the coefficient of variation as indicators of the firm's risk at a zero debt ratio: σ = $2.96 and CV$_{EPS}$ = 1.23.

Financial Leverage
The extent to which fixed-income securities (debt and preferred stock) are used in a firm's capital structure.

Table 14-1	Interest Rates for Bigbee with Different Debt/Assets Ratios

Amount Borrowed[a]	Debt/Assets Ratio	Interest Rate, r$_d$, on All Debt
$ 20,000	10%	8.0%
40,000	20	8.3
60,000	30	9.0
80,000	40	10.0
100,000	50	12.0
120,000	60	15.0

[a]We assume that the firm must borrow in increments of $20,000. We also assume that Bigbee is unable to borrow more than $120,000, which is 60% of its $200,000 of assets, due to restrictions in its corporate charter.

Table 14-2	**Effects of Financial Leverage: Bigbee Electronics Financed with Zero Debt or 50% Debt**

Section I. Zero Debt

Debt ratio	0%
Assets	$200,000
Debt	$ 0
Equity	$200,000
Shares outstanding	10,000

Demand For Product (1)	Probability (2)	EBIT (3)	Interest (4)	Pretax Income (5)	Taxes (40%) (6)	Net Income (7)	ROE (8)	EPS[a] (9)
Terrible	0.05	($ 60,000)	$0	($ 60,000)	($24,000)	($36,000)	(18.00)%	($3.60)
Poor	0.20	(20,000)	0	(20,000)	(8,000)	(12,000)	(6.00)	(1.20)
Normal	0.50	40,000	0	40,000	16,000	24,000	12.00	2.40
Good	0.20	100,000	0	100,000	40,000	60,000	30.00	6.00
Wonderful	0.05	140,000	0	140,000	56,000	84,000	42.00	8.40
Expected value		$ 40,000	$0	$ 40,000	$16,000	$24,000	12.00%	$2.40
Standard deviation							14.82%	$2.96
Coefficient of variation							1.23	1.23

Section II. 50% Debt

Debt ratio	50.00%
Assets	$200,000
Debt	$100,000
Interest rate	12.00%
Equity	$100,000
Shares outstanding	5,000

Demand For Product (1)	Probability (2)	EBIT (3)	Interest (4)	Pretax Income (5)	Taxes (40%) (6)	Net Income (7)	ROE (8)	EPS[a] (9)
Terrible	0.05	($ 60,000)	$12,000	($ 72,000)	($28,800)	($43,200)	(43.20)%	($ 8.64)
Poor	0.20	(20,000)	12,000	(32,000)	(12,800)	(19,200)	(19.20)	(3.84)
Normal	0.50	40,000	12,000	28,000	11,200	16,800	16.80	3.36
Good	0.20	100,000	12,000	88,000	35,200	52,800	52.80	10.56
Wonderful	0.05	140,000	12,000	128,000	51,200	76,800	76.80	15.36
Expected value		$ 40,000	$12,000	$ 28,000	$11,200	$16,800	16.80%	$ 3.36
Standard deviation							29.64%	5.93
Coefficient of variation							1.76	1.76

Assumptions: 1. In terms of its operating leverage, Bigbee has chosen Plan B. The probability distribution and EBIT are obtained from Figure 14-2.

2. Sales and operating costs (and hence EBIT) are not affected by the financing decision. Therefore, EBIT under both financing plans is identical and is taken from the EBIT column for Plan B in Figure 14-2.

3. All losses can be carried back to offset income in the prior year.

[a]The EPS figures can also be obtained using the following formula in which the numerator amounts to an income statement at a given sales level displayed horizontally:

$$EPS = \frac{(Sales - Fixed\ costs - Variable\ costs - Interest)(1 - Tax\ rate)}{Shares\ outstanding} = \frac{(EBIT - I)(1 - T)}{Shares\ outstanding}$$

For example, with zero debt and sales = $200,000, EPS is $2.40:

$$EPS_{D/A = 0} = \frac{(\$200,000 - \$60,000 - \$100,000 - 0)(0.6)}{10,000} = \$2.40$$

With 50% debt and sales = $200,000, EPS is $3.36:

$$EPS_{D/A = 0.5} = \frac{(\$200,000 - \$60,000 - \$100,000 - \$12,000)(0.6)}{5,000} = \$3.36$$

Refer to the tabular data given in Figure 14-2 to arrive at sales, fixed costs, and variable costs that are used in the preceding equations.
Note: Because the demand for the product has a normal distribution, the probability distribution is symmetrical. Consequently, the expected values equal the values under normal demand. This would not occur under an asymmetrical probability distribution.

Now look at Section II, the situation if Bigbee decides to use 50% debt with an interest rate of 12%. Neither sales nor operating costs will be affected; hence, the EBIT column is the same for zero debt and 50% debt. However, the company will now have $100,000 of debt with a cost of 12%; hence, its interest expense will be $12,000. This interest must be paid regardless of the state of the economy—if it is not paid, the company will be forced into bankruptcy and stockholders will be wiped out. Therefore, we show a $12,000 cost in Column 4 as a fixed number for all sales levels. Column 5 shows pretax income; Column 6, the applicable taxes; and Column 7, the resulting net income. When net income is divided by the equity investment—which now will be only $100,000 because $100,000 of the $200,000 total assets were financed with debt—we find the ROE under each demand state. If demand is terrible and sales are zero, a very large loss will be incurred and the ROE will be −43.2%. However, if demand is wonderful, ROE will be 76.8%. The expected ROE is the probability-weighted average, which is 16.8% if the company uses 50% debt.

Typically, using debt increases the expected rate of return for an investment. However, debt also increases risk to the common stockholders. This situation holds with our example—financial leverage raises the expected ROE from 12% to 16.8%, but it also increases the risk of the investment as measured by the coefficient of variation, which rises from 1.23 to 1.76.

Figure 14-4 graphs the data in Table 14-2. It demonstrates that using financial leverage increases the expected ROE but that it also flattens out the probability distribution, increases the probability of a large loss, and thus increases the risk borne by stockholders.

We can also calculate Bigbee's EPS if it uses 50% debt. With Debt = $0, 10,000 shares would be outstanding; but if half the equity was replaced by debt (Debt = $100,000), only 5,000 shares would be outstanding. We can determine the EPS that would result at each of the possible demand levels under the different capital structures.[4] With no debt, EPS would be −$3.60 if demand was terrible, $2.40 if demand was normal; and $8.40 if demand was wonderful. With 50% debt, EPS would be −$8.64 if demand was terrible, $3.36 if demand was normal, and $15.36 if demand was wonderful. Expected EPS would be $2.40 with no debt but $3.36 with 50% financial leverage.

FIGURE 14-4	ROE Probability Distributions for Bigbee Electronics, with and without Leverage

---

[4]We assume in this example that the firm could change its capital structure by repurchasing common stock at its book value of $100,000/5,000 shares = $20 per share. However, the firm may have to pay a higher price to repurchase its stock on the open market. If Bigbee had to pay $22 per share, it could repurchase only $100,000/$22 = 4,545 shares; and in this case, expected EPS would be only $16,800/(10,000 − 4,545) = $16,800/5,455 = $3.08 rather than $3.36.

The EPS distributions under the two financial structures are graphed in Figure 14-5, where we use continuous distributions rather than the discrete distributions contained in Table 14-2. Although expected EPS would be much higher if financial leverage was employed, the graph makes it clear that the risk of low, or even negative, EPS would also be higher if debt was used.

Another view of the relationships among expected EPS, risk, and financial leverage is presented in Figure 14-6. The tabular data in the lower section were calculated in the manner set forth in Table 14-2, and the graphs plot these data. Here we see that expected EPS rises until the firm is financed with 50% debt. Interest charges rise, but this effect is more than offset by the declining number of shares outstanding as debt is substituted for equity. However, EPS peaks at a debt ratio of 50%, beyond which interest rates rise so rapidly that EPS falls in spite of the falling number of shares outstanding.

The right panel of Figure 14-6 shows that risk, as measured by the coefficient of variation of EPS, rises continuously and at an increasing rate as debt is substituted for equity.

These examples make it clear that using leverage has both positive and negative effects: Higher leverage increases expected EPS (in this example, until the debt ratio equals 50%), but it also increases risk. When determining its optimal capital structure, Bigbee needs to balance these positive and negative effects of leverage. This issue is discussed in the following sections.

SELF TEST

What is business risk, and how can it be measured?

What are some determinants of business risk?

Why does business risk vary from industry to industry?

What is operating leverage?

How does operating leverage affect business risk?

What is financial risk, and how does it arise?

Explain this statement: Using leverage has both good and bad effects.

| **FIGURE 14-5** | EPS Probability Distributions for Bigbee Electronics, with and without Leverage |

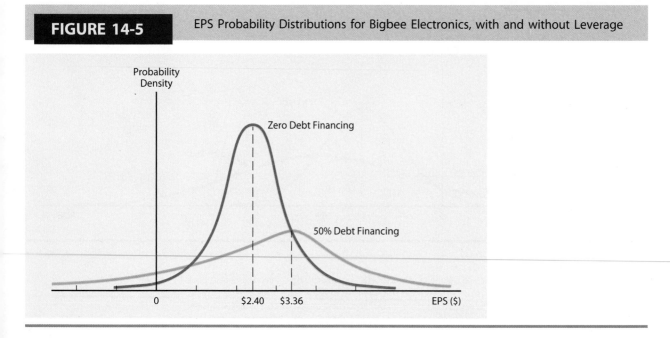

FIGURE 14-6	Relationships among Expected EPS, Risk, and Financial Leverage

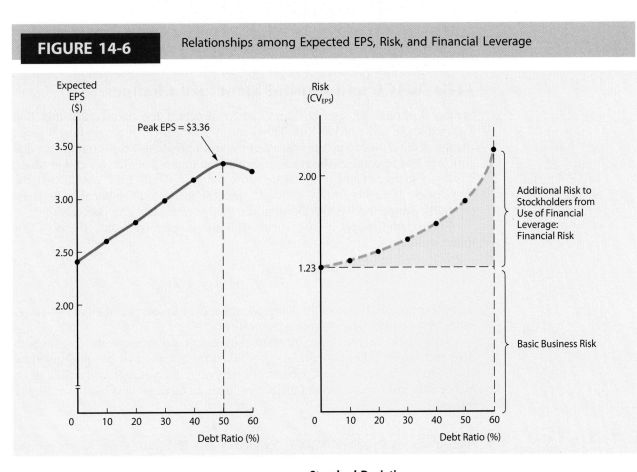

Debt Ratio	Expected EPS	Standard Deviation of EPS	Coefficient of Variation
0%[a]	$2.40[a]	$2.96[a]	1.23[a]
10	2.56	3.29	1.29
20	2.75	3.70	1.35
30	2.97	4.23	1.43
40	3.20	4.94	1.54
50[a]	3.36[a]	5.93[a]	1.76[a]
60	3.30	7.41	2.25

[a]Values for debt ratios = 0% and 50% were taken from Table 14-2. Values at other debt ratios were calculated similarly.

14-3 DETERMINING THE OPTIMAL CAPITAL STRUCTURE

As we saw in Figure 14-6, Bigbee's expected EPS is maximized at a debt ratio of 50%. Does that mean that Bigbee's optimal capital structure calls for 50% debt? The answer is a resounding "**No!**" *The optimal capital structure is the one that maximizes the price of the firm's stock, and this generally calls for a debt ratio that is lower than the one that maximizes expected EPS.*

We know that stock prices are positively related to expected earnings but negatively related to higher risk. Therefore, to the extent that higher debt levels raise expected EPS, leverage works to increase the stock price. However, higher debt levels also increase the firm's risk, which raises the cost of equity and works to reduce the stock price. So even though increasing the debt ratio from 40% to 50% raises EPS, in our example, the higher EPS is more than offset by the corresponding increase in risk.

14-3a WACC and Capital Structure Changes

Managers should set as the target capital structure the debt-equity mix that maximizes the firm's stock price. However, it is difficult to estimate how a given change in the capital structure will affect the stock price. As it turns out, the capital structure that maximizes the stock price also minimizes the WACC; and at times, it is easier to predict how a capital structure change will affect the WACC than the stock price. Therefore, many managers use the estimated relationship between capital structure and the WACC to guide their capital structure decisions.

Recall from Chapter 10 that when a firm uses no preferred stock, the WACC is found as follows:

$$\text{WACC} = w_d(r_d)(1 - T) + w_c(r_s)$$
$$= (D/A)(r_d)(1 - T) + (E/A)(r_s)$$

In this expression, D/A and E/A represent the debt-to-assets and equity-to-assets ratios, respectively, and they must sum to 1.0.

Note that in Table 14-3, an increase in the debt ratio increases the costs of both debt and equity. [The cost of debt, r_d, is taken from Table 14-1 but multiplied by $(1 - T)$ to put it on an after-tax basis.] Bondholders recognize that if a firm has a higher debt ratio, this increases the risk of financial distress, which leads to higher interest rates.

Table 14-3			**Bigbee's Stock Price and WACC Estimates with Different Debt/Assets Ratios**						
Debt/ Assets (1)	Debt/ Equity[a] (2)	A-T r_d (3)	Expected EPS (and DPS)[b] (4)	Estimated Beta[c] (5)	$r_s = [r_{RF} +$ $(RP_M)b]$[d] (6)	Estimated Price[e] (7)	Resulting P/E Ratio (8)	WACC[f] (9)
0%	0.00%	4.8%	$2.40	1.50	12.0%	$20.00	8.33×	12.00%
10	11.11	4.8	2.56	1.60	12.4	20.65	8.06	11.64
20	25.00	5.0	2.75	1.73	12.9	21.33	7.75	11.32
30	42.86	5.4	2.97	1.89	13.5	21.90	7.38	11.10
40	**66.67**	**6.0**	**3.20**	**2.10**	**14.4**	**22.22**	**6.94**	**11.04**
50	100.00	7.2	3.36	2.40	15.6	21.54	6.41	11.40
60	150.00	9.0	3.30	2.85	17.4	18.97	5.75	12.36

[a]$D/E = \dfrac{D/A}{1 - D/A}$

[b]Bigbee pays all of its earnings out as dividends, so EPS = DPS.

[c]The firm's unlevered beta, b_U, is 1.5. The remaining betas were calculated using the Hamada equation, given the unlevered beta, tax rate, and D/E ratio as inputs.

[d]We assume that $r_{RF} = 6\%$ and $RP_M = 4\%$. Therefore, at D/A = 0, $r_s = 6\% + (4\%)1.5 = 12\%$. Other values of r_s are calculated similarly.

[e]Since all earnings are paid out as dividends, no retained earnings will be plowed back into the business and growth in EPS and DPS will be zero. Hence, the zero growth stock price model developed in Chapter 9 can be used to estimate the price of Bigbee's stock. For example, at D/A = 0,

$$P_0 = \frac{\text{DPS}}{r_s} = \frac{\$2.40}{0.12} = \$20$$

Other prices were calculated similarly.

[f]Column 9 values are found with the weighted average cost of capital (WACC) equation developed in Chapter 10:

$$\text{WACC} = w_d r_d(1 - T) + w_c r_s$$
$$= (D/A)(r_d)(1 - T) + (1 - D/A)r_s$$

For example, at D/A = 40%,

$$\text{WACC} = 0.4(10\%)(0.6) + 0.6(14.4\%) = 11.04\%$$

We use book weights here, but market value weights theoretically would be better. See Eugene F. Brigham and Phillip R. Daves, *Intermediate Financial Management*, 9th ed. (Mason, OH: South-Western College Publishing, 2007), Chapter 10, for a discussion of this point.

In practice, financial managers use financial statement forecasting models to determine how changes in the debt ratio will affect the current ratio, times-interest-earned ratio, and EBITDA coverage ratio.[5] They then discuss their projected ratios with bankers and bond rating agencies, which ask probing questions and may make their own adjustments to the firm's forecasts. The bankers and rating agencies compare the firm's ratios with those of other firms in its industry and arrive at a "what if" rating and corresponding interest rate. Moreover, if the company plans to issue bonds to the public, the SEC requires that it inform investors what the coverages will be after the new bonds have been sold. Recognizing all this, sophisticated financial managers use their forecasted ratios to predict how bankers and other lenders will judge their firms' risks and thus their costs of debt. Experienced financial managers and investment bankers can judge quite accurately the effects of capital structure on the cost of debt.

14-3b The Hamada Equation

Increasing the debt ratio increases the risks that bondholders face and thus the cost of debt. More debt also raises the risk borne by stockholders, which raises the cost of equity, r_s. It is harder to quantify leverage's effects on the cost of equity, but a theoretical formula can help measure the effect.

To begin, recall from Chapter 8 that a stock's beta is the relevant measure of risk for a diversified investor. Moreover, beta increases with financial leverage, and Robert Hamada formulated the following equation to quantify this effect.[6]

$$b_L = b_U[1 + (1 - T)D/E] \qquad \textbf{14-2}$$

Here b_L is the firm's current beta, which we now assume is based on the existence of some financial leverage, and b_U is the firm's beta if the firm was debt-free, or unlevered.[7] If the firm was debt-free, its beta would depend entirely on its business risk and thus would be a measure of the firm's "basic business risk." D/E is the measure of financial leverage as used in the Hamada equation, and T is the corporate tax rate.[8]

Now recall the CAPM version of the cost of equity:

$$r_s = r_{RF} + (RP_M)b_i$$

---

[5]We discuss financial statement forecasts in Chapter 17.

[6]See Robert S. Hamada, "Portfolio Analysis, Market Equilibrium, and Corporation Finance," *Journal of Finance*, March 1969, pp. 13–31.

[7]Note that Equation 14-2 is the original equation that Hamada put forward, and it was based on a set of assumptions. The most notable were (a) that the beta of the company's debt is zero, (b) that the level of debt is constant, and (c) that the values of the company's interest tax shields are discounted at the before-tax cost of debt. Other researchers have derived alternative equations that are based on different assumptions. For example, one commonly used alternative assumes that the company's debt ratio remains constant and that the interest tax shields are discounted at the unlevered cost of equity. In this case, the resulting equation is as follows:

$$b_L = b_U[1 + D/E]$$

See Eugene F. Brigham and Phillip R. Daves, *Intermediate Financial Management*, 9th ed. (Mason, OH: Thomson/South-Western, 2007), Chapter 15, for further discussion of the Hamada equation and the different approaches for levering and unlevering betas.

[8]Recall from Chapter 4 that the debt/equity ratio, D/E, is directly related to the D/A ratio:

$$\frac{D}{E} = \frac{D/A}{1 - D/A}$$

For example, if the firm has $40 of debt and $60 of equity, D/A = 0.4, E/A = 0.6, and

$$\frac{D}{E} = \frac{0.4}{1 - 0.4} = 0.4/0.6 = 0.6667$$

Thus, any D/A ratio can be directly translated into a D/E ratio. Note also that Hamada's equation assumes that assets are reported at market values rather than accounting book values. This point is discussed at length in Brigham and Daves, op cit., where feedbacks among capital structure, stock prices, and capital costs are examined.

Note that beta is the only variable in the equity cost equation that is under management's control. The other two variables, r_{RF} and RP_M, are determined by market forces that are beyond the firm's control; but b_L is determined by the firm's operating decisions, which as we saw earlier, affect its basic business risk, and by its capital structure decisions as reflected in its D/A (or D/E) ratio.

Unlevered Beta, b_U
The firm's beta coefficient if it has no debt.

We can solve Equation 14-2 to find the **unlevered beta, b_U**, obtaining Equation 14-2a:

14-2a $$b_U = b_L / [1 + (1 - T)(D/E)]$$

Since the current (levered) beta is known, as are the tax rate and the debt/equity ratio, we can insert values for these known variables and find the unlevered beta. The unlevered beta can then be used in Equation 14-2 with different debt levels to find the levered betas that would exist at those different debt levels. The resulting betas can be used to find the cost of equity at different debt levels.

We can illustrate all this with Bigbee Electronics. First, assume that the risk-free rate of return, r_{RF}, is 6% and that the market risk premium, RP_M, is 4%. Next, we need the unlevered beta, b_U. Because Bigbee has no debt, its D/E = 0. Therefore, its current 1.5 beta is also its unlevered beta; hence, $b_U = 1.5$. With b_U, r_{RF}, and RP_M specified, we can use Equation 14-2 to estimate Bigbee's betas at different degrees of financial leverage and its resulting cost of equity at each debt ratio.

Bigbee's betas at different debt/equity ratios are shown in Column 5 of Table 14-3. The current cost of equity is 12% as shown at the top of Column 6:

$$r_s = r_{RF} + \text{Risk premium}$$
$$= 6\% + (4\%)(1.5)$$
$$= 6\% + 6\% = 12\%$$

The first 6% is the risk-free rate; the second is the firm's risk premium. Because Bigbee currently uses no debt, it has no financial risk. Therefore, the 6% risk premium is attributable entirely to business risk.

If Bigbee changes its capital structure by adding debt, this would increase the risk stockholders would have to bear. That, in turn, would result in a higher risk premium. Conceptually, a firm's cost of equity consists of the following components:

$$r_s = r_{RF} + \text{Premium for business risk} + \text{Premium for financial risk}$$

Figure 14-7, which is based on data shown in Column 6 of Table 14-3, graphs Bigbee's cost of equity at different debt ratios. As the figure shows, r_s consists of the 6% risk-free rate, a constant 6% premium for business risk, and a premium for financial risk that starts at zero but rises at an increasing rate as the firm's debt ratio increases.

14-3c The Optimal Capital Structure

Column 9 of Table 14-3 also shows Bigbee's WACC at different capital structures. Currently, it has no debt; so its debt ratio is zero and its WACC is $r_s = 12\%$. As Bigbee begins to substitute lower-cost debt for higher-cost equity, its WACC declines. However, as the debt ratio rises, the costs of both debt and equity rise, at first slowly but then at a faster and faster rate. Eventually, the increasing costs of the two components offset the fact that more low-cost debt is being used. Indeed, at 40% debt, the WACC hits a minimum of 11.04%; after that, it rises with further increases in the debt ratio.

Another way of looking at this is to note that even though the component cost of equity is higher than that of debt, using only lower-cost debt would not

| FIGURE 14-7 | Bigbee's Required Rate of Return on Equity at Different Debt Levels |

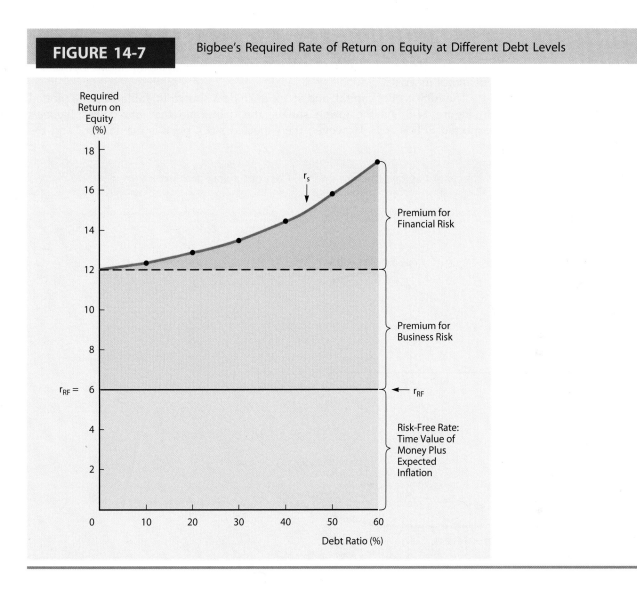

maximize value because of the feedback effects of debt on the costs of debt and equity. For example, if Bigbee used more than 40% debt (say, 50%), it would have more of the cheaper capital; but this benefit would be more than offset by the fact that the additional debt raises the costs of debt and equity.

These thoughts were echoed in a statement made by the Georgia-Pacific Corporation:

On a market-value basis, our debt-to-capital ratio is 47%. By employing this capital structure, we believe that our weighted average cost of capital is minimized, at approximately 10%. Although reducing debt would reduce our marginal cost of debt, this action would likely increase our weighted average cost of capital because we would then have to use more higher-cost equity.

Finally, and very importantly, recall that the capital structure that minimizes the WACC is also the capital structure that maximizes the firm's stock price. Bigbee pays out all of its earnings as dividends, so it plows zero earnings back into the business, which leads to an expected growth rate in earnings and dividends of zero. Thus, in Bigbee's case, we can use the zero growth stock price model developed in Chapter 9 to estimate the stock price at each different capital structure. These estimates are shown in Column 7 of Table 14-3. Here we see that the stock price first rises with financial leverage, hits a peak of $22.22 at a debt ratio of 40%, and then begins to decline. *Thus, Bigbee's optimal capital structure occurs at a debt ratio of 40%, and that debt ratio both maximizes its stock price and minimizes its WACC.*[9]

The EPS, cost of capital, and stock price data shown in Table 14-3 are plotted in Figure 14-8. As the graph shows, the debt ratio that maximizes Bigbee's expected EPS is 50%. However, the expected stock price is maximized, and the

FIGURE 14-8	Effects of Capital Structure on EPS, Cost of Capital, and Stock Price

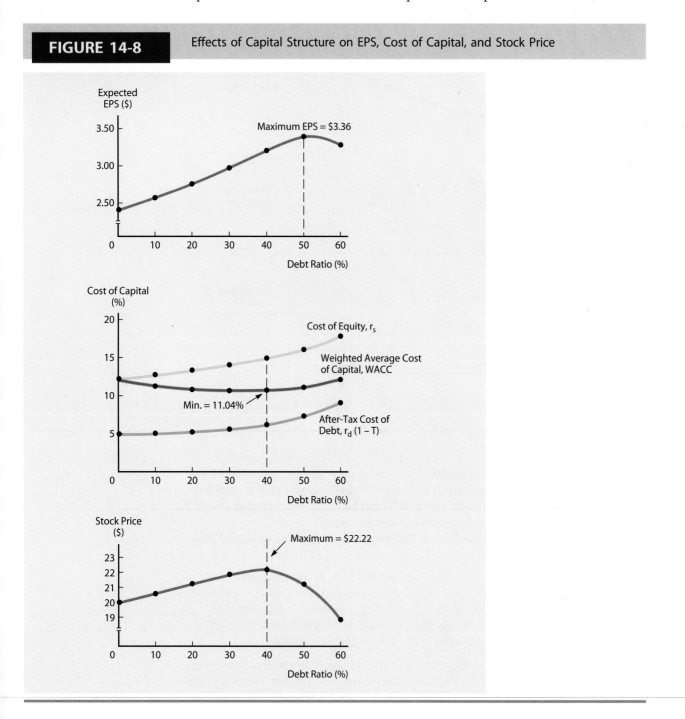

[9]We could also estimate the stock price if some earnings were retained and the expected growth rate was positive. However, this would complicate the analysis, and it is another reason we generally analyze the optimal capital structure decision using the WACC rather than the stock price.

WACC is minimized at a 40% debt ratio. Thus, Bigbee's optimal capital structure calls for 40% debt and 60% equity. Management should set its target capital structure at these ratios; and if the existing ratios are off target, it should move toward that target when new securities are issued.

SELF TEST

What happens to the component costs of debt and equity when the debt ratio is increased? Why does this occur?

Using the Hamada equation, explain the effects of financial leverage on beta.

What is the equation for calculating a firm's unlevered beta?

Use the Hamada equation to calculate the unlevered beta for Firm X with the following data: $b_L = 1.25$, T = 40%, Debt/Assets = 0.42, and Equity/Assets = 0.58. (**$b_U = 0.8714$**)

What would be the cost of equity for Firm X at Equity/Assets ratios of 1.0 (no debt) and 0.58 assuming that $r_{RF} = 5\%$ and $RP_M = 4\%$? (**8.49%, 10%**)

Using a graph and illustrative data, discuss the premiums for financial risk and business risk at different debt levels. Do these premiums vary depending on the debt level? Explain.

Is expected EPS generally maximized at the optimal capital structure? Explain.

14-4 CAPITAL STRUCTURE THEORY

Business risk is an important determinant of the optimal capital structure. Moreover, firms in different industries have different business risks. So we would expect capital structures to vary considerably across industries, and this is the case. For example, pharmaceutical companies generally have very different capital structures than airlines. In addition, capital structures vary among firms within a given industry, which is a bit harder to explain. What factors can explain these differences? In an attempt to answer that question, academics and practitioners have developed a number of theories.

Modern capital structure theory began in 1958 when Professors Franco Modigliani and Merton Miller (hereafter, MM) published what has been called the most influential finance article ever written.[10] MM proved, under a restrictive set of assumptions, that a firm's value should be unaffected by its capital structure. Put another way, MM's results suggest that it does not matter how a firm finances its operations—hence, that capital structure is irrelevant. However, the assumptions upon which MM's study was based are not realistic, so their results are questionable. Here is a partial listing of their assumptions:

1. There are no brokerage costs.
2. There are no taxes.
3. There are no bankruptcy costs.
4. Investors can borrow at the same rate as corporations.
5. All investors have the same information as management about the firm's future investment opportunities.
6. EBIT is not affected by the use of debt.

---

[10]Franco Modigliani and Merton H. Miller, "The Cost of Capital, Corporation Finance, and the Theory of Investment," *American Economic Review*, June 1958. Both Modigliani and Miller won Nobel Prizes for their work.

YOGI BERRA ON THE MM PROPOSITION

When a waitress asked Yogi Berra (Baseball Hall of Fame catcher for the New York Yankees) whether he wanted his pizza cut into four pieces or eight, Yogi replied: "Better make it four. I don't think I can eat eight."[a]

Yogi's quip helps convey Modigliani and Miller's basic insight. The firm's choice of leverage divides future cash flows in a way that's like slicing a pizza. MM recognized that if a company's future investments are fixed, it's like fixing the size of the pizza: No information costs means that everyone sees the same pizza; no taxes means that the IRS

gets none of the pie; and no "contracting" costs means that nothing sticks to the knife.

So just as the substance of Yogi's meal is unaffected by whether the pizza is sliced into four pieces or eight, the economic substance of the firm is unaffected by whether the liability side of the balance sheet is sliced to include more or less debt under the MM assumptions. Note, though, that whereas the IRS may get none of Yogi's pizza, it is very likely to get some of the firm's income. Yogi's assumptions are more realistic than MM's.

[a]Lee Green, *Sportswit* (New York: Fawcett Crest, 1984), p. 228.
Source: Michael J. Barclay, Clifford W. Smith, and Ross L. Watts, "The Determinants of Corporate Leverage and Dividend Policies," *Journal of Applied Corporate Finance*, Vol. 7, no. 4 (Winter 1995), pp. 4–19. Used by permission.

Despite the fact that some of these assumptions are unrealistic, MM's irrelevance result is extremely important. By indicating the conditions under which capital structure is irrelevant, MM provided clues about what is required to make capital structure relevant and hence to affect a firm's value. MM's work marked the beginning of modern capital structure research, and subsequent research has focused on relaxing the MM assumptions to develop a more robust and realistic theory. Research in this area is quite extensive, but the highlights are summarized in the following sections.

14-4a The Effect of Taxes[11]

MM's original 1958 paper was criticized harshly, and they published a follow-up in 1963 that relaxed the assumption of no corporate taxes.[12] They recognized that the Tax Code allows corporations to deduct interest payments as an expense, but dividend payments to stockholders are not deductible. This differential treatment encourages corporations to use debt in their capital structures. Indeed, MM demonstrated that if all their other assumptions hold, this differential treatment leads to an optimal capital structure of 100% debt.

MM's 1963 work was modified several years later by Merton Miller (this time without Modigliani), when he brought in the effects of personal taxes.[13] Miller noted that bonds pay interest, which is taxed as personal income at rates going up to 35%, while income from stocks comes partly from dividends and partly from capital gains. Further, most long-term capital gains are taxed at a maximum rate of 15%, and this tax can be deferred until the stock is sold and the gain realized. If a stock is held until the owner dies, no capital gains tax must be paid. So on balance, returns on common stocks are taxed at lower effective rates than returns on debt.[14]

---

[11]This section is relatively technical, and it can be omitted without loss of continuity.
[12]Franco Modigliani and Merton H. Miller, "Corporate Income Taxes and the Cost of Capital: A Correction," *American Economic Review*, Vol. 53 (June 1963), pp. 433–443.
[13]Merton H. Miller, "Debt and Taxes," *Journal of Finance*, Vol. 32 (May 1977), pp. 261–275.
[14]When Miller wrote his article, dividends were taxed at a maximum rate of 70% and capital gains at a much lower rate. Today (2008) dividends and most capital gains are taxed at a maximum rate of 15%, but interest is taxed at a maximum rate of 35%. [Capital gains can be caught by the Alternative Minimum Tax (AMT), in which case they are taxed at either 26% or 28% depending on one's income bracket.] These tax law changes would not affect Miller's final conclusion.

Because of the tax situation, Miller argued that investors are willing to accept relatively low before-tax returns on stocks as compared to the before-tax returns on bonds. For example, an investor in the 35% tax bracket might require a 10% pretax return on Bigbee's bonds, which would result in a $10\%(1 - T) = 10\%(0.65) = 6.5\%$ after-tax return. Bigbee's stock is riskier than its bonds, so the investor would require a higher after-tax return (say, 8.5%) on the stock. Because the stock's returns (either dividends or capital gains) would be taxed at only 15%, a pretax return of $8.5\%/(1 - T) = 8.5\%/0.85 = 10.0\%$ would provide the required 8.5% after-tax return. In this example, the interest rate on the bonds would be 10%, the same as the required return on the stock, r_s. Thus, the more favorable treatment of income on the stock would cause investors to accept the same before-tax returns on the stock and on the bond.[15]

As Miller pointed out, (1) the *deductibility of interest* favors the use of debt financing, but (2) the *more favorable tax treatment of income from stocks* lowers the required rates of return on stocks and thus favors the use of equity. It is difficult to specify the net effect of these two factors. However, most observers believe that interest deductibility has a stronger effect and hence that our tax system favors the corporate use of debt. Still, that effect is certainly reduced by the lower taxes on stock income. Indeed, Duke University professor John Graham estimated the overall tax benefits of debt financing.[16] He concluded that the tax benefits associated with debt financing represent about 7% of the average firm's value; so if a leverage-free firm decided to use an average amount of debt, its value would rise by 7%.

We can observe changes in corporate financing patterns following major changes in tax rates. For example, in 1993, the top personal tax rate on interest and dividends was raised sharply, but the capital gains tax rate was not increased. This resulted in a greater use of equity, especially retained earnings. Subsequent reductions in tax rates on both dividends and capital gains have continued the benefits of equity financing over debt financing, which has continued the trend toward a greater reliance on equity financing.

14-4b The Effect of Potential Bankruptcy

MM's irrelevance results also depend on the assumption that firms don't go bankrupt and hence that bankruptcy costs are irrelevant. However, in practice, bankruptcy exists and it can be quite costly. Firms in bankruptcy have high legal and accounting expenses, and they have a hard time retaining customers, suppliers, and employees. Moreover, bankruptcy often forces a firm to liquidate assets for less than they would be worth if the firm continued to operate. Assets such as plant and equipment are often illiquid because they are configured to a company's individual needs and because they are difficult to disassemble and move.

Note too that the *threat of bankruptcy*, not just bankruptcy per se, brings about these problems. If they become concerned about the firm's future, key employees start "jumping ship," suppliers start refusing to grant credit, customers begin seeking more stable suppliers, and lenders start demanding higher interest rates and imposing stricter loan covenants.

Bankruptcy-related problems are likely to increase the more debt a firm has in its capital structure. Therefore, bankruptcy costs discourage firms from pushing their use of debt to excessive levels. Note too that bankruptcy-related costs have two components: (1) the probability of their occurrence and (2) the costs that will be incurred if financial distress arises. A firm whose earnings are relatively volatile,

---

[15]The situation here is similar to that involving tax-exempt municipal bonds versus taxable bonds.
[16]John R. Graham, "How Big Are the Tax Benefits of Debt?" *Journal of Finance*, Vol. 55 (2000), pp. 1901–1941; and "Estimating the Tax Benefits of Debt," *Journal of Applied Corporate Finance*, Vol. 14, no. 1 (Spring 2001), pp. 42–54.

all else equal, faces a greater chance of bankruptcy and thus should use less debt than a more stable firm. This is consistent with our earlier point that firms with high operating leverage (and thus greater business risk) should limit their use of financial leverage. Likewise, firms whose assets are illiquid and would have to be sold at "fire sale" prices should limit their use of debt financing.

14-4c Trade-Off Theory

Trade-Off Theory
The capital structure theory that states that firms trade off the tax benefits of debt financing against problems caused by potential bankruptcy.

The preceding arguments led to the development of what is called "the trade-off theory of leverage." This theory states that firms trade off the tax benefits of debt financing against problems caused by potential bankruptcy. A summary of the **trade-off theory** is expressed graphically in Figure 14-9. Here are some observations about the figure:

1. The fact that interest paid is a deductible expense makes debt less expensive than common or preferred stock. In effect, the government pays part of the cost of debt—or to put it another way, debt provides *tax shelter benefits.* As a result, using more debt reduces taxes and thus allows more of the firm's operating income (EBIT) to flow through to investors. This factor, on which MM focused, tends to raise the stock's price. Indeed, under the assumptions of MM's original paper, the stock price would be maximized at 100% debt. The line labeled "MM Result Incorporating the Effects of Corporate Taxation" in Figure 14-9 expresses the relationship between stock prices and debt under their assumptions.

2. In the real world, firms have target debt ratios that call for less than 100% debt. The reason is to hold down the adverse effects of potential bankruptcy.

3. There is some threshold level of debt, labeled D_1 in Figure 14-9, below which the probability of bankruptcy is so low as to be immaterial. Beyond D_1, however, bankruptcy-related costs become increasingly important and they

| FIGURE 14-9 | Effect of Leverage on the Value of Bigbee's Stock |

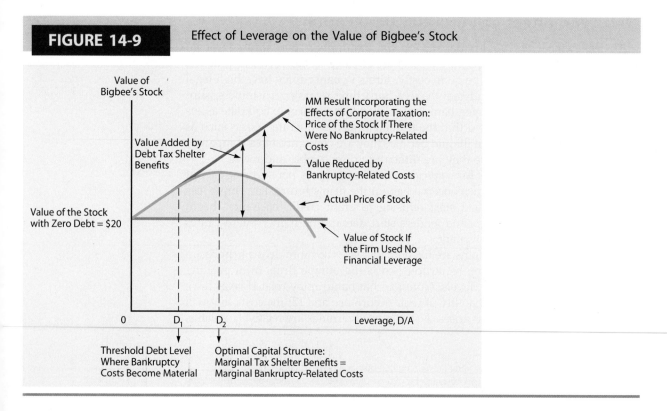

begin to offset the tax benefits of debt. In the range from D_1 to D_2, bankruptcy-related costs reduce but do not completely offset the tax benefits of debt; so the firm's stock price continues to rise (but at a decreasing rate) as its debt ratio increases. However, beyond D_2, bankruptcy-related costs exceed the tax benefits; so from this point on, increasing the debt ratio lowers the stock price. Therefore, D_2 is the optimal capital structure, the one where the stock price is maximized. Of course, D_1 and D_2 vary from firm to firm depending on business risk and bankruptcy costs, and they can change for a given firm over time.

4. While theoretical and empirical work supports the general shape of the curves in Figures 14-8 and 14-9, these graphs must be taken as approximations, not as precisely defined functions. The numbers in Figure 14-8 are rounded to two decimal places, but that is merely for illustrative purposes—the numbers are not nearly that accurate since the graph is based on judgmental estimates.

5. Another disturbing aspect of capital structure theory expressed in Figure 14-9 is the fact that many large, successful firms such as Intel and Microsoft use far less debt than the theory suggests. This point led to the development of signaling theory, which is discussed in the next section.

14-4d Signaling Theory

MM assumed that everyone—investors and managers alike—has the same information about a firm's prospects. This is called **symmetric information**. However, in fact, managers often have better information than outside investors. This is called **asymmetric information**, and it has an important effect on the optimal capital structure. To see why, consider two situations, one where the company's managers know that its prospects are extremely favorable (Firm F) and one where the managers know that the future looks unfavorable (Firm U).

Now suppose Firm F's R&D labs have just discovered a nonpatentable cure for the common cold. They want to keep the new product a secret as long as possible to delay competitors' entry into the market. New plants must be built to make the new product, so capital must be raised. But how should Firm F raise the needed capital? If it sells stock, when profits from the new product start flowing in, the price of the stock will rise sharply and purchasers of the new stock will make a bonanza. The current stockholders (including the managers) also will do well, but not as well as they would have done if the company had not sold stock before the price increased. In that case, they would not have had to share the benefits of the new product with the new stockholders. *Therefore, we would expect a firm with very favorable prospects to avoid selling stock and instead raise any required new capital by using new debt even if this moved its debt ratio beyond the target level.*[17]

Now consider Firm U. Suppose its managers have information that new orders are off sharply because a competitor has installed new technology that improved the quality of its products. Firm U must upgrade its own facilities at a high cost just to maintain current sales. As a result, its return on investment will fall (but not by as much as if it took no action, which would lead to a 100% loss through bankruptcy). How should Firm U raise the needed capital? Here the situation is just the reverse of that facing Firm F—Firm U will want to sell stock so that some of the adverse consequences will be borne by new investors. *Therefore, a firm with unfavorable prospects would want to finance with stock, which would mean bringing in new investors to share the losses.*[18]

Symmetric Information
The situation where investors and managers have identical information about firms' prospects.

Asymmetric Information
The situation where managers have different (better) information about firms' prospects than do investors.

[17]It would be illegal for Firm F's managers to personally purchase more shares on the basis of their inside knowledge of the new product. They could be sent to jail if they did.
[18]Of course, Firm U would have to make certain disclosures when it offered new shares to the public, but it might be able to meet the legal requirements without fully disclosing management's worst fears.

The conclusion from all this is that firms with extremely bright prospects prefer not to finance through new stock offerings, whereas firms with poor prospects do like to finance with outside equity. How should you, as an investor, react to this conclusion? You ought to say, "If I see that a company plans to issue new stock, I should worry because I know that management would not want to issue stock if future prospects looked good. However, management would want to issue stock if things looked bad. Therefore, I should lower my estimate of the firm's value, other things held constant, if it plans to issue new stock."

If you gave that answer, your views are consistent with those of sophisticated portfolio managers. *In a nutshell, the announcement of a stock offering is generally taken as a* **signal** *that the firm's prospects as seen by its management are not bright.* This, in turn, suggests that when a firm announces a new stock offering, more often than not, the price of its stock will decline.[19] Empirical studies have shown that this situation does exist.[20]

What are the implications of all this for capital structure decisions? Issuing stock emits a negative signal and thus tends to depress the stock price; so even if the company's prospects are bright, a firm should, in normal times, maintain a **reserve borrowing capacity** that can be used in the event that some especially good investment opportunity comes along. *This means that firms should, in normal times, use more equity and less debt than is suggested by the tax benefit/bankruptcy cost trade-off model illustrated in Figure 14-9.*

14-4e Using Debt Financing to Constrain Managers

In Chapter 1, we stated that conflicts of interest may arise if managers and shareholders have different objectives. Such conflicts are particularly likely when the firm has more cash than is needed to support its core operations. Managers often use excess cash to finance their pet projects or for perquisites such as plush offices, corporate jets, and skyboxes at sports arenas, all of which may do little to benefit stock prices.[21] By contrast, managers with more limited free cash flow are less able to make wasteful expenditures.

Firms can reduce excess cash flow in a variety of ways. One way is to funnel some of it back to shareholders through higher dividends or stock repurchases. Another alternative is to tilt the target capital structure toward more debt in the hope that higher debt service requirements will force managers to become more disciplined. If debt is not serviced as required, the firm will be forced into bankruptcy, in which case its managers would lose their jobs. Therefore, a manager is less likely to buy an expensive corporate jet if the firm has large debt service requirements.

A leveraged buyout (LBO) is a good way to reduce excess cash flow. In an LBO, debt is used to finance the purchase of a high percentage of the company's shares. Indeed, the projected savings from reducing frivolous waste has motivated quite a few leveraged buyouts. As noted, high debt payments after the LBO force managers to conserve cash by eliminating unnecessary expenditures.

Of course, increasing debt and reducing free cash flow has its downside: It increases the risk of bankruptcy. A former professor (who is currently the Federal Reserve chairman) has argued that adding debt to a firm's capital structure is like putting a dagger into the steering wheel of a car.[22] The dagger—which points

---

[19]Stock issues are more of a negative signal for mature companies than for new, rapidly growing firms, where investors expect rapid growth to require additional equity.

[20]See Paul Asquith and David W. Mullins, Jr., "The Impact of Initiating Dividend Payments on Shareholders' Wealth," *Journal of Business*, January 1983, pp. 77–96.

[21]If you don't believe that corporate managers can waste money, read Bryan Burrough, *Barbarians at the Gate* (New York: Harper & Row, 1990), the story of the takeover of RJR-Nabisco.

[22]Ben Bernanke, "Is There Too Much Corporate Debt?" Federal Reserve Bank of Philadelphia *Business Review*, September/October 1989, pp. 3–13.

toward your chest—motivates you to drive more carefully; but you may get stabbed if someone runs into you, even if you are being careful. The analogy applies to corporations in the following sense: Higher debt forces managers to be more careful with shareholders' money; but even well-run firms can face bankruptcy (get stabbed) if some event beyond their control, such as a war, an earthquake, a strike, or a recession, occurs. To complete the analogy, the capital structure decision comes down to deciding how big a dagger stockholders should use to keep managers in line.

If you find the discussion of capital structure theory imprecise and somewhat confusing, you're not alone. In truth, not even the chairman of the Federal Reserve Board knows how to identify a firm's precise optimal capital structure or how to measure the effects of capital structure changes on stock prices and the cost of capital. In practice, capital structure decisions must be made using a combination of judgment and numerical analysis. Still, an understanding of the theoretical issues presented here can help you make better judgments about capital structure issues.

SELF TEST

Why does MM's theory with taxes lead to 100% debt?

How would an increase in corporate taxes tend to affect an average firm's capital structure? What about an increase in the personal tax rate?

Explain what asymmetric information means and how signals affect capital structure decisions.

What is meant by reserve borrowing capacity, and why is it important to firms?

How can the use of debt serve to discipline managers?

14-5 CHECKLIST FOR CAPITAL STRUCTURE DECISIONS

In addition to the types of analysis discussed previously, firms generally consider the following factors when making capital structure decisions:

1. *Sales stability.* A firm whose sales are relatively stable can safely take on more debt and incur higher fixed charges than a company with unstable sales. Utility companies, because of their stable demand, have historically been able to use more financial leverage than can industrial firms.

2. *Asset structure.* Firms whose assets are suitable as security for loans tend to use debt relatively heavily. General-purpose assets that can be used by many businesses make good collateral, whereas special-purpose assets do not. Thus, real estate companies are usually highly leveraged, whereas companies involved in technological research are not.

3. *Operating leverage.* Other things the same, a firm with less operating leverage is better able to employ financial leverage because it will have less business risk.

4. *Growth rate.* Other things the same, faster-growing firms must rely more heavily on external capital. Further, the flotation cost involved in selling common stock exceeds that incurred when selling debt, which encourages rapidly growing firms to rely more heavily on debt. At the same time, however, those firms often face higher uncertainty, which tends to reduce their willingness to use debt.

5. *Profitability.* It is often observed that firms with very high rates of return on investment use relatively little debt. Although there is no theoretical justification for this fact, one practical explanation is that very profitable firms such as Intel, Microsoft, and Google do not need to do much debt financing. Their

high rates of return enable them to do most of their financing with internally generated funds.

6. *Taxes.* Interest is a deductible expense, and deductions are most valuable to firms with high tax rates. Therefore, the higher a firm's tax rate, the greater the advantage of debt.

7. *Control.* The effect of debt versus stock on a management's control position can influence capital structure. If management currently has voting control (more than 50% of the stock) but is not in a position to buy any more stock, it may choose debt for new financings. On the other hand, management may decide to use equity if the firm's financial situation is so weak that the use of debt might subject it to serious risk of default. The reason? If the firm goes into default, managers will probably lose their jobs. However, if too little debt is used, management runs the risk of a takeover. Thus, control considerations can lead to the use of debt or equity because the type of capital that best protects management varies from situation to situation. In any event, if management is at all insecure, it will consider the control situation.

8. *Management attitudes.* No one can prove that one capital structure will lead to higher stock prices than another. Management, then, can exercise its own judgment about the proper capital structure. Some managers tend to be relatively conservative and thus use less debt than an average firm in the industry, whereas aggressive managers use a relatively high percentage of debt in their quest for higher profits.

9. *Lender and rating agency attitudes.* Regardless of a manager's analysis of the proper leverage factors for his or her firm, the attitudes of lenders and rating agencies frequently influence financial structure decisions. Corporations often discuss their capital structures with lenders and rating agencies and give much weight to their advice. For example, Moody's and Standard & Poor's recently told one large utility that its bonds would be downgraded if it issued more bonds. This influenced its decision, and its next financing was with common equity.

10. *Market conditions.* Conditions in the stock and bond markets undergo long- and short-run changes that can have an important bearing on a firm's optimal capital structure. For example, during a recent credit crunch, the junk bond market dried up and there simply was no market at a "reasonable" interest rate for any new long-term bonds rated below BBB. Therefore, low-rated companies in need of capital were forced to go to the stock market or to the short-term debt market, regardless of their target capital structures. When conditions eased, however, these companies sold long-term bonds to get their capital structures back on target.

11. *The firm's internal condition.* A firm's own internal condition can also have a bearing on its target capital structure. For example, suppose a firm just successfully completed an R&D program, and it forecasts higher earnings in the immediate future. However, the new earnings are not yet anticipated by investors and hence are not reflected in the stock price. This company would not want to issue stock—it would prefer to finance with debt until the higher earnings materialize and are reflected in the stock price. Then it could sell an issue of common stock, use the proceeds to retire the debt, and return to its target capital structure. This point was discussed earlier in connection with asymmetric information and signaling.

12. *Financial flexibility.* An astute corporate treasurer made this statement to the authors:

> *Our company can earn a lot more money from good capital budgeting and operating decisions than from good financing decisions. Indeed, we are not sure exactly how financing decisions affect our stock price, but we know for*

sure that having to turn down promising ventures because funds are not available will reduce our long-run profitability. For this reason, my primary goal as treasurer is to always be in a position to raise the capital needed to support operations.

We also know that when times are good, we can raise capital with either stocks or bonds, but when times are bad, suppliers of capital are much more willing to make funds available if we give them a stronger position, and this means debt. Further, when we sell a new issue of stock, this sends a negative "signal" to investors, so stock sales by a mature company such as ours are not desirable.

Putting all these thoughts together gives rise to the goal of maintaining financial flexibility, which from an operational viewpoint means maintaining adequate "reserve borrowing capacity." Determining the "adequate" reserve is judgmental; but it clearly depends on the firm's forecasted need for funds, predicted capital market conditions, management's confidence in its forecasts, and the consequences of a capital shortage.

SELF TEST

How does sales stability affect the target capital structure?

How do the types of assets used affect a firm's capital structure?

How do taxes affect the target capital structure?

How do the attitudes of lenders and rating agencies affect capital structure?

How does the firm's internal condition affect its actual capital structure?

What is financial flexibility, and is it increased or decreased by a high debt ratio?

14-6 VARIATIONS IN CAPITAL STRUCTURES

As might be expected, wide variations in the use of financial leverage occur across industries and among the individual firms in each industry. Table 14-4 illustrates differences for selected industries; the ranking is in descending order of the common equity ratio, as shown in Column 1.[23]

Pharmaceutical and aerospace/defense companies use relatively little debt because their industries tend to be cyclical, oriented toward research, or subject to huge product liability suits. Utility companies, on the other hand, use debt relatively heavily because their fixed assets make good security for mortgage bonds and because their relatively stable sales make it safe to carry more than average debt.

The times-interest-earned (TIE) ratio gives an indication of how vulnerable the company is to financial distress. This ratio depends on three factors: (1) the percentage of debt, (2) the interest rate on the debt, and (3) the company's profitability. Generally, low-leveraged industries such as pharmaceuticals and aerospace/defense have high coverage ratios, whereas industries such as utilities, which finance heavily with debt, have low coverages.

---

[23]Information on capital structures and financial strength is available from a multitude of sources. We used the *MSN Money* web site to develop Table 14-4, but published sources include *The Value Line Investment Survey, Robert Morris Association Annual Studies,* and *Dun & Bradstreet Key Business Ratios.*

Table 14-4	Capital Structure Percentages, 2008: Six Industries Ranked by Common Equity Ratios

Industry[a]	Common Equity Ratio[b] (1)	Long-Term Debt Ratio (2)	Times-Interest-Earned Ratio (3)	Return on Equity (4)
Pharmaceuticals	70.42%	29.58%	16.6	23.70%
Aerospace/Defense	62.11	37.89	33.7	24.00
Railroads	59.17	40.83	7.7	15.90
Computers	55.56	44.44	18.8	30.30
Steel	52.63	47.37	15.2	32.80
Utilities	46.30	53.70	5.9	14.40

[a]Capital structure ratios are calculated as a percentage of total capital, where total capital is defined as long-term debt plus equity, with both measured at book value.

[b]These ratios are based on accounting (or book) values. Stated on a market-value basis, the equity percentages would rise because most stocks sell at prices that are much higher than their book values. *Source: MSN Money;* http://moneycentral.msn.com; May15, 2008.

Wide variations also exist among firms in given industries. For example, although the average ratio of common equity to total capital in 2008 for the pharmaceutical industry was 70.4%, GlaxoSmithKline had a ratio of only 47.4%. Thus, factors unique to individual firms, including managerial attitudes, play an important role in setting target capital structures.

GLOBAL PERSPECTIVES

TAKING A LOOK AT GLOBAL CAPITAL STRUCTURES

To what extent does capital structure vary among different countries? The following table, which is taken from a study by Raghuram Rajan and Luigi Zingales, both of the University of Chicago, shows the median debt ratios of firms in the largest industrial countries.

Rajan and Zingales show that there is considerable variation in capital structure among firms within each of the seven countries. They also show that capital structures for the firms in each country are generally determined by a similar set of factors: firm size, profitability, market-to-book ratio, and the ratio of fixed assets to total assets. All in all, the Rajan-Zingales study suggests that the points developed in this chapter apply to firms all around the world.

Median Percentage of Debt to Total Assets in Different Countries

Country	Book Value Debt Ratio
United Kingdom	10%
Germany	11
France	18
Italy	21
Japan	21
United States	25
Canada	32

Source: Raghuram G. Rajan and Luigi Zingales, "What Do We Know about Capital Structure? Some Evidence from International Data," *Journal of Finance*, Vol. 50, no. 5 (December 1995), pp. 1421–1460. Used with permission.

Why do wide variations in the use of financial leverage occur across industries and among individual firms in each industry?

TYING IT ALL TOGETHER

When we studied the cost of capital in Chapter 10, we took the firm's capital structure as given and calculated the cost of capital based on that structure. Then in Chapters 11, 12, and 13, we described capital budgeting techniques, which use the cost of capital as input. Capital budgeting decisions determine the types of projects that a firm accepts, which affect the nature of the firm's assets and its business risk. In this chapter, we reverse the process, taking the firm's assets and business risk as given and then seeking to determine the best way to finance those assets. More specifically, in this chapter, we examined the effects of financial leverage on earnings per share, stock prices, and the cost of capital and we discussed various capital structure theories.

The different theories lead to different conclusions about the optimal capital structure, and no one has been able to prove that one theory is better than the others. Therefore, we cannot estimate the optimal capital structure with much precision. Accordingly, financial executives generally treat the optimal capital structure as a range—for example, 40% to 50% debt—rather than as a precise point, such as 45%. The concepts discussed in this chapter are used as a guide, and they help managers understand the factors to consider when they are setting their target capital structures.

SELF-TEST QUESTIONS AND PROBLEMS
(Solutions Appear in Appendix A)

ST-1   **KEY TERMS**   Define each of the following terms:

a. Optimal capital structure; target capital structure

b. Business risk; financial risk

c. Financial leverage; operating leverage; operating breakeven

d. Hamada equation; unlevered beta

e. Symmetric information; asymmetric information

f. Modigliani-Miller theories

g. Trade-off theory; signaling theory

h. Reserve borrowing capacity

ST-2   **OPERATING LEVERAGE AND BREAKEVEN ANALYSIS**   Olinde Electronics Inc. produces stereo components that sell at $P = \$100$ per unit. Olinde's fixed costs are $200,000, variable costs are $50 per unit, 5,000 components are produced and sold each year, EBIT is currently $50,000, and Olinde's assets (all equity-financed) are $500,000. Olinde can change its production process by adding $400,000 to assets and $50,000 to fixed operating costs. This change would (1) reduce variable costs per unit by $10 and (2) increase output by 2,000 units, but (3) the sales price on all units would have to be lowered to $95 to permit sales of the additional output. Olinde has tax loss carry-forwards that cause its tax rate to be zero, it uses no debt, and its average cost of capital is 10%.

a. Should Olinde make the change? Why or why not?

b. Would Olinde's breakeven point increase or decrease if it made the change?

c. Suppose Olinde was unable to raise additional equity financing and had to borrow the $400,000 at an interest rate of 10% to make the investment. Use the DuPont equation to find the expected ROA of the investment. Should Olinde make the change if debt financing must be used? Explain.

ST-3 **FINANCIAL LEVERAGE** Gentry Motors Inc., a producer of turbine generators, is in this situation: EBIT = $4 million, tax rate = T = 35%, debt outstanding = D = $2 million, r_d = 10%, r_s = 15%, shares of stock outstanding = N_0 = 600,000, and book value per share = $10. Because Gentry's product market is stable and the company expects no growth, all earnings are paid out as dividends. The debt consists of perpetual bonds.

a. What are Gentry's earnings per share (EPS) and its price per share (P_0)?

b. What is Gentry's weighted average cost of capital (WACC)?

c. Gentry can increase its debt by $8 million to a total of $10 million, using the new debt to buy back and retire some of its shares at the current price. Its interest rate on debt will be 12% (it will have to call and refund the old debt), and its cost of equity will rise from 15% to 17%. EBIT will remain constant. Should Gentry change its capital structure? Why or why not?

d. If Gentry did not have to refund the $2 million of old debt, how would this affect the situation? Assume that the new and the still outstanding debt are equally risky, with r_d = 12%, but that the coupon rate on the old debt is 10%.

e. What is Gentry's TIE coverage ratio under the original situation and under the conditions in Part c of this question?

QUESTIONS

14-1 Changes in sales cause changes in profits. Would the profit change associated with sales changes be larger or smaller if a firm increased its operating leverage? Explain your answer.

14-2 Would each of the following increase, decrease, or have an indeterminant effect on a firm's breakeven point (unit sales)?

a. The sales price increases with no change in unit costs.

b. An increase in fixed costs is accompanied by a decrease in variable costs.

c. A new firm decides to use MACRS depreciation for both book and tax purposes rather than the straight-line depreciation method.

d. Variable labor costs decline; other things are held constant.

14-3 Discuss the following statement: All else equal, firms with relatively stable sales are able to carry relatively high debt ratios. Is the statement true or false? Why?

14-4 If Congress increased the personal tax rate on interest, dividends, and capital gains but simultaneously reduced the rate on corporate income, what effect would this have on the average company's capital structure?

14-5 Which of the following would likely encourage a firm to increase the debt in its capital structure?

a. The corporate tax rate increases.

b. The personal tax rate increases.

c. Due to market changes, the firm's assets become less liquid.

d. Changes in the bankruptcy code make bankruptcy less costly to the firm.

e. The firm's sales and earnings become more volatile.

14-6 Why do public utilities generally use different capital structures than pharmaceutical companies?

14-7 Why is EBIT generally considered independent of financial leverage? Why might EBIT actually be affected by financial leverage at high debt levels?

14-8   Is the debt level that maximizes a firm's expected EPS the same as the debt level that maximizes its stock price? Explain.

14-9   If a firm goes from zero debt to successively higher levels of debt, why would you expect its stock price to rise first, then hit a peak, and then begin to decline?

14-10   When the Bell System was broken up, the old AT&T was split into a new AT&T in addition to seven regional telephone companies. The specific reason for forcing the breakup was to increase the degree of competition in the telephone industry. AT&T had a monopoly on local service, long distance, and the manufacture of all equipment used by telephone companies; and the breakup was expected to open most of those markets to competition. In the court order that set the terms of the breakup, the capital structures of the surviving companies were specified and much attention was given to the increased competition telephone companies could expect in the future. Do you think the optimal capital structure after the breakup was the same as the pre-breakup optimal capital structure? Explain your position.

14-11   A firm is about to double its assets to serve its rapidly growing market. It must choose between a highly automated production process and a less automated one. It also must choose a capital structure for financing the expansion. Should the asset investment and financing decisions be jointly determined, or should each decision be made separately? How would these decisions affect one another? How could the leverage concept be used to help management analyze the situation?

PROBLEMS

Easy Problems 1–5

14-1   **BREAKEVEN ANALYSIS**   A company's fixed operating costs are $500,000, its variable costs are $3.00 per unit, and the product's sales price is $4.00. What is the company's breakeven point; that is, at what unit sales volume will its income equal its costs?

14-2   **OPTIMAL CAPITAL STRUCTURE**   Jackson Trucking Company is in the process of setting its target capital structure. The CFO believes that the optimal debt ratio is somewhere between 20% and 50%, and her staff has compiled the following projections for EPS and the stock price at various debt levels:

Debt Ratio	Projected EPS	Projected Stock Price
20%	$3.20	$35.00
30	3.45	36.50
40	3.75	36.25
50	3.50	35.50

Assuming that the firm uses only debt and common equity, what is Jackson's optimal capital structure? At what debt ratio is the company's WACC minimized?

14-3   **RISK ANALYSIS**

a.   Given the following information, calculate the expected value for Firm C's EPS. Data for Firms A and B are as follows: $E(EPS_A) = \$5.10$, and $\sigma_A = \$3.61$; $E(EPS_B) = \$4.20$, and $\sigma_B = \$2.96$.

			PROBABILITY		
	0.1	0.2	0.4	0.2	0.1
Firm A: EPS_A	($1.50)	$1.80	$5.10	$8.40	$11.70
Firm B: EPS_B	(1.20)	1.50	4.20	6.90	9.60
Firm C: EPS_C	(2.40)	1.35	5.10	8.85	12.60

b.   You are given that $\sigma_C = \$4.11$. Discuss the relative riskiness of the three firms' earnings.

14-4 **UNLEVERED BETA** Harley Motors has $10 million in assets, which were financed with $2 million of debt and $8 million in equity. Harley's beta is currently 1.2, and its tax rate is 40%. Use the Hamada equation to find Harley's unlevered beta, b_U.

14-5 **FINANCIAL LEVERAGE EFFECTS** Firms HL and LL are identical except for their leverage ratios and the interest rates they pay on debt. Each has $20 million in assets, has $4 million of EBIT, and is in the 40% federal-plus-state tax bracket. Firm HL, however, has a debt ratio (D/A) of 50% and pays 12% interest on its debt, whereas LL has a 30% debt ratio and pays only 10% interest on its debt.

    a. Calculate the rate of return on equity (ROE) for each firm.

    b. Observing that HL has a higher ROE, LL's treasurer is thinking of raising the debt ratio from 30% to 60% even though that would increase LL's interest rate on all debt to 15%. Calculate the new ROE for LL.

Intermediate Problems 6–9

14-6 **BREAKEVEN ANALYSIS** The Weaver Watch Company sells watches for $25, the fixed costs are $140,000, and variable costs are $15 per watch.

    a. What is the firm's gain or loss at sales of 8,000 watches? at 18,000 watches?

    b. What is the breakeven point? Illustrate by means of a chart.

    c. What would happen to the breakeven point if the selling price was raised to $31? What is the significance of this analysis?

    d. What would happen to the breakeven point if the selling price was raised to $31 but variable costs rose to $23 a unit?

14-7 **FINANCIAL LEVERAGE EFFECTS** The Neal Company wants to estimate next year's return on equity (ROE) under different leverage ratios. Neal's total assets are $14 million, it currently uses only common equity, and its federal-plus-state tax rate is 40%. The CFO has estimated next year's EBIT for three possible states of the world: $4.2 million with a 0.2 probability, $2.8 million with a 0.5 probability, and $700,000 with a 0.3 probability. Calculate Neal's expected ROE, standard deviation, and coefficient of variation for each of the following debt ratios; then evaluate the results:

Debt Ratio	Interest Rate
0%	—
10	9%
50	11
60	14

14-8 **HAMADA EQUATION** Cyclone Software Co. is trying to establish its optimal capital structure. Its current capital structure consists of 25% debt and 75% equity; however, the CEO believes that the firm should use more debt. The risk-free rate, r_{RF}, is 5%; the market risk premium, RP_M, is 6%; and the firm's tax rate is 40%. Currently, Cyclone's cost of equity is 14%, which is determined by the CAPM. What would be Cyclone's estimated cost of equity if it changed its capital structure to 50% debt and 50% equity?

14-9 **RECAPITALIZATION** Tapley Inc. currently has assets of $5 million, has zero debt, is in the 40% federal-plus-state tax bracket, has a net income of $1 million, and pays out 40% of its earnings as dividends. Net income is expected to grow at a constant rate of 5% per year, 200,000 shares of stock are outstanding, and the current WACC is 13.40%.

    The company is considering a recapitalization where it will issue $1 million in debt and use the proceeds to repurchase stock. Investment bankers have estimated that if the company goes through with the recapitalization, its before-tax cost of debt will be 11% and its cost of equity will rise to 14.5%.

    a. What is the stock's current price per share (before the recapitalization)?

    b. Assuming that the company maintains the same payout ratio, what will be its stock price following the recapitalization?

Challenging Problems 10–13

14-10 **BREAKEVEN AND OPERATING LEVERAGE**

    a. Given the following graphs, calculate the total fixed costs, variable costs per unit, and sales price for Firm A. Firm B's fixed costs are $120,000, its variable costs per unit are $4, and its sales price is $8 per unit.

    b. Which firm has the higher operating leverage at any given level of sales? Explain.

    c. At what sales level, in units, do both firms earn the same operating profit?

COMPREHENSIVE/SPREADSHEET PROBLEM

14-14 **WACC AND OPTIMAL CAPITAL STRUCTURE** Elliott Athletics is trying to determine its optimal capital structure, which now consists of only debt and common equity. The firm does not currently use preferred stock in its capital structure, and it does not plan to do so in the future. Its treasury staff has consulted with investment bankers. On the basis of those discussions, the staff has created the following table showing the firm's debt cost at different levels:

Debt-to-Assets Ratio (w_d)	Equity-to-Assets Ratio (w_c)	Debt-to-Equity Ratio (D/E)	Bond Rating	Before-Tax Cost of Debt (r_d)
0.0	1.0	0.00	A	7.0%
0.2	0.8	0.25	BBB	8.0
0.4	0.6	0.67	BB	10.0
0.6	0.4	1.50	C	12.0
0.8	0.2	4.00	D	15.0

Elliott uses the CAPM to estimate its cost of common equity, r_s, and estimates that the risk-free rate is 5%, the market risk premium is 6%, and its tax rate is 40%. Elliott estimates that if it had no debt, its "unlevered" beta, b_U, would be 1.2.

a. What is the firm's optimal capital structure, and what would be its WACC at the optimal capital structure?

b. If Elliott's managers anticipate that the company's business risk will increase in the future, what effect would this likely have on the firm's target capital structure?

c. If Congress were to dramatically increase the corporate tax rate, what effect would this likely have on Elliott's target capital structure?

d. Plot a graph of the after-tax cost of debt, the cost of equity, and the WACC versus (1) the debt/assets ratio and (2) the debt/equity ratio.

INTEGRATED CASE

CAMPUS DELI INC.

14-15 **OPTIMAL CAPITAL STRUCTURE** Assume that you have just been hired as business manager of Campus Deli (CD), which is located adjacent to the campus. Sales were $1,100,000 last year, variable costs were 60% of sales, and fixed costs were $40,000. Therefore, EBIT totaled $400,000. Because the university's enrollment is capped, EBIT is expected to be constant over time. Because no expansion capital is required, CD pays out all earnings as dividends. Assets are $2 million, and 80,000 shares are outstanding. The management group owns about 50% of the stock, which is traded in the over-the-counter market.

CD currently has no debt—it is an all-equity firm—and its 80,000 shares outstanding sell at a price of $25 per share, which is also the book value. The firm's federal-plus-state tax rate is 40%. On the basis of statements made in your finance text, you believe that CD's shareholders would be better off if some debt financing was used. When you suggested this to your new boss, she encouraged you to pursue the idea but to provide support for the suggestion.

In today's market, the risk-free rate, r_{RF}, is 6% and the market risk premium, RP_M, is 6%. CD's unlevered beta, b_U, is 1.0. CD currently has no debt, so its cost of equity (and WACC) is 12%.

If the firm was recapitalized, debt would be issued and the borrowed funds would be used to repurchase stock. Stockholders, in turn, would use funds provided by the repurchase to buy equities in other fast-food companies similar to CD. You plan to complete your report by asking and then answering the following questions.

a. (1) What is business risk? What factors influence a firm's business risk?

(2) What is operating leverage, and how does it affect a firm's business risk?

b. (1) What do the terms *financial leverage* and *financial risk* mean?

(2) How does financial risk differ from business risk?

c. To develop an example that can be presented to CD's management as an illustration, consider two hypothetical firms: Firm U with zero debt financing and Firm L with $10,000 of 12% debt. Both firms have $20,000 in total assets and a 40% federal-plus-state tax rate, and they have the following EBIT probability distribution for next year:

Probability	EBIT
0.25	$2,000
0.50	3,000
0.25	4,000

(1) Complete the partial income statements and the firms' ratios in Table IC14-1.

(2) Be prepared to discuss each entry in the table and to explain how this example illustrates the effect of financial leverage on expected rate of return and risk.

d. After speaking with a local investment banker, you obtain the following estimates of the cost of debt at different debt levels (in thousands of dollars):

Amount Borrowed	D/A Ratio	D/E Ratio	Bond Rating	r_d
$ 0	0	0	—	—
250	0.125	0.1429	AA	8.0%
500	0.250	0.3333	A	9.0
750	0.375	0.6000	BBB	11.5
1,000	0.500	1.0000	BB	14.0

Now consider the optimal capital structure for CD.

(1) To begin, define the terms *optimal capital structure* and *target capital structure*.

(2) Why does CD's bond rating and cost of debt depend on the amount of money borrowed?

Table IC 14-1 **Income Statements and Ratios**

	Firm U			Firm L		
Assets	$20,000	$20,000	$20,000	$20,000	$20,000	$20,000
Equity	$20,000	$20,000	$20,000	$10,000	$10,000	$10,000
Probability	0.25	0.50	0.25	0.25	0.50	0.25
Sales	$ 6,000	$ 9,000	$12,000	$ 6,000	$ 9,000	$12,000
Operating costs	4,000	6,000	8,000	4,000	6,000	8,000
Earnings before interest and taxes	$ 2,000	$ 3,000	$ 4,000	$ 2,000	$ 3,000	$ 4,000
Interest (12%)	0	0	0	1,200		1,200
Earnings before taxes	$ 2,000	$ 3,000	$ 4,000	$ 800	$	$ 2,800
Taxes (40%)	800	1,200	1,600	320		1,120
Net income	$ 1,200	$ 1,800	$ 2,400	$ 480	$	$ 1,680
Basic earning power (BEP = EBIT/Assets)	10.0%	15.0%	20.0%	10.0%	%	20.0%
ROE	6.0%	9.0%	12.0%	4.8%	%	16.8%
TIE	∞	∞	∞	1.7×	×	3.3×
Expected basic earning power		15.0%			%	
Expected ROE		9.0%			10.8%	
Expected TIE		∞			2.5×	
σ_{BEP}		3.5%			%	
σ_{ROE}		2.1%			4.2%	
σ_{TIE}		0			0.6×	

(3) Assume that shares could be repurchased at the current market price of $25 per share. Calculate CD's expected EPS and TIE at debt levels of $0, $250,000, $500,000, $750,000, and $1,000,000. How many shares would remain after recapitalization under each scenario?

(4) Using the Hamada equation, what is the cost of equity if CD recapitalizes with $250,000 of debt? $500,000? $750,000? $1,000,000?

(5) Considering only the levels of debt discussed, what is the capital structure that minimizes CD's WACC?

(6) What would be the new stock price if CD recapitalizes with $250,000 of debt? $500,000? $750,000? $1,000,000? Recall that the payout ratio is 100%, so g = 0.

(7) Is EPS maximized at the debt level that maximizes share price? Why or why not?

(8) Considering only the levels of debt discussed, what is CD's optimal capital structure?

(9) What is the WACC at the optimal capital structure?

e. Suppose you discovered that CD had more business risk than you originally estimated. Describe how this would affect the analysis. How would the analysis be affected if the firm had less business risk than originally estimated?

f. What are some factors a manager should consider when establishing his or her firm's target capital structure?

g. Put labels on Figure IC14-1 and then discuss the graph as you might use it to explain to your boss why CD might want to use some debt.

h. How does the existence of asymmetric information and signaling affect capital structure?

FIGURE IC 14-1   Relationship between Capital Structure and Stock Price

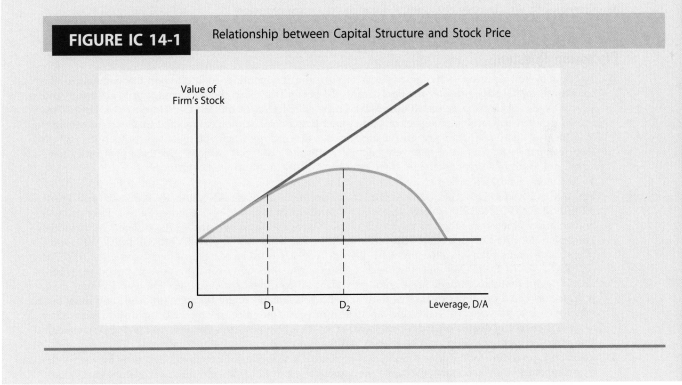

THOMSON ONE | Business School Edition

Access the Thomson ONE problems through the CengageNOW™ web site. Use the Thomson ONE—Business School Edition online database to work this chapter's questions.

Exploring the Capital Structures for Four of the World's Leading Auto Companies

This chapter provides an overview of the effects of leverage and describes the process that firms use to determine their optimal capital structure. The chapter also indicates that capital structures tend to vary across industries and across countries. If you are interested in exploring these differences in more detail, Thomson ONE provides information about the capital structures of each of the companies it follows.

The following discussion questions demonstrate how we can use this information to evaluate the capital structures for four of the world's leading automobile companies: General Motors (GM-N), Ford (F-N), BMW (BMW-FF), and Toyota (7203-TO). (The combination of letters and numbers in parentheses are the Thomson ONE quote symbols.) As you gather information about these companies, be mindful of the currencies in which these companies' financial data are reported.

Discussion Questions

1. To get an overall picture of each company's capital structure, it is helpful to look at a chart that summarizes the company's capital structure over the past decade. To obtain this chart, choose a company to start with and select FINANCIALS. Next, select MORE>THOMSON REPORTS & CHARTS>CAPITAL STRUCTURE. This should generate a chart that plots the company's long-term debt, common equity, and total current liabilities over the past decade. What, if any, are the major trends that emerge when you're looking at these charts? Do these companies tend to have relatively high or relatively low levels of debt? Do these companies have significant levels of current liabilities? Have their capital structures changed over time?

2. To get more details about the companies' capital structures over the past 5 years, select FINANCIALS>FINANCIAL RATIOS>THOMSON RATIOS. From here, you can select ANNUAL RATIOS and/or 5 YEAR AVERAGE RATIOS REPORT. In each case, you can scroll down and look for "Leverage Ratios." Here you will find a variety of leverage ratios for the past 5 years. (Notice that these two pages offer different information. The ANNUAL RATIOS page offers year-end leverage ratios, while the 5 YEAR AVERAGE RATIOS REPORT offers the average ratio over the previous 5 years for each calendar date. In other words, the 5 YEAR AVERAGE RATIOS REPORT smooths the changes in capital structure over the reporting period.) Do these ratios suggest that the company has significantly changed its capital structure over the past 5 years? If so, what factors could possibly explain this shift? (Financial statements might be useful to detect any shifts that may have led to the company's changing capital structure. You may also consult the company's annual report to see if there is any discussion and/or explanation for these changes. Both the historical financial statements and annual report information can be found via Thomson ONE.)

3. Repeat this procedure for the other three auto companies. Do you find similar capital structures for each of the four companies? Do you find that the capital structures have moved in the same direction over the past 5 years, or have the different companies changed their capital structures in different ways over the past 5 years?

4. The financial ratios investigated thus far are based on book values of debt and equity. Determine whether using the market value of equity (market capitalization found on the OVERVIEW page) makes a significant difference in the most recent year's "LT Debt Pct Common Equity" and "Total Debt Pct Total Assets." (Note: "LT Debt" is defined by Thomson ONE as the "Long Term Debt" listed on the balance sheet, while "Total Debt" is defined as "Long Term Debt" plus "ST Debt & Current Portion Due LT Debt.") Are there big differences between the capital structures measured on a book or market basis?

5. You can also use Thomson ONE to search for companies with very large or very small debt ratios. For example, if you want to find the top 50 companies with the highest debt ratio, select "SCREENING & TARGETING". Now select ADVANCED SEARCH, ALL COMPANIES, THOMSON FINANCIAL, RATIOS, and LEVERAGE. From here, select "LT Debt Pct Total Cap 5 Yr. Avg." (This will focus on the average capital structure over the past 5 years, which should give us a better indication of the company's long-run target capital structure.) Once you click on SELECT, you should see the "Search Expression Builder" screen. From here, click on "Rank" and select the top 50 by typing 50 in the box below rank; then click on ADD. You can easily change this to select the bottom 50 (or perhaps the bottom 5% or 10%). Take a close look at the resulting firms by clicking on SEARCH. Do you observe any differences between the types of firms that have high debt levels and the types of firms that have low debt levels? Are these patterns similar to what you expect after reading the chapter? (As a quick review, you may want to look at the average capital structures for different industries, which is summarized in the text.) *Note: The searches are cumulative. So if you ask for the top 10% of the database and follow that by asking for the bottom 5%, you will be shown the bottom 5% of the top 10%. In other words, you will see only a small subset of the firms you are asking for. Hence, before beginning a new search, clear all existing searches.*

6. From the submenu just above the list of firms, you may choose a number of options. "Companies" displays a list of the firms and allows you to access a firm report. "Profiles" provides key information about the firms, such as ticker, country, exchange, and industry code. "Financials" gives a couple of key financial figures (expressed in U.S. dollars) from the firms' balance sheets and income statements. "Market Data" includes the firms' market capitalization, current price, P/E ratio, EPS, and so forth. Finally, "Report Writer" allows you to create customized company reports.

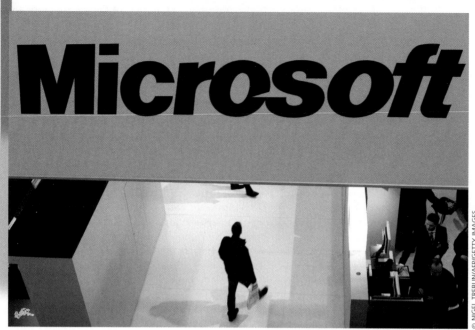

© NIGEL TREBLIN/AFP/GETTY IMAGES

Microsoft

15 Distributions to Shareholders: Dividends and Share Repurchases

Microsoft Shifts Gears and Begins to Unload Part of Its Vast Cash Hoard

Profitable companies regularly face three important questions: (1) How much of our free cash flow should we pass on to shareholders? (2) Should we provide this cash to stockholders by raising the dividend or by repurchasing stock? (3) Should we maintain a stable, consistent payment policy; or should we let the payments vary as conditions change?

In this chapter, we discuss many of the issues that affect firms' cash distribution policies. As we will see, mature companies with stable cash flows and limited growth opportunities tend to return a significant amount of their cash to shareholders either by paying dividends or by using the cash to repurchase common stock. By contrast, rapidly growing companies with good investment opportunities are prone to invest most of their available cash in new projects rather than paying dividends or repurchasing stock. Microsoft, which has long been regarded as the epitome of a growth company, illustrates this tendency. Its sales grew from $786 *million* in 1989 to a projected $60.3 *billion* in 2008, which

translates to an annual growth rate of nearly 26%. Much of this growth came from large, long-term investments in new products and technology; and given the firm's emphasis on growth, it paid no dividends over most of its life.

However, over time, this quintessential growth company began to evolve into a mature "cash cow." Its Windows® and Office products have saturated the market, and they help the company produce large amounts of free cash flow each month. Moreover, until 2003, the company did not pay any dividends to its shareholders because management wanted to keep the cash available for acquisitions and other investments. As a result, the company reported a staggering $49 billion in cash on its balance sheet as of June 30, 2003.

Since then, Microsoft has shifted gears; and it now pays a significant portion of its cash to shareholders. First, in 2003, it initiated a regular quarterly dividend of 8 cents a share. That regular dividend was doubled in 2004. However, the cash kept pouring in; and by mid-2004,

Microsoft's cash hoard had grown to more than $60 billion. At that point, the company took some larger steps to return cash to its shareholders. Once again, the regular quarterly dividend was doubled to 32 cents a share. More dramatically, Microsoft announced plans to pay a one-time special dividend of $3 a share. In addition, it announced plans to repurchase up to $30 billion worth of stock in the open market. All told, this meant that $62.62 billion would be provided to its shareholders.

Microsoft continued to generate a great deal of cash, and its reported cash holdings in March 2008 were around $25 billion. But the company's aggressive use of dividends and share repurchases to return cash to shareholders in recent years represents an important shift in policy. When managers decide how and when to distribute cash to shareholders, they face a fundamental question: Could we earn more on the available cash if we kept it in the firm and used it to invest in new projects, or would shareholders earn more if they received the cash and invested it in alternative investments with the same risk? If the company could earn more, it would make sense to retain the cash. However, if investors could earn more, the company would increase shareholder value paying out more dividends and/or repurchasing more shares.

PUTTING THINGS IN PERSPECTIVE

Successful companies earn income. That income can be reinvested in operating assets, used to retire debt, or distributed to stockholders. If the decision is made to distribute income to stockholders, three key issues arise: (1) How much should be distributed? (2) Should the distribution be in the form of dividends, or should the cash be passed on to shareholders by buying back stock? (3) How stable should the distribution be? That is, should the funds paid out from year to year be stable and dependable, which stockholders like; or should they be varied depending on the firms' cash flows and investment requirements, which managers tend to like? Those three issues are the primary focus of this chapter; and by the time you complete it, you should be able to:

- Explain why some investors like the firm to pay more dividends while other investors prefer reinvestment and the resulting capital gains.
- Discuss the various trade-offs that companies face when trying to establish their optimal dividend policy.
- Differentiate between stock splits and stock dividends.
- List the advantages and disadvantages of stock repurchases vis-à-vis dividends from both investors' and companies' perspectives.

15-1 DIVIDENDS VERSUS CAPITAL GAINS: WHAT DO INVESTORS PREFER?

When deciding how much cash to distribute, financial managers must keep in mind that the firm's objective is to maximize shareholder value. Consequently, the **target payout ratio**—defined as the percentage of net income to be paid out as cash dividends—should be based in large part on investors' preferences for dividends versus capital gains: Do investors prefer to receive dividends; or would they rather have the firm plow the cash back into the business, which presumably will produce capital gains? This preference can be considered in terms of the constant growth stock valuation model.

Target Payout Ratio
The target percentage of net income paid out as cash dividends.

$$\hat{P}_0 = \frac{D_1}{r_s - g}$$

If the company increases the payout ratio, this will raise D_1, which, taken alone, will cause the stock price to rise. However, if D_1 is raised, less money will be available for reinvestment, which will cause the expected growth rate to decline; and that will tend to lower the stock's price. Therefore, any change in the payout policy will have two opposing effects. As a result, the **optimal dividend policy** must strike the balance between current dividends and future growth that maximizes the stock price. In the following sections, we discuss the major theories that have been advanced to explain how investors regard current dividends versus future growth.

15-1a Dividend Irrelevance Theory

Professors Merton Miller and Franco Modigliani (MM) advanced the **dividend irrelevance theory**, which stated that dividend policy has no effect on either the price of a firm's stock or its cost of capital.[1] MM developed their theory under a stringent set of assumptions; and under those assumptions, they proved that a firm's value is determined only by its basic earning power and its business risk. In other words, the value of the firm depends only on the income produced by its assets, not on how that income is split between dividends and retained earnings. Note, though, that MM assumed, among other things, that no taxes are paid on dividends, that stocks can be bought and sold with no transactions costs, and that everyone—investors and managers alike—has the same information regarding firms' future earnings.

Given their assumptions, MM argued that each shareholder can construct his or her own dividend policy. For example, if a firm does not pay dividends, a shareholder who wants a 5% dividend can "create" it by selling 5% of his or her stock. Conversely, if a company pays a higher dividend than an investor wants, the investor can use the unwanted dividends to buy additional shares of the company's stock. Note, though, that in the real world, individual investors who want additional dividends would have to incur transactions costs to sell shares, and investors who do not want dividends would have to pay taxes on the unwanted dividends and then incur transactions costs to purchase shares with the after-tax dividends. Because taxes and transactions costs do exist, dividend policy may well be relevant and investors may prefer policies that help them reduce taxes and transactions costs.

In defense of their theory, MM noted that many stocks are owned by institutional investors who pay no taxes and who can buy and sell stocks with very low transactions costs. For such investors, dividend policy might well be irrelevant; and if these investors dominate the market and represent the "marginal investor," MM's theory could be valid in spite of its unrealistic assumptions. Note too that for tax-paying investors, the taxes and transactions costs depend on what the individual investor's income is and how long he or she plans to hold the stock. As a result, when it comes to investors' preferences for dividends, one size does not fit all. Next, we discuss why some investors prefer dividends whereas others prefer capital gains.

15-1b Reasons Some Investors Prefer Dividends

The principal conclusion of MM's dividend irrelevance theory is that dividend policy does not affect either stock prices or the required rate of return on equity, r_s. Early critics of MM's theory suggested that investors preferred a sure dividend today to an uncertain future capital gain. In particular, Myron Gordon and John Lintner argued that r_s declines as the dividend payout is increased because

---

[1]Merton H. Miller and Franco Modigliani, "Dividend Policy, Growth, and the Valuation of Shares," *Journal of Business,* October 1961, pp. 411–433.

investors are less certain of receiving the capital gains that should result from retaining earnings than they are of receiving dividend payments.[2]

MM disagreed. They argued that r_s is independent of dividend policy, which implies that investors are indifferent between dividends and capital gains, that is, between D_1/P_0 and g. MM called the Gordon-Lintner argument the **bird-in-the-hand fallacy** because in MM's view, most investors plan to reinvest their dividends in the stock of the same or similar firms and, in any event, the riskiness of the firm's cash flows to investors in the long run is determined by the riskiness of operating cash flows, not by dividend payout policy.

Keep in mind, however, that MM's theory relied on the assumption that there are no taxes or transactions costs, which means that investors who prefer dividends could simply create their own dividend policy by selling a percentage of their stock each year. In reality, most investors face transactions costs when they sell stock; so investors who are looking for a steady stream of income would logically prefer that companies pay regular dividends. For example, retirees who have accumulated wealth over time and now want annual income from their investments probably prefer dividend-paying stocks.

Bird-in-the-Hand Fallacy
MM's name for Gordon-Lintner's theory that a firm's value will be maximized by setting a high dividend payout ratio.

15-1c Reasons Some Investors Prefer Capital Gains

While dividends reduce transactions costs for investors who are looking for steady income from their investments, dividends increase transactions costs for other investors who are less interested in income and more interested in saving money for the long-term future. These long-term investors want to reinvest their dividends, and that creates transactions costs. Given this concern, a number of companies have established dividend reinvestment plans that help investors automatically reinvest their dividends. (We discuss dividend reinvestment plans in Section 15-4 of this chapter.)

In addition (and perhaps more importantly), the Tax Code encourages many individual investors to prefer capital gains to dividends. Prior to 2003, dividends were taxed at the ordinary income tax rate, which went up to 38% versus a rate of 20% on capital gains. Since 2003, the maximum tax rate on dividends and long-term capital gains has been set at 15%.[3] This change lowered the tax disadvantage of dividends, but reinvestment and the accompanying capital gains still have two tax advantages over dividends. First, taxes must be paid on dividends the year they are received, whereas taxes on capital gains are not paid until the stock is sold. Due to time value effects, a dollar of taxes paid in the future has a lower effective cost than a dollar of taxes paid today. Moreover, if a stock is held by someone until he or she dies, there is no capital gains tax at all—the beneficiaries who receive the stock can use the stock's value on the death day as their cost basis, which permits them to escape the capital gains tax completely.

Because of these tax advantages, some investors prefer to have companies retain most of their earnings. Those investors might be willing to pay more for low-payout companies than for otherwise similar high-payout companies.

Finally, the provision in the 2003 Tax Act that lowered the maximum tax rate on dividends is set to expire in 2010 unless Congress votes to extend it or to make it permanent. Now in the middle of the 2008 election cycle, it is not clear what will happen, particularly after a new Congress and a new president are elected. If

[2]Myron J. Gordon, "Optimal Investment and Financing Policy," *Journal of Finance*, May 1963, pp. 264–272; and John Lintner, "Dividends, Earnings, Leverage, Stock Prices, and the Supply of Capital to Corporations," *Review of Economics and Statistics*, August 1962, pp. 243–269.
[3]However, long-term capital gains are classified as income subject to the Alternative Minimum Tax (AMT), and the AMT rate in 2008 was 26% or 28% depending on your income bracket. The AMT was supposed to hit only the very wealthy, but it was not indexed for inflation. However, by 2008, many not-so-wealthy individuals are being hit. Given the AMT situation, many investors would prefer dividends to capital gains from a tax standpoint.

Congress chooses to let this provision expire and dividends are once again treated as ordinary income, even more investors will prefer capital gains over dividends. At this point, only time will tell.

SELF TEST

Explain briefly the ideas behind the dividend irrelevance theory.

What did Modigliani and Miller assume about taxes and brokerage costs when they developed their dividend irrelevance theory?

Why did MM refer to the Gordon-Lintner dividend argument as the bird-in-the-hand fallacy?

Why do some investors prefer high-dividend-paying stocks?

Why might other investors prefer low-dividend-paying stocks?

15-2 OTHER DIVIDEND POLICY ISSUES

Before we discuss how dividend policy is set in practice, we need to examine two other issues that affect dividend policy: (1) the *information content*, or *signaling, hypothesis* and (2) the *clientele effect*.

15-2a Information Content, or Signaling, Hypothesis

An increase in the dividend is often accompanied by an increase in the stock price, while a dividend cut generally leads to a stock price decline. This observation was used to refute MM's irrelevance theory—their opponents argued that stock price actions after changes in dividend payouts demonstrate that investors prefer dividends to capital gains. However, MM argued differently. They noted that corporations are reluctant to cut dividends and hence that corporations do not raise dividends unless they anticipate higher earnings in the future to support the higher dividends. Thus, MM argued that a higher-than-expected dividend increase is a **signal** to investors that management forecasts good future earnings.[4] Conversely, a dividend reduction, or a smaller-than-expected increase, is a signal that management forecasts poor future earnings. If the MM position is correct, stock price changes after dividend increases or decreases do not demonstrate a preference for dividends over retained earnings. Rather, such price changes simply indicate that dividend announcements have **information content, or signaling**, about future earnings.

Managers often have better information about future prospects for dividends than public stockholders, so there is clearly some information content in dividend announcements. However, it is difficult to tell whether the stock price changes that follow dividend increases or decreases reflect only signaling effects (as MM argue) or both signaling and dividend preference. Still, a firm should consider signaling effects when it is contemplating a change in dividend policy. For example, if a firm has good long-term prospects but also has a need for cash to fund current

Signal

An action taken by management that provides clues to investors about how management views the firm's prospects.

Information Content (Signaling)

The theory that investors regard dividend changes as signals of management's earnings forecasts.

---

[4]Stephen Ross has suggested that managers can use capital structure as well as dividends to give signals concerning a firm's future prospects. For example, a firm with good earnings prospects can carry more debt than a similar firm with poor earnings prospects. This theory, called *incentive signaling*, rests on the premise that signals with cash-based variables (either debt interest or dividends) cannot be mimicked by unsuccessful firms because those firms do not have the future cash-generating power to maintain the announced interest or dividend payment. Thus, investors are more likely to believe a glowing verbal report when it is accompanied by a dividend increase or a debt-financed expansion program. See Stephen A. Ross, "The Determination of Financial Structure: The Incentive-Signaling Approach," *The Bell Journal of Economics*, Spring 1977, pp. 23–40.

investments, it might be tempted to cut the dividend to increase funds available for investment. However, this action might cause the stock price to decline because the dividend reduction is taken as a signal that future earnings are likely to decline, when just the reverse is actually true. So managers should consider signaling effects when they set dividend policy.

15-2b Clientele Effect

As we indicated earlier, different groups, or **clienteles**, of stockholders prefer different dividend payout policies. For example, retired individuals, pension funds, and university endowment funds generally prefer cash income; so they often want the firm to pay out a high percentage of its earnings. Such investors are frequently in low or even zero tax brackets, so taxes are of little concern. On the other hand, stockholders in their peak-earning years might prefer reinvestment because they have less need for current investment income and simply reinvest dividends received after incurring income taxes and brokerage costs.

If a firm retains and reinvests income rather than paying dividends, those stockholders who need current income will be disadvantaged. The value of their stock might increase, but they will be forced to go to the trouble and expense of selling off some of their shares to obtain cash. Also, some institutional investors (or trustees for individuals) might be legally precluded from selling stock and then "spending capital." On the other hand, stockholders who are saving rather than spending dividends favor the low-dividend policy: The less the firm pays out in dividends, the less these stockholders have to pay in current taxes and the less trouble and expense they must go through to reinvest their after-tax dividends. Therefore, investors who want current investment income should own shares in high-dividend-payout firms, while investors with no need for current investment income should own shares in low-dividend-payout firms. For example, investors seeking high cash income might invest in electric utilities, which had an average payout of 60% in 2008, while investors favoring growth could invest in the software industry, which paid out only 18% that same year.

All of this suggests that a **clientele effect** exists, which means that firms have different clienteles and that the clienteles have different preferences—hence, that a change in dividend policy might upset the majority clientele and have a negative effect on the stock's price.[5] This suggests that a company should follow a stable, dependable dividend policy so as to avoid upsetting its clientele.

Clienteles
Different groups of stockholders that prefer different dividend payout policies.

Clientele Effect
The tendency of a firm to attract a set of investors that like its dividend policy.

SELF TEST   Define (1) information content and (2) the clientele effect and explain how they affect dividend policy.

15-3 ESTABLISHING THE DIVIDEND POLICY IN PRACTICE

Investors may or may not prefer dividends to capital gains; however, because of the clientele effect, they almost certainly prefer *predictable* dividends. Given this situation, how should firms set their basic dividend policies? In particular, how

---

[5]For example, see R. Richardson Pettit, "Taxes, Transactions Costs and the Clientele Effect of Dividends," *The Journal of Financial Economics*, December 1977, pp. 419–436.

should a company establish the specific percentage of earnings it will distribute, the form of that distribution, and the stability of its distributions over time? In this section, we describe how most firms answer those questions.

15-3a Setting the Target Payout Ratio: The Residual Dividend Model[6]

When a firm is deciding how much cash to distribute to stockholders, it should consider two points: (1) The overriding objective is to maximize shareholder value; and (2) the firm's cash flows really belong to its shareholders, so management should not retain income unless they can reinvest those earnings at higher rates of return than shareholders can earn themselves. On the other hand, recall from Chapter 10 that internal equity (retained earnings) is cheaper than external equity (new common stock); so if good investments are available, it is better to finance them with retained earnings than with new stock.

When a dividend policy is established, one size does not fit all. Some firms produce a large amount of cash but have limited investment opportunities—this is true for firms in profitable but mature industries where few growth opportunities exist. Such firms typically distribute a large percentage of their cash to shareholders, thereby attracting investor clienteles who prefer high dividends. Other firms have many good investment opportunities but currently generate little or no excess cash. Such firms generally distribute little or no cash but enjoy rising earnings and stock prices, thereby attracting investors who prefer capital gains.

The past few decades have seen increasing numbers of young, high-growth firms trading on the stock exchanges. A study by Eugene Fama and Kenneth French showed that the proportion of firms paying dividends has fallen sharply over time. In 1978, 66.5% of firms on the major stock exchanges paid dividends. By 1999, that proportion had fallen to 20.8%. Fama and French's analysis suggested that part of this decline was due to the changing composition of firms on the exchanges. However, their analysis also indicated that all firms, new and old, have become less likely to pay dividends.[7]

As a result of the 2003 tax changes, which lowered the tax rate on dividends, many companies initiated dividends or increased their payouts. For example, in 2002, only 113 companies raised or initiated dividends; however, in 2003 that number doubled to 229. Previously, those companies would have been more inclined to buy back shares. As of 2007, 389 companies in the S&P 500 paid dividends; this is a historic high.

As Table 15-1 suggests, dividend payouts and dividend yields for large corporations vary considerably. Generally, firms in stable, cash-producing industries such as utilities, food, and tobacco pay relatively high dividends, whereas companies in rapidly growing industries such as computer software and biotechnology tend to pay lower dividends. Average dividends also differ significantly across countries. Higher payout ratios in some countries can be partially explained by lower tax rates on earnings distributed as cash dividends relative to applicable rates on reinvested income. This biases the dividend policy toward higher payouts.

---

[6]The term *payout* ratio can be interpreted two ways: (1) in the conventional way, which is that the payout ratio means the percentage of net income paid out as *cash dividends* or (2) as the percentage of net income distributed to stockholders *through dividends and share repurchases*. In this section, we assume that no repurchases occur. Increasingly, though, firms are using the residual model to determine "distributions to shareholders" and then making a separate decision as to the form of those distributions. Further, over time, an increasing percentage of the total distribution has been in the form of share repurchases.

[7]Eugene F. Fama and Kenneth R. French, "Disappearing Dividends: Changing Firm Characteristics or Lower Propensity to Pay?" *Journal of Applied Corporate Finance*, Vol. 14, no. 1 (Spring 2001), pp. 67–79; and "Disappearing Dividends: Changing Firm Characteristics or Lower Propensity to Pay?" *Journal of Financial Economics*, Vol. 60 (April 2001), pp. 3–43. The last citation is a longer and more technical version of the first paper cited.

Table 15-1	Dividend Payouts in 2008		
Company	Industry	Dividend Payout	Dividend Yield
I. COMPANIES THAT PAY HIGH DIVIDENDS			
Verizon Communications	Telecommunications	83.63%	4.50%
Bank of America Corporation	Banking	72.61	6.86
Southern Copper	Mining	71.02	5.85
Pfizer, Inc.	Pharmaceuticals	52.24	6.41
AT&T Inc.	Telecommunications	51.31	4.12
II. COMPANIES THAT PAY NO DIVIDENDS			
Amazon.com	Online retail	0.00%	0.00%
Cisco Systems	Computer hardware/software	"	"
Dell Inc.	Personal computers	"	"
eBay Inc.	Internet software and services	"	"
Genentech Inc.	Biotechnology	"	"

Source: Value Line Investment Survey, May 15, 2008.

For a given firm, the optimal payout ratio is a function of four factors: (1) management's opinion about its investors' preferences for dividends versus capital gains, (2) the firm's investment opportunities, (3) the firm's target capital structure, and (4) the availability and cost of external capital. These factors are combined in what we call the **residual dividend model**. First, under this model, we assume that investors are indifferent between dividends and capital gains. Then the firm follows these four steps to establish its target payout ratio: (1) It determines the optimal capital budget; (2) given its target capital structure, it determines the amount of equity needed to finance that budget; (3) it uses retained earnings to meet equity requirements to the extent possible; and (4) it pays dividends only if more earnings are available than are needed to support the optimal capital budget. The word *residual* implies "leftover," and the residual policy implies that dividends are paid out of "leftover" earnings.

Residual Dividend Model
A model in which the dividend paid is set equal to net income minus the amount of retained earnings necessary to finance the firm's optimal capital budget.

If a firm rigidly follows the residual dividend policy, dividends paid in any given year can be expressed in the following equation:

$$\text{Dividends} = \text{Net income} - \frac{\text{Retained earnings required to help}}{\text{finance new investements}}$$

$$\text{Dividends} = \text{Net income} - [(\text{Target equity ratio})(\text{Total capital budget})]$$

For example, suppose the company has $100 million of earnings, it has a target equity ratio of 60%, and it plans to spend $50 million on capital projects. In that case, it would need $50(0.6) = $30 million of common equity plus $20 million of new debt to finance the capital budget. That would leave $100 − $30 = $70 million available for dividends, which would result in a 70% payout ratio.

Note that the amount of equity needed to finance the capital budget might exceed net income; in the preceding example, if the capital budget was $100/Equity percentage = $100/0.6 = $166.67 million, no dividends would be paid. If the capital budget exceeded $166.67, the company would have to issue new common stock in order to maintain its target capital structure.

Most firms have a target capital structure that calls for at least some debt, so new financing is done partly with debt and partly with equity. As long as a firm finances with the optimal mix of debt and equity and uses only internally generated equity (retained earnings), the marginal cost of each new dollar of capital will be minimized. So internally generated equity is available for financing a certain amount of new investment; but beyond that amount, the firm must turn to more expensive new common stock. At the point where new stock must be sold, the cost of equity (and consequently the marginal cost of capital) rises.

To illustrate these points, consider the case of Texas and Western (T&W) Transport Company. T&W's overall composite cost of capital is 10%. However, this cost assumes that all new equity comes from retained earnings. If the company must issue new stock, its cost of capital will be higher. T&W has $60 million of net income and a target capital structure with 60% equity and 40% debt. Provided it does not pay any cash dividends, T&W could make net investments (investments in addition to asset replacements from depreciation) of $100 million, consisting of $60 million from retained earnings plus $40 million of new debt supported by the retained earnings, at a 10% marginal cost of capital. If the capital budget exceeded $100 million, the required equity component would exceed net income, which is, of course, the maximum possible amount of retained earnings. In this case, T&W would have to issue new common stock, thereby pushing its cost of capital above 10%.[8]

At the beginning of its planning period, T&W's financial staff considers all proposed projects for the upcoming period. All independent projects are accepted if their estimated IRRs exceed their risk-adjusted costs of capital. In choosing among mutually exclusive projects, the project with the highest positive NPV is accepted. The capital budget represents the amount of capital that is required to finance all accepted projects. If T&W follows a strict residual dividend policy, we can see from Table 15-2 that the estimated capital budget will have a profound effect on its dividend payout ratio. If investment opportunities are poor, the capital budget will be only $40 million. To maintain the target capital structure, 0.6 ($40) = $24 million must be equity, with the remaining $16 million coming as debt. If T&W followed a strict residual policy, it would pay out $60 − $24 = $36 million as dividends; hence, its payout ratio would be $36/$60 = 0.6 = 60%.

Table 15-2	**T&W's Dividend Payout Ratio with $60 Million of Net Income When Faced with Different Investment Opportunities (Dollars in Millions)**		
	INVESTMENT OPPORTUNITIES		
	Poor	**Average**	**Good**
Capital budget	$40	$70	$150
Net income (NI)	$60	$60	$ 60
Required equity (0.6 × Capital budget)	24	42	90
Dividends paid (NI − Required equity)	$36	$18	($ 30)[a]
Dividend payout ratio (Dividends/NI)	60%	30%	0%

[a]With a $150 million capital budget, T&W would retain all of its earnings and issue $30 million of new stock.

---

[8]If T&W does not retain all of its earnings, its cost of capital will rise above 10% before its capital budget reaches $100 million. For example, if T&W chose to retain $36 million, its cost of capital would increase once the capital budget exceeded $36/0.6 = $60 million. To understand this point, note that a capital budget of $60 million would require $36 million of equity. If the capital budget rose above $60 million, the company's required equity capital would exceed its retained earnings, thereby requiring it to issue new common stock.

If the company's investment opportunities were average, its capital budget would be $70 million. This would require $42 million of equity; so dividends would be $60 − $42 = $18 million, for a payout of $18/$60 = 30%. Finally, if investment opportunities were good, the capital budget would be $150 million and 0.6($150) = $90 million of equity would be required. Therefore, all of the net income would be retained, dividends would be zero, and the company would have to issue some new common stock to maintain the target capital structure.

We see then that under the residual model, dividends and the payout ratio would vary with investment opportunities. Dividend variations would also occur if earnings fluctuated. Because investment opportunities and earnings vary from year to year, strict adherence to the residual dividend policy would result in unstable dividends. One year the firm might pay zero dividends because it needed the money to finance good investment opportunities, but the next year it might pay high dividends because investment opportunities were poor and it didn't need to retain much. Similarly, fluctuating earnings would also lead to variable dividends, even if investment opportunities were stable. *Therefore, following the residual dividend policy would almost certainly lead to fluctuating, unstable dividends.* This would not be bad if investors were not bothered by fluctuating dividends; but since investors do prefer stable, dependable dividends, it would not be optimal to follow the residual model in a strict sense. Therefore, firms should operate as follows:

1. Estimate earnings and investment opportunities, on average, over the next 5 or so years.
2. Use this forecasted information to find the average residual model amount of dividends (and the payout ratio) during the planning period.
3. Set a target payout policy based on the projected data.

Thus, firms should use the residual policy to help set their long-run target payout ratios, but not as a guide to the payout in any one year.

Most large companies use the residual dividend model in a conceptual sense, then implement it with a computerized financial forecasting model. Information on projected capital expenditures and working capital requirements is entered into the model, along with sales forecasts, profit margins, depreciation, and the other elements required to forecast cash flows. The target capital structure is also specified; the model then generates the amount of debt and equity that will be required to meet the capital budgeting requirements while maintaining the target capital structure.

Dividend payments are introduced; and the higher the payout ratio, the greater the required external equity. Most companies use the model to find a dividend payout over the forecast period (generally 5 years) that will provide sufficient equity to support the capital budget without having to sell new common stock or take the capital structure ratios outside the optimal range. This chapter's Excel model includes an illustration of this process. In addition, Web Appendix 15A discusses this approach in more detail. The end result might be a memo such as the following from the CFO to the chairperson of the board:

> *We forecasted the total market demand for our products, what our share of the market is likely to be, and our required investments in capital assets and working capital. Using this information, we developed projected balance sheets and income statements for the period 2009–2013.*
>
> *Our 2008 dividends totaled $50 million, or $2.00 per share. On the basis of projected earnings, cash flows, and capital requirements, we can increase the dividend by 6% per year. This would be consistent with a payout ratio of 42%, on average, over the forecast period. Any faster dividend growth rate would require us to sell common stock, cut the capital budget, or raise the debt ratio.*

GLOBAL PERSPECTIVES

DIVIDEND YIELDS AROUND THE WORLD

Average dividend yields have varied over time, and they vary considerably in different countries around the world. The accompanying graph, obtained from a recent study by Elroy Dimson, Paul Marsh, and Mike Staunton of the London Business School, shows how the average dividend yield for 16 different countries has changed over the past century. In both 1900 and 1950, dividend yields varied from nation to nation, but the average around the world was about 5%. However, by 2004, the yield in most countries had declined significantly and the average had fallen to about 3%. For the United States, the average dividend yield was 4.3% in 1900, 7.2% in 1950, and 1.7% in 2004. Thus, U.S. stocks went from having one of the highest yields in 1900 to the second lowest in 2004.

DIVIDEND YIELDS AROUND THE WORLD: 1900, 1950, AND 2004

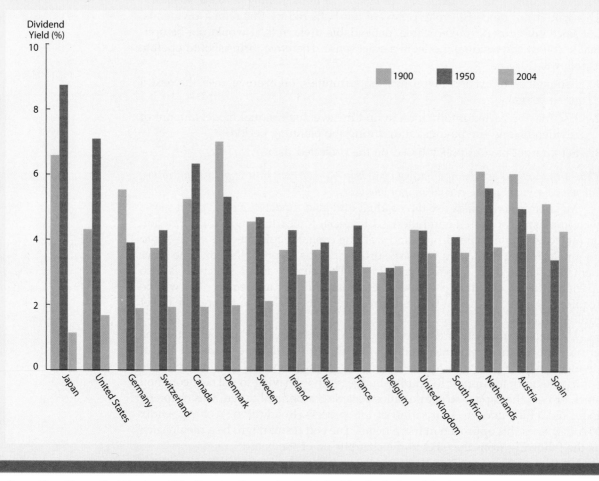

Source: Elroy Dimson, Paul Marsh, and Mike Staunton, "Forecasting the Market," London Business School, Working Paper Draft 1, March 10, 2004.

Any slower growth rate would lead to increases in the common equity ratio. Therefore, I recommend that the Board increase the dividend for 2009 by 6%, to $2.12, and that it plan for similar increases in the future.

Events over the next 5 years will undoubtedly lead to differences between our forecasts and actual results. If and when such events occur, we should reexamine our position. However, I am confident that we can meet random cash shortfalls by increasing our borrowings—we have unused debt capacity that gives us flexibility in this regard.

We ran the corporate model under several scenarios. If the economy totally collapses, our earnings will not cover the dividend. However, in all likely scenarios our cash flows would cover the recommended dividend. I know the Board does not want to push the dividend up to a level where we would have to cut it under bad conditions. Our model runs indicate, though, that the $2.12 dividend could be maintained under any reasonable set of forecasts. Only if we increased the dividend to over $3.00 would we be seriously exposed to the danger of having to reduce it.

I might also note that most analysts' reports are forecasting that our dividends will grow in the 5% to 6% range. Thus, if we go to $2.12, we will be at the high end of the range, which should give our stock a boost. With takeover rumors so widespread, getting the stock up a bit would make us all breathe a little easier.

Finally, we considered distributing cash to shareholders through a stock repurchase program. Here we would reduce the dividend payout ratio and use the funds generated to buy our stock on the open market. Such a program has several advantages, but it would also have drawbacks. I do not recommend that we institute a stock repurchase program at this time. However, if our free cash flows exceed our forecasts, I would recommend that we use these surpluses to buy back stock. Also, I plan to continue looking into a regular repurchase program, and I may recommend such a program in the future.

This company has very stable operations, so it can plan its dividends with a fairly high degree of confidence. Other companies, especially those in cyclical industries, have difficulty maintaining a dividend in bad times that would be too low in good times. Such companies often set a very low "regular" dividend and then supplement it with an "extra" dividend when times are good. General Motors, Ford, and other auto companies have followed such **low-regular-dividend-plus-extras** policies in the past. Each company announced a low regular dividend that it was confident it could maintain "through hell or high water," one that stockholders could count on under all conditions. Then when times were good and profits and cash flows were high, the company would pay a clearly designated extra dividend. Because investors recognized that the extras might not be maintained in the future, they did not interpret them as a signal that the companies' earnings were permanently higher nor did they take the elimination of the extra as a negative signal.

Low-Regular-Dividend-Plus-Extras
The policy of announcing a low regular dividend that can be maintained no matter what and then when times are good, paying a designated "extra" dividend.

15-3b Earnings, Cash Flows, and Dividends

We normally think of earnings as being the primary determinant of dividends, but cash flows are actually more important. This is demonstrated in Figure 15-1, which plots data for Chevron Corporation from 1985 through 2007. Panel A shows that Chevron's dividends per share (DPS) rose slowly but steadily from 1985 to 2007. Earnings per share (EPS) also grew slowly; but they were more volatile, rising and falling with the price of oil. The earnings payout ratio (defined as DPS/EPS) averaged 70% over the entire 23 years, but it exceeded 100% on several occasions.

Cash flow per share (CFPS) tracked EPS very closely—the two were correlated at 0.99. However, CFPS was always higher than EPS, and it always exceeded the dividend by a substantial margin. Moreover, cash dividends are paid in cash; so even when earnings were insufficient to cover the dividend, cash flows took up the slack and enabled the company to maintain a stable dividend policy.

FIGURE 15-1	Chevron Corp.: Earnings, Cash Flows, and Dividends, 1985–2007

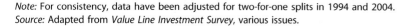

Note: For consistency, data have been adjusted for two-for-one splits in 1994 and 2004.
Source: Adapted from *Value Line Investment Survey*, various issues.

Now look at Panel B. Here we see that the earnings payout is extremely volatile, but the cash flow payout (defined as DPS/CFPS) is relatively stable and always well below 100%. Those stable (and high) cash flows indicate that Chevron's dividend is relatively safe, and investors can count on receiving it going forward. Indeed, given the very high cash flows per share, continued substantial dividend increases (or large share repurchases) are likely—provided something bad doesn't happen in the oil market.

Chevron is typical of most large, strong companies. Its dividend is dependable, and it grows at a steady rate. Earnings are relatively volatile; but cash flows are more stable, and those stable cash flows are responsible for the steady dividends. When earnings change dramatically, either up or down, dividends are likely to follow with a lag while management determines whether the earnings change is likely to continue. Thus, the dip in Chevron's earnings in 2001 and 2002 turned out to be temporary, so the dividend was maintained and even increased during those years. The huge earnings and cash flow gains after 2002—which have continued into 2008—suggest that dividends, repurchases, and profitable new investments will continue on into the future. But Chevron does deal with oil; and with that commodity, strange things can happen!

15-3c Payment Procedures

Companies normally pay dividends quarterly; and if conditions permit, the dividend is increased once each year. For example, Katz Corporation paid $0.50 per quarter in 2008, or at an annual rate of $2.00. In common financial parlance, we say that Katz's 2008 *regular quarterly dividend* was $0.50 and its *annual dividend* was $2.00. In late 2008, Katz's board of directors met, reviewed projections for 2009, and decided to keep the 2009 dividend at $2.00. The directors announced the $2.00 rate, so stockholders could count on receiving it unless the company experienced unanticipated operating problems.

The actual payment procedure is as follows:

1. *Declaration date.* On the **declaration date**—say, November 7—the directors meet and declare the regular dividend, issuing a statement similar to the following: "On November 7, 2008, the directors of Katz Corporation met and declared the regular quarterly dividend of 50 cents per share, payable to holders of record at the close of business on December 5, payment to be made on January 2, 2009." For accounting purposes, the declared dividend becomes an actual liability on the declaration date. If a balance sheet was constructed, the amount ($0.50) × (Number of shares outstanding) would appear as a current liability and retained earnings would be reduced by a like amount.

2. *Holder-of-record date.* At the close of business on the **holder-of-record date**, December 5, the company closes its stock transfer books and makes up a list of shareholders as of that date. If Katz Corporation is notified of the sale before 5 p.m. on December 5, the new owner will receive the dividend. However, if notification is received on or after December 6, the previous owner will receive the dividend check.

3. *Ex-dividend date.* Suppose Jean Buyer buys 100 shares of stock from John Seller on December 2. Will the company be notified of the transfer in time to list Buyer as the new owner and thus pay the dividend to her? To avoid conflict, the securities industry has set up a convention under which the right to the dividend remains with the stock until 2 business days prior to the holder-of-record date; on the second business day before that date, the right to the dividend no longer goes with the shares. The date when the right to the dividend leaves the stock is called the **ex-dividend date**. In this case, the ex-dividend date is 2 business days prior to December 5, or December 3:

Dividend goes with stock if it is bought on or before this date	December 2
Ex-dividend date: Buyer does not receive the dividend	December 3
Buyer does not receive the dividend	December 4
Holder-of-record date; not normally of concern to stockholder	December 5

Therefore, if Buyer is to receive the dividend, Buyer must buy the stock on or before December 2. If Buyer buys it on December 3 or later, Seller will receive the dividend because he or she will be the official holder of record.

Katz's dividend amounts to $0.50, so the ex-dividend date is important. Barring fluctuations in the stock market, we would normally expect the price of a stock to drop by approximately the amount of the dividend on the

Declaration Date
The date on which a firm's directors issue a statement declaring a dividend.

Holder-of-Record Date
If the company lists the stockholder as an owner on this date, then the stockholder receives the dividend.

Ex-Dividend Date
The date on which the right to the current dividend no longer accompanies a stock; it is usually 2 business days prior to the holder-of-record date.

ex-dividend date. Thus, if Katz closed at $30.50 on December 2, it would probably open at about $30 on December 3.[9]

4. *Payment date.* The company actually mails the checks to the holders of record on January 2, the **payment date.**

Payment Date
The date on which a firm actually mails dividend checks.

Explain the logic of the residual dividend model, the steps a firm would take to implement it, and the reason it is more likely to be used to establish a long-run payout target than to set the actual year-by-year payout ratio.

How do firms use long-run planning models to help set dividend policy?

Which are more critical to the dividend decision, earnings or cash flow? Explain.

Explain the procedures used to actually pay the dividend.

What is the ex-dividend date, and why is it important to investors?

A firm has a capital budget of $30 million, net income of $35 million, and a target capital structure of 45% debt and 55% equity. If the residual dividend policy is used, what is the firm's dividend payout ratio? **(52.86%)**

15-4 DIVIDEND REINVESTMENT PLANS

Dividend Reinvestment Plan (DRIP)
A plan that enables a stockholder to automatically reinvest dividends received back into the stock of the paying firm.

During the 1970s, most large companies instituted **dividend reinvestment plans (DRIPs)**, under which stockholders can automatically reinvest their dividends in the stock of the paying corporation.[10] Today most large companies offer DRIPs, but participation rates vary considerably. There are two types of DRIPs: (1) plans that involve only old, already-outstanding stock and (2) plans that involve newly issued stock. In either case, the stockholder must pay taxes on the amount of the dividends even though stock rather than cash is received.

Under both types of DRIPs, stockholders choose between continuing to receive dividend checks versus having the company use the dividends to buy more stock in the corporation for the investor. Under an "old stock" plan, the company gives the money that stockholders who elect to use the DRIP would

---

[9]Tax effects cause the price decline, on average, to be less than the full amount of the dividend. If you bought Katz's stock on December 2, you would receive the dividend, but you would almost immediately pay 15% of it in taxes. Thus, you would want to wait until December 3 to buy the stock if you thought you could get it for $0.50 less per share. Your reaction (and that of others) would influence stock prices around dividend payment dates. Here is what would happen:

1. Other things held constant, a stock's price should rise during the quarter, with the daily price increase (for Katz) equal to $0.50/90 = $0.005556. Therefore, if the price started at $30 just after its last ex-dividend date, it would rise to $30.50 on December 2.
2. In the absence of taxes, the stock's price would fall to $30 on December 3 and then start up as the next dividend accrual period began. Thus, over time, if everything else was held constant, the stock's price would follow a sawtooth pattern if it was plotted on a graph.
3. Because of taxes, the stock's price would neither rise by the full amount of the dividend nor fall by the full dividend amount when it goes ex-dividend.
4. The amount of the rise and subsequent fall would be the Dividend × (1 − T), where generally T = 15%, the tax rate on individual dividends.

See Edwin J. Elton and Martin J. Gruber, "Marginal Stockholder Tax Rates and the Clientele Effect," *Review of Economics and Statistics*, February 1970, pp. 68–74, for an interesting discussion of the subject.

[10]See Richard H. Pettway and R. Phil Malone, "Automatic Dividend Reinvestment Plans," *Financial Management*, Winter 1973, pp. 11–18, for an old but still excellent discussion of the subject.

have received to a bank, which acts as a trustee. The bank then uses the money to purchase the corporation's stock on the open market and allocates the shares purchased to the participating stockholders' accounts on a pro rata basis. The transactions costs of buying shares (brokerage costs) are low because of volume purchases, so these plans benefit small stockholders who do not need current cash dividends.

A "new stock" DRIP invests the dividends in newly issued stock; hence, these plans raise new capital for the firm. AT&T, Xerox, and many other companies have used new stock plans to raise substantial amounts of equity. No fees are charged to stockholders, and some companies have offered stock at discounts of 2% to 5% below the actual market price. The companies offer discounts because they would have incurred flotation costs if the new stock had been raised through investment bankers.

One interesting aspect of DRIPs is that they are forcing corporations to reexamine their basic dividend policies. A high participation rate in a DRIP suggests that stockholders might be better served if the firm simply reduced cash dividends, which would save stockholders some personal income taxes. Quite a few firms have surveyed their stockholders to learn more about their preferences and to find out how they would react to a change in dividend policy. A more rational approach to basic dividend policy decisions may emerge from this research. Companies switch from old stock to new stock DRIPs depending on their need for equity capital.

Many companies offering DRIPs have expanded their programs by moving to "open enrollment," whereby anyone can purchase the firm's stock directly and thus bypass brokers' commissions. ExxonMobil not only allows investors to buy their initial shares at no fee but also lets them pick up additional shares through automatic bank account withdrawals. Several plans, including ExxonMobil's, offer dividend reinvestment for individual retirement accounts; and some allow participants to invest weekly or monthly rather than on the quarterly dividend schedule. With all of these plans (and many others), stockholders can invest more than the dividends they are forgoing—they simply send a check to the company and buy shares without a brokerage commission.

SELF TEST

What are dividend reinvestment plans?

What are their advantages and disadvantages from both stockholders' and firms' perspectives?

15-5 SUMMARY OF FACTORS INFLUENCING DIVIDEND POLICY

In earlier sections, we described the theories of investor preference for dividends and the potential effects of dividend policy on the value of a firm. We also discussed the residual dividend model for setting a firm's long-run target payout ratio. In this section, we discuss several other factors that affect the dividend decision. These factors may be grouped into four broad categories: (1) constraints on dividend payments, (2) investment opportunities, (3) availability and cost of alternative sources of capital, and (4) effects of dividend policy on r_s. We discuss these factors next.

15-5a Constraints

1. *Bond indentures.* Debt contracts often limit dividend payments to earnings generated after the loan was granted. Also, debt contracts often stipulate that no dividends can be paid unless the current ratio, times-interest-earned ratio, and other safety ratios exceed stated minimums.

2. *Preferred stock restrictions.* Typically, common dividends cannot be paid if the company has omitted its preferred dividend. The preferred arrearages must be satisfied before common dividends can be resumed.

3. *Impairment of capital rule.* Dividend payments cannot exceed the balance sheet item "retained earnings." This legal restriction, known as the impairment of capital rule, is designed to protect creditors. Without the rule, a company that is in trouble might distribute most of its assets to stockholders and leave its debtholders out in the cold. (Liquidating dividends can be paid out of capital; but they must be indicated as such, and they must not reduce capital below the limits stated in debt contracts.)

4. *Availability of cash.* Cash dividends can be paid only with cash. Thus, a shortage of cash in the bank can restrict dividend payments. However, the ability to borrow can offset this factor.

5. *Penalty tax on improperly accumulated earnings.* To prevent wealthy individuals from using corporations to avoid personal taxes, the Tax Code provides for a special surtax on improperly accumulated income. Thus, if the IRS can demonstrate that a firm's dividend payout ratio is deliberately being held down to help its stockholders avoid personal taxes, the firm is subject to heavy penalties. This factor is relevant primarily to privately owned firms.

15-5b Investment Opportunities

1. *Number of profitable investment opportunities.* As we saw in our discussion of the residual model, if a firm has a large number of profitable investment opportunities, this will tend to produce a low target payout ratio and vice versa if the firm has few good investment opportunities.

2. *Possibility of accelerating or delaying projects.* The ability to accelerate or postpone projects permits a firm to adhere more closely to a stable dividend policy.

15-5c Alternative Sources of Capital

1. *Cost of selling new stock.* If a firm needs to finance a given level of investment, it can obtain equity by retaining earnings or by issuing new common stock. If flotation costs (including any negative signaling effects of a stock offering) are high, r_e will be well above r_s, making it better to set a low payout ratio and to finance through retention rather than through the sale of new common stock. On the other hand, a high dividend payout ratio is more feasible for a firm whose flotation costs are low. Flotation costs differ among firms—for example, the flotation percentage is especially high for small firms, so they tend to set low payout ratios.

2. *Ability to substitute debt for equity.* A firm can finance a given level of investment with debt or equity. As noted, low stock flotation costs permit a more flexible dividend policy because equity can be raised by retaining earnings or by selling new stock. A similar situation holds for debt policy: If the firm can adjust its debt ratio without raising its WACC sharply, it can pay the expected dividend, even if earnings fluctuate, by additional borrowing.

3. *Control.* If management is concerned about maintaining control, it may be reluctant to sell new stock; hence, the company may retain more earnings than

it otherwise would. However, if stockholders want higher dividends and a proxy fight looms, the dividend might be increased.

15-5d Effects of Dividend Policy on r_s

The effects of dividend policy on r_s may be considered in terms of four factors: (1) stockholders' desire for current versus future income, (2) the perceived riskiness of dividends versus capital gains, (3) the tax advantage of capital gains, and (4) the information content of dividends (signaling). We discussed each of those factors earlier, so we only note here that the importance of each factor varies from firm to firm depending on the makeup of its current and possible future stockholders.

It should be apparent that dividend policy decisions are based more on informed judgment than on quantitative analysis. Even so, to make rational dividend decisions, financial managers must take account of all the points discussed in the preceding sections.

SELF TEST

Identify the four broad sets of factors that affect dividend policy.

What constraints affect dividend policy?

How do investment opportunities affect dividend policy?

How does the availability and cost of outside capital affect dividend policy?

15-6 STOCK DIVIDENDS AND STOCK SPLITS

Stock dividends were originally used by firms that were short of cash in lieu of regular cash dividends. Today, though, the primary purpose of dividends is to increase the number of shares outstanding and thus to lower the stock's price in the market. Stock splits have a similar purpose.

Stock dividends and splits can best be explained through an example. We use Porter Electronic Controls Inc., a $700 million electronic components manufacturer, for this purpose. Since its inception, Porter's markets have been expanding and the company has enjoyed growth in sales and earnings. Some of its earnings have been paid out in dividends; but some also were retained each year, causing its earnings per share and the stock price to grow. The company began its life with only a few thousand shares outstanding; and, after some years of growth, each of Porter's shares had a very high EPS and DPS. When a "normal" P/E ratio was applied, the resulting market price was so high that few people could afford to buy a "round lot" of 100 shares. This limited demand for the stock and thus kept the firm's total market value below what it would have been if more shares at a lower price had been outstanding. To correct this situation, Porter "split its stock," as described in the next section.

15-6a Stock Splits

Although there is little empirical evidence to support the contention, there is nevertheless a widespread belief in financial circles that *an optimal price range* exists for stocks. *Optimal* means that if the price is within this range, the price/earnings ratio (and hence the firm's value) will be maximized. Many observers, including Porter's management, believe that the best range for most stocks is from $20 to $80 per share. Accordingly, if the price of Porter's stock rose to $80, management would probably declare a two-for-one **stock split**, thus doubling the number of

Up-to-date information about changes in stock splits and stock repurchases is now just a few clicks away. A good place to get started is The Online Investor at www.theonlineinvestor.com. The Online Investor's home page includes recent stock repurchase and stock split announcements at "Buybacks" and "Stock Splits."

Stock Split
An action taken by a firm to increase the number of shares outstanding, such as doubling the number of shares outstanding by giving each stockholder two new shares for each one formerly held.

shares outstanding, halving the earnings and dividends per share, and thereby lowering the stock price. Each stockholder would have more shares, but each share would be worth less. In Yogi Berra's terms (refer to Chapter 14's feature box "Yogi Berra on the M&M Proposition"), a stock split just divides the corporate value pie into more slices. If the post-split price was $40, Porter's stockholders would be exactly as well off as they were before the split. However, if the stock price was to stabilize above $40, stockholders would be better off. Stock splits can be of any size—for example, the stock can be split two-for-one, three-for-one, one-and-a-half-for-one, or any other way.[11]

15-6b Stock Dividends

Stock Dividend

A dividend paid in the form of additional shares of stock rather than in cash.

Stock dividends are similar to stock splits because they "divide the pie into smaller slices" without affecting the fundamental position of the current stockholders. On a 5% stock dividend, the holder of 100 shares would receive an additional 5 shares (without cost); on a 20% stock dividend, the same holder would receive 20 new shares; and so forth. Again, the total number of shares is increased; so earnings, dividends, and price per share all decline.

If a firm wants to reduce the price of its stock, should it use a stock split or a stock dividend? Stock splits are generally used after a sharp price run-up to produce a large price reduction. Stock dividends used on a regular annual basis keep the stock price more or less constrained. For example, if a firm's earnings and dividends were growing at about 10% per year, its stock price would tend to increase at about that same rate and it would soon be outside the desired trading range. A 10% annual stock dividend would maintain the stock price within the optimal trading range. Note, though, that because small stock dividends create bookkeeping problems and unnecessary expenses, firms use stock splits far more often than stock dividends.[12]

15-6c Effect on Stock Prices

If a company splits its stock or declares a stock dividend, will this increase the market value of its stock? Several empirical studies have addressed this question. Here is a summary of their findings.[13]

1. On average, the price of a company's stock rises shortly after it announces a stock split or dividend.

2. One reason that stock splits and stock dividends may lead to higher prices is that investors often take stock splits/dividends as signals of higher future

---

[11]*Reverse splits,* which reduce the shares outstanding, can also be used. For example, a company whose stock sells for $5 might employ a one-for-five reverse split, exchanging one new share for five old ones and raising the value of the shares to about $25, which is within the optimal price range. LTV Corporation did this after several years of losses had driven its stock price below the optimal range.

[12]Accountants treat stock splits and stock dividends somewhat differently. For example, in a two-for-one stock split, the number of shares outstanding is doubled and the par value is halved, and that is about all there is to it. With a stock dividend, a bookkeeping entry is made transferring "retained earnings" to "common stock." For example, if a firm had 1,000,000 shares outstanding, if the stock price was $10, and if it wanted to pay a 10% stock dividend, (1) each stockholder would be given 1 new share of stock for each 10 shares held and (2) the accounting entries would involve showing 100,000 more shares outstanding and transferring 100,000($10) = $1,000,000 from "retained earnings" to "common stock." The retained earnings transfer limits the size of stock dividends, but that is not important because companies can split their stock any way they choose.

[13]See Eugene F. Fama, Lawrence Fisher, Michael C. Jensen, and Richard Roll, "The Adjustment of Stock Prices to New Information," *International Economic Review,* February 1969, pp. 1–21; Mark S. Grinblatt, Ronald M. Masulis, and Sheridan Titman, "The Valuation Effects of Stock Splits and Stock Dividends," *Journal of Financial Economics,* December 1984, pp. 461–490; Ravi Dahr, William N. Goetzmann, Shane Shepherd, and Ning Zhu, "The Impact of Clientele Changes: Evidence from Stock Splits," Yale International Center for Finance Working Paper No. 03-14, March 2004; and Thomas E. Copeland, "Liquidity Changes Following Stock Splits," *Journal of Finance,* March 1979, pp. 115–141.

earnings. Because only companies whose managements believe that things look good tend to split their stocks, the announcement of a stock split is taken as a signal that earnings and cash dividends are likely to rise. Thus, the price increases associated with stock splits/dividends may be the result of a favorable signal for earnings and dividends.

3. If a company announces a stock split or dividend, its price will tend to rise. However, if during the next few months it does not announce an increase in earnings and dividends, the stock price generally will drop back to the earlier level. This supports the signaling effect discussed earlier.

4. By creating more shares and lowering the stock price, stock splits may also increase the stock's liquidity. This tends to increase the firm's value.

5. There also is evidence that stock splits change the mix of shareholders. The proportion of trades made by individual investors tends to increase after a stock split, whereas the proportion of trades made by institutional investors tends to fall. We are not sure how this affects the stock's value.

What do we conclude from all this? From a pure economic standpoint, stock dividends and splits are just additional pieces of paper. However, they provide management with a relatively low-cost way of signaling that the firm's prospects look good. Further, we should note that since few large, publicly owned stocks sell at prices above several hundred dollars, we simply do not know what the effect would be if Chevron, Microsoft, Xerox, Hewlett-Packard, and other highly successful firms had never split their stocks and consequently sold at prices in the thousands or even millions of dollars per share.[14]

SELF TEST

What are stock dividends and stock splits?

How do stock dividends and splits affect stock prices?

In what situation should a firm pay a stock dividend?

In what situation should a firm split its stock?

Suppose you have 100 common shares of Tillman Industries. The EPS is $4.00, the DPS is $2.00, and the stock sells for $60 per share. Now Tillman announces a two-for-one split. Immediately after the split, how many shares will you have, what will be the adjusted EPS and DPS, and what would you expect the stock price to be? **(200 shares; $2.00; $1.00; probably a little over $30)**

15-7 STOCK REPURCHASES

Several years ago, a *Fortune* article entitled "Beating the Market by Buying Back Stock" reported that during a one-year period, more than 600 major corporations repurchased significant amounts of their own stock. It also gave illustrations of some specific companies' repurchase programs and the effects of these programs on stock prices. The article's conclusion was that "buybacks have made a mint for shareholders who stay with the companies carrying them out."

---

[14]It is interesting to note that Berkshire Hathaway, which is controlled by billionaire Warren Buffett, one of the most successful financiers of the 20th century, has never had a stock split and its stock sold on the NYSE for $123,000 per share in May 2008. But in response to investment trusts that were being formed to sell fractional units of the stock—and thus, in effect, to split it—Buffett himself created a new class of Berkshire Hathaway stock (Class B) worth about 1/30 of a Class A (regular) share.

More recently, as we noted in the opening vignette, Microsoft announced plans to establish a dividend and to repurchase shares of its common stock. Microsoft's recent actions are part of a larger trend in which many leading companies have repurchased stock. How do stock repurchase programs work, and why have they become so prevalent over the past several years? We discuss these questions in the remainder of this section.

There are three principal types of **stock repurchases:** (1) situations where the firm has cash available for distribution to its stockholders and it distributes this cash by repurchasing shares rather than by paying cash dividends, (2) situations where the firm concludes that its capital structure is too heavily weighted with equity and it sells debt and uses the proceeds to buy back its stock, and (3) situations where the firm has issued options to employees and it uses open market repurchases to obtain stock for use when the options are exercised.

Stock that has been repurchased by a firm is called *treasury stock*. If some of the outstanding stock is repurchased, fewer shares will remain outstanding. Assuming that the repurchase does not adversely affect the firm's future earnings, the earnings per share on the remaining shares will increase, resulting in a higher market price per share. As a result, capital gains will have been substituted for dividends.

Stock Repurchase
A transaction in which a firm buys back shares of its own stock, thereby decreasing shares outstanding, increasing EPS, and often increasing the stock price.

15-7a The Effects of Stock Repurchases

Many companies have been repurchasing their stock in recent years. Until the 1980s, most repurchases amounted to a few million dollars. But in 1985, Phillips Petroleum announced plans for the largest repurchase on record at that time—81 million of its shares with a market value of $4.1 billion. Even more dramatic, in 2004, Microsoft announced plans for a $30 billion stock repurchase that would take place over a number of years. Other large repurchases have been made by Procter & Gamble, Dell, Home Depot, Texas Instruments, IBM, Coca-Cola, Teledyne, Atlantic Richfield, Goodyear, and Xerox. Indeed, since 1985, more shares have been repurchased than issued.

The effects of a repurchase can be illustrated with data on American Development Corporation (ADC). The company expects to earn $4.4 million in 2009, and 50% of this amount (or $2.2 million) has been allocated for distribution to common shareholders. There are 1.1 million shares outstanding, and the market price is $20 a share. ADC believes that it can use the $2.2 million to repurchase 100,000 of its shares through a tender offer at $22 a share or pay a cash dividend of $2 a share.[15]

The effect of the repurchase on the EPS and market price per share of the remaining stock can be analyzed as follows:

1. $\text{Current EPS} = \dfrac{\text{Total earnings}}{\text{Number of shares}} = \dfrac{\$4.4 \text{ million}}{1.1 \text{ million}} = \$4.00 \text{ per share}$

---

[15]Stock repurchases are generally made in one of three ways: (1) A publicly owned firm can simply buy its own stock through a broker on the open market. (2) It can make a *tender offer*, under which it permits stockholders to send in (that is, "tender") their shares to the firm in exchange for a specified price per share. In this case, the firm generally indicates that it will buy up to a specified number of shares within a particular time period (usually about 2 weeks); if more shares are tendered than the company wants to purchase, purchases are made on a pro rata basis. (3) The firm can purchase a block of shares from one large holder on a negotiated basis. If a negotiated purchase is employed, care must be taken to ensure that this one stockholder does not receive preferential treatment over other stockholders or that any preference given can be justified by "sound business reasons." A number of years ago Texaco's management was sued by stockholders who were unhappy over the company's repurchase of about $600 million of stock from the Bass Brothers at a substantial premium over the market price. The suit charged that Texaco's management, afraid the Bass Brothers would attempt a takeover, used the buyback to "get them off its back." Such payments have been dubbed *greenmail*.

2. P/E ratio $= \dfrac{\$20}{\$4} = 5\times$

3. EPS after repurchasing 100,000 shares $= \dfrac{\$4.4 \text{ million}}{1 \text{ million}} = \$4.40 \text{ per share}$

4. Expected market price after repurchase $= (P/E)(EPS) = (5)(\$4.40) = \$22 \text{ per share}$

It should be noted from this example that in any case, investors would receive before-tax benefits of $2 per share either in the form of a $2 cash dividend or a $2 increase in the stock price. This result would occur because we assumed, first, that shares could be repurchased at exactly $22 a share and, second, that the P/E ratio would remain constant. If shares could be bought for less than $22, the operation would be even better for *remaining* stockholders; but the reverse would hold if ADC had to pay more than $22 a share. Furthermore, the P/E ratio might change as a result of the repurchase operation, rising if investors viewed it favorably and falling if they viewed it unfavorably. Some factors that might affect P/E ratios are considered next.

15-7b Advantages of Repurchases

The advantages of repurchases are as follows:

1. A repurchase announcement may be viewed as a positive signal by investors because repurchases are often motivated by managements' belief that their firms' shares are undervalued.

2. The stockholders have a choice when the firm distributes cash by repurchasing stock—they can sell or not sell. With a cash dividend, on the other hand, stockholders must accept a dividend payment and pay the tax. Thus, those stockholders who need cash can sell back some of their shares, while those who do not want additional cash can simply retain their stock. From a tax standpoint, a repurchase permits both types of stockholders to get what they want.

3. A repurchase can remove a large block of stock that is "overhanging" the market and keeping the price per share down.

4. Dividends are "sticky" in the short run because managements are reluctant to raise the dividend if the increase cannot be maintained in the future—managements dislike cutting cash dividends because of the negative signal a cut gives. Therefore, if excess cash flows are expected to be temporary, managements may prefer to make distributions as share repurchases rather than to declare increased cash dividends that cannot be maintained.

5. Companies can use the residual model to set a target cash distribution level, then divide the distribution into a *dividend component* and a *repurchase component*. The dividend payout ratio will be relatively low; but the dividend itself will be relatively secure, and it will grow as a result of the declining number of shares outstanding. This gives the company more flexibility in adjusting the total distribution than if the entire distribution were in the form of cash dividends because repurchases can be varied from year to year without giving off adverse signals. This procedure has much to recommend it, and it is an important reason for the dramatic increase in the volume of share repurchases. IBM, FPL, and most other large companies use repurchases in this manner.

6. Repurchases can be used to produce large-scale changes in capital structure. For example, a number of years ago Consolidated Edison decided that its debt ratio was so low that it was not minimizing its WACC. It then borrowed $400 million and used the funds to repurchase shares of its common stock. This resulted in an immediate shift from a nonoptimal to an optimal capital structure.

7. Companies that use stock options as an important component of employee compensation can repurchase shares and then reissue those shares when employees exercise their options. This avoids having to issue new shares, which dilutes earnings per share. Microsoft and other high-tech companies have used this procedure in recent years.

15-7c Disadvantages of Repurchases

Disadvantages of repurchases include the following:

1. Stockholders may not be indifferent between dividends and capital gains, and the price of the stock might benefit more from cash dividends than from repurchases. Cash dividends are generally dependable, but repurchases are not.

2. The *selling* stockholders may not be fully aware of all the implications of a repurchase, or they may not have all the pertinent information about the corporation's present and future activities. This is especially true in situations where management has good reason to believe that the stock price is well below its intrinsic value. However, firms generally announce repurchase programs before embarking on them to avoid potential stockholder suits.

3. The corporation may pay too high a price for the repurchased stock, to the disadvantage of remaining stockholders. If its shares are not actively traded and if the firm seeks to acquire a relatively large amount of its stock, the price may be bid above its intrinsic value and then fall after the firm ceases its repurchase operations.

15-7d Conclusions on Stock Repurchases

When all the pros and cons on stock repurchases have been totaled, where do we stand? Our conclusions may be summarized as follows:

1. Because of the deferred tax on capital gains, repurchases have a tax advantage over dividends as a way to distribute income to stockholders. This advantage is reinforced by the fact that repurchases provide cash to stockholders who want cash but also allow those who do not need current cash to delay its receipt. On the other hand, dividends are more dependable and are thus better suited for those who need a steady source of income.

2. Because of signaling effects, companies should not pay fluctuating dividends—that would lower investors' confidence in the company and adversely affect its cost of equity and its stock price. However, cash flows vary over time, as do investment opportunities; so the "proper" dividend in the residual model sense varies. To get around this problem, a company can set its dividend at a level low enough to keep dividend payments from constraining operations and then use repurchases on a more or less regular basis to distribute excess cash. Such a procedure would provide regular, dependable dividends in addition to additional cash flows to those stockholders who want it.

3. Repurchases are also useful when a firm wants to make a large, rapid shift in its capital structure, wants to distribute cash from a one-time event such as the sale of a division, or wants to obtain shares for use in an employee stock option plan.

In earlier editions of this book, we argued that companies ought to be doing more repurchasing and paying out less cash as dividends. Increases in the size and frequency of repurchases in recent years suggest that companies have finally reached this same conclusion.

Explain how repurchases can (1) help stockholders hold down taxes and (2) help firms change their capital structures.

What is treasury stock?

What are three procedures a firm can use to repurchase its stock?

What are some advantages and disadvantages of stock repurchases?

How can stock repurchases help a company operate in accordance with the residual dividend model?

TYING IT ALL TOGETHER

Once a company becomes profitable, it must decide what to do with the cash it generates. It may choose to retain cash and use it to purchase additional operating assets, to repay outstanding debt, or to acquire other companies. Alternatively, it may choose to return cash to shareholders. Keep in mind that every dollar that management chooses to retain is a dollar that shareholders could have received and invested elsewhere. Therefore, managers should retain earnings if and only if they can invest the money within the firm and earn more than stockholders can earn outside the firm. Consequently, high-growth companies with many good projects tend to retain a high percentage of earnings, whereas mature companies with a great deal of cash but limited investment opportunities tend to have generous cash distribution policies.

SELF-TEST QUESTIONS AND PROBLEMS
(Solutions Appear in Appendix A)

ST-1 **KEY TERMS** Define each of the following terms:
   a. Target payout ratio; optimal dividend policy
   b. Dividend irrelevance theory; bird-in-the-hand fallacy
   c. Information content (signaling) hypothesis; clientele effect; signal; clienteles
   d. Residual dividend model
   e. Low-regular-dividend-plus-extras
   f. Declaration date; holder-of-record date; ex-dividend date; payment date
   g. Dividend reinvestment plan (DRIP)
   h. Stock split; stock dividend
   i. Stock repurchase

ST-2 **ALTERNATIVE DIVIDEND POLICIES** Components Manufacturing Corporation (CMC) has an all-common-equity capital structure. It has 200,000 shares of $2 par value common stock outstanding. When CMC's founder, who was also its research director and most successful inventor, retired unexpectedly to the South Pacific in late 2008, CMC was left suddenly and permanently with materially lower growth expectations and relatively few attractive new investment opportunities. Unfortunately, there was no way to replace the founder's contributions to the firm. Previously, CMC found it necessary to plow back most of its earnings to finance growth, which averaged 12% per year. Future growth at a 6% rate is considered realistic, but that level would call for an increase in the dividend payout. Further, it now appears that new investment projects with at least the 14% rate of return required by CMC's stockholders ($r_s = 14\%$) would amount to only $800,000 for 2009 compared to a projected $2,000,000 of net income. If the existing 20% dividend payout was continued, retained earnings would be $1.6 million in 2009; but as noted, investments that yield the 14% cost of capital would amount to only $800,000.

The one encouraging point is that the high earnings from existing assets are expected to continue, and net income of $2 million is still expected for 2009. Given the dramatically changed circumstances, CMC's management is reviewing the firm's dividend policy.

a.   Assuming that the acceptable 2009 investment projects would be financed entirely by earnings retained during the year and assuming that CMC uses the residual dividend model, calculate DPS in 2009.

b.   What payout ratio does your answer to Part a imply for 2009?

c.   If a 60% payout ratio is maintained for the foreseeable future, what is your estimate of the present market price of the common stock? How does this compare with the market price that should have prevailed under the assumptions existing just before the news about the founder's retirement? If the two values of P_0 are different, comment on why.

d.   What would happen to the stock price if the old 20% payout was continued? Assume that if this payout is maintained, the average rate of return on the retained earnings will fall to 7.5% and the new growth rate will be as follows:

$$g = (1.0 - \text{Payout ratio})(\text{ROE})$$
$$= (1.0 - 0.2)(7.5\%)$$
$$= (0.8)(7.5\%) = 6.0\%$$

QUESTIONS

15-1   Discuss the pros and cons of having the directors formally announce what a firm's dividend policy will be in the future.

15-2   The cost of retained earnings is less than the cost of new outside equity capital. Consequently, it is totally irrational for a firm to sell a new issue of stock and to pay dividends during the same year. Discuss the meaning of those statements.

15-3   Would it ever be rational for a firm to borrow money in order to pay dividends? Explain.

15-4   Modigliani and Miller (MM) on the one hand and Gordon and Lintner (GL) on the other hand have expressed strong views regarding the effect of dividend policy on a firm's cost of capital and value.

a.   In essence, what are MM's and GL's views regarding the effect of dividend policy on the cost of capital and stock prices?

b.   How could MM use the information content, or signaling, hypothesis to counter their opponents' arguments? If you were debating MM, how would you counter them?

c.   How could MM use the clientele effect concept to counter their opponents' arguments? If you were debating MM, how would you counter them?

15-5   How would each of the following changes tend to affect aggregate (that is, the average for all corporations) payout ratios, other things held constant? Explain your answers.

a.   An increase in the personal income tax rate

b.   A liberalization of depreciation for federal income tax purposes—that is, faster tax write-offs

c.   A rise in interest rates

d.   An increase in corporate profits

e.   A decline in investment opportunities

f.   Permission for corporations to deduct dividends for tax purposes as they now deduct interest charges

g.   A change in the Tax Code so that realized and unrealized capital gains in any year are taxed at the same rate as dividends

15-6   One position expressed in the financial literature is that firms set their dividends as a residual after using income to support new investment.

   a.   Explain what a residual dividend policy implies, illustrating your answer with a table showing how different investment opportunities can lead to different dividend payout ratios.

   b.   Think back to Chapter 14 where we considered the relationship between capital structure and the cost of capital. If the WACC-versus-debt-ratio plot was shaped like a sharp V, would this have a different implication for the importance of setting dividends according to the residual policy than if the plot was shaped like a shallow bowl (a flattened U)?

15-7   Executive salaries have been shown to be more closely correlated to the size of the firm than to its profitability. If a firm's board of directors is controlled by management rather than outside directors, this might result in the firm's retaining more earnings than can be justified from the stockholders' point of view. Discuss those statements, being sure (a) to discuss the interrelationships among cost of capital, investment opportunities, and new investment and (b) to explain the implied relationship between dividend policy and stock prices.

15-8   What is the difference between a stock dividend and a stock split? As a stockholder, would you prefer to see your company declare a 100% stock dividend or a two-for-one split? Assume that either action is feasible.

15-9   Most firms like to have their stock selling at a high P/E ratio, and they also like to have extensive public ownership (many different shareholders). Explain how stock dividends or stock splits may help achieve those goals.

15-10   Indicate whether the following statements are true or false. If the statement is false, explain why.

   a.   If a firm repurchases its stock in the open market, the shareholders who tender the stock are subject to capital gains taxes.

   b.   If you own 100 shares in a company's stock and the company's stock splits 2-for-1, you will own 200 shares in the company following the split.

   c.   Some dividend reinvestment plans increase the amount of equity capital available to the firm.

   d.   The Tax Code encourages companies to pay a large percentage of their net income in the form of dividends.

   e.   If your company has established a clientele of investors who prefer large dividends, the company is unlikely to adopt a residual dividend policy.

   f.   If a firm follows a residual dividend policy, holding all else constant, its dividend payout will tend to rise whenever the firm's investment opportunities improve.

PROBLEMS

Easy Problems 1–3

15-1   **RESIDUAL DIVIDEND MODEL**   Axel Telecommunications has a target capital structure that consists of 70% debt and 30% equity. The company anticipates that its capital budget for the upcoming year will be $3,000,000. If Axel reports net income of $2,000,000 and it follows a residual dividend payout policy, what will be its dividend payout ratio?

15-2   **STOCK SPLIT**   Gamma Medical's stock trades at $90 a share. The company is contemplating a 3-for-2 stock split. Assuming that the stock split will have no effect on the market value of its equity, what will be the company's stock price following the stock split?

15-3   **STOCK REPURCHASES**   Beta Industries has net income of $2,000,000, and it has 1,000,000 shares of common stock outstanding. The company's stock currently trades at $32 a share. Beta is considering a plan in which it will use available cash to repurchase 20% of its shares in the open market. The repurchase is expected to have no effect on net income or the company's P/E ratio. What will be Beta's stock price following the stock repurchase?

Intermediate Problems 4–6

15-4   **STOCK SPLIT**   After a 5-for-1 stock split, Strasburg Company paid a dividend of $0.75 per new share, which represents a 9% increase over last year's pre-split dividend. What was last year's dividend per share?

15-5   **EXTERNAL EQUITY FINANCING**   Northern Pacific Heating and Cooling Inc. has a 6-month backlog of orders for its patented solar heating system. To meet this demand, management plans to expand production capacity by 40% with a $10 million investment in plant and machinery. The firm wants to maintain a 40% debt-to-total-assets ratio in its capital structure. It also wants to maintain its past dividend policy of distributing 45% of last year's net income. In 2008, net income was $5 million. How much external equity must Northern Pacific seek at the beginning of 2009 to expand capacity as desired? Assume that the firm uses only debt and common equity in its capital structure.

15-6   **RESIDUAL DIVIDEND MODEL**   Welch Company is considering three independent projects, each of which requires a $5 million investment. The estimated internal rate of return (IRR) and cost of capital for these projects are presented here:

Project H (high risk):	Cost of capital = 16%	IRR = 20%
Project M (medium risk):	Cost of capital = 12%	IRR = 10%
Project L (low risk):	Cost of capital = 8%	IRR = 9%

Note that the projects' costs of capital vary because the projects have different levels of risk. The company's optimal capital structure calls for 50% debt and 50% common equity. Welch expects to have net income of $7,287,500. If Welch establishes its dividends from the residual model, what will be its payout ratio?

Challenging Problems 7–9

15-7   **DIVIDENDS**   Bowles Sporting Inc. is prepared to report the following income statement (shown in thousands of dollars) for the year 2009.

Sales	$15,200
Operating costs including depreciation	11,900
EBIT	$ 3,300
Interest	300
EBT	$ 3,000
Taxes (40%)	1,200
Net income	$ 1,800

Prior to reporting this income statement, the company wants to determine its annual dividend. The company has 500,000 shares of stock outstanding, and its stock trades at $48 per share.

a.   The company had a 40% dividend payout ratio in 2008. If Bowles wants to maintain this payout ratio in 2009, what will be its per-share dividend in 2009?

b.   If the company maintains this 40% payout ratio, what will be the current dividend yield on the company's stock?

c.   The company reported net income of $1.5 million in 2008. Assume that the number of shares outstanding has remained constant. What was the company's per-share dividend in 2008?

d.   As an alternative to maintaining the same dividend payout ratio, Bowles is considering maintaining the same per-share dividend in 2009 that it paid in 2008. If it chooses this policy, what will be the company's dividend payout ratio in 2009?

e.   Assume that the company is interested in dramatically expanding its operations and that this expansion will require significant amounts of capital. The company would like to avoid transactions costs involved in issuing new equity. Given this scenario, would it make more sense for the company to maintain a constant dividend payout ratio or to maintain the same per-share dividend?

15-8   **ALTERNATIVE DIVIDEND POLICIES**   Rubenstein Bros. Clothing is expecting to pay an annual dividend per share of $0.75 out of annual earnings per share of $2.25. Currently, Rubenstein Bros.' stock is selling for $12.50 per share. Adhering to the company's target capital structure, the firm has $10 million in assets, of which 40% is funded by debt. Assume that the firm's book value of equity equals its market value. In past years, the firm has earned a return on equity (ROE) of 18%, which is expected to continue this year and into the foreseeable future.

a.   Based on that information, what long-run growth rate can the firm be expected to maintain? (Hint: g = Retention rate × ROE.)

b.   What is the stock's required return?

c. If the firm changed its dividend policy and paid an annual dividend of $1.50 per share, financial analysts would predict that the change in policy will have no effect on the firm's stock price or ROE. Therefore, what must be the firm's new expected long-run growth rate and required return?

d. Suppose instead that the firm has decided to proceed with its original plan of disbursing $0.75 per share to shareholders, but the firm intends to do so in the form of a stock dividend rather than a cash dividend. The firm will allot new shares based on the current stock price of $12.50. In other words, for every $12.50 in dividends due to shareholders, a share of stock will be issued. How large will the stock dividend be relative to the firm's current market capitalization? (Hint: Remember that market capitalization = P_0 × number of shares outstanding.)

e. If the plan in Part d is implemented, how many new shares of stock will be issued and by how much will the company's earnings per share be diluted?

15-9 **ALTERNATIVE DIVIDEND POLICIES** In 2008, Keenan Company paid dividends totaling $3,600,000 on net income of $10.8 million. Note that 2008 was a normal year and that for the past 10 years, earnings have grown at a constant rate of 10%. However, in 2009, earnings are expected to jump to $14.4 million and the firm expects to have profitable investment opportunities of $8.4 million. It is predicted that Keenan will not be able to maintain the 2009 level of earnings growth—the high 2009 earnings level is attributable to an exceptionally profitable new product line introduced that year—and the company will return to its previous 10% growth rate. Keenan's target capital structure is 40% debt and 60% equity.

a. Calculate Keenan's total dividends for 2009 assuming that it follows each of the following policies:

(1) Its 2009 dividend payment is set to force dividends to grow at the long-run growth rate in earnings.

(2) It continues the 2008 dividend payout ratio.

(3) It uses a pure residual dividend policy (40% of the $8.4 million investment is financed with debt and 60% with common equity).

(4) It employs a regular-dividend-plus-extras policy, with the regular dividend being based on the long-run growth rate and the extra dividend being set according to the residual policy.

b. Which of the preceding policies would you recommend? Restrict your choices to the ones listed but justify your answer.

c. Assume that investors expect Keenan to pay total dividends of $9,000,000 in 2009 and to have the dividend grow at 10% after 2009. The stock's total market value is $180 million. What is the company's cost of equity?

d. What is Keenan's long-run average return on equity? [Hint: g = Retention rate × ROE = (1.0 – Payout rate)(ROE).]

e. Does a 2009 dividend of $9,000,000 seem reasonable in view of your answers to Parts c and d? If not, should the dividend be higher or lower? Explain your answer.

COMPREHENSIVE/SPREADSHEET PROBLEM

15-10 **RESIDUAL DIVIDEND MODEL** Buena Terra Corporation is reviewing its capital budget for the upcoming year. It has paid a $3.00 dividend per share (DPS) for the past several years, and its shareholders expect the dividend to remain constant for the next several years. The company's target capital structure is 60% equity and 40% debt, it has 1,000,000 shares of common equity outstanding, and its net income is $8 million. The company forecasts that it will require $10 million to fund all of its profitable (that is, positive NPV) projects for the upcoming year.

a. If Buena Terra follows the residual dividend model, how much retained earnings will it need to fund its capital budget?

b. If Buena Terra follows the residual dividend model, what will be the company's dividend per share and payout ratio for the upcoming year?

c. If Buena Terra maintains its current $3.00 DPS for next year, how much retained earnings will be available for the firm's capital budget?

d. Can the company maintain its current capital structure, maintain the $3.00 DPS, and maintain a $10 million capital budget without having to raise new common stock?

e. Suppose that Buena Terra's management is firmly opposed to cutting the dividend; that is, it wants to maintain the $3.00 dividend for the next year. Also assume that the company was committed to funding all profitable projects and was willing to issue more debt (along with the available retained earnings) to help finance the company's capital budget. Assume that the resulting change in capital structure has a minimal effect on the company's composite cost of capital so that the capital budget remains at $10 million. What portion of this year's capital budget would have to be financed with debt?

f. Suppose once again that Buena Terra's management wants to maintain the $3.00 DPS. In addition, the company wants to maintain its target capital structure (60% equity and 40% debt) and maintain its $10 million capital budget. What is the minimum dollar amount of new common stock that the company would have to issue to meet each of its objectives?

g. Now consider the case where Buena Terra's management wants to maintain the $3.00 DPS and its target capital structure, but it wants to avoid issuing new common stock. The company is willing to cut its capital budget to meet its other objectives. Assuming that the company's projects are divisible, what will be the company's capital budget for the next year?

h. What actions can a firm that follows the residual dividend policy take when its forecasted retained earnings are less than the retained earnings required to fund its capital budget?

INTEGRATED CASE

SOUTHEASTERN STEEL COMPANY

15-11 **DIVIDEND POLICY** Southeastern Steel Company (SSC) was formed 5 years ago to exploit a new continuous casting process. SSC's founders, Donald Brown and Margo Valencia, had been employed in the research department of a major integrated-steel company; but when that company decided against using the new process (which Brown and Valencia had developed), they decided to strike out on their own. One advantage of the new process was that it required relatively little capital compared to the typical steel company, so Brown and Valencia have been able to avoid issuing new stock and thus own all of the shares. However, SSC has now reached the stage in which outside equity capital is necessary if the firm is to achieve its growth targets yet still maintain its target capital structure of 60% equity and 40% debt. Therefore, Brown and Valencia have decided to take the company public. Until now, Brown and Valencia have paid themselves reasonable salaries but routinely reinvested all after-tax earnings in the firm; so dividend policy has not been an issue. However, before talking with potential outside investors, they must decide on a dividend policy.

Assume that you were recently hired by Arthur Adamson & Company (AA), a national consulting firm, which has been asked to help SSC prepare for its public offering. Martha Millon, the senior AA consultant in your group, has asked you to make a presentation to Brown and Valencia in which you review the theory of dividend policy and discuss the following questions:

a. (1) What is meant by the term *dividend policy*?

(2) Explain briefly the dividend irrelevance theory that was put forward by Modigliani and Miller. What were the key assumptions underlying their theory?

(3) Why do some investors prefer high-dividend-paying stocks, while other investors prefer stocks that pay low or nonexistent dividends?

b. Discuss (1) the information content, or signaling, hypothesis; (2) the clientele effect; and (3) their effects on dividend policy.

c. (1) Assume that SSC has an $800,000 capital budget planned for the coming year. You have determined that its present capital structure (60% equity and 40% debt) is optimal, and its net income is forecasted at $600,000. Use the residual dividend model approach to determine SSC's total dollar dividend and payout ratio. In the process, explain how the residual dividend model works. Then explain what would happen if net income was forecasted at $400,000 and at $800,000.

    (2) In general terms, how would a change in investment opportunities affect the payout ratio under the residual payment policy?

    (3) What are the advantages and disadvantages of the residual policy? (Hint: Don't neglect signaling and clientele effects.)

d. What is a dividend reinvestment plan (DRIP), and how does it work?

e. Describe the series of steps that most firms take in setting dividend policy in practice.

f. What are stock repurchases? Discuss the advantages and disadvantages of a firm's repurchasing its own shares.

g. What are stock dividends and stock splits? What are the advantages and disadvantages of stock dividends and stock splits?

THOMSON ONE | Business School Edition

Access the Thomson ONE problems through the CengageNOW™ web site. Use the Thomson ONE—Business School Edition online database to work this chapter's questions.

Microsoft's Dividend Policy

In this chapter's opening vignette, we discussed Microsoft's decision to establish a dividend payout policy in 2003. Let's find out what has happened to Microsoft's (MSFT) dividend policy since the time of this announcement. We can address this issue by relying on the data that are provided in Thomson ONE.

Discussion Questions

1. To get information about MSFT's dividend policy, enter its ticker quote (MSFT-O) and select OVERVIEW> FULL REPORTS>THOMSON FULL REPORTS>FULL COMPANY REPORT. Click on STOCK & EARNINGS DATA and scroll down to the "Annual Historical Data" section. What has happened to MSFT's dividend per share, dividend yield, and dividend payout over the past 5 years? Provide an explanation for what took place.

2. Compare this information with other firms in the same industry. To see how MSFT stacks up against its peers, select COMPARABLES>OVERVIEWS>PER SHARE DATA to get MSFT's peers' last annual dividends. Accessing COMPARABLES>OVERVIEWS>ABSOLUTE RANKINGS will give their dividend yields. You can also get this information from the VALUATION COMPARISON in this same section. Has MSFT behaved differently from its peers, or have there been industry-wide shifts?

3. Refer back to the FULL COMPANY REPORT used in Question 1. Manually plot earnings and dividends over time. In the text, we point out that dividends are often more stable than earnings. Do you see a similar pattern for MSFT? Explain.

4. In the "Interim Financial Data" section of the FULL COMPANY REPORT, identify the dividend declared date, ex-date, and pay date. Explain the significance of those dates. Go back to "Overview" and access the "Interactive Price Chart." Can you observe price shifts around these dates? Explain what price shifts you might expect to see.

5. Investors are more concerned with future dividends than historical dividends, so go to ESTIMATES and scroll down to the "Consensus Estimates" section. Click on the "Available Measures" menu to toggle between earnings per share and dividends per share. How do analysts expect MSFT's payout policy to behave in the future?

6. Refer back to the FULL COMPANY REPORT and scroll down to the "5 Yr Annual Balance Sheet" section. Does it appear that MSFT has been repurchasing any stock, or has it been issuing new stock?

PART 6

WORKING CAPITAL MANAGEMENT AND FINANCIAL FORECASTING

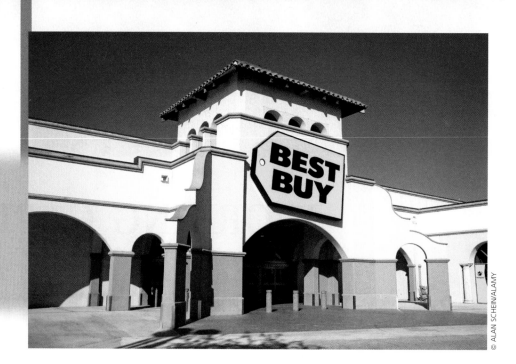

CHAPTER

16 Working Capital Management

Best Buy Manages Its Working Capital Well

Best Buy Company, North America's largest consumer electronics retailer, has performed extremely well over the past decade. Its stock sold for $50 in late 2007, up from $2 only 10 years earlier. This excellent performance stemmed from sound financial and operating practices, especially its working capital management, the focus of this chapter.

Working capital management involves finding the optimal levels for cash, marketable securities, accounts receivable, and inventory and then financing that working capital for the least cost. Most of Best Buy's customers use credit cards, so neither in-store cash nor accounts receivable is significant. Therefore, Best Buy's working capital policy focuses on its inventories. To maintain sales, its stores must be well stocked with the goods customers are seeking at the time they are shopping. This involves determining what new products are hot, determining where they can be obtained at the lowest cost, and delivering them to stores in a timely manner.

Dramatic improvements in communications and computer technology have transformed the way Best Buy manages its inventories. It now collects real-time data from each store on how each product is selling, and its computers place orders automatically to keep the shelves full. Moreover, if sales of an item are slipping, prices are lowered to reduce stocks of that item before the situation gets so bad that drastic price cuts are necessary. After studying this chapter, you will have a good understanding of how working capital should be managed so as to maximize profits and stock prices.

PUTTING THINGS IN PERSPECTIVE

About 50% of the typical industrial or retail firm's assets are held as working capital, and many students' first jobs focus on working capital management. This is particularly true in smaller businesses, where the majority of new jobs are being created. When you finish this chapter, you should be able to:

- Explain how different amounts of current assets and current liabilities affect firms' profitability and thus their stock prices.
- Discuss how the cash conversion cycle is determined, how the cash budget is constructed, and how each is used in working capital management.
- Explain how companies decide on the proper amount of each current asset—cash, marketable securities, accounts receivable, and inventory.
- Discuss how companies set their credit policies and explain the effect of credit policy on sales and profits.
- Describe how the costs of trade credit, bank loans, and commercial paper are determined and how that information impacts decisions for financing working capital.
- Explain how companies use security to lower their costs of short-term credit.

16-1 BACKGROUND ON WORKING CAPITAL

The term *working capital* originated with the old Yankee peddler who would load up his wagon and go off to peddle his wares. The merchandise was called "working capital" because it was what he actually sold, or "turned over," to produce his profits. The wagon and horse were his fixed assets. He generally owned the horse and wagon (so they were financed with "equity" capital), but he bought his merchandise on credit (that is, by borrowing from his supplier) or with money borrowed from a bank. Those loans were called *working capital loans*, and they had to be repaid after each trip to demonstrate that the peddler was solvent and worthy of a new loan. Banks that followed this procedure were said to be employing "sound banking practices." The more trips the peddler took per year, the faster his working capital turned over and the greater his profits.

This concept can be applied to modern businesses, as we demonstrate in this chapter. We begin with a review of two basic definitions that were covered in Chapter 3:

1. **Working capital.** Current assets are often called *working capital* because these assets "turn over" (i.e., are used and then replaced all during the year).[1]
2. **Net working capital.** When a firm buys inventory on credit, its suppliers in effect lend it the money used to finance the inventory. The firm could have borrowed from its bank or sold stock to obtain the money, but it received the funds from its suppliers. These loans are recorded as accounts payable, and they are typically "free" in the sense that they do not bear interest. Similarly, Allied pays its workers every 2 weeks and pays taxes quarterly, so its labor force and the tax authorities provide it with loans equal to its accrued wages and taxes. If we subtract the sum of payables plus accruals from current assets, the difference is called *net working capital*, which represents the amount of

---

[1]Any current assets not used in normal operations, such as excess cash held to pay for a plant under construction, are deducted and thus not included in working capital. Allied Food Products uses all of its current assets in operations.

money that the firm must obtain from non-free sources to carry its current assets. Here is the 2008 net working capital for Allied Food Products, the firm we discussed in Chapter 3:

$$\text{Net working capital} = (\text{Current assets}) - (\text{Payables} + \text{Accruals})$$
$$= \$1,000 - (\$60 + \$140) = \$800 \text{ million}$$

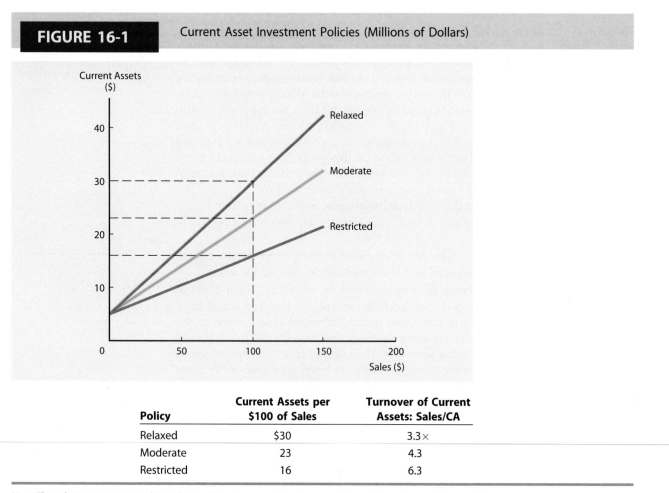

SELF TEST

How did the term *working capital* originate?

Differentiate between working capital and net working capital.

16-2 CURRENT ASSET INVESTMENT POLICIES

In this section, we discuss how the amount of current assets held affects profitability. To begin, Figure 16-1 shows three alternative policies regarding the size of current asset holdings. The top line has the steepest slope, which indicates that the

FIGURE 16-1   Current Asset Investment Policies (Millions of Dollars)

Policy	Current Assets per $100 of Sales	Turnover of Current Assets: Sales/CA
Relaxed	$30	3.3×
Moderate	23	4.3
Restricted	16	6.3

Note: The sales/current assets relationship is shown here as being linear, but the relationship could be curvilinear.

firm holds a great deal of cash, marketable securities, receivables, and inventories relative to its sales. When receivables are high, the firm has a liberal credit policy, which results in a high level of accounts receivable. This is a **relaxed investment policy**. On the other hand, when a firm has a **restricted** (or *tight* or *"lean-and-mean"*) **investment policy**, holdings of current assets are minimized. A **moderate investment policy** lies between the two extremes.

We can use the DuPont equation to demonstrate how working capital management affects ROE:

$$\text{ROE} = \text{Profit margin} \times \text{Total assets turnover} \times \text{Leverage factor}$$

$$= \frac{\text{Net income}}{\text{Sales}} \times \frac{\text{Sales}}{\text{Assets}} \times \frac{\text{Assets}}{\text{Equity}}$$

A restricted (lean-and-mean) policy means a low level of assets (hence, a high total assets turnover ratio), which results in a high ROE, other things held constant. However, this policy also exposes the firm to risks because shortages can lead to work stoppages, unhappy customers, and serious long-run problems. The relaxed policy minimizes such operating problems; but it results in a low turnover, which in turn lowers ROE. The moderate policy falls between the two extremes. The optimal strategy is the one that maximizes the firm's long-run earnings and the stock's intrinsic value.

Note that changing technologies can lead to changes in the optimal policy. For example, when a new technology makes it possible for a manufacturer to produce a given product in 5 rather than 10 days, work-in-progress inventories can be cut in half. Similarly, retailers such as Wal-Mart and Home Depot have inventory management systems in which bar codes on all merchandise are read at the cash register. This information is transmitted electronically to a computer that records the remaining stock of each item, and the computer automatically places an order with the supplier's computer when the stock falls to a specified level. This process lowers the "safety stocks" that would otherwise be necessary to avoid running out of stock, which lowers inventories to profit-maximizing levels.

Relaxed Current Asset Investment Policy
Relatively large amounts of cash, marketable securities, and inventories are carried; and a liberal credit policy results in a high level of receivables.

Restricted Current Asset Investment Policy
Holdings of cash, marketable securities, inventories, and receivables are constrained.

Moderate Current Asset Investment Policy
Between the relaxed and restricted policies.

SELF TEST

Identify and explain three alternative current asset investment policies.

Use the DuPont equation to show how working capital policy affects a firm's expected ROE.

16-3 CURRENT ASSET FINANCING POLICIES

Investments in current assets must be financed; and the primary sources of funds include bank loans, credit from suppliers (accounts payable), accrued liabilities, long-term debt, and common equity. Each of those sources has advantages and disadvantages, so each firm must decide which sources are best for it.

To begin, note that most businesses experience seasonal and/or cyclical fluctuations. For example, construction firms tend to peak in the summer, retailers peak around Christmas, and the manufacturers who supply both construction companies and retailers follow related patterns. Similarly, the sales of virtually all businesses increase when the economy is strong; hence, they build up current assets at those times but let inventories and receivables fall when the economy weakens. Note, though, that current assets rarely drop to zero—companies maintain some **permanent current assets**, which are the current assets needed at the low point of the business cycle. Then as sales increase during an upswing, current assets are increased, and these extra current assets are defined as **temporary current assets** as opposed to permanent current assets. The way these two types of current assets are financed is called the firm's **current assets financing policy**.

16-3a Maturity Matching, or "Self-Liquidating," Approach

The **maturity matching, or "self-liquidating," approach** calls for matching asset and liability maturities as shown in Panel a of Figure 16-2. All of the fixed assets plus the permanent current assets are financed with long-term capital, but temporary current assets are financed with short-term debt. Inventory expected to be sold in 30 days would be financed with a 30-day bank loan, a machine expected to last for 5 years would be financed with a 5-year loan, a 20-year building would be financed with a 20-year mortgage bond, and so forth. Actually, two factors prevent an exact maturity matching: (1) There is uncertainty about the lives of assets. For example, a firm might finance inventories with a 30-day bank loan, expecting to sell the inventories and use the cash to retire the loan. But if sales are slow, the cash would not be forthcoming and the firm might not be able to pay off the loan when it matures. (2) Some common equity must be used, and common equity has no maturity. Still, when a firm attempts to match asset and liability maturities, this is defined as a *moderate current asset financing policy*.

16-3b Aggressive Approach

Panel b of Figure 16-2 illustrates the situation for a more aggressive firm that finances some of its permanent assets with short-term debt. Note that we used the term *relatively* in the title of Panel b because there can be different *degrees* of aggressiveness. For example, the dashed line in Panel b could have been drawn *below* the line designating fixed assets, indicating that all of the current assets—both permanent and temporary—and part of the fixed assets were financed with short-term credit. This policy would be a highly aggressive, extremely nonconservative position; and the firm would be subject to dangers from loan renewal as well as problems with rising interest rates. However, short-term interest rates are generally lower than long-term rates, and some firms are willing to sacrifice some safety for the chance of higher profits.

The reason for adopting the aggressive policy is to take advantage of the fact that the yield curve is generally upward-sloping; hence, short-term rates are generally lower than long-term rates. However, a strategy of financing long-term assets with short-term debt is really quite risky. To illustrate, suppose a company borrows $1 million on a 1-year basis and uses the funds to buy machinery that will lower labor costs by $200,000 per year for 10 years.[2] Cash flows from the equipment would not be sufficient to pay off the loan at the end of only 1 year, so the loan would have to be renewed. If the company encountered temporary financial problems, the lender might refuse to renew the loan, which could lead to bankruptcy. Had the firm matched maturities and financed the plant with a 10-year

---

[2]We are oversimplifying here. Few lenders would explicitly lend money for 1 year to finance a 10-year asset. What would actually happen is that the firm would borrow on a 1-year basis for "general corporate purposes" and then use the money to purchase the 10-year machinery.

FIGURE 16-2 Alternative Current Asset Financing Policies

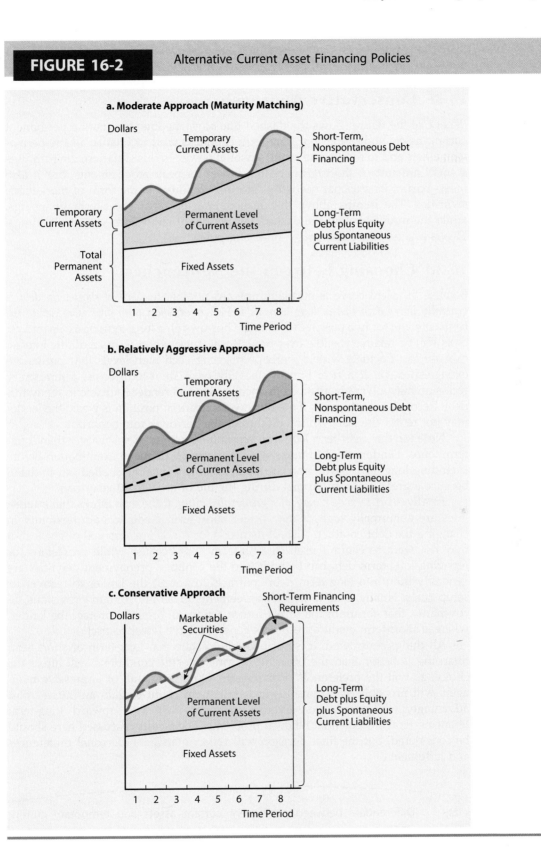

loan, the required loan payments would have been better matched with the cash flows and the loan renewal problem would not have arisen.

16-3c Conservative Approach

Panel c of the figure shows the dashed line *above* the line designating permanent current assets, indicating that long-term capital is used to finance all the permanent assets and to meet some of the seasonal needs. In this situation, the firm uses a small amount of short-term credit to meet its peak requirements, but it also meets part of its seasonal needs by "storing liquidity" in the form of marketable securities. The humps above the dashed line represent short-term financings, while the troughs below the dashed line represent short-term security holdings. This is a very safe, conservative financing policy.

16-3d Choosing between the Approaches

Because the yield curve is normally upward-sloping, the *cost of short-term debt is generally lower than that of long-term debt.* However, *short-term debt is riskier to the borrowing firm* for two reasons: (1) If a firm borrows on a long-term basis, its interest costs will be relatively stable over time. But if it uses short-term credit, its interest expense can fluctuate widely, perhaps reaching such high levels that profits are extinguished. (2) If a firm borrows heavily on a short-term basis, a temporary recession may adversely affect its financial ratios and render it unable to repay this debt. Recognizing this point, if the borrower's financial position is weak, the lender may not renew the loan, which could force the borrower into bankruptcy.

Note too that *short-term loans can generally be negotiated much faster* than long-term loans. Lenders need to make a more thorough financial examination before extending long-term credit, and the loan agreement must be spelled out in detail because a great deal can happen during the life of a 10- to 20-year loan.

Finally, *short-term debt may offer greater flexibility.* If the firm thinks that interest rates are abnormally high, it may prefer short-term credit to gain flexibility in changing the debt contract. Also, if its needs for funds are seasonal or cyclical, it may not want to commit itself to long-term debt because while provisions for repaying long-term debt can be built into the contract, prepayment penalties are generally built into long-term debt contracts to permit the lender to recover its setup costs. Finally, long-term loan agreements generally contain provisions, or covenants, that constrain the firm's future actions in order to protect the lender, whereas short-term credit agreements generally have fewer restrictions.

All things considered, it is not possible to state that long-term or short-term financing is better than the other. The firm's specific conditions will affect the choice, as will the preferences of managers. Optimistic and/or aggressive managers will probably lean more toward short-term credit to gain an interest cost advantage, while more conservative managers will lean toward long-term financing to avoid potential renewal problems. The factors discussed here should be considered, but the final decision will reflect managers' personal preferences and judgments.

SELF TEST

Differentiate between permanent current assets and temporary current assets.

What does maturity matching mean, and what is the advantage of this financing policy?

What are advantages and disadvantages of short-term versus long-term debt?

16-4 THE CASH CONVERSION CYCLE

All firms follow a "working capital cycle" in which they purchase or produce inventory, hold it for a time, and then sell it and receive cash. This process is similar to the Yankee peddler's trips, and it is known as the **cash conversion cycle (CCC)**.

16-4a Calculating the Targeted CCC

Assume that Great Fashions Inc. (GFI) is a start-up business that buys ladies' golf outfits from a manufacturer in China and sells them through pro shops at high-end golf clubs in the United States, Canada, and Mexico. The company's business plan calls for it to purchase $100,000 of merchandise at the start of each month and have the merchandise sold within 60 days. The company will have 40 days to pay its suppliers, and it will give its customers 60 days to pay for their purchases. GFI expects to just break even during its first few years; so its monthly sales will be $100,000, the same as its purchases. Any funds required to support operations will be obtained from the bank, and those loans must be repaid as soon as cash is available.

This information can be used to calculate GFI's cash conversion cycle, which nets out the following three time periods:[3]

1. **Inventory conversion period.** For GFI, this is the 60 days it takes to sell the merchandise.[4]
2. **Average collection period (ACP).** This is the length of time customers are given to pay for goods following a sale. The ACP is also called the days' sales outstanding (DSO). GFI's business plan calls for an ACP of 60 days, which is consistent with its 60-day credit terms.
3. **Payables deferral period.** This is the length of time GFI's suppliers give GFI to pay for its purchases (40 days in our example).

On Day 1, GFI buys merchandise and expects to sell the goods and thus convert them to accounts receivable in 60 days. It should take another 60 days to collect the receivables, making a total of 120 days between receiving merchandise and collecting cash. However, GFI is able to defer its own payments for 40 days.

We combine these three periods to find the planned cash conversion cycle, shown here as an equation and in Figure 16-3 as an illustration.

Inventory conversion period		Average collection period		Payables deferral period		Cash conversion cycle	16-1
60	+	60	−	40	=	80 days	

Although GFI must pay $100,000 to its suppliers after 40 days, it will not receive any cash until $60 + 60 = 120$ days into the cycle. Therefore, it will have to borrow the $100,000 cost of the merchandise from its bank on Day 40, and it will not be able to repay the loan until it collects on Day 120. Thus, for $120 − 40 = 80$ days—which is the cash conversion cycle (CCC)—it will owe the bank $100,000 and will be paying interest on this debt. The shorter the cash conversion cycle, the better because that will lower interest charges.

Note that if GFI could sell goods faster, collect receivables faster, or defer its payables longer without hurting sales or increasing operating costs, its CCC

Cash Conversion Cycle (CCC)
The length of time funds are tied up in working capital or the length of time between paying for working capital and collecting cash from the sale of the working capital.

Inventory Conversion Period
The average time required to convert raw materials into finished goods and then to sell them.

Average Collection Period (ACP)
The average length of time required to convert the firm's receivables into cash, that is, to collect cash following a sale.

Payables Deferral Period
The average length of time between the purchase of materials and labor and the payment of cash for them.

---

[3]See Verlyn D. Richards and Eugene J. Laughlin, "A Cash Conversion Cycle Approach to Liquidity Analysis," *Financial Management*, Spring 1980, pp. 32–38.
[4]If GFI were a manufacturer, the inventory conversion period would be the time required to convert raw materials into finished goods and then to sell those goods.

FIGURE 16-3   The Cash Conversion Cycle

would decline, its interest charges would be reduced, and its profits and stock price would be improved.

16-4b Calculating the CCC from Financial Statements

The preceding section illustrates the CCC in theory; but in practice, we would calculate the CCC based on the firm's financial statements. Moreover, the actual CCC would almost certainly differ from the theoretically forecasted value because of real-world complexities such as shipping delays, sales slowdowns, and customer delays in making payments. Moreover, a firm such as GFI would start a new cycle before the earlier one ended, and this too would muddy the waters.

To see how the CCC is calculated in practice, assume that GFI has been in business for several years and is now in a stable position—placing orders, making sales, obtaining collections, and making payments on a recurring basis. The following data were taken from its latest financial statements:

Annual sales	$1,216,666
Cost of goods sold	1,013,889
Inventory	250,000
Accounts receivable	300,000
Accounts payable	150,000

We begin with the inventory conversion period:

16-2 $$\text{Inventory conversion period} = \frac{\text{Inventory}}{\text{Cost of goods sold per day}}$$

$$= \frac{\$250,000}{\$1,013,889/365} = 90 \text{ days}$$

Thus, it takes GFI an average of 90 days to sell its merchandise, not the 60 days called for in the business plan. Note also that inventory is carried at cost; so the denominator of the equation should be the cost of goods sold, not sales.

The average collection period (or days sales outstanding) is calculated next:

16-3 $$\text{Average collection period} = \frac{\text{Receivables}}{\text{Sales}/365}$$

$$= \frac{\$300,000}{\$1,216,666/365} = 90 \text{ days}$$

So it takes GFI 90 days after a sale to receive cash, not the 60 days called for in the business plan. Because receivables are recorded at the sales price, we use sales rather than cost of goods sold in the denominator.

SOME FIRMS OPERATE WITH NEGATIVE WORKING CAPITAL!

Some firms are able to operate with zero or even negative net working capital. Dell and Amazon.com are examples. When customers order computers from Dell's web site or books from Amazon, they must provide a credit card number. Dell and Amazon then receive next-day cash, even before the product is shipped and before they have paid their own suppliers. This results in a negative CCC, which means that working capital provides, does not use, cash.

To grow, companies normally need cash for working capital. However, when the CCC is negative, growth in sales *provides* cash rather than *uses* it. This cash can be invested in plant and equipment as well as research and development or used for any other corporate purpose. Analysts recognize this point when they value Dell and Amazon, and it helps the companies' stock prices.

The payables deferral period is found as follows, again using cost of goods sold in the denominator because payables are recorded at cost:

$$\frac{\text{Payables}}{\text{deferral period}} = \frac{\text{Payables}}{\text{Purchases per day}} = \frac{\text{Payables}}{\text{Cost of goods sold}/365} \qquad \textbf{16-4}$$

$$= \frac{\$150,000}{\$1,013,889/365} = 54 \text{ days}$$

GFI is supposed to pay its suppliers after 40 days; but it is a slow payer, delaying payment on average until Day 54.

We can combine the three periods to calculate GFI's actual cash conversion cycle:

$$\text{Cash conversion cycle (CCC)} = 90 \text{ days} + 90 \text{ days} - 54 \text{ days} = 126 \text{ days}$$

GFI's actual 126-day CCC is quite different from the planned 80 days. It takes longer than planned to sell merchandise, customers don't pay as fast as they should, and GFI pays its suppliers slower than it should. The end result is a CCC of 126 days versus the planned 80 days.

When the planned 80-day CCC is "reasonable," the actual 126 days is too high. The CFO should push salespeople to speed up sales and the credit manager to accelerate collections. Also, the purchasing department should try to get longer payment terms. If GFI could take those steps without hurting sales and operating costs, the firm would help its profits and stock price.

Two professors, Hyun-Han Shin and Luc Soenen, studied more than 2,900 companies over a 20-year period. They found that shortening the cash conversion cycle resulted in higher profits and better stock price performances.[5] Their study demonstrates that good working capital management is important.

SELF TEST

Define the following terms: *inventory conversion period, average collection period,* and *payables deferral period.* Explain how these terms are used to form the cash conversion cycle.

How would a reduction in the cash conversion cycle increase profitability?

What are some actions a firm can take to shorten its cash conversion cycle?

---

[5]See Hyun-Han Shin and Luc Soenen, "Efficiency of Working Capital Management and Corporate Profitability," *Financial Practice and Education,* Fall/Winter 1998, pp. 37–45.

16-5 THE CASH BUDGET

Cash Budget
A table that shows cash receipts, disbursements, and balances over some period.

Firms need to forecast their cash flows. If they are likely to need additional cash, they should line up funds well in advance. On the other hand, if they are likely to generate surplus cash, they should plan for its productive use. The primary forecasting tool is the **cash budget**, illustrated in Table 16-1, which is a printout from the chapter's Excel model.

Table 16-1

Allied Food Products 2009 Cash Budget (Dollars in Millions)

	A	B	C	D	E	F	G	H	I	J	K	L	M	N
4														
5	Input Data													
6	Collections during month of sale						20%		Assumed constant. Don't change.					
7	Collections during 1st month after sale						70%		Assumed constant. Don't change.					
8	Collections during 2nd month after sale						10%		Equal to 100% - (20% + 70%) - Bad debt %					
9	Percent bad debts						0%		Can change to see effects					
10	Discount on first month collections						2%		Can change to see effects					
11	Purchases as a % of next month's sales						70%		Can change to see effects					
12	Lease payments						$ 15		Can change to see effects					
13	Construction cost for new plant (Oct)						$100		Can change to see effects					
14	Target cash balance						$ 10		Can change to see effects					
15	Sales adjustment factor (change from base)						0%		% increase or decrease from base to see effects					
16														
17														
18	THE CASH BUDGET													
19							May	June	July	August	Sept	Oct	Nov	Dec
20	*Sales (gross)*						$200	$250	$300	$400	$500	$350	$250	$200
21	*Collections*													
22	During month of sale: 0.2(Sales)(0.98)								$ 59	$ 78	$ 98	$ 69	$ 49	$ 39
23	During 1st month after sale: 0.7(prior month's sales)								175	210	280	350	245	175
24	During 2nd month after sale: 0.1(sales 2 months ago)								20	25	30	40	50	35
25	Total collections								$254	$313	$408	$459	$344	$249
26	*Purchases: 70% of next month's sales*							$210	$280	$350	$245	$175	$140	
27	*Payments*													
28	Payment for materials: Last month's purchases								$210	$280	$350	$245	$175	$140
29	Wages and salaries								30	40	50	40	30	30
30	Lease payments								15	15	15	15	15	15
31	Other expenses								10	15	20	15	10	10
32	Taxes										30			20
33	Payment for plant construction											100		
34	Total payments								$265	$350	$465	$415	$230	$215
35	*Net cash flows:*													
36	Net cash flow (NCF) for month: Row 25 minus Row 34								($ 11)	($ 37)	($ 57)	($ 44)	($114)	($ 34)
37	Cumulative NCF: Prior month's cum. NCF plus this month's NCF								($ 11)	($ 48)	($105)	($ 61)	($ 53)	($ 87)
38	*Cash surplus (or loan requirement)*													
39	Target cash balance								$ 10	$ 10	$ 10	$ 10	$ 10	$ 10
40	Surplus cash (or loan needed): Row 37 minus Row 39								($ 21)	($ 58)	($115)	($ 71)	($ 43)	($ 77)
41	Maximum required loan (shown as a negative)								($115)					
42	Maximum available for investment								$ 77					

Notes:

a. Although the budget period is July through December, sales and purchases data for May and June are needed to determine collections and payments during July and August.

b. Firms can both borrow and pay off commercial loans on a daily basis. So the $21 million loan shown for July would likely be borrowed gradually on a daily basis as needed; and during October, the $115 million loan that existed at the beginning of the month would be reduced daily to the $71 million ending balance, which, in turn, would be completely paid off sometime during November.

Cash budgets can be of any length, but firms typically develop a monthly cash budget like Table 16-1 for the coming year and a daily cash budget at the start of each month. The monthly budget is good for annual planning, while the daily budget gives a more precise picture of the actual cash flows and is good for scheduling actual payments on a day-by-day basis.

The monthly cash budget begins with a forecast of sales for each month and a projection of when actual collections will occur. Then there is a forecast of materials purchases, followed by forecasted payments for materials, labor, leases, new equipment, taxes, and other expenses. When the forecasted payments are subtracted from the forecasted collections, the result is the expected net cash gain or loss for each month. This gain or loss is added to or subtracted from the beginning cash balance, and the result is the amount of cash the firm would have on hand at the end of the month if it neither borrowed nor invested.

We use Allied Foods to illustrate cash budgets. To shorten the example, we deal only with the last half of 2009. Allied sells mainly to grocery chains, and its projected 2009 sales are $3,300 million. As Table 16-1 shows, sales increase during the summer, peak in September, and then decline during the fall. All sales are on terms of 2/10, net 30, meaning that a 2% discount is allowed if payment is made within 10 days. But if the discount is not taken, the full amount is due in 30 days. However, like most companies, Allied finds that some customers pay late. Experience shows that 20% of customers pay during the month of the sale—these are the discount customers. Another 70% pay during the month immediately following the sale; and 10% are late, paying in the second month after the sale.[6]

The costs to Allied for foodstuffs, spices, preservatives, and packaging materials average 70% of sales revenues. Purchases are generally made 1 month before the firm expects to sell the finished products, but Allied's suppliers allow it to delay payments for 30 days. July sales are forecasted at $300 million; so purchases during June should amount to $210 million, and this amount must be paid in July.

Wages and lease payments are also built into the cash budget, as are Allied's estimated tax payments—$30 million due September 15 and $20 million due December 15. Also, a $100 million payment for a new plant must be made in October, and miscellaneous other required payments are shown in the budget. Allied's **target cash balance** is $10 million, and it plans to borrow to meet this target or to invest surplus funds if it generates more cash than is needed.

Target Cash Balance
The desired cash balance that a firm plans to maintain in order to conduct business.

We use this information at the top of Table 16-1 to forecast monthly cash surpluses or shortfalls from July through December, along with the amount Allied will need to borrow or will have available to invest so as to keep the end-of-month cash balance at the target level.

Inputs used in the forecast—which are assumptions that may not be correct—are given in Rows 6 through 15. These values are used in the calculations shown here. Row 20 gives the sales forecast for the period May through December. May and June sales are needed to determine collections for July and August. Rows 22 through 25 relate to collections. Row 22 shows that 20% of the sales during any given month are collected during that month. However, customers who pay the first month take the discount; so collections for that month are reduced by 2%. For example, collections for July are calculated as 20% of the $300 million sales for that month minus the 2% discount, or $0.2(\$300) - 0.2(\$300)(0.02) = \$58.8$ million, rounded to $59 million. Row 23 shows the collections for the previous month's sales. For example, in July, 70% of the $250 million June sales, or $175 million,

---

[6]A negligible percentage of sales results in bad debts. The low bad debt losses result from Allied's careful screening of customers and its generally tight credit policies. However, the cash budget model can show the effects of bad debts, so Allied's CFO could show top management how cash flows would be affected if the firm relaxed its credit policy to stimulate sales.

should be collected. Row 24 shows collections from sales 2 months earlier. Thus, in July, collections for May sales should be (0.10)($200) = $20 million. The collections during each month are summed and shown on Row 25. Thus, the July collections include 20% of July sales (minus the discount) and 70% of June sales plus 10% of May sales, or $254 million in total.

Raw material costs, which are 70% of next month's sales, are shown on Row 26. July sales are forecasted at $300 million, so June purchases are 0.7($300) = $210 million. The $210 million must be paid in July, so that amount is shown on Row 28. Continuing, forecasted sales for August are $400 million; so Allied must purchase 0.7($400) = $280 million of materials in July, and that amount must be paid in August.

Other required payments—labor costs, lease payments, taxes, construction costs, and miscellaneous expenses—are shown on Rows 29 through 33; and the total of all payments is shown on Row 34.

Next, on Row 36, we show the net cash flow (NCF) for each month, calculated as collections on Row 25 minus total payments on Row 34. The NCF for July is –$11 million; and cash flows remain negative due to the fall harvest and processing until October, when positive cash flows begin.

The monthly cash flows are then used to calculate the cumulative net cash flows as shown on Row 37. Here we add the NCF for each month to the cumulative NCF from the prior month. Since there was no prior cumulative NCF at the beginning of July, the cumulative NCF for July is simply the NCF for that month, –$11 million. For August, we add the NCF for that month, –$37 million, to the prior cumulative NCF, the –$11 million at the end of July, to get the –$48 million cumulative NCF at the end of August. There is another negative cash flow during September, so the cumulative NCF rises to a peak of –$105 million. However, in October, the NCF is positive; so the cumulative figure declines to –61 million, and it changes from negative amounts to positive amounts in November and December.

Allied's target cash balance is $10 million—it wants to maintain that balance at all times. It plans to borrow $10 million at the start of the analysis, and we show that amount on Row 39. Because there is a projected cash loss of $11 million during July and because Allied borrowed $10 million at the start of the month, at the end of July, its loan outstanding will total $21 million as shown on Row 40.[7] It will incur additional cash shortfalls in August and September; and the required loan will continue to increase, peaking at $115 million at the end of September. However, positive cash flows begin in October; and they will be used to reduce the loan, which will be completely paid off by the end of November, at which time the company will have funds to invest. Indeed, by the end of December, Allied should have no loans outstanding and $77 million available for investment.

Row 41 shows the maximum required loan, $115 million; and Row 42 shows the maximum projected surplus, $77 million. Allied's treasurer will need to arrange a line of credit so that the firm can borrow up to $115 million, increasing the loan over time as funds are needed and repaying it later when cash flows become positive. The treasurer would show the cash budget to the bankers when negotiating for the line of credit. Lenders would want to know how much Allied expects to need, when the funds will be needed, and when the loan will be repaid. The lenders—and Allied's top executives—would question the treasurer about the budget. They would want to know how the forecasts would be affected if sales were higher or lower than those projected, how changes would affect the forecasts when customers pay, and the like. The questioning would focus on these two questions: *How accurate is the forecast likely to be? What would be the effects of significant errors?*

---

[7] If Allied had begun with a positive cash balance, that amount would have been deducted from the initial loan needed. Note too that our cash budget is simplified because it does not show interest expense for the loan or interest income on investments. Those items could be added easily to the cash budget.

Note that if cash inflows and outflows do not occur uniformly during each month, the actual funds needed might be quite different from the indicated amounts. The data in Table 16-1 show the situation on the last day of each month, and we see that the maximum projected loan is $115 million. However, if all payments had to be made on the 1st of the month but most collections came on the 30th, Allied would have to make $265 million of payments in July before it received the $254 million from collections. In that case, the firm would need to borrow about $275 million, not the $21 million shown in Table 16-1. A daily cash budget would reveal that situation.

Table 16-1 was prepared using Excel, which makes it easy to change the assumptions. Therefore, we could examine the cash flow effects of changes in sales, the target cash balance, customers' payments, and so forth. Also, the effects of changes in credit policy and inventory management could be examined through the cash budget.

SELF TEST

How could the cash budget be used when the terms of a bank loan are negotiated?

Suppose a firm's cash flows do not occur uniformly throughout the month. What effect would this have on the accuracy of the forecasted borrowing requirements based on a monthly cash budget? How could the firm deal with this problem?

16-6 CASH AND MARKETABLE SECURITIES

When most of us use the term *cash,* we mean currency (paper money and coins) in addition to bank demand deposits. However, when corporate treasurers use the term, they often mean currency and demand deposits *in addition to very safe, highly liquid marketable securities that can be sold quickly at a predictable price and thus be converted to bank deposits.*[8] Therefore, "cash" as reported on balance sheets generally includes short-term securities, which are also called "cash equivalents."

Note that a firm's marketable security holdings can be divided into two categories: (1) *Operating short-term securities,* which are held primarily to provide liquidity and are bought and sold as needed to provide funds for operations, and (2) *other short-term securities,* which are holdings in excess of the amount needed to support normal operations. Highly profitable firms such as Microsoft often hold far more securities than are needed for liquidity purposes. Those securities will eventually be liquidated; and the cash will be used for such things as paying a large one-time dividend, repurchasing stock, retiring debt, acquiring other firms, or financing major expansions. This breakdown is not reported on the balance sheet, but financial managers know how much of their securities will be needed for operating versus other purposes. In our discussion of net working capital, the focus is on securities held to provide operating liquidity.

---

[8]The reason corporate treasurers think of cash as they do is that from their perspective, there is little difference between demand deposits and liquid marketable securities. They can call a dealer, sell securities, and have the proceeds deposited in the firm's bank account in an hour or so. Also, many types of short-term securities are available. Treasury bills are an obvious example; but as we discussed in Chapter 2, there are many other safe, liquid, short-term, marketable securities.

16-6a Currency

Fast-food operators, casinos, hotels, movie theaters, and a few other businesses hold substantial amounts of currency; but the importance of currency has decreased over time due to the rise of credit cards, debit cards, and other payment mechanisms. Companies such as McDonald's need to hold enough currency to support operations; but if they held more, this would raise capital costs and tempt robbers. Each firm decides its own optimal level; but even for retailers, currency generally represents a small part of total cash holdings.[9]

16-6b Demand Deposits

Demand (or checking) deposits are far more important than currency for most businesses. These deposits are used for *transactions*—paying for labor and raw materials, purchasing fixed assets, paying taxes, servicing debt, paying dividends, and so forth. However, commercial demand deposits typically earn no interest; so firms try to minimize their holdings while still ensuring that they are able to pay suppliers promptly, take trade discounts, and take advantage of bargain purchases. The following techniques are used to optimize demand deposit holdings:

1. *Hold marketable securities rather than demand deposits to provide liquidity.* When the firm holds marketable securities, the need for demand deposits is reduced. For example, if a large bill requiring immediate payment comes in unexpectedly, the treasurer can simply call a securities dealer, sell some securities, and have funds deposited in the firm's checking account that same day. Securities pay interest whereas demand deposits do not, so holding securities in lieu of demand deposits increases profits.

2. *Borrow on short notice.* Firms can establish lines of credit under which they can borrow with just a telephone call if and when they need extra cash. Note, though, that they may have to pay fees for those commitments; and the cost of those fees must be considered when deciding to use borrowing capacity rather than securities to provide liquidity.

3. *Forecast payments and receipts better.* The better the firm can forecast its cash inflows and outflows, the smaller its needs for funds to meet unexpected requirements. Therefore, improving inflow/outflow forecasts lessens the need to hold liquid assets and thus reduces the required amount of working capital. The cash budget is the key tool used to improve cash forecasts.

4. *Speed up payments.* Firms can take actions to get their cash receipts faster. For example, they can use **lockboxes**, which are post office boxes operated by banks. Suppose a New York firm sells to customers all across the country. If it sends out bills and has customers make payments to its New York headquarters, time will be lost in waiting on the mail, in opening envelopes, in depositing checks in the bank, and in waiting for the bank to clear the checks to make sure they are good. To speed up this process, the firm can direct customers to send payments to a post office box in the customer's local area, then have a bank empty the box several times each day and start the collection process. If a firm's receipts average $1 million per day and if the use of lockboxes can reduce the delay in obtaining usable cash from 5 days to 1 day, the firm will reduce funds in transit from $5 million to $1 million and thus

Lockbox
A post office box operated by a bank to which payments are sent. Used to speed up effective receipt of cash.

---

[9]In "olden days," currency was also held as a store of value, for use during emergencies, for use in making bargain purchases, and the like. That is true today only in undeveloped parts of the world.

receive an effective cash infusion of $4 million. This is a one-time benefit, but the firm will be earning a continuing return on the $4 million.[10]

5. *Use credit cards, debit cards, wire transfers, and direct deposits.* If a firm switches from selling on credit to accepting credit or debit cards, it will receive next-day cash and thus the same cash flow benefits as described earlier. Similarly, requiring customers to pay via wire deposits speeds up collections, increases free cash flows, and reduces required cash holdings.

6. *Synchronize cash flows.* If a firm can synchronize its cash inflows and outflows, the firm will reduce its need for cash balances. For example, utilities, oil companies, department stores, and the like generally use "billing cycles" under which different customers are billed on different days, causing cash to flow in evenly during the month. These firms can then set up their own payment schedules to match their inflows. This reduces average cash balances, just as your personal average monthly balance can be reduced when your income comes in at the same time as your required payments.

Banks have experts who help firms optimize their cash management procedures. The banks charge a fee for this service, but the benefits of a good cash management system are well worth the cost.

16-6c Marketable Securities

Marketable securities held for operations are managed in conjunction with demand deposits—the management of one requires coordination with the other. Firms also purchase marketable securities as cash builds up from operations and then sell those securities when they need cash. Microsoft is a good example. It had accumulated more than $60 billion of cash (mostly marketable securities) by the end of 2004. It needed to hold some of those securities for liquidity purposes, but mainly the funds built up because Microsoft generated more cash from operations than it needed. Investors urged management to use this "cash" in a more productive manner or to pay it out as dividends so stockholders could invest it. Partly because of this pressure, in the fall of 2004, Microsoft announced a one-time dividend of $30 billion; it also stepped up its stock repurchase program. By the end of 2007, Microsoft's holdings of cash and equivalents had been reduced to a more "reasonable" $6.6 billion.

Given the size and importance of marketable securities holdings, how they are managed can have a significant effect on profits. A trade-off between risk and return is involved—the firm wants to earn high returns; but since most marketable securities are held to provide liquidity, treasurers want to hold securities that can be sold very quickly at a known price. That means high-quality, short-term instruments. Long-term Treasury bonds are safe, but they are not well suited for the marketable securities portfolio because their prices decline when interest rates rise. Similarly, short-term securities issued by risky companies are not suitable because their prices decline when the issuers' problems grow worse. Treasury bills, most commercial paper (discussed in Section 16-11), bank certificates of deposit, and money market funds are suitable holdings.

It's worth noting that so-called safe securities don't always turn out to be safe. In 2007, billions of dollars of Aaa-rated commercial paper was actually backed by

[10]We should mention the term *float*, as it often comes up in connection with cash management. If you write a check and it takes 5 days for the recipient to receive and deposit the check and for it to be deducted from your account, you have 5 days of float, or the use of the money for 5 days before you have to deposit funds in your account. That's *payment float*. On the other hand, if someone sends you a check and it takes 6 days for you to receive and deposit it and for the bank to clear the funds, that's 6 days of *collection float*. Your "net float" would be −1 day. Positive net float is good, but negative net float is bad from the standpoint of minimizing required cash holdings.

subprime mortgages; and when those mortgages started defaulting, this commercial paper caused their holders a great deal of trouble. One issue of commercial paper was downgraded from Aaa to Ba in just one day, and those people holding what they thought was safe and highly liquid paper found it to be totally illiquid and of doubtful value. As you might guess, before it defaulted, the mortgage-backed commercial paper paid a somewhat higher return, about 3.505% versus about 3.467% for paper backed by T-bills. Those seeking higher returns generally have to accept more risk.

A firm's relationship with its bank—especially its ability to borrow on short notice—can have a significant effect on its need for both demand deposits and marketable securities. If a company has a firmly committed line of credit under which it can obtain funds with a simple telephone call, it won't need much in the way of liquid reserves.

Finally, larger corporations shop for securities all around the world, buying wherever risk-adjusted rates are highest. This shopping tends to equalize world-wide rates—if interest rates in Europe are higher than rates in the United States for equally risky securities, companies will buy European securities, driving their prices up and their yields down, until an equilibrium has been established. We truly live in a global economy.[11]

SELF TEST

What two definitions of cash are commonly encountered?

Differentiate between marketable securities held for operating (transactions) purposes and securities held for other reasons.

How has the development of credit and debit cards affected firms' currency holdings?

How would the use of credit cards affect a firm's cash conversion cycle assuming it previously allowed customers 30 days to pay for their purchases?

How does a firm's ability to borrow affect its optimal holdings of cash and securities?

Common stocks that are traded on the NYSE are liquid in the sense that they can be sold and converted to cash on short notice. Are stocks a good choice for a firm's marketable securities portfolio? Explain.

16-7 INVENTORIES

Inventories, which can include (1) *supplies,* (2) *raw materials,* (3) *work in process,* and (4) *finished goods,* are an essential part of virtually all business operations. Optimal inventory levels depend on sales, so sales must be forecasted before target inventories can be established. Moreover, because errors in setting inventory levels lead to lost sales or excessive carrying costs, inventory management is quite important. Therefore, firms use sophisticated computer systems to monitor their inventory holdings.

Retailers such as Best Buy, Wal-Mart, and Home Depot use computers to keep track of each inventory item by size, shape, and color; and bar code information collected at checkout updates inventory records. When inventories shown in the computer decline to a set level, the computer sends an order to the supplier's computer,

---

[11]Companies can also buy securities that are denominated in different currencies. Thus, if a firm's treasurer thinks that the euro is likely to appreciate against the dollar, he or she might purchase securities denominated in euros; and if things work out as expected, the firm will earn interest and enjoy an additional gain from the change in exchange rates. Again, these actions help to keep world financial markets in equilibrium.

SUPPLY CHAIN MANAGEMENT

Herman Miller, Inc., manufactures a wide variety of office furniture; and a typical order from a single customer might require work at five different plants. Each plant uses components from different suppliers, and each plant works on orders for many customers. Imagine all the coordination that's required. The sales force generates the order, the purchasing department orders components from suppliers, and the suppliers must order materials from their own suppliers. Then the suppliers ship the components to the appropriate Herman Miller plant, the plants build the products, the different products are gathered together to complete the order, and the order is shipped to the customer. If one part of that process malfunctions, the entire order will be delayed, inventory will pile up, and extra costs to expedite the order will be incurred. Moreover, the company's reputation will be damaged, hurting future sales.

To prevent such consequences, Herman Miller employs a process called supply chain management (SCM). The key element in SCM is sharing information all the way from the point of sale at the retailer to suppliers and even back to suppliers' suppliers. SCM requires sophisticated software; but even more important, SCM requires cooperation among the different companies and departments in the supply chain. A new culture of open communication is required, and this is often difficult for many companies because they are reluctant to divulge operating information. Many of Herman Miller's suppliers were initially wary of these new relationships. However, SCM has been a win-win situation, with increases in value for Herman Miller and its suppliers.

SCM enabled Herman Miller to sharply reduce its inventory, to cut 2 weeks off delivery times to customers, and to operate its plants at a 20% higher volume without further capital expenditures. The results were much higher earnings, cash flows, and stock price.

Sources: Elaine L. Appleton, "Supply Chain Brain," CFO, July 1997, pp. 51–54; and Kris Frieswick, "Up Close and Virtual," *CFO*, April 1998, pp. 87–91.

specifying exactly what is needed. The computer also reports how fast items are moving. If an item is moving too slowly, the computer will suggest a price cut to lower the inventory stock before the item becomes obsolete. Manufacturers such as GE use similar systems to keep track of items and to place orders as they are needed.

Although inventory management is important, it is under the operational control of production managers and marketing people rather than financial managers. Still, financial managers are involved in several ways. First, it is expensive to install and maintain the computer systems used to track inventories; and the capital budgeting analysis discussed earlier in the text must be used to determine which system is best. Second, if the firm decides to increase its inventory holdings, the financial manager must raise the capital needed to acquire the additional inventory. And third, the financial manager is responsible for identifying any area of weakness that affects the firm's overall profitability, using ratios and other procedures for comparing the firm to its benchmark companies. Therefore, the CFO will compare the firm's inventory-to-sales ratio with those of its benchmarks to see if things look "reasonable."

Since inventory management is outside the mainstream of finance, we cover it in Web Appendix 16A rather than in the text chapter. However, "Supply Chain Management," provided at the top of this page, discusses how inventories are managed by modern corporations.

SELF TEST What are the three primary tasks of the financial manager regarding inventory management?

16-8 ACCOUNTS RECEIVABLE

Account Receivable
Funds due from a customer.

Although some sales are made for cash, today the vast majority of sales are on credit. Thus, in the typical situation, goods are shipped, inventories are reduced, and an **account receivable** is created.[12] Eventually, the customer pays, the firm receives cash, and its receivables decline. The firm's credit policy is the primary determinant of accounts receivable, and it is under the administrative control of the CFO. Moreover, credit policy is a key determinant of sales, so sales and marketing executives are concerned with this policy. Therefore, we begin our discussion of accounts receivable by discussing credit policy.

16-8a Credit Policy

Credit Policy
A set of rules that includes the firm's credit period, discounts, credit standards, and collection procedures offered.

Credit Period
The length of time customers have to pay for purchases.

Discounts
Price reductions given for early payment.

Credit policy consists of these four variables:

1. **Credit period** is the length of time buyers are given to pay for their purchases. For example, the credit period might be 30 days. Customers prefer longer credit periods, so lengthening the period will stimulate sales. However, a longer credit period lengthens the cash conversion cycle; hence, it ties up more capital in receivables, which is costly. Also, the longer a receivable is outstanding, the higher the probability that the customer will default and that the account will end up as a bad debt.

2. **Discounts** are price reductions given for early payment. The discount specifies what the percentage reduction is and how rapidly payment must be made to be eligible for the discount. For example, a 2% discount is often given if the customer pays within 10 days. Offering discounts has two benefits. First, the discount amounts to a price reduction, which stimulates sales. Second, discounts encourage customers to pay earlier than they otherwise would, which shortens the cash conversion cycle. However, discounts mean lower prices—and lower revenues unless the quantity sold increases by enough to offset the price reduction. The benefits and costs of discounts must be balanced when credit policy is being established.

Credit Standards
The financial strength customers must exhibit to qualify for credit.

3. **Credit standards**, which refer to the required financial strength of acceptable credit customers. With regard to credit standards, factors considered for business customers include ratios such as the customer's debt and interest coverage ratios, the customer's credit history (has the customer paid on time in the past or tended to be delinquent), and the like. For individual customers, their credit score as developed by credit rating agencies is the key item. In both cases, the key question is this: Is the customer likely to be willing and able to make the required payment on schedule? Note that when standards are set too low, bad debt losses will be too high; on the other hand, when standards are set too high, the firm loses too many sales and thus profits. So a balance must be struck between the costs and benefits of tighter credit standards.

Collection Policy
The degree of toughness in enforcing the credit terms.

4. **Collection policy** refers to the procedures used to collect past due accounts, including the toughness or laxity used in the process. At one extreme, the firm might write a series of polite letters after a fairly long delay; while at the other extreme, delinquent accounts may be turned over to a collection agency relatively quickly. Companies should be somewhat firm, but excessive pressure

---

[12]Whenever goods are sold on credit, two accounts are created—an asset item entitled *account receivable* appears on the books of the selling firm, and a liability item called an *account payable* appears on the books of the purchaser. At this point, we are analyzing the transaction from the viewpoint of the seller; so we are focusing on the variables under the seller's control—in this case, receivables. In Section 16-9, we will examine the transaction from the viewpoint of the purchaser when we discuss accounts payable as a source of funds and consider their cost relative to the cost of funds obtained from other sources.

can lead customers whose business is profitable to take their business elsewhere. Again, a balance must be struck between the costs and benefits of different collection policies.

Firms generally publish their **credit terms**, defined as a statement of their credit period and discount policy. Thus, Allied Foods might have stated credit terms of 2/10, net 30, which means that it allows a 2% discount if payment is received within 10 days of the purchase; if the discount is not taken then, the full amount is due in 30 days. Credit standards and collection policies are relatively subjective, so they are not generally discussed in the published credit terms.

Credit Terms
Statement of the credit period and any discount offered.

16-8b Setting and Implementing the Credit Policy

Credit policy is important for three main reasons: (1) It has a major effect on sales, (2) it influences the amount of funds tied up in receivables, and (3) it affects bad debt losses. Because of the importance of the policy, the firm's executive committee, which normally consists of the president in addition to the vice presidents of finance and marketing, has the final say on setting the credit policy. Once the policy has been established, the credit manager, who typically works under the CFO, must carry it out and monitor its effects. Managing a credit department requires fast, accurate, and up-to-date information. Several organizations, including Experian, Equifax, and TransUnion, use computer-based networks to collect, store, and distribute credit information. For businesses, Dun & Bradstreet provides detailed credit reports over the Internet for a fee. The reports include the following types of information:

1. A summary balance sheet and income statement
2. A number of key ratios with trend information
3. Data obtained from the firm's suppliers telling whether it pays promptly or slowly and whether it has recently failed to make any payments
4. A verbal description of the physical condition of the firm's operations
5. A verbal description of the backgrounds of the firm's owners, including any previous bankruptcies, lawsuits, or divorce settlement problems
6. A summary rating ranging from A for the best credit risks down to F for those firms that are deemed likely to default

For individuals, **credit scores**, which are numerical scores from 0 to 10 that are based on a statistical analysis, provide a summary assessment of the likelihood that a potential customer will default on a required payment. Computerized analytical systems assist in making better credit decisions; but in the final analysis, most credit decisions are exercises in informed judgment.[13]

Credit Score
A numerical score from 0 to 10 that indicates the likelihood that a person or business will pay on time.

We have emphasized the costs of granting credit. *However, if it is possible to sell on credit and to impose a carrying charge on the receivables that are outstanding, credit sales can actually be more profitable than cash sales.* This is especially true for consumer durables (e.g., automobiles and appliances), but it is also true for certain types of industrial equipment. Thus, GM's General Motors Acceptance Corporation (GMAC) unit, which finances automobiles, is highly profitable, as are other

---

[13]Credit analysts use procedures ranging from highly sophisticated computerized *credit-scoring* systems, which calculate the statistical probability that a given customer will default, to informal procedures, which involve going through a checklist of factors that should be considered when a credit application is processed. The credit-scoring systems use various financial ratios, such as the current ratio and the debt ratio (for businesses), and income, years with the same employer, and the like (for individuals), to determine the statistical probability of default. Credit is then granted to those with low default probabilities. The informal procedures often involve examining the "5 Cs of Credit": character, capacity, capital, collateral, and conditions. Character is obvious; capacity is a subjective estimate of ability to repay; capital means how much net worth the borrower has; collateral means assets pledged to secure the loan; and conditions refers to business conditions, which affect ability to repay.

companies' credit subsidiaries.[14] Some companies actually earn more on credit than cash sales, and their salespeople earn higher commissions when they make a credit sale.

The carrying charges on outstanding consumer credit are generally about 18% on a nominal basis: 1.5% per month, so $1.5\% \times 12 = 18\%$. This is equivalent to an effective annual rate of $(1.015)^{12} - 1.0 = 19.6\%$. Having receivables outstanding that earn more than 18% is highly profitable unless there are too many bad debt losses.

Legal considerations must also be taken into account when setting credit policy. Under the Robinson-Patman Act, it is illegal for a firm to charge prices that discriminate between customers unless the different prices are cost-justified. The same holds true for credit—it is illegal to offer more favorable credit terms to one customer or class of customers than to another unless the differences are cost-justified.

16-8c Monitoring Accounts Receivable

The total amount of accounts receivable outstanding at any given time is determined by the volume of credit sales and the average length of time between sales and collections. For example, suppose Boston Lumber Company (BLC), a wholesale distributor of lumber products, has sales of $1,000 per day (all on credit) and it requires payment after 10 days. BLC has no bad debts or slow-paying customers. Under those conditions, it must have the capital to carry $10,000 of receivables:

16-5
$$\text{Accounts receivable} = \text{Sales per day} \times \text{Length of collection period}$$
$$= \$1{,}000 \times 10 \text{ days} = \$10{,}000$$

If either sales or the collection period changes, so will accounts receivable. For example, if sales doubled to $2,000/day, receivables would also double; and the firm would need an additional $10,000 to finance this increase. Similarly, if the collection period lengthened to 20 days, this too would double the receivables and require additional capital.

If management is not careful, the collection period will creep up, as good customers take longer to pay and as sales are made to weaker customers, who tend to pay slowly or not at all and thus create bad debts. So it is important to monitor receivables. One easy-to-use monitoring technique employs the DSO. Here's Allied Foods' DSO as calculated back in Chapter 4:

$$\text{DSO} = \frac{\text{Days sales outstanding}}{} = \frac{\text{Receivables}}{\text{Average sales per day}} = \frac{\text{Receivables}}{\text{Annual sales}/365}$$
$$= \frac{\$375}{\$3{,}000/365} = \frac{\$375}{\$8.2192} = 45.625 \text{ days} \approx 46 \text{ days}$$

Industry average = 36 days

Allied has an average daily sales (ADS) of $8.2192 million, and those sales are outstanding for 45.625 days. If we multiply the DSO by the average daily sales, we determine the capital tied up in receivables:

$$\text{Receivables} = (\text{ADS})(\text{DSO})$$
$$= (\$8.2192)(45.625) = \$375 \text{ million}$$

---

[14]Companies that do a large volume of sales financing typically set up subsidiary companies called *captive finance companies* to do the actual financing. For example, General Motors, Chrysler, and Ford have captive finance companies, as do Sears, IBM, and General Electric.

Note, though, that if Allied collected its receivables faster and reduced its DSO to the 36-day industry average, its receivables would decline to $295.89 million, or by $79.11 million. The DSO can also be compared to the firm's own credit terms. Allied sells on terms of net 30, so its DSO should be no greater than 30 days. Obviously, some customers are paying late, so there is room for improvement in its collections policy and practices.[15]

SELF TEST

What are credit terms?

What are the four credit policy variables?

Define days sales outstanding (DSO). What can be learned from it, and how is it affected by seasonal sales fluctuations?

What is credit quality, and how is it assessed?

How does collection policy influence sales, the collection period, and the bad debt loss percentage?

How can cash discounts be used to influence sales volume and the DSO?

How do legal considerations affect a firm's credit policy?

16-9 ACCOUNTS PAYABLE (TRADE CREDIT)

Firms generally make purchases from other firms on credit and record the debt as an *account payable*. Accounts payable, or **trade credit**, is the largest single category of short-term debt, representing about 40% of the average corporation's current liabilities. This credit is a spontaneous source of financing in the sense that *it arises spontaneously from ordinary business transactions.* For example, if a firm makes a purchase of $1,000 on terms of net 30, it must pay for goods 30 days after the invoice date. This instantly and spontaneously provides $1,000 of credit for 30 days. If the firm purchases $1,000 of goods each day, on average, it will be receiving 30 times $1,000, or $30,000, of credit from its suppliers. If sales, and consequently purchases, double, its accounts payable also will double, to $60,000. So simply by growing, the firm spontaneously generates another $30,000 of financing. Similarly, if the terms under which it buys are extended from 30 to 40 days, its accounts payable will expand from $30,000 to $40,000. Thus, expanding sales and lengthening the credit period generate additional financing.

Trade credit may be free, or it may be costly. If the seller does not offer discounts, the credit is free in the sense that there is no cost for using it. However, if discounts are available, a complication arises. To illustrate, suppose PCC Inc. buys 20 microchips each day with a list price of $100 per chip on terms of 2/10, net 30. Under those terms, the "true" price of the chips is 0.98($100) = $98 because the chips can be purchased for only $98 by paying within 10 days. Thus, the $100 list price has two components:

List price = $98 "true" price + $2 finance charge

> **Trade Credit**
> *Debt arising from credit sales and recorded as an account receivable by the seller and as an account payable by the buyer.*

---

[15]Another technique used to monitor receivables is the *Aging Schedule,* which shows the dollar amount and percentage of receivables that have been outstanding for different lengths of time. See Brigham and Daves, *Intermediate Financial Management,* 9th ed., (Mason, OH: Thomson/South-Western, 2007), Chapter 21, pp. 737–738.

If PCC decides to take the discount, it will pay at the end of Day 10 and show $19,600 of accounts payables:[16]

$$\text{Accounts payable}_{\text{(Take discounts)}} = (10 \text{ days})(20 \text{ chips}) (\$98 \text{ per chip})$$
$$= \$19,600$$

If it decides to delay payment until the 30th day, its trade credit will be $58,800:

$$\text{Accounts payable}_{\text{(No discounts)}} = (30 \text{ days})(20 \text{ chips})(\$98 \text{ per chip})$$
$$= \$58,800$$

By not taking discounts, PCC can obtain an additional $39,200 of trade credit, *but this $39,200 is costly credit because the firm must give up the discounts to get it.* Therefore, PCC must answer this question: Could we obtain the additional $39,200 at a lower cost from some other source (e.g., a bank)?

To illustrate the situation, assume that PCC operates 365 days per year and buys 20 chips per day at a "true" price of $98 per chip. Therefore, its total chip purchases are 20($98)(365) = $715,400 per year. If it does not take discounts, its chips will cost 20($100)(365) = $730,000, or an additional $14,600. *This $14,600 is the annual cost of the $39,200 of extra credit.* Dividing the $14,600 cost by the $39,200 additional credit yields the nominal annual cost of the additional trade credit, 37.24%:

$$\text{Nominal annual cost of trade credit} = \frac{\$14,600}{\$39,200} = 37.24\%$$

If PCC can borrow from its bank or some other source for less than 37.24%, it should take the discount and use only $19,600 of trade credit.

The same result can be obtained with the following equation:

16-6

$$\begin{array}{c}\text{Nominal annual} \\ \text{cost of} \\ \text{trade credit}\end{array} = \frac{\text{Discount \%}}{100 - \text{Discount \%}} \times \frac{365}{\begin{array}{c}\text{Days credit is} - \text{Discount} \\ \text{outstanding} \quad \text{period}\end{array}}$$

$$= \frac{2}{98} \times \frac{365}{20} = 2.04\% \times 18.25 = 37.24\%$$

The numerator of the first term, Discount %, is the cost per dollar of credit, while the denominator, 100 − Discount %, represents the funds made available by not taking the discount. Thus, the first term, 2.04%, is the cost per period for the trade credit. The denominator of the second term is the number of days of extra credit obtained by not taking the discount. So the entire second term shows how many times per year the cost is incurred, 18.25 times in this example.[17]

---

[16]A question arises here: Should accounts payable reflect gross purchases or purchases net of discounts? Generally accepted accounting principles permit either treatment if the difference is not material; but if the discount is material, the account payable must be recorded net of discounts, or at the "true" price. Then the cost of not taking discounts is reported as an additional expense called "discounts lost." This procedure highlights the often high cost of not taking discounts. In PCC's case, it would record payables of 20($98) = $1,960, not $2,000, per day; and if it did not take the discount and had to pay the full $2,000, it would show the $40 discount lost per day as an expense.

[17]The nominal annual cost formula does not take account of compounding; and in effective annual interest terms, the cost of trade credit is even higher. The discount is equivalent to interest; and with terms of 2/10, net 30, the firm gains the use of funds for 30 − 10 = 20 days. So there are 365/20 = 18.25 "interest periods" per year. Remember that the first term in Equation 16-6, (Discount %)/(100 − Discount %) = 0.02/0.98 = 0.0204, is the periodic interest rate. That rate is paid 18.25 times each year, so the effective annual cost of trade credit is 44.6%:

$$\text{Effective annual rate} = (1.0204)^{18.25} - 1.0 = 1.4459 - 1.0 = 44.6\%$$

Thus, the 37.2% nominal cost calculated with Equation 16-6 understates the effective cost.

With this background, we can define two types of trade credit: free and costly:

1. **Free trade credit** is the trade credit that is obtained without a cost, and it consists of all trade credit that is available without giving up discounts. In PCC's case, when it buys on terms of 2/10, net 30, the first 10 days of purchases, or $19,600, are free.

2. **Costly trade credit** is any trade credit over and above the free trade credit. For PCC, the additional 20 days, or $39,200, are not free because getting the additional credit means giving up the discount.

Firms should always use the free component, but they should use the costly component only if they cannot obtain funds at a lower cost from another source.[18]

Free Trade Credit
Credit received during the discount period.

Costly Trade Credit
Credit taken in excess of free trade credit, whose cost is equal to the discount lost.

SELF TEST

What is trade credit?

What is the difference between free trade credit and costly trade credit?

What is the formula for finding the nominal annual cost of trade credit?

Does the nominal cost of trade credit understate the effective cost? Explain.

16-10 BANK LOANS

The key features of bank loans, another important source of short-term financing for businesses and individuals, are discussed in this section.

16-10a Promissory Note

The terms of a bank loan are spelled out in a **promissory note.** Here are some key features of most promissory notes:[19]

1. *Amount.* The amount borrowed is indicated.

2. *Maturity.* Although banks do make longer-term loans, *the bulk of their lending is on a short-term basis*—about two-thirds of all bank loans mature in a year or less. Long-term loans always have a specific maturity date, while a short-term loan may or may not have a specified maturity. For example, a loan may mature in 30 days, 90 days, 6 months, or 1 year; or it may call for payment "on demand," in which case the loan can remain outstanding as long as the borrower wants to continue using the funds and the bank agrees. Bank loans to businesses are frequently written as 90-day notes, so the loan must be repaid or renewed at the end of 90 days. It is often expected that the loan will be renewed; but if the borrower's financial position deteriorates, the bank can refuse to renew it. This can lead to bankruptcy. Because banks usually don't

Promissory Note
A document specifying the terms and conditions of a loan, including the amount, interest rate, and repayment schedule.

---

[18]Note that the cost of trade credit can be reduced by paying late. If PCC could get away with paying in 60 days rather than the specified 30 days, the effective credit period would become $60 - 10 = 50$ days, the number of times the discount would be lost would fall to $365/50 = 7.3$, and the nominal cost would drop from 37.2% to $2.04\% \times 7.3 = 14.9\%$. This is called *stretching accounts payable,* and it damages the firm's reputation and can cause problems later.

[19]Sometimes the note will also specify that the firm must maintain a *compensating balance* equal to 10% to 20% of the face amount of the loan. This balance generally has the effect of increasing the effective cost of the loan. Compensating balances are much less common today than they were a few years ago.

demand payment unless the borrower's creditworthiness has deteriorated, some "short-term loans" remain outstanding for years, with the interest rate floating with rates in the economy.

3. *Interest rate.* The interest rate can be *fixed* or *floating.* For larger loans, it is typically indexed to the bank's prime rate, to the T-bill rate, or to the London Interbank Offer Rate (LIBOR). The note will also indicate whether the bank uses a *360-* or *365-day year* for purposes of calculating interest. The indicated rate is a *nominal rate,* and the effective annual rate is generally higher.

4. *Interest only versus amortized.* Loans are either *interest only,* meaning that only interest is paid during the life of the loan, with all principal repaid when the loan matures, or *amortized,* meaning that some of the principal is repaid on each payment date. Amortized loans are also called *installment loans.*

5. *Frequency of interest payments.* If the note is on an interest-only basis, it will indicate *how frequently interest must be paid.* Interest is typically calculated daily but paid monthly.

6. *Discount interest.* Most loans call for interest to be paid only after it has been earned; but banks also lend on a *discount basis,* where interest is paid in advance. On a discount loan, the borrower actually receives less than the face amount of the loan; and this increases its effective cost. We discuss discount loans in Web Appendix 16B.

7. *Add-on loans.* Auto loans and other consumer installment loans are generally set up on an "add-on basis," which means that interest charges over the life of the loan are calculated and then added to the face amount of the loan. Thus, the borrower signs a promissory note calling for payment of the funds received plus all interest that must be paid over the life of the loan. The add-on feature raises the effective cost of a loan.

8. *Collateral.* If a loan is secured by equipment, buildings, accounts receivable, or inventories, this fact is indicated in the note. Security for loans is discussed in more detail in Section 16-13.

9. *Restrictive covenants.* The note may also specify that the borrower must maintain certain ratios at or better than specified levels, and it spells out what happens if the borrower defaults on those covenants. Default provisions often allow the lender to demand immediate payment of the entire loan balance. Also, the interest rate on the loan might be increased.

10. *Loan guarantees.* If the borrower is a small corporation, the bank will probably insist that its larger stockholders *personally guarantee* the loan. Troubled companies' owners have been known to divert assets from the company to relatives or other entities they own, so banks protect themselves by obtaining personal guarantees.

16-10b Line of Credit

Line of Credit
An arrangement in which a bank agrees to lend up to a specified maximum amount of funds during a designated period.

A **line of credit** is an agreement between a bank and a borrower indicating the maximum amount of credit the bank will extend to the borrower. For example, in December, a bank loan officer might indicate to a financial manager that the bank regards the firm as being "good for" up to $80,000 during the coming year, provided the borrower's financial condition does not deteriorate. If on January 10, the financial manager signs a promissory note for $15,000 for 90 days, this would be called "taking down" $15,000 of the credit line. The $15,000 would be credited to the firm's checking account; and before it was repaid, the firm could borrow an additional $65,000 for a total of $80,000. Such a line of credit would be informal and nonbinding; but formal and binding lines are available, as discussed next.

16-10c Revolving Credit Agreement

A **revolving credit agreement** is a formal line of credit. To illustrate, in 2008, a Texas petroleum company negotiated a revolving credit agreement for $100 million with a group of banks. The banks were formally committed for 4 years to lend the firm up to $100 million if the funds were needed. The company, in turn, paid an annual commitment fee of one-fourth of 1% on the unused balance of the commitment to compensate the banks for making the commitment. Thus, if the firm did not take down any of the $100 million commitment during a year, it would still be required to pay a $250,000 annual fee, normally in monthly installments of $20,833.33. If it borrowed $50 million on the first day of the agreement, the unused portion of the line of credit would fall to $50 million and the annual fee would fall to $125,000. Of course, interest would also have to be paid on the money the firm actually borrowed. In this case, the interest rate on the "revolver" was pegged to the LIBOR rate, being set at LIBOR minus 0.5 percentage point; so the cost of the loan would vary over time as interest rates changed.[20]

> **Revolving Credit Agreement**
> *A formal, committed line of credit extended by a bank or another lending institution.*

Note that a revolving credit agreement is similar to an informal line of credit, but with an important difference: The bank has a *legal obligation* to honor a revolving credit agreement, and it receives a commitment fee. Neither the legal obligation nor the fee exists under informal lines of credit.

16-10d Costs of Bank Loans

The costs of bank loans vary for different types of borrowers at any given point in time and for all borrowers over time. Interest rates are higher for riskier borrowers, and rates are higher on smaller loans because of the fixed costs involved in making and servicing loans. If a firm can qualify as a "prime credit" because of its size and financial strength, it can borrow at the **prime rate**, which at one time was the lowest rate banks charged. Rates on other loans are generally scaled up from the prime rate. But loans to large, strong customers are made at rates tied to LIBOR; and the costs of such loans are generally well below prime:

> **Prime Rate**
> *A published interest rate charged by commercial banks to large, strong borrowers.*

Rates on April 28, 2008 : Prime : 5.25%. 1-Year LIBOR : 3.17875%.

The rate to smaller, riskier borrowers is generally stated something like "prime plus 2.5%"; but for a larger borrower such as the Texas oil company, it is generally stated something like "LIBOR plus 2.5%."

Bank rates vary widely over time depending on economic conditions and Federal Reserve policy. When the economy is weak, loan demand is usually slack, inflation is low, and the Fed makes plenty of money available to the system. As a result, rates on all types of loans are relatively low. Conversely, when the economy is booming, loan demand is typically strong, the Fed restricts the money supply to fight inflation, and the result is high interest rates. As an indication of the kinds of fluctuations that can occur, the prime rate during 1980 rose from 11% to 21% in just 4 months and it rose from 6% to 9% during 1994.

Calculating Banks' Interest Charges: Regular (or Simple) Interest

Banks calculate interest in several different ways. In this section, we explain the procedure used for most business loans. We discuss procedures used for consumer and small business loans in Web Appendix 16B. For illustrative purposes,

---

[20]Each bank sets its own prime rate; but because of competitive forces, most banks' prime rates are identical. Further, most banks follow the rate set by the large New York City banks.

In recent years, many banks have been lending to large, strong companies at rates below the prime rate. As we discuss in Section 16-11, larger firms have ready access to the commercial paper market; and if banks want to do business with these companies, they must match (or at least come close to) the commercial paper rate.

Regular, or Simple, Interest
The situation when only interest is paid monthly.

we assume a loan of $10,000 at the prime rate (currently 5.25%) with a 360-day year. Interest must be paid monthly, and the principal is payable "on demand" if and when the bank wants to end the loan. Such a loan is called a **regular,** or **simple, interest** loan.

We begin by dividing the nominal interest rate (5.25% in this case) by 360 to get the rate per day. The rate is expressed as a *decimal fraction,* not as a percentage:

$$\text{Simple interest rate per day} = \frac{\text{Nominal rate}}{\text{Days in year}}$$
$$= 0.0525/360 = 0.00014583333$$

To find the monthly interest payment, the daily rate is multiplied by the amount of the loan, then by the number of days during the payment period. For our illustrative loan, the daily interest charge would be $1.458333333 and the total for a 30-day month would be $43.75:

$$\text{Interest charge for month} = (\text{Rate per day})(\text{Amount of loan})(\text{Days in month})$$
$$= (0.00014583333)(\$10,000)(30 \text{ days}) = \$43.75$$

The *effective interest rate* on a loan depends on how frequently interest must be paid—the more frequently interest is paid, the higher the effective rate. If interest is paid once a year, the nominal rate also will be the effective rate. However, if interest must be paid monthly, the effective rate will be $(1 + 0.0525/12)^{12} - 1 = 5.3782\%$.

Calculating Banks' Interest Charges: Add-On Interest

Add-On Interest
Interest that is calculated and added to funds received to determine the face amount of an installment loan.

Banks and other lenders typically use **add-on interest** for automobiles and other types of installment loans. The term *add-on* means that the interest is calculated and then added to the amount borrowed to determine the loan's face value. To illustrate, suppose you borrow $10,000 on an *add-on* basis at a nominal rate of 7.25% to buy a car, with the loan to be repaid in 12 monthly installments. At a 7.25% add-on rate, you would make total interest payments of $10,000 (0.0725) = $725. However, since the loan is paid off in monthly installments, you would have the use of the full $10,000 for only the first month; and the outstanding balance would decline until, during the last month, only 1/12 of the original loan was still outstanding. Thus, you would be paying $725 for the use of only about half the loan's face amount, as the average usable funds would be only about $5,000. Therefore, we can calculate the approximate annual rate as 14.5%:

16-7
$$\text{Approximate annual rate}_{\text{Add-on}} = \frac{\text{Interest paid}}{(\text{Amount received})/2}$$
$$= \frac{\$725}{\$10,000/2} = 14.5\%$$

The annual percentage rate (APR) the bank would provide to the borrower would be 13.12%, and the true effective annual rate would be 13.94%. Both of those rates are far higher than the nominal 7.25%.[21]

---

[21]To find the annual percentage rate and the effective rate on an add-on loan, we first find the payment per month, $10,725/12 = $893.75. With a financial calculator, enter N = 12, PV = 10000, PMT = −893.75, FV = 0; then press I/YR to obtain 1.093585%. This is a monthly rate; so multiply by 12 to get 13.12%, which is the APR the bank would report to the borrower. The effective annual rate would be $(1.010936)^{12} - 1 = 13.94\%$, quite a bit above the APR.

What is a promissory note, and what terms are normally included in promissory notes?

What is a line of credit? a revolving credit agreement?

What's the difference between simple interest and add-on interest as bankers use these terms?

If a firm borrowed $500,000 at a rate of 10% simple interest with monthly interest payments and a 365-day year, what would be the required interest payment for a 30-day month? If interest must be paid monthly, what would be the effective annual rate? **($4,109.59; 10.47%)**

If this loan had been made on a 10% add-on basis payable in 12 end-of-month installments, what would be the monthly payments? What is the annual percentage rate? the effective annual rate? **($45,833.33; 17.97% 19.53%)**

How does the cost of costly trade credit generally compare with the cost of short-term bank loans?

16-11 COMMERCIAL PAPER

Commercial paper is a promissory note issued by a large, strong firm—most often a financial institution—that wants to borrow on a short-term basis. Commercial paper is sold primarily to other business firms, insurance companies, pension funds, money market mutual funds, and banks in denominations of at least $100,000. It is generally unsecured; but "asset-backed paper" secured by credit card debt and other small, short-term loans has also been issued. Also (and with very bad consequences) in 2007, subsidiaries of financial institutions such as Citigroup sold a great deal of commercial paper and used it to buy bonds backed by subprime mortgages. This created a situation where short-term commercial paper was backed by long-term debt—and very poor quality debt at that. When the real situation was learned, holders of commercial paper refused to roll it over when it matured and the financial institutions that had sold it were forced to sell the mortgages that backed the paper, often at huge losses. That forced Citi and other institutions to bail out their subsidiaries and to take losses in the tens of billions of dollars.

A large majority of the commercial paper outstanding has been issued by financial institutions. Nonfinancial companies also issue a great deal of paper, but they generally rely more heavily on bank loans for short-term funding. For example, in March 2008, the Federal Reserve reported that commercial paper issued by nonfinancial firms totaled slightly more than $177 billion—that same month the total amount of commercial and industrial loans held by commercial banks was nearly 1.5 trillion dollars.

Commercial Paper
Unsecured, short-term promissory notes of large firms, usually issued in denominations of $100,000 or more with an interest rate somewhat below the prime rate.

What is commercial paper?

What types of companies use commercial paper to meet their short-term financing needs?

16-12 ACCRUALS (ACCRUED LIABILITIES)

Accruals
Continually recurring short-term liabilities, especially accrued wages and accrued taxes.

Spontaneous Funds
Funds that are generated spontaneously as the firm expands.

As we discussed in Chapter 3, firms generally pay employees on a weekly, biweekly, or monthly basis; so the balance sheet typically shows some accrued wages. Similarly, the firm's own estimated income taxes, Social Security and income taxes withheld from employee payrolls, and sales taxes collected are generally paid on a weekly, monthly, or quarterly basis. Therefore, the balance sheet typically shows some accrued wages and taxes, which we refer to as **accruals**.

Accruals arise automatically from a firm's operations; hence, they are **spontaneous funds**. For example, if sales grow by 50%, accrued wages and taxes should also grow by about 50%. Accruals are "free" in the sense that no interest is paid on them. However, firms cannot control their accruals because the timing of wage payments is set by contract or industry custom and tax payments are set by law. Thus, firms use all the accruals they can, but they have little **control over their levels.**

SELF TEST

What types of short-term credit are classified as accrued liabilities?

What is the cost of accrued liabilities? If accruals have such a low cost, why don't firms use them even more?

16-13 USE OF SECURITY IN SHORT-TERM FINANCING

Secured Loan
A loan backed by collateral, often inventories or accounts receivable.

Other things held constant, borrowers prefer to use unsecured short-term debt because the bookkeeping costs associated with **secured loans** are high. However, firms may find that they can borrow only if they put up collateral to protect the lender or that securing the loan enables them to borrow at a lower rate.

Stocks and bonds, equipment, inventory, accounts receivable, land, and buildings can be used as collateral. However, few firms that need loans hold portfolios of stocks and bonds. Land, buildings, and equipment are good forms of collateral; but they are generally used to secure long-term loans rather than short-term working capital loans. Therefore, most secured short-term business loans use accounts receivable and inventories as collateral.

To understand the use of security, consider the case of a Chicago hardware dealer who wanted to modernize and expand his store. He requested a $200,000 loan. After examining his financial statements, the bank indicated that it would lend him a maximum of $100,000 on an unsecured basis and that the interest rate would be 10%. However, the company had about $300,000 of accounts receivable that could be used as collateral; and with the receivables as security, the bank agreed to lend the full $200,000 and at the prime rate of 5.25%. Processing costs for administering the loan were fairly high; but even so, the secured loan was less expensive than an unsecured loan would have been.[22]

---

[22]The term *asset-based financing* is often used as a synonym for *secured financing*. In recent years, accounts receivable have been used as security for long-term bonds, which has permitted corporations to borrow from lenders such as pension funds rather than being restricted to banks and other traditional short-term lenders.

When the collateral securing a loan is to be kept on the borrower's premises, a form called a UCC-1 (Uniform Commercial Code Form 1) is filed with the secretary of the state in which the collateral is located, along with a *Security Agreement* (also part of the Uniform Commercial Code) that describes the nature of the agreement. The UCC-1 prevents the borrower from using the same collateral to secure loans from different lenders, and the security agreement spells out conditions under which the lender can seize the collateral.

SELF TEST

From the borrower's standpoint, what are the advantages and disadvantages of securing a loan?

What two types of current assets are frequently used as security for short-term loans?

How could borrowers take advantage of lenders if UCC-1s did not exist?

TYING IT ALL TOGETHER

This chapter discussed the management of current assets, including cash, marketable securities, inventory, and receivables. Current assets are essential, but there are costs associated with holding them. So if a company can reduce its current assets without hurting sales, this will increase its profitability. The investment in current assets must be financed; and this financing can be in the form of long-term debt, common equity, and/or short-term credit. Firms typically use trade credit and accruals; they also may use bank debt or commercial paper.

Although current assets and procedures for financing them can be analyzed as we did in this chapter, decisions are normally made within the context of the firm's overall financial plan. We take up financial planning in the next chapter; hence, we continue our discussion of working capital there.

SELF-TEST QUESTIONS AND PROBLEMS
(Solutions Appear in Appendix A)

ST-1 **KEY TERMS** Define each of the following terms:
   a. Working capital; net working capital
   b. Relaxed current asset policy; restricted current asset policy; moderate current asset policy
   c. Permanent current assets; temporary current assets
   d. Current asset financing policy; maturity matching (self-liquidating) approach to financing working capital
   e. Cash conversion cycle; inventory conversion period; average collection period; payables deferral period
   f. Cash budget; target cash balance
   g. Lockbox; account receivable

h.   Credit policy; credit period; discounts; credit standards; collection policy; credit terms; credit score

i.   Trade credit; free versus costly trade credit

j.   Promissory note; line of credit; revolving credit agreement

k.   Prime rate; simple interest; add-on interest

l.   Commercial paper; accruals; spontaneous funds

m.   Secured loan

ST-2   **WORKING CAPITAL POLICY**   Calgary Company is thinking of modifying its working capital assets policy. Fixed assets are $600,000, sales are projected at $3 million, the EBIT/sales ratio is projected at 15%, the interest rate is 10% on all debt, the federal-plus-state tax rate is 40%, and Calgary plans to maintain a 50% debt-to-assets ratio. Three alternative current asset policies are under consideration: 40%, 50%, and 60% of projected sales. What is the expected return on equity under each alternative?

ST-3   **CURRENT ASSET FINANCING**   Vanderheiden Press Inc. and Herrenhouse Publishing Company had the following balance sheets as of December 31, 2008 (thousands of dollars):

	Vanderheiden Press	**Herrenhouse Publishing**
Current assets	$100,000	$ 80,000
Fixed assets (net)	100,000	120,000
Total assets	$200,000	$200,000
Current liabilities	$ 20,000	$ 80,000
Long-term debt	80,000	20,000
Common stock	50,000	50,000
Retained earnings	50,000	50,000
Total liabilities and equity	$200,000	$200,000

Earnings before interest and taxes for both firms are $30 million, and the effective federal-plus-state tax rate is 40%.

a.   What is the return on equity for each firm if the interest rate on current liabilities is 10% and the rate on long-term debt is 13%?

b.   Assume that the short-term rate rises to 20%. While the rate on new long-term debt rises to 16%, the rate on existing long-term debt remains unchanged. What would be the returns on equity for Vanderheiden Press and Herrenhouse Publishing under these conditions?

c.   Which company is in a riskier position? Why?

QUESTIONS

16-1   What are some pros and cons of holding high levels of current assets in relation to sales? Use the DuPont equation to help explain your answer.

16-2   Define cash conversion cycle (CCC) and explain why, holding other things constant, a firm's profitability would increase if it lowered its CCC.

16-3   What are the two definitions of cash, and why do corporate treasurers often use the second definition?

16-4   What is a cash budget, and how can this statement be used to help reduce the amount of cash that a firm needs to carry? What are the advantages and disadvantages of daily over monthly cash budgets, and how might a cash budget be used when a firm is negotiating a loan from its bank?

16-5   What are the four key factors in a firm's credit policy? How would an easy policy differ from a tight policy? Give examples of how the four factors might differ between the two policies. How would the easy versus the tight policy affect sales? profits?

16-6   What does it mean to adopt a maturity matching approach to financing assets, including current assets? How would a more aggressive or a more conservative approach differ from the maturity matching approach, and how would each affect expected profits and risk? In general, is one approach better than the others?

16-7   Why is some trade credit called free while other credit is called costly? If a firm buys on terms of 2/10, net 30, pays at the end of the 30th day, and typically shows $300,000 of accounts payable on its balance sheet, would the entire $300,000 be free credit, would it be costly credit, or would some be free and some costly? Explain your answer. No calculations are necessary.

16-8   Define each of the following loan terms and explain how they are related to one another: the prime rate, the rate on commercial paper, the simple interest rate on a bank loan calling for interest to be paid monthly, and the rate on an installment loan based on add-on interest. If the stated rate on each of these loans was 6%, would they all have equal, effective annual rates? Explain.

16-9   Why are accruals called spontaneous sources of funds, what are their costs, and why don't firms use more of them?

16-10 Indicate using a (+), (−), or (0) whether each of the following events would probably cause accounts receivable (A/R), sales, and profits to increase, decrease, or be affected in an indeterminate manner:

	A/R	Sales	Profits
The firm tightens its credit standards.	_____	_____	_____
The terms of trade are changed from 2/10, net 30, to 3/10, net 30.	_____	_____	_____
The terms are changed from 2/10, net 30, to 3/10, net 40.	_____	_____	_____
The credit manager gets tough with past due accounts.	_____	_____	_____

PROBLEMS

Easy Problems 1–3

16-1   **CASH CONVERSION CYCLE**   Primrose Corp has $15 million of sales, $2 million of inventories, $3 million of receivables, and $1 million of payables. Its cost of goods sold is 80% of sales, and it finances working capital with bank loans at an 8% rate. What is Primrose's cash conversion cycle (CCC)? If Primrose could *lower* its inventories and receivables by 10% each and increase its payables by 10%, all without affecting sales or cost of goods sold, what would be the new CCC, how much cash would be freed up, and how would that affect pretax profits?

16-2   **RECEIVABLES INVESTMENT**   Lamar Lumber Company has sales of $10 million per year, all on credit terms calling for payment within 30 days; and its accounts receivable are $2 million. What is Lamar's DSO, what would it be if all customers paid on time, and how much capital would be released if Lamar could take action that led to on-time payments?

16-3   **COST OF TRADE CREDIT AND BANK LOAN**   Lamar Lumber buys $8 million of materials (net of discounts) on terms of 3/5, net 60; and it currently pays after 5 days and takes discounts. Lamar plans to expand, which will require additional financing. If Lamar decides to forgo discounts, how much additional credit could it get and what would be the nominal and effective cost of that credit? If the company could get the funds from a bank at a rate of 10%, interest paid monthly, based on a 365-day year, what would be the effective cost of the bank loan? Should Lamar use bank debt or additional trade credit? Explain.

Intermediate Problems 4–6

16-4   **CASH CONVERSION CYCLE**   Zocco Corporation has an inventory conversion period of 75 days, an average collection period of 38 days, and a payables deferral period of 30 days.

a.   What is the length of the cash conversion cycle?

b.   If Zocco's annual sales are $3,421,875 and all sales are on credit, what is the investment in accounts receivable?

c.   How many times per year does Zocco turn over its inventory?

16-5   **RECEIVABLES INVESTMENT**   McDowell Industries sells on terms of 3/10, net 30. Total sales for the year are $912,500; 40% of the customers pay on the 10th day and take discounts, while the other 60% pay, on average, 40 days after their purchases.

a.   What is the days' sales outstanding?

b.   What is the average amount of receivables?

c.   What is the percentage cost of trade credit to customers who take the discount?

d.   What is the percentage cost of trade credit to customers who do not take the discount and pay in 40 days?

e.   What would happen to McDowell's accounts receivable if it toughened up on its collection policy with the result that all nondiscount customers paid on the 30th day?

16-6   **WORKING CAPITAL INVESTMENT**   Prestopino Corporation produces motorcycle batteries. Prestopino turns out 1,500 batteries a day at a cost of $6 per battery for materials and labor. It takes the firm 22 days to convert raw materials into a battery. Prestopino allows its customers 40 days in which to pay for the batteries, and the firm generally pays its suppliers in 30 days.

a.   What is the length of Prestopino's cash conversion cycle?

b.   At a steady state in which Prestopino produces 1,500 batteries a day, what amount of working capital must it finance?

c.   By what amount could Prestopino reduce its working capital financing needs if it was able to stretch its payables deferral period to 35 days?

d.   Prestopino's management is trying to analyze the effect of a proposed new production process on its working capital investment. The new production process would allow Prestopino to decrease its inventory conversion period to 20 days and to increase its daily production to 1,800 batteries. However, the new process would cause the cost of materials and labor to increase to $7. Assuming the change does not affect the average collection period (40 days) or the payables deferral period (30 days), what will be the length of its cash conversion cycle and its working capital financing requirement if the new production process is implemented?

Challenging Problems 7–10

16-7   **WORKING CAPITAL CASH FLOW CYCLE**   Christie Corporation is trying to determine the effect of its inventory turnover ratio and days sales outstanding (DSO) on its cash flow cycle. Christie's 2008 sales (all on credit) were $150,000; and it earned a net profit of 6%, or $9,000. It turned over its inventory 6 times during the year, and its DSO was 36.5 days. The firm had fixed assets totaling $35,000. Christie's payables deferral period is 40 days.

a.   Calculate Christie's cash conversion cycle.

b.   Assuming Christie holds negligible amounts of cash and marketable securities, calculate its total assets turnover and ROA.

c.   Suppose Christie's managers believe that the inventory turnover can be raised to 7.3 times. What would Christie's cash conversion cycle, total assets turnover, and ROA have been if the inventory turnover had been 7.3 for 2008?

16-8   **WORKING CAPITAL POLICY**   Rentz Corporation is investigating the optimal level of current assets for the coming year. Management expects sales to increase to approximately $2 million as a result of an asset expansion presently being undertaken. Fixed assets total $1 million, and the firm plans to maintain a 60% debt ratio. Rentz's interest rate is currently 8% on both short-term and longer-term debt (which the firm uses in its permanent structure). Three alternatives regarding the projected current assets level are under consideration: (1) a tight policy where current assets would be only 45% of projected sales, (2) a moderate policy where current assets would be 50% of sales, and (3) a relaxed policy where current assets would be 60% of sales. Earnings before interest and taxes should be 12% of total sales, and the federal-plus-state tax rate is 40%.

a.   What is the expected return on equity under each current asset level?

b.   In this problem, we assume that expected sales are independent of the current asset policy. Is this a valid assumption? Why or why not?

c.   How would the firm's risk be affected by the different policies?

16-9   **LOCKBOX SYSTEM**   Hardin-Gehr Corporation (HGC) began operations 5 years ago as a small firm serving customers in the Detroit area. However, its reputation and market area grew quickly. Today HGC has customers all over the United States. Despite its broad customer base, HGC has maintained its headquarters in Detroit; and it keeps its central billing system there. On average, it takes 5 days from the time customers mail in payments until HGC can receive, process, and deposit them. HGC would like to set up a lockbox collection system, which it estimates would reduce the time lag from customer mailing to deposit by 3 days—bringing it down to 2 days. HGC receives an average of $1,400,000 in payments per day.

a.   How much free cash would HGC generate if it implemented the lockbox system? Would this be a one-time cash flow or a recurring one, assuming the company ceases to grow? How would growth affect your answer?

b.   If HGC has an opportunity cost of 10%, how much is the lockbox system worth on an annual basis?

c.   What is the maximum monthly charge HGC should pay for the lockbox system?

16-10   **CASH BUDGETING**   Helen Bowers, owner of Helen's Fashion Designs, is planning to request a line of credit from her bank. She has estimated the following sales forecasts for the firm for parts of 2009 and 2010:

May 2009	$180,000
June	180,000
July	360,000
August	540,000
September	720,000
October	360,000
November	360,000
December	90,000
January 2010	180,000

Estimates regarding payments obtained from the credit department are as follows: collected within the month of sale, 10%; collected the month following the sale, 75%; collected the second month following the sale, 15%. Payments for labor and raw materials are made the month after these services were provided. Here are the estimated costs of labor plus raw materials:

May 2009	$ 90,000
June	90,000
July	126,000
August	882,000
September	306,000
October	234,000
November	162,000
December	90,000

General and administrative salaries are approximately $27,000 a month. Lease payments under long-term leases are $9,000 a month. Depreciation charges are $36,000 a month. Miscellaneous expenses are $2,700 a month. Income tax payments of $63,000 are due in September and December. A progress payment of $180,000 on a new design studio must be paid in October. Cash on hand on July 1 will be $132,000, and a minimum cash balance of $90,000 should be maintained throughout the cash budget period.

a.   Prepare a monthly cash budget for the last 6 months of 2009.

b.   Prepare monthly estimates of the required financing or excess funds—that is, the amount of money Bowers will need to borrow or will have available to invest.

c.   Now suppose receipts from sales come in uniformly during the month (that is, cash receipts come in at the rate of $\frac{1}{30}$ each day), but all outflows must be paid on the 5th. Will this affect the cash budget? That is, will the cash budget you prepared be valid under these assumptions? If not, what could be done to make a valid estimate of the peak financing requirements? No calculations are required, although if you prefer, you can use calculations to illustrate the effects.

d. Bowers' sales are seasonal; and her company produces on a seasonal basis, just ahead of sales. Without making any calculations, discuss how the company's current and debt ratios would vary during the year if all financial requirements were met with short-term bank loans. Could changes in these ratios affect the firm's ability to obtain bank credit? Explain.

COMPREHENSIVE/SPREADSHEET PROBLEM

16-11 **CASH BUDGETING** Rework Problem 16-10 using a spreadsheet model. After completing Parts a through d, respond to the following: If Bowers' customers began to pay late, collections would slow down, thus increasing the required loan amount. If sales declined, this also would have an effect on the required loan. Do a sensitivity analysis that shows the effects of these two factors on the maximum loan requirement.

INTEGRATED CASE

SKI EQUIPMENT INC.

16-12 **MANAGING CURRENT ASSETS** Dan Barnes, financial manager of Ski Equipment Inc. (SKI), is excited, but apprehensive. The company's founder recently sold his 51% controlling block of stock to Kent Koren, who is a big fan of EVA (Economic Value Added). EVA is found by taking the after-tax operating profit and subtracting the dollar cost of all the capital the firm uses:

$$\text{EVA} = \text{EBIT}(1 - T) - \text{Capital costs}$$
$$= \text{EBIT}(1 - T) - \text{WACC}(\text{Capital employed})$$

If EVA is positive, the firm is creating value. On the other hand, if EVA is negative, the firm is not covering its cost of capital and stockholders' value is being eroded. Koren rewards managers handsomely if they create value, but those whose operations produce negative EVAs are soon looking for work. Koren frequently points out that if a company can generate its current level of sales with fewer assets, it will need less capital. That would, other things held constant, lower capital costs and increase EVA.

Shortly after he took control of SKI, Koren met with SKI's senior executives to tell them of his plans for the company. First, he presented some EVA data that convinced everyone that SKI had not been creating value in recent years. He then stated, in no uncertain terms, that this situation must change. He noted that SKI's designs of skis, boots, and clothing are acclaimed throughout the industry but that something is seriously amiss elsewhere in the company. Costs are too high, prices are too low, or the company employs too much capital; and he expects SKI's managers to correct the problem.

Barnes has long believed that SKI's working capital situation should be studied—the company may have the optimal amounts of cash, securities, receivables, and inventories; but it may also have too much or too little of these items. In the past, the production manager resisted Barnes's efforts to question his holdings of raw materials inventories, the marketing manager resisted questions about finished goods, the sales staff resisted questions about credit policy (which affects accounts receivable), and the treasurer did not want to talk about her cash and securities balances. Koren's speech made it clear that such resistance would no longer be tolerated.

Barnes also knows that decisions about working capital cannot be made in a vacuum. For example, if inventories could be lowered without adversely affecting operations, less capital would be required, the dollar cost of capital would decline, and EVA would increase. However, lower raw materials inventories might lead to production slowdowns and higher costs, while lower finished goods inventories might lead to the loss of profitable sales. So before inventories are changed, it will be necessary to study operating as well as financial effects. The situation is the same with regard to cash and receivables.

a. Barnes plans to use the ratios in Table IC 16-1 as the starting point for discussions with SKI's operating executives. He wants everyone to think about the pros and cons of changing each type of current asset and the way changes would interact to affect profits and EVA. Based on the data in Table IC16-1, does SKI seem to be following a relaxed, moderate, or restricted working capital policy?

b. How can we distinguish between a relaxed but rational working capital policy and a situation where a firm has a large amount of current assets simply because it is inefficient? Does SKI's working capital policy seem appropriate? Explain.

c. SKI tries to match the maturity of its assets and liabilities. Describe how SKI could adopt a more aggressive or a more conservative financing policy.

d. Assume that SKI's payables deferral period is 30 days. Now calculate the firm's cash conversion cycle.

e. What might SKI do to reduce its cash and securities without harming operations?

In an attempt to better understand SKI's cash position, Barnes developed a cash budget. Data for the first 2 months of the year are shown in Table IC 16-2. (Note that Barnes's preliminary cash budget does not account for interest income or interest expense.) He has the figures for the other months, but they are not shown in Table IC16-2.

f. In his preliminary cash budget, Barnes has assumed that all sales are collected and, thus, that SKI has no bad debts. Is this realistic? If not, how would bad debts be dealt with in a cash budgeting sense? (Hint: Bad debts affect collections but not purchases.)

g. Barnes's cash budget for the entire year, although not given here, is based heavily on his forecast for monthly sales. Sales are expected to be extremely low between May and September but then increase dramatically in the fall and winter. November is typically the firm's best month, when SKI ships equipment to retailers for the holiday season. Interestingly, Barnes's forecasted cash budget indicates that the company's cash holdings will exceed the targeted cash balance every month except October and November, when shipments will be high but collections will not be coming in until later. Based on the ratios in Table IC16-1, does it appear that SKI's target cash balance is appropriate? In addition to possibly lowering the target cash balance, what actions might SKI take to better improve its cash management policies and how might that affect its EVA?

h. Is there any reason to think that SKI may be holding too much inventory? If so, how would that affect EVA and ROE?

i. If the company reduces its inventory without adversely affecting sales, what effect should this have on the company's cash position (1) in the short run and (2) in the long run? Explain in terms of the cash budget and the balance sheet.

j. Barnes knows that SKI sells on the same credit terms as other firms in the industry. Use the ratios presented in Table IC16-1 to explain whether SKI's customers pay more or less promptly than those of its competitors. If there are differences, does that suggest that SKI should tighten or loosen its credit policy? What four variables make up a firm's credit policy, and in what direction should each be changed by SKI?

k. Does SKI face any risks if it tightens its credit policy? Explain.

l. If the company reduces its DSO without seriously affecting sales, what effect will this have on its cash position (1) in the short run and (2) in the long run? Answer in terms of the cash budget and the balance sheet. What effect should this have on EVA in the long run?

m. Assume that SKI buys on terms of 1/10, net 30, but that it can get away with paying on the 40th day if it chooses not to take discounts. Also assume that it purchases $3 million of components per year, net of discounts. How much free trade credit can the company get, how much costly trade credit can it get, and what is the percentage cost of the costly credit? Should SKI take discounts? Why or why not?

n. Suppose SKI decided to raise an additional $100,000 as a 1-year loan from its bank, for which it was quoted a rate of 8%. What is the effective annual cost rate assuming simple interest and add-on interest on a 12-month installment loan?

Table IC 16-1   **Selected Ratios: SKI and Industry Average**

	SKI	Industry
Current	1.75	2.25
Debt/assets	58.76%	50.00%
Turnover of cash and securities	16.67	22.22
Days sales outstanding (365-day basis)	45.63	32.00
Inventory turnover	4.82	7.00
Fixed assets turnover	11.35	12.00
Total assets turnover	2.08	3.00
Profit margin	2.07%	3.50%
Return on equity (ROE)	10.45%	21.00%

| Table IC 16-2 | SKI's Cash Budget for January and February |

	Nov	Dec	Jan	Feb	Mar	Apr
I. COLLECTIONS AND PURCHASES WORKSHEET						
(1) Sales (gross)	$71,218	$68,212.00	$65,213.00	$52,475.00	$42,909	$30,524
Collections						
(2) During month of sale (0.2 × 0.98 × month's sales)			12,781.75	10,285.10		
(3) During first month after sale (0.7 × previous month's sales)			47,748.40	45,649.10		
(4) During second month after sale (0.1 × sales 2 months ago)			7,121.80	6,821.20		
(5) Total collections (Lines 2 + 3 + 4)			$67,651.95	$62,755.40		
Purchases						
(6) (0.85 × forecasted sales 2 months from now)		$44,603.75	$36,472.65	$25,945.40		
(7) Payments (1-month lag)			44,603.75	36,472.65		
II. CASH GAIN OR LOSS FOR MONTH						
(8) Collections (from Section I)			$67,651.95	$62,755.40		
(9) Payments for purchases (from Section I)			44,603.75	36,472.65		
(10) Wages and salaries			6,690.56	5,470.90		
(11) Rent			2,500.00	2,500.00		
(12) Taxes						
(13) Total payments			$53,794.31	$44,443.55		
(14) Net cash gain (loss) during month (Line 8 – Line 13)			$13,857.64	$18,311.85		
III. CASH SURPLUS OR LOAN REQUIREMENT						
(15) Cash at beginning of month if no borrowing is done			$ 3,000.00	$16,857.64		
(16) Cumulative cash [cash at start + gain or − loss = (Line 14 + Line 15)]			$16,857.64	$35,169.49		
(17) Target cash balance			1,500.00	1,500.00		
(18) Cumulative surplus cash or loans outstanding to maintain $1,500 target cash balance (Line 16 – Line 17)			$15,357.64	$33,669.49		

CHAPTER 17

Financial Planning and Forecasting

The Miss That Hit Like a Bombshell

In March 2008, CEO Jeffrey Immelt announced to security analysts that GE's divisions were hitting their earnings targets and that the firm would enjoy double-digit growth for the year. According to Immelt, GE's global portfolio of businesses, which ranged from nuclear power plants to TV networks and movie studios, stabilized earnings and protected the company from economic shocks such as the subprime mortgage debacle. GE's stock responded nicely, rising from $32 to $38 per share. However, less than a month later Immelt held another televised news conference where he announced that GE's first-quarter earnings were down 5.8%, with similar declines likely for the rest of 2008. GE's stock plunged, lowering stockholder wealth by about $50 billion in just one day.

Immelt's announcement delivered a blow to GE's reputation and credibility. Investors set stock prices based on information and recommendations from the security analysts who work for the large investment banks and brokerages. Analysts study historical data, but they recognize

that companies' managers have the best information about future earnings. Therefore, if a company is "credible" and can be trusted, analysts base their forecasts heavily on information like Immelt provided in his March forecast. Each analyst produces a "target price," which is essentially his or her estimate of the stock's intrinsic value. The brokers of the analysts' firms then use that information when they make recommendations to their customers. Immelt's initial forecast led to buy recommendations and GE purchases, but the quick retraction led to substantial losses and unhappy customers. Those customers let their brokers know how they felt, and those feelings were relayed to the analysts and then to Immelt; and he probably called some of his subordinates to task. The whole episode was embarrassing to Immelt and to GE. GE's board must have been unhappy, which is not good for a CEO in an era when CEOs can be easily replaced.

GE was founded to commercialize Thomas Edison's inventions in lightbulb and power plant

525

technologies, but today its divisions extend far beyond its base. A number of analysts have questioned GE's diversification strategy and have argued that the company should spin off unrelated units and return to its roots. They point out that GE's stock price in 2008 is about 30% below its 2001 level; and they ask why, if the company has such a good strategic plan, its stock price has not done better. Here's the comment of one analyst, Citigroup's Jeff Sprague: "We believe the evidence is mounting that GE is too big and complex to manage effectively." Sprague and others believe that stockholders would be better served if GE was split into several smaller, more focused companies. Then each company's CEO would presumably understand his or her particular business and could focus exclusively on running it. Businesses that are related could be kept together, but unrelated ones would be spun off. If that was done, perhaps forecasting would be easier, Immelt would end up less chagrined, and GE's stockholders would be wealthier.

Source: "GE Shocks Market with Profit Drop, Shares Tumble," April 11, 2008, http://moneycentral.msn.com.

PUTTING THINGS IN PERSPECTIVE

Yogi Berra, the former player and manager for the New York Yankees, once said, "If you don't know where you're going, you probably won't get there." That's certainly true for a company—it needs a plan, one that starts with the firm's general goals and details the steps that will be taken to get there. When you finish this chapter, you should be able to:

- **Discuss the importance of strategic planning and the central role that financial forecasting plays in the overall planning process.**
- **Explain how firms forecast sales.**
- **Use the Additional Funds Needed (or AFN) equation and discuss the relationship between asset growth and the need for funds.**
- **Explain how spreadsheets are used in the forecasting process, starting with historical statements, ending with projected statements, and including a set of financial ratios based on those projected statements.**
- **Discuss how planning is an iterative process.**

Financial planners begin with a set of assumptions, see what is likely to happen based on those assumptions, and then see if modifications can help the firm achieve better results. GE's critics suggest that the company should make forecasts based on its current structure and on an "if broken up" basis, then go forward with the breakup if that indicates the higher shareholder value.[1]

Although we focus on forecasting from the corporation's standpoint, top security analysts go through the same process. Analysts with hedge and private equity funds are especially active as forecasters, and they are particularly interested in the iterative process of forecasting.

---

[1]GE's executives have undoubtedly done these analyses. However, since executive compensation is a function of the size of the corporation, there is a bias against voluntary divestitures. Hedge funds and buyout funds have no such bias, so the majority of breakups are led by activist investors.

17-1 STRATEGIC PLANNING

Management textbooks often list the following as the key elements of a strategic plan:

- *Mission Statement.* Many but not all firms articulate a **mission statement.** GE does not have one, but it states that its chairman's letter in the annual report serves this purpose. In his letter, Jeff Immelt discusses his goals for GE's major businesses and for the firm as a whole. Not surprisingly, Immelt indicated that he wants the various businesses to achieve high growth rates, high profit margins, and high rates of return on invested capital, all with the ultimate goal of increasing GE's stock price.

  Mission Statement
  A condensed version of a firm's strategic plan.

- *Corporate Scope.* **Corporate scope** defines the lines of business the firm plans to pursue and the geographic areas in which it will operate. Some firms deliberately limit their scope on the theory that it is better for top managers to focus sharply on a narrow range of functions as opposed to spreading the company over many different types of businesses. Academics have studied which is the better choice. Some studies suggest that investors generally value focused firms more highly than diversified ones.[2] However, if a firm is successful in combining a group of diversified businesses so that they help one another, as GE tries to do, the result may be synergistic effects that raise the value of the overall enterprise.[3] In any event, the stated corporate scope should be logical and consistent with the firm's capabilities.

  Corporate Scope
  Defines a firm's lines of business and geographic areas of operation.

- *Statement of Corporate Objectives.* A firm's **statement of coporate objectives** is that part of the corporate plan that sets forth the specific goals that operating managers are expected to meet. Like most firms, GE has both qualitative and quantitative objectives. For example, here is a key statement from Immelt's 2006 letter to stockholders:

  Statement of Corporate Objectives
  Sets forth specific goals to guide management.

  We expect our businesses to achieve 10%+ earnings growth most years, with long-term returns on equity of 20%. We expect our businesses to be industry leaders in market share, value, and profitability.

  GE has a history of selling off units that do not meet its objectives and of replacing underperforming managers, but GE also rewards managers generously when they meet their targets.

- *Corporate Strategies.* GE has several broad **corporate strategies**. One is to be highly diversified by both products and geographic scope in order to achieve earnings stability and financial strength. Its management believes that financial strength will lead to a low cost of capital, which will benefit all its units. Also, since GE's management believes that the company should be at the forefront in addressing environmental issues, it is investing heavily in

  Corporate Strategies
  Broad approaches developed for achieving a firm's goals.

---

[2]See, for example, Philip G. Berger and Eli Ofek, "Diversification's Effect on Firm Value," *Journal of Financial Economics,* Vol. 37, no. 1 (1995), pp. 39–66; and Larry Lang and René Stulz, "Tobin's Q, Corporate Diversification, and Firm Performance," *Journal of Political Economy,* Vol. 102, Issue 6 (1994), pp. 1248–1280.

[3]The dictionary definition of *synergy* is a situation where the whole is greater than the sum of the parts, and it's sometimes called the $2 + 2 = 5$ effect. GE has a jet engine business and another business that produces gas turbines for electric power generation. Those businesses are similar enough so that new developments in one can benefit the other. One has to wonder, though, how GE's jet engine business benefits its Universal-NBC entertainment unit. GE's management argues that its diversification stabilizes its revenues and profits and that this resulted in a triple-A bond rating and a relatively low cost of capital for all its businesses. A number of academic studies dispute this conclusion, though, with the academics arguing that it is easy for stockholders to diversify and better to have top managers focus on one business. Interestingly, GE's April 2008 earnings shortfall brought forth calls for the company to be broken up into more cohesive units whose managers could focus on products and markets that they knew very well.

infrastructure technologies to purify air and water. Immelt expects to "do good by doing good."

Operating Plan
Provides management with detailed implementation guidance based on the corporate strategy to help meet the corporate objectives.

Financial Plan
The document that includes assumptions, projected financial statements, and projected ratios and ties the entire planning process together.

- *Operating Plan.* Each of GE's units must develop a detailed **operating plan** that is consistent with the corporate strategy to help it achieve the firm's objectives. Operating plans can be developed for any time horizon, but most companies use a 5-year horizon. The plan explains in considerable detail those people responsible for each particular function, deadlines for specific tasks, sales and profit targets, and the like.

- *Financial Plan.* Financial planning is a multistep process. Allied's **financial plan** involves four steps. First, assumptions are made about the future levels of sales, costs, interest rates, and so forth, for use in the forecast. Second, a set of projected financial statements is developed. Third, projected ratios such as those we discussed in Chapter 4 are calculated and analyzed. Fourth, the entire plan is reexamined, the assumptions are reviewed, and the management team considers how additional changes in operations might improve results. This last step requires reconsideration of all the earlier parts of the overall plan, from the mission statement to the operating plan. Thus, the financial plan ties the entire planning process together.

  Financial planning as described previously is often called "value-based management," meaning that the effects of various decisions on the firm's financial position and value are studied by simulating their effects within the firm's financial model. For example, if GE was considering a shift in appliance manufacturing from Kentucky to Mexico, it would simulate the effects through its financial model and then make the move if it appeared that profits and thus shareholder wealth would be increased.[4]

What are the key elements of a corporation's strategic plan?

How is the financial plan related to the other parts of a firm's overall strategic plan?

How can the financial plan be used to help management provide guidance to security analysts?

17-2 THE SALES FORECAST

Financial plans generally begin with a *sales forecast*, which starts with a review of sales during the past 5 years, shown as a graph such as the one in Figure 17-1 for Allied Foods. These numbers are based on Allied's financial statements, which were first presented in Chapter 3. The data below the graph show 5 years of historical sales.

Allied had its ups and downs from 2004 to 2008. In 2006, poor weather in California's fruit-producing regions resulted in below-average crops, which caused 2006 sales to fall below the 2005 level. Then a bumper crop in 2007 pushed sales up by 15%, an unusually high growth rate for a mature food processor. As shown in the chapter's Excel model, the compound annual growth rate over the 4-year period was 9.88%.[5] Due to planned new products, planned increased

---

[4]Note, though, that there would surely be political ramifications to such a move. These effects would be studied by use of the model, and the computer-generated results would be an input in the decision. However, the ultimate decision would be made by GE's top executives and board, not, in essence, by a computer.
[5]Note that you need 5 years of data to find the 4-year growth rate from 2004 to 2008.

FIGURE 17-1	Allied Food Products: 2009 Sales Projection (Millions of Dollars)

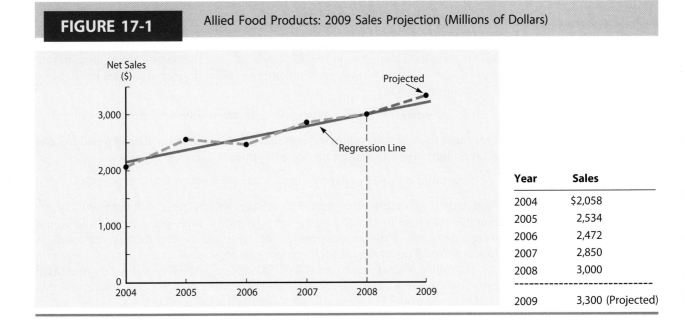

Year	Sales
2004	$2,058
2005	2,534
2006	2,472
2007	2,850
2008	3,000
2009	3,300 (Projected)

production, planned distribution capacity, a new advertising campaign, and other factors, management expects the growth rate to increase slightly, to 10%, in 2009. Therefore, sales should rise from $3,000 million to $3,300 million.

Of course, management likes higher sales growth, but not at any cost. For example, sales could be increased by cutting prices, spending more on advertising, granting easier credit, and the like. However, all of those actions would have a cost. Also, sales growth cannot occur without a concurrent increase in capacity, and that too is costly. So the sales growth must be balanced against the cost of achieving that growth.

If the sales forecast is off, the consequences can be serious. First, if the market expands by more than Allied expects, it will not be able to meet demand, its customers will buy from competitors, and it will lose market share. On the other hand, if its projections are overly optimistic, Allied could end up with too much plant, equipment, and inventory, leading to low turnover ratios, high costs for depreciation and storage, and write-offs of spoiled inventory. This would result in low profits and a depressed stock price. Moreover, if Allied financed its expansion with debt, high interest charges would compound the firm's problems.

Finally, note that the sales forecast is the most important input in the firm's forecast of financial statements, including the projected EPS, which we will cover in Section 17-4. The importance of the sales forecast is highlighted when we forecast the financial statements.

SELF TEST   Why is an accurate sales forecast critical for financial planning?

17-3 THE AFN EQUATION

We saw in Chapter 3 that in 2008, Allied had assets of $2,000 million and sales of $3,000 million. Thus, it required $2,000/$3,000 = $0.6667 of assets to generate each dollar of sales. Moreover, the company plans to increase sales by 10%, or $300 million, in 2009:

$$\text{Increase in Sales} = \Delta\text{Sales} = 0.10(\$3{,}000 \text{ million}) = \$300 \text{ million}$$

Assuming the assets-to-sales ratio remains constant, Allied will need an additional $200 million of assets to support the $300 million increase in sales:

$$\text{Required increase in assets} = 0.6667(\Delta\text{Sales}) = 0.6667(\$300) = \$200 \text{ million}$$

Note that if growth is low (say, 0%), ΔSales will be zero and there will be no required increase in assets. On the other hand, if sales grow very rapidly, the requirement for additional assets will be large. Thus, the increase in assets is fundamentally dependent on the growth rate in sales.

Naturally, if assets are to grow by $200 million, liabilities and equity must also grow by the same amount—the balance sheet must balance. But where will this capital come from? Here are a firm's primary capital sources:

Spontaneously Generated Funds
Funds that arise out of normal business operations from its suppliers, employees, and the government (such as accounts payable and accrued wages and taxes) that reduce the firm's need for external financing.

1. *Spontaneous Increases in Accounts Payable and Accruals.* Allied must make additional purchases to increase its inventories, and it must hire more workers. Its purchases will automatically lead to additional accounts payable, which amount to "loans" from its suppliers. Also, hiring more workers will automatically lead to higher accrued wages, which amount to short-term "loans" from its workers. Hence, some of the required $200 million will come *spontaneously* from suppliers and workers—this is called **spontaneously generated funds**. Also, assuming profit margins are maintained, higher sales will mean higher profits and thus higher taxes and accrued taxes. So "spontaneous" increases in payables, accrued wages, and accrued taxes will take care of part of the required $200 million.

Retention Ratio
The proportion of net income that is reinvested in the firm and is calculated as 1 minus the dividend payout ratio.

2. *Addition to Retained Earnings.* Assuming Allied has positive earnings and does not pay out all of those earnings as dividends, its retained earnings will grow. The addition to retained earnings depends on the firm's profit margin and its **retention ratio**, which is the proportion of net income that is reinvested in the firm. This addition to retained earnings will help finance growth.

Additional Funds Needed (AFN)
The amount of external capital (interest-bearing debt and preferred and common stock) needed to acquire the needed assets.

3. *AFN: Additional Funds Needed.* It is possible that spontaneous funds and additional retained earnings will offset the forecasted increase in assets. Normally, though, that situation does not occur—normally, there is a short-fall, called **Additional Funds Needed (AFN)**, which has to be made up by additional borrowing and/or the sale of new stock. Note, though, that if a company is growing very slowly and thus not increasing assets very much, its spontaneous funds plus its addition to retained earnings may be larger than the required increase in assets. In that case, the AFN is negative, indicating that a surplus of capital is forecasted.

AFN Equation
An equation that shows the relationship of external funds needed by a firm to its projected increase in assets, the spontaneous increase in liabilities, and its increase in retained earnings.

We can combine these concepts to develop Equation 17-1, the **AFN equation**. AFN is the total amount of new interest-bearing debt and preferred and common stock the firm must issue to support its planned growth.[6]

---

[6]The term *additional funds needed* was developed to show how much additional capital a firm needs to support its planned growth. However, as we see later, a firm may be able to grow without any additional outside capital. In fact, the firm may even generate excess capital that can be used to retire debt, repurchase stock, and raise the dividend. In this case, the calculated AFN will be negative. Also, in this chapter we do quite a few calculations and generally round when we show results. This may lead to minor "rounding differences," which you should disregard.

$$
\begin{array}{cccc}
\text{Additional} & \text{Projected} & \text{Spontaneous} & \text{Increase in} \\
\text{funds} = \text{increase} & - & \text{increase in} & - & \text{retained} \\
\text{needed, or AFN} & \text{in assets} & \text{liabilities} & \text{earnings} \\
\end{array}
$$

$$
= (A_0^*/S_0)\Delta S - (L_0^*/S_0)\Delta S \quad - \quad MS_1(1 - \text{Payout}) \quad \boxed{17\text{-}1}
$$

Allied Foods' CFO used Equation 17-1 in the following manner. Every fall the company's Executive Committee, which includes the CEO, the CFO, and other top executives, meets to consider plans for the coming year. The meeting this year is especially important for two reasons: (1) The national credit crunch is constraining the firm's ability to raise capital, so the amounts needed and available must be determined. (2) Corporate raiders and private equity firms have targeted a number of food processors; and when they take over, heads roll in the acquired firm. Allied's executives are aware of both factors.

Allied's CFO plans to proceed in two steps. First, he will use the AFN equation to give the others an idea of how much new capital the firm will need to support the targeted 10% growth rate, assuming the various operating ratios remain constant. Second, he will present the results of a full-scale financial planning model. The model will show forecasted financial statements in addition to a set of forecasted ratios like those discussed in Chapter 4, along with an estimate of the 2009 EPS. The CFO hopes the EPS forecast will help the company avoid the embarrassment suffered by GE's Jeff Immelt, which was discussed in this chapter's opening vignette.

The CFO brought copies of Table 17-1, which is based on Equation 17-1, and data from the financial statements presented in Chapter 3 to the Executive Committee.[7] Part I of the table picks up selected data from the 2008 balance sheet and income statement. Part II uses the Part I data to calculate inputs for Equation 17-1. Note that all the calculations in Part II assume that the company's operating ratios in 2009 continue at 2008 levels. Part III uses the items calculated in Part II to calculate the AFN. To increase sales by $300 million, Allied must increase assets by $200 million. The asset increase will be supported by $20 million from spontaneous increases in payables and accruals, and another $66 million will come from retained earnings. In total, $114 million of new outside funds will be needed; and since Allied does not use preferred stock, the amount must come from interest-bearing debt in addition to new common stock.

As noted, the AFN equation assumes that the 2009 ratios will remain constant at the 2008 levels. If economic conditions or managerial decisions cause the ratios to change, the forecasted AFN will change. Part IV of the table shows how some specific input changes will change the forecasted AFN. For example, if the target growth rate was increased from 10% to 15% with other things held constant, the AFN would increase from $114 million to $201 million. On the other hand, if the target growth rate was lowered to 5%, the AFN would be only $27 million. Also, as shown in Part V, if the company grew at a rate of 3.45% while other things were held constant, AFN would be zero. Thus, 3.45% is called Allied's **sustainable growth rate**.

Finally, note that if the growth rate slowed and other inputs were changed in the manner specified in Part IV of the table, Allied would end up with a large *negative* AFN, indicating that retained earnings and spontaneous capital were far more than sufficient to finance the now smaller amount of additional assets needed.

Sustainable Growth Rate
The maximum achievable growth rate without the firm having to raise external funds. In other words, it is the growth rate at which the firm's AFN equals zero.

---

[7]The CFO also loaded the Excel model on his laptop so he could do on-the-spot sensitivity analyses. For example, he could change the growth rate and instantly find the new AFN. Similarly, he could change the dividend payout ratio, the profit margin, and the other variables to see how those changes would affect the firm's capital requirements. Still, the analysis in Table 17-1 provided a useful starting point.

Table 17-1	Additional Funds Needed (AFN) Model ($ in Millions)

	A	B	C	D	E	F	G	H	I	J
1										
2	Part I. 2008 Data from Chapter 3, Tables 3-1 and 3-2									
3	A_0^* = Assets at 12/31/08; all assets were needed for 2008 sales							$2,000		
4	S_0 = 2008 Sales							$3,000		
5	2008 Net Income							$117.5		
6	2008 Dividends							$57.5		
7	L_0^* = 2008 payables + accruals, which increase spontaneously with sales							$200		
8	Part II. Data Used in the AFN Equation: 2008 Ratios Held Constant									
9	AFN = Additional Funds Needed to buy assets needed to support growth. AFN is in addition to funds raised internally (i.e., AFN represents required external funds).							Base Case: 2008 Data		
10	g = Target growth rate in sales							10.00%		
11	A_0^*/S_0 = Assets required per $1 of sales = $2,000/$3,000. Shows the required new assets for the coming year when multiplied by the increase in sales. Also called the *capital intensity ratio*. The higher this ratio, the more new assets the firm will need to support a given amount of growth.							0.6667		
12	S_1 = 2009 Sales = $(1 + g)(S_0) = (1.1)(\$3,000)$							$3,300		
13	ΔS = Growth in sales = $S_1 - S_0$ = $3,300 - $3,000. It can also be found as $\Delta S = g(S_0)$.							$300		
14	L_0^*/S_0 = Spontaneously generated funds per dollar of new sales. When multiplied by ΔS, we find the new payables and accruals that are available to support growth.							0.0667		
15	M = Profit margin on sales = 2008 net income/S_0 = $117.5/$3,000. Multiply by S_1 (not S_0) to find the net income available in 2009 for dividends or growth.							0.0392		
16	RR = Retention Rate = (1 - Dividend Payout Ratio) = (1 - Dividends/Net Income) = (1 - $57.5/$117.50). The higher the retention rate, the greater the proportion of net income that is retained to support growth.							0.5106		
17	Part III. The AFN Equation									
18	AFN	=	Required increase in assets	-	Spontaneous increase in Payables and Accruals	-	Funds obtained as new Retained Earnings Based on 2009 Sales			
19		=	$(A_0^*/S_0)\Delta S$	-	$(L_0^*/S_0)\Delta S$	-	$MS_1(RR)$			
20		=	0.6667($300)	-	0.0667($300)	-	0.0392($3,300)(0.5106)			
21		=	$200	-	$20	-	$66			
22	AFN	=	$114 million							
23	Part IV. Sensitivity Analysis: AFN with Changed Input Values							AFN (Old = $114)		
24								New	Change: New - Old	
25	Higher Growth:	15%, up from 10%. With faster growth, the firm needs more new assets.						$201	$87	
26	Lower Growth:	5%, down from 10%. With slower growth, the firm needs less new assets. At g < 3.45%, new retained earnings plus spontaneous funds exceed required new assets.						$27	-$87	
27	A_0^*/S_0:	0.5000, down from 0.6667. This factor is called the capital intensity ratio. We lowered it in this example; and with a lower value, fewer assets are required for any given level of sales. If Allied's management can increase the total assets turnover ratio, the A_0^*/S_0 ratio will decline, which will reduce AFN.						$64	-$50	
28	L_0^*/S_0:	0.0800, up from 0.0667. Allied spontaneously generates funds from accounts payable and accruals; and the larger the L_0^*/S_0 ratio, the smaller the need for external financing. With a higher value, more spontaneous funds are available; so the AFN declines.						$110	-$4	

(Continued)

29	M:	0.1000, up from 0.0392. If the profit margin increases, more earnings will be available to support growth and thus the smaller the AFN. With a higher profit margin, more net income is earned; so the AFN declines.	$12	-$102
30	Payout:	20%, down from 48.94%. If Allied lowers the dividend payout ratio, more of its earnings will be retained and thus the smaller the AFN. Here we lower the payout, so the AFN declines.	$77	-$37
31		Change all variables simultaneously to g = 5% and the other values as indicated above. The result is a large but negative AFN, indicating that the firm is generating a substantial amount of capital—more than sufficient to meet its forecasted asset requirements.	-$189	-$303
32				
33		Part V. Sustainable Growth Rate. Maximum achievable growth rate without raising external funds (i.e., g that forces AFN = 0, holding other variables at base-case levels). Use g = 3.45%, and you will see that AFN = 0.		3.45%

17-3a Excess Capacity Adjustments

The AFN equation includes the term A_0^*/S_0, which is called the **capital intensity ratio**. For Allied, this ratio is calculated as $2,000/$3,000 = 0.6667. When multiplied by ΔS = $300 million, this ratio indicated that Allied must increase its assets by $200 million. However, the CFO thought that in 2008, Allied had more fixed assets than it really needed; he wanted to demonstrate to the Executive Committee how **excess capacity adjustments** might affect the firm's need for external funds. He noted that Allied had $1,000 million of current assets and $1,000 million of fixed assets; so he broke A_0^*/S_0 into two parts, one for fixed assets and one for current assets:

$$\text{Current assets}: A_{0C}^*/S_0 = \$1,000/\$3,000 = 0.333 = 33.3\%$$
$$\text{Fixed assets}: A_{0F}^*/S_0 = \$1,000/\$3,000 = 0.333 = 33.3\%$$

> **Capital Intensity Ratio**
> *The ratio of assets required per dollar of sales (A_0^*/S_0).*

> **Excess Capacity Adjustments**
> *Changes made to the existing asset forecast because the firm is not operating at full capacity.*

Now suppose that the current assets were used at full capacity but that fixed assets had been used at only 96% of capacity in 2008. Therefore, if fixed assets had been used to full capacity, sales could have reached $3,125 million before any additions to fixed assets were required versus the actual $3,000 million of sales. In this example, the calculated $3,125 million sales is Allied's full capacity sales:

$$\text{Full capacity sales} = \frac{\text{Actual sales}}{\text{Percentage of capacity at which fixed assets were operated}}$$
$$= \$3,000 \text{ million}/0.96 = \$3,125 \text{ million}$$

This indicates that Allied's Target fixed assets/Sales ratio should be 32% rather than the indicated 33.3% calculated previously:

$$\text{Target fixed assets/Sales} = \frac{\text{Actual fixed assets}}{\text{Full capacity sales}}$$
$$= \$1,000/\$3,125 = 0.32 = 32\%$$

Under these conditions, sales could increase to $3,125 million with no increase in fixed assets and a sales increase to $3,300 million would require only $1,056 million of fixed assets, or an additional $56 million of fixed assets:

$$\frac{\text{Required level}}{\text{of fixed assets}} = (\text{Target fixed assets/Sales})(\text{Projected sales})$$
$$= 0.32(\$3,300) = \$1,056 \text{ million}$$

$$\text{Earlier estimate of AFN} = 1.1(\$1,000) = \$1,100 \text{ million}$$
$$\text{Difference} = -\$44 \text{ million}$$

Thus, the existence of excess capacity would lower Allied's required AFN from $114 million to $114 million − $44 million = $70 million.

A similar situation could occur with respect to inventories, cash, or any other asset. Moreover, the L_0^*/S_0 ratio could be increased if the firm negotiated longer credit terms for its purchases. Similarly, it might be possible for Allied to improve its profit margin or to lower its dividend payout ratio. Because so many conditions can change, it is useful to go beyond the AFN equation analysis and construct Allied's **forecasted financial statements**, the topic of the next section. Also, we want to know how good or bad the firm's financial ratios will be and what the impact will be on its EPS. The AFN tells us nothing about those things, but the forecasted financial statements do.

Forecasted Financial Statements
Financial statements that project the company's financial position and performance over a period of years.

SELF TEST

If the key ratios are expected to remain constant, the AFN equation can be used to forecast the need for external funds. Write out the equation and explain its logic.

How would an *increase* in each of the following factors affect the AFN?
(1) Payout ratio
(2) Capital intensity ratio, A_0^*/S_0
(3) Profit margin
(4) Days sales outstanding, DSO
(5) Sales growth rate

Is it possible for the AFN to be negative? If so, what would that indicate?

If excess capacity exists, how would that affect the calculated AFN?

17-4 FORECASTED FINANCIAL STATEMENTS[8]

The AFN equation provides useful insights into the forecasting process—if you understand the AFN, you will find it easier to understand forecasted financial statements. Therefore, Allied's CFO used the AFN calculations in Table 17-1 as a warm up for his presentation of the forecasted 2009 financial statements. We describe how he developed the forecast presented in Table 17-2 in this section. Following is a brief discussion of the table.

17-4a Part I. Inputs

Rows 2 through 9 show the basic inputs, or assumptions, used in the forecast. The CFO had met previously with the CEO and other top executives. They had reviewed the ratio analysis developed in Chapter 4 and concluded that improvements must be made in 2009. Otherwise, a private equity buyer or hedge fund might decide to take over the firm; and if that occurred, the executives would probably lose their jobs.

---

[8]This section is relatively straightforward, but it does involve a number of steps. The table can be developed with a calculator, but it's far easier to do using Excel. We recommend that everyone read the section and look at Table 17-2 while doing so. Finance majors should read the section especially carefully. It also would help if they accessed the chapter model and worked through it.

Adjustable Inputs. The inputs in Column C show key 2008 ratios that management controls and that may be adjusted in the future. Column D gives the values the CFO used for the initial 2009 forecast, and Column E gives industry-average numbers. The first input shown is the growth rate. This number can be changed; but throughout Table 17-2, a 10% growth rate is assumed. Next, we have the Operating costs/Sales ratio. Allied's ratio in 2008 was 90.54%, which is higher than the industry's 87% ratio. A reduction toward the industry average would lead to a substantial improvement in net income, and the CFO used as a tentative target for 2009 a ratio of 89.5%. Next, we saw in Chapter 4 that Allied's receivables and inventories were too high relative to its sales. If those accounts can be reduced, the result will be lower bad debts and storage costs and thus increased profits. Also, the excess capital invested in receivables and inventories can be released and used to pay off debt and/or to repurchase common stock, both of

Table 17-2		Forecasted Financial Statements (Total Dollars and Shares in Millions)				
	A	B	C	D	E	F	G

	A / B	C	D	E	F	G
1						
2	Part I. Inputs					
3		Adjustable Inputs				
4		2008	2009	Industry	Fixed Inputs	
5	Growth rate, g	NA	10.00%	NA	Tax rate (T)	40%
6	Operating costs/Sales	90.54%	89.50%	87.00%	Interest rate	10.00%
7	Receivables/Sales	12.50%	11.00%	9.86%	Shares out'ing	50
8	Inventories/Sales	20.50%	19.00%	9.17%	Price per share	$23.06
9	Debt ratio	53.00%	49.00%	40.00%	FA/Sales	33.33%
	Payout ratio	48.94%	47.00%	45.00%		
10	Part II. Income Statements	2008		Change		2009
11	Sales	$3,000.0		(1 + g)		$3,300.0
12	Operating costs (includes depreciation)	2,716.2		0.895		2,953.5
13	Earnings before interest and taxes (EBIT)	$ 283.8				$ 346.5
14	Less interest expense	88.0		See notes		80.9
15	Earnings before taxes (EBT)	$ 195.8				$ 265.6
16	Taxes	78.3		EBT(T)		106.2
17	Net income (NI)	$ 117.5				$ 159.3
18	Dividends	$ 57.5		NI(Payout)		$ 74.9
19	Addition to retained earnings	$ 60.0				$ 84.4
20	Part III. Balance Sheets	2008		Change		2009
21	*Assets*					
22	Cash	$ 10.0		(1 + g)		$ 11.0
23	Accounts receivable	375.0		0.1100		363.0
24	Inventories	615.0		0.1900		627.0
25	Fixed assets (grow with sales)	1,000.0		(1 + g)		1,100.0
26	Total assets	$2,000.0				$2,101.0
27	*Liabilities and Equity*					
28	Payables + accruals (both grow with sales)	$ 200.0		(1 + g)		$ 220.0
29	Short-term bank loans	110.0		See notes		103.5
30	Total current liabilities	$ 310.0				$ 323.5
31	Long-term bonds	750.0		See notes		706.0
32	Total debt	$1,060.0				$1,029.5
33	Common stock	130.0		See notes		177.1
34	Retained earnings	810.0		$84.4		894.4
35	Total common equity	$ 940.0				$1,071.5
36	Total liabilities and equity	$2,000.0				$2,101.0

(Continued)

| | _Table 17-2_ | _(Continued)_ | | |

	Part IV. Ratios and EPS	2008	2009E	Industry
37				
38	Operating costs/Sales	90.54%	89.50%	87.00%
39	Receivables/Sales	12.50%	11.00%	9.86%
40	Inventory/Sales	20.50%	19.00%	9.17%
41	Debt ratio	53.00%	49.00%	40.00%
42	Payout ratio	48.94%	47.00%	45.00%
43	Inventory turnover	4.88×	5.26×	10.90×
44	Days sales outstanding (DSO)	45.63 days	40.15 days	36.00 days
45	Total assets turnover	1.50×	1.57×	1.80×
46	Assets/Equity (equity multiplier)	2.13×	1.96×	1.67×
47	Times interest earned (TIE)	3.23×	4.28×	6.00×
48	Profit margin	3.92%	4.83%	5.00%
49	Return on assets (ROA)	5.88%	7.58%	9.00%
50	Return on equity (ROE)	12.50%	14.87%	15.00%

	DuPont Calculations	Profit Margin N/S	Total Assests Turnover (S/A)	Equity Multiplier (A/E)	= ROE
51					
52	Actual for 2008	3.92%	1.50	2.13	12.5%
53	Forecasted for 2009	4.83%	1.57	1.96	14.9%
54	Industry-average data	5.00%	1.80	1.67	15.0%
55	**Earnings per share (EPS)**	**$2.35**	**$3.06**		

56	Part V. Notes on Calculations	
57	Assets in 2009 will change to this amount, from the balance sheet	$2,101.0
58	Target debt ratio	49.00%
59	Resulting total debt: (Target ratio)(2009 Assets)	$1,029.5
60	Less: Payables and accruals	-$ 220.0
51	Bank loans and bonds (= Interest-bearing debt)	$ 809.5
62	Allocated to bank loans, based on 2008 proportions	12.79%	$ 103.5
63	Allocated to bonds, based on 2008 proportions	87.21%	$ 706.0
64	Interest expense: (Interest rate)(2009 Bank loans plus bonds)	$ 80.9
65	Target equity ratio = 1 - Target debt ratio	51%
66	Required total equity: (2009 Assets)(Target equity ratio)	$1,071.5
67	Retained earnings, from 2009 balance sheet	$ 894.4
68	Required common stock = Required equity - Retained earnings	$ 177.1
69	Old shares outstanding (millions)	50
70	Increase in common stock = 2009 Stock - 2008 Stock	$ 47.1
71	Initial price per share from input section	$ 23.06
72	Change in shares = Change in stock/Initial price per share	2.04
73	New shares outstanding = Old shares + Δ Shares	52.04
74	Old EPS = 2008 Net income/Old shares outstanding	$ 2.35
75	New EPS = 2009 Net income/New shares outstanding	$ 3.06

which would improve the firm's ROE and EPS. Again, the CFO set initial targets between Allied's 2008 ratios and the industry averages.

In addition, Allied's debt ratio, at 53%, greatly exceeds the 40% industry average; and the firm's bankers have complained and indicated that the cost of debt would decline if this ratio was lowered. Security analysts also have stated that Allied's stock is riskier than it would be if it had less debt, and that adversely affects its price/earnings (P/E) ratio.

Similarly, Allied's dividend payout ratio is above average, and the CEO and several board members think that it should be lowered. This would provide more funds to support growth, which stockholders may want.

Fixed Inputs. Some other inputs required for the forecast are not under management's direct control or are not expected to change. These inputs are shown in Column G—the tax rate; the interest rate; the shares initially outstanding; the initial stock price; and the Fixed assets/Sales ratio, which the CFO concluded was fine. The number of shares outstanding will change in 2009 depending on how much new equity the firm must raise; but in this analysis, the other variables are held constant. Of course, management hopes the stock price will increase as a result of the firm's actions and improved financial position, but the CFO wisely decided not to make a prediction at this point.

17-4b Part II. Forecasted Income Statement

The forecasted 2009 income statement starts with the 2008 income statement, but forecasts that 2009 sales will grow by 10%. Next, the assumed new operating cost ratio is multiplied by the new sales level to calculate the forecasted 2009 operating costs, which are subtracted from sales to obtain the forecasted EBIT. Interest expenses are calculated in Part V, the Notes section, after the interest-bearing debt has been determined in the balance sheet developed in Part III. Once the interest expense has been calculated and entered in the income statement, the forecasted net income is determined. Dividends for 2009 are found by multiplying the target payout ratio by the 2009 forecasted net income. Dividends are then subtracted from net income to find the 2009 addition to retained earnings.

17-4c Part III. Forecasted Balance Sheet

The forecasted 2009 balance sheet is developed from the 2008 statement. Cash and fixed assets are multiplied by 1.10 because they increase at the same rate as sales growth. Accounts receivable are found by multiplying the assumed 11% Receivables/Sales ratio (given in Part I) by sales, and inventories are found by multiplying the 19% Inventories/Sales ratio (also given in Part I) by sales. We then sum the four asset accounts to find forecasted 2009 total assets.

On the liabilities side, because payables and accruals grow at the same rate as sales, we multiply the 2008 values by 1.10. Also, 2009 retained earnings are found by adding the 2009 addition to retained earnings from the income statement to 2008 retained earnings. To complete the balance sheet, we need to find the amounts for short-term bank debt, bonds, and new common stock. To obtain those values, we skip down to Part V, the Notes section. Here we multiply the target debt ratio times the just calculated total assets to obtain the forecasted total debt amount. We then subtract payables and accruals from this amount to find the forecast for interest-bearing debt (which includes bank loans and bonds). Next, we multiply the interest-bearing debt by the 2008 proportions of bank debt and long-term bonds to find the forecasted amounts for those two items. Similarly, we find the required amount of 2009 total equity by multiplying (1 − target debt ratio) times the forecasted assets. We then subtract forecasted retained earnings to find 2009 common stock, which we insert in the balance sheet. When we sum the liability and equity accounts, the total matches the forecasted assets, which it must.

17-4d Part IV. Ratios and EPS

With the 2009 income statement and balance sheet forecasted, we can calculate the forecasted 2009 ratios and EPS; those calculations are done in Part IV. The first five ratios shown are the same ones given in the Part I Inputs section. We calculated them from the forecasted statement as a check on the accuracy of the model.

An interesting aspect of Part IV is the DuPont calculations. In 2008, Allied's profit margin and turnover were quite low, but its equity multiplier was relatively high. The result was a low but risky 12.5% ROE. The forecast for 2009 shows improvements in the profit margin and turnover, which boost ROE, and a lowering of the equity multiplier, which holds down the ROE but indicates less financial risk. The result is a much better and less risky 14.9% ROE, which is very close to the industry average.

The final item in Part IV is the forecasted EPS, which jumps from $2.35 in 2008 to $3.06 in 2009. The CFO calculated the following data for use in his talk but decided not to include it in the table:

> P/E ratio   9.8x versus   11.3x for the industry
> Current stock price $23.06

Allied's estimated stock price is then calculated by multiplying its forecasted EPS by the industry average P/E ratio:

$$\$3.06(11.3) = \$34.58$$

Percentage gain: $34.58/$23.06 − 1 = 49.96%, or approximately 50%

17-4e Using the Forecast to Improve Operations

Allied's CFO generated Table 17-2 with a straightforward Excel model. The table could have been worked with a calculator, but it was easier to do the work using Excel. Moreover and very importantly, once he set up the model, he could make all kinds of changes to see the forecasted results under alternative scenarios. It's trivially easy to change the growth rate and the five key input variables in Part I. It would be easy to change the financing assumptions, perhaps using more bank debt and fewer bonds. It also would be easy to show the results of financing only with debt or only with stock. With any such input changes, the model instantly provides modified results. Indeed, the CFO had the model on his laptop, took it to the meeting, and answered a number of "what if" questions.

Of course, it's much easier to change inputs in a spreadsheet model than it is to change actual operations so that the forecasted results are generated. However, as we said earlier in the chapter, if you don't know where you're going, it's hard to get there. Allied's ratio analysis in Chapter 4 pointed out the firm's weaknesses, and the model shown in Table 17-2 demonstrates how improvements in the driver variables will affect the firm's ROE, its EPS, and (of course) its stock price. Allied's managers' compensation is partly based on the firm's financial results, including its ROE and stock price, so they are keenly interested in the model and its results. The threat of firing is also a strong motivator, and getting poor results while operating good assets makes the firing of management a real possibility.

SELF TEST

What advantages does the forecasted financial statement method have over the AFN equation for forecasting financial requirements?

Why should a marketing or management major be interested in financial forecasting?

Would financial forecasting be relevant for such people when they graduate and enter the work force? Explain.

17-5 USING REGRESSION TO IMPROVE FORECASTS[9]

In financial statement forecasts, it is often appropriate to assume that most of the assets increase at the same rate as sales. However, that is often not the case. We noted in our discussion of the AFN equation that excess capacity might exist, in which case assets would increase less rapidly than sales. Similarly, economies of scale might exist, and this too could enable sales to increase less rapidly than assets. We can use regression techniques to investigate the existence of such situations and thus improve the financial forecasts.

To illustrate **regression analysis**, consider Figure 17-2, which shows Allied's sales, inventories, and receivables during the last 5 years and scatter diagrams of inventories and receivables versus sales. Estimated regression equations, found with a financial calculator or spreadsheet, can be developed. For example, here is the estimated relationship between inventories and sales (in millions of dollars):

Regression Analysis
A statistical technique that fits a line to observed data points so that the resulting equation can be used to forecast other data points.

$$\text{Inventories} = -\$35.7 + 0.186(\text{Sales})$$

We can use the regression equation to estimate the 2009 inventory level. Since 2009 sales are projected at $3,300 million, according to the regression, 2009 inventories should be $578 million:

$$\text{Inventories} = -\$35.7 + 0.186(\$3,300) = \$578 \text{ million}$$

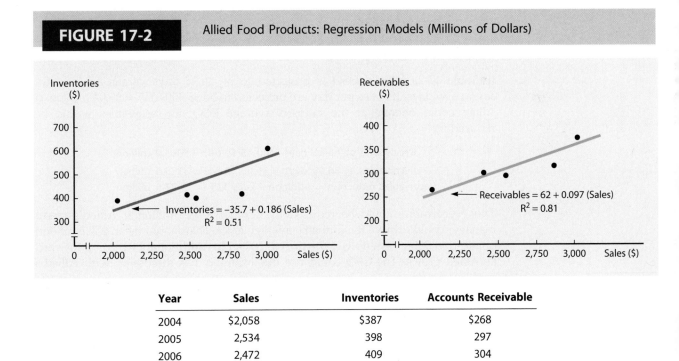

| **FIGURE 17-2** | Allied Food Products: Regression Models (Millions of Dollars) |

Year	Sales	Inventories	Accounts Receivable
2004	$2,058	$387	$268
2005	2,534	398	297
2006	2,472	409	304
2007	2,850	415	315
2008	3,000	615	375
2009	3,300 (Projected)		

---

[9]This section is relatively technical, but it can be omitted without loss of continuity.

This is $49 million less than the $627 million forecast used in the projected financial statements. Note also that although our graph shows a linear relationship, we could have used a nonlinear regression model had we believed that such a relationship was more appropriate. Also, we could have used a multiple regression equation, which would have brought other factors that affect inventories into the picture.

Examine the following statement: Using regression to predict items such as inventories is better than basing such predictions on last year's Inventory/Sales ratio because regression helps smooth out the effects of random fluctuations. Do you agree or disagree? Explain.

17-6 ANALYZING THE EFFECTS OF CHANGING RATIOS

When we forecasted the 2009 financial statements, we assumed that the 2009 operating ratios would move closer to the industry averages and we based asset levels on those assumptions. However, it is often preferable to base forecasted assets on a regression analysis. Also, it is often useful to examine specific asset ratios to get a better idea of the effects on the firm's financial position given various changes to these ratios. In this section, we explore the effects of modifying receivable and inventory ratios.

17-6a Modifying Accounts Receivable

In Table 17-2, Allied's DSO is projected to be 40.15 days versus an industry average 36 days. Its sales per day are projected to be $3,300/365 = $9.04 million. If Allied could operate at the industry-average DSO, its receivables would be reduced by

$$\text{Receivables at 40.15 days} = 40.15(\$9.04) = \underline{\$363.0 \text{ million}}$$
$$\text{Receivables at 36.00 days} = 36.00(\$9.04) = \underline{\$325.5 \text{ million}}$$
$$\text{Receivables reduction} = \text{Additional 2009 FCF} = \underline{\$ \; 37.5 \text{ million}}$$

Thus, receivables could be reduced by another $37.5 million if Allied's credit manager could achieve the industry-average DSO. That would mean $37.5 million of additional free cash flow to the firm in 2009, plus additional FCF going forward as Allied grows. The CFO could use this example in a discussion with Allied's credit manager.

17-6b Modifying Inventories

Inventories can be analyzed in a similar manner. First, note that Allied's forecasted inventory turnover is 5.26 times versus 10.9 times for the industry. Moreover, in Table 17-2, Allied's forecasted 2009 inventory is $627 million versus $3,300 million of sales. Given this information, we can find Allied's inventories if Allied is able to achieve the industry-average inventory turnover:

$$\text{Currently forecasted inventory turnover} = \$3,300/5.26 = \underline{\$627 \text{ million}}$$
$$\text{Inventory at industry-average turnover} = \$3,300/10.9 = \underline{\$303 \text{ million}}$$
$$\text{Inventory reduction} = \text{Additional 2009 FCF} = \underline{\$324 \text{ million}}$$

Thus, inventories could be reduced by another $324 million if Allied's inventory turnover could be increased to the industry average. That would mean another $324 million of free cash flow in 2009, plus further additions going forward. Again, the CFO could use this example in a discussion with the inventory manager.

17-6c Other "Special Studies"

Once a firm has developed a model to forecast its financial statements, it can do all types of special "what if" studies. For example, the model that Allied's CFO used to make Table 17-2 (which is part of the chapter Excel model) could be used to find the results shown in the two preceding sections for receivables and inventories. The model also could be used to estimate the effects of changing the dividend policy on the statements and on the required AFN. Indeed, the AFN equation could be modified to obtain a "quick and dirty" estimate of the effects of the dividend payout on the AFN. As we saw earlier in Section 17-3 in the discussion of the AFN equation, Allied has a payout ratio of 0.4894; and when that number was used in the equation, an AFN of $114 million resulted:

$$\text{AFN} = 0.6667(\Delta S) - 0.06667(\Delta S) - 0.0392(S_1)(0.5106)$$
$$= 0.6667(\$300) - 0.06667(\$300) - 0.0392(\$3,300)(0.5106)$$
$$= \$200 - \$20 - \$66$$
$$= \$114 \text{ million}$$

Now suppose Allied anticipated problems raising $114 million to carry out its business plan. The CFO might then suggest to the directors a reduction of the payout ratio to 20%. That would result in an AFN of about $77 million (shown in Part IV of Table 17-1), which is about $37 million less than the original AFN calculated. Of course, as we saw in the dividend chapter, lowering the dividend might create problems of its own; but at times, such an action may be necessary to maximize a firm's intrinsic value and long-run stock price.

TYING IT ALL TOGETHER

This chapter described techniques for forecasting financial statements, which is a crucial part of the financial planning process. Both investors and corporations regularly use forecasting techniques to help value a company's stock; to estimate the benefits of potential projects; and to estimate how changes in capital structure, dividend policy, and working capital policy influence shareholder value.

The type of forecasting described in this chapter is important for several reasons. First, if the projected operating results are unsatisfactory, management can "go back to the drawing board," reformulate its plans, and develop more reasonable targets for the coming year. Second, the funds required to meet the sales forecast simply may not be obtainable. If not, it is obviously better to know this in advance and to scale back projected operations than to suddenly run out of cash and have operations grind to an abrupt halt. And third, firms often give guidance to analysts regarding likely future earnings; and as GE's Jeff Immelt learned, it is beneficial to be able to provide reasonably accurate forecasts.

SELF-TEST QUESTIONS AND PROBLEMS
(Solutions Appear in Appendix A)

ST-1 **KEY TERMS** Define each of the following terms:

   a. Mission statement; corporate scope; statement of corporate objectives; corporate strategies

   b. Operating plan; financial plan

   c. Spontaneously generated funds

   d. Additional Funds Needed (AFN); AFN equation

   e. Capital intensity ratio; sustainable growth rate

   f. Forecasted financial statements; retention ratio

   g. Excess capacity adjustments

   h. Regression analysis

ST-2 **SUSTAINABLE GROWTH RATE** Weatherford Industries Inc. has the following ratios: $A_0^*/S_0 = 1.6$; $L_0^*/S_0 = 0.4$; profit margin $= 0.10$; and retention ratio $= 0.55$, or 55%. Sales last year were $100 million. Assuming that these ratios will remain constant, use the AFN equation to determine the maximum growth rate (the sustainable growth rate) Weatherford can achieve without having to employ nonspontaneous external funds.

ST-3 **ADDITIONAL FUNDS NEEDED** Suppose Weatherford's financial consultants report (1) that the inventory turnover ratio is Sales/Inventory $= 3$ times versus an industry average of 4 times and (2) that Weatherford can reduce inventories and thus raise its turnover to 4 without affecting sales, the profit margin, or the other asset turnover ratios. Under those conditions, use the AFN equation to determine the amount of additional funds Weatherford will require next year if sales grow by 20%.

QUESTIONS

17-1 What are the key factors on which external financing depends, as indicated in the AFN equation?

17-2 Assume that an average firm in the office supply business has a 6% profit margin, a 40% debt/assets ratio, a total assets turnover of 2 times, and a dividend payout ratio of 40%. Is it true that if such a firm is to have any sales growth ($g > 0$), it will be forced to borrow or to sell common stock (that is, it will need some nonspontaneous external capital even if g is very small)? Explain.

17-3 Would you agree that computerized corporate planning models were a fad during the 1990s but that because of a need for flexibility in corporate planning, they are no longer used by most firms?

17-4 Certain liability and net worth items generally increase spontaneously with increases in sales. Put a check mark (✓) next to those items that typically increase spontaneously.

Accounts payable	_____
Notes payable to banks	_____
Accrued wages	_____
Accrued taxes	_____
Mortgage bonds	_____
Common stock	_____
Retained earnings	_____

17-5 Suppose a firm makes the following policy changes. If the change means that external nonspontaneous financial requirements (AFN) will increase, indicate this with a (+);

indicate a decrease with a (–); and indicate an indeterminate or negligible effect with a (0). Think in terms of the immediate short-run effect on funds requirements.

a. The dividend payout ratio is increased.   _____

b. Rather than produce computers in advance, a computer company decides to produce them only after an order has been received.   _____

c. The firm decides to pay all suppliers on delivery, rather than after a 30-day delay, to take advantage of discounts for rapid payment.   _____

d. The firm begins to sell on credit. (Previously, all sales had been on a cash basis.)   _____

e. The firm's profit margin is eroded by increased competition; sales are steady.   _____

f. Advertising expenditures are stepped up.   _____

g. A decision is made to substitute long-term mortgage bonds for short-term bank loans.   _____

h. The firm begins to pay employees on a weekly basis. (Previously, it had paid employees at the end of each month.)   _____

PROBLEMS

Easy Problems 1–6

17-1   **AFN EQUATION**   Carter Corporation's sales are expected to increase from $5 million in 2008 to $6 million in 2009, or by 20%. Its assets totaled $3 million at the end of 2008. Carter is at full capacity, so its assets must grow in proportion to projected sales. At the end of 2008, current liabilities are $1 million, consisting of $250,000 of accounts payable, $500,000 of notes payable, and $250,000 of accrued liabilities. Its profit margin is forecasted to be 5%, and the forecasted retention ratio is 30%. Use the AFN equation to forecast the additional funds Carter will need for the coming year.

17-2   **AFN EQUATION**   Refer to Problem 17-1. What additional funds would be needed if the company's year-end 2008 assets had been $4 million? Assume that all other numbers are the same. Why is this AFN different from the one you found in Problem 17-1? Is the company's "capital intensity" the same or different? Explain.

17-3   **AFN EQUATION**   Refer to Problem 17-1 and assume that the company had $3 million in assets at the end of 2008. However, now assume that the company pays no dividends. Under these assumptions, what additional funds would be needed for the coming year? Why is this AFN different from the one you found in Problem 17-1?

17-4   **PRO FORMA INCOME STATEMENT**   Austin Grocers recently reported the following 2008 income statement (in millions of dollars):

Sales	$700
Operating costs including depreciation	500
EBIT	$200
Interest	40
EBT	$160
Taxes (40%)	64
Net income	$ 96
Dividends	$ 32
Addition to retained earnings	$ 64

This year the company is forecasting a 25% increase in sales; and it expects that its year-end operating costs, including depreciation, will equal 70% of sales. Austin's tax rate, interest expense, and dividend payout ratio are all expected to remain constant.

a. What is Austin's projected 2009 net income?

b. What is the expected growth rate in Austin's dividends?

17-5   **EXCESS CAPACITY** Walter Industries has $5 billion in sales and $1.7 billion in fixed assets. Currently, the company's fixed assets are operating at 90% of capacity.

    a.   What level of sales could Walter Industries have obtained if it had been operating at full capacity?

    b.   What is Walter's Target fixed assets/Sales ratio?

    c.   If Walter's sales increase 12%, how large of an increase in fixed assets will the company need to meet its Target fixed assets/Sales ratio?

17-6   **REGRESSION AND INVENTORIES** Jasper Furnishings has $300 million in sales. The company expects that its sales will increase 12% this year. Jasper's CFO uses a simple linear regression to forecast the company's inventory level for a given level of projected sales. On the basis of recent history, the estimated relationship between inventories and sales (in millions of dollars) is as follows:

$$\text{Inventories} = \$25 + 0.125(\text{Sales})$$

Given the estimated sales forecast and the estimated relationship between inventories and sales, what are your forecasts of the company's year-end inventory level and its inventory turnover ratio?

Intermediate Problems 7–12

17-7   **PRO FORMA INCOME STATEMENT** At the end of last year, Roberts Inc. reported the following income statement (in millions of dollars):

Sales	$3,000
Operating costs excluding depreciation	2,450
EBITDA	$ 550
Depreciation	250
EBIT	$ 300
Interest	125
EBT	$ 175
Taxes (40%)	70
Net income	$ 105

Looking ahead to the following year, the company's CFO has assembled this information:

- Year-end sales are expected to be 10% higher than the $3 billion in sales generated last year.

- Year-end operating costs, excluding depreciation, are expected to equal 80% of year-end sales.

- Depreciation is expected to increase at the same rate as sales.

- Interest costs are expected to remain unchanged.

- The tax rate is expected to remain at 40%.

On the basis of that information, what will be the forecast for Roberts' year-end net income?

17-8   **LONG-TERM FINANCING NEEDED** At year-end 2008, total assets for Ambrose Inc. were $1.2 million and accounts payable were $375,000. Sales, which in 2008 were $2.5 million, are expected to increase by 25% in 2009. Total assets and accounts payable are proportional to sales, and that relationship will be maintained; that is, they will grow at the same rate as sales. Ambrose typically uses no current liabilities other than accounts payable. Common stock amounted to $425,000 in 2008, and retained earnings were $295,000. Ambrose plans to sell new common stock in the amount of $75,000. The firm's profit margin on sales is 6%; 60% of earnings will be retained.

    a.   What was Ambrose's total debt in 2008?

    b.   How much new long-term debt financing will be needed in 2009? (Hint: AFN − New stock = New long-term debt.)

17-9   **SALES INCREASE** Pierce Furnishings generated $2 million in sales during 2008, and its year-end total assets were $1.5 million. Also, at year-end 2008, current liabilities were $500,000, consisting of $200,000 of notes payable, $200,000 of accounts payable, and $100,000 of accrued liabilities. Looking ahead to 2009, the company estimates that its assets must increase by $0.75 for every $1.00 increase in sales. Pierce's profit margin is 5%, and its retention ratio is 40%. How large of a sales increase can the company achieve without having to raise funds externally?

17-10 **REGRESSION AND RECEIVABLES** Edwards Industries has $320 million in sales. The company expects that its sales will increase 12% this year. Edwards' CFO uses a simple linear regression to forecast the company's receivables level for a given level of projected sales. On the basis of recent history, the estimated relationship between receivables and sales (in millions of dollars) is as follows:

$$\text{Receivables} = \$9.25 + 0.07(\text{Sales})$$

Given the estimated sales forecast and the estimated relationship between receivables and sales, what are your forecasts of the company's year-end balance for receivables and its year-end days sales outstanding (DSO) ratio? Assume that DSO is calculated on the basis of a 365-day year.

17-11 **REGRESSION AND INVENTORIES** Charlie's Cycles Inc. has $110 million in sales. The company expects that its sales will increase 5% this year. Charlie's CFO uses a simple linear regression to forecast the company's inventory level for a given level of projected sales. On the basis of recent history, the estimated relationship between inventories and sales (in millions of dollars) is as follows:

$$\text{Inventories} = \$9 + 0.0875(\text{Sales})$$

Given the estimated sales forecast and the estimated relationship between inventories and sales, what are your forecasts of the company's year-end inventory level and its inventory turnover ratio?

17-12 **EXCESS CAPACITY** Edney Manufacturing Company has $2 billion in sales and $0.6 billion in fixed assets. Currently, the company's fixed assets are operating at 80% of capacity.

a. What level of sales could Edney have obtained if it had been operating at full capacity?

b. What is Edney's Target fixed assets/Sales ratio?

c. If Edney's sales increase 30%, how large of an increase in fixed assets will the company need to meet its Target fixed assets/Sales ratio?

Challenging Problems 13–14

17-13 **ADDITIONAL FUNDS NEEDED** Morrissey Technologies Inc.'s 2008 financial statements are shown here.

Morrissey Technologies Inc.: Balance Sheet as of December 31, 2008

Cash	$ 180,000	Accounts payable	$ 360,000
Receivables	360,000	Notes payable	56,000
Inventories	720,000	Accrued liabilities	180,000
Total current assets	$1,260,000	Total current liabilities	$ 596,000
		Long-term debt	100,000
Fixed assets	1,440,000	Common stock	1,800,000
		Retained earnings	204,000
Total assets	$2,700,000	Total liabilities and equity	$2,700,000

Morrissey Technologies Inc.: Income Statement for December 31, 2008

Sales	$3,600,000
Operating costs including depreciation	3,279,720
EBIT	$ 320,280
Interest	20,280
EBT	$ 300,000
Taxes (40%)	120,000
Net Income	$ 180,000
Per Share Data:	
Common stock price	$ 45.00
Earnings per share (EPS)	$ 1.80
Dividends per share (DPS)	$ 1.08

Suppose that in 2009, sales increase by 10% over 2008 sales. The firm currently has 100,000 shares outstanding. It expects to maintain its 2008 dividend payout ratio and believes that its assets should grow at the same rate as sales. The firm has no excess capacity. However, the firm would like to reduce its Operating costs/Sales ratio to 87.5% and increase its total debt ratio to 30%. (It believes that its current debt ratio is too low relative to the industry average.) The firm will raise 30% of 2009 forecasted total debt as notes payable, and it will issue long-term bonds for the remainder. The firm forecasts that its before-tax cost of debt (which includes both short-term and long-term debt) is 12.5%. Assume that any common stock issuances or repurchases can be made at the firm's current stock price of $45.

a. Construct the forecasted financial statements assuming that these changes are made. What are the firm's forecasted notes payable and long-term debt balances? What is the forecasted addition to retained earnings?

b. If the profit margin remains at 5% and the dividend payout ratio remains at 60%, at what growth rate in sales will the additional financing requirements be exactly zero? In other words, what is the firm's sustainable growth rate? (Hint: Set AFN equal to zero and solve for g.)

17-14 **EXCESS CAPACITY** Krogh Lumber's 2008 financial statements are shown here.

Krogh Lumber: Balance Sheet as of December 31, 2008 (Thousands of Dollars)

Cash	$ 1,800	Accounts payable	$ 7,200
Receivables	10,800	Notes payable	3,472
Inventories	12,600	Accrued liabilities	2,520
Total current assets	$25,200	Total current liabilities	$13,192
		Mortgage bonds	5,000
		Common stock	2,000
Net fixed assets	21,600	Retained earnings	26,608
Total assets	$46,800	Total liabilities and equity	$46,800

Krogh Lumber: Income Statement for December 31, 2008 (Thousands of Dollars)

Sales	$36,000
Operating costs including depreciation	30,783
Earnings before interest and taxes	$ 5,217
Interest	1,017
Earnings before taxes	$ 4,200
Taxes (40%)	1,680
Net income	$ 2,520
Dividends (60%)	$ 1,512
Addition to retained earnings	$ 1,008

a. Assume that the company was operating at full capacity in 2008 with regard to all items *except* fixed assets; fixed assets in 2008 were being utilized to only 75% of capacity. By what percentage could 2009 sales increase over 2008 sales without the need for an increase in fixed assets?

b. Now suppose 2009 sales increase by 25% over 2008 sales. Assume that Krogh cannot sell any fixed assets. All assets other than fixed assets will grow at the same rate as sales; however, after reviewing industry averages, the firm would like to reduce its Operating costs/Sales ratio to 82% and increase its debt ratio to 42%. The firm will maintain its 60% dividend payout ratio, and it currently has 1 million shares outstanding. The firm plans to raise 35% of its 2009 total debt as notes payable, and it will issue bonds for the remainder. Its before-tax cost of debt is 11%. Any stock issuances or repurchases will be made at the firm's current stock price of $40. Develop the projected financial statements as shown in Table 17-2. What are the balances of notes payable, bonds, common stock, and retained earnings?

COMPREHENSIVE/SPREADSHEET PROBLEM

17-15 FORECASTING FINANCIAL STATEMENTS Use a spreadsheet model to forecast the financial statements in Problems 17-13 and 17-14.

INTEGRATED CASE

NEW WORLD CHEMICALS INC.

17-16 FINANCIAL FORECASTING Sue Wilson, the new financial manager of New World Chemicals (NWC), a California producer of specialized chemicals for use in fruit orchards, must prepare a formal financial forecast for 2009. NWC's 2008 sales were $2 billion, and the marketing department is forecasting a 25% increase for 2009. Wilson thinks the company was operating at full capacity in 2008, but she is not sure. The first step in her forecast was to assume that key ratios would remain unchanged and that it would be "business as usual" at NWC. The 2008 financial statements, the 2009 initial forecast, and a ratio analysis for 2008 and the 2009 initial forecast are given in Table IC 17-1.

Assume that you were recently hired as Wilson's assistant and that your first major task is to help her develop the formal financial forecast. She asks you to begin by answering the following questions.

a. Assume (1) that NWC was operating at full capacity in 2008 with respect to all assets, (2) that all assets must grow at the same rate as sales, (3) that accounts payable and accrued liabilities also will grow at the same rate as sales, and (4) that the 2008 profit margin and dividend payout will be maintained. Under those conditions, what would the AFN equation predict the company's financial requirements to be for the coming year?

b. Consultations with several key managers within NWC, including production, inventory, and receivable managers, have yielded some very useful information.

   (1) NWC's high DSO is largely due to one significant customer who battled through some hardships the past 2 years but who appears to be financially healthy again and is generating strong cash flow. As a result, NWC's accounts receivable manager expects the firm to lower receivables enough to make the DSO equal to 34 days without adversely affecting sales.

   (2) NWC was operating a little below capacity; but its forecasted growth will require a new facility, which is expected to increase NWC's net fixed assets to $700 million.

   (3) A relatively new inventory management system (installed last year) has taken some time to catch on and to operate efficiently. NWC's inventory turnover improved slightly last year, but this year NWC expects even more improvement as inventories decrease and inventory turnover is expected to rise to 10×.

   Incorporate that information into the 2009 initial forecast results, as these adjustments to the initial forecast represent the final forecast for 2009. (Hint: Total assets do not change from the initial forecast.)

c. Calculate NWC's forecasted ratios based on its final forecast and compare them with the company's 2008 historical ratios, the 2009 initial forecast ratios, and the industry averages. How does NWC compare with the average firm in its industry, and is the company's financial position expected to improve during the coming year? Explain.

d. Based on the final forecast, calculate NWC's free cash flow for 2009. How does this FCF differ from the FCF forecasted by NWC's initial "business as usual" forecast?

e. Initially, some NWC managers questioned whether the new facility expansion was necessary, especially since it results in increasing net fixed assets from $500 million to $700 million (a 40% increase). However, after extensive discussions about NWC needing to position itself for future growth and being flexible and competitive in today's marketplace, NWC's top managers agreed that the expansion was necessary. Among the issues raised by opponents was that NWC's fixed assets were being operated at only 85% of capacity. Assuming that its fixed assets were operating at only 85% of capacity, by how much could sales have increased, both in dollar terms and in percentage terms, before NWC reached full capacity?

f. How would changes in these items affect the AFN: (1) the dividend payout ratio, (2) the profit margin, (3) the capital intensity ratio, and (4) NWC beginning to buy from its suppliers on terms that permit it to pay after 60 days rather than after 30 days? (Consider each item separately and hold all other things constant.)

Table IC 17-1	**Financial Statements and Other Data on NWC (Millions of Dollars)**

A. Balance Sheets

	2008	2009E
Cash and equivalents	$ 20	$ 25
Accounts receivable	240	300
Inventories	240	300
Total current assets	$ 500	$ 625
Net fixed assets	500	625
Total assets	$1,000	$1,250
Accounts payable and accrued liabilities	$ 100	$ 125
Notes payable	100	190
Total current liabilities	$ 200	$ 315
Long-term debt	100	190
Common stock	500	500
Retained earnings	200	245
Total liabilities and equity	$1,000	$1,250

B. Income Statements

	2008	2009E
Sales	$2,000.00	$2,500.00
Less: Variable costs	1,200.00	1,500.00
Fixed costs	700.00	875.00
Earnings before interest and taxes (EBIT)	$ 100.00	$ 125.00
Interest	16.00	16.00
Earnings before taxes (EBT)	$ 84.00	$ 109.00
Taxes (40%)	33.60	43.60
Net income	$ 50.40	$ 65.40
Dividends (30%)	$ 15.12	$ 19.62
Addition to retained earnings	$ 35.28	$ 45.78

C. Key Ratios

	NWC (2008)	NWC (2009E)	Industry	Comment
Basic earning power	10.00%	10.00%	20.00%	
Profit margin	2.52	2.62	4.00	
Return on equity	7.20	8.77	15.60	
Days sales outstanding (365 days)	43.80 days	43.80 days	32.00 days	
Inventory turnover	8.33×	8.33×	11.00×	
Fixed assets turnover	4.00	4.00	5.00	
Total assets turnover	2.00	2.00	2.50	
Debt/assets	30.00%	40.34%	36.00%	
Times interest earned	6.25×	7.81×	9.40×	
Current ratio	2.50	1.99	3.00	
Payout ratio	30.00%	30.00%	30.00%	

THOMSON ONE | Business School Edition

Access the Thomson ONE problems through the CengageNOW™ web site. Use the Thomson ONE—Business School Edition online database to work this chapter's questions.

Forecasting the Future Performance of Abercrombie & Fitch

Clothing retailer Abercrombie & Fitch enjoyed phenomenal success in the late 1990s. Between 1996 and 2000, its sales grew almost fourfold—from $335 million to more than $1.2 billion—and its stock price soared by more than 500%. However, in 2002, its growth rate had begun to slow down and Abercrombie had a hard time meeting its quarterly earnings targets. As a result, the stock price in late 2002 was about half of what it was 3 years earlier. Abercrombie's struggles resulted from increased competition, a sluggish economy, and the challenges of staying ahead of the fashion curve. Since 2002, the company's stock has rebounded strongly, but questions remain about the firm's long-term growth prospects.

Given the questions about Abercrombie's future growth rate, analysts have focused on the company's earnings reports. Thomson ONE provides a convenient and detailed summary of the company's recent earnings history along with a summary of analysts' earnings forecasts.

To access this information, begin by entering the company's ticker symbol, ANF, on Thomson ONE's main screen and then selecting "GO." This takes you to an overview of the company's recent performance. After checking out the overview, you should click on "Estimates." Click on "View Forecasts" (in the middle of your screen) to see details of the EPS summary report. On both of these screens, you will find a wide range of information about the company's past and projected earnings.

Discussion Questions

1. What are the mean and median forecasts for Abercrombie's earnings per share over the next fiscal year?
2. Based on analysts' forecasts, what is the expected long-term growth rate in earnings?
3. Have analysts made any significant changes to their forecasted earnings for Abercrombie & Fitch in the past few months? Explain.
4. Historically, have Abercrombie's reported earnings generally met, exceeded, or fallen short of analysts' forecasted earnings?
5. How has Abercrombie's stock performed this year relative to the S&P 500?

PART 7

SPECIAL TOPICS IN FINANCIAL MANAGEMENT

© RICHARD LEVINE/ALAMY

CHAPTER 18
Derivatives and Risk Management

Using Derivatives to Manage Risk

Consumer products giant Procter & Gamble (P&G) has more than 5 billion customers in 180 countries. Its products include such well-known brands as Crest, Tide, Pampers, Gillette, and Charmin. Its products are consumed regularly; and its sales and earnings are fairly immune to changes in the economic cycle, making it a relatively low-risk company. Indeed, Value Line estimates that P&G's beta is 0.65, which suggests that its risk is 35% below that of an average stock.

Low risk does not mean the company is riskless, and P&G's managers devote considerable time and effort at managing the risks the company does face. For example, in a recent annual report, management described in detail how the company deals with risks resulting from changes in interest rates, exchange rates, and commodity prices. In each instance, P&G first examines its net exposure to the risk factor and then uses derivatives such as options, futures,

and swaps to hedge and thus reduce those risks. Here is a statement from its annual report:

As a multinational company with diverse product offerings, we are exposed to market risks such as changes in interest rates, currency exchange rates, and commodity prices. To manage the volatility related to these exposures, we evaluate our exposures on a global basis to take advantage of the direct netting opportunities and of currency, interest rate, and commodity correlations that exist within the portfolio. For the remaining exposures, we enter into various derivative transactions in accordance with the company's hedging policies that are designed to partially, or entirely, offset changes in the underlying exposures being hedged. We do not hold or issue derivative financial instruments for speculative purposes. Note 6 to the Consolidated Financial Statements includes a detailed discussion of our accounting policies for financial instruments.

Derivative positions are monitored using techniques including market value, sensitivity analysis, and value-at-risk modeling. The tests for interest rate and currency rate exposures are based on the CorporateManager™ value-at-risk model using a 1-year horizon and a 95% confidence level. The model incorporates the impact of correlation (the degree to which exposures move together over time) and diversification (from holding multiple currency and interest rate instruments) and assumes that financial returns are normally distributed.

Source: Procter & Gamble's 2007 Annual Report, p. 47.

It is clear from P&G's annual report that the company spends a great deal of time and energy managing its various risks. However, nothing is completely riskless; and in some instances, the steps taken to control risk have backfired. Indeed, P&G incurred huge losses in the 1990s on derivative transactions that were supposedly undertaken to reduce risk.

This chapter first discusses the reasons firms manage risk instead of passing it off to its shareholders. Next, the chapter provides an overview of options, futures, and swaps and describes how companies use those instruments to help minimize their risks. Finally, the chapter concludes with an overview of firms' risk management policies, the nature of risk management, and the general process that firms follow when managing risks.

PUTTING THINGS IN PERSPECTIVE

In this chapter, we discuss risk management, a topic of increasing importance to financial managers. The term *risk management* can mean many things; but in business, it involves identifying events that could have adverse financial consequences and then taking actions to prevent and/or minimize the damage caused by those events. Years ago corporate risk managers dealt primarily with insurance—they made sure the firm was adequately insured against fire, theft, and other casualties and that it had adequate liability coverage. More recently, the scope of risk management has broadened to include such responsibilities as controlling the costs of key inputs such as petroleum by purchasing oil futures or protecting against changes in interest rates or exchange rates through dealings in the interest rate or foreign exchange markets. In addition, risk managers try to ensure that actions designed to hedge against risk are not actually increasing risk.

When you finish this chapter, you should be able to:

- Identify the circumstances in which it makes sense for companies to manage risk.
- Describe the various types of derivatives and explain how they can be used to manage risk.
- Value options using the Black-Scholes Option Pricing Model.
- Discuss the various elements of risk management and the different processes that firms use to manage risks.

18-1 REASONS TO MANAGE RISK

We know that investors dislike risk. We also know that most investors hold well-diversified portfolios; so at least in theory, the only "relevant risk" is systematic risk. If you asked corporate executives what type of risk they were concerned about, you might expect their answer to be, "beta." However, this is almost certainly not the answer you would get. The most likely answer, if you asked a CEO to define risk, is something like this: "Risk is the possibility that our future earnings and free cash flows will be significantly lower than we expect." For example, consider Plastics Inc., which manufactures dashboards, interior door panels, and other plastic components used by auto companies. Petroleum is the key feedstock for plastic and thus makes up a large percentage of its costs. Plastics Inc. has a 3-year contract with an auto company to deliver 500,000 door panels each year at a price of $60 each. When the company signed this contract, oil sold for $120 per barrel, and oil was expected to stay at that level for the next 3 years. If oil prices fall, Plastics will have higher-than-expected profits and free cash flows; but if oil prices rise, profits will fall. Plastics' value depends on its profits and free cash flows, so a change in the price of oil will cause stockholders to earn more or less than they anticipated.

Suppose Plastics announces that it plans to lock in a 3-year supply of oil at a guaranteed price of $120 per barrel and the cost of the guarantee is zero. Would that cause its stock price to rise? At first glance, it may seem that the answer is yes; but maybe that's not correct. Recall that the long-run value of a stock depends on the present value of its expected future free cash flows discounted at the weighted average cost of capital (WACC). Locking in the cost of oil will cause an increase in Plastics' stock price if and only if (1) it causes the expected future free cash flows to increase or (2) it causes the WACC to decline.

First, consider the free cash flows. Before the announcement of guaranteed oil costs, investors had formed an estimate of the expected future free cash flows based on an expected oil price of $120 per barrel. Therefore, while locking in the cost of oil at $120 per barrel will lower the riskiness of the expected future free cash flows, it will not change the *size* of the cash flows because investors already expected a price of $120 per barrel.

Now what about the WACC? It will change only if locking in the cost of oil causes a change in the cost of debt or equity or the target capital structure. Assuming that the foreseeable increases in the price of oil were not enough to cause bankruptcy, Plastics' cost of debt should not change and neither should its target capital structure. Regarding the cost of equity, recall from Chapter 8 that most investors hold well-diversified portfolios, which means that the cost of equity should depend only on systematic risk. Moreover, even though an increase in oil prices would have a negative effect on Plastics' stock price, it would not have a negative effect on all stocks. Indeed, oil producers should have higher-than-expected returns and stock prices. Assuming that Plastics' investors hold well-diversified portfolios, including stocks of oil-producing companies, there would not appear to be much reason to expect its cost of equity to decline. The bottom line is this: If Plastics' expected future cash flows and WACC will not change significantly due to an elimination of the risk of oil price increases, neither should the value of its stock.

We discuss futures contracts and hedging in detail in the next section, but for now let's assume that Plastics has *not* locked in oil prices. Therefore, if oil prices increase, its stock price will fall. However, because its stockholders know this, they can build portfolios that contain oil futures whose values will rise or fall with oil prices and thus offset changes in the price of Plastics' stock. By choosing the correct number of futures contracts, investors can "hedge" their portfolios and completely eliminate the risk due to changes in oil prices. There will be a cost to hedging; but that cost to large, sophisticated investors should be about the same as the cost to Plastics. If stockholders can hedge away oil price risk, why should they pay a higher price for Plastics' stock just because the company hedged away the risk?

This discussion suggests that unless something else is going on, it doesn't make sense for firms to hedge risk. At the same time, a 1995 survey reported that

59% of firms with market values greater than $250 million engage in risk management; and that percentage is surely much higher today.[1] One explanation is that corporate managers frequently hedge risk even though it does little to increase corporate value. The other (perhaps more likely) explanation is that hedging creates other benefits that ultimately lead to higher cash flows and/or a lower WACC. Here are some of the reasons that have been suggested for why it might make sense for companies to manage risks:

1. *Debt capacity.* Risk management can reduce the volatility of cash flows, and this decreases the probability of bankruptcy. As we discussed in Chapter 14, firms with lower operating risks can use more debt, which can lead to higher stock prices due to the interest tax savings.

2. *Maintaining the optimal capital budget over time.* Recall from Chapters 10, 13, and 14 that firms are reluctant to raise external equity due to high flotation costs and market pressure. This means that the capital budget must generally be financed with debt plus internally generated funds, mainly retained earnings and depreciation. In years when internal cash flows are low, they may be too small to support the optimal capital budget, causing firms to slow investment below the optimal rate or to incur the high costs associated with external equity. By smoothing out the cash flows, risk management can alleviate this problem.

3. *Financial distress.* Financial distress (and its results—which can range from worried stockholders to higher interest rates on debt to customer defections to bankruptcy) is associated with having cash flows fall below expected levels. Risk management can reduce the likelihood of low cash flows and hence of financial distress.

4. *Comparative advantages in hedging.* Many investors cannot implement a home-made hedging program as efficiently as a company can. First, firms generally have lower transactions costs due to a larger volume of hedging activities. Second, there is the problem of asymmetric information—managers know more about the firm's risk exposure than outside investors; hence, managers can create more effective hedges. And third, effective risk management requires specialized skills and knowledge that firms are more likely to have.

5. *Borrowing costs.* As discussed later in the chapter, firms can sometimes reduce input costs, especially the interest rate on debt, through the use of derivative instruments called "swaps." Any such cost reduction adds value to the firm.

6. *Tax effects.* Companies with volatile earnings pay more taxes than do more stable companies due to the treatment of tax credits and the rules governing corporate loss carry-forwards and carry-backs. Moreover, when volatile earnings lead to bankruptcy, tax loss carry-forwards are generally lost. Therefore, our tax system encourages risk management to stabilize earnings.[2]

7. *Compensation systems.* Many compensation systems establish "floors" and "ceilings" on bonuses, or they reward managers for meeting targets. To illustrate, suppose a firm's compensation system calls for a manager to receive no bonus when net income is below $1 million, a bonus of $10,000 when income is between $1 million and $2 million, and a bonus of $20,000 when income is $2 million or more. Moreover, the manager will receive an additional $10,000 when actual income is at least 90% of the forecasted level, which is $1 million. Now consider the following two situations. First, if income is stable at $2 million each year, the manager receives a $30,000 bonus each year, for a 2-year total of $60,000. However, if income is zero the first year and

[1]See Gordon M. Bodnar, Gregory S. Hayt, and Richard C. Marston, "1995 Wharton Survey of Derivative Usage by U.S. Non-Financial Firms," *Financial Management,* Winter 1996, pp. 113–133.
[2]See Clifford W. Smith and René Stulz, "The Determinants of Firms' Hedging Policies," *The Journal of Financial and Quantitative Analysis,* December 1985, pp. 395–406.

$4 million the second year, the manager receives no bonus the first year and $30,000 the second year, for a 2-year total of $30,000. So even though the company has the same total income ($4 million) over the 2 years, the manager's bonus is higher when earnings are stable. So even if hedging does not add much value for stockholders, it still may be beneficial to managers.

Perhaps the most important aspect of risk management involves derivative securities. The next section explains **derivatives**, which are securities whose values are determined by the market price of some other asset.

Derivatives include *options,* whose values depend on the price of some underlying asset; *interest rate and exchange rate futures* and *swaps,* whose values depend on interest rate and exchange rate levels; and *commodity futures,* whose values depend on commodity prices.

Derivatives
Securities whose values are determined by the market price or interest rate of some other asset.

SELF TEST

Explain why finance theory, combined with well-diversified investors and "homemade hedging," might suggest that risk management does not add much value to a company.

List and explain some reasons companies might employ risk management techniques.

18-2 BACKGROUND ON DERIVATIVES

The Chicago Board of Trade has an excellent web site at **www.cmegroup.com**. *Make sure you check out the wealth of information on the history and operations of the exchange by clicking on "About CME Group."*

A historical perspective is useful when studying derivatives. One of the first formal markets for derivatives was the futures market for wheat. Farmers were concerned about the price they would receive for their wheat when they sold it in the fall, and millers were concerned about the price they would have to pay. The risks that both parties faced could be reduced if they established a price earlier in the year. Accordingly, mill agents would go out to the wheat belt and make contracts with farmers that called for the farmers to deliver grain at a predetermined price. Both parties benefited from the transaction in the sense that their risks were reduced. The farmers could concentrate on growing their crop without worrying about the price of grain, and the millers could concentrate on their milling operations. Thus, *hedging with futures* lowered aggregate risk in the economy.

These early futures dealings were between two parties who arranged transactions between themselves. Soon, though, middlemen came into the picture, and trading in futures was established. The Chicago Board of Trade was an early marketplace for this dealing, and *futures dealers* helped make a market in futures contracts. Thus, farmers could sell futures on the exchange, and millers could buy them there. This improved the efficiency and lowered the cost of hedging operations.

Quickly, a third group—*speculators*—entered the scene. As we will see in the next section, most derivatives, including futures, are highly leveraged, meaning that a small change in the value of the underlying asset will produce a large change in the price of the derivative. This leverage appealed to speculators. At first, one might think that the appearance of speculators would increase risk, but that is not true. Speculators add capital and players to the market, which tends to stabilize the market. Of course, derivatives markets are inherently volatile due to the leverage involved; hence, risk to the speculators is high. Still, by speculators bearing that risk, the derivatives markets become stable for the hedgers.

Natural hedges are defined as situations in which aggregate risk can be reduced by derivatives transactions between two parties (called *counterparties*). They exist for many commodities, foreign currencies, interest rates on securities with different maturities, and even common stocks where portfolio managers want to "hedge their bets." Natural hedges occur when futures are traded between

Natural Hedges
Situations in which aggregate risk can be reduced by derivatives transactions between two parties known as counterparties.

cotton farmers and cotton mills, copper mines and copper fabricators, importers and foreign manufacturers for currency exchange rates, electric utilities and coal miners, and oil producers and oil users. In all of those situations, hedging reduces aggregate risk and thus benefits the economy.

Hedging also can be done in situations where no natural hedge exists. In these situations, one party wants to reduce some type of risk and another party agrees to sell a contract that protects the first party from that specific event or situation. Insurance is an obvious example of this type of hedge. Note, though, that with *nonsymmetric hedges,* risks are generally *transferred* rather than *eliminated.* Even in these instances, though, insurance companies can reduce certain types of risk through diversification.

For a number of reasons, the derivatives markets have grown more rapidly than any other major market in recent years. First, analytical techniques such as the Black-Scholes Option Pricing Model, which is discussed in Section 18-5, have been developed to establish "fair" prices. Having a better basis for pricing hedges makes the counterparties more comfortable with deals. Second, computers and electronic communications make it much easier for counterparties to deal with one another. Third, globalization has greatly increased the importance of currency markets and the need for reducing the exchange rate risks brought on by global trade. Recent trends and developments are sure to continue if not accelerate, so the use of derivatives for risk management is bound to grow.

Note, though, that derivatives have a potential downside. These instruments are highly leveraged, so small miscalculations can lead to huge losses. Also, because they are complicated, most people do not understand them well. Consequently, mistakes are more likely to occur than with less complex instruments, and it makes it harder for a firm's top management to exercise proper control over derivatives transactions. One relatively low-level employee operating in the Far East entered into transactions that led to the bankruptcy of Britain's oldest bank (Barings Bank), the institution that held the accounts of the Queen of England. (See the following Global Perspectives.) Just prior to the problems at Barings, Orange County, California, went bankrupt due to its treasurer's speculation in derivatives and Procter & Gamble got into a nasty fight with Bankers Trust over derivative-related losses. A few years later in 1998, the high-profile hedge fund Long-Term Capital Management LP nearly collapsed because of bad bets made in the derivatives market. More recently, it has been argued that extensive derivative positions enabled Enron to hide some of its losses and to hide debt that had been incurred on some of its unprofitable businesses.

The P&G, Orange County, Barings Bank, Long-Term Capital Management, and Enron affairs make the headlines, causing some people to argue that derivatives should be regulated out of existence to "protect the public." However, derivatives are used far more often to hedge risks than they are used in harmful speculations, but these beneficial transactions do not make the headlines. So while the horror stories point out the need for top managers to exercise control over the personnel who deal with derivatives, they do not justify the elimination of derivatives. In the balance of this chapter, we discuss how firms can manage risks and how derivatives are used in risk management.

SELF TEST

What is a "natural hedge"? Give some examples of natural hedges.

How does a nonsymmetric hedge differ from a natural hedge? Provide an example of a nonsymmetric hedge.

List three reasons the derivatives markets have grown more rapidly than any other major market in recent years.

GLOBAL PERSPECTIVES

BARINGS AND SUMITOMO SUFFER LARGE LOSSES IN THE DERIVATIVES MARKET

Barings, a conservative English bank with a long, impressive history dating back to its financing of the Louisiana Purchase in the 19th century, collapsed in 1995 when one of its traders lost $1.4 billion in derivatives trades. Nicholas Leeson, a 28-year-old trader in Barings' Singapore office, had speculated in Japanese stock index and interest rate futures without his superiors' knowledge. A lack of internal controls at the bank allowed him to accumulate large losses without being detected. Leeson's losses caught many by surprise, and the losses provide ammunition to those who argue that derivatives trading should be more highly regulated if not sharply curtailed.

Most argue that the blame goes beyond Leeson—that both the bank and the exchanges were at fault for failing to provide sufficient oversight. For misreporting his trades, Leeson was sentenced to a 6½-year term in a Singapore prison. What remained of Barings was ultimately sold to a Dutch banking concern.

Many analysts, including those who argued that the Barings episode was an unsettling although isolated incident, were startled by a similar case a year and a half after the Barings debacle. In June 1996, Japan's Sumitomo Corporation disclosed that its well-respected chief copper trader, Yasuo Hamanaka, had been conducting unauthorized speculative trades for more than a decade. The cumulative loss on the trades was $2.6 billion.

These two events illustrate the dangers of derivatives and the importance of internal controls. While it is unsettling to learn that the actions of a single, relatively low-level employee can suddenly cripple a giant corporation, these losses should be placed in perspective. The overwhelming majority of firms that use derivatives have been successful in enhancing performance and/or reducing risk. For this reason, most analysts argue that it would be a huge mistake to use the rare instances where fraud occurred to limit a market that has, for the most part, been a resounding success. However, given the volume of business in this market, in the future, we can expect to see other problems similar to those encountered by Barings and Sumitomo.

18-3 OPTIONS

Option

A contract that gives its holder the right to buy (or sell) an asset at a predetermined price within a specified period of time.

An **option** is a contract that gives its holder the right to buy (or sell) an asset at some predetermined price within a specified period of time. Financial managers should understand option theory for risk management. Also, such an understanding will help them structure warrant and convertible financings, discussed in Chapter 20.

18-3a Option Types and Markets

Strike (Exercise) Price

The price that must be paid for a share of common stock when an option is exercised.

Call Option

An option to buy, or "call," a share of stock at a certain price within a specified period.

There are many types of options and option markets.[3] To illustrate how options work, suppose you owned 100 shares of IBM, which on Wednesday, July 23, 2008, sold for $128.77 per share. You could sell to someone the right to buy your 100 shares at any time during the next 4 months at a price of, say, $130 per share. The $130 is called the **strike,** or **exercise, price**. Such options exist; and they are traded on a number of exchanges, with the Chicago Board Options Exchange (CBOE) being the oldest and the largest. This type of option is defined as a **call option** because the purchaser has a "call" on 100 shares of stock. The seller of an option is called the option *writer*. An investor who "writes" call options against stock held in his or her portfolio is said to be selling *covered options*. Options sold without the stock to back them up are called *naked options*. When the exercise price exceeds the

---

[3]For an in-depth treatment of options, see Don M. Chance, *An Introduction to Derivatives and Risk Management* (Mason, OH: Thomson/South-Western, 2004).

current stock price, a call option is said to be *out-of-the-money*. When the exercise price is below the current price of the stock, the option is *in-the-money*.

Table 18-1 is a listing of selected options quotations (calls and puts) for IBM obtained from the MSN Money web site on July 23, 2008. As shown in the first column, IBM's last stock price was $128.77. This implies that the first call option listed with a $125 strike price was selling in-the-money, while the last two options listed were trading out-of-the-money. Taking a closer look, we see that IBM's September $135 call option sold for $1.75. Thus, for $1.75(100) = $175, you could buy options until September 20, 2008, that would give you the right to purchase 100 shares of IBM stock at a price of $135 per share.[4] If the stock price stayed below $135 during that period, you would lose your $175; but if it rose to $145, your $175 investment would increase in value to ($145 – $135)(100) = $1,000 in less than 60 days. That translates into a very healthy annualized return. Incidentally, if the stock price did increase, you would not exercise your options and buy the stock— rather, you would sell the options, which would then have a value of $1,000 versus the $175 you paid, to another option buyer or back to the original seller.

In this example, you can see that investors in call options profit when the value of the underlying asset (in this case, IBM stock) increases. Alternatively, if investors believe that IBM stock is going to decline, it makes sense to sell call options on the stock. In this case, the buyer of the option pays you the current option price today; and in return, you agree to sell shares of stock to the buyer at the strike price. As stated in the previous paragraph, the buyer of the option will choose to exercise the option only if the stock sells for more than the strike price. For example, if you sold the September $135 option, you would receive $175 immediately for being the writer of the option. If IBM stock remains below $135 through September, the option will expire worthless and you will earn $175 profit from selling the option. However, if the stock price rose to $145, the option holder would choose to exercise his or her option to buy 100 shares of the stock for $135 per share—which means as the seller (or writer) of the option, you would be forced to sell 100 shares of stock for $135 even though they are worth $145 in the market. In this case, the seller of the call option would realize a net payoff of −$825. (This is the sum of the $175 received for writing the call option and the $1,000 lost when the option was exercised.)

Another way to profit from a decline in the stock price is to buy an option that gives you the right to *sell* a stock at a specified price within some future period—this is called a **put option**. For example, suppose you think that IBM's stock price is likely to decline from its current level of $128.77 sometime during the next 2 months. Table 18-1 provides data on IBM's put options. You could buy a 2-month put option (the September put option) for $299 ($2.99 × 100) that

You can obtain information for a specific company's call and put options at http://moneycentral.msn.com/investor/options. Just type the firm's ticker symbol and click "Go." Shaded options are "in-the-money."

Put Option
An option to sell a share of stock at a certain price within a specified period.

Table 18-1	Selected IBM Options Quotations, July 23, 2008						
		CALLS—LAST QUOTE			PUTS—LAST QUOTE		
Last Price	**Strike Price**	**Sept.**	**Oct.**	**Jan.**	**Sept.**	**Oct.**	**Jan.**
128.77	125	6.60	8.10	11.80	2.99	4.30	6.90
128.77	130	3.58	5.20	8.20	5.00	6.40	9.10
128.77	135	1.75	3.00	5.82	8.00	9.30	11.20

Note: Table 18-1 was created from data for July 23, 2008, from the MSN Money web site at http://moneycentral.msn.com/investor/options. The data provided on this web site are constantly updated during the day, so we have "captured" this data at one point during the trading day.

---

[4]Actually, the *expiration date*, which is the last date the option can be exercised, is the Friday before the third Saturday of the exercise month. Also note that option contracts are generally written in 100-share multiples.

would give you the right to sell 100 shares (that you would not necessarily own) at a price of $125 per share. ($125 is the strike price.) Suppose you bought this 100-share contract for $299 and then IBM's stock fell to $120. You could buy a share of stock for $120 and exercise your put option by selling the stock for $125. Your profit from exercising the option would be ($125 − $120)(100) = $500. After subtracting the $299 you paid for the option, your profit (before taxes and commissions) would be $201.

In addition to options on individual stocks, options also are available on several stock indexes such as the NYSE Index, Dow Jones Industrials, the S&P 100, and the S&P 500, just to name a few. Index options permit a person to hedge (or bet) on a rise or fall in the general market as well as on individual stocks.

Option trading is one of the hottest financial activities in the United States. The leverage involved makes it possible for speculators with just a few dollars to make a fortune almost overnight. Also, investors can sell options against their stocks and earn the value of the option (less brokerage commissions) even if the stock's price remains constant. Most importantly, though, options can be used to create *hedges* that protect the value of an individual stock or portfolio. We will discuss hedging strategies in more detail later in the chapter.[5]

Long-term Equity AnticiPation Security (LEAPS)

A long-term option that is listed on the exchanges and tied to individual stocks and stock indexes.

Conventional options are generally written for 7 months or less, but another type of option called a **Long-term Equity AnticiPation Security (LEAPS)** is also traded. Like conventional options, LEAPS are listed on exchanges and are tied to individual stocks and to stock indexes. The major difference is that LEAPS are long-term options having maturities of up to 3 years. One-year LEAPS cost about twice as much as the matching 3-month option; but because of their much longer time to expiration, LEAPS provide buyers with more potential for gains and offer better long-term protection for a portfolio.

Corporations on whose stocks options are written have nothing to do with the option market. Corporations do not raise money in the option market, nor do they have any direct transactions in it. Moreover, option holders do not vote for corporate directors or receive dividends. Studies have been conducted by the SEC and others as to whether option trading stabilizes or destabilizes the stock market and whether this activity helps or hinders corporations seeking to raise new capital. The studies have not been conclusive; but option trading is here to stay, and many regard it as the "most exciting game in town."

18-3b Factors That Affect the Value of a Call Option

A study of Table 18-1 provides some insights into call option valuation. First, we see that at least three factors affect a call option's value: (1) The higher the stock's market price in relation to the strike price, the higher the call option price. Thus, IBM's $135 September call option sells for $1.75, whereas IBM's $125 September option sells for $6.60. This difference arises because IBM's current stock price is $128.77. (2) The higher the strike price, the lower the call option price. Thus, all of IBM's call options shown, regardless of exercise month, decline as the strike price increases. (3) The longer the option period, the higher the option price. This occurs because the longer the time before expiration, the greater the chance that the stock price will climb substantially above the exercise price. Thus, option prices increase as the expiration date is lengthened. As shown in Table 18-1, all of the January 2009 options are higher in price than either the September or October options.

---

[5]Insiders who trade illegally generally buy options rather than stock because the leverage inherent in options increases the profit potential. Note, though, that it is illegal to use insider information for personal gain; an insider using such information would be taking advantage of the option seller. Insider trading, in addition to being unfair and essentially equivalent to stealing, hurts the economy: Investors lose confidence in the capital markets and raise their required returns because of an increased element of risk, which raises the cost of capital and thus reduces the level of real investment.

Other factors that affect option values, especially the volatility of the underlying stock, are discussed in later sections.

18-3c Exercise Value versus Option Price

How is the actual price of a call option determined in the market? In Section 18-5, we present a widely used model (the Black-Scholes model) for pricing call options; but first it is useful to establish some basic concepts. To begin, we define a call option's **exercise value** as follows:

$$\text{Exercise value} = \text{Current stock price} - \text{Strike price} \qquad \text{18-1}$$

Exercise Value
For a call option, it is the difference between the current stock price and the option's strike price.

The exercise value is what the option would be worth if you had to exercise it immediately. For example, if a stock sells for $50 and its option has a strike price of $20, you could buy the stock for $20 by exercising the option. You would own a stock worth $50, but you would have to pay only $20. Therefore, the option would be worth $30 if you had to exercise it immediately. Note that the calculated exercise value of a call option could be negative, but realistically the minimum "true" value of an option is zero because no one would exercise an out-of-the-money option. Note also that an option's exercise value is only a first approximation value—it merely provides a starting point for finding the actual value of the option.

Now consider Figure 18-1, which presents some data on Space Technology Inc. (STI), a company that recently went public and whose stock price has fluctuated widely during its short history. The third column in the tabular data shows the exercise values for STI's call option when the stock was selling at different prices, the fourth column gives the actual market prices for the option, and the fifth column shows the premium of the actual option price over its exercise value. At any stock price below $20, the exercise value is set at zero; but above $20, each $1 increase in the price of the stock brings with it a $1 increase in the option's exercise value. Note, however, that the actual market price of the call option lies above the exercise value at each price of the common stock, although the premium declines as the price of the stock increases above the strike price. For example, when the stock sold for $20 and the option had a zero exercise value, its actual price, and the premium, was $9. Then as the price of the stock rose, the *exercise value's increase* matched the stock's increase dollar for dollar, but the *market price* of the option climbed less rapidly, causing the premium to decline. The premium was $9 when the stock sold for $20 a share, but it had declined to $1 by the time the stock price had risen to $73 a share. Beyond that point, the premium virtually disappeared.

Why does this pattern exist? Why should a call option ever sell for more than its exercise value, and why does the premium decline as the price of the stock increases? The answer lies, in part, in the speculative appeal of options—they enable someone to gain a high degree of personal leverage when buying securities. To illustrate, suppose STI's option sold for the same amount as its exercise value. Now suppose you were thinking of investing in the company's common stock at a time when it was selling for $21 a share. If you bought a share and the price rose to $42, you would have made a 100% capital gain. However, had you bought the option at its exercise value ($1 when the stock was selling for $21), your capital gain would have been $22 − $1 = $21 on a $1 investment, or 2,100%. At the same time, your total loss potential with the option would be only $1 versus a potential loss of $21 if you purchased the stock. The huge capital gains potential, combined with the loss limitation, is clearly worth something—the exact amount it is worth to investors is the amount of the premium. Note, however, that buying the option is riskier than buying STI's stock because there is a higher probability of losing money on the option. If STI's stock price fell to $20, you would have a 4.76% loss if

| FIGURE 18-1 | Space Technology Inc.: Option Price and Exercise Value |

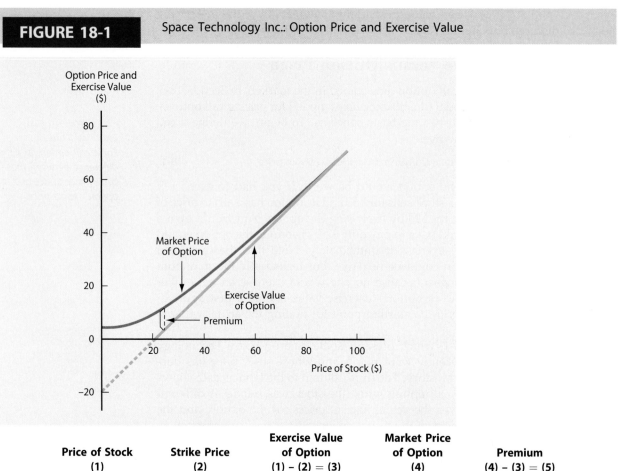

Price of Stock (1)	Strike Price (2)	Exercise Value of Option (1) – (2) = (3)	Market Price of Option (4)	Premium (4) – (3) = (5)
$20.00	$20.00	$ 0.00	$ 9.00	$9.00
21.00	20.00	1.00	9.75	8.75
22.00	20.00	2.00	10.50	8.50
35.00	20.00	15.00	21.00	6.00
42.00	20.00	22.00	26.00	4.00
50.00	20.00	30.00	32.00	2.00
73.00	20.00	53.00	54.00	1.00
98.00	20.00	78.00	78.50	0.50

you bought the stock (ignoring transactions costs), but you would have a 100% loss on the option investment.

Why does the premium decline as the stock price rises? Part of the answer is that both the leverage effect and the loss protection feature decline at high stock prices. For example, if you were thinking of buying STI stock when its price was $73 a share, the exercise value of the option would be $53. If the stock price doubled to $146, you would have a 100% gain on the stock. Now note that the exercise value of the option would go from $53 to $126, for a percentage gain of 138% versus 2,100% in the earlier case. Also note that the potential loss per dollar of potential gain on the option is much greater when the option is selling at high prices. These two factors, the declining leverage impact and the increasing danger of larger losses, help explain why the premium diminishes as the common stock price rises.

In addition to the stock price and the exercise price, the price of an option depends on three other factors: (1) the option's term to maturity, (2) the variability of the stock price, and (3) the risk-free rate. We will explain precisely how these factors affect call option prices later; but for now, note these points:

1. The longer a call option has to run, the greater its value and the larger its premium. If an option expires at 4 p.m. today, there is not much chance that the stock price will increase very much; so the option must sell at close to its exercise value, and its premium must be small. On the other hand, if the expiration date is a year away, the stock price could rise sharply, pulling the option's value up with it.

2. An option on an extremely volatile stock is worth more than an option on a very stable stock. When the stock price rarely moves, there is only a small chance of a large gain. However, when the stock price is highly volatile, the option may easily become very valuable. At the same time, losses on options are limited—you can make an unlimited amount, but you can lose only what you paid for the option. Therefore, a large decline in a stock's price does not have a corresponding bad effect on option holders. As a result of the unlimited upside but limited downside, the more volatile a stock, the higher the value of its options.

3. The effect of the risk-free rate on a call option isn't as obvious. The expected growth rate of a firm's stock price increases as interest rates increase, but the present value of future cash flows decreases. The first effect tends to increase the call option's price, while the second tends to decrease it. As it turns out, the first effect dominates the second one; so the price of a call option always increases as the risk-free rate increases. We illustrate this fact in Table 18-2 in Section 18-5.

Because of Points 1 and 2, in a graph such as Figure 18-1, the longer an option's life, the higher its market price line above the exercise value line. Similarly, the more volatile the price of the underlying stock, the higher the market price line. When we discuss the Black-Scholes Option Pricing Model, we will see precisely how these factors (and the discount rate) affect option values.

SELF TEST

What is an option? a call option? a put option?

Define a call option's exercise value. Why is the actual market price of a call option usually above its exercise value?

What are some factors that affect a call option's value?

Underwater Technology stock is currently trading at $30 a share. A call option on the stock with a $25 strike price currently sells for $12. What are the exercise value and the premium of the call option? **($5; $7)**

18-4 INTRODUCTION TO OPTION PRICING MODELS[6]

Nearly all option pricing models are based on the concept of a **riskless hedge**. To illustrate how a riskless hedge works, consider an example where an investor buys shares of stock in Western Cellular and simultaneously sells a call option on the stock. If the stock's price increases, the investor will earn a profit on the stock but will lose money from selling the call option. (Recall that when an investor agrees to sell or write a call option, he or she makes money when the stock's price falls and loses money when the stock price increases.) Conversely, if the stock price declines, the investor will lose on his or her investment in the stock but gain from selling the call option. As we demonstrate, it is possible to set things up such that

Riskless Hedge
A hedge in which an investor buys a stock and simultaneously sells a call option on that stock and ends up with a riskless position.

---

[6]Sections 18-4 and 18-5 are relatively technical, and they can be omitted without loss of continuity.

the investor will end up with a riskless position—regardless of what the stock price does, the value of the investor's portfolio will remain constant. Thus, a riskless investment will have been created.

If an investment is riskless, it must, in equilibrium, yield the risk-free rate. If it offered a higher return, arbitrageurs would buy it and, in the process, push the return down—and vice versa if it offered less than the risk-free rate. Given the stock price, its potential volatility, the option's exercise price, the life of the option, and the risk-free rate, there is but one price for the option if it is to meet the equilibrium condition, namely, that a portfolio that consists of the stock and the call option will earn the risk-free rate. Building on this idea, we show the steps that are used to estimate the current value of the call option:

1. *Assumptions of the example.* The stock of Western Cellular, a manufacturer of cell phones, sells for $40 per share. Options exist that permit the holder to buy one share of Western at an exercise price of $35. These options will expire at the end of 1 year, at which time Western's stock will be selling at one of two prices, $30 or $50. Also, the risk-free rate is 8%. Based on these assumptions, we must find the value of the options.

2. *Find the range of values at expiration.* When the option expires at the end of the year, Western's stock will sell for $30 or $50, and here is the situation with regard to the value of the options:

	Ending Stock Price	−	Strike Price Value	=	Ending Option Value	
	$30.00	−	$35.00	=	$ 0.00	(Option is worthless; lowest value is zero.)
	50.00	−	35.00	=	15.00	
Range	$20.00				$15.00	

3. *Equalize the range of payoffs for the stock and the option.* As just shown, the ranges of payoffs for the stock and the option are $20 and $15, respectively. To construct the riskless portfolio, we need to equalize these ranges. We do so by buying 0.75 share and selling one option (or 75 shares and 100 options) to produce the following situation, where the range for both the stock and the option is $15:

	Ending Stock Price	×	0.75	=	Ending Value of Stock	Ending Value of Option
	$30.00	×	0.75	=	$22.50	$ 0.00
	50.00	×	0.75	=	37.50	15.00
Range	$20.00				$15.00	$15.00

4. *Create a riskless hedged investment.* We can now create a riskless investment portfolio by buying 0.75 share of Western's stock and selling one call option. Here is the situation:

	Ending Stock Price	×	0.75	=	Ending Value of Stock in the Portfolio	+	Ending Value of Option in the Portfolio	=	Ending Total Value of the Portfolio
	$30.00	×	0.75	=	$22.50	+	$ 0.00	=	$22.50
	50.00	×	0.75	=	37.50	+	−15.00	=	22.50

EXPENSING EXECUTIVE STOCK OPTIONS

In Chapter 1, we noted that many companies give senior managers stock options as part of their compensation packages. One reason for doing so is that options give managers a strong incentive to increase their companies' stock prices. Another benefit is that options are a substitute for salaries, which reduces a firm's cash requirements. Reducing the need for cash payments is particularly important for young start-up companies where cash for salaries is generally in short supply. However, options are not free to the issuing company—they have a very real cost because they lead to an increase in the number of shares outstanding, which in turn reduces the company's earnings per share.

In the past, there was another important reason companies liked to issue stock options. Cash paid as salaries must be reported as salary expense on the income statement, thus lowering reported profits. By contrast, until recently, stock options, even though they may have a true value in the millions of dollars, did not have to be reported on the income statement and thus did not reduce reported profits.[a] While some companies such as Microsoft, Cisco, Citigroup, and GE took steps to voluntarily expense their executive stock options, many other companies resisted.

Companies had been reluctant to expense options for two reasons. First, managers generally dislike any action

that reduces reported profits because their own salaries, bonuses, and future options are generally based on reported profits. Recent studies indicate that expensing options reduces the reported profits of an average S&P 500 company by about 15%; and for some companies, the reduction is more than 50%. Second, companies weren't sure how to value them. The Black-Scholes model is used most frequently, but it has limitations. In particular, some executive stock options are worth less than the valuations implied by Black-Scholes because grantees must wait several years before they can exercise their options.

Despite their reluctance, accountants and corporate managers faced intense pressure from investors who argued that it is better to be approximately correct than exactly wrong (that is, expensing options using Black-Scholes for an approximate valuation rather than not expensing them and getting an obviously incorrect result). Responding to this pressure, the Financial Accounting Standards Board (FASB) recently put new guidelines in place that require public companies to deduct as an expense the value of their stock options granted each year. Some critics have complained that the new guidelines still give companies too much discretion in deciding how to value these options, but many contend that this is at least a step in the right direction.

[a]Although options were not reported as an expense on firms' income statements, they had to be reported in the notes to the financial statements.
Sources: Elizabeth MacDonald, "A Volatile Brew: Easing the Impact of Strict New Stock Option Rules," *Forbes*, August 15, 2005, pp. 70–71; and Anthony Bianco, "The Angry Market," *Business Week*, July 29, 2002, pp. 32–51.

The stock in the portfolio will have a value of $22.50 or $37.50 depending on what happens to the price of the stock. The call option that was sold will have no effect on the value of the portfolio if Western's price falls to $30 because it will not be exercised—it will expire worthless. However, if the stock price ends at $50, the holder of the option will exercise it, paying the $35 exercise price for stock that would cost $50 on the open market; so in that case, the option would have a cost of $15 to the holder of the portfolio.

Now note that the value of the portfolio is $22.50 regardless of whether Western's stock price increases or decreases. So the portfolio is riskless. A hedge has been created that protects against increases or decreases in the price of the stock.

5. *Pricing the call option.* To this point, we have not mentioned the price of the call option that was sold to create the riskless hedge. How much should it sell for? Obviously, the seller would like to receive a high price for it, but the buyer would want to pay a low price. What is the *fair,* or *equilibrium,* price? To find this price, we proceed as follows:

   a. The value of the portfolio will be $22.50 at the end of the year regardless of what happens to the stock price. This $22.50 is riskless.

b. The risk-free rate is 8%, so the present value of the riskless $22.50 year-end value is as follows:

$$PV = \$22.50/1.08 = \$20.83$$

c. Because Western's stock is currently selling for $40 and because the portfolio contains 0.75 share, the cost of the stock in the portfolio is as follows:

$$0.75(\$40) = \$30.00$$

d. If you paid $30 for the stock and if the present value of the portfolio was $20.83, the option would have to sell for at least $9.17.

$$\text{Price of option} = \text{Cost of stock} - \text{PV of portfolio}$$
$$= \$30 - \$20.83 = \$9.17$$

If this option sold at a price higher than $9.17, other investors could create riskless portfolios as described and earn more than the risk-free rate. Investors would create such portfolios—and options—until their price fell to $9.17, at which point the market would be in equilibrium. Conversely, if the options sold for less than $9.17, investors would refuse to create them and the resulting supply shortage would drive up the price to $9.17. Thus, investors (or arbitrageurs) would buy and sell in the market until the options were priced at their equilibrium level.

Clearly, this example is overly simplistic—Western's stock price could be almost anything after 1 year, and you could not purchase 0.75 share of stock (but you could do so in effect by buying 75 shares and selling 100 options). Still, the example does illustrate that investors can, in principle, create riskless portfolios by buying stocks and selling call options against those stocks; the return on such portfolios should be the risk-free rate. If call options are not priced to reflect this condition, arbitrageurs will actively trade stocks and options until option prices reflect equilibrium conditions. In the next section, we discuss the Black-Scholes Option Pricing Model, which is based on the general premise developed here—the creation of a riskless portfolio—but is applicable to "real-world" option pricing because it allows for a complete range of ending stock prices.

SELF TEST Describe how a risk-free portfolio can be created using stocks and options.

How can such a portfolio be used to help estimate a call option's value?

18-5 THE BLACK-SCHOLES OPTION PRICING MODEL (OPM)

Black-Scholes Option Pricing Model (OPM)
Derived from the concept of a riskless hedge, this model calculates the value of an option as the difference between the expected PV of the terminal stock price and the PV of the exercise price.

The **Black-Scholes Option Pricing Model (OPM)**, developed in 1973, helped give rise to the rapid growth in options trading.[7] This model, which has even been programmed into the permanent memories of some hand-held calculators, is widely used by option traders. Next, we show how the OPM can be used to value call options. In Appendix 18A, we show in more detail what the connection is between call and put values and how the OPM can be used to value put options.

---

[7]See Fischer Black and Myron Scholes, "The Pricing of Options and Corporate Liabilities," *Journal of Political Economy,* May/June 1973, pp. 637–659.

18-5a OPM Assumptions and Equations

In deriving their option pricing model, Fischer Black and Myron Scholes made the following assumptions:

1. The stock underlying the call option provides no dividends or other distributions during the life of the option.
2. There are no transactions costs for buying or selling the stock or the option.
3. The short-term, risk-free interest rate is known and is constant during the life of the option.
4. Any purchaser of a security may borrow any fraction of the purchase price at the short-term, risk-free interest rate.
5. Short selling is permitted, and the short seller will receive immediately the full cash proceeds of today's price for a security sold short.[8]
6. The call option can be exercised only on its expiration date.
7. Trading in all securities takes place continuously, and the stock price moves randomly.

The derivation of the Black-Scholes model rests on the concept of a riskless hedge such as the one set up in the last section. By buying shares of a stock and simultaneously selling call options on that stock, an investor can create a risk-free investment position, where gains on the stock will exactly offset losses on the option. This riskless hedged position must earn a rate of return equal to the risk-free rate. Otherwise, an arbitrage opportunity would exist and people trying to take advantage of this opportunity would drive the price of the option to the equilibrium level as specified by the Black-Scholes model.

The Black-Scholes model consists of the following three equations.

$$V = P[N(d_1)] - Xe^{-r_{RF}t}[N(d_2)] \qquad \text{18-2}$$

$$d_1 = \frac{\ln(P/X) + [r_{RF} + (\sigma^2/2)]t}{\sigma\sqrt{t}} \qquad \text{18-3}$$

$$d_2 = d_1 - \sigma\sqrt{t} \qquad \text{18-4}$$

Here

V = current value of the call option

P = current price of the underlying stock

$N(d_i)$ = probability that a deviation less than d_i will occur in a standard normal distribution. Thus, $N(d_1)$ and $N(d_2)$ represent areas under a standard normal distribution function.

X = exercise, or strike, price of the option

$e \approx 2.7183$

r_{RF} = risk-free interest rate

---

[8]Suppose an investor (or a speculator) does not own any IBM stock. If the investor anticipates a rise in the stock price and consequently buys IBM stock, he or she is said to have *gone long* in IBM. On the other hand, if the investor thinks that IBM's stock is likely to fall, he or she could *go short*, or *sell IBM short*. Since the short seller has no IBM stock, he or she would have to borrow the shares sold short from a broker. If the stock price falls, the short seller could, later on, buy shares on the open market and pay back the ones borrowed from the broker. The short seller's profit, before commissions and taxes, would be the difference between the price received from the short sale and the price paid later to purchase the replacement stock.

$$t = \text{time until the option expires (the option period)}$$
$$\ln(P/X) = \text{natural logarithm of } P/X$$
$$\sigma^2 = \text{variance of the rate of return on the stock}$$

Note that the value of the option is a function of the variables we discussed earlier: (1) P, the stock's price; (2) t, the option's time to expiration; (3) X, the strike price; (4) σ^2, the variance of the underlying stock; and (5) r_{RF}, the risk-free rate. We do not derive the Black-Scholes model—the derivation involves extremely complicated mathematics that go far beyond the scope of this text. However, it is not difficult to use the model. Under the assumptions set forth previously, if the option price is different from the one found by Equation 18-2, this will provide the opportunity for arbitrage profits, which will force the option price back to the value indicated by the model.[9] As noted earlier, the Black-Scholes model is widely used by traders; so actual option prices conform reasonably well to values derived from the model.

In essence, the first term of Equation 18-2, $P[N(d_1)]$, can be thought of as the expected present value of the terminal stock price, while the second term, $Xe^{-r_{RF}t}[N(d_2)]$, can be thought of as the present value of the exercise price. However, rather than try to figure out what the equations mean, it is more productive to insert some numbers to see how changes in the inputs affect the value of an option.

Robert's Online Option Pricer can be accessed at www.intrepid.com/~robertl/option-pricer1.html. The site is designed to provide an online financial service to small investors for option pricing, giving anyone a means to price option trades without the need to buy expensive software and hardware.

18-5b OPM Illustration

The current stock price (P), the exercise price (X), and the time to maturity (t) can be obtained from a newspaper such as *The Wall Street Journal* or on leading financial web sites such as Yahoo! Finance and MSN Money. The risk-free rate, r_{RF}, is the yield on a Treasury bill with a maturity equal to the option expiration date. The annualized variance of stock returns, σ^2, can be estimated by multiplying the variance of the percentage change in daily stock prices for the past year [that is, the variance of $(P_t - P_{t-1})/P$] by 365 days.

Assume that the following information has been obtained:

$$P = \$21$$
$$X = \$21$$
$$t = 0.36 \text{ year}$$
$$r_{RF} = 5\% = 0.05$$
$$\sigma^2 = 0.09. \text{ Note that } \sigma^2 = 0.09, \text{ then } \sigma = \sqrt{0.09} = 0.3.$$

Given that information, we now can use the OPM by solving Equations 18-2, 18-3, and 18-4. Since d_1 and d_2 are required inputs for Equation 18-2, we solve Equations 18-3 and 18-4 first as follows:

$$d_1 = \frac{\ln(\$21/\$21) + [0.05 + (0.09/2)](0.36)}{0.3(0.6)}$$
$$= \frac{0 + 0.0342}{0.18} = 0.19$$
$$d_2 = d_1 - 0.3\sqrt{0.36} = 0.19 - 0.18 = 0.01$$

---

[9]*Programmed trading,* in which stocks are bought and options are sold (or vice versa), is an example of arbitrage between stocks and options.

Note that $N(d_1) = N(0.19)$ and $N(d_2) = N(0.01)$ represent areas under a standard normal distribution function. From Appendix C at the end of the book, we see that the value $d_1 = 0.19$ implies a probability of $0.0753 + 0.5000 = 0.5753$; so $N(d_1) = 0.5753$. Similarly, $N(d_2) = 0.504$. We can use those values to solve Equation 18-2:

$$
\begin{aligned}
V &= \$21[N(d_1)] - \$21e^{-(0.05)(0.36)}[N(d_2)] \\
&= \$21[N(0.19)] - \$21(0.98216)[N(0.01)] \\
&= \$21(0.5753) - \$20.625(0.504) \\
&= \$12.081 - \$10.395 = \$1.686
\end{aligned}
$$

Thus, the value of the option, under the assumed conditions, is $1.686. Suppose the actual option price was $2.25. Arbitrageurs could simultaneously sell the option, buy the underlying stock, and earn a riskless profit. Such trading would occur until the price of the option was driven down to $1.686. The reverse would occur if the option sold for less than $1.686. Thus, because investors would be unwilling to pay more than $1.686 for the option and they could not buy it for less, $1.686 is the *equilibrium value* of the option.

To see how the five OPM factors affect the value of the option, consider Table 18-2. Here the top row shows the base-case input values that were used previously to illustrate the OPM and the resulting option value, $V = \$1.686$. In each of the subsequent rows, the boldfaced factor is increased while the other four are held constant at their base-case levels. The resulting value of the call option is given in the last column. Now let's consider the effects of the changes:

1. *Current stock price.* If the current stock price, P, increases from $21 to $25, the option value increases from $1.686 to $4.672. Thus, the value of the option increases as the stock price increases, but by less than the stock price increase, $2.986 versus $4.00. Note, though, that the percentage increase in the option value, ($4.672 – $1.686)/$1.686 = 177%, far exceeds the percentage increase in the stock price, ($25 – $21)/$21 = 19%.

2. *Exercise price.* If the exercise price, X, increases from $21 to $25, the value of the option declines. Again, the decrease in the option value is less than the exercise price increase, but the percentage change in the option value (in absolute value terms), ($0.434 – $1.686)/$1.686 = –74%, exceeds the percentage change in the exercise price, ($25 – $21)/$21 = 19%.

3. *Option period.* As the time to expiration increases from $t = 0.36$ year to $t = 0.50$ year, the value of the option increases from $1.686 to $2.023. This occurs because the value of the option depends on the chances for an increase in the price of the underlying stock; and the longer the option has before its expiration, the higher the stock price may climb.

4. *Risk-free rate.* As the risk-free rate increases from 5% to 8%, the value of the option increases slightly, from $1.686 to $1.802. Equations 18-2, 18-3, and 18-4

Table 18-2	Effects of OPM Factors on the Value of a Call Option					
	INPUT FACTORS					OUTPUT
Case	P	X	t	r_{RF}	σ^2	V
Base case	$21	$21	0.36	5%	0.09	$1.686
Increase P by $4	**25**	21	0.36	5	0.09	4.672
Increase X by $4	21	**25**	0.36	5	0.09	0.434
Increase t to 0.5	21	21	**0.50**	5	0.09	2.023
Increase r_{RF} to 8%	21	21	0.36	**8**	0.09	1.802
Increase σ^2 to 0.16	21	21	0.36	5	**0.16**	2.181

suggest that the principal effect of an increase in r_{RF} is to reduce the present value of the exercise price, $Xe^{-r_{RF}t}$, hence to increase the current value of the option.[10] The risk-free rate also plays a role in determining the values of the normal distribution functions $N(d_1)$ and $N(d_2)$, but this effect is of secondary importance. Indeed, option prices in general are not very sensitive to interest rate changes, at least not to changes within the ranges normally encountered.

5. *Variance.* As the variance increases from the base case 0.09 to 0.16, the value of the option increases from $1.686 to $2.181. Therefore, the riskier the underlying security, the more valuable the option. This result is logical. First, if you bought an option to buy a stock that sells at its exercise price and if $\sigma^2 = 0$, there would be a zero probability of the stock price increasing, hence a zero probability of making money on the option. On the other hand, if you bought an option on a high-variance stock, there would be a fairly high probability that the stock price would go way up, hence that you would make a large profit on the option. Of course, a high-variance stock could go way down; but as an option holder, your losses would be limited to the price paid for the option—only the right-hand side of the stock's probability distribution counts. Put another way, an increase in the price of the stock helps option holders more than a decrease hurts them; so the greater the variance, the greater the value of the option. This makes options on risky stocks more valuable than those on safer low-variance stocks.

Myron Scholes and Robert Merton were awarded the 1997 Nobel Prize in Economics, and Fischer Black would have been a corecipient had he still been alive.[11] Their work provided analytical tools and methodologies that are widely used to solve many types of financial problems, not just option pricing. Indeed, the entire field of modern risk management is based primarily on their contributions. This concludes our discussion of options and option pricing theory. The next section discusses some other types of derivative securities.

SELF TEST

What is the purpose of the Black-Scholes Option Pricing Model?

Explain what a "riskless hedge" is and how the riskless hedge concept is used in the Black-Scholes OPM.

Describe the effect of a change in each of the following factors on the value of a call option:

1. Stock price
2. Exercise price
3. Option life
4. Risk-free rate
5. Stock price variance (that is, riskiness of stock)

What is the value of a call option with these data: P = $25, X = $25, r_{RF} = 8%, t = 0.5 (6 months), σ^2 = 0.09, $N(d_1)$ = 0.61586, and $N(d_2)$ = 0.53287? **($2.60)**

---

[10]At this point, you may be wondering why the first term in Equation 18-2, $P[N(d_1)]$, is not discounted. In fact, it has been because the current stock price, P, already represents the present value of the expected stock price at expiration. In other words, P is a discounted value and the discount rate used in the market to determine today's stock price includes the risk-free rate. Thus, Equation 18-2 can be thought of as the present value of the end-of-option period spread between the stock price and the strike price, adjusted for the probability that the stock price will be higher than the strike price.

[11]See Robert C. Merton, "Theory of Rational Option Pricing," *Bell Journal of Economics and Management Science,* Vol. 4 (1973), pp. 141–183.

18-6 FORWARD AND FUTURES CONTRACTS

Forward contracts are agreements where one party agrees to buy a commodity at a specific price on a specific future date and the other party agrees to make the sale. *Goods are actually delivered under forward contracts.* Unless both parties are financially strong, there is a danger that one party will default on the contract, especially if the price of the commodity changes markedly after the agreement is reached.

A **futures contract** is similar to a forward contract but with three key differences: (1) Futures contracts are "marked to market" on a daily basis, meaning that gains and losses are noted and money must be put up to cover losses. This greatly reduces the risk of default that exists with forward contracts. (2) With futures, physical delivery of the underlying asset is never taken—the two parties simply settle up with cash for the difference between the contracted price and the actual price on the expiration date. (3) Futures contracts are generally standardized instruments that are traded on exchanges, whereas forward contracts are generally tailor-made, are negotiated between two parties, and are not traded after they have been signed.

Futures and forward contracts were originally used for commodities such as wheat, where farmers would sell forward contracts to millers, enabling both parties to lock in prices and thus reduce their risk exposure. Commodities contracts are still important, but today more trading is done in foreign exchange and interest rate futures. To illustrate how foreign exchange contracts are used, suppose GE arranges to buy electric motors from a German manufacturer on terms that call for GE to pay 1 million euros in 180 days. GE would not want to give up the free trade credit; but if the euro appreciated against the dollar during the next 6 months, the dollar cost of the million euros would rise. GE could hedge the transaction by buying a forward contract under which it agreed to buy the million euros in 180 days at a fixed dollar price. This would lock in the dollar cost of the motors. This transaction would probably be conducted through a money center bank, which would try to find a German company (a "counterparty") that needed dollars in 6 months. Alternatively, GE could buy a futures contract on an exchange.

Interest rate futures represent another huge and growing market. For example, suppose Simonset Corporation decides to build a new plant at a cost of $20 million. It plans to finance the project with 15-year bonds that would carry an 8% interest rate if they were issued today. However, the company will not need the money for about 6 months. Simonset could sell 15-year bonds now, locking in the 8% rate, but it would have the money before it was needed; so it would have to invest in short-term securities that would yield less than 8%. However, if Simonset waited 6 months to sell the bond issue, interest rates might be higher than they are today, in which case the firm would have to pay higher interest costs on the bonds, perhaps to the point of making it unprofitable to build the plant.

One solution to Simonset's dilemma involves *interest rate futures*, which are based on a hypothetical 15-year Treasury bond with a 6% semiannual coupon. If interest rates in the economy rise, the value of the hypothetical T–bond will fall and vice versa. In our example, Simonset is worried about an increase in interest rates. Should rates rise, the hypothetical Treasury bond's value would decline. Therefore, Simonset could sell T-bond futures for delivery in 6 months to hedge its position. If interest rates rise, Simonset will have to pay more when it issues its own bonds. However, it will make a profit on its futures position because it will have presold the bonds at a higher price than it will have to pay to cover (repurchase) them. Of course, if interest rates decline, Simonset will lose on its futures position, but this will be offset by the fact that it will pay a lower interest rate when it issues its bonds.

Forward Contract
A contract under which one party agrees to buy a commodity at a specific price on a specific future date and the other party agrees to make the sale. Physical delivery occurs.

Futures Contract
Standardized contracts that are traded on exchanges and are "marked to market" daily, but where physical delivery of the underlying asset is never taken.

In 2008, futures contracts were available on more than 40 real and financial assets traded on 10 U.S. exchanges—the largest in the United States is the Chicago Mercantile Exchange (CME).[12] There are more than 75 futures and futures options exchanges worldwide—of which the Eurex Exchange is the largest and the CME is the second largest.

Futures contracts are divided into two classes, **commodity futures** and **financial futures.** Commodity futures, which cover oil, various grains, oilseeds, livestock, meats, fibers, metals, and wood, were first traded in the United States in the mid-1800s. Financial futures, which were first traded in 1975, include Treasury bills, notes, bonds, certificates of deposit, eurodollar deposits, foreign currencies, and stock indexes.

To illustrate how futures contracts work, consider the CBOT's contract on Treasury bonds. The basic contract is for $100,000 of a hypothetical 6% coupon, semiannual payment Treasury bond with 15 years to maturity. Table 18-3 shows an extract from the Treasury bond futures table that appeared on *The Wall Street Journal* web site on July 23, 2008.

The first column gives the delivery month, and the next two columns give the last trading price and the change from the previously traded price. The next three columns give the open, high, and low prices, respectively, for that contract on that day. Column 7 shows the volume of trading in that contract for the day; and Column 8 shows the "open interest," which is the number of contracts outstanding. Since the web site shows trades throughout the day, the last price shown is not necessarily the settlement price, which is the price at the close of trading. In Table 18-3, all of the last prices shown are settlement prices, indicated by the *s* following the price. The last price for the September 2008 futures, 113'19.5, means 113 plus $^{19.5}/_{32}$, or 113.609375% of par.

To illustrate, we focus on the Treasury bonds for December 2008 delivery. The settlement price was 112'20.5, or 112 plus $^{20.5}/_{32}$% of the $100,000 contract value. Thus, the price at which one could buy $100,000 face value of 6%, 15-year Treasury bonds to be delivered in December 2008 was 112.640625% of par, or 1.12640625 ($100,000) = $112,640.625. The contract price fell by $^{17}/_{32}$ of 1% of $100,000, or by $531.25, from the previous day. So if you had bought the contract yesterday, you would have lost $531.25. There were 3,620 contracts outstanding, representing a total value of about $407.76 million.

Note that the contract price fell by $^{17}/_{32}$% on this particular day. Why would the value of the bond futures contract fall? Since bond prices decline when interest rates rise, we know that interest rates rose that day. Moreover, we can calculate

Commodity Futures
A contract that is used to hedge against price changes for input materials.

Financial Futures
A contract that is used to hedge against fluctuating interest rates, stock prices, and exchange rates.

Table 18-3	Interest Rate Futures

TREASURY BONDS (CBT)—$100,000; PTS. 32nds OF 100%

Delivery Month (1)	Last (2)	Change (3)	Open (4)	High (5)	Low (6)	Volume (7)	Open Interest (8)
Sep '08	113'19.5s	−0'17.5	114'04.5	114'05.5	113'11.0	292770	879590
Dec '08	112'20.5s	−0'17.0	113'05.0	113'05.0	112'13.5	131	3620
Mar '09	111'18.0s	−0'17.0	111'18.0	111'18.0	111'18.0	0	17
Jun '09	110'20.5s	−0'17.0	110'20.5	110'20.5	110'20.5	0	20
Sep '09	110'20.5s	−0'17.0	110'20.5	110'20.5	110'20.5	0	0

Source: www.wsj.com, July 23, 2008.

---

[12]In July 2007, the CME merged with the Chicago Board of Trade to become CME Group Inc.; and in July 2008, CME and the New York Mercantile Exchange agreed to a strategic combination.

the implied rates inherent in the futures contracts. Recall that the contract relates to a hypothetical 15-year, semiannual payment, 6% coupon bond. The closing price (settlement price) was $112^{20.5}/_{32}$, or 112.640625% of par. Using a financial calculator, we can solve for r_d in the following equation:

$$\sum_{t=1}^{30} \frac{\$30}{(1 + r_d/2)^t} + \frac{\$1,000}{(1 + r_d/2)^{30}} = \$1,126.40625$$

The solution value for the 6-month rate is 2.40378%, which is equivalent to a nominal annual rate of 4.80756%, or 4.81%. Because the price of the bond fell by $^{17}/_{32}$ that day, we could find the previous day's closing (settlement) price and its implied interest rate, which would turn out to be 4.76%. Therefore, interest rates rose by 5 basis points, which was enough to decrease the value of the contract by $531.25.

Thus, the futures contract for December 2008 delivery of this hypothetical bond sold for $112,640.625 for one bond with a par value of $100,000, which translates to a yield to maturity of about 4.8%. This yield reflects investors' beliefs about what the interest rate level will be in December 2008. The spot yield on T-bonds was about 4.6% in July 2008, so the marginal trader in the futures market was predicting about a 20-basis-point increase in yields over the next 5 months. That prediction could, of course, turn out to be incorrect.

Now suppose that 2 months later interest rates in the futures market had fallen from the earlier levels, say, from 4.8% to 4.5%. Falling interest rates mean rising bond prices, and we could calculate that the December contract would then be worth about $116,234. Thus, the contract's value would have increased by $116,234.00 − $112,640.63 = $3,593.37.

When futures contracts are purchased, the purchaser does not have to put up the full amount of the purchase price; rather, the purchaser is required to post an initial *margin*, which for CBT Treasury bond contracts is $2,430 per $100,000 contract. However, investors are required to maintain a certain value in the margin account, called a *maintenance margin*. The maintenance margin for CBT Treasury bond contracts is $1,800 per $100,000 contract. If the value of the contract declines, the owner may be required to add additional funds to the margin account; and the more the contract value falls, the more money that must be added. The value of the contract is checked at the end of every working day, and margin account adjustments are made at that time. This is called "marking to market." If an investor purchased our illustrative contract and then sold it for $116,234, he or she would have made a profit of $3,593.37 on a $2,430 investment, or a return of about 48% in only 2 months. It is clear, therefore, that futures contracts offer a considerable amount of leverage. Of course, if interest rates had risen, the value of the contract would have declined and the investor could easily have lost his or her $2,430, or more. Futures contracts are not settled by delivery of the securities involved. Rather, the transaction is completed by reversing the trade, which amounts to selling the contract back to the original seller.[13] The actual gains and losses on the contract are realized when the futures contract is closed.

Our examples show that forward contracts and futures can be used to hedge, or reduce, risks. Later, in Section 18-8, we describe in more detail how futures can be used to hedge various types of risk. It has been estimated that more than 95% of all futures transactions are designed as hedges, with banks and futures dealers

---

[13]The buyers and sellers of most financial futures contracts do not actually trade with each other—each trader's contractual obligation is with a futures exchange. This feature helps to guarantee the fiscal integrity of the trade. Incidentally, commodities futures traded on the exchanges are settled the same way as financial futures; but in the case of commodities, much of the contracting is done off the exchange, between farmers and processors, as *forward contracts*, in which case actual deliveries occur.

serving as middlemen between hedging counterparties. Interest rate and exchange rate futures can, of course, be used for speculative as well as hedging purposes. We can buy a T-bond contract on $100,000 of bonds with only $2,430 down, in which case a small change in interest rates will result in a very large gain or loss. Still, the primary motivation behind the vast majority of these transactions is to hedge risks, not to create them.

Futures contracts and options are similar to each other—so similar that people often confuse the two. Therefore, it is useful to compare the two instruments. A *futures contract* is a definite agreement on the part of one party to buy something on a specific date at a specific price, and the other party agrees to sell on the same terms. No matter how low or how high the price goes, the two parties must settle the contract at the agreed-upon price. An *option,* on the other hand, gives someone the right to buy (call) or sell (put) an asset, but the holder of the option does not have to complete the transaction. Note also that options exist for both individual stocks and "bundles" of stocks such as those in the S&P and Value Line indexes, but generally not for commodities. Futures, on the other hand, are used for commodities, debt securities, and stock indexes.

SELF TEST

What is a forward contract?

What is a futures contract? What are the key differences between forward and futures contracts?

What is the key difference between futures contracts and options?

What is the difference between the initial margin and the maintenance margin on a futures contract?

Suppose you buy a March futures contract on a hypothetical 15-year, 6% semiannual coupon bond with a settlement price today of $109^9/_{32}$. You post the initial margin required for this transaction ($2,430 per $100,000 contract). What nominal yield to maturity is implied by the settlement price? If interest rates fall to 4.5%, what return would you earn on one futures contract? If interest rates rose to 5.5%, what is the return on one futures contract? **(5.11%, 186%, −273.62%)**

18-7 OTHER TYPES OF DERIVATIVES

Options, forwards, and futures are among the most important classes of derivative securities; but there are other types of derivatives, including swaps, structured notes, inverse floaters, and a host of other "exotic" contracts.

18-7a Swaps

Swap
Two parties agree to exchange obligations to make specified payment streams.

A **swap** is just what the name implies—two parties agree to swap something, generally obligations to make specified payment streams. Most swaps today involve interest payments or currencies. To illustrate an interest rate swap, suppose Company S has a 20-year, $100 million floating-rate bond outstanding, while Company F has a $100 million, 20-year, fixed-rate issue outstanding. Thus, each company has an obligation to make a stream of interest payments, but one payment stream is fixed while the other will vary as interest rates change in the future.

Now suppose Company S has stable cash flows, and it wants to lock in its cost of debt. Company F has cash flows that fluctuate with the economy, rising when the economy is strong and falling when it is weak. Recognizing that interest rates also move up and down with the economy, Company F has concluded that it would be better off with variable-rate debt. If the companies swapped their payment obligations, an *interest rate swap* would occur. Company S would now have to make fixed payments, which is consistent with its stable cash inflows; and Company F would have a floating stream, which for it, is less risky.

Note, though, that swaps can involve *side payments*. For example, if interest rates had fallen sharply since Company F issued its bonds, its old payment obligations would be relatively high and it would have to make a side payment to get S to agree to the swap. Similarly, if the credit risk of one company was higher than that of the other, the stronger company would be concerned about the ability of its weaker "counterparty" to make the required payments. This too would lead to the need for a side payment.

Currency swaps are similar to interest rate swaps. To illustrate, suppose Company A, an American firm, had issued $100 million of dollar-denominated bonds in the United States to fund an investment in Germany. Meanwhile, Company G, a German firm, had issued $100 million of euro-denominated bonds in Germany to make an investment in the United States. Company A would earn euros but be required to make payments in dollars, and Company G would be in the opposite situation. Thus, both companies would be exposed to exchange rate risk. However, both companies' risks would be eliminated if they swapped payment obligations. As with interest rate swaps, differences in interest rates or credit risks would require side payments.

Originally, swaps were arranged between companies by money center banks, which would match up counterparties. Such matching still occurs; but today most swaps are between companies and banks, with the banks then taking steps to ensure that their own risks are hedged. For example, Citibank might arrange a swap with Company A, which would agree to make specified payments in euros to the bank, and the bank would make the dollar payments that Company A would otherwise owe. Citibank would charge a fee for setting up the swap, and these charges would reflect the creditworthiness of Company A. To protect itself against exchange rate movements, the bank would hedge its position by lining up a German company that needed to make dollar payments or by using currency futures.

18-7b Structured Notes

The term **structured note** often means a debt obligation that is derived from some other debt obligation. For example, in the early 1980s, investment bankers began buying large blocks of 30-year noncallable Treasury bonds and then *stripping* them to create a series of zero coupon bonds. The zero with the shortest maturity was backed by the first interest payment on the T-bond issue, the second shortest zero was backed by the next interest payment, and so forth, on out to a 30-year zero backed by the last interest payment plus the maturity value of the T-bond. Zeros formed by stripping T-bonds were one of the first types of structured notes.

Another important type of structured note is backed by the interest and principal payments on mortgages. In the 1970s, Wall Street firms began to buy large packages of mortgages backed by federal agencies and place these packages, or "pools," with a trustee. Then bonds called *collateralized mortgage obligations (CMOs)*, backed by the mortgage pool held in trust, were sold to pension funds, individuals for their IRA accounts, and other investors who were willing to invest in CMOs but who would not have purchased individual mortgages. This *securitization* of mortgages made billions of dollars of new capital available to home buyers.

For several reasons, CMOs are more difficult to evaluate than straight bonds. First, the underlying mortgages can be prepaid at any time; and when this occurs, the prepayment proceeds are used to retire part of the CMO debt. Therefore, the holder of a CMO never knows when his or her bond will be called. This situation

Structured Note
A debt obligation derived from another debt obligation.

is further complicated by the fact that when interest rates decline, bond prices rise. However, declining rates also lead to mortgage prepayments, which cause the CMOs to be called especially rapidly.

A variety of structured notes can be created, ranging from notes whose cash flows can be predicted with virtual certainty to other notes whose payment streams are highly uncertain. For example, investment bankers can (and do) create notes called *IOs* (for *interest only*), which provide cash flows from the interest component of the mortgage amortization payments, and *POs* (for *principal only*), which are paid from the principal repayment stream. In each case, the value of the note is found as the PV of an expected payment stream, but the length and size of the stream are uncertain. Suppose, for example, that you are offered an IO that you expect to provide payments of $100 for 10 years. (You expect the mortgages to be refinanced after 10 years, at which time your payments will cease.) Suppose further that you discount the expected payment stream at a rate of 10% and determine the value to be $614.46. You have $614.46 to invest; so you buy the IO, expecting to earn 10% on your money.

Now suppose interest rates decline. If rates fall, the discount rate will drop, which usually implies an increase in the IO's value. However, if rates decline sharply, a rash of mortgage refinancings will result, in which case your payments, which come from interest only, will cease (or be greatly reduced) and the value of your IO will fall sharply. On the other hand, a sharp increase in interest rates reduces refinancings, lengthens your expected payment stream, and probably increases the value of your IO.

Investment bankers can "slice and dice" a pool of mortgages into a bewildering array of structured notes ranging from "plain vanilla" ones with highly predictable cash flows to "exotic" ones (sometimes called "toxic waste") whose risks are almost incalculable but are surely large.

Securitizing mortgages through CMOs serves a useful economic function—it provides an investment outlet for pension funds and others with money to invest, and it makes more money available to homeowners at a reasonable cost. Also, some investors want relatively safe investments, while other investors are willing to buy more speculative securities for the higher expected returns they provide. Structured notes permit a partitioning of risks to give investors what they want. There are dangers though. Naive officials managing money for local governments such as Orange County, California, often buy the "toxic waste" when they really ought to be holding only safe securities.

More recently, Wall Street firms have put together a similar set of instruments called *collateralized debt obligations (CDOs)*. CDOs are similar to CMOs; but instead of assembling a portfolio of mortgages, the issuing firm assembles a portfolio of debt instruments. Once again the overall risk is partitioned into several classes. If you are holding the senior class, you are first in line to receive cash flows from the portfolio; as a result, your risk may not be all that great. On the other hand, if you buy one of the riskier classes that have lower priority, you can expect higher returns but much more risk.

18-7c Inverse Floaters

A floating-rate note has an interest rate that rises and falls with some interest rate index. For example, the interest rate on a $100,000 note at prime plus 1% will be 7.50% when the prime rate is 6.50%, and the note's rate will move up and down with the prime rate. Because the cash flows associated with the note and the discount rate used to value it rise and fall together, the market value of the note is relatively stable.

With an **inverse floater**, the rate paid on the note moves counter to market rates. Thus, if interest rates in the economy rose, the interest rate paid on an inverse floater would fall, lowering its cash interest payments. At the same time,

Inverse Floater
A note in which the interest rate paid moves counter to market rates.

CREDIT INSTRUMENTS CREATE NEW OPPORTUNITIES AND RISKS

While market participants have traditionally used derivatives to hedge interest rate risk and currency risk, they still often face credit risk. Perhaps not surprisingly, a new set of derivative instruments has evolved to help market participants manage this credit risk.

One example of a credit derivative is a credit swap (sometimes called a credit default swap). In its simplest form, one party agrees to bear the credit risk of another party in exchange for an ongoing payment. For example, say that Company Z agrees to sell a credit swap to Bank A, which recently made a loan to Company L. Under the terms of the agreement, Bank A agrees to make regular payments to Company Z. In return, Company Z agrees to compensate Bank A if Company L defaults on the loan. In effect, the seller of the swap is providing a form of insurance to Bank A by agreeing to bear all or part of the loan's credit risk.

Credit derivatives provide value to the extent that they increase market liquidity and help financial institutions manage risk. On the other hand, the value of these positions can change dramatically in a short period of time. Moreover, there are concerns where a sudden loss could create a chain reaction. For example, a hedge fund losing big money on its credit derivative positions could have a negative effect on the banks that have lent money to the hedge fund.

Trying to put this in perspective, a Wall Street veteran quoted in a recent issue of *BusinessWeek* compared credit derivatives to fertilizer: "It can help your garden grow or can be made into bombs."

Indeed, renewed concerns about the widespread use of credit derivatives have recently resurfaced in the midst of the recent financial crisis that led to the decline and ultimate buyout of Bear Stearns. Throughout this crisis, regulators were concerned that Bear Stearns' problems could quickly spread to other key financial players that had entered into credit swaps with Bear Stearns.

Source: Mara Der Hovanesian, Chester Dawson, and Kerry Capell, "Taking Risk to Extremes: Will Derivatives Cause a Major Blowup in the World's Credit Markets?" *Business Week*, May 23, 2005, p. 96.

the discount rate used to value the inverse floater's cash flows would rise along with other rates. The combined effect of lower cash flows and a higher discount rate would lead to a very large decline in the value of the inverse floater. Thus, inverse floaters are exceptionally vulnerable to increases in interest rates. Of course, if interest rates fall, the value of an inverse floater will soar.

We have discussed the most important types of derivative securities, but not all types. However, this discussion should give you a good idea of how and why derivatives are created and how they can be used and misused.

SELF TEST

Briefly describe the following types of derivative securities:

1. Swaps
2. Structured notes
3. Inverse floaters

18-8 USING DERIVATIVES TO REDUCE RISKS

Firms are subject to numerous risks related to interest rate, stock price, and exchange rate fluctuations in the financial markets. For an investor, one of the most obvious ways to reduce financial risks is to hold a broadly diversified portfolio of stocks and debt securities, including international securities and debt of varying maturities. However, derivatives also can be used to reduce the risks associated with financial and commodity markets.[14]

---

[14]In Chapter 19, we discuss the risks involved with holding foreign currencies and the procedures for reducing such risks.

18-8a Security Price Exposure

Firms are exposed to losses due to changes in security prices when securities are held in investment portfolios, and firms are exposed to losses when securities are being issued. In addition, firms are exposed to risk if they use floating-rate debt to finance an investment that produces a fixed income stream. Risks such as these can often be mitigated by using derivatives. As we discussed earlier, derivatives are securities whose values stem, or are derived, from the values of other assets. Thus, options and futures contracts are derivatives because their values depend on the prices of some underlying assets. Now we will further explore the use of two types of derivatives, futures and swaps, to help in managing certain types of risk.

18-8b Futures

Speculation
With futures, it involves betting on future price movements.

Hedging
Using transactions to lower risk.

Long Hedges
Futures contracts are bought in anticipation of (or to guard against) price increases.

Short Hedges
Futures contracts are sold to guard against price declines.

Futures are used for both speculation and hedging. **Speculation** involves betting on future price movements, and futures are used because of the leverage inherent in the contract. **Hedging**, on the other hand, is done by a firm or an individual to protect against a price change that would otherwise negatively affect profits. For example, rising interest rates and commodity (raw material) prices can hurt profits, as can adverse currency fluctuations. If two parties have mirror-image risks, they can enter into a transaction that eliminates, as opposed to transfers, risks. This is a "natural hedge." Of course, one party to a futures contract could be a speculator and the other a hedger. Thus, to the extent that speculators broaden the market and make hedging possible, they help decrease risk to those who seek to avoid it.

There are two basic types of hedges: (1) **long hedges**, in which futures contracts are *bought* in anticipation of (or to guard against) price increases, and (2) **short hedges**, where a firm or an individual *sells* futures contracts to guard against price declines. Recall that rising interest rates lower bond prices and thus decrease the value of bond futures contracts. Therefore, if a firm or an individual needs to guard against an *increase* in interest rates, a futures contract that makes money if rates rise should be used. That means selling, or going short, on a futures contract. To illustrate, assume that in July, Carson Foods is considering a plan to issue $10,000,000 of 15-year bonds in December to finance a capital expenditure program. The interest rate would be 7% with semiannual payments if the bonds were issued today; and at that rate, the project would have a positive NPV. However, interest rates may rise over the next 5 months; and when the issue is sold, the interest rate might be substantially above 7%, which would make the project a bad investment. Carson can protect itself against a rise in rates by hedging in the futures market.

In this situation, Carson would be hurt by an increase in interest rates; so it would use a short hedge. It would choose a futures contract on that security most similar to the one it plans to issue, long-term bonds. In this case, Carson would probably hedge with Treasury bond futures. Since it plans to issue $10,000,000 of bonds, it would sell $10,000,000/$100,000 = 100 Treasury bond contracts for delivery in December. Carson would have to put up 100($2,430) = $243,000 in margin money and pay brokerage commissions. For illustrative purposes, we use the numbers in Table 18-3. We can see that each December contract has a value of 112 plus $^{20.5}/_{32}$%, so the total value of the 100 contracts is 1.12640625($100,000) (100) = $11,264,062. Now suppose renewed fears of inflation push the interest rate on Carson's debt up by 100 basis points, to 8%, over the next 4 months. If Carson issued 7% semiannual coupon bonds, they would bring only $913.54 per bond because investors now require an 8% return. Thus, Carson would lose $86.46 per bond times 10,000 bonds, or $864,600, as a result of delaying the financing. However, the increase in interest rates would also bring about a change in the value of Carson's short position in the futures market. Interest rates have increased, so the value of the futures contract would fall; and if the interest rate on the futures contract increased by the same full percentage point, from 4.8% to 5.8%, the contract value would fall to $10,198,562. Carson would then close its position in the futures market by repurchasing for $10,198,562 the contracts that it earlier sold short for $11,264,062, giving it a profit of $1,065,500, less commissions.

Thus, if we ignored commissions and the opportunity cost of the margin money, Carson would offset the loss on the bond issue. In fact, in our example, Carson more than offsets the loss, pocketing an additional $200,900. Of course, if interest rates had fallen, Carson would have lost on its futures position; but this loss would have been offset by the fact that Carson could now sell its bonds with a lower coupon.

If futures contracts existed on Carson's own debt and interest rates moved identically in the spot and futures markets, the firm could construct a **perfect hedge**, in which gains on the futures contract would exactly offset losses on the bonds. In reality, it is virtually impossible to construct perfect hedges because in most cases, the underlying asset is not identical to the futures asset and even when they are, prices (and interest rates) may not move exactly together in the spot and futures markets.

Note too that if Carson had been planning an equity offering and if its stock tended to move fairly closely with one of the stock indexes, the company could have hedged against falling stock prices by selling short the index future. Even better, if options on Carson's stock were traded in the option market, it could have used options rather than futures to hedge against falling stock prices.

The futures and options markets permit flexibility in the timing of financial transactions because the firm can be protected, at least partially, against changes that occur between the time a decision is reached and the time the transaction is completed. However, this protection has a cost—the firm must pay commissions. Whether the protection is worth the cost is a matter of judgment. The decision to hedge also depends on management's risk aversion as well as the company's strength and ability to assume the risk in question. In theory, the reduction in risk resulting from a hedge transaction should have a value equal to the cost of the hedge. Thus, a firm should be indifferent to hedging. However, many firms believe that hedging is worthwhile. Trammell Crow, a large Texas real estate developer, has used T-bill futures to lock in interest costs on floating-rate construction loans, while Dart & Kraft has used eurodollar futures to protect its marketable securities portfolio. Citi Smith Barney and other investment banking houses hedge in the futures and options markets to protect themselves when they are engaged in major underwritings.

> **Perfect Hedge**
> *Occurs when the gain or loss on the hedged transaction exactly offsets the loss or gain on the unhedged position.*

18-8c Swaps

A *swap* is another method for reducing financial risks. As noted earlier, a swap is an exchange.[15] In finance, it is an exchange of cash payment obligations in which each party to the swap prefers the payment type or pattern of the other party. In other words, swaps occur because the counterparties prefer the terms of the other's debt contract and the swap enables each party to obtain a preferred payment obligation. Generally, one party has a fixed-rate obligation and the other party has a floating-rate obligation or one party has an obligation denominated in one currency and the other party's obligation is denominated in another currency.

Major changes have occurred over time in the swaps market. First, standardized contracts have been developed for the most common types of swaps, and

---

[15]For more information on swaps, see Clifford W. Smith, Jr., Charles W. Smithson, and Lee MacDonald Wakeman, "The Evolving Market for Swaps," *Midland Corporate Finance Journal*, Winter 1986, pp. 20–32; and Mary E. Ruth and Steve R. Vinson, "Managing Interest Rate Uncertainty Amidst Change," *Public Utilities Fortnightly*, December 22, 1988, pp. 28–31.

this has had two effects: (1) Standardized contracts lower the time and effort involved in arranging swaps and thus lower transactions costs. (2) The development of standardized contracts has led to a secondary market for swaps, which has increased the liquidity and efficiency of the swaps market. A number of international banks now make markets in swaps and offer quotes on several standard types. Also, as noted previously, because the banks now take counterparty positions in swaps, it is not necessary to find another firm with mirror-image needs before a swap transaction can be completed. The bank would generally find a final counterparty for the swap at a later date, so its positioning helps make the swap market more operationally efficient.

To further illustrate a swap transaction, consider the following situation. An electric utility currently has outstanding a 5-year floating-rate note tied to the prime rate. The prime rate could rise significantly over the period, so the note carries a high degree of interest rate risk. The utility could, however, enter into a swap with a counterparty (say, Citibank) wherein the utility would pay Citibank a fixed series of interest payments over the 5-year period and Citibank would make the company's required floating-rate payments. As a result, the utility would have converted a floating-rate loan to a fixed-rate loan and the risk of rising interest rates would have been passed from the utility to Citibank. Such a transaction can lower both parties' risks—because banks' revenues rise as interest rates rise, Citibank's risk would be lower if it had floating-rate obligations.

Longer-term swaps can also be made. Recently, Citibank entered into a 17-year swap in an electricity cogeneration project financing deal. The project's sponsors were unable to obtain fixed-rate financing on reasonable terms, and they were afraid that interest rates would increase and make the project unprofitable. However, the project's sponsors were able to borrow from local banks on a floating-rate basis and then arrange a simultaneous swap with Citibank for a fixed-rate obligation.

18-8d Commodity Price Exposure

As noted earlier, futures markets were established for many commodities long before they began to be used for financial instruments. We can use Porter Electronics, which uses large quantities of copper as well as several precious metals, to illustrate inventory hedging. Suppose that in July 2008, Porter foresaw a need for 100,000 pounds of copper in June 2009 for use in fulfilling a fixed-price contract to supply solar power cells to the U.S. government. Porter's managers are concerned that a strike by Chilean copper miners will occur, which could raise the price of copper in world markets and turn the expected profit on the solar cells into a loss.

Porter could, of course, buy the copper it will need to fulfill the contract; but if it does, it will incur substantial carrying costs. As an alternative, the company could hedge against increasing copper prices in the futures market. The New York Mercantile Exchange (which as of July 2008 is part of the Chicago Mercantile Exchange) trades standard copper futures contracts of 25,000 pounds each. Thus, Porter could buy four contracts (go long) for delivery in June 2009. Assume that these contracts were trading in July for about $3.496 per pound and that the spot price at that date was about $3.677 per pound. If copper prices continue to rise appreciably over the next 10 months, the value of Porter's long position in copper futures will increase, thus offsetting some of the price increase in the commodity. Of course, if copper prices fall, Porter will lose money on its futures contract. But the company will be buying the copper on the spot market at a cheaper price, so it will make a higher-than-anticipated profit on its sale of solar cells. Thus, hedging in the copper futures market locks in the cost of raw materials and removes some risk to which the firm would otherwise be exposed.

Many other manufacturers, such as Alcoa with aluminum and Archer Daniels Midland with grains, routinely use the futures markets to reduce the risks associated with input price volatility.

18-8e The Use and Misuse of Derivatives

Most of the news stories about derivatives are related to financial disasters. Much less is heard about the benefits of derivatives. However, because of these benefits, more than 90% of large U.S. companies use derivatives on a regular basis. In today's market, sophisticated investors and analysts are demanding that firms use derivatives to hedge certain risks. For example, Prudential Securities reduced its earnings estimate for Cone Mills, a North Carolina textile company, because Cone did not sufficiently hedge its exposure to changing cotton prices. This example leads us to one conclusion: If a company can safely and inexpensively hedge its risks, it should do so.

There can, however, be a downside to the use of derivatives. Hedging is invariably cited by authorities as a "good" use of derivatives, whereas speculating with derivatives is often cited as a "bad" use. Some people and organizations can afford to bear the risks involved in speculating with derivatives, but others are not sufficiently knowledgeable about the risks they are taking or should not be taking those risks in the first place. Most would agree that the typical corporation should use derivatives only to hedge risks, not to speculate in an effort to increase profits. Recall from the opening vignette to this chapter that in its annual report, Procter & Gamble indicated that it used derivatives to hedge its various risks. It specifically stressed that it did not use derivatives for speculative purposes. Hedging allows managers to concentrate on running their core businesses without having to worry about interest rate, currency, and commodity price variability. However, problems can arise quickly when hedges are improperly constructed or when a corporate treasurer, eager to report relatively high returns, uses derivatives for speculative purposes.

SELF TEST

Explain how a company can use the futures market to hedge against rising interest rates.

What is a swap? Describe the mechanics of a fixed-rate swap and a floating-rate swap.

Explain how a company can use the futures market to hedge against rising raw materials prices.

How should derivatives be used in risk management? What problems can occur?

18-9 RISK MANAGEMENT

As businesses become increasingly complex, it is becoming more difficult for CEOs and directors to know what problems might lie in wait. Therefore, companies need to have someone systematically look for potential problems and design safeguards to minimize potential damage. For that reason, most larger firms have designated "risk managers" who report to the chief financial officer (CFO), while the CFOs of smaller firms personally assume risk management responsibilities. In any event, because **risk management** is becoming increasingly

Risk Management
Involves the management of unpredictable events that have adverse consequences for a firm.

important, it is something finance students should understand. Therefore, in the remainder of this chapter, we discuss the basics of risk management, with particular emphasis on how derivatives can be used to hedge financial risks.

It is useful to begin our discussion of risk management by defining some commonly used terms that describe different risks. Some of these risks can be mitigated, or managed, which is what risk management is all about.

1. *Pure risks* offer only the prospect of a loss. Examples include the risk that a plant will be destroyed by fire or that a product liability suit will result in a large judgment against the firm.

2. *Speculative risks* offer the chance of a gain but might result in a loss. Thus, investments in new projects and marketable securities involve speculative risks.

3. *Demand risks* are associated with the demand for a firm's products or services. Because sales are essential to all businesses, demand risk is one of the most significant risks that firms face.

4. *Input risks* are associated with input costs, including labor and materials. Thus, a company that uses copper as a raw material in its manufacturing process faces the risk that the cost of copper will increase and that it will not be able to pass this increase on to its customers.

5. *Financial risks* result from financial transactions. As we have seen, if a firm plans to issue new bonds, it faces the risk that interest rates will rise before the bonds can be brought to market. Similarly, if the firm enters into contracts with foreign customers or suppliers, it faces the risk that fluctuations in exchange rates will result in unanticipated losses.

6. *Property risks* are associated with destruction of productive assets. Thus, the threat of fire, floods, and riots imposes property risks on a firm.

7. *Personnel risks* result from employees' actions. Examples include the risks associated with employee fraud or embezzlement and suits based on charges of age or sex discrimination.

8. *Environmental risks* include risks associated with polluting the environment. Public awareness in recent years, coupled with the huge costs of environmental cleanup, has increased the importance of this risk.

9. *Liability risks* are associated with product, service, or employee actions. Examples include the very large judgments assessed against asbestos manufacturers and some health care providers as well as costs incurred as a result of improper actions of employees, such as driving corporate vehicles in a reckless manner.

10. *Insurable risks* can be covered by insurance. In general, property, personnel, environmental, and liability risks can be transferred to insurance companies. Note, though, that the *ability* to insure a risk does not necessarily mean that the risk *should* be insured. Indeed, a major function of risk management involves evaluating all alternatives for managing a particular risk, including self-insurance, and then choosing the optimal alternative.

The risk classifications we used are somewhat arbitrary, and different classifications are commonly used in different industries. However, the list does provide an idea of the wide variety of risks to which a firm can be exposed.

18-9a An Approach to Risk Management

Firms often use the following process for managing risks.

1. *Identify the risks that the firm faces.* Here the risk manager identifies the potential risks that his or her firm faces. (See "Microsoft's Goal: Manage Every Risk!")

2. *Measure the potential effect of each risk.* Some risks are so small as to be immaterial, whereas others have the potential for dooming the company. It is useful to segregate risks by potential effect and then focus on the most serious threats.

3. *Decide how each relevant risk should be handled.* In most situations, risk exposure can be reduced through one of the following techniques:

    a. *Transfer the risk to an insurance company.* Often it is advantageous to insure against (hence, transfer) a risk. However, insurability does not necessarily mean that a risk should be covered by insurance. In many instances, it might be better for the company to *self-insure*, which means bearing the risk directly rather than paying another party to bear it.

    b. *Transfer the function that produces the risk to a third party.* For example, suppose a furniture manufacturer is concerned about potential liabilities arising from its ownership of a fleet of trucks used to transfer products from its manufacturing plant to various locations across the country. One way to eliminate this risk would be to contract with a trucking company to do the shipping, thus passing the risks to a third party.

    c. *Purchase derivative contracts to reduce risk.* As indicated earlier, firms use derivatives to hedge risks. Commodity derivatives can be used to reduce input risks. For example, a cereal company may use corn or wheat futures to hedge against increases in grain prices. Similarly, financial derivatives can be used to reduce risks that arise from changes in interest rates and exchange rates.

    d. *Reduce the probability of the occurrence of an adverse event.* The expected loss arising from any risk is a function of the probability of occurrence and the dollar loss if the adverse event occurs. In some instances, it is possible to reduce the probability that an adverse event will occur. For example, the probability that a fire will occur can be reduced by instituting a fire prevention program, by replacing old electrical wiring, and by using fire-resistant materials in areas with the greatest fire potential.

    e. *Reduce the magnitude of the loss associated with an adverse event.* Continuing with the fire risk example, the dollar cost associated with a fire can be reduced by such actions as installing sprinkler systems, designing facilities with self-contained fire zones, and locating facilities close to a fire station.

    f. *Totally avoid the activity that gives rise to the risk.* For example, a company might discontinue a product or service line because the risks outweigh the rewards, as with the decision by Dow Corning to discontinue its manufacture of silicone breast implants.

Note that risk management decisions, like all corporate decisions, should be based on a cost/benefit analysis for each feasible alternative. For example, suppose it would cost $50,000 per year to conduct a comprehensive fire safety training program for all personnel in a high-risk plant. Presumably, this program would reduce the expected value of future fire losses. An alternative to the training program would be to place $50,000 annually in a reserve fund set aside to cover future fire losses. Both alternatives involve expected cash flows; and from an economic standpoint, the choice should be made on the basis of the lowest present value of future costs. Thus, the same financial management techniques applied to other corporate decisions can also be applied to risk management decisions. Note, though, that if a fire occurs and a life is lost, the trade-off between fire prevention and expected losses may not sit well with a jury. The same thing holds true for product liability, as Ford, GM, and other corporations have learned.

MICROSOFT'S GOAL: MANAGE EVERY RISK!

Twenty years ago risk management meant buying insurance against fire, theft, and liability losses. Today, though, due to globalization, volatile markets, and lawyers looking for someone to sue, a multitude of risks can adversely affect companies. Microsoft addressed these risks by creating a virtual consulting practice, called Microsoft Risk Co., to help manage the risks that its sales, operations, and product groups face.

In an article in *CFO*, Scott Lange, who was head of Microsoft Risk at the time the article appeared, identified these 12 major sources of risk:

1. *Business partners* (interdependency, confidentiality, cultural conflict, contractual risks).

2. *Competition* (market share, price wars, industrial espionage, antitrust allegations).

3. *Customers* (product liability, credit risk, poor market timing, inadequate customer support).

4. *Distribution systems* (transportation, service availability, cost, dependence on distributors).

5. *Financial* (foreign exchange, portfolio, cash, interest rate, stock market).

6. *Operations* (facilities, contractual risks, natural hazards, internal processes and control).

7. *People* (employees, independent contractors, training, staffing inadequacy).

8. *Political* (civil unrest, war, terrorism, enforcement of intellectual property rights, change in leadership, revised economic policies).

9. *Regulatory and legislative* (antitrust, export licensing, jurisdiction, reporting and compliance, environmental).

10. *Reputations* (corporate image, brands, reputations of key employees).

11. *Strategic* (mergers and acquisitions, joint ventures and alliances, resource allocation and planning, organizational agility).

12. *Technological* (complexity, obsolescence, workforce skill sets).

According to Lange, it is important to resist the idea that risk should be categorized by how the insurance industry views it. Insurance coverage lines are a tiny subset of the risks that a modern enterprise faces in the pursuit of its business objectives. Lange also defined the role of finance in risk management: The role of finance is to put on paper all of the risks that can be identified and to try to quantify them. When possible, use a number—one number perhaps or a probability distribution. For example, what is the probability of losing $1 million on a product? $10 million? At Microsoft, the finance department works with the product groups to determine the exposure. "We try to use common sense," Lange says.

In many ways, risk management mirrors the quality movement of the 1980s and 1990s. The goal of the quality movement was to take the responsibility for quality out of a separate Quality Control Department and to make all managers and employees responsible for quality. Lange had a similar goal for Microsoft—to have risk management permeate the thinking of all Microsoft managers and employees.

Source: Edward Teach, "Microsoft's Universe of Risk," *CFO*, March 1997, pp. 69–72.

SELF TEST   Define the following terms:

1. Pure risks
2. Speculative risks
3. Demand risks
4. Input risks
5. Financial risks
6. Property risks
7. Personnel risks
8. Environmental risks
9. Liability risks
10. Insurable risks
11. Self-insurance

Should a firm insure itself against all insurable risks that it faces? Explain.

TYING IT ALL TOGETHER

Companies face a variety of risks every day, for it is hard to succeed without taking some chances. In Chapter 8, we discussed the trade-off between risk and return. When some action can lower risk without lowering returns too much, the action can enhance value. Based on that fact, this chapter described the various types of risks that companies face and the basic principles of corporate risk management. One important tool for managing risk is the derivatives market, and this chapter provided an introduction to derivative securities.

SELF-TEST QUESTIONS AND PROBLEMS
(Solutions Appear in Appendix A)

ST-1   **KEY TERMS**   Define each of the following terms:

a.   Derivative; natural hedge

b.   Option; call option; put option

c.   Long-term Equity AnticiPation Security (LEAPS)

d.   Exercise value; strike (exercise) price

e.   Black-Scholes Option Pricing Model (OPM); riskless hedge

f.   Futures contract; forward contract

g.   Commodity futures; financial futures

h.   Swap; structured note

i.   Inverse floater

j.   Risk management

k.   Speculation

l.   Hedging; long hedges; short hedges; perfect hedge

ST-2   **BLACK-SCHOLES MODEL**   An analyst is interested in using the Black-Scholes model to value call options on the stock of Ledbetter Inc. The analyst has accumulated the following information:

- The price of the stock is $33.

- The strike price is $33.

- The option matures in 6 months (t = 0.50).

- The standard deviation of the stock's returns is 0.30, and the variance is 0.09.

- The risk-free rate is 10%.

Given that information, the analyst is able to calculate some other necessary components of the Black-Scholes model:

- $d_1 = 0.34177$

- $d_2 = 0.12964$

- $N(d_1) = 0.63369$

- $N(d_2) = 0.55155$

$N(d_1)$ and $N(d_2)$ represent areas under a standard normal distribution function. Using the Black-Scholes model, what is the value of the call option?

QUESTIONS

18-1 List seven reasons risk management might increase the value of a firm.

18-2 Why do options typically sell at prices higher than their exercise values?

18-3 Discuss some of the techniques available to reduce risk exposure.

18-4 Explain how the futures markets can be used to reduce interest rate and input price risk.

18-5 How can swaps be used to reduce the risks associated with debt contracts?

18-6 Give two reasons stockholders might be indifferent between owning the stock of a firm with volatile cash flows and the stock of a firm with stable cash flows.

PROBLEMS

Easy Problems 1–3

18-1 **OPTIONS** A call option on Bedrock Boulders stock has a market price of $7. The stock sells for $30 a share, and the option has an exercise price of $25 a share.

    a. What is the exercise value of the call option?

    b. What is the premium on the option?

18-2 **OPTIONS** The exercise price on one of Flanagan Company's call options is $15, its exercise value is $22, and its premium is $5. What are the option's market value and the stock's current price?

18-3 **OPTIONS** Which of the following events are likely to increase the market value of a call option on a common stock? Explain.

    a. An increase in the stock's price

    b. An increase in the volatility of the stock price

    c. An increase in the risk-free rate

    d. A decrease in the time until the option expires

Intermediate Problems 4–5

18-4 **BLACK-SCHOLES MODEL** Assume that you have been given the following information on Purcell Industries:

Current stock price = $15	Exercise price of option = $15
Time to maturity of option = 6 months	Risk-free rate = 10%
Variance of stock price = 0.12	$d_1 = 0.32660$
$d_2 = 0.08165$	$N(d_1) = 0.62795$
$N(d_2) = 0.53252$	

Using the Black-Scholes Option Pricing Model, what is the value of the option?

18-5 **FUTURES** What is the implied nominal interest rate on a Treasury bond ($100,000) futures contract that settled at 100'16.0 (or 100-160)? If interest rates increased by 1%, what would be the contract's new value?

Challenging Problems 6–8

18-6 **HEDGING** The Zinn Company plans to issue $20,000,000 of 10-year bonds in December to help finance a new research and development laboratory. It is now August, and the current cost of debt to the high-risk biotech company is 11%. However, the firm's financial manager is concerned that interest rates will climb even higher in coming months.

    a. Use data in Table 18-3 to create a hedge against rising interest rates.

    b. Assume that interest rates generally increase by 200 basis points. How well did your hedge perform?

    c. What is a perfect hedge? Are most real-world hedges perfect? Explain.

18-7 **OPTIONS** Audrey is considering an investment in Morgan Communications, whose stock currently sells for $60. A put option on Morgan's stock, with an exercise price of $55, has a market value of $3.06. Meanwhile, a call option on the stock with the same exercise price and time to maturity has a market value of $9.29. The market believes that at the expiration of the options, the stock price will be $70 or $50 with equal probability.

a. What is the premium associated with the put option? the call option?

b. If Morgan's stock price increases to $70, what would be the return to an investor who bought a share of the stock? if the investor bought a call option on the stock? if the investor bought a put option on the stock?

c. If Morgan's stock price decreases to $50, what would be the return to an investor who bought a share of the stock? if the investor bought a call option on the stock? if the investor bought a put option on the stock?

d. If Audrey buys 0.6 share of Morgan Communications and sells one call option on the stock, has she created a riskless hedged investment? What is the total value of her portfolio under each scenario?

e. If Audrey buys 0.75 share of Morgan Communications and sells one call option on the stock, has she created a riskless hedged investment? What is the total value of her portfolio under each scenario?

18-8 **RISKLESS HEDGE** Stewart Enterprises' current stock price is $60 per share. Call options for this stock exist that permit the holder to purchase one share at an exercise price of $50. These options will expire at the end of 1 year, at which time Stewart's stock will be selling at one of two prices, $45 or $70. The risk-free rate is 7%. As an assistant to the firm's treasurer, you have been asked to perform the following tasks to arrive at the value of the firm's call options.

a. Find the range of values for the ending stock price and the call option at the option's expiration in 1 year.

b. Equalize the range of payoffs for the stock and the option.

c. Create a riskless hedged investment.

d. What is the cost of the stock in the riskless portfolio?

e. What is the present value of the riskless portfolio?

f. From your answers in Parts d and e, what is the value of the firm's call option?

COMPREHENSIVE/SPREADSHEET PROBLEM

18-9 **BLACK-SCHOLES MODEL**

a. Rework Problem 18-4 using the spreadsheet model.

b. Construct data tables for the intrinsic value and Black-Scholes exercise value for this option and graph the relationship. Include possible stock price values ranging up to $30.

c. Suppose this call option is purchased today. Draw the profit diagram of this option position at expiration.

d. Given the following information, create a riskless hedge to determine the value of the firm's call option given the following information:

Current stock price = $25   Exercise price = $30

Option expiration = 6 months   Risk-free rate = 5%

At the end of the 6 months, the firm's stock will be worth $20 or $40. What is the value of the firm's call option?

INTEGRATED CASE

TROPICAL SWEETS INC.

18-10 **DERIVATIVES AND CORPORATE RISK MANAGEMENT** Assume that you have just been hired as a financial analyst by Tropical Sweets Inc., a midsized California company that specializes in creating exotic candies from tropical fruits such as mangoes, papayas, and dates. The firm's CEO, George Yamaguchi, recently returned from an industry corporate executive conference in San Francisco. One of the sessions he attended was on the pressing need for smaller companies to institute corporate risk management programs. As no one at Tropical Sweets is familiar with the basics of derivatives and corporate risk management, Yamaguchi has asked you to prepare a brief report that the firm's executives can use to gain at least a cursory understanding of the topics.

To begin, you gather some outside materials on derivatives and corporate risk management and use those materials to draft a list of pertinent questions that need to be answered. In fact, one possible approach to the paper is to use a question-and-answer format. Now that the questions have been drafted, you must develop the answers.

a. Why might stockholders be indifferent to whether a firm reduces the volatility of its cash flows?

b. What are seven reasons risk management might increase the value of a corporation?

c. What is an option? What is the single most important characteristic of an option?

d. Options have a unique set of terminology. Define the following terms:

    (1) Call option

    (2) Put option

    (3) Exercise price

    (4) Striking, or strike, price

    (5) Option price

    (6) Expiration date

    (7) Exercise value

    (8) Covered option

    (9) Naked option

    (10) In-the-money call

    (11) Out-of-the-money call

    (12) LEAPS

e. Consider Tropical Sweets' call option with a $25 strike price. The following table contains historical values for this option at different stock prices:

Stock Price	Call Option Price
$25	$ 3.00
30	7.50
35	12.00
40	16.50
45	21.00
50	25.50

    (1) Create a table that shows the (a) stock price, (b) strike price, (c) exercise value, (d) option price, and (e) premium of option price over exercise value.

    (2) What happens to the premium of option price over exercise value as the stock price rises? Why?

f. In 1973, Fischer Black and Myron Scholes developed the Black-Scholes Option Pricing Model (OPM).

    (1) What assumptions underlie the OPM?

    (2) Write the three equations that constitute the model.

    (3) What is the value of the following call option according to the OPM?

        Stock price = $27

        Exercise price = $25

        Time to expiration = 6 months

        Risk-free rate = 6.0%

        Stock return variance = 0.11

g. Disregard the information in Part f. Determine the value of a firm's call option by creating a riskless hedge given the following information. A firm's current stock price is $15 per share. Options exist that permit the holder to buy one share of the firm's stock at an exercise price of $15. These options expire in 6 months, at which time the firm's stock will be selling at one of two prices, $10 or $20. The risk-free rate is 6%. What is the value of this firm's call option?

  h. What effect does each of the following call option parameters have on the value of a call option?

   (1) Current stock price

   (2) Exercise price

   (3) Option's term to maturity

   (4) Risk-free rate

   (5) Variability of the stock price

  i. What are the differences between forward and futures contracts?

  j. Explain briefly how swaps work.

  k. Explain briefly how a firm can use futures and swaps to hedge risk.

  l. What is corporate risk management? Why is it important to all firms?

APPENDIX 18A

Valuation of Put Options

A put option gives its owner the right to sell a share of stock. If the stock pays no dividends and the option can be exercised only upon its expiration date, what is its value? Consider the payoffs for two portfolios at expiration date T shown in Table 18A-1. The first portfolio consists of a put option and a share of stock; the second has a call option (with the same strike price and expiration date as the put option) and some cash. The amount of cash is equal to the present value of the exercise cost, discounted at the continuously compounded risk-free rate, which is $Xe^{-r_{RF}t}$. At expiration, the value of this cash will equal the exercise cost, X.

If the stock price at expiration date T, P_T, is less than the strike price, X, when the option expires, the value of the put option at expiration is $X - P_T$. Therefore, the value of Portfolio 1, which contains the put and the stock, is equal to $X - P_T$ plus P_T, or just X. For Portfolio 2, the value of the call is zero at expiration (because the call option is out-of-the-money) and the value of the cash is X, for a total value of X. Notice that both portfolios have the same payoffs when the stock price is less than the strike price.

What if the stock price is greater than the strike price at expiration? In this case, the put is worth nothing; so the payoff of Portfolio 1 is equal to the stock price at expiration, P_T. The call option is worth $P_T - X$, and the cash is worth X; so the payoff of Portfolio 2 is P_T. Therefore, the payoffs of the two portfolios are equal whether the stock price is below or above the strike price.

If the two portfolios have identical payoffs, they must have identical values. This is known as the *put-call parity relationship:*

Put option + Stock = Call option + PV of exercise price

If V is the Black-Scholes value of the call option, the value of a put is as follows:[1]

$$\text{Put option} = V - P + Xe^{-r_{RF}t}$$

Table 18A-1	**Portfolio Payoffs**		
		STOCK PRICE AT EXPIRATION IF:	
		$P_T < X$	$P_T \geq X$
Put		$X - P_T$	0
Stock		P_T	P_T
	Portfolio 1:	X	P_T
Call		0	$P_T - X$
Cash		X	X
	Portfolio 2:	X	P_T

---

[1]This model cannot be applied to an American put option or to a European option on a stock that pays a dividend prior to expiration. For an explanation of valuation approaches in these situations, refer to Don M. Chance, *An Introduction to Derivatives and Risk Management* (Mason, OH: Thomson/South-Western, 2004) or John C. Hull, *Options, Futures, and Other Derivatives* (Upper Saddle River, NJ: Prentice-Hall, 2006).

For example, consider a put option written on the stock discussed in Section 18-5b. If the put option has the same exercise price and expiration date as the call, its price is as follows:

$$\text{Put option} = \$1.69 - \$21 + \$21e^{-.05(0.36)}$$
$$= \$1.69 - \$21 + \$20.62 = \$1.31$$

QUESTION

18A-1   In words, what is put-call parity?

PROBLEMS

18A-1   **PUT-CALL PARITY**   A put option written on the stock of Ellis Enterprises (EE) has an exercise price of $30 and 9 months remaining until expiration. The risk-free rate is 5%. A call option written on EE has the same exercise price and expiration date as the put option. EE's stock price is $45. If the call option has a price of $18.99, what is the price (i.e., value) of the put option?

18A-2   **PUT-CALL PARITY**   The current price of a stock is $50, and the annual risk-free rate is 5.5%. A call option with a strike price of $46 and 6 months until expiration has a current value of $9.59. What is the value of a put option written on the stock with the same strike price and expiration date as the call option?

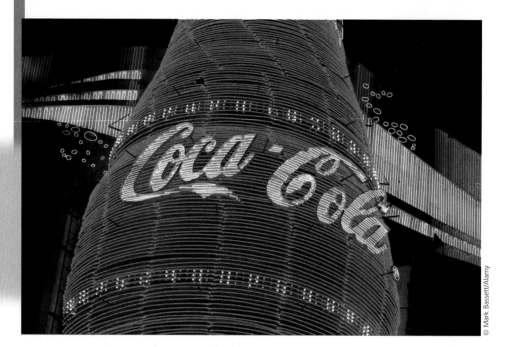
© Mark Bassett/Alamy

CHAPTER 19

Multinational Financial Management[1]

Coca-Cola

U.S. Firms Look Overseas to Enhance Shareholder Value

From the end of World War II until the 1970s, the United States dominated the world economy. However, that situation no longer exists. Raw materials, finished goods, services, and money flow freely across most national boundaries, as do innovative ideas and new technologies. World-class U.S. companies are making breakthroughs in foreign labs, obtaining capital from foreign investors, and putting foreign employees on the fast track to the top. Dozens of top U.S. manufacturers, including Dow Chemical, Colgate-Palmolive, IBM, and Hewlett-Packard, sell more of their products outside the United States than they do at home. Likewise, service firms such as Citigroup, McDonald's, and AFLAC receive more than half their revenues from foreign sales.

The trend is even more pronounced in profits. In recent years, Coca-Cola and many other companies have made more money in the Pacific Rim and Western Europe than in the United States. All told, Coca-Cola now reports that more than 75%

of its operating profits come from outside North America. As a result, economic events around the globe and changing exchange rates now have a profound effect on the company's bottom line. In particular, profits earned in foreign currencies are worth more when the U.S. dollar declines. Consequently, the sharp decline in the U.S. dollar in recent years has helped boost Coca-Cola's profits and helps explain why the stock has outperformed the overall stock market.

Successful global companies such as Coca-Cola must conduct business in different economies, and they must be sensitive to the many subtleties of different cultures and political systems. Accordingly, they find it useful to blend into the foreign landscape to help win product acceptance and avoid political problems. At the same time, foreign-based multinationals are arriving on American shores in ever greater numbers. Sweden's ABB, the Netherlands's Philips, France's Thomson, and Japan's Fujitsu and Honda

---

[1]This chapter was coauthored with Professor Roy Crum of the University of Florida.

are all waging campaigns to be identified as American companies that employ Americans, transfer technology to America, and help the U.S. trade balance.

The emergence of "world companies" raises a host of questions for governments. For example, should domestic firms be favored, or does it make no difference what a company's nationality is as long as the firm provides domestic jobs? Should a company make an effort to keep jobs in its home country, or should it produce where total production costs are lowest? What nation controls the technology developed by a multinational corporation, particularly when

the technology can be used in military applications? Must a multinational company adhere to rules imposed in its home country with respect to its operations outside the home country? And if a U.S. firm such as Xerox produces copiers in Japan and then ships them to the United States, should they be reflected in the trade deficit in the same way as Toshiba copiers imported from Japan? Keep those questions in mind as you read this chapter. When you finish, you should have a better appreciation of the problems that governments face and the difficult but profitable opportunities that managers of multinational companies face.

PUTTING THINGS IN PERSPECTIVE

Managers of multinational companies must deal with a wide range of issues that are not present when a company operates in a single country. In this chapter, we highlight the key differences between multinational and domestic corporations and we discuss the impact these differences have on the financial management of multinational businesses. By the time you complete this chapter, you should be able to:

- Identify the primary reasons companies choose to go "global."
- Explain how exchange rates work and interpret different exchange rate quotations.
- Discuss the intuition behind interest rate parity and purchasing power parity.
- Explain the different opportunities and risks that investors face when they invest overseas.
- Identify some specific challenges that a multinational corporation faces and discuss how they influence its capital budgeting, capital structure, and working capital policies.

19-1 MULTINATIONAL, OR GLOBAL, CORPORATIONS

The term **multinational**, or **global, corporation** describes a firm that operates in an integrated fashion in a number of countries. During the past 20 years, a new and fundamentally different form of international commercial activity has developed that has greatly increased worldwide economic and political interdependence. Rather than merely buy resources from and sell goods to foreign nations, multinational firms now make direct investments in fully integrated operations—from extraction of raw materials through the manufacturing process and finally to the distribution of products to consumers throughout the world. Today multinational corporate networks control a large and growing share of the world's technological, marketing, and productive resources.

Companies, both U.S. and foreign, go "global" for seven primary reasons:

1. *To seek production efficiency.* As competition increases in their domestic marketplace and as demand increases in other markets, companies often conclude that they must produce their products overseas. Companies based in high-cost countries have strong incentives to shift production to lower-cost regions, assuming an adequate supply of labor with the requisite skills and an adequate

Multinational, or Global, Corporation
A firm that operates in an integrated fashion in a number of countries.

transportation infrastructure. For example, GE has production and assembly plants in Mexico, South Korea, and Singapore. Even Japanese manufacturers have started to shift some of their production to lower-cost countries in the Pacific Rim and the Americas. BMW, in response to high production costs in Germany, has built assembly plants in the United States, among other countries. Those examples illustrate how companies strive to remain competitive by locating manufacturing facilities wherever in the world they can produce and transport their products to meet the demand in their major markets at the lowest total unit landed costs.

2. *To avoid political, trade, and regulatory hurdles.* Governments sometimes impose tariffs, quotas, and other restrictions on imported goods and services. They often do so to raise revenues, to protect domestic industries, and to pursue various political and economic policy objectives. To circumvent government hurdles, firms often develop production facilities abroad. For example, the primary reason Japanese auto companies moved production to the United States was to get around U.S. import quotas. Now Honda, Nissan, Toyota, Mazda, and Mitsubishi are assembling vehicles in the United States. This was also the situation in the 1970s when India followed a development strategy to compete domestically with imported products. One reason that prompted U.S. pharmaceutical maker SmithKline and Britain's Beecham to merge was to avoid licensing and regulatory delays in their largest markets, Western Europe and the United States. GlaxoSmithKline (the result of a 2000 merger between Glaxo Wellcome and SmithKline Beecham) now identifies itself as an inside player in Europe and the United States.

3. *To broaden their markets.* After a company's home market matures, growth opportunities are often better in foreign markets. According to economic product life-cycle theory, a firm first produces in its home market, where it can better develop its product and satisfy local customers. This attracts competitors; but when the home market is expanding rapidly, new customers provide the necessary sales growth. However, as the home market matures and the growth of total demand slows, competition becomes more intense. At the same time, demand for the product develops abroad, which creates conditions favoring production in foreign countries to satisfy foreign demand and to cut production and transportation costs so that the company can remain competitive. Thus, such homegrown firms as IBM, Coca-Cola, and McDonald's are aggressively expanding into overseas markets. In addition, foreign firms such as Sony and Toshiba now play an important role in the U.S. consumer electronics market. Also, as products become more complex and development becomes more expensive, it is necessary to sell more units to cover overhead costs; so larger markets are critical.

4. *To seek raw materials and new technology.* Supplies of many essential raw materials are geographically dispersed; so companies must go where the materials are found, no matter how challenging it may be to operate in some of the locations. For example, major deposits of oil are located on the northern coast of Alaska, in Siberia, in the deserts of the Middle East, and in the Canadian tar sands, all of which present unique challenges. Thus, U.S. oil companies such as ExxonMobil need major production facilities around the world to ensure access to the basic input resources needed to sustain the companies in the future. Because ExxonMobil has refineries, distribution facilities, and oil production fields, this type of investment is referred to as a **vertically integrated investment**, whereby the firm undertakes an investment to secure its supply of inputs at stable prices.

Vertically Integrated Investment
Occurs when a firm undertakes an investment to secure its input supply at stable prices.

5. *To protect processes and products.* Firms often possess special intangible assets such as brand names, technological and marketing know-how, managerial

expertise, and superior research and development (R&D) capabilities. Unfortunately, property rights involving intangible assets are often difficult to protect, particularly in foreign markets. Firms sometimes invest abroad rather than license local foreign firms in order to protect the secrecy of their production processes, distribution systems, or the product itself. Once a firm's formula or production process is revealed to other local firms, those firms may more easily develop similar products or processes, which will hurt the original firm's sales. For example, to protect its formula, Coca-Cola builds bottling plants and distribution networks in foreign markets but imports the concentrate or syrup required to make the product from the United States. In the 1960s, Coca-Cola faced strong pressure from the Indian government to reveal its formula in order to continue its operations in India. Rather than reveal its formula, the company withdrew its operations from India until the foreign investment climate improved.

6. *To diversify.* By establishing worldwide production facilities and markets, firms can cushion the effect of adverse economic conditions in any single country. For example, in recent years, the decline in the U.S. dollar has benefited U.S. corporations with significant overseas operations, which helps soften the blow from a weakening U.S. economy. In general, geographic diversification of inputs and outputs works because the economic fluctuations or political vagaries of different countries are not perfectly correlated. Therefore, companies investing overseas can benefit from diversification in the same way that individuals benefit from investing in a broad portfolio of stocks. However, because individual shareholders can diversify their investments internationally on their own, it makes less sense for firms to undertake foreign investments solely for diversification purposes. Note, though, that in countries that place constraints on foreign stock ownership or that do not have internationally traded companies, corporate diversification might make sense because then companies can do something that shareholders cannot easily duplicate in their individual portfolios.

7. *To retain customers.* If a company goes abroad and establishes production or distribution operations, it will need inputs and services at the new locations. If it can obtain what it needs from a supplier that also operates in the same set of countries, managing the relationship will be much easier and economies of scale and other synergies will likely be obtained. Therefore, suppliers of inputs or services can better retain the business of their customers who are "going global" if they follow their customers abroad. Large U.S. banks such as Citibank and JPMorgan Chase initially expanded abroad to supply banking services to their long-time customers, although they quickly capitalized on their global network to develop new customer relationships. The same history is also true for accounting, law, advertising, and similar service providers.

The past 10 to 20 years has seen an increasing amount of investment in the United States by foreign corporations and in foreign nations by U.S. corporations. This trend is shown in Figure 19-1, and it is important because of its implications for eroding the traditional doctrine of independence and self-reliance that has been a hallmark of U.S. policy. Just as U.S. corporations with extensive overseas operations are said to use their economic power to exert substantial economic and political influence over host governments in many parts of the world, it is feared that foreign corporations are gaining similar sway over U.S. policy. These developments suggest an increasing degree of mutual influence and interdependence among business enterprises and nations, to which the United States is not immune.

FIGURE 19-1   Direct Investment Positions on a Current-Cost Basis, 1982–2006

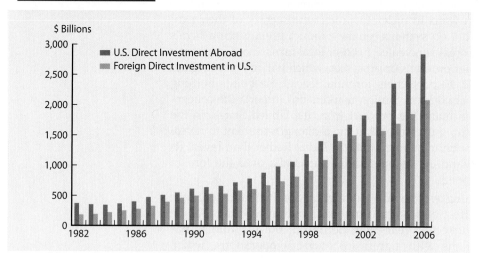

Sources: Marilyn Ibarra and Jennifer Koncz, "Direct Investment Positions for 2006: Country and Industry Detail," *Survey of Current Business*, July 2007, pp. 21–36; Elena L. Nguyen, "The International Investment Position of the United States at Yearend 2002," *Survey of Current Business*, July 2003, pp. 12–21; Patricia E. Abaroa, "The International Investment Position of the United States at Yearend 2003," *Survey of Current Business*, July 2004, pp. 30–39; and Bureau of Economic Analysis, "U.S. Net International Investment Position at Yearend 2004," *BEA News*, June 30, 2005.

SELF TEST

What is a multinational corporation?

Why do companies "go global"?

Discuss the following statement: The United States is not immune to the influence of foreign corporations over U.S. economic and political policies.

19-2 MULTINATIONAL VERSUS DOMESTIC FINANCIAL MANAGEMENT

In theory, the concepts and procedures discussed in the first 18 chapters are valid for both domestic and multinational operations. However, some additional factors need to be considered when firms operate globally. Five of these factors are listed here:

1. *Different currency denominations.* Cash flows in various parts of a multinational corporate system will be denominated in different currencies. Hence, exchange rates must be included in all financial analyses.

2. *Political risk.* Nations are free to place constraints on the transfer or use of corporate resources, and they can change regulations and tax rules at any time. They can even expropriate assets within their boundaries. Therefore, political risks can take on many forms. Of course, political risks are present for companies operating in a single country. But for multinational firms, political risks exist in various forms from country to country; and they must be addressed explicitly in any financial analysis.

3. *Economic and legal ramifications.* Each country has its own unique economic and legal systems, and these differences can cause significant problems when a corporation tries to coordinate and control its worldwide operations. For example, differences in tax laws among countries can cause a given economic transaction to have strikingly different after-tax consequences depending on where the transaction occurs. Similarly, differences in legal systems of host nations, such as the Common Law of Great Britain versus the French Civil Law, complicate matters ranging from the simple recording of business transactions to the role the judiciary plays in resolving conflicts. Such differences can restrict multinational corporations' flexibility in deploying resources and make procedures that are required in one part of the company illegal in others. These differences also make it difficult for executives trained in one country to move easily to another.

4. *Role of governments.* Most financial models developed in the United States assume the existence of a competitive marketplace in which the participants determine the terms of trade. The government, through its power to establish basic ground rules, is involved in the process; but other than taxes, its role is minimal. Thus, the market provides the primary barometer of success, and it gives the best clues about what must be done to remain competitive. This view of the process is reasonably correct for the United States and Western Europe, but it does not accurately describe the situation in the rest of the world. Although market imperfections can complicate the decision process, they can also be valuable to the extent that they can be overcome by one firm but still serve as barriers to entry by competitors. Frequently, the terms under which companies compete, the actions that must be taken or avoided, and the terms of trade on various transactions are determined not in the marketplace, but by direct negotiation between host governments and multinational enterprises. This is essentially a political process, and it must be treated as such. Thus, traditional financial models have to be recast to include political and other noneconomic aspects of the decision.

5. *Language and cultural differences.* The ability to communicate is critical in all business transactions. In this regard, U.S. citizens are often at a disadvantage because they generally are fluent only in English. On the other hand, European and Japanese businesspeople are usually fluent in several languages, including English. At the same time, even within geographic regions that are considered relatively homogenous, different countries have unique cultural heritages that shape values and influence the conduct of business. Multinational corporations find that matters such as defining the appropriate goals of the firm, attitudes toward risk, performance evaluation and compensation systems, interactions with employees, and the ability to curtail unprofitable operations vary dramatically from one country to the next.

Those five factors complicate financial management and increase the risks that multinational firms face. However, the prospects for high returns and other factors make it worthwhile for firms to accept these risks and learn how to manage them.

SELF TEST   Identify and briefly discuss five major factors that complicate financial management in multinational firms.

19-3 THE INTERNATIONAL MONETARY SYSTEM

International Monetary System
The framework within which exchange rates are determined. It is the blueprint for international trade and capital flows.

Every nation has a monetary system and a monetary authority. In the United States, the Federal Reserve is the monetary authority; and its task is to hold down inflation while promoting economic stability and growth. If countries are to trade with one another, some sort of system must be designed to facilitate payments between nations. The **international monetary system** is the framework within which exchange rates are determined; and it ties global currency, money, capital, real estate, commodity, and real asset markets into a network of institutions and instruments regulated by intergovernmental agreements and driven by each country's unique political and economic objectives.[2]

19-3a International Monetary Terminology

In a discussion of the international monetary system, it is useful to begin by introducing some important concepts and terminology:

Exchange Rate
The number of units of a given currency that can be purchased for one unit of another currency.

1. An **exchange rate** is the price of one country's currency in terms of another country's currency. For example, on Monday, May 26, 2008, one U.S. dollar would buy 0.5046 British pound, 0.6340 euro, or 0.9919 Canadian dollar.

2. A *spot exchange rate* is the quoted price for a unit of foreign currency to be delivered "on the spot" or within a very short period of time. The pound rate quoted, £0.5046/$, is a spot rate as of the close of business on May 26, 2008.

3. A *forward exchange rate* is the quoted price for a unit of foreign currency to be delivered at a specified date in the future. If today was May 26, 2008, and we wanted to know how many pounds we could expect to receive for a dollar on November 26, 2008, we would look at the 6-month forward rate, which was £0.5122/$ versus the £0.5046/$ spot rate. Thus, the dollar is expected to *appreciate* relative to the British pound during the next 6 months. Note also that the *forward exchange contract* on May 26 would lock in this exchange rate but no money would change hands until November 26. The spot rate on November 26 might be quite different from £0.5122, in which case we would have a profit or a loss on the forward purchase.

For a listing of world currencies, currency symbols, and their regimes, go to the University of British Columbia Sauder School of Business Pacific Exchange Rate Service web site, at http://fx.sauder. ubc.ca/currencies.html.

4. A *fixed exchange rate* for a currency is set by the government and is allowed to fluctuate only slightly (if at all) around the desired rate, which is called the *par value*. For example, Belize has fixed the exchange rate for the Belizean dollar at BZD 2.00/$1, and it has maintained this fixed rate for the past few years.

5. A *floating* or *flexible exchange rate* is not regulated by the government, so supply and demand in the market determine the currency's value. The U.S. dollar and the euro are examples of free-floating currencies. If U.S. customers are importing more goods from Europe than they are exporting to Europe, they will have to make net purchases of euros and sales of dollars, which will cause the euro to appreciate relative to the dollar. Note, though, that central banks do intervene in the market from time to time to nudge exchange rates up or down even though they basically float.

6. *Devaluation* or *revaluation of a currency* is the technical term referring to the decrease or increase in the stated par value of a currency whose value is fixed. This decision is made by the government, usually without warning.

---

[2]For a comprehensive history of the international monetary system and details of how it has evolved, consult one of the many economics books on the subject, including Robert Carbaugh, *International Economics,* 11th ed. (Mason, OH: Thomson/South-Western, 2007); Mordechai Kreinin, *International Economics: A Policy Approach,* 10th ed. (Mason, OH: Thomson/South-Western, 2006); Beth V. Yarbrough and Robert M. Yarbrough, *The World Economy: Trade and Finance,* 7th ed. (Mason, OH: Thomson/South-Western, 2006); and Joseph P. Daniels and David D. VanHoose, *Global Economic Issues and Policies with Economic Applications* (Mason, OH: Thomson/South-Western, 2004).

For example, on July 21, 2005, the Chinese government suddenly announced that it was revaluing the yuan to make it 2.1% stronger against the U.S. dollar. (The new exchange rate was CNY 8.1097/$.) Even though it was widely believed that the yuan was significantly undervalued, this revaluation caught many by surprise since the exchange rate had been pegged at a fixed rate of CNY 8.2781/$ for nearly a decade. Just as importantly, on that date, the Chinese government abandoned the strict peg to the U.S. dollar and instead adopted a more flexible system where the yuan is now linked to a basket of foreign currencies including the dollar. Since then, the yuan has steadily appreciated relative to the U.S. dollar. On May 26, 2008, the exchange rate was CNY 6.9365/$; so it cost 14.5% fewer yuan to buy a dollar than previously.

7. *Depreciation* or *appreciation of a currency* refers to a decrease or increase, respectively, in the foreign exchange value of a floating currency. These changes are caused by market forces rather than by governments.

19-3b Current Monetary Arrangements

At the most basic level, we can divide currency regimes into two broad groups: floating rates and fixed rates. Within the two regimes, there are gradations among subregimes in terms of how rigidly they adhere to the basic positions. Looking first at the floating-rate category, the two main subgroups are as follows:

1. *Freely floating.* Here the exchange rate is determined by the supply and demand for the currency. Under a **freely-floating regime**, governments may occasionally intervene in the market to buy or sell their currency to stabilize fluctuations, but they do not attempt to alter the absolute level of the rate. This policy exists at one end of the continuum of exchange-rate regimes. For example, the currencies of Australia, Brazil, and the Philippines, among many others, are allowed to float with a minimum of intervention.

2. *Managed floating.* Here there is significant government intervention to manage the exchange rate by manipulating the currency's supply and demand. For example, the governments of Colombia, Israel, and Poland manage their respective currency's float. Governments rarely reveal their target exchange rate levels when they use a **managed-float regime** because doing so would make it too easy for currency speculators to profit.

Most developed countries follow either a freely-floating or a managed-float regime. A few developing countries do so as well, often reluctantly and as a result of a market that forces them to abandon a fixed-rate regime.

Types of fixed-exchange-rate regimes include the following:

1. *No local currency.* The most extreme position is for the country to have no local currency of its own, using another country's currency as its legal tender (such as the U.S. dollar in the Panama Canal Zone, in Ecuador, and in the Turks and Caicos Islands) or belonging to a group of countries that shares a common currency (such as the euro). With this arrangement, the local government surrenders the ability to use exchange rates to tinker with its economy.

2. *Currency board arrangement.* Under a variation of the first subregime, a country technically has its own currency but commits to exchange it for a specified foreign money unit at a fixed exchange rate. This requires the country to impose domestic currency restrictions unless it has enough foreign currency reserves to cover all requested exchanges. This is called a **currency board arrangement**. Argentina had a currency board arrangement before its crisis of January 2002, when it was forced to devalue the peso and default on its debt.

3. *Fixed-peg arrangement.* In a **fixed-peg arrangement**, the country locks, or "pegs," its currency to another currency or basket of currencies at a fixed

Freely-Floating Regime
Occurs when the exchange rate is determined by supply and demand for the currency.

Managed-Float Regime
Occurs when there is significant government intervention to control the exchange rate via manipulation of the currency's supply and demand.

Currency Board Arrangement
Occurs when a country has its own currency but commits to exchange it for a specified foreign money unit at a fixed exchange rate and legislates domestic currency restrictions unless it has the foreign currency reserves to cover requested exchanges.

Fixed-Peg Arrangement
Occurs when a country locks its currency to a specific currency or basket of currencies at a fixed exchange rate.

exchange rate. This allows the currency to vary only slightly from its desired rate; and if it moves outside the specified limits (often set at ±1% of the target rate), its central bank intervenes to force the currency back within the limits. An example is China, where the yuan is no longer pegged to the U.S. dollar but rather to a basket of currencies. Additional examples include Bhutan's ngultrum, which is pegged to the Indian rupee; the Falkland Islands' pound, which is pegged to the British pound; and Barbados's dollar, which is pegged to the U.S. dollar.

Other variations have been used, and new ones are developed from time to time. A majority of the world's countries employ a system that includes a fixed-exchange-rate arrangement along with occasional interventions. So while the most important currencies (as measured by volume of transactions) are allowed to float and the international monetary system is often called a floating regime, most currencies are partially fixed but occasionally are manipulated in some manner.

SELF TEST

What is an international monetary system?

What is the difference between spot and forward exchange rates?

What is the basic difference between floating and fixed exchange rates?

Differentiate between devaluation/revaluation of a currency and depreciation/appreciation of a currency.

What are the two broad categories of the various currency regimes? What are the subgroups of those two broad categories?

19-4 FOREIGN EXCHANGE RATE QUOTATIONS

Foreign exchange rate quotations can be found in *The Wall Street Journal* and in other leading print publications and on web sites. Exchange rates are given two different ways. As shown in Table 19-1, which is an excerpt from *The Wall Street Journal Online,* in Column 1, they are quoted as "USD equivalent"; in Column 2, they are quoted as "Currency per USD." For example, 1 Canadian dollar is worth (or can be exchanged for) 1.0082 U.S. dollars, or 1 U.S. dollar can buy 0.9919 Canadian dollar.

Note that if the foreign exchange markets are in equilibrium, which is usually the case for the major traded currencies, the two quotations must be reciprocals of each other, as shown here for the Canadian dollar.

Canadian dollar: $1/1.0082 = 0.9919$

$1/0.9919 = 1.0082$

19-4a Cross Rates

All of the exchange rates given in Table 19-1 are relative to the U.S. dollar. Suppose, though, that a German executive is flying to Tokyo on business. The exchange rate in which he or she is interested is not euros or yen per dollar—rather, the issue is how many yen can be purchased with a euro. This is called a **cross rate**, and it can be calculated from the following data from Column 2 of Table 19-1:

For up-to-date currency quotations on the web, visit two popular sites: **www.bloomberg.com/markets/currencies/fxc.html** *and* **http://finance.yahoo.com/currency**.

Cross Rate
The exchange rate between any two currencies.

	Spot Rate
Euro	€0.6340/$1
Yen	¥103.44/$1

Table 19-1	Sample Exchange Rates: Monday, May 26, 2008	
	Direct Quotation: U.S. Dollars Required to Buy One Unit of Foreign Currency (1)	**Indirect Quotation:** Number of Units of Foreign Currency per U.S. Dollar (2)
Brazilian real	$ 0.6028	1.6589
British pound	1.9816	0.5046
Canadian dollar	1.0082	0.9919
Chinese yuan	0.1442	6.9365
Danish krone	0.2114	4.7304
Euro	1.5772	0.6340
Hungarian forint	0.006456	154.89
Israeli shekel	0.3018	3.3135
Japanese yen	0.009667	103.44
Mexican peso	0.0962	10.3983
South African rand	0.1299	7.6982
Swedish krona	0.1693	5.9067
Swiss franc	0.9760	1.0246
Venezuelan bolivar fuerte	0.46628742	2.1446

Note: Column 2 equals 1.0 divided by Column 1. However, rounding differences do occur.
Source: Adapted from *The Wall Street Journal Online*, http://online.wsj.com, May 27, 2008.

Because the quotations have the same denominator—one U.S. dollar—we can calculate the cross rate between these (and other) currencies by using the Column 2 quotations. For our German national, the cross rates are found as follows:

$$\text{Euro/yen exchange rate} = \frac{\text{Euro/\$}}{\text{Yen/\$}}$$

And when we cancel the dollar signs, we are left with the number of euros that one yen could purchase:

$$€0.6340/¥103.44 = €0.0061/¥$$

Alternatively, we could find the number of yen that one euro could buy:

$$\text{Yen/euro exchange rate} = \frac{\text{Yen/\$}}{\text{Euro/\$}}$$

$$¥103.44/€0.6340 = ¥163.15/€$$

Note that those two cross rates are reciprocals of each other.

Financial publications such as *The Wall Street Journal* and web sites such as Bloomberg, Yahoo, and *The Wall Street Journal Online* provide tables of key currency cross rates. Table 19-2 gives the table from *The Wall Street Journal Online* for May 26, 2008. Notice that there may be slight differences when you calculate cross rates due to the rounding of individual quotations. Currency traders carry quotations out to 12 decimal places.

19-4b Interbank Foreign Currency Quotations

The quotations from *The Wall Street Journal Online* given in Tables 19-1 and 19-2 are sufficient for many purposes. For other purposes, however, additional terminology and conventions are useful. There are two ways to state the exchange rate between two currencies, in either **American** or **European terms**. Accordingly, we need to designate one of the currencies as the "home" currency and the other

American Terms
The foreign exchange rate quotation that represents the number of American dollars that can be bought with one unit of local currency.

European Terms
The foreign exchange rate quotation that represents the units of local currency that can be bought with one U.S. dollar. "European" is intended as a generic term that applies globally.

Table 19-2	Key Currency Cross Rates						
	US Dollar (1)	Euro (2)	Pound (3)	SFranc (4)	Peso (5)	Yen (6)	Cdn Dlr (7)
Canada	0.9919	1.5644	1.9655	0.9681	0.0954	0.0096	—
Japan	103.44	163.15	204.99	100.96	9.9483	—	104.29
Mexico	10.398	16.400	20.605	10.149	—	0.1005	10.484
Switzerland	1.0246	1.6160	2.0303	—	0.0985	0.0099	1.0330
United Kingdom	0.5046	0.7959	—	0.4925	0.0485	0.0049	0.5088
Euro	0.6340	—	1.2564	0.6188	0.0610	0.0061	0.6392
United States	—	1.5772	1.9816	0.9760	0.0962	0.0097	1.0082

Notes: Column 1 shows how many units of each foreign currency a U.S. dollar will buy. Column 2 shows how many units a euro will buy, and so forth.

Source: Adapted from "Key Currency Cross Rates," *The Wall Street Journal Online,* http://online.wsj.com, May 27, 2008.

Direct Quotation

The home currency price of one unit of the foreign currency.

Indirect Quotation

The foreign currency price of one unit of the home currency.

as the "foreign" currency. This designation is arbitrary. The *home* currency price of one unit of the *foreign* currency is called a **direct quotation**. Thus, to a person who considers the United States to be "home," American terms represent a direct quotation. On the other hand, the *foreign* currency price of one unit of the *home* currency is called an **indirect quotation**. European terms represent indirect quotations to people in the United States. Note that if the perspective changes and the "home" currency is no longer the U.S. dollar, the designations of direct and indirect will change. For the remainder of this chapter, unless specifically stated otherwise, we will assume that the United States is the "home" country and thus that the U.S. dollar is the home currency.

SELF TEST

Explain the difference between direct and indirect quotations.

What is a cross rate?

Assume that today 1 Canadian dollar is worth 0.75 U.S. dollar. How many Canadian dollars would you receive for 1 U.S. dollar? (1.333)

Assume that 1 U.S. dollar can be exchanged for 105 Japanese yen or for 0.80 euro. What is the euro/yen exchange rate? **(€0.007619/¥)**

19-5 TRADING IN FOREIGN EXCHANGE

Importers, exporters, tourists, and governments buy and sell currencies in the foreign exchange market. For example, when a U.S. trader imports automobiles from Japan, payment is probably made in Japanese yen. The importer buys yen (through its bank) in the foreign exchange market, much as one buys common stocks on the New York Stock Exchange or pork bellies on the Chicago Mercantile Exchange. However, whereas stock and commodity exchanges have organized trading floors, the foreign exchange market consists of a network of brokers and banks based in New York, London, Tokyo, and other financial centers. Most buy and sell orders are conducted by computer and telephone.[3]

---

[3]For a more detailed explanation of exchange rate determination and operations of the foreign exchange market, see Roy L. Crum, Eugene F. Brigham, and Joel F. Houston, *Fundamentals of International Finance* (Mason, OH: Thomson/South-Western, 2005).

19-5a Spot Rates and Forward Rates

The exchange rates shown earlier in Tables 19-1 and 19-2 are known as **spot rates**, which means the rate paid for delivery of the currency "on the spot" or, in reality, no more than 2 days after the day of the trade. For most of the world's major currencies, it also is possible to buy (or sell) currencies for delivery at some agreed-upon future date, usually 30, 90, or 180 days from the day the transaction is negotiated. This rate is known as the **forward exchange rate**.

For example, suppose a U.S. firm must pay 500 million yen to a Japanese firm in 30 days and the current spot rate is 103.44 yen per dollar. Unless spot rates change, the U.S. firm will pay the Japanese firm the equivalent of $4.834 million (500 million yen divided by 103.44 yen per dollar) in 30 days. But if the spot rate falls to 100 yen per dollar, for example, the U.S. firm will have to pay the equivalent of $5 million. The treasurer of the U.S. firm can avoid this risk by entering into a 30-day forward exchange contract. This contract promises delivery of yen to the U.S. firm in 30 days at a guaranteed price of 103.26 yen per dollar. No cash changes hands at the time the treasurer signs the forward contract, although the U.S. firm might have to put down some collateral as a guarantee against default. Because the firm can use an interest-bearing instrument for the collateral, though, this requirement is not costly. The counterparty to the forward contract must deliver the yen to the U.S. firm in 30 days, and the U.S. firm is obligated to purchase the 500 million yen at the previously agreed-upon rate of 103.26 yen per dollar. Therefore, the treasurer of the U.S. firm is able to lock in a payment equivalent to $4.842 million no matter what happens to spot rates. This technique, which is called "hedging," was discussed in Chapter 18.

Forward rates for 30-, 90-, and 180-day delivery, along with the current spot rates for some commonly traded currencies, are given in Table 19-3. If we can obtain *more* of the foreign currency for a dollar in the forward market than in the spot market, the forward currency is less valuable than the spot currency and the forward currency is said to be selling at a **discount**. Conversely, if we can obtain *less* of the foreign currency for a dollar in the forward market than in the spot market, the forward currency is more valuable than the spot currency and the forward currency is said to be selling at a **premium**. Thus, because a dollar buys *fewer* yen and Swiss francs in the forward market than in the spot market, the forward yen and Swiss francs are selling at a premium. On the other hand, a dollar would buy more pounds and Canadian dollars in the forward market than

Spot Rate
The effective exchange rate of a foreign currency for delivery on (approximately) the current day.

Forward Exchange Rate
An agreed-upon price at which two currencies will be exchanged at some future date.

Discount on Forward Rate
The situation when the spot rate is less than the forward rate.

Premium on Forward Rate
The situation when the spot rate is greater than the forward rate.

Table 19-3	Selected Spot and Forward Exchange Rates (Number of Units of Foreign Currency per U.S. Dollar)				
	Spot Rate	**FORWARD RATES**			**Forward Rate at a Premium or Discount**
		30 Days	**90 Days**	**180 Days**	
British pound	0.5046	0.5060	0.5084	0.5122	Discount
Canadian dollar	0.9919	0.9925	0.9930	0.9938	Discount
Japanese yen	103.44	103.26	102.95	102.48	Premium
Swiss franc	1.0246	1.0244	1.0241	1.0241	Premium

Notes:
a. These are representative quotes as provided by a sample of New York banks. Forward rates for other currencies and for other lengths of time can often be negotiated.
b. When it takes more units of a foreign currency to buy one dollar in the future, the value of the foreign currency is less in the forward market than in the spot market; hence, the forward rate is at a discount to the spot rate. Likewise, when it takes fewer units of a foreign currency to buy one dollar in the future, the value of the foreign currency is more in the forward market than in the spot market; hence, the forward rate is at a premium to the spot rate.

Source: Adapted from *The Wall Street Journal Online,* http://online.wsj.com, May 27, 2008.

in the spot market, so the forward pounds and Canadian dollars are selling at a discount.

Explain what it means for a forward currency to sell at a discount and at a premium.

Suppose a U.S. firm must pay 200 million Swiss francs to a Swiss firm in 90 days. Briefly explain how the firm would use forward exchange rates to "lock in" the price of the payable due in 90 days.

19-6 INTEREST RATE PARITY

Market forces determine whether a currency sells at a forward premium or discount, and the general relationship between spot and forward exchange rates is specified by a concept called "interest rate parity."

Interest Rate Parity
Specifies that investors should expect to earn the same return in all countries after adjusting for risk.

Interest rate parity holds that investors should earn the same return on interest-bearing investments in all countries after adjusting for risk. It recognizes that when you invest in a country other than your home country, you are affected by two forces—returns on the investment itself and changes in the exchange rate. It follows that your overall return will be higher than the investment's stated return if the currency in which your investment is denominated appreciates relative to your home currency. Likewise, your overall return will be lower if the foreign currency you receive declines in value.

The relationship between spot and forward exchange rates and interest rates, which is known as interest rate parity, is expressed in the following equation:

$$\frac{\text{Forward exchange rate}}{\text{Spot exchange rate}} = \frac{(1 + r_h)}{(1 + r_f)}$$

Both the forward and spot rates are expressed in terms of the amount of home currency received per unit of foreign currency; and r_h and r_f are the periodic interest rates in the home country and the foreign country, respectively. If this relationship does not hold, currency traders will buy and sell currencies—that is, engage in *arbitrage*—until it does hold.

To illustrate interest rate parity, consider the case of a U.S. investor who can buy default-free 90-day Japanese bonds that promise a 4% nominal return. The 90-day interest rate, r_f, is 4%/4 = 1% because 90 days is one-fourth of a 360-day year. Assume also that the spot exchange rate is $0.009667, which means that you can exchange 0.009667 dollar for 1 yen, or 103.44 yen per dollar. Finally, assume that the 90-day forward exchange rate is $0.009713, which means that you can exchange 1 yen for 0.009713 dollar, or receive 102.95 yen per dollar exchanged, 90 days from now.

The U.S. investor can receive a 4% annualized return denominated in yen; but if he or she ultimately wants to consume goods in the United States, those yen must be converted to dollars. The dollar return on the investment depends, therefore, on what happens to exchange rates over the next 3 months. However, the investor can lock in the dollar return by selling the foreign currency in the forward market. For example, the investor can do the following simultaneously:

- Convert $1,000 to 103,440 yen in the spot market.
- Invest the 103,440 yen in 90-day Japanese bonds that have a 4% annualized return or a 1% quarterly return and hence will pay (103,440)(1.01) = 104,474.40 yen in 90 days.

- Agree today to exchange the 104,474.40 yen 90 days from now at the 90-day forward exchange rate of 102.95 yen per dollar, for a total of $1,014.81.

This investment, therefore, has an expected 90-day return of $14.81/$1,000 = 1.481%, which translates into a nominal return of 4(1.481%) = 5.92%. In this case, 4% of the expected 5.92% return is coming from the bond itself and 1.92% arises because the market believes the yen will strengthen relative to the dollar. Note that by locking in the forward rate today, the investor has eliminated any exchange rate risk. And because the Japanese bond is assumed to be default-free, the investor is assured of earning a 5.92% dollar return.

Interest rate parity implies that an investment in the United States with the same risk as a Japanese bond should have an annual return of 5.92%. Solving for r_h in the parity equation, we indeed find that the predicted annual interest rate in the United States is 5.92%.

Interest rate parity shows why a particular currency might be at a forward premium or discount. Note that a currency is at a forward premium whenever domestic interest rates are higher than foreign interest rates. Discounts will prevail if domestic interest rates are lower than foreign interest rates. If these conditions do not hold, arbitrage will soon force interest rates back to parity.

SELF TEST

What is interest rate parity?

Assume that interest rate parity holds. When a currency trades at a forward premium, what does that imply about domestic rates relative to foreign interest rates? when a currency trades at a forward discount?

Assume that 90-day U.S. securities have a 3.5% annualized interest rate, whereas 90-day Canadian securities have a 4% annualized interest rate. In the spot market, 1 U.S. dollar can be exchanged for 1.4 Canadian dollars. If interest rate parity holds, what is the 90-day forward exchange rate between U.S. and Canadian dollars? **($0.7134/C$ or C$1.40173/$)**

On the basis of your answer to the previous question, is the Canadian dollar selling at a premium or discount on the forward rate? **(Discount)**

19-7 PURCHASING POWER PARITY

We have discussed exchange rates in some detail, and we have considered the relationship between spot and forward exchange rates. However, we have not yet addressed this fundamental question: What determines the spot level of exchange rates in each country? While exchange rates are influenced by a multitude of factors that are difficult to predict, particularly on a day-to-day basis, over the long run, market forces work to ensure that similar goods sell for similar prices in different countries after exchange rates are taken into account. This relationship is known as "purchasing power parity."

Purchasing power parity (PPP), sometimes referred to as the *law of one price,* implies that the level of exchange rates adjusts so as to cause identical goods to cost the same amount in different countries. For example, if a pair of tennis shoes costs $100 in the United States and 50 pounds in Britain, PPP implies that the exchange rate will be $2 per pound. Consumers can purchase the shoes in Britain for 50 pounds, or they can exchange their 50 pounds for $100 and purchase the same shoes in the United States at the same effective cost, assuming no

Purchasing Power Parity (PPP)
The relationship in which the same products cost roughly the same amount in different countries after the exchange rate is taken into account.

transactions or transportation costs. The equation for purchasing power parity is shown here:

$$P_h = (P_f)(\text{Spot rate})$$

or

$$\text{Spot rate} = \frac{P_h}{P_f}.$$

HUNGRY FOR A BIG MAC? GO TO CHINA!

Purchasing power parity (PPP) implies that the same product will sell for the same price in every country after adjusting for current exchange rates. One problem when testing to see if PPP holds is that it assumes that goods consumed in different countries are of the same quality. For example, if you find that a product is more expensive in Switzerland than it is in Canada, one explanation is that PPP fails to hold but another explanation is that the product sold in Switzerland is of a higher quality and therefore deserves a higher price.

One way to test for PPP is to find goods that have the same quality worldwide. With this in mind, *The Economist* magazine occasionally compares the prices of a well-known good whose quality is the same in 120 different countries: the McDonald's Big Mac hamburger.

The tables shown in Panels A and B on the next page provide information collected during 2007. The Panel A table gives the price of a Big Mac in each country's local currency and the actual dollar exchange rate when these data were collected. In Panel B, the first numeric column calculates the price of the Big Mac in terms of the U.S. dollar—this is obtained by dividing the local price by the actual exchange rate at that time. For example, a Big Mac costs 6.30 Swiss francs in Zurich, which is shown in Panel A. Given an exchange rate of 1.21 Swiss francs per dollar (as shown in Panel A), this implies that the dollar price of a Big Mac is 6.30 Swiss francs/1.21 Swiss francs per dollar ≈ $5.20, shown in Panel B.

The second numeric column in Panel B backs out the implied exchange rate that would hold under PPP. This is obtained by dividing the price of the Big Mac in each local currency by its U.S. price. For example, as shown in Panel A, a Big Mac costs 52 rubles in Russia and $3.41 in the United States. If PPP holds, the exchange rate should be approximately 15.2 rubles per dollar (52 rubles/$3.41), which is shown in Panel B.

Comparing the implied exchange rate (shown in Panel B) to the actual exchange rate (shown in Panel A), we see the extent to which the local currency is under- or overvalued relative to the dollar. Given that the actual exchange rate at the time was 25.6 rubles per dollar, this rate implies that the ruble was 41% undervalued, which is shown in the last column of Panel B.

The evidence suggests that strict PPP does not hold, but recent research suggests that the Big Mac test may shed some insights about where exchange rates are headed. The average price of a Big Mac in the European Monetary Union (EMU) is 3.06 euros. This implies that the euro's PPP is $1.12; so at its current rate of $1.36, the euro is overvalued by 22%.

Norway, Sweden, Switzerland, and Denmark—four European countries that are not part of the EMU—have currencies that are significantly overvalued against the dollar. The Norwegian kroner is overvalued by 102%, the Swedish krona is overvalued by 42%, the Swiss franc is overvalued by 53%, and the Danish krone is overvalued by 49%. In contrast, the Japanese yen is the most undervalued rich-world currency—by 33%.

According to the Big Mac Index, relative to the U.S. dollar, the euro is overvalued by 22%. A particularly bad year for the U.S. dollar was 2007. At year-end, the U.S. dollar was at its lowest point in a decade. This decline occurred primarily because the U.S. had imported so much more than it had exported, paying for the deficit by borrowing from foreigners. At some point, we will have to pay off that debt, which means selling dollars and buying foreign currencies. Those transactions will lower the value of the dollar relative to the values of foreign currencies. The Big Mac Index anticipates those actions.

One last benefit of the Big Mac test is that it tells us the cheapest places to find a Big Mac. According to the data, if you are looking for a Big Mac, head to China but avoid Iceland because the Chinese yuan is the most undervalued currency and the Icelandic kronur is the most overvalued.

Sources: Adapted from "Sizzling: The Big Mac Index (Food for Thought about Exchange Rate Controversies), *The Economist*, Vol. 384, July 7, 2007, pp. 74–76; and Li Lian Ong, "Burgernomics: The Economics of the Big Mac Standard," *Journal of International Money and Finance*, Vol. 16, no. 6 (1997), pp. 867–878.

PANEL A			PANEL B			
	Big Mac Prices in Local Currency	**Actual Dollar Exchange Rate, 7/2/07**		**Big Mac Prices in Dollars[a]**	**Implied PPP of the Dollar[b]**	**Under(−) Over (+)Valuation against the Dollar, %**
United States[c]	$3.41	—	United States[c]	$3.41	—	—
Argentina	Peso8.25	3.09	Argentina	2.67	2.42	−22
Australia	A$3.45	1.17	Australia	2.95	1.01	−14
Brazil	Real6.90	1.91	Brazil	3.61	2.02	6
Britain	£1.99	2.01[d]	Britain	4.01	1.71[d]	18
Canada	C$3.88	1.05	Canada	3.68	1.14	8
Chile	Peso1,565	527	Chile	2.97	459	−13
China	Yuan11.0	7.60	China	1.45	3.23	−58
Czech Republic	Koruna52.9	21.1	Czech Republic	2.51	15.5	−27
Denmark	DKr27.75	5.46	Denmark	5.08	8.14	49
Egypt	Pound9.54	5.69	Egypt	1.68	2.80	−51
Euro area	€3.06	1.36[e]	Euro area	4.17[f]	1.12[e]	22
Hong Kong	HK$12.0	7.82	Hong Kong	1.54	3.52	−55
Hungary	Forint600	180	Hungary	3.33	176	−2
Iceland	Kronur469	61.7	Iceland	7.61	138	123
Indonesia	Rupiah15,900	9,015	Indonesia	1.76	4,663	−48
Japan	¥280	122	Japan	2.29	82.1	−33
Malaysia	Ringgit5.50	3.43	Malaysia	1.60	1.61	−53
Mexico	Peso29.0	10.8	Mexico	2.69	8.50	−21
New Zealand	NZ4.60	1.28	New Zealand	3.59	1.35	5
Norway	Kroner40.0	5.81	Norway	6.88	11.7	102
Peru	NewSol9.50	3.17	Peru	3.00	2.79	−12
Philippines	Peso85.0	45.9	Philippines	1.85	24.9	−46
Poland	Zloty6.90	2.75	Poland	2.51	2.02	−26
Russia	Rouble52.0	25.6	Russia	2.03	15.2	−41
Singapore	S$3.95	1.52	Singapore	2.59	1.16	−24
South Africa	Rand15.5	6.97	South Africa	2.22	4.55	−35
South Korea	Won2,900	923	South Korea	3.14	850	−8
Sweden	SKr33.0	6.79	Sweden	4.86	9.68	42
Switzerland	SFr6.30	1.21	Switzerland	5.20	1.85	53
Taiwan	NT$75.0	32.8	Taiwan	2.29	22.0	−33
Thailand	Baht62.0	34.5	Thailand	1.80	18.2	−47
Turkey	Lira4.75	1.30	Turkey	3.66	1.39	7
Venezuela	Bolivar7,400	2,147	Venezuela	3.45	2,170	1

Notes:
[a]At current exchange rate.
[b]Purchasing power parity: Local price divided by price in the United States.
[c]Average of New York, Chicago, San Francisco, and Atlanta.
[d]Dollars per pound.
[e]Dollars per euro.
[f]Weighted average of member countries.
Sources: McDonald's; and "Sizzling: The Big Mac Index (Food for Thought about Exchange Rate Controversies)," *The Economist,* Vol. 384, July 7, 2007, pp. 74–76.

Here:

P_h = Price of the good in the home country ($100, assuming the United States is the home country)

P_f = Price of the good in the foreign country (50 pounds)

Note that the spot market exchange rate is expressed as the number of units of home currency that can be exchanged for one unit of foreign currency ($2 per pound).

PPP assumes that market forces will eliminate situations in which the same product sells at a different price overseas. For example, if the tennis shoes cost $90 in the United States, trading companies could purchase them in the United States for $90, sell them for 50 pounds in Britain, exchange the 50 pounds for $100 in the foreign exchange market, and earn a profit of $10 on every pair of shoes. Ultimately, this trading activity would increase the demand for tennis shoes in the United States and thus raise P_h, increase the supply of tennis shoes in Britain and thus reduce P_f, and increase the demand for dollars in the foreign exchange market and thus reduce the spot rate. Each of those actions works to restore PPP.

Note that PPP assumes that there are no transportation or transactions costs (or import restrictions) that would limit the ability to ship goods between countries. In many cases, these assumptions are incorrect, which explains why PPP is often violated. An additional complication, when empirically testing to see whether PPP holds, is that products in different countries are rarely identical. Frequently, there are real or perceived differences in quality, which can lead to price differences in different countries.

Still, the concepts of interest rate parity and purchasing power parity are critically important to those engaged in international activities. Companies and investors must anticipate changes in interest rates, inflation, and exchange rates; and they often try to hedge the risks of adverse movements in those factors. The parity relationships are extremely useful when anticipating future conditions.

SELF TEST

What is purchasing power parity?

A television set sells for 1,000 U.S. dollars. In the spot market, $1 = 110 Japanese yen. If purchasing power parity holds, what should be the price (in yen) of the same television set in Japan? (**¥110,000**)

Price differences in "similar" products in different countries often exist. What can explain those differences?

19-8 INFLATION, INTEREST RATES, AND EXCHANGE RATES

Relative inflation rates, or the rates of inflation in foreign countries compared with that in the home country, have two key implications for multinational firms: (1) Relative inflation rates influence future production costs at home and abroad, and (2) inflation has an important effect on relative interest rates and exchange rates. Both of those factors influence multinational corporations' financing decisions and the profitability of foreign investments.

The currencies of countries with higher inflation rates than the U.S. inflation rate, by definition, *depreciate* over time against the dollar. Countries in which this has occurred include Mexico and all the South American nations. On the other hand, the currencies of Switzerland and Japan, which have had less inflation than the United States, have *appreciated* against the dollar. *In fact, a foreign currency will, on average, depreciate or appreciate at a percentage rate approximately equal to the amount by which its inflation rate is over or under the U.S. inflation rate.*

Relative inflation also affects interest rates. Indeed, the interest rate in any country is largely determined by its inflation rate. So countries with higher inflation rates than the U.S. inflation rate also have higher interest rates, and the reverse is true for countries with lower inflation rates.

It is tempting for a multinational corporation to borrow in countries with the lowest interest rates. However, this is not always a good strategy. Suppose, for example, that interest rates in Switzerland are lower than those in the United States because of Switzerland's lower inflation rate. A U.S. multinational firm could therefore reduce its interest expense by borrowing in Switzerland. However, because of relative inflation rates, the Swiss franc will probably appreciate in the future, causing the dollar cost of annual interest and principal payments on Swiss debt to rise over time. Thus, *the lower interest rate could be more than offset by losses from currency appreciation.* Similarly, multinational corporations should not necessarily avoid borrowing in a country such as Brazil, where interest rates have been very high, because future depreciation of the Brazilian real could make such borrowing relatively inexpensive.

SELF TEST

What effects do relative inflation rates have on relative interest rates?

What happens over time to the currencies of countries with higher inflation rates than U.S. inflation rates? to the currencies of countries with lower inflation rates?

Why might a multinational corporation decide to borrow in a country such as Brazil, where interest rates are high, rather than in a country such as Switzerland, where interest rates are low?

19-9 INTERNATIONAL MONEY AND CAPITAL MARKETS

One way for U.S. citizens to invest in world markets is to buy the stocks of U.S. multinational corporations that invest directly in foreign countries. Another way is to purchase foreign securities—stocks, bonds, or money market instruments issued by foreign companies. Security investments are known as *portfolio investments,* and they are distinguished from *direct investments* in physical assets by U.S. corporations.

For a time after World War II, the U.S. capital markets dominated world markets. Today, however, the value of U.S. securities represents less than one-fourth of the value of all securities. Given this situation, it is important for both corporate managers and investors to understand international markets. Moreover, these markets often offer better opportunities for raising or investing capital than are available domestically.

19-9a International Credit Markets

There are three major types of international credit markets. The first type is the market for floating-rate bank loans, called **Eurocredits**, whose rates are tied to LIBOR, which stands for *London Interbank Offer Rate.* LIBOR is the interest rate offered by the largest and strongest banks on large deposits. On May 26, 2008, the 3-month LIBOR rate was 2.65%. Eurocredits tend to be issued for a fixed term with no early repayment. The oldest example of a Eurocredit is a **Eurodollar** deposit,

Eurocredits
Floating-rate bank loans that are available in most major trading currencies and that are tied to LIBOR.

Eurodollar
A U.S. dollar deposited in a bank outside the United States.

STOCK MARKET INDICES AROUND THE WORLD

In Chapter 2, we described the major U.S. stock market indices. As discussed herein, similar market indices also exist for each major world financial center. The accompanying figure compares four of these indices (Japan, Germany, Great Britain, and India) against the U.S. Dow Jones Industrial Average.

Hong Kong

In Hong Kong, the primary stock index is the Hang Seng. Created by HSI Services Limited, the Hang Seng Index reflects the performance of the Hong Kong stock market. It is comprised of 33 domestic stocks (accounting for about 70% of the market's capitalization), which are divided into four subindices: Commerce and Industry, Finance, Utilities, and Properties.

Germany

The major indicator of the German stock market, the XETRA DAX, is comprised of 30 German blue chip stocks. These stocks are listed on the Frankfurt Exchange, and they are representative of the industrial structure of the German economy.

Great Britain

The FT-SE 100 Index (pronounced "footsie") is the most widely followed indicator of equity investments in Great Britain. It is a value-weighted index comprised of the 100 largest companies on the London Stock Exchange, and its value is calculated every minute during the trading session.

Japan

In Japan, the principal barometer of stock performance is the Nikkei 225 Index. The index's value, which is calculated every minute throughout daily trading, consists of a collection of highly liquid equity issues thought to be representative of the Japanese economy.

Chile

The Santiago Stock Exchange has three main share indices: the General Stock Price Index (IGPA), the Selective Stock Price Index (IPSA), and the INTER-10 Index. The IPSA, which reflects the price variations of the most active stocks, is comprised of 40 of the most actively traded stocks on the exchange.

India

Of the 22 stock exchanges in India, the Bombay Stock Exchange (BSE) is the largest, with more than 6,000 listed stocks and approximately two-thirds of the country's total trading volume. Established in 1875, the exchange is also the oldest in Asia. Its yardstick is the BSE Sensex, an index of 30 publicly traded Indian stocks that account for one-fifth of the BSE's market capitalization.

Spain

In Spain, the IBEX 35 is the official index for measuring equity market performance. This index is comprised of the 35 most actively traded securities on the Joint Stock Exchange System (comprising the four Spanish stock exchanges).

Eurobond

An international bond underwritten by an international syndicate of banks and sold to investors in countries other than the one in whose money unit the bond is denominated.

Foreign Bond

A type of international bond issued in the domestic capital market of the country in whose currency the bond is denominated and underwritten by investment banks from the same country.

which is a U.S. dollar deposited in a bank outside the United States. Today Eurocredits exist for most major trading currencies.

The second type of market is the Eurobond market. A **eurobond** is an international bond underwritten by an international bank and sold to investors in countries other than the one in whose currency the bond is denominated. Thus, U.S. dollar-denominated eurobonds are not sold in the United States, pound eurobonds are not sold in the United Kingdom, and yen eurobonds are not sold in Japan. These bonds are true international debt instruments and are usually issued in bearer form, which means that the owner's identity is not registered and thus is not known. To receive interest payments, the owner must clip a coupon and present it for payment at one of the designated payor banks. Most eurobonds are not rated by the rating agencies such as S&P and Moody's, although a number of eurobonds are starting to be rated. Eurobonds can be issued with either a fixed-coupon rate or a floating-rate coupon depending on the preferences of the issuer, and they have medium- or long-term maturities.

The third type of market is the foreign bond market. **Foreign bonds** are issued in the country in whose currency the bond is denominated, and they are underwritten by investment banks in that country. However, the borrower is headquartered in a different country. For instance, a Canadian company might issue a U.S. dollar-denominated bond in New York to fund its U.S. operations. Foreign bonds issued in the United States are sometimes called "Yankee bonds." Similarly,

Selected International Stock Indices—Compound Returns Since January 1995

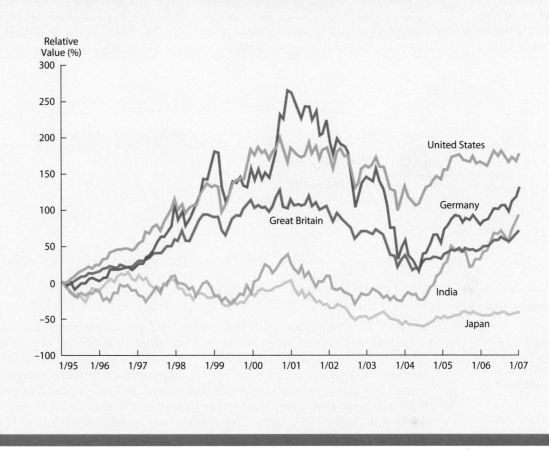

Source: Adapted from Yahoo Finance historical quotes obtained from the web site at http://finance.yahoo.com.

"bulldogs" are foreign bonds issued in London, and "samurai bonds" are foreign bonds issued in Tokyo. Foreign bonds can have a fixed-rate coupon or a floating-rate coupon, and they have the same maturities as the purely domestic bonds with which they must compete for funds.

19-9b International Stock Markets

New issues of stock are sold in international markets for a variety of reasons. For example, a Turkish firm might sell an equity issue in the United States because it can tap a much larger source of capital than in its home country. Also, a U.S. firm might tap the Turkish market because it wants to create an equity market presence to accompany its operations in that country. Occasionally, large multinational companies also issue new stock simultaneously in multiple countries. For example, Alcan Aluminum, a Canadian company, simultaneously issued new stock in Canada, Europe, and the United States using different underwriting syndicates in each market.

In addition to new issues, outstanding stocks of large multinational companies are occasionally listed on several international exchanges. For example, Coca-Cola's stock is traded on six stock exchanges in the United States, four exchanges in Switzerland, and the Frankfurt Exchange in Germany. Some 500 foreign stocks are listed in the United States—one example is Royal Dutch Petroleum, which is listed on the NYSE. U.S. investors also can invest in foreign companies through **American Depository Receipts (ADRs)**, which are certificates representing ownership of foreign stock held in trust. About 1,700 ADRs are now available in the United States, with most of them traded on the over-the-counter (OTC) market. However, more and more ADRs are being listed on the New York Stock Exchange, including England's British Airways, Japan's Honda Motors, and Italy's Fiat Group.

American Depository Receipts (ADRs)
Certificates representing ownership of foreign stock held in trust.

SELF TEST

What are the three major types of international credit markets?

What is LIBOR?

What are ADRs?

19-10 INVESTING OVERSEAS

Investors should consider additional risk factors if they invest overseas. First, there is **country risk**, which refers to the risk involved in investing in a particular country. This risk depends on the country's economic, political, and social environment. Some countries provide a safer investment climate and therefore less country risk than others. Examples of country risk include the risk that property will be expropriated without adequate compensation in addition to risks associated with changes in tax rates, regulations, and currency repatriation. Country risk also includes changes in host-country requirements regarding local production and employment as well as the danger of damage due to internal strife, ranging from crippling strikes to terrorism and civil war.

It is especially important to keep in mind when investing overseas that securities are often denominated in a currency other than the dollar, which means that returns on the investment depend on what happens to exchange rates. This is known as **exchange rate risk**. For example, if a U.S. investor purchases a Japanese bond, interest will probably be paid in yen, which must then be converted into dollars before the investor can spend his or her money in the United States. If the yen weakens relative to the dollar, it will buy fewer dollars; hence, fewer dollars will be received when funds are repatriated. However, if the yen strengthens, the effective investment return will increase. It therefore follows that returns on a foreign investment depend on the in-country performance of the foreign security and on changes in exchange rates.

Country Risk
The risk that arises from investing or doing business in a particular country.

Exchange Rate Risk
The risk that exchange rate changes will reduce the number of dollars provided by a given amount of a foreign currency.

SELF TEST

What is country risk?

What is exchange rate risk?

On what two factors does the return on a foreign investment depend?

GLOBAL PERSPECTIVES

MEASURING COUNTRY RISK

Various forecasting services measure the level of country risk in different countries and provide indexes that indicate factors such as each country's expected economic performance, access to world capital markets, political stability, and level of internal conflict. Country risk analysts use sophisticated models to measure risk, thus providing corporate managers and investors with a way to judge both the relative and absolute risk of investing in different countries. A sample of recent country risk estimates compiled by *Institutional Investor* is presented in the accompanying table. The higher a country's score, the lower its country risk. The maximum possible score is 100.

Rank	Country	Total Score
1	Switzerland	96.4
7	Germany	94.8
11	France	94.1
12	United Kingdom	94.0
13	United States	93.8
17	Japan	91.4
29	South Korea	79.9
33	Chile	77.4
34	China	76.5
44	Russia	69.4

Rank	Country	Total Score
46	Mexico	69.3
52	South Africa	65.8
55	India	62.7
60	Brazil	60.6
70	Turkey	52.0
84	Argentina	41.9
92	Iran	35.7
118	Tanzania	27.9
161	Iraq	13.9
174	Zimbabwe	5.8

The countries with the least country risk have strong market-based economies, ready access to worldwide capital markets, relatively little social unrest, a stable political climate, relatively low inflation, and a sound currency. Switzerland's top ranking may surprise you, but that country's ranking is the result of its strong economic performance and political stability. You also may be surprised that the United States was ranked 13th. At the lower end of the range, there are fewer surprises. Each of those countries has considerable social and political unrest and no market-based economic system. An investment in any of these countries is clearly a risky proposition.

Source: Excerpted from Harvey P. Shapiro, "Feeling the U.S.'s Pain," *Institutional Investor,* March 2008, pp. 107–110.

GLOBAL PERSPECTIVES

INVESTING IN INTERNATIONAL STOCKS

The U.S. stock market represents approximately 35% of the world stock market; and as a result, many U.S. investors hold at least some foreign stock. Analysts have long touted the benefits of investing overseas, arguing that foreign stocks improve diversification and provide good growth opportunities.

When investing in international stocks, you need to recognize that you are investing in both the foreign *market* and the foreign *currency.* Table 19-4 indicates how stocks in each country performed in 2007. Column 2 indicates how stocks in each country performed in terms of the U.S. dollar, while Column 3 shows how the country's stocks performed in terms of its local currency. For example, in 2007, Brazilian stocks rose by 42.6%, but the Brazilian real increased by about 20% versus the U.S. dollar. Therefore, if a U.S. investor had bought Brazilian stocks, he or she would have made 42.6% in Brazilian real terms; but those Brazilian reals would have bought 20% more U.S. dollars, so the effective return would have been 71.1%. Thus, the results of foreign investments depend on the foreign market and on what happens to the exchange rate. Indeed, when you invest overseas, you are making two bets: (1) that foreign stocks will increase in their local markets and (2) that the currencies in which you will be paid will rise relative to the dollar. For Brazil and most of the other countries shown in Table 19-4, both of those factors were favorable in 2007.

(Continued)

Table 19-4	Dow Jones Global Stock Indexes in 2007 (Ranked by Performance in U.S.-Dollar Terms)	
Country	**Return in U.S. Dollars**	**Return in Local Currency**
Brazil	+71.1%	+42.6%
Malaysia	+44.6	+35.5
Hong Kong	+44.5	+44.9
Thailand	+39.0	+29.5
Indonesia	+39.0	+45.1
Finland	+39.0	+25.3
Philippines	+36.7	+15.1
South Korea	+33.6	+34.5
Germany	+30.5	+17.7
Greece	+29.8	+17.1
Singapore	+27.6	+19.7
Canada	+27.1	+7.8
Norway	+26.8	+10.6
Australia	+25.3	+12.4
Portugal	+24.5	+12.3
Chile	+23.0	+15.1
Spain	+17.8	+6.2
Denmark	+17.6	+6.1
Iceland	+13.1	−0.2
South Africa	+12.6	+9.1
Netherlands	+12.0	+1.0
France	+11.3	+0.4
Mexico	+10.8	+11.7
Taiwan	+6.5	+6.0
Belgium	+5.6	−4.7
Switzerland	+5.6	−2.0
United Kingdom	+3.8	+2.1
United States	+3.8	+3.8
New Zealand	+2.2	−6.4
Italy	+1.7	−8.3
Austria	+1.6	−8.4
Sweden	−3.1	−8.5
Japan	−6.0	−11.9
Ireland	−19.2	−27.1
World	+8.4	—
World except U.S.	+11.8	—

Source: "Ups and Downs Around the World," *The Wall Street Journal*, January 2, 2008, p. R4.

19-11 INTERNATIONAL CAPITAL BUDGETING

Up to now, we have discussed the general environment in which multinational firms operate. In the remainder of the chapter, we discuss how international factors affect key corporate decisions. We begin with capital budgeting. Although the same basic principles of capital budgeting apply to both foreign and domestic operations, there are some key differences. First, cash flow estimation is more complex for overseas investments. Most multinational firms set up separate subsidiaries for each foreign country in which they operate, and the relevant cash flows for the parent company are the dividends and royalties paid by the subsidiaries to the parent. Second, these cash flows must be converted into the parent company's currency, so they are subject to exchange rate risk. For example, General Motors' German subsidiary may make a profit of 100 million euros in 2008, but the value of this profit to GM will depend on the dollar/euro exchange rate: How many *dollars* will 100 million euros buy?

Dividends and royalties are normally taxed by both foreign and home-country governments. Furthermore, a foreign government may restrict the **repatriation of earnings** to the parent company. For example, some governments place a ceiling, often stated as a percentage of the company's net worth, on the amount of cash dividends that a subsidiary can pay to its parent. Such restrictions are normally intended to force multinational firms to reinvest earnings in the foreign country, although restrictions are sometimes imposed to prevent large currency outflows that might disrupt the exchange rate.

Repatriation of Earnings
The process of sending cash flows from a foreign subsidiary back to the parent company.

Whatever the host country's motivation for blocking repatriation of profits, the result is that the parent corporation cannot use cash flows blocked in the foreign country to pay dividends to its shareholders or to invest elsewhere in the business. Hence, from the perspective of the parent organization, *the cash flows that are relevant for foreign investment analysis are those that the subsidiary is actually expected to send back to the parent*. The present value of those cash flows is found by applying an appropriate discount rate, and this present value is then compared with the parent's required investment to determine the project's NPV.

In addition to the complexities of the cash flow analysis, *the cost of capital may be different for a foreign project than for an equivalent domestic project because foreign projects may be more or less risky*. Higher risks might arise from (1) exchange rate risk and (2) political risk. A lower risk might result from the benefits of international diversification.

The foreign currency cash flows to be turned over to the parent must be converted into U.S. dollars by translating them at expected future exchange rates. An analysis should be conducted to ascertain the effects of exchange rate variations; and on the basis of this analysis, an exchange rate risk premium should be added to the domestic cost of capital to reflect this risk. It is sometimes possible to hedge against exchange rate fluctuations; but this may not be possible, especially on long-term projects. If hedging is used, the costs of doing so must be subtracted from the project's cash flows.

Political risk refers to potential actions by a host government that would reduce the value of a company's investment. It includes at one extreme the expropriation without compensation of the subsidiary's assets; but it also includes less drastic actions that reduce the value of the parent firm's investment in the foreign subsidiary, including higher taxes, tighter repatriation or currency controls, and restrictions on prices charged. The risk of expropriation is small in traditionally friendly and stable countries such as Great Britain and Switzerland. However, in Latin America, Africa, the Far East, and Eastern Europe, the risk may be substantial. Past expropriations include those of ITT and Anaconda Copper in Chile; Gulf Oil in Bolivia; Occidental Petroleum in Libya; and the assets of many companies in Iraq, Iran, and Cuba.

Political Risk
Potential actions by a host government that would reduce the value of a company's investment.

Note that companies can take several steps to reduce the potential loss from expropriation: (1) finance the subsidiary with local capital, (2) structure operations so that the subsidiary has value only as a part of the integrated corporate system, and (3) obtain insurance against economic losses due to expropriation from a source such as the Overseas Private Investment Corporation (OPIC). In the latter case, insurance premiums would have to be added to the project's cost.

Several organizations rate the country risk, or the risk associated with investing in a particular country. These ratings are based on the country's social, political, and economic environment—its **business climate**. Perhaps surprisingly, many of these studies suggest that the United States does not have the lowest level of country risk. This is particularly significant because even though people in the United States often assume that its bonds have no country risk, others do not agree. Foreign investors are concerned about how changes in U.S. policies (e.g., tax or Federal Reserve policies) might affect their investments. To the extent that these perceptions about U.S. country risk influence investors' willingness to hold U.S. securities, they will have an effect on U.S. interest rates.

SELF TEST

List some key differences in capital budgeting as applied to foreign versus domestic operations.

What are the relevant cash flows for an international investment—the cash flows produced by the subsidiary in the country in which it operates or the cash flows in dollars that it sends to its parent company? Explain.

Why might the cost of capital for a foreign project differ from that of an equivalent domestic project? Could it be lower? Explain.

What adjustments might be made to the domestic cost of capital for a foreign investment due to exchange rate risk, political risk, and country risk?

19-12 INTERNATIONAL CAPITAL STRUCTURES

Capital structures vary across countries. For example, the Organization for Economic Cooperation and Development (OECD) recently reported that, on average, Japanese firms have 85% debt to total assets (in book value terms), German firms have 64%, and U.S. firms have 55%. One problem, however, when interpreting these numbers is that different countries often use different accounting conventions with regard to (1) reporting assets on a historical-cost versus a replacement-cost basis, (2) treating leased assets, (3) reporting pension plan liabilities, and (4) capitalizing versus expensing R&D costs. These differences make it difficult to compare capital structures.

A study by Raghuram Rajan and Luigi Zingales of the University of Chicago attempted to control for different accounting practices. In their study, Rajan and Zingales used a database that covers fewer firms than the OECD but one that provides a more complete breakdown of balance sheet data. They concluded that differences in accounting practices can explain much but not all of the cross-country variations.

Rajan and Zingales's results are summarized in Table 19-5. There are a number of different ways to measure capital structure. One way is the average ratio of total liabilities to total assets—this is similar to the measure used by the OECD, and it is reported in Column 1. Based on this measure, German and Japanese firms appear to be more highly leveraged than U.S. firms. However, if you look at Column 2, where capital structure is measured by interest-bearing debt to total assets, it appears that German firms use less leverage than U.S. and Japanese firms. What explains this difference? Rajan and Zingales argue that much of this difference is explained by the way German firms account for pension liabilities. German firms generally include all pension liabilities (and their offsetting assets) on the balance sheet, whereas firms in other countries (including the United States) generally "net out" pension assets and liabilities on their balance sheets. To see the importance of this difference, consider a firm with $10 million in liabilities (not including pension liabilities) and

Table 19-5	**Median Capital Structures among Large Industrialized Countries (Measured in Terms of Book Value)**				
Country	**Total Liabilities to Total Assets (Unadjusted for Accounting Differences) (1)**	**Debt to Total Assets (Unadjusted for Accounting Differences) (2)**	**Total Liabilities to Total Assets (Adjusted for Accounting Differences) (3)**	**Debt to Total Assets (Adjusted for Accounting Differences) (4)**	**Times Interest Earned (TIE) Ratio (5)**
Canada	56%	32%	48%	32%	1.55x
France	71	25	69	18	2.64
Germany	73	16	50	11	3.20
Italy	70	27	68	21	1.81
Japan	69	35	62	21	2.46
United Kingdom	54	18	47	10	4.79
United States	58	27	52	25	2.41
Mean	64%	26%	57%	20%	2.69×
Standard deviation	8%	7%	10%	8%	1.07×

Source: Raghuram Rajan and Luigi Zingales, "What Do We Know about Capital Structure? Some Evidence from International Data," *Journal of Finance,* Vol. 50, no. 5 (December 1995), pp. 1421–1460. Used with permission.

$20 million in assets (not including pension assets). Assume that the firm has $10 million in pension liabilities that are fully funded by $10 million in pension assets. Therefore, net pension liabilities are zero. If this firm was in the United States, it would report a ratio of total liabilities to total assets equal to 50% ($10 million/$20 million). By contrast, if this firm operated in Germany, both its pension assets and liabilities would be reported on the balance sheet. The firm would have $20 million in liabilities and $30 million in assets—or a 67% ($20 million/$30 million) ratio of total liabilities to total assets. Total debt is the sum of short-term debt and long-term debt and excludes other liabilities including pension liabilities. Therefore, the measure of total debt to total assets provides a more comparable measure of leverage across different countries.

Rajan and Zingales also make a variety of adjustments that attempt to control for other differences in accounting practices. The effects of these adjustments are reported in Columns 3 and 4. Overall, the evidence suggests that companies in Germany and the United Kingdom tend to have less leverage, whereas firms in Canada appear to have more leverage relative to firms in the United States, France, Italy, and Japan. This conclusion is supported by data in the final column, which shows the average times-interest-earned ratio for firms in a number of different countries. Recall from Chapter 4 that the TIE ratio is the ratio of operating income (EBIT) to interest expense. This measure indicates how much cash the firm has available to service its interest expense. In general, firms with more leverage have a lower times-interest-earned ratio. The data indicate that this ratio is highest in the United Kingdom and Germany and lowest in Canada.

SELF TEST   Do international differences in financial leverage exist? Explain.

TYING IT ALL TOGETHER

Over the past two decades, the global economy has become increasingly integrated and more companies generate more of their profits from overseas operations. In many respects, the concepts developed in the first 18 chapters still apply to multinational firms. However, multinational companies have more opportunities but also face different risks than do companies that operate only in their home market. The chapter discussed many of the key trends affecting the global markets today, and it described the most important differences between multinational and domestic financial management.

SELF-TEST QUESTIONS AND PROBLEMS
(Solutions Appear in Appendix A)

ST-1 **KEY TERMS** Define each of the following terms:

a. Multinational, or global, corporation

b. Vertically integrated investment

c. International monetary system

d. Exchange rate

e. Freely-floating regime; managed-float regime

f. Currency board arrangement

g. Fixed-peg arrangement

h. Cross rate

i. American terms; European terms

j. Direct quotation; indirect quotation

k. Spot rate; forward exchange rate

l. Discount on forward rate; premium on forward rate

m. Interest rate parity; purchasing power parity

n. Eurocredits; Eurodollar

o. Eurobond; foreign bond

p. American Depository Receipts (ADRs); repatriation of earnings

q. Country risk; exchange rate risk; political risk; business climate

ST-2 **CROSS RATES** Suppose the exchange rate between the U.S. dollar and the EMU euro is €0.65 = $1.00 and the exchange rate between the U.S. dollar and the Canadian dollar is $1.00 = C$0.98. What is the cross rate of euros to Canadian dollars?

QUESTIONS

19-1 Why do U.S. corporations build manufacturing plants abroad when they can build them at home?

19-2 If the euro depreciates against the U.S. dollar, can a dollar buy more or fewer euros as a result?

19-3   If the United States imports more goods from abroad than it exports, foreigners will tend to have a surplus of U.S. dollars. What will this do to the value of the dollar with respect to foreign currencies? What is the corresponding effect on foreign investments in the United States?

19-4   Should firms require higher rates of return on foreign projects than on identical projects located at home? Explain.

19-5   Does interest rate parity imply that interest rates are the same in all countries?

19-6   Why might purchasing power parity fail to hold?

19-7   What is a Eurodollar? If a French citizen deposits $10,000 in Chase Manhattan Bank in New York, have Eurodollars been created? What if the deposit is made in Barclay's Bank in London? Chase Manhattan's Paris branch? Does the existence of the Eurodollar market make the Federal Reserve's job of controlling U.S. interest rates easier or more difficult? Explain.

PROBLEMS

Easy Problems 1–4

19-1   **EXCHANGE RATE**   If British pounds sell for $2 (U.S.) per pound, what should dollars sell for in pounds per dollar?

19-2   **CROSS RATE**   A currency trader observes that in the spot exchange market, 1 U.S. dollar can be exchanged for 3.50 Israeli shekels or for 104.00 Japanese yen. What is the cross-exchange rate between the yen and the shekel; that is, how many yen would you receive for every shekel exchanged?

19-3   **INTEREST RATE PARITY**   Six-month T-bills have a nominal rate of 7%, while default-free Japanese bonds that mature in 6 months have a nominal rate of 5.5%. In the spot exchange market, 1 yen equals $0.009. If interest rate parity holds, what is the 6–month forward exchange rate?

19-4   **PURCHASING POWER PARITY**   A television costs $500 in the United States. The same television costs 312.5 euros. If purchasing power parity holds, what is the spot exchange rate between the euro and the dollar?

Intermediate Problems 5–11

19-5   **EXCHANGE RATES**   Table 19-1 lists foreign exchange rates for May 26, 2008. On that day, how many dollars would be required to purchase 1,000 units of each of the following: British pounds, Canadian dollars, EMU euros, Japanese yen, Mexican pesos, and Swedish kronas?

19-6   **EXCHANGE RATES**   Use the foreign exchange section of a current issue of *The Wall Street Journal* to look up the six currencies in Problem 19-5.

   a.   What is the current exchange rate for changing dollars into 1,000 units of pounds, Canadian dollars, euros, yen, Mexican pesos, and Swedish kronas?

   b.   What is the percentage gain or loss between the May 26, 2008, exchange rate and the current exchange rate for each of the currencies in Part a?

19-7   **CURRENCY APPRECIATION**   Suppose that 1 Danish krone could be purchased in the foreign exchange market today for $0.20. If the krone appreciated 10% tomorrow against the dollar, how many krones would a dollar buy tomorrow?

19-8   **CROSS RATES**   Suppose the exchange rate between the U.S. dollar and the Swedish krona was 6 krona = $1 and the exchange rate between the dollar and the British pound was £1 = $2. What was the exchange rate between Swedish kronas and pounds?

19-9   **CROSS RATES**   Use the foreign exchange section of a current issue of *The Wall Street Journal* to look up the three currencies in Problem 19-8. What is the current exchange rate between Swedish kronas and pounds?

19-10   **INTEREST RATE PARITY**   Assume that interest rate parity holds. In both the spot market and the 90-day forward market, 1 Japanese yen = 0.0086 dollar. And 90-day risk-free securities yield 4.6% in Japan. What is the yield on 90-day risk-free securities in the United States?

19-11   **PURCHASING POWER PARITY**   In the spot market, 10.5 Mexican pesos can be exchanged for 1 U.S. dollar. A compact disc costs $15 in the United States. If purchasing power parity (PPP) holds, what should be the price of the same disc in Mexico?

Challenging Problems 12–17

19-12   **INTEREST RATE PARITY**   Assume that interest rate parity holds and that 90-day risk-free securities yield 5% in the United States and 5.3% in Britain. In the spot market, 1 pound = $2.

a.   Is the 90-day forward rate trading at a premium or a discount relative to the spot rate?

b.   What is the 90-day forward rate?

19-13   **SPOT AND FORWARD RATES**   Chamberlain Canadian Imports has agreed to purchase 15,000 cases of Canadian beer for 4 million Canadian dollars at today's spot rate. The firm's financial manager, James Churchill, has noted the following current spot and forward rates:

	U.S. Dollar/Canadian Dollar	Canadian Dollar/U.S. Dollar
Spot	1.0526	0.9500
30-day forward	1.0504	0.9520
90-day forward	1.0471	0.9550
180-day forward	1.0444	0.9575

On the same day, Churchill agrees to purchase 15,000 more cases of beer in 3 months at the same price of 4 million Canadian dollars.

a.   What is the price of the beer in U.S. dollars if it is purchased at today's spot rate?

b.   What is the cost in U.S. dollars of the second 15,000 cases if payment is made in 90 days and the spot rate at that time equals today's 90-day forward rate?

c.   If the exchange rate for the Canadian dollar is 0.90 to $1 in 90 days, how much will Churchill have to pay for the beer (in U.S. dollars)?

19-14   **EXCHANGE GAINS AND LOSSES**   You are the vice president of International InfoXchange, headquartered in Chicago, Illinois. All shareholders of the firm live in the United States. Earlier this month you obtained a loan of 5 million Canadian dollars from a bank in Toronto to finance the construction of a new plant in Montreal. At the time the loan was received, the exchange rate was $1.05 to the Canadian dollar. By the end of the month, it has unexpectedly dropped to 95 cents. Has your company made a gain or a loss as a result, and by how much?

19-15   **RESULTS OF EXCHANGE RATE CHANGES**   Early in September 1983, it took 245 Japanese yen to equal $1. Nearly 25 years later, in May 2008, that exchange rate had fallen to 103.5 yen to $1. Assume that the price of a Japanese-manufactured automobile was $9,000 in September 1983 and that its price changes were in direct relation to exchange rates.

a.   Has the price, in dollars, of the automobile increased or decreased during the 25-year period because of changes in the exchange rate?

b.   What would the dollar price of the automobile be in May 2008, again assuming that the car's price changes only with exchange rates?

19-16   **FOREIGN INVESTMENT ANALYSIS**   After all foreign and U.S. taxes, a U.S. corporation expects to receive 3 pounds of dividends per share from a British subsidiary this year. The exchange rate at the end of the year is expected to be $2 per pound, and the pound is expected to depreciate 5% against the dollar each year for an indefinite period. The dividend (in pounds) is expected to grow at 10% a year indefinitely. The parent U.S. corporation owns 10 million shares of the subsidiary. What is the present value in dollars of its equity ownership of the subsidiary? Assume a cost of equity capital of 15% for the subsidiary.

19-17   **FOREIGN CAPITAL BUDGETING**   Solitaire Machinery is a Swiss multinational manufacturing company. Currently, Solitaire's financial planners are considering undertaking a 1-year project in the United States. The project's expected dollar-denominated cash flows consist of an initial investment of $1,000 and a cash inflow the following year of $1,200. Solitaire estimates that its risk-adjusted cost of capital is 14%. Currently, 1 U.S. dollar will buy 1.025 Swiss francs. In addition, 1-year risk-free securities in the United States are yielding 7.25%, while similar securities in Switzerland are yielding 4.5%.

a.   If this project was instead undertaken by a similar U.S.-based company with the same risk-adjusted cost of capital, what would be the net present value and rate of return generated by this project?

b.   What is the expected forward exchange rate 1 year from now?

c.   If Solitaire undertakes the project, what is the net present value and rate of return of the project for Solitaire?

COMPREHENSIVE/SPREADSHEET PROBLEM

19-18   **MULTINATIONAL FINANCIAL MANAGEMENT**   Yohe Telecommunications is a multinational corporation that produces and distributes telecommunications technology. Although its corporate headquarters are located in Maitland, Florida, Yohe usually buys its raw materials in several different foreign countries using several different foreign currencies. The matter is further complicated because Yohe often sells its products in other foreign countries. One product in particular, the SY-20 radio transmitter, draws Component X, Component Y, and Component Z (its principal components) from Switzerland, France, and England, respectively. Specifically, Component X costs 165 Swiss francs, Component Y costs 20 euros, and Component Z costs 105 British pounds. The largest market for the SY-20 is Japan, where the product sells for 42,000 Japanese yen. Naturally, Yohe is intimately concerned with economic conditions that could adversely affect dollar exchange rates. You will find Tables 19-1, 19-2, and 19-3 useful for completing this problem.

a.   How much in dollars does it cost Yohe to produce the SY-20? What is the dollar sale price of the SY-20?

b.   What is the dollar profit that Yohe makes on the sale of the SY-20? What is the percentage profit?

c.   If the U.S. dollar was to weaken by 10% against all foreign currencies, what would be the dollar profit for the SY-20?

d.   If the U.S. dollar was to weaken by 10% only against the Japanese yen and remained constant relative to all other foreign currencies, what would be the dollar and percentage profits for the SY-20?

e.   Using the 180-day forward exchange information from Table 19-3, calculate the return on 1-year securities in Switzerland assuming the rate of return on 1-year securities in the United States is 4.9%.

f.   Assuming that purchasing power parity (PPP) holds, what would be the sale price of the SY-20 if it was sold in England rather than Japan?

INTEGRATED CASE

CITRUS PRODUCTS INC.

19-19   **MULTINATIONAL FINANCIAL MANAGEMENT**   Citrus Products Inc. is a medium-sized producer of citrus juice drinks with groves in Indian River County, Florida. Until now, the company has confined its operations and sales to the United States; but its CEO, George Gaynor, wants to expand into the Pacific Rim. The first step is to set up sales subsidiaries in Japan and Australia, then to set up a production plant in Japan, and finally to distribute the product throughout the Pacific Rim. The firm's financial manager, Ruth Schmidt, is enthusiastic about the plan; but she is worried about the implications of the foreign expansion on the firm's financial management process. She has asked you, the firm's most recently hired financial analyst, to develop a 1-hour tutorial package that explains the basics of multinational financial management. The tutorial will be presented at the next board of directors meeting. To get you started, Schmidt has given you the following list of questions.

a.   What is a multinational corporation? Why do firms expand into other countries?

b.   What are the five major factors that distinguish multinational financial management from financial management as practiced by a purely domestic firm?

c.   Consider the following illustrative exchange rates:

	U.S. Dollars Required to Buy One Unit of Foreign Currency
Japanese yen	0.009
Australian dollar	0.650

(1) Are these currency prices direct quotations or indirect quotations?

(2) Calculate the indirect quotations for yen and Australian dollars.

(3) What is a cross rate? Calculate the two cross rates between yen and Australian dollars.

(4) Assume that Citrus Products can produce a liter of orange juice and ship it to Japan for $1.75. If the firm wants a 50% markup on the product, what should the orange juice sell for in Japan?

(5) Now assume that Citrus Products begins producing the same liter of orange juice in Japan. The product costs 250 yen to produce and ship to Australia, where it can be sold for 6 Australian dollars. What is the U.S. dollar profit on the sale?

(6) What is exchange rate risk?

d. Briefly describe the current international monetary system. What are the different types of exchange rate systems?

e. What is the difference between spot rates and forward rates? When is the forward rate at a premium to the spot rate? at a discount?

f. What is interest rate parity? Currently, you can exchange 1 yen for 0.0095 U.S. dollar in the 30-day forward market, and the risk-free rate on 30-day securities is 4% in both Japan and the United States. Does interest rate parity hold? If not, which securities offer the highest expected return?

g. What is purchasing power parity (PPP)? If grapefruit juice costs $2 a liter in the United States and purchasing power parity holds, what should be the price of grapefruit juice in Australia?

h. What effect does relative inflation have on interest rates and exchange rates?

i. (1) Briefly explain the three major types of international credit markets.

(2) Briefly explain how ADRs work.

j. To what extent do average capital structures vary across different countries?

k. What is the effect of multinational operations on capital budgeting decisions?

CHRIS KLEPONIS/Bloomberg News/Landov

CHAPTER 20

Hybrid Financing: Preferred Stock, Leasing, Warrants, and Convertibles

Now Enticing: Convertible Securities

Convertible bonds and preferred stocks make fixed interest or dividend payments but can be exchanged at the holder's option for a given number of shares of common stock. For example, in April 2008, CIT Corporation, a multi-billion dollar financial company, sold $558 million of preferred stock with an 8.75% coupon. The holder of the preferred could convert it into 79 shares of the common stock per $1,000 of par value. The "conversion price," or effective price a convertible holder would be paying for the common, was $1,000/79 = $12.65. Therefore, if the common, which sold for $11 per share when the preferred was issued, rises above $12.65 per share, holders of the preferred can earn a capital gain by converting. If CIT had used straight preferred stock (i.e., stock without the conversion option), a dividend rate of about 13% would have been required. Therefore, the conversion option lowered the company's cash dividend requirement by a substantial amount.

Companies such as CIT use convertibles for two main reasons. First, they can obtain funds with lower required cash payments. Second, CIT's conversion price was set at 15% above the price of the common stock on the issue date, which means that common will, in effect, be sold at a price that is 15% above what it would have brought on the issue date. CIT's stock had fallen from $60 to $11 per share in the 12 months before this issue, and management believed that the stock was well below its intrinsic value. Therefore, management wanted to get equity at the highest possible price to avoid further dilution. Fannie Mae, the world's largest mortgage company; Bank of America; and many other financial institutions also used convertibles in 2008 to raise the cash needed to continue operations.

Who purchases convertibles? Historically, convertibles were bought by individuals who wanted securities that were less risky than the issuing company's common stock but that provided a higher expected return than the issuer's straight debt or preferred stock. Unless CIT's fortunes take a further turn for the worse, a holder of its convertibles will earn an 8.75% rate from the dividend plus an uncertain but perhaps positive capital gain from eventual conversion.

Individual investors still buy convertibles; but in 2008, the largest buyers were hedge funds engaged in arbitrage operations. A fund would buy a firm's convertibles and simultaneously short its common stock. If the stock rises or falls, the convertible also will rise or fall. Meanwhile, the hedge fund holder will collect the interest or dividend and, if things work out as expected, will earn a relatively high but safe return. Hedge funds use mathematical models, factoring in the prices of the securities, the coupon rate on the convertibles, and other variables. Investing in convertibles is getting increasingly complex; but when you finish this chapter, you should have a good understanding of what convertibles are, how they are valued, why a firm might choose to issue a convertible bond rather than straight debt or common stock, and how to make money by investing in these convertibles.

Sources: Tom Lauricella, "Now Enticing: Convertible Securities," *The Wall Street Journal*, May 16, 2008, p. C1; and "CIT Prices $1.5 Billion in Concurrent Offerings of Common Stock and Convertible Preferred," *Reuters*, April 22, 2008.

PUTTING THINGS IN PERSPECTIVE

In previous chapters, we examined common stocks and the various types of long-term debt. In this chapter, we examine four other types of long-term capital: (1) *preferred stock,* which is a hybrid security that represents a cross between debt and common equity; (2) *leasing,* which is used by financial managers as an alternative to borrowing to finance fixed assets; (3) *warrants,* which are derivative securities issued by firms to facilitate the issuance of some other type of security; and (4) *convertibles,* which combine the features of debt (or preferred stock) and warrants. When you finish this chapter, you should understand what these financing instruments are, how they can be used to raise capital efficiently and at a relatively low cost, and how investors should evaluate their use.

When you finish this chapter, you should be able to:

- Identify the basic features of preferred stock and explain its advantages and disadvantages.
- Differentiate among the types of leases, discuss the financial statement effects of leasing, and evaluate a lease.
- Explain what warrants are and how they are used and analyze their cost to the firm.
- Explain what convertibles are and how they are used and analyze their cost to the firm.

20-1 PREFERRED STOCK

Preferred stock is a hybrid—it is similar to bonds in some respects and to common stock in other ways. Accountants classify preferred stock as equity; hence, they show it on the balance sheet as an equity account. However, from a finance perspective, preferred stock lies somewhere between debt and common equity. It imposes a fixed charge. Thus, it increases the firm's financial leverage; yet omitting the preferred dividend does not force a company into bankruptcy. We describe the basic features of preferred, explain its advantages and disadvantages, and then discuss some different types of preferred.

20-1a Basic Features

Preferred stock has a par (or liquidating) value, often $25 or $100. The dividend is stated as a percentage of par, or as so many dollars per share, or both ways. For example, several years ago Klondike Paper Company sold 150,000 shares of $100 par value perpetual preferred stock for a total of $15 million. This preferred had a stated annual dividend of $12 per share, so the preferred dividend yield was $12/$100 = 0.12, or 12%, at the time of issue. The dividend was set when the stock was issued; it will not be changed in the future. Therefore, if the required rate of return on preferred, r_p, changes from 12% after the issue date—as it actually did—the market price of the preferred stock will increase or decrease. Currently, r_p for Klondike Paper's preferred is 9% and the price of the preferred has risen from $12/0.12 = $100 to $12/0.09 = $133.33.

If the preferred dividend is not earned, the company does not have to pay it. However, most preferred issues are **cumulative**, meaning that the total of all unpaid preferred dividends must be paid before dividends can be paid on the common stock. Unpaid preferred dividends are called **arrearages**. Dividends in arrears do not earn interest; thus, arrearages do not grow in a compound interest sense—they grow only from additional nonpayments of the preferred dividend. Also, many preferred stocks accrue arrearages for only a limited number of years (say, 3 years), meaning that the cumulative feature ceases after 3 years. However, the dividends in arrears continue in force until they are paid.

Preferred stock normally has no voting rights. However, most preferred issues stipulate that the preferred stockholders can elect a minority of the directors—say, three out of ten—if the preferred dividend is passed (omitted). Jersey Central Power & Light, one of the companies that owned a share of the Three Mile Island (TMI) nuclear plant, had preferred stock outstanding that could elect a *majority* of the directors if the preferred dividend was passed for four successive quarters. Jersey Central kept paying its preferred dividends even during the dark days following the TMI accident. Had the preferred not been entitled to elect a majority of the directors, the dividend probably would have been passed.

Although nonpayment of preferred dividends will not bankrupt a company, corporations issue preferred with every intention of paying the dividend. Even if passing the dividend does not give the preferred stockholders control of the company, failure to pay a preferred dividend precludes payment of common dividends. In addition, passing the dividend makes it difficult to raise capital by selling bonds and virtually impossible to sell more preferred or common stock. However, having preferred stock outstanding does give a firm the chance to overcome its difficulties—if bonds had been used instead of preferred stock, Jersey Central would have been in danger of being forced into bankruptcy before it had a chance to straighten out its problems. *Thus, from the viewpoint of the corporation, preferred stock is less risky than bonds.*

However, for investors, preferred stock is riskier than bonds: (1) Preferred stockholders' claims are subordinated to those of bondholders in the event of liquidation, and (2) bondholders are more likely to continue receiving income during hard times than are preferred stockholders. Accordingly, investors require a higher after-tax rate of return on a given firm's preferred stock than on its bonds. However, since 70% of preferred dividends is exempt from corporate taxes, preferred stock is attractive to corporate investors. In recent years, high-grade preferred stock, on average, has sold on a lower pretax yield basis than

Cumulative
A protective feature on preferred stock that requires preferred dividends previously not paid to be paid before any common dividends can be paid.

Arrearages
Unpaid preferred dividends.

high-grade bonds. As an example, BNC Inc.'s preferred stock recently had a market yield of about 5.4%, whereas its bonds provided a yield of 5.9%, or 0.5 percentage point *more* than its preferred. The tax treatment accounted for this differential; the *after-tax yield* to corporate investors was 4.83% on the preferred versus 3.84% on the bonds.[1]

About half of all preferred stock issued in recent years has been converted into common stock. As discussed in this chapter's opening vignette, in the spring of 2008, CIT Corporation issued $558 million of convertible preferred stock with an 8.75% annual dividend rate. The issue can be converted into common stock at the rate of 79 shares of common per $1,000 par value of preferred.

Some preferred stocks are similar to perpetual bonds in that they have no maturity date, but most new issues now have specified maturities. For example, many preferred shares have a sinking fund provision that calls for the retirement of 2% of the original issue each year, meaning that the issue will "mature" in a maximum of 50 years. Also, many preferred issues are callable by the issuing corporation, which also can limit the life of the preferred.[2]

Virtually all nonconvertible preferred stock is owned by corporations, which can take advantage of the 70% dividend exclusion to obtain a higher after-tax yield on preferred stock than on bonds. Individuals should not own preferred stocks (except convertible preferreds). Because they can get higher yields on safer bonds, it is not logical for them to hold preferreds. As a result of this ownership pattern, the volume of preferred stock financing is geared to the supply of money in the hands of corporate investors. When the supply of such money is plentiful, the prices of preferred stocks are bid up, their yields fall, and investment bankers suggest that companies that need financing consider issuing preferred stock.

For issuers, preferred stock has a tax *disadvantage* relative to debt—interest expense is deductible, but preferred dividends are not. Still, firms with low tax rates may have an incentive to issue preferred stock that can be bought by corporate investors with high tax rates, who can take advantage of the 70% dividend exclusion. If a firm has a lower tax rate than potential corporate buyers, the firm might be better off issuing preferred stock than debt. The key here is that the tax advantage to a high-tax-rate corporation is greater than the tax disadvantage to a low-tax-rate issuer. To illustrate, assume that risk differentials between debt and preferred would require an issuer to set the interest rate on new debt at 10% and the dividend yield on new preferred at 12% in a no-tax world. However, when taxes are considered, a corporate buyer with a high tax rate (say, 40%) might be willing to buy the preferred stock if it had an 8% before-tax yield. This would produce an $8\%(1 - \text{Effective T}) = 8\%[1 - 0.30(0.40)] = 7.04\%$ after-tax return on the preferred versus $10\%(1 - 0.40) = 6.0\%$ on the debt. If the issuer has a low tax rate (say, 10%), its after-tax costs would be $10\%(1 - T) = 10\%(0.90) = 9\%$ on the bonds and 8% on the preferred. Thus, the security with lower risk to the issuer, preferred

---

[1]The after-tax yield on a 5.9% bond to a corporate investor in the 35% marginal tax rate bracket is $5.9\%(1 - T) = 5.9\%(0.65) = 3.84\%$. The after-tax yield on a 5.4% preferred stock is $5.4\%(1 - \text{Effective T}) = 5.4\%[1 - (0.30)(0.35)] = 5.4\%(0.895) = 4.83\%$. Also note that tax law prohibits firms from issuing debt and then using the proceeds to purchase another firm's preferred or common stock. If debt is used for stock purchases, the 70% dividend exclusion will be voided. This provision is designed to prevent a firm from engaging in "tax arbitrage," using tax-deductible debt to purchase largely tax-exempt preferred stock.

[2]Prior to the late 1970s, virtually all preferred stock was perpetual and almost no issues had sinking funds or call provisions. Then insurance company regulators, worried about the unrealized losses the companies had been incurring on preferred holdings as a result of rising interest rates, put into effect some regulatory changes that essentially mandated that insurance companies buy only limited life preferreds. From that time on, virtually no new preferred has been perpetual. This example illustrates the way securities change as a result of changes in the economic environment.

stock, also has a lower cost. Such situations can make preferred stock a logical financing choice.[3]

20-1b Adjustable Rate Preferred Stock

In addition to the "plain vanilla" variety of preferred stocks, several variations also are used. One of these is **adjustable rate preferred stock,** which has dividends tied to the LIBOR rate, the rate on Treasury securities, or, in some instances, to periodic auctions. (See "A Good Idea That Went Bad: Auction Rate Preferred Stock (ARPS)," which follows, for more on auction rate preferreds.) Also, about half of all "regular, fixed rate" preferred stock issued in recent years has been converted into the issuing firm's common stock. See the section on convertibles later in this chapter for a more detailed discussion.

Adjustable Rate Preferred Stock
Preferred stock with a dividend that is adjusted at regular intervals.

20-1c Advantages and Disadvantages of Preferred Stock

There are advantages and disadvantages to financing with preferred stock. Here are the major advantages from the issuers' standpoint:

1. Passing a preferred dividend cannot force a firm into bankruptcy, whereas failure to pay interest on a bond can lead to bankruptcy.

2. By issuing preferred stock, the firm avoids the dilution of common equity that occurs when common stock is sold.

3. Since preferred stock sometimes has no maturity and since preferred sinking fund payments, if present, are typically spread over a long period, preferred issues can reduce the cash flow drain from repayment of principal that occurs with debt issues.

There are two major disadvantages:

1. Preferred stock dividends are not deductible to the issuer; consequently, the after-tax cost of preferred is typically higher than the after-tax cost of debt. However, the tax advantage of preferreds to corporate purchasers lowers its pretax cost and thus its effective cost.

2. Although preferred dividends can be passed, investors expect them to be paid and firms intend to pay the dividends if conditions permit. Thus, preferred dividends are considered a fixed cost. Therefore, their use, like that of debt, increases the firm's financial risk and thus its cost of common equity.

SELF TEST

Should preferred stock be considered as equity or debt? Explain.

Who are the major purchasers of "regular" preferred stock? How do tax considerations affect these purchases?

Briefly explain the mechanics of auction rate preferred stock. If you were buying an adjustable rate preferred stock, would you rather buy one whose rate was indexed to Treasury bonds or set in an auction? Explain.

What are the advantages and disadvantages of preferred stock from the perspective of its issuer?

---

[3]For a more rigorous treatment of the tax hypothesis of preferred stock, see Iraj Fooladi and Gordon S. Roberts, "On Preferred Stock," *Journal of Financial Research,* Winter 1986, pp. 319–324. For an example of an empirical test of the hypothesis, see Arthur L. Houston, Jr., and Carol Olson Houston, "Financing with Preferred Stock," *Financial Management,* Autumn 1990, pp. 42–54.

A GOOD IDEA THAT WENT BAD: AUCTION RATE PREFERRED STOCK (ARPS)[4]

Investment bankers created and began selling *auction rate preferred stock (ARPS)* in the 1980s. These securities pay interest that is determined at periodic auctions, generally weekly. They were promoted as being both ultrasafe and highly liquid. Indeed, potential investors were told that they were essentially equivalent to money market funds but with slightly higher rates.

Holders who wanted their cash could sell shares at the weekly auctions. Buyers would submit bids, indicating the yields they were willing to accept for the next weekly period. The yield for the next week was supposed to be the lowest rate sufficient to cause all of the shares offered to be sold (i.e., for the market to clear). For example, if the minimum yield required to sell all of the offered shares was 4.2%, all holders of the securities—those who retained their shares and the new purchasers—would receive the 4.2% rate for the coming week, which would be the cost to the issuer. However, to limit the cost to the issuer, the ARPS had a maximum rate, generally one based on a market index such as LIBOR. If the bids at or above the maximum rate were insufficient to permit all of the offered shares to be purchased, the auction would "fail." Then none of the offered shares would be sold, and those who wanted to cash out would simply be out of luck. After a failed auction, the rate was set at the maximum rate plus a penalty that was spelled out in the securities' prospectuses.

From the time ARPSs were first introduced until February 2008, no auction failed. This enabled investment banks and their brokers to promote the auctions as being safe and liquid. However, it turned out that auctions had been successful because the investment banks that underwrote the ARPS would step in and buy sufficient quantities to prevent failed auctions. But in 2008, the banks, facing liquidity problems due to the mortgage market meltdown, stopped buying and making the markets clear, which left investors holding some $360 billion of totally illiquid securities that were paying rates well below a "fair" market-clearing rate. Interestingly, some of the brokerages had large holdings of the ARPS in their own accounts prior to February 2008, but they reduced or eliminated their holdings shortly before the freeze.

Under SEC rules, purchasers of new securities must be provided with a prospectus, but buyers in the secondary market do not get one. The original buyers—who were exclusively institutional investors—received prospectuses and presumably studied them. However, since ARPSs are designed to be short-term investments, few if any of the holders in 2008 had ever seen a prospectus—they had simply relied on their brokers' representations that these securities were safe and liquid. Note though that brokers generally received higher commissions when they sold ARPS than when they placed funds in money funds, and brokerage firms earned higher fees on ARPS. Thus, brokers and their firms had an incentive to steer investors into ARPS. *BusinessWeek* reported that one man sold

his house; went to a bank to buy a CD to hold his funds temporarily; and was then sent from the CD department to the bank's brokerage division, which sold him $150,000 of ARPS.

All ARPS shares were not created equal. Almost all are safe in the sense of being creditworthy—they were AAA-rated and backed by high-grade assets. However, their auctions were conducted in different ways, and the penalty rates imposed if auctions failed differed radically. In some cases, the penalty rates were as high as 10%, while others were as low as 0.2% or 0.3%. The prospectuses spelled out these differences, but most holders in 2008 had never seen a prospectus, much less compared the ones for different ARPS. They simply bought whichever ARPS their broker recommended.

When ARPS were first offered, they generally had par values of $100,000 to $250,000, which was the minimum purchase size. Also, sales were initially limited to institutional investors, who received the relatively lengthy and complex prospectuses. As time went by, the shares were split, lowering the required minimum investment to $25,000, and brokers began to market them to the general public. Thus, what had originally been a reasonable security and marketing process was transformed into a highly questionable one.

As one might guess, investors have filed hundreds of arbitration cases and class action suits have been filed against all of the big Wall Street investment banks, ranging from Merrill Lynch and Citigroup to the Royal Bank of Canada. It's impossible to know how the ARPS problem will be resolved, but several points can be made:

- Wall Street is constantly trying to invent new securities with the goal of making more money. Those securities can turn out to be good or bad for investors.

- The ability to see what's actually involved with a security, or its *transparency,* is critically important. The investment banking firms provided transparency initially, but not in the ARPS market as it had evolved by 2008.

- Brokers and brokerage firms are in business to make money. Companies that issue ARPS want to hold down their costs, but investors want to earn high returns with little risk. This means that brokers and their firms have a *conflict of interest.* If they persuade their investor-customers to buy securities that pay low returns, the issuer-customers benefit; and if they can get issuers to sell securities that provide higher yields, investors benefit. The market is supposed to resolve such conflicts and to produce rates of return that are "fair" to all parties. However, the ARPS market in 2008 suggests that this doesn't always happen.

We don't know how the ARPS debacle will turn out. The matter will probably be resolved in the courts, not in the market; but it's a safe bet that investors will look more closely and ask more questions the next time their brokers offer them a new and "innovative" security.

---

[4]See Aaron Pressman, "Auction-Rate Securities: How to Get Unstuck," *BusinessWeek,* June 2, 2008, pp. 76–78, for a discussion of these securities.

20-2 LEASING

Firms generally own fixed assets and report them on their balance sheets; but it is the *use* of buildings and equipment that is important, not their ownership per se. One way of obtaining the use of assets is to buy them, but an alternative is to lease them. Leasing was originally associated with real estate—land and buildings. Today, however, it is possible to lease virtually any kind of fixed asset; and in 2008, about 30% of all new capital equipment acquired by businesses was leased.[5]

20-2a Types of Leases

Leasing takes three different forms: (1) *sale-and-leaseback* arrangements; (2) *operating leases*; and (3) straight *financial,* or *capital, leases.*

Sale and Leaseback

Under a **sale and leaseback,** a firm that owns land, buildings, or equipment sells the property and simultaneously executes an agreement to lease the property back for a specified period under specific terms. The purchaser could be an insurance company, a commercial bank, a specialized leasing company, or even an individual investor. The sale-and-leaseback plan is an alternative to taking out a mortgage loan.

The firm that is selling the property, or the **lessee,** immediately receives the purchase price put up by the buyer, or the **lessor.**[6] At the same time, the seller-lessee firm retains the use of the property as if it had borrowed and mortgaged the property to secure the loan. Note that under a mortgage arrangement, the financial institution would normally receive a series of equal payments that amortized the loan while providing a specified rate of return to the lender on the outstanding balance. Under a sale-and-leaseback arrangement, the lease payments are set up exactly the same way; the payments return the purchase price to the investor-lessor while providing a specified rate of return on the lessor's outstanding investment.

Sale and Leaseback
An arrangement whereby a firm sells land, buildings, or equipment and simultaneously leases the property back for a specified period under specific terms.

Lessee
The party that uses, rather than the one who owns, the leased property.

Lessor
The owner of the leased property.

Operating Leases

Operating leases, sometimes called *service leases,* provide for both *financing* and *maintenance.* IBM is one of the pioneers of the operating lease contract; and computers and office copying machines, together with automobiles and trucks, are the primary types of equipment involved. Ordinarily, these leases call for the lessor to maintain and service the leased equipment and the cost of providing maintenance is built into the lease payments.

Another important characteristic of operating leases is the fact that they are frequently *not fully amortized;* in other words, the payments required under the lease contract are not sufficient to recover the full cost of the equipment. However, the lease contract is written for a period considerably shorter than the expected economic life of the leased equipment; and the lessor expects to recover all investment costs through subsequent renewal payments, through subsequent leases to other lessees, or through the sale of the leased equipment.

A final feature of operating leases is that they frequently contain a *cancellation clause,* which gives the lessee the right to cancel the lease before the expiration of the basic agreement. This is important to the lessee, for it means that the equipment can be returned if it is rendered obsolete by technological developments or is no longer needed because of a decline in the lessee's business.

Operating Lease
A lease under which the lessor maintains and finances the property; also called a service lease.

---

[5]For a detailed treatment of leasing, see James S. Schallheim, *Lease or Buy? Principles for Sound Decision Making* (Boston: Harvard Business School Press, 1994).
[6]The term *lessee* is pronounced "less-ee," not "lease-ee"; *lessor* is pronounced "less-or."

Financial Lease

A lease that does not provide for maintenance services, is not cancelable, and is fully amortized over its life; also called a capital lease.

Financial, or Capital, Leases

Financial leases, sometimes called *capital leases,* are differentiated from operating leases in three respects: (1) They do *not* provide for maintenance services, (2) they are *not* cancelable, and (3) they *are* fully amortized (i.e., the lessor receives rental payments that are equal to the full price of the leased equipment plus a return on the investment). In a typical financial lease, the firm that will use the equipment (the lessee) selects the specific items it requires and negotiates the price and delivery terms with the manufacturer. The user firm then negotiates terms with a leasing company and once the lease terms are set, arranges to have the lessor buy the equipment from the manufacturer or the distributor. When the equipment is purchased, the user firm simultaneously signs the lease contract.

Financial leases are similar to sale-and-leaseback arrangements, the major difference being that the leased equipment is new and the lessor buys it from a manufacturer or a distributor instead of from the user-lessee. A sale and leaseback may thus be thought of as a special type of financial lease, and both sale and leasebacks and financial leases are analyzed in the same manner.[7]

20-2b Financial Statement Effects

Off Balance Sheet Financing

Financing in which the assets and liabilities involved do not appear on the firm's balance sheet.

Lease payments are shown as operating expenses on a firm's income statement; but under certain conditions, neither the leased assets nor the liabilities under the lease contract appears on the firm's balance sheet. For this reason, leasing is often called **off balance sheet financing**. This point is illustrated in Table 20-1 by the balance sheets of two hypothetical firms, B (for Buy) and L (for Lease). Initially, the balance sheets of both firms are identical, and both have debt ratios of 50%. Each firm then decides to acquire fixed assets that cost $100. Firm B borrows $100 to make the purchase; so both an asset and a liability are recorded on its balance sheet, and its debt ratio is increased to 75%. Firm L leases the equipment, so its balance sheet is unchanged. The lease may call for fixed charges as high as or even higher than those on the loan, and the obligations assumed under the lease may be equally or more dangerous from the standpoint of financial safety; but the firm's debt ratio remains at 50%.

SFAS #13

Statement of Financial Accounting Standards issued by the Financial Accounting Standards Board that details the conditions and procedures for capitalizing leases.

To correct this problem, the Financial Accounting Standards Board issued **SFAS #13**, which requires that for an unqualified audit report, firms that enter into financial (or capital) leases must restate their balance sheets to (1) report leased assets as fixed assets and (2) show the present value of future lease payments as liabilities. This process is called *capitalizing the lease,* and its net effect is to cause Firm L to report a balance sheet similar to that for Firm B after the asset increase.[8]

The logic behind SFAS #13 is simple. If a firm signs a lease contract, its obligation to make lease payments is just as binding as if it had signed a loan agreement. The failure to make lease payments can bankrupt a firm as surely as failure to make principal and interest payments on a loan. Therefore, for all intents

---

[7]For a lease transaction to qualify as a lease for *tax purposes,* and thus for the lessee to be able to deduct the lease payments, the life of the lease must not exceed 80% of the expected life of the asset and the lessee cannot be permitted to buy the asset at a nominal value. These conditions are IRS requirements, and they should not be confused with the FASB requirements discussed later in the chapter concerning the capitalization of leases. It is important to consult lawyers and accountants to ascertain whether a prospective lease meets current IRS regulations.

[8]SFAS #13, "Accounting for Leases," November 1976, spells out in detail the conditions under which leases must be capitalized and the procedures for doing so. Also, see Schallheim, *op. cit.,* Chapter 4, for more on the accounting treatment of leases. The FASB issued SFAS #157, "Fair Value Measurements," on September 15, 2006; however, SFAS #13 remains intact. FASB and IASB have put leasing on their agenda, and a preliminary view document that will review guidance under SFAS #13 is expected out late 2008/early 2009. So any decision on the international convergence project on leasing is still a ways off.

Table 20-1	Balance Sheet Effects of Leasing

BEFORE ASSET INCREASE				AFTER ASSET INCREASE							
Firms B and L				**Firm B, Which Borrows and Buys**				**Firm L, Which Leases**			
Current assets	$ 50	Debt	$ 50	Current assets	$ 50	Debt	$150	Current assets	$ 50	Debt	$ 50
Fixed assets	50	Equity	50	Fixed assets	150	Equity	50	Fixed assets	50	Equity	50
Total	$100		$100	Total	$200		$200	Total	$100		$100
	Debt ratio: 50%				Debt ratio: 75%				Debt ratio: 50%		

and purposes, a financial lease is identical to a loan.[9] That being the case, when a firm signs a lease agreement, it has, in effect, raised its "true" debt ratio and thereby has changed its "true" capital structure. Accordingly, if the firm had previously established a target capital structure and if there is no reason to think that the optimal capital structure has changed, then using lease financing requires additional equity just as debt financing does.

If disclosure of the lease in the Table 20-1 example is not made, investors could be deceived into thinking that Firm L's financial position is stronger than it actually is. Even if the lease was disclosed in a footnote, investors might not fully recognize its impact and might not see that Firms B and L are in essentially the same financial position. If this was the case, Firm L would have increased its true amount of debt through a lease arrangement; but its required returns on debt and equity, r_d and r_s, and consequently its weighted average cost of capital, would not have increased as much as those of Firm B, which borrowed directly. Thus, investors would be willing to accept a lower return from Firm L because they would mistakenly view it as being in a stronger financial position than Firm B. These benefits of leasing would accrue to stockholders at the expense of new investors, who were, in effect, being deceived by the fact that the firm's balance sheet did not fully reflect its true liability situation. That is why SFAS #13 was issued.

A lease must be classified as a capital lease—and hence be capitalized and shown directly on the balance sheet—if any one of the following conditions exists:

- Under the terms of the lease, ownership of the property is effectively transferred from the lessor to the lessee.

- The lessee can purchase the property or renew the lease at less than a fair market price when the lease expires.

- The lease runs for a period equal to or greater than 75% of the asset's life.

- The present value of the lease payments is equal to or greater than 90% of the initial value of the asset.[10]

---

[9]There are certain legal differences between loans and leases. In a bankruptcy liquidation, the lessor is entitled to take possession of the leased asset; and if the value of the asset is less than the required payments under the lease, the lessor can claim (as a general creditor) 1 year's lease payments. In a bankruptcy reorganization, the lessor receives the asset plus 3 years' lease payments, if needed, to bring the value of the asset up to the remaining investment in the lease. Under a secured loan arrangement, on the other hand, the lender has a security interest in the asset, meaning that if it is sold, the lender will be given the proceeds and the full unsatisfied portion of the lender's claim will be treated as a general creditor obligation. (See Web Appendix 7B.) It is not possible to state as a general rule whether a supplier of capital is in a stronger position as a secured creditor or as a lessor. Since one position is usually regarded as being about as good as the other at the time the financial arrangements are being made, a lease is about as risky as a secured term loan from both the lessor-lender's and the lessee-borrower's viewpoints.

[10]The discount rate used to calculate the present value of the lease payments must be the lower of (1) the rate used by the lessor to establish the lease payments or (2) the interest rate that the lessee would have paid for new debt with a maturity equal to that of the lease.

These rules, together with strong footnote disclosures for operating leases, are sufficient to ensure that no one will be fooled by lease financing. Thus, leases are recognized to be essentially the same as debt, and they have the same effects as debt on the firm's required rate of return. Therefore, leasing will not generally permit a firm to use more financial leverage than could be obtained with conventional debt.

20-2c Evaluation by the Lessee

Any prospective lease must be evaluated by the lessee and the lessor. The lessee must determine whether leasing an asset will be less costly than buying it, and the lessor must decide whether the lease will provide a reasonable rate of return. Since our focus is primarily on financial management as opposed to investments, we restrict our analysis to that conducted by the lessee.[11]

In the typical case, the events leading to a lease arrangement follow the sequence described in the following list. A great deal of theoretical literature exists about the correct way to evaluate lease-versus-purchase decisions, and some very complex decision models have been developed to aid in the analysis. The analysis given here, however, leads to the correct decision in every case we have encountered.

1. The firm decides to acquire a particular building or piece of equipment. This decision is based on regular capital budgeting procedures, and the decision to acquire the asset is a "done deal" before the lease analysis begins. Therefore, in a lease analysis, we are concerned simply with whether to finance the machine by a lease or by a loan.

2. Once the firm has decided to acquire the asset, the next question is how to finance it. Well-run businesses do not have excess cash lying around, so new assets must be financed in some manner.

3. Funds to purchase the asset could be obtained by borrowing, by retaining earnings, or by issuing new stock. Alternatively, the asset could be leased. Because of SFAS #13 capitalization/disclosure provisions for leases, a lease would have the same capital structure effect as a loan.

As indicated earlier, a lease is comparable to a loan in the sense that the firm must make a specified series of payments, and failure to make those payments may result in bankruptcy. Thus, it is most appropriate to compare the cost of leasing with that of debt financing.[12] The lease-versus-borrow-and-purchase analysis is illustrated with data on the Mitchell Electronics Company, and the following conditions are assumed:

1. Mitchell plans to acquire equipment with a 5-year life that has a cost of $10,000,000 delivered and installed.

2. Mitchell can borrow the required $10 million using a 10% loan to be amortized over 5 years.

3. Alternatively, Mitchell can lease the equipment for 5 years at a rental charge of $2,800,000 per year payable at the end of the year. The lessor will own the asset at the expiration of the lease.[13] The lease payment schedule is established by the potential lessor; and Mitchell can accept it, reject it, or negotiate the terms.

---

[11]The lessee is typically offered a set of lease terms by the lessor, which is generally a bank, a finance company such as GE Commercial Finance (the largest U.S. lessor), or some other institutional lender. The lessee can accept or reject the lease or shop around for a better deal. In this chapter, we take the lease terms as given for purposes of our analysis. See Chapter 19 of Eugene F. Brigham and Phillip R. Daves, *Intermediate Financial Management*, 9th ed. (Mason, OH: Thomson/South-Western, 2007), for a discussion of lease analysis from the lessor's standpoint, including a discussion of how a potential lessee can use such an analysis in bargaining for better terms.

[12]The analysis should compare the cost of leasing to the cost of debt financing *regardless* of how the asset is financed. The asset may be purchased with available cash if it is not leased; but because leasing is a substitute for debt financing, a comparison between the two is still appropriate.

[13]Lease payments can occur at the beginning of the year or at the end of the year. In this example, we assume end-of-year payments, but we demonstrate beginning-of-year payments in Self-Test Problem ST-2.

4. The equipment will be used for 5 years, at which time its estimated net salvage value will be $715,000. Mitchell plans to continue using the equipment beyond Year 5. So (1) if it purchases the equipment, the company will keep it; and (2) if it leases the equipment, the company will exercise an option to buy it at its estimated salvage value, $715,000.

5. The lease contract stipulates that the lessor will maintain the equipment. However, if Mitchell borrows and buys, it will have to bear the cost of maintenance. This service will be performed by the equipment manufacturer at a fixed contract rate, $500,000 per year, payable at year-end.

6. The equipment falls into the MACRS 5-year class life, and Mitchell's effective federal-plus-state tax rate is 40%. Also, the depreciable basis is the original cost of $10,000,000. The MACRS depreciation rates are 20%, 32%, 19%, 12%, 11%, and 6%.

NPV Analysis

Table 20-2 shows the cash flows that would be incurred each year under the two financing plans. The table is set up to produce two cash flow time lines, one for

| Table 20-2 | | Lease vs. Purchase Analysis (Dollars in Thousands) | | | | | | |

	A	B	C	D	E	F	G	H	I
36									
37	Inputs								
38	New equipment cost		$10,000		Tax rate		40%		
39	New equipment life		5		Loan interest rate		10%		
40	Salv. value = purch. option		$715		After-tax cost rate		6.0% = G39*(1 - G38)		
41	Annual maintenance		$500		Annual lease pymt		$2,800		
42									
43	Loan payments		$2,637.97 = -PMT(G39,C39,C38)						
44									
45	Depreciation			1	2	3	4	5	6
46	Depreciation rate			20%	32%	19%	12%	11%	6%
47	Depreciation expense			$2,000	$3,200	$1,900	$1,200	$1,100	$600
48	Depreciation tax savings = Deprn(T)*			800	1,280	760	480	440	240
49									
50	*Cost of Owning* Year =		0	1	2	3	4	5	
51	Net purchase price		($10,000)						
52	Maintenance cost			($500)	($ 500)	($500)	($500)	($500)	
53	Maint. Tax sav. = Maint.(T)			200	200	200	200	200	
54	Tax savings from deprn.			800	1,280	760	480	440	
55	Net cash flow		($10,000)	$500	$ 980	$460	$180	$140	
56	PV ownership cost @ 6%		($ 8,023)						
57									
58	*Cost of Leasing*								
59	Lease payment			($2,800)	($2,800)	($2,800)	($2,800)	($2,800)	
60	Tax saving = Lease pymt(T)			1,120	1,120	1,120	1,120	1,120	
61	Cost to purchase							(715)	
62	Net cash flow			($1,680)	($1,680)	($1,680)	($1,680)	($2,395)	
63	PV of leasing @ 6%		($7,611)						
64									
65	*Cost Comparison*								
66	PV ownership cost @ 6%			($8,023)					
67	PV of leasing @ 6%			($7,611)					
68	Net Advantage to Leasing (NAL)			$ 412	Leasing costs less, so lease should be done.				
69									
70	*Depreciation is a non-cash charge, so its only cash flow effect is the tax savings it provides.								

owning as shown on Row 55 and one for leasing as shown on Row 62. All cash flows occur at the end of the year.

The top section of the table (Rows 37 to 41) shows the inputs required for the analysis. Row 43 shows the loan payment required to amortize a $10 million loan at a 10% interest rate. It could be found with a calculator by inputting N = 5, I/YR = 10, PV = −10000, and FV = 0, with PMT = 2,637.97 (in thousands) or with Excel as we did in the table.

Depreciation and the tax savings resulting from it are shown on Rows 45 through 48. Next, Rows 50 through 56 show the cost of owning analysis, which represents the firm's borrowing and buying the equipment. Rows 51 through 54 show the individual cash flow items, and Row 55 is a time line that summarizes the annual net cash flows if Mitchell finances the equipment with a loan. The present values of these cash flows are found and shown on Row 56; they represent the *present value of the cost of owning*. (Note that we could do the same analysis with a financial calculator. We would input the cash flows as shown on Row 55 into the cash flow register; input the interest rate, I/YR = 6; and press the NPV key to obtain the PV cost of owning the equipment.)

On Rows 58 through 63, we calculate the present value cost of leasing. The lease payments are $2,800 (shown in thousands) per year. This payment, which in this example (but not in all cases) includes maintenance, was established by the prospective lessor and then offered to Mitchell Electronics. If Mitchell accepts the lease, the full amount of the lease payment will be a deductible expense, so the tax savings will be (Tax rate)(Lease payment) = (0.4)($2,800) = $1,120. These amounts are shown on Rows 59 and 60. Next, Row 61 shows the $715 that Mitchell will have to pay in Year 5 to purchase the equipment. We include this amount as a cost of leasing because Mitchell plans to continue the operation and thus will be forced to purchase the equipment from the lessor. If Mitchell did not plan to continue the operation, no entry would have appeared on this line, but we would have included the $715, minus any applicable taxes, as a Year 5 inflow in the cost of owning analysis. Row 62 shows the annual net cash flows associated with leasing, and Row 63 shows the PV cost of leasing. (As indicated earlier in the cost of owning analysis, using a financial calculator, we would input the cash flows as shown on Row 62 into the cash flow register, input the interest rate (I/YR = 6), and then press the NPV key to obtain the PV cost of leasing the equipment.)

The rate used to discount the cash flows is a critical issue. We know that the riskier a cash flow, the higher the discount rate used to find its present value. This principle applies in lease analysis. But just how risky are these cash flows? Most of them are relatively certain, at least when compared with the types of cash flow estimates used in capital budgeting analysis. For example, the lease, loan, and maintenance payments are set by contract, and the depreciation expenses are established by law and are not likely to change. The tax savings are somewhat uncertain because tax rates may change, but tax rates do not change very often. The $715 estimated salvage value is the least certain of the cash flows, but even here the estimate is based on historical experience.

Since the cash flows under both the lease and the borrow-and-purchase alternatives are reasonably certain, they should be discounted at a relatively low rate. Most analysts recommend that the company's cost of debt be used, and this rate seems reasonable in our example. Further, since all the cash flows are on an after-tax basis, *the after-tax cost of debt, which is 6%, should be used*. Accordingly, in Table 20-2, we used a 6% discount rate to obtain the present values. The financing method that results in the smaller present value of costs is the one that should be selected. In our example, leasing has a net advantage over buying: The present value of the cost of leasing is $412,000 less than that of buying, so Mitchell should lease.

20-2d Other Factors That Affect Leasing Decisions

The basic analysis set forth in Table 20-2 is sufficient to handle most situations. However, two factors warrant additional comments.

Estimated Residual Value

It is important to note that the lessor will own the property upon the expiration of the lease. The estimated end-of-lease salvage value is called the **residual value**. Superficially, it would appear that if estimated residual values are expected to be large, owning would have an advantage over leasing. However, if expected residual values are large—as they may be under inflation for certain types of equipment as well as for real property—competition among leasing companies will force leasing rates down to the point where potential residual values will be fully recognized in the lease contract rates. Thus, the existence of large residual values on equipment is not likely to bias the decision against leasing.

Residual Value
The value of leased property at the end of the lease term.

Increase Credit Availability

As noted in our earlier discussion of Table 20-1, leasing could have an advantage for firms that are seeking the maximum degree of financial leverage. Because some leases are not shown on the balance sheet, lease financing can give the firm a stronger appearance in a superficial credit analysis, thus permitting it to use more leverage than it could if it did not lease. This may be true for smaller firms; but now that larger firms are required to capitalize major leases and to report them on their balance sheets, this point is of questionable validity.[14]

SELF TEST

Define each of these terms: (1) sale and leaseback; (2) operating lease; and (3) financial, or capital, lease.

What is off balance sheet financing, what is SFAS #13, and how are the two related?

List the sequence of events, for the lessee, leading to a lease arrangement.

Why is it appropriate to compare the cost of lease financing with that of debt financing?

20-3 WARRANTS

A **warrant** is a long-term option from a company that gives the holder the right to buy a stated number of shares of the firm's stock at a specified price for a specified length of time. Generally, warrants are distributed with debt, and they are used to induce investors to buy long-term debt that carries a lower coupon rate than would otherwise be required. For example, when Infomatics Corporation, a rapidly growing high-tech company, wanted to sell $50 million of 20-year bonds in 2008, the investment bankers informed management that the bonds would be difficult to sell and that a 10% coupon rate would be required. However, as an alternative, the bankers suggested that investors would be willing to buy the bonds with a coupon rate of only 8% if the company offered 20 warrants with each $1,000 bond, each

Warrant
A long-term option to buy a stated number of shares of common stock at a specified price.

---

[14]Enron, in a widely publicized financial fraud that was uncovered in 2000, used illegal leases to hide debts with the assistance of its accounting firm, Arthur Andersen. Both Enron and Andersen were put out of business, and some high-ranking officers received long jail sentences and huge fines.

warrant having a 10-year life and entitling the holder to buy one share of common stock at an exercise price of $22 per share at any time during their 10-year life. The stock was selling for $20 per share at the time, and the warrants would expire in 2018 if they were not previously exercised.

Thus, investors were willing to buy Infomatics' bonds with a yield of only 8% in a 10% market because warrants were offered as part of the package. The warrants are long-term *call options* that have value because holders can buy the firm's common stock at the exercise price regardless of how high the market price climbs. This option offsets the low interest rate on the bonds and makes the package of low-yield bonds and warrants attractive to investors. (See Chapter 18 for a more complete discussion of options.)

20-3a Initial Market Price of a Bond with Warrants

The Infomatics bonds, if they had been issued as straight debt, would have carried a 10% interest rate. However, with warrants attached, the bonds were sold to yield 8%. Someone buying the bonds at their $1,000 initial offering price would thus be receiving a package consisting of an 8%, 20-year bond plus 20 warrants. Since the going interest rate on bonds as risky as those of Infomatics was 10%, we can find the straight-debt value of the bonds, assuming an annual coupon for ease of illustration, as follows:

PV = $829.73 {add approximately equal to sign} $830

Using a financial calculator, input N = 20, I/YR = 10, PMT = 80, and FV = 1000. Then press the PV key to obtain the bond's value, $829.73, or approximately $830. Thus, a person buying the bonds in the initial underwriting would pay $1,000 and receive in exchange a straight bond worth about $830 plus 20 warrants presumably worth about $1,000 − $830 = $170.

20-1	Price paid for bond with warrants	=	Straight-debt value of bond	+	Value of warrants
	$1,000	=	$830	+	$170

Since investors receive 20 warrants with each bond, each warrant has an implied value of $170/20 = $8.50.

Detachable Warrant
A warrant that can be detached from a bond and traded independently of the bond.

Typically, the 20 warrants would be **detachable warrants;** that is, they can be detached from the bond and the two securities traded separately. If the bonds and warrants were priced correctly, the bonds would sell for $830 in the aftermarket, the warrants would sell for $8.50 each, and the package would be in equilibrium at the $1,000 offering price.

However, it is possible for the bankers to price the issue incorrectly. They can estimate the straight-debt value quite accurately, but it is more difficult to estimate the proper value of the warrants. For example, if the bankers estimate the warrants' value too low, they may think that each warrant will sell for $6 and will attach $170/$6 = 28.3333 warrants to each bond. Then when the issue is offered to the public, its price will rise from the $1,000 offer price to:

Market price of bond = $830 + $8.50(28.3333) = $1,070.83

Thus, the firm would have sold for $1,000 something that should have been sold for $1,070.83. More warrants would be outstanding than necessary; so when those warrants are exercised, there would be more dilution of the original shareholders' equity than was necessary. On the other hand, if the bankers overestimated the value of the warrants (perhaps valuing them at $10 versus the true $8.50), the issue would fail—it could not be sold at the $1,000 offering price, and the firm would not obtain the money it needed. So valuing the warrants correctly is important.

We discussed in Chapter 18 the Black-Scholes Option Pricing Model (OPM) for finding the value of a call option. It is tempting to use this model to find the value of a warrant, since call options are similar to warrants in many respects: Both give the investor the right to buy a share of stock at a fixed exercise price on or before the expiration date. However, there is a major difference between call options and warrants. When call options are exercised, the stock provided to the option holder comes from the secondary market; but when warrants are exercised, the shares provided are newly issued. This means that the exercise of warrants dilutes the value of the original equity, which could cause the value of the original warrant to differ from the value of a similar call option. Therefore, investment bankers cannot use the Black-Scholes model to determine the value of warrants.

Even though the Black-Scholes model cannot be used, investment bankers can query potential buyers and compare the new warrants with others that are outstanding to estimate their value. The querying would be done during the "road show," where the firm's officers travel around the country with the investment bankers and hold meetings with potential investors. The company officers provide facts about the firm and the issue, answer questions, and get a sense from the potential buyers how many shares (or bonds in this case) they would buy under different offering terms (coupon rates, number of warrants, life of warrants, and so forth). The bankers "make a book," taking down names and prices of potential customers. And since this information is used when the issue is allocated to buyers, the potential buyers tell the truth about their intentions. In any event, good investment bankers can set new issue prices close to equilibrium prices.

20-3b Use of Warrants in Financing

Small, rapidly growing firms generally use warrants as "sweeteners" when they sell debt or preferred stock. Such firms frequently are regarded by investors as being highly risky, so their bonds can be sold only with high coupon rates and very restrictive indenture provisions. To avoid this, firms such as Infomatics often offer warrants along with the bonds. Getting warrants along with bonds enables investors to share in the company's growth, assuming it does in fact grow and prosper. Therefore, they are willing to accept a lower interest rate and less restrictive indenture provisions. A bond with warrants has some characteristics of debt and some characteristics of equity. It is a hybrid security that provides the financial manager with an opportunity to expand the firm's mix of securities and thus to appeal to a broader group of investors.

Virtually all warrants today are detachable. Thus, after a bond with attached warrants is sold, the warrants can be detached and traded separately from the bond. Further, even after the warrants have been exercised, the bond (with its low coupon rate) remains outstanding.

The exercise price on warrants is generally set at some 15% to 30% above the market price of the stock on the date the bond is issued. If the firm grows and prospers and if its stock price rises above the exercise price at which shares may be purchased, warrant holders can exercise their warrants and buy stock at the stated price. However, as we saw in connection with pure options, without some incentive, warrants would never be exercised prior to maturity—their value in the open market at least would be equal to and probably would be greater than their value if exercised; so holders would sell warrants rather than exercise them. Three

Stepped-Up Exercise Price

An exercise price that is specified to rise if a warrant is exercised after a designated date.

conditions encourage holders to exercise their warrants: (1) Warrant holders will exercise and buy stock if the warrants are about to expire and the market price of the stock is above the exercise price. (2) Warrant holders will exercise voluntarily if the company raises the dividend on the common stock by a sufficient amount. No dividend is earned on the warrant, so it provides no current income. However, if the common stock pays a high dividend, it provides an attractive dividend yield, and the dividend limits future price growth because less earnings will be retained. This induces warrant holders to exercise their option to buy the stock. (3) Warrants sometimes have **stepped-up exercise prices**, which prod owners into exercising them. For example, Williamson Scientific Company has warrants outstanding with an exercise price of $25 until December 31, 2012, at which time the exercise price rises to $30. If the price of the common stock is over $25 just before December 31, 2012, many warrant holders will exercise their options before the stepped-up price takes effect and the value of the warrants falls.

Another desirable feature of warrants is that they generally bring in funds only when funds are needed. If the company grows, it will probably need new equity capital. At the same time, growth will cause the price of the stock to rise and the warrants to be exercised; hence, the firm will obtain additional cash. If the company is not successful and it cannot profitably employ additional money, the price of its stock probably will not rise sufficiently to induce exercise of the warrants.

20-3c The Component Cost of Bonds with Warrants

When Infomatics issued its debt with warrants, the firm received $50 million, or $1,000 for each bond. Simultaneously, the company assumed an obligation to pay $80 interest for 20 years plus $1,000 at the end of 20 years. The pretax cost of the money would have been 10% if no warrants had been attached; but each Infomatics bond had 20 warrants, each of which entitled its holder to buy one share of stock for $22. What is the percentage cost of the $50 million? *As we shall see, the cost is well above the 8% coupon rate on the bonds.*

First, note that when the warrants expire 10 years from now, the stock is expected to sell for $51.87, given the $20 initial price and the 10% expected growth rate:

$$P_{10} = \$20(1.10)^{10} = \$51.87$$

Therefore, investors could exercise their warrants and receive one share of stock worth $51.87 for each warrant exercised. Thus, if the investor held the complete package, he or she would realize a profit in Year 10 of $51.87 − $22 = $29.87 on each warrant. Since each bond has 20 warrants attached, investors would have a gain of 20($29.87) = $597.40 per bond at the end of Year 10. Here is a time line of the cash flow stream to an investor:

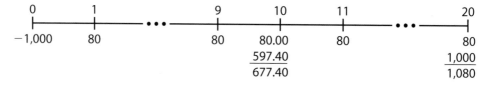

The IRR of this stream is 10.66%, which is the investor's overall pretax rate of return on the issue. This return is 66 basis points higher than the return on straight debt. That reflects the fact that the issue is riskier to investors than a straight-debt issue because part of the return is expected to come in the form of stock price appreciation, and that part of the return is riskier than the interest payments.

The before-tax cost to the company is the same as the before-tax return to investors—this was true of common stocks, straight bonds, and preferred stocks; and it is also true of bonds sold with warrants.

20-3d Problems with Warrant Issues

Although warrants are bought by investors with the expectation of receiving a total return commensurate with the overall riskiness of the package of securities being purchased, things do not always work out as expected. For example, in 1989, Sony paid $3.4 billion for Columbia Pictures, a U.S. movie studio. To help finance the deal, in 1990, Sony sold $470 million of 4-year bonds with warrants at an incredibly low 0.3% coupon interest rate. The rate was so low because the warrants, which also had a maturity of 4 years, allowed investors to purchase Sony stock at 7,670 yen per share, only 2.5% above the share price at the time the package was issued.

Investors snapped up the issue, and many of the warrants were "peeled off" and sold separately on the open market. The warrant buyers obviously believed that Sony's stock would climb well above the exercise price. From Sony's point of view, the bond-with-warrants package provided a very low-cost "bridge loan" (the bonds) that would be replaced with equity financing when the warrants were exercised, presumably in 4 years. This very low-cost capital encouraged Japanese firms to acquire foreign companies and to invest huge amounts in new plant and equipment.

However, the willingness of investors to buy Japanese warrants suffered a severe blow when the Japanese stock market fell by 40%. By 1994, when the warrants expired, Sony's stock sold for only 5,950 yen versus the 7,670 yen exercise price; so the warrants were not exercised. Thus, Sony's planned infusion of equity capital never materialized, and it had to refinance the 4-year bond issue at much higher rates.

Both Sony and its investors lost on the deal. The investors lost because they did not earn the return they had expected on the issue. Sony lost because it had to alter its financing plans and ended up paying a high rate on its debt. In spite of presumably good planning by the company and investors, this bond-with-warrants issue, and many like it, did not work out as anticipated.

SELF TEST

What is a warrant?

Describe how a new bond issue with warrants is valued.

How are warrants used in corporate financing?

The use of warrants lowers the coupon rate on the corresponding debt issue. Does this mean that the component cost of a debt-plus-warrants package is less than the cost of straight debt? Explain.

A company recently issued bonds with attached warrants. The bond-plus-warrants package sells at a price equal to its $1,000 face value. The bonds mature in 10 years and have a 6% annual coupon. The company also has 10-year straight debt (with no warrants attached) outstanding. The straight debt has a yield to maturity of 8%. What is the straight-debt value of the bonds? What is the value of the warrants? **($865.80, $134.20)**

20-4 CONVERTIBLES

Convertible securities are bonds or preferred stocks that, under specified terms and conditions, can be exchanged for common stock at the option of the holder. Unlike the exercise of warrants, which brings in additional funds to the firm, conversion does not provide capital: Debt (or preferred stock) is simply replaced on the balance sheet by common stock. Of course, reducing the debt or preferred stock will improve the firm's financial strength and make it easier to raise additional capital, but that requires a separate action.

Convertible Security
A security, usually a bond or preferred stock, that can be exchanged at the option of the holder for the common stock of the issuing firm.

20-4a Conversion Ratio and Conversion Price

Conversion Ratio, CR
The number of shares of common stock that are obtained by converting a convertible bond or share of convertible preferred stock.

Conversion Price, P$_C$
The effective price paid for common stock obtained by converting a convertible security.

One of the most important provisions of a convertible security is the **conversion ratio, CR**, defined as the number of shares of stock a bondholder will receive upon conversion. Related to the conversion ratio is the **conversion price, P$_c$**, which is the effective price investors pay for common stock bought through a convertible. The relationship between the conversion ratio and the conversion price can be illustrated by the Silicon Valley Software Company's $1,000 par value convertible debentures issued in August 2008. At any time prior to maturity on August 15, 2028, a debenture holder can exchange a bond for 20 shares of common stock; therefore, the conversion ratio, CR, is 20. The bond cost purchasers $1,000, the par value, when it was issued. Dividing the $1,000 par value by the 20 shares received gives a conversion price of $50 a share.

20-2
$$\text{Conversion price} = P_c = \frac{\text{Par value of bond given up}}{\text{Shares received}}$$

$$= \frac{\$1,000}{CR} = \frac{\$1,000}{20} = \$50$$

Conversely, by solving for CR, we obtain the conversion ratio.

20-3
$$\text{Conversion ratio} = CR = \frac{\$1,000}{P_c}$$

$$= \frac{\$1,000}{\$50} = 20 \text{ shares}$$

Once CR is set, the value of P$_c$ is established and vice versa.

Like a warrant's exercise price, the conversion price is typically set at from 15% to 30% above the market price of the common stock at the time the issue is sold. Exactly how the conversion price is established can best be understood after examining some of the reasons firms use convertibles.

Generally, the conversion price and conversion ratio are fixed for the life of the bond, although sometimes a stepped-up conversion price is used. For example, the 2008 convertible debentures for Breedon Industries are convertible into 12.5 shares until 2018; into 11.76 shares from 2019 until 2028; and into 11.11 shares from 2027 until maturity in 2038. The conversion price thus starts at $80, rises to $85, and then goes to $90. Breedon's convertibles, like most, have 10 years of call protection.

Another factor that may cause a change in the conversion price and ratio is a standard feature of almost all convertibles—the clause protecting the convertible against dilution from stock splits, stock dividends, and the sale of common stock at a price below the conversion price. The typical provision states that if common stock is sold at a price below the conversion price, the conversion price must be lowered to the price at which the new stock was issued and the conversion ratio raised correspondingly. Also, if the stock is split or if a stock dividend is declared, the conversion price must be lowered by the percentage amount of the stock dividend or split. For example, if Breedon Industries were to have a 2-for-1 stock split during the first 10 years of its convertible's life, the conversion ratio would automatically be adjusted from 12.5 to 25 and the conversion price lowered from $80 to $40. If this protection was not contained in the contract, a company could completely thwart conversion by the use of stock splits and stock dividends. Warrants are similarly protected against dilution.

The standard protection against dilution from selling new stock at prices below the conversion price can, however, get a company into trouble. For example, assume that Breedon's stock was selling for $65 per share at the time the convertible was issued. Further, suppose the market dropped sharply and Breedon's stock price fell to $50 per share. If Breedon needed new equity to support operations, a new common stock sale would require the company to lower the conversion price on the convertible debentures from $80 to $50. That would raise the value of the convertibles and, in effect, transfer wealth from current shareholders to convertible holders. Firms considering the use of convertibles or bonds with warrants should remember potential problems such as this.

20-4b The Component Cost of Convertibles

In spring 2008, Silicon Valley Software was evaluating the use of the convertible bond issue described earlier. The issue would consist of 20-year convertible bonds offered at a price of $1,000 per bond; this $1,000 would also be the bond's par (and maturity) value. The bond would pay a 10% annual coupon interest rate, or $100 per year. Each bond would be convertible into 20 shares of stock, so the conversion price would be $1,000/20 = $50. The stock was expected to pay a dividend of $2.80 during the coming year, and it sold at $35 per share. Further, the stock price was expected to grow at a constant rate of 8% per year. Therefore, $r_s = \hat{r}_s = D_1/P_0 + g = \$2.80/\$35 + 8\% = 8\% + 8\% = 16\%$. If the bonds were not made convertible, they would have to offer a yield of 13%, given their riskiness and the general level of interest rates. The convertible bonds would not be callable for 10 years, after which they could be called at a price of $1,050, with this price declining by $5 per year thereafter. If, after 10 years, the conversion value exceeds the call price by at least 20%, management would probably call the bonds.

Figure 20-1 shows the expectations of an average investor and the company.[15]

1. The horizontal line at M = $1,000 represents the par (and maturity) value. Also, $1,000 is the price at which the bond is initially offered to the public.

2. The bond is protected against call for 10 years. It is initially callable at a price of $1,050, and the call price declines thereafter by $5 per year. Thus, the call price is represented by the solid section of the line V_0M''.

3. Since the convertible has a 10% annual coupon rate and since the yield on a nonconvertible bond of similar risk was stated to be 13%, the expected "straight-bond" value of the convertible, B_t, must be less than par. At the time of issue, B_0 is $789 as follows:

$$\text{Pure-debt value at time of issue} = B_0 = \sum_{t=1}^{N} \frac{\text{Coupon interest}}{(1+r_d)^t} + \frac{\text{Maturity value}}{(1+r_d)^N} \qquad \text{20-4}$$

$$= \sum_{t=1}^{20} \frac{\$100}{(1.13)^t} + \frac{\$1,000}{(1.13)^{20}} = \$789$$

Note, however, that the bond's straight-debt value must be $1,000 just prior to maturity, so the straight-debt value rises over time. B_t follows the line B_0M'' in the graph.

4. The bond's initial **conversion value, C_t,** or the value of the stock the investor would receive if the bonds were converted at t = 0, is $700: The bond's conversion value is $P_t(CR)$; so at t = 0, conversion value = $P_0(CR) = \$35(20$ shares) = $700. Since the stock price is expected to grow at an 8% rate, the conversion value should rise at this same rate over time. For example, in Year 5, it should be $P_5(CR) = \$35(1.08)^5(20) = \$1,029$. The expected conversion value over time is given by the line C_t in Figure 20-1.

5. The actual market price of the bond cannot fall below the higher of its straight-debt value or its conversion value. If the market price dropped below the

Conversion Value, C_t
The value of common stock obtained by converting a convertible security.

[15]For a more complete discussion of how the terms of a convertible offering are determined, see M. Wayne Marr and G. Rodney Thompson, "The Pricing of New Convertible Bond Issues," *Financial Management,* Summer 1984, pp. 31–37.

FIGURE 20-1	Silicon Valley Software: Convertible Bond Model

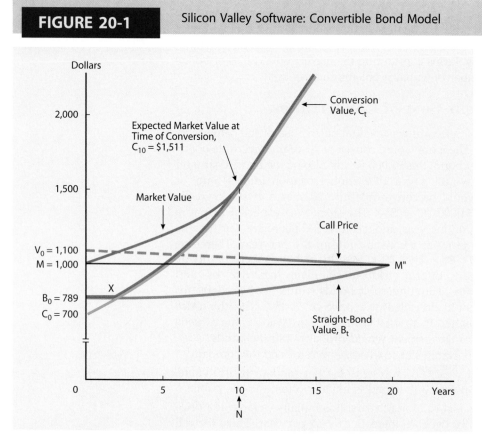

Year	Pure-Bond Value, B_t	Conversion Value, C_t	Maturity Value, M	Market Value	Floor Value	Premium
0	$ 789	$ 700	$1,000	$1,000	$ 789	$211
1	792	756	1,000	1,023	792	231
2	795	816	1,000	1,071	816	255
3	798	882	1,000	1,147	882	265
4	802	952	1,000	1,192	952	240
5	806	1,029	1,000	1,241	1,029	212
6	811	1,111	1,000	1,293	1,111	182
7	816	1,200	1,000	1,344	1,200	144
8	822	1,296	1,000	1,398	1,296	102
9	829	1,399	1,000	1,453	1,399	54
10	837	1,511	1,000	1,511	1,511	0
11	846	1,632	1,000	1,632	1,632	0
⋮	⋮	⋮	⋮	⋮	⋮	⋮
20	1,000	3,263	1,000	3,263	3,263	0

straight-bond value, those who wanted bonds would recognize the bargain and buy the convertible as a bond. Similarly, if the market price dropped below the conversion value, people would buy the convertibles, exercise them to get stock, and then sell the stock at a profit. Therefore, the higher of the bond value and conversion value curves in the graph represents a *floor price* for the bond. In Figure 20-1, the floor price is represented by the thicker shaded line B_0XC_t.

6. The bond's market value will typically exceed its floor value. It will exceed the straight-bond value because the option to convert is worth something—a 10% bond with conversion possibilities is worth more than a 10% bond without this option. The convertible's price will also exceed its conversion value because holding the convertible is equivalent to holding a call option; and prior to expiration, the option's true value is higher than its expiration (or conversion) value. We cannot say exactly where the market value line will lie, but we do know that it will be at or above the floor set by the straight-bond and conversion value lines.

7. At some point, the market value line will touch the conversion value line. This convergence will occur for two reasons. First, the stock should pay higher dividends as the years go by, but the interest payments on the convertible are fixed. For example, Silicon's convertibles would pay $100 in interest annually, while the dividends on the 20 shares received upon conversion would initially be 20($2.80) = $56. However, at an 8% growth rate, the dividends after 10 years would be up to $120.90, while the interest would still be $100. Thus, at some point, rising dividends could be expected to push against the fixed interest payments, causing the premium to disappear and investors to convert voluntarily. Second, once the bond becomes callable, its market value cannot exceed the higher of the conversion value and the call price without exposing investors to the danger of a call. For example, suppose that 10 years after issue (when the bonds were callable), the market value of the bond was $1,600, the conversion value was $1,500, and the call price was $1,050. If the company called the bonds the day after you bought 10 bonds for $16,000, you would be forced to convert into stock worth only $15,000; so you would suffer a loss of $100 per bond, or $1,000, in one day. Recognizing this danger, you and other investors would not pay much of a premium over the higher of the call price or the conversion value once the bond becomes callable. Therefore, in Figure 20-1, we assume that the market value line hits the conversion value line in Year 10, when the bond becomes callable.

8. Let N represent the year when investors expect conversion to occur, either voluntarily because of rising dividends or because the company calls the convertibles to strengthen its balance sheet by substituting equity for debt. In our example, we assume that N = 10, the first call date.

9. Since N = 10, the expected market value at Year 10 is $35(1.08)^{10}(20) = $1,511$. An investor can find the expected rate of return on the convertible bond, r_c, by finding the IRR of the following cash flow stream:

The solution is $r_c = IRR = 12.8\%$

10. The return on a convertible is expected to come partly from interest income and partly from capital gains; in this case, the total expected return is 12.8%, with 10% representing interest income and 2.8% representing the expected capital gain. The interest component is relatively assured, while the capital gain component is riskier. Therefore, a convertible's expected return is riskier than that of a straight bond. This leads us to conclude that r_c should be larger than the cost of straight debt, r_d. Thus, it would seem that the expected rate of return on Silicon's convertibles, r_c, should lie between its cost of straight debt, $r_d = 13\%$, and its cost of common stock, $r_s = 16\%$.

11. Investment bankers use the type of model described here in addition to a knowledge of the market to set the terms on convertibles (the conversion ratio,

coupon interest rate, and years of call protection) such that the security will just "clear the market" at its $1,000 offering price. In our example, the required conditions do not hold—the calculated rate of return on the convertible is only 12.8%, which is less than the 13% cost of straight debt. Therefore, the terms on the bond must be made more attractive to investors. Silicon Valley Software would have to increase the coupon interest rate on the convertible above 10%, raise the conversion ratio above 20 (and thereby lower the conversion price from $50 to a level closer to the current $35 market price of the stock), lengthen the call-protected period, or use a combination of those three such that the expected return on the convertible ends up between 13% and 16%.[16]

20-4c Use of Convertibles in Financing

Convertibles have two important advantages from the issuer's standpoint: (1) Convertibles, like bonds with warrants, offer a company the chance to sell debt with a low interest rate in exchange for a chance to participate in the company's success if it does well. (2) In a sense, convertibles provide a way to sell common stock at prices higher than those currently prevailing. Some companies want to sell common stock, not debt, but believe that the price of their stock is temporarily depressed. Management may know, for example, that earnings are depressed because of start-up costs associated with a new project, but they expect earnings to rise sharply during the next year or so, pulling the price of the stock up with them. Thus, if the company sold stock now, it would be giving up more shares than necessary to raise a given amount of capital. However, if it set the conversion price 20% to 30% above the present market price of the stock, 20% to 30% fewer shares would be given up when the bonds were converted than if stock were sold directly at the current time. Note, however, that management is counting on the stock's price to rise above the conversion price to make the bonds attractive in conversion. If earnings do not rise and pull the stock price up (hence, conversion does not occur), the company will be saddled with debt in the face of low earnings, which could be disastrous.

How can the company make sure that conversion will occur if the price of the stock rises above the conversion price? Typically, convertibles contain a call provision that enables the issuing firm to force holders to convert. Suppose the conversion price is $50, the conversion ratio is 20, the market price of the common stock has risen to $60, and the call price on a convertible bond is $1,050. If the company calls the bond, bondholders can convert into common stock with a market value of 20($60) = $1,200 or allow the company to redeem the bond for $1,050. Naturally, bondholders prefer $1,200 to $1,050, so conversion would occur. The call provision gives the company a way to force conversion, provided the market price of the stock is greater than the conversion price. Note, however, that most convertibles have a fairly long period of call protection—10 years is typical. Therefore, if the company wants to be able to force conversion fairly early, it must set a short call-protection period. This will, in turn, require that it set a higher coupon rate or a lower conversion price.

From the standpoint of the issuer, convertibles have three important disadvantages: (1) Although the use of a convertible bond may give the company the opportunity to sell stock at a price higher than the price at which it could be sold currently, if the stock greatly increased in price, the firm would probably find that it would have been better off had it used straight debt in spite of its higher cost and then later sold common stock and refunded the debt. (2) Convertibles typically have a low coupon interest rate, and the advantage of this low-cost debt will be lost when conversion occurs. (3) If the company truly wants to raise equity capital and if the

---

[16]In this discussion, we ignore the tax advantages to investors associated with capital gains. In some situations, tax effects could result in r_c being less than r_d.

price of the stock does not rise sufficiently after the bond is issued, the company will be stuck with debt.

20-4d Convertibles Can Reduce Agency Costs

A potential agency problem between bondholders and stockholders is asset substitution. Stockholders have an "option-related" incentive to take on projects with high upside potential even though they increase the risk of the firm. When such an action is taken, the potential exists for a wealth transfer from bondholders to stockholders. However, when convertible debt is issued, actions that increase the risk of the company may also increase the value of the convertible debt. Thus, some of the gains to shareholders from taking on high-risk projects must be shared with convertible bondholders. This sharing of benefits lowers agency costs. The same general logic applies to convertible preferred and to warrants.

SELF TEST

What is a conversion ratio? a conversion price? a straight-bond value?

What is meant by a convertible's floor value?

What are the advantages and disadvantages of convertibles to issuers? to investors?

How do convertibles reduce agency costs?

A convertible bond has a par value of $1,000 and a conversion price of $40. The stock currently trades for $30 a share. What are the bond's conversion ratio and conversion value at $t = 0$? **(CR = 25; P_0(CR) = $30 × 25 = $750)**

20-5 A FINAL COMPARISON OF WARRANTS AND CONVERTIBLES

Convertible debt can be thought of as straight debt with nondetachable warrants. Thus, at first, it might appear that debt with warrants and convertible debt are more or less interchangeable. However, a closer look reveals one major and several minor differences between the two securities.[17] First, as we discussed previously, the exercise of warrants brings in new equity capital, while the conversion of convertibles results only in a switch from debt to equity.

A second difference involves flexibility. Most convertible issues contain a call provision that allows the issuer to refund the debt, which could force conversion if the conversion value exceeds the call price. However, most warrants are not callable, so firms generally must wait until maturity for the warrants to generate new equity capital. Also, maturities generally differ between warrants and convertibles— warrants typically have much shorter lives than convertibles, and warrants typically expire before their accompanying debt matures. Further, warrants provide for fewer future common shares than do convertibles because with convertibles, all of the debt is converted to common, whereas debt remains outstanding when warrants are exercised. Together these facts suggest that debt-plus-warrant issuers are more interested in selling debt than in selling equity and that the warrants are primarily a sweetener to induce investors to buy the debt.

---

[17]For a more detailed comparison of warrants and convertibles, see Michael S. Long and Stephen F. Sefcik, "Participation Financing: A Comparison of the Characteristics of Convertible Debt and Straight Bonds Issued in Conjunction with Warrants," *Financial Management*, Autumn 1990, pp. 23–34.

In general, firms that issue bonds with warrants are smaller and riskier than those that issue convertibles. One possible rationale for the use of option securities, especially the use of debt with warrants by small firms, is the difficulty investors have assessing the risk of small companies. If a start-up with a new, untested product seeks debt financing, it is very difficult for potential lenders to judge the risk of the venture; hence, it is difficult to set a fair interest rate. Under these circumstances, many potential investors would be reluctant to invest, making it necessary to set very high interest rates to attract debt capital. However, such high interest rates can bankrupt a new firm trying to develop and market a new product. By issuing debt with warrants, investors obtain a package that offers upside potential to offset the risks of loss.

Finally, there is a significant difference in issuance costs between debt with warrants and convertible debt. Bonds with warrants typically require flotation costs that are about 1.2% more than the flotation costs for convertibles. In general, bond-with-warrant financings have underwriting fees that closely reflect the weighted average of the fees associated with debt and equity issues, while underwriting costs for convertibles are substantially lower.

SELF TEST

What are some differences between debt-with-warrant financing and convertible debt?

Explain how bonds with warrants might help small, risky firms sell debt securities.

20-6 REPORTING EARNINGS WHEN WARRANTS OR CONVERTIBLES ARE OUTSTANDING[18]

If warrants or convertibles are outstanding, a firm can theoretically report earnings per share in one of three ways:

1. *Basic EPS,* where earnings available to common stockholders are divided by the average number of shares outstanding during the period.

2. *Primary EPS,* where earnings available are divided by the average number of shares that would have been outstanding if warrants and convertibles "likely to be converted in the near future" had been exercised or converted. In calculating primary EPS, earnings are adjusted by "backing out" the interest on the convertibles, after which the adjusted earnings are divided by the adjusted number of shares. Accountants have a formula that compares the conversion or exercise price with the actual market value of the stock to determine the likelihood of conversion when deciding on the need to use this adjustment procedure.

3. *Diluted EPS,* which is similar to primary EPS except that *all* warrants and convertibles are assumed to be exercised or converted, regardless of the likelihood of exercise or conversion.

Under SEC rules, firms are required to report both basic and diluted EPS. For firms with large numbers of option securities outstanding, there can be a substantial difference between the basic and diluted EPS figures. For financial statement purposes, firms reported diluted EPS until 1997, when the Financial Accounting

---

[18]As part of the FASB's short-term convergence project with the IASB to improve U.S. financial reporting while concurrently eliminating individual differences between U.S. GAAP and international financial reporting standards, the FASB issued a revised exposure draft of EPS reporting on August 7, 2008. The FASB expects to issue a final document in the second half of 2009 that will make additional changes to SFAS #128 (issued in February 1997), which is discussed in this section.

Standards Board (FASB) changed to basic EPS. According to FASB, the change was made to give investors a simpler picture of a company's underlying performance. Also, the change makes it easier for investors to compare the performance of U.S. firms with their foreign counterparts, which tend to use basic EPS.

SELF TEST

What are the three possible methods for reporting EPS when warrants and convertibles are outstanding?

Which methods are most used in practice?

Why should investors be concerned about a firm's outstanding warrants and convertibles?

TYING IT ALL TOGETHER

While common stock and long-term debt provide most of the capital that corporations use, companies also use several forms of "hybrid securities." The hybrids include preferred stock, leasing, convertibles, and warrants, each of which has some characteristics of debt and some of equity. We discussed the pros and cons of the hybrids from the standpoints of issuers and investors, the way to determine when to use them, and the factors that affect their values. The basic rationale for these securities and the procedures used to evaluate them are based on concepts developed in earlier chapters.

SELF-TEST QUESTIONS AND PROBLEMS
(Solutions Appear in Appendix A)

ST-1 **KEY TERMS** Define each of the following terms:

a. Cumulative; adjustable rate preferred stock

b. Arrearages; auction rate preferred stock (ARPS)

c. Lessee; lessor

d. Sale and leaseback; operating lease; financial lease

e. Off balance sheet financing; SFAS #13

f. Residual value

g. Warrant; detachable warrant; stepped-up exercise price

h. Convertible security; conversion ratio, CR; conversion price, P_c; conversion value, C_t

i. Basic EPS; primary EPS; diluted EPS

ST-2 **LEASE ANALYSIS** The Olsen Company has decided to acquire a new truck. One alternative is to lease the truck on a 4-year contract for a lease payment of $10,000 per year, with payments to be made at the beginning of each year. The lease would include maintenance. Alternatively, Olsen could purchase the truck outright for $40,000, financing with a bank loan for the net purchase price, amortized over a 4-year period at an interest rate of 10% per year, payments to be made at the end of each year. Under the borrow-to-purchase arrangement, Olsen would have to maintain the truck at a cost of $1,000 per year, payable at year-end. The truck falls into the MACRS 3-year class. The applicable MACRS depreciation rates are 33%, 45%, 15%, and 7%. The truck has a salvage value of $10,000, which is the expected market value after 4 years, at which time Olsen plans to replace the truck regardless of whether the firm leases the truck or purchases it. Olsen has a federal-plus-state tax rate of 40%.

a. What is Olsen's PV cost of leasing?

b. What is Olsen's PV cost of owning? Should the truck be leased or purchased?

c. The appropriate discount rate for use in Olsen's analysis is the firm's after-tax cost of debt. Why?

d. The salvage value is the least certain cash flow in the analysis. How might Olsen incorporate the higher riskiness of this cash flow into the analysis?

QUESTIONS

20-1 For purposes of measuring a firm's leverage, should preferred stock be classified as debt or equity? Does it matter if the classification is being made (a) by the firm's management, (b) by creditors, or (c) by equity investors?

20-2 You are told that one corporation just issued $100 million of preferred stock and another purchased $100 million of preferred stock as an investment. You are also told that one firm has an effective tax rate of 20%, whereas the other is in the 35% bracket. Which firm is more likely to have bought the preferred? Explain.

20-3 One often finds that a company's bonds have a higher yield than its preferred stock even though an investor considers the bonds to be less risky than the preferred. What causes this yield differential?

20-4 Why would a company choose to issue floating-rate as opposed to fixed-rate preferred stock?

20-5 Distinguish between operating leases and financial leases. Would a firm be more likely to finance a fleet of trucks or a manufacturing plant with an operating lease? Explain.

20-6 One alleged advantage of leasing voiced in the past was that it kept liabilities off the balance sheet, thus making it possible for a firm to obtain more leverage than it otherwise could have. This raised the question of whether the lease obligation and the asset involved should be capitalized and shown on the balance sheet. Discuss the pros and cons of capitalizing leases and related assets.

20-7 Suppose there were no IRS restrictions on what constitutes a valid lease. Explain in a manner that a legislator might understand why some restrictions should be imposed.

20-8 Suppose Congress changed the tax laws in a way that (1) permitted equipment to be depreciated over a shorter period, (2) lowered corporate tax rates, and (3) reinstated the investment tax credit. Discuss how each of these changes would affect the relative use of leasing versus conventional debt in the U.S. economy.

20-9 What effect does the expected growth rate of a firm's stock price (subsequent to issue) have on its ability to raise additional funds through (a) convertibles and (b) warrants?

20-10 a. How would a firm's decision to pay out a higher percentage of its earnings as dividends affect each of the following?

(1) The value of its long-term warrants

(2) The likelihood that its convertible bonds will be converted

(3) The likelihood that its warrants will be exercised

b. If you owned the warrants or convertibles of a company, would you be pleased or displeased if it raised its payout rate from 20% to 80%? Why?

20-11 Evaluate the following statement: Issuing convertible securities represents a means by which a firm can sell common stock at a price above the existing market price.

20-12 Suppose a company simultaneously issues $50 million of convertible bonds with a coupon rate of 9% and $50 million of pure bonds with a coupon rate of 12%. Both bonds have the same maturity. Does the fact that the convertible issue has the lower coupon rate suggest that it is less risky than the pure bond? Would you regard the cost of capital as being lower on the convertible than on the pure bond? Explain. (Hint: Although it might appear at first glance that the convertible's cost of capital is lower, this is not necessarily the case because the interest rate on the convertible understates its cost. Think about this.)

PROBLEMS

**Easy
Problems
1–3**

20-1 **LEASING** Connors Construction needs a piece of equipment that can be leased or purchased. The equipment costs $100. One option is to borrow $100 from the local bank and use the money to buy the equipment. The other option is to lease the equipment. If Connors chooses to lease the equipment, it *will not* capitalize the lease on the balance sheet. Following is the company's balance sheet *prior* to the purchase or leasing of the equipment.

Current assets	$300	Debt	$400
Fixed assets	500	Equity	400
Total assets	$800	Total liabilities and equity	$800

What would be the company's debt ratio if it chose to purchase the equipment? What would be the company's debt ratio if it chose to lease the equipment? Would the company's financial risk be different depending on whether the equipment was leased or purchased? Explain.

20-2 **WARRANTS** Gregg Company recently issued two types of bonds. The first issue consisted of 20-year straight (no warrants attached) bonds with an 8% annual coupon. The second issue consisted of 20-year bonds with a 6% annual coupon with warrants attached. Both bonds were issued at par ($1,000). What is the value of the warrants that were attached to the second issue?

20-3 **CONVERTIBLES** Petersen Securities recently issued convertible bonds with a $1,000 par value. The bonds have a conversion price of $40 a share. What is the bonds' conversion ratio, CR?

**Intermediate
Problems
4–7**

20-4 **BALANCE SHEET EFFECTS OF LEASING** Two textile companies, McDaniel-Edwards Manufacturing and Jordan-Hocking Mills, began operations with identical balance sheets. A year later both required additional manufacturing capacity at a cost of $200,000. McDaniel-Edwards obtained a 5-year, $200,000 loan at an 8% interest rate from its bank. Jordan-Hocking, on the other hand, decided to lease the required $200,000 capacity from National Leasing for 5 years; an 8% return was built into the lease. The balance sheet for each company, before the asset increases, is as follows:

		Debt	$200,000
		Equity	200,000
Total assets	$400,000	Total liabilities and equity	$400,000

a. Show the balance sheet of each firm after the asset increase and calculate each firm's new debt ratio. (Assume that Jordan-Hocking's lease is kept off the balance sheet.)

b. Show how Jordan-Hocking's balance sheet would have looked immediately after the financing if it had capitalized the lease.

c. Would the rate of return (1) on assets and (2) on equity be affected by the choice of financing? If so, how?

20-5 **LEASE VERSUS BUY** Morris-Meyer Mining Company must install $1.5 million of new machinery in its Nevada mine. It can obtain a bank loan for 100% of the required amount. Alternatively, a Nevada investment banking firm that represents a group of investors believes that it can arrange for a lease financing plan. Assume that the following facts apply:

(1) The equipment falls in the MACRS 3-year class. The applicable MACRS rates are 33%, 45%, 15%, and 7%.

(2) Estimated maintenance expenses are $75,000 per year.

(3) Morris-Meyer's federal-plus-state tax rate is 40%.

(4) If the money is borrowed, the bank loan will be at a rate of 15%, amortized in 4 equal installments to be paid at the end of each year.

(5) The tentative lease terms call for end-of-year payments of $400,000 per year for 4 years.

(6) Under the proposed lease terms, the lessee must pay for insurance, property taxes, and maintenance.

(7) Morris-Meyer must use the equipment if it is to continue in business, so it will almost certainly want to acquire the property at the end of the lease. If it does, under the lease terms, it can purchase the machinery at its fair market value at that time. The best

estimate of this market value is the $250,000 salvage value, but it may be much higher or lower under certain circumstances.

To assist management in making the proper lease-versus-buy decision, you are asked to answer the following questions.

a. Assuming that the lease can be arranged, should Morris-Meyer lease or borrow and buy the equipment? Explain.

b. Consider the $250,000 estimated salvage value. Is it appropriate to discount it at the same rate as the other cash flows? What about the other cash flows—are they all equally risky? Explain. (Hint: Riskier cash flows are normally discounted at higher rates; but when the cash flows are *costs* rather than *inflows,* the normal procedure must be reversed.)

20-6   **WARRANTS**   Pogue Industries Inc. has warrants outstanding that permit its holders to purchase 1 share of stock per warrant at a price of $21. (Refer to Chapter 18 for Parts a, b, and c.)

a. Calculate the exercise value of Pogue's warrants if the common stock sells at each of the following prices: $18, $21, $25, and $70.

b. At what approximate price do you think the warrants would sell under each condition indicated in Part a? What premium is implied in your price? Your answer will be a guess, but your prices and premiums should bear reasonable relationships to each other.

c. How would each of the following factors affect your estimates of the warrants' prices and premiums in Part b?

(1) The life of the warrant is lengthened.

(2) The expected variability (σ_p) in the stock's price decreases.

(3) The expected growth rate in the stock's EPS increases.

(4) The company announces the following change in dividend policy: Whereas it formerly paid no dividends, henceforth it will pay out *all* earnings as dividends.

d. Assume that Pogue's stock now sells for $18 per share. The company wants to sell some 20-year, annual interest, $1,000 par value bonds. Each bond will have 50 warrants, each exercisable into 1 share of stock at an exercise price of $21. Pogue's pure bonds yield 10%. Regardless of your answer to Part b, assume that the warrants will have a market value of $1.50 when the stock sells at $18. What annual coupon interest rate and annual dollar coupon must the company set on the bonds with warrants if the bonds are to clear the market? Round to the nearest dollar or percentage point.

20-7   **CONVERTIBLES**   In the summer of 2008, the Hadaway Company was planning to finance an expansion with a convertible security. They considered a convertible debenture but feared the burden of fixed interest charges if the common stock did not rise enough to make conversion attractive. They decided on an issue of convertible preferred stock, which would pay a dividend of $1.05 per share.

The common stock was selling for $21 a share at the time. Management projected earnings for 2008 at $1.50 a share and expected a future growth rate of 10% a year in 2009 and beyond. The investment bankers and management agreed that the common stock would continue to sell at 14 times earnings, the current price/earnings ratio.

a. What conversion price should the issuer set? The conversion rate will be 1.0; that is, each share of convertible preferred can be converted into 1 share of common. Therefore, the convertible's par value (as well as the issue price) will be equal to the conversion price, which, in turn, will be determined as a percentage over the current market price of the common. Your answer will be a guess, but it should be a reasonable one.

b. Should the preferred stock include a call provision? Why or why not?

Challenging Problems 8–10

20-8   **LEASE ANALYSIS**   As part of its overall plant modernization and cost reduction program, the management of Tanner-Woods Textile Mills has decided to install a new automated weaving loom. In the capital budgeting analysis of this equipment, the IRR of the project was found to be 20% versus a project required return of 12%.

The loom has an invoice price of $250,000, including delivery and installation charges. The funds needed could be borrowed from the bank through a 4-year amortized loan at a 10% interest rate, with payments to be made at the end of each year. In the event the loom is purchased, the manufacturer will contract to maintain and service it for a fee of

$20,000 per year paid at the end of each year. The loom falls in the MACRS 5-year class, and Tanner-Woods's marginal federal-plus-state tax rate is 40%. The applicable MACRS rates are 20%, 32%, 19%, 12%, 11%, and 6%.

United Automation Inc., maker of the loom, has offered to lease the loom to Tanner-Woods for $70,000 upon delivery and installation (at t = 0) plus 4 additional annual lease payments of $70,000 to be made at the end of Years 1 through 4. (Note that there are 5 lease payments in total.) The lease agreement includes maintenance and servicing. Actually, the loom has an expected life of 8 years, at which time its expected salvage value is zero; however, after 4 years, its market value is expected to equal its book value of $42,500. Tanner-Woods plans to build an entirely new plant in 4 years, so it has no interest in leasing or owning the proposed loom for more than that period.

a. Should the loom be leased or purchased?

b. The salvage value is clearly the most uncertain cash flow in the analysis. Assume that the appropriate salvage value pretax discount rate is 15%. What would be the effect of a salvage value risk adjustment on the decision?

c. The original analysis assumed that Tanner-Woods would not need the loom after 4 years. Now assume that the firm will continue to use the loom after the lease expires. Thus, if it leased, Tanner-Woods would have to buy the asset after 4 years at the then existing market value, which is assumed to equal the book value. What effect would this requirement have on the basic analysis? (No numerical analysis is required; just verbalize.)

20-9   **FINANCING ALTERNATIVES**   The Howe Computer Company has grown rapidly during the past 5 years. Recently, its commercial bank urged the company to consider increasing its permanent financing. Its bank loan under a line of credit has risen to $150,000, carrying a 10% interest rate, and Howe has been 30 to 60 days late in paying trade creditors.

Discussions with an investment banker have resulted in the decision to raise $250,000 at this time. Investment bankers have assured Howe that the following alternatives are feasible (flotation costs will be ignored):

*   *Alternative 1:* Sell common stock at $10 per share.

*   *Alternative 2:* Sell convertible bonds at a 10% coupon, convertible into 80 shares of common stock for each $1,000 bond (i.e., the conversion price is $12.50 per share).

*   *Alternative 3:* Sell debentures with a 10% coupon; each $1,000 bond will have 80 warrants to buy 1 share of common stock at $12.50.

Keith Howe, the president, owns 80% of Howe's common stock and wants to maintain control of the company; 50,000 shares are outstanding. The following are summaries of Howe's latest financial statements:

Balance Sheet

		Current liabilities	$200,000
		Common stock, $1 par	50,000
		Retained earnings	25,000
Total assets	$275,000	Total liabilities and equity	$275,000

Income Statement

Sales	$550,000
All costs except interest	495,000
EBIT	$ 55,000
Interest	15,000
EBT	$ 40,000
Taxes (40%)	16,000
Net income	$ 24,000
Shares outstanding	50,000
Earnings per share	$0.48
Price/earnings ratio	18×
Market price of stock	$8.64

a. Show the new balance sheet under each alternative. For Alternatives 2 and 3, show the balance sheet after conversion of the debentures or exercise of the warrants. Assume that $150,000 of the funds raised will be used to pay off the bank loan and the rest used to increase total assets.

b. Show Keith Howe's control position under each alternative, assuming that he does not purchase additional shares.

c. What is the effect on earnings per share of each alternative if it is assumed that earnings before interest and taxes will be 20% of total assets?

d. What will be the debt ratio under each alternative?

e. Which of the three alternatives would you recommend to Keith Howe? Why?

20-10 **CONVERTIBLES** O'Brien Computers Inc. needs to raise $35 million to begin producing a new microcomputer. O'Brien's straight, nonconvertible debentures currently yield 12%. Its stock sells for $38 per share, the last dividend was $2.46, and the expected growth rate is a constant 8%. Investment bankers have tentatively proposed that O'Brien raise the $35 million by issuing convertible debentures. These convertibles would have a $1,000 par value, carry an annual coupon rate of 10%, have a 20-year maturity, and be convertible into 20 shares of stock. The bonds would be noncallable for 5 years, after which they would be callable at a price of $1,075; this call price would decline by $5 per year in Year 6 and each year thereafter. Management has called convertibles in the past (and presumably will call them again in the future), once they were eligible for call, as soon as their conversion value was about 20% above their par value (not their call price).

a. Draw an accurate graph similar to Figure 20-1 representing the expectations set forth in the problem.

b. Suppose the previously outlined projects work out on schedule for 2 years, but then O'Brien begins to experience extremely strong competition from Japanese firms. As a result, O'Brien's expected growth rate drops from 8% to zero. Assume that the dividend at the time of the drop is $2.87. The company's credit strength is not impaired, and its value of r_s is also unchanged. What would happen (1) to the stock price and (2) to the convertible bond's price? Be as precise as you can.

COMPREHENSIVE/SPREADSHEET PROBLEMS

20-11 **LEASE ANALYSIS** Use the spreadsheet model to rework Parts a and b of Problem 20-8. Then answer the following question.

c. Accepting that the corporate WACC should be used equally to discount all anticipated cash flows, at what cost of capital would the firm be indifferent between leasing and buying?

20-12 **WARRANTS** Storm Software wants to issue $100 million in new capital to fund new opportunities. If Storm raised the $100 million of new capital in a straight-debt 20-year bond offering, Storm would have to offer an annual coupon rate of 12%. However, Storm's advisers have suggested a 20-year bond offering with warrants. According to the advisers, Storm could issue 9% annual coupon-bearing debt with 20 warrants per $1,000 face value bond. Storm has 10 million shares of stock outstanding at a current price of $25. The warrants can be exercised in 10 years (on December 31, 2018) at an exercise price of $30. Each warrant entitles its holder to buy one share of Storm Software stock. After issuing the bonds with warrants, Storm's operations and investments are expected to grow at a constant rate of 11.4% per year.

a. If investors pay $1,000 for each bond, what is the value of each warrant attached to the bond issue?

b. What is the component cost of these bonds with warrants? What premium is associated with the warrants?

INTEGRATED CASE

FISH & CHIPS, INC., PART I

20-13   **LEASE ANALYSIS**   Martha Millon, financial manager for Fish & Chips Inc., has been asked to perform a lease-versus-buy analysis on a new computer system. The computer costs $1,200,000; and if it is purchased, Fish & Chips could obtain a term loan for the full amount at a 10% cost. The loan would be amortized over the 4-year life of the computer, with payments made at the end of each year. The computer is classified as special purpose; hence, it falls into the MACRS 3-year class. The applicable MACRS rates are 33%, 45%, 15%, and 7%. If the computer is purchased, a maintenance contract must be obtained at a cost of $25,000, payable at the beginning of each year.

After 4 years, the computer will be sold. Millon's best estimate of its residual value at that time is $125,000. Because technology is changing rapidly, however, the residual value is uncertain.

As an alternative, National Leasing is willing to write a 4-year lease on the computer, including maintenance, for payments of $340,000 at the beginning of each year. Fish & Chips' marginal federal-plus-state tax rate is 40%. Help Millon conduct her analysis by answering the following questions.

a. (1) Why is leasing sometimes referred to as "off balance sheet" financing?

   (2) What is the difference between a capital lease and an operating lease?

   (3) What effect does leasing have on a firm's capital structure?

b. (1) What is Fish & Chips' present value cost of owning the computer? (Hint: Set up a table whose bottom line is a "time line" that shows the net cash flows over the period t = 0 to t = 4. Then find the PV of these net cash flows, or the PV cost of owning.)

   (2) Explain the rationale for the discount rate you used to find the PV.

c. (1) What is Fish & Chips' present value cost of leasing the computer? (Hint: Again, construct a time line.)

   (2) What is the net advantage to leasing? Does your analysis indicate that the firm should buy or lease the computer? Explain.

d. Now assume that Millon believes that the computer's residual value could be as low as $0 or as high as $250,000, but she stands by $125,000 as her expected value. She concludes that the residual value is riskier than the other cash flows in the analysis, and she wants to incorporate this differential risk into her analysis. Describe how this can be accomplished. What effect will it have on the lease decision?

e. Millon knows that her firm has been considering moving its headquarters to a new location, and she is concerned that these plans may come to fruition prior to the expiration of the lease. If the move occurs, the company would obtain new computers; hence, Millon would like to include a cancellation clause in the lease contract. What effect would a cancellation clause have on the riskiness of the lease?

FISH & CHIPS, INC., PART II

20-14   **PREFERRED STOCK, WARRANTS, AND CONVERTIBLES**   Martha Millon, financial manager of Fish & Chips Inc., is facing a dilemma. The firm was founded 5 years ago to develop a new fast-food concept; and although Fish & Chips has done well, the firm's founder and chairman believes that an industry shake-out is imminent. To survive, the firm must capture market share now, which requires a large infusion of new capital.

Because the stock price may rise rapidly, Millon does not want to issue new common stock. On the other hand, interest rates are currently very high by historical standards; and with the firm's B rating, the interest payments on a new debt issue would be too much to handle if sales took a downturn. Thus, Millon has narrowed her choice to bonds with warrants or convertible bonds. She has asked you to help in the decision process by answering the following questions.

a. How does preferred stock differ from common equity and debt?

b. What is adjustable-rate preferred?

c. How can a knowledge of call options help a person understand warrants and convertibles?

d. One of Millon's alternatives is to issue a bond with warrants attached. Fish & Chips' current stock price is $10, and the company's investment bankers estimate its cost of 20-year annual coupon debt without warrants to be 12%. The bankers suggest attaching 50 warrants to each bond, with each warrant having an exercise price of $12.50. It is estimated that each warrant, when detached and traded separately, will have a value of $1.50.

    (1) What coupon rate should be set on the bond with warrants if the total package is to sell for $1,000?

    (2) Suppose the bonds are issued and the warrants immediately trade for $2.50 each. What does this imply about the terms of the issue? Did the company "win" or "lose"?

    (3) When would you expect the warrants to be exercised?

    (4) Will the warrants bring in additional capital when exercised? If so, how much and what type of capital?

    (5) Because warrants lower the cost of the accompanying debt, shouldn't all debt be issued with warrants? What is the expected cost of the bond with warrants if the warrants are expected to be exercised in 5 years, when Fish & Chips' stock price is expected to be $17.50? How would you expect the cost of the bond with warrants to compare with the cost of straight debt? with the cost of common stock?

e.   As an alternative to the bond with warrants, Millon is considering convertible bonds. The firm's investment bankers estimate that Fish & Chips could sell a 20-year, 10% annual coupon, callable convertible bond for its $1,000 par value, whereas a straight-debt issue would require a 12% coupon. Fish & Chips' current stock price is $10, its last dividend was $0.74, and the dividend is expected to grow at a constant rate of 8%. The convertible could be converted into 80 shares of Fish & Chips stock at the owner's option.

    (1) What conversion price, P_c, is implied in the convertible's terms?

    (2) What is the straight-debt value of the convertible? What is the implied value of the convertibility feature?

    (3) What is the formula for the bond's conversion value in any year? its value at Year 0? at Year 10?

    (4) What is meant by the term *floor value* of a convertible? What is the convertible's expected floor value in Year 0? in Year 10?

    (5) Assume that Fish & Chips intends to force conversion by calling the bond when its conversion value is 20% above its par value, or at 1.2($1,000) = $1,200. When is the issue expected to be called? Answer to the closest year.

    (6) What is the expected cost of the convertible to Fish & Chips? Does this cost appear consistent with the riskiness of the issue? Assume conversion in Year 5 at a conversion value of $1,200.

f.   Millon believes that the cost of the bond with warrants and the cost of the convertible bond are essentially equal, so her decision must be based on other factors. What are some factors she should consider when making her decision?

CHAPTER
21 Mergers and Acquisitions

Mergers: Reshaping the Corporate Landscape

Over the past several years, a series of large mergers have reshaped the corporate landscape. These mergers include the $85 billion merger between Exxon and Mobil in 1998, Procter & Gamble's $55 billion bid for Gillette in 2005, and the infamous $160 billion deal between America Online and Time Warner in 2000.

More recently, two unsolicited merger bids made big headlines. First, in February 2008, Microsoft offered to acquire Yahoo for $44.6 billion, which translated into $31 a share. Microsoft's offer represented more than a 50% premium to Yahoo's shareholders. (Prior to the offer, Yahoo's stock was trading at just below $20 a share.) Despite the substantial premium, Yahoo's management rejected the offer. Three months later Microsoft raised the price to $33 a share, but Yahoo's management once again rejected the offer and said that they wouldn't sell for less than $37 a share. At that point, Microsoft withdrew its offer; and by early July, Yahoo's stock was once again trading at around $20 a share. Many of Yahoo's shareholders, most

notably Carl Icahn, have sharply criticized Yahoo's management for rejecting the deal. Facing this difficult economic environment, it remains to be seen what steps Yahoo will take to try to improve its slumping stock price.

Around the same time that Microsoft's bid for Yahoo was taking place, the Belgian/Brazilian brewer InBev made an unsolicited bid for Anheuser-Busch. InBev's $46.35 billion cash offer translated into $65 a share, which represented a 35% premium over the stock price for which Anheuser-Busch was trading the month prior to the announced offer. Despite this premium, Anheuser-Busch's management immediately rejected the deal. In response, InBev raised the bid to $52 billion, or $70 a share. Facing pressure from its board and shareholders, Anheuser-Busch's management reluctantly agreed to sell the company.

While it will be interesting to see how this deal turns out, it's worth noting that while target shareholders generally benefit when their firm is acquired, the track record for acquiring firms in large deals has not been very successful.

In an article written for *The Wall Street Journal,* shortly after the P&G–Gillette announced deal, David Harding and Sam Rovit discussed the potential pitfalls of large acquisitions. They estimated that only 3 out of 10 large deals in recent years have created meaningful benefits for the acquiring firm's shareholders. Harding and Rovit (who are Bain & Company partners and coauthors of a recent book entitled *Mastering the Merger: Four Critical Decisions That Make or Break a Deal*) argue that five major criteria will determine whether a merger is successful:

1. *Is management successful in deal making?* Experienced acquirers tend to do better than firms that make infrequent acquisitions.

2. *Will the acquisition strengthen the buyer's core?* Firms tend to do better when they acquire companies that operate in businesses they understand.

3. *Did management do its homework?* Successful acquirers take time to do the necessary due diligence.

4. *Is the company addressing merger integration issues up front?* Deals can often unravel because there is no clear plan for how the two management teams are going to be integrated after the acquisition.

5. *Is the executive team prepared for the unexpected?* History shows that nothing turns out the way it was planned. Successful acquirers anticipate the unexpected and are able to adapt well to changing circumstances.

Sources: David Kesmodel, Dana Cimilluca, and Dennis Berman, "Anheuser Deal Recognizes Its Tough Spot," *The Wall Street Journal,* July 15, 2008, p. B3; Matthew Dalton, "InBev Stands Firm On Bid for Anheuser," *http://online.wsj.com,* July 1, 2008; Benjamin Pimentel, "Yahoo Shares Head Back to Pre-Microsoft Days," *www.marketwatch.com,* July 1, 2008; Benjamin Pimentel, "Yahoo Doubts Microsoft Really Wanted Marriage," *www.marketwatch.com,* June 30, 2008; David Harding and Sam Rovit, "Five Ways to Spot a Good Deal," *The Wall Street Journal,* March 29, 2005, p. B2; and David Harding and Sam Rovit, *Mastering the Merger: Four Critical Decisions That Make or Break the Deal,* (Boston, MA: Bain and Company, Inc., 2004).

PUTTING THINGS IN PERSPECTIVE

Most corporate growth occurs by internal expansion, which takes place when a firm's existing divisions grow through normal capital budgeting activities. However, the most dramatic examples of growth, and often the largest increases in firms' stock prices, result from mergers. In this chapter, we will describe various aspects related to corporate mergers.

When you finish this chapter, you should be able to:

- Identify the different types of mergers and the various rationales for mergers.
- Conduct a simple analysis to evaluate the potential value of a target firm and discuss the various considerations that influence the bid price.
- Explain whether the typical merger creates value for the participating shareholders.
- Discuss the value of other transactions such as leveraged buyouts (LBOs), corporate alliances, and divestitures.

21-1 RATIONALE FOR MERGERS

Merger
The combination of two or more firms to form a single firm.

Financial managers and theorists have proposed many reasons for the high level of U.S. merger activity. The primary motives behind corporate **mergers** are presented in this section.[1]

---
[1] As we use the term, *merger* means any combination that forms one economic unit from two or more previous ones. For legal purposes, there are distinctions among the various ways these combinations can occur; but our focus is on the fundamental economic and financial aspects of mergers.

21-1a Synergy

The primary motivation for most mergers is to increase the value of the combined enterprise. If Companies A and B merge to form Company C, and if C's value exceeds that of A and B taken separately, then **synergy** is said to exist. Such a merger should be beneficial to both A's and B's stockholders.[2] Synergistic effects can arise from four sources: (1) *operating economies*, which result from economies of scale in management, marketing, production, or distribution; (2) *financial economies*, including lower transactions costs and better coverage by security analysts; (3) *differential efficiency*, which implies that the management of one firm is more efficient and that the weaker firm's assets will be more productive after the merger; and (4) *increased market power* due to reduced competition. Operating and financial economies are socially desirable, as are mergers that increase managerial efficiency; but mergers that reduce competition are socially undesirable and often illegal.[3]

Synergy
The condition wherein the whole is greater than the sum of its parts; in a synergistic merger, the postmerger value exceeds the sum of the separate companies' premerger values.

21-1b Tax Considerations

Tax considerations have stimulated a number of mergers. For example, a profitable firm in the highest tax bracket could acquire a firm with large accumulated tax losses. These losses could then be turned into immediate tax savings rather than carried forward and used in the future.[4] Also, mergers can serve as a way of minimizing taxes when disposing of excess cash. For example, if a firm has a shortage of internal investment opportunities compared with its free cash flow, it could (1) pay an extra dividend, (2) invest in marketable securities, (3) repurchase its own stock, or (4) purchase another firm. If it pays an extra dividend, its stockholders would have to pay immediate taxes on the distribution. Marketable securities often provide a good place to keep money temporarily, but they generally earn a rate of return less than that required by stockholders. A stock repurchase might result in a capital gain for the remaining stockholders. However, using surplus cash to acquire another firm would avoid all these problems, and this has motivated a number of mergers.

21-1c Purchase of Assets below Their Replacement Cost

Sometimes a firm will be touted as an acquisition candidate because the cost of replacing its assets is considerably higher than its market value. For example, in the early 1980s, oil companies could acquire reserves cheaper by buying other oil companies than by conducting exploratory drilling. Thus, Chevron acquired Gulf Oil to augment its reserves. Similarly, in the 1980s, several steel company executives stated that it was cheaper to buy an existing steel company than to construct a new mill. For example, LTV (the fourth largest steel company) acquired Republic Steel (the sixth largest) to create the second largest firm in the industry.

21-1d Diversification

Managers often cite diversification as a reason for mergers. They contend that diversification helps stabilize a firm's earnings and thus benefits its owners.

---

[2]When synergy exists, the whole is greater than the sum of the parts. Synergy is also called the "2 plus 2 equals 5 effect." The distribution of the synergistic gain between A's and B's stockholders is determined by negotiation. This point is discussed later in the chapter.

[3]In the 1880s and 1890s, many mergers occurred in the United States and some of them were obviously directed toward gaining market power rather than increasing efficiency. As a result, Congress passed a series of acts designed to ensure that mergers are not used as a method of reducing competition. The principal acts include the Sherman Act (1890), the Clayton Act (1914), and the Celler Act (1950). These acts make it illegal for firms to merge if the merger tends to lessen competition. The acts are enforced by the antitrust division of the Justice Department and by the Federal Trade Commission.

[4]Mergers undertaken only to use accumulated tax losses would probably be challenged by the IRS. In recent years, Congress has made it increasingly difficult for firms to pass along tax savings after mergers.

Stabilization of earnings is certainly beneficial to employees, suppliers, and customers; but its value is less certain from the standpoint of stockholders. Why should Firm A acquire Firm B to stabilize earnings when stockholders can simply buy the stock of both firms? Indeed, research of U.S. firms suggests that in most cases, diversification does not increase the firm's value. To the contrary, many studies find that diversified firms are worth significantly less than the sum of their individual parts.[5]

21-1e Managers' Personal Incentives

Financial economists like to think that business decisions are based only on economic considerations, especially maximization of firms' values. However, many business decisions are based more on managers' personal motivations than on economic analyses. Business leaders like power, and more power is attached to running a larger corporation than a smaller one. Obviously, no executive would admit that his or her ego was the primary reason behind a merger, but egos do play a prominent role in many mergers.

It has also been observed that executive salaries are highly correlated with company size—the bigger the company, the higher the salaries of its top officers. This too could play a role in corporate acquisition programs.

Personal considerations deter as well as motivate mergers. After most takeovers, some managers of the acquired companies lose their jobs—or at least their autonomy. Therefore, managers who own less than 51% of their firms' stock look to devices that will lessen the chances of a takeover. Mergers can serve as such a device. For example, several years ago Paramount made a bid to acquire Time Inc. Time's managers received a great deal of criticism when they rejected Paramount's bid and chose instead to enter into a heavily debt-financed merger with Warner Brothers that enabled them to retain power. Such **defensive mergers** are hard to defend on economic grounds. The managers involved invariably argue that synergy, not a desire to protect their own jobs, motivated the acquisition; but observers suspect that many mergers were designed more to benefit managers than stockholders.

Defensive Merger
A merger designed to make a company less vulnerable to a takeover.

21-1f Breakup Value

Firms can be valued by book value, economic value, or replacement value. Recently, takeover specialists have begun to recognize breakup value as another basis for valuation. Analysts estimate a company's breakup value, which is the value of the individual parts of the firm if they are sold off separately. If this value is higher than the firm's current market value, a takeover specialist could acquire the firm at or even above its current market value, sell it off in pieces, and earn a substantial profit.

SELF TEST

Define *synergy*. Is synergy a valid rationale for mergers? Describe several situations that might produce synergistic gains.

Give two examples of how tax considerations can motivate mergers.

Suppose your firm could purchase another firm for only half its replacement value. Would that be a sufficient justification for the acquisition? Explain.

Discuss the pros and cons of diversification as a rationale for mergers.

What is breakup value?

[5]See, for example, Philip Berger and Eli Ofek, "Diversification's Effect on Firm Value," *Journal of Financial Economics*, Vol. 37 (1995), pp. 37–65; and Larry Lang and René Stulz, "Tobin's Q, Corporate Diversification, and Firm Performance," *Journal of Political Economy*, Vol. 102 (1994), pp. 1248–1280.

21-2 TYPES OF MERGERS

Economists classify mergers into four types: (1) horizontal, (2) vertical, (3) congeneric, and (4) conglomerate. A **horizontal merger** occurs when one firm combines with another in its same line of business—the recently proposed merger between Sirius Satellite Radio and XM Satellite Ratio is an example. An example of a **vertical merger** is a steel producer's acquisition of one of its own suppliers, such as an iron or coal mining firm, or an oil producer's acquisition of a petrochemical firm that uses oil as a raw material. *Congeneric* means "allied in nature or action"; hence, a **congeneric merger** involves related enterprises but not producers of the same product (horizontal) or firms in a producer-supplier relationship (vertical). The recent Bank of America and Countrywide Financial merger is such an example. A **conglomerate merger** occurs when unrelated enterprises combine. Conglomerate mergers tend to produce few, if any synergies, and have become less popular in recent years.

Operating economies (and anticompetitive effects) are at least partially dependent on the type of merger involved. Vertical and horizontal mergers generally provide the greatest synergistic operating benefits, but they are also the mergers most likely to be attacked by the Department of Justice as anticompetitive. In any event, it is useful to think of these economic classifications when analyzing prospective mergers.

Horizontal Merger
A combination of two firms that produce the same type of good or service.

Vertical Merger
A merger between a firm and one of its suppliers or customers.

Congeneric Merger
A merger of firms in the same general industry but for which no customer or supplier relationship exists.

Conglomerate Merger
A merger of companies in totally different industries.

SELF TEST

What are the four economic types of mergers?

21-3 LEVEL OF MERGER ACTIVITY

Five major "merger waves" have occurred in the United States. The first was in the late 1800s, when consolidations occurred in the oil, steel, tobacco, and other basic industries. The second was in the 1920s, when the stock market boom helped financial promoters consolidate firms in a number of industries, including utilities, communications, and autos. The third was in the 1960s, when conglomerate mergers were the rage. The fourth occurred in the 1980s, when LBO and other firms began using junk bonds to finance acquisitions. The fifth, which involves strategic alliances designed to enable firms to compete better in the global economy, is in progress today.

As can be seen from Table 21-1, which lists some of the more recent larger mergers, some huge mergers have occurred in recent years.[6] In addition, a number of high-profile global mergers have taken place recently, including the mergers of Daimler-Benz and Chrysler, Deutschebank and Bankers Trust, and British Petroleum and Amoco. In general, those mergers have been significantly different from mergers of the 1980s. Most mergers in the 1980s were financial transactions in which buyers sought companies that were selling at less than their true value as a

---

[6]For detailed reviews of the 1980's merger wave, see Andrei Shleifer and Robert W. Vishny, "The Takeover Wave of the 1980s," *Journal of Applied Corporate Finance,* Fall 1991, pp. 49–56; Edmund Faltermayer, "The Deal Decade: Verdict on the '80s," *Fortune,* August 26, 1991, pp. 58–70; and "The Best and Worst Deals of the '80s: What We Learned from All Those Mergers, Acquisitions, and Takeovers," *BusinessWeek,* January 15, 1990, pp. 52–57.

Table 21-1	A Sample of Large Mergers Announced in Recent Years		
Buyer	**Target**	**Announcement Date**	**Value (Billions, U.S. $)**
America Online	Time Warner	January 10, 2000	$160.0
Vodafone AirTouch	Mannesmann	November 14, 1999	148.6
BHP Billiton	Rio Tinto	May 11, 2007	145.3
RBS, Fortis, & Banco Santander	ABN-AMRO Holding	July 16, 2007	99.4
Pfizer	Warner-Lambert	November 4, 1999	90.0
Exxon	Mobil	December 1, 1998	85.2
Bell Atlantic	GTE	July 28, 1998	85.0
SBC Communications	Ameritech	May 11, 1998	80.6
Vodafone	AirTouch	January 18, 1999	74.4
Royal Dutch Petroleum	Shell Trans. & Trading	October 28, 2004	74.3
British Petroleum	Amoco	August 11, 1998	61.7
AT&T	MediaOne Group	May 6, 1999	61.0
Sanofi-Synthelabo	Aventis	January 26, 2004	60.2
Pfizer	Pharmacia Corporation	July 15, 2002	60.0
JP Morgan Chase	Bank One	January 14, 2004	58.8
Procter & Gamble	Gillette	January 28, 2005	55.0
Comcast	AT&T Broadband	July 8, 2001	47.0

Source: Adapted from recent "Year-End Review" articles from *The Wall Street Journal.*

result of incompetent or sluggish management. If a target company could be managed better, if redundant assets could be sold, and if operating and administrative costs could be cut, profits and stock prices would rise. On the other hand, most of the more recent mergers have been strategic in nature—companies are merging to gain economies of scale or scope and thus to be better able to compete in the world economy. Indeed, many recent mergers have involved companies in the financial, defense, media, computer, telecommunications, and health care industries, all of which are experiencing structural changes and intense competition.

Recently, there has also been an increase in cross-border mergers. Many of these mergers have been motivated by large shifts in the value of the world's leading currencies. For example, many suggest that the recent decline in the U.S. dollar has helped spur InBev's bid for Anheuser-Busch.

SELF TEST

What five major "merger waves" have occurred in the United States?

What are some reasons for the current wave?

21-4 HOSTILE VERSUS FRIENDLY TAKEOVERS

In the vast majority of merger situations, one firm (generally the larger of the two) decides to buy another company, negotiates a price with the management of the target firm, and then acquires the target company. Occasionally, the acquired firm will initiate the action, but it is more common for a firm to seek acquisitions than to seek to be acquired.[7] Following convention, we call a company that seeks to acquire another firm the **acquiring company** and the firm that it seeks to acquire the **target company**.

Once an acquiring company has identified a possible target, it must (1) establish a suitable price or range of prices and (2) tentatively set the terms of payment—will it offer cash, its own common stock, bonds, or some combination of cash and securities? Next, the acquiring firm's managers must decide how to approach the target company's managers. If the acquiring firm has reason to believe that the target's management will approve the merger, it will propose a merger and try to work out suitable terms. If an agreement is reached, the two management groups will issue statements to their stockholders indicating that they approve the merger and the target firm's management will recommend to its stockholders that they agree to the merger. Generally, the stockholders are asked to *tender* (or send in) their shares to a designated financial institution, along with a signed power of attorney that transfers ownership of the shares to the acquiring firm. The target firm's stockholders then receive the specified payment—common stock of the acquiring company (in which case the target company's stockholders become stockholders of the acquiring company), cash, bonds, or some mix of cash and securities. This is a **friendly merger**.

Often, however, the target company's management resists the merger. Perhaps they think that the price offered is too low, or perhaps they want to keep their jobs. In either case, the acquiring firm's offer is said to be *hostile* rather than friendly and the acquiring firm must make a direct appeal to the target firm's stockholders. In a **hostile merger**, the acquiring company will again make a **tender offer** and again ask the stockholders of the target firm to tender their shares in exchange for the offered price. This time, though, the target firm's managers will urge stockholders not to tender their shares, generally stating that the price offered (cash, bonds, or stocks in the acquiring firm) is too low.

While most mergers are friendly, a number of interesting cases have involved high-profile firms that have attempted hostile takeovers. For example, Warner-Lambert tried to fight off a hostile bid by Pfizer; however, the merger was completed in 2000. Overseas, Olivetti successfully conducted a hostile takeover of Telecom Italia; and in another telecommunications merger, Britain's Vodafone AirTouch made a hostile bid for its German rival, Mannesmann AG, which was successful.

Acquiring Company
A company that seeks to acquire another firm.

Target Company
A firm that another company seeks to acquire.

Friendly Merger
A merger whose terms are approved by management of both companies.

Hostile Merger
A merger in which the target firm's management resists acquisition.

Tender Offer
The offer of one firm to buy the stock of another firm by going directly to the stockholders, frequently (but not always) over the opposition of the target company's management.

 SELF TEST

What's the difference between a hostile and a friendly merger?

21-5 MERGER ANALYSIS

In theory, merger analysis is quite simple. The acquiring firm performs an analysis to value the target company and then determines whether the target can be bought at that value or, preferably, for less than the estimated value. The target

---

[7]However, if a firm is in financial difficulty, if its managers are elderly and do not think that suitable replacements are on hand, or if it needs the support (often the capital) of a larger company, it may seek to be acquired. Thus, when a number of Texas, Ohio, and Maryland financial institutions were in trouble in the 1980s, they lobbied to get their state legislatures to pass laws that would make it easier for them to be acquired. Out-of-state banks then moved in to help salvage the situation and minimize depositor losses.

company, on the other hand, should accept the offer if the price exceeds either its value if it continued to operate independently or the price it could receive from some other bidder. Theory aside, however, some difficult issues are involved. In this section, we discuss valuing the target firm, which is the initial step in a merger analysis. Then we discuss setting the bid price and post-merger control.

21-5a Valuing the Target Firm

Several methodologies are used to value target firms, but we will confine our discussion to the two most common: (1) the discounted cash flow approach and (2) the market multiple method. However, regardless of the valuation methodology, it is crucial to recognize two facts. First, the target company typically does not continue to operate as a separate entity but becomes part of the acquiring firm's portfolio of assets. Therefore, changes in operations affect the value of the business and must be considered in the analysis. Second, the goal of merger valuation is to value the target firm's equity because a firm is acquired from its owners, not from its creditors. Thus, although we use the expression *valuing the firm*, our focus is on the value of the equity rather than on total value.

Discounted Cash Flow Analysis

The discounted cash flow (DCF) approach to valuing a business involves the application of capital budgeting procedures to an entire firm rather than to a single project. To apply this method, two key items are needed: (1) pro forma statements that forecast the incremental free cash flows expected to result from the merger and (2) a discount rate, or cost of capital, to apply to the projected cash flows.

Pro Forma Cash Flow Statements Obtaining accurate post-merger cash flow forecasts is by far the most important task in the DCF approach. In a pure **financial merger**, in which no synergies are expected, the incremental post-merger cash flows are simply the expected cash flows of the target firm. In an **operating merger**, where the two firms' operations are to be integrated, forecasting future cash flows is more difficult.

Table 21-2 shows the projected cash flow statements for Apex Corporation, which is being considered as a target by Hightech, a large conglomerate. The projected data are for the post-merger period, and all synergistic effects have been included. Apex currently uses 50% debt; and if it is acquired, Hightech will keep the debt ratio at 50%. Both Hightech and Apex have a 40% marginal federal-plus-state tax rate.

Lines 1 through 4 of the table show the operating information that Hightech expects for the Apex subsidiary if the merger takes place, and Line 5 contains the earnings before interest and taxes (EBIT) for each year. Unlike a typical capital budgeting analysis, a merger analysis usually incorporates interest expense into the cash flow forecast, as shown on Line 6. This is done for three reasons: (1) Acquiring firms often assume the debt of the target firm, so old debt at different coupon rates is often part of the deal; (2) the acquisition is often financed partially by debt; and (3) if the subsidiary is to grow in the future, new debt must be issued over time to support the expansion. Thus, debt associated with a merger is typically more complex than the single issue of new debt associated with a normal capital project, and the easiest way to properly account for the complexities of merger debt is to specifically include each year's expected interest expense in the cash flow forecast. Therefore, we are using what is called the **equity residual method** to value the target firm. Here the estimated net cash flows are a residual that belongs solely to the acquiring firm's shareholders. Therefore, the estimates should be discounted at the cost of equity. This is in contrast to the corporate value model of Chapter 9, where the free cash flows (which belong to all investors, not

Financial Merger
A merger in which the firms involved will not be operated as a single unit and from which no operating economies are expected.

Operating Merger
A merger in which operations of the firms involved are integrated in the hope of achieving synergistic benefits.

Equity Residual Method
A method used to value a target firm using net cash flows that are a residual and belong solely to the acquiring firm's shareholders.

Table 21-2	Projected Post-Merger Cash Flow Statements for the Apex Subsidiary as of December 31 (Millions of Dollars)				
	2009	**2010**	**2011**	**2012**	**2013**
1. Net sales	$105.0	$126.0	$151.0	$174.0	$191.0
2. Cost of goods sold	75.0	89.0	106.0	122.0	132.0
3. Selling and administrative expenses	10.0	12.0	13.0	15.0	16.0
4. Depreciation	8.0	8.0	9.0	9.0	10.0
5. EBIT	$ 12.0	$ 17.0	$ 23.0	$ 28.0	$ 33.0
6. Interest[a]	8.0	9.0	10.0	11.0	11.0
7. EBT	$ 4.0	$ 8.0	$ 13.0	$ 17.0	$ 22.0
8. Taxes (40%)[b]	1.6	3.2	5.2	6.8	8.8
9. Net income	$ 2.4	$ 4.8	$ 7.8	$ 10.2	$ 13.2
10. Plus depreciation	8.0	8.0	9.0	9.0	10.0
11. Cash flow	$ 10.4	$ 12.8	$ 16.8	$ 19.2	$ 23.2
12. Less retentions needed for growth[c]	4.0	4.0	7.0	9.0	12.0
13. Plus terminal value[d]					127.8
14. Net cash flow to Hightech[e]	$ 6.4	$ 8.8	$ 9.8	$ 10.2	$139.0

Notes:
[a]Interest payments are estimates based on Apex's existing debt plus additional debt required to finance growth.
[b]Hightech will file a consolidated tax return after the merger. Thus, the taxes shown here are the full corporate taxes attributable to Apex's operations: No additional taxes on any cash flows will be passed from Apex to Hightech.
[c]Some of the cash flows generated by the Apex subsidiary after the merger must be retained to finance asset replacements and growth, while some will be transferred to Hightech to pay dividends on its stock or for redeployment within the corporation. These retentions are net of any additional debt used to help finance growth.
[d]Apex's available cash flows are expected to grow at a constant 5% rate after 2013. The value of all post-2013 cash flows as of December 31, 2013, is estimated by use of the constant growth model to be $127.8 million.

$$V_{2013} = \frac{CF_{2014}}{r_s - g} = \frac{(23.2 - \$12.0)(1.05)}{0.142 - 0.05} = \$127.8 \text{ million}$$

In the next section, we discuss the estimated 14.2% cost of equity. The $127.8 million is the PV at the end of 2013 of the stream of cash flows for Year 2014 and thereafter.
[e]There are the net cash flows projected to be available to Hightech by virtue of the acquisition. The cash flows could be used to make dividend payments to Hightech's stockholders, to finance asset expansion in Hightech's other divisions and subsidiaries, and so forth.

just shareholders) are discounted at the WACC. Both methods lead to the same estimate of equity value.

Line 7 contains the earnings before taxes (EBT), and Line 8 gives taxes based on Hightech's 40% marginal rate. Line 9 lists each year's net income; and depreciation is added back on Line 10 to obtain each year's cash flow, as shown on Line 11. Because some of Apex's assets will wear out or become obsolete and because Hightech plans to expand the Apex subsidiary should the acquisition occur, some equity funds must be retained and reinvested in the business. These retentions, which are not available for transfer to the parent, are shown on Line 12. Finally, we have projected only 5 years of cash flows, but Hightech would likely operate the Apex subsidiary for many years—in theory, forever. Therefore, we applied the constant growth model to the 2013 cash flow to estimate the value of all cash flows beyond 2013. (See Note d in Table 21-2.) This "terminal value" represents Apex's projected value at the end of 2013, and it is shown on Line 13.

The net cash flows shown on Line 14 would be available to Hightech's stockholders, and they are the basis of the valuation.[8] Of course, the post-merger

---

[8]We purposely made the cash flows relatively simple to keep the focus on key issues. In an actual merger valuation, the cash flows would be more complex, normally including items such as additional capital furnished by the acquiring firm, tax loss carry-forwards, tax effects of plant and equipment valuation adjustments, and cash flows from the sale of some of the subsidiary's assets.

cash flows are extremely difficult to estimate; and in a complete merger valuation, just as in a complete capital budgeting analysis, sensitivity, scenario, and simulation analyses should be conducted. Indeed, in a friendly merger, the acquiring firm would send a team consisting of dozens of accountants, engineers, and so forth, to the target firm's headquarters. They would go over its books, estimate required maintenance expenditures, set values on assets such as real estate and petroleum reserves, and the like. Such an investigation, which is called *due diligence,* is an essential part of any merger analysis.

Estimating the Discount Rate The bottom-line net cash flows shown on Line 14 are after interest and taxes; hence, they represent equity. Therefore, they should be discounted at the cost of equity rather than at the overall cost of capital. Further, the discount rate used should reflect the risk of the cash flows in the table. The most appropriate discount rate is Apex's cost of equity, not that of Hightech or the consolidated post-merger firm.

Although we will not illustrate it here, Hightech could perform a risk analysis on the Table 21-2 cash flows just as it does on any set of capital budgeting flows. Sensitivity analysis, scenario analysis, and/or Monte Carlo simulation could be used to give Hightech's management a feel for the risks involved with the acquisition. Apex is a publicly traded company, so we can assess directly its market risk. Apex's market-determined pre-merger beta was 1.63. Because the merger would not change Apex's capital structure or tax rate, the firm's post-merger beta would remain at 1.63. However, if Apex's capital structure had changed, the Hamada equation (which was discussed in Chapter 14) could have been used to determine the firm's new beta corresponding to its changed capital structure.

We use the Security Market Line to estimate Apex's post-merger cost of equity. If the risk-free rate is 6% and the market risk premium is 5%, Apex's cost of equity, r_s, after the merger with Hightech, will be about 14.2%.[9]

$$r_s = r_{RF} + (RP_M)b = 6\% + (5\%)1.63 = 14.15\% \approx 14.2\%$$

Valuing the Cash Flows The current value of Apex's stock to Hightech is the present value of the cash flows expected from Apex, discounted at 14.2% (in millions of dollars):

$$V_{2008} = \frac{\$6.4}{(1.142)^1} + \frac{\$8.8}{(1.142)^2} + \frac{\$9.8}{(1.142)^3} + \frac{\$10.2}{(1.142)^4} + \frac{\$139.0}{(1.142)^5} \approx \$96.5$$

Thus, the value of Apex's stock to Hightech is $96.5 million.

Note that in a merger analysis, the value of the target consists of the target's pre-merger value plus any value created by operating or financial synergies. In this example, we held the target's capital structure and tax rate constant. Therefore, the only synergies were operating synergies, and these effects were incorporated into the forecasted cash flows. If there had been financial synergies, the analysis would had to have been modified to reflect this added value. For example, if Apex had

---

[9]In this example, we used the Capital Asset Pricing Model to estimate Apex's cost of equity; thus, we assumed that investors require a premium for market risk only. We also could have conducted a corporate risk analysis in which the relevant risk would be the contribution of Apex's cash flows to the total risk of the post-merger firm.

In actual merger situations among large firms, companies usually hire an investment banker to help develop valuation estimates. For example, when General Electric acquired Utah International (UI), GE hired Morgan Stanley to determine UI's value. We discussed the valuation process with the Morgan Stanley analyst in charge of the appraisal, and he confirmed that Morgan Stanley applied all of the standard procedures discussed in this chapter. Note, though, that merger analysis, like the analysis of any other complex issue, requires judgment and people's judgments differ as to how much weight to give to different methods in any given situation.

been operating with only 30% debt and if Hightech could have lowered Apex's overall cost of capital by increasing the debt ratio to 50%, Apex's merger value would have exceeded the $96.5 million calculated previously.

Market Multiple Analysis

The second method of valuing a target company is **market multiple analysis**, which applies a market-determined multiple to net income, earnings per share, sales, or book value or for businesses such as cable TV or cell phone systems, the number of subscribers. While the DCF method applies valuation concepts in a precise manner, focusing on expected cash flows, market multiple analysis is more judgmental. To illustrate the concept, note that Apex's forecasted net income is $2.4 million in 2009, and it rises to $13.2 million in 2013, for an average of $7.7 million over the 5-year forecast period. The average P/E ratio for publicly traded companies similar to Apex is 12.5.

To estimate Apex's value using the market P/E multiple approach, multiply its $7.7 million average net income by the market multiple of 12.5 to obtain the value of $7.7(12.5) = $96.25 million. This is the equity, or ownership, value of the firm. Note that we used the average net income over the next 5 years to value Apex. The market P/E multiple of 12.5 is based on the current year's income of comparable companies, but Apex's current income does not reflect synergistic effects or managerial changes that will be made. By averaging future net income, we are attempting to capture the value added by Hightech to Apex's operations.

Note that measures other than net income can be used in the market multiple approach. For example, another commonly used measure is *earnings before interest, taxes, depreciation, and amortization (EBITDA)*. The procedure is identical to the one just described, except that the market multiple is price divided by EBITDA rather than earnings per share, and this multiple is multiplied by Apex's EBITDA.

As noted, in some businesses such as cable TV and cell phones, an important element in the valuation process is the company's number of customers. The acquirer has an idea of the cost required to obtain a new customer and the average cash flow per customer. Managed care companies such as HMOs have applied similar logic in acquisitions, basing their valuations on the number of people insured.

Market Multiple Analysis
A method of valuing a target company that applies a market-determined multiple to net income, earnings per share, sales, book value, and so forth.

21-5b Setting the Bid Price

Using the DCF valuation results, $96.5 million is the most Hightech could pay for Apex—if it pays more, Hightech's own value will be diluted. On the other hand, if Hightech can acquire Apex for less than $96.5 million, Hightech's stockholders will gain value. Therefore, Hightech will bid something less than $96.5 million when it makes an offer for Apex.

Figure 21-1 graphs the merger situation. The $96.5 million is shown as a point on the horizontal axis, and it is the maximum price that Hightech can afford to pay. If Hightech pays less (say, $86.5 million), its stockholders will gain $10 million from the merger; while if Hightech pays more, its stockholders will lose. What we have then is a 45-degree line that cuts the x-axis at $96.5 million, and that line shows how much Hightech's stockholders can expect to gain or lose at different acquisition prices.

Now consider the target company, Apex. It has 10 million shares of stock that sell for $6.25, so its value as an independent operating company is presumably $62.5 million. [In making this statement, we assume (1) that the company's present management is doing a good job of operating the company and (2) that the $6.25 market price per share does not include a "speculative merger premium" in addition to the PV of its operating cash flows.] If Apex is acquired at a price greater than $62.5 million, its stockholders will gain value, while they will lose

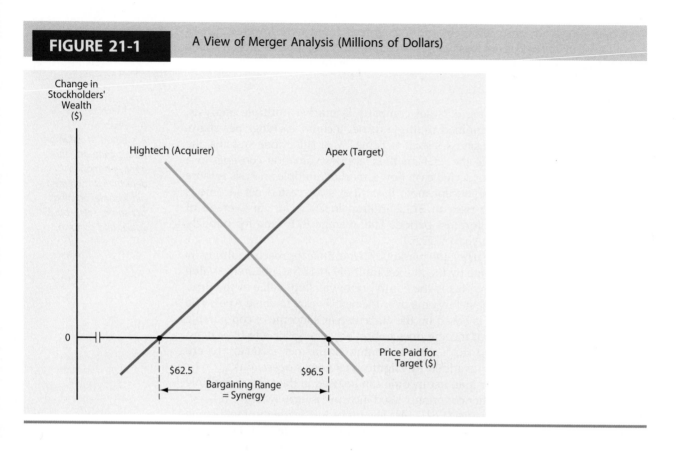

| FIGURE 21-1 | A View of Merger Analysis (Millions of Dollars) |

value at any lower price. Thus, we can draw another 45-degree line, this one with an upward slope, to show how the merger price affects Apex's stockholders.

The difference between $62.5 and $96.5 million, or $34 million, represents synergistic benefits expected from the merger. Here are some points to note:

1. If there were no synergistic benefits, the maximum bid would be equal to the current value of the target company. The greater the synergistic gains, the greater the gap between the target's current price and the maximum the acquiring company could pay.

2. The greater the synergistic gain, the more likely a merger is to be consummated.

3. The issue of how to divide the synergistic benefits is critically important. Obviously, both parties want to get as much as possible. In our example, if Apex's management knew the maximum price that Hightech could pay, it would argue for a price close to $96.5 million. Hightech, on the other hand, would try to get Apex at a price as close to $62.5 million as possible.

4. Within the $62.5 to $96.5 million range, where will the actual price be set? The answer depends on a number of factors, including whether Hightech offers to pay with cash or securities, the negotiating skills of the two management teams, and (most importantly) the bargaining positions of the two parties as determined by fundamental economic conditions. To illustrate the latter point, suppose Hightech could acquire many companies similar to Apex but no company other than Hightech could gain synergies by acquiring Apex. In this case, Hightech would probably make a relatively low, take-it-or-leave-it offer, and Apex would probably take it because some gain is better than none. On the other hand, if Apex has some unique technology or some other asset that many companies want, once Hightech announces its offer, other firms will probably make competing bids and the

MORE THAN JUST FINANCIAL STATEMENTS

When corporations merge, they combine more than just their financial statements. Mergers bring together two organizations with different histories and corporate cultures. Deals that look good on paper can fail if the individuals involved are unwilling or unable to work together to generate the potential synergies. Consequently, when analyzing a potential merger, it is important to determine whether the two companies are compatible.

Many deals fall apart because, during the "due diligence" phase, synergistic benefits are revealed to be less than was originally anticipated, so there is little economic rationale for the merger. Other negotiations break off because the two parties cannot agree on the price to be paid for the acquired firm's stock. In addition, merger talks often collapse because of "social issues." These social issues include both the "chemistry" of the companies and their personnel and such basic issues as these: What will be the name of the combined company? Where will headquarters be located? And, most important: Who will run the combined company? Robert Kindler, a partner at Cravath,

Swaine & Moore, a prominent New York law firm that specializes in mergers, summarizes the importance of these issues as follows: "Even transactions that make absolute economic sense don't happen unless the social issues work."

Investment bankers, lawyers, and other professionals state that mergers tend to be most successful if there is a clear and well-arranged plan spelling out who will run the company. This issue is straightforward if one firm is clearly dominant and is acquiring the other. However, in cases where there is "a merger of equals," senior personnel issues often become sticky. This situation is made considerably easier if one of the chief executives is at or near the retirement age.

Some analysts believe that social issues often play too large a role, derailing mergers that should take place. In other cases where a merger occurs, concerns about social issues preclude managers from undertaking the necessary changes—like laying off redundant staff—for the deal to benefit shareholders.

Source: "In Many Merger Deals, Ego and Pride Play Big Roles in Which Way Talks Go," *The Wall Street Journal*, August 22, 1996, p. C1. Reprinted by permission of *The Wall Street Journal*, Copyright © 2002 Dow Jones & Company, Inc. All Rights Reserved Worldwide.

final price will probably be close to or even above $96.5 million. A price above $96.5 million would presumably be paid by some other company that had a better synergistic fit or perhaps whose management was more optimistic about Apex's cash flow potential. In Figure 21-1, this situation would be represented by a line parallel to that for Hightech but shifted to the right of the Hightech line.

5.   Hightech would, of course, want to keep its maximum bid secret; and it would plan its bidding strategy carefully and consistently with the situation. If it thought that other bidders would emerge or that Apex's management might resist to preserve their jobs, it might make a high "preemptive" bid in hopes of scaring off competing bids and/or management resistance. On the other hand, it might make a lowball bid in hopes of "stealing" the company.

We will have more to say about these points in the sections that follow, and you should keep Figure 21-1 in mind as you go through the rest of the chapter.

21-5c Post-Merger Control

The employment/control situation is often of vital interest in a merger analysis. First, consider the situation in which a small, owner-managed firm sells out to a larger concern. The owner-manager may be anxious to retain a high-status position, and he or she may also have developed a camaraderie with the employees and thus be concerned about their retention after the merger. If so, these points would be stressed during the merger negotiations.[10] When a publicly owned firm that is not owned by its managers is merged with another company, the acquired firm's managers will be worried about their post-merger positions. If the acquiring firm agrees to retain the old management, management may be willing to support the merger and to recommend its acceptance to the stockholders. If the old management is to be removed, management will probably resist the merger.[11]

SELF TEST

What is the difference between an operating merger and a financial merger?

Describe the way post-merger cash flows are estimated in a DCF analysis.

What is the basis for the discount rate in a DCF analysis? Describe how this rate might be estimated.

Describe the market multiple approach.

What are some factors that acquiring firms consider when they set a bid price?

How do control issues affect mergers?

Assuming the following facts, what is the value of XYZ Corporation to JKL Enterprises? XYZ's post-merger cash flows in Years 1–3 are estimated to be $7 million, $10 million, and $12 million, respectively. In addition, its terminal value in Year 3 is $318 million. The firm's cost of equity is 10%, and its growth rate is 6%. **($262.56 million)**

21-6 THE ROLE OF INVESTMENT BANKERS

Investment bankers are involved with mergers in a number of ways: (1) They help arrange mergers, (2) they help target companies develop and implement defensive tactics, (3) they help value target companies, (4) they help finance mergers, and (5) they invest in the stocks of potential merger candidates. These merger-related activities have been quite profitable. For example, Thomson Financial estimated that financial advisers received nearly $16 billion in fees from worldwide merger activity generated during just the first half of 2008. No wonder investment banking houses are able to make top offers to finance graduates!

---

[10]The acquiring firm may also be concerned about this point, especially if the target firm's management is quite good. Indeed, a condition of the merger may be that the management team agrees to stay on for a period such as 5 years after the merger. In this case, the price paid may be contingent on the acquired firm's performance subsequent to the merger. For example, when International Holdings acquired Walker Products, the price paid was an immediate 100,000 shares of International Holdings stock worth $63 per share plus an additional 30,000 shares each year for the next 3 years, provided Walker Products earned at least $1 million during each of those years. Since Walker's managers owned the stock and would receive the bonus, they had a strong incentive to stay on and help the firm meet its targets.

Finally, if the managers of the target company are highly competent but do not want to remain on after the merger, the acquiring firm may build into the merger contract a noncompete agreement with the old management. Typically, the acquired firm's principal officers must agree not to affiliate for a specified period with a new business that is competitive with the one they sold (e.g., 5 years). Such agreements are especially important with service-oriented businesses.

[11]Managements of firms that are thought to be attractive merger candidates often arrange *golden parachutes* for themselves. Golden parachutes are extremely lucrative retirement plans that take effect if a merger is consummated. Thus, when Bendix Corp. was acquired by Allied Automotive, Bill Agee, Bendix's chairman, "pulled the ripcord of his golden parachute" and walked away with $4 million. If a golden parachute is large enough, it can also function as a poison pill—for example, where the president of a firm worth $10 million would have to be paid $8 million if the firm is acquired, this will prevent a takeover. Stockholders are increasingly resisting such arrangements, but some still exist.

21-6a Arranging Mergers

The major investment banking firms have merger and acquisition groups that operate within their corporate finance departments. (Corporate finance departments offer advice, as opposed to underwriting or brokerage services, to business firms.) Members of these groups identify firms with excess cash that might want to buy other firms; companies that might be willing to be bought; and firms that might, for a number of reasons, be attractive to others. Also, if an oil company, for instance, decided to expand into coal mining, it might enlist the aid of an investment banker to help it acquire a coal company. Similarly, dissident stockholders of firms with poor track records might work with investment bankers to oust management by helping to arrange a merger. Investment bankers are reported to have offered packages of financing to corporate raiders, where the package included designing the securities to be used in the tender offer, as well as lining up people and firms to buy the target firm's stock and then tendering it once the final offer was made.

Investment bankers have occasionally taken illegal actions in the merger arena. For example, they are reported to have parked stock—purchasing it for a raider under a guaranteed buy-back agreement—to help the raider de facto accumulate more than 5% of the target's stock without disclosing the position. People have gone to jail for this.

21-6b Developing Defensive Tactics

Target firms that do not want to be acquired generally enlist the help of an investment banking firm, along with a law firm that specializes in mergers. Defenses include such tactics as (1) changing the by-laws so that only one-third of the directors are elected each year and/or so that a 75% approval (a *supermajority*) versus a simple majority is required to approve a merger; (2) trying to convince the target firm's stockholders that the price being offered is too low; (3) raising antitrust issues in the hope that the Justice Department will intervene; (4) repurchasing stock in the open market in an effort to push the price above that being offered by the potential acquirer; (5) getting a **white knight** who is acceptable to the target firm's management to compete with the potential acquirer; (6) getting a **white squire** who is friendly to current management to buy enough of the target firm's shares to block the merger; and (7) taking a *poison pill*, as described next.

Poison pills—which occasionally amount to committing economic suicide to avoid a takeover—are tactics such as borrowing on terms that require immediate repayment of all loans if the firm is acquired, selling off at bargain prices the assets that originally made the firm a desirable target, granting such lucrative **golden parachutes** to their executives that the cash drain from these payments render the merger infeasible, and planning defensive mergers that leave the firm with new assets of questionable value and a huge debt load. Currently, the most popular poison pill is for a company to give its stockholders stock purchase rights that allow them to buy the stock of an acquiring firm at half price should the firm be acquired. The blatant use of poison pills is constrained by directors' awareness that excessive use may trigger stockholders to bring personal suits against directors who voted for them and perhaps, in the near future, by laws that further limit management's use of pills. Still, investment bankers and antitakeover lawyers are busy thinking up new poison pill formulas, and others are just as busy trying to come up with antidotes.[12]

---

[12]It has become extremely difficult and expensive for companies to buy "directors' insurance," which protects the board from such contingencies as stockholders' suits; and even when insurance is available, it often does not pay for losses if the directors have not exercised due caution and judgment. This exposure is making directors extremely leery of actions that might trigger stockholder suits.

A video clip entitled "T. Boone Pickens on White Knights," which discusses mergers and takeovers, is available at Ohio State University's web site at **www.cob.ohio-state.edu/ fin/clips.htm**. *The clip requires a QuickTime video player for Windows or Macintosh (which you can download for free at* **www. apple.com/quicktime**). *One caveat is that the video clip is in excess of 5 MB in size and therefore should be accessed only with a fast Internet connection.*

White Knight
A company that is acceptable to the management of a firm under threat of a hostile takeover and that will compete with the potential acquirer.

White Squire
An individual or a company that is friendly to current management and will buy enough of the target firm's shares to block a hostile takeover.

Poison Pill
An action that will seriously hurt a company if it is acquired by another.

Golden Parachutes
Large payments made to the managers of a target firm when it is acquired.

Another takeover defense that is being used is the employee stock ownership plan (ESOP). ESOPs are designed to give lower-level employees an ownership stake in the firm, and current tax laws provide generous incentives for companies to establish such plans and fund them with the firm's common stock.

21-6c Establishing a Fair Value

If a friendly merger is being worked out between two firms' managements, it is important to document that the agreed-upon price is a fair one; otherwise, the stockholders of either company may sue to block the merger. Therefore, in most large mergers, each side hires an investment banking firm to evaluate the target company and to help establish the fair price. A recent study of fairness opinions in mergers suggests that advisers working for the acquiring firms tend to produce overly optimistic valuations of the target firm, whereas the advisers working for the target firms tend to produce more accurate estimates of the target's value. The study also concludes that the market often gains useful information from the fairness opinions provided by the target's advisers.[13]

21-6d Financing Mergers

Many mergers are financed with the acquiring company's excess cash. However, if the acquiring company has no excess cash, it will require a source of funds. Perhaps the single most important factor behind the 1980s merger wave was the development of junk bonds for use in financing acquisitions.

Drexel Burnham Lambert was the primary developer of *junk bonds,* defined as bonds rated below investment grade (BBB/Baa). Prior to Drexel's actions, it was almost impossible to sell low-grade bonds to raise new capital. Drexel then pioneered a procedure under which a target firm's situation would be appraised very closely and a cash flow projection similar to that in Table 21-2 (but more detailed) would be developed.

To be successful in the mergers and acquisitions (M&A) business, an investment banker must be able to offer a financing package to clients, whether they are acquirers who need capital to take over companies or target companies trying to finance stock repurchase plans or other defenses against takeovers. Drexel was the leading player in the merger financing game during the 1980s; but since Drexel's bankruptcy, Goldman Sachs, UBS, Morgan Stanley, and others are vying for the title.

21-6e Arbitrage Operations

Arbitrage

The simultaneous buying and selling of the same commodity or security in two different markets at different prices and pocketing a risk-free return.

Arbitrage generally means simultaneously buying and selling the same commodity or security in two different markets at different prices and pocketing a risk-free return. However, the major brokerage houses, as well as some wealthy private investors, are engaged in a different type of arbitrage called *risk arbitrage.* The *arbitrageurs,* or "arbs," speculate in the stocks of companies that are likely takeover targets. Vast amounts of capital are required to speculate in a large number of securities and thus reduce risk—and to make money on narrow spreads. However, the large investment bankers have the wherewithal to play the game. To be successful, arbs need to be able to sniff out likely targets, assess the probability of offers reaching fruition, and move in and out of the market quickly incurring low transactions costs.

---

[13]Matthew D. Cain, "The Information Content of Fairness Opinions in Negotiated Mergers," 2007 PhD dissertation, Purdue University.

What are some defensive tactics that firms can use to resist hostile takeovers?

What role did junk bonds play in the merger wave of the 1980s?

What is the difference between pure arbitrage and risk arbitrage?

21-7 DO MERGERS CREATE VALUE? THE EMPIRICAL EVIDENCE

All the recent merger activity has raised two questions: (1) Do corporate acquisitions create value? (2) If so, how do the parties share the value?

Most researchers agree that takeovers increase the wealth of the shareholders of target firms; otherwise, they would not agree to the offer. However, there is a debate as to whether mergers benefit the acquiring firm's shareholders. In particular, managements of acquiring firms may be motivated by factors other than shareholder wealth maximization. For example, they may want to merge merely to increase the size of the corporations they manage because increased size usually brings larger salaries in addition to job security, perquisites, power, and prestige.

The validity of the competing views on who gains from corporate acquisitions can be tested by examining the stock price changes that occur around the time of a merger or takeover announcement. Changes in the stock prices of the acquiring and target firms represent market participants' beliefs about the value created by the merger and about how that value will be divided between the target and acquiring firms' shareholders. So examining a large sample of stock price movements can shed light on the issue of who gains from mergers.

THE TRACK RECORD OF RECENT LARGE MERGERS

Academics have long known that acquiring firm's shareholders rarely reap the benefits of mergers. However, this important information never seemed to make it up to the offices of corporate America's decision makers; the 1990s saw bad deal after bad deal, with no apparent learning on the part of acquisitive executives. *BusinessWeek* published an analysis of 302 large mergers from 1995 to 2001, and it found that 61% of them led to losses by the acquiring firms' shareholders. Indeed, those losing shareholders' returns during the first post-merger year averaged 25 percentage points less than the returns on other companies in the industry. The average returns for all the merging companies, both winners and losers, were 4.3% below industry averages and 9.2% below the S&P 500. The article cited four common mistakes:

1. The acquiring firms often overpaid. Generally, the acquirers gave away all of the synergies from the mergers to the acquired firms' shareholders, and then some.

2. Management overestimated the synergies (cost savings and revenue gains) that would result from the merger.

3. Management took too long to integrate operations between the merged companies. This irritated customers and employees alike, and it postponed any gains from the integration.

4. Some companies cut costs too deeply, at the expense of maintaining sales and production infrastructures.

The worst performance came from companies that paid for their acquisitions with stock. The best performance, albeit a paltry 0.3% better than industry averages, came from companies that used cash for their acquisitions. On the bright side, the shareholders of the companies that were acquired fared quite well, earning, on average, 19.3% more than their industry peers; and all of those gains came in the 2 weeks surrounding the merger announcement.

Source: David Henry, "Mergers: Why Most Big Deals Don't Pay Off," *BusinessWeek*, October 14, 2002, pp. 60–70.

We cannot simply examine stock prices around merger announcement dates because other factors influence stock prices. For example, if a merger was announced on a day when the entire market advanced, the fact that the target firm's price rose would not necessarily signify that the merger was expected to create value. Hence, studies examine *abnormal returns* associated with merger announcements, where abnormal returns are defined as that part of a stock price change caused by factors other than changes in the general stock market.

Many studies have examined both acquiring and target firms' stock price responses to mergers and tender offers.[14] Jointly, these studies have covered nearly every acquisition involving publicly traded firms from the early 1960s to the present, and they are remarkably consistent in their results: On average, the stock prices of target firms increase by about 30% in hostile tender offers, while in friendly mergers, the average increase is about 20%. However, for both hostile and friendly deals, the stock prices of acquiring firms, on average, remain constant. However, as the accompanying box entitled "The Track Record of Recent Large Mergers" suggests, abnormal returns vary considerably among mergers and it is not unusual for acquiring firms to see their stock prices fall when mergers are announced. On balance, the evidence indicates (1) that acquisitions do create value but (2) that shareholders of target firms reap virtually all the benefits.

In hindsight, these results are not too surprising. First, because target firm's shareholders can always say no, they are in the driver's seat. Second, takeovers are a competitive game; so if one potential acquiring firm does not offer full value for a potential target, another firm will generally jump in with a higher bid. Finally, managements of acquiring firms might be willing to give up all the value created by the merger because the merger would enhance the acquiring managers' personal positions without harming their shareholders.

It has also been argued that acquisitions may increase shareholder wealth at the expense of bondholders—in particular, there is concern that leveraged buyouts dilute the claims of bondholders. Specific instances can be cited in which bonds were downgraded and bondholders did suffer losses, sometimes quite large ones, as a direct result of an acquisition. However, most studies find no evidence to support the contention that bondholders, on average, lose in corporate acquisitions.

Explain how researchers can study the effects of mergers on shareholder wealth.

Do mergers create value? If so, who profits from this value?

Do the research results discussed in this section seem logical? Explain.

21-8 CORPORATE ALLIANCES

Corporate, or Strategic, Alliance
A cooperative deal that stops short of a merger.

Mergers are one way for two companies to join forces; but many companies are striking cooperative deals, called **corporate, or strategic, alliances**, which stop far short of merging. Whereas mergers combine all of the assets of the firms involved, as well as their ownership and managerial expertise, alliances allow firms to create combinations that focus on specific business lines that offer the most potential synergies. These alliances take many forms, from simple marketing agreements to joint ownership of worldwide operations.

---

[14]For an excellent summary of the effects of mergers on value, see Michael C. Jensen and Richard S. Ruback, "The Market for Corporate Control: The Scientific Evidence," *Journal of Financial Economics*, April 1983, pp. 5–50.

One form of corporate alliance is the **joint venture**, in which parts of companies are joined to achieve specific, limited objectives.[15] A joint venture is controlled by a management team consisting of representatives of the two (or more) parent companies. Joint ventures have been used often by U.S., Japanese, and European firms to share technology and/or marketing expertise. For example, Whirlpool announced a joint venture with the Dutch electronics giant Philips to produce appliances under Philips's brand names in five European countries. By joining with their foreign counterparts, U.S. firms are attempting to gain a stronger foothold in Europe. Although alliances are new to some firms, they are established practices to others. For example, Corning Glass now obtains more than half of its profits from 23 joint ventures, two-thirds of them with foreign companies representing almost all of Europe as well as Japan, China, South Korea, and Australia.

Joint Venture

A corporate alliance in which two or more independent companies combine their resources to achieve a specific, limited objective.

SELF TEST

What is the difference between a merger and a corporate alliance?

What is a joint venture? Give some reasons joint ventures may be advantageous to the parties involved.

21-9 PRIVATE EQUITY INVESTMENTS

Not all target firms are acquired by publicly traded corporations. In recent years, an increasing number of firms including Outback Steakhouse, Hertz, Toys "R" Us, and Neiman Marcus have been acquired by private equity firms. Private equity firms raise capital from wealthy individuals and look for opportunities to make profitable investments. Today's leading private equity firms include the Blackstone Group, the Carlyle Group, Bain Capital, and Kohlberg Kravis Roberts (KKR). In many cases, these firms engage in a **leveraged buyout (LBO)** where a small group of investors, which usually includes current management, acquires a firm in a transaction financed largely by debt. The debt is serviced with funds generated by the acquired company's operations and often by the sale of some of its assets. Sometimes the acquiring group plans to run the acquired company for a number of years, boost its sales and profits, and then take it public again as a stronger company. In other instances, the LBO firm plans to sell off divisions to other firms that can gain synergies. In either case, the acquiring group expects to make a substantial profit from the LBO, but the inherent risks are great due to the heavy use of financial leverage.

Leveraged Buyout (LBO)

A situation in which a small group of investors (which usually includes the firm's managers) borrows heavily to buy all the shares of a company.

SELF TEST

What is an LBO?

What actions do companies typically take to meet the large debt burdens resulting from LBOs?

To see *Fortune's* ranking of leading private equity firms, go to **http://money.cnn.com/galleries/2007/fortune/0702/gallery.powerlist.fortune/index.html**.

---

[15]Cross-licensing, consortia, joint bidding, and franchising are still other ways for firms to combine resources. For more information on joint ventures, see Sanford V. Berg, Jerome Duncan, and Phillip Friedman, *Joint Venture Strategies and Corporate Innovation* (Cambridge, MA: Oelgeschlager, Gunn and Hain, 1982).

21-10 DIVESTITURES

Although corporations do more buying than selling of productive facilities, a good bit of selling does occur. In this section, we briefly discuss the major types of divestitures, after which we present some examples and rationales for divestitures.

21-10a Types of Divestitures

Divestiture

The sale of some of a company's operating assets.

Spin-Off

A divestiture in which the stock of a subsidiary is given to the parent company's stockholders.

Carve-Out

A minority interest in a corporate subsidiary is sold to new shareholders, so the parent gains new equity financing yet retains control.

Liquidation

Occurs when the assets of a division are sold off piecemeal rather than as an operating entity.

There are four types of **divestitures**: (1) selling an operating unit to another firm, (2) setting up the business to be divested as a separate corporation and then "spinning it off" to the divesting firm's stockholders, (3) following the steps for a spin-off but selling only some of the shares, and (4) liquidating assets outright.

Sale to another firm generally involves the sale of an entire division or unit, usually for cash but sometimes for stock of the acquiring firm. In a **spin-off**, the firm's existing stockholders are given new stock representing separate ownership rights in the division that was divested. The division establishes its own board of directors and officers, and it becomes a separate company. The stockholders end up owning shares of two firms instead of one, but no cash has been transferred. In a **carve-out**, a minority interest in a corporate subsidiary is sold to new shareholders, so the parent gains new equity financing yet retains control. Finally, in a **liquidation**, the assets of a division are sold off piecemeal rather than as an operating entity. To illustrate the different types of divestitures, we present some high-profit examples in the next section.

21-10b Divestiture Illustrations

1. Pepsi spun off its fast-food business, which included Pizza Hut, Taco Bell, and Kentucky Fried Chicken. The spun-off businesses operated under the name Tricon Global Restaurants (which was later changed to Yum! Brands, Inc.). Pepsi originally acquired the chains because it wanted to increase the distribution channels for its soft drinks. Over time, however, Pepsi began to realize that the soft-drink and restaurant businesses were quite different and synergies between them were less than anticipated. The spin-off was part of Pepsi's attempt to focus on its core business. However, Pepsi will try to maintain these distribution channels by signing long-term contracts that ensure that Pepsi products will be sold exclusively in each of the three spun-off chains.

2. United Airlines sold its Hilton International Hotels subsidiary to Ladbroke Group PLC of Britain for $1.1 billion and sold its Hertz rental car unit and its Westin hotel group. The sales culminated a disastrous strategic move by United to build a full-service travel empire. The failed strategy resulted in the firing of Richard J. Ferris, the company's chairman. The move into nonairline travel-related businesses had been viewed by many analysts as a mistake because there were few synergies to be gained. Further, analysts feared that United's managers, preoccupied by running hotels and rental car companies, would not maintain the company's focus in the highly competitive airline industry. The funds raised by the divestitures were paid out to United's shareholders as a special dividend.

3. General Motors (GM) spun off its Electronic Data Systems (EDS) subsidiary. EDS, a computer services company founded in 1962 by Ross Perot, prospered as an independent company until it was acquired by GM in 1984. The rationale for the acquisition was that EDS's expertise would help GM operate better in the information age and build cars that encompassed leading-edge computer technology. However, the spread of desktop computers and the movement of companies to downsize their internal computer staffs caused EDS's non-GM business to soar. Ownership by GM hampered EDS's ability to

strike alliances and, in some cases, to enter into business agreements. The best way for EDS to compete in its industry was as an independent; hence, it was spun off.

4. AT&T was broken up in 1983 to settle a Justice Department antitrust suit filed in the 1970s.[16] For almost 100 years, AT&T had operated as a holding company that owned Western Electric (its manufacturing subsidiary), Bell Labs (its research arm), a huge long-distance network that was operated as a division of the parent company, and 22 Bell operating companies (e.g., Pacific Telephone, New York Telephone, Southern Bell, and Southwestern Bell). In 1984, AT&T was reorganized into eight separate companies—a slimmed-down AT&T, which kept Western Electric, Bell Labs, and the long-distance operations, in addition to seven regional telephone holding companies that were created from the 22 old operating telephone companies. The stock of the seven telephone companies was then spun off to the old AT&T's stockholders. After the divestiture, a person who held 100 shares of old AT&T stock owned 100 shares of the "new" AT&T and 10 shares of each of the seven operating companies. These 170 shares were backed by the same assets that had previously backed 100 shares of old AT&T common.

   The AT&T divestiture resulted from a suit by the Justice Department, which wanted to divide the Bell System into a regulated monopoly segment (the seven regional telephone companies) and a manufacturing/long-distance segment that would be exposed to competition. The breakup was designed to strengthen competition and thus speed up technological change in those parts of the telecommunications industry that were not natural monopolies. Ironically, on November 18, 2005, SBC Communications, which can trace its roots back to the original Bell Telephone Co., acquired AT&T for $16 billion. The "new" firm, AT&T Inc., is a global telecommunications company.

5. Some years ago Woolworth liquidated all of its 336 Woolco discount stores. This made the company, which had sales of $7.2 billion before the liquidation, 30% smaller. Woolco had posted operating losses of $19 million the year before the liquidation, and its losses in the latest 6 months had climbed to an alarming $21 million. Woolworth's CEO, Edward F. Gibbons, was quoted as saying, "How many losses can you take?" Woolco's problems necessitated a write-off of $325 million, but management believed it was better to go ahead and "bite the bullet" rather than let the losing stores "bleed the company to death." Competition led to a continuing decline of the company; so in 1997, its remaining retail stores were closed.

6. As a result of some imprudent loans to oil companies and to developing nations, Continental Illinois, one of the largest U.S. bank holding companies at the time, was threatened with bankruptcy. Continental then sold off several profitable divisions, such as its leasing and credit card operations, to raise funds to cover bad loan losses. In effect, Continental sold assets in order to stay alive. Ultimately, Continental was bailed out by the Federal Deposit Insurance Corporation and the Federal Reserve, which arranged a $7.5 billion rescue package and provided a blanket guarantee for all of Continental's $40 billion of deposits, which kept deposits in excess of $100,000 from fleeing the bank because of their uninsured status.

As the preceding examples illustrate, the reasons for divestitures vary widely. Sometimes stock analysts and investors feel more comfortable when firms "stick to their knitting"; the Pepsi and United Airlines divestitures are examples. Other

---

[16]Another forced divestiture involved DuPont and General Motors. In 1921, GM was in serious financial trouble and DuPont supplied capital in exchange for 23% of the stock. In the 1950s, the Justice Department won an antitrust suit that required DuPont to spin off (to DuPont's stockholders) its GM stock.

companies need cash to finance expansion in their primary business lines or to reduce a large debt burden, and divestitures can be used to raise this cash; Continental Bank illustrates this point. The divestitures also show that running a business is a dynamic process—conditions change and corporate strategies change in response; as a result, firms alter their asset portfolios by acquisitions and/or divestitures. Some divestitures, such as Woolworth's liquidation of its Woolco stores, are to unload losing assets that are dragging the company down. The AT&T example is one of the many instances in which a divestiture is the result of an antitrust settlement. The GM spin-off illustrates a situation in which parts of the business can operate more efficiently alone than together.

SELF TEST

Identify and briefly explain the four types of divestitures.

TYING IT ALL TOGETHER

This chapter included discussions of mergers, divestitures, and LBOs. The majority of the discussion in this chapter was about mergers. We discussed the rationale for mergers, different types of mergers, the level of merger activity, and merger analysis. We showed how to use two different approaches to value the target firm: discounted cash flow and market multiple analyses. We also explained how the acquiring firm can structure its takeover bid and investment bankers' roles in arranging and financing mergers. In addition, we discussed two cooperative arrangements that fall short of mergers: corporate, or strategic, alliances and joint ventures.

SELF-TEST QUESTIONS AND PROBLEMS
(Solutions Appear in Appendix A)

ST-1 **KEY TERMS**   Define each of the following terms:

a.   Synergy; merger

b.   Horizontal merger; vertical merger; congeneric merger; conglomerate merger

c.   Friendly merger; hostile merger; defensive merger; tender offer; target company; breakup value; acquiring company

d.   Operating merger; financial merger; equity residual method; market multiple analysis

e.   White knight; white squire; poison pill; golden parachute

f.   Arbitrage

g.   Joint venture; corporate, or strategic, alliance

h.   Divestiture; spin-off; leveraged buyout (LBO); carve-out; liquidation

ST-2 **MERGER VALUE** Pizza Place, a national pizza chain, is considering purchasing a smaller chain, Western Mountain Pizza. Pizza Place's analysts project that the merger will result in incremental net cash flows of $1.5 million in Year 1, $2 million in Year 2, $3 million in Year 3, and $5 million in Year 4. In addition, Western's Year 4 cash flows are expected to grow at a constant rate of 5% after Year 4. Assume that all cash flows occur at the end of the year. The acquisition will be made immediately if it is undertaken. Western's post-merger beta is estimated to be 1.5, and its post-merger tax rate would be 40%. The risk-free rate is 6%, and the market risk premium is 4%. What is the value of Western Mountain Pizza to Pizza Place?

QUESTIONS

21-1 Four economic classifications of mergers are (1) horizontal, (2) vertical, (3) conglomerate, and (4) congeneric. Explain the significance of these terms in merger analysis with regard to (a) the likelihood of governmental intervention and (b) possibilities for operating synergy.

21-2 Firm A wants to acquire Firm B. Firm B's management agrees that the merger is a good idea. Might a tender offer be used? Why or why not?

21-3 Distinguish between operating mergers and financial mergers.

21-4 In the spring of 1984, Disney Productions' stock was selling for about $3.125 per share. (All prices have been adjusted for 4-for-1 splits in 1986 and 1992.) Then Saul Steinberg, a New York financier, began acquiring it; and after he had 12%, he announced a tender offer for another 37% of the stock—which would bring his holdings up to 49%—at a price of $4.22 per share. Disney's management then announced plans to buy Gibson Greeting Cards and Arvida Corporation, paying for them with stock. It also lined up bank credit and (according to Steinberg) was prepared to borrow up to $2 billion and use the funds to repurchase shares at a higher price than Steinberg was offering. All of these efforts were designed to keep Steinberg from taking control. In June, Disney's management agreed to pay Steinberg $4.84 per share, which gave him a gain of about $60 million on a 2-month investment of about $26.5 million.

When Disney's buyback of Steinberg's shares was announced, the stock price fell almost instantly from $4.25 to $2.875. Many Disney stockholders were irate, and they sued to block the buyout. Also, the Disney affair added fuel to the fire in a congressional committee that was holding hearings on proposed legislation that would (1) prohibit someone from acquiring more than 10% of a firm's stock without making a tender offer for all the remaining shares, (2) prohibit poison pill tactics such as those Disney's management had used to fight off Steinberg, (3) prohibit buybacks such as the deal eventually offered to Steinberg (greenmail) unless there was an approving vote by stockholders, and (4) prohibit (or substantially curtail) the use of golden parachutes (the one thing Disney's management did not try).

Set forth the arguments for and against this type of legislation. What provisions, if any, should it contain? Also, look up Disney's current stock price to see how its stockholders have fared. Note that Disney's stock was split 3-for-1 in July 1998.

21-5 Two large, publicly owned firms are contemplating a merger. No operating synergy is expected. However, since returns on the two firms are not perfectly positively correlated, the standard deviation of earnings would be reduced for the combined corporation. One group of consultants argues that this risk reduction is sufficient grounds for the merger. Another group thinks that this type of risk reduction is irrelevant because stockholders can hold the stock of both companies and thus gain the risk-reduction benefits without all the hassles and expenses of the merger. Whose position is correct? Explain.

PROBLEMS

Easy Problems 1–3

The following information is required to work Problems 21-1, 21-2, and 21-3.

Harrison Corporation is interested in acquiring Van Buren Corporation. Assume that the risk-free rate of interest is 5% and that the market risk premium is 6%.

21-1 **VALUATION** Van Buren currently expects to pay a year-end dividend of $2.00 a share ($D_1 = $2.00). Van Buren's dividend is expected to grow at a constant rate of 5% a year, and its beta is 0.9. What is the current price of Van Buren's stock?

21-2 **MERGER VALUATION** Harrison estimates that if it acquires Van Buren, the year-end dividend will remain at $2.00 a share, but synergies will enable the dividend to grow at a constant rate of 7% a year (instead of the current 5%). Harrison also plans to increase the debt ratio of what would be its Van Buren subsidiary—the effect of this would be to raise Van Buren's beta to 1.1. What is the per-share value of Van Buren to Harrison Corporation?

21-3 **MERGER BID** On the basis of your answers to Problems 21-1 and 21-2, if Harrison were to acquire Van Buren, what would be the range of possible prices it could bid for each share of Van Buren common stock?

Intermediate Problems 4–5

21-4 **MERGER ANALYSIS** Apilado Appliance Corporation is considering a merger with the Vaccaro Vacuum Company. Vaccaro is a publicly traded company, and its current beta is 1.30. Vaccaro has been barely profitable, so it has paid an average of only 20% in taxes during the last several years. In addition, it uses little debt, having a debt ratio of just 25%.

If the acquisition were made, Apilado would operate Vaccaro as a separate, wholly owned subsidiary. Apilado would pay taxes on a consolidated basis, and the tax rate would therefore increase to 35%. Apilado also would increase the debt capitalization in the Vaccaro subsidiary to 40% of assets, which would increase its beta to 1.47. Apilado's acquisition department estimates that Vaccaro, if acquired, would produce the following net cash flows to Apilado's shareholders (in millions of dollars):

Year	Net Cash Flows
1	$1.30
2	1.50
3	1.75
4	2.00
5 and beyond	Constant growth at 6%

These cash flows include all acquisition effects. Apilado's cost of equity is 14%, its beta is 1.0, and its cost of debt is 10%. The risk-free rate is 8%.

a. What discount rate should be used to discount the estimated cash flows? (Hint: Use Apilado's r_s to determine the market risk premium.)

b. What is the dollar value of Vaccaro to Apilado?

c. Vaccaro has 1.2 million common shares outstanding. What is the maximum price per share that Apilado should offer for Vaccaro? If the tender offer is accepted at this price, what will happen to Apilado's stock price?

21-5 **CAPITAL BUDGETING ANALYSIS** The Stanley Stationery Shoppe wants to acquire The Carlson Card Gallery for $400,000. Stanley expects the merger to provide incremental earnings of about $64,000 a year for 10 years. Ken Stanley has calculated the marginal cost of capital for this investment to be 10%. Conduct a capital budgeting analysis for Stanley to determine whether he should purchase The Carlson Card Gallery.

Challenging Problem 21–6

21-6 **MERGER ANALYSIS** TransWorld Communications Inc., a large telecommunications company, is evaluating the possible acquisition of Georgia Cable Company (GCC), a regional cable company. TransWorld's analysts project the following post-merger data for GCC (in thousands of dollars):

	2009	2010	2011	2012
Net sales	$450	$518	$555	$600
Selling and administrative expense	45	53	60	68
Interest	18	21	24	27
Tax rate after merger	35%			
Cost of goods sold as a percent of sales	65%			
Beta after merger	1.50			
Risk-free rate	8%			
Market risk premium	4%			
Terminal growth rate of cash flow available to TransWorld	7%			

If the acquisition is made, it will occur on January 1, 2009. All cash flows shown in the income statements are assumed to occur at the end of the year. GCC currently has a capital structure of 40% debt, but TransWorld would increase that to 50% if the acquisition were made. GCC, if independent, would pay taxes at 20%; but its income would be taxed at 35% if it were consolidated. GCC's current market-determined beta is 1.40, and its investment bankers think that its beta would rise to 1.50 if the debt ratio were increased to 50%. The cost of goods sold is expected to be 65% of sales, but it could vary somewhat. Depreciation-generated funds would be used to replace worn-out equipment, so they would not be available to TransWorld's shareholders. The risk-free rate is 8%, and the market risk premium is 4%.

a. What is the appropriate discount rate for valuing the acquisition?

b. What is the terminal value?

c. What is the value of GCC to TransWorld?

COMPREHENSIVE/SPREADSHEET PROBLEM

21-7   **MERGER ANALYSIS**   Use the spreadsheet model to rework Problem 21-6 and then answer the following question:

d. Suppose GCC has 120,000 shares outstanding. What is the maximum per-share price TransWorld should offer for GCC?

INTEGRATED CASE

SMITTY'S HOME REPAIR COMPANY

21-8   **MERGER ANALYSIS**   Smitty's Home Repair Company, a regional hardware chain that specializes in do-it-yourself materials and equipment rentals, is cash-rich because of several consecutive good years. One of the alternative uses for the excess funds is an acquisition. Linda Wade, Smitty's treasurer and your boss, has been asked to place a value on a potential target, Hill's Hardware, a small chain that operates in an adjacent state; and she has enlisted your help.

The following table indicates Wade's estimates of Hill's earnings potential if it comes under Smitty's management (in millions of dollars). The interest expense listed here includes the interest (1) on Hill's existing debt; (2) on new debt that Smitty's would issue to help finance the acquisition; and (3) on new debt expected to be issued over time to help finance expansion within the new "H division," the code name given to the target firm. The retentions represent earnings that will be reinvested within the H division to help finance its growth.

Hill's Hardware currently uses 40% debt financing, and it pays federal-plus-state taxes at a 30% rate. Security analysts estimate Hill's beta to be 1.2. If the acquisition were to take place, Smitty's would increase Hill's debt ratio to 50%, which would increase Hill's beta to 1.3. Further, because Smitty's is highly profitable, taxes on the consolidated firm would be 40%. Wade realizes that Hill's Hardware also generates depreciation cash flows, but she believes that these funds would have to be reinvested within the division to replace worn-out equipment.

Wade estimates the risk-free rate to be 9% and the market risk premium to be 4%. She also estimates that net cash flows after 2012 will grow at a constant rate of 6%. Smitty's management is new to the merger game, so Wade has been asked to answer some basic questions about mergers as well as to perform the merger analysis. To structure the task, Wade has developed the following questions, which you must answer and then defend to Smitty's board.

a. Several reasons have been proposed to justify mergers. Among the more prominent are (1) tax considerations, (2) risk reduction, (3) control, (4) purchase of assets at below-replacement cost, and (5) synergy. In general, which of the reasons are economically justifiable? Which are not? Which fit the situation at hand? Explain.

b. Briefly describe the differences between a hostile merger and a friendly merger.

c. Use the data developed in the table to construct the H division's cash flow statements for 2009 through 2012. Why is interest expense deducted in merger cash flow statements, whereas it is not normally deducted in a capital budgeting cash flow analysis? Why are earnings retentions deducted in the cash flow statement?

	2009	2010	2011	2012
Net sales	$60.0	$90.0	$112.5	$127.5
Cost of goods sold (60%)	36.0	54.0	67.5	76.5
Selling/administrative expense	4.5	6.0	7.5	9.0
Interest expense	3.0	4.5	4.5	6.0
Necessary retained earnings	0.0	7.5	6.0	4.5

d. Conceptually, what is the appropriate discount rate to apply to the cash flows developed in Part c? What is your actual estimate of this discount rate?

e. What is the estimated terminal value of the acquisition; that is, what is the estimated value of the H division's cash flows beyond 2012? What is Hill's value to Smitty's? Suppose another firm were evaluating Hill's as an acquisition candidate. Would it obtain the same value? Explain.

f. Assume that Hill's has 10 million shares outstanding. These shares are traded relatively infrequently; but the last trade, made several weeks ago, was at a price of $9 per share. Should Smitty's make an offer for Hill's? If so, how much should it offer per share?

g. What merger-related activities are undertaken by investment bankers?

Solutions to Self-Test Questions and Problems

Note: Except for Chapter 1, no answers are provided for ST-1 problems because they are verbal rather than quantitative in nature.

CHAPTER 1

ST-1   Refer to the marginal glossary definitions or to relevant chapter sections to check your responses.

CHAPTER 3

ST-2   **a.**

EBIT	$5,000,000
Interest	1,000,000
EBT	$4,000,000
Taxes (40%)	1,600,000
Net income	$2,400,000

b. NWC = Current assets − (Payables + Accruals)

    = $14,000,000 − ($3,000,000 + $1,000,000)

    = $10,000,000

c. $\text{FCF} = \left(\text{EBIT}(1 - \text{T}) + \text{Depreciation} \right) - \left(\begin{array}{c} \text{Capital} \\ \text{expenditures} \end{array} + \begin{array}{c} \text{Increase in net} \\ \text{working captial} \end{array} \right)$

    = [$5,000,000(0.6) + $1,000,000] − [$3,000,000 + 0]

    = $4,000,000 − $3,000,000

    = $1,000,000

d. Retained earnings at the end of the year can be calculated as follows:

Balance of retained earnings$_{\text{BOY}}$	$4,500,000
Add: Net income*	2,400,000
Less: Common dividends	1,200,000
Balance of retained earnings$_{\text{EOY}}$	$5,700,000

    *Net income was calculated in Part a.

CHAPTER 4

ST-2   Billingsworth paid $2 in dividends and retained $2 per share. Since total retained earnings rose by $12 million, 6 million shares must be outstanding. With a book value of $40 per share, total common equity must be $40(6 million) = $240 million. Since Billingsworth has $120 million of debt, its debt ratio must be 33.3%:

$$\frac{\text{Debt}}{\text{Assets}} = \frac{\text{Debt}}{\text{Debt} + \text{Equity}} = \frac{\$120 \text{ million}}{\$120 \text{ million} + \$240 \text{ million}}$$

$$= 0.333 = 33.3\%$$

ST-3 **a.** When answering questions such as this, always begin by writing down the relevant definitional equations, then start filling in numbers. Note that the extra zeros indicating millions have been deleted in the following calculations.

(1) $$DSO = \frac{Accounts\ receivable}{Sales/365}$$

$$40.55 = \frac{A/R}{Sales/365}$$

$$A/R = 40.55(\$2.7397) = \$111.1\ million$$

(2) $$Current\ ratio = \frac{Current\ assets}{Current\ liabilities} = 3.0$$

$$= \frac{Current\ assets}{\$105.5} = 3.0$$

$$Current\ assets = 3.0(\$105.5) = \$316.50\ million$$

(3) $$Total\ assets = Current\ assets + Fixed\ assets$$
$$= \$316.5 + \$283.5 = \$600\ million$$

(4) $$ROA = Profit\ margin \times Total\ assets\ turnover$$
$$= \frac{Net\ income}{Sales} \times \frac{Sales}{Total\ assets}$$
$$= \frac{\$50}{\$1,000} \times \frac{\$1,000}{\$600}$$
$$= 0.05 \times 1.667 = 0.083333 = 8.3333\%$$

(5) $$ROE = ROA \times \frac{Assets}{Equity}$$

$$12.0\% = 8.3333\% \times \frac{\$600}{Equity}$$

$$Equity = \frac{(8.3333\%)(\$600)}{12.0\%}$$
$$= \$416.67\ million$$

(6) $$Current\ assets = Cash\ and\ equivalents + Accounts\ receivable + Inventories$$
$$\$316.5 = \$100.0 + \$111.1 + Inventories$$
$$Inventories = \$105.4\ million$$

$$Quick\ ratio = \frac{Current\ assets - Inventories}{Current\ liabilities}$$

$$= \frac{\$316.5 - \$105.4}{\$105.5} = 2.00$$

(7) $$Total\ assets = Total\ claims = \$600\ million$$
$$Current\ liabilities + Long\text{-}term\ debt + Equity = \$600\ million$$
$$\$105.5 + Long\text{-}term\ debt + \$416.67 = \$600\ million$$
$$Long\text{-}term\ debt = \$600 - \$105.5 - \$416.67 = \$77.83\ million$$

Note: We could have found equity as follows:

$$ROE = \frac{Net\ income}{Equity}$$

$$12.0\% = \frac{\$50}{Equity}$$

$$Equity = \$50/0.12$$
$$= \$416.67\ million$$

Then we could have gone on to find long-term debt.

b. Kaiser's average sales per day were $1,000/365 = 2.74 million. Its DSO was 40.55, so $A/R = 40.55(\$2.74) = \$111.1$ million. Its new DSO of 30.4 would cause $A/R = 30.4(\$2.74) = \$83.3$ million. The reduction in receivables would be $\$111.1 - \$83.3 = \$27.8$ million, which would equal the amount of cash generated.

(1)   New equity = Old equity − Stock bought back

$$= \$416.7 - \$27.8$$
$$= \$388.9 \text{ million}$$

Thus,

$$\text{New ROE} = \frac{\text{Net income}}{\text{New equity}}$$
$$= \frac{\$50}{\$388.9}$$
$$= 12.86\% \text{ (versus old ROE of 12.0\%)}$$

(2)   New ROA $= \dfrac{\text{Net income}}{\text{Total assets} - \text{Reduction in A/R}}$

$$= \frac{\$50}{\$600 - \$27.8}$$
$$= 8.74\% \text{ (versus old ROA of 8.33\%)}$$

(3) The old debt is the same as the new debt:

$$\text{Debt} = \text{Total claims} - \text{Equity}$$
$$= \$600 - \$416.7 = \$183.3 \text{ million}$$

New total assets = Old total assets − Reduction in A/R

$$= \$600 - \$27.8$$
$$= \$572.2 \text{ million}$$

Therefore,

$$\frac{\text{Debt}}{\text{Old total assets}} = \frac{\$183.3}{\$600} = 30.6\%$$

while

$$\frac{\text{New debt}}{\text{New total assets}} = \frac{\$183.3}{\$572.2} = 32.0\%$$

CHAPTER 5

ST-2 **a.**

```
1/1/09    8%   1/1/10      1/1/11      1/1/12
├─────────────┼───────────┼───────────┤
−1,000                              FV = ?
```

$1,000 is being compounded for 3 years; so your balance on January 1, 2012, is $1,259.71:

$$FV_N = PV(1 + I)^N = \$1,000(1 + 0.08)^3 = \$1,259.71$$

Alternatively, using a financial calculator, input $N = 3$, $I/YR = 8$, $PV = -1000$, $PMT = 0$, and $FV = ?$ Solve for $FV = \$1,259.71$.

b.

```
1/1/09   2%   1/1/10          1/1/11          1/1/12
├┼┼┼┼┼┼┼┼┼┼┼┼┼┼┼┼┼┼┼┼┼┼┼┼┤
−1,000                                    FV = ?
```

$$FV_N = PV\left(1 + \frac{I_{NOM}}{M}\right)^{NM} = FV_{12} = \$1,000(1.02)^{12} = \$1,268.24$$

Alternatively, using a financial calculator, input N = 12, I/YR = 2, PV = −1000, PMT = 0, and FV = ? Solve for FV = $1,268.24.

c.

1/1/09		1/1/10	1/1/11	1/1/12
	8%			

−333.333   −333.333   −333.333
                                    FV = ?

Using a financial calculator, input N = 3, I/YR = 8, PV = 0, PMT = −333.333, and FV = ? Solve for FV = $1,082.13.

d.

1/1/09		1/1/10	1/1/11	1/1/12
	8%			

−333.333   −333.333   −333.333   FV = ?

Using a financial calculator in begin mode, input N = 3, I/YR = 8, PV = 0, PMT = −333.333, and FV = ? Solve for FV = $1,168.70.

e.

1/1/09		1/1/10	1/1/11	1/1/12
	8%			

                    ?   ?   ?
                                       FV = 1,259.71

Using a financial calculator, input N = 3, I/YR = 8, PV = 0, FV = 1259.71, and PMT = ? Solve for PMT = −$388.03. Therefore, you would have to make 3 payments of $388.03 each beginning on January 1, 2010.

ST-3   **a.** Set up a time line like the one in the preceding problem.

1/1/09		1/1/10	1/1/11	1/1/12	1/1/13
	8%				

PV = ?   FV = 1,000

Note that your deposit will grow for 4 years at 8%. The deposit on January 1, 2009, is the PV; and the FV is $1,000. Using a financial calculator, input N = 4, I/YR = 8, PMT = 0, FV = 1000, and PV = ? Solve for PV = −$735.03.

$$PV = \frac{FV_N}{(1+I)^N} = \frac{\$1,000}{(1.08)^4} = \$735.03$$

b.

1/1/09		1/1/10	1/1/11	1/1/12	1/1/13
	8%				

                    ?   ?   ?   ?
                                                    FV = 1,000

Here we are dealing with a 4-year annuity whose first payment occurs 1 year from today, on 1/1/10, and whose future value must equal $1,000. You should modify the time line to help visualize the situation. Using a financial calculator, input N = 4, I/YR = 8, PV = 0, FV = 1000, and PMT = ? Solve for PMT = −$221.92.

c. This problem can be approached in several ways. Perhaps the simplest is to ask this question: If I received $750 on 1/1/10 and deposited it to earn 8%, would I have the required $1,000 on 1/1/13? The answer is no.

1/1/09		1/1/10	1/1/11	1/1/12	1/1/13
	8%				

                 −750   FV = ?

$$FV_3 = \$750(1.08)(1.08)(1.08) = \$944.78$$

This indicates that you should let your father make the payments of $221.92 rather than accept the lump sum of $750.

You could also compare the $750 with the PV of the payments as shown here:

1/1/09		1/1/10	1/1/11	1/1/12	1/1/13

8%

−221.92   −221.92   −221.92   −221.92

PV = ?

Using a financial calculator, input N = 4, I/YR = 8, PMT = −221.92, FV = 0, and PV = ? Solve for PV = $735.03.

This is less than the $750 lump sum offer, so your initial reaction might be to accept the lump sum of $750. However, that would be a mistake. The problem is that when you found the $735.03 PV of the annuity, you were finding the value of the annuity *today*, on January 1, 2009. You were comparing $735.03 today with the lump sum of $750 one year from now. This is, of course, invalid. What you should have done was take the $735.03; recognize that this is the PV of an annuity as of January 1, 2009; multiply $735.03 by 1.08 to get $793.83; and compare $793.83 with the lump sum of $750. You would then take your father's offer to make the payments of $221.92 rather than take the lump sum on January 1, 2010.

d.

1/1/09	1/1/10	1/1/11	1/1/12	1/1/13

I = ?

−750   1,000

Using a financial calculator, input N = 3, PV = −750, PMT = 0, FV = 1000, and I/YR = ? Solve for I/YR = 10.0642%.

e.

1/1/09	1/1/10	1/1/11	1/1/12	1/1/13

I = ?

−200   −200   −200   −200

FV = 1,000

Using a financial calculator, input N = 4, PV = 0, PMT = −200, FV = 1000, and I/YR = ? Solve for I/YR = 15.09%.

You might be able to find a borrower willing to offer you a 15% interest rate, but some risk would be involved—he or she might not actually pay you your $1,000!

f.

4%

−400   ?   ?   ?   ?   ?   ?

FV = 1,000

Find the future value of the original $400 deposit:

$$FV_6 = PV(1.04)^6 = \$400(1.2653) = \$506.13$$

This means that on January 1, 2013, you need an additional sum of $493.87:

$$\$1,000.00 - \$506.13 = \$493.87$$

This will be accumulated by making 6 equal payments that earn 8% compounded semiannually, or 4% each 6 months. Using a financial calculator, input N = 6, I/YR = 4, PV = 0, FV = 493.87, and PMT = ? Solve for PMT = −$74.46.

Alternatively, input N = 6, I/YR = 4, PV = −400, FV = 1000, and PMT = ? Solve for PMT = −$74.46.

g. Effective annual rate $= \left(1 + \dfrac{I_{NOM}}{M}\right)^M - 1.0$

$$= \left(1 + \dfrac{0.08}{2}\right)^2 - 1 = (1.04)^2 - 1$$

$$= 1.0816 - 1 = 0.0816 = 8.16\%$$

$$APR = I_{PER} \times M$$

$$= 0.04 \times 2 = 0.08 = 8\%$$

ST-4   Bank A's effective annual rate is 8.24%:

$$\text{Effective annual rate} = \left(1 + \dfrac{0.08}{4}\right)^4 - 1.0$$

$$= (1.02)^4 - 1$$

$$= 1.0824 - 1$$

$$= 0.0824 = 8.24\%$$

Now Bank B must have the same effective annual rate:

$$\left(1 + \dfrac{I_{NOM}}{12}\right)^{12} - 1.0 = 0.0824$$

$$\left(1 + \dfrac{I_{NOM}}{12}\right)^{12} = 1.0824$$

$$1 + \dfrac{I_{NOM}}{12} = (1.0824)^{1/12}$$

$$1 + \dfrac{I_{NOM}}{12} = 1.00662$$

$$\dfrac{I_{NOM}}{12} = 0.00662$$

$$I_{NOM} = 0.07944 = 7.94\%.$$

Thus, the two banks have different quoted rates—Bank A's quoted rate is 8%, while Bank B's quoted rate is 7.94%. However, both banks have the same effective annual rate of 8.24%. The difference in their quoted rates is due to the difference in compounding frequency.

CHAPTER 6

ST-2   a. Average inflation over 4 years $= (2\% + 2\% + 2\% + 4\%)/4 = 2.5\%$

b. $T_4 = r_{RF} + MRP_4$
$= r^* + IP_4 + MRP_4$
$= 3\% + 2.5\% + (0.1)3\%$
$= 5.8\%$

c. $C_{4,\,BBB} = r^* + IP_4 + MRP_4 + DRP + LP$
$= 3\% + 2.5\% + 0.3\% + 1.3\% + 0.5\%$
$= 7.6\%$

d. $T_8 = r^* + IP_8 + MRP_8$
$= 3\% + (3 \times 2\% + 5 \times 4\%)/8 + 0.7\%$
$= 3\% + 3.25\% + 0.7\%$
$= 6.95\%$

e. $C_{8, BBB} = r^* + IP_8 + MRP_8 + DRP + LP$

$= 3\% + 3.25\% + 0.7\% + 1.3\% + 0.5\%$

$= 8.75\%$

f. $T_9 = r^* + IP_9 + MRP_9$

$7.3\% = 3\% + IP_9 + 0.8\%$

$IP_9 = 3.5\%$

$3.5\% = (3 \times 2\% + 5 \times 4\% + X)/9$

$31.5\% = 6\% + 20\% + X$

$5.5\% = X$

$X = \text{Inflation in Year 9} = 5.5\%$

ST-3 $T_1 = 6\%; T_2 = 6.2\%; T_3 = 6.3\%; MRP = 0$

a.   Yield of 1-year security 1 year from now is calculated as follows:

$$(1.062)^2 = (1.06)(1 + X)$$

$$\frac{(1.062)^2}{1.06} = 1 + X$$

$$1.064 = 1 + X$$

$$X = 6.4\%$$

b.   Yield of 1-year security 2 years from now is calculated as follows:

$$(1.063)^3 = (1.062)^2(1 + X)$$

$$\frac{(1.063)^3}{(1.062)^2} = 1 + X$$

$$1.065 = 1 + X$$

$$6.5\% = X$$

c.   Yield of 2-year security 1 year from now is calculated as follows:

$$(1.063)^3 = (1.06)(1 + X)^2$$

$$\frac{(1.063)^3}{1.06} = (1 + X)^2$$

$$1.1332 = (1 + X)^2$$

$$1 + X = (1.1332)^{1/2}$$

$$1 + X = 1.0645$$

$$X = 6.45\%$$

CHAPTER 7

ST-2   a.   Pennington's bonds were sold at par; therefore, the original YTM equaled the coupon rate of 12%.

b. $$V_B = \sum_{t=1}^{50} \frac{\$120/2}{\left(1 + \dfrac{0.10}{2}\right)^t} + \frac{\$1,000}{\left(1 + \dfrac{0.10}{2}\right)^{50}}$$

With a financial calculator, input the following: N = 50, I/YR = 5, PMT = 60, FV = 1000, and PV = ? Solve for PV = $1,182.56.

c.   Current yield = Annual coupon payment/Price

$= \$120/\$1,182.56$

$= 0.1015 = 10.15\%$

Capital gains yield = Total yield − Current yield

$= 10\% - 10.15\% = -0.15\%$

Total return = 10%

d. With a financial calculator, input the following: $N = 13$, $PV = -916.42$, $PMT = 60$, $FV = 1000$, and $r_d/2 = I/YR = ?$ Calculator solution $= r_d/2 = 7.00\%$; therefore, $r_d = YTM = 14.00\%$.

$$\text{Current yield} = \$120/\$916.42 = 13.09\%$$

$$\text{Capital gains yield} = 14\% - 13.09\% = 0.91\%$$

e. The following time line illustrates the years to maturity of the bond:

Thus, on March 1, 2008, $13\frac{2}{3}$ periods were left before the bond matured. Bond traders use the following procedure to determine the price of the bond:

(1) Find the price of the bond on the next coupon date, July 1, 2008. Using a financial calculator, input $N = 13$, $I/YR = 7.75$, $PMT = 60$, $FV = 1000$, and $PV = ?$ Solve for $PV = \$859.76$.

(2) Add the coupon, $60, to the bond price to get the total value, TV, of the bond on the next interest payment date:

$$\text{TV} = \$859.76 + \$60.00 = \$919.76.$$

(3) Discount this total value back to the purchase date (March 1, 2008): Using a financial calculator, input $N = 4/6$, $I/YR = 7.75$, $PMT = 0$, $FV = 919.76$, and $PV = ?$ Solve for $PV = \$875.11$.

(4) Therefore, you would have written a check for $875.11 to complete the transaction. Of this amount, $20 = (\frac{1}{3})(\$60)$ would represent accrued interest and $855.11 would represent the bond's basic value. This breakdown would affect your taxes and those of the seller.

(5) This problem could be solved *very* easily using a spreadsheet or a financial calculator with a bond valuation function, such as the HP-12C or the HP-17BII. This is explained in the calculator manual under the heading "Bond Calculations."

ST-3 a. (1) $\$100,000,000/10 = \$10,000,000$ per year, or $5 million each 6 months. Since the $5 million will be used to retire bonds immediately, no interest will be earned on it.

(2) VDC will purchase bonds on the open market if they're selling at less than par. So the sinking fund payment will be less than $5,000,000 each period.

b. The debt service requirements will decline. As the amount of bonds outstanding declines, so will the interest requirements (amounts given in millions of dollars). If the bonds are called at par, the total bond service payments are calculated as follows:

Semiannual Payment Period (1)	Sinking Fund Payment (2)	Outstanding Bonds on Which Interest Is Paid (3)	Interest Payment[a] (4)	Total Bond Service (2) + (4) = (5)
1	$5	$100	$6.0	$11.0
2	5	95	5.7	10.7
3	5	90	5.4	10.4
⋮	⋮	⋮	⋮	⋮
20	5	5	0.3	5.3

[a]Interest is calculated as $(0.5)(0.12)$ (Column 3).; for example: Interest in Period 2 = $(0.5)(0.12)$ ($95) = $5.7.

The company's total cash bond service requirement will be $21.7 million per year for the first year. For both options, interest will decline by 0.12 ($10,000,000) = $1,200,000 per year for the remaining years. The total debt service requirement for the open market purchases cannot be precisely determined, but the amounts would be less than what's shown in Column 5 of the preceding table.

c. Here we have a 10-year 7% annuity whose compound value is $100 million; and we are seeking the annual payment, PMT. The solution can be obtained with a financial calculator. Input N = 10, I/YR = 7, PV = 0, and FV = 100000000 and press the PMT key to obtain $7,237,750. This amount is not known with certainty as interest rates over time will change, so the amount could be higher (if interest rates fall) or lower (if interest rates rise).

d. Annual debt service costs will be $100,000,000(0.12) + $7,237,750 = $19,237,750.

e. If interest rates rose, causing the bond's price to fall, the company would use open market purchases. This would reduce its debt service requirements.

CHAPTER 8

ST-2   a. The average rate of return for each stock is calculated by averaging the returns over the 5-year period. The average return for Stock A is:

$$r_{Avg\ A} = (-24.25\% + 18.50\% + 38.67\% + 14.33\% + 39.13\%)/5$$
$$= 17.28\%$$

The average return for Stock B is:

$$r_{Avg\ B} = (5.50\% + 26.73\% + 48.25\% + -4.50\% + 43.86\%)/5$$
$$= 23.97\%$$

The realized rate of return on a portfolio made up of Stock A and Stock B would be calculated by finding the average return in each year as r_A(% of Stock A) + r_B(% of Stock B) and then averaging those annual returns:

Year	Portfolio AB's Return, r_{AB}
2004	(9.38%)
2005	22.62
2006	43.46
2007	4.92
2008	41.50
	r_{Avg} = 20.62%

b. The standard deviation of returns is estimated, using Equation 8-2a, as follows:

$$\text{Estimated } \sigma = \sqrt{\frac{\sum_{t=1}^{N} (\bar{r}_t - \bar{r}_{Avg})^2}{N-1}} \qquad \text{8-2a}$$

For Stock A, the estimated σ is 25.84%:

$$\sigma_A = \sqrt{\frac{(-24.25\% - 17.28\%)^2 + (18.50\% - 17.28\%)^2 + (38.67\% - 17.28\%)^2 + (14.33\% - 17.28\%)^2 + (39.13\% - 17.28\%)^2}{5-1}}$$
$$= 25.84\%$$

The standard deviations of returns for Stock B and the portfolio are similarly determined; they are as follows:

	Stock A	Stock B	Portfolio AB
Standard deviation	25.84%	23.15%	22.96%

c.   Since the risk reduction from diversification is small (σ_{AB} falls only to 22.96%), the most likely value of the correlation coefficient is 0.8. If the correlation coefficient was −0.8, the risk reduction would be much larger. In fact, the correlation coefficient between Stocks A and B is 0.76.

d.   If more randomly selected stocks were added to a portfolio, σ_p would decline to somewhere in the vicinity of 20%. (See Figure 8-6.) σ_p would remain constant only if the correlation coefficient was +1.0, which is most unlikely. σ_p would decline to zero only if the correlation coefficient, ρ, was equal to zero and a large number of stocks were added to the portfolio or if the proper proportions were held in a two-stock portfolio with $\rho = -1.0$.

ST-3   a. $b = (0.6)(0.70) + (0.25)(0.90) + (0.1)(1.30) + (0.05)(1.50)$
$= 0.42 + 0.225 + 0.13 + 0.075 = 0.85$

b. $r_{RF} = 6\%$; $RP_M = 5\%$; $b = 0.85$
$r_p = 6\% + (5\%)(0.85)$
$= 10.25\%$

c. $b_N = (0.5)(0.70) + (0.25)(0.90) + (0.1)(1.30) + (0.15)(1.50)$
$= 0.35 + 0.225 + 0.13 + 0.225$
$= 0.93$

$r = 6\% + (5\%)(0.93)$
$= 10.65\%$

CHAPTER 9

ST-2   a.   This is not necessarily true. Because G plows back two-thirds of its earnings, its growth rate should exceed that of D; but D pays higher dividends ($3 versus $1). We cannot say which stock should have the higher price.

b.   Again, we do not know which price would be higher.

c.   This is false. The changes in r_d and r_s would have a greater effect on G; its price would decline more.

d.   The total expected return for D is $\hat{r}_D = D_1/P_0 + g = 12\% + 0\% = 12\%$. The total expected return for G will have D_1/P_0 less than 12% and g greater than 0%; but $\hat{r}_G$ should be neither greater than nor smaller than D's total expected return, 12%, because the two stocks are stated to be equally risky.

e.   We have eliminated a, b, c, and d; so e should be correct. On the basis of the available information, D and G should sell at about the same price, $25; thus, $\hat{r}_s = 12\%$ for both D and G. G's current dividend yield is $1/$25 = 4%. Therefore, g = 12% − 4% = 8%.

ST-3   The first step is to solve for g, the unknown variable, in the constant growth equation. Since D_1 is unknown but D_0 is known, substitute $D_0(1 + g)$ for D_1 as follows:

$$\hat{P}_0 = P_0 = \frac{D_1}{r_s - g} = \frac{D_0(1 + g)}{r_s - g}$$

$$\$36 = \frac{\$2.40(1 + g)}{0.12 - g}$$

Solving for g, we find the growth rate to be 5%:

$$\$4.32 - \$36g = \$2.40 + \$2.40g$$
$$\$38.4g = \$1.92$$
$$g = 0.05 = 5\%$$

The next step is to use the growth rate to project the stock price 5 years hence:

$$\hat{P}_5 = \frac{D_0(1+g)^6}{r_s - g}$$
$$= \frac{\$2.40(1.05)^6}{0.12 - 0.05}$$
$$= \$45.95$$

[**Alternatively,** $\hat{P}_5 = \$36(1.05)^5 = \$45.95$.]

Therefore, the firm's expected stock price 5 years from now, $\hat{P}_5$, is $45.95.

ST-4 **a.** **(1)** Calculate the PV of the dividends paid during the supernormal growth period:

$$D_1 = \$1.1500(1.15) = \$1.3225$$
$$D_2 = \$1.3225(1.15) = \$1.5209$$
$$D_3 = \$1.5209(1.13) = \$1.7186$$
$$PV\ D = \frac{\$1.3225}{1.12} + \frac{\$1.5209}{(1.12)^2} + \frac{\$1.7186}{(1.12)^3}$$
$$= \$1.1808 + \$1.2125 + \$1.2233$$
$$= \$3.6166 \approx \$3.62$$

(2) Find the PV of the firm's stock price at the end of Year 3:

$$\hat{P}_3 = \frac{D_4}{r_s - g} = \frac{D_3(1+g)}{r_s - g}$$
$$= \frac{\$1.7186(1.06)}{0.12 - 0.06}$$
$$= \$30.36$$

$$PV\ \hat{P}_3 = \frac{\$30.36}{(1.12)^3} = \$21.61$$

(3) Sum the two components to find the value of the stock today:

$$\hat{P}_0 = \$3.62 + \$21.61 = \$25.23$$

Alternatively, the cash flows can be placed on a time line as follows:

Enter the cash flows into the cash flow register and I/YR = 12 and press the NPV key to obtain P_0 = $25.23.

b.

$$\hat{P}_1 = \frac{\$1.5209}{1.12} + \frac{\$1.7186}{(1.12)^2} + \frac{\$30.36}{(1.12)^2}$$
$$= \$1.3579 + \$1.3701 + \$24.2028$$
$$= \$26.9308 \approx \$26.93$$

(Calculator solution: $26.93)

$$\hat{P}_2 = \frac{\$1.7186}{1.12} + \frac{\$30.36}{1.12}$$
$$= \$1.5345 + \$27.1071$$
$$= \$28.6416 \approx \$28.64$$

(Calculator solution : $28.64)

c.

Year	Dividend Yield	+	Capital Gains Yield	= Total Return
1	$\frac{\$1.3225}{\$25.23} \approx 5.24\%$		$\frac{\$26.93 - \$25.23}{\$25.23} \approx 6.74\%$	$\approx 12\%$
2	$\frac{\$1.5209}{\$26.93} \approx 5.65\%$		$\frac{\$28.64 - \$26.93}{\$26.93} \approx 6.35\%$	$\approx 12\%$
3	$\frac{\$1.7186}{\$28.64} \approx 6.00\%$		$\frac{\$30.36 - \$28.64}{\$28.64} \approx 6.00\%$	$\approx 12\%$

CHAPTER 10

ST-2   **a.**   Component costs are as follows:

Common : $r_s = \dfrac{D_1}{P_0} + g = \dfrac{D_0(1+g)}{P_0} + g$

$= \dfrac{\$3.60(1.09)}{\$54} + 0.09$

$= 0.0727 + 0.09 = 16.27\%$

Preferred : $r_p = \dfrac{\text{Preferred dividend}}{P_p} = \dfrac{\$11}{\$95} = 11.58\%$

Debt at $r_d = 12\%$: $r_d(1 - T) = 12\%(0.6) = 7.20\%$

b.   WACC calculation:

$$WACC = w_d r_d (1 - T) + w_p r_p + w_c r_s$$
$$= 0.25(7.2\%) + 0.15(11.58\%) + 0.60(16.27\%) = 13.30\%$$

c.   LEI should accept Projects A, B, C, and D. It should reject Project E because its rate of return does not exceed the WACC of funds needed to finance it.

CHAPTER 11

ST-2   **a.**   *Net present value (NPV):*

$$NPV_X = -\$10,000 + \frac{\$6,500}{(1.12)^1} + \frac{\$3,000}{(1.12)^2} + \frac{\$3,000}{(1.12)^3} + \frac{\$1,000}{(1.12)^4} = \$966.01$$

$$NPV_Y = -\$10,000 + \frac{\$3,500}{(1.12)^1} + \frac{\$3,500}{(1.12)^2} + \frac{\$3,500}{(1.12)^3} + \frac{\$3,500}{(1.12)^4} = \$630.72$$

Alternatively, using a financial calculator, input the cash flows into the cash flow register, enter I/YR = 12, and then press the NPV key to obtain $NPV_X = \$966.01$ and $NPV_Y = \$630.72$.

Internal rate of return (IRR):
To solve for each project's IRR, find the discount rates that equate each NPV to zero:

$$IRR_X = 18.0\%$$
$$IRR_Y = 15.0\%$$

Modified internal rate of return (MIRR):
To obtain each project's MIRR, begin by finding each project's terminal value (TV) of cash inflows:

$$TV_X = \$6,500(1.12)^3 + \$3,000(1.12)^2 + \$3,000(1.12)^1 + \$1,000 = \$17,255.23$$
$$TV_Y = \$3,500(1.12)^3 + \$3,500(1.12)^2 + \$3,500(1.12)^1 + \$3,500 = \$16,727.65$$

Now each project's MIRR is the discount rate that equates the PV of the TV to each project's cost, $10,000:

$$MIRR_X = 14.61\%$$
$$MIRR_Y = 13.73\%$$

Payback:
To determine the payback, construct the cumulative cash flows for each project:

CUMULATIVE CASH FLOWS

Year	Project X	Project Y
0	($10,000)	($10,000)
1	(3,500)	(6,500)
2	(500)	(3,000)
3	2,500	500
4	3,500	4,000

$$Payback_X = 2 + \frac{\$500}{\$3,000} = 2.17 \text{ years}$$

$$Payback_Y = 2 + \frac{\$3,000}{\$3,500} = 2.86 \text{ years}$$

Discounted payback:
To determine the discounted payback, construct the cumulative discounted cash flows at the firm's WACC of 12% for each project:

Project X

Years	0	1	2	3	4
Cash Flow	−10,000	6,500	3,000	3,000	1,000
Discounted Cash Flow	−10,000	5,803.57	2,391.58	2,135.34	635.52
Cumulative Discounted Cash Flow	−10,000	−4,196.43	−1,804.85	+330.49	+966.01

Discounted Payback$_X$ = 2 + $1,804.85/$2,135.34 = 2.85 years

Project Y

Years	0	1	2	3	4
Cash Flow	−10,000	3,500	3,500	3,500	3,500
Discounted Cash Flow	−10,000	3,125.00	2,790.18	2,491.23	2,224.31
Cumulative Discounted Cash Flow	−10,000	−6,875.00	−4,084.82	−1,593.59	+630.72

Discounted Payback$_Y$ = 3 + $1,593.59/$2,224.31 = 3.72 years

b. The following table summarizes the project rankings by each method:

	Project That Ranks Higher
NPV	X
IRR	X
MIRR	X
Payback	X
Discounted payback	X

Note that all methods rank Project X over Project Y. In addition, both projects are acceptable under the NPV, IRR, and MIRR criteria. Thus, both projects should be accepted if they are independent.

c. In this case, we would choose the project with the higher NPV at r = 12%, or Project X.

d. To determine the effects of changing the cost of capital, plot the NPV profiles of each project. The crossover rate occurs at about 6% to 7% (6.2%). See the graph below.

   If the firm's cost of capital is less than 6.2%, a conflict exists because $NPV_Y > NPV_X$, but $IRR_X > IRR_Y$. Therefore, if r is 5%, a conflict exists. Note, however, that when r = 5.0%, $MIRR_X = 10.64\%$ and $MIRR_Y = 10.83\%$; hence, the modified IRR ranks the projects correctly, even if r is to the left of the crossover point.

e. The basic cause of the conflict is differing reinvestment rate assumptions between NPV and IRR. NPV assumes that cash flows can be reinvested at the cost of capital, while IRR assumes reinvestment at the (generally) higher IRR. The high reinvestment rate assumption under IRR makes early cash flows especially valuable; hence, short-term projects look better under IRR.

NPV Profiles for Projects X and Y

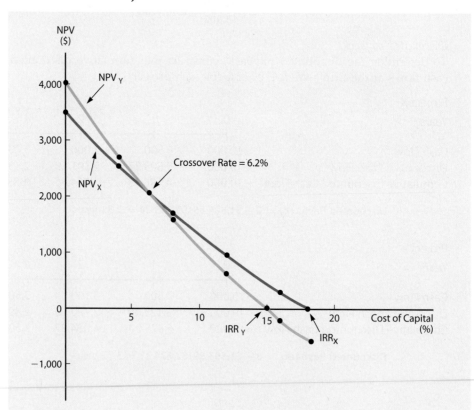

Cost of Capital	NPV$_X$	NPV$_Y$
0%	$3,500	$4,000
4	2,545	2,705
8	1,707	1,592
12	966	631
16	307	(206)
18	5	(585)

CHAPTER 12

ST-2 **a.** Estimated investment requirements:

Price	($55,000)
Installation	(10,000)
Change in net working capital	(2,000)
Total investment	($67,000)

b. Depreciation schedule:

Equipment cost = $65,000; MACRS 3-year class

	YEARS		
	1	**2**	**3**
MACRS depreciation rates	33%	45%	15%
Equipment depreciation expense	$21,450	$29,250	$9,750

Note that the remaining book value of the equipment at the end of the project's life is $0.07 \times \$65,000 = \$4,550$.

c.

	Year 0	Year 1	Year 2	Year 3
Equipment purchase	($65,000)			
Change in NWC	(2,000)			
Revenues (4,000 × $50)		$200,000	$200,000	$200,000
Variable costs (70%)		140,000	140,000	140,000
Fixed costs		30,000	30,000	30,000
Depreciation		21,450	29,250	9,750
EBIT		$ 8,550	$ 750	$ 20,250
Taxes (40%)		3,420	300	8,100
AT operating income		$ 5,130	$ 450	$ 12,150
Add back: Depreciation		21,450	29,250	9,750
Salvage value				10,000
Tax on salvage value				(2,180)
Recovery of NWC				2,000
Project cash flows	($67,000)	$ 26,580	$ 29,700	$ 31,720

```
0        1        2        3
|--11%---|--------|--------|
-67,000  26,580   29,700   31,720
```

d. From the time line shown in Part c, the project's NPV can be calculated as follows:

$$\text{NPV} = -\$67,000 + \$26,580/(1.11)^1 + \$29,700/(1.11)^2 + \$31,720/(1.11)^3$$
$$= \$4,245$$

Alternatively, using a financial calculator, you would enter $\text{CF}_0 = -67000$, $\text{CF}_1 = 26580$, $\text{CF}_2 = 29700$, $\text{CF}_3 = 31720$, and $\text{I/YR} = 11$ and then solve for $\text{NPV} = \$4,245$.

Since the NPV is positive, the project should be accepted.

e. Project analysis if unit sales turned out to be 20% below forecast:
Initial projection = 4,000 units; however, if unit sales turn out to be only 80% of forecast, unit sales = 3,200.

	Year 0	Year 1	Year 2	Year 3
Equipment purchase	($65,000)			
Change in NWC	(2,000)			
Revenues (3,200 × $50)		$160,000	$160,000	$160,000
Variable costs (70%)		112,000	112,000	112,000
Fixed costs		30,000	30,000	30,000
Depreciation		21,450	29,250	9,750
EBIT		($ 3,450)	($ 11,250)	$ 8,250
Taxes (40%)		(1,380)	(4,500)	3,300
AT operating income		($ 2,070)	($ 6,750)	$ 4,950
Add back: Depreciation		21,450	29,250	9,750
Salvage value				10,000
Tax on salvage value				(2,180)
Recovery of NWC				2,000
Project cash flows	($67,000)	$ 19,380	$ 22,500	$ 24,520

NPV Calculation:

$$\text{NPV} = -\$67,000 + \$19,380/(1.11)^1 + \$22,500/(1.11)^2 + \$24,520/(1.11)^3$$
$$= -\$13,350$$

Alternatively, using a financial calculator, you would enter $\text{CF}_0 = -67000$, $\text{CF}_1 = 19380$, $\text{CF}_2 = 22500$, $\text{CF}_3 = 24520$, and $\text{I/YR} = 11$ and then solve for $\text{NPV} = -\$13,350$.

Since the NPV is negative, the project should not be accepted. If unit sales were 20% below the forecasted level, the project would no longer be accepted.

f. *Best-case scenario:* Unit sales = 4,800; Variable cost % = 65%

	Year 0	**Year 1**	**Year 2**	**Year 3**
Equipment purchase	($65,000)			
Change in NWC	(2,000)			
Revenues (4,800 × $50)		$240,000	$240,000	$240,000
Variable costs (65%)		156,000	156,000	156,000
Fixed costs		30,000	30,000	30,000
Depreciation		21,450	29,250	9,750
EBIT		$ 32,550	$ 24,750	$ 44,250
Taxes (40%)		13,020	9,900	17,700
AT operating income		$ 19,530	$ 14,850	$ 26,550
Add back: Depreciation		21,450	29,250	9,750
Salvage value				10,000
Tax on salvage value				(2,180)
Recovery of NWC				2,000
Project cash flows	($67,000)	$ 40,980	$ 44,100	$ 46,120

Project NPV:

$$\text{NPV} = -\$67,000 + \$40,980/(1.11)^1 + \$44,100/(1.11)^2 + \$46,120/(1.11)^3$$
$$= \$39,434$$

Alternatively, using a financial calculator, you would enter $CF_0 = -67000$, $CF_1 = 40980$, $CF_2 = 44100$, $CF_3 = 46120$, and I/YR = 11 and then solve for NPV = $39,434.

Base-case scenario: The NPV was calculated in Part d as $4,245.

Worst-case scenario: Unit sales = 3,200; Variable cost % = 75%

	Year 0	**Year 1**	**Year 2**	**Year 3**
Equipment purchase	($65,000)			
Change in NWC	(2,000)			
Revenues (3,200 × $50)		$160,000	$160,000	$160,000
Variable costs (75%)		120,000	120,000	120,000
Fixed costs		30,000	30,000	30,000
Depreciation		21,450	29,250	9,750
EBIT		($ 11,450)	($ 19,250)	$ 250
Taxes (40%)		(4,580)	(7,700)	100
AT operating income		($ 6,870)	($ 11,550)	$ 150
Add back: Depreciation		21,450	29,250	9,750
Salvage value				10,000
Tax on salvage value				(2,180)
Recovery of NWC				2,000
Project cash flows	($67,000)	$ 14,580	$ 17,700	$ 19,720

Project NPV:

$$\text{NPV} = -\$67,000 + \$14,580/(1.11)^1 + \$17,700/(1.11)^2 + \$19,720/(1.11)^3$$
$$= -\$25,080$$

Alternatively, using a financial calculator, you would enter $CF_0 = -67000$, $CF_1 = 14580$, $CF_2 = 17700$, $CF_3 = 19720$, and I/YR = 11 and then solve for NPV = –$25,080.

Scenario	Probability	NPV
Best case	25%	$39,434
Base case	50	4,245
Worst case	25	– 25,080
	Expected NPV =	$ 5,711

$$\sigma_{\text{NPV}} = [0.25(\$39,434-\$5,711)^2 + 0.50(\$4,245-\$5,711)^2 + 0.25(-\$25,080-\$5,711)^2]^{1/2}$$
$$\sigma_{\text{NPV}} = [\$284,310,182 + \$1,074,578 + \$237,021,420]^{1/2}$$
$$\sigma_{\text{NPV}} = \$22,856$$
$$\text{CV}_{\text{NPV}} = \$22,856/\$5,711 = 4.0$$

g. The project's CV = 4.0, which is significantly larger than the firm's typical project CV. So the WACC for this project should be adjusted upward, 11% + 3% = 14%.

   To calculate the expected NPV, standard deviation, and coefficient of variation, you would recalculate each scenario's NPV by discounting the project cash flows by 14% rather than 11%.

Best-case scenario:

$$\text{NPV} = -\$67,000 + \$40,980/(1.14)^1 + \$44,100/(1.14)^2 + \$46,120/(1.14)^3$$
$$= \$34,011$$

Alternatively, using a financial calculator, you would enter $CF_0 = -67000$, $CF_1 = 40980$, $CF_2 = 44100$, $CF_3 = 46120$, and I/YR = 14 and then solve for NPV = $34,011.

Base-case scenario:

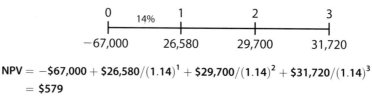

$$\text{NPV} = -\$67,000 + \$26,580/(1.14)^1 + \$29,700/(1.14)^2 + \$31,720/(1.14)^3$$
$$= \$579$$

Alternatively, using a financial calculator, you would enter $CF_0 = -67000$, $CF_1 = 26580$, $CF_2 = 29700$, $CF_3 = 31720$, and I/YR = 14 and then solve for NPV = $579.

Worst-case scenario:

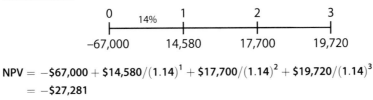

$$NPV = -\$67,000 + \$14,580/(1.14)^1 + \$17,700/(1.14)^2 + \$19,720/(1.14)^3$$
$$= -\$27,281$$

Alternatively, using a financial calculator, you would enter $CF_0 = -67000$, $CF_1 = 14580$, $CF_2 = 17700$, $CF_3 = 19720$, and $I/YR = 14$ and then solve for $NPV = -\$27,281$.

Scenario	Probability	NPV
Best case	25%	$34,011
Base case	50	579
Worst case	25	− 27,281
	Expected NPV =	$ 1,972

$$\sigma_{NPV} = [0.25(\$34,011 - \$1,972)^2 + 0.50(\$579 - \$1,972)^2 + 0.25(-\$27,281 - \$1,972)^2]^{1/2}$$
$$\sigma_{NPV} = [\$256,624,380 + \$970,225 + \$213,934,502]^{1/2}$$
$$\sigma_{NPV} = \$21,715$$
$$CV_{NPV} = \$21,715/\$1,972 = 11.01$$

Because the expected NPV of the project is still positive, the project would be accepted; but it is risky.

ST-3 **a.** Machine W:

```
0      10%     1              2
|--------------|--------------|
-500,000   300,000       300,000
```

$$NPV_W = -\$500,000 + \frac{\$300,000}{(1.10)^1} + \frac{\$300,000}{(1.10)^2}$$
$$= \$20,661.16$$

Machine WW:

```
0      10%    1          2          3          4
|------------|----------|----------|----------|
-500,000  165,000   165,000    165,000    165,000
```

$$NPV_{WW} = -\$500,000 + \frac{\$165,000}{(1.10)^1} + \frac{\$165,000}{(1.10)^2} + \frac{\$165,000}{(1.10)^3} + \frac{\$165,000}{(1.10)^4}$$
$$= \$23,027.80$$

Since the projects are independent and both have positive NPVs, both projects should be accepted.

b. Since the projects are mutually exclusive, only one project can be accepted. Since the projects are not repeatable, the NPVs calculated in Part a can be used to answer this question. Machine WW has the higher NPV and should be chosen.

c. **(1)** Machine W's NPV needs to be recalculated under the assumption that it is repeated in Year 2.

Replacement chain analysis:

Machine W:

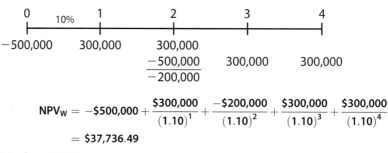

$$NPV_W = -\$500,000 + \frac{\$300,000}{(1.10)^1} + \frac{-\$200,000}{(1.10)^2} + \frac{\$300,000}{(1.10)^3} + \frac{\$300,000}{(1.10)^4}$$

$$= \$37,736.49$$

Machine WW:

$NPV_{WW} = \$23,027.80$ (NPV remains the same since it's calculated over a 4-year life.)

Since the projects are mutually exclusive but repeatable, Machine W should be chosen because its 4-year NPV is higher than Machine WW's.

(2) *Equivalent annual annuity analysis:*

Machine W:

Using a financial calculator, enter N = 2, I/YR = 10, PV = –20661.16, and FV = 0 and then solve for EAA_W = PMT = $11,904.76.

Machine WW:

Using a financial calculator, enter N = 4, I/YR = 10, PV = –23027.80, and FV = 0 and then solve for EAA_{WW} = PMT = $7,264.60.

The equivalent annual annuity analysis arrives at the same decision as the replacement chain method. EAA_W = $11,904.76 and EAA_{WW} = $7,264.60; therefore, Machine W should be chosen if the projects are mutually exclusive and can be repeated indefinitely because $EAA_W > EAA_{WW}$.

d.   Yes. If the two projects can be repeated indefinitely over time but the cash flows are expected to change, the replacement chain analysis can be used. The analysis would be similar to what was done in Part c(1) except that the repeated cash flows would not be identical to the original cash flows.

CHAPTER 13

ST-2   a.   No abandonment considered; WACC = 12%

Years:	0	1	2	3	NPV
25%	−25,000	18,000	18,000	18,000	$18,233
50%	−25,000	12,000	12,000	12,000	3,822
25%	−25,000	−8,000	−8,000	−8,000	−44,215
				Expected NPV =	−$ 4,585

b.   Abandonment considered; WACC = 12%

Years:	0	1	2	3	NPV
25%	−25,000	18,000	18,000	18,000	$18,233
50%	−25,000	12,000	12,000	12,000	3,822
25%	−25,000	−8,000			
	Abandon project	15,000		0	−20,185
				Expected NPV =	$ 1,423

c. Value of the abandonment option:

NPV with abandonment	$1,423
NPV without abandonment	(4,585)
Value of abandonment option	$6,008

CHAPTER 14

ST-2 a. The following information is given in the problem:

$$Q = \text{Units of output (sales)} = 5,000$$
$$P = \text{Average sales price per unit of output} = \$100$$
$$F = \text{Fixed operating costs} = \$200,000$$
$$V = \text{Variable costs per unit} = \$50$$
$$EBIT = \text{Operating income} = \$50,000$$
$$\text{Total assets} = \$500,000$$
$$\text{Common equity} = \$500,000$$

(1) Determine the new EBIT level if the change is made:

$$\text{New EBIT} = P_2(Q_2) - F_2 - V_2(Q_2)$$
$$\text{New EBIT} = \$95(7,000) - \$250,000 - \$40(7,000)$$
$$= \$135,000$$

(2) Determine the incremental EBIT:

$$\Delta EBIT = \$135,000 - \$50,000 = \$85,000$$

(3) Estimate the approximate rate of return on the new investment:

$$\Delta ROA = \frac{\Delta EBIT}{\text{Investment}} = \frac{\$85,000}{\$400,000} = 21.25\%$$

Since the ROA exceeds Olinde's average cost of capital, this analysis suggests that the firm should make the investment.

b. The change would increase the breakeven point. Still, with a lower sales price, it might be easier to achieve the higher new breakeven volume.

$$\text{Old: } Q_{BE} = \frac{F}{P - V} = \frac{\$200,000}{\$100 - \$50} = 4,000 \text{ units}$$

$$\text{New: } Q_{BE} = \frac{F}{P_2 - V_2} = \frac{\$250,000}{\$95 - \$40} = 4,545 \text{ units}$$

c. The incremental ROA is:

$$ROA = \frac{\Delta \text{Profit}}{\Delta \text{Sales}} \times \frac{\Delta \text{Sales}}{\Delta \text{Assets}}$$

Using debt financing, the incremental profit associated with the investment is equal to the incremental profit found in Part a minus the interest expense incurred as a result of the investment:

$$\Delta \text{Profit} = \text{New profit} - \text{Old profit} - \text{Interest}$$
$$= \$135,000 - \$50,000 - 0.10(\$400,000)$$
$$= \$45,000$$

The incremental sales is calculated as:

$$\Delta\text{Sales} = P_2Q_2 - P_1Q_1$$
$$= \$95(7{,}000) - \$100(5{,}000)$$
$$= \$665{,}000 - \$500{,}000$$
$$= \$165{,}000$$

$$\text{ROA} = \frac{\$45{,}000}{\$165{,}000} \times \frac{\$165{,}000}{\$400{,}000} = 11.25\%$$

The return on the new investment still exceeds the average cost of capital, so the firm should make the investment.

ST-3 **a.**

EBIT	$4,000,000
Interest ($2,000,000 × 0.10)	200,000
Earnings before taxes (EBT)	$3,800,000
Taxes (35%)	1,330,000
Net income	$2,470,000

$$\text{EPS} = \$2{,}470{,}000/600{,}000 = \$4.1167$$
$$P_0 = \$4.1167/0.15 = \$27.44$$

b.

$$\text{Equity} = 600{,}000 \times \$10 = \$6{,}000{,}000$$
$$\text{Debt} = \$2{,}000{,}000$$
$$\text{Total capital} = \$8{,}000{,}000$$
$$\text{WACC} = w_d r_d(1 - T) + w_c r_s$$
$$= (2/8)(10\%)(1 - 0.35) + (6/8)(15\%)$$
$$= 1.625\% + 11.25\%$$
$$= 12.875\%$$

c.

EBIT	$4,000,000
Interest ($10,000,000 × 0.12)	1,200,000
Earnings before taxes (EBT)	$2,800,000
Taxes (35%)	980,000
Net income	$1,820,000

Shares bought and retired:

$$\Delta N = \Delta\text{Debt}/P_0 = \$8{,}000{,}000/\$27.44 = 291{,}545$$

New outstanding shares:

$$N_1 = N_0 - \Delta N = 600{,}000 - 291{,}545 = 308{,}455$$

New EPS:

$$\text{EPS} = \$1{,}820{,}000/308{,}455 = \$5.90$$

New price per share:

$$P_0 = \$5.90/0.17 = \$34.71 \text{ versus } \$27.44$$

Therefore, Gentry should change its capital structure.

d. In this case, the company's net income would be higher by $(0.12 - 0.10)$ $(\$2,000,000)(1 - 0.35) = \$26,000$ because its interest charges would be lower. The new price would be as follows:

$$P_0 = \frac{(\$1,820,000 + \$26,000)/308,455}{0.17} = \$35.20$$

In the first case, in which debt had to be refunded, the bondholders were compensated for the increased risk of the higher debt position. In the second case, the old bondholders were not compensated; their 10% coupon perpetual bonds would now be worth $\$100/0.12 = \$833.33$. That is $\$1,666,667$ in total, down from the old $2 million, or a loss of $333,333.

The stockholders would have a gain of $(\$35.20 - \$34.71)(308,455) = \$151,143$. This gain would, of course, be at the expense of the old bondholders. (There is no reason to think that bondholders' losses would exactly offset stockholders' gains.)

e.
$$TIE = \frac{EBIT}{I}$$

$$Original\ TIE = \frac{\$4,000,000}{\$200,000} = 20\ times$$

$$New\ TIE = \frac{\$4,000,000}{\$1,200,000} = 3.33\ times$$

CHAPTER 15

ST-2 **a.**

Projected net income	$2,000,000
Less projected capital investments	800,000
Available residual	$1,200,000
Shares outstanding	200,000

$$DPS = \$1,200,000/200,000\ shares = \$6 = D_1$$

b.
$$EPS = \$2,000,000/200,000\ shares = \$10$$
$$Payout\ ratio = DPS/EPS = \$6/\$10 = 60\%$$
$$Total\ dividends/NI = \$1,200,000/\$2,000,000 = 60\%$$

c.
$$Currently,\ P_0 = \frac{D_1}{r_s - g} = \frac{\$6}{0.14 - 0.06} = \frac{\$6}{0.08} = \$75$$

Under the former circumstances, D_1 would be based on a 20% payout on $10 EPS, or $2. With $r_s = 14\%$ and $g = 12\%$, we solve for P_0:

$$P_0 = \frac{D_1}{r_s - g} = \frac{\$2}{0.14 - 0.12} = \frac{\$2}{0.02} = \$100$$

Although CMC has suffered a severe setback, its existing assets will continue to provide a good income stream. More of these earnings should be passed on to the shareholders, as the slowed internal growth has reduced the need for funds. However, the net result is a 25% decrease in the value of the shares.

d. If the payout ratio was continued at 20%, even after internal investment opportunities had declined, the price of the stock would drop to $2/(0.14 − 0.06) = $25 rather than to $75. Thus, an increase in the dividend payout is consistent with maximizing shareholder wealth.

Because of the diminishing nature of profitable investment opportunities, the greater the firm's level of investment, the lower the average ROE. Thus, the more money CMC retains and invests, the lower its average ROE will be. We can determine the average ROE under different conditions as follows:

Old situation (with founder active and a 20% payout):

$$g = (1.0 - \text{Payout ratio})(\text{Average ROE})$$
$$12\% = (1.0 - 0.2)(\text{Average ROE})$$
$$\text{Average ROE} = 12\%/0.8 = 15\% > r_s = 14\%$$

Note that the *average* ROE is 15%, whereas the *marginal* ROE is presumably equal to 14%.

New situation (with founder retired and a 60% payout as explained in Part c):

$$g = 6\% = (1.0 - 0.6)(\text{ROE})$$
$$\text{ROE} = 6\%/0.4 = 15\% > r_s = 14\%$$

This suggests that a new payout of 60% is appropriate and that the firm is taking on investments down to the point at which marginal returns are equal to the cost of capital. Note that if the 20% payout was maintained, the *average* ROE would be only 7.5%, which would imply a marginal ROE far below the 14% cost of capital.

CHAPTER 16

ST-2   The Calgary Company: Alternative Balance Sheets

	Restricted (40%)	Moderate (50%)	Relaxed (60%)
Current assets	$1,200,000	$1,500,000	$1,800,000
Fixed assets	600,000	600,000	600,000
Total assets	$1,800,000	$2,100,000	$2,400,000
Debt	$ 900,000	$1,050,000	$1,200,000
Equity	900,000	1,050,000	1,200,000
Total liabilities and equity	$1,800,000	$2,100,000	$2,400,000

The Calgary Company: Alternative Income Statements

	Restricted	Moderate	Relaxed
Sales	$3,000,000	$3,000,000	$3,000,000
EBIT	450,000	450,000	450,000
Interest (10%)	90,000	105,000	120,000
Earnings before taxes	$ 360,000	$ 345,000	$ 330,000
Taxes (40%)	144,000	138,000	132,000
Net income	$ 216,000	$ 207,000	$ 198,000
ROE	24.0%	19.7%	16.5%

ST-3   **a. and b.**

Income Statements for Year Ended December 31, 2008 (Thousands of Dollars)

	VANDERHEIDEN PRESS		HERRENHOUSE PUBLISHING	
	a	b	a	b
EBIT	$ 30,000	$ 30,000	$ 30,000	$ 30,000
Interest	12,400	14,400	10,600	18,600
Taxable income	$ 17,600	$ 15,600	$ 19,400	$ 11,400
Taxes (40%)	7,040	6,240	7,760	4,560
Net income	$ 10,560	$ 9,360	$ 11,640	$ 6,840
Equity	$100,000	$100,000	$100,000	$100,000
ROE	10.56%	9.36%	11.64%	6.84%

The Vanderheiden Press has a higher ROE when short-term interest rates are high, whereas Herrenhouse Publishing does better when rates are lower.

c. Herrenhouse's position is riskier. First, its profits and return on equity are more volatile than Vanderheiden's. Second, Herrenhouse must renew its large short-term loan every year; and if the renewal comes up at a time when money is tight, when its business is depressed, or both, Herrenhouse may be denied credit, which may put it out of business.

CHAPTER 17

ST-2   To solve this problem, we will define ΔS as the change in sales and g as the growth rate in sales. Then we use the following three equations:

$$\Delta S = S_0 g$$
$$S_1 = S_0(1 + g)$$
$$AFN = (A_0^*/S_0)(\Delta S) - (L_0^*/S_0)(\Delta S) - MS_1(RR)$$

Set $AFN = 0$; substitute known values for A_0^*/S_0, L_0^*/S_0, M, RR, and S_0; and solve for g:

$$0 = 1.6(\$100g) - 0.4(\$100g) - 0.10[\$100(1 + g)](0.55)$$
$$0 = \$160g - \$40g - 0.055(\$100 + \$100g)$$
$$0 = \$160g - \$40g - \$5.5 - \$5.5g$$
$$\$114.5g = \$5.5$$
$$g = \$5.5/\$114.5 = 0.048 = 4.8\%$$
$$= \text{Maximum growth rate without external financing}$$

ST-3   Assets consist of cash, marketable securities, receivables, inventories, and fixed assets. Therefore, we can break the A_0^*/S_0 ratio into its components—cash/sales, inventories/sales, and so forth. Then

$$\frac{A_0^*}{S_0} = \frac{A_0^* - \text{Inventories}}{S_0} + \frac{\text{Inventories}}{S_0} = 1.6$$

We know that the inventory turnover ratio is Sales/Inventories = 3 times, so Inventories/Sales = 1/3 = 0.3333. Further, if the inventory turnover ratio can be increased to 4 times, the Inventory/Sales ratio will fall to 1/4 = 0.25, a difference of $0.3333 - 0.2500 = 0.0833$. This, in turn, causes the A_0^*/S_0 ratio to fall from $A_0^*/S_0 = 1.6$ to $A_0^*/S_0 = 1.6 - 0.0833 = 1.5167$.

This change has two effects: First, it changes the AFN equation. Second, it means that Weatherford currently has excessive inventories. Because it is costly to hold excess inventories, Weatherford will want to reduce its inventory holdings by not replacing inventories until the excess amounts have been used. We can account for this by setting up the revised AFN equation (using the new A_0^*/S_0 ratio), estimating the funds that will be needed next year if no excess inventories are currently on hand and then subtracting the excess inventories that are currently on hand:

Present conditions:

$$\frac{\text{Sales}}{\text{Inventories}} = \frac{\$100}{\text{Inventories}} = 3$$

So

$$\text{Inventories} = \$100/3 = \$33.3 \text{ million at present}$$

New conditions:

$$\frac{\text{Sales}}{\text{Inventories}} = \frac{\$100}{\text{Inventories}} = 4$$

So

$$\text{New level of inventories} = \$100/4 = \$25 \text{ million}$$

Therefore,

$$\text{Excess inventories} = \$33.3 - \$25 = \$8.3 \text{ million}$$

Forecast of funds needed:

$$\Delta S = 0.2(\$100 \text{ million}) = \$20 \text{ million}$$
$$\text{AFN} = 1.5167(\$20) - 0.4(\$20) - 0.1(\$120)(0.55) - \$8.3$$
$$= \$30.3 - \$8 - \$6.6 - \$8.3$$
$$= \$7.4 \text{ million}$$

CHAPTER 18

ST-2

$$V = P[N(d_1)] - Xe^{-r_{RF}t}[N(d_2)]$$
$$= [\$33(0.63369)] - [\$33(0.95123)(0.55155)]$$
$$= \$20.91 - \$17.31$$
$$= \$3.60$$

CHAPTER 19

ST-2

$$\frac{\text{Euros}}{\text{C\$}} = \frac{\text{Euros}}{\text{US\$}} \times \frac{\text{US\$}}{\text{C\$}}$$
$$= \frac{0.65}{\$1} \times \frac{\$1}{0.98} = \frac{0.65}{0.98} = 0.6633 \text{ euro per Canadian dollar}$$

CHAPTER 20

ST-2

a. Cost of leasing

	BEGINNING OF YEAR			
	0	**1**	**2**	**3**
Lease payment (AT)[a]	($ 6,000)	($6,000)	($6,000)	($6,000)
Total PV cost of leasing =	($22,038)			

[a]After-tax payment = $10,000(1 − T) = $10,000(0.6) = $6,000

Using a financial calculator, input the following data after switching your calculator to "BEG" mode: $N = 4, I/YR = 6, PMT = 6000$, and $FV = 0$. Then press the PV key to arrive at the answer of ($22,038). Switch your calculator back to "END" mode. Note that the interest rate used is the after-tax cost of debt, $10\%(1 - T) = 6\%$.

b. Cost of owning:

Depreciable basis = $40,000

Here are the cash flows under the borrow-and-buy alternative:

		END OF YEAR			
	0	**1**	**2**	**3**	**4**
1. Depreciation schedule					
(a) Depreciable basis		$40,000	$40,000	$40,000	$40,000
(b) Allowance		0.33	0.45	0.15	0.07
(c) Depreciation		13,200	18,000	6,000	2,800
2. Cash flows					
(d) Net purchase price	($40,000)				
(e) Depreciation tax savings		5,280[a]	7,200	2,400	1,120
(f) Maintenance (AT)		(600)	(600)	(600)	(600)
(g) Salvage value (AT)					6,000
(h) Total cash flows	($40,000)	$ 4,680	$ 6,600	$ 1,800	$ 6,520

Total PV cost of owning = ($23,035)

[a] Depreciation(T) = $13,200(0.40) = $5,280

Input the cash flows for the individual years into the cash flow register and enter $I/YR = 6$. Then press the NPV key to arrive at the answer of ($23,035). Because the present value of the cost of leasing is less than that of owning, the truck should be leased: $23,035 − $22,038 = $997, net advantage to leasing.

c. The discount rate is based on the cost of debt because most cash flows are fixed by contract and, consequently, are relatively certain. Thus, the lease cash flows have about the same risk as the firm's debt. Also, leasing is considered to be a substitute for debt. We use an after-tax cost rate because the cash flows are stated net of taxes.

d. The firm could increase the discount rate on the salvage value cash flow. This would increase the PV cost of owning and make leasing even more advantageous.

CHAPTER 21

ST-2 Time line numbers are in millions of dollars:

```
0        1        2        3        4
|---12%--|--------|--------|--------|
PV = ?   1.5      2.0      3.0      5.0
                                 TV = 75.0*
                                      80.0
```

$r_s = 6\% + 4\%(1.5)$

$= 12\%$

*Terminal CF $= \dfrac{\$5(1.05)}{0.12 - 0.5} = \$75.00$

To solve this problem, use your financial calculator to enter $CF_0 = 0, CF_1 = 1.5, CF_2 = 2.0, CF_3 = 3.0, CF_4 = 80$, and $I/YR = 12$. Then solve for $NPV = \$55.91$ million.

APPENDIX B

Answers to Selected End-of-Chapter Problems

Appendix B provides some intermediate steps and final answers to selected end-of-chapter problems. Please note that your answer may differ slightly from those provided here due to rounding differences. Also, although it was not the intent, some of the problems may have more than one correct solution depending on what assumptions were made in working the problem. Finally, many of the problems involve some verbal discussion as well as numerical calculations; the verbal material is not presented here.

3-2 $2,500,000

3-4 a, possibly c

3-6 **a.** $50,000
    b. $115,000

3-8 $12,681,482

3-10 **a.** $NWC_{08} = \$192,000,000$
       $NWC_{07} = \$210,000,000$
    b. FCF = $58,000,000

4-2 $D/A = 58.33\%$

4-4 $M/B = 4.2667$

4-6 ROE = 8%

4-8 15.31%

4-10 $NI/S = 2\%$; $D/A = 40\%$

4-12 TIE = 3.86

4-14 $\Delta ROE = +5.54\%$; QR = 1.2

4-16 a.

4-18 $262,500

4-20 $50

4-22 **a.** Current ratio = 1.98; DSO = 76.3 days;
       Total assets turnover = 1.70;
       Debt ratio = 61.9%

5-2 PV = $1,292.10

5-4 N = 11.01 years

5-6 $FVA_5 = \$1,725.22$; $FVA_{5\ Due} = \$1,845.99$

5-8 PMT = $444.89; EAR = 12.6825%

5-10 **a.** $895.42
    b. $1,552.92
    c. $279.20
    d. $499.99; $867.13

5-12 **a.** 7%
    b. 7%
    c. 9%
    d. 15%

5-14 **a.** $6,374.97
    b. $1,105.13
    c. $2,000.00
    d. (1) $7,012.47
        (2) $1,160.38
        (3) $2,000.00

5-16 $PV_{7\%} = \$1,428.57$; $PV_{14\%} = \$714.29$

5-18 **a.** Stream A: $1,251.25
       Stream B: $1,300.32
    b. Stream A and Stream B: $1,600

5-20 Contract 2; PV = $10,717,847.14

5-22 **a.** $802.43
    b. Pymt 1: Int = $500; Princ pymt = $302.43.
       Pymt 2: Int = $484.88; Princ pymt = $317.55
    c. $984.88

5-24 **a.** $279.20
    b. $276.84
    c. $443.72

5-26 $17,290.89; $19,734.26

5-28 $I_{NOM} = 7.8771\%$

5-30 **a.** E = 63.74 yrs.; K = 41.04 yrs.
    b. $35,825.33

5-32 $496.11

5-34 **a.** PMT = $10,052.87
    b. Yr 3: Int/Pymt = 9.09%;
       Princ/Pymt = 90.91%

5-36 **a.** $5,308.12
    b. $4,877.09

5-38 $309,015

5-40 $9,385

6-2 2.25%

6-4 1.5%

6-6 21.8%

6-8 8.5%

6-10 6.0%

6-12 0.35%

6-14 **a.** r_1 in Year 2 = 6%
    b. $I_1 = 2\%$; $I_2 = 5\%$

6-16 14%

6-18 **a.** $r_1 = 9.20\%$; $r_5 = 7.20\%$

7-2 **a.** 7.22%
    b. $988.46

7-4 YTM = 6.62%; YTC = 6.49%;
    most likely yield = 6.49%

7-6 **a.** $C_0 = \$1{,}012.79$; $Z_0 = \$693.04$
$C_1 = \$1{,}010.02$; $Z_1 = \$759.57$
$C_2 = \$1{,}006.98$; $Z_2 = \$832.49$
$C_3 = \$1{,}003.65$; $Z_3 = \$912.41$
$C_4 = \$1{,}000.00$; $Z_4 = \$1{,}000.00$

7-8 15.03%

7-10 **a.** YTM $= 9.69\%$
b. CY $= 8.875\%$; CGY $= 0.816\%$

7-12 **a.** YTM $= 8\%$; YTC $= 6.1\%$

7-14 **a.** 5 years
b. YTC $= 6.47\%$

7-16 \$1,067.95

7-18 **a.** TLGK $= 6.1\%$; UPS $= 3.65\%$

8-2 $b_p = 1.12$

8-4 $r_M = 11\%$; $r = 12.2\%$

8-6 **a.** $\hat{r}_Y = 14\%$
b. $\sigma_X = 12.20\%$

8-8 $b = 1.33$

8-10 4.2%

8-12 **a.** $r_i = 15.5\%$
b. (1) $r_M = 15\%$; $r_i = 16.5\%$
(2) $r_M = 13\%$; $r_i = 14.5\%$
c. (1) $r_i = 18.1\%$
(2) $r_i = 14.2\%$

8-14 $b_N = 1.16$

8-16 $r_p = 11.75\%$

8-18 **a.** \$0.5 million
d. (1) \$75,000
(2) 15%

8-20 **a.** $r_A = 11.30\%$; $r_B = 11.30\%$
b. $r_{p\ Avg} = 11.30\%$
c. $\sigma_A = 20.8\%$; $\sigma_B = 20.8\%$; $\sigma_p = 20.1\%$
d. $CV_A = CV_B = 1.84$; $CV_p = 1.78$

9-2 $\hat{P}_0 = \$6.25$

9-4 **a.** end of Year 2
b. \$37.80
c. \$34.09

9-6 $r_p = 8.33\%$

9-8 **a.** \$125
b. \$83.33

9-10 \$23.75

9-12 **a. (1)** \$9.50
(2) \$13.33
(3) \$21.00
(4) \$44.00
b. (1) Undefined
(2) $-\$48.00$, which is nonsense

9-14 $P_0 = \$19.89$

9-16 6.25%

9-18 **a.** $P_0 = \$54.11$; $D_1/P_0 = 3.55\%$; CGY $= 6.45\%$

9-20 \$35.00

10-2 $r_p = 8\%$

10-4 **a.** $r_s = 15\%$
b. $r_e = 16.11\%$

10-6 **a.** $r_s = 16.3\%$
b. $r_s = 15.4\%$
c. $r_s = 16\%$
d. $r_{s\ Avg} = 15.9\%$

10-8 $r_s = 16.51\%$; WACC $= 12.79\%$

10-10 WACC $= 11.4\%$

10-12 **a.** $r_s = 14.40\%$
b. WACC $= 10.62\%$
c. Project A

10-14 11.94%

10-16 **a.** $g = 8\%$
b. $D_1 = \$2.81$
c. $r_s = 15.81\%$

10-18 **a.** $r_d(1 - T) = 7\%$; $r_p = 10.20\%$; $r_s = 15.72\%$
b. WACC $= 13.86\%$
c. Projects 1 and 2 will be accepted.

10-20 **a.** $r_d(1 - T) = 5.4\%$; $r_s = 14.6\%$
b. WACC $= 10.92\%$

11-2 IRR $= 16\%$

11-4 4.34 years

11-6 **a.** 5%: $NPV_A = \$3.52$; $NPV_B = \$2.87$
10%: $NPV_A = \$0.58$; $NPV_B = \$1.04$
15%: $NPV_A = -\$1.91$; $NPV_B = -\$0.55$
b. $IRR_A = 11.10\%$; $IRR_B = 13.18\%$
c. 5%: Choose A; 10%: Choose B; 15%:
Do not choose either one.

11-8 **a.** Without mitigation: NPV $= \$12.10$ million;
IRR $= 19.86\%$
With mitigation: NPV $= \$5.70$ million;
IRR $= 15.24\%$

11-10 Project A; $NPV_A = \$30.16$

11-12 $IRR_L = 11.74\%$

11-14 **a.** HCC; PV of costs $= -\$805{,}009.87$
c. LCC; PV of costs $= -\$686{,}627.14$

11-16 **a.** $NPV_A = \$14{,}486{,}808$; $NPV_B = \$11{,}156{,}893$;
$IRR_A = 15.03\%$; $IRR_B = 22.26\%$
b. Crossover rate $\approx 12\%$

11-18 **a.** No; $PV_{Old} = -\$89{,}910.08$;
$PV_{New} = -\$94{,}611.45$
b. \$2,470.80
c. 22.94%

11-20 \$10,239.20

11-22 \$250.01

12-2 **a.** $2,600,000
 b. $2,000,000
 c. $2,700,000

12-4 Yes, NPV = $15,301.10

12-6 **a.** SL: Deprec. = $200,000/yr.
 b. MACRS: $264,000; $360,000;
  $120,000; $56,000
 c. MACRS; $12,781.64

12-8 **a.** −$178,000
 b. $52,440; $60,600; $88,960
 c. No, NPV = −$19,549.

12-10 Yes, NPV = $921.36.

12-12 **a.** A: $6,750; B: $7,650;
  $\sigma_A = \$474.34$; $CV_A = 0.0703$
 b. Project B

12-14 Model 360-6;
  $NPV_{360-6} = \$22,256$;
  $EAA_{360-6} = \$5,723.30$

12-16 Machine B;
  $NPV_B = \$3.67$ million

12-18 $NPV_5 = \$2,211$; $NPV_4 = -\$2,081$;
  $NPV_8 = \$13,329$; $E(NPV) = \$4,486.46$

12-20 **a.** −$98,500
 b. $46,675; $52,975; $37,225; $33,025; $22,850
 c. Yes, NPV = $34,073.20.

13-2 Projects A, B, C, and D; $3,900,000

13-4 **a.** No, $NPV_3 = \$1,307.29$.

13-6 **a.** NPV = $4.6795 million
 b. No, NPV = $3.2083 million.

14-2 30% debt and 70% equity

14-4 $b_U = 1.0435$

14-6 **a. (1)** −$60,000
  (2) $40,000
 b. $Q_{BE} = 14,000$
 c. $Q_{BE} = 8,750$
 d. $Q_{BE} = 17,500$

14-8 $r_s = 17\%$

14-10 **a.** $FC_A = \$80,000$; $V_A = \$4.80$/unit;
  $P_A = \$8.00$/unit; $FC_B = \$120,000$;
  $V_B = \$4.00$/unit; $P_B = \$8.00$/unit
 b. Firm B
 c. 50,000 units

14-12 **a.** $EPS_{Old} = \$2.04$; New: $EPS_D = \$4.74$;
  $EPS_S = \$3.27$
 b. 339,750 units
 c. $Q_{Old} = 316,957$ units
  $Q_{New, \, Debt} = 272,250$ units
  $Q_{New, \, Stock} = 204,750$ units

15-2 $P_0 = \$60$

15-4 $D_0 = \$3.44$

15-6 Payout = 31.39%

15-8 **a.** 12%
 b. 18%
 c. g = 6%; $r_s = 18\%$
 d. 6%
 e. 28,800 new shares; $0.13 per share

16-2 73 days; 30 days; $1,178,082

16-4 **a.** 83 days
 b. $356,250
 c. 4.87×

16-6 **a.** 32 days
 b. $288,000
 c. $45,000
 d. (1) 30
  (2) $378,000

16-8 **a.** $ROE_T = 11.75\%$; $ROE_M = 10.80\%$;
  $ROE_R = 9.16\%$

16-10 **a.** Oct. loan = $22,800

17-2 AFN = $610,000

17-4 **a.** $133.50 million
 b. 39.06%

17-6 $67 million; 5.01×

17-8 **a.** $480,000
 b. $18,750

17-10 $34.338 million; 34.97 ≈ 35 days

17-12 **a.** $2,500,000,000
 b. 24%
 c. $24,000,000

17-14 **a.** 33%
 b. NP = $3,553.2; Bonds = $6,598.8;
  Stock = $2,514; RE = $28,284

18-2 V = $27; $P_0 = \$37$

18-4 $1.82

18-6 **b.** Futures = +$4,018,098; Bond = −$2,203,701;
  Net = $1,814,397

18-8 **a.** Stock range: $70 − $45 = $25
  Option range: $20 − $0 = $20
 b. Buy 0.8 share and sell one option.
 c. Value of portfolio = $36
 d. $48
 e. $33.64
 f. $14.36

19-2 29.7143 yen per shekel

19-4 1 euro = $1.6 or $1 = 0.625 euro

19-8 12 kronas per pound

19-10 $r_{NOM-U.S.} = 4.6\%$

19-12 **a.** Discount
b. $1.9985

19-14 +$500,000

19-16 $586,046,512

20-2 $196.36

20-4 **a.** $D/A_{J-H} = 50\%$; $D/A_{M-E} = 67\%$

20-6 **a.** $0; $0; $4; $49
d. 9%

20-8 **a.** Purchase; NPV = $-$185,112

21-2 $P_0 = \$43.48$

21-4 **a.** 16.8%
b. V = $14.93 million
c. $12.44

21-6 **a.** 14%
b. TV = $1,143.4
c. V = $877.2

Selected Equations and Tables

CHAPTER 3

Stockholders' equity = Paid-in capital + Retained earnings

Stockholders' equity = Total assets − Total liabilities

Net working capital = Current assets − (Payables + Accruals)

Operating income (or EBIT) = Sales revenues − Operating costs

$$FCF = \left(EBIT(1 - T) + Depreciation \right) - \left(\begin{array}{c} Capital \\ expenditures \end{array} + \begin{array}{c} Increase\ in\ net \\ working\ capital \end{array} \right)$$

Individual Tax Rates in April 2008
Single Individuals

If Your Taxable Income Is	You Pay This Amount on the Base of the Bracket	Plus This Percentage on the Excess over the Base (Marginal Rate)	Average Tax Rate at Top of Bracket
Up to $7,825	$ 0	10.0%	10.0%
$7,825–$31,850	782.50	15.0	13.8
$31,850–$77,100	4,386.25	25.0	20.4
$77,100–$160,850	15,698.75	28.0	24.3
$160,850–$349,700	39,148.75	33.0	29.0
Over $349,700	101,469.25	35.0	35.0

Married Couples Filing Joint Returns

If Your Taxable Income Is	You Pay This Amount on the Base of the Bracket	Plus This Percentage on the Excess over the Base (Marginal Rate)	Average Tax Rate at Top of Bracket
Up to $15,650	$ 0	10.0%	10.0%
$15,650–$63,700	1,565.00	15.0	13.8
$63,700–$128,500	8,772.50	25.0	19.4
$128,500–$195,850	24,972.50	28.0	22.4
$195,850–$349,700	43,830.50	33.0	27.0
Over $349,700	94,601.00	35.0	35.0

Corporate Tax Rates as of January 2008

If a Corporation's Taxable Income Is	It Pays This Amount on the Base of the Bracket	Plus This Percentage on the Excess over the Base (Marginal Rate)	Average Tax Rate at Top of Bracket
Up to $50,000	$ 0	15%	15.0%
$50,000–$75,000	7,500	25	18.3
$75,000–$100,000	13,750	34	22.3
$100,000–$335,000	22,250	39	34.0
$335,000–$10,000,000	113,900	34	34.0
$10,000,000–$15,000,000	3,400,000	35	34.3
$15,000,000–$18,333,333	5,150,000	38	35.0
Over $18,333,333	6,416,667	35	35.0

CHAPTER 4

$$\text{Current ratio} = \frac{\text{Current assets}}{\text{Current liabilities}}$$

$$\text{Quick, or acid test, ratio} = \frac{\text{Current assets} - \text{Inventories}}{\text{Current liabilities}}$$

$$\text{Inventory turnover ratio} = \frac{\text{Sales}}{\text{Inventories}}$$

$$\text{Days, sales, outstanding (DSO)} = \frac{\text{Receivables}}{\text{Average sales per day}} = \frac{\text{Receivables}}{\text{Annual sales}/365}$$

$$\text{Fixed assets turnover ratio} = \frac{\text{Sales}}{\text{Net fixed assets}}$$

$$\text{Total assets turnover ratio} = \frac{\text{Sales}}{\text{Total assets}}$$

$$\text{Debt ratio} = \frac{\text{Total debt}}{\text{Total assets}}$$

$$\text{Times-interest-earned (TIE) ratio} = \frac{\text{EBIT}}{\text{Interest charges}}$$

$$\text{D}/\text{E} = \frac{\text{D}/\text{A}}{1 - \text{D}/\text{A}} \quad \text{and} \quad \text{D}/\text{A} = \frac{\text{D}/\text{E}}{1 + \text{D}/\text{E}}$$

$$\text{EBITDA coverage} = \frac{\text{EBITDA} + \text{Lease payments}}{\text{Interest} + \text{Principal payments} + \text{Lease payments}}$$

$$\text{Operating margin} = \frac{\text{Operating income (EBIT)}}{\text{Sales}}$$

$$\text{Profit margin} = \frac{\text{Net income}}{\text{Sales}}$$

$$\text{Return on total assets (ROA)} = \frac{\text{Net income}}{\text{Total assets}}$$

$$\text{Basic earning power (BEP)} = \frac{\text{EBIT}}{\text{Total assets}}$$

$$\text{Return on investors' 'capital (ROIC)} = \frac{\text{Net income} + \text{Interest}}{\text{Debt} + \text{Equity}}$$

$$\text{Return on common equity (ROE)} = \frac{\text{Net income}}{\text{Common equity}}$$

$$\text{Price}/\text{Earnings (P}/\text{E) ratio} = \frac{\text{Price per share}}{\text{Earnings per share}}$$

$$\text{Book value per share} = \frac{\text{Common equity}}{\text{Shares outstanding}}$$

$$\text{Market}/\text{book ratio (M}/\text{B)} = \frac{\text{Market price per share}}{\text{Book value per share}}$$

$$\text{ROE} = \text{Profit margin} \times \text{Total assets turnover} \times \text{Equity multiplier}$$
$$= \frac{\text{Net income}}{\text{Sales}} \times \frac{\text{Sales}}{\text{Total assets}} \times \frac{\text{Total assets}}{\text{Total common equity}}$$

$$\text{EVA} = \text{EBIT}(1 - \text{Corporate tax rate}) - (\text{Total investors' capital}) \times (\text{After-tax cost of capital})$$

$$\text{EVA} = \text{Net income} - [\text{Equity capital} \times \text{Cost of equity capital}]$$
$$= (\text{Equity capital})(\text{Net income}/\text{Equity capital} - \text{Cost of equity capital})$$
$$= (\text{Equity capital})(\text{ROE} - \text{Cost of equity capital})$$

CHAPTER 5

Future value $= FV_N = PV(1 + I)^N$

Present value $= PV = \dfrac{FV_N}{(1 + I)^N}$

$FVA_N = PMT(1 + I)^{N-1} + PMT(1 + I)^{N-2} + PMT(1 + I)^{N-3} + \cdots + PMT(1 + I)^0$

$\quad = PMT\left[\dfrac{(1 + I)^N - 1}{I}\right]$

$FVA_{due} = FVA_{ordinary}(1 + I)$

$PVA_N = PMT/(1 + I)^1 + PMT/(1 + I)^2 + \cdots + PMT/(1 + I)^N$

$\quad = PMT\left[\dfrac{1 - \frac{1}{(1+I)^N}}{I}\right]$

$PVA_{due} = PVA_{ordinary}(1 + I)$

PV of a perpetuity $= \dfrac{PMT}{I}$

$PV = \dfrac{CF_1}{(1 + I)^1} + \dfrac{CF_2}{(1 + I)^2} + \cdots + \dfrac{CF_N}{(1 + I)^N} = \displaystyle\sum_{t=1}^{N} \dfrac{CF_t}{(1 + I)^t}$

Periodic rate $(I_{PER}) = \dfrac{\text{Stated annual rate}}{\text{Number of payments per year}} = I/M$

Number of periods $= (\text{Number of years})(\text{Periods per year}) = NM$

Effective annual rate $(EFF\%) = \left(1 + \dfrac{I_{NOM}}{M}\right)^M - 1.0$

CHAPTER 6

Quoted interest rate $(r) = r^* + IP + DRP + LP + MRP$

$\qquad\qquad\qquad\quad = r_{RF} \quad + DRP + LP + MRP$

$r_{T\text{-bill}} = r_{RF} = r^* + IP$

$r_{T\text{-bond}} = r_t^* + IP_t + MRP_t$

$r_{C\text{-bond}} = r_t^* + IP_t + MRP_t + DRP_t + LP_t$

r_{RF} with cross-product term $= r^* + I + (r^* \times I)$

CHAPTER 7

Bond's value $(V_B) = \dfrac{INT}{(1 + r_d)^1} + \dfrac{INT}{(1 + r_d)^2} + \cdots + \dfrac{INT}{(1 + r_d)^N} + \dfrac{M}{(1 + r_d)^N}$

$\qquad\qquad\quad = \displaystyle\sum_{t=1}^{N} \dfrac{INT}{(1 + r_d)^t} + \dfrac{M}{(1 + r_d)^N}$

Price of callable bond $= \displaystyle\sum_{t=1}^{N} \dfrac{INT}{(1 + r_d)^t} + \dfrac{\text{Call price}}{(1 + r_d)^N}$

$V_B = \displaystyle\sum_{t=1}^{2N} \dfrac{INT/2}{(1 + r_d/2)^t} + \dfrac{M}{(1 + r_d/2)^{2N}}$

CHAPTER 8

Expected rate of return $(\hat{r}) = P_1 r_1 + P_2 r_2 + \cdots + P_N r_N$

$$= \sum_{i=1}^{N} P_i r_i$$

Standard deviation $= \sigma = \sqrt{\sum_{i=1}^{N} (r_i - \hat{r})^2 P_i}$

Estimated $\sigma = \sqrt{\dfrac{\sum_{t=1}^{N} (\bar{r}_t - \bar{r}_{Avg})^2}{N - 1}}$

Coefficient of variation $= CV = \dfrac{\sigma}{\hat{r}}$

$\hat{r}_p = w_1 \hat{r}_1 + w_2 \hat{r}_2 + \cdots + w_N \hat{r}_N$

$= \sum_{i=1}^{N} w_i \hat{r}_i$

$b_p = w_1 b_1 + w_2 b_2 + \cdots + w_N b_N$

$= \sum_{i=1}^{N} w_i b_i$

$RP_i = (RP_M) b_i$

$r_i = r_{RF} + (r_M - r_{RF}) b_i$

CHAPTER 9

Value of stock $(\hat{P}_0) = $ PV of expected future dividends

$$= \frac{D_1}{(1 + r_s)^1} + \frac{D_2}{(1 + r_s)^2} + \cdots + \frac{D_\infty}{(1 + r_s)^\infty}$$

$$= \sum_{t=1}^{\infty} \frac{D_t}{(1 + r_s)^t}$$

Constant growth stock: $\hat{P}_0 = \dfrac{D_0(1 + g)^1}{(1 + r_s)^1} + \dfrac{D_0(1 + g)^2}{(1 + r_s)^2} + \cdots + \dfrac{D_0(1 + g)^\infty}{(1 + r_s)^\infty}$

$$= \frac{D_0(1 + g)}{r_s - g} = \frac{D_1}{r_s - g}$$

$$\begin{matrix} \text{Expected rate} \\ \text{of return} \end{matrix} = \begin{matrix} \text{Expected} \\ \text{dividend yield} \end{matrix} + \begin{matrix} \text{Expected growth rate, or} \\ \text{capital gains yield} \end{matrix}$$

$$\hat{r}_s = \frac{D_1}{P_0} + g$$

Growth rate $= (1 - \text{Payout ratio}) \text{ROE}$

Zero growth stock: $\hat{P}_0 = \dfrac{D}{r_s}$

Horizon value $= \hat{P}_N = \dfrac{D_{N+1}}{r_s - g}$

Nonconstant: $\hat{P}_0 = \dfrac{D_1}{(1 + r_s)^1} + \dfrac{D_2}{(1 + r_s)^2} + \cdots + \dfrac{D_N}{(1 + r_s)^N} + \dfrac{D_{N+1}}{(1 + r_s)^{N+1}} + \cdots + \dfrac{D_\infty}{(1 + r_s)^\infty}$

$$= \frac{D_1}{(1 + r_s)^1} + \frac{D_2}{(1 + r_s)^2} + \cdots + \frac{D_N}{(1 + r_s)^N} + \frac{\hat{P}_N}{(1 + r_s)^N}$$

$$= \text{PV of nonconstant dividends} + \text{PV of horizon value, } \hat{P}_N$$

$$\text{Market value of company } (V_{Company}) = \text{PV of expected future free cash flows}$$

$$= \frac{FCF_1}{(1 + WACC)^1} + \frac{FCF_2}{(1 + WACC)^2} + \cdots + \frac{FCF_\infty}{(1 + WACC)^\infty}$$

Horizon value $(V_{Company\ at\ t=N}) = FCF_{N+1}/(WACC - g_{FCF})$

Market value of equity $=$ Book value $+$ PV of all future EVAs

$$V_p = \frac{D_p}{r_p}$$

$$\hat{r}_p = \frac{D_p}{V_p}$$

CHAPTER 10

$$\text{WACC} = \begin{pmatrix} \% \\ \text{of} \\ \text{debt} \end{pmatrix} \begin{pmatrix} \text{After-tax} \\ \text{cost of} \\ \text{debt} \end{pmatrix} + \begin{pmatrix} \% \text{ of} \\ \text{preferred} \\ \text{stock} \end{pmatrix} \begin{pmatrix} \text{Cost of} \\ \text{preferred} \\ \text{stock} \end{pmatrix} + \begin{pmatrix} \% \text{ of} \\ \text{common} \\ \text{equity} \end{pmatrix} \begin{pmatrix} \text{Cost of} \\ \text{common} \\ \text{equity} \end{pmatrix}$$

$$= w_d r_d (1 - T) \qquad + \qquad w_p r_p \qquad + \qquad w_c r_s$$

After-tax cost of debt $=$ Interest rate on new debt $-$ Tax savings

$$= r_d - r_d T$$

$$= r_d (1 - T)$$

Component cost of preferred stock $= r_p = \dfrac{D_p}{P_p}$

Required rate of return $=$ Expected rate of return

$$r_s = r_{RF} + RP = D_1/P_0 + g = \hat{r}_s$$

$$r_s = r_{RF} + (RP_M)b_i$$

$$= r_{RF} + (r_M - r_{RF})b_i$$

$$\hat{P}_0 = \frac{D_1}{(1 + r_s)^1} + \frac{D_2}{(1 + r_s)^2} + \cdots + \frac{D_\infty}{(1 + r_s)^\infty}$$

$$= \sum_{t=1}^{\infty} \frac{D_t}{(1 + r_s)^t}$$

$$\hat{P}_0 = \frac{D_1}{r_s - g}$$

$$r_s = \hat{r}_s = \frac{D_1}{P_0} + \text{Expected } g$$

Cost of equity from new stock $= r_e = \dfrac{D_1}{P_0(1 - F)} + g$

Retained earnings breakpoint $= \dfrac{\text{Addition to retained earnings for the year}}{\text{Equity fraction}}$

CHAPTER 11

$$\text{NPV} = CF_0 + \frac{CF_1}{(1 + r)^1} + \frac{CF_2}{(1 + r)^2} + \cdots + \frac{CF_N}{(1 + r)^N}$$

$$= \sum_{t=0}^{N} \frac{CF_t}{(1 + r)^t}$$

$$CF_0 + \frac{CF_1}{(1 + IRR)^1} + \frac{CF_2}{(1 + IRR)^2} + \cdots + \frac{CF_N}{(1 + IRR)^N} = 0$$

$$\sum_{t=0}^{N} \frac{CF_t}{(1 + IRR)^t} = 0$$

$$\sum_{t=0}^{N} \frac{COF_t}{(1+r)^t} = \frac{\sum_{t=0}^{N} CIF_t(1+r)^{N-t}}{(1+MIRR)^N}$$

$$PV\ costs = \frac{TV}{(1+MIRR)^N}$$

$$Payback = \begin{array}{c} Number\ of \\ years\ prior\ to \\ full\ recovery \end{array} + \frac{\begin{array}{c} Unrecovered\ cost \\ at\ start\ of\ year \end{array}}{\begin{array}{c} Cash\ flow\ during \\ full\ recovery\ year \end{array}}$$

CHAPTER 13

Value of option = Expected NPV with option − Expected NPV without option

CHAPTER 14

$$EBIT = PQ - VQ - F = 0$$

$$Q_{BE} = \frac{F}{P - V}$$

$$b_L = b_U[1 + (1-T)(D/E)]$$

$$b_U = b_L/[1 + (1-T)(D/E)]$$

CHAPTER 15

$$Dividends = Net\ income - \begin{array}{c} Retained\ earnings\ required\ to\ help \\ finance\ new\ investments \end{array}$$

$$= Net\ income - [(Target\ equity\ ratio)(Total\ capital\ budget)]$$

CHAPTER 16

$$\begin{array}{c} Inventory \\ conversion \\ period \end{array} + \begin{array}{c} Average \\ collection \\ period \end{array} - \begin{array}{c} Payables \\ deferral \\ period \end{array} = \begin{array}{c} Cash \\ conversion \\ cycle \end{array}$$

$$Inventory\ conversion\ period = \frac{Inventory}{Cost\ of\ goods\ sold\ per\ day}$$

$$Average\ collection\ period\ (ACP\ or\ DSO) = \frac{Receivables}{Sales/365}$$

$$Payables\ deferral\ period = \frac{Payables}{Purchases\ per\ day} = \frac{Payables}{Cost\ of\ goods\ sold/365}$$

Accounts receivable = Sales per day × Length of collection period

Receivables = (ADS)(DSO)

$$\begin{array}{c} Nominal\ annual \\ cost\ of \\ trade\ credit \end{array} = \frac{Discount\ \%}{100 - Discount\ \%} \times \frac{365}{\begin{array}{c} Days\ credit\ is \\ outstanding \end{array} - \begin{array}{c} Discount \\ period \end{array}}$$

$$Simple\ interest\ rate\ per\ day = \frac{Nominal\ rate}{Days\ in\ year}$$

Interest charge for month = (Rate per day)(Amount of loan)(Days in month)

$$Approximate\ annual\ rate_{Add-on} = \frac{Interest\ paid}{(Amount\ received)/2}$$

CHAPTER 17

$$\text{AFN} = \begin{matrix}\text{Projected}\\\text{asset}\\\text{increase}\end{matrix} - \begin{matrix}\text{Spontaneous}\\\text{liabilities}\\\text{increase}\end{matrix} - \begin{matrix}\text{Increase in}\\\text{retained}\\\text{earnings}\end{matrix}$$

$$= (A_0^*/S_0)\Delta S - (L_0^*/S_0)\Delta S - MS_1(1-\text{Payout})$$

$$\begin{matrix}\text{Full}\\\text{capacity}\\\text{sales}\end{matrix} = \frac{\text{Actual sales}}{\begin{matrix}\text{Percentage of capacity}\\\text{at which fixed assets}\\\text{were operated}\end{matrix}}$$

$$\text{Target fixed assets}/\text{Sales} = \frac{\text{Actual fixed assets}}{\text{Full capacity sales}}$$

$$\begin{matrix}\text{Required level}\\\text{of fixed assets}\end{matrix} = (\text{Target fixed assets}/\text{Sales})(\text{Projected sales})$$

CHAPTER 18

Exercise value = Current stock price − Strike price

$$V = P[N(d_1)] - Xe^{-r_{RF}t}[N(d_2)]$$

$$d_1 = \frac{\ln(P/X) + [r_{RF} + (\sigma^2/2)]t}{\sigma\sqrt{t}}$$

$$d_2 = d_1 - \sigma\sqrt{t}$$

Values of the Areas under the Standard Normal Distribution Function

z	0.00	0.01	0.02	0.03	0.04	0.05	0.06	0.07	0.08	0.09
0.0	.0000	.0040	.0080	.0120	.0160	.0199	.0239	.0279	.0319	.0359
0.1	.0398	.0438	.0478	.0517	.0557	.0596	.0636	.0675	.0714	.0753
0.2	.0793	.0832	.0871	.0910	.0948	.0987	.1026	.1064	.1103	.1141
0.3	.1179	.1217	.1255	.1293	.1331	.1368	.1406	.1443	.1480	.1517
0.4	.1554	.1591	.1628	.1664	.1700	.1736	.1772	.1808	.1844	.1879
0.5	.1915	.1950	.1985	.2019	.2054	.2088	.2123	.2157	.2190	.2224
0.6	.2257	.2291	.2324	.2357	.2389	.2422	.2454	.2486	.2517	.2549
0.7	.2580	.2611	.2642	.2673	.2704	.2734	.2764	.2794	.2823	.2852
0.8	.2881	.2910	.2939	.2967	.2995	.3023	.3051	.3078	.3106	.3133
0.9	.3159	.3186	.3212	.3238	.3264	.3289	.3315	.3340	.3365	.3389
1.0	.3413	.3438	.3461	.3485	.3508	.3531	.3554	.3577	.3599	.3621
1.1	.3643	.3665	.3686	.3708	.3729	.3749	.3770	.3790	.3810	.3830
1.2	.3849	.3869	.3888	.3907	.3925	.3944	.3962	.3980	.3997	.4015
1.3	.4032	.4049	.4066	.4082	.4099	.4115	.4131	.4147	.4162	.4177
1.4	.4192	.4207	.4222	.4236	.4251	.4265	.4279	.4292	.4306	.4319
1.5	.4332	.4345	.4357	.4370	.4382	.4394	.4406	.4418	.4429	.4441
1.6	.4452	.4463	.4474	.4484	.4495	.4505	.4515	.4525	.4535	.4545
1.7	.4554	.4564	.4573	.4582	.4591	.4599	.4608	.4616	.4625	.4633
1.8	.4641	.4649	.4656	.4664	.4671	.4678	.4686	.4693	.4699	.4706
1.9	.4713	.4719	.4726	.4732	.4738	.4744	.4750	.4756	.4761	.4767
2.0	.4773	.4778	.4783	.4788	.4793	.4798	.4803	.4808	.4812	.4817
2.1	.4821	.4826	.4830	.4834	.4838	.4842	.4846	.4850	.4854	.4857
2.2	.4861	.4864	.4868	.4871	.4875	.4878	.4881	.4884	.4887	.4890
2.3	.4893	.4896	.4898	.4901	.4904	.4906	.4909	.4911	.4913	.4916

z	0.00	0.01	0.02	0.03	0.04	0.05	0.06	0.07	0.08	0.09
2.4	.4918	.4920	.4922	.4925	.4927	.4929	.4931	.4932	.4934	.4936
2.5	.4938	.4940	.4941	.4943	.4945	.4946	.4948	.4949	.4951	.4952
2.6	.4953	.4955	.4956	.4957	.4959	.4960	.4961	.4962	.4963	.4964
2.7	.4965	.4966	.4967	.4968	.4969	.4970	.4971	.4972	.4973	.4974
2.8	.4974	.4975	.4976	.4977	.4977	.4978	.4979	.4979	.4980	.4981
2.9	.4981	.4982	.4982	.4982	.4984	.4984	.4985	.4985	.4986	.4986
3.0	.4987	.4987	.4987	.4988	.4988	.4989	.4989	.4989	.4990	.4990

CHAPTER 19

Direct quotation: $\dfrac{\text{U.S. \$ required}}{\text{1 unit of foreign currency}}$

Indirect quotation: $\dfrac{\text{Units of foreign currency}}{\text{1 U.S. \$}}$

$\dfrac{\text{Forward exchange rate}}{\text{Spot exchange rate}} = \dfrac{(1 + r_h)}{(1 + r_f)}$

$P_h = (P_f)(\text{Spot rate})$

$\text{Spot rate} = \dfrac{P_h}{P_f}$

CHAPTER 20

Price paid for bond with warrants = Straight-debt value of bond + Value of warrants

$\text{Conversion price } (P_c) = \dfrac{\text{Par value of bond given up}}{\text{Shares received}}$

$\text{Conversion ratio } (CR) = \dfrac{\text{Par value of bond given up}}{P_c}$

FUNDAMENTALS OF FINANCIAL MANAGEMENT

Concise Sixth Edition

Eugene F. Brigham
UNIVERSITY OF FLORIDA

Joel F. Houston
UNIVERSITY OF FLORIDA

SOUTH-WESTERN
CENGAGE Learning™

Australia • Brazil • Japan • Korea • Mexico • Singapore • Spain • United Kingdom • United States

BRIEF CONTENTS

CONTENTS

Chapter 12 for

FUNDAMENTALS OF FINANCIAL MANAGEMENT: CONCISE, SIXTH EDITION

Chapter 12 of *Fundamentals of Financial Management: Concise 6e* is reproduced in the following 35 pages. *Concise 6e* is virtually the same as chapter 12 in *Fundamentals of Financial Management, 12e* through coverage of "Within-Firm and Beta Risk". The coverage of "Unequal Project Lives", however, is not present in *Concise 6e*. The topics "Real Options", "The Optimal Capital Budget", and "The Post Audit" (which are found in Chapter 13 of *Fundamentals of Financial Management, 12e*) are briefly covered at the end of *Concise 6e*'s Chapter 12.

CHAPTER
12

Cash Flow Estimation and Risk Analysis

Home Depot Keeps Growing

Home Depot Inc. (HD) has grown phenomenally in recent years, and that growth continues. At the beginning of 1990, HD had 118 stores with annual sales of $2.8 billion. By early 2008, it had 2,234 stores and annual sales of $77 billion. Stockholders have benefited mightily from this growth as the stock's price has increased from a split-adjusted $1.87 in 1990 to $40 in early 2007, or by 2,039%.

However, the more recent news has not been as good. In the face of a declining housing market, the company has struggled. In May 2008, it announced the closing of 12 underperforming stores. Still, despite the poor housing market, the company continues to open new stores in areas it thinks the stores will do well. It costs, on average, over $20 million to purchase land, construct a new store, and stock it with inventory. Therefore, it is critical that the company perform a financial analysis to determine whether a potential store's expected cash flows will cover its costs.

Home Depot uses information from its existing stores to forecast its new stores' expected

cash flows. Thus far, its forecasts have been outstanding, but there are always risks. First, a store's sales might be less than projected, especially if the economy weakens. Second, some of HD's customers might bypass the store altogether and buy directly from manufacturers through the Internet. Third, its new stores could "cannibalize," or take sales away from, its existing stores. To avoid cannibalization while still opening enough new stores to generate substantial growth, HD has been developing complementary formats. For example, it recently rolled out its Expo Design Center chain, which offers one-stop sales and service for kitchen and bath and other remodeling and renovation work; and in 2007, it acquired a Chinese home improvement chain to jump-start its operations in that nation.

Rational expansion decisions require detailed assessments of the forecasted cash flows, along with a measure of the risk that forecasted sales might not be realized. That information can then be used to determine the risk-adjusted NPV associated with each potential project. In this chapter, we describe techniques for estimating projects' cash flows, as well as projects' risks. Companies such as Home Depot use these techniques on a regular basis when making capital budgeting decisions.

PUTTING THINGS IN PERSPECTIVE

The basic principles of capital budgeting were covered in Chapter 11. Given a project's expected cash flows, it is easy to calculate the primary decision criterion—the NPV—as well as the supplemental criteria, IRR, MIRR, payback, and discounted payback. However, in the real world, cash flows are not just handed to you—rather, they must be estimated based on information from various sources. Moreover, uncertainty surrounds the forecasted cash flows, and some projects are more uncertain and thus riskier than others. In this chapter, we review examples that illustrate how project cash flows are estimated, discuss techniques for measuring and then dealing with risk, and discuss how projects are evaluated once they go into operation.

When you finish this chapter, you should be able to:

- Identify "relevant" cash flows that should and should not be included in a capital budgeting analysis.
- Estimate a project's relevant cash flows and put them into a time line format that can be used to calculate a project's NPV, IRR, and other capital budgeting metrics.
- Explain how risk is measured and use this measure to adjust the firm's WACC to account for differential project riskiness.
- Discuss how some projects can be altered after they have been accepted and how these alterations can change a project's cash flows and thus its realized NPV.
- Describe the post-audit, which is an important part of the capital budgeting process, and discuss its relevance in capital budgeting decisions.

12-1 CONCEPTUAL ISSUES IN CASH FLOW ESTIMATION

Before the cash flow estimation process is illustrated, we need to discuss several important conceptual issues. A failure to handle these issues properly can lead to incorrect NPVs and thus bad capital budgeting decisions.

12-1a Cash Flow versus Accounting Income

We saw in Chapter 3 that there is a difference between cash flows and accounting income. We also saw that *cash* is what people and firms spend or reinvest; so the present value of *cash flows*, not accounting income, is the basis of a firm's value. That's why, in the last chapter, we discounted net cash flows, not net income, to find projects' NPVs.

Many things can lead to differences between net cash flows and net income. First, depreciation is not a cash outlay, but it is deducted when net income is calculated. Second, net income is based on the depreciation rate the firm's accountants decide to use, not necessarily the depreciation rate allowed by the IRS, and it is the IRS rate that determines cash flows. Moreover, if a project requires an addition to working capital, this directly affects cash flows but not net income. Other factors also differentiate net income from cash flow, but the important thing to keep in mind is this: *For capital budgeting purposes, the project's cash flows, not its accounting income, is the key item.*

12-1b Timing of Cash Flows

In theory, capital budgeting analyses should deal with cash flows exactly when they occur; hence, daily cash flows theoretically would be better than annual flows. However, it would be costly to estimate and then analyze daily flows, and they would probably be no more accurate than annual estimates because we simply cannot forecast accurately at a daily level out 10 years or so into the future. Therefore, we generally assume that all cash flows occur at the end of the year. Note, though, for projects with highly predictable cash flows, it might be useful to assume that cash flows occur at midyear (or even quarterly or monthly); but for most purposes, we assume end-of-year flows.

12-1c Incremental Cash Flows

Incremental Cash Flow
A cash flow that will occur if and only if the firm takes on a project.

Incremental cash flows are flows that will occur *if and only if* some specific event occurs. In capital budgeting, the event is the firm's acceptance of a project and the project's incremental cash flows are ones that occur as a result of this decision. Cash flows such as investments in buildings, equipment, and working capital needed for the project are obviously incremental, as are sales revenues and operating costs associated with the project. However, some items are not so obvious, as we explain later in this section.

12-1d Replacement Projects

Two types of projects can be distinguished: expansion projects, where the firm makes an investment, such as a new Home Depot store, and replacement projects, where the firm replaces existing assets, generally to reduce costs. For example, suppose Home Depot is considering replacing some of its delivery trucks. The benefit would be lower fuel and maintenance expenses, and the shiny new trucks also might improve the company's image and reduce pollution. Replacement analysis is complicated by the fact that almost all of the cash flows are incremental, found by subtracting the new cost numbers from the old numbers. Thus, the fuel bill for a more efficient new truck might be $10,000 per year versus $15,000 for the old truck. The $5,000 savings is the incremental cash flow that would be used in the replacement analysis. Similarly, we would need to find the difference in depreciation and other factors that affect cash flows. Once we have found the incremental cash flows, we use them in a "regular" NPV analysis to decide whether to replace the asset or to continue using it.

12-1e Sunk Costs

Sunk Cost
A cash outlay that has already been incurred and that cannot be recovered regardless of whether the project is accepted or rejected.

A **sunk cost** is an outlay that was incurred in the past and cannot be recovered in the future regardless of whether the project under consideration is accepted. In capital budgeting, we are concerned with *future incremental cash flows*—we want to know if the *new* investment will produce enough incremental cash flow to justify the incremental investment. *Because sunk costs were incurred in the past and cannot be recovered regardless of whether the project is accepted or rejected, they are not relevant in the capital budgeting analysis.*

To illustrate this concept, suppose Home Depot spent $2 million to investigate a potential new store and obtain the permits required to build it. That $2 million would be a sunk cost—the money is gone, and it won't come back regardless of whether or not the new store is built.

Not handling sunk costs properly can lead to incorrect decisions. For example, suppose Home Depot completed the analysis and found that it must spend an additional $17 million, on top of the $2 million site study, to open the store. Suppose it then used as the required investment $19 million and found a projected NPV of −$1 million. This would indicate that HD should reject the new store. *However, that would be a bad decision.* The real issue is whether the *incremental* $17 million would result in *incremental* cash inflows sufficient to produce a positive NPV. If the $2 million sunk cost is disregarded, as it should be, the true NPV will be a *positive* $1 million. Therefore, the failure to deal properly with the sunk cost would lead to turning down a project that would add $1 million to stockholders' value.

12-1f Opportunity Costs Associated with Assets the Firm Owns

Another issue relates to **opportunity costs** associated with assets the firm already owns. For example, suppose Home Depot owns land with a market value of $2 million and that land will be used for the new store if HD decides to build it. If HD decides to go forward with the project, only another $15 million will be required, not the typical $17 million because HD would not need to buy the required land. Does this mean that HD should use $15 million as the cost of the new store? The answer is no. If the new store is not built, HD could sell the land and get a cash flow of $2 million. This $2 million is an *opportunity cost*—something that HD would not receive if the land was used for the new store. Therefore, the $2 million must be charged to the new project, and a failure to do so would artificially and incorrectly increase the new project's NPV.

If this is not clear, consider the following example. Assume that a firm owns a building and equipment with a market (resale) value of $10 million. The property is not being used, and the firm is considering using it for a new project. The only required additional investment would be $100,000 for working capital, and the new project would produce a cash inflow of $50,000 forever. If the firm has a WACC of 10% and evaluates the project using only the $100,000 of working capital as the required investment, it would find an NPV of $50,000/0.10 = $500,000. Does this mean that the project is a good one? The answer is no. The firm can sell the property for $10 million, which is much better than $500,000.

12-1g Externalities

Another potential problem involves **externalities,** which are defined as the effects of a project on other parts of the firm or the environment. The three types of externalities are explained next.

Negative Within-Firm Externalities

As noted earlier, retailers such as Home Depot opening new stores that are too close to their existing stores takes customers away from their existing stores. In this case, even though the new store has positive cash flows, its existence reduces some of the firm's current cash flows. This type of externality is called **cannibalization** because the new business eats into the company's existing business. Manufacturers also can experience cannibalization effects. Thus, if Cengage Learning, the publisher of this book, decides to publish another introductory finance text, that new book will presumably reduce sales of this one. Those lost cash flows should be taken into account, and that means charging them as a cost when analyzing the proposed new book.

Dealing properly with negative externalities can be tricky. If Cengage decided not to publish the new book because of its cannibalization effect, might another publisher publish it, causing our book to lose sales regardless of what Cengage does? Logically, Cengage must look at the total situation, which is more than a simple mechanical analysis. Experience and knowledge of the industry is required to make good decisions.

Opportunity Cost
The best return that can be earned on assets the firm already owns if those assets are not used for the new project.

Externality
An effect on the firm or the environment that is not reflected in the project's cash flows.

Cannibalization
The situation when a new project reduces cash flows that the firm would otherwise have had.

One of the best examples of a company fouling up as a result of not dealing correctly with a cannibalization situation was IBM's response when transistors made personal computers possible in the 1970s. IBM's mainframe computers were the biggest game in town, and they generated huge profits. But IBM had the technology, got into PCs, and for a time was the leading PC company. However, top management decided to rein back the PC division because managers were afraid it would hurt the more profitable mainframe business. That decision opened the door for Microsoft, Intel, Dell, Hewlett-Packard and others; and IBM went from being the most profitable firm in the world to one whose very survival was threatened. This experience highlights the fact that while it is essential to understand the theory of finance, it is equally important to understand the business environment, including how competitors are likely to react to a firm's actions. A great deal of judgment goes into making good financial decisions.

Positive Within-Firm Externalities

Cannibalization occurs when new products compete with old ones. However, a new project also can be *complementary* to an old one, in which case cash flows in the old operation will be *increased* when the new one is introduced. For example, Apple's iPod was a profitable product; but when Apple made an investment in another project, its music store, that investment boosted sales of the iPod. So if an analysis of the proposed music store indicated a negative NPV, the analysis would not be complete unless the incremental cash flows that would occur in the iPod division were credited to the music store. That might well change an NPV from negative to positive.

Environmental Externalities

The most common type of negative externality has to do with the environment. Government rules and regulations constrain what companies can do, but firms have some flexibility in dealing with the environment. For example, suppose a manufacturer is studying a proposed new plant. The company could meet the environmental regulations at a cost of $1 million, but the plant would still emit fumes that might cause ill feelings in its neighborhood. Those ill feelings would not show up in the cash flow analysis, but they still should be considered. Perhaps a relatively small additional expenditure would reduce the emissions substantially, make the plant look good relative to other plants in the area, and provide goodwill that would help the firm's sales and negotiations with governmental agencies in the future.

Of course, everyone's profits depend on the earth remaining healthy, so companies have an incentive to do things to protect the environment even though those actions are not required. However, if one firm decides to take actions that are good for the environment but costly, its products must reflect the higher costs. If its competitors decide to get by with less costly but less environmentally friendly processes, they can price their products lower and make more money. Of course, the more environmentally friendly companies can advertise their environmental efforts, and this might—or might not—offset the higher costs. All of this illustrates why government regulations are necessary, both nationally and internationally. Finance, politics, and the environment are all interconnected.

SELF TEST

Why should companies use a project's cash flows rather than accounting income when finding a project's NPV?

Explain the following terms: incremental cash flow, sunk cost, opportunity cost, externality, and cannibalization.

Give an example of a "good" externality, that is, one that increases a project's true NPV.

12-2 ANALYSIS OF AN EXPANSION PROJECT

In Chapter 11, we analyzed two projects, S and L. We were given the cash flows and used them to illustrate how the NPV, IRR, MIRR, and payback are calculated. Now we demonstrate how cash flows are actually estimated, using our old Project S to demonstrate the procedure. We explain the process in Table 12-1. Look at it as we discuss the analysis. Note that the dollars are in thousands; we omitted

Table 12-1   **Cash Flow Estimation and Analysis for Expansion Project S**

	A	B	C	D	E	F	G	H	I
1									
2					0	1	2	3	4
3	*Investment Outlays at Time = 0*								
4	Equipment				-$900				
5	Net WC				-100				
6	*Net Cash Flows Over the Project's Life*								
7	Unit sales					537	520	505	490
8	Sales price					$10.00	$10.00	$10.00	$10.00
9	Variable cost per unit					$5.092	$5.391	$5.228	$6.106
10	Sales revenues = Units × Price					$5,370	$5,200	$5,050	$4,900
11	Variable costs = Units × Cost/unit					2,735	2,803	2,640	2,992
12	Fixed operating costs except depr'n					2,000	2,000	2,000	2,000
13	Depreciation: <u>Accelerated</u> from table below					297	405	135	63
14	Total operating costs					$5,032	$5,208	$4,775	$5,055
15	EBIT (or operating income)					$338	-$8	$275	-$155
16	Taxes on operating income		40%			135	-3	110	-62
17	After-tax project operating income					$203	-$5	$165	-$93
18	Add back depreciation					297	405	135	63
19	Salvage value (taxed as ordinary income)								50
20	Tax on salvage value (SV is taxed at 40%)								-20
21	Recovery of net working capital								100
22	Project net cash flows (Time Line)				-$1,000	$500	$400	$300	$100
23	*Depreciation*			Accelerated		1	2	3	4
24		Cost:	$900	Rate		33%	45%	15%	7%
25				Depreciation		$297	$405	$135	$63
26	Alternative *depreciation*			Straight line					
27		Cost:	$900	Rate		25%	25%	25%	25%
28				Depreciation		$225	$225	$225	$225
29	*Project Evaluation @ WACC =*			*10%*					
30			Accelerated			Formulas		Straight line	
31		NPV	$78.82		=NPV(D29,F22:I22)+E22			$64.44	
32		IRR	14.489%		=IRR(E22:I22)			13.437%	
33		MIRR	12.106%		=MIRR(E22:I22,D29,D29)			11.731%	
34		Payback	2.33		=G2+(-E22-F22-G22)/H22			2.60	

35	1. Accelerated depreciation rates are set by Congress. We show the <u>approximate</u> rates for a 4-year asset in 2008. Companies also have the option of using straight-line depreciation. Under IRS rules, salvage value is not deducted when establishing the depreciable basis. However, if a salvage payment is received, it is called a recapture of depreciation and is taxed at the 40% rate.
36	2. If the firm owned assets that would be used for the project but would be sold if the project is not accepted, the after-tax value of those assets would be shown as an "opportunity cost" in the "Investment Outlays" section.
37	3. If this project would reduce sales and cash flows from one of the firm's other divisions, then the after-tax cannibalization effect, or "externality," would be deducted from the net cash flows shown on Row 22.
38	4. If the firm had previously incurred costs associated with this project, but those costs could not be recovered regardless of whether this project is accepted, then they are "sunk costs" and should not enter the analysis.

three zeros to streamline the presentation. Also note that we used Excel to make Table 12-1. We could have used a calculator and plain paper, but Excel is much better when dealing with arithmetic. You don't need to know Excel to understand the discussion; but if you plan to work in finance—or in almost any business function—you should learn something about it.

The column headers in the table, the A through I, and the row headers, 1 through 38, designate cells, which contain the data. For example, the equipment needed for Project S will cost $900, and that number is shown in Cell E4 as a negative. The equipment is expected to have a salvage value of $50 at the end of the project's 4-year life; this is shown in Cell I19.[1] The new project will require $100 of working capital; this is shown in Cell E5 as a negative number because it is a cost and then as a positive number in Cell I21 because it is recovered at the end of Year 4. The total investment at Time 0 is $1,000, which is shown in Cell E22.

Unit sales of Project S are shown on Row 7; they are expected to decline somewhat over the project's 4-year life. The sales price, a constant $10, is shown on Row 8. The projected variable cost per unit is given on Row 9; it generally increases over time due to expected increases in materials and labor. Sales revenue, which is calculated as units multiplied by price, is given on Row 10. Variable costs, equal to units multiplied by VC/unit, are given on Row 11; and fixed costs excluding depreciation, which are a constant $2,000, are shown on Row 12.

Depreciation is found as the annual rate allowed by the IRS times the depreciable basis. As noted in Chapter 3, Congress sets the depreciation rates that can be used for tax purposes and these are the tax rates used in capital budgeting. Congress permits firms to depreciate assets by the straight-line method or by an accelerated method. As we will see, profitable firms are better off using accelerated depreciation. We discuss depreciation more fully in Appendix 12A; but to simplify things for this chapter, we assume that the applicable accelerated rates for a project with a 4-year life are as given on Row 24 of the depreciation section of the table and that straight-line rates are as given on Row 27. Thus, we assume that if the firm uses accelerated depreciation, it will write off 33% of the basis during Year 1, another 45% in Year 2, and so forth. These are the rates used to obtain the cash flows shown in the table.

The depreciable basis is the cost of the equipment including any shipping or installation costs, or $900 as shown in Cells E4, C24, and C27. The total depreciation over the 4 years equals the cost of the equipment.

If for some reason the firm decided to use straight-line depreciation, it could write off a constant $225 per year. Its total cash flows over the entire 4 years would be the same as under accelerated depreciation; but under straight line, those cash flows would come in a bit slower because the firm would have higher tax payments in the early years and lower tax payments later on.

We calculate the annual cash flows for Project S over the 4 years in Columns F, G, H, and I, ending with the net cash flows shown on Row 22. The numbers in Cells E22 through I22 amount to a cash flow time line, and they are the same numbers used in Chapter 11 for Project S. Since the numbers are the same, the NPV, IRR, MIRR, and payback shown in Cells C31 through C34 are the same as those we calculated in Chapter 11.

The Excel model used to make Table 12-1 is part of the chapter Excel model available on the text's web site. We recommend that anyone with a computer and

---

[1] The equipment will be fully depreciated after 4 years. Therefore, the $50 estimated salvage value will exceed the book value, which will be zero. This $50 gain is classified as a recapture of depreciation, and it is taxed at the same rate as ordinary income.

some familiarity with Excel access the model and work through it to see how the table was generated. Anyone doing real-world capital budgeting today would use such a model; and our model provides a good template, or starting point, if and when you need to analyze an actual project.

12-2a Effect of Different Depreciation Rates

If we replaced the accelerated depreciation numbers in Table 12-1 with the constant $225 values that would exist under straight line, the result would be a cash flow time line on Row 22 that has the same total flows. However, in the early years, the cash flows resulting from straight-line depreciation would be lower than those now in the table; and the later years' cash flows would show higher numbers. You know that dollars received earlier have a higher present value than dollars received later. Therefore, Project S's NPV is higher if the firm uses accelerated depreciation. The exact effect is shown in the Project Evaluation section of Table 12-1—the NPV is $78.82 under accelerated depreciation and $64.44, or 18% less, with straight line.

Now suppose Congress wants to encourage companies to increase their capital expenditures to boost economic growth and employment. What change in depreciation would have the desired effect? The answer is to make accelerated depreciation even more accelerated. For example, if the firm could write off this 4-year equipment at rates of 50%, 35%, 10%, and 5%, its early tax payments would be lower, early cash flows would be higher, and the project's NPV would be higher than that shown in Table 12-1.

12-2b Cannibalization

Project S does not involve any cannibalization effects. Suppose, however, that Project S would reduce the net after-tax cash flows of another division by $50 per year. No other firm would take on this project if our firm turns it down. In this case, we would add a row at about Row 18 and deduct $50 for each year. If this were done, Project S would end up with a negative NPV; hence, it would be rejected. On the other hand, if Project S would cause additional flows in some other division (a positive externality), those after-tax inflows should be attributed to Project S.

12-2c Opportunity Costs

Now suppose the $900 initial cost shown in Table 12-1 was based on the assumption that the project would save money by using some equipment the company now owns and that equipment would be sold for $100, after taxes, if the project is rejected. The $100 is an opportunity cost, and it should be reflected in our calculations. We would add $100 to the project's cost. The result would be an NPV of $78.82 − $100 = − $21.18, so the project would be rejected.

12-2d Sunk Costs

Now suppose the firm had spent $150 on a marketing study to estimate potential sales. This $150 could not be recovered regardless of whether the project is accepted or rejected. Should the $150 be charged to Project S when determining its NPV for capital budgeting purposes? The answer is no. We are interested only in *incremental costs*. The $150 is not an incremental cost; it is a *sunk cost*. Therefore, it should not enter into the analysis.

One additional point should be made about sunk costs. If the $150 expenditure was actually made, in the final analysis, Project S would turn out to be a loser: Its NPV would be $78.82 − $150 = −$71.18. If we could somehow back up and reconsider the project *before* the $150 had been spent, we would see that the project should be rejected. However, we can't back up—at this point, we can either abandon the project or spend $1,000 and go forward with it. If we go forward, we will receive an incremental NPV of $78.82, which would reduce the loss from −$150 to −$71.18.

12-2e Other Changes to the Inputs

Variables other than depreciation also could be varied, and these changes would alter the calculated cash flows and thus NPV and IRR. For example, we could increase or decrease the projected unit sales, the sales price, the variable and/or the fixed costs, the initial investment cost, the working capital requirements, the salvage value, and even the tax rate if we thought Congress was likely to raise or lower taxes. Such changes could be made easily in an Excel model, making it possible to see the resulting changes in NPV and IRR immediately. This is called *sensitivity analysis,* and we discuss it later in the chapter when we take up procedures for measuring projects' risks.

SELF TEST

In what ways is the setup for finding a project's cash flows similar to the projected income statements for a new single-product firm? In what ways would the two statements be different? **(One would find cash flows; the other, net income.)**

Would a project's NPV for a typical firm be higher or lower if the firm used accelerated rather than straight-line depreciation? Why?

How could the analysis in Table 12-1 be modified to consider cannibalization, opportunity costs, and sunk costs?

Why does working capital appear as both a negative and a positive number in Table 12-1?

12-3 REPLACEMENT ANALYSIS[2]

In the last section, we assumed that Project S was an entirely new project. So all of its cash flows were incremental—they occurred only if the firm accepted the project. This is true for expansion projects; but for replacement projects, we must find cash flow *differentials* between the new and old projects and these differentials are the incremental flows that we analyze.

We evaluate a replacement decision in Table 12-2, which is set up much like Table 12-1, but with data on both a new highly efficient machine (which will be depreciated on an accelerated basis) and the old machine (which is depreciated on a straight-line basis). Here we find the firm's cash flows when it continues using the old machine, then the cash flows when it decides to use the new one. Finally, we subtract the old flows from the new to arrive at the *incremental cash flows.* We used Excel to do the analysis; but again, we could have used a calculator or pencil and paper. Here are the key inputs used in the analysis. No additional working capital is needed.

---

[2] This section is somewhat technical, but it can be omitted without loss of continuity.

Data applicable to both machines:

Sales revenues, which would remain constant	$2,500
Expected life of the new and old machines	4 years
WACC for the analysis	10%
Tax rate	40%

Data for old machine:

Market (salvage) value of the old machine today	$400
Old labor, materials, and other costs per year	$1,000
Old machine's annual depreciation	$100

Data for new machine:

Cost of new machine	$2,000
New labor, materials, and other costs per year	$400

The key here is to find the *incremental* cash flows. As noted previously, we find the cash flows from the operation with the old machine, then find the cash flows with the new machine, then find the differences in the cash flows. This is what we do in Parts I, II, and III of Table 12-2. Since there will be an additional expenditure to buy the new machine, that cost is shown in Cell E13. However, we can sell the old machine for $400, so that is shown as an inflow in Cell E14. The net cash outlay at Time 0 is $1,600, as shown in Cell E23.

The net cash flows based on the old machine are shown on Row 11 and those for the new machine are on Row 23. Then on Row 25, we show the differences in the cash flows with and without replacement—these are the incremental cash flows used to find the NPV. When we evaluate the incremental cash flows, we see that the replacement has an NPV of $80.28, so the old machine should be replaced.[3]

In some instances, replacements add capacity as well as lower operating costs. When this is the case, sales revenues in Part II would be increased; and if that led to a need for more working capital, that number would be shown as a Time 0 expenditure along with a recovery at the end of the project's life. These changes would, of course, be reflected in the differential cash flows on Row 25.

SELF TEST

What role do incremental cash flows play in a replacement analysis?

If you were analyzing a replacement project and you suddenly learned that the old equipment could be sold for $1,000 rather than $100, would this new information make the replacement look better or worse? **(Better; the net initial investment would be lower.)**

In Table 12-2, we assumed that output would not change if the old machine was replaced. Suppose output would actually double. How would this change be dealt with in the framework of Table 12-2?

---

[3] We could have found the incremental cash flows by calculating the differences in the only factors that change, the net cost of the new machine, operating cost savings reduced for the taxes, and the differences in depreciation, which save some taxes. This procedure is shown in the lower section of the table. The two procedures produce the same incremental cash flows and NPV, as they must.

Table 12-2 — **Replacement Project R**

	A	B	C	D	E	F	G	H	I
1					0	1	2	3	4
2	*Part I. Net Cash Flows Before Replacement*								
3	Sales revenues					$2,500	$2,500	$2,500	$2,500
4	Costs except depreciation					1,000	1,000	1,000	1,000
5	Depreciation					100	100	100	100
6	Total operating costs					$1,100	$1,100	$1,100	$1,100
7	Operating income					$1,400	$1,400	$1,400	$1,400
8	Taxes 40%					560	560	560	560
9	After-tax operating income					$840	$840	$840	$840
10	Add back depreciation					100	100	100	100
11	Net cash flows before replacement					$940	$940	$940	$940
12	*Part II. Net Cash Flows After Replacement*								
13	New machine cost				-$2,000				
14	After-tax salvage value, old machine				$400				
15	Sales revenues					$2,500	$2,500	$2,500	$2,500
16	Costs except depreciation					400	400	400	400
17	Depreciation					660	900	300	140
18	Total operating costs					$1,060	$1,300	$700	$540
19	Operating income					$1,440	$1,200	$1,800	$1,960
20	Taxes 40%					576	480	720	784
21	After-tax operating income					$864	$720	$1,080	$1,176
22	Add back depreciation					660	900	300	140
23	Net cash flows after replacement				-$1,600	$1,524	$1,620	$1,380	$1,316
24	Part III. Incremental Cash Flows and Evaluation								
25	*Incremental CFs = CF After - CF Before*				-$1,600	$584	$680	$440	$376
26									
27	*Project Evaluation @ WACC = 10%*								
28	NPV =				$80.28				
29	IRR =				12.51%				
30	MIRR =				11.35%				
31	Payback =				2.76				
32	*Part IV. Alternative (Streamlined) Calculation for NCF*								
33	New machine cost				-$2,000				
34	Salvage value, old machine				400				
35	Net cost of new machine				-$1,600				
36	Cost savings = Old - New					$600	$600	$600	$600
37	A-T savings = Cost savings × (1 - Tax rate)					360	360	360	360
38	△ Depreciation = (New - old)					560	800	200	40
39	Depr'n tax savings = △ Depreciation × Tax rate					224	320	80	16
40	NCF = A-T cost savings + Depr'n tax savings				-$1,600	$584	$680	$440	$376

12-4 RISK ANALYSIS IN CAPITAL BUDGETING[4]

Projects differ in risk, and risk should be reflected in capital budgeting decisions. However, it is difficult to measure risk, especially for new projects where no history exists. For this reason, managers deal with risk in many different ways, ranging from almost totally subjective adjustments to highly sophisticated analyses that involve computer simulation and high-powered statistics.

---

[4] Some professors may choose to cover some of the risk sections (12-4 through 12-6) and skip others. We offer a range of choices, and we tried to make the exposition clear enough that interested and self-motivated students can read sections on their own even if the sections are not assigned.

Three separate and distinct types of risk are involved:

1. **Stand-alone risk,** which is a project's risk assuming (a) that it is the only asset the firm has and (b) that the firm is the only stock in each investor's portfolio. Stand-alone risk is measured by the variability of the project's expected returns. *Diversification is totally ignored.*

2. **Corporate, or within-firm, risk,** which is a project's risk to the corporation as opposed to its investors. Within-firm risk takes account of the fact that the project is only one asset in the firm's portfolio of assets; hence, some of its risk will be eliminated by diversification within the firm. This type of risk is measured by the project's impact on uncertainty about the firm's future returns.

3. **Market, or beta, risk,** which is the riskiness of the project as seen by a well-diversified stockholder who recognizes (a) that the project is only one of the firm's assets and (b) that the firm's stock is but one part of his or her stock portfolio. The project's market risk is measured by its effect on the firm's beta coefficient.

Taking on a project with a great deal of stand-alone or corporate risk will not necessarily affect the firm's beta. However, if the project has high stand-alone risk and if its returns are highly correlated with returns on the firm's other assets and with returns on most other stocks in the economy, the project will have a high degree of all three types of risk. Market risk is theoretically the most relevant of the three because it is the one reflected in stock prices. Unfortunately, market risk is also the most difficult to estimate, primarily because new projects don't have "market prices" that can be related to stock market returns. Therefore, most decision makers do a *quantitative* analysis of stand-alone risk and then consider the other two risk measures in a *qualitative* manner.

Projects are generally classified into several categories. Then with the firm's overall WACC as a starting point, a **risk-adjusted cost of capital** is assigned to each category. For example, a firm might establish three risk classes, assign the corporate WACC to average-risk projects, add a 5% risk premium for higher-risk projects, and subtract 2% for low-risk projects. Under this setup, if the company's overall WACC was 10%, 10% would be used to evaluate average-risk projects, 15% for high-risk projects, and 8% for low-risk projects. While this approach is probably better than not making any risk adjustments, these adjustments are highly subjective and difficult to justify. Unfortunately, there's no perfect way to specify how high or low the adjustments should be.[5]

Stand-Alone Risk
The risk an asset would have if it were a firm's only asset and if investors owned only one stock. It is measured by the variability of the asset's expected returns.

Corporate (Within-Firm) Risk
Risk considering the firm's diversification but not stockholder diversification. It is measured by a project's effect on uncertainty about the firm's expected future returns.

Market (Beta) Risk
Considers both firm and stockholder diversification. It is measured by the project's beta coefficient.

Risk-Adjusted Cost of Capital
The cost of capital appropriate for a given project, given the riskiness of that project. The greater the risk, the higher the cost of capital.

SELF TEST

What are the three types of project risk?

Which type is theoretically the most relevant? Why?

What is one classification scheme that firms often use to obtain risk-adjusted costs of capital?

---

[5] We should note that the CAPM approach can be used for projects provided there are specialized publicly traded firms in the same business as that of the project under consideration. For further information on estimating the risk-adjusted cost of capital, see Web Appendix 12C; and for more information on measuring market (or beta) risk, see Web Appendix 12D.

12-5 MEASURING STAND-ALONE RISK

A project's stand-alone risk reflects uncertainty about its cash flows. The required investment, unit sales, sales prices, and operating costs shown in Table 12-1 for Project S are subject to uncertainty. First-year sales were projected at 537 units (actually, 537,000; but we shortened it to 537 to streamline the analysis) to be sold at a price of $10 per unit. However, unit sales would almost certainly be somewhat higher or lower than 537, and the price would probably turn out to be different from the projected $10 per unit. Similarly, the other variables would probably differ from their indicated values. *Indeed, all the inputs are expected values, and actual values can vary from expected values.*

Three techniques are used to assess stand-alone risk: (1) sensitivity analysis, (2) scenario analysis, and (3) Monte Carlo simulation. We discuss them in the following sections.

12-5a Sensitivity Analysis

Sensitivity Analysis
Percentage change in NPV resulting from a given percentage change in an input variable, other things held constant.

Intuitively, we know that a change in a key input variable such as units sold or sales price will cause the NPV to change. **Sensitivity analysis** *measures the percentage change in NPV that results from a given percentage change in an input, other variables held at their expected values.* This is by far the most commonly used type of risk analysis, and it is used by most firms. It begins with a *base-case* situation, where the project's NPV is found using the base-case value for each input variable. Here's a list of the key inputs for Project S:

- Equipment cost
- Required working capital
- Unit sales
- Sales price
- Variable cost per unit
- Fixed operating costs
- Tax rate
- WACC

Base-Case NPV
The NPV when sales and other input variables are set equal to their most likely (or base-case) values.

The data we used in Table 12-1 were the *most likely, or base-case, values*; and the resulting NPV, $78.82, is the **base-case NPV.** It's easy to imagine changes in the inputs, and those changes would result in different NPVs.

When senior managers review capital budgeting studies, they are interested in the base-case NPV, but they always go on to ask the financial analyst a series of "what if" questions: What if unit sales turn out to be 25% below the base case level? What if market conditions force us to price the product at $9, not $10? What if variable costs are higher than we forecasted? Sensitivity analysis is designed to provide answers to such questions. Each variable is increased or decreased from its expected value, holding other variables constant at their base-case levels. Then the NPV is calculated using the changed input. Finally, the resulting set of NPVs is plotted to show how sensitive NPV is to changes in each variable.

Figure 12-1 shows Project S's sensitivity graph for six key variables. The table below the graph gives the NPVs based on different values of the inputs, and those NPVs were then plotted to make the graph. Figure 12-1 shows that as unit sales and price increase, the project's NPV increases, whereas the opposite is true for the other four input variables. An increase in variable costs, fixed costs, equipment costs, and WACC lowers the project's NPV. The ranges shown at the bottom of the table and the slopes of the lines in the graph indicate how sensitive NPV is to changes in each input. When the data are plotted in

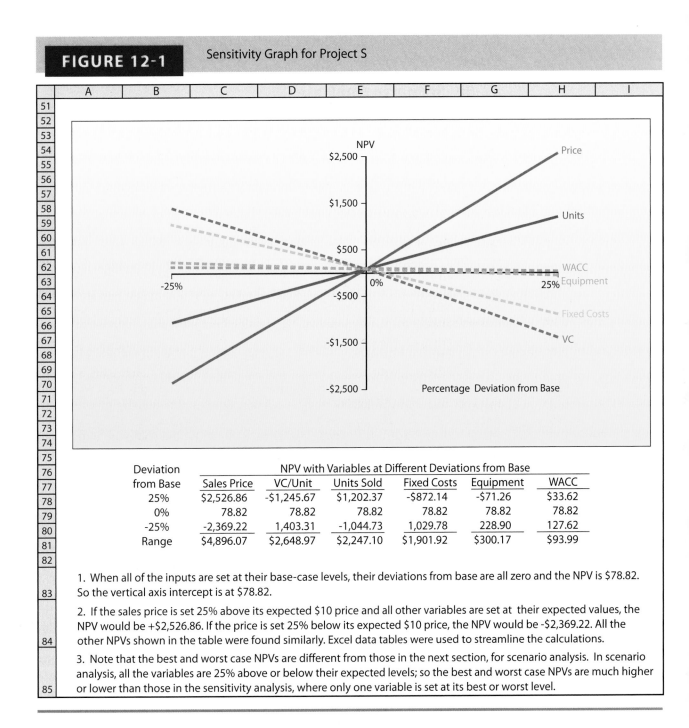

FIGURE 12-1	Sensitivity Graph for Project S

	A	B	C	D	E	F	G	H	I

| Deviation | NPV with Variables at Different Deviations from Base | | | | | |
from Base	Sales Price	VC/Unit	Units Sold	Fixed Costs	Equipment	WACC
25%	$2,526.86	-$1,245.67	$1,202.37	-$872.14	-$71.26	$33.62
0%	78.82	78.82	78.82	78.82	78.82	78.82
-25%	-2,369.22	1,403.31	-1,044.73	1,029.78	228.90	127.62
Range	$4,896.07	$2,648.97	$2,247.10	$1,901.92	$300.17	$93.99

1. When all of the inputs are set at their base-case levels, their deviations from base are all zero and the NPV is $78.82. So the vertical axis intercept is at $78.82.

2. If the sales price is set 25% above its expected $10 price and all other variables are set at their expected values, the NPV would be +$2,526.86. If the price is set 25% below its expected $10 price, the NPV would be -$2,369.22. All the other NPVs shown in the table were found similarly. Excel data tables were used to streamline the calculations.

3. Note that the best and worst case NPVs are different from those in the next section, for scenario analysis. In scenario analysis, all the variables are 25% above or below their expected levels; so the best and worst case NPVs are much higher or lower than those in the sensitivity analysis, where only one variable is set at its best or worst level.

Figure 12-1, the slopes of the lines in the graph indicate how sensitive NPV is to each input: *The larger the range, the steeper the variable's slope and the more sensitive the NPV is to this variable.* We see that NPV is very sensitive to changes in the sales price, fairly sensitive to changes in variable costs, a bit less sensitive to units sold and fixed costs, but not very sensitive to changes in the equipment cost or the WACC.

If we were comparing two projects, the one with the steeper sensitivity lines would be riskier, other things held constant, because relatively small changes in the input variables would produce large changes in the NPV. Thus, sensitivity analysis provides useful insights into a project's risk.[6]

12-5b Scenario Analysis

In sensitivity analysis, we change one variable at a time. However, it is useful to know what would happen to the project's NPV if all of the inputs turned out to be better or worse than expected. Also, we can assign probabilities to the good, bad, and most likely (or base-case) scenarios, then find the expected value and the standard deviation of the NPV. **Scenario analysis** allows for these extensions—it allows us to change more than one variable at a time, and it incorporates the probabilities of changes in the key variables.

In a scenario analysis, we begin with the **base-case scenario,** which uses the most likely set of input values. We then ask marketing, engineering, and other operating managers to specify a **worst-case scenario** (low unit sales, low sales price, high variable costs, and so forth) and a **best-case scenario.** Often the best and worst cases are defined as having a 25% probability of conditions being that good or bad, with a 50% probability for the base-case conditions. Obviously, conditions can take on many more than three values, but such a scenario setup is useful to provide an idea about the project's riskiness.

The best-case, base-case, and worst-case values for Project S are shown in Figure 12-2, along with plots of the data. If the project is highly successful, the combination of a high sales price, low production costs, and high unit sales will result in a very high NPV, $7,450.38. However, if things turn out badly, the NPV will be a negative $4,782.40. The graphs show the wide range of possibilities, suggesting that this is a risky project. If the bad conditions materialize, the company will not go bankrupt—this is just one project for a large company. Still, losing $4,782.40 (or $4,782,400 since we are working in thousands) would hurt the stock price.

If we multiply each scenario's probability by the NPV under that scenario and then sum the products, we will have the project's expected NPV, $706.40 as shown in Figure 12-2. Note that the *expected* NPV differs from the *base-case* NPV. This is not an error—mathematically, they are not equal. We also calculate the standard deviation of the expected NPV; it is $5,028.94. When we divide the standard deviation by the expected NPV, we get the coefficient of variation, 7.12, which is a measure of stand-alone risk. The firm's average project has a coefficient of variation of about 2.0, so the CV of 7.12 indicates that this project is much riskier than most of the firm's other projects.

Our firm's WACC is 10%, so that rate should be used to find the NPV of an average-risk project. Project S is riskier than average, so a higher discount rate should be used to find its NPV. There is no way to determine the "correct" discount rate—this is a judgment call. However, some firms increase the corporate WACC when they evaluate projects deemed to be relatively risky and reduce it for low-risk projects. When the NPV was recalculated using a 12.5% WACC, the base-case NPV fell from $78.82 to $33.62; so the project still passed the NPV test.

Note that the base-case results are the same in our sensitivity and scenario analyses; but in the scenario analysis, the worst case is much worse than in the sensitivity analysis and the best case is much better. This is because in scenario analysis, all of the variables are set at their best or worst levels, while in sensitivity analysis, only one variable is adjusted and all the others are left at their base-case levels.

---

[6] Sensitivity analysis is tedious using a regular calculator but easy using a spreadsheet. We used the chapter's Excel model to calculate the NPVs and to draw the graph in Figure 12-1. To conduct such an analysis by hand would be quite time-consuming, and if the basic data were changed even slightly—say the cost of the equipment was increased slightly—all of the calculations would have to be redone. With a spreadsheet, by simply typing over the old input with the new one, the analysis changes instantaneously.

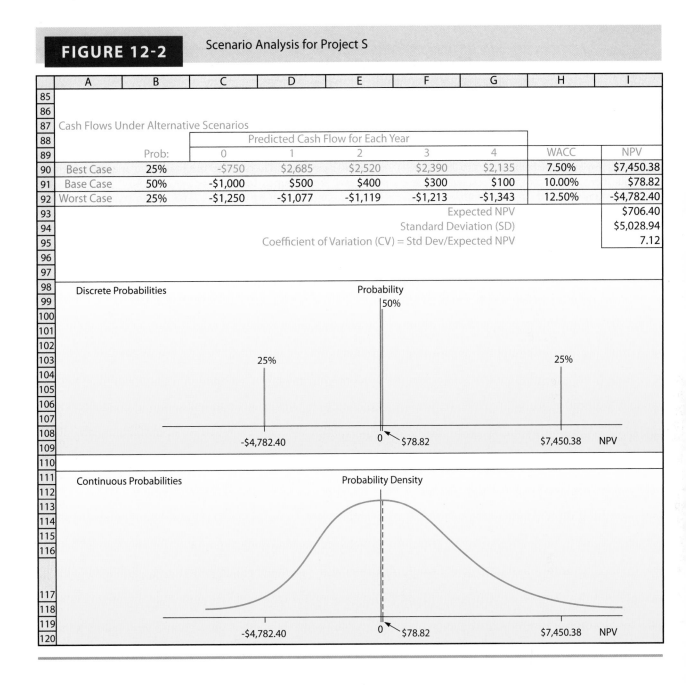

FIGURE 12-2 Scenario Analysis for Project S

	A	B	C	D	E	F	G	H	I
85									
86									
87	Cash Flows Under Alternative Scenarios								
88			Predicted Cash Flow for Each Year						
89		Prob:	0	1	2	3	4	WACC	NPV
90	Best Case	25%	-$750	$2,685	$2,520	$2,390	$2,135	7.50%	$7,450.38
91	Base Case	50%	-$1,000	$500	$400	$300	$100	10.00%	$78.82
92	Worst Case	25%	-$1,250	-$1,077	-$1,119	-$1,213	-$1,343	12.50%	-$4,782.40
93							Expected NPV		$706.40
94							Standard Deviation (SD)		$5,028.94
95						Coefficient of Variation (CV) = Std Dev/Expected NPV			7.12

12-5c Monte Carlo Simulation

Monte Carlo simulation, so named because this type of analysis grew out of work on the mathematics of casino gambling, is a sophisticated version of scenario analysis. Here the project is analyzed under a large number of scenarios, or "runs." In the first run, the computer randomly picks a value for each variable—units sold, sales price, variable costs per unit, and so forth. Those values are then used to calculate an NPV, and that NPV is stored in the computer's memory. Next, a second set of input values is selected at random and a second NPV is calculated. This process is repeated perhaps 1,000 times, generating 1,000 NPVs. The mean of the 1,000 NPVs is determined and used as a measure of the project's expected profitability, and the standard deviation (or perhaps the coefficient of variation) of the NPVs is used as a measure of risk.

Monte Carlo Simulation
A risk analysis technique in which probable future events are simulated on a computer, generating estimated rates of return and risk indexes.

GLOBAL PERSPECTIVES

CAPITAL BUDGETING PRACTICES IN THE ASIAN/PACIFIC REGION

A recent survey of executives in Australia, Hong Kong, Indonesia, Malaysia, the Philippines, and Singapore asked several questions about companies' capital budgeting practices. The study yielded the results summarized here.

Techniques for Evaluating Corporate Projects
Consistent with U.S. companies, most companies in this region evaluate projects using IRR, NPV, and payback. IRR usage ranged from 96% (in Australia) to 86% (in Hong Kong). NPV usage ranged from 96% (in Australia) to 81% (in the Philippines). Payback usage ranged from 100% (in Hong Kong and the Philippines) to 81% (in Indonesia).

Techniques for Estimating the Cost of Equity Capital
Recall from Chapter 10 that three basic approaches can be used to estimate the cost of equity: CAPM, dividend

yield plus growth rate (DCF), and cost of debt plus a risk premium. The use of these methods varied considerably from country to country. (See Table A.) The CAPM is used most often by U.S. firms. This is also true for Australian firms, but not for the other Asian/Pacific firms, which instead are more likely to use the DCF and risk premium approaches.

Techniques for Assessing Risk
Firms in the Asian/Pacific region rely heavily on scenario and sensitivity analyses. They also use decision trees and Monte Carlo simulation, but less frequently. (See Table B.)

Table A

Method	Australia	Hong Kong	Indonesia	Malaysia	Philippines	Singapore
CAPM	72.7%	26.9%	0.0%	6.2%	24.1%	17.0%
Dividend yield plus growth rate	16.4	53.8	33.3	50.0	34.5	42.6
Cost of debt plus risk premium	10.9	23.1	53.4	37.5	58.6	42.6

Table B

Risk Assessment Technique	Australia	Hong Kong	Indonesia	Malaysia	Philippines	Singapore
Scenario analysis	96%	100%	94%	80%	97%	90%
Sensitivity analysis	100	100	88	83	94	79
Decision tree analysis	44	58	50	37	33	46
Monte Carlo simulation	38	35	25	9	24	35

Source: Adapted from George W. Kester et al., "Capital Budgeting Practices in the Asia-Pacific Region: Australia, Hong Kong, Indonesia, Malaysia, Philippines, and Singapore," *Financial Practice and Education*, Vol. 9, no. 1 (Spring/Summer 1999), pp. 25–33.

Monte Carlo simulation is technically more complex than scenario analysis, but simulation software makes the process manageable. Simulation is useful; but because of its complexity, a detailed discussion is best left for advanced finance courses.[7]

---

[7] To use Monte Carlo simulation, one needs probability distributions for the inputs and correlation coefficients between each pair of inputs. It is often difficult to obtain "reasonable" values for the correlations, especially for new projects where no historical data are available. This limits the use of simulation analysis.

Explain briefly how a sensitivity analysis is done and what the analysis is designed to show.

What is a scenario analysis, what is it designed to show, and how does it differ from a sensitivity analysis?

What is Monte Carlo simulation? How does a simulation analysis differ from a regular scenario analysis?

12-6 WITHIN-FIRM AND BETA RISK[8]

Sensitivity analysis, scenario analysis, and Monte Carlo simulation as described in the preceding section dealt with stand-alone risk. They provide useful information about a project's risk; but if the project is negatively correlated with the firm's other projects, it might actually stabilize the firm's total earnings and thus be relatively safe. Similarly, if a project is negatively correlated with returns on most stocks, it might reduce the firm's beta and thus be correctly evaluated with a relatively low WACC. So in theory, we should be more concerned with within-firm and beta risk than with stand-alone risk.

Although managers recognize the importance of within-firm and beta risk, they generally end up dealing with these risks subjectively, or judgmentally, rather than quantitatively. The problem is that to measure diversification's effects on risk, we need the *correlation coefficient between a project's returns and returns on the firm's other assets*, which requires historical data that obviously does not exist for new projects. Experienced managers generally have a "feel" for how a project's returns will relate to returns on the firm's other assets. Generally, positive correlation is expected; and if the correlation is high, stand-alone risk will be a good proxy for within-firm risk. Similarly, managers can make judgmental estimates about whether a project's returns will be high when the economy and the stock market are strong (hence, what the project's beta should be). But for the most part, those estimates are subjective, not based on actual data.

However, projects occasionally involve an entirely new product line, such as a steel company going into iron ore mining. In such cases, the firm may be able to obtain betas for "*pure-play*" companies in the new area. For example, this steel company might get the average beta for a group of mining companies such as Rio Tinto and BHP, assume that its mining subsidiary has similar characteristics, and use the average beta of the "comparables" to calculate a WACC for the mining subsidiary. While the pure-play approach makes sense for some projects, it is actually rare. Just think about it. How would you find a pure-play proxy for a new inventory control system, machine tool, truck, or most other projects? The answer is, you couldn't.

Our conclusions regarding risk analysis are as follows:

- It is very difficult, if not impossible, to quantitatively measure projects' within-firm and beta risks.
- Most projects' returns are positively correlated with returns on the firm's other assets and with returns on the stock market. This being the case, stand-alone risk is correlated with within-firm and market risk; so not much is lost by focusing just on stand-alone risk.

---

[8] This section is relatively technical, but it can be omitted without a loss of continuity.

- Experienced managers make many judgmental assessments, including those related to risk; and they work them into the capital budgeting process. Introductory students like neat, precise answers; and they want to make decisions on the basis of calculated NPVs. Experienced managers consider quantitative NPVs, but they also bring subjective judgment into the decision process.

- If a firm does not use the types of analyses covered in this book, it will have trouble. On the other hand, if a firm tries to quantify everything and let a computer make its decisions, it too will have trouble. Good managers understand and use the theory of finance, but they apply it with judgment.

SELF TEST

Is it easier to measure the stand-alone, within-firm, or beta risk for projects such as a new delivery truck or a Home Depot warehouse?

If a firm cannot measure a potential project's risk with precision, should it abandon the project? Explain your answer.

12-7 REAL OPTIONS[9]

Traditional discounted cash flow (DCF) analysis—where cash flows are estimated and then discounted to obtain the expected NPV—has been the cornerstone of capital budgeting since the 1950s. However, in recent years, it has been shown that DCF techniques do not always lead to proper capital budgeting decisions.

DCF techniques were originally developed to value securities such as stocks and bonds. These are *passive* investments—once the investment has been made, most investors can take no actions that influence the cash flow the investment produces.[10] However, capital budgeting projects are not passive investments— managers can often take *positive actions* after the investment has been made that alter the cash flow stream. Opportunities for such actions are called **real options**— "real" to distinguish them from financial options, such as an option to buy shares of GE stock, and "options" because they offer the right but not the obligation to take the future action to increase cash flows. Real options are valuable, but this value is not captured by conventional NPV analysis. Therefore, a project's real options must be considered separately.

Real Option
The right but not the obligation to take some action in the future.

12-7a Types of Real Options

There are several types of real options, including (1) *abandonment,* where the project can be shut down if its cash flows are low; (2) *timing,* where a project can be delayed until more information about demand and/or costs can be obtained; (3) *expansion,* where the project can be expanded if demand turns out to be stronger than expected; (4) *output flexibility,* where the output can be changed if market conditions change; and (5) *input flexibility,* where the inputs used in the production

---

[9] This section is relatively technical, but it can be omitted without loss of continuity if there is insufficient time to cover it.

[10] Large investors such as Warren Buffett and some hedge fund operators can buy stock in companies and then influence the firms' operations and cash flows. However, the average stockholder does not have such influence.

process (e.g., coal versus natural gas for generating electricity) can be changed if input prices and/or availability change. We illustrate abandonment options here in the text, and we cover other types of options in Web Appendix 12F.

12-7b Abandonment Options

In capital budgeting, we generally assume that a project will be operated for its full physical life. However, this is not always the best course of action. If the firm's project has an **abandonment option** that can be implemented if things don't go well, this can lower its risk, increase its expected profitability, and raise its calculated NPV.

Table 12-3 gives a picture of the **decision tree** for Project S. In the scenario analysis in Section 12-5, we examined Project S under the best-case, base-case, and worst-case assumptions. In the worst-case situation, the project has negative cash flows for its full 4-year life. However, if the company can abandon the project after Year 1, when it sees that the project is not a success, its expected NPV can be improved. The earlier analysis is reproduced in the top section of Table 12-3, labeled "No Abandonment." In Column C, which is Time 0, we see that the firm must invest between $750 and $1,250. Columns D through G show the annual cash flows under each scenario; and in Column H, we show the WACCs for each scenario. Then in Column I, we show the NPV under each scenario when the cash flows are discounted at their respective WACCs. The sum of the products obtained by multiplying each probability times each branch NPV is the expected NPV, which is $706.40. The standard deviation and the coefficient of variation are also calculated to provide an idea of the project's risk. This project has a positive expected NPV; hence, by the NPV criterion, it should be accepted.

Now suppose the company could make a second decision, at t = 1, to abandon (or shut down) the project if things go badly during Year 1. To see what would happen, we add another branch to the tree, as shown in the Worst #2 row in Table 12-3 under the "Can Abandon" situation. Here we assume that the company abandons the project at the end of Year 1, when information about the actual production costs and demand conditions become available. If things were going well, the project would be continued. However, if things were going badly, the firm would close the operation and not suffer the indicated losses during the next 3 years.[11]

Given the "Can Abandon" option, the firm would clearly prefer to abandon the project than to continue. Therefore, we assign a zero probability to continuing after a bad start. Therefore, the 25% probability associated with the worst case is used for "Worst #2," and a 0% probability is assigned to "Worst #1."

The option to abandon raises the expected NPV from $706.40 to $1,350.09, and it lowers the standard deviation. Those changes combine to lower the coefficient of variation. The coefficient of variation is 3.05, which is above the company's average of 2.0, which indicates that the project is still riskier than most, even after the abandonment option has been factored in. Therefore, the 12.50% WACC is still appropriate. Also note that the difference between the expected NPVs with and without abandonment represents the **option value** to abandon this project. As shown in the lower part of Table 12-3, this option is worth $643.68.

In this case, the ability to abandon makes the NPV look better; but it does not reverse the accept/reject decision. However, it often turns out that if we fail to consider abandonment, the bad case is so bad that the expected NPV is negative.

Abandonment Option
The option to abandon a project if operating cash flows turn out to be lower than expected. This option can raise expected profitability and lower project risk.

Decision Tree
A diagram that lays out different branches that are the result of different decisions made or the result of different economic situations.

Option Value
The difference between the expected NPVs with and without the relevant option. It is the value that is not accounted for in a traditional NPV analysis. A positive option value expands the firm's opportunities.

---

[11] If the assets devoted to the project could be sold, this would be a cash inflow at the time of the sale, presumably at the end of Year 1.

Table 12-3 — **Decision Tree for Abandonment Option (Dollars in Thousands)**

	A	B	C	D	E	F	G	H	I	J
21										
22										
23	Situation 1. No Abandonment									
24				Predicted Cash Flow for Each Year						
25		Prob:	0	1	2	3	4	WACC	NPV	
26	Best Case	25%	-$750	$2,685	$2,520	$2,390	$2,135	7.50%	$7,450.38	
27	Base Case	50%	-$1,000	$500	$400	$300	$100	10.00%	$78.82	
28	Worst Case	25%	-$1,250	-$1,077	-$1,119	-$1,213	-$1,343	12.50%	-$4,782.40	
29						Expected NPV			$706.40	
30						Standard Deviation (SD)			$5,028.94	
31				Coefficient of Variation (CV) = Std Dev/Expected NPV					7.12	
32										
33	Situation 2. Can Abandon									
34				Predicted Cash Flow for Each Year						
35		Prob.	0	1	2	3	4	WACC	NPV	
36	Best Case	25%	-$750	$2,685	$2,520	$2,390	$2,135	7.50%	$7,450.38	
37	Base Case	50%	-$1,000	$500	$400	$300	$100	10.00%	$78.82	
38	Worst #1	0%	-$1,250	-$1,077	-$1,119	-$1,213	-$1,343	12.50%	-$4,782.40	Don't use
39	Worst #2	25%	-$1,250	-$1,077	$0	$0	$0	12.50%	-$2,207.67	Use
40				Expected NPV (includes #2, excludes #1)					$1,350.09	
41						Standard Deviation (SD)			$4,121.03	
42				Coefficient of Variation (CV) = Std Dev/Expected NPV					3.05	
43										
44				Value of the Real Option to Abandon						
45				Expected NPV with Abandonment					$1,350.09	
46				Expected NPV without Abandonment					$706.40	
47				Difference = Value of the Option					$643.68	

But when abandonment is considered, the expected NPV becomes positive. Clearly, abandonment must be considered to obtain valid assessments for different projects, and the opportunity to abandon is an important way to limit downside losses.

Note too that it might be necessary for the firm to make arrangements so that it has the option of abandoning a project when it is making the initial decision. This might require contractual arrangements with suppliers, customers, and its union; and there might be some costs to obtaining the advance permissions. Any such costs could be compared with the value of the option as we calculated it, which would enter into the initial decision.

SELF TEST

Why might DCF techniques not lead to proper capital budgeting decisions?

What is a real option?

What are some types of real options? Briefly explain each one.

Would you expect an abandonment option to increase or decrease a project's NPV and its risk as measured by the coefficient of variation? Why or why not?

How can the value of an option be estimated?

12-8 THE OPTIMAL CAPITAL BUDGET

Thus far, we have described various factors that managers consider when they evaluate individual projects. For planning purposes, managers must also forecast the total capital budget because the amount of capital raised affects the WACC and thus influences projects' NPVs. We use Data Devices Inc. (DDI), a manufacturer and distributor of storage devices, to illustrate how this process works.

Step 1. The treasurer obtains an estimate of the firm's overall composite WACC. As we discussed in Chapter 10, this composite WACC is based on market conditions, the firm's capital structure, and the riskiness of its assets. DDI's projects are roughly similar from year to year in terms of their risks.

Step 2. The corporate WACC is scaled up or down for each of the firm's divisions to reflect the division's risk. DDI, for example, assigns a factor of 0.9 to its stable, low-risk replacement battery division, but a factor of 1.1 to its large disk drives (an extremely competitive business), which it sells to computer manufacturers. Therefore, if the corporate cost of capital is determined to be 10.50%, the cost of capital for the battery division is 0.9(10.50%) = 9.45%, while that for the disk-drive division is 1.1(10.50%) = 11.55%.

Step 3. Financial managers within each of the firm's divisions estimate the relevant cash flows and risks of each of their potential projects. The estimated cash flows should consider any embedded real options. Then within each division, projects are classified into one of three groups—high risk, average risk, and low risk—and the same 0.9 and 1.1 factors are used to adjust the divisional cost of capital estimates. (A factor of 1.0 would be used for an average-risk project.) For example, a low-risk project in the battery division would be assigned a cost of capital of 0.9(9.45%) = 8.51%, while a high-risk project in the disk-drive division would have a cost of 1.1(11.55%) = 12.71%.

Step 4. Each project's NPV is determined using its risk-adjusted cost of capital. The optimal capital budget consists of all independent projects with positive NPVs plus those mutually exclusive projects with the highest positive NPVs.

In estimating its **optimal capital budget,** we assumed that DDI will be able to obtain financing for all of its profitable projects. This assumption is reasonable for large, mature firms with good track records. However, smaller firms, new firms, and firms with dubious track records may have difficulties raising capital, even for projects that the firm concludes would have highly positive NPVs. In such circumstances, the size of the capital budget may be constrained, a situation called **capital rationing.** When capital is limited, it should be used in the most efficient way possible. Procedures have been developed for allocating capital so as to maximize the aggregate NPV subject to the constraint that the capital rationing ceiling is not exceeded. However, because these procedures are extremely complicated, they are best left for advanced finance courses.

The procedures discussed in this section cannot be implemented with precision. However, they do force the firm to think carefully about each division's relative risk, about the risk of each project within the divisions, and about the relationship between the total amount of capital raised and the cost of that capital. Further, the process forces the firm to adjust its capital budget to reflect capital market conditions. If the costs of debt and equity rise, this fact will be reflected in the cost of capital used to evaluate projects. Thus, projects that would be marginally acceptable when capital costs were low would (correctly) be ruled unacceptable when capital costs become high.

Optimal Capital Budget
The annual investment in long-term assets that maximizes the firm's value.

Capital Rationing
The situation in which a firm can raise only a specified, limited amount of capital regardless of how many good projects it has.

Explain how a financial manager might estimate his or her firm's optimal capital budget.

What is capital rationing?

What factors must be considered when a firm is developing its optimal capital budget?

How does a firm's annual capital budget reflect market conditions?

12-9 THE POST-AUDIT

Post-Audit

A comparison of actual versus expected results for a given capital project.

A final aspect of the capital budgeting process is the **post-audit,** which involves (1) comparing actual results with those predicted by the project's sponsors and (2) explaining why any differences occurred. For example, many firms require that the operating divisions send a monthly report for the first 6 months after a project goes into operation and a quarterly report thereafter until the project's results meet expectations. From then on, reports on the operation are reviewed on a regular basis like those of other operations. The post-audit has two main purposes:

1. *Improve forecasts.* When decision makers are forced to compare their projections with actual outcomes, there is a tendency for estimates to improve. Conscious or unconscious biases are observed and eliminated; new forecasting methods are sought as the need for them becomes apparent; and people simply tend to do everything better, including forecasting, when they know that their actions are being monitored.

2. *Improve operations.* Businesses are run by people, and people can perform at higher or lower levels of efficiency. When a divisional team has made a forecast about an investment, the team members are, in a sense, putting their reputations on the line. Accordingly, if costs are above and sales are below predicted levels, executives in production, marketing, and other areas will strive to improve operations and to bring results in line with forecasts. In a discussion related to this point, one executive made this statement: "You academicians only worry about making good decisions. In business, we also worry about making decisions good."

The post-audit is not a simple process. First, we must recognize that each element of the cash flow forecast is subject to uncertainty, so a percentage of all projects undertaken by any reasonably aggressive firm will necessarily go awry. This fact must be considered when appraising the performances of the operating executives who sponsor projects. Second, projects sometimes fail to meet expectations for reasons beyond the control of their sponsors and for reasons that no one could be expected to anticipate. For example, the unanticipated run-up in oil prices in 2007 adversely affected many projects. Third, it is often difficult to separate the operating results of one investment from those of a larger system. Although some projects stand alone and permit ready identification of costs and revenues, the cost savings that result from assets such as new computers may be very hard to measure. Fourth, it is often hard to hand out blame or praise because the executives who were responsible for launching a given investment have moved on by the time the results are known.

Because of these difficulties, some firms tend to play down the importance of the post-audit. However, observations of both businesses and governmental units suggest that the best-run and most successful organizations put a great deal of emphasis on post-audits. Accordingly, we regard the post-audit as an important element in a good capital budgeting system.

SELF TEST

What is done in the post-audit?

Identify several benefits of the post-audit.

What are some factors that complicate the post-audit process?

TYING IT ALL TOGETHER

This chapter focused on estimating the cash flows that are used in a capital budgeting analysis, appraising the riskiness of those flows, finding NPVs when risk is present, and determining the values of real options, which can raise expected returns and lower risks. Here is a summary of our primary conclusions:

- Some cash flows are *relevant* (hence, should be included in a capital budgeting analysis), while others should not be included. The key question is this: Is the cash flow *incremental* in the sense that it will occur if and only if the project is accepted?
- *Sunk costs* are not incremental costs—they are not affected by accepting or rejecting the project. *Cannibalization* and other *externalities,* on the other hand, are incremental—they will occur if and only if the project is accepted.
- The cash flows used to analyze a project are different from a project's *net income.* One important factor is that *depreciation* is deducted when accountants calculate net income; but because it is a noncash charge, it must be added back to find cash flows.
- Many projects require additional *net working capital.* Net working capital is a negative flow when the project is started but a positive flow at the end of the project's life, when the capital is recovered.
- We considered two types of projects—expansion and replacement. For a replacement project, we find the difference in the cash flows when the firm continues to use the old asset versus the new asset. If the NPV of the differential flows is positive, the replacement should be made.
- The forecasted cash flows (and hence NPV and other outputs) are only estimates—they may turn out to be incorrect, and this means *risk.*
- There are three types of risk: *stand-alone, within-firm, and market (or beta) risk.* In theory, market risk is most relevant; but since it cannot be measured for most projects, stand-alone risk is the one on which we generally focus. However, firms subjectively consider within-firm and market risk, which they definitely should not ignore. Note, though, that since the three types of risk are generally positively correlated, stand-alone risk is often a good proxy for the other risks.
- Stand-alone risk can be analyzed using *sensitivity analysis, scenario analysis, and/or Monte Carlo simulation.*
- Once a decision has been made about a project's relative risk, we determine a *risk-adjusted WACC* for evaluating it.

- *Real options* enable firms to take actions to alter the originally forecasted cash flows after a project is in operation. These options can increase NPVs.
- The post-audit, which compares the project's actual performance to its expected results, is an important part of the capital budgeting process.

SELF-TEST QUESTIONS AND PROBLEMS (Solutions Appear in Appendix A)

ST-1   **KEY TERMS**   Define the following terms:

a. Incremental cash flow; sunk cost; opportunity cost; externality; cannibalization

b. Stand-alone risk; corporate (within-firm) risk; market (beta) risk

c. Risk-adjusted cost of capital

d. Sensitivity analysis; base-case NPV

e. Scenario analysis; base-case scenario; worst-case scenario; best-case scenario

f. Monte Carlo simulation

g. Real option; abandonment option; decision tree

h. Option value

i. Optimal capital budget; capital rationing

j. Post-audit

ST-2   **PROJECT AND RISK ANALYSIS**   As a financial analyst, you must evaluate a proposed project to produce printer cartridges. The equipment would cost $55,000, plus $10,000 for installation. Annual sales would be 4,000 units at a price of $50 per cartridge, and the project's life would be 3 years. Current assets would increase by $5,000 and payables by $3,000. At the end of 3 years, the equipment could be sold for $10,000. Depreciation would be based on the MACRS 3-year class; so the applicable rates would be 33%, 45%, 15%, and 7%. Variable costs would be 70% of sales revenues, fixed costs excluding depreciation would be $30,000 per year, the marginal tax rate is 40%, and the corporate WACC is 11%.

a. What is the required investment, that is, the Year 0 project cash flow?

b. What are the annual depreciation charges?

c. What are the project's annual net cash flows?

d. If the project is of average risk, what is its NPV? Should it be accepted?

e. Suppose management is uncertain about the exact unit sales. What would the project's NPV be if unit sales turned out to be 20% below forecast but other inputs were as forecasted? Would this change the decision? Explain.

f. The CFO asks you to do a scenario analysis using these inputs:

	Probability	Unit Sales	VC%
Best case	25%	4,800	65%
Base case	50	4,000	70
Worst case	25	3,200	75

Other variables are unchanged. What are the expected NPV, its standard deviation, and the coefficient of variation? [Hint: To do the scenario analysis, you must change unit sales and VC% to the values specified for each scenario, get the scenario cash flows, and then find each scenario's NPV. Then you must calculate the project's expected NPV, standard deviation (SD), and coefficient of variation (CV). This is not difficult, but it requires many calculations. You might want to look at the answer, but make sure you understand how it was computed.]

g. The firm's project CVs generally range from 1.0 to 1.5. A 3% risk premium is added to the WACC if the initial CV exceeds 1.5, and the WACC is reduced by 0.5% if the CV is 0.75 or less. Then a revised NPV is calculated. What WACC should be used for this project? What are the revised values for the expected NPV, standard deviation, and coefficient of variation? Would you recommend that the project be accepted? Why or why not?

QUESTIONS

12-1   Operating cash flows rather than accounting income are listed in Table 12-1. Why do we focus on cash flows as opposed to net income in capital budgeting?

12-2   Explain why sunk costs should not be included in a capital budgeting analysis but opportunity costs and externalities should be included. Give an example of each.

12-3   Explain why working capital is included in a capital budgeting analysis and how it is recovered at the end of a project's life.

12-4   Why are interest charges not deducted when a project's cash flows for use in a capital budgeting analysis are calculated?

12-5   Most firms generate cash inflows every day, not just once at the end of the year. In capital budgeting, should we recognize this fact by estimating daily project cash flows and then using them in the analysis? If we do not, are our results biased? If so, would the NPV be biased up or down? Explain.

12-6   What are some differences in the analysis for a replacement project versus that for a new expansion project?

12-7   Distinguish among beta (or market) risk, within-firm (or corporate) risk, and stand-alone risk for a project being considered for inclusion in the capital budget.

12-8   In theory, market risk should be the only "relevant" risk. However, companies focus as much on stand-alone risk as on market risk. What are the reasons for the focus on stand-alone risk?

12-9   Define (a) sensitivity analysis, (b) scenario analysis, and (c) simulation analysis. If GE was considering two projects (one for $500 million to develop a satellite communications system and the other for $30,000 for a new truck), on which project would the company be more likely to use a simulation analysis?

12-10   If you were the CFO of a company that had to decide on hundreds of potential projects every year, would you want to use sensitivity analysis and scenario analysis as described in the chapter or would the amount of arithmetic required take too much time and thus not be cost-effective? What involvement would nonfinancial people such as those in marketing, accounting, and production have in the analysis?

PROBLEMS

Easy
Problems 1–4

12-1   **REQUIRED INVESTMENT** Truman Industries is considering an expansion. The necessary equipment would be purchased for $9 million, and the expansion would require an additional $3 million investment in working capital. The tax rate is 40%.

a.   What is the initial investment outlay?
b.   The company spent and expensed $50,000 on research related to the project last year. Would this change your answer? Explain.
c.   The company plans to use another building that it owns to house the project. The building could be sold for $1 million after taxes and real estate commissions. How would that fact affect your answer?

12-2   **PROJECT CASH FLOW** Eisenhower Communications is trying to estimate the first-year net cash flow (at Year 1) for a proposed project. The financial staff has collected the following information on the project:

Sales revenues	$10 million
Operating costs (excluding depreciation)	7 million
Depreciation	2 million
Interest expense	2 million

The company has a 40% tax rate, and its WACC is 10%.

a. What is the project's net cash flow for the first year (t = 1)?
b. If this project would cannibalize other projects by $1 million of cash flow before taxes per year, how would this change your answer to Part a?
c. Ignore Part b. If the tax rate dropped to 30%, how would that change your answer to Part a?

12-3 **NET SALVAGE VALUE** Kennedy Air Services is now in the final year of a project. The equipment originally cost $20 million, of which 80% has been depreciated. Kennedy can sell the used equipment today for $5 million, and its tax rate is 40%. What is the equipment's after-tax net salvage value?

12-4 **REPLACEMENT ANALYSIS** The Chang Company is considering the purchase of a new machine to replace an obsolete one. The machine being used for the operation has a book value and a market value of zero. However, the machine is in good working order and will last at least another 10 years. The proposed replacement machine will perform the operation so much more efficiently that Chang's engineers estimate that it will produce after-tax cash flows (labor savings and depreciation) of $9,000 per year. The new machine will cost $40,000 delivered and installed, and its economic life is estimated to be 10 years. It has zero salvage value. The firm's WACC is 10%, and its marginal tax rate is 35%. Should Chang buy the new machine?

Intermediate Problems 5–11

12-5 **DEPRECIATION METHODS** Kristin is evaluating a capital budgeting project that should last 4 years. The project requires $800,000 of equipment. She is unsure what depreciation method to use in her analysis, straight-line or the 3-year MACRS accelerated method. Under straight-line depreciation, the cost of the equipment would be depreciated evenly over its 4-year life. (Ignore the half-year convention for the straight-line method.) The applicable MACRS depreciation rates are 33%, 45%, 15%, and 7% as discussed in Appendix 12A. The company's WACC is 10%, and its tax rate is 40%.

a. What would the depreciation expense be each year under each method?
b. Which depreciation method would produce the higher NPV, and how much higher would it be?

12-6 **SCENARIO ANALYSIS** Huang Industries is considering a proposed project whose estimated NPV is $12 million. This estimate assumes that economic conditions will be "average." However, the CFO realizes that conditions could be better or worse, so she performed a scenario analysis and obtained these results:

Economic Scenario	Probability of Outcome	NPV
Recession	0.05	($70 million)
Below average	0.20	(25 million)
Average	0.50	12 million
Above average	0.20	20 million
Boom	0.05	30 million

Calculate the project's expected NPV, standard deviation, and coefficient of variation.

12-7 **NEW PROJECT ANALYSIS** You must evaluate a proposed spectrometer for the R&D Department. The base price is $140,000, and it would cost another $30,000 to modify the equipment for special use by the firm. The equipment falls into the MACRS 3-year class and would be sold after 3 years for $60,000. The applicable depreciation rates are 33%, 45%, 15%, and 7% as discussed in Appendix 12A. The equipment would require an $8,000 increase in working capital (spare parts inventory). The project would have no effect on revenues, but it should save the firm $50,000 per year in before-tax labor costs. The firm's marginal federal-plus-state tax rate is 40%.

a. What is the net cost of the spectrometer; that is, what is the Year 0 project cash flow?
b. What are the project's annual net cash flows in Years 1, 2, and 3?
c. If the WACC is 12%, should the spectrometer be purchased? Explain.

12-8 **NEW PROJECT ANALYSIS** You must evaluate a proposal to buy a new milling machine. The base price is $108,000, and shipping and installation costs would add another $12,500. The machine falls into the MACRS 3-year class, and it would be sold after 3 years for $65,000. The applicable depreciation rates are 33%, 45%, 15%, and 7% as discussed in Appendix 12A. The machine would require a $5,500 increase in working capital (increased inventory less increased accounts payable). There would be no effect on revenues, but pretax labor costs would decline by $44,000 per year. The marginal tax rate is 35%, and the WACC is 12%. Also, the firm spent $5,000 last year investigating the feasibility of using the machine.

   a. How should the $5,000 spent last year be handled?
   b. What is the net cost of the machine for capital budgeting purposes, that is, the Year 0 project cash flow?
   c. What are the project's annual net cash flows during Years 1, 2, and 3?
   d. Should the machine be purchased? Explain your answer.

12-9 **REPLACEMENT ANALYSIS** The Dauten Toy Corporation uses an injection molding machine that was purchased 2 years ago. This machine is being depreciated on a straight-line basis, and it has 6 years of remaining life. Its current book value is $2,100, and it can be sold for $2,500 at this time. Thus, the annual depreciation expense is $2,100/6 = $350 per year. If the old machine is not replaced, it can be sold for $500 at the end of its useful life.
   Dauten is offered a replacement machine that has a cost of $8,000, an estimated useful life of 6 years, and an estimated salvage value of $800. This machine falls into the MACRS 5-year class; so the applicable depreciation rates are 20%, 32%, 19%, 12%, 11%, and 6%. The replacement machine would permit an output expansion, so sales would rise by $1,000 per year. Even so, the new machine's greater efficiency would cause operating expenses to decline by $1,500 per year. The new machine would require that inventories be increased by $2,000, but accounts payable would simultaneously increase by $500. Dauten's marginal federal-plus-state tax rate is 40%, and its WACC is 15%. Should the company replace the old machine?

12-10 **REPLACEMENT ANALYSIS** Mississippi River Shipyards is considering replacing an 8-year-old riveting machine with a new one that will increase earnings before depreciation from $27,000 to $54,000 per year. The new machine will cost $82,500, and it will have an estimated life of 8 years and no salvage value. The new machine will be depreciated over its 5-year MACRS recovery period; so the applicable depreciation rates are 20%, 32%, 19%, 12%, 11%, and 6%. The applicable corporate tax rate is 40%, and the firm's WACC is 12%. The old machine has been fully depreciated and has no salvage value. Should the old riveting machine be replaced by the new one? Explain your answer.

12-11 **PROJECT RISK ANALYSIS** The Butler-Perkins Company (BPC) must decide between two mutually exclusive projects. Each costs $6,750 and has an expected life of 3 years. Annual project cash flows begin 1 year after the initial investment and are subject to the following probability distributions:

PROJECT A		PROJECT B	
Probability	Cash Flows	Probability	Cash Flows
0.2	$6,000	0.2	$ 0
0.6	6,750	0.6	6,750
0.2	7,500	0.2	18,000

BPC has decided to evaluate the riskier project at 12% and the less risky project at 10%.

   a. What is each project's expected annual cash flow? Project B's standard deviation (σ_B) is $5,798, and its coefficient of variation (CV_B) is 0.76. What are the values of σ_A and CV_A?
   b. Based on the risk-adjusted NPVs, which project should BPC choose?
   c. If you knew that Project B's cash flows were negatively correlated with the firm's other cash flows whereas Project A's flows were positively correlated, how might this affect the decision? If Project B's cash flows were negatively correlated with gross domestic product (GDP) while A's flows were positively correlated, would that influence your risk assessment? Explain.

Challenging 12-12 **SCENARIO ANALYSIS** Your firm, Agrico Products, is considering a tractor that would
Problems   have a net cost of $36,000, would increase pretax operating cash flows before taking
12–15   account of depreciation by $12,000 per year, and would be depreciated on a straight-line

basis to zero over 5 years at the rate of $7,200 per year beginning the first year. (Thus, annual cash flows would be $12,000 before taxes plus the tax savings that result from $7,200 of depreciation.) The managers are having a heated debate about whether the tractor would last 5 years. The controller insists that she knows of tractors that have lasted only 4 years. The treasurer agrees with the controller, but he argues that most tractors do give 5 years of service. The service manager then states that some last as long as 8 years.

Given this discussion, the CFO asks you to prepare a scenario analysis to determine the importance of the tractor's life on the NPV. Use a 40% marginal federal-plus-state tax rate, a zero salvage value, and a 10% WACC. Assuming each of the indicated lives has the same probability of occurring (probability = 1/3), what is the tractor's expected NPV? (Hint: Use the 5-year straight-line depreciation for all analyses and ignore the MACRS half-year convention for this problem.)

12-13   **NEW PROJECT ANALYSIS**   Holmes Manufacturing is considering a new machine that costs $250,000 and would reduce pretax manufacturing costs by $90,000 annually. Holmes would use the 3-year MACRS method to depreciate the machine, and management thinks the machine would have a value of $23,000 at the end of its 5-year operating life. The applicable depreciation rates are 33%, 45%, 15%, and 7% as discussed in Appendix 12A. Working capital would increase by $25,000 initially, but it would be recovered at the end of the project's 5-year life. Holmes's marginal tax rate is 40%, and a 10% WACC is appropriate for the project.

    a.   Calculate the project's NPV, IRR, MIRR, and payback.

    b.   Assume that management is unsure about the $90,000 cost savings—this figure could deviate by as much as plus or minus 20%. What would the NPV be under each of these situations?

    c.   Suppose the CFO wants you to do a scenario analysis with different values for the cost savings, the machine's salvage value, and the working capital (WC) requirement. She asks you to use the following probabilities and values in the scenario analysis:

Scenario	Probability	Cost Savings	Salvage Value	WC
Worst case	0.35	$ 72,000	$18,000	$30,000
Base case	0.35	90,000	23,000	25,000
Best case	0.30	108,000	28,000	20,000

Calculate the project's expected NPV, its standard deviation, and its coefficient of variation. Would you recommend that the project be accepted? Why or why not?

12-14   **REPLACEMENT ANALYSIS**   The Erley Equipment Company purchased a machine 5 years ago at a cost of $90,000. The machine had an expected life of 10 years at the time of purchase, and it is being depreciated by the straight-line method by $9,000 per year. If the machine is not replaced, it can be sold for $10,000 at the end of its useful life.

A new machine can be purchased for $150,000, including installation costs. During its 5-year life, it will reduce cash operating expenses by $50,000 per year. Sales are not expected to change. At the end of its useful life, the machine is estimated to be worthless. MACRS depreciation will be used. The machine will be depreciated over its 3-year class life rather than its 5-year economic life; so the applicable depreciation rates are 33%, 45%, 15%, and 7%.

The old machine can be sold today for $55,000. The firm's tax rate is 35%. The appropriate WACC is 16%.

    a.   If the new machine is purchased, what is the amount of the initial cash flow at Year 0?

    b.   What are the incremental net cash flows that will occur at the end of Years 1 through 5?

    c.   What is the NPV of this project? Should Erley replace the old machine? Explain.

12-15   **REPLACEMENT ANALYSIS**   The Bigbee Bottling Company is contemplating the replacement of one of its bottling machines with a newer and more efficient one. The old machine has a book value of $600,000 and a remaining useful life of 5 years. The firm does not expect to realize any return from scrapping the old machine in 5 years, but it can sell it now to another firm in the industry for $265,000. The old machine is being depreciated by $120,000 per year using the straight-line method.

The new machine has a purchase price of $1,175,000, an estimated useful life and MACRS class life of 5 years, and an estimated salvage value of $145,000. The applicable depreciation rates are 20%, 32%, 19%, 12%, 11%, and 6%. The machine is expected to economize on electric power usage, labor, and repair costs as well as to reduce the number of defective bottles. In total, an annual savings of $255,000 will be realized if the new machine is installed. The company's marginal tax rate is 35%, and it has a 12% WACC.

a. What initial cash outlay is required for the new machine?
b. Calculate the annual depreciation allowances for both machines and compute the change in the annual depreciation expense if the replacement is made.
c. What are the incremental net cash flows in Years 1 through 5?
d. Should the firm purchase the new machine? Support your answer.
e. In general, how would each of the following factors affect the investment decision, and how should each be treated?
   (1) The expected life of the existing machine decreases.
   (2) The WACC is not constant but is increasing as Bigbee adds more projects to its capital budget for the year.

COMPREHENSIVE/SPREADSHEET PROBLEM

12-16   **NEW PROJECT ANALYSIS**   You must analyze a potential new product—a caulking compound that Cory Materials' R&D people developed for use in the residential construction industry. Cory's marketing manager thinks the company can sell 115,000 tubes per year at a price of $3.25 each for 3 years, after which the product will be obsolete. The required equipment would cost $150,000, plus another $25,000 for shipping and installation. Current assets (receivables and inventories) would increase by $35,000, while current liabilities (accounts payable and accruals) would rise by $15,000. Variable costs would be 60% of sales revenues, fixed costs (exclusive of depreciation) would be $70,000 per year, and fixed assets would be depreciated under MACRS with a 3-year life. (Refer to Appendix 12A for MACRS depreciation rates.) When production ceases after 3 years, the equipment should have a market value of $15,000. Cory's tax rate is 40%, and it uses a 10% WACC for average-risk projects.

a. Find the required Year 0 investment and the project's annual net cash flows. Then calculate the project's NPV, IRR, MIRR, and payback. Assume at this point that the project is of average risk.
b. Suppose you now learn that R&D costs for the new product were $30,000 and that those costs were incurred and expensed for tax purposes last year. How would this affect your estimate of NPV and the other profitability measures?
c. If the new project would reduce cash flows from Cory's other projects and if the new project would be housed in an empty building that Cory owns and could sell, how would those factors affect the project's NPV?
d. Are this project's cash flows likely to be positively or negatively correlated with returns on Cory's other projects and with the economy, and should this matter in your analysis? Explain.
e. **Spreadsheet assignment: at instructor's option**   Construct a spreadsheet that calculates the cash flows, NPV, IRR, payback, and MIRR.
f. The CEO expressed concern that some of the base-case inputs might be too optimistic or too pessimistic. He wants to know how the NPV would be affected if these six variables were 20% better or 20% worse than the base-case level: unit sales, sales price, variable costs, fixed costs, WACC, and equipment cost. Hold other things constant when you consider each variable and construct a sensitivity graph to illustrate your results.
g. Do a scenario analysis based on the assumption that there is a 25% probability that each of the six variables itemized in Part f will turn out to have their best-case values as calculated in Part f, a 50% probability that all will have their base-case values, and a 25% probability that all will have their worst-case values. The other variables remain at base-case levels. Calculate the expected NPV, the standard deviation of NPV, and the coefficient of variation.
h. Does Cory's management use the risk-adjusted discount rate to adjust for project risk? Explain.

INTEGRATED CASE

ALLIED FOOD PRODUCTS

12-17 **CAPITAL BUDGETING AND CASH FLOW ESTIMATION** Allied Food Products is considering expanding into the fruit juice business with a new fresh lemon juice product. Assume that you were recently hired as assistant to the director of capital budgeting and you must evaluate the new project.

The lemon juice would be produced in an unused building adjacent to Allied's Fort Myers plant; Allied owns the building, which is fully depreciated. The required equipment would cost $200,000, plus an additional $40,000 for shipping and installation. In addition, inventories would rise by $25,000, while accounts payable would increase by $5,000. All of these costs would be incurred at t = 0. By a special ruling, the machinery could be depreciated under the MACRS system as 3-year property. The applicable depreciation rates are 33%, 45%, 15%, and 7%.

The project is expected to operate for 4 years, at which time it will be terminated. The cash inflows are assumed to begin 1 year after the project is undertaken, or at t = 1, and to continue out to t = 4. At the end of the project's life (t = 4), the equipment is expected to have a salvage value of $25,000.

Unit sales are expected to total 100,000 units per year, and the expected sales price is $2.00 per unit. Cash operating costs for the project (total operating costs less depreciation) are expected to total 60% of dollar sales. Allied's tax rate is 40%, and its WACC is 10%. Tentatively, the lemon juice project is assumed to be of equal risk to Allied's other assets.

You have been asked to evaluate the project and to make a recommendation as to whether it should be accepted or rejected. To guide you in your analysis, your boss gave you the following set of tasks/questions:

a. Allied has a standard form that is used in the capital budgeting process. (See Table IC12-1.) Part of the table has been completed, but you must replace the blanks with the missing numbers. Complete the table using the following steps:
   (1) Fill in the blanks under Year 0 for the initial investment outlay.
   (2) Complete the table for unit sales, sales price, total revenues, and operating costs excluding depreciation.
   (3) Complete the depreciation data.
   (4) Complete the table down to after-tax operating income and then down to the project's operating cash flows.
   (5) Fill in the blanks under Year 4 for the terminal cash flows and complete the project cash flow line. Discuss working capital. What would have happened if the machinery were sold for less than its book value?
b. (1) Allied uses debt in its capital structure, so some of the money used to finance the project will be debt. Given this fact, should the projected cash flows be revised to show projected interest charges? Explain.
   (2) Suppose you learned that Allied had spent $50,000 to renovate the building last year, expensing these costs. Should this cost be reflected in the analysis? Explain.
   (3) Suppose you learned that Allied could lease its building to another party and earn $25,000 per year. Should that fact be reflected in the analysis? If so, how?
   (4) Assume that the lemon juice project would take profitable sales away from Allied's fresh orange juice business. Should that fact be reflected in your analysis? If so, how?
c. Disregard all the assumptions from Part b and assume there is no alternative use for the building over the next 4 years. Now calculate the project's NPV, IRR, MIRR, and payback. Do these indicators suggest that the project should be accepted? Explain.
d. If this project had been a replacement rather than an expansion project, how would the analysis have changed? Think about the changes that would have to occur in the cash flow table.
e. (1) What three levels, or types, of project risk are normally considered?
   (2) Which type is most relevant?
   (3) Which type is easiest to measure?
   (4) Are the three types of risk generally highly correlated?
f. (1) What is sensitivity analysis?
   (2) How would you perform a sensitivity analysis on the unit sales, salvage value, and WACC for the project? Assume that each of these variables deviates from its base-case, or expected, value by plus or minus 10%, 20%, and 30%. Explain how you would calculate the NPV, IRR, MIRR, and payback for each case; but don't do the analysis unless your instructor asks you to.
   (3) What is the primary weakness of sensitivity analysis? What are its primary advantages?

Work out quantitative answers to the remaining questions only if your instructor asks you to. Also note that it will take a *long time* to do the calculations unless you are using an *Excel* model.

g. Assume that inflation is expected to average 5% over the next 4 years and that this expectation is reflected in the WACC. Moreover, inflation is expected to increase revenues and variable costs by this same 5%. Does it appear that inflation has been dealt with properly in the initial analysis to this point? If not, what should be done and how would the required adjustment affect the decision?

h. The expected cash flows, considering inflation (in thousands of dollars), are given in Table IC12-2. Allied's WACC is 10%. Assume that you are confident about the estimates of all the variables that affect the cash flows except unit sales. If product acceptance is poor, sales would be only 75,000 units a year, while a strong consumer response would produce sales of 125,000 units. In either case, cash costs would still amount to 60% of revenues. You believe that there is a 25% chance of poor acceptance, a 25% chance of excellent acceptance, and a 50% chance of average acceptance (the base case). Provide numbers only if you are using a computer model.

   (1) What is the worst-case NPV? the best-case NPV?

   (2) Use the worst-case, most likely case (or base-case), and best-case NPVs with their probabilities of occurrence to find the project's expected NPV, standard deviation, and coefficient of variation.

i. Assume that Allied's average project has a coefficient of variation (CV) in the range of 1.25 to 1.75. Would the lemon juice project be classified as high risk, average risk, or low risk? What type of risk is being measured here?

j. Based on common sense, how highly correlated do you think the project would be with the firm's other assets? (Give a correlation coefficient or range of coefficients based on your judgment.)

k. How would the correlation coefficient and the previously calculated σ combine to affect the project's contribution to corporate, or within-firm, risk? Explain.

l. Based on your judgment, what do you think the project's correlation coefficient would be with respect to the general economy and thus with returns on "the market"? How would correlation with the economy affect the project's market risk?

m. Allied typically adds or subtracts 3% to its WACC to adjust for risk. After adjusting for risk, should the lemon juice project be accepted? Should any subjective risk factors be considered before the final decision is made? Explain.

Table IC 12-1 **Allied's Lemon Juice Project (Total Cost in Thousands)**

End of Year:	0	1	2	3	4
I. Investment Outlay					
Equipment cost					
Installation					
Increase in inventory					
Increase in accounts payable	_____				
Total net investment	_____				
II. Project Operating Cash Flows					
Unit sales (thousands)			100		
Price/unit		$ 2.00	$ 2.00	_____	_____
Total revenues		_____	_____	_____	$200.0
Operating costs excluding depreciation			$ 120.0		
Depreciation				36.0	16.8
Total costs		$199.2	$ 228.0	_____	_____
Operating income before taxes (EBIT)				$44.0	
Taxes on operating income		0.3	_____		25.3
After-tax operating income				$26.4	
Depreciation		79.2		36.0	
Project operating cash flows	$ 0.0	$ 79.7			$ 54.7
III. Project Termination Cash Flows					
Return of net working capital					
Salvage value					
Tax on salvage value					
Total project termination cash flows					_____
IV. Project Net Cash Flows					
Project net cash flows	($260.0)	_____	_____	_____	$ 89.7
V. Results					
NPV =					
IRR =					
MIRR =					
Payback =					

| Table IC 12-2 | Allied's Lemon Juice Project Considering 5% Inflation (in Thousands) | | | | |

	YEAR				
	0	**1**	**2**	**3**	**4**
Investment in:					
Fixed assets	($240)				
Net working capital	(20)				
Unit sales (thousands)		100	100	100	100
Sales price (dollars)		$ 2.100	$ 2.205	$ 2.315	$ 2.431
Total revenues		$210.0	$220.5	$231.5	$243.1
Cash operating costs (60%)		126.0	132.3	138.9	145.9
Depreciation		79.2	108.0	36.0	16.8
Operating income before taxes (EBIT)		$ 4.8	($ 19.8)	$ 56.6	$ 80.4
Taxes on operating income (40%)		1.9	(7.9)	22.6	32.1
After-tax operating income		$ 2.9	($ 11.9)	$ 34.0	$ 48.3
Plus depreciation		79.2	108.0	36.0	16.8
Project operating cash flows		$ 82.1	$ 96.1	$ 70.0	$ 65.1
Salvage value					25.0
Tax on SV (40%)					(10.0)
Recovery of NWC					20.0
Project net cash flows	($260)	$ 82.1	$ 96.1	$ 70.0	$100.1
Cumulative cash flows for payback:	(260.0)	(177.9)	(81.8)	(11.8)	88.3
Compounded inflows for MIRR:		109.2	116.3	77.0	100.1
Sum of compounded inflows:					402.6

NPV = $15.0
IRR = 12.6%
MIRR = 11.6%

APPENDIX 12A

Tax Depreciation

Because depreciation is covered in detail in accounting courses, here we provide only some basic information that is needed for capital budgeting. First, note that accountants generally calculate each asset's depreciation in two ways—they use straight line to figure the depreciation used for reporting profits to investors; but they use depreciation rates provided by the Internal Revenue Service (IRS), called MACRS (Modified Accelerated Cost Recovery System) rates, when they calculate depreciation for tax purposes. In capital budgeting, we are concerned with tax depreciation; so the relevant rates are the MACRS rates.

Under MACRS, each type of fixed asset is assigned to a "class" and is then depreciated over the asset's **class life.** Table 12A-1 provides class lives for different types of assets as they existed in 2008. Next, as shown in Table 12A-2, MACRS specifies **annual depreciation rates** for assets in each class life. Real properties (buildings) are depreciated on a straight-line basis over 27.5 or 39 years; but all other assets are depreciated over shorter periods and on an accelerated basis, with high depreciation charges in the early years and less depreciation in the later years. The IRS tables are based on the **half-year convention,** where it is assumed that the asset is placed in service halfway through the first year and is taken out of service halfway through the year after its class life.

In the following example, we calculate depreciation on equipment that would be classified as a 5-year asset with a cost of $8 million. In developing the tables, the IRS assumes that the machinery would be used for only 6 months of the year in which it is acquired, for 12 months in each of the next 4 years, and then for 6 months of the sixth year. Here are the depreciation charges, in thousands, that could be deducted for tax purposes based on MACRS:

Year	1	2	3	4	5	6
Rate	20%	32%	19%	12%	11%	6%
Depreciation	$1,600	$2,560	$1,520	$960	$880	$480

The total of the annual depreciation charges equals the $8 million cost of the asset, but it would be taken over 6 years and thus would affect cash flows over those 6 years.

Class Life
The specified life of assets under the MACRS system.

Annual Depreciation Rates
The annual expense accountants charge against income for "wear and tear" of an asset. For tax purposes, the IRS provides that appropriate MACRS rates be used that are dependent on an asset's class life.

Half-Year Convention
Assumes assets are used for half the first year and half the last year.

T a b l e 1 2 A - 1	Major Classes and Asset Lives for MACRS

Class	Type of Property
3-year	Certain special manufacturing tools
5-year	Automobiles, light-duty trucks, computers, and certain special manufacturing equipment
7-year	Most industrial equipment, office furniture, and fixtures
10-year	Certain longer-lived types of equipment
27.5-year	Residential rental real property such as apartment buildings
39-year	All nonresidential real property, including commercial and industrial buildings

| Table 12A-2 | Recovery Allowance Percentage for Personal Property |

	CLASS OF INVESTMENT			
Ownership Year	**3-Year**	**5-Year**	**7-Year**	**10-Year**
1	33%	20%	14%	10%
2	45	32	25	18
3	15	19	17	14
4	7	12	13	12
5		11	9	9
6		6	9	7
7			9	7
8			4	7
9				7
10				6
11				3
	100%	100%	100%	100%

Notes:

a. We developed these recovery allowance percentages based on the 200% declining balance method prescribed by MACRS, with a switch to straight-line depreciation at some point in the asset's life. For example, consider the 5-year recovery allowance percentages. The straight-line percentage would be 20% per year, so the 200% declining balance multiplier is 2.0(20%) = 40% = 0.4. However, because the half-year convention applies, the MACRS percentage for Year 1 is 20%. For Year 2, 80% of the depreciable basis remains to be depreciated; so the recovery allowance percentage is 0.40(80%) = 32%. In Year 3, 20% + 32% = 52% of the depreciation has been taken, leaving 48%; so the percentage is 0.4(48%) = 19%. In Year 4, the percentage is 0.4(29%) = 12%. After 4 years, straight-line depreciation exceeds the declining balance depreciation; so a switch is made to straight-line. (This is permitted under the law.) However, the half-year convention must also be applied at the end of the class life, and the remaining 17% of depreciation must be taken (amortized) over 1.5 years. Thus, the percentage in Year 5 is 17%/1.5 ≈ 11% and in Year 6 is 17% − 11% = 6%. Although the tax tables carry out the allowance percentages to two decimal places, we have rounded to the nearest whole number for ease of illustration.

b. Residential rental property (apartments) is depreciated over a 27.5-year life, whereas commercial and industrial structures are depreciated over 39 years. In both cases, straight-line depreciation must be used. The depreciation allowance for the first year is based, pro rata, on the month the asset was placed in service, with the remainder of the first year's depreciation being taken in the 28th or 40th year.